SAINT LOUIS

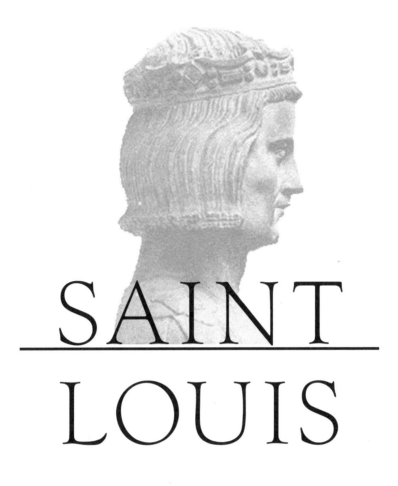

SAINT
LOUIS

JACQUES LE GOFF

Translated by Gareth Evan Gollrad

University of Notre Dame Press
Notre Dame, Indiana

English Language Edition Copyright © 2009 by
University of Notre Dame
Notre Dame, Indiana 46556
All Rights Reserved
www.undpress.nd.edu

Manufactured in the United States of America

Translated by Gareth Evan Gollrad from *Saint Louis*, by Jacques Le Goff,
published by Éditions Gallimard, Paris, France. © Éditions Gallimard, 1996.

Representation of Saint Louis. Early fourteenth-century statue from the church of
Mainneville, Eure, France. Artist unknown.

The publication of this book was generously supported by the
Laura Shannon Fund for French Medieval Studies.

Library of Congress Cataloging-in-Publication Data

Le Goff, Jacques, 1924-
[Saint Louis. English]
Saint Louis / by Jacques Le Goff ; translated by Gareth Evan Gollrad.
    p.   cm.
Includes bibliographical references and index.
ISBN-13: 978-0-268-03381-1 (cloth : alk. paper)
ISBN-10: 0-268-03381-1 (cloth : alk. paper)
1. Louis IX, King of France, 1214–1270.   2. Christian saints—France—Biography.
3. France—Kings and rulers—Biography.   I. Gollrad, Gareth Evan.   II. Title.
DC91.L39513   2008
944'.023092—dc22
[B]

2008027215

Sa piété, qui était celle d'un anachorète, ne lui ôta aucune vertu de roi. Une sage économie ne déroba rien à sa libéralité. Il sut accorder une politique profonde avec une justice exacte et peut-être est-il le seul souverain qui mérite cette louange: prudent et ferme dans le conseil, intrépide dans les combats sans être emporté, compatissant comme s'il n'avait jamais été que malheureux. Il n'est pas donné à l'homme de porter plus loin la vertu.

Voltaire

Essai sur les moeurs, Chapter 58

Contents

Translator's Note

Le Goff's work is a living monument, an epically proportioned historical narrative that explores every knowable aspect of Saint Louis' life. At the same time, this work offers a complete historical analysis, not only bringing Louis IX to life for us but distinguishing between the living king familiar to his friends and inner circle and the narrative constructions of more distant authors and their traditional models of kingship and sainthood or modern scholarly criticism. Le Goff's book is also a brilliant prism, as through the life of Saint Louis the reader discovers almost every important dimension of life in thirteenth-century France, presented in moving depth and intricate detail.

I am grateful to many for having received the opportunity to translate this *Saint Louis,* above all to Barbara Hanrahan, the Director of the University of Notre Dame Press. On the same note, I thank Françoise Meltzer, my former mentor in the Department of Romance Languages and Literatures at the University of Chicago. Not least of all, I thank the author himself for providing such an interesting, complex, and richly nuanced work to translate.

I would also like to thank those who helped me at different stages of the translation—above all the ever-affable Peter Dembowski, medievalist *extraordinaire,* who helped me with some of the most challenging Old French words that surfaced in the original, and Carole Roos for all her helpful, highly focused, and encouraging work as my copyeditor. Likewise, I thank those who have taken an interest in this work during my years in law school at Chicago-Kent College of Law, most notably my professors there Hank Perritt and Dan Hamilton.

Finally, I thank all those closest to me who have steadfastly sustained me over the years with their friendship, love, and support—most of all the love of my life Jessica Buben, my mother Julie, my sister Karen, and my father Evan who is sadly missed.

Gareth Evan Gollrad

Acknowledgments

The elaboration and composition of this book lasted roughly fifteen years. I benefited from a lot of precious assistance over this long period. My thanks first go out to the École des hautes études en sciences sociales (which succeeded the VIth section of the École pratique des hautes études in 1975). For thirty-five years the École allowed me to closely combine research and teaching within an interdisciplinary dialogue. My debt is particularly great to my young colleagues and fellow researchers, both French and foreign, who actively participated in my seminar.

I would also like to thank all those who contributed to the completion of this work through their research and the information they provided, particularly Collete Ribaucourt, Philippe Buc, Jacques Dalarun, and, especially, Marie-Claire and Pierre Gasnault. For their readings of my manuscript, their criticisms, corrections, and suggestions, I am immensely grateful to my dear friends and colleagues Jean-Claude Schmitt and Jacques Revel.

Jacques Revel carried out minute work of exceptional quality on the first version of my text. The time that he dedicated to this work and the intelligence that he manifested in this veritable collaboration are such that my acknowledgment cannot do them justice.

Throughout this process, I put the expertise, devotion, and labor of my excellent secretary Christine Bonnefoy to the test. I thank her too with all my heart.

I would also like to express my gratitude to my old and dear friend Pierre Nora who accepted this book for his prestigious "Bibliothèque des histoires." In this endeavor, I include two people at Gallimard who did a magnificent job preparing the final version of my manuscript and whose work was as intelligent as it was meticulous: Isabelle Châtelet who was an exemplary reader and my dear friend Louis Évrard. The end of this work was marked by great sadness. As I was reading Louis Évrard's final notes and corrections, I learned of his sudden and unexpected death. I would like to express my admiration and affectionate homage here for this man whose integrity and moral and intellectual rigor were unparalleled; he was a humanist of outstanding erudition and culture, an unobtrusive and generous man to whom so many books and authors owe so much. My thanks also go out to Nicole Évrard and to my daughter Barbara who established the Indexes.

I did not manage to keep this long labor away from my wife and children. Over the course of the years, I spoke to them a lot about Saint Louis, too much no doubt. Having had their fill of my reflections, I am not so sure that they would choose him as their favorite historical figure. I thank them for their patience, support, and affection.

Introduction

Sometimes called "the century of Saint Louis," the thirteenth century has attracted historians less than the creative and turbulent twelfth century and less than the fourteenth century that sank into the great crisis at the close of the Middle Ages. Between his grandfather Philip Augustus and his grandson Philip the Fair, who have both garnered extensive interest from modern historians, we find to our great surprise that Louis IX has been "the least known of the great kings of medieval France." One recent work by the American historian William Chester Jordan and another by the French historian Jean Richard present him as a man driven by a single idea, his fascination with the crusades and his obsession with the Holy Land. I believe that Saint Louis was a far more complex character. His long reign of forty-four years contained more changes and the period in which he lived was less stable than the term often used to describe it, "apogee" of the Middle Ages, implies.

The thirteenth century, however, is not the object of this study. We will have to deal with it, of course, since Louis lived during this period that constitutes the matter of his life and his actions. Still, this book is about the man himself and deals with the age only to the extent that it allows us to explain him. My topic is not "the reign of Saint Louis," nor is it "Saint Louis and his kingdom," nor "Saint Louis and Christendom," nor "Saint

Louis and his age," even if I will have to explore these themes. Speaking of the saintly king may sometimes lead me to cover extensive ground in great depth and detail, as, along with Emperor Frederick II, he was the most important political figure of the thirteenth century in Western Christendom. However, while Frederick II whose reign we see today as one of the precursors of the modern state remained a marginal figure fascinated by the Mediterranean cultural frontier, geographically, chronologically, and ideologically speaking, Louis IX was the central figure of Christendom in the thirteenth century. This led me to the idea of writing his biography, although this may not seem like a logical conclusion.

WHEN MORE THAN TEN YEARS AGO I SLOWLY DECIDED TO BEGIN research on one of the major figures of the medieval West and to give this investigation a biographical form, I imagined that it would be a difficult undertaking for any historian and would take me away from the way I had been practicing history until then. I was right about the first point and wrong about the second.

This feeling of difficulty that I mention here may seem paradoxical at first. With the proliferation of biographical publications that has taken place in recent years, the genre being very much in fashion, one might think of this as a leisurely exercise for which it would suffice to have access to the right documents, which is quite possible, and to possess an adequate talent for writing. My dissatisfaction with most of those anachronistically psychological, rhetorical, superficial, or excessively anecdotal works, as with those that too easily employ the notion of "mentality" in order to play upon the exoticism of the past without any real explanation or critical spirit, forced me to reflect on the implications and demands of historical biography. Thus I became convinced of this intimidating truth: historical biography is one of the most difficult ways to produce history.

On the other hand, while I thought I was drifting away from my prior interests and methods, I discovered almost all of the great problems of historical writing and research I had been facing before. Of course, my idea that biography is a particular way of producing history had been confirmed. Nevertheless, it required other methods in addition to the intrinsic methods of the historian's practice. This task demanded first of all the positing of a problem, the search for and criticism of sources, the treatment of the subject within a time period long enough to capture the dialectic of continuity and change, a style of writing capable of highlighting the attempt to explain, an awareness of the current stakes in dealing with the question to be treated. In other words, the task also required an awareness of the distance that separates us from the question to be dealt with. Biography confronts today's historian with the essential though classic problems of the profession in an especially poignant and complex manner. However, it does this in a form that is often no longer familiar to us.

In spite of several brilliant exceptions, there was an eclipse of historical biography in the middle of the twentieth century. This is especially evident in the movement stemming from the *Annales*. Historians more or less abandoned the genre to novelists, their old rivals in this domain. Marc Bloch once stated as much, and without the customary scorn for this historiographical form. He expressed it with regret in fact, and probably with the feeling that biography, like political history, was not yet ready to assimilate new forms of historical thinking and practice. Commenting on the definition given by one of the father's of the new history, Fustel de Coulanges, who wrote, "History is the science of human societies," Bloch observed that "this may excessively reduce the individual's part in history."

Today when history along with the social sciences is going through a period of intense critical revision of its fundamental assumptions, and while this is taking place in the midst of the crisis of a general transformation of Western societies, I have the impression that biography has been partly freed from the traps in which false problems had confined it. It may even become a privileged position for making useful observations on the conventions and ambitions of the historian's profession, on the limits of his given knowledge, and on the redefinitions that he needs.

As I present this book and define what I have set out to do, I will have to explain what historical biography should not be today. In fact, these objections have helped me rediscover my own ways of producing history in a state of transformation on what have been especially difficult grounds. All this is perhaps more obvious here than anywhere else.

ACCUSTOMED BY MY TRAINING AS A HISTORIAN TO ATTEMPT TO WRITE a global history, I was soon struck by how biography imposed the necessity of turning its character into what Pierre Toubert and I have called a "globalizing" subject around which the entire field of research is organized. So, what object crystallizes the whole of its environment and the areas dissected by the historian in the field of historical knowledge more and better than an actual character? Saint Louis participated simultaneously in the economic, the social, the political, the religious, and the cultural; he acted in all of these domains, while thinking of them in a way that the historian must analyze and explain—even if the search for complete knowledge of the individual in question remains a "utopian quest." In effect, it is necessary here—more than for any other object of historical study—to know how to respect the absences and lacunae left by the documentation and to resist wanting to reconstitute what the silences of and about Saint Louis hide, the disjunctions and discontinuities that break the flow and apparent unity of a life. A biography, however, is not only the collection of everything we can and should know about a historical character.

If a character then "globalizes" a sum of diverse phenomena, it is not because it is more "concrete" in relation to the historian's other objects. For example, some have quite correctly denounced the false opposition between "a concrete falsehood of biography" and "an abstract falsehood" of political history. But more than other historical methods, the biographical method strives to produce "reality effects" [*effets de réel*]. What makes it even more similar to the methods of the novelist is that these "reality effects" do not result from the style and writing of the historian alone. Due to his familiarity with the sources and with the period in which his character lived, thanks to an "appropriate dismantling" [*démontage approprié*], the historian must be capable of placing these "reality effects," whose truth can be inferred, in the documents themselves. Or, more simply, he must be capable of taking these documents apart in order to conjure whatever produces a reasonable conviction of historical reality. As we shall see, Saint Louis benefits from having an exceptional witness, Joinville, who often makes the historian say, "Ah yes, now, that is the 'real' Saint Louis!" However, the historian must not let his guard down.

He effectively chooses to submit to one major constraint: the limitation of the documentation that dictates the ambition and the scope of his investigation. He is different from the novelist in this regard, even when the novelist becomes preoccupied with information about the truth he pretends to describe. It just so happens that Saint Louis is (along with Saint Francis of Assisi) the one character of the thirteenth century about whom we know the most through primary sources. There can be no doubt that this is because he was king and because he was a saint. History has spoken of great men most of all, and for a long time was interested in them only as individuals. This was especially true in the Middle Ages. However, the apparent advantage the case of Saint Louis presents for the historian is by and large offset by the doubts that can arise about the reliability of the sources. These, more than other sources, run the risk, if not of lying, then at least of presenting us with an imagined or imaginary figure.

One main reason for this risk is the quality and objectives of the old biographers of Louis who are almost all hagiographers (the most important ones in any case). They do not only want to make him into a sainted king. They want to make him into a king and a saint according to the particular ideals of the ideological groups to which they belong. So, there is a Saint Louis of the new Mendicant orders—the Dominicans and Franciscans—and a Saint Louis of the Benedictines of the royal abbey of Saint-Denis. He was more of a mendicant for the first groups, and more of a "national" model of the king for the second. Another cause of manipulation is that the sources that present the king to us are essentially literary sources. These are the *Vitae* in particular, the Lives of saints written in Latin. Medieval literature was divided between genres that obeyed certain rules. Even if the conception of saintliness in the thirteenth century admitted a bit more freedom, the hagiographical genre was still full of stereotypes. Is the Saint Louis of our sources only an assemblage of commonplace ideas? I had to commit the entire central section of my study to evaluating the reliability of these sources. I did this by studying the conditions for the production of the memory of Saint Louis in the thirteenth through the beginning of the fourteenth century. I did this not only in employing classical methods for the criticism of sources, but, more radically, as a systematic production of memory. I had to ask myself if it were possible to get closer to a Saint Louis who could be called "true," truly historical, through the sources.

The nature of these Lives comprised both a justification and a new danger for my project. The hagiographical Life was a history, even if the narrative was organized around manifestations of virtues and piety, including a catalog of miracles usually appearing in a separate section. Moving from the hagiographical biography of the thirteenth century to the historical biography of the late twentieth century, I was able to test the false opposition that has recently been raised between historical narrative and a "structuralist" narrative that would have previously been called sociological and, in an even earlier time, institutional. But all history is narrative because, placing itself in time by definition, in succession, it is necessarily associated with narration. But that is not all. First, contrary to what many—even many historians—believe, there is nothing immediate about the narrative. It is the result of an entire series of intellectual and scientific operations that one has every reason to expose, in other words, to justify. It also induces an interpretation and represents a serious danger. Jean-Claude Passeron has pointed out the risk of "the excess of meaning and coherence inherent in any biographical approach." What he calls the "biographical utopia" not only consists in the risk of believing that "nothing is meaningless" in biographical narrative without selection and criticism, but perhaps even more in the illusion that it authentically reconstitutes someone's destiny. So, a life and, perhaps even more, the life of a character endowed with a power as rich in symbolic and political reality as a king doubling as a saint can be conceived through some form of illusion predetermined by its function and its final perfection. In following this plan, are we not adding a model suggested by the historian's rhetoric and that Giovanni Levi has defined as associating "an organized chronology, a coherent and stable personality, actions without inertia, decisions without uncertainty" to the models that inspired the hagiographers?

I have tried several times to escape the constraining logic of this "biographical illusion" denounced by Pierre Bourdieu. Saint Louis did not ineluctably proceed toward his destiny as a saintly king in the conditions of the thirteenth century and in following the dominant models of his time. He formed himself and formed his era as much as he was formed by it. This construction was made up of chance and hesitation over different choices. It is vain to try to imagine a biography, or any other historical phenomenon, in any other way than we know that it occurred. We do not write history with too many "ifs." However, we should understand that on numerous occasions Saint Louis, even in believing that he was history itself led by Providence, could have acted differently than he did. For a Christian, there can be different ways of reacting to the provocations of Providence without disobeying it. I have tried to show that Louis defined himself little by little through a series of unpredictable choices. And I have constantly interrupted the thread of his biographical trajectory while seeking to account for the problems that he encountered at different points in his life. I have also tried to define the difficulties the recuperation of these moments of life present for the historian. The pair of governing figures, unique in

French history, that he formed for a long time with his mother, Blanche of Castile, makes it impossible for the historian to date a "rise to power" of Louis IX as can be done for Louis XIV. When he learned of the Mongol raid into central Europe, when illness cast him down at death's door, when he was freed from captivity by the Muslims in Egypt, when he returned to his kingdom from the Holy Land after a six-year absence, Louis had to choose. He had to make decisions that unpredictably formed the character that finally was Saint Louis. I mention here only a few of the important events that required him to make decisions weighted with consequences. It was in the daily nature of exercising his royal function and in the secret, unconscious and uncertain construction of his sainthood that the existence of Saint Louis became a life the biographer can attempt to explain.

Giovanni Levi accurately stated that "biography constitutes . . . the ideal place for verifying the interstitial and nevertheless important character of the freedom that agents have at their disposal, and for observing how normative systems function in concrete situations that are never exempt from contradiction." I have tried to appreciate the extent of the power that nature and the plasticity of monarchical institutions provided Saint Louis in the middle of the thirteenth century. I have attempted to explain the growing prestige of a sacred royalty that was nonetheless still far from absolute and whose thaumaturgical power was strictly limited. And I have striven to depict his struggle with time and space and an economy that he did not even know how to name. I have made no attempt to conceal the contradictions that weighed on Saint Louis' character: between his penchants for the flesh and fine living and his ideals of mastery over sexuality and gluttony, between the "hilarious" piety of the mendicants and the rigorous ascetic practice of monastic tradition, between the pomp of royal duty and the humility of a sovereign who wanted to behave, if not as the most humble of laymen, then at least as a Christian as humble as he should be, between a king who declared that "no one holds more fast to life than I," and who often exposed himself to death, thinking constantly of his death and the dead, between a king who became more and more the king of France and who wanted to be a king for all Christendom.

This problem of the uncertainties and contradictions of a life that any attempt at biographical history encounters is actually modified by the particular characteristics of Saint Louis' case. Almost all his former biographers affirmed the existence of a turning point or even a rupture in his life at some point during the crusade. Before 1254 we would be dealing with a normally pious king, like any Christian king. After this date, we would be facing a penitential and eschatological sovereign who prepared himself—and wanted to prepare his subjects—for eternal salvation by establishing a moral and religious order in his kingdom while readying himself to be a Christlike king. This version of the life and the reign of Louis IX follows the hagiographical model that sought a moment of conversion in the lives of saints at the same time as a model of biblical kingship that would make Louis IX into a new Josiah whose rule the Old Testament divided around the rediscovery and the reapplication [*réactualisation*] of the Pentateuch. My own work adds a hypothesis that may fortify this thesis about the turning point of 1254: in effect, I attribute great importance to the meeting that took place that year between Louis, who was debarking in Provence while returning from the Holy Land, and a Franciscan, Friar Hugh of Digne who professed millenarian ideas calling for the realization on earth of a long state of peace and justice prefiguring Heaven. However, was the change that great between the king who bowed devoutly before the relics of the Passion acquired in 1239, the ruler who commissioned investigators for redressing offenses in 1247, and the legislator of the "great ordinance" of the end of 1254 which was supposed to instill a moral order in his kingdom? Moreover, what enables the historian to partly escape any abusive explanations in the unfolding life of Saint Louis is that in keeping with the scholastic and intellectual practices of the thirteenth century his biographers had recourse to three kinds of arguments whose intersections allowed one to avoid any single type of explanation. There were the *authorities:* Holy Scripture and the writings of the Church Fathers that allowed the biographers to apply biblical models. Then, there were the *reasons* derived from the methods of the new Scholasticism. While the third type, that of the *exempla,* edifying anecdotes, circulated a large number of commonplaces, it also introduced a narrative element of fantasy that broke down the rigidity of the first two types of demonstration.

The main problem here arises from a particular reaction. Without the sources stating it explicitly, we have the impression that, without ever being so proud as to want to be a saint, very early on Louis IX had been in some way "programmed" by his mother and the advisors of his youth, and that from this early age he modeled himself to become an incarnation of the ideal Christian king. His life then ended up being only the impassioned and voluntary realization of this project. Against William C. Jordan who, not without talent and subtlety, sees in Saint Louis a king torn between his royal duties and a sense of devotion patterned after the Mendicant orders, I believe that Saint Louis had mentally and practically reconciled politics and religion as well as realism and morality without any tormenting internal conflict. I believe that he accomplished this with an aptitude that is all the more extraordinary since he had assimilated it to the point of making it unconscious. We will have many occasions to verify this in the course of the book.

This tendency to form a project does not free his linear biography from his hesitations, his sticking points, his moments of repentance and the contradictions involved in conforming to royal rectitude as defined in that day and age by Isidore of Séville according to whom the word "king" [*roi*] came from "to rule rightly" [*rex a recte regendo*]. If Louis escaped certain dramas, his constant aspiration to be an embodiment of the ideal king casts a shadow of uncertainty upon his biography, which remains impassioning from beginning to end. Furthermore, certain testimonials seem to hold up a mirror for us in which the image of the saintly king has been incredibly deformed.

ANOTHER THING THAT KEPT ME FROM GETTING LOST IN COMPOSING a biography of Saint Louis is that I was quickly able to eliminate another false problem. This was the presumed opposition between individual and society, the vacuity of which has already been exposed by Pierre Bourdieu. The individual exists only within a network of diversified social relations, and this diversity also allows him to develop his role. An understanding of society is needed in order to see how an individual figure lives and forms himself within it. In my previous works, I studied the appearance of two new social groups in the thirteenth century: the merchants, which led me to scrutinize the relations between economy and morality, a problem that Saint Louis also encountered; and university members, whom I then called "intellectuals" and who provided ecclesiastical institutions and, in a less pronounced manner, governments with their leading members. Furthermore, they promoted the rise of a third power, institutionalized knowledge (*studium*) that stood alongside ecclesiastical power (*sacerdotium*) and princely power (*regnum*). Louis had limited relations with the intellectuals and this new power. Finally, I studied the members of a much larger society: one found in the recently discovered "beyond" of the thirteenth century. I am referring to the dead in Purgatory and their relations with the living. Saint Louis had constant contact with death, the dead, and the beyond. The social setting in which the saintly king lived was therefore to a large extent familiar to me. It was likewise my task to recover what was both normal and exceptional in his path of development, for with him I attained the summit of political power and heavenly Paradise.

I gained access to an individual or, rather, I had to ask myself if I was able to gain access to him, as the personal problem opened up into a general process of questioning. Saint Louis lived at a time in which certain historians have thought they could detect the emergence or the invention of the individual. I discuss this at great length in the course of this book. Without waiting any longer, it is, however, very important to remember that Louis lived in a century whose beginnings saw the introduction of the examination of conscience (a canon of the Fourth Lateran Council of 1215 imposed obligatory auricular confession for all Christians), but also, toward its end, the birth of the individual portrait in art. In what sense was Louis an individual? Recalling a judicious distinction made by Marcel Mauss between the "sense of the self" [*le sens du moi*] and the concept of the individual, I believe that Saint Louis was in possession of the first but that he was not aware of the second. In any case, he was without a doubt the first king of France to make a royal virtue of conscience, an individual disposition.

Finally, in biographical inquiry I discovered one of the essential preoccupations of the historian: time. In what is first of all a plural form, I believe that today we have discovered the diversity of times, after a phase in which the West was dominated by the unified time of the mechanical clock and the watch, a time broken down into pieces by the crises of our societies and the social sciences. Saint Louis himself lived in a period that was prior to this time in the process of being unified and on the basis of which princes would attempt to establish their power. In the thirteenth century, there was no one time but only times of the king. Compared to other men, the sovereign existed in relation to a greater number of times, and the relationships that he had with them, although subjected to the conditions of the age, sometimes surpassed the limits of the ordinary. The time of power had its own rhythms particular to its schedule, travel, and the exercise of power. Within certain limits, it could determine the measures of time, and the king also measured time through the burning of candles, the observation of sundials, the ringing of bells, and the changes of the liturgical calendar. Above all though, the biographical work has taught me to recognize a kind of time I was not accustomed to — the time of a life that, for a king and his historian, cannot be confused with the time of his reign. Even if Louis IX had been a king at twelve and remained on the throne for his entire life, to restore an individual, let alone a king, to this measure of social, biological time that runs "from the cradle to the grave" as the ethnologists like to say, opens new perspectives on chronology and periodization. This is a unit of measure for a time that is above all political and even more acute [*plus chaude*] if this time is dynastic, as was the case with Louis. It is a form of time unpredictable in its beginning and end, but a time which the king and only the king carries within himself as an individual in all places and at all times. The sociologist Jean-Claude Chamboredon has pertinently explained the relation of the time of biography to the times of history. I have paid close attention to how the periods and the general manner of evolution in the time of the life of Saint Louis developed in relation to the diverse temporal junctures of the thirteenth century such as the economic, the social, the political, the intellectual, and the religious. Saint Louis was a contemporary of the end of the great economic expansion, the end of peasant servitude and the rise of the urban bourgeoisie, the construction of the modern feudal state, the triumph of Scholasticism, and the establishment of Mendicant piety. The rhythm of these great events marked the youth, the maturity, and the old age of the king in different ways, including the major phases coming before and after his illness in 1244 and before and after his return from the crusade in 1254. Sometimes these events marked his life at specific points, often in coinciding harmonies, and sometimes in shifts that did not entirely correspond. Sometimes he seems to accelerate history and sometimes he seems to slow its advance.

TO WRAP UP THIS INTRODUCTION, I WILL LIMIT MYSELF TO THREE remarks. First of all, we must not forget that whether as individuals or in groups, men acquire a considerable amount of their knowledge and their habits during their childhood and their youth when they were exposed to the influence of older people such as parents, masters, and the elderly. These individuals all had much more importance in a world where age was a sign of authority and where memory itself was more powerful than in societies dominated by writing. Their chronological compass had therefore opened well before their births. If Marc Bloch was right to say that "men are more the sons of their time than of their fathers," we might add: of their time and of the time of their fathers. Born in 1214, the first king of France who knew his grandfather (Philip Augustus), Louis was in many ways as much a man of the twelfth as of the thirteenth century.

Saint Louis' biography presents one other original problem. The king was canonized after his death. We will examine the difficulties that delayed this promotion. Because of these difficulties, twenty-seven years had passed between the dates of his death (1270) and his canonization (1297). During this time, the supporters of his canonization kept him alive in so many ways so that he would not disappear from the memories of the witnesses and the pontifical curia. This period comprised a sort of supplement to the life of the king that I had to take into account. It was also the time of a forceful re-working of his life story.

My goal is then to present a "total" history of Saint Louis, to present it successively following the events of his life and according to the sources and the fundamental themes of the personality of the king in himself and in his time.

Finally, as Borges stated, a man is never really dead until the last man who knew him is dead in turn, so if we do not know this man directly and entirely, we are at least lucky enough to know the person who died last among those who knew Saint Louis well: Joinville. Joinville dictated his out-standing testimony more than thirty years after Louis' death. He died at the age of ninety-three, forty-seven years after his royal friend. The biography I have written therefore continues up to Saint Louis' definitive death, and no further. Writing the life of Saint Louis after Saint Louis, a history of the historical image of the sainted king, would be a fascinating subject, but one that arises from a different set of historiographical problems.

SO, I CONCEIVED THIS BOOK KEEPING TWO PRIORITIZING [*préjudicielles*] questions at the forefront of my mind. Each is actually a different side of the same question: is it possible to write a biography of Saint Louis? Did Saint Louis exist?

In the first part of my work, I have presented the results of my attempt at biography. This section is more clearly narrative in style although suffused with the problems presented in the first stages of this life as Louis formed it.

I have dedicated the second part of this work to the critical study of the production of the memory of the saintly king by his contemporaries. Here I engage in justifying the ultimately affirmative response I give to the question "Did Saint Louis exist?" In the third and final section, I have tried to fray a path toward the inner life of Saint Louis' character by exploring the main perspectives that made him a unique and ideal king for the thirteenth century, a king who realized his identity as a Christly king but who could only receive the halo of sainthood—a magnificent compensation in itself.

This structure and conception of biography led me to cite many texts. I wanted the reader to see and hear my character as I have seen and heard him myself because Saint Louis was the first king of France who spoke in the sources. And of course he spoke with a voice from a time when orality could only be heard through writing. I was finally encouraged to adopt passages from certain texts and certain themes at different moments of my story according to the successive approaches I used to get closer to my character. Echoing these texts is one part of the method I employed in my attempt to end up with a form of Saint Louis that would be convincing and in order to give the reader access to this form. I hope that my readers find some interest in this work and that they experience several surprises as they join me in this investigation.[1]

PART

I

The Life of Saint Louis

From Birth to Marriage
(1214 – 1234)

LIKE HIS DESTINY, THE BIRTH OF ONE OF THE MOST FAMOUS KINGS of France is shrouded in uncertainties. Louis, the second known son of Louis, the elder son and heir of the king of France, Philip Augustus II,[1] and of Louis' wife, Blanche of Castile, was born on April 25, most probably in the year 1214 at Poissy about thirty kilometers from Paris. His father had received this fiefdom from his grandfather in 1209, the year he was knighted at the relatively late age of twenty-two. With the death of his father in 1226, the child became King Louis IX. He would die in 1270. From the date of his canonization in 1297, he would be known as Saint Louis. As a king, Saint Louis often liked to refer to himself as Louis de Poissy, not only because it was a common habit of great persons of the time to affix the name of the place they were born to their first name, but especially because, as a good Christian, Saint Louis dated his true birth to the day of his baptism at Poissy.

The birth of Saint Louis by itself therefore expresses certain fundamental characteristics of the structures in which the history of the French monarchy evolved at the beginning of the thirteenth century. The first of these structures is the importance of biological chance in determining the fate of families and, more particularly, that of the royal family. The fertility of couples, the number and gender of children in a dynasty in which, without proclaiming it as law,[2] tradition pushed daughters and their sons away from succession to the throne, and the mortality of infants and young children were all decisive factors in the transmission of royal power.

In this society, there was no civil state to record the memory of premature deaths (though still rare, the first parish records appeared only in the fourteenth century). As Philippe Ariès has shown so well, it was a society in which the child did not represent any special value that inspired interest, even if his parents cherished him. The number and identity of children of the royal family who passed away early in life remain unknown to us. As it often happened in this time of high infant mortality that did not spare even powerful families, Louis and Blanche, Saint Louis' parents, must have had two or three first children who died at a tender age. We do not know their names, number, sex, and dates of birth and death. At the time of their marriage in 1200, Louis was thirteen and Blanche was twelve. Philip, their first known son, the one who would have inherited the throne, was born in 1209 and died at the age of nine in 1218. Saint Louis only became the eldest surviving son and therefore the successor to the crown at four years of age. The death of eldest sons was not rare for the Capetians: Henri I, the only king from 1031 to 1060, had an older brother, Hugues, who died before their father Robert the Pious. Louis VII, the only king from 1137 to 1180, had an older brother Philip who died before his father Louis VI. Saint Louis himself was succeeded by his second-born son, Philip III, who became heir to the throne in 1260 after the death of his older brother Louis, dead at the age of sixteen. An heir at four, in Saint Louis' case the death of his older brother must not have left any deep psychological marks. As a child he probably had only the faintest memory of the brief time during which he was not destined to be king. Nonetheless, these premature deaths of the elder sons of the royal family obscure the list of kings' names for posterity, since, as Andrew Lewis has shown, royal dynasties and especially the Capetian dynasty did not choose the given names of kings by chance. The basic choices were provided by the names of the Robertan-Capetians, Robert and Hugh (Hugues), and, after that, Eudes and Henri. Then, probably due to the influence of Anne of Kiev, the Russian wife of Henri I, we begin to see the Greek name Philip (Philippe). Later, when the taboos placed on the names of the great Carolingians disappeared with the recognition of the Carolin-gian ancestry of the Capetians, the name Louis (a form of Clovis), which also tied the Capetians to the Merovingians, appeared with Louis VI who was born in 1081. Finally, we also get the name Charles—with Pierre Char-lot, the bastard son of Philip Augustus. Among the brothers of Saint Louis, a Jean and an Alphonse were added to the list, introduced by the queen mother Blanche of the royal family of Castile.

In the Capetian family at the end of the twelfth century, there was a pro-nounced tendency to give the eldest son the name of his grandfather and the name of the father to the second son. Thus Saint Louis' older brother had been given the name of his grandfather Philip (Augustus), while Louis re-ceived the name of his father, the future Louis VIII. We can only read the code for naming the kings of France by keeping track of the eventual deaths of the oldest sons. Saint Louis was born into a dynasty whose emblems—in this case that of royal names—were in the process of being defined.

Otherwise, aside from certain exceptions, people were not interested in children's exact and complete dates of birth, even in the case of children of the royal family. For instance we know that Saint Louis' grandfather, Philip Augustus, was born on the night of August 21 and 22 in 1165 because his long anticipated birth appeared to be a miracle and had been recorded by the chroniclers as an event. Before him, his father Louis VII had had only girls from his three successive marriages and, at forty-five years of age, was considered an old man who might have been unable to procreate—even though his third wife was very young. On the other hand, contemporaries saw nothing memorable in the birth of the future Louis VIII, nor in the births of his two sons, the first-born Philip, dead at nine, and the second-born Saint Louis. Therefore we do not know Saint Louis' birth date with any certainty. As credible sources tell us that he died in 1270 at the age of fifty-six or in his fifty-sixth year, we must hesitate between 1214 and 1215. Some have also thought it was in 1213 or 1216, although this is not very likely. Like most historians today, I think that the correct date is 1214. The reader will immediately make the connection with the date of the great victory of his grandfather, Philip Augustus, at Bouvines on July 27 of the same year.[3] Saint Louis was probably born three months before this impor-tant event, one of the major dates in the historical memory of the French. Although the victory at Bouvines was widely celebrated, no historian of the time, not even any popular historian, ever made this connection. What people consider memorable has changed in nature between the thirteenth century and the end of the twentieth century.

Most of Saint Louis' earliest biographers did, however, note the day of his birth on April 25. This was first of all because Christianity considered the day of one's birth essential due to the idea that the festival or the patron of the day seemed to foretell the destiny of the newborn or, at least, to assure him of a privileged protector before God. This attitude existed outside of any horoscope of birth or "nativity," a type of text that only began to appear in the fourteenth century.

Saint Louis' biographers explained the meaning of this birth on April 25, Saint Mark's Day. Joinville, Saint Louis' close companion, provides one of the best explanations of his day of birth.

> So, as I have heard it told, he was born after Easter on the day of Saint Mark the Evangelist. On this day, people carry the cross in processions in many places, and in France they are called black crosses. So, this was like a prophecy of the great multitude of people who died on these two crusades, the one in Egypt and the other when he died in Carthage for there was much great mourning over these in this world and many great joys that arise from them in heaven for those who died as true crusaders on these two great pilgrimages.[4]

Starting with his birth, thanks to this text that is not an isolated source we have not only been informed about a processional practice concerning the dead, which came from a pagan, folkloric, barely christianized tradition, but also come face to face with an image of Saint Louis that may seem strange to us. Medieval tradition has not transmitted it to our current field of historical memory. Here we get a glimpse of Saint Louis not only as a denizen of heaven, but a Saint Louis who in his closeness to death appeared as a king of the dead and of death, as a funerary king.

THE CHILD HEIR

In 1218, at the age of four Louis became the probable heir to the throne after his father Louis, if God gives them life. The death of his older brother Philip failed to capture the interest of the chroniclers, no doubt because he was very young. He was only nine years old and seemed somewhat far from being king with his grandfather Philip Augustus still on the throne. In 1131, almost a century earlier, another Philip had died at the age of fifteen. He was the older brother of Louis VI, a king crowned as coadjutor with his father. This Philip had been buried in the necropolis of the kings at Saint-Denis, whereas Saint Louis' older brother was buried only in Notre-Dame de Paris where his father Louis VIII and his mother Blanche of Castile erected a chapel for him in 1225.[5]

When the young Louis became *primogenitus,* the official term for the first-born, the heir to the throne, this was not noted as a memorable event. No specific information prior to 1226 about this event has reached us. His parents, and especially his mother, paid special attention to his education, as befitting a future king, not only because it was thought that a sovereign should be morally and religiously formed for royal duties, prepared to protect the Church and to follow its advice, but also because the maxim put forth by the bishop of Chartres, the Englishman John of Salisbury, in his *Policraticus* (1159) that "an illiterate king is only a crowned ass"[6] was inspiring Christian courts and dynasties more and more, inviting them to give future kings a solid Latin education based on the classical liberal arts. We can guess that like the young aristocrats of his time the child had more contact with his mother than with his father who probably took over when he began his military training. As he liked to recall as an adult, the child also grew up in contact with his aging grandfather, the great Philip Augustus who, after his brilliant victory at Bouvines in July 1214, left his son, Louis' father, the responsibility of making war, which he did with limited success. He typically had less success in England for example, but had greater success in Languedoc. Fifty years old in 1215, the king would prefer from this point on to rest on the laurels of the victorious ruler. The new conqueror of Normandy, the victor of Bouvines, became Philip the Conqueror. Several experienced and faithful advisors wisely and firmly governed the kingdom of this sovereign who brought his people the most beautiful gift a king can give—peace. At their head, Friar Guérin, the hospitaler monk who became bishop of Senlis, was almost a vice-king but with no personal ambitions and, because he was a cleric, with no dynastic progeny. Philip Augustus must have loved the presence of his grandson, who would eventually become the first king of France to have known his grandfather. This could only reinforce the dynasty, especially since his grandfather had such a strong personality.

Dynastic power surrounded the child Louis. His father was rarely seen, but bore the nickname the Lion. His two parents had a strong presence in the child's life—the grandfather had been strong and still remained powerful, while his mother would appear as a strong woman of Scripture. There were no models of weakness around the child.

On July 14, 1223, Philip Augustus died of malaria at the age of fifty-seven. His death introduced two innovations into the history of the Capetian kings. The first of these concerned funerals, which took on an exceptionally sumptuous nature. For the first time in France, Philip Augustus was buried following the "royal custom" (*more regio*) inspired by Byzantine ceremony and even more by the funerals of the English Plantagenet kings. The body was exposed with the royal insignia, the regalia. The king was dressed in the royal vestments, a tunic and a dalmatic covered in a sheet of gold. He held the crown and scepter. Buried in Saint-Denis, carried there by a cortege of barons and bishops, his face was left uncovered the day after his death.[7] The king's body was both collective—as an effect of the insignia—and individual due to the appearance of his face, and he was thus solemnly interred. The child, who could neither follow the cortege nor attend the funeral, must have heard about the ceremony. He learned that a king of France was not buried in just any place or in just any way. The king was established as a king more than ever in death.

If we believe the accounts of several chroniclers, the second innovation was that some people at the royal court and in the Church of France thought of having Philip Augustus recognized as a saint. It seems that the only prior case of this involved the Benedictine monk Helgaud de Fleury-sur-Loire who had tried to make the son of Hugh Capet into a saint nearly two centuries earlier. He had not succeeded. The sycophants of Philip Augustus came no closer. However, they claimed that certain miracles had been performed by the king and that, because his birth had been miraculous (he was also Philip Dieudonné), his death was accompanied by signs that mark the death of saints: a comet announced it, and an Italian knight had a vision of it and was healed so that he could bear news of it to a cardinal and the pope, who, having verified the report, declared it in the middle of a session of the papal council. Nevertheless, in 1223 rumors of miracles, comets, and visions were no longer enough to confer sainthood. The proclamation of sainthood could only result from a canonization proceeding carried out by the court in Rome. How could the pope have recognized the sainthood of a king that his predecessor had excommunicated for a conjugal life deemed scandalous in Rome?[8] Whether the child had heard of the aborted attempt to canonize his grandfather or not, and, if this were the case, whether he thought about it consciously or unconsciously, in any case, he would succeed where Philip Augustus had failed. People were able to make a different case in his favor on two essential points. He did not accomplish miracles during his life but after his death, in conformity with Pope Innocent III's decision at the beginning of the thirteenth century to officially recognize only posthumous miracles as true miracles. Innocent III implemented this decision in order to thwart false miracle workers and to keep Christians from following the false prophets and sorcerers who invented imaginary miracles.[9] Saint Louis would also be proclaimed a saint for his virtues and his Christian lifestyle, particularly in married life. The content of sainthood changed in the course of the thirteenth century. People had tried to make Philip Augustus a saint on the basis of an older model of sainthood. Saint Louis would become a modern saint with everything traditional that this included as well.[10]

In any case, Saint Louis enjoyed telling stories about his grandfather. If he happened to lose his temper with a servant, he remembered that Philip Augustus would do the same and that it was only justice being served. Guillaume de Saint-Pathus tells of one evening at bedtime when Saint Louis wanted to see the sore on his wounded leg. An old servant who held a candle above the king's leg in order to cast light on it let a drop of burning wax fall on it: "The saint who was sitting on the bed because of the pain he felt stretched out on the bed and said, 'Ah! Jean!' And the servant Jean answered, 'Ha! I hurt you!' And the saintly king responded: 'Jean, my ancestor threw you out of our house for less than that.' Jean had in fact told the saint king and others that King Philip once kicked him out of the manor because he had put logs on the fire that crackled as they burned." According to his entourage and his hagiographer, Saint Louis did not punish Jean and kept him in his service, thereby proving his goodness and his superiority over his grandfather.[11]

Joinville reports a similar episode, although Saint Louis does not appear superior to his grandfather in it. While the king was in Hyères upon returning from his first crusade in 1254, he was out walking, but the path became so narrow that he wanted to mount his palfrey. When no one brought it to him, he had to mount Joinville's. When Ponce, his squire, finally arrived with his palfrey, the king "bore down on him with anger and reprimanded him severely." Joinville then said, "Sire, you should go easy on Ponce the squire because he has served your grandfather and your father and you." Refusing to disarm, the king replied to Joinville: "Seneschal, he has not served us; it is we who have served him when we put up with having him around us with the bad qualities that he has. For King Philip my grandfather told me that we must reward these people, some more, some less, according to how they serve, and he used to say that no one can be a good ruler on this earth if he does not also know how to boldly and harshly refuse what he can give."[12]

Thus the child began to learn the skills of kingship around his grandfather who was the one that he wanted his readers to think of in his *Enseignements à son fils,* this Mirror for Princes, a moral testament that he composed only a short time before his death for the future Philip III.

> I want you to remember the words of King Philip my grandfather that a member of his council who heard them reported to me. One day, the king was with his private council, and the members of his council told him that the clerics were doing him great wrong and that people were astonished by the way he was putting up with it. And he responded: "I know perfectly well that they are doing me great wrong, but when I think of the honors that Our Lord has done me, I prefer to tolerate the harm rather than cause a scandal between myself and the Holy Church.[13]

Philip Augustus was laid to rest next to his forefathers in the royal necropolis of Saint-Denis. Louis was heir to the throne of France from that point on. Three years later, in 1226, his own father, Louis VIII, joined his grandfather in the cemetery of kings. The child Louis became king of France at the age of twelve.

THE WORLD AROUND THE CHILD KING

Now we must situate the young king in the world around him. We must even situate him in relation to places he would never go and among his great contemporaries, the ones he knew and the ones he would never know, in addition to his interlocutors, his antagonists, and his enemies. In order to understand Saint Louis' place in the history of his time, we must situate him on the broadest horizons. If we circumscribed this history within the narrow space of its hero's life, even within the Kingdom of France, it would not be fully understood because it would lack the necessary references and the appropriate scale. This is particularly important as Louis acted outside the borders of the Kingdom of France within the larger space of Christendom, even if he did not physically appear everywhere within it. He would also leave France to visit the hostile world of Islam in person, venturing forth to North Africa and the Middle East and even, through the intermediary of his plans, his dreams, and his envoys, into the very heart of the Orient, that endless source of marvels and nightmares.

The Oriental Horizon: Byzantium, Islam, the Mongol Empire

Three great entities comprised the essential expanse of the world in which Saint Louis had just become king of France. In appearance, these three entities outshone the small plot of Latin Christendom that included the Kingdom of France. But one of them, Byzantium, had begun its slow decline; the other, Islam, had entered a period of stagnation and fragmentation; the third, that of the Mongol conquest, seemed both vague and splendid in its unifying and devastating power.

The closest force was the Byzantine world. It seemed close in geographical space as well as by its religion and recent military and political history. The Byzantine Empire was like a shrinking skin, eaten away in Asia Minor by the Seljuk Turks, while the Serbs and the Bulgars broke away from it in the Balkans. The Bulgars founded a second empire with the Asenid dynasty, which reached its apogee under the kings Kalojan (1196–1207) and John III Asen (1218–1241). Their religion, Greek Christianity, which was considered the only Christian orthodoxy since the schism between Greeks and Latins in 1054, was more of a cause of conflict than a tie between the two Christendoms. Of course, the Turkish threat made the reunion of the two Churches a priority. This objective gave rise to long negotiations between the papacy and the Byzantines throughout the time of Saint Louis, leading to an official reconciliation at the Second Council of Lyon (1274) four years after his death. However, the agreement was more political than religious and, being superficial, did not last.

One fantasy obsessed Latin Christendom in the first half of the thirteenth century, the fantasy of retaking Constantinople from the Byzantine Greeks and founding a Latin Christian empire there. The dream seemed to come true around the time of Saint Louis' birth. In 1204, pushed by the Byzantine emperor's Venetian creditors, the crusaders of the Fourth Crusade captured Constantinople and founded a Latin empire there the following year. The first emperor, Baudouin I, the count of Flanders, was taken prisoner by the Bulgars at Adrianopolis in 1205 and died in captivity. The Latin Empire held up in Byzantium. Beginning in 1228, the emperor was Baudouin II of Courtenay. Deep in debt, he sold the relics of the Passion to Saint Louis in 1239. In 1261, Michael VIII Paleologus chased him from Constantinople. Obsessed by the crusade to the Holy Land, Saint Louis was in no hurry to help Baudouin II retake Constantinople. The dream of a Latin empire on the shores of the Bosphorus was dead. The hope for Latin Christian domination over the Greek Orthodox subjects of the former Byzantine Empire and for the reunification of an emperor of the Germanic Holy Roman Empire in the West with a Latin emperor in Constantinople, for the old empire under obedience to Rome and the spiritual guidance of the pope, faded. The Peloponnesian remained in the hands of the Latin princes of Morea, while the Venetians and Genoese snatched up the commerce in the remaining parts of the Byzantine Empire. Ultimately, Byzantium would play only a very marginal role in the thoughts and politics of Saint Louis.

At the same time, the Muslim world was undergoing conflicting movements, spurts of power and a slow process of decline, even though this decline was not as marked as Western historiography makes it out to be. In the West, there was the collapse of the great Western Muslim empire that was founded in the twelfth century by the Berber Almohads of Morocco who had extended their domination over the entire Maghreb and the southern half of Spain. After the key victory of the league of kings at Las Navas de Tolosa in 1212, the Christian reconquest brought the fall of Beha to Portugal (1235), of the Baleares (1235) and Valencia (1238) to Aragon, and of Córdoba (1236), Murcia (1243), Cartagena (1244), Séville (1248), and Cádiz (1265) to Castile. Only the Muslim enclaves of Grenada and Málaga remained. The Maghreb split into three domains, that of the Hafsids in Tunis, the Zayanids in the Central Atlas, and the Marinids in the south of Morocco. There would be no Spanish horizon for Saint Louis' crusade since the Spanish took charge of it themselves, while the king of France could cling to the illusion that the sultan of Tunis would be easily converted or just as easily conquered.

In the Middle East, after the death of Saladin the Great (1193) who had retaken Jerusalem from the Christians, his successors, the Ayyubids, divided the sultanate and attacked each other in Syria and Egypt. This did not stop them from defeating the imprudent crusaders who set forth into Egypt on the expedition of Jean de Brienne, the king of Jerusalem, from 1217 to 1221, nor from retaking Jerusalem in 1244, which had been ceded to Emperor Frederick II in 1229 for a considerable sum. The power of the mercenary slaves (Slavic, Greek, Circassian, and Turkish), the Mamelukes, began to rise. They replaced the Ayyubids in 1250. One of them, Baybars (d. 1277) took control of the sultanate in 1260 after chasing the Mongols out of Syria. He razed Saint-Jean-d'Acre, and its capture in 1292 put an end to the incursion of Latins in the Holy Land, as the Latin kingdom, still called the Kingdom of Jerusalem, continued to shrink. Not even a palace revolt, which occurred while Saint Louis was their prisoner in Egypt in 1250, prevented them from defeating the king of France and imposing their own peace conditions on him. The Islamic world, in which Sunni orthodoxy reigned supreme and from which the Mongols took Baghdad in 1258, had lost its political unity and economic dynamism. As Saint Louis could attest, it was still a formidable enemy for the Christian world.

The one great world event in the thirteenth century, however, was the formation of the Mongol Empire. The brilliant giant that rose up on the cusp of the century is Temujin, who named himself the supreme leader, Genghis Khan (Cinggis qan). For the pagan Mongols he was the object of a cult as soon as he died. After the example of all the great Turkic and Mongol families of ancient Central Asia, he transmitted a mythical story of his origins to his descendants: "The origin of Genghis Khan is the blue wolf, born with his destiny fixed in the upper realms of Heaven, and his wife is the wild hind."[14] Genghis Khan transformed the nomadic Mongol world from an empire of the steppes into a universal empire. Born around 1160, he brought to conclusion a social and political evolution that began decades earlier. He eliminated his superiors and rivals and, in 1206, in the course of an assembly reuniting the chiefs of all the Mongol tribes, "he founds the

Mongol State," and took the name of Genghis Khan. He completed the military organization of the Mongols and gave them a civil administration, "with the vocation of governing the world." He believed that he had been elected by "the eternal blue Sky," the supreme supernatural power of Turco-Mongol religion, in order to conquer the world. He marched forth to conquer it in 1207, seven years before the birth of Saint Louis. He overcame the peoples of the Siberian forest in 1207; between 1207 and 1212 he conquered the sedentary peoples of Manchuria and the Chinese marches of the north. The remaining Turkish empires to the west from the shores of the Ili and Lake Balkhash fell under his control. Starting in 1209, he conquered Tibet, the north of China including Beijing (Tahing, 1215), and Korea. He began to attack Muslim countries in 1211, and his great invasion of the West lasted from 1219 to 1223 with the destruction of the kingdoms of Qara-Khitay and the Turks of Khwarizm, the annexation of eastern Turkestan, Afghanistan, and Persia. His lieutenants surveyed, raided, and pillaged between the Caspian Sea and the Black Sea, across the steppes of Qipchaq or Cummans and into the Bulgar kingdom of the Volga. In 1226, Genghis Khan continued to campaign toward the south and definitively captured the Chinese kingdom of Si-Hia and its capital Tchong-hing (currently Ningxia) on the Huang he. He died the following year in 1227. He had planned to split this immense empire among his four sons, but with a unity maintained by the preeminence of one of them, his third son, Ogodei. I will not enter into the complex details of the political history of the Mongols after Genghis Khan. It would take us too far from Saint Louis and would only bring vague and fragmentary information about all this extraordinary history that disturbed and reshaped the larger part of the Asian continent of which tiny Christian Europe was only an appendage. From this enormous movement, Europe encountered only the final release to the west of the extreme Mongol waves in Russia, where they ravaged Riazan, Vladimir, Moscow, Tver, Novgorod, Kiev, and the Ukraine from 1237 to 1240, and the south of Poland (Kraków remembers it to this day), Hungary, and Austria, right to the outskirts of Vienna in 1241. After the Huns of Attila in the fifth century and the Avars from the sixth century until the eighth century when Charlemagne vanquished them, this was the greatest Asian peril that Western Christendom had ever known. Europe was terrified by it.[15]

In this confusion of peoples, Christian clerics found the hells of Antiquity. Westerners identified these Mongols, whom they named "Tartars," with the peoples of Gog and Magog mentioned in the Apocalypse (20:7–8) as the hordes that Satan would unleash from the four corners of the earth at the end of time in order to torment humans in the age of the Antichrist. The High Middle Ages made them out to be the voracious, exterminating cannibals that Alexander had imprisoned behind high walls at the extreme eastern end of the Asian continent and who would be released in this final moment of terrestrial horror.[16] According to the pessimists, these "new demons" would unite with the demoniacal Saracens who were also the heirs of a sacred tradition proclaiming the coming of infernal powers to strike the Christians. "The Mongol invasions, extending the Mediterranean zone of the crusades and the encounter with Muslim civilization, made the threat of the monstrous forces of destruction appearing in biblical and koranic traditions even more palpable to the Western world."[17] An echo of this fear animates the work of the English Franciscan Roger Bacon, who, although marked by the spirit of Oxford, had lived for a long time in Paris. Bacon wrote his major work, the *Majus Opus,* between 1265 and 1268 at the behest of his protector, Guy Foulcois (or Foulques), an advisor to Saint Louis who became Pope Clement IV in 1265. "The entire world is practically in a state of damnation," he cries out. "Whatever role the Tartars and the Saracens may play in it, it is certain that the Antichrist and his legions will achieve this end. And if the Church does not make haste to oppose and destroy these machinations with holy measures, it will be struck down in some intolerable way by these scourges upon Christians. All knowledgeable men believe that we are no longer very far from the times of the Antichrist."[18] The English monk Matthew Paris described them as "inhuman and bestial men that we must call monsters rather than men, thirsty blood-drinkers who rip apart and devour the flesh of dogs and men alike."[19] The imaginary bestiary gets mixed up with reality. Following the usual habit of men of the Middle Ages, the border between dreams and lived experience disappeared. The nightmares were quite real.

Confronted with the threats of Gog and Magog, in other words with the Mongols, the Saracens, and the Antichrist, Roger Bacon saw only one weapon, one possible defense: *Reformatio,* reformation, so that the Church, Christians, and the republic of the faithful could return to the path of "the true law." During the same period, Saint Louis had the same attitude. The misfortunes of Christians, his own people, and the people of the Kingdom of France had their deepest cause in sin, and in order to avoid succumbing to the peoples who were the scourges of God, they would have to do penance to purify and reform themselves.

Confronted with the Mongols, Saint Louis himself at first had been stricken with panic. At the time of the farthest Mongol advance into Central Europe in 1241, the Benedictine monk Matthew Paris attributed this dialogue to him and his mother, while Christendom was submerged in fasting and prayer in order to appease God and assure that he would "crush the pride of the Tartars."

> While this terrible scourge of godly anger was threatening our peoples, I have been assured that the mother of the French king, a venerable woman beloved by God, the queen Blanche said, "Where are you my son, King Louis?" And he came running: "What is wrong, Mother?" Heaving great sighs, she broke out in tears and, although she was a woman, measuring these imminent perils in a manner that was not womanly, said: "What must be done, dear son, against such a dismal event whose terrifying news has crossed our borders?" Hearing these words, with tears in his voice but under divine inspiration, the king replied: "Take courage, dear Mother. Let us rise up to the call of celestial consolation. May a single thing come from these two things. If they fall upon us, we will either throw them down to the Tartarian[20] realms from which they came, these beings that we call Tartars, or they will be the ones who deliver us all to heaven." He meant to say: "Either we will repulse them, or, if we should be vanquished, we will pass on toward God as confessors in Christ or martyrs."[21]

These words would have given courage to the French and their neighbors. In preparation, Emperor Frederick II sent out a letter on the Tartar peril to other Christian princes, evoking "this barbarous people that has emerged from the extremities of the earth, whose origins we ignore, sent by God to correct his people and, let us hope, not to destroy all Christendom but preserve us for the end of all time."[22]

Faced with the Mongols, there were optimists as well, especially once it seemed clear that their incursions into Europe would not continue after 1239–1241. They drew hope from two sources: religion and diplomacy.

The Mongols were pagans and tolerant in religious matters. Several grandsons of Genghis Khan married Nestorian Christian princesses.[23] One of them became a Buddhist. Nothing more was needed to awaken one of the great Christian fantasies of the thirteenth century entertained by Saint Louis more than anyone else: the conversion of the Mongol princes. It was reported that the Mongol rulers followed the more or less serious practice—as was very fashionable in the thirteenth century from the Atlantic Ocean to the Sea of China—of having Christians, Muslims, Buddhists, and Taoists debate for them (Saint Louis had Christian clerics and rabbis argue for him), apparently in the hope of finding a more convincing religion to adopt.

Certain Western Christians also hoped that, whether they converted or not, the Mongols would become their allies against the Muslims in Syria and Egypt, whom they could then take from the rear. In effect, they had captured Damascus in 1260, but the Mamelukes of Egypt sent them packing almost immediately. The year 1260 saw the Mongol conquest grind to a halt everywhere other than southern China. For Christians, the Asian peril would soon become the Turks.

The optimists, however—and Saint Louis was one of them—thought of sending messengers to the Mongol princes in the hope of converting them to Christianity and making them allies against the Muslims. The Mongol khans did the same, although they were less interested in making allies than in finding new subjects. This followed their habitual preference for peaceful submission over military conquest whenever possible.

In the eyes of the Mongols who were used to vast spaces and confrontations with great powers, the Christian West was only a group of weak peoples governed by insignificant rulers. They were not worthy partners in dialogue. Pope Innocent IV had sent Christian ambassadors to the "Tartars" in 1245 as an opening bid for negotiations. In December 1248, while wintering in Cyprus as he waited to debark for Egypt, Saint Louis received a Mongol ambassador from the representative of the Great Khan in Iran, Guyuk, a grandson of Genghis Khan, who requested the meeting. His letter stressed the complete freedom and equality granted to all Christians in the Mongol Empire. Saint Louis responded by sending a messenger to Guyuk. The messenger was the Dominican André de Longjumeau, who bore gifts including a magnificent scarlet tent intended to serve as a chapel. When he reached the court of the khan Guyuk, the regent, his mother, answered by insisting on the expected submission of the French king and demanded an annual tribute. Upon hearing this response in the Holy Land in 1253, Joinville tells us that Saint Louis regretted ever having sent the messenger on this mission. However, when he was still in the Holy Land, a rumor circulated that a descendant of Genghis Khan, Sartaq, had converted to Christianity. Without making him an actual ambassador, Saint Louis sent the Franciscan Guillaume de Rubrouck with a letter for Sartaq that vaguely alluded to the possibility of a common alliance between Christians and Mongols. The messenger and the letter were finally dispatched to the court of the Great Khan Möngke in his capital of Karakorum in Mongolia. The letter had been lost. Guillaume de Rubrouck unsuccessfully explained the Christian faith to Möngke, who sent Saint Louis his own letter in which he repeatedly called for his submission. When the Franciscan returned to Cyprus, Saint Louis had already returned to France, and the diplomatic correspondence between Saint Louis and the Mongols came to an end.[24] However, in 1262, after the death of Möngke in 1259, his brother Hülegü sent a large embassy to Paris (the Tartar monsters had become "twenty-four noble Tartars, accompanied by two Friar Preachers who were their interpreters"). He sent thanks for the gift of the scarlet tent, which had been greatly appreciated, and proposed an alliance in due and proper form with the king of France against the Muslims in Syria. (By this point, the Mongols had figured out the difference between the pope, the spiritual sovereign, and the king of France, the temporal sovereign whom they considered the most powerful of the Christian princes.) The Mongols would provide a standing army, and the king of France would furnish the navy that they lacked. It would be an alliance between the Asian continent and the Christian Mediterranean. Jerusalem and the other holy sites would be returned to the Christians.[25] This opening of a dialogue and these abortive attempts at communication in which the Mendicant friars who specialized in languages could have played a greater role shows the impotence of medieval Christendom, Saint Louis' included, in opening up to a world in which they did not hold a strong position. It seems that Saint Louis and his advisors halted before this call—that was perhaps only symbolic, although in the medieval world symbols meant a lot—for the submission of the king of France to the Mongol khan. They gave no follow-up to this letter. Negotiations dragged on between the pope and the Mongols for several more years with no results.

The entire Orient was a group of mirages for Saint Louis. There was the mirage of a Latin empire in Constantinople and of the union of the Latin and Greek Churches, a goal that was pursued particularly, at the behest of the papacy, by a man who was close to the king of France, Cardinal Eudes de Châteauroux, a Franciscan who had been the chancellor of the

Church of Paris. There was the mirage of the weakening of the Muslim rulers who had been torn apart by internal rivalries and who, nevertheless, had vanquished Saint Louis and recaptured the Holy Land that he had wanted to defend. There was the mirage of a possible Mongol conversion to Christianity and a Franco-Mongol alliance against the Muslims. At a time when Christendom was recentering itself and disengaging little by little from the crusades, when the Mendicant orders themselves were torn between their apostolic mission in the Christian world and missionary work in Africa and Asia, Saint Louis vacillated between his concern for his kingdom and his eccentric dreams. He would never be able to be more than a king who brought crusading to an end and a prince of unreality when confronted with the distant horizons of Christendom. From the Orient, Saint Louis would only acquire remarkable relics and a martyr's halo that the Roman Church would fail to recognize in the end.

CHRISTENDOM

Christendom made up Saint Louis' world as much as France itself.[26] He ruled France as a sovereign and was one of the leaders of the Christian world that surrounded his kingdom. There was no contradiction between these two allegiances, and he felt none. The notion that the unity of the Far West was built around the Christian religion existed in the thirteenth century. In general, it found expression in the terms "Christian people" (*populus christianus*) and "Christian world" (*orbus christianus*). The term "Christendom" (*Chrétienté, Christianitas*) was also used and appeared in Old French around 1040 in the *Chanson d'Alexis*. One day, while speaking in the name of the prelates of the Kingdom of France, Bishop Gui d'Auxerre, addressing Saint Louis, said, "Sire, these archbishops and bishops who are here have asked me to tell you that Christendom [*cretientés*] is waning and being lost in your hands."[27] At the beginning of the first Council of Lyon, Pope Innocent IV defined Christendom in opposition to its adversaries: the insolence of the Saracens, the schism of the Greeks, and the ferocity of the Tartars.[28] This Christendom, a spiritual republic, was also defined by the space it occupied. Innocent IV wanted to shut the Mongols out of the "doors of Christendom" (*januae christianitis*) and set three kingdoms against them: Poland, Lithuania, and Volhynia.[29] A single choice emerged for the Christians (and this was one of the great debates underlying the century of Saint Louis):

whether to give priority to the defense of the Holy Land and crusading, or to stick to the defense of Europe, which implied the conversion of the pagan peoples of Eastern Europe—the Lithuanians, the Prussians, and, farther south, the Cumanians who were threatening Hungary. Was the frontier of Latin Christendom still on the Jordan or on the Dnieper? Saint Louis did not seem to hesitate between the two and opted for what had been the traditional response since 1095 when Urban II preached the crusade at Clermont.

THE RESULTS OF EXPANSION

The tendency of the Christian world was to fall back upon Europe. The spirit of the crusades began to waver. The key to this change in attitudes can be found in the very prosperity of the West. Expansion brought an influx of Christians into the Orient, and the same expansion brought them back to Europe. At the end of the eleventh century, the excessively rapid demographic growth of the Christian world could not be absorbed by Europe, and so this youthful Christendom in which young men were deprived of land, women, and power broke out in internal violence. The first wave of savage feudalism could not be contained by any peaceful inclinations. The Church turned it against the Muslims, and because the Spanish Reconquest could not absorb the surplus of Latin men, greed, and energy, the Church directed them toward the East. However, in the thirteenth century internal prosperity reached its zenith in the West. The "agricultural revolution" and land clearings dissipated famine. There would no longer be any widespread famine in the West.

Progress in the rural economy favored social progress. Although the seigniorial system reined men in within a tight-knit social framework, the freeing of serfs accelerated, and although the air of the city did not make people as free as a German proverb claims,[30] the urban explosion brought people into the towns and revived artisanship and commerce, including commerce with far-off places. Textile production underwent spectacular progress, building continued at an impressive pace, and stone replaced wood with growing frequency. The percent of money used in exchange rose dramatically, and the masters of the mint coined more pieces of high value, the silver "*gros.*" The thirteenth century saw a return to minting in gold, which had disappeared in the West since the times of Charlemagne. Saint Louis was the first French king to mint a gold coin, the *écu,* in 1266. This prosperity forced the feudal lords to grant more freedoms and impose limits on violence. The doctrines of limiting war to "just" wars and confining war to small areas in times of restraint transformed peace from an ideal into a reality. Protection for merchants arose alongside protection for widows and orphans, and because the new society produced a larger number of poor people, it was necessary to address their situation by increasing the number of hospitals and leper-houses. This was done with an ambiguous solicitude that wavered between charity and imprisonment. Alongside the Church, the brotherhoods, and the corporations, a state that bore a slight resemblance to the *welfare state* started to take shape. Saint Louis distinguished himself in this area.

City life introduced new cultural needs and new means to satisfy them. Schools were established in growing numbers and, in the course of the thirteenth century, they taught a growing number of young city-dwellers to read and write. They did not only educate future clerics but also a growing number of lay students. These were mostly boys who learned how to read, write, and count, although there were also some schoolmistresses. Teaching corporations were founded, which took the general name of "university,"[31] and in the Christian society of Saint Louis they formed a new power alongside the Kingdom (*Regnum*) and the Priesthood: the Knowledge (*Studium*) embodied by the universities. The universities gave the Latin language a second life as the international language of knowledge, scholastic Latin forged for the most part within the university colleges. Outside these orders, use of the common language made rapid progress. The vernacular languages became literary languages. Under Saint Louis, the administration of the Kingdom of France began to write in French. He was the first king of France that we can hear expressing himself in French. The theater was reborn as it left the Church and took to the stage in the city. Church festivals spread into the streets, combining studious liturgies with more or less pagan rites from the countryside that began to invade the city. Carnival battles and beats back Lent. A fabliau from 1250 transports the imagination to a new country far from Christian asceticism, a land of plenty, the "*pays de Cocagne.*" Though still in the service of God and the powerful, art sought to satisfy more common aesthetic tastes in addition to its function as a manifestation of power, bringing heaven to the earth as much as it elevated earth to the heavens. The triumph of stained glass bathed the churches in colored light. Sculpture displayed a "beautiful God" at Amiens and made the angels smile at Reims.

The gothic was a festival. On earth as in heaven, the values expressed were still profoundly Christian. Terrestrial gardens—where, thanks to love, one could pluck the rose—were a new version of the Garden of Eden where Eve picked the fatal apple. The earth was no longer a mere reflection of Paradise lost and consumed by sin. Made in the image of God and collaborating in this world on the divine work of the Creation, man could produce and enjoy the goods that would multiply in the Paradise regained at the end of time: knowledge, beauty, honestly acquired wealth, lawful calculations, the body that is born again, even laughter which the Church had frowned upon for a long time, all set off on their eternal course in this world through the work of man.[32] In the thirteenth century, Christendom seemed to lose its barbaric trappings. God's judgment softened as the Fourth Lateran Council (1215) outlawed the ordeal, although it was still slow to disappear in practice.[33] If trials by fire, water, and hot irons disappeared rather quickly, judgment by duels and "battle wagers," the forms of the ordeal preferred by warriors, would only be eliminated much later. Saint Louis would try to abolish them without success.

Attached to the new well-being of their European homes, it became increasingly difficult for Christians to leave for the dubious rewards of crusading. One man who considered himself one of Saint Louis' closest friends, a devoted admirer and a Christian knight whose impetuous nature the saintly king sometimes had to mollify, Joinville refused to follow him on his second crusade:

> I was hard pressed by the king of France and the king of Navarre[34] to take part in the crusade. To this, I replied that for as long as I had been in the service of God and of the king overseas, and since I had returned, the sergeants of the French king and of the king of Navarre had ruined me and impoverished my people to such an extent that there will never be another time when either of us, they or I, could be worse off. And so I told them that if I wanted to do God's will, I would remain here to help and defend my people, for if I entrusted my body to the adventure of the pilgrimage of the cross, when I could clearly see that there would be harm and loss for my people, I would provoke the wrath of God who gave his body to save his people. I thought that all the people who advised him to make this journey were committing a mortal sin, because as long as he was

in France the entire kingdom existed in good peace both within itself and with its neighbors, and for as long as he was gone the state
of the kingdom was only in decline.[35]

So, the seneschal refused to go on the crusade, repatriating his duty to his domain in Champagne. From that point on he believed that the act of following
and imitating God did not involve running away on "the adventure of the
pilgrimage of the cross," but resided in "helping and defending his people"
on his land. And from whom or from what will he save them? From Satan,
the Saracens, or the Tartars? No. He will save his people from the "sergeants
of the king of France and of the king of Navarre," in order to protect the
benefits of Christendom's expansion for his dependents. The seneschal pretended to act like the lord of his vassals and peasants when he was actually
behaving like these new men who rejected prowess and adventure, like the
bourgeois. When he followed the king into the Holy Land twenty years earlier, he wrote that, "I never wanted to set eyes on Joinville again for fear
that my heart would soften me toward the castle and the two children I was
leaving behind."[36] Twenty years later, he was forty-three years old. His children had grown up, but his castle still kept the lord of Joinville squarely in
the middle of this Christian world that he did not wish to leave anymore.

Saint Louis still loved life and this terrestrial existence. Would he have
to be enchanted by this terrestrial image of a celestial Jerusalem in order to
leave again as he did, turning his back on his own century and carrying his
cross toward this Jerusalem that his Christian contemporaries so easily separated from their own sufficient Christianity? Among the prayers attributed
to Saint Louis as he was dying, we find: "Lord God, give us the power to
scorn the riches of this world."[37] He lived out the religious anxieties of his
times to a profound degree.[38]

RELIGIOUS ANXIETIES

The very prosperity of the thirteenth-century Christian world no doubt
contributed to the worries that tormented it.

Since around 1000, the increasing enrichment of the powerful, whether
ecclesiastical or secular, and the increasingly strong attachment to a society
layered in more numerous social classes provoked diverse reactions of

concern and rejection. An intense reaction of spiritual opposition arose both inside and outside of the Church among monastic, ecclesiastical, and secular groups. Its general target was the Church itself and its rapacity, which demanding Christians judged particularly scandalous in the contemporary practice of buying ecclesiastical positions—beginning with bishoprics. People called this practice Simonism after the name of Simon the Magician who had tried to buy spiritual gifts from the apostles. The offensive also targeted the head of the Church, the papacy, the first power to form a monarchical state, claiming financial dues that became heavier and heavier with time, harvesting and manipulating larger and larger sums of money. The cleric-critics composed satirical texts that were sometimes very violent in opposing the Roman curia. They managed to circulate these in ecclesiastical milieus and among powerful lay figures. For example, one of these satires was *L'Évangile selon le marc d'argent*.[39] Wandering preachers spread these ideas, although their behavior was suspicious in a society where every person was supposed to occupy a fixed position. Along with criticism of money, the Church, and the Roman pontiff appeared contestations of certain elements of Christian dogma and of certain religious practices imposed by the Church. Some people challenged any hierarchy at all, as well as the sacraments, including marriage and the sexual morality underlying it, the cult of images and of the crucifix in particular, the monopoly held by the clergy over preaching and the ability to read Scripture directly, and the luxury of the churches. Some demanded a return to the strict practice of the Gospels and the manners of the ancient Church. Men and women were asked "to follow Christ naked as he was naked." Some refused to take any oaths, which undermined one of the foundational principles of feudal society. Saint Louis himself refused to swear, even in ways condoned by the Church. This defiance was usually limited to criticism of power, money, and excess in the use of earthly goods. It called for reform. Sometimes it became more radical, either by rejecting the Church or by attacking essential elements of Christian dogma. This is what the Church called heresy. The Church condemned these anti-establishment movements in absolute terms. The heretic must renounce his error or be completely cut off from Christian society.[40] Heresy was not a crisis of unbelief, but, on the contrary, a fever of faith, the desire to live out the "scorn for the world" that monasticism and the Church advocated, perhaps a bit imprudently, in the High Middle Ages. The movement affected clerics and laymen at all levels of society. The

Kingdom of France could not escape its agitations. The first "popular" heretic known to have existed, some time around the year 1000, was a peasant from Vertus-en-Champagne. He was struck with a religious fit while tending his vines. Heretical clerics were burned in Orléans in 1022. A heretical group surfaced in Arras in 1025. Some of these heretical groups seem to have had ties with the Capetian royal family. This was the case in Orléans in 1020 and in Paris in 1210. Saint Louis despised heresy, although what separated heresy from orthodoxy was not always very clear. Some people will mention his encounter at Hyères with a Franciscan professing the suspect ideas of Joachim de Fiore, a meeting that, to me, seems to be of great significance.[41]

Saint Louis' personal devotion was in line with his aspiration to imitate Christ, if not in his poverty, which would have been difficult for a French king to practice, then in his humility. He was a practitioner of the important movement for penitence that enflamed many who aspired to evangelical perfection. Like many of his contemporaries, he was fascinated with the hermits whose numbers were increasing in the forested and insular wastelands of Christendom. They embodied this flight from the world (*fuga mundi*), from a world perverted by the West's economic expansion. In the eleventh and twelfth centuries, new religious orders strove to reform monasticism, which had become wrapped up in wealth, power, and the abandonment of manual labor. The most appealing was the order of Cîteaux to which Saint Bernard (d. 1153) brought the halo of his immense prestige. By the end of the twelfth century, people were already accusing the Cistercians of having been seduced in turn by the temptations of the world. In the thirteenth century, however, they were still symbols of a reformed and purified monasticism. Alongside the Mendicants, as newly reformed monastic clergy in the thirteenth century the Cistercians held on to Saint Louis' favor. To this day his name is still linked with Royaumont, a Cistercian monastery he founded that was his favorite place to visit.

Nevertheless, the wave of heresy continued to grow at the beginning of the thirteenth century. These heresies are often difficult to identify by the ancient and fantastic names the Church gave them either out of ignorance of their true nature or due to a desire to discredit them as repetitions of old errors condemned ages ago. Among them, the most spectacular and the one that appeared most threatening to the Church and the rulers who defended it was the one we call "Catharism" today. The most common name that people gave to the Cathars in thirteenth-century France is "*aubi-geois*" (*albigeois*). Because they were numerous in the south of France, people called them *Albigeois* in the same way they called the Christian bankers that they considered usurers *Cahorsins.* Catharism was a dualist and non-monotheistic religion. The Cathars believed in the existence of two Gods, one who was good and invisible and who saved souls, the king of an entirely spiritual world, the other an evil god, the ruler of the visible material world who damned bodies and souls. The Cathars identified this evil god with Satan and the vengeful God of the Old Testament. The Church was his instrument in this world, identified with the Beast of the Apocalypse. For the Christian Church, this was an absolute danger. Between this religion that had its own rites, its own clergy, its own hierarchy (the "parfaits" or perfect ones) and official Christianity, there could be no compromise, even though many Albigenses concealed their activities in a mantle of clandestine relations while accepting the façade of orthodoxy. Dualist heresy was a widespread phenomenon throughout the Christian world, in the East as well as the West. Through the twelfth and thirteenth centuries it cropped up in Aquitaine, in Champagne, in Flanders, in the Rhineland, and in Piedmont, but it had two important centers in the East, Bulgaria and Bosnia, and two in the West, Lombardy and Languedoc.[42] Saint Louis would come across it in his kingdom. While his grandfather Philip Augustus had refused to crusade against the Albigenses, his father, Louis VIII had already carried out the largest part of the military campaign against these heretics in southern France. In 1226, Saint Louis led the decisive phase of the crusade against the Albigenses.[43]

Favorable to the Cathars and hostile to his Capetian overlord, the attitude of Raimond VI, the count of Toulouse, certainly played a role in shaping these events, but there is no doubt that the king wanted to take back the initiative from the lords and knights of the North who for their own profit had attacked the lords of the South under the pretext of a crusade. Louis VIII also wanted to put himself on better terms than his father had been with the papacy.

In order to stamp out the vibrant remains of the heresy, the Church invented a special tribunal, the Inquisition. In this court, the Church developed a new and perverse kind of judicial proceeding dubbed "inquisitorial." It was set in motion when a judge was alerted by a denunciation in the form of public rumor or the discovery of a material element revealing a crime or an offense. It tended to replace the accusatory proceeding in which the victim or his supporters called upon the judge and were responsible for providing evidence of the crime. At least in theory, the inquisitorial proceeding had two advantages: the only crimes that it left unpunished were unknown, and one of its purposes was to obtain a confession from the guilty party,[44] which was considered the most objective and irrefutable form of proof. However, as implemented by the Inquisition, the inquisitorial proceeding was secret; it was held without any witnesses or lawyers for the accused who did not know the names of his accusers if he had been denounced. Those accused of heresy were suspected of being liars and dissimulators. The will of many inquisitors to force them to confess led to the use of torture, which became more common in the course of the thirteenth century. When the Tribunal of the Inquisition issued a harsh sentence—which happened frequently—such as a particularly cruel form of imprisonment, sometimes for life, death by immurement, or burning at the stake, the Church tried to keep its hands clean and left the responsibility of executing the sentence to the civil powers. People called this "abandonment to the secular arm." After Gregory IX's institution of the Inquisition in 1233, Saint Louis was the first king to put condemned heretics to death under its law.[45]

The outburst of heresy in thirteenth-century Christendom was only one aspect of a more widespread religious unrest. This ferment had at least two other significant manifestations that for the most part remained internal to Christian orthodoxy.

The first of these was the birth of new religious orders that met new spiritual needs, satisfying the desire certain men and women of high spirituality had to be apostles for society in response to the social and economic expansion. These were the Mendicant orders. As a reaction against the decline of monasticism, which, in the form of solitude especially satisfied the aspirations of aristocratic and chivalric society, the friars, who were not monks, did not live in solitude in the forest that was the desert of the West but among people in the towns. The main target of their apostolic mission was the new urban society corrupted by heresy. Their main weapon was their example of living in humility and poverty, which justified their dependence on charity. In this world in which the spirit of wealth, the lure of profit, and greed (*avaritia*) assumed new forms in response to the increasing pervasiveness of money, they decided to become "mendicants." And the reform embodied in their lifestyle was an advantage that they could use to dedicate themselves efficiently to the goal of social reform.

In the twelfth century, at the end of a long development that transformed the concepts of sin and penitence and that reorganized spiritual life around intentions instead of acts, the Fourth Lateran Council (1215) made individual auricular confession obligatory for all Christians at least once a year. (This would become the Easter confession.) This opened the door to a crisis in psychological and spiritual life through the practice of the examination of conscience, and the discovery of this form of confession that involved repentance gave new meaning to penitence. The Mendicant friars taught the priests how to take confessions, and they taught believers how to make them.[46] They used speech in order to convince. They resuscitated and renewed the art of preaching. They made the sermon a medium that attracted the crowds.[47] Some of them became stars of preaching. A great admirer of sermons, Saint Louis would call the Franciscan Saint Bonaventure to preach before him and his family.

Christians had always been preoccupied with salvation and, more particularly, with the form of the afterlife. At the end of the twelfth century and the beginning of the thirteenth century, the geography of the afterlife changed. A new space for the afterlife, Purgatory, sprung up between Heaven and Hell. It was dually intermediary because it would only last for the duration of history and then be absorbed into eternity. In this place, sinners who had died and who had not been hardened could expiate and redeem the remainder of their penitential debt with their suffering and the *suffrages* of the living before going to Heaven.[48] The Mendicant brothers spread the belief in Purgatory and taught Christians to prepare for death in a different way because it would lead to an immediate individual judgment while waiting for the collective final judgment. To the great displeasure of parish priests, they opened up sepulchres in churches for some people, or at least for the families of important bourgeois.

There were two important and very different characters at the origin of the Mendicant orders: the Spaniard Dominic of Calaruega, the founder of the Friar Preachers (who would be named Dominicans after him) and the Italian Francis of Assisi, the founder of the Minors (who would similarly be called the Franciscans).[49] Alongside these two main Mendicant orders in the course of the thirteenth century, the Carmelites were formed, first in 1229 and then definitively in 1250, and the Augustinians in 1256. Saint Louis was seven years old in 1221 when Saint Dominic died before being canonized in 1234. He was twelve years old when he became king in 1226, the same year that Saint Francis died before being canonized in 1228. Saint Louis would become king of the Mendicant orders. Some people would even suspect him of wanting to become a Mendicant friar.[50]

The other expression of religious unrest in the thirteenth century was the emergence of laymen in the Church.[51] The development of brotherhoods went hand in hand with the spread of piety among laymen.[52] They got caught up in a great movement for penitence that also raised their status in the Church. Conjugality, the normal status of laymen, inspired new religious ideals like conjugal chastity. Women in particular benefited from this promotion of laymen. Saint Claire was more than a copy of Saint Francis; she was the first woman to give her rule to a female order. However, an even newer innovation followed. The Mendicant orders not only gave rise to secondary female orders but also to tertiary secular orders. Under the distrustful surveillance of the Church, which was always careful to control the devotion of laymen and women, laymen embraced a life that straddled the border that separated them from the clerics. In the towns, women especially led a life of religious devotion, although without becoming nuns. They pursued this life in modest lodgings that were often grouped together in a single place. These women were the Beguines, newcomers to thirteenth-century religious life.[53]

These laypersons would often be receptive to the mystical trends in Christianity. Although the millenarian ideas[54] of the Cistercian abbot Joachim de Fiore (d. 1202) stirred up only certain particular religious milieus, the Franciscans for instance, concern about final ends, fear of the end of time, and belief in the closeness of the Last Judgment spurred certain laymen to extreme religious experiences like the processions of the Flagellants in 1260.[55] Sainthood, which previously had been the almost exclusive monopoly of clerics and monks, now included laymen, men and women alike. A merchant from Cremona named Homebon who died in 1197 was canonized by Innocent III in 1199 two years after his death.[56] However, the most famous saint drawn from the laity would be Saint Louis, this Saint Louis who protected the Parisian Beguines, who was a paragon for Christian spouses, and who was at least touched by Joachimism. All things considered, Saint Louis was an eschatological king, a king obsessed with the idea of the end of time. Like most Christians of his time, Saint Louis lived torn between the fear[57] maintained by the Church, disturbed to see the faithful become more and more attached to the material world, and the hope, like the "wait for good things to come," for an earthly life that would be as much an impetus as an obstacle to the future life.[58] The very Christian Saint Louis was also one of the great political actors in thirteenth-century Christendom.

POLITICAL ORGANIZATION: THE EMERGENCE OF THE MONARCHICAL STATE

In Saint Louis' time, the political order of Western Christendom was disturbed again by the resumption of the great conflict between the two heads of Christian society, the pope and the emperor. This conflict became violently intense under the pontificate of Innocent IV (1243–1254), who was confronted with the other great secular figure of the thirteenth century along with Saint Louis, Emperor Frederick II. The emperor was an extraordinary man who was Saint Louis' opposite in many ways.[59] In this conflict, Saint Louis maintained a certain respect for each of these traditional powers. But in this time when the game of chess was starting to become fashionable among the ruling elite,[60] he moved his pawns forward under the cover of neutrality, the pawns of the French monarchy.

The great political movement in the thirteenth-century Christian world was in fact the irresistible rise of monarchy and the state that it built. Begun in the previous century, especially in England, this movement continued in the thirteenth century with the pontifical monarchy, which possessed the increasingly centralizing and bureaucratic nature of the modern state, although it lacked its territorial base (despite the States of the Patrimony of Saint Peter in central Italy) and lacked even more its "national" foundations like those being claimed in Castile, Aragon, and, especially, in France. Saint Louis' widely admired grandfather, Philip Augustus, had taken a decisive step.[61] In a less spectacular way that has received less attention from historians, Saint Louis would take other essential steps in forming a French monarchical state. Although we will discuss this topic again in relation to King Louis IX, this monarchical state, far from being incompatible with feudalism, combined with feudal structures and mentalities. This was the basis of its strength.[62]

What the French or the Spanish managed to accomplish successfully, the English seemed to complete only halfway. The English monarchy that was so strong and resurgent under Henry II (1154–1189) seems to decline under his sons Richard the Lion-Hearted (1189–1199) and even more under John Lackland (1199–1216), and then under his grandson Henry III (1216–1272), the contemporary friend and enemy of Saint Louis. One year after the birth of Saint Louis in 1215, John Lackland granted the Magna Carta under pressure from the English barons. This fundamental article of English political history did not replace royal power with the power of the barons. Instead, it placed a dual limit on royal power. It recognized the privileges not only of the barons but also of the middle and low nobility, the Church, the towns, and bourgeois. It also confirmed that the king was subject to the laws, which were above him, whether these were "existing laws" or the moral law that imposed "reasonable" measures upon the sovereign and prohibited him from acting arbitrarily.[63]

In Germany, on the other hand, despite the efforts and posturing of Frederick II, royal power was in decline. Of course, Frederick II did form a central power in southern Italy and Sicily that might have lasted if it had not been imposed by a foreign presence.[64] However, not only did he fail to reestablish the Holy Roman Empire against the papacy, despite being crowned in Rome by the Pope Honorius III in 1220, he also had to abandon any real power to the German princes in his "Act in Favor of the Princes" (*Statutum in favorem principum*) in 1231.

A form of non-centralized, non-monarchical power extended its influence in Italy. To impose order in the towns, communal power often sought out a foreign power to govern the city with the title of potentate. In this age when religious and secular power were not clearly distinguished, in which people confused moral order with order in itself (Saint Louis himself tended to do away with this distinction toward the end of his reign), sometimes a city would take a man of the Church as potentate. In 1233 in Parma, for example, a movement to instill peace and justice — for instance by fighting against usury, as Saint Louis would do — gave absolute power to a Franciscan, Friar Gherardo da Modena. This was the short-lived but important Movement of the Alleluia.[65] More generally, in the northern part of Central Italy, the most economically, socially, and culturally vibrant region outside of the Kingdom of Naples and Sicily, the Patrimony of Saint Peter, and the feudal Alpine and sub-Alpine states, a division of townspeople into two parties, the Guelphs and Gibellines, began to take shape. They fought endlessly for power and banished one another in succession with the support of the emperor or the pope. This political anarchy contrasted starkly with the region's economic prosperity. As Pisa began to decline, Genoa, Florence, and Venice asserted their economic power in the thirteenth century. They would be eminent partners for Saint Louis, especially Genoa, which would furnish him with most of the ships he needed for the crusade (as it had done for Philip Augustus) and a part of his financial backing.

In Portugal and Spain, the Reconquest of the Muslims dominated the political landscape. Under their warring and conquering kings, Castile and Aragon proceeded to build a monarchical state. Saint Louis' first cousin, Ferdinand III, definitively reunited León with Castile in 1230.[66] In the states of the Crown of Aragon, the influence of Barcelona and the prosperity of Catalonia continued to grow.

In the Scandinavian kingdoms, where cities were few and far between and not very powerful, the royal dynasties struggled against the nobility. In Iceland, the thirteenth century was the great age of the sagas. The first "true" sagas appeared at the beginning of the thirteenth century and they were sagas of "royalty," the political idol of the century in a land that had no royalty.[67] In Poland and Hungary, the nobles had the upper hand, especially in Poland where the rulers had to fight against two forms of German colonization: the intrusion of German colonists on undeveloped lands and in cities, and the formation of a troublesome state of monk-knights whose mission to the pagans (Lithuanians and Prussians) melded with a pure and simple will to conquer animated by a feeling of belonging to Germanic culture. The eastern expansion of the Teutonic Knights[68] was stopped by the Russian prince of Novgorod, Alexander Nevski, at the Battle of Lake Chudskoye or Peipus in 1242.[69] Thus Christendom advanced as it continued to share the same values under the leadership of the Church and a resurgent papacy. Deeply defined and reformed by the Mendicant orders, it was invigorated by the universities and scholasticism with a new intellectual force. It struggled against heresy, imposed order on the economy, knowledge, and religious practice, and even formed a prototype of world economy (*Weltwirtschaft*), and, on a higher level, a common market whose year-round center existed at the fairs of Champagne. It formulated its principles at the ecumenical councils, although only in the Roman West (Lateran IV in 1215, Lyon I in 1245, Lyon II in 1274, dates that circumscribe the reign of Saint Louis). Despite all this, the Christian West suffered increasing political division. The unified imperial power declined (the interregnum lasted from 1250 to 1273). In Germany and especially in Italy, power belonged first of all to the cities that incorporated the more or less extensive surrounding territories, forming city-states in many places. The future, however, seems to belong to the monarchies that built the modern state around the king. Saint Louis' France was on the cutting edge of this movement.

FRANCE

Let us look now on this land of the Christian Far West that made up the Kingdom of France that the young Louis inherited in 1226.[70]

First, France was overall the most prosperous region of the Christian world, particularly in its western regions of Flanders, Artois, Picardy, Champagne, Île de France, and Normandy. The countrysides and the towns were both flourishing. France was also the most populous Christian country with a population estimated at ten million inhabitants among Europe's sixty million people.[71]

Ten million Frenchmen in the thirteenth century, ten million peasants, writes Robert Fossier, who is hardly exaggerating. While the towns and the urban population played a considerable role and would continue to grow under Saint Louis, this happened in spite of their fairly modest number of inhabitants. Under Philip Augustus, the population of Paris surpassed 100,000, which made it the most populous city in all Christendom. At the beginning of the following century, it probably reached 200,000, making it a demographic monster. After Paris, however, Gand and Montpellier had close to 40,000 inhabitants. Toulouse must have had close to 25,000.[72] The other "important" cities of the kingdom—Bruges, Rouen, Tours, Orléans, Amiens, Reims,[73] and Bordeaux—each had roughly 20,000 inhabitants. Certainly, in the urban world we must include those towns that had the status and functions (markets, most notably) of *bourgs* even if on a very modest scale, although their small populations and submergence in the surrounding countryside hardly correspond to our modern criteria. In this society in which land was still almost everything, people belonged almost exclusively to either the minority of lords or the mass of peasants. Saint Louis was fundamentally a king of peasants. These *"vilains"* (the term globally designated the different social categories of the countryside, even though the rate of emancipations was accelerating and even though the number of serfs continued to decrease under Saint Louis) will be almost entirely absent from this book. The sources from the period that inform us about the king are almost entirely silent on the world of the peasants. Although certain charters in the royal acts dealt with them, though they dwelt on the deepest level of the social hierarchy and were ultimately affected by a number of the royal ordinances, the king's name was an abstraction in their world. It is almost impossible to know what the French peasants knew or thought about Saint Louis. I would like my readers to remember the silent presence of these peasant masses. They do not show up in the glorious reign of Saint Louis, although his rule was founded on their labor.

Other material and spiritual goods circulated in this society; they comprised and explained this French prosperity. The fairs of Champagne are generally credited for serving as a "nascent clearing house" for the financing of commercial exchange throughout the West in the thirteenth century. Under Philip Augustus, the fairs took on most of their important characteristics including the regular cycle of six fairs, their major role as a center of financial credit, and their policy of protecting merchants.[74] Philip Augustus profited from the fairs by forcing the merchants traveling between Flanders, Paris, and Champagne to take the "royal road" and pay tolls for safe passage, notably at Bapaume.

The intellectual and artistic movements of this time are no less important. While Bologna became a great center for the study of law, the University of Paris was in the process of becoming the major center for the study of theology, the highest science in Christianity. It received its first known charters from Cardinal Robert de Courson in 1215. Gothic architecture, which some have called a "French art," was reaching its highest point. To mention only those cathedrals where Saint Louis carried out some of the most important acts of his rule, let us note that the façade of Notre-Dame de Paris had been under construction since around 1205. The Portal of the Virgin was made between 1210 and 1220, and the Western Window was completed around 1220. The reconstruction of the cathedral of Reims began in 1210–1211. Most of the new cathedral of Chartres was completed around 1220, and the stained glass windows were put into place between roughly 1210 and 1236. Finally, the construction of the cathedral of Amiens began in 1220. Saint Louis was the king of the great construction sites of the cathedrals. He was also the king of precious manuscripts illuminated in the workshops of Paris.[75]

Under Philip Augustus, Paris had effectively become the primary residence of the king, if not the capital. As a center for the memory and continuity of royal power, it was there that the archives of the kingdom were permanently housed in a small room attached to the chapel of the royal palace. Previously, someone in the king's retinue carried them around, following all his movements, and they once fell into the hands of Richard the Lion-Hearted at the battle of Fréteval in 1194. According to Robert-Henri Bautier, "the great novelty of the reign is precisely its constant recourse to writing."[76] Saint Louis continued this practice, forging a balance between advances in writing and renewed spoken usage.

Paris figured at the center of a system of symbolic sites for the monarchy. This system took shape under Philip Augustus. There is Reims where the king was crowned and where they kept the Holy Ampulla. There is Saint-Denis where the king was buried in the abbatial basilica where Philip Augustus placed the regalia, the emblems of royal power used in the coronation of Reims. Then, there is Paris, where the king most often resided in the Palais de la Cité.

Paris was the heart of what was then called France and would be called the Île de France beginning in the fifteenth century.

The regions that made up the royal domain where the king was the immediate lord comprised one of the wealthiest areas of this prosperous nation. This was particularly true of its center, the Île de France. Louis VII had left Philip Augustus a royal domain that stretched in a long band from north to south, from Compiègne and Senlis all the way to Bourges by way of Paris and Orléans. At the time of his death, Philip Augustus had added Valois, Vermandois, Amiénois, Artois, Gien, Bas-Berry, and Auvergne to his domain. More importantly, he had taken Normandy, Maine, Touraine, Anjou, and Saintonge from the king of England. The royal domain had become four times larger. In a more general sense, the grandfather's reign was a major turning point for the French monarchy.

THE GRANDFATHER'S HERITAGE

In addition to this significant territorial expansion, what Philip Augustus left to his son and his grandson can be grouped into three categories: the administrative, the financial, and the moral. All three contributed to the development of the monarchical state.

Administrative innovation paved the way for monarchical centralism. The master work here was the creation of the bailiffs [*baillis*], direct representatives of the king and his curia in matters of applying his decisions, carrying out the orders delegated to them, overseeing the collection of large revenues, and leading investigations [*enquêtes*] that were assigned to them. They were the prefects of their time. Other envoys were appointed to carry out investigations within the domain and sometimes outside of it. They represented themselves as "defenders of the truth, of the law, and of peace" (C. Petit-Dutaillis). Saint Louis would only generalize this procedure and give it a "mystical" allure: their actions were supposed to assure the salvation of the king and of his subjects. In the domains previously held by the Plantagenets, Philip Augustus kept the seneschals, but used them as bailiffs. The benefit, however, was political. Thus, "kingdom and domain tended to come together" (Robert-Henri Bautier).

In the financial domain, progress came first of all with a considerable increase in revenue resulting from territorial growth, but also from better accounting and better surveillance of income. Upon leaving for the crusade in 1190, Philip Augustus had ordered his bailiffs to go three times a year to the Temple in Paris, where the knights of the order kept the royal treasure, in order to keep an account of it. A portion of the revenues was always supposed to be set aside for unpredictable expenses. After 1204 and the conquest of the Plantagenet lands, Normandy in particular, ordinary revenues probably increased by 80,000 Parisian pounds a year.[77] In the course of the reign, royal revenues seem to have doubled, passing from 228,000 pounds at the beginning of the reign to 438,000 at its end. Philip Augustus's testament in 1222 showed significant treasury reserves in addition to the considerable inheritance that the king left to his successor.[78] Saint Louis would soon inherit this treasury. A king of economic prosperity, he would be a king of financial riches. His political initiatives and his prestige owed a lot to what the kingdom produced in the period that preceded his rule and to the money his grandfather left him. One contemporary source referred to him, quite correctly, as "the rich king." He was a privileged heir.

The society in which Saint Louis was born and would live was one of warriors as much as of peasants. Philip Augustus did not change royal military power as much as the administration. However, he reinforced and adapted it to the development of the economy. First of all, he defined and strengthened the observation of the military obligations owed to him by his vassals and towns. These measures were all the more necessary since the size of the armies grew under his rule. The drafting of sergeants (*la prisée des sergents*), established in 1194 and revised in 1204, enumerates, for example, the number of men that the provostships [*prévôtés*] of the former domain had to provide.

He relied more and more on paid combatants, on mercenaries, both as a response to the spread of the monetary economy and to the feudal lords' growing resistance to military service and to the growing number of men drawn away from rural and urban work by heightened demographic movement. This weighed more and more heavily on the royal finances and released into the kingdom men of war with no fixed position who were violent, unstable, and hard to control outside of periods of military activity.

At the same time, Philip Augustus reinforced and built powerful fortresses that stood against Flanders and the English possessions in the West. One of them, Vernon, on the outskirts of Normandy, was one of Saint Louis' favorite places to stay.[79] He surrounded the cities of the domain with powerful ramparts that could shelter the surplus population resulting from the demographic growth of the eleventh and twelfth centuries. Paris is the most well-known example. Saint Louis would rule in a recently fortified Paris whose walls pressed up against the fortresses of the Louvre and whose two Châtelets faced each other on the two shores of the Seine between the Right Bank and the Cité.

Finally, Philip Augustus left him a moral legacy based on the development of the "royal religion,"[80] advances in the juridical status of the kingdom—even if there were no "fundamental laws"—and the patriotic aura of victory. We have seen that in addition to the traditional coronation, the depositing of the regalia at Saint-Denis and the royal funeral rites of 1223 had manifested the spread of the royal symbols and of the sacred character of the monarch and the monarchy. Still, no document tells us that Philip Augustus "touched" the scrofulous and healed them as Saint Louis would do to his great credit. The great political aspiration of the Capetians was to get away from the supremacy of the emperor, however theoretical it may have been. In 1202, Pope Innocent III declared with the decree *Per venerabilem* that the king of France "recognizes no superior" in the temporal realm. Under Saint Louis, some recalled that "the king holds [his power] from no one other than God and himself."[81]

Finally, Philip the Conqueror had been the victor of Bouvines. The king's return to Paris was an occasion for all the orders of French society to rejoice. We cannot describe this joy as an expression of national sentiment (which did not really exist in the Middle Ages, because there was no French "nation") but it was the first great "patriotic" festival. The main beneficiary was the king and, through him, the monarchy itself, "so much that nothing but their love of the king made the people abandon themselves with joy in all the villages," says Guillaume le Breton in his *Philippide*.[82] The young Louis IX would soon enjoy the Parisians fidelity to the monarchy.

In opposition to these essential gains, Philip Augustus left one big problem for his successors. In 1154, Henry Plantagenet, who had just married Eleanor of Aquitaine, from whom the king of France, Louis VII had separated, became king of England. His French possessions (almost all of the west from Normandy to Aquitaine) made him a more powerful king in France than the king of France. Along with these grounds for rivalry, there was the problem of Flanders, which strained under French sovereignty and whose economic interests (the need for English wool as primary material for its cloth and the need for an English market for it) led it to have better relations with England. The "first Hundred Years' War" soon began. Despite Philip Augustus's spectacular successes over the king of England in the west of France, despite Bouvines where the count of Flanders was taken prisoner, the French had not gotten rid of the English. The heir to the throne, Louis, Saint Louis' father, managed to land in England and have himself crowned in London but he had to beat a hasty retreat. Truces were signed, but there was no peace. Saint Louis would have to fight the English and struggle to put an end to the first Hundred Years' War.

The Brief Reign of the Father

The short reign of Louis VIII (1223–1226)[83] passed on three important legacies to his young son Louis.

The first was his engagement in the south of France. Philip Augustus never wanted to intervene in the region of Toulouse, although he refused to give up his rights to the county [*comté*] of Toulouse.[84] Louis VIII did not share his scruples. He accepted the rights of Amaury de Montfort and headed up the crusade against the Albigenses. Thus he resolutely threw the French monarchy into the Midi, and his son Louis along with it.

The art of governing pragmatically as well as theoretically excited the Capetians and included precautions taken against unpredictable events. This led them to dictate their wills at dates that were more or less removed from

a death that they considered near or far in time and, in any case, as unpredictable. For a Christian of the Middle Ages, and even more for a king who
was answerable to God by virtue of the oaths taken for his coronation, his
kingdom, and his people, the worst death was a sudden one that threatened
to unexpectedly send him before the heavenly Judge still burdened with sins
unabsolved by penitence, and therefore condemned to eternal damnation
and prey to hell. Since the reign of Louis VII, who left on the Second Crusade in 1147, kings made it a custom to draw up a text before leaving for the
crusades. This text was specifically intended to make provisions for the kingdom's government in their absence. Historians inaccurately called this text a
testament. The most well known was drawn up by Philip Augustus in 1190
before he left on the Third Crusade. Some people have interpreted it as an
edict because it made a number of decrees, in particular some concerning
the bailiffs, that set rules for administering the kingdom beyond the time of
the king's absence. Alongside these false testaments for the crusades, we
have to look at other pseudo-testaments. From a familial point of view, these
texts organized the division of the kings' inheritance among their children.
In the case of kings, the family was a dynasty, and these decisions had both
a familial "feudal" character and a general political character. In anticipation
of their deaths, they also drew up commendations for their children (like
the *Enseignements* that Saint Louis dictated at the end of his life for his son
and daughter) or "last wills," dictated on their deathbeds—orally for the
most part—in front of qualified witnesses. Whether truly spoken or merely
attributed to him, the ones that Louis VIII pronounced proved very important. Among all these decisions for the future that historians have not
so metaphorically christened "testaments," we must single out actual testaments intended primarily to indicate the bequests to be given to institutions
and individuals in exchange for prayers to be made by the beneficiaries on
behalf of the deceased. All of these royal decisions took on more or less
obligatory characteristics. The "testaments" of the crusades had a particularly imperative quality. In effect, they were included in the special laws of
the crusades and benefited from the absolute backing of the Church. The
"testament" dictated by Louis VIII in 1225 resembles a "*testament de croisade,*"
as the king dictated it only shortly before leaving to fight the Albigenses, although the crusade against Raimond VII of Toulouse, the protector of the
heretics, had not yet been declared. Furthermore, in a single text Louis VIII's
testament united a familial inheritance arrangement and a testament in the

true sense of the word.[85] In it, he gave the gold and stones from his crown and other jewels (except for certain particularly symbolic and sacred pieces[86]) to the Order of Saint Victor for the foundation of a new abbey, arranged for various charitable gifts and restitutions (the repayment of debts and restitution for exactions), and designated four executors of his will who were all faithful supporters of his father. Respecting the rule of handing down the undivided kingdom to the eldest son, the traditional right of primogeniture, Louis VIII reserved for his successor Louis, who had become the eldest after the death of his brother, "all the land held by our very dear father, Philip, pious in memory, to hold in the same way that he held it, in fiefs and domains, except those lands and fiefs and domains that we exempt on the present page."

The second thing that Louis VIII left to his son for the defense of the kingdom was the Royal Treasury, the gold and the silver kept in the tower of the Louvre near Saint Thomas.[87] However, as we just read, he excluded certain "fiefs and domains." These lands were given to his younger sons following a Capetian tradition of Frankish origin that divided the patrimonial lands among the sons. However, the dynastic tradition limited these bequests in order to preserve the territorial integrity of the kingdom for the oldest son. This tradition was not declared "inalienable" until the fourteenth century. Nevertheless, Saint Louis benefited from the practice that slowly substituted a "stately" notion of the royal territory for a familial and patrimonial one. However, as we shall see, the difference between the wills of Louis VIII and those of his predecessors lay in the fact that the latter, possessing a limited domain, so as not to weaken their heirs, only granted the younger sons (who were few, if there were any) scant lands generally taken from the territories united with the royal domain under their own rule. In 1225, Louis VIII held a royal domain that had grown considerably, quadrupled in size by his father. He thus planned to provide lands for his three younger sons in addition to his heir, Louis. He had three living sons at this date, and would have a fourth born posthumously. He therefore gave them important territories. With this situation that the risks of history (the biological risk and the risk of conquest) made unusual, historians have decided that Louis VIII had innovated and run a serious risk of weakening and dismembering the kingdom. They credit him with creating a perilous phenomenon in medieval French history—the *apanages,* a term that appears only at the end of the thirteenth century.[88]

Louis VIII was in fact conforming to the custom in use among the important aristocratic families of the time. The royal family was an exceptional one in spite of everything else. He declared his purpose in his testament: "Desirous to provide, in all things, he who will succeed us in our kingdom in the future, and in such a way that the peace of the said kingdom will not be disturbed, we have disposed of all our lands and of all our movable goods in the following manner. . . ." His concern was not just theoretical. The past, even the recent past in certain cases, even in France and especially in England and Castile, had shown the harm that could be done by dynastic familial quarrels between fathers and sons and between brothers within a kingdom. Still, Louis VIII left the young Louis with a delicate problem: will the inheritance of the sons cause peace or dissension? In any case, this is another reason for us to carefully follow the relations between Saint Louis and his brothers. How was this system devised for the "sons of the king of France"—crowned or not—going to work?

On the other hand, the third thing that Louis VIII left to his son was a dynastic tradition that was more strongly rooted in the continuity of the French monarchy. In his own time and in a certain historiographical tradition, Hugh Capet had the reputation of being a usurper. One particularly hostile interpretation of this usurpation, echoed in Dante (*Divine Comedy, Purgatory* 20.52), made Hugh into a butcher's son. Even the people who recognized the legitimacy of his selection by the assembly of barons and prelates in 987 considered his ascension as a sign that the Carolingians had been replaced by a new dynasty. For the Capetians, identifying themselves with the Carolingians was a political and ideological objective of the utmost importance. It meant erasing the accusation that they were usurpers, pushing the origins of their dynasty further back into the past, and, especially, claiming direct descent from this character of mythified history, Charlemagne. Thus, they would also be able to reclaim him from the Germans, who benefited by their association with this figure, although the attempted canonization of the emperor carried out at the insistence of Frederick Bàrbarossa at Aix-la-Chapelle in 1165 had been a partial failure because an antipope had pronounced it.[89] However, this goal of the Capetians to be recognized as direct descendants of Charlemagne would only become a "Carolingian fervor," in Bernard Guenée's words, under Philip Augustus.[90] According to Guenée, the "epic literature had prepared the triumph of Charlemagne." The institution of the Twelve Peers appeared for the first time under Philip Augustus,

and it was very likely inspired by the *chansons de geste* from the cycle of Charlemagne.[91] Imagination created the historical reality, the institutional reality.
We find other evidence of this in the fascination with the prophetic spirit
that, as Elizabeth Brown has shown, permeated the reign of Philip Augustus.[92] The political history of Christendom had been dominated for a long
time by prophecies promising that either the emperor or the king of France
was the sovereign who would rule at the end of time. These millenarian
prophecies that had adopted the ancient sibyls, notably the sibyl of Tibur,
into Christian monarchical ideology, combined with others that announced
to certain founders of dynasties that their descendants would end only with
the world itself. According to works like the *Histoire de l'Église de Reims* by
Flodoard in the tenth century, this had also been the case for Clovis to
whom Saint Rémi, under the influence of a miraculous illumination, was
said to have predicted that his lineage would rule forever. Saint Louis would
make a point of expressing his ancestral ties with the Merovingians as well
as the Carolingians, establishing continuity between what people would later
refer to as the three races, the Capetians being the third. The royal given
name Louis, moreover, related the Capetians not only to the Carolingians
from Louis the Pious through Louis V (who died in 987 and was succeeded
by Hugh Capet), but also to Clovis whose Latin name (*Hludovicus* or *Chlodovi-
cus*) was the same as Louis (*Ludovicus*).

In the time of Philip Augustus, another prophecy demanded a "return to the race of Charlemagne" (*reditus ad stirpem Karoli*). The prophecy of
Saint Valéry stated that this saint had promised Hugh the Great that his son
Hugh Capet and his lineage would hold the Kingdom of France "until the
seventh succession." But Philip Augustus was the seventh Capetian king.
Would the dynasty falter? The return to the race of Charlemagne was supposed to allow the Capetians to cross these dangerous straits beyond the
seventh reign. Some claimed that Philip Augustus's Carolingian ancestry
also came through his mother, Adèle de Champagne.[93] This thesis was advanced by the *Histoire des Francs jusqu'en 1214* (*Gesta Francorum usque ad annum
1214*). In 1208, Philip Augustus named his newly born bastard son Charlot, a diminutive that was evidently neither pejorative nor disrespectful. (He
would later become the bishop of Noyon.) After 1214, Guillaume le Breton
gave the nickname *Carolides* to the victor of Bouvines. However, the genealogical reference that succeeded best was the one put forth by André de
Marchiennes (an abbot whose patrons were the counts of Hainaut) in his

Histoire succincte des faits de la succession des rois de France (*Historia succincta de gestis et successione regnum Francorum*) in 1196. The author emphasized the Carolingian ancestry of Isabelle (or Elisabeth) de Hainaut, Philip Augustus's first wife and the mother of their oldest son Louis. Isabelle descended from the second-to-last Carolingian king, Louis IV, and his son Charles de Lorraine who was pushed aside by Hugh Capet. If Louis (who in effect would become King Louis VIII) became king, the kingdom would have reverted to the race of Charlemagne.[94] This was what happened in 1223 with the accession of Louis VIII, the eighth Capetian king. Saint Valéry's prophecy had come true. Three years later, the child Louis in turn became the king descended from Charlemagne. This return to Charlemagne was credited to his rule first in 1244 in the *Speculum historiale* (*Miroir de l'histoire*) written in Latin by the Dominican Vincent de Beauvais working under the king's protection. It was subsequently confirmed by the rearrangement of the royal tombs in Saint-Denis,[95] which took place between 1263 and 1267 at Saint Louis' request. It was finally proclaimed in 1274 in the French version of the *Grandes Chroniques de France* composed by the monk Saint-Denis Primat, as at the end of his life Saint Louis had asked him to do this.[96]

THE DEATH OF THE FATHER

Let us return to the child who, at twelve years of age, became king of France. His father, Louis VIII, had taken the cross against the count of Toulouse, the protector of the heretics, on January 30, 1226. He decided to attack first in Provence, taking the road of Lyon and Provence. Meeting with resistance at Avignon, he laid siege to the city and took it in August. He then easily obtained the surrender of Languedoc (Béziers, Carcassonne, Pamiers) and decided to return to Paris in October by way of Auvergne. At the end of the month, he was stricken with dysentery and had to stop at Montpensier.[97] The illness quickly took hold, and his death approached. At thirty-eight years of age (he would be thirty-nine in 1226), in his testament of 1225 he had made no provisions for the government of the kingdom in his absence or in case of death.[98] This customary precaution taken by the kings of France upon leaving overseas for the crusades must not have seemed necessary to him in this case of a crusade within the borders of the kingdom.

He had to call a council. The automatic succession of the young Louis who had become *primogenitus,* the eldest son of the king, did not seem safe. For the first time since the beginnings of the Capetian dynasty, in other words in more than two centuries, a ruling king, Philip Augustus, had not crowned his eldest son king while he was still alive. The continuity of the dynasty seemed safe at the time, and on this point the Carolingian model (the Carolingian sovereigns had generally crowned their inheritors king during their lives) had been ignored. Still, a certain number of risks appeared. The heir was still a child. The dying king had a half brother, the son of Philip Augustus and Agnès de Méran, Philip Hurepel (the *Hérissé* or "Bristling One"), count of Boulogne. He was in the age of strength, twenty-five years old, while a number of powerful barons and vassals were displaying a lack of enthusiasm for serving the king. Thibaud the count of Champagne, Pierre Mauclerc the count of Bretagne, and Hugues de Lusignan the count of the March had left the royal army in late July after the expiration of their forty days of obligatory service, before the end of the siege of Avignon. Finally, certain lords were unhappy with the fact that one of the most powerful barons of the kingdom, the count of Flanders, Ferrand de Portugal, one of the losers at Bouvines, was still harshly imprisoned in the tower of the Louvre twelve years later.

On November 3rd, Louis VIII summoned his barons, prelates, and other important figures in the army into the room where he was dying. There were twenty-six people in all, including the archbishops of Sens and Bourges, the bishops of Beauvais, Noyon, and Chartres, his half brother Philip Hurepel the count of Boulogne, the counts of Blois, Monfort, Soissons, and Sancerre, the lords of Bourbon and de Coucy, and certain high dignitaries in his retinue. He made them promise to swear in person, upon his death, homage and loyalty to his son Louis, or to his second-born Robert in case of Louis' death, and to have Louis crowned king as quickly as possible.[99]

This is the only decision Louis VIII made that is supported by an irrefutable document. Other less definite texts relate additional information about the subsequent acts of the dying king. According to the chronicler Philippe Mousket (or Mouskès), the bishop of Tournai who died in 1241, Louis VIII summoned three of his most faithful supporters, old advisors to his father Philip Augustus, Barthélemy de Roye and Jean de Nesle, to whom, along with several others, his father had confided the surveillance of the two most important prisoners taken at Bouvines, the count of Boulogne and the count of Flanders. He also summoned Friar Guérin who, more than a gray eminence, had been a kind of acting vice-king at the end of his father's rule. According to Mousket, he implored them to "take his children under their protection."[100] This was not an official mission, but, as François Olivier-Martin describes it, "the king simply wanted to confide the lives and well-being of his children to very dear friends and very reliable companions."[101] These two circles comprised Saint Louis' entourage: one was filled with the powerful men who made up his "council," or who rather prefigured this group, drawn from the royal curia of barons, prelates, and individuals elevated by the king's favor in order to assist him in making important decisions; the other circle was made up of intimate friends in whom he confided more secret information, whom he charged with more personal missions, and whom he sometimes consulted for less interested and more friendly advice.

After putting this request to his faithful supporters, Louis VIII still said nothing about one essential problem. Who would govern the kingdom in the name of this child king? There were no texts and no traditions that anticipated this question. In this case, it was no longer a matter of indicating who would be responsible for ruling during the absence of a king who left on a crusade. That situation had arisen twice. In 1147, when Louis VII left on the Second Crusade, he had selected a triumvirate consisting in his closest councilor, Suger, the abbot of Saint-Denis, the archbishop of Reims (Saint-Denis and Reims are already paired together!), and a layman, the count of Nevers, who withdrew to a cloister almost immediately after and was replaced by the count of Vermandois, a close relative of the king. The archbishop of Reims withdrew into the background. The count of Vermandois wanted to pursue his own personal ambitions. Suger pushed him aside, and the abbot of Saint-Denis directed the government of the kingdom by himself in the absence of the king.

In 1190 on the eve of his departure for the Third Crusade, Philip Augustus had confided the kingdom to his mother, Adèle de Champagne, the widow of Louis VII, and to Louis VII's brother, his maternal uncle, Guillaume aux Blanches Mains, the archbishop of Reims. The widow of the previous king, the current king's mother, could therefore exercise a function that later historians have inaccurately called a "regency." This term only appeared at the end of the fourteenth century and from that point on designated a more official function with a much clearer juridical definition. In the twelfth and thirteenth centuries, this position was merely one of "guardianship and tutelage," even if the people designated by the king or by some other member of the group were effectively called upon to govern.

In one single previous case, the selection of temporary rulers involved the government of the kingdom during the minority of a king. When his father, Henri I, died in 1060, Philip I had been crowned at Reims the previous year. He was only seven or eight years old.[102] Henri had confided the protection of his son and the kingdom to his brother-in-law, Baudouin V, the count of Flanders. Since there was no problem of succession, and because traces of the "post-Carolingian" lineage were still heralded, the choice of king had clearly been dictated by a desire to assure the young successor and the government of the kingdom of the power and authority of one of the most powerful lords among all those that a text from 1067 referred to as "the princes of the royal palace" (*principes regalis palatii*).[103]

In the days following the death of Louis VIII at Montpensier on November 8th and after his funeral rites at Saint-Denis on November 15th, people noticed that the tutelage of the young king and the kingdom had passed into the hands of Louis VIII's widow, the queen mother Blanche of Castile who was thirty-eight years old.

This arrangement appeared legal due to an unquestionably authentic though unusual act. In this act conserved in the Treasury of charters, in other words, in the royal archives, the archbishop of Sens and the bishops of Chartres and Beauvais informed unnamed addressees, most likely the entire group of the prelates of the kingdom for whom Louis VIII spoke on his deathbed, of his will to place his son and successor, the kingdom, and his other children under the "bail and tutelage" of Queen Blanche, their mother, until Louis reached the "legal age."[104] This act is dated 1226, but with no indication of the month or day. It most certainly dates from after November 8th, the date of Louis VIII's death. He is mentioned in the act as already deceased. It must also precede April 19, 1227, Easter Day and the beginning of the New Year according to the official custom of the time.

First of all, it was strange that Louis VIII had never indicated in his testament or in his solemn declaration made before the group of powerful figures assembled around him on November 3, 1226, whom he designated to rule or at least wished to exercise what we would now call regency. Maybe he was paralyzed by this odd timidity that seems to have afflicted the Capetians when they were faced with hard decisions concerning not only the government of the kingdom but also familial, dynastic problems. A second strange condition appeared in the fact that he identified three of the five bishops who had been present at his declaration of November 3rd as the only witnesses of his decision, or what passed for it. As far as we can tell, they had not yet left Montpensier. The eminent archbishop of Sens, a superior to the bishop of Paris and an equal of the archbishop of Reims (although the last man to hold this title had recently died and no replacement had been named) figured alone here as the royal prelate par excellence.

Historians have come up with various hypotheses to explain this document that was essential for the life of the future Saint Louis, as his mother's tutelage shaped his personality more than anything else. For some, the act relates what really happened—the archbishop of Sens and the two bishops only transcribed the last wishes that were truly uttered by Louis VIII. Others have considered this act a fabrication intended to lend the weight of the king's decision to the actual situation that arose after his death, interpreting it as a major coup that Blanche of Castile pulled off in order to seize power. A variation on this second hypothesis seems to me most likely to be closest to the truth, although it cannot be proven. Certain terms in the declaration of the three prelates can be interpreted in a very different sense that opposes the authenticity of Louis VIII's decision. They stress that the king, although he was dying, was fulfilling the conditions that made the expression of his last wishes legal and enforceable. He apparently made things known to them that cannot be considered simple intentions or recommendations, but which are presented only as sovereign decisions ("he wanted and decided"[105]), and they stress that the king made his decision "after lengthy deliberation"[106] and that he was therefore "of a sane mind,"[107] emphasizing this in a way that sounds as dubious as it appears convincing. This allows us to piece together the following scenario: those faithful to the king, devoted above all to the dynasty and the continuity and consolidation of the monarchical government, lacking any official will from the dying king, came together to address the situation. This meeting became particularly necessary due to the fact that one group of the faithful, Barthélemy de Roye, Jean de Nesle, the chancellor Guérin, and the bishop of Senlis were in Montpensier, while the others remained in Paris. Their goal was to assure the continuity of the government that they themselves had in fact exercised since the reign of Philip Augustus and during the brief reign of Louis VIII, although none of them had a "social position" that would allow him to impose his will, alone or with others, as the guardian of the young king and kingdom. No doubt, they wanted to avoid two possible outcomes. The first and most obvious, which perhaps led Louis VIII to maintain a guarded silence, was the idea of confiding the "regency" to the adult male who was closest by blood to the young king, his uncle, the half brother of the dead king, the son of Philip Augustus, Philip Hurepel, count of Boulogne. Philip Hurepel was a powerful baron at the height of his strength at twenty-five years of age. His position was strengthened even more by his marriage and his father's generous gifts, which had provided him with five counties. To give him the "regency" would threaten the tradition that had been patiently established in favor of the oldest son of the king.

The second possibility to be avoided was the constitution of an assembly of barons who would have governed in young Louis' name. According to a contemporary chronicler of Saint Louis, Hugues de la Ferté-Bernard,[108] the Minstrel of Reims, a troubadour-knight, this was in effect demanded by the interested parties. It therefore seems that the "governing team"[109] had the idea of entrusting the tutelage of the king and the kingdom to Queen Blanche who, as a woman and a foreigner, would be obligated to follow their council. They could have persuaded the archbishop of Sens and the bishops of Chartres and Beauvais to send the letter in which they declared having been witness to Louis VIII's naming of Blanche of Castile as guardian. They would have been ready to protect the royal succession according to the traditional custom of primogeniture, as were most of the prelates who had supported the Capetian dynasty since the time of Hugh Capet. Even if this scene were true, it is not hard to imagine that the "governing team," far from having chosen Blanche for her supposed weakness, on the contrary, had confided this weighty responsibility to her because they considered her worthy of it and already appreciated her determination. Blanche had left for Montpensier after hearing the announcement of her husband's sickness and met only with his coffin on the way to Saint-Denis. The chroniclers show her suffering from a violent grief that she finally expressed during the funeral ceremony. However, once Louis VIII was buried, she committed herself entirely to the claim and defense of her son, the child king, and to maintaining and reinforcing the power of the French monarchy. She seized on the power that the king or the governing team had given her during the time of Louis' minority, exercised it with strength, and never let it fall.

A Plague on the Land Whose Ruler Is a Child

Now we have a twelve-year-old child at the head of the kingdom. There had been no child king for over a century and a half. The feeling that spread among the subjects of the kingdom—including, no doubt, among those who hoped to take advantage of the situation—was at the very least one of worry and maybe even outright distress.[110]

One essential function of the king was to connect the society that he ruled to the divinity. Although singled out by his birth and a dynastic tradition, the medieval king was still the elect of God, and this was particularly true of the king of France. Through his coronation, he was the anointed of the Lord. Even when God was angered with the people of a Christian kingdom, the king shielded his people from harm. Moreover, communication between God and the people and the kingdom passed through him. Even though he was legitimately royal and anointed, a child was a fragile intermediary in this position. The minority of a king was a trial to be endured.

Now, we must examine the evidence about childhood in the Middle Ages, because it explains Louis' entry into royalty.

Historians have discussed the place of children in medieval society and the image of the child in the value system of the time. This place and this image evolved, but along with Philippe Ariès, I believe that childhood itself had little value in the Middle Ages. Of course, it was not that people did not love children. But, aside from the part of human nature that pushes parents to love their children,[111] people loved the man or woman in them that they would become.[112] The childhood of the model man in the Middle Ages, the saint, was negated and denied. A future saint expressed his saintliness by acting like a precocious adult.

The saint in the Middle Ages embodied a commonplace privileged since late Antiquity, that of the *puer-senex,* the elderly child. According to Curtius, "this topos is a reflection of the dominant mentality at the end of Antiquity. In their beginnings and near their end, all civilizations sing the praise of youth and venerate old age at the same time. However, only a civilization in decline could cultivate a human ideal that tended to destroy the opposition between age and youth by uniting them in a kind of compromise."[113] This topos evolved in the course of the Middle Ages. It was adapted to Christianity. It developed at the end of the sixth century through the important example of Gregory the Great, one of the great authorities in medieval times. Gregory applied this topos to one of the figures that would come to dominate the medieval imagination, Saint Benoît, the second father of Latin monasticism after Saint Martin. In his life of Saint Benoît, Gregory says of him: "He was a venerable man in his life . . . from childhood on he had the heart of an old man." This is exactly what people would say about Saint Louis. Geoffroy de Beaulieu recalled that as a child "he became a more perfect man with every passing day."[114] Henri-Irène Marrou had spoken of "man against child" in Antiquity. I would like to point out that in the Middle Ages there were small adults and no children.[115] Childhood was a bad time that everyone had to survive. "This is childhood," Jean-Charles Payen has emphasized, it means "acting in unreasonable ways." The attitude of adults toward children gave the impression that they felt they were very close to the original sin. Adults had always received baptism in the Christian tradition; from that time on it was administered as quickly as possible after birth as if to give the child the strength to resist Satan and the bad instincts that seem to be the "natural" tendencies of youth. How could a king who was either a priest-king or a warrior-king or a benefactor—or all three at once—be embodied in a child who was incapable of dealing with the sacred, being a conqueror, and creating riches?

In every state, the man of the Middle Ages and his ideological mentor, the Church, looked to Scripture in order to understand the child in depth. What do they find in Scripture that explained the status of children?

In the thirteenth century, in matters of political theory the authoritative text for clerics that dealt with the problem of the child king was the *Policraticus* (1159) by John of Salisbury. This Englishman was a collaborator of Thomas Becket. He spent the larger part of his life in France at the schools of Paris and Reims with his friend the abbot of Saint-Rémi, Pierre de Celle, and finally in Chartres, which, along with Paris, was the great scholarly center of the twelfth century. He was bishop of Chartres until his death in 1180.[116] John of Salisbury was one of the great representatives of Christian humanism in the twelfth century, one of the great intellectuals who developed a synthesis between the idea of nature that was reborn in Chartres,[117] the thought of Classical Antiquity reintegrated into Christian philosophy, and the great movement of Christian theology that was in the midst of a major renewal.

John of Salisbury treated the subject of the child king in a chapter on the king as head of state. John introduced the theme of society as a human body into medieval Christian political thought. The fact and the principle that John dealt with here was hereditary succession, which was justified by divine promise and familial right, although it followed from nature. The king's natural successor must respond to the need for justice like his predecessor. A rupture in divine legitimacy arises when the father or the son go against this need. Any wrong done by the unjust royal father is sanctioned by God who refuses him any progeny. The Bible and ancient history show that bad kings do not benefit from the gift of succession. For instance, Saul and his three sons perished in the battle of Gilboa against the Philistines (1 Samuel 31); Alexander and Caesar had no royal descendants.[118]

Let's look at the biblical sources on the child king or on the king as he exists between youth and old age. His youth is hard to distinguish from his maturity because the philosophical and ideological division between them is unclear. The record includes three documents. The first is the example of Roboam. The son of Solomon lost a large part of his kingdom as punishment by God for scorning the council of the elders and following the council of youth. Afterward, he ruled over only Judah, while Jeroboam became king of the other tribes of Israel (1 Kings 12). We can identify the moral of the story with the help of the second document, the imprecation of Ecclesiastes (10:16–17): "Woe to thee, O land, when thy king is a child."[119] From Roboam, we move to the third document in the group and the example of Job (Job 28–29) who recalls happy times in the past: "When I went out to the gate through the city, when I prepared my seat in the street! The young men saw me, and hid themselves: and the aged arose, and stood up."

In his *Conquest of Ireland* (*Expugnatio Hibernica* 2.35) written in 1209, Giraud de Galles (also known as the Cambrian) explained the decline of Ireland and the failure of the government of Prince John, the son of Henry II, as a result of his young age: "If a country is governed by a prince, even if it formerly enjoyed a prosperous situation, it will be cursed [allusion to Ecclesiastes 10:16–17], especially if, primitive and lacking in education, it is confided to a primitive being who needs to be educated."

This was the ideological context made up of bad examples and biblical angst predominant among the clerics when Louis became king at the age of twelve. They could not possibly guess that the king was a future saint and apply the topos of the elderly child to him. Their only hope was that his mother and his entourage would continue to give him a good education and reinforce it, which alone could successfully combat the weaknesses and dangers of childhood and especially of the childhood of kings. John of Salisbury had already appealed to the need for the king to provide for the education of his heir.[120] However, it was under Saint Louis and at the request of the royal family that Vincent de Beauvais would define the education of royal children in a way that gave new value to the image of the child in the middle of the thirteenth century.[121]

Louis' accession to the throne threw his kingdom and its subjects into a dangerous period in which the king's role as mediator between them and God was in danger of being weakened. Thinking of this young, fragile king, did they know when his childhood, or to speak in juridical terms, his minority would end?

In the decision that the three prelates attributed to his dying father, Louis VIII remained unclear about this subject. He supposedly confided the tutelage of the young king to his mother until he reached "the legal age" (*ad aetatem legitimam*). To the best of our knowledge, there was no legal age of majority for kings in France. We must wait for Charles V in 1374 for a king that set it at fourteen.[122] Canonical law offered no ruling on the topic.[123] No text of Roman law on the subject was still valid. The customs varied, and the historical examples were not very clear.[124] The old Germanic majority was fourteen years, but the Carolingian kings were crowned at thirteen. The age of the majority became twenty-one for nobles in most principalities beginning in the eleventh century, while it was still fourteen for commoners. Montesquieu thought that the production of heavier arms set the age for military service and therefore the age of majority back. However, the dubbing of young nobles usually took place earlier, although the father of Saint Louis, the future Louis VIII, had only been knighted at the age of twenty-one (or twenty-two) in 1209, as we have seen.

In 1215, a letter from the future Louis VIII mentioned that the age of majority was fixed at twenty-one in the Kingdom of France. The duke of Burgundy Hugues IV, the count of Champagne Thibaud IV, and the count of Brittany, Jean le Roux only attained their majority at twenty-one years of age. Saint Louis' *Établissements* (1270) and Philippe de Beaumanoir's *Coutumes du Beauvaisis* (ca. 1280) indicated that nobles only became adults at the age of twenty-one. However, a document from 1235 declared that in Flanders the sons of the countess Jean d'Avesnes and his brother Baudouin, fifteen and sixteen years old, must be considered major ("their age is sufficient") according to the customs of Flanders. Saint Louis' brothers were knighted and granted possession of their "apanages" (privileges, lands) at twenty-one, Robert in 1237, Alphonse in 1241, and Charles in 1247. The son and successor of Saint Louis, the future Philip III the Bold, was similarly knighted at twenty-one in 1267.

It still seems that the general tendency had been to recognize the majority of the Capetian kings somewhat earlier at fourteen or shortly thereafter. In effect, there was a desire to limit as much as possible the period in which the king, as guarantor of the kingdom and its divine protection, was not in complete control of his powers. Hence for nearly two centuries the very early coronation that took place before the father's death and then as soon as possible thereafter advanced the age of majority to the time of adolescence. Philip I governed alone around the age of fourteen, and Philip Augustus was also considered major as king, ruling on his own at fourteen.

For Saint Louis, the situation was still unique and unclear. We do not know when he was considered major and began to act accordingly. It certainly was not at fourteen. This was because, since his accession to the throne, a woman, his mother, Blanche of Castile held power and clearly had no desire to give it up. Saint Louis seems to have adapted to the situation. Perhaps his mother kept him waiting in the wings. Instead, I believe that there was such an understanding between mother and son that a form of shared government between them almost imperceptibly succeeded the mother's tutelage, without allowing us to say that the son ruled without governing because his authority became apparent early on. On at least three occasions that we will return to here, the campaign of Brittany in 1231, the resolution of the conflict between the University of Paris and the royal provost [*prévôt*] in the same year (he was seventeen at the time), and the conflict with the bishop of Beauvais in 1233, Louis seems to have acted on his own and even taken a stance opposed to his mother in the University affair.

After his marriage at twenty in 1234 and his twenty-first birthday the following year, Saint Louis probably governed on his own, even if it were still with his mother at his side. The acts mention them together on the same level for a long time. If his name appeared alone in certain acts beginning in 1235, other parallel acts show the king's correspondents soliciting the mother at the same time, usually to get her to use her influence on her son. It seems that this was not simply for formality's sake, but rather the recognition of a unique situation and an appeal to the continuity of authority. Blanche was the queen. For a time there were three queens in France, the widow of Philip Augustus, the Danish Ingeburg, who had been shunned for

so long and who was living for the most part in her domain of the Orléanais where she died in 1236, Blanche, and Marguerite de Provence whom
Saint Louis married in 1234. Blanche was the only one who was always called
only "the queen" (*regina*), while Ingeburg was referred to as the "queen of
Orléans" (*regina Aurelianensis*), and Marguerite as the "young queen" (*juvenis
regina*).

Since 1227, however, Saint Louis, though still a child, received homage
from his vassals and the declaration of loyalty from his lords on his own.
More importantly, he had been crowned since the end of 1226.

THE CORONATION OF THE CHILD KING

After receiving homage from the barons and prelates, the first act on behalf
of his son that Louis VIII had called for was his coronation. He had asked
that it be carried out as quickly as possible. For the sake of his royal nature,
it was important that the child become a full-fledged king as soon as possible both to make any challenge to his legitimacy more difficult and, more
essentially, to put an end to the period of anxiety that took hold when one
king had died and the next had not entirely become his successor.

A miniature from the *Heures de Jeanne de Navarre* executed in the first
half of the fourteenth century shows the young Louis and his mother in
a litter on their way to Reims for the coronation.[125] The image shows the
queen already exercising her tutelage over the child king and in possession
of power, the crown on her head, as he moves forward to sacred status. He
appears with a halo on his head because the miniature, executed after his
canonization, is meant to show the historical eternity of the saintly king, a
saint since childhood, rather than the historical, chronological truth. He was
already the king Saint Louis who was going to be anointed and crowned.
The childhood of the king was hidden away.[126]

Later on I will discuss the coronation of French kings in the thirteenth
century, because the documents pertaining to Saint Louis' coronation date
from after his consecration. We have no account of his coronation and are
not sure what liturgical ordinance (*ordo*) presided over it.

The chroniclers noted three aspects of Louis IX's coronation. The
first was the haste with which it was carried out. We have already seen why:
the anxiety in the time of the interregnum (the second that occurred in the

Kingdom of France when a new king had not been anointed during his father's life) increased due to the age of the young king and the fact that the Capetian dynasty had not yet become all-powerful. The interregnum was not an opportune moment to dispute a successor because the right of the first-born son of the dead king was well established, but to place pressure on the incomplete king and his entourage. At a time when the notion of the crime of lese-majesty toward the king was being developed, the interregnum was a gap in time when the majesty of the new king had not yet been instituted or in which agitation or rebellion was not looked upon as such a serious offense. Louis VIII died on November 8. He was buried on November 15. Louis IX was crowned on November 29. Three weeks was a major accomplishment given the weak mastery of space and the complexity that the planning of a royal coronation had attained at the time.

A second problem, which highlighted the risks that a child king represented for the kingdom, was that at twelve years of age Louis IX had not yet been knighted. The king of France must be a knight. The liturgy of the coronation that developed under Louis IX definitively added a specific dubbing that became the first section of the ceremony itself. On the way to Reims, the royal child was dubbed during a brief stop in Soissons.[127]

The third aspect of the coronation underscored by the chroniclers was the absence of the ecclesiastical and lay elite (archbishops and important feudal lords). Nevertheless, Blanche of Castile and the handful of powerful men who were present during Louis VIII's last days at Montpensier sent many invitations to the coronation at Reims, and to be even more persuasive, included Louis VIII's instructions from his deathbed. The lists drawn up by the chroniclers of those who attended and who did not attend contradict one another. Philippe Mousket, for example, placed the duke of Burgundy and the count de Bar at the scene, while Matthew Paris, the tributary of his predecessor Roger of Wendover, excluded them. It matters little. It is clear that the attendance of the powerful was spotty and less than brilliant. Furthermore, as happened fairly often at the coronations of French kings, there was no archbishop in Reims. The successor of the deceased prelate had not yet taken his post. This situation had been provided for. The bishop of Soissons, the first suffragan of the archbishop of Reims, was the consecrating prelate, and this in no way diminished the legitimacy of the ceremony, although, no doubt, it somewhat reduced its brilliance.

The English chroniclers leave us with a curious and interesting piece of additional information about the circumstances of the coronation. On the occasion of this royal inauguration, several of the lords in attendance called for the liberation of all the prisoners who were still incarcerated in the royal fortress of the Louvre since Bouvines. They especially sought the liberation of the counts of Flanders and Boulogne. They had been imprisoned there for twelve years, the entire length of the new king's life.[128] I am struck by the institutional nature of this request more than by its political aspect. This is the first known allusion to any sort of political amnesty related to the coronation, in other words to a kind of right of pardon of the kings of France at the moment of their consecration. This right of pardon attributed to monarchs on the occasion of their accession to the throne was only established with regularity in the seventeenth century and seems to have been imposed with some difficulty. As sacred, thaumaturgical, and all-powerful as they were, the kings of France still submitted to God and the laws. The right of pardon that was granted to the presidents of the Republic without any difficulty was conceded only reluctantly to kings. The kings of France only slowly attained full sovereignty. Moreover, in this episode of 1226 we can see the ambiguous position that the powerful members of society held in relation to the king. They struggled to impose their will on him, but credited him with an exorbitant power.

Before examining the political aspects of the coronation, let us imagine the first steps of the young king insofar as the limitations of the texts and facts allow.

Here at the age of twelve, he was thrust upon the scene by the unexpected death of a father. We see him first on the road to Auvergne, trying to reach his dying father on horseback, then learning the fatal news from the mouth of Friar Guérin who wisely made him return to Paris. He attended his father's funeral ceremony within the impressive royal funeral liturgy under the gothic vaults of Saint-Denis, and then returned on the dusty and winding road to Reims via Soissons atop a car that resembled a merchant's cart. The medieval roads were neither paved nor straight, and the child king clearly had to travel more than the 157 kilometers that make up this itinerary today. At Soissons, the child underwent the rites that were customarily reserved for the adolescent children of men of quality, those Christian warriors that the young Percival in the *Conte du Graal* encountered with terror. In Reims, the liturgy, with its gestures that must have been striking for a child, went on for long hours in a cathedral still under construction.

He was weighed down with a heavy coat, cumbersome insignia, and a weighty crown amid the dizzying prayers, chants, incense, and rites that were incomprehensible even to a gifted child. People had no doubt explained to him everything that this could represent for a child of his age. It was a cold ceremony, overshadowed by the troublesome absence of the prelates and great lords who should have rushed to rally around the child king. Then, there was the return to Paris that the chroniclers passed over in silence. Their account does not even show the least excitement of the people or the least cry of joy or encouragement. Yet, everywhere, at each moment, there was a presence, the presence of the loving mother. Strong and protective, she was already the strong woman of the Gospel that Pope Boniface VIII spoke of during Saint Louis' canonization.

A child, even if he were a king, would certainly keep a weighty and poignant memory of these hours, of these days when so many events, countrysides, decorations, and gestures paraded in the fading light of short, late autumn days. The chroniclers do not even mention the weather at the time. Such a test would toughen or weaken a man according to his particular qualities. Louis would be a son worthy of his father, a warrior without equal, worthy of his grandfather, the victor of Bouvines at fifty years of age, and the worthy son of his mother, the Spaniard. Strong like them, he learned the duties of a king in a different way. The ideology of the time began to think of the king's role as an onerous calling. In his memories and in life, he would continue to honor this omnipresent mother until his death.

A Difficult Minority

The chroniclers attributed political motives to the absence of powerful figures at the coronation of Louis IX. They may have exaggerated. The ceremony was unusually rushed. In the thirteenth century, it took a long time to receive news, prepare for a voyage, and to be ready to leave on time. And then, of course, the coronation of a child did not seem particularly appealing to these prelates and great lords who were used to living in the society of accomplished men. To a significant extent, the chroniclers' interpretations of these absences arose from the events that followed the coronation and that they projected back onto it in order to explain these episodes. The powerful, however, certainly stayed away from the coronation, and at least some of them had political motives for their absence.

Here, I am relating only what allows us to better understand Louis IX's life, the things that explain the function and the figure of the king. His guardian and advisors rushed to deal with certain delicate individual cases, and their solutions may have already been deployed—according to some— in the final months of the reign of Louis VIII.

The tradition of succession in the Capetian family and the "wills" of Louis VIII that had assured the accession of the young Louis IX were not so firmly established that they made useless any precautions regarding certain members of the royal family. The young king had two uncles aged twenty-five and seventeen in 1226. The latter presented no particular problems. He was a bastard, although he bore the weighty name of Charles, Pierre Charlot. His father, Philip Augustus, had managed to have him recognized by the Pope Honorious III as capable of receiving ecclesiastical benefices despite his illegitimate birth. He was destined for the Church. The first case, that of Philip "Hurepel," was more threatening. In the eyes of the Church, he too was a bastard, since the pope had not recognized the legitimacy of Philip Augustus's third marriage with Agnès de Méran, Philip's mother. This was because the Church considered the king of France as still married to Ingeburg of Denmark, who did not die until 1236. She had been repudiated the day after her unfortunate wedding night. Philip Hurepel had been legitimated by Pope Innocent III, and, as his mother had been accepted into the French aristocracy and tacitly by the French prelates as the legitimate queen of France, his position was much more honorable than that of his half brother. Even in appearance, legally, the status of Philip Hurepel was entirely normal. I wonder, however, if the vague memory of illegitimacy that weighed on him did not contribute to dissuading him from making any serious attempt to dispute the French throne with his nephew.[129]

His father Philip Augustus and his brother Louis VIII had richly endowed Philip Hurepel with lands and fiefdoms, although the lands that they gave him had belonged to Renaud de Boulogne, one of the two main traitors of Bouvines who was imprisoned in the Louvre. The two kings had considered these lands as confiscated by the crown and therefore they were supposed to revert to it if Philip died without any male progeny, which actually happened in 1236. In order to reconcile Philip Hurepel, the young king (or rather his mother and the advisors who were acting in his name) immediately gave him two or three castles that Louis VIII had kept among his lands. These castles were Mortain and Lillebonne, along with the allegiance of the county of Saint-Pol, although they came with the condition that they too would revert to the crown. At the beginning of the following year, Philip was granted a *rente viagère,* an annual life payment of 6,000 pounds *tournois,* but which engaged him to claim no more lands for himself or his eventual heirs as part of his inheritance.

Among the barons, the most urgent case was that of Ferrand of Flanders (or Portugal, his country of origin). This traitor of Bouvines was still imprisoned in the Louvre, and Louis VIII had promised to free him. This was mentioned explicitly in the lords' request to the young king for a pardon of prisoners, a request presented at the coronation ceremony. Ferrand was released during Epiphany on January 6, 1227. He paid a large ransom and gave guarantees to the king with conditions that appear to have been less harsh than those envisaged by Louis VIII. He would remain faithful to the king. As for Renaud de Boulogne, the other traitor of Bouvines, he died in his prison at the Louvre around Easter in 1227.

The new rulers next turned to deal with the most troublesome lords who held large fiefdoms, the count of Brittany and Hugues de Lusignan, or Hugh the Brown, count of the March. They were always ready to play their interests off between the king of France and the king of England and had left the royal host in the summer of 1226 during the siege of Avignon. In this world in which family relations — along with land — played such an important role in maintaining alliances, a project to marry Jean, the second brother of Louis IX born in 1219, and Yolande, the daughter of the count of Brittany, Pierre Mauclerc, was conceived in March 1227. Jean would die in 1232. Louis VIII had planned to give him Maine and Anjou. As a gage for accepting the agreement, Pierre would receive Angers, Le Mans, Baugé, and Beaufort-en-Vallée. During these negotiations in Vendôme in the spring of 1227, Hugh the Brown agreed to marry one of the daughters of Alphonse, Louis IX's third brother born in 1220, the future holder of Poitou and Auvergne. He was the future Alphonse de Poitiers. Pierre also agreed to marry one of his sons to Isabelle, the king's sister born in 1225. He returned certain lands that Louis VIII had given him in exchange for a ten-year annual payment of 10,000 pounds *tournois* for forfeiting Saint-Jean-d'Angély and a part of Aunis.

The governing group's most important efforts targeted the most threatening figure for the Kingdom of France, the king of England, Henry III. He was only twenty years old at the time. Deprived of a large part of his

French territories by Louis IX's grandfather, he still held lands in the southwest and made no secret of his intention to reconquer at least some of the lands that he had lost in France. The church of the abbey of Fontrevault in Maine, which had been reconquered by Philip Augustus, housed the necropolis of his Plantagenet ancestors, his grandfather Henry II, his grandmother the famous Eleanor of Aquitaine who had been divorced from the French king Louis VII, and his uncle Richard the Lion-Hearted. His representative on the continent was his brother Richard of Cornwall. In April 1227, a first truce was concluded between Richard and the king of France. In May, Henry III asked Louis IX for an official truce, and it was settled in June. In the meantime, Blanche of Castile had negotiated a peace with one of the most powerful of the malcontented lords, Thibaud IV, the count of Champagne.

On the eve of the summer of 1227, after ruling for six months, the young king seems to have secured his position in his kingdom.

And yet everything began to waver almost immediately. Joinville exposes the young king's anxiety for us. The king was a child. His mother was a "foreign woman" who "had neither relatives nor friends in the Kingdom of France."[130] A significant number of barons met at Corbeil and decided to abduct the young king. They did not necessarily want to imprison or harm him, and they had no intention to dethrone him, but they wanted to separate him from his mother and his advisors, to take him hostage in order to govern in his name and claim power, land, and wealth for themselves. They selected two prestigious chiefs who did not hesitate to play a leading role in this plan of revolt against Louis and his mother. In order to give their project some semblance of dynastic legitimacy, they elected Philip Hurepel, count of Boulogne, who "bristled" with as little brains as malice, weakly allowing himself to be manipulated in this affair. For their military leader, they took Pierre Mauclerc, the duke of Brittany, the most powerful and the least faithful of all the vassals of the king of France. He belonged to the line of Dreux and, manipulating the solidarity of lineage relations, would play a key role in the revolt against Louis and his mother. The young king, who had gone to Vendôme with his mother to negotiate with the hesitant barons of the west, returned to Paris through Orléans. He took the road of Orléans, a great artery of the royal domain since the time of Hugh Capet, back to Paris. At Montlhéry, the troops of the barons massed in Corbeil blocked his route. Here, in this time of "need," Joinville tells us, "the king had the help of God." Through Joinville, we hear the young king speak for the first time at the age of thirteen. The direct memory of Saint Louis that we have inherited starts here:

> And the saintly king told me that neither he nor his mother who were in Montlhéri dared return to Paris until the armed inhabitants of Paris came looking for them. And he told me that from Montlhéri on the entire road was full of people, armed and unarmed, who were all crying out to Our Lord to grant him a good and long life and to defend him and protect him from his enemies.[131]

Popular loyalty to the king had just been unleashed. New memories took shape in the mind of the child king. After the cold voyage from Reims, here was the heated ride from Montlhéry to Paris, a memory that would comfort and reassure Louis IX about his duty to be worthy of the confidence and love of his people. In this world of gifts and counter-gifts, the young king had emotionally experienced the fact that this system of reciprocity did not only play out on the higher level of relations with his vassals (for whom loyalty was not always part of the deal), but also on the level of his people. God had helped the king, but Queen Blanche and his advisors stirred up this help by first of all helping themselves. In the name of the young king, they sent messages calling upon the loyalty and support of the Parisians and the bourgeois from other towns in the domain. Did the memory of Bouvines come into play here? There, Philip Augustus had called upon the foot soldiers of the communes who fought valiantly, and, on the return trip to Paris, Saint Louis' grandfather had heard the cheers of the people. Thus there really were certain moments of unity between the people and their kings in the history of France.

The young king benefited from two important factors put into play by his mother and his advisors. Freed and extremely loyal to the king, Count Ferrand of Flanders and the recently reconciled count of Champagne, Thibaud IV, came to his aid, displaying a degree of support that would not falter until his death.

In 1228, the second year of Louis IX's rule, the coalition of barons reunited with even greater determination. This coalition seems to have had Enguerran de Coucy as its ringleader. With the support of Philip Hurepel, it did not take on the king and his protectress directly, but moved against their most powerful supporter, Thibaud de Champagne. Their campaign began by firing off a number of pamphlets that for the most part contained demeaning or downright injurious anecdotes that circulated in written and oral form against Blanche of Castile. This seems to me to be the first appearance of public opinion, of open expressions of popular collective judgments, spontaneous or not, on affairs of government and the behavior of the governing body. A campaign like this presupposes the emergence of public opinion. This French public opinion that was also expressed in song, as we shall see, moved to the front of the stage under the reign of Saint Louis' grandson Philip the Fair at the very end of the thirteenth and at the beginning of the fourteenth century. For purposes of understanding Saint Louis' conduct, it is no trivial matter to propose that French public opinion began to express itself under his rule.

And for what did they blame the regent? They claimed that she was emptying the royal coffers to profit her Castilian parents. They insisted that she was putting off the marriage of the young king in order to better dominate him and govern for herself. Most of all, they employed the traditional moral attack claiming that she engaged in immoral behavior. They accused her of being the mistress of the pontifical legate Romain Frangipani, Romain de Saint-Ange, on whom she relied for maintaining relations between the monarchy and the papacy and the Church and in continuing the crusade against the Albigenses in which her husband, Louis VIII, had played such an important role. They also accused her of being the mistress of the count of Champagne, her eager supporter Thibaud IV. A great courtly poet, he sang of a lady in whom they saw the queen. There is no document that can give the historian access to Blanche of Castile's bed, but if he trusts his intuition, which is necessary sometimes, and relies on his scientific familiarity with the period and its characters, he can determine that these were, as I believe, nothing but pure slanders. The intent of these slanders, moreover, was not foolish: woman was dangerous in the Middle Ages and had to be watched and kept in check insofar as she was capable of seducing men and behaving like one of Eve's descendants. However, the widow who can no longer have sexual relations or bear children may become a man if her character allows. This was what the hagiographers of Saint Louis would say. The slanderers wanted to degrade her by reducing her to the status of a woman who was still lustful and sexual and therefore unworthy of respect and power, a false widow and an unworthy guardian. The interesting thing here, and I would like to repeat it, was that there were ears to take in these calumnies, not individual ears listening to some oral confidence at the court, in an assembly, or in the gossip of lords or clerics, but ears that are collective in a manner of speaking, members of a network of people informed by written news that was not destined for long-term posterity like the chronicle, but for short-term useage like the pamphlet, created for immediate diffusion within narrowly defined circumstances. Along with the preachers, minstrels, and others belonging to this milieu of gossipmongers that seems to have been composed of the Parisian students, these medieval reporters were particularly caustic toward the queen. The Minstrel of Reims would later report that the queen undressed in public in order to prove that she was not pregnant.[132]

Fortunately for the kingdom, the barons were flexible (the game of feudalism involved juggling one's rights and duties as a vassal) and impressed with royalty, whether a child or a woman represented it, just as their ancestors had been impressed with the first weak Capetians in spite of everything else. According to the interests and whims of the vassals in this impassioned class of lords with unstable feelings, the complex practice of vassalic loyalty could brusquely transform those faithful to the king into rebels, or instead bring them back to a state of obedience in which, in the guise of the feudal mentality, they returned to the fundamental prestige of the king and royalty.

Joinville writes, "And many people say that the count of Brittany would have beaten the queen and king if the king had not had God's help in this time of need." Without disrespecting the notion of divine Providence, we can translate this to mean that Pierre Mauclerc was afraid of the king and by extension of royalty. He was afraid, in other words, of what was a divine and sacred institution for the French in the thirteenth century.

Nevertheless, it was still necessary to engage in military operations. At sixteen years of age, the young king led the royal host in three campaigns in 1230. He led two in the west against the count of Brittany and his accomplices, and one in the east in Champagne in order to protect the count against his enemies. When the king called upon his vassals to fulfill their military service, which they owed at certain times, usually in the spring and for a period of time that was fixed by custom, they had their backs against the wall. A refusal to respond to the king's summons, to desert the royal host, was a serious act of disobedience that freed the king from his duty to protect the rebellious vassals, exposing them to his reprisals.

Returning to his game of switching sides, Pierre Mauclerc had sworn allegiance to the king of England in October 1229 and refused to show up at the convening of the army by the king of France at Melun at the end of December. Louis IX then raised the royal host against him. Without disobeying their feudal obligation, the barons sent only small contingents of troops, with the exception of the count of Champagne thanks to whom the royal army was victorious. The campaign in January ended with the retaking of the strongholds of Anjou, which had been ceded to the Briton in 1227, and of Angers, Baugé, and Beaufort. Bellême was also taken. The count of Brittany had called for assistance from the king of England, Henry III, who disembarked at Saint-Mâlo, although he did not dare to engage in hostilities and shut himself up in Nantes without fighting. Louis IX marched at the head of another army, which, thanks to the help of Hugues de Lusignan, the count of the March, took Clisson and laid siege to Ancenis. The castle of la Haye-Pesnel near Avranches, which belonged to one of the leaders of the rebel lords, Fouques Pesnel, was taken and razed. The fief was confiscated, and the king gave it to the rebel's brother. However, the Briton and the English still held their positions, while the barons left the royal host, as they had announced, in order to turn against the count of Champagne. Louis IX had to launch a new campaign in the west in the spring of 1231. In the spring of 1231, he imposed a three-year truce on Pierre Mauclerc in Saint-Aubin-du-Cormier.

In the meantime, with the help of the faithful convert Ferrand of Flanders who kept Philip Hurepel in check, Louis IX struck camp in Champagne, and not daring to oppose the king, the barons fighting Thibaud IV abandoned all hostilities.

The French monarchy also met with great success in an area where it had only recently begun to intervene with strength under the short reign of Louis VIII (1223–1226), the Occitan Midi. In 1229, the royal government managed to end the Albigensian Crusade and to make peace with the indomitable and troublesome count of Toulouse, Raimond VII (1197–1249). He was the faithful successor of his father Raimond VI (1156–1222) in his struggle against the crusaders from the North and the monarchy's invasion of the Midi. Under the skillful guidance of the pontifical legate, Cardinal Romain de Saint-Ange, who was devoted not only to Blanche of Castile but also to the French royal power, the crusaders adopted a scorched earth policy after the death of Louis VIII. Although less glorious, it was far more efficient. They ravaged the fields and the harvests, hobbling the economy in Raimond VII's lands and especially in the region of Toulouse. The count had to make peace with the royal government, which was also ready to negotiate a compromise. The negotiations opened at Sens, then moved to Senlis, and finally to Meaux, a possession of the count of Champagne who served as an arbiter. In this conflict, the young king did not take part in the military operations, and we do not know what role he played in ending the crusade.

The treaty was sworn at Meaux on April 11, 1229 and immediately confirmed in Paris. Raimond retained most of his lands including everything in the dioceses of Toulouse, Cahors, and Agen, as well as everything in the southern Albigeois south of the Tarn with the exception of Mirepoix, which was ceded to Guy de Lévis. The king of France received the northern part of the Albigeois including the town of Albi. The pope acquired the lands that the house of the Toulousan count of Saint-Gilles had held east of the Rhone in the kingdom of Arles. The only daughter of Raimond VII, Jeanne, would marry a brother of the king of France and would bring him Toulouse and the surrounding region as a dowry.[133] She would inherit the other lands of her father if he died without having any son. The king received a gage of seven castles, including the citadel of Toulouse, the Narbonnais castle.

Raimond VII agreed to found a university in Toulouse in order to help extirpate the heresy. He also agreed to take up the cross. Kept as a hostage in the Louvre, Raimond reconciled with the Church and the monarchy on April 13. In a penitent's habit, a shirt and a cord around his neck, he made honorable amends at the hands of the acting cardinal at Notre-Dame, then, the same day, swore liege-homage (to the exclusion of any other or at least with priority over any other) to Louis IX. At fifteen and a knight for three years, the young king then knighted his vassal Raimond, a thirty-two-year-old man. In exchange, he gave him the seigniory of Rouergue.

Here are more images that made an impression on the memory of the young king: the infamy of heresy and the support for heresy that was purified by a humiliating and impressive ceremony; within the bounds of the cathedral of his "capital" the solemn exercise of his royal suzerainty through the symbolic and striking gestures of giving homage and dubbing; perhaps also, for the feudal king in all his glory, a dream sparked by the count's promise to crusade, an image of the voyage over the sea and of Jerusalem where every sin is finally washed away.

In any case, even if it were impossible for the protagonists of 1229 to know that the marriage of Jeanne de Toulouse and Alphonse de Poitiers would lead to the incorporation of Occitania into the French royal domain less than fifty years later, this represented a major leap forward for the Capetian monarchical power. It was a leap into the feared and alluring South whose disturbing seductions had always been followed by disappointments up to this point. Louis IX was the first king of France to actually rule over these two remarkably different halves of the Kingdom of France, the North and the South. To the kingdom's major western extension carried out by his grandfather, he added an appreciable new expanse of this space toward the south. To the clauses of the Treaty of Meaux-Paris and their consequences, we must add the articles of the Treaty of Melun that was concluded in this same year, 1229, with the rebellious lord of the Midi, Raimond Trencavel, viscount of Béziers and Narbonne. Again, we find a compromise. Trencavel kept Béziers but gave up Carcassonne. This viscounty, along with Beaucaire that was added to the commune of Avignon by Louis VIII in 1226, and the viscounties of Nîmes and Agde, ceded to Simon de Montfort by one of Trencavel's cousins, Bernard Aton, formed the two new seneschalcies [*sénéchaussées*] of Beaucaire and Carcassonne. (The *sénéchaussées* were the southern equivalent of the *bailliages,* administrative jurisdictions assigned to a *bailli* or bailiff, a representative of the crown.) Simon's heir, his son Amaury, ceded all his rights and lands in the Midi to the king of France in 1229. For the first time in its history, the Kingdom of France extended to the Mediterranean, and, although it was only on a narrow front, this was still extremely important. The dream of the crusade now had a material launching point: Aigues-Mortes. Saint Louis was the first king of France who would be able to leave on a crusade from his own soil instead of from a foreign land. Even if the uniqueness of southern France—more or less respected by the French monarchy by choice or necessity—subsisted for a very long time, the unity of the two Frances was realized by force from the North. Having had little experience there, it appears that Saint Louis was never very interested in this new half of his kingdom. It seemed so far away to this king who saw it only from his residences in Paris and the Île-de-France. His brother, Alphonse de Poitiers, would be the immediate ruler of the South until his death, although he lived most of his life close to Saint Louis. Thanks to his advisors in the South he became more interested in the administration of eastern Languedoc within the framework of a general reform of the kingdom after his return from the crusade. However, Saint Louis would generally think of this new part of the royal domain as a new Capetian road for leaving on and returning from the crusades.

The first years of Louis' reign were undoubtedly years of danger and difficulty, as we have generally chosen to present them here. However, they were also years that saw decisive advances in royal power and personal prestige for the young king. Thanks to his presence in the theaters of military operation and at the assemblies of the powerful lords, thanks, of course, to the skillful and energetic policies of his mother and his advisors, Louis appeared as a warrior and a sovereign. The youth knighted at Soissons had become a warrior king, a leader at war. The adolescent who was shocked at Montlhéry summoned his barons, and with the sole exception of the Briton (of course Brittany would be a thorn in the side of the Kingdom of France for a long time), they all came and obeyed.

In addition, we have not sufficiently stressed two revealing events concerning the progress of royal power. The war between the count of Champagne and the barons was a private war. Louis IX was not afraid to get involved in it, and when he did, the nature of the conflict changed. The barons had to abandon their ambitions. The king intervened in the private domain and did not appear on the scene as a mere ally or opponent. In the all-important field of war, private interests retreated before the royal interest, which the historian can now begin to identify as public.

During the same period, Louis summoned all the barons of the kingdom to the assembly of Melun in December 1230. All of them came or nearly all, as no notable absence was recorded. They were called to confirm and extend the measures taken by Louis' father and grandfather against the Jews, and here the young king issued the first known ordinance, in other words the first royal act pronounced as a function of the royal sovereign and, therefore, of sovereignty. It applied *to the entire kingdom* and not only to the royal domain.

In our brief consideration of 1230–1231, we must go beyond the simple claim that "the crisis was surmounted." Often, when weak periods in historical evolution are not followed by decline, they reveal the progress of the powerful forces at work in the long duration and the depth of structures. The break in the flow of these forces allows a leap forward and a stronger rebound to take place. Beneath the troubled surface of events appears the general thrust of the currents.

During this prolonged minority, the young king seems to gradually assume the rights and powers of his function. However, at the same time, Blanche of Castile continued to appear at center stage with their advisors in the background. Their presence was rarely recorded in the documents. In this period, as Louis IX saw several key figures leave the scene, some of the defining traits of his character and political behavior began to appear.

The three main advisors held over from the governments of Philip Augustus and Louis VIII disappeared rather quickly. They had played an important role at the time of the latter's death and during the accession of the new king. The bishop of Senlis, Friar Guérin, gave up his seals in 1227 and died before the end of the year. Barthélemy de Roye, the chamberlain who died in 1237, seems to have gradually faded away. Jean de Nesle appeared only intermittently. One of the main supporters of the royal family stayed in place: Gautier Cornut, the archbishop of Sens, the first prelate named on the hierarchical lists of the ecclesiastics.

The disappearance of these elders paralleled the deaths of the young princes of the royal family. The king's second brother Jean who was promised to the daughter of the count of Brittany in 1227 at the age of nine died shortly thereafter. The fourth brother Philippe Dagobert died in 1235 at approximately twelve years of age. Charles, the only surviving brother after Robert and Alphonse, received Maine and Anjou in "apanage" as specified in the will of Louis VIII. The group of "sons of the king of France" grew tighter.

Other changes in the leadership of the large fiefdoms took place. Among the more "political" changes figures the death of Ferrand, count of Flanders in 1233. He had been a firm supporter of the king and his mother since 1227. Then, Philip Hurepel, "the *Hérissé*," the young king's uncle, neither glorious nor loyal, followed Ferrand to the tomb several months later in January 1234. Despite everything, this death removed the only possible obstacle within the family. Robert de Dreux, another leader of the revolt at the beginning of Saint Louis' reign, died two months later. The matter of the succession of Champagne was also resolved in the king's favor. The enemy barons opposing Thibaud de Champagne failed miserably in their military operations, but encountered more success in their dynastic machinations. Thibaud IV had to confront a pretender to his title, his cousin Alix, the queen of Cyprus. Her rights to the county of Champagne were defensible, because, as the oldest daughter of Count Henri II, she was entitled to receive the inheritance of the county. It was only the Capetian royal family that excluded women from its succession. The conflict between Thibaud and his cousin reached a boiling point when Alix returned to France in 1233. An agreement was finally reached in 1234. The queen of Cyprus abandoned her personal claims to the county of Champagne in exchange for a sum of 40,000 pounds *tournois* and a payment of 2,000 pounds a year. This was an enormous sum, and, in spite of all his wealth—Champagne was the location of the largest commercial fairs in all of Christendom and Thibaud had just become king of Navarre in 1233 upon the death of his uncle Sanche, his mother's brother—he was unable to pay it. He approached the king, became his friend, and the royal government agreed to pay Queen Alix for him, although in exchange Thibaud had to surrender his control of the counties of Blois, Chartres, and Sancerre and the viscounty of Châteaudun. This put an end to the threat of the principality of Blois-Champagne that affected the royal dynasty due to the fact that it surrounded the Île-de-France and the Orléanais, the heart of the royal domain.

The Affair of the University of Paris

With the renewal of his entourage and the end of all the major feudal threats with the significant exception of England, the young king's position was strengthened at the end of the crisis. Moreover, from 1227 to 1234 and especially from 1231 to 1234, the young king expressed some of the character traits and political conduct that were subsequently associated with the image and the memory of Saint Louis. It was in his relations with the University of Paris, with the bishops, the emperor, and especially in the matter of his religious devotion that the future Saint Louis began to acquire a voice.

The University of Paris was a young institution in 1229. Emerging from the interaction of the various schools that masters had opened on the Sainte-Geneviève Hill in the course of the tumultuous twelfth century and that had begun to form corporations at the turn of the century, the University received privileges from Philip Augustus and governing statutes from the papacy. The University's corporation was comprised of a community of clerics and a Christian institution at the very beginning of the century. Saint Louis' grandfather no doubt immediately sensed the importance for the French monarchy of having a center for advanced studies in Paris, his

virtual capital, which could bring glory, knowledge, and high-ranking clerical and lay officials to the monarchy.[134] However, it is also clear that Philip
Augustus had no "university policy," and this would also be Saint Louis'
position in relation to the University. Although they understood the benefits and prestige that the University of Paris brought to the monarchy, they
intervened within it in order to restore public order when things got out
of hand, or acted as a "secular arm" when ecclesiastical condemnations required some intercession. In 1219, Pope Honorius III forbade the teaching
of Roman law at the University of Paris with the bull *Super speculam*. We have
to grasp that there was more to this than the French king's intervention in
a matter where he was merely anxious to prevent the teaching of a fundamentally imperial law in his capital at a time when he aspired to be recognized as independent of the emperor's superiority. It was rather a question
of the pope's desire to assure that the attraction of the study of law would
not overshadow theology. He wanted to make Paris the theological center of
all Christianity. In addition, Honorious III forbade the teaching of medicine,
another possible competitor. This obligated the monarchy to recruit its jurists in Toulouse and especially more and more in Orléans. The importance
of the University of Paris for the Capetian power can be measured by the
very strong theme of the *translatio studii* among the clerics of the thirteenth
century. If there had been a transfer of imperial power from Antiquity to the
Middle Ages—a *translatio imperii* from the empires of the East to the Roman
Empire and then to the Holy Roman Empire—then there was a transfer of
intellectual power—*translatio studii*—from Athens to Rome and from Rome
to Paris. Rome was the political capital and Paris was the intellectual capital
of Christendom. These were the myths of power, anchored in institutional
realities, which the young king of France inherited. To lose the University
of Paris would be to throw away one of the major foundations of his prestige and power. Italy, people still said, had the pope, Germany had the emperor, and France had the university. The two strong points of the University of Paris were the Faculty of the Arts with its propaedeutic teaching of
the seven liberal arts, a place for general education, the most open to innovations, the most teeming with ideas and discussions, and, alongside it, the Faculty of Theology, a summit of knowledge, the center for the new scholastic
project. This was a meeting place for young clerics who were protected by
the privileges of clerical status without being bound by the obligations of
the priesthood. They were exempt from taxation and exclusively exercised
judicial authority over their corporation and episcopal offices in matters

of dogma and faith. The place comprised a tumultuous milieu, giving rise to all kinds of moral offenses—robberies, rapes, all sorts of youthful violence and plain old rowdy behavior: drunkenness, song, and uproar.

This milieu moved under the watchful eyes of the royal power, the bishop-chancellor, and the townspeople. A student brawl got out of hand in a cabaret adjacent to the Saint-Marcel Church in the faubourg of the same name. The royal sergeants and their archers, the policemen of the time, showed up to restore order. They did it brutally, killing and wounding a number of students. Thus began a bitter conflict between the University, the townspeople, and the royal power exercised by Blanche of Castile who adopted a harsh attitude toward the students and who was, once more, supported by the pontifical legate. Courses stopped and there was a strike, the first important strike to occur in the West. The strike was accompanied by a secession, which had already occurred in the past, a departure of masters and students to another city. Prior to this, however, secessions of masters and students had never been accompanied by a general stoppage of teaching. This was an opportunity for other rulers and cities to provoke a *brain drain* of the Parisian intellectual elite. The king of England tried to attract Parisians to the recently founded University of Oxford. Thanks to the strike, the count of Brittany dreamt of establishing a university in Nantes. The authorities in Toulouse tried to debauch the Parisians to get them to come help start up the university that Raimond VII had just sworn to establish: they invoked the charms of Toulousain women as much as the promise of being able to explain Aristotle's books, which were banned in Paris. Despite these temptations, most of the secessionists did not go very far. They wanted to be able to return to Paris where living conditions and educational conditions were so favorable for them. The nascent power of the University needed to feed off all of the powers assembled in Paris. Most of the students and masters withdrew to Angers and Orléans.

It would take two years for the dust to settle. Both parties hardened their positions. The stakes were high for both of them. For the University, its independence and judicial privileges were in question. For the royal power, its authority and its right to enforce public order in Paris were the issue. The cooling off began with Pope Gregory IX's intervention. He was concerned that the Church might have to do without a major theological center outside of the territories ruled directly by the emperor. He spurred the negotiations forward and pulled the bishop of Paris, the pontifical legate, and Blanche of Castile back into line.

It seems, however, that after Blanche of Castile's long bout of stubbornness, Louis IX personally intervened so that the royal power could respond favorably to the pontifical request and make the necessary concessions. Had he acted in a manner worthy of his grandfather by understanding the value that the University represented for the French monarchy? Guillaume de Nangis emphatically attributed this foresight to the young king, although he may have been retrospectively transposing the French monarchy's attitude at the end of the century upon the events of 1230. He perfectly exposed the ideology behind the relations between the University of Paris and the Kingdom of France in a text that no doubt expresses the ideas of a mere monk of Saint Denis, but which, it is my hypothesis, explains what really happened along with the actual motives of the young Saint Louis.

> In this same year [1229], a great dispute arose in Paris between the clerics and the townspeople, and the townspeople killed some of the clerics. Because of this, the university people left Paris and went to various provinces. When the king saw that the study of letters and philosophy, through which the treasures of the intelligence [*sens*] and knowledge [*sapience*] are acquired, had ceased, treasures that are worth more than all others, and that it had left Paris, having come from Greece and Rome to France with the title of chivalry, the gentle and debonair king was very worried and feared that such great and rich treasures would leave his kingdom, because the riches of salvation are full of sense and knowledge, and because he didn't want any lord to reproach him by saying, "Because you threw science away and chased it from your kingdom, know that you have pushed me away from you." The king rushed to reconcile the clerics and the townspeople, and he did it so well that the townspeople paid the clerics back for the wrongs that they had committed against them. And the king did this especially because knowledge is a precious jewel, and because the study of letters and philosophy came first from Greece to Rome and from Rome to France with the title of chivalry following Saint Denis who preached the faith in France. . . .[135]

The historiographer of Saint-Denis inscribed the Parisian university within the order of royal symbols, making knowledge, along with faith and chivalry, the three symbols of the three lilies of the monarchy. Of course, the monk of Saint-Denis still had a thesaurus-like concept of knowledge that was somewhat archaic in relation to the concepts the ordinary and mendicant masters of the University had of teaching and the diffusion of knowledge. Still, we can see how he managed to introduce Saint-Denis and his monastery into the mythical genesis of the *translatio studii*. Here, we can grasp the developmental process of the French "national" myth produced by the pairing of Saint-Denis and royalty, of Saint-Denis and Paris.

The king paid a fine for the violence inflicted on the students by the royal sergeants, renewed the University's privileges, promised to make Parisian landlords respect the fixed price for renting rooms to students, and created a committee made up of two masters and two townspeople to oversee the implementation of this measure. He ordered the bourgeois to pay reparations for the murders and injuries of students, and made them swear to the bishop of Paris, the abbots of Saint-Geneviève and Saint-Germain-des-Prés, and the canons of the chapter of Saint-Marcel never to do any more harm to the members of the University.

The pope validated the diplomas obtained by the students who had sought refuge in Angers and Orléans during the secession on condition that they return to Paris. He recognized the right of masters and students to strike if, fifteen days after the murder of any member of their community, the guilty had not made compensation for his act. By the papal bull *Parens scientiarum* of April 1231, subsequently referred to as the Charter [*la Charte*] of the University of Paris, Gregory definitively granted the University its autonomy and privileges. Here is a *Grande Charte,* which, unlike the English one, did not oppose royal power, but actually served it. The young Louis IX was thankful for it.

LOUIS AND EMPEROR FREDERICK II

In the important area of relations between the king of France and the emperor, we get another premonition from a precocious personal intervention the young king made.

Even though Hugh Capet had played on his Ottonian ancestry, for a long time, forever in fact, the Capetians tried to free their kingdom from any dependence on the emperor, sometimes with an uproar like Louis VI in 1124, but usually more discreetly. They also knew how to take advantage of the violent conflicts that sometimes opposed the popes and the emperors from the eleventh to the fourteenth century.

Saint Louis kept up this resistance—and not without success. At the same time, he made an effort to respect the imperial rank. He felt he was the member of a body, Christendom, and it had two heads, the pope and the emperor. The pope was master of spiritual things, and outside the Germanic Holy Empire the emperor had a right to special honors. In all temporal matters, however, neither the Church (popes and bishops) nor the emperor had any special legal rights or juridical powers in the Kingdom of France. In France, this order combined with the desire to maintain an equal balance between the pope and the emperor whenever possible in order to safeguard the symbolic unity of a bicephalous Christendom. As Saint Louis matured and advanced in age he would try more and more to establish justice and peace, and in the conflict between the pope and the emperor his conduct would be driven by a growing desire for fairness and reconciliation.

A kind of sympathy seems to have existed between these two great political figures of the thirteenth century, if only from afar. This sympathy existed despite the fact that they were so different from each other and so often opposed, with Emperor Frederick II thinking only of his imperial dream and Louis IX of his eschatological dream. However, both men shared a common vision of the Christian world that extended to the far reaches of Eastern Europe and Jerusalem. One of them dreamed of achieving this by all means available to the human hero, the other by all paths open to the Christian hero.

It seems that the French initiatives addressed to Frederick II in 1232 bore the personal mark of the young king of France as he began to distance himself politically from his mother and his advisors in this matter. In May and June, Louis renewed his "treaties" with Frederick and his son Henry, the king of the Romans. The Hohenstaufens promised him that they would keep an eye on the anti-French actions of the king of England and not allow any private wars to develop between imperial vassals and French vassals. Frederick II ratified this agreement while he presided over an assembly of German princes in Frioul. He treated Louis like a brother, and the two rulers exchanged the mutual promises of loyalty and assistance vassals customarily swore to their lords.

Conflicts with the Bishops: The Beauvais Affair

In dealing with another series of problems, the young king clearly appeared at the front of the stage and, this time, not as a mere participant or figurehead. This occurred in the legal conflicts with the bishops. Alongside their accepted ecclesiastical and spiritual power, the bishops exercised a temporal power, which was typically a judicial power that they held through seigniorial titles or that they pretended to derive from their episcopal functions. In the 1230s, royal power came into conflict over this with the archbishops of Rouen and Reims. However, the longest and most serious dispute occurred with the bishop of Beauvais.

This conflict pitted the king against a person who should have had his ear. Milon de Nanteuil had been elected bishop of Beauvais in 1217 and was consecrated in Rome by Pope Honorius III in 1222. He was one of Philip Augustus's companions on the crusade and had been taken prisoner. He had also been a close associate of Louis VIII whom he accompanied on the crusade against the Albigenses and later visited at Montpensier during his mortal illness.[136]

The conflict was triangulated, opposing the town commune, the bishop—who was also a count—and the king. The townspeople were divided into two classes, the *populares,* who composed twenty-one trades, and the *majores,* which included only the moneychangers who were numerous and powerful because the bishop had the right to mint money. An agreement between Philip Augustus and the commune entrusted the election of the mayor to twelve peers, six of them named by the *populares* and six by the *majores.* Each group selected a candidate, and the bishop would name one of them mayor. In 1232, it became obvious that this agreement could never work. The king declared, more than once in fact, that the *majores* were dominating the city by committing a large number of injustices in fiscal affairs. Imitating the Italian communes that called on a supposedly neutral foreigner to rule them, Louis appointed a bourgeois of Senlis as mayor. The inhabitants of Beauvais revolted against this intruder, and the riot resulted in a number of deaths.

During an interview between the king, his mother, and Bishop Milon in Bresles, the bishop asked the king not to get involved in an affair that, according to him, did not concern royal justice but only episcopal justice. The king answered that he would deal with the Beauvais affair himself and in a curt tone told him, "You will see what I will do." The measures taken by Louis IX were spectacular. He arrested a large number of the inhabitants of the town and imprisoned them first in market stalls that were converted into cells and then in new prisons built solely for that purpose. The king's forces razed fifteen houses that belonged to the most compromised bourgeois and, according to one document, placed 1,500 others under house arrest in Paris. Louis IX and his followers stayed in Beauvais for four days. According to an agreement negotiated with Philip Augustus, the bishop of Beauvais was supposed to pay the king 100 Parisian pounds a year. This was supposed to redeem the king's rights of residence [*droits de résidence*] in the town, in other words to pay for the expenses of the king and his followers during his stay. Claiming that his stay was exceptional, the king demanded 800 pounds from the bishop for his rights of residence. The astonished bishop requested a delay to make payment. The king immediately seized the bishop's temporal holdings, in other words sources of his income that were not related to his religious function. For example, all of the bishop's wine was taken from his cellars and sold on the public square. This act was obviously dictated by the king's will to vigorously show his determination to defend his rights.

The bishop organized resistance to the king and called on his superior, the archbishop of Reims, the other bishops of the province, and even the pope. They all took his side against the king. The bishop issued an interdiction, in other words he suspended the administration of the sacraments in the diocese. Councils or, rather, provincial synods of bishops condemned the king's position. Pope Gregory IX wrote him one letter after another in order to sway him, and even wrote to the queen to get her to use her influence on her son. After the death of Milon de Nanteuil (September 1234), the conflict spread to the province of Reims. In Reims, the townspeople revolted against the archbishop, thinking they would benefit from the king's support. In April 1235, the pope appointed a mediator, Pierre de Colmieu, the *prévôt* of Saint-Omer who was on the verge of becoming archbishop of Rouen. Nothing swayed the king. In response to the prelates, he summoned an assembly of all the French nobility to Saint-Denis in September 1235. He had them sign a letter to the pope that protested the pretensions of all the bishops in general and of the archbishop of Reims and the bishop of Beauvais in particular. The letter declared that episcopal temporal rights only derived from secular, royal, and seigniorial justice. The pope protested vehemently, threatened the king with excommunication, and reminded him of all the precedents from the time of his predecessor Honorius III. The king did not budge and more than once pointed out the inefficiency of excommunications and interdictions issued right and left.

The whole affair gradually settled and came to a close. A new bishop was elected in 1238, and he took a more conciliatory position. Involved in a heated conflict with Emperor Frederick II, the popes Gregory IX (dead in 1241) and Innocent IV (elected in 1243) showed more and more consideration for the king of France, especially in matters of ecclesiastical temporal powers. The superior authority of royal tribunals over episcopal officials was no longer contested by the 1240s.[137]

The affair revealed something important about the institutional development of the kingdom and also afforded some insight into Saint Louis' conduct. The king's respect for the papacy and the Church did not go so far as to abandon the rights of royalty in temporal matters. More than a simple return to tradition, this showed the progress of royal power. The affair of Beauvais and Reims and the texts and declarations that it gave rise to prefigured — or actually initiated? — the conflict that opposed Saint Louis' grandson Philip the Fair and Pope Boniface VIII seventy years later. In a letter dated March 22, 1236, the pope wrote: "The wrong done to the Church of Beauvais is a wrong done to the entire 'Gallican' Church and even to the universal Church." If Saint Louis was inflexible and biting when the rights of the king and the kingdom were at stake, it was because at the age of eighteen the very Christian king already had no weaknesses in relation to the threats of the papacy and the bishops against the functions of royal justice. He had no tolerance for ecclesiastical abuses of excommunication and interdiction.[138] One thing was also clear in addition to his character and his politics: an overwhelming process of development brought him closer to consolidating the prerogatives of royal justice and realizing the increasing assertiveness of the state.

THE DEVOUT KING: THE FOUNDATION OF ROYAUMONT

Another characteristic and behavioral trait that heralded the future Saint Louis revealed itself between 1229 and 1234, between his fifteenth and twentieth birthdays: he was a devout king.

In his testament, his father Louis VIII had left a large sum for the foundation of a monastery in Paris. The royal family would have close relations with this monastery, which, more than others, would pray for them. In this intention, we come across the old alliance between monasticism and royal power that the Capetian dynasty had tried to cultivate with several important monasteries like Tours, Fleury-sur-Loire (where Philip I was buried), Barbeau (that Louis VII chose for his sepulchre), and of course Saint-Denis. These alliances began under Hugh Capet, continuing a tradition started by his Robertian ancestors, and this was one of the main reasons for their success. Louis VIII had confided this establishment to the monastic canons of Saint-Victor of Paris, a suburban monastery built on the slopes of Mount Sainte-Geneviève. It played an important role in the scholarly and theological movement of the twelfth century. It was still prestigious, although today's historians can guess that it had already begun its long decline brought on by competition from the University and the Mendicants. Then in 1229, when Louis IX and Blanche of Castile enacted the foundation of the late king, they gave it to the order of Cîteaux. This shift appears all the more surprising since the abbot of Saint-Victor, designated in Louis VIII's testament as the guarantor of the execution of the foundation, seems to have been in close contact with the young king and his mother. Still, the attraction of reformed Cistercian monasticism had a stronger influence on the young king, as we have already seen. For Saint Louis, as for many Christians of the time, Cîteaux represented a sort of transition toward the Mendicant orders, whose members did not yet make up the core of his entourage.

With the foundation of Royaumont, we discover not only Louis IX's love of religious buildings, but also his piety, mixed with humility, and his authoritarianism in matters of worship.

Joinville bears witness to his precocious love of religious buildings: "Since the earliest times that he held his kingdom and knew what he wanted to do, he began to build churches and other religious houses. Between them all, Royaumont takes the prize in beauty and grandeur."[139] The construction of Royaumont was also an occasion for the young king to experience humility and penitence. In a symbolic fashion, Louis put himself to work in the monastic tradition of primitive Benedictism restored to honor by Cîteaux in the twelfth century. In the biography he wrote based on the documents for the canonization proceeding at the end of the thirteenth century, Guillaume de Saint-Pathus showed the king at work: "And as the monks were coming out to labor after the third canonical hour of the day according to the custom of the order of Cîteaux, carrying stones and mortar to the spot where they were building the wall, the gentle king lifted a stretcher full of stones and carried it in front while a monk carried it from behind, and the gentle king had done this more than once during this period."[140] And since Guillaume de Saint-Pathus related this pious behavior in his chapter on Saint Louis' love for all those who were dear to him, he added, "And also at this time the gentle king made his brothers Lord Alphonse, Lord Robert, and Lord Charles carry the stretcher too. And there was a monk with each one of them carrying the other side of the stretcher. And the saintly king made other lords of his following [*compagnie*] do the same thing. And when his brothers sometimes wanted to speak, yell, and play,[141] the gentle king told them: 'The monks observe silence here, and we must observe it too'. And when the gentle king's brothers filled their stretchers[142] with heavy loads and wanted to stop when they were halfway there, he told them, 'The monks don't rest, and you shouldn't be taking any rests either.' Thus the saintly king taught his people [*sa mesnie:* his family and his entourage] to do good." Saint Louis' family and friends were beginning to learn the price of being around him and enjoying his affection.

In order to build the abbey that Louis VIII wanted and that they gave to the Cistercians, the king and his mother chose a spot near Asnières-sur-Oise in the diocese of Beauvais where the young king stayed once in a while. They had already acquired it for this purpose. The place was named Cuimont, although it was unchristened so that it could be named Royaumont ("royal mount"), a name that expressed the close ties between the monastery and the royalty. Beginning in 1232 at the request of the monks of Saint-Denis, the general chapter of Cîteaux decided that the festival of Saint-Denis would be celebrated in all the monasteries of the order with two masses and the solemnities of the other public holidays, except that the laypersons would not stop working. Information like this helps us better understand how the favors Saint Louis granted to the Cistercians, who had just become associated with him through a kind of alliance of prayer, forged a spiritual relationship between the monks of the abbey, the dynasty, and royal power. Through this alliance and through Royaumont, Cîteaux became part of this royal network that had Saint-Denis at its center.

THE DEVOUT KING AND THE LOSS OF THE HOLY NAIL

The other devotional event of the early years was the loss and recovery of a distinguished relic from Saint-Denis: the Holy Nail. Let's listen to Guillaume de Nangis tell of this event. He was a monk at Saint-Denis and gave the event—a news event—the proportions of a cosmic drama:

> In the following year [1232], at this same church [Saint-Denis] it happened that the very Holy Nail, one of those with which our Lord was crucified, that was brought there in the time of Charles the Bald, king of France and emperor of Rome who gave it to the church named above, fell from the vase in which it was kept while they were giving it to some pilgrims to kiss, and it was lost among the throngs of people who were kissing it on the third day of the calends of March [February 28]. But afterward it was found thanks to a great miracle and it was returned to the church with great joy and great jubilation on the following first of April [Good Friday that year]. The sorrow and compassion that the saintly King Louis and his noble mother Queen Blanche had from such a great loss must be mentioned. When they learned of the loss of this very high treasure and of what happened to the Holy Nail under their rule, King Louis and his mother Queen Blanche felt great sadness and said no one could have brought them crueler news that could make them suffer any more cruelly. Because of the great pain he had, the very good and very noble King Louis could not contain himself and he began to scream aloud that he would have rather had the best city of his kingdom ruined and destroyed. When he learned of the pain and the crying the abbot and the monks of Saint-Denis went through night and day without any possible consolation, he sent them wise and well-spoken [*bien parlants*] men to comfort them, and he wanted to come in person, but his people kept him from doing that. He commanded and had it cried out in all Paris, in the streets and the public places, that if anyone knew something about the loss of the Holy Nail and if anyone had found it or hidden it, he should return it immediately and he would have 100 pounds from the purse of the king. What more can we say? The anguish and sadness caused by the loss of the Holy Nail everywhere was so great that it can hardly be told. When the people of Paris heard the king's message and the news of the loss of

the Holy Nail, they were very tormented, and many men, women, children, clerics, and students began to wail and scream from the depth of their hearts, crying and in tears. They ran into all their churches to call on God's help in such great peril. It was not only Paris that was crying, but everyone in the Kingdom of France who learned of the loss of the holy and precious nail was crying too. Many wise men feared that because this cruel loss happened in the beginning of the reign, great misfortunes or epidemics may occur, and that this may have been a prelude to the destruction—and God save it—of the entire body of the Kingdom of France.[143]

The influence of the relics over an entire people, the public revelation of the intense fascination that they exercised over the young king, the excessive emotional expression of a religious feeling very close to magic, the practice of a devotion founded on material objects sacralized by the Church in which we can still discern Saint-Denis' long-term policy that tied Saint Louis' France to Jesus through the pseudo-apostle Denys and the Carolingian dynasty: this episode sheds raw light on Christian piety in the thirteenth century. Saint Louis was no more an exception; he was the royal sublimation of the religious heart of a people that could still be shaken by relics and miracles. Among the most simple, the most wise, and the most powerful, the belief in the sacred virtue of objects that safeguard the prosperity of a kingdom remained unshakeable. Their accidental loss could foretell its ruin. Romans did not examine the flight and appetite of birds and the livers of their prey with more anxiety than the French investigating the loss of a holy nail in the thirteenth century. The young Louis shared and excited the profound religious feelings of his people, feelings that seem "primitive" to us. He began to form his image and his policies around the intense public expression of these feelings. However, some members of his entourage considered these manifestations of piety excessive and unworthy of a king, who was supposed to display moderation and give the example of reason. Louis already shocked everyone who had a traditional idea of how a king was supposed to behave. Was royal majesty compatible with these signs of piety that combined gestures expressing the intensity of belief in a very ancient sacredness (the cult of the relics, veneration for places of worship such as churches and monasteries) with gestures of a new individual devotion proclaiming humility, the fear of sin, and the need for penitence? For Louis, there would not be any personal problem here. Without contradiction, he felt and thought of himself both as king of France, conscious of his duties—in both appearances and symbolic acts—and as a Christian who, in order to be an example and assure his own salvation and that of his people, must show his faith according to old and new practices. He must do this not only "from his heart," an expression that was dear to him, in his conscience, but also with his body, in his visible behavior. But two groups surrounded him: his advisors who expected him to share the values and attitudes of the social ranks to which he belonged (the aristocracy and the prelates), and the people who saw him as a secular leader. Wouldn't these two groups, these two parts of an emerging public opinion, be split between two feelings: admiration and embarrassment? Should we anticipate some condemnation of an attitude deemed scandalous and dangerous, unworthy of the royal function and perilous for the kingdom and its subjects? Louis' reign would unfold in the disparity between the king's conduct trusting in the compatibility, or better, in the necessary fusion of his two major concerns: on the one hand, the good of the kingdom and his people, his personal salvation that because he was king must be inseparable from the salvation of the kingdom and his subjects; on the other, unrest in French public opinion as it was torn between its fascination with the king's piety and its fear that this piety might not involve behavior required of a king. Louis himself had moments of doubt, even periods of doubt, especially after the failure of his crusade, but he always regained self-control, convinced that he was on the "right" path that defined the royal function.[144] Nevertheless, it was a great sin to fail to assume one's place in this society in a clear way, to transgress the *state* [*status*] in which God placed us, to straddle clear social boundaries of God's creation, and especially the boundaries that separate clerics and laymen. In this society that would never accept a Melchisedech, a priest-king, for its leader, Louis himself believed in the need for this distinction and struggled to remain within the limits of the secular state, even when he marched to the very edge of the border beyond which one enters the world of the clerics and the monks. The king's behavior disturbed people. Wasn't he basically a scandalous hybrid, a monk-king, or, later when he surrounded himself with friars of the new Mendicant orders, a friar-king? In the end, the majority of public opinion found the right solution, and it was sanctioned by the Church: he would be a sainted king, a king who was secular and saintly, though only through the random avatars of a long reign and a life, which, for the thirteenth century, was a very long one.

From Marriage to the Crusade
(1234–1248)

WE DO NOT KNOW WHEN LOUIS' MAJORITY WAS FIRST RECOGNIZED. It had to have taken place in 1234 when he was twenty years old or later in 1235 when he was twenty-one. The age of majority for French kings was not set until 1375 by Charles V, and it was fixed at fourteen years of age. Louis' case was an exception. Blanche de Castile governed so well during her son's youth and, it seems, had acquired such a taste for power that with the support not only of her advisors but with the approval of the other powerful figures within the kingdom she prolonged her tutelage over her son and the kingdom. As we have seen, the young king undoubtedly began to intervene in certain affairs, expressing his will, if not his power. Furthermore, he seems to have done this with remarkable efficiency on several occasions: during the strike of the University of Paris and during the conflicts with the bishops. The threshold marking his passage to adulthood and personal rule can be detected neither in the sources nor in the facts. This is because an unusual situation had arisen in which there were no signs of discontinuity. In practice there was a kind of "co-royalty," the sharing of royal power between Louis and his mother. This "co-royalty" was unequal but, as we shall see, tacitly shared.[1]

The Marriage of Louis IX (1234)

In 1234, Louis IX was nineteen years old. He had not been married, nor even engaged, which was unusual for such an important figure at this time. This must have set the young king's entourage abuzz with accusations that his mother was delaying a union that was bound to decrease her influence over her son and limit her power in the affairs of the kingdom. Later on, her treatment of her daughter-in-law would give some credence to this suspicion. We must not forget that the marriage of a king of France was no trifling matter either, and that they had to find him a partner with a sufficiently high social rank who would bring significant political advantages including the ability—which was much harder to predict—to bear her husband numerous or at least male offspring. (On this last point, people in the Middle Ages believed in their ability to formulate more or less well-founded speculations.) In order to protect family interests, which were dynastic and political in the case of a sovereign, parents in the Middle Ages arranged marriages between powerful persons without allowing the future spouses to have any say in the matter. Typically, the two future spouses never even met until they were married.[2] Love took refuge in abduction, concubinage, adultery, and literature. Marriage for the sake of love had no meaning in the Middle Ages. Modern love as we know it in the West was born and for a long time lived only in the imagination and in illicit relations before it ever existed in conjugal practice. It came into existence through the many obstacles that opposed the feeling of love.

According to Guillaume de Nangis, the marriage was a result of the king's wish, although Louis was probably only complying with custom. The date of the wedding ceremony had to have been the result of an agreement between the king, his mother, their main advisors, and the availability of an appropriate young lady: "In the year of the grace of our Lord, 1234, the eighth year of the reign of the king Saint Louis and the nineteenth year of his life, he desired to have a fruit from his body that would rule the kingdom after him [in other words, a male heir], and he wanted to be married, not for reasons of luxury but to procreate his lineage."[3]

The choice fell on the oldest daughter of Raimond Bérenger V who had been count of Provence since 1209. He was the first count of the Aragonese dynasty of Provence to reside in his lands there on a more or less regular basis, usually at Aix-en-Provence or Brignoles. The marriage introduced the king into a region that interested the French crown in three distinct ways. It completed the Capetian penetration into the former domains of the count of Toulouse in the South that had been dominated for such a long time by the heretics. It reinforced the presence of the French monarchy on the shores of the Mediterranean. In February 1234, Louis IX had just mediated a dispute there between his future father-in-law and the count of Toulouse, Raimond VII, over the possession of Marseille. This also made the French monarchy's presence felt in the imperial lands on the left bank of the Rhone in the Kingdom of Arles, whose curacy had been granted to Richard the Lion-Hearted by Emperor Henry IV at the end of the twelfth century. Thus, in a single stroke, the Provençal marriage also became a part of the anti-English strategy of the French royal power.

After Marguerite, who would marry the king of France, Raimond Bérenger V had three other daughters. His two sons had died at a young age, so he had no male heir.[4] His second daughter, Éléonore or Aliénor, would marry King Henry III of England in 1236. This was the English response to the marriage of Louis and Marguerite. The third daughter, Sanchie or Sanche, would marry Henry III's brother Richard of Cornwall in 1241. She was crowned queen of the Romans at his side at Aix-la-Chapelle in 1257, but would not become empress as her husband failed to become emperor. She would die in 1261. To prevent Provence from being absorbed by France or England, the two powerful kingdoms in the West, Raimond Bérenger V dictated a testament before he died in 1245, designating his fourth daughter Beatrice as heiress to the county. His testament also specified that if Beatrice had no children and if Sanchie had no sons, Provence would go to King James of Aragon. However, Beatrice married the youngest brother of the king of France, Charles d'Anjou, in 1246.[5] When he became king of Naples and Sicily with the help of the papacy, Beatrice was crowned queen in 1265 although she would die less than a year later. Provence then became a possession of the Kingdom of Naples and Sicily.[6]

It would be tempting to say more about this count who had four daughters, all four of them queens, and who became the father-in-law of Christendom, albeit posthumously. It is more important, however, to describe the network of alliances that Louis entered into in 1234 and that would come together between 1236 and 1246. In contrast to Louis IX and his three brothers, Marguerite and her three sisters did not form a solid group. Although the two older sisters, the queen of France and the queen of England, seem to have been very close, they were not very close with their two younger sisters. Born years apart, they did not grow up together through infancy and adolescence. The older sisters also held a grudge against the youngest for inheriting from their father. The relations between France and England showed both the efficiency and the limitations of the system of marital alliances between medieval royal families. Powerless to prevent armed conflict from breaking out between the two kings, Louis IX and Henry III, at the beginning of the 1240s, these family ties would play a positive role in resolving the conflict. Louis would rely on them once he definitively took on the role of peacemaker.

Louis and Marguerite were related in the fourth degree, but on January 2, 1234, Pope Gregory IV lifted the interdiction on consanguine marriages due to "the urgent and clearly useful necessity" for a union that would help bring peace to a region ravaged by heresy and the war against the heretics. Marguerite was barely nubile. She was thirteen years old, and this may be a reason for Louis' relatively late marriage as he would have had to wait for the desired spouse to reach an age at which she was physically capable of being married. The two parties decided the marriage would take place in Sens, a city that was easily accessible from Paris and from Provence and the seat of the prestigious archbishopric on which the bishopric of Paris depended. At the time, Sens was home to one of the main advisors of the royal power, Gautier Cornut. The city also took great pride in its cathedral, one of the first and most beautiful gothic cathedrals in the land.

Everything happened in May. Two envoys from the young king, the Archbishop Gautier Cornut and Jean de Nesle, the faithful advisor held over from the reigns of Philip Augustus and Louis VIII, were responsible for meeting the fiancée in Provence and bringing her to Sens. In Lyon they drafted the king's marriage vows that engaged him to marry Marguerite before Ascension Day, which took place that year on June 1. The engagement agreement was a response to an act sealed on April 30 in Sisteron in which the count and countess of Provence promised to pay the king of France a sum of 8,000 silver marcs payable over a period of five years as a dowry for Marguerite. They also agreed to hand over the castle of Tarascon as a gage. On May 17, the count also agreed to pay the king a supplement of 2,000 marcs.[7] Led by her uncle, Guillaume de Savoie, bishop of Valence, Marguerite passed through Tournus on May 19 and arrived in Sens just before May 28. On May 24, Louis was still at Fontainebleau. On the 25th, he arrived at Pont-sur-Yonne and stopped at the Abbey of Sainte-Colombe near Sens, where he spent the next three days. The marriage took place on Saturday May 27, the day before the Sunday preceding the Ascension.[8]

The attendance was brilliant. Louis' retinue included his mother, Blanche of Castile, his brothers Robert and Alphonse, his cousin Alphonse de Portugal (the future Alphonse III) Blanche of Castile's nephew, various nobles including the faithful Barthélemy de Roye the old servant of Philip Augustus, and several ladies who made up the retinue of Marguerite. Among the guests who responded to the summons of the king, there was the archbishop of Tours; the bishops of Auxerre, Chartres, Meaux, Orléans, Paris, and Troyes; the abbots of Saint-Denis and the monasteries of Sens, Saint-Jean, Saint-Rémi, and Saint-Pierre-le-Vif, as well as the archdeacon and the canons of the chapter of Sens; Jeanne the countess of Flanders and Hainaut; Hugues X the count of the March, the lord of Lusignan; Archambaud IX, the lord of Bourbon; the duke of Burgundy Hugues IV and his wife; Mathilde d'Artois; the countess of Courtenay and Nevers and her husband Guiges V the count of Forez; and, last but not least, the count of Toulouse Raimond VII. So, there were the prelates who were more or less closely tied to the monarchy, including the bishop of Paris and the abbot of Saint-Denis (the archbishop of Reims did not take part in the event), the important lords of the regions, and the holders of the three largest counties in the kingdom, Flanders, the March, and Toulouse. Hugues de Lusignan and Raimond VII were the two most powerful vassals who were often the least inclined to express their loyalty to the king.

The marriage ceremony unfolded in two series of events.[9] It first took place on a platform in front of the outside of the church. Marriage in the Middle Ages had long been only a private contract. In the thirteenth century it was in the process of becoming a sacrament coming under the control of the Church. The external ceremony thus also served as a final public announcement of the marriage (after the publication of bans that was made obligatory by the Fourth Lateran Council twenty years earlier in 1215). The audience was asked one last time if they had any reason to object to the union; the pontifical dispensation had already taken care of the potential objection. The archbishop exhorted the fiancés and passed to the essential rite. In this society of solemn gestures, the ritual act was expressed through a symbolic gesture, the linking of the partners' right hands [dextrarum junctio], which recalled the gesture of a vassal's homage in which the vassal placed his hands between the hands of his lord. This gesture signified the mutual consent of the two spouses because the woman was more or less the equal of the man in the marriage liturgy. Normally, the father of the bride united the hands of the two spouses. In the absence of the count of Provence, Marguerite's uncle, Guillaume de Savoie, the bishop of Valence, was probably the one who carried out this gesture.

Invoking the Holy Spirit, the archbishop blessed and incensed a ring that he then handed to the king who placed it on Marguerite's right hand. First, he placed it on her thumb, saying "*In nomine Patris*" (in the name of the Father), then on her index finger, continuing with "*et filii*" (and of the Son), and finally on the middle finger, ending with "*et Spiritus Sancti, Amen*" (and of the Holy Spirit, Amen). Louis then gave thirteen deniers to Marguerite who gave them back to the archbishop along with the nuptial charter confirming the conclusion of the marriage. The exact meaning of this gesture, the *treizain,* is unknown. In the Middle Ages, writing often completes the gesture. The archbishop's prayers, a benediction, and an incensement of the marriage partners ended this first phase. The young newlyweds then entered the church.

The second phase of the marriage was essentially a mass. Several texts adapted for the event were read or sung: a passage from the First Epistle of Saint Paul to the Corinthians ("Know ye not that your bodies are the members of Christ? . . . Flee fornication! . . . Know ye not that your body is the temple of the Holy Ghost?" 6:15–20); from the Gospel of Mark ("God made them man and woman. . . . And they twain shall be one flesh. . . . Whosoever shall put away his wife, and marry another, commiteth adultery against her. And if a woman shall put away her husband, and be married to another, she committeth adultery" 10:6–12); and a preface thanking God: "You who bound the nuptial ring with the soft yoke of love and the indissolvable tie of peace so that the multiplication of the sons of adoption may be accomplished by the chaste fecundity of the holy nuptials."

Two rites carried out in the course of the mass were particularly significant. After the Preface, the two spouses bowed down at the feet of the archbishop, and someone spread a nuptial veil [*velatio nuptialis*] over the "prostrate" Louis and Marguerite, while the archbishop called on the grace of God for the couple. A similar rite, which was a rite of passage or initiation (in this case representing the passage from celibacy to conjugality) took place during ordinations (marking the passage from the laity to the clergy or of the priest into a bishop) and during the royal coronation (to affect the transformation of the king in practice into a consecrated and therefore a crowned and sacralized king). The ritual ended after a long prayer that voiced the wish for the wife to be kind to her husband like Rachel, wise like Rebecca, and faithful like Sarah.

At the moment of the invocation—"May the Lord's peace always be with you" (*Pax Domini sit semper vobiscum*)—the king mounted the altar to receive the kiss of peace from the archbishop, which he then returned to his new wife. One contemporary, the Dominican Gullaume Peyraut, underscored the importance of this kiss (another ritual of vassalage) with which the husband promised love and protection to his wife: "The husband promised to love his wife when he gave her this kiss during the mass in the presence of the body of the Lord, a kiss that is always a sign of love and peace." Then, Louis and Marguerite took communion.

After the mass, two rites completed the couple's passage into the conjugal state. We have no record of them in the marriage of Louis and Marguerite, but they must have taken place. Some bread and a goblet of wine were blessed by the officiant and symbolically shared by the two partners. These were substitutes for the two forms of communion taken by the king alone among all laymen, in the fashion of the priests, at his coronation mass. Finally, there was the officiant's blessing of the nuptial chamber, and after this the two newlyweds sat or lay down on the bed. As the evidence suggests, this was a fertility rite that underscored the procreative purpose of marriage, its reason for being.

Through one of Marguerite's confidential statements, we learn much later that the young royal spouse did not touch his wife on their wedding night. Like the very devout and formal Christian husbands of the age, he respected the three "nights of Tobias" recommended by the Church, following the virtuous example of Tobias in the Old Testament.

On the day after the wedding, Sunday May 28, 1234, the new young queen was crowned. The inauguration—to borrow an English term that unfortunately does not apply to people in French—of queens in France underwent a noticeable decline in the Middle Ages. Queens were still anointed in the thirteenth century, although not with the miraculous oil of the Holy Ampulla, which was strictly reserved for the king. They were also crowned during the king's coronation if he was already married, or crowned in a special ceremony held shortly after their wedding if their husband was already king. Beginning in the fifteenth century, they were no longer crowned with the king, and during the sixteenth century their crowning was reduced to a minor ceremony.[10] The customary place for the individual crowning of the queen was Saint-Denis, never Reims, although Saint-Denis was not the only place that the ceremony was held. The church of Sens was prestigious enough for its cathedral to provide the setting for the ceremony. The fact that Marguerite's coronation followed immediately after the wedding, the next day, was probably a sign of Louis IX's special consideration for his young wife.

The ceremony must have followed the *ordo* contained in a manuscript dating from approximately 1250. In the third part of this book, I will analyze the two ceremonies, the king's coronation and the crowning of the queen. We should also mention that a great feast followed it and that Louis XI also dubbed several knights and may have used his thaumaturgical power of laying on hands to heal victims of scrofula.[11] With the queen's crowning, the king again adopted a set of rites based on his own coronation and that also resulted from it. On the other hand, I do not believe that Louis IX also created a new order of knighthood in Sens, the *Coste de Geneste,* as some have written.[12] Records of this order only appear a century and a half later during the reign of Charles VI, who unsuccessfully tried to develop it and who probably created it himself. To make it seem more illustrious, someone invented an origin legend for it that extended back to Saint Louis, the "great man" (and the saint) of the dynasty. The creation of a chivalric order like this corresponds neither to the spirit of the thirteenth century nor to Saint Louis' behavior, whatever kind of chivalrous king might he have been or wanted to be.[13]

We are lucky enough to possess the records of the royal accounts paid for the wedding in Sens. They afford us a glimpse of some of the material, economic, and symbolic aspects of the event.[14]

The festivities in Sens apparently cost 2,526 pounds from the Royal Treasury. This sum paid for the transportation of the royal cortege and its baggage in carts and by boat, the harnessing for the horses, the carpets, the wooden platforms, and the leaf-gilt lodge where Louis sat on a silk sheet during the external ceremony, the jewels, the gifts — including a golden cup for the master cupbearer — the tablecloths and napkins for the feast, and most of all the many sumptuous clothes for the ceremony including many of woolen cloth, silk, and various furs.[15] Here we find the great vestimentary luxury of the Middle Ages. For the king and his retinue, people made "felt hats wrapped in cloth the color of peacocks' feathers or ornamented with peacock feathers and cotton." For the queen, they chose "furs of ermine and sable." Marguerite wore a dress of brownish pink, and her gold crown cost 58 pounds. "Monsignor Alphonse de Portugal, the nephew," was dressed in purple. They spent 98 pounds for bread, 307 pounds for wine, 667 pounds for the cooked dishes, and 50 pounds for wax. Marguerite brought six trumpet players and the count of Provence's minstrel with her. Other minstrels came to perform for the games and dances.

Saint Louis' wedding was held with all the splendor of the royal weddings of the age. The young king was always careful to carry himself with the dignity of his position. Although he would increasingly limit the external signs of his wealth and power, at this time he was still immersed in the tradition of royal luxury.

On June 8, Louis and Marguerite entered Paris amidst new festivities.[16]

The "Chivalry" of Brothers. Joinville's Appearance

These lavish customs appeared in three family ceremonies that completed the unity and rank of the quartet of "sons of the king" that Louis formed with his three surviving brothers. We are talking about "chivalry," in other words, about the dubbing of the brothers, which was an occasion for great festivities. For these young men, this was a triple entry into their rights of majority, in this case at twenty years of age, their entrance into the superior society of laymen, into knighthood, and into the governance of their inherited lands. The event was carried out according to the testament of Louis VIII, but it was presented as the personal decision of Louis IX.

Robert was dubbed in 1237 and assumed possession of Artois. Alphonse was dubbed in 1241 and received Poitou. In 1246, Charles was dubbed and took over Anjou. One exceptional account records the memory of the knighting of Alphonse de Poitiers in Saumur on June 24, 1241. He was dubbed on Saint John's Day when Christian knights celebrated their initiation into knighthood on the same day that ancient pagan rituals, the fires of Saint John, recalled the memory of the summer solstice festivals and the year's passage to its zenith.

This privileged witness was the young Joinville. At seventeen, he was still a squire and one of the modest participants, fascinated by this festival that brought him closer to the royal family. It was probably the first time that he set eyes on the king who was ten years his senior. Several years later, he would become part of his circle, one of his close companions smitten with admiration and affection. He would leave us with a treasured memory of the king in an extraordinary and inestimable biography.

The king summoned his court to Saumur in Anjou, and I was there and I can testify that it was the best organized meeting that I had ever seen: at the king's table right next to him sat the count of Poitiers whom he had made into a knight on Saint John's Day, and next to him was the count Jean de Dreux whom he had also just knighted; next to Jean de Dreux sat the count of the March, and next to the count of the March was the good count Pierre de Bretagne. And in front of the king's table, across from the count de Dreux, sat His Royal Highness the king of Navarre in a tunic and a satin cloak, nicely outfitted with a buckle, a clasp, and a piece of gold brocade, and I was sitting right across from him.

The count d'Artois served the food in front of the king, his brother. The good count Jean de Soissons sliced the meat before the king. To guard the king's table, there was Lord Imbert de Beaujeu, who had since been constable of France, and Lord Enguerran de Coucy and Lord Archambaud de Bourbon. Behind these three barons, there were about thirty of their knights, dressed in silk tunics, to protect them; and behind these knights was a large number of sergeants dressed in the arms of the count de Poitiers applied in taffeta. The king was wearing a blue satin tunic and an overcoat and a cloak of vermilion satin trimmed with ermine, and on his head a cotton hat that suited him poorly because he was still a young man.

The king held this feast in the halls of Saumur, and people said that the great King Henry of England had made them to hold his great feasts. These halls are made in the same way as the cloisters of the Cistercians, but I believe that there are none as big as these because at the wall of the cloister where the king was eating, where he was surrounded with knights and sergeants who took up a great space, there were still twenty bishops and archbishops eating at a table nearby, and further down next to this table there was another where Queen Blanche, the king's mother, was eating at the other end of the cloister from her son.[17]

Here we glimpse the scene through the eyes of a bedazzled young man. He was a "provincial" to boot, from a modest familial castle in Champagne. For us, it is one of the first "true" looks at the external appearance of Saint Louis. He was still a sumptuous king in terms of his environment and his personal appearance, although one detail reveals the twenty-seven-year-old king's inclination toward humility and aversion to worldly appearances: his head was poorly dressed. He was wearing a cotton hat that clashed with his other clothes and that made him look older and more homely. The burgeoning seduction that Saint Louis exerted on the young Joinville, who had been raised to respect propriety and chivalric decorum, allowed him to see things clearly and made him sensitive to the meaningful details craved by the vampiric historian who traffics in the fresh flesh of history too often refused him.

THE KING AS FATHER

Since May 27, 1234, Louis had been married to a young girl who, along with her sisters, was praised by contemporaries for her beauty. She had been married in order to procreate. This was both the teaching of the Church, the requirement of dynastic existence, and the fulfillment of an attitude that, in order to conform to the morality and the rules of Christian conjugality, would not take any less advantage of everything "conceded" to the flesh. This was clearly the version of marriage according to Saint Paul: "Better to marry than to burn."

Nevertheless, the couple would have no offspring until 1240, six years after the wedding. This might have been because the young queen's fertility was slow to develop. There were probably also miscarriages or even children who died in infancy, which the documents and chroniclers of the time never mention. Blanche of Castile lost several children like this in the early years of her marriage. The only ones who left any trace of their existence were those who reached an age at which there was some reasonable hope of seeing them play a role in the dynasty's matrimonial strategy, either by attaining the age of the majority or by being engaged. We really do not know.

They had two daughters to begin with, which did nothing to assure the dynasty's future. Blanche was born on July 12, 1240, but she died three years later. Then Isabelle was born on March 18, 1242. Finally, they had three sons. Louis was born on February 25, 1244, Philip on May 1, 1245, and Jean, who was born and died almost immediately after in 1248. When the king left on the crusade in August 1248, the future seemed safe with the two remaining sons. The royal couple would engender six more children, three of them in the Orient and three after their return to France. Seven of Louis and Marguerite's eleven children would survive their father, including four sons. This was the demography of a typically fertile royal couple in the thirteenth century.

THE KING OF RELICS: THE CROWN OF THORNS

In thirteenth-century Christendom, one important expression of devotion was the possession of distinguished relics, which was also a sign of great prestige. The fortunes of a city, a domain, or even a kingdom could depend on them. A relic was an active treasure that engendered benefits and protection. Saint Louis experienced this with the theft of the Holy Nail of Saint-Denis.

Baudouin the younger, the nephew of Baudouin IX of Flanders, became the first Latin emperor of Constantinople after the taking of the city by the Western crusaders. He was the son of Pierre Courtenay, who preceded him as emperor of Constantinople from 1216 to 1219. In 1237, Emperor Baudouin came to France to seek help from the king and Christendom against the Greeks. He was nineteen years old and upon reaching his majority had to don the imperial diadem that was owed him as his birthright, but that his father-in-law Jean de Brienne had worn in waiting. However, continually eaten away by the Greeks who left them only the city and its immediate surroundings, the Latin empire of Constantinople was no longer anything more than a shrinking skin.

During his stay in France where he was well cared for by his cousin Louis,[18] Baudouin received two pieces of bad news. First, he learned of the death of Jean de Brienne. Second, he learned of the intention of the Latin barons of Constantinople, hard pressed by a serious lack of money, to sell the most precious relic of the city to a group of foreigners. This relic was the Crown of Thorns that Jesus wore as a sign of humility during his Passion. The new emperor Baudouin II begged Louis and Blanche of Castile to help him prevent the holy crown from falling into foreign hands.

The king and his mother were immediately impassioned. What a marvelous opportunity it was to acquire this crown that would gratify their piety and flatter their glory! A crown of humility, the relic was a crown after all. It was a royal relic. It embodied the humble and suffering royalty that the image of Christ had become in the mournful worship of the thirteenth century. Their imagination placed it on the king's head, an image of Jesus on this earth, an image of the kingdom in suffering and of the triumph over death through suffering. Whatever the strength and authenticity of Louis' feelings might have been in this affair, one cannot help but remark that it was a "real coup." The young king of France made his mark upon Christendom. The political and ideological stakes clearly did not escape the king and his mother. After the *translatio imperii* and the *translatio studii* from the East to the West, now we had the *translatio Sacratissimae Passionis instrumentorum,* the "transfer of the implements of the Most Holy Passion." And the destination of this distinguished relic, its fated resting place, was France, which began to look more and more like the favored land of God and Jesus. Gautier Cornut, the archbishop of Sens, the friend and servant of the king, the head of the "Gallican" Church, emphasizes this:

> Just as our Lord Jesus Christ chose the Land of the promise [the Holy Land] to reveal the mysteries of his redemption, it very much seems and people believe that in order to more piously venerate the triumph of his Passion, he specifically chose our France [*nostram Galliam*] so that from the East to the West the name of our Lord would be praised by the transfer of the implements of his very Holy Passion carried out by our Lord and Redeemer from the region [*a climate*] of Greece, that people say is the closest to the Orient, to France that extends to the frontiers of the West.[19]

France was becoming a new Holy Land. Of Louis himself, the prelate says: "He rejoiced that our Lord would have chosen his France [*suam Galliam*] in order to grant an honor of this importance, France where faith in his clemency is so strong and where the mysteries of our salvation are celebrated with such great devotion."[20]

Thus began the adventures and tribulations of the Crown of Thorns, including its long and marvelous voyage from Constantinople to Paris.

Baudoin II sent a messenger with a letter from Paris, ordering that the Crown of Thorns be entrusted to the messengers sent by Louis, two Dominicans, Jacques and André. Jacques had been a Dominican prior in Constantinople and would be able to certify the relic's authenticity. In effect, we have to understand the attitudes of Western Christians toward the relics in general and this extraordinary one in particular. They had no doubt that Christ's actual Crown of Thorns could have been preserved in Constantinople. Saint Helen was the mother of Emperor Constantine in the fourth century and the inventor of the True Cross in the Christian tradition. Her travels in the Holy Land and the records indicating that Emperor Heraclius brought this True Cross from Jerusalem to Constantinople in 630 lent some historical credence to this belief. The "criticism" of the relics that developed in the West in the eleventh and twelfth centuries inspired the Benedictine abbot Guibert de Nogent to write his famous treatise, "Des reliques des saints" (*De pignoribus sanctorum*) at some time between 1119 and 1129.[21] This critique called for all kinds of precautions to be taken during the lengthy transfer of the very holy relic. At each stage of the journey, they had to carefully check to make sure that a false copy had not replaced the holy object while it was being transported in its special reliquary (just as the miraculous water of Reims was kept in the Holy Ampulla).

When the messengers of Emperor Baudouin II and of King Louis IX arrived in Constantinople, they learned that the government's need for money had become so urgent that the Latin barons borrowed from Venetian merchant bankers and gave them the Crown of Thorns as a gage. If no one bought the relic back before the festival of the holy martyrs Gervais and Protais (June 18), it would become the property of the Venetians and transferred to the City by the Lagoon. It turned out that the Venetian merchants were working in the service of the pope's policy on relics. In the ninth century, the pope had already pulled off another sensational deal by purchasing the relics of Saint Mark in Alexandria. They would make up an important part of the prestige of the republic of the doges. The search for the Crown had a dramatic ending. The messengers from Baudouin and Louis arrived just before the fateful date. Having already paid for the Crown of Thorns, the king of France made his claim prevail. They entered into negotiations. The Venetians agreed to hand over the distinguished relic to the king of France on one condition: they insisted that the Crown of Thorns go to Venice first and that the city of the doges reap the benefits, however temporary, from the material presence of the prodigious relic in Venice. Touched by the relic, the republic would derive a certain degree of protection, benefits, and prestige from it.

The end of the negotiations takes us to Christmas Day, 1238. Was it safe to transport this precious treasure by sea during the winter when it was so difficult to navigate? In addition, they learned that the Greeks had used their spies to find out about the relic's sale and its imminent transport by sea. They spread word of the possible itineraries among their galleys in order to seize the holy merchandise. Nevertheless, amid the tears and sighs of Constantinople's residents, the Crown of Thorns set out to sea. God protected it and it arrived safely in Venice where it was displayed in the palace chapel, Saint Mark's. Brother André stayed in Venice to look after the relic, while Friar Jacques traveled ahead to relay the good news to Louis and his mother. He returned quickly to Venice with the enormous sum of money needed to make the purchase. (We don't know what the exact price was today.) He also returned with Baudouin II's envoys. They oversaw the exchange and assured the approval of the emperor of Constantinople. New negotiations opened in which French merchants in Venice played an active role. In the end, the Venetians did not dare oppose Baudouin's will or the determination of the French king. Venice shed its own tears as it reluctantly watched the Crown depart for its final destination.

This time, the relic was transported over land, although the fears were no less great. The relic continued to make its protection felt, proving that the king of France benefited from divine protection. To assure its safety, the voyagers had been given an imperial pass of safe-conduct from Frederick II. This was the greatest legal guarantee in all of Christendom in matters of temporal security. The relic's miraculous powers also influenced the weather conditions. Not a drop of rain fell during the Crown's transport by day. On the other hand, when the relic was sheltered in hospices for the night, the rain fell in droves. The sign of divine protection was therefore obvious.

Louis set forth to greet the holy acquisition, just as he had set out in advance five years earlier to greet his fiancée. With him he brought his mother, his brothers, the archbishop of Sens Gautier Cornut who was very active in this stage of the journey, the bishop of Auxerre Bernard, and numerous other barons and knights. He met with the holy object at Villeneuve-l'Archevêque.

There was intense emotion when they presented the golden shrine containing the relic to the king. They checked to make sure that the seals of the Latin barons of Constantinople and the doge of Venice who sent it were still intact. They opened the lid and uncovered the priceless treasure [*inaestimabilis margarita*]. The king, the queen mother, and their companions were choked up with emotion. They cried abundant tears and moaned. "They stood dumbstruck at the sight of the lovingly desired object. Their devout spirits were transfixed with such fervor that they thought they saw the Lord before them in person carrying the Crown of Thorns at that very moment."[22] In a sharp study on the mentality of the crusaders who during the taking of Jerusalem in 1099 believed that they were punishing the very people who had crucified Christ, Paul Rousset has analyzed the complete negation of historical time that this type of behavior entailed.[23] Facing the Crown of Thorns, Saint Louis and his companions spontaneously found themselves in the same state of mind. This was what the flexibility of the Christian medieval sense of time was like. Overcome with strong emotion born from the resurrection of the memory of Christ, earthly time came to a stop and became concentrated in this moment that Saint Augustine so movingly described as the extreme limit of the feeling of eternity. Nine years before his departure on the crusade, Saint Louis experienced the crusader's ecstasy. This happened on Saint Lawrence's eve, August 9, 1239.

Next came the penitential procession that accompanied the distinguished sign of Christ's humiliated kingship, the union of the king and his companions with the Passion of Jesus, and their participation in the return of the Incarnation. The king and his oldest brother Robert carried the shrine barefoot and in their shirts (in other words, wearing only a single tunic on their bodies) from Villeneuve-l'Archevêque to Sens. They were surrounded by other knights who had taken off their shoes. When they arrived in the town in the midst of an immense applauding crowd escorted by clerics dressed in silk and monks and other religious carrying all the relics of all the saints of the city and the region who had all come together to somehow salute the living Lord in his relic, the procession advanced to the ringing of bells and the blaring of organs through the streets and squares that had been decorated with carpets and wall hangings. At nightfall, the cortege marched by torchlight, its path lit by twisted candles [*cum candelis tortilibus*]. They finally deposited the relic in Saint-Étienne's cathedral for the night. In reading Gautier Cornut's account of all this, we can sense that the archbishop was overcome with joy. These hours that the Crown of Thorns had been in his city and in his church were an extraordinary recompense for a life spent in the service of God and the royal family.

The last stage of the voyage began the next day. They spent eight days traveling by boat on the Yonne and the Seine to Vincennes where the king had his palace outside the city. The shrine was displayed on a high platform near Saint-Antoine's church so that all the people from Paris who had come out to see it could admire it. Once more, the entire clergy came bearing the relics of the Parisian saints. Preachers exalted the honor that had fallen on the Kingdom of France. Then, as in Sens, Louis and his brother Robert carried the shrine into the walls of the city, barefoot and wearing only their shirts, followed by the prelates, clerics, religious, and knights all barefoot, too.

They stopped for a few moments with the relic in Saint-Mary's cathedral (Notre-Dame) so that worship of Christ's mother could be expressed in unison with the worship of her son. Finally, the Crown of Thorns reached its final destination after its long voyage from the shores of the Bosphorus to the shores of the Seine, the royal palace. They deposed it in the palace chapel, the chapel of Saint-Nicolas. Protecting the kingdom, the Crown was first of all a distinguished possession of the king. The relic was a royal but private possession, although its protection extended over the king, his kingdom, and his subjects.

As the emperor of Constantople's misfortunes and desperate need for money continued to grow, Louis spent an amazing amount to complete his collection of relics of the Passion. In 1241, he acquired a part of the True Cross, the Holy Sponge that Christ's cruel tormentors gave him to drink vinegar from on the cross, and the iron from the Holy Lance that Longinus used to pierce his side.

The Sainte-Chapelle

The palatine chapel of Saint-Nicolas was a very modest place to keep treasures like this. For the relics of the Passion, for the crown of Christ, they needed a church that would be a glorious shrine, a palace worthy of the Lord. Louis decided to build a new chapel, the one that would keep the simple name Sainte-Chapelle that referred to all palatine chapels. In effect, according to Louis' wishes, the Sainte-Chapelle would become both "a monumental reliquary" and a "royal sanctuary" (Louis Grodecki). Louis never missed an opportunity to associate the glory of the king with the glory of God.

In May 1243, Pope Innocent IV granted the privileges for the future chapel. In January 1246, Louis founded a college of canons for keeping the relics and celebrating the cults. In 1246 and 1248, royal charters set aside the resources needed for the construction and especially for the stained glass windows. The solemn consecration took place in the king's presence on April 26, 1248, two months before Saint Louis' departure for the crusade. The chapel's construction, including the windows and probably the sculptures too, was thus completed in record time. According to the inquiry into Saint Louis' canonization, the Sainte-Chapelle cost 40,000 pounds *tournois* and the shrine for the relics of the Passion cost 100,000. We do not know the name of the main architect and his assistants.[24]

Since the time of Louis IX, the Sainte-Chapelle has passed for a chef-d'oeuvre. The English chronicler Matthew Paris calls it, "a chapel of marvelous beauty worthy of this royal treasure."[25] No one has described the charm of this church better than Henri Focillon:

> the dimensions of the Sainte-Chapelle, so much larger than the apsidal chapels at Amiens, gave the strangest and most paradoxical authority to a scheme which seems to defy gravity, at least when viewed from within. The wall mass, having been eliminated to make room for the stained-glass windows, reappears outside in the massive buttresses, as if the sidewalls had been turned on hinges to a position at right angles to their original one. In addition the archivolts of the windows receive a new load, to prevent them from yielding to the thrust of the vaults, in the form of a stone triangle, the gable, whose weight bears relatively lightly on the flanks of the arch but is concentrated over the keystone, playing a part analogous to that of the pinnacles of the buttresses. Everything, indeed, in this building betrays the refinement of its solutions, from the system of equilibrium, which we have briefly analyzed, devised for the sake of the interior effect, to the vaulting of the undercroft on which it stands. There is a severity in its grace, which has nothing of mediocrity. This conception delighted its century, and was acclaimed a masterpiece.[26]

Whatever boldness and beauty the Sainte-Chapelle may offer, we have also stressed the fact that it did not present any real innovations. It simply brought the architecture of traditional gothic apsidal chapels, the lengthening of high windows and the classical gothic art of stained glass window making, to completion. It also bore the signs of the limitations its functions imposed on it: dimensions that were still modest because it was only a palatine chapel, and the rupturing of certain lines and spaces necessitated by the presentation of the relics. The high chapel was designed for these relics that form the *palladium* ("the holy shield") of the Kingdom of France, to use a fitting expression coined by Jean Richard.[27] Some have described the so-called window "of the relics" as "the key to the entire iconographic program."[28] Doesn't this monument so closely tied to Saint Louis' personality and his objectives in worship and power definitively resemble him? Doesn't it embody the union of his modesty and his boldness and his ostentation, the supreme surge of tradition breaking on the shores of innovation?

AN ESCHATOLOGICAL KING: THE MONGOL APOCALYPSE

We have already seen that on the global scale the most important event of the thirteenth century was the formation of the Mongol Empire.[29] Louis IX would only have distant contacts with the Mongols through the intermediary of ambassadors carrying vague propositions weakened by mutual ignorance and delusion. At the time, the French king shared all Christendom's anxiety when the Mongols advanced into Hungary and the south of Poland after laying waste to Russia and the Ukraine, reaching Kraków and the outskirts of Vienna in 1241. Let's remember the essential part of this literally apocalyptic episode: in the form of a vision it showed Louis the ultimate perspectives on his destiny and its profound relation to the fate of Christendom and humanity. This was a new, extremely intense religious experience that Saint Louis saw. These hordes might be the peoples of Gog and Magog that had escaped the bounds of their confinement in the far eastern reaches of the earth and who brought the massacres and destruction announced in the Apocalypse as a prelude to the end of the world. Distraught but of sound mind, if it was true as Matthew Paris tells it, in the midst of the tears he always cried in these moments of extreme emotion, joy, or fear, he wrote to his mother: "Have courage. . . . If they fall upon us, we will either throw them down to the Tartarian realms from which they came, these beings that we call Tartars, or they will be the ones who deliver us all to heaven."

Two fates—and perhaps two desires—appeared to the young twenty-seven-year-old king: the eschatological destiny of the end of time and the destiny of a martyr.

THE CONQUERING KING: THE WAR AGAINST THE ENGLISH

Despite the Mongol menace, less exotic dangers were threatening the kingdom. During Louis IX's childhood and adolescence, the English monarchy had never ceased from being the French monarchy's main enemy and the greatest threat facing the construction of the French monarchical state.

At nine years of age, Henry III had succeeded his father John Lackland in 1216. Upon reaching adulthood, he had never renounced his claim to the English territories in France that had been reconquered by Philip Augustus. He also disputed the judgment rendered by the court of French peers that had recognized the legitimacy of the king of France's confiscation of John Lackland's fiefs in the west of France. However, he was torn between the English barons who had limited his powers by forcing his father to grant the Magna Carta and the French barons like the count of Brittany and the count of the March who counted on him to emancipate them from their submission to the king of France. He also vacillated between his prudent advisor Hubert de Burgh and his hotheaded brother Richard of Cornwall. In the middle of these opposing parties, for a long time, Henry III made only weak moves to reconquer those lands. The support the popes Honorius III and Gregory IX had successively given to his claims had no effect on Blanche of Castile, the young Louis, and their advisors. We might recall that the pitiful English campaign of 1231–1232 had ended in a number of truces, and that in November 1234 Henry III's main ally in France, the count of Brittany, Pierre Mauclerc had rallied to the king of France. Pope Gregory IX wanted to maintain the balance of power between the two kingdoms. He especially wanted to show consideration for the king of France so as to secure his support against the emperor who was opening hostilities against him. In 1238, he got Henry III and Louis IX to agree to renew their truces for another five years.

The break in the peace came from one of the major traditional players on the political theater of western France, Hugues de Lusignan or Hugh the Brown, the count of the March. Beginning in 1238, he found himself confronted by a new antagonist in the region, the king's own brother Alphonse. When Blanche of Castile and her advisors had managed to neutralize Hugues de la Marche in 1227, the peace agreement stipulated that one of Hugues X's daughters would marry one of Louis IX's brothers — Alphonse. But, in 1229 Alphonse was engaged to Jeanne, daughter of the count of Toulouse as stipulated by one of the provisions of the Treaty of Meaux-Paris that had ended the Albigensian Crusade. During renegotiations of the agreement between the king and the count of the March in 1230, they decided that the king's sister Isabelle was supposed to marry Hugues, the oldest son and heir of Hugues X. However, in 1238, Hugues de la Marche the younger married Yolande, the daughter of Pierre Mauclerc, the count of Brittany, while between 1238 and 1241, at an unknown date, Alphonse actually married Jeanne de Toulouse. Upon reaching the age of majority and entering knighthood, Alphonse received the county of Poitiers and Auvergne as specified in Louis VIII's testament.

The new count's lands surrounded the county of the March, and what's more, Hugues X was supposed to transfer his fealty as a vassal from the king of France, a very honorable lord, to Alphonse de Poitiers, a lord of lower rank. After the festivals of Saumar, however, Hugues X pledged fealty to Alphonse de Poitiers. This situation displeased his wife even more. She was Isabelle d'Angoulême, the widow of John Lackland who, having remarried with the count of the March, wanted to at least preserve her status as a queen. Here was what provoked the rupture: in 1230 when he promised to marry his sister Isabelle to the young Hugues de la Marche, Louis IX had surrendered Aunis and Saint-Jean-d'Angély to Hugues X as a gage. Now that Alphonse had taken control of the county of Poitou that included these gages in its territory, the king of France insisted upon the return of Aunis and Saint-Jean-d'Angély to Alphonse, basing his claim on the dissolution of the previous marriage agreement (although we do not know who was responsible for that).

Hugues X decided to break with the king, symbolically destroying the house that he held in Poiters for the purpose of swearing allegiance to his lord. Then, during the solemn assembly of the vassals of the count of Poitou in Poitiers on Christmas Day in 1241, he publicly denounced his previous allegiance. After vainly attempting to make him reverse his decision, Louis submitted his case to the court of the peers of France who judged in favor of confiscating the rebel's fiefs.

Wasting no time, the count of the March had already formed a league against the king of France. Most of the barons of Poitou, the seneschal of Guyenne, the cities of Bordeaux, Bayonne, La Réole, and Saint-Émilion, Raimond VII the count of Toulouse, and most of the barons of Languedoc joined it. Thus a formidable alliance reuniting a large number of the seigniories and cities south of the Loire had taken shape. From its inception, the king of England had an interest in this coalition, although at first he was held back by the agreements he made in the truces of 1238 and by the reluctance of the English barons. Some contemporaries suspected Emperor Frederick II of encouraging these allies and of making overtures to Henry III of England, his brother-in-law.[30] It appears that the emperor had actually been more cautious than this, and Louis IX kept up their contacts. In this same year of 1241, Pope Gregory IX offered Louis IX to give the Roman crown to his brother Robert d'Artois. He had already excommunicated Frederick II for the second time in 1239. This gesture implied the promise of the imperial crown with royal authority in Germany. The king of France did not want to get mixed up in this affair and wanted to maintain good relations with the emperor, although without abandoning his interventions in the Kingdom of Arles. He declined the offer for his brother, authorized some of his vassals to swear allegiance to Frederick II, and refused to join the coalition that the pope was trying to form against him.

He sent his reassurances to the emperor while humbling him at the same time. Louis' envoys announced to Frederick II that: "The Lord does not wish us ever to attack a Christian without good reason. We are not motivated by ambition. We believe, in effect, that our sire the king of France, that a lineage of royal blood has promoted to govern the Kingdom of France, is superior to any emperor who has only been promoted by a voluntary election. It is enough for the count Robert to be the brother of such a great king."[31] Gregory IX died on August 22, 1241. The pontifical throne would remain empty until the election of Innocent IV almost two years later on June 25, 1243.[32]

After the rejection of Hugues de la Marche, the king of England decided to join the coalition in order to reclaim his rights in France. On the other hand, the count of Brittany, Pierre Mauclerc, had just returned from the Holy Land where he took part in the "Crusade of the Barons" (1239–1241) that was funded by a loan from Saint Louis. He refused to budge.

The war would last one year, from April 28, 1242 to April 7, 1243.[33] It occurred in three phases. From April 28 to July 20, 1242, the king of France was only opposed by the count of the March and his allies, and the war consisted in a series of sieges. From July 21 to August 4, 1242, Louis IX marched against the English, defeated them outside of Saintes, and pursued them all the way to Blaye. From August 4, 1242 to April 7, 1243, the war continued against the count of Toulouse, Raimond VII, who surrendered on October 20. In October and November, the English tried to blockade La Rochelle and failed as Henry III made fruitless attempts to rebuild his army and his alliances.

I will discuss only a few details about the first two phases of the war, because this was where Louis acquired his reputation as a military leader, which assumed a new dimension here.

Eight days after Easter, which fell on April 20 in 1242, Louis summoned the royal host to meet on April 28 in Chinon. From Poitiers where he was staying with his brothers, Louis gave the signal for the campaign to begin on May 4. He led a powerful army with 4,000 knights, 20,000 squires, sergeants, and crossbowmen, and 1,000 wagons. The towns would provide the necessary provisions. The army set out on the campaign in a perfectly orderly manner, "as was the custom among the French," writes the English Benedictine monk Matthew Paris. One after another, the army lay siege to and captured the castles of Montreuil-Bonin, Béruge, Fontenay, Prez, Saint-Gelais, Tonnay-Boutonne, Matus, Thoré, and Saint-Affaire.[34] The French were well equipped with siege engines including wooden towers, catapults, and "raised engines." This military equipment and the spirited discipline of the French troops urged on by their king explained these repeated successes. There were many prisoners, and the king sent them to Paris and other locations in the kingdom. Then, near Taillebourg, the French and English armies met.

Henry III left Portsmouth on May 9 and debarked at Royan on the 13th.[35] With little conviction, both sides joined in useless talks that went nowhere. Henry III declared war on the king of France on June 16. He had to make hasty preparations because he had come with too few troops. In the meantime, the French were mopping up in Poitou.

On July 20, the French were searching out the English and arrived at Taillebourg. The town surrendered immediately. Nearby, there were two bridges over the Charente. One was made of stone and extended by an embankment. The other was a wooden bridge linking Taillebourg and Saintes. On July 21, the two armies faced off at this point looking across the Charente, which was not fordable at this time of year. The French pushed the English back across the stone bridge, and the English beat a rapid retreat to Saintes. The next day, July 22, Louis IX crossed the Charente and the battle took place outside of Saintes: "There," writes Guillaume de Nangis, there was a marvelous and mighty battle and a great slaughter of people and the bitter and hard-fought battle lasted a long time, but in the end, the English could not sustain the French attacks and fled. When the English king saw what was happening, he was shocked and retreated as quickly as he could toward the town of Saintes. Seeing that they were retreating, the French pursued them in great haste and killed many and took a great many prisoners. . . . On the night after the battle, the king of England and the count of the March fled with the rest of their people and evacuated the city and the castle of Saintes. The next morning, on July 24, the citizens of Saintes came and turned over the keys of the city and the castle to Louis. King Louis stationed a garrison there.[36]

Henry III retreated to Pons, but on July 25, the lord of Pons Renaud surrendered to Louis IX, who had reached Colombières. On July 26, Hugues de Lusignan surrendered in turn. Henry III barely escaped capture in Barbezieux where he had taken refuge. He barely escaped between the night of July 26 and the morning of July 27, abandoning his baggage and his chapel. He reached Blaye but was forced to evacuate before the approach of the French king who entered the town on August 4, while Henry III was returning to Bordeaux.

Hugues de Lusignan's surrender was an amazing spectacle. He showed up with his wife and his three sons. The king of England had just knighted his two youngest sons. Sobbing and crying, he knelt before the king of France and begged aloud for his forgiveness. The king lifted him up on his feet and offered to pardon him on two conditions: that he return all the castles that he had taken from Alphonse de Poitiers, and that he give him, the king, three castles in gage. To avenge an offense that Hugues had committed against him, Geoffrey de Rançon, lord of Taillebourg, had turned the town over to Louis IX and vowed that he would not cut his hair until he got even. He had his hair cut in public on this occasion. Hugues de la Marche's prestige had been squandered in this affair and to add insult to injury, a younger French knight with a great military reputation threw down the glove to challenge him to a duel. Fearing for the loss of their leader, Hugues' entourage asked the king to intervene to protect him. Moved to pity, Louis persuaded the challenger to renounce the duel.

Although Louis IX's losses in the battle were relatively low, he next dealt with an outbreak of dysentery that was decimating his army. He became sick himself, and several members of his entourage were alarmed, recalling the similar epidemic that took Louis VIII's life at Montpensier during his return from the Albigensian Crusade. The medieval warrior, spared in battle, often fell victim to outbreaks of disease. Weakened but healed, Louis finally returned to Tours at the end of August, and from there he continued on to Paris. The war seemed to be over on this front. Henry III was still in Bordeaux and ordered the blockade of La Rochelle, which failed. His brother, Richard of Cornwall, had already returned to England in October 1242. The king of England had sent a message to Emperor Frederick from Saintes in June, seeking an alliance against the king of France. He now wrote to him to announce the end of his hopes. In March, he wrote Louis IX to request a five-year truce, and Louis granted it without hesitation.

Even more than in our memory of the king's campaigns as an adolescent after his succession to the throne, a king who was more present than active on the field of battle, in all this we find the image of the warrior king, of the king who was a leader in war, a chivalrous king, and, as appropriate for a sacred king, a king who was a conqueror. The king thrived in fulfilling this second function that all of his ancestors had exercised with more or less brilliance. The king who worshipped the relics also knew how to accomplish great feats in these battles that made the hearts of the medieval nobility pound with excitement and that even a monk like Guillaume de Nangis described as "marvelous."

Next, the king of France scored yet another decisive victory in Languedoc over the count of Toulouse, Raimond VII. The lords of the South seem to have benefited for a long time from Blanche of Castile's personal indulgence. The king allowed the Church to impose the Inquisition in 1233 and played no direct role in the persecution of the heretics. However, in 1240 the viscount of Béziers Trencavel wanted to take back the lands that had been confiscated from his father in 1209 during the expedition of the crusaders from the North against the heretics of the South. The Treaty of Meaux-Paris in 1229 had made these lands the definitive possessions of the king of France, who brought them together under the seneschalcy of Béziers-Carcassonne. Trencavel tried to seize Carcassonne, but the royal seneschal, the archbishop of Narbonne, and the nobles of the region shut themselves up inside the city and held their ground until a royal army was able to relieve them and force Trencavel to lift the siege.

This was when Raimond VII of Toulouse allied himself with the coalition of barons of Poitou and the king of England in 1242, although he had already renewed his allegiance to the king of France in 1241. The counts of Foix, Comminges, Armagnac, Rodez, and the viscounts of Narbonne and Béziers all rallied behind the count of Toulouse, while other families like the knights of Carcassès and the lords of Anduze residing in the foothills of the Cévennes remained loyal to the king. A bit of help from the people of Montségur was enough to light the fuse. On May 29, 1242, they assassinated two inquisitors and the archdeacon of Toulouse in one of the count of Toulouse's houses in Avignonet. After joining Henry III in Blaye in late July, Raimond VII returned to the region after the English king's defeat at Saintes. He retook Narbonne, captured by the viscount Aimery on August 17, and Albi and proclaimed the return of these two towns into his holdings.

Louis sent two armies into Languedoc after imposing peace on the West and the king of England. The count of Foix immediately abandoned the count of Toulouse. The king released him from his allegiance to Raimond VII, whom he promptly turned against on October 15. Raimond VII was soon obliged to request the king's pardon. He asked Blanche of Castile to intervene on his son's behalf. The king granted his request and made a new treaty with the count of Toulouse in Lorris in January 1243. Raimond abandoned his claims to Narbonne and Albi, promised to raze certain castles, agreed to immediately undertake the extirpation of heretics on his lands, and finally to carry out his oath to take part in a crusade.

The "pacification" of the Midi would take several more years to completely eliminate the remaining pockets of resistance. One legendary event from this ongoing campaign was the siege of Montségur in 1243–1244. The bailiff Hugues d'Arcis laid siege to the citadel because its lord refused to recognize the treaty of Lorris and continued his rebellion against the king. Apparently, the French promised not to harm the inhabitants during their surrender. However, only the mere rebels were pardoned, while the people who admitted to being heretics were burned at the stake. These were the last gasps of opposition to the French monarchy in the Midi. Saint Louis would confide the job of helping the Church combat the last heretics to his officers and his brother Alphonse de Poitiers who succeeded his father-in-law Raimond VII in 1249. Still, unlike his father, he did not show any particular desire to get involved personally in this region. Except for the new and out of the way town of Aigues-Mortes, he would never visit it.

The King's Illness and His Vow to Crusade

After becoming gravely ill two years earlier at the end of the war in Poitou, the king fell sick again in 1244. It was probably dysentery, which quite often afflicted men and women in the Middle Ages. Its recurrence marked Saint Louis' life at several points.[37] He fell ill at Pontoise around Saint-Luces Day, December 10. His condition rapidly deteriorated and everyone feared the worst. Obeying his constant concern, which became more acute with the risk of death, on December 14 he named two judges to arbitrate his disputes with the chapter of Notre-Dame in order to reconcile himself with God, the Church, and his conscience. People throughout the entire kingdom were ordered to participate in campaigns consisting in quests, prayers, and solemn processions. His mother had the precious relics from the royal chapel brought to Pontoise so that he could touch them, which would become a custom for the kings of France when they were dying. One day, they actually believed that he was dead. This scene unfolded in Paris as Joinville tells it:

> He was in such an extreme condition, as they called it, that one of the ladies who was looking after him wanted to pull the sheet over his face and said he was dead. But another lady who was on the other side of the bed wouldn't stand for it and said he still had his soul in his body. And just as he heard the debate between these two women, Our Lord came to him and sent health to him straight away because before he was mute and could not speak. So, straight away he was able to speak, and he asked for them to bring him the cross. . . .[38]

People's reactions were mixed when they learned of the king's vow, just as Christendom itself had mixed feelings about the crusades in this thirteenth-century milieu.[39] The enthusiasm that people felt about the crusades in the twelfth century—which had not always been shared by Christian rulers—had waned.[40] Repeated failures had discouraged people. There was the failure of the crusade of Frederick Barbarossa, Richard the Lion-Hearted, and Philip Augustus from 1189 to 1192; the Fourth Crusade of the French barons that had been diverted to Constantinople (1204); and the Fifth Crusade (1217–1221). The Crusade of Children in 1212 was no more than a moving, dramatic, and catastrophic event. The Sixth Crusade of Frederick II in 1228–1229 resulted in the scandalous success of the return of Jerusalem to the Christians in exchange for a shameful treaty with the Muslims.

One troubadour, however, became an apologist for Saint Louis' crusade. He was astonished that a "loyal and complete, upstanding prud'homme" leading a "holy, clean, pure life without sin and filth" could take the vow to crusade when this was normally done to make penitence. He claimed that the king had a vision during his illness and he had him say: "For a long time my mind has been Overseas, and this body of mine will go there, as God wishes it, and will conquer the land from the Saracens." Contrary to what we know from other sources, he affirmed that "everyone was joyful and lighthearted when they heard the king."[41] This propagandistic minstrel was undoubtedly expressing the feelings of the idealistic majority of the populace. But, among the political rulers and in certain other milieus, there were different opinions. The reigning "reason" among the rulers and other educated social groups increasingly opposed the traditional, unreflective enthusiasm of the people and the faithful supporters of the crusades. Certain indirect arguments held little weight in the end.

The crusades were sometimes attacked, almost reflexively, in the form of criticism of pontifical fiscal policy and of the papacy's growing influence over Christendom. This criticism became more pointed in light of the popes' tendency to stretch the idea of the crusade by applying it not only to the struggle against heretics in the West—as in the crusade against the Albigenses—or to the attack on Greek Orthodox Christians in 1204, but also to the essentially political conflict that opposed them to the Staufen and especially to Frederick II (who died in 1250) at the end of Gregory IX's pontificate (1227–1241) and under Innocent IV (1243–1254). Especially in France, England, and Spain (which had the excuse that it was already financing another crusade, the Reconquista), the clergy would have had trouble bearing the brunt of the tithes that Innocent IV granted Louis IX for his crusade. However, these criticisms did not actually target the crusades but pontifical fiscal policy. In addition, some of the critics accused the papacy of having weakened or killed off the spirit of the crusade with their cupidity.

We should not grant too much importance to the hostility of the heretics. Although for history it represents the existence of a movement of dissent that was both strongly rooted in the past and sometimes very modern in character, this hostility scarcely existed outside its limited area of influence in these milieus. The people of Vaud condemned the crusade as something opposed to the spirit and the letter of Christianity, which forbade murder. The Cathars were also hostile to war and saw the preachers of the crusade as assassins. The marginal Joachim de Fiore who died in 1202 was perhaps more influential. He inspired the millenarian movement of the thirteenth century[42] and believed that the crusades went against God's plan and that God wanted to convert the Muslims rather than exterminate them.[43]

I think that the reason for the decline of the spirit of the crusades was more profound. For many, the war front for Christian combat was limited to Europe at its geographical boundaries where it was threatened by the Prussians, the Tartars, the Cumanians, in the Iberian peninsula where the Reconquista made decisive progress, and also on the inner borders where heresy had not yet been completely eliminated. Furthermore, it seems that the internal revolution of conscience that was transforming the minds and hearts of Christians in the West for roughly a century profoundly modified the conditions of the crusades. More than some external illumination, conversion became the internal crystallization of a long process of education and desire. The "converted" Christian could discover an entire Jerusalem within himself, which made the reconquest of the terrestrial Jerusalem less necessary. The conversion of the infidel became an increasingly important goal alongside the desire to chase him off, to subjugate him, or to kill him. The missionary spirit mixed in with the spirit of the crusades.[44] The Franciscans and Saint Francis himself expressed this new demand in the Holy Land and even in the lands of the infidels. Surrounded by Mendicant friars, Louis IX must have heard this new music, even though he never renounced the armed expedition. At the Council of Lyon in 1245, Pope Innocent IV insisted on the importance of preaching to the infidels, even as he made his struggle against Emperor Frederick II into an internal crusade. Most of all, Western men and women became increasingly attached to material and moral goods as they became more available in the West in the course of the thirteenth century. Their spread was part of growing economic prosperity, cultural and artistic development, and the increasing security in better-governed seigniories and forming states. European Christianity demanded and sustained the passions of Christians more. From this point on a Christian king had the special function of governing his kingdom well, of taking care of its physical body as well as its political body, and of staying among his subjects. Blanche of Castile and the majority of the king's ecclesiastical and secular entourage managed to implement this change. Louis did not.

A staunch Christian who embodied this new Christian political attitude, Blanche of Castile reacted negatively to the announcement of Louis' vow to take up the cross. Joinville attests to this: "When the queen his mother heard people saying that he had renounced his decision, she was overcome with joy, and when she learned that he had taken up the cross, as he was saying himself, she looked as doleful as if she had actually seen his dead body." Her attitude was also no doubt that of a passionately loving mother tormented by the vision of a long separation from her son and the considerable dangers of the journey overseas. According to Matthew Paris, Blanche of Castile and Guillaume d'Auvergne, the bishop of Paris who received the king's vow, both made one last effort to dissuade him from crusading once he recovered from his illness. They pointed out that his vow was not legitimate because he made it when he was sick and, therefore, not in possession of his complete mental faculties. With a mixture of harshness, humor, and theatrical flourish that seems characteristic of Saint Louis, he violently ripped off the cross stitched on his clothing and ordered the bishop of Paris to give it back to him, "so that no one can keep saying that he took it without knowing what he was doing" since this time he was of sane mind and body.

Pushing the faith that had been instilled in him to the extreme, for Louis the crusade represented a crowning achievement for the conduct of a Christian prince. Would he just leave the glory of the passage and the battle for the Holy Land to his ancestors and a number of his contemporaries? In his judgment, the tradition of crusading was not outdated. The terrestrial Jerusalem was still a desirable goal. Christendom was not just limited to the European West but included the places where Christ lived and died. He was one of those Christians for whom the Passion of Christ was an ever-contemporary event that was supposed to become an action in the present, not just found within a sacred past. He wanted to inscribe his name in the Book of Judgment as a crusader like the members of his family and kingdom who went before him. The religious present and the dynastic past came together in Louis' decision to take up the cross.[45]

When he made his vow to crusade, Louis had a traditional attitude. His great grandfather, Louis VII had made the pilgrimage to Jerusalem

(1147–1149). This was a typical example of a penitential crusade as the king went to the Holy Land to seek absolution for two enormous sins. In 1142, the royal armies under his command had burned down the church of Vitry during his expedition against the count of Champagne, killing nearly 1,300 people. He also refused to allow Pierre de La Châtre to assume his elected position as the archbishop of Bourges, an offense that convinced Pope Innocent II to issue an interdiction against the kingdom. After these events, Saint Bernard and the new pope, Eugene III, a Cistercian with close ties to the abbey of Clairvaux, both pressured the king of France to adopt his penitential mission. There was no Saint Bernard at Louis IX's side; his desire to crusade came only from himself. Philip Augustus, Louis' grand-father who was so different and yet so loved and admired, also took the cross. This was in 1188 after Saladin recaptured Jerusalem from the Christians in 1187. He was not very strongly motivated when he arrived in Acre in 1191 and returned to the West in early August of the same year. He left people with the memory of a king who deserted the crusade, a "king who failed." Perhaps Louis IX wanted to erase this memory of his grandfather's dishonor. His father, Louis VIII, carried out a "crusade of substitution" against the Albigenses, and his mother Blanche of Castile must have told him stories about the Reconquista, the "Spanish crusades." Then again, leg-end associated the ruler identified by Capetian propaganda as its great an-cestor, Charlemagne, with pilgrimage to the Holy Land.[46] In 1239, an odd assortment of barons with close ties to the king, including Thibaud IV de Champagne and Richard of Cornwall, the king of England's brother, took up the cross.[47] However, there can be no doubt that Louis IX had a unique personal attitude toward the crusade. Wasn't it his master plan, or, if not his master plan, at least an essential part of it?[48]

In any case, although Saint Louis undoubtedly knew of the dangers threatening the holy sites in the form of the Khwarizmian Turks who had been chased out of Mesopotamia by the Mongols and called upon by Ayyub, the sultan of Egypt, to fight the Christians, he had only recently learned of the Turks' sack of Jerusalem on August 23, 1244 and the catastrophic defeat inflicted on the Franks and their Muslim allies from Syria on October 17 at Forbie by an Egyptian army reinforced by the Khwarizmians. Saint Louis made his decision to crusade before any news of these events had reached his land. The king's decision was not dictated by these events. He made it entirely on his own.

THE KING, THE POPE, AND THE EMPEROR

The renewal of the greatest conflict disturbing the Christian world from the eleventh to the thirteenth century, the struggle between its two leaders, the emperor and the pope, eventually affected the king of France. Louis IX's attitude in relation to these two superpowers was both constant and consistent. As the monarch of what would henceforth be the most powerful kingdom in all Christendom, the king of France had the means to uphold this policy. It was a question of giving each of them what he believed his due: a filial and obedient respect in spiritual matters for the pope, courtesy and formal recognition of the emperor's symbolic preeminence. However, the king of France denied them both any right to become involved in any temporal matters that depended on his sole authority, imposing respect for his independence in all temporal affairs. In relation to the unruly Frederick II, Louis held a strong position resulting from Pope Innocent III's recognition, given at the beginning of the century, that the king of France "knows no superior in his own kingdom." Louis maintained an attitude of respectful neutrality but, as with the pope, he knew how to shift between deference and firmness whenever necessary. He thought that this must be the right way for Christian princes to treat each other.[49]

We have seen how Louis IX allowed French knights to fight alongside imperial troops in Lombardy, and how he refused to allow his brother, Robert d'Artois, to accept the German crown that the pope offered him. On May 3, 1241, a Genoese flotilla carrying a large number of prelates to the council called by Gregory IX was defeated by a flotilla from Pisa in the service of the emperor. Many of the ecclesiastical dignitaries were captured and held prisoner by Frederick II. Among them were a number of important French prelates including the archbishops of Auch, Bordeaux, and Rouen, the bishops of Agde, Carcassonne, and Nîmes, and the abbots of Cîteaux, Clairvaux, Cluny, Fécamp, and La Merci-Dieu. Several months earlier, Louis had met with Frederick II at Vaucouleurs, so he thought that he could count on his good will. As soon as he learned of the situation, he delegated the mission to reclaim these prisoners from the emperor to the abbot of Corbie and one of the knights of his house, Gervais d'Escrennes. However, as Guillaume de Nangis tells it, Frederick II had already unconditionally asked the king of France not to allow the prelates of his kingdom to leave it to answer the pontifical summons. Frederick II kept his captives in a prison

in Naples and sent an insolent reply to the king of France: "Your royal highness should not be surprised if Caesar holds harshly and in torment those
who had come to torment Caesar." Stupefied, Louis dispatched the abbot of
Cluny with a message for the emperor (Frederick had released him shortly
after his imprisonment):

> Until now, our faith and our hope have held together firmly. They
> have held together so well that any subject of quarrel, complaint, or
> hatred between our kingdom and your empire [note the terms that
> imply both an inequality in honor and equality in fact] has never been
> able to last very long. Why? Because our predecessors who held the
> Kingdom of France have always loved and honored the solemn
> greatness of the Empire of Rome, and we who come after them, we
> firmly hold to the principles of our predecessors without chang-
> ing them. But it seems to us that you, you are breaking the friendship
> and the alliance of peace and concord. You are holding our prelates
> who had gone to the [pontifical] seat of Rome in faith and obedience,
> unable to reject the pope's orders, and you have captured them on the
> sea, which we can only tolerate with pain and sadness. Rest assured
> that we know from their letters that they never thought of doing any-
> thing to oppose you. Therefore, as they have done nothing to your
> detriment, it behooves your majesty to release them and give them up.
> Think about it and consider our message with good judgment and do
> not hold the prelates by force and your will alone because the King-
> dom of France has not been weakened so much that it can be led
> about beneath your spurs.[50]

This brilliant declaration sent Frederick II backpedaling. As the chronicler tells us: "When the emperor heard the words in King Louis' letters, he
released the prelates from his kingdom against his heart and against his will
because he hesitated to make him angry."[51]

Despite these distractions, Louis kept working to impose order within
his kingdom. In order to keep the peace between Christian rulers, he apparently believed that no lord could be a vassal to two different kings ruling two different kingdoms at the same time. Thus, in 1244, he ordered
the lords who were both his vassals and vassals of the king of England for
their landholdings there to choose between the two of them. There were

quite a few of these lords in Normandy. Henry III retaliated by confiscating the English lands of French lords. Saint Louis demonstrated his idea of what a feudal monarchy was supposed to be: a state in which vassalage and loyalty to the kingdom were closely tied together and in which lords were both vassals and subjects of the king.

He also wanted to forge close ties between the French monarchy and the order of Cîteaux. He had as much veneration for this order as for the new Mendicant orders. He decided to come to Cîteaux in great splendor for the meeting of the general chapter in the fall of 1244 on Saint Michael's eve. As was his custom, he took advantage of this trip to visit the sites of pilgrimage, relics, and monasteries along his route. He stopped at the Church of Madeleine in Vézelay and at the monastery of Vitteaux-en-Auxois. His mother Queen Blanche, who had received the privileged authorization from the pope to enter the Cistercian convents with twelve other women, accompanied him. His brothers Robert d'Artois and Alphonse de Poitiers, the duke of Burgundy, and six other French counts also accompanied him. As soon as they came within an arrow shot of the monastery, they dismounted out of deference and walked praying as they continued the rest of the way to the church. Out of respect for the king and his mother and in consideration of the long voyage, the monks allowed them to eat meat, but only in the house of the duke of Burgundy that lay outside their enclosure. They allowed the women authorized by the pope to enter the monastery but only on condition that they did not sleep there. The general chapter decided to honor the names of Louis and his mother with a memento for the living in all the houses in the order in France. Similar bonds of prayer united the king with the Dominicans, the Franciscans, the Premonstrants, and the Grandmontines. These ties of prayer were bound to assure the salvation of the king and his mother. However, in the piety of a medieval king for whom almost every act of worship was political, prayer commitments forged bonds between the dynasty and the religious orders, these two spiritual and temporal powers with which he built "artificial" familial relations, which in the Middle Ages were almost as solid as physical familial ties.

In June 1243, Innocent IV succeeded Celestin IV whose pontificate lasted all of twelve days and who had replaced Gregory IX who died in August 1241.[52] The conflict between Frederick and the papacy immediately took a rough turn.

When he was visiting the Cistercian general chapter, Louis received messengers from the pope. They bore a letter asking the king of France to grant him safe residence in France to shelter him from Frederick II's attacks. He would thus repeat the action of his ancestor, Louis VII, who had hosted Pope Alexander III when he was persecuted by the current emperor's grandfather, Frederick I Barbarossa. Louis IX answered them with great deference. However, he firmly responded that he must follow his barons' council and that they had formally advised him not to allow the pope to take refuge in France. Clearly, he did not want to occupy any position that came between the pope and the emperor. Innocent IV would still continue to depend on the French king's support. Fleeing the insecurity of Italy, he took refuge in Lyon, which was technically part of the Empire, although it was almost independent in practice, under the authority of its archbishop and in close proximity to France, which exerted an important influence there.[53]

Innocent IV arrived in Lyon on December 2. He learned of the French king's serious illness, but was soon reassured about his condition. On December 27, 1244, he announced the convocation of an ecumenical council in Lyon for Saint John's Day of the coming year. He also summoned the emperor to appear before the council to explain his conduct and to hear his sentence.

According to the custom, the secular rulers were also invited to the council, but Louis was still reluctant to get too involved and did not come to Lyon. The council presented a deposition against Frederick II in July 1245. They declared him stripped of both the empire and all his kingdoms. Louis, who was still thinking primarily of his crusade, proposed an interview with Innocent IV at Cluny in the hope of laying the grounds for some reconciliation between the emperor and the pope. He also sought some assurance from the pope about the support for his crusade that the pope had announced during the council. Matthew Paris asserts that the king of France forbade the pope to enter his kingdom any further than Cluny, but such a rude gesture seems unlikely. Louis IX and Innocent IV arrived at Cluny at the head of a large procession of members of the royal family and barons on one side and with cardinals and prelates on the other.[54] Only the pope, the king of France, and his mother Blanche of Castile—who still seemed to govern the kingdom along with her son—participated in the talks. The negotiations themselves remained secret. We can at least suppose that despite their occasionally animated disagreements,[55] relations between the pope and the king of France remained friendly, that Innocent renewed his support for Louis' crusade, but that he rejected Louis' attempts to reconcile him with Frederick II.

Louis IX continued to solidify his neutral position. In his letters, he addressed Frederick as his "very excellent and very dear friend, the ever august emperor, the king of Sicily and of Jerusalem." In 1246, he tried again without success to negotiate a solution with the pope in Frederick's favor, but then, in 1247, learned that Frederick had assembled a large army to march against the pope in Lyon and sent a large number of troops to defend the pontiff. Frederick II retreated to Parma after advancing as far as the Alps. Despite this, relations between the emperor and the king of France remained cordial. After saving the pope, Louis stuck with his policy of maintaining a balance of power and supported a revolt of French secular lords against the clergy. He addressed a statement to the pope that vigorously protested the pontifical curacy's treatment of the Church and Kingdom of France in violating their jurisdictions and burdening them with excessive exactions.[56]

SAINT LOUIS AND THE MEDITERRANEAN

This complex political game did not distract the king in any way from his larger plans. By deciding to leave on a crusade, he wrote a new page in the history of relations between the French monarchy and the Mediterranean.[57] Up to this point, the landlocked sea had never been a political horizon for Gaul or the western Kingdom of Francia, the ancestors of France. Conquered from the Ostrogoths by the Merovingians in the sixth century, Provence repeatedly rebelled until it was brutally put down by Charles Martel in the 730s. Later on, however, the Carolingians moved the vital center of their empire from the Mediterranean to the north, and with the division agreed to at Verdun, Provence passed into the domain of Lotharingia. From the Rhone to the Alps, the Mediterranean coast remained part of the empire until the end of the fifteenth century. Between the Rhone and the Pyrenees, the Mediterranean coast was at least theoretically part of the Kingdom of Western Francia. It therefore became part of the Capetian kingdom beginning in 987, although until the thirteenth century the lords of Languedoc hardly recognized Capetian suzerainty even in theory, and the influence of Aragon remained strong from Roussillon to Montpellier. It was only with the end of the Albigensian Crusade and the rule of Louis IX that the Mediterranean region became part of the territorial realities and the political horizon of the French monarchy. In 1229, Amaury de Montfort surrendered all his rights in the Midi to the king of France. The royal domain expanded with the additions of the seneschalcy of Beaucaire (the city had been purchased by Louis VIII in 1226 from the commune of Avignon) and of Carcassonne. For the first time, the French royal domain reached the Mediterranean Sea. Because Saint-Gilles, a very active port in the twelfth century, no longer had open waters with access to the sea, Saint Louis decided to build the port of Aigues-Mortes.

The crusading expeditions of Louis VII and Philip Augustus were not part of any Mediterranean policy. The kings depended on Marseille and Genoa for transporting their armies over sea. However, outside any royal action, there was already an important French presence in the eastern Mediterranean, and it would be a key element in the situation defining Louis IX's crusade.

The French aristocratic and chivalric orders had already played a crucial role in the early crusades, and particularly in the First Crusade. They played an essential part in the creation of the Latin Kingdom of Jerusalem and in the establishment of other Christian principalities in the Holy Land. The titles of the chronicles that recount the taking of Jerusalem and conquest of the Holy Land testify to this. For example, we have the *Gesta Francorum Jerusalem expugnantium* (Great Deeds of the French Conquerors of Jerusalem) written by an unknown cleric, although its hero was the Norman Bohémond. There is also the famous *Gesta Dei per Francos* (Great Feats of God Carried out by the Francs) by the abbot Guibert de Nogent. From the onset the French were credited with an "eschatological vocation" for the crusades.[58] Saint Louis would soak all this up and live it.

The "Franks," French people for the most part, had actually been the main occupiers and colonizers of the Mediterranean coast in the Middle East. Penetrated with both rural and urban colonization and smattered with "new towns," which were really so many French *bourgades* in a "New France," Syria in the twelfth century can be compared to Canada in the seventeenth and eighteenth centuries or Algeria in the nineteenth century.[59]

Among French advantages in the Mediterranean, we must not forget the language. In the thirteenth century, vernacular languages were making remarkable breakthroughs not only in literature but also in written documents of law and government. Behind Latin, and in a more vibrant way, French appeared as the new international language of Christendom. French was spoken more and more all around the Mediterranean Sea. In southern Italy and Sicily, the French spoken by the Normans was obviously in decline, although in Cyprus, which was conquered by Richard the Lion-Hearted in 1191, and where the Lusignans set up their dynasty in 1192, the governing class spoke French and the general populace spoke a *lingua franca* made up of French, Italian, and Greek.[60] Especially in the Latin states overseas, the French language and French customs and fashions took root. The second generation of "Franks" born in the Levant grew up in what was truly a second "France overseas."[61] As a common language, French was also the language used for recording customs, which were written down in thirteenth-century European Christendom, as we find in the *Livre au roi,* the *Assises de la Cour aux bourgeois,* and the *Livre de Jean d'Ibelin* to name only a few.[62]

In the thirteenth century, the Mediterranean world that Louis IX confronted was a place of meetings, exchanges, and confrontations between three great political and cultural forces: Latin Christendom, Greek Byzantine Christendom, and the Muslim world that extended along its entire southern shore from Egypt to Morocco and into southern Spain. During most of Louis IX's reign, the Latins who founded the Latin Kingdom of Constantinople during the Fourth Crusade in 1204 governed Constantinople, the European part of the Byzantine Empire, and northwest Anatolia. The Greeks would reconquer all these lands in 1261. However, the Christian Reconquista over the Muslims in Spain moved forward quickly.[63]

The Mediterranean region was first of all a physical space that was difficult to master in technological and psychological terms. The West made major advances in maritime navigation in the thirteenth century, but we do not know how much they influenced travel and trade on the Mediterranean Sea. The mobile stem rudder placed in the back of the ship and running parallel to it only seems to have reached the Mediterranean from the North Sea at the beginning of the fourteenth century. The Genoese and Venetian ships outfitted by Saint Louis used two side rudders, as was the custom. Use of the compass, first known in the West around 1190, spread only very slowly.[64] Genoa and Venice built ships with large dimensions for their trade. These ships were easily transformed for military transport carrying large numbers of men on their two bridges and horses, provisions, and drinking water in their holds. At Marseilles, Joinville watched with admiring astonishment as they loaded the horses into these veritable shipping naves: "On the day we went into our boats, they opened the boat's door and put in all the horses that we had to take overseas. Then, they closed the door and sealed it tightly, just like when we 'drown' a barrel, because when the ship is on the high seas, the whole door is in the water."[65]

The Venetian "*nave*" (*nef,* ship), the *Roccaforte,* chartered by Saint Louis, measured 38.19 meters long and 14.22 meters wide in the middle of the hull and 13.70 meters wide beneath the castles. Its tonnage is estimated at nearly 600 tons and its displacement, in other words the volume of water that it took up at sea, was nearly 1,200 tons.[66] One major flaw of these large ships was their significant leeway, their tendency to drift.[67] Maritime cartography had only made slow progress at this time. The oldest nautical map from the Middle Ages that we know of was used on board the ship that Saint Louis took to Tunis in 1270 according to the testimony of the chronicler of Saint-Denis, Guillaume de Nangis.[68]

For Saint Louis, there would be no shortage of adventures and storms at sea. They had to wait for good weather before they could set sail. Saint Louis embarked at Aigues-Mortes on August 25, 1248. He arrived at the port of Limassol on the island of Cyprus during the night of September 17 or 18. Fear of bad weather delayed their departure for Egypt until the spring of the following year. Their precautions did nothing to prevent strong winds from blowing a number of the ships far off course when the French fleet arrived off the coast of Egypt in May 1249. Separated from their king, they would not return for a long time, although he still had 700 ships carrying most of the 2,800 knights that he brought with him.

On the return trip in the spring of 1254, the king's ship got lost in the fog and wrecked on a sandbar off the coast of Cyprus. Later, the entire navy got caught in a storm so violent that the queen promised Joinville to donate a prestigious ex-voto in the form of a silver ship of five marcs to Saint-Nicolas-de-Varangéville (Saint-Nicolas-du-Port in Lorraine).[69]

The Mediterranean held dangerous waters, especially for the French who were almost all accustomed to life on land. Frederick Barbarossa also feared the sea and for that reason chose the overland route for the Third Crusade, which proved fatal. On this same crusade, Philip Augustus was seasick and seems to have always retained some serious anxiety about the sea. Joinville identifies the king's fearlessness in confronting their fortunes at sea as one of the great examples of his courage, recalling that he never lost his composure during their shipwreck or during the squall that followed.[70] In writing down his memories, he was amazed to recall how well the king braved the sea: "He who dares put himself in such peril with the well-being of others or in mortal sin is madly bold, for they go to sleep at night in one place without knowing that they won't be at the bottom of the sea in the morning."[71]

The idea that Saint Louis overcame the fear of the sea, which was so common on the penitential pilgrimage of the crusade in the thirteenth century, would be counted later as evidence of his sainthood.[72]

The thirteenth-century Mediterranean world was also an economic space. Its Christian shores were dominated by the Italian city-states. Amalfi's time had passed. It was the age of Pisa, Genoa, and Venice. When Louis IX built the port of Aigues-Mortes on the coastal land recently added to the royal domain, it was for the economic interest first of all. He wanted to develop it as a commercial center and to attract Italian and Genoese merchants. With this in mind, he also acquired the lands of the abbey of Psalmodi at the mouth of the lagoon of Aigues-Mortes.[73] In 1239, part of the "barons' crusade" led by Thibaud IV of Champagne and king of Navarre and Duke Hugues de Bourgogne was able to embark at the still crudely formed port of Aigues-Mortes, although most of them still left from Marseilles. With Aigues-Mortes, Louis IX made the Mediterranean into a new frontier and a new horizon for the French kingdom.

The Mediterranean was finally and above all a religious space for Louis IX. Different religions crossed this space with the men who bore them. Since the end of the eleventh century, the crusading expeditions had turned the Mediterranean Sea into a battlefront for Latin Christians. It was a front for them to reconquer by force or persuasion, by crusading or preaching. For these Christians, this space was comprised of Latin Europe with the Iberian Peninsula, whose conquest was yet to be completed, and the holy sites of Palestine and Jerusalem. The Mediterranean came to play a key role in this religious expansion, just as in Western Europe's economic expansion. A traditional form of worship, whether it was penitential or not, the pilgrimage to Jerusalem assumed the violent, military form of the crusade at the end of the eleventh century.[74] Beginning in the thirteenth century, an entire series of reasons we have considered here led western Christians to multiply their efforts to convert other people by preaching and by example, if not to replace crusading entirely with peaceful missions.[75] The Franciscans were at the forefront of these missionary efforts in the Levant and the Holy Land. Francis of Assisi himself and his "second" brother Elijah made the voyage. Franciscan monasteries were founded in the Latin states of Syria and Palestine, in Antioch, Tripoli, Beirut, Tyre, Sidon, Acre, Jaffa, and in Cyprus. Other Franciscan missions went to Africa, like the voyage of Friar Gilles to Tunis in 1219. However, they all failed and sometimes ended in bloody slaughters like the massacre of the martyrs of Ceuta in 1220.[76] After Saint Louis' death (1270), new conversion projects would be methodically organized by the Mendicant orders,[77] feeding the hopes of Raymond Lulle. The tradition of the pilgrimage across the sea would continue after the military front of the crusades shut down in the fourteenth century.

For Latin Christians in the thirteenth century and especially for Saint Louis, the Mediterranean was the space of a great fantasy, the fantasy of conversion: the conversion of the Muslims, the conversion of the Mongols, and the return of Greek Orthodox Christians to Latin Roman Christianity through the unification of the two Churches.[78]

THE PREPARATIONS FOR THE CRUSADE

Their first problem was figuring out how to master the space of the Mediterranean. The first question was choosing a port to embark from; they chose to leave from Aigues-Mortes. They chose Aigues-Mortes over Narbonne and Montpellier, which were politically unreliable—the first because of its relations with the dynasty of the count of Toulouse, the second due to the Aragonese influence there. They also chose it over ports outside of the kingdom: Marseilles, although many crusaders left from its port, including Joinville, and Genoa, the port of departure for Philip Augustus. On his return from the Holy Land, Saint Louis landed at Salins d'Hyères after some hesitation. Provence was under the solid control of his brother, Charles d'Anjou who inherited it in 1246 through his marriage with Beatrice de Provence. Before his departure, Louis went forward with his brother's initiation ("dubbing") into knighthood at Melun on Easter Day, 1246. During the solemn ceremony he put his brother in possession of the counties of Anjou and Maine that their father, Louis VIII, had reserved for him. The important accomplishment was the construction of the port of

Aigues-Mortes before Saint Louis' departure; this was one of the most amazing urban achievements of medieval France. Aigues-Mortes was destined to be the launching pad and terminal point of the *iter hierosolymitanum,* "the road to Jerusalem."[79]

The next material preparations involved buying or renting the ships to transport the army of crusaders. Genoa and Venice and, to a lesser extent, Marseilles, furnished the largest number of the boats.[80] They also had to amass enough supplies. Joinville describes the "great profusion of the king's supplies" in Cyprus in 1249. He recalled the wine gathered in large "storerooms" in the middle of the fields and in barrels stacked high on the seashore along with stockpiles of grain and barley and wheat forming "mountains" in the countryside around Limassol.[81] An enterprise of this kind presented enormous logistical problems. On the work at Aigues-Mortes, William Jordan has shown the exceptionally careful and daring planning with which Louis prepared for the crusade. In order to bring the large quantity of raw materials required for equipping and supplying the crusading army to Aigues-Mortes, especially salt and wood, Louis granted special privileges to the inhabitants of Montpellier in order to get them to accept the new competing port. He had the road of the Cévennes rerouted with a mixture of "coaxing, concessions, and force," suppressing all tolls and deforesting the region. As late as 1253 young newlyweds in Alès, where the king requisitioned all the experienced carpenters and cut down all the surrounding forests, could not find enough wood to make torches for their customary wedding festivities.[82]

The financial preparation was no less detailed; it relied heavily on contributions from the cities and the Church of France. The cities made donations and gave forced contributions; the Church accepted an increase in the tithe for the crusades from one-twentieth to one-tenth of its revenue.[83] The king also made arrangements with the Templars and Italian bankers, which allowed him to transfer large sums of money from the Royal Treasury and to secure loans.[84] Overall, this system of financing worked quite well. They would be able to pay the king's ransom without any trouble, although it is true that it was not a particularly exorbitant sum: 200,000 pounds—less than one year of the kingdom's revenue, while Richard the Lion-Hearted's ransom, calculated at the same rate, was at least as high as 500,000 pounds, a sum equal to four years' revenue of the English crown.[85] Likewise, the considerable expenses that Louis paid in the Holy

Land for fortifying towns and castles would be paid without any great difficulty. Whether the king's prolonged absence was harmful to his kingdom or not is debatable. However, in terms of finance, it does not seem to have incurred any significant losses.[86]

In contrast to these efforts, the diplomatic preparations for the crusade were a failure. Emperor Frederick II and Pope Innocent IV pretended to support Louis' project, but the emperor warned his Muslim friends in the East about the king's plans, while the pope diverted funding for the crusade agreed to at the Council of Lyon in 1245 in order to support his struggle against Frederick II in Europe. The kings of Castile and Aragon were completely wrapped up in the reconquest of the Iberian Peninsula and did not do a thing to help. Several English detachments were the only non-French forces to join Saint Louis' army. Crusading was clearly turning its back on the Orient in order to carry on the fight in Europe, continuing in Spain and Portugal as it had also been carried out against the Albigenses. The Aragonese had not yet really begun their Mediterranean expansion. Only the Italian city-states continued their economic and territorial colonization of the East. Saint Louis' Mediterranean policy was isolated from the overall politics of the crusades that was in the process of turning away from the region. It was also an anomaly in relation to Christendom's policy of economic and territorial expansion (which was Italian before becoming Spanish) that was in the process of separating itself more and more from any religious goals. Louis prolonged the age of crusading in the Mediterranean. After him, the West would think of the region as more of a pipeline to the spices of the East.

It is not surprising then that his preparation for the crusade also involved a religious preparation in a way that seemed necessary to him. This religious preparation took on three basic forms: a campaign of sermons and prayers in which the Cistercians and the Dominicans distinguished themselves, a kind of penitential political policy of the royal government marked by the investigation [*enquête*] of 1247 that was confided primarily to the Dominicans and Franciscans with the purpose of repairing the sins of the administration by making restitution for exactions and redressing miscarriages of justice, and, finally, measures taken against the Jews and more specifically usurers.

According to the custom, Louis IX asked Innocent IV to designate a pontifical legate to take charge of preaching on the crusade. During the

Council of Lyon in 1245, the pope chose a personage of the highest order known by the king, Eudes de Châteauroux, the former canon of Notre-Dame de Paris and the chancellor of the University of Paris from 1238 to 1244, the date on which Innocent IV made him a cardinal.[87] At the same time, the pope made the Council readopt the measures in favor of crusading and crusaders passed by the Fourth Lateran Council in 1215. These measures were varied but they all had the purpose of assuring the success of the crusade by purifying the crusaders and all Christians residing in the West of their sins and by granting material and spiritual privileges to those who would leave.

The pride manifest in luxury would have to be curbed by the "states," the social categories that had that particular sin: the nobles and the wealthy. They would have to eat and dress modestly. Tournaments, festivals that appealed to all the vices[88] and that the Church had unsuccessfully forbidden since the Fourth Lateran Council of 1215, were once more prohibited throughout Christendom for three years. They prohibited wars for four years too, and during this time everyone was supposed to observe these prescriptions for peace. The crusaders would benefit from an exemption from all tithes, and any interest on their debts would be abolished. There would be a remission for the sins of anyone who would furnish ships for the crusade and for all who preached the crusade. The men leaving on the crusade would be able to draw the revenue from their ecclesiastical benefices for three years. The ten percent tithe on revenues for the pope and the cardinals would be turned over as a subsidy for the Holy Land. Any pirates who attacked the crusaders' ships would be excommunicated, as would any Christians who did business with the Saracens, especially any who sold them arms, and any crusaders who foreswore their vows to crusade. On the other hand, there was the promise of eternal salvation for the crusaders and for everyone who helped make the crusade a reality.[89]

In Louis' mind, the one important political and religious measure that ended up contributing to the success of the crusade in France was the great campaign of the royal investigators in 1247. The purpose of the investigation was to draw up a list of all the injustices committed by the agents of the king or in the name of the king in order to wipe them out and satisfy any royal subjects who had been wronged. This was actually a penitential measure reinforced by reparations. By these actions, the king would be able to leave his kingdom in peace, relieved of the grievances that could have led some of his subjects to cause disturbances in his absence. Cleansed of the sin of having poorly carried out his royal function by allowing his agents to commit violations of justice, the king could hope that God would grant him success in this endeavor.

We should also remember that the alms and privileges the king granted to religious establishments in exchange for prayers for the crusade were added to the royal penitential restitutions and all the measures taken to assure that justice and peace would prevail in the kingdom. Another example of such measures was the resolution of the succession of Flanders through arbitration between the competing sons who were the offspring from the two successive marriages of the countess and their families, the Avesnes and the Dampierres (1246).

As for the Jews, aside from the increased repression of their money-lending practices, they had to submit to new attacks orchestrated by the pontifical legate against the Talmud. Apparently these attacks were not always followed by the confiscation and destruction of copies of the Talmud, which had taken place earlier from 1240 to 1244.[90]

Finally, it seems that Saint Louis had not been very well prepared nor even seriously thought about preparing to acquire knowledge about the Muslims whom he was about to attack. He did not think of them as pagans but as members of an absurd, evil sect. Of course, he must have heard the ideas that one the advisors of his youth, Guillaume d'Auvergne, the bishop of Paris from 1228 to 1249, professed about them in his book, *De fide et legibus*. According to him, Saracen law was a mixture of good and evil, and Christians should have no soft spot for this sect. In Egypt, Saint Louis would get a chance to form his own opinion based on experience.[91]

The Crusade and the
Stay in the Holy Land
(1248-1254)

In his solid and brilliant book, William Jordan reaches the conclusion that
Saint Louis was fascinated by the idea of the crusades and that this idea
dominated his rule and his politics.[1] Jean Richard, the author of another recent remarkable biography of the king, comes close to sharing this opinion.
I believe that this idea is an exaggeration. It seems to me that Saint Louis
wanted most of all to realize and embody the model of the ideal Christian
king in order to attain his salvation by serving Christendom and the Kingdom of France. The crusade was a part of this goal, a part of this program.
In this sense, Saint Louis would be a traditional crusader just like his great-
grandfather Louis VII and his grandfather Philip Augustus, although his
crusading ambition grew out of a more modern and more Christlike devotion and a more impassioned personal engagement. He was "the crusader
in the old-fashioned mold, refusing any diplomatic negotiations for the pur-

pose of obtaining treaties or truces, whereas Frederick II had the style of a political missionary for the papacy with his attempt at peaceful infiltration."[2] Louis nevertheless tried to combine war and conversion in his crusade. Without being his ultimate objective, the crusade was one of the great guiding ideas of his rule.

SAINT LOUIS AND THE ORIENT

The crusade of 1248, however, arose from certain original ideas.[3] In choosing Egypt as his destination, Louis plainly adhered to the tradition of Baudouin I (1118), Amaury I (1163–1169), and Jean de Brienne (1218–1221). The Christians viewed Egypt and Damietta as the military and political key to holding Palestine.[4] According to Matthew Paris, however, King Louis' ideas had moved beyond this point as he contemplated establishing Christian settlements in Egypt: "After the taking of Damietta, nothing bothered the king of France more than the fact that he did not have enough men with him to keep and populate the conquered countries as well as those left to conquer. He had brought plows, harrows, spades, and other plowing implements." Colonization, no doubt limited to Damietta and several important strategic sectors of Egypt, was supposed to go hand in hand with the reconquest of Jerusalem or rather precede it so as to better assure the subsequent defense of the Holy Land.[5] The design and construction of a Christian church in Damietta after it was taken confirm his intention of setting up a permanent Christian population in Egypt.[6]

Along with this project for an establishment in northern Egypt, Saint Louis probably anticipated a lengthy stay in the Holy Land, while it seems that most of the other Christian kings who had crusaded before him, including the kings of France, had planned to return to their European kingdoms as quickly as possible. It is hard to say whether King Louis had foreseen the long stay he would choose to undertake in circumstances beyond his control after his defeat, captivity, and liberation in 1250. Some historians see it as an improvised decision brought on by events. They even consider it a "turning point in the Eastern policy of the Capetian kings," a transition from sporadic crusading to an attempt to provide permanent protection for the holy sites of Christendom.[7] Instead, I think that Saint Louis had planned to stay in the Orient after the expected military success in

Egypt in order to organize and lead the defense of the Christian territories. His defeat in Egypt only made him believe more strongly in the need for his presence in the Holy Land. He held this view for moral and religious as well as military reasons, although his stay would end with the announcement of the death of Blanche of Castile, precipitating his return to France in 1254. The transformation in Saint Louis' oriental and Mediterranean policy came about slowly from roughly 1239 to 1248.

Saint Louis imposed a major change on the ideology of the crusades. Beyond the Holy Sepulcher, the tomb of Christ, beyond Jerusalem and the memory of Christ's Passion, it was Christ himself that Louis would search for in the Orient. From the sign of the cross, Louis wanted to reach the Crucified Christ himself. As a suffering king who would gradually seem more and more like a sacrificial king, a Christlike king whose image would be diffused by his biographers and hagiographers, beginning in 1239 with the theft of the Holy Nail, Saint Louis affirmed his devotion for the Christ of the Passion, the man crucified in Jerusalem. His devotion was like the first step on the path of the King on the cross, which would lead him to the East, into captivity, to Africa, and to his death.

In 1239, the finest and fittest of the French barons left for the Holy Land under the leadership of Thibaud IV of Champagne. The young king supported the crusaders by authorizing their departure and facilitating the financing of their expedition. He even gave their army a "royal" presence by allowing the constable Amaury de Montfort to carry the fleur-de-lis on the journey. Richard of Cornwall, the brother of the king of England, joined the army of the barons, and in 1241 they negotiated an agreement that returned Jerusalem to the Christians. Perhaps Saint Louis was inspired to emulate the success of this expedition.

We might recall that the troubadour who recounted and praised the way Saint Louis took up the cross as he emerged from his illness had him say, "for a long time my spirit has been Overseas."[8] Thus the land overseas was also an oneiric horizon for the king, a dream fed by "collective images and representations" of the crusades[9] and most of all by the imaginary double image of Jerusalem as a terrestrial and celestial city, as well as by the tomb of Christ and the multitude of visions and prophecies that accompanied the various episodes of the crusades.[10] In Saint Louis' emotional life, in his life of passion, and in his heart, Jerusalem, a distant princess, was no doubt Blanche of Castile's great rival.

From Paris to Aigues-Mortes

Just as during the reception of the relics of the Passion, but this time with the rituals of crusading including the departure from the kingdom for the holy war, the great penitential liturgy began again. On the Friday after Pentecost, June 12, 1248, Louis went to Saint-Denis to receive the oriflamme, the scarf, and the staff from the hand of the cardinal-legate Eudes. He thereby associated the royal insignia of the king of France leaving on a war expedition with the insignia of the pilgrim setting out on the pilgrimage of the crusade. He then returned to Paris and accompanied by a large procession walked barefoot to the royal abbey of Saint-Antoine-des-Champs, which had been founded in 1198 by Foulques, the priest of Neuilly and famous preacher of the First Crusade. He solicited the prayers of the nuns there and then left the place on horseback to spend the night at the royal palace of Corbeil. He remained there for several days and officially promoted his mother as regent of the kingdom in his absence, granting her extensive but clearly defined powers.[11] Here, we can grasp the utility for the government of the kingdom that resulted from the role Blanche of Castile played up to this point. Although she was subordinate to her son, the king (how could this have happened any other way in the Capetian monarchy that excluded women from its succession?), as his associate she continued to occupy an important position that lasted well beyond his majority. In addition to her strong character, she possessed an extensive knowledge of governmental affairs that made any briefing entirely unnecessary. This was an advantage for the king who also counted on the advisors he left with his mother and to whom, he knew, she would not defer easily.[12]

The departure from Paris on June 12, 1248 marked another turning point in Saint Louis' life that struck his entourage and others beyond it. This involved a change in the king's image, although, as was often the case, the change in appearance expressed a much deeper break with the past. We have seen how the rules for the crusades that were restated at the Council of Lyon in 1245 urged the crusaders to adhere to modesty in dress. It is easy to imagine that the strict Saint Louis respected these measures and made others respect them as well. In effect, Joinville informs us that for as long as he was in the Orient he never saw any pieces of embroidery in anyone's battle dress in the entire army. As was Saint Louis' habit, he was not merely content to strictly follow the prescriptions of the Church in this matter but had to go much further. Relying on original sources, Le Nain de Tillemont successfully describes this change in the king's appearance:

> Since he had left Paris, he stopped wearing scarlet clothes and furs of scarlet, green, or any other stunning color, nor blue Siberian squirrel and fine vair nor any other precious things that Westerners used to adorn their battle dress. He always wanted to be dressed simply in blue[13] and blue-green camlet[14] or brownish black or black silk, and all the furs on his robes and coverings were of rabbit or hare's fur, sheepskin, or even squirrel. He also gave up all the gold and silver ornamentation on his saddles, bridles, and things of this nature. He did not even want the reins and chest covers of his horses to be made of silk, nor his stirrups, bits, and spurs to be of gold, wanting only simple iron.[15]

The most remarkable thing was that Saint Louis would maintain this appearance after returning from the crusade, keeping this look until the end of his life except on special rare occasions. Most historians agree and interpret this renunciation of luxurious dress as the sign of a turning point in the king's life marking a transition from a style of living and governing that simply complied with the recommendations of the Church to a truly religious personal and political form of conduct, from simple conformity to a true "moral order." Historians generally situate this turning point at his return from the crusade in 1254. However, the external signs of this transformation first appeared in 1248. I believe that there was an initial transformation in 1247–1248, marked by the dispatch of the royal investigators, the policy of penitential reparations for royal abuses of power, and the renunciation of sumptuous dress. The change was closely linked to the crusade and the legislation governing it. Of course, a second more decisive turning point would occur in 1254. It would signal the internalization and generalization in all the king's governing actions of a development that had remained primarily external in 1247–1248. These two moments constitute Louis IX's march toward a purifying and even an eschatological life and rule.

At Corbeil, Louis finally bade his mother adieu and moved on toward the south, making a long stop at Sens where the general chapter of the Franciscan order was meeting. His arrival on foot, dressed as a pilgrim, marked another stage in his penitential mission. A special witness there, the Franciscan friar Salimbene of Parma, left us with a most striking physical portrait of the king.[16] Another important step was taken in Lyon. The pope still resided there and held a long interview with the king. He granted Louis full and complete absolution for his sins and promised to protect the Kingdom of France against any eventual machinations by the king of England as the truces between the two rulers had not been renewed. Louis failed, however, in his final attempt to reconcile Innocent IV and Emperor Frederick II.

Louis sailed down the Rhone from Lyon and was stopped at the formidable keep of Roche-de-Glun. Roger de Clérieu, a "very mean man," exacted a toll from everyone who passed through, including pilgrims. He robbed anyone who refused to pay and went so far as to kill certain travelers. With one hand in brigandage and another in predatory taxation, he was one of those thieving lords so common in the history and legends of the Middle Ages. The king refused to pay the toll. Roger took hostages, and Louis laid siege to the castle, taking it and demolishing it in just a few days.

Louis IX finally arrived at Aigues-Mortes in the middle of August. On August 25, he embarked with all his followers. With the exception of his mother, his young children, and his sister-in-law, the countess d'Artois whose pregnancy had nearly come to term, he had ordered nearly all members of his immediate family to accompany him. He also wanted the crusade to be a kind of familial expedition showing the engagement of his kin, whom he considered a single entity formed of his brothers and their wives. His queen Marguerite de Provence accompanied him along with his brothers Robert d'Artois, Charles d'Anjou, and his wife Beatrice.[17] His brother Alphonse de Poitiers was supposed to leave from Marseilles[18] with his father-in-law the count of Toulouse, Raimond VII who came to salute the king at Aigues-Mortes but returned to Marseilles so that he could leave on the beautiful ship that he had sent from England through the Straits of Gibraltar.

Although it may be difficult to calculate the figures, and although historians disagree on this point, we can estimate the crusading army's numbers at over 2,500 knights with an equal number of squires and valets, 10,000 foot soldiers, and 5,000 crossbowmen. This brings the figure to a total of roughly 25,000 men, plus 7,000 or 8,000 horses. These are amazing numbers for the times. The majority of the army, including the knights, was in the king's pay. According to Le Nain de Tillemont, the royal navy numbered thirty-eight large ships and hundreds of smaller vessels. According to Matthew Paris, there were not enough boats to embark all the soldiers they had recruited. The king left about 1,000 mercenaries at Aigues-Mortes; most of them were Italians from Genoa and Pisa and, although the incident is not well known, they spread unrest in the town. It is possible that Louis did not want to take men in whom he had little confidence and who were not animated with the religious spirit that he wanted to see. Maybe Matthew Paris exaggerated the importance of the incident.

The king, his family, and most of the army left from Aigues-Mortes on August 25, 1248. Exactly twenty-two years later, this would be the day of Louis' death on his second crusade. A lack of wind delayed the departure of the royal fleet, which finally left Aigues-Mortes on August 28.

I have chosen not to recount Louis IX's crusade and stay in the Holy Land in any detail. Joinville's version makes much better reading. Here, I have chosen to stick to everything that can directly or indirectly shed light on Saint Louis' character and allow us to appreciate his role, his historical importance, and the essence of his life.

I have already mentioned how poor mastery of the seas at this time excessively prolonged the trip to Egypt.[19] The fear of sailing in winter delayed Louis, his navy, and his army in Cyprus for more than eight months. When they finally debarked in early June 1249, strong winds blew a number of knights and their ships far off course.

The Voyage and the Campaign in Egypt

For the most part, the voyage for the crusade of 1248–1249 took on a traditional form. Although Saint Louis' departure from Aigues-Mortes represented an important development in the Mediterranean politics of the kings of France and in the paths of the crusades, other crusaders embarked from ports used in the past like Marseilles, from which Joinville departed. Since Richard the Lion-Hearted conquered Cyprus in 1191 and the "Latin" dynasty of the Lusignan had been established there, the island had been destined to serve as a base of operations for the crusades. René Grousset has quite rightly said that the Latin Kingdom of Cyprus played an essential role in helping prolong the existence of the Latin states in the Holy Land for an extra century. Emperor Frederick II had debarked from Cyprus in 1228 for his strange crusade and managed to put the island under his control, although his suzerainty there ended in 1233. First under his mother's regency, then with his sole authority, the young Henri I de Lusignan ruled the island from 1246 until his death in 1253, although it seems that he let the aristocracy and clergy there govern the island. Joinville does not even mention this phantom king. In 1247, however, Pope Innocent IV released him from his vow of service to the emperor and placed his kingdom under the protection of the Holy See. The island perfectly fulfilled its role as a crusading base for Louis IX. He had been amassing fresh supplies there since 1246, disembarked there on September 17, 1248, and had to winter there until May 30, 1249.

Similarly, the landing near Damietta and the city's capture on June 5, 1249 only repeated its fall to Jean de Brienne in 1218.[20] However, in the months that followed things started to go wrong. First, Saint Louis and his army suffered an outbreak of epidemics: dysentery, typhoid, and scurvy. The plague had disappeared from the Mediterranean in the course of the eighth century and only reappeared in the middle of the fourteenth century.[21]

Of course, there was also the Muslim's military superiority in certain domains. The power that the Christians gained from their siege engines was almost completely negated by the Muslims' Greek fire.[22] Joinville experienced it firsthand. With his usual gift for description, he shows Louis and his army powerless under attack from Greek fire:

> One night when we were guarding the *chats-châteaux*,[23] they brought one of the siege engines called perrier [a kind of catapult] toward us, which they had not yet done, and they put Greek fire in the catapult of the machine. When the good knight Sir Gauthier d'Ecurey who was with me saw this, he told us, "Sirs, we are in the greatest danger we have ever been in, because if they burn our castles and we stay, we are lost and burned alive, and if we leave these posts that we have been ordered to keep, we will be dishonored. That is why no one but God can defend us from this peril. I advise you and am of the opinion that every time they throw the fire on us, we should get down on our knees and elbows and pray to Our Lord to protect us from this danger." As soon as they shot the fire at us, we got down on our elbows and knees as he advised us. The first shot landed between our two *chats-châteaux*.

So, the Muslims managed to destroy the crusaders' two *chats-châteaux* and they would later destroy a third that the king had built with wood from some of the supply ships after the destruction of the first two.[24] After this, disease broke out in the French camp, aggravating the situation and the suffering of the king and the army:

> Because of this misfortune and because of the harshness of this country where a drop of water never falls, we were stricken with the scourge of the army, which was so bad that the flesh of our legs became entirely dry and our skin became spotted black like the color of soil or like an old boot. And when we caught this disease, our flesh rotted to the very gums, and no one escaped this illness, and many died from it. The sign of death was that when someone began to bleed from his nose, we knew he would die.
>
> Because of the wounds I received on Shrovetide, the sickness of the army struck me in the mouth and the legs, and a double triple fever and a head cold so great that the cold flowed out of my brain through my nostrils. Because of these ills, I stayed in bed sick on the third Thursday of Lent, and the priest came to say the mass for me in my pavilion, and he was sick just like me.
>
> The disease began to attack the whole camp so badly that some had so much dead flesh in their gums that the barbers had to cut away the dead flesh just so they could chew and swallow. It was a pitiful sound to hear the people whose flesh was being cut away groaning in the camp, for they groaned like women who are having trouble giving birth.

They then attempted to retreat by land and water:

> The king had a bad case of the army's disease and dysentery. He could have easily saved himself by leaving on the galleys if he had wanted, but he said that he would not leave his own people, God willing. He fainted several times that evening and because of his miserable dysentery he had to cut the bottom of his undergarment so many times that he had to go back to his wardrobe.[25]

The defeat of the chivalrous king and of the *"furia"* of French knighthood soon followed. It was the outcome of a series of events. According to Joinville, the victory of Mansourah on February 9, 1250, was Saint Louis' high point as a chivalrous king: "The king came with his battle group with great screams and the din of trumpets and bells, and he stopped on a raised path. I never saw such a beautiful knight, because he appeared above all his people by a shoulder's length with a golden helm on his head and a German sword in his hand."[26] As for the battle: "it was a very beautiful feat of arms because no one drew a bow or a crossbow and it was all combat with cudgels and swords."[27] Here is the mentality of the French knighthood that would lead to the great disasters of the Hundred Years' War. Thus Robert d'Artois ignored the battle plan agreed upon and fell upon a group of Turks, leading the knights of the Temple behind him and, abandoning all caution in pursuing the Muslims, fell into a trap. He was massacred.[28]

Finally, the army, weakened by its own victory, exhausted by the outbreak of disease ("the disease of the army," as Joinville calls it) had to retreat because Saint Louis and his circle had forgotten to safeguard their control of the Nile to protect their supply routes. The Muslims cut the great river off from them. The retreating army of crusaders was crushed at Fariskur on April 6, 1250. The king had proven a good knight but a weak strategist. A large part of his army was taken prisoner. Many of the wounded and sick were massacred by the Saracens just as Richard the Lion-Hearted had slaughtered 2,700 Muslim prisoners on the outskirts of Acre in 1191.

The King Imprisoned

Being taken prisoner was the worst misfortune that could befall a king. Richard the Lion-Hearted went through it. But to be taken prisoner by infidels was the worst misfortune that could happen to a Christian king.

Saint Louis, however, knew how to turn this disastrous situation to his own benefit. First of all, Queen Marguerite, who became chief of the naval forces at sea, collected the 400,000 bezants (200,000 pounds) needed for the first ransom payment in record time. She paid the ransom, and Louis was freed on May 6. His imprisonment only lasted a month. He displayed great courage and dignity in prison, as told by his chaplain Guillaume de Chartres who never left his side during this harsh trial. He thought first and foremost of the other crusaders who were being held prisoner and he refused to make any statements opposed to his Christian faith. This gave him the courage to face torture and death. When he learned that his principals managed to cheat the Muslims out of 20,000 pounds while paying the ransom, he became enraged, thinking that his word should be kept even though it had been given to miscreants. This fact attested to by Joinville during the inquiry concerning his canonization gained recognition as one of the most virtuous deeds expressing Louis IX's saintliness. The preacher Jean de Semois mentioned this during the solemn raising of Saint Louis' body at Saint-Denis after his canonization.[29] In the course of discussions with his Muslim captors, Saint Louis learned that dialogue with them was possible even if he still detested their false religion. When one emir told him that only a crazy man would run the risk of crossing the sea as he had done (the Muslims of the time were no sailors either), especially since Christians feared the Mediterranean Sea, he laughed out loud in agreement. He especially admired the sultan's library of religious works even though it was full of books of abomination and error. After his return, he was the first king of France to establish his own library of religious manuscripts—Christian manuscripts, of course—housed in the Sainte-Chapelle.[30]

The Distant King

Unlike other Christian rulers who had always stayed less than two years in the Holy Land whether they succeeded or failed on their crusades, Saint Louis decided to stay there for an unspecified length of time. He announced this sad news to his people through a message that expressed an entirely new character insofar as it was addressed to French public opinion—whose existence is proven once more here by the care the king took to inform it.[31] He composed this letter in August 1250 and sent it from Acre. His brothers Alphonse de Poitiers and Charles d'Anjou carried it to France. The letter gave a truthful account of the successes and failures of the Egyptian campaign including the death of his brother, his captivity, and the ten-year truce negotiated with the sultan. He claimed that he was determined to return to France after his liberation but renounced this decision after seeing how the Muslims violated the agreement they had made. He therefore decided to stay in the Holy Land after consulting with the barons of France and the Kingdom of Jerusalem as well as the knights of the different military orders. He would stay there in the hope of accomplishing "something good, the deliverance of the captives, the preservation of the castles and fortresses of the Kingdom of Jerusalem, and [of obtaining] other advantages for Christendom, especially since a conflict had broken out between the sultan of Aleppo and the people who were governing in Cairo." He finally called upon his subjects to take up the cross and join him in the Holy Land.[32] Of course, this was not the first time that the Kingdom of France had been orphaned by a king who had left on a crusade. However, none of the other kings' absences lasted as long as Louis', which continued for nearly six years from August 1248 to July 1254.

It is true that in addition to her effectiveness and good qualities, the regent Blanche had the necessary means to govern. Her son had left her extensive powers that were clearly defined, excellent and experienced ecclesiastical and secular advisors, and adequate financial resources. In 1250, when Louis decided to stay longer in the Holy Land, he stressed these facts: "I realized that if I were to stay, I can see no risk involved for my kingdom because Madame the queen has more than enough people to defend it."[33] He sent his two surviving brothers back to France to bolster their mother. Alphonse de Poitiers had just received his inheritance from his father-in-law Raimond VII, the count of Toulouse, who died in 1249. Charles d'Anjou, the count of Provence, would actually pursue his personal interests and ambitions, sometimes to the great annoyance of his royal brother. Alphonse, on the other hand, would fulfill his duties and sometimes preside over the royal council in Paris.

The Affair of the Shepherds

In 1251, Blanche of Castile found herself facing an exceptional, unexpected, and serious event: the movement of the shepherds [*pastoureaux*]. This affair is worth discussing because it is one of the most beautiful examples of the role that imagination can play in history, and it is closely tied to a certain image of Saint Louis that dwelt among and animated the popular masses. The whole affair shocked the clerics and intellectuals of the time: it was "an amazing and extraordinary wonder" (*mirabile prodigium et novitas*), says Guillaume de Nangis; "an amazing event" (*quoddam mirabile*), writes Matthew Paris.[34]

Let's listen to Guillaume de Nangis tell it:

1251. An amazing and extraordinary wonder transpired in the Kingdom of France. In order to seduce simple-minded people and spread a desire among them for false imaginings [*falsis adinvention-ibus*], the leaders of certain groups of brigands pretended to have seen visions of angels and apparitions of the blessed Virgin Mary who they said commanded them to take up the cross and form a kind of army with shepherds [*pastores*] and other commoners among the people chosen by God in order to save the Holy Land and to go help the king of France there. They represented the content of this vision with embroidered images that they carried as banners in front of their marches. First they crossed Flanders and Picardy and attracted shepherds and the simplest people with their false cries like magnets attract iron as they crossed villages and fields. When they reached France [Île-de-France] they had become so numerous that they came forward grouped by the hundreds and the thousands like an army, and when they went through the country near flocks and herds of sheep, the shepherds abandoned their flocks and pushed by some kind of frenzy joined their criminal expedition without even warning their families. Although the shepherds and simple people acted in this way without knowing what they were doing but with good intentions, on the other hand there were a great number of bandits and assassins among them who were aware of the criminal purpose that they were following in secret, and the instructions of these leaders guided the whole troop. Brandishing daggers, axes, and other arms as they crossed villages and cities, they terrorized their populations so completely that no one vested with judicial power dared oppose them, and they had fallen so deep in error that they arranged marriages, passed out crosses, and pronounced absolution from sins at the drop of a hat, and, what's worse, led the good people so far into their fabrication that most of them claimed and others believed that the food and wine that were given them not only would not go missing but were replenished in greater quantities. When they learned that the people had fallen into such great error, the clergy were filled with sadness; they wanted to oppose it and in doing so provoked such hatred that when they were discovered in the countryside many of them were killed and became martyrs. Queen Blanche, who was governing the kingdom alone at that time with astonishing efficiency, let them go on, certainly not because she shared their error, but because she hoped they would bring help to her son, the holy king Louis, and the Holy Land. After passing through Paris, they thought that they no longer had a thing to fear, boasting that they were men of good, which they supported with rational arguments, because when they had been in Paris, which is the source of all knowledge, no one ever contradicted them.[35] So, they developed their errors free of all restraint and began to systematically rob and pillage. When they reached Orléans, they attacked the clerics of the university and killed many of them, although a number of them were killed as well. Their leader,[36] whom they called the Master of Hungary,[37] arrived from Orléans with his troops at Bourges, and invaded the synagogues of the Jews, destroyed their books, and unjustly robbed them of their possessions. As he left the town with the people who were with him, the armed inhabitants of Bourges followed them and killed the master and most of his companions. After their fall, others dispersed to other places and were killed or hung for their misdeeds. The rest of them disappeared like smoke.

The English Benedictine Matthew Paris adds other details and makes the Master of Hungary into an old man who, as he tells it, had already started the Crusade of Children in 1212, converted to Islam in Toledo, and was sent by the sultan of Babylon (the sultan of Egypt) in order to deliver France to the Muslims once it was emptied of its crusaders and widowed of its king. According to him, the shepherds did not disappear as quickly as Guillaume de Nangis claims. He says that they broke up into smaller groups and describes how one of their leaders was apparently seized and drowned in the Garonne. He claims another fled to Germany and was cut to pieces in Storeham. In Paris's version, one survivor finally repented and, due to his penitence, actually joined Saint Louis in the Holy Land and placed himself in his service.

I will not go into any depth to analyze this movement that combined class struggle, anti-clericalism, anti-semitism, millenarianism, the role of charismatic leaders, the misleading of the masses, and recurrent, disturbing episodes of fanatic and criminal bestiality concealed behind the appearance of an ideal and a faith. Nevertheless, as it surpasses the limits of any biography of Saint Louis, this episode deserves its own specialized study. It should be mentioned here because it was probably provoked by the letter that the king sent to his people from the Holy Land. It reveals some of the troubling undercurrents in Saint Louis' kingdom and the perversions that his charisma and policy of crusading could arouse.

Blanche of Castile was not able to react quickly in dealing with this affair. Caught off balance, it seems she may have met with the Master of Hungary, perhaps at the abbey of Maubuisson. Although she was not extremely old (she was sixty-three years old in 1251, which was old in the Middle Ages), her health was in decline and she had probably begun to suffer from serious ailments.

In addition, the governing action of the regent and the council had begun to function at a slower pace in the absence of any urgent or important problems. It was also true that the king continued to take part in the government of his kingdom from the Holy Land. Some people have observed that the documents preserved in the archives of the curia that came from the Holy Land are much more numerous than those drawn up in Paris.[38]

Beginning in 1253, as others have already shown, the prince Louis (Saint Louis' son) seems to exercise power through the documents in the archives whose seals have disappeared, which, however, prevents us from knowing whether the king's personal seal was used on them or someone else's. The title he received expressed a more pronounced affirmation of the dynastic hierarchy: he was the "first-born" (*primogenitus*) of the king. Acts and deeds originated in his authority; letters were addressed to him: for example, one written by the abbot of Cluny is addressed "to Louis, by the grace of God, the first-born of our illustrious lord Louis and to his council."[39] Clearly, this child of eight years did not actually govern. But again in this case, the distance of the king made an innovation possible. The "council" that assisted the young prince was no longer the former judiciary council (curia), but a government council. By making or letting the council in Paris that assumed the functions of government take the name of a royal council in the name of his son, a name that up until now had been reserved exclusively for the king's person (who was in the Holy Land at this time), Louis IX reinforced an awareness of the existence of a state that was becoming detached from the physical person of the king. The king was far away; the state became present.

Louis IX in the Holy Land

Louis' long stay in the Holy Land, which lasted from May 1250 to April 1254, was marked by three important decisions that reveal shifts in the king of France's Mediterranean policy for the crusade. By remaining in the Holy Land in order to organize its defense and by committing most of the manpower and the majority of the expenses to the fortification of castles and towns, Louis moved from a policy of conquest or reconquest to one of resistance.

The declarations made on the occasion of Louis' renunciation of the pilgrimage of Jerusalem still left the door open to the idea of reconquering the holy city. In effect, when in Jaffa the king learned that the sultan of Damascus was willing to grant him a pass of safe conduct to visit Jerusalem, people reminded him that in 1192 Richard the Lion-Hearted refused to go to any place from which he could see Jerusalem because he did not want to see the holy city of God without being able to deliver it from his enemies. His entourage therefore convinced him that "if he, the greatest king of the Christians, made his pilgrimage without freeing the city from God's enemies, then all the other kings and all the other pilgrims who came after him would be content simply to carry out their pilgrimage as the king of France had done, without worrying about the liberation of Jerusalem." Thus, the king of France upheld this privileged characteristic in the leadership of the crusade and kept open its possibilities. He must renounce seeing Jerusalem in order to sustain the will and the hope of holding it and possessing it.

Finally, during the course of his stay in the Holy Land, Saint Louis saw his Mongol fantasy, the hope of converting the Asiatic invaders or at least of cooperating with them to encircle the Muslims, disappear. The king had sent the Dominican André de Longjumeau to the court of the Great Khan. He returned from Asia and rejoined the king, who was in Caesaria at the time, in the spring of 1251. He was accompanied by Mongol envoys that demanded a large tribute from Louis as a sign of submission to the khan. The king told Joinville that he "strongly regrets having sent" this embassy. He would nonetheless try one more time to convert the Great Khan by sending him the Franciscan Guillaume de Rubrouck in 1253. He returned to Nicosia in June 1255. The king of France had already returned to France by this time, and when Guillaume wrote him to report on his mission, the king recognized its failure: the conversion of the khan was only a false hope and a delusion.[40]

The Crusade, Louis IX, and the West

In light of the Sixth Crusade, Saint Louis' crusade and the last Western crusade to the Holy Land, and in light of its results, rather than assess the immediate effects of this expedition, which, paradoxically, by its very failure, helped bolster Louis IX's image, can we weigh its long-term effects on the Western enterprise of crusading? The crusade of Tunis would only be a footnote, an appendix, whose consequences would be limited to Louis and his family. Considering that after 1254 the curtain fell on this century-and-a-half–long phenomenon of the Christian crusades, the historian should step back and examine this long episode in its larger perspective in order to better assess Saint Louis' place in it as well as what his crusade meant to him.[41]

Materially, there were no significant results. With the exception of Cyprus, no lands had been conquered and held for a long period of time. Cyprus was conquered from the Byzantines who had seized it from the Muslims in the tenth century. There was no significant immigration or settlement of Christians in the East either. The idea that an excessive population and especially one of landless young nobles ready for adventure (Georges Duby's "young people") created ideal conditions for crusading may have played a role in setting off the First Crusade. However, in this case, the papacy's main motive had been to end internal wars between Christians by redirecting hostilities against the infidels, shifting them to the Orient, and leaving them there. Moreover, this idea cannot explain the crusades that followed. The effects on economic activity were generally negative because, as one would expect, war tended to limit commerce more than it encouraged it. One proof of this is the insignificant role the Italians — the great promoters of economic expansion — played in the crusades, with the exception of the Normans in Sicily. The West was benefiting everywhere from this economic growth. For all their efforts, the crusaders ultimately left only the ruins of imposing monuments, notably in Jerusalem and Acre. Moreover, on the eastern borders of the Holy Land they left those impressive fortresses that, like so many monumental expressions of war, were powerless to stop the course of history. The fate of these grandiose ruins has only been to testify to the vanities of war.[42]

Should we therefore conclude that the crusades siphoned off men and wealth from the Christian West? I do not think so. We cannot really judge the importance of the death toll of Christians on the crusades: their deaths were just and glorious to their contemporaries, while they are at best useless in the eyes of history, although it is clear they did not weaken the Christian world. The only actual result of the crusades that was truly important for society was to decapitate or uproot the lineage of certain nobles, accelerating the extinction of certain noble families. As for the economic cost, we must make two observations. First of all, the cost of the crusade was limited by the monarchy. The cost of the crusade of 1248 to 1254 has been estimated at 1,537,540 pounds *tournois,* and the apparent exactness of this figure should not fool us.[43] It is only a very rough estimate as the kinds of numeric records that allow us to take a quantitative approach to historical realities were still at a very crude stage in the middle of the thirteenth century. However, if we compare this rough figure to the more reliable figure of the king's annual revenue of 250,000 pounds *tournois,* we would have to conclude that Louis IX would have emptied the coffers that his grandfather, Philip Augustus, had filled to capacity. His father Louis VIII's reign was too brief (1223–1226) to have any significant impact on the Royal Treasury. Two facts contradict this hypothesis. First of all, only one part of the considerable expenses for the crusade fell on the Royal Treasury. Most of the money came from the cities and especially from the clergy. Joinville reports that during a council meeting with the legate and other important figures in Acre after the king's liberation during the summer of 1250, while discussing the question of whether the king should stay or return to France, he opposed those who wanted the king to return to France for economic reasons by mentioning that he thought that the king still had a lot of money because the crusade was largely financed by the clergy. He said to the king: "Sire, people say, and I don't know if it's true, that the king has not yet spent any of his deniers, but only the deniers of the clergy."[44] The king did not answer. It is certain that this opinion was partly false. The king had spent money and would continue to spend his own money for the crusade, mainly in assuring the subsistence of some of the crusaders. Joinville knew this and had learned it the hard way. He, too, had been taken prisoner when he was on a ship in the Nile. Before surrendering, he threw his own personal treasure (a box full of money and valuable jewels) along with the precious relics he carried with him into the river. He owed his life to the protection of a Saracen who passed him off as the king's cousin. When the king signed the treaty with the Muslims, Joinville was released with the prisoners who were not massacred and was then reunited with his suzerain and friend. He had lost everything. "The king said: 'Come to me seneschal.' I went to him and kneeled before him, and he sat me down and said to me: 'Seneschal, you know that I have always loved you very much, and my people tell me that they find you hardened. How is this?"—'Sire, I can't take it anymore [*je n'en puis mais*], for you know that I was captured on the water and that I have nothing left and that I lost everything I had.' And he asked me what I wanted, and I told him that I wanted to ask for 2,000 pounds to last me until Easter for the two thirds of the year."[45]

Louis IX was no spendthrift and did not like to be asked for money. He calculated Joinville's monetary needs on the spot. He would need three knights that would have to be paid 400 pounds each. The king "counted on his fingers": "Your new knights will cost 1,200 pounds." He would need 800 more "to be mounted and armed and to feed his knights." The accounting was done, and Louis thought the figure was reasonable: "Truly, I see no excess here and I retain you." In exchange, Joinville, who was a seneschal of the count of Champagne and not of the king to whom he was only a rear vassal, became the direct vassal of the king and had to swear allegiance to him. At the end of the contract's term on Easter 1251, Louis asked him what he wanted in order to stay with him for another year. Joinville proposed "another deal," and as he was comfortable speaking openly with the king, he said to him, "'Because you anger whenever anyone asks you for something, I want you to agree with me that if I ask you for something during the year to come, you will not become angry, and if you refuse me, I won't get angry either.' When he heard this he burst out laughing [*si commença à rire moult clairement*] and told me that he would retain me on that condition. Then he took me by the hand and led me before the legate and toward his council and repeated the agreement we had made to them, and they were joyed by it because I was the richest man in the entire camp."[46]

The king's two other major expenses were for the purchase of ships and the reconstruction of keeps in the Holy Land. However, we should try to think of this problem in different terms. In the thirteenth century, there were neither material nor mental constructs corresponding to what we call economy.[47] Just as some historians conclude that royal revenues were wasted on the crusade, other contemporary historians have imagined that the construction of cathedrals diverted great sums of money from productive investments and slowed or even killed off economic prosperity. However, this notion of "productive investments" does not correspond to any mental or economic reality of the time. In the absence of any regular tax, with the revenue he received from his domain, to which exceptional revenues drawn from the cities and clergy were added, it was in a very small number of cases like the crusade that the king had to pay for his living expenses and the living expenses of his people along with any military activities. Louis did not lead a life of luxury full of sumptuous expenses. If the crusade had never taken place, the sums spent on it would have stayed in his Treasury under the watch of the Templars who kept it in the dungeon of the Temple of Paris, and it would have eventually been spent on other war efforts. Apart from the crusade, the war against the English and the count of Toulouse in 1242 and the expeditions against the uprising of the barons at the beginning of his reign and then again in Languedoc in 1240, Louis IX did a remarkable job of establishing peace throughout his kingdom until the brief and catastrophic crusade of 1270. Of course he did not fill the Royal Treasury as his grandfather had done, but, between his crusading expeditions and the periods of peace, financial crisis was essentially unknown.

In terms of culture, the crusade involved a rejection of dialogue. It was no occasion for cultural exchange. War prevented any acculturation on both sides. On the one hand, the Christians brought almost nothing with them to the East and left nothing there. This surprises the great American historian of the Middle East, Bernard Lewis: "The impact of the Crusaders on the countries they had ruled for up to two centuries was in most ways remarkably slight."[48] On the other hand, Western Christian borrowings from oriental culture rarely came about through the crusades. It is a myth frequently reproduced in writing that during the twelfth and thirteenth centuries one novelty or another had been brought to the West from the Orient by the crusaders. These novelties were either inventions or innovations that were actually created in the West by Christians, or, if they were actual borrowings from the East, more often than not they came through trade or through intermediary zones of contact between the two cultures in the Mediterranean: from Sicily and especially from Spain where cultural exchanges coexisted with ongoing hostilities. If a certain mutual respect existed, it was limited to a specific community that adhered to the chivalric ideal, which, especially in the twelfth century, influenced the Frankish lords in the Orient and their Muslim homologues in Syria and Palestine.[49] In the eyes of history, this was a pathetic form of respect between two backward-looking social classes, one that contributed heavily to the sterilization of Muslim culture in the Middle East, halting its progress, the other that failed to slow a development in the West that worked against it to a significant extent.

Some historians have adopted the complaint that I once voiced in the past: "As I see it, the apricot is the only fruit that Christians could have brought back from the crusades."[50] I may be even more pessimistic today. The crusades fed the Islamic spirit of holy war, the *jihad,* and brought it back to life.[51] Reaction against the medieval crusades developed in the nineteenth century even more than in the Middle Ages, and the outcry against them can still be heard in the aggression of the "fundamentalist" revival in contemporary Islam. The crusade, which still has some nostalgic partisans in the West, and the *jihad* are a perverted form of faith. I share Steven Runciman's opinion about this: "High ideals were besmirched by cruelty and greed, enterprise and endurance by a blind and narrow self-righteousness; and the Holy War itself was nothing more than a long act of intolerance in the name of God, which is the sin against the Holy Ghost."[52]

Some historians have also viewed the medieval crusade as the first Western act of colonization.[53] For example, a certain similarity exists between the *poulains* [colts] and the *pieds-noirs* of contemporary North Africa. In opposition to the crusaders who are by definition only "passing through," this term designated the Franks who were born in the Holy Land and who resided there permanently. They were the "little ones" of the first "horses" [*chevaux*], the first generation of knights [*chevaliers*] who conquered the Holy Land and took up residence there. At the beginning of the twelfth century the meaning of the word changed in the same measure that relations between the Christian West and the Latin States of Syria-Palestine declined. The Westerners reproached the "*poulains*" for adopting manners similar to the Muslims', for their tendency to get along with them, in other words for no longer acting as defenders of their faith and for practicing what we know today as tolerance, a word and a reality unknown to Western Christians of the twelfth and thirteenth centuries outside of certain rare and exceptional circumstances. In the thirteenth century, the term gradually became an insult on the lips of the Westerners as the distance between the *poulains* and the crusaders grew wider. Joinville provides us with a significant and colorful example. During the week when Louis IX consulted his advisors about the decision to return to France or stay in the Holy Land, Joinville argued against the majority opinion, passionately debating in favor of staying in the Orient. He was harshly attacked. The discussions took such a violent turn that one old and renowned knight anxious to return to France, Sir Jean de Beaumont, called his nephew, Sir Guillaume de Beaumont, who held the opposite opinion, a "piece of filth" [*sale ordure*]! As Joinville tells it: "They call the peasants of the land *poulains,* and Sir Pierre d'Avallon, who lived in Sur (Tyre), heard someone call me a *poulain* because I had advised the king to stay with the *poulains.* And Sir Pierre d'Avallon urged me to defend myself against the people who called me a *poulain* and to tell them that I would rather be a *poulain* than a worn-out warhorse like them."[54]

Some have argued that the crusades helped Western Christendom develop self-awareness and that they expressed a new religious sensibility. If this were true, then they constituted a warped response to the important growth of the eleventh and twelfth centuries. It was a delayed response. At least in the thirteenth century crusading also contradicted Christendom's internal development at a time when, despite the other perversion of the Inquisition from which Saint Louis kept his distance except in the case of the Jews, it was discovering a richer, more peaceful voice in the internalization of individual consciousness. Saint Louis took part in this movement too.

The crusading king was thus nostalgic for the past, half of himself testifying to Westerners' inability to use their progress to aid in the transformation of the West in which his other half took part. Just as *La Mort le roi Artu* (The Death of King Arthur) marked the dismal apotheosis of chivalry, Saint Louis' crusades sounded the death knell of crusading, the end of this aggressive phase of a penitential and self-sacrificing Christendom. He embodied the egotism of faith at its highest ultimate point, which since the price of the believer's sacrifice was to achieve his salvation at the expense of the "other" bore the seeds of intolerance and death.

However, in the medieval world where the ideals of the crusade continued to inspire profound admiration even among those who no longer believed in them (a Rutebeuf or a Joinville for example), Saint Louis emerged with his image enhanced by these catastrophic crusades. His image was illuminated by "the beauty of death" and initiated a process of "death and transfiguration." From this point of view, the crusade of Tunis would be a crowning achievement in all its dazzling and mortal brevity.

THE DEATH OF HIS MOTHER

A terrible event in Louis' life put a brutal end to his stay in the Holy Land. He was at Sidon in the spring of 1253 when he learned of his mother's death. She passed away on November 27, 1252. The interruption of maritime communications during the winter was responsible for this delay that only increased the king's sadness. Worries latched on to his pain, reinforced perhaps by certain words from the messengers. Was anyone governing his kingdom? With the regent gone, a young prince only ten years old, his uncles more preoccupied with their own lands than with the kingdom, his advisors were undoubtedly distraught and probably not up to dealing with the problems of governing the kingdom, which was, however, in a state of peace and endowed with an effective administration. The course of action was immediately clear. After abandoning himself for several days to extreme bouts of sadness,[55] the king decided to return to France. Louis gave several final orders to reinforce the Christian defenses in the Holy Land. It was simply a matter of holding out for as long as possible. Then Louis set out to sea. He left the terrestrial Jerusalem once and for all, never to see it again.

From One Crusade to
the Next and Death
(1254–1270)

Louis set sail from Acre on April 24 or 25, 1254. Several days later, the king's ship rammed a sandbar off the shores of Cyprus, which damaged the boat's keel. They were afraid the ship would sink, and this was an occasion for the king to display his composure and sense of duty as he refused to leave the ship because the other boats could not take everyone else aboard.

In his life of Saint Louis, which is a chronological succession of images of the king based on exemplary anecdotes like all the biographies of the time, Joinville gives us two images of Saint Louis on the return home.

The first is an image of the king on a walk and his idyllic meeting with a hermit. The second anecdote illustrates Louis' intransigence as a severe judge confronting the careless conduct of an adolescent who was guilty of a double offense in his eyes: guilty of committing what he considered a capital sin, while the rest of his entourage thought it only a venial offense, and guilty of putting the French fleet in danger. The king acted here as the defender of morality and the common interest that had arisen through a sense of God's anger, which could be provoked by faulty and undisciplined conduct.

> We saw an island called Lampedusa, a place where we had taken many rabbits, and we found an ancient hermitage among the rocks and found a garden there made by the hermits who dwelled there in ancient times: there were olive trees, fig trees, vine stocks, and other trees. A fountain stream flowed through the garden. We went with the king to the back of the garden where we found an oratory whitened with lime and a cross, reddened with earth, under the first vault.
>
> We entered under the second archway and found two dead bodies whose flesh was rotting; their ribs still held together, and the bones of their hands were held on their chests. They were laying facing the east in the same way that bodies are laid in the ground. When it was time to go back aboard our ship, one of our sailors was missing, which made the captain of our ship think that he had stayed behind in order to become a hermit, and because of this Nicolas de Soisi, who was the king's head sergeant, left three sacks of biscuits on the shore so that he could find them and live off them.[1]

The voyage by sea was a trial that hit them with alternating storms and lack of winds, fierce waves and rocks and fearsome men. When the fleet arrived off the coast of Provence, the entire entourage including "the queen and all his councilors" asked Louis to put ashore without delay. The land was part of the Empire, but it belonged to Louis' brother, Charles d'Anjou, count of Provence. Louis, however, still insisted on going all the way to "his" port, Aigues-Mortes, "which was his land."[2] They finally convinced him to land at Salins d'Hyères on July 10. The possibility afforded him of meeting a famous Franciscan residing in the monastery of Hyères at that time must have played some part in his reluctant decision.

THE MEETING WITH HUGH OF DIGNE

Hugh of Digne (or de Barjols) belonged to the Rigorist movement of the Spiritual Franciscans. He was a follower of the millenarian ideas of Joachim de Fiore, who died in 1202 and who called for the establishment of an eternal Gospel on earth. These ideas seemed suspect to the guardians of orthodoxy in the Franciscan order and the Church. The order was in the midst of a great Joachimite ferment. Its leader, the general minister John of Parma, was elected in 1247 and was a fervent Joachimite. In the same year of 1254 that Saint Louis met Hugh of Digne,[3] another Joachimite Franciscan, Gerardo da Borgo san Donnino, wrote his *Introduction to the Eternal Gospel* (*Liber Introductorius ad Evangelium Eternum*). This book spread the abbot of Fiore's ideas. It immediately provoked violent reactions, especially at the University of Paris where a bitter conflict opposed the Mendicant (Dominican and Franciscan) masters in theology to certain ordinary masters. In 1256, Pope Alexander IV condemned Joachim de Fiore's arguments and Gerardo da Borgo san Donnino's book. Hugh of Digne probably died that same year or before February 2, 1257 in any case. He thus escaped any condemnation. Although his admirers trumpeted the many miracles that took place at his tomb in Marseilles, Hugh was not proclaimed a saint. His more fortunate sister, Douceline, whom he served as spiritual advisor [*directeur de conscience*], was also a Joachimite and the founder of a community of Beguines near Hyères (1240) and of another in Marseilles (1255). She died in 1274 after receiving the grace of visions and ecstasies.[4] In 1257, John of Parma resigned from his functions and surrendered the general leadership of the Franciscans to the young future Saint Bonaventure. He was judged for heresy and escaped a harsh condemnation thanks only to the solid support of Cardinal Ottobono Fieschi, the future and briefly reigning Pope Hadrian V (1276). Hugh of Digne retained his great prestige in the Franciscan order despite his imprudent actions. Saint Bonaventure adopted—often literally—a large part of his commentary on the Rule of Saint Francis, and his fellow friar, Salimbene of Parma, the same one who had watched Saint Louis depart on his crusade from the general chapter of Sens in 1248, dedicated sparkling pages in his chronicle to Hugh. Hugh's talent as a preacher particularly fascinated him: his voice would ring out like a trumpet and strike his listeners in waves.[5]

This was the same Franciscan guru who fascinated the young king of France in the summer of 1254. Joinville was there:

> The king had heard about a Franciscan monk called Brother Hugh. Because of his great reputation, the king sent for this Cordelier so that he could see him and hear him speak. On the day he came to Hyères we looked out on the path by which he was coming and

saw that a very large crowd of men and women followed him on foot. The king had him preach. The beginning of the sermon was on the members of the religious orders and congregations, and he thus said: "Seigneurs, I see too many religious members at the king's court and in his company." And with these words, he added, "beginning with me."[6]

However, the sermon was addressed especially to the king:

> In his sermon he taught the king how he had to conduct himself in accordance with the will of his people, and at the end of his sermon he thus said that he had read the Bible and the books that go with it and that he had never seen, neither in the book of the faithful nor in the books of the unbelievers, that any kingdom or domain had ever been lost or transferred from one lord's seigniory to another's or from one king to another but for lack of justice. So, he said, since he is returning to France, the king must take care to execute justice well enough for his people to keep the love of God and in such a way that God will not take the Kingdom of France away from him with his life.[7]

Carried away by the Franciscan, the king wanted him to join his retinue in complete disregard of what he had said in his sermon. Hugh refused. Joinville, however, spurred the king on, and he pressed his request: the abbot might accompany him as far and as long as he could. Hugh of Digne angrily repeated his refusal. He consented at the very most to spend a day with the king.

Whether it was premeditated or improvised, I believe that his meeting with Hugh of Digne was of the utmost importance in the saintly king's life. Weighed down with the failure of his crusade, Louis tried to identify its causes and asked himself what he had to do to please God to gain his own salvation and that of his people and to serve Christendom. Hugh showed him a way: by establishing the rule of justice here on earth in anticipation of the "last time," for the promotion of an evangelical city on earth; in other words, Hugh showed him the possibility of becoming an eschatological king. I believe that this religious program corresponded to Louis' deepest thoughts and wishes and that it ended up defining the political program of the final period of his reign. With a message transmitted through less mystical Mendicants in the king's entourage (Bonaventure preached before him several times), Hugh of Digne had an inspiring influence on Louis IX's political and religious thinking in the final phase of his life. This influence lasted long after their amazing meeting and after Hugh's death, influencing the king just as Guillaume d'Auvergne, the Cistercians of Royaumont, and the Dominicans of Saint-Jacques had before the crusade.

It is also possible to connect Hugh of Digne's influence to an episode that took place shortly after the Franciscan's death. The dispute between the ordinary clergy and the Mendicants was exacerbated in 1255 by the ordinary master Guillaume de Saint-Amour's pamphlet against the Mendicants entitled *Tractatus brevis de periculis novissimorum temporum* (Short Treatise on the Perils of the Last Times). In 1257, Pope Alexander IV condemned Guillaume de Saint-Amour and asked Louis IX to expel him from France. The king first tried to reconcile the two parties and received Guillaume, but it was not enough for him to simply hold his position. He went even further in criticizing the friars and even attacked the king of France, accusing him of acting like a Mendicant instead of a king. In his function as secular arm of the Church, Louis IX then complied with the pope's request. Any requests to pardon Guillaume fell on deaf ears until the king's death, which was followed closely by Guillaume's in 1272, exiled all that time in his native town of Saint-Amour.[8]

The Return of a Grief-Stricken Crusader

Departing from Hyères, Joinville accompanied the king to Aix-en-Provence. From that point they left on the pilgrimage of Saint-Marie-Madeleine in Saint-Baume ("we were under a very high column of rock there on which they said that Mary Magdalene had been on a retreat for seventeen years"). They then proceeded to Beaucaire where Louis IX reentered the territory of the Kingdom of France. Joinville left him at this point to return to Champagne. Louis then stopped at Aigues-Mortes, Saint-Gilles, Nîmes, Alès, Le Puy, Brioude, Issoire, Clermont, Saint-Pourçain, Saint-Benoît-sur-Loire, his royal castle at Vincennes, Saint-Denis, where he deposited the banner and the cross that he had kept during the return trip, and finally to Paris, which he entered on September 7, 1254.

According to Matthew Paris, Louis was well received by his people but seemed overwhelmed with sadness:

> The king of France, his face and mind disturbed, would not accept any consolations. Neither music nor any pleasing or consoling words could please him or make him laugh. Neither the return trip through his home country and kingdom, nor the respectful greetings of the crowd that came to greet him, or the homage he received accompanied with gifts given to his seigniory consoled him. His eyes lowered, frequently sobbing, he thought about his capture and the general confusion that it had wrought on Christendom. To console him, one pious bishop who was full of tact said: "My very dear Lord and king, do not fear falling into a sadness and a state of disgust for life that annihilate spiritual joy. They are the cruel stepmothers of the soul. That is the greatest sin, because it wrongs the Holy Spirit. Let your sight and thought recall the patience of Job and the suffering of Eustache." And he retraced their history up to the final rewards that God granted them. Then the king, the most pious of all the kings on earth, answered: "If I were the only one to have to put up with the shame and adversity, and if my sins did not fall upon the universal Church, I would bear them more serenely. But, unfortunately for me, it is all Christendom that has been exposed to embarrassment because of me." They sang a mass in honor of the Holy Spirit so that he might receive its consoling, which is stronger than anything. And, henceforth, through the grace of God, he accepted the salutary council of consolation.[9]

Matthew Paris undoubtedly exaggerates and gives in to the rhetoric of mourning. However, all of the other testimony is in agreement insofar as it recognized a profound change in Louis, a kind of conversion to a greater practice of austerity after the crusade. After this point, he only rarely gave up the harsh clothing he had adopted as a good crusader, simple clothing that he did not abandon with the cross at Saint-Denis.

Again, Joinville attests to this:

> After the king returned from overseas, he lived so devoutly that he would never wear furs or vair or Siberian squirrel or scarlet or

golden spurs or stirrups. His clothes were all of camlet and rough cloth; the furs of his coverings and clothes were all of deerskin or hare's foot or sheepskin. He was so sober in his eating that he never ordered dishes other than what his cook brought for him, and when they put it before him he would eat it. He watered down his wine in a glass goblet, and, according to the strength of the wine, he would add water in proportion and hold the goblet in his hand while they watered down the wine behind his table. He always gave his poor something to eat, and gave them deniers after the meal.[10]

His confessor, Geoffroy de Beaulieu, goes even further in describing his behavior:

> After his happy return to France, witnesses of his life and confidents of his conscience saw the point to which he strove to be devout toward God, just toward his subjects, merciful toward the misfortunate, humble toward himself, and to use all his strength to make progress in every kind of virtue. For as much as gold exceeds silver in value, his new way of living after returning from the Holy Land exceeded the holiness of his previous life, and, yet, in his youth he had always been good, innocent, and of exemplary character.[11]

Louis passed from the simplicity that he had always advocated to strict austerity. He also made this austerity the guiding principle in his politics, which henceforth followed a program of penitence, purification, and moral and religious order for the kingdom and his subjects. His attempts to achieve religious objectives and his actions for reinforcing monarchical power were once more inextricably entwined.

THE KINGDOM'S REFORMER

The main implement of royal political power consisted in a series of edicts, in other words, texts issued from the royal *potestas* that possessed the force of law. The increasing number of these royal acts attested to the progress of monarchical power insofar as they tended to apply more and more to the entire kingdom, even though certain edicts were only applicable to specific areas, limited to territories that benefited from a particular status (Normandy[12] or the lands of Languedoc, for example).

Beginning in December 1254, Louis promulgated a text that historians have often called "the Great Edict" due to its completeness and the significance of the measures that it decreed. It aimed to reform the practices that count the most in royal government and thus to thoroughly reform the government. The reform of the Church, which had been a watchword for the papacy and the clerics for nearly two centuries, seems to be transferred to the Kingdom of France in the form of a complete program.

However, it has already been shown that the "Great Edict" of December 1254 was in fact an amalgam of several texts issued from Louis IX's authority between late July and December 1254.[13] Taken together the document is so imposing that it comprised a novelty in its very completeness and to such an extent that it has been considered as "the first royal edict"[14] and as "the charter of French liberties."[15] In the Middle Ages it was called the *statutum generale* (general statute) or, in the plural, the *statuta sancti Ludovici* (the statutes of Saint Louis), while in French it was referred to as the "*establissement le roi.*"[16]

Shortly after his return to the royal domain, Louis took measures for reforming the kingdom's administration in the Midi. There are two mandates both local and regional in character that date from his stays in Saint-Gilles and Nîmes; they applied to the cities of Beaucaire and Nîmes and to the seneschalcy of Beaucaire. These measures were issued on the spot and were probably taken in response to requests from the inhabitants of those jurisdictions. Louis decided that his decisions should be widely publicized and ordered that they be proclaimed *en place publique*. They took the earlier results of his investigations of 1247 into account. These texts abolished measures taken by royal seneschals in violation of previously existing local customs [*coutumes des lieux*]. The king followed a Capetian practice that contributed significantly to the reinforcement of monarchical power by forging a curious alliance between tradition and progress. The idea of innovation was generally looked down upon by populations who were attached to maintaining customs that they considered privileges and that dazzled them with the additional prestige of having been handed down through the ages. In fact, the claim that something marked a return to the past was quite often a means of legitimating and softening administrative and political changes. This was especially true in the Midi where direct royal government was very recent and where the king wanted to make a point not only of stressing continuity with the past but also of making advances that respected local and regional traditions. From then on, the royal officers (administrators) "must render justice without any special consideration for the persons involved." They could not accept any gifts (bread, wine, or fruit) worth more than ten shillings and they had to refuse any gifts for their wives or children. Likewise, they could no longer give any gifts to those appointed to examine their accounts or to their superiors, their wives, or their children. All of this amounted to a moralization of royal government.

The Great Edict of December also added a series of measures concerning morality in itself. Blasphemy, any "impious words against God, the Virgin, and the saints," dice games, and visits to brothels[17] and taverns were all forbidden to royal officers. The practice of usury by any of them became an offense equal to theft. The edict also contained other measures for reforming the administrative practices of the royal officers. They were no longer able to buy buildings in the territory where they exercised their functions, nor marry their children there, nor leave any of them in convents or monasteries within their territory. They could not imprison anyone for debts, except for debts owed to the king. They could not level any fines against the accused until they had been judged, and they had to presume any accused person innocent if he had not yet been found guilty. They could not sell their offices. They could not impede the transport of grains—a measure meant to fight famine and prevent the hoarding of grains. Upon leaving office, they had to stay within their jurisdiction or leave prosecutors there for forty days so that they could eventually respond to any complaints about them. Another article outlawed the abusive requisition of horses.

And these were not the only things the edict dealt with: dice games and even making dice were forbidden for everyone in the entire kingdom as were "table" games like backgammon and checkers, which were dually condemnable as games of chance and of money. Prostitutes were to be expelled from the "good towns."[18] In particular, they were chased off the streets at the center of town ("streets that are at the heart of the aforementioned good towns") and relegated to places outside the city walls, far from churches and cemeteries.[19] People who rented houses to them were subject to a confiscation of one year's rent. Access to taverns was henceforth prohibited for the regular population living in towns, while their free use was reserved for travelers (the "*trespassants,*" those passing through).

This legislation, which no doubt expressed Saint Louis' ideas and wishes, may seem like it was hard to implement due to its odd combination of moral prescriptions, rules for good administration, and modern principles of justice. The measures repressing blasphemy, gambling, prostitution, and the frequentation of taverns have an archaic aspect related to the Christian idea of a king's function and the remarkably strict way that Louis IX defined it after returning from his ill-fated crusade. The prescriptions against Jews expressed medieval Christendom's evolution from anti-Judaism to anti-Semitism. Our anti-racist societies recognize everything in this that we must reject in medieval Christianity's descent into persecutions and crimes that culminated in the anti-Semitic crimes of our twentieth century whose historical roots we must denounce. The act of requiring people suspected of delinquency and crime to be granted dependable public justice and the affirmation of the presumption of innocence are modern principles of justice that mark a turning point for ideas and practices in relation to "feudal" justice. We know that it has always been difficult to assure the observance of the presumption of innocence for suspects and the accused. Finally, there was the code of good conduct for "administrators" at the heart of this legislation, intended to assure the successful workings of the public (royal) administration as much as to impress a positive image of it in people's minds. This might seem like a concern belonging to another time and another society if the struggle against the corruption of political representatives were not emerging again as one of the primary needs and responsibilities of our contemporary societies. The Middle Ages are a present past. If the twenty-first century, among others, turns out to be a century of ethical urgency, then it will have to draw part of its inspiration from the long view of historical time. The great ages of history were all periods of moralization.

Upon returning from his crusade, Saint Louis was influenced by the trends of his century, and the different texts that made up the Great Edict of 1254 were a collective work. However, there can be no doubt that this important text carried the strong imprint of the will and ideas of the king. He wanted to realize this Christian political ideal that he did not invent but whose successful implementation appeared to him like a duty and requirement of his royal function. This would offer redemption from the failure of the crusade. His kingdom had to be saved, and he must be, too, body and soul. If his own salvation did not depend entirely on the success of this political program, it could at least be won through his unwavering commitment to the attempt to make it work.

The Great Edict extended measures first decreed for the south of France to the entire kingdom. It was finally completed with the readoption of older decrees: in particular with an act from the beginning of Louis' reign (December 1230) that had the king ratify measures taken by an assembly of barons against the Jews and their usurious practices, and with a now lost edict of 1240 that renewed the condemnation of Jewish usurers and that banned the Talmud for passages that were blasphemous toward God and the Virgin Mary.[20]

THE KING'S NEW MEN

Louis made the decisions although he also knew how to listen to the opinions of the expert advisors that he was able to keep in his service, whether they were clerics in his chancery, "grand officers" running his "*hôtel*," members of his Parlement, or members of the council.

Some of them formed a group of insiders who were sometimes summoned to the council, but more often they were simply guests with whom the king liked to speak on familiar terms at the table after meals or at other times of the day. Two of them were famous, and Louis enjoyed inciting their jealousy, which was suffused with friendship and esteem: the lord de Joinville, seneschal of Champagne,[21] and Robert de Sorbon, the canon of Notre-Dame-de-Paris. Another of these insiders was the young count of Champagne, Thibaud V, king of Navarre, who became the king's son-in-law when he married his daughter Isabelle in 1255. Following the tradition of the Capetian court, we also find churchmen and secular lords among them. They were usually from the lesser nobility, and we know less about them, although Joinville is an exception. While speaking about the king, he also spoke a lot about himself and probably exaggerated his role.

In the first group, there was Guy Foulcois (or Foulques), who joined the orders after he became a widower, becoming a cleric in the service of Alphonse de Poitiers. Louis met Guy at Saint-Gilles after his return to France and took him into his service. He influenced the composition of the first two texts that formed the Great Edict of 1254. In 1257, he became bishop of Puy, then archbishop of Narbonne, cardinal-bishop of Sabine, and finally was elected pope under the name Clement IV (1265–1268). In this position he obviously remained favorable to the king of France. Two of Louis IX's other advisors became cardinals during the same promotion of 1261: Raoul Grosparmi, keeper of the king's seals during the crusade, and Simon Monpris de Brie, a Franciscan who succeeded Raoul as keeper of the seals and who also became pope under the name Martin IV (1281–1285). It was under his pontificate that the canonization proceedings for Louis IX made decisive progress. Another Franciscan, Eudes Rigaud, was even closer to the king. He was one of the "Four Masters" who had drawn up the official commentary on the Franciscan rule in 1242. He later became the master regent of the convent of the Cordeliers in Paris, a master in theology at the University, and, finally, archbishop of Rouen.[22]

Finally, there were the Mendicant friars who were the king's spiritual advisors. At the head of their ranks was the Dominican Geoffroy de Beaulieu, Louis' confessor. After Louis' death he was his first biographer in the hagiographical pursuit of his canonization.

It is also important to mention the beginnings of a change in the size of the royal council and the Parlement after the king's return. Certainly, this change started with the period of the crown prince Louis' "government" from 1252 to 1254. A certain number of the "parliamentarians" were qualified as "masters." Most of them held university titles and were masters in law or civil law. They invented a monarchical law formed through an application of Roman law to customary law. The monarchical law was expressed more and more in written form. It gradually achieved an efficient synthesis between Roman law, dissociated from the imperial monopoly on it, and feudal law. This synthesis helped build the monarchical state.[23] Their contemporaries called these "masters" *legists,* and they reached the height of their influence during the reign of Saint Louis' grandson, Philip IV the Fair. They were not educated at the University of Paris because the papacy had refused to give the new university a school of civil (Roman) law. This might have been at the instigation of the French king who may not have wanted law that confirmed imperial authority taught in his capital. More often than not these masters received their formation at the University of Orléans because the invasion of southern legists formed in Toulouse had not yet begun, although a certain juridical culture that Guy Foulcois had already acquired and placed respectively in the service of Alphonse de Poitiers, Louis IX, and the pontifical throne obviously came from the Midi. Unlike the real legists like Jacques de Révigny, a professor at Orléans from 1260 to 1280,[24] these men were practitioners like Pierre de Fontaines, who relied on his experience as the bailiff of Vermandois to reconcile Roman law and customary law. At the king's request, he wrote the *Conseil à un ami* between 1254 and 1258 for the heir to the throne, using specific examples from a bailiff's administration to show that one could not solely and entirely follow the written law, *the* law or custom, nor *law* properly speaking.[25]

Finally, these new men in the king's service were bailiffs and seneschals who represented royal authority in the jurisdictions of the domain and the kingdom. They worked as both the instrument and the embodiment of royal justice. In order to avoid the temptations of corruption and favoritism born from a long frequentation that was capable of leading to friendship without conscious complicity, changes in assignments or replacements were frequent among them. Louis IX's rule went through two "strong periods" in this respect: from 1254 to 1256 and from 1264 to 1266. The reasons for the replacements and displacements are hard to identify. The latter were less numerous than the former during the second period. During the first period they were clearly the result of the return of the king and his investigations.[26]

JUSTICE IN THE CITIES

The Great Edict was readopted in 1256. The new draft introduced certain important differences in relation to the texts of 1254. The measures adopted by the king up to this point were implemented in four different forms—and even in a fifth beginning in February 1255. They were composed in French and in Latin, and this was done specifically for the areas speaking *langue d'oïl* as well as those speaking *langue d'oc* [*langue d'oïl* was the language spoken in northern France that eventually became modern French; *langue d'oc* was the term for the language of southern France including Provençal, Languedoc, which gave its name to the region, and other regional dialects.—Trans.] and ultimately for the entire kingdom.

The Edict of 1256 resulted from a change in the texts of 1254 that transformed them from what they were, essentially a series of instructions to the bailiffs and seneschals, into an actual general edict for the kingdom. The new text included only twenty-six articles instead of thirty. The articles on the Jews and commerce were omitted. The first of these was included in anti-Jewish legislation that henceforth comprised a separate chapter in the kingdom's acts. The measures governing the circulation of grains were circumstantial acts more than general rules. The articles calling for religious and moral order against gambling, blasphemy, and prostitution form a coherent whole that may be a better reflection of Louis' political stance, although he also had to accept the softening of certain measures, especially the ones against prostitution. Prostitutes were chased from the town centers and from areas near holy places, but otherwise tolerated. This was an outline for creating ghettos for prostitution. No doubt Louis had to resign himself to the advice of his entourage who favored control rather than a strict interdiction of prostitution as they thought of it as a necessary outlet for the carnal weakness of the sons of Adam. On the other hand, the text omitted the reference to torture, the first in a French royal edict, which had appeared in a single text of 1254 addressed to the bailiffs and the seneschals of the South.[27] This is an important detail because it reminds us that the use of torture that would spread later on came from the Inquisition, the Church, and the South when the struggle against heresy united with all the means supplied by the rebirth of Roman law. This law inspired the king to insist upon the recognition of the presumption of innocence as a fundamental judicial principle: "no one may be deprived of his rights without proof of his crime and without a trial" (*nemo sine culpa vel causa privandus est jure suo*).

Here we can sense Louis' firm position and profound commitment, his desire for justice, and his resolve to purify the kingdom. The Edict of 1256 extended the instructions of 1254 to the entire hierarchy of royal agents down to its lowest levels: provosts, viscounts, local judges [*viguiers*], mayors, foresters, sergeants, and "others." We also get a sense of what partially escaped his competence and his interest: legal practices and the program's application to the concrete conditions of social life.

The King as Investigator

The king virtually transformed himself into an investigator. He expressed two aspects of his function to his subjects: the judge who traveled the country to hear cases and who dispensed justice on his path, and the king in all his majesty who, following the example of divine Majesty, sublimated all forms of law and sovereignty, of *potestas* and *auctoritas,* offering himself to pure contemplation. After traveling through part of Languedoc upon his return from the Holy Land, Louis visited Chartres, Tours, the important pilgrimage sites (the Virgin and Saint Martin were the dynasty's protectors), Picardy, Artois, Flanders, and Champagne in 1255. These were the wealthy regions of rural and urban prosperity on the important border with the Empire. In 1256 he visited Normandy, the jewel that his grandfather Philip Augustus had wrested from the English.

THE KING AND THE INVESTIGATIONS IN LANGUEDOC

Languedoc presented ideal grounds for legal inquiry. Here more than anywhere else the Capetian monarchy could attempt to undo the traces and memories of the shameless and unrestrained offenses committed by the officers of the crown after 1229 and again after 1240–1242. They had taken advantage of their distance from Paris and the repressive conditions of dealing with the heresy. They had profited to the detriment of the local populations whom they treated like vanquished people in a conquered land.

Joseph Strayer has painstakingly identified the detailed investigations carried out between 1258 and 1262 in the seneschalcy of Carcassonne-Béziers, as they took place under the direction of "the king's conscience."[28] These investigations were initiated after the ones carried out in Beaucaire from 1254 to 1257, where the problems were less serious and less difficult to resolve because there had been few heretics in the region and because its inhabitants had not participated in the revolts of 1240 and 1242.[29] The records of these investigations afford us a fairly clear insight into the thoughts and actions of the king. It is interesting to examine them in greater detail.

From the beginning of their mission, the investigating officers encountered difficult problems on which they consulted with the king. In April 1259, he responded with a long letter.[30] In this letter he recommended a certain indulgence, not as a juridical principle but from a moral point of view, reminding them that mercy should temper strict justice. He admitted that he had been harsher when he was younger but now tended to be less severe. This claim may appear strange as he seemed more concerned with moral order since his return from the crusade. However, there is really no contradiction here. His program was to establish the rule of true justice and peace.

Although justice and peace were to be pursued more zealously, they would only exist more effectively when justice was moderate and accepted and peace achieved by reconciliation as much as by punishment. The eschatological king wanted to use consent to purify flawed behavior.

The king reaffirmed the presumption of the innocence of the accused party who had neither fled nor been tried and condemned. It was particularly important to assure that those suspected of heresy were in fact heretics. The rights of women to their inheritances and dowries had to be thoroughly respected. Woman was a weak being, and it was the special task of royal justice to protect the weak including women, widows, and the poor. In particular, the king refused to allow women to be punished for the offenses of their husbands. He did not accept collective responsibility when there had been no complicity.[31] Louis was more ambiguous about the clergy: people were supposed to "do it justice" [*lui rendre justice*], which can be understood in different ways. We know that in relation to people of the Church Louis followed two convictions that led to very different attitudes without necessarily contradicting each other. He had profound respect for the "Holy Church" and its members and expected others to show the same consideration; however, he was hostile to the material forms of its power. Hugh of Digne must have reinforced this attitude in him. In 1247, he supported France's secular nobility against the Church. In any case, he believed that the Church should not be wealthy.[32]

The investigators' sentences followed these royal directives. They treated the plaintiffs with a large degree of understanding. Among the 145 plaintiffs individually named in 130 rulings, seventy-five received a judgment that was entirely or almost entirely favorable. Thirty-three received a sentence that was partly favorable. There were only thirty-three others who received unfavorable judgments. For the most part, these were declared heretics and their accomplices. In four cases, the investigators deemed themselves incapable of reaching a verdict. Among the sixty-five requests made by men, thirty-seven received a favorable judgment, and for the fifty-five made by women, the success rate rose to forty-five.

The sentences pronounced were more favorable to villages than to cities. Many of the cities had been especially ill treated in the course of the struggle against the heresy for which many of them had been centers of resistance. Many of these southern cities were perched on hilltops or hillsides. The invaders destroyed these sites of resistance by removing their inhabitants to locations on the plains. Cities built high in the hills were forcibly abandoned in favor of low-lying towns. The wealthy inhabitants often received an indemnity if they were not heretics. In his letter of April 1259, the king personally intervened to assure that someone would indemnify the owners of lands seized for the construction of the new bourg of Carcassonne. However, most of the urban communities had their petitions "nonsuited." The bishops received the harshest treatment. The king had been very upset and even scandalized by the virtual independence and power of the bishops in the South. Despite a letter from Saint Louis in support of the bishop of Béziers, the investigators did not reward him the goods he claimed as his rightful restitution, while the king did not seem to have kept his agents in check. The same thing happened to the bishop and chapter of Lodève, although the bishop produced four charters granted by Philip Augustus confirming his rights to exercise judicial authority. The investigating officers claimed that only a general ruling (*ordinatio generalis*) from the king could decide such an important matter; however, no royal decision was forthcoming, depriving the bishop of his former right.

Joseph Strayer assesses the investigators' judgments and actions in an overall favorable manner: "They worked cautiously and intelligently. They sought out all relevant testimony. They passed sentences only after conducting careful examinations." However, the American historian adds, "They were not too indulgent, except perhaps for women, and they would do nothing that could weaken royal power." The king's execution of justice in Languedoc corresponded to Saint Louis' general position: submission to morality and religion went hand in hand with the interests of the king, in other words, with the interests of the nascent state.

THE KING AND THE TOWNS

Louis IX's reign occupied a key period in the history of French cities, and the king seems to have played an important role in this development. In the thirteenth century—and especially in France—this milieu was the culminating point for the great movement of urbanization in the West. Until this time, this movement had occurred in a more or less anarchical way, even though we can also observe a similar process taking place everywhere along two lines. There was an economic evolution through which the cities emerged as markets and centers of artisanal production, and a social and political evolution through which the "bourgeois" or "citizens," the upper and middle levels of urban society, more or less easily and completely seized power in urban affairs from the lords of the cities whether they were secular or ecclesiastical (bishops) lords, or, in the royal domain, from the king himself.[33]

In the twelfth century, the Capetians implemented an urban policy dominated by three concerns that were not always compatible. They tried to support economic activity that depended more and more on the towns; they wanted to garner the support of urban communities against the feudal lords of different domains, great or small; and they were careful not to alienate the Church. The reign of Philip Augustus represented a turning point in this regard. First of all, his reign marked the end or what was nearly the end of the communal movement, the conquest of administrative autonomy by the towns. The last important series in the creation of new communes dates from the decade preceding the battle of Bouvines (1214) in which military contingents from the cities played an important role. Philip Augustus laid claim to *service* from the towns, which was first and foremost military service in the form of the *ost* and the *chevauchée* [the *ost*, i.e., the army, the manpower needed to form an army; the *chevauchée,* horses and tack for war and transport.—Trans.]. He also demanded their *fidélité.* This feudal vocabulary masked a new reality, the reality of the monarch's power and the fact that he now acted as the king of France rather than as a feudal lord in his domain and a suzerain in the kingdom. Philip Augustus wanted to integrate the cities into the monarchical "state" system by exploiting the two services he had a right to demand from nonreligious groups—military service and economic service.

Under Louis IX, this process reached a new decisive stage. The most important cities in the kingdom came to form a kind of objective community, and this occurred spontaneously in some ways but also under pressure from royal power. They formed the network of "good towns" [*bonnes villes*], a term that appeared at the opening of the thirteenth century and whose use was becoming common in the acts of the royal chancery and in the texts of Louis IX himself. "A good town," as they put it, "is one that represents an interest for the king."[34] Louis was the first king of the "good towns." As the same historian describes this relation, the king "sees everything in his good towns, a real administrative agent, a community that always needs to be controlled, and an incomparable political force that has to be handled carefully in all circumstances. . . . Saint Louis treats them as one of the essential elements of the relations that he wants to establish with the entire country. In his eyes they are privileged communities that have a right to speak out but that he must also . . . keep under his control." A king of cities, Saint Louis cultivated this element of modernity. He firmly controlled the cities but gently coddled them. According to a version included in his *Enseignements* written for his son, not the original version that he wrote or dictated but one that was retouched by several of his biographers from Geoffroy de Beaulieu to Guillaume de Nangis without betraying his original thoughts or expressions,[35] we read: "I fondly remember that Paris and the good towns of my kingdom helped me against the barons when I was newly crowned."[36] And again we read, "Above all, keep the good towns and communes of your kingdom in the condition and openness in which your predecessors kept them, and if there is something to amend, amend it and correct it to keep them in your favor, and do it with love, for both your subjects and foreigners, especially your peers and your barons, will fear to commit any acts against you because of the strength and the wealth of the large cities." The tithe levied on the cities of northern France was intended to pay the hefty sum promised to King Henry III of England in 1257 during the negotiations ending in the treaty of Paris in 1258.[37] This sum was compensation for the territories abandoned by the impecunious English. It provided Louis with an opportunity to reform the administration of the towns and their relations with the royal government. The sum owed amounted to roughly 134,000 pounds *tournois,* which, according to William Jordan, must have represented the French crown's entire revenue for at least a half a year. Many of the cities refused to pay this tax, arguing that they were too poor and unable to pay it. The king then decided to launch an investigation into their finances, and his agents found that most of the towns were unable to provide their accounts in an acceptable form. The result of the inquiries was recorded in a group of municipal *rationes* (accounts or reports) in 1259–1260.[38] As Jordan supposes, the king in all likelihood was shocked by the discovery of this disorder, and he then undertook a major reorganization of urban finances that was the object of two edicts of 1262, one for Normandy and another for Francia, in other words, greater Île-de-France.[39]

One consideration of a social and moral nature probably influenced Louis IX's thinking in this matter. The king was always concerned with protecting the weak. In his *Enseignements* he advises his son: "If any quarrel arises between a poor man and a rich one, side with the poor man over the rich man whenever possible until you know the truth, and once you know it, do justice." He must have been shocked by the typical attitudes of the rich who ruled over the poor. Shortly after Louis IX's death, the royal bailiff Philippe de Beaumanoir writes in chapter one of his famous *Coutumes de Beauvaisis* (which he completed in 1283) a number of observations that seem to have been directly inspired by the deceased king:

> It is necessary, he states, to take care to do no wrong to the cities and their common people [*li communs peuples*] and to respect and assure respect for their charters and privileges. The lord of a town should check the "state of the town" [*l'estat de la ville*] each year and control the action of the mayor and of the people who govern the city so that the rich be warned that they will be severely punished if they commit any misdeeds and do not allow the poor to earn a peaceful living. If there are conflicts in the cities between the poor and the rich and among the rich themselves, and if they do not manage to elect a mayor, prosecutors, and lawyers, the lord of the town must name someone capable of governing the city for one year. If the conflicts are about the accounts, the lord should summon all those who made out the receipts and expenses, and they should provide an account of them to him. There are cities where the government has been taken over by the wealthy and their families and where the poor and middle classes have been excluded from it. The lord should make them give public accounts in the presence of delegates of the common people.[40]

According to the investigations, what weighed down urban finances were the excessive travel of municipal officers, the lack of training for employees who were nonetheless well paid, excessive generosity toward distinguished visitors, and the burden of debts, which was the cause of usury practices — one of the king's bêtes noires. The main measure taken by the edicts of 1262 was to require the mayor of every *bonne ville* to come to Paris each year with three or four other people of his on Saint Martin's Day (November 18) in order to give an annual account of the financial management of the city to the royal administration. Gifts, expenditures, and salaries were severely restricted. Usury practices were outlawed, and the city's money had to be kept in the communal treasury.

These edicts do not seem to have been strictly observed, but royal intervention in the cities grew considerably as a result of them, and, despite its deficiencies, the government of the royal cities appeared as a model to be imitated at the end of the reign.

Examining the royal interventions that took place in even the most trivial matters, William Jordan cites the example of an order given by the king when he assumed authority for the municipal council in the city of Bourges in order "to drive out the wandering pigs who have been polluting the entire town." When the municipality of Beaune consulted the royal commune of Soissons in 1264 on a point in their communal charter disputed by the duke of Burgundy, this showed the success of royal interventions. In its response, the municipality of Soissons stressed the superior authority of royal government over ducal government in matters like these. At the very least, this illustrates the case of a "good town" that the king made proud and happy with his leadership.[41]

The recognition of the superiority of the "king's laws," in other words of the "state's laws," dates from the reign of Saint Louis, although it was probably only theoretical in certain situations. However, the king also called for the cities to associate themselves with the "law of state" and to collaborate on its elaboration in economic matters. The towns became indispensable agents in the diffusion and application of royal law, and this law's efficiency depended to a great extent on the collaboration of the towns. This was especially true in the Midi, which had only recently been united with the rest of the kingdom.[42]

LOUIS AND PARIS

Although it could not accurately be called a capital, ever since the Capetians made Paris their primary place of residence in the twelfth century and set up the central bodies of the kingdom there, and ever since Philip Augustus built a wall around the city and constructed the fortress of the Louvre there, a special relationship bound the city and the king.[43] Louis IX added his feelings of gratitude toward the Parisians who supported him and his mother during the tough times at the beginning of his reign. In consideration of this unique situation, Paris had no bailiff. The king who usually resided in Paris with his court did not need any separate agent to represent him there. The chief royal officer was the provost whose authority extended over the provostship and viscounty of Paris, which also included various domains in the outlying areas. The origins of the Parisian municipality are obscure, although it seems that merchants who engaged in commerce on the Seine, the "water merchants," exercised some authority over commercial matters at least since the time of Philip Augustus, and that a provost represented them. However, the first provost of the merchants of Paris whose name has reached us is one Evrouin de Valenciennes, mentioned in a document dating from April 1263.[44]

The government of Paris started to cause big problems for the king in the middle of the thirteenth century. Due to constant immigration, the city's population never stopped growing and reached at least 160,000 around 1250.[45] Crime spread rapidly in these conditions and reached staggering proportions. The absence of a clearly defined municipality with representation for the townspeople, uncertainty over who held the royal provostship, and especially the fact that the provost's position was awarded to the highest bidder, all paradoxically made the king's main city of residence the least safe and the most arbitrarily governed city in the kingdom. Upon returning from the crusade, Louis took matters in his own hands and applied a general correction that ended in the appointment of a royal provost paid by the king, the strong character Étienne Boileau.

Louis IX's Parisian "reform" and the strong character of Étienne Boileau made a strong impression on contemporaries. In his chronicle, Guillaume de Nangis writes: "At this time, the provostship of Paris was for sale; the consequences were that indigents were oppressed, the rich were allowed to get away with everything, and foreigners could do whatever they wanted with impunity. The king forbade the sale of the provost's position and created an annual income for the man who would be provost and he named Étienne Boileau as provost. Boileau took over the position and in a matter of days made the city a much more peaceful place to live."[46] This is the gilded legend of the virtually miraculous transformation of Paris by Saint Louis and Étienne Boileau.

We can hear Joinville echo the same sentiment in greater detail. In addition, he was a source here for Guillaume de Nangis and his *Grandes Chroniques de France* more than thirty years after Saint Louis' death.

> The provostship of Paris used to be sold to the bourgeois of Paris, or to several of them; when it happened that some of them had bought it, they supported their children and their nephews in their misdeeds because the young people could count on their parents and

their friends who held the provostship. This is why the little people were always walked upon and could get no justice in disputes with rich folk because of the presents and gifts that they would give to the provosts.

At that time, when someone spoke the truth before the provost or wanted to keep his oath so as not to commit perjury about some debt or anything else for which he had to answer, the provost would impose a fine on him, and he would be punished. Because of the great injustices and rapacious confiscations made in the provost's jurisdiction, the little people did not dare remain on royal lands and went to live in other provostships and in the lands of other lords. And the king's lands were so deserted that when the provost held court, no more than ten or twelve people would come.

In addition, there were so many thieves and miscreants in and around Paris that the entire land was full of them. The king, who was very concerned about keeping the little people on his lands, learned the truth. He decided that he did not want the provostship of Paris to be sold anymore, but he gave great and generous wages to the people who would hold it. He abolished all the negative impositions that could burden the little people, and he asked around the entire country and kingdom where he could find a man who upheld good, honest justice and who would not spare the rich man any more than the poor.

Then, they pointed Étienne Boileau out to him, a man who governed the provostship so well that no criminal, thief, or murderer dared stay in Paris who was no sooner killed or hung. Neither family nor lineage, nor silver or gold could save him from justice. The king's lands began to change, and the people came back so that they could benefit from the justice carried out there. Then, its population grew so much and changed so that sales, submissions of cases to the court, purchases, and other things were worth twice as much to the king as before.[47]

One preliminary remark: the last part of the sentence can be understood in two ways. Either it means that economic relations in Paris produced twice as much as before, which seems to me to be the actual meaning: there was an economic boom in Paris after peace was reimposed by the king and the new provost, Étienne Boileau. Or, if we choose to adopt Natalis de Wailly's translation, Joinville is relating two events that had no real connection, interpreting the doubling of the prices of objects of economic activity in Paris as a sign of progress, which, on the contrary, would actually be a sign of crisis. We cannot altogether exclude this possibility because we know there were early signs of the great crisis of the fourteenth century during the final years of Louis IX's reign.

In any case, it was during the 1260s that the king dealt with the essential problems of governing Paris.

He allowed or, more accurately, incited the bourgeois to organize. Every two years a hierarchy of electors chose four aldermen from the ranks of the "water merchants," the "Hanseatic merchants of Paris." They also selected a merchant provost who, according to Arié Serper, "took over leadership in municipal affairs." The aldermen and provost had to be born in Paris. They occupied a city hall called the *parloir aux bourgeois*. The provost presided over a tribunal comprised of a certain number of bourgeois who made decisions about necessary measures for governing the city on a level that did not directly depend on the king and the various lords who had rights in different parts of the town. The tribunal also exercised seigniorial jurisdiction over a certain number of streets owned by the "hanse" (corporation) of the water merchants. Still, most of its prerogatives were of an economic order. The tribunal ruled on cases related to commerce and navigation. It was the guardian of the corporation's privileges and judged the trials concerning the water merchants. It had the right to arrest offenders and confiscate their merchandise because the water merchants alone held the right to transport commodities on the Seine from the downstream bridge of Mantes up to the bridges of Paris. The bourgeois patrol, still called the "seated watch" or "sleeping watch," was set up at fixed positions and enforced respect for the jurisdiction of municipal authority around the docks, fountains, sewers, rivers, and ports. The merchant provost also exercised justice over measurements, wine criers, and weighers. The names for the agents who took orders from the bourgeois plainly indicate the nature of the domain confided to their municipal jurisdiction: receivers or brokers [*courtiers*], measurers, weighers, criers, taverners, and salt porters.

As we shall see, the king was not absent from the "economic" domain, although it was not what interested him the most. Saint Louis' third function in relation to material prosperity (ranked behind the first two, which involved his religious, judicial, and war-making functions) was one in which his presence was the weakest, although it was also one in which he acquired more and more influence.[48]

The provost of Paris was transformed from a "local administrator with a judicial function restricted to the domain into an administrator functioning as a bailiff." In the second half of the thirteenth century, he administered justice and taxation, oversaw the trade guilds, and upheld the privileges of the University of Paris. He was in control of the military, financial, and police administrations that lay outside the authority of the provost of the merchants and the lords of the "towns and lands" who occupied limited territories. The watch [*le guet*] was an important part of police activity. The royal watch [*le guet royal*], created by Louis IX in 1254, had more extensive authority and was more powerful than the bourgeois watch. It was not located in a certain place but moved wherever it was needed. In 1254, it was composed of twenty mounted sergeants and forty foot sergeants, all in the pay of the king. They followed orders given by the knight of the watch, a royal officer under the authority of the royal provost. The provost's building was an imposing keep, the Châtelet, located just a stone's throw from the royal palace on the right bank of the Seine.

Étienne Boileau was named provost in 1261. He soon had the reputation of being an excellent administrator and a solid judge. Although the reestablishment of control over the city did not happen overnight with the wave of a magic wand, as Guillaume de Nangis would have us believe, Boileau did manage to accomplish this in notable ways. He restored safety to the city and reorganized its trades [*métiers*], in other words its corporations, in a way that corresponded to the king's principles, combining protection and control as was the case for the other towns overall. The tool for implementing this policy was the recording of the customs and statutes of the roughly one hundred Parisian trade corporations. We still possess this incredible document entitled *Le Livre des métiers* (The Book of Trades) attributed to Étienne Boileau and composed around 1268. It holds a significant place in the important trend of recording customs in writing. The king was concerned with the fate of simple workers, but he laid the groundwork for a hierarchical structure that granted a nearly discretionary power to the masters of the guilds. The first part of *Le Livre des métiers* was essentially a guide for policing the corporations, followed by a fiscal report including a summary of the various taxes levied on the corporations and on the populace of Paris as a whole.

Louis IX thus brought the Parisian municipality under royal control while playing a key role in its organization. The royal provost could review decisions made by the merchant provost. Moreover, the merchants requested royal intervention in their affairs several times at the end of the reign. At the end of the 1260s, they asked for Louis' support against foreign merchants, and in 1269 he reconfirmed their privileges at their request, thereby underscoring "royal power's control over municipal institutions."[49]

As Louis IX shaped it without exactly having created it, the structure of political power in Paris closely corresponded to the exceptional status of this quasi-capital among the cities of France. Apart from the hiatus of the French Revolution, this structure has remained the same until almost the present day.[50] The city would have no bailiff, in other words no prefect, but instead would have a provost with the functions of a bailiff, in other words a *préfet de police* (police chief or commissioner). It would have no mayor either, but instead would have a quasi-mayor, the merchant provost. This bicephalous structure actually left power in the hands of a single master, the king.

THE UNCOMPROMISING DISPENSER OF JUSTICE: TWO SPECTACULAR CASES

It was not enough for Louis IX to define principles of justice through edicts and to implement it through his bailiffs, seneschals, investigators, and the provost of Paris. He enjoyed dispensing justice himself in exemplary cases. Between the years 1254 and 1260 he did not always display the leniency that he mentioned in his letter to his investigators in Languedoc in 1259, nor the forgiveness that political treatises called for the prince to provide in order to lighten the burden of justice after the example of the supreme Judge, the God of justice and mercy. Two cases that made a powerful impression on Louis' contemporaries attest to this. In his *Vie de Saint Louis*, Guillaume de Nangis reports events of 1255:

> After King Louis IX had established the aforementioned institutions [the Great Edict] and after they had been published through-

out the Kingdom of France, it so happened that a man of Paris of the middle class swore violently against the name of Our Lord and spoke great blasphemy.[51] For this, the good king Louis who was very upstanding had the man seized and branded with a red-hot iron on his lips so that he would always remember his sin and so that others would hesitate to villainously swear on their Creator. Many people [the Latin text calls them "wise men according to the century"] cursed the king and whispered against him when they learned of this and saw it. However, remembering the passages from Scripture that state, "You will be happy when men curse you because of me,"[52] and, "Lord God, they will curse me, and you will bless me," the good king said a very Christian thing: that he would be glad to be marked with a red-hot iron on condition that all vile swear words be removed from his kingdom. After this, the king granted a new benefit to the people of Paris, from whom he received many prayers, but when the king learned of their praise, he stated that he would rather receive more praise from Our Lord for the curses that had been addressed to him on account of the man he had branded with a hot iron for having scorned God than praise addressed to him from people for what he had done for the common good of Paris.[53]

When it came to blasphemy, one of Louis' worst bêtes noires, he confused justice with severity. Some of his contemporaries would even say that he confused justice "with cruelty." Our chronicler-biographer, the monk of Saint-Denis, Guillaume de Nangis, relates this to the second example:

> And because the wise man says that the throne of kings is adorned and reinforced by justice, we, in order to praise the fervor of justice that he had, are going to tell the affair of the lord of Coucy. It happened that at this time[54] in the abbey of Saint-Nicolas in the woods near the city of Laon, there lived three young nobles [children] who were natives of Flanders and who came to learn the language of France.[55] One day, these young people went to play in the woods of the abbey with bows and iron tipped arrows made for shooting and killing rabbits. While following prey that they had flushed out of the woods of the abbey, they entered a wood belonging to Enguerran, the lord of Coucy. They were captured and held

by the sergeants who were guarding his woods. When Enguerran learned what they had done from his foresters, the cruel pitiless man had these young people hung on the spot. However, when the abbot of Saint-Nicolas who had them in his care learned of this, and lord Gilles le Brun, the constable of France who was from the same lineage as these young people, they went to King Louis and asked him to execute justice on the lord of Coucy.[56] As soon as he learned of the lord of Coucy's cruelty, the good upstanding king summoned him to his court in order to answer in this miserable case. When the lord of Coucy heard the king's order, he came to the court and said that he should not have to be pressured to reply without council, and that he wanted to be judged by the peers of France according to the custom of the baronage. But it was proven against the lord of Coucy by the recorder of the court of France that he did not hold his lands in a barony, because the lands of Bove and Gournay which conferred lordly status and the honor of barony were separated from the land of Coucy due to the division of the lands between him and his brothers; this is why they told the lord of Coucy that he did not hold his land as a barony. Having heard these facts established before him, King Louis had the lord of Coucy seized and arrested, and this was done not by his barons or knights but by his sergeants at arms [*gendarmes*]. He had him imprisoned in the tower of the Louvre and fixed the date on which he would have to respond in the presence of the barons. On that day, the barons of France came to the king's palace and when they were assembled, the king summoned the lord of Coucy and forced him to respond in the aforementioned case. Obeying the king's will, the lord of Coucy then called all the barons of his lineage to his council, and they almost all came forward and drew themselves aside, so that the king was practically alone except for several gentlemen of his council. Nevertheless, the king's intention was to remain inflexible and to pronounce a just judgment [*justum judicium judicare*], in other words to punish the lord according to the law of the talion and to condemn him to a similar death [similar to that of the young people he had hung]. When the barons realized the king's intention, they gently prayed and implored him to have pity on the lord of Coucy and to impose a fine of his choice on him. The king, who was itching to do justice [*qui moult fut échaffé de justice faire*], answered before all the barons that although he believed that Our Lord had given him the ability to hang him just as well as to release him, he would hang him without worrying about the barons of his lineage. The king finally gave in to the humble prayers of the barons and decided that the lord of Coucy could redeem his life by paying a fine of 10,000 pounds and by building two chapels in which prayers would be sung every day for the souls of the three young people he had killed. He would also provide wood for the abbey where the young people had been hung and had to promise to spend three years in the Holy Land.[57] The good upstanding king took the money for the fine but rather than put it in his treasury he put it directly to good works. This was done promptly and should serve as a great example for everyone who upholds and respects justice, because a very noble man of such high lineage who was accused only by poor people managed only with difficulty to save his life before he who maintained and upheld justice.[58]

This was an exemplary occurrence. The significant commentary by a monk of Saint-Denis amplifies royal policy with no fear of exaggerating when it opposes the rank of Enguerran de Coucy and his barons to the victims presented as "poor people," though in fact they were young nobles related to the constable of France who was an intimate of the king. This affair, however, which had strong reverberations in the historical memories of the chroniclers and illuminators, truly characterizes the principles and attitudes of Saint Louis as a dispenser of justice. Among the principles and attitudes at work here we find the king's desire to minimize feudal proceedings in favor of royal justice (the arrest made by royal sergeants instead of knights is significant in this regard), his insistence on balancing respect for customs with the royal power's superiority in making rulings, and his tendency to identify justice with severity and then to moderate it with a leniency that corresponded to the royal ideals of mercy and the king's benevolence toward his barons. We get the impression here that Saint Louis assumed a mask of inflexibility in order to be able to better force his barons into a position of humility and to garner more appreciation for his own goodness.

Two value systems—social and juridical—are confirmed and opposed to one another here. We see feudal justice that was arbitrary as soon as the crime, however tenuous it might have been, violated the *potestas,* the power of the lord who exercised or believed that he could exercise high justice on his land. And we see royal justice, equally arbitrary in the end, but that was imposed by virtue of the superior judicial power of the sovereign, *a fortiori* in the case of Enguerran, since the king personally expressed a rigorous faith in this ideal of justice. He was a law-abiding king who embodied the idea of the equality of justice for the powerful and the poor even if monarchical propaganda leaned toward reality. This progress in terms of justice could also present a serious threat. In order to prove a more or less fallacious accusation of lese-majesty (the notion of this crime became clearer under Saint Louis' rule[59]), royal justice could be even more frighteningly arbitrary. His grandson, Philip the Fair, the king of trials of lese-majesty in the name of reasons of state, got his start under Saint Louis. Under Saint Louis, these trials had not quite reached this point. Clearly, what shocked Saint Louis and provoked his ire were not simply the disproportion and the cruelty of the punishment, but the fact that the young victims were hung without any trial or judgment. The king truly wanted to be the guarantor of justice within his kingdom. Contrary to the arguments of certain historians, Enguerran de Coucy's trial did not result from the new inquisitional procedure adopted from Romano-Catholic law,[60] which royalty employed after the ecclesiastical inquisition in order to summon the accused without ever receiving any accusation from a victim or one of his relatives or associates. On the contrary, the traditional accusatory procedure led to the royal intervention since the abbot of Saint-Nicolas-au-Bois and the constable Gilles le Brun had appealed directly to the king.

NEW MEASURES FOR PURIFICATION: AGAINST ORDEALS AND USURY, AGAINST JEWS AND LOMBARDS

The inquisitorial investigation introduced by Roman canonical law also differed from other judiciary traditions. It was especially different from the ordeals or judgments of God. The Fourth Lateran Council of 1215 had forbidden them. They included trials by fire or water from which the accused was supposed to emerge unscathed, and one-on-one combats (*gages de bataille,* battle wagers) from which the accused or his champion was supposed to emerge victorious. These forms of justice continued to be practiced, particularly among the nobles.[61] The Church tried to replace them with "rational" proof and, in particular, with evidence established by witnesses. The state in turn embarked on this path under Louis IX. A royal edict of 1261 outlawed "battle wagers" and replaced them with the procedure of investigation and proof established by witnesses. As an anonymous chronicler at the end of the thirteenth century says of the king: "Know that for as long as he lived he would not tolerate any trials by battle of champions or knights of the Kingdom of France for murder or treason or inheritance or debt, but he made sure that everything was done by investigations conducted by tribunals or people of sworn loyalty."[62]

While rationalizing judiciary practices, Louis continued to pursue his correction of usury practices. An edict of 1257 or 1258 named a commission responsible for correcting the excessive application of measures previously taken against the Jews.[63]

The words designating usurers here, with no other defining terms, seems to signal an important development in royal policy, which no longer focused exclusively on Jewish usurers usually considered the main specialists in these practices. The policy now also went after Christian usurers whose numbers were increasing. Their usurious loans generally represented much larger sums than those lent by Jewish lenders. They therefore also imposed interest that had a higher absolute value, sometimes a percentage, than interest demanded by Jewish lenders. In general, Jewish lenders dealt only in loans for low-value consumption, although they simultaneously imposed measures resented as excessively onerous such as the seizure of collateral in the form of clothing, furniture, or livestock.

The extension of measures taken against non-Jewish usurers seems, however, to have been limited to Christian moneylenders who were foreigners. An edict of 1268 expelled Lombard (Italian), Cahorsin,[64] and other foreign usurers from the kingdom. According to this law, they all had to leave in three months' time. During this period, their debtors were supposed to be able to earn back their collateral by repaying their loans minus the usurious fees. Sometimes these merchants were authorized to do business in France on condition that they abstained from usury and any other prohibited commercial practices. The motive given to justify this edict was not of a moral order but of an economic and political one: usurious extortion "greatly impoverishes our kingdom," in the king's opinion. He also articulated a need to put an end to the misdeeds that these foreigners were suspected of committing in their homes and workplaces.[65] The first expression seems to give voice to a nascent awareness of a "national" economic patrimony and of the economic borders of the kingdom. This awareness led Saint Louis' grandson to establish customs barriers and to outlaw the export of certain collective forms of wealth like precious metals. The second expression is disturbing since in the name of state interests the king was inviting his subjects to transform rumors into wild accusations. To sum things up, reasons of state were already taking precedence in making and justifying government policies.[66] In any case, what we must remember about these two edicts, it seems, is that usury was what was being condemned rather than the merchant, the foreigner, or the Jew.

THE "GOOD" MONEY

The end of Louis IX's reign saw a number of important monetary reforms. They were first of all a consequence of economic development and the spread of the monetary economy. I will not enter into any detail on aspects of these facts that would take us away from the individual history of the king. I will analyze the psychological, moral, and ideological aspects of these measures. They comprised a part of the program for cleaning up the kingdom from a religious perspective. I refer my readers to the subsequent part of this work where I deal with Saint Louis' actions and ideas as part of "the king's third function,"[67] which involves the problem of determining how the French people in the middle of the thirteenth century—including the king and the governing and intellectual elites—understood what we now call the "economy."

The king's monetary reforms extended from 1262 to 1270.[68] They included an edict of 1262 that banned the counterfeit of royal coinage and that established a monopoly favoring the circulation of royal money in the kingdom with the exception of coins produced by lords authorized to mint them that could henceforth only circulate on their own lands. There were two other edicts that banned the use of English coins, the "esterlins" [sterling], throughout the kingdom. The first of these edicts, published between 1262 and 1265, has been lost. It commanded the king's subjects, including churchmen, to give up the use of sterlings. The other edict of 1265 set the final date of their circulation for mid-August 1266. Another edict of 1265 reiterated the measures taken in the edict of 1262 that prohibited the imitation of royal coins, reserving the privilege of circulation throughout the entire kingdom to royal coinage. This time, however, a notable exception was made for the coins of Nantes, Angers, and Le Mans. The explanation for tolerating these coins was that "people do not believe that there is enough [royal] money in pounds of Tours and Paris." Another edict of July 1266, of which we possess only a fragment, ordered the resumption of the minting of the Parisian denier with specifications for a new weight and color in precious metal as well as the creation of a new larger pound of Tours. Finally, another lost edict, issued between 1266 and 1270, created a new gold coin, the ecu.[69] If we stick to a modern "economic" point of view, these measures have threefold significance.

The return to minting *parisis* at a heavier weight than before (to 1.2881 grams from 1.2237 for the *parisis* of Philip Augustus) but with a lower fineness of precious metal (0.4791 grams of silver down from 0.5009 grams of silver) actually amounted to a devaluation of the currency. This was a more or less conscious response to what we call inflation, the continued decline of the coin's value since at least the twelfth century. This evolution resulted from the growing need for monetary currencies to respond to growth in the monetary economy and to the increase in the minting of coins by the king and the lords who had a right to strike money. This growth in monetary circulation resulted from both a rising economic demand and from the desire to increase the benefits of seigniorage, the lord's immediate profit on the minting of coins.[70] In the course of the thirteenth century, the portion of seigniorage in the receipts collected by the Royal Treasury never stopped growing.[71] The ban on imitations of royal coins and the limit imposed on the circulation of seigniorial coins also partly responded to this desire to reduce or abolish inflation.

Two other measures marked an especially significant date in France's monetary history. The most impressive was the readoption of a gold mint after five centuries, a return to the bi-metal coinage of Antiquity and the High Middle Ages. This measure admitted Latin Christianity into the exclusive club of two-metal economic and political systems alongside Byzantium and Islam. Beginning in 1175, King Alphonso of Castile, the last Norman kings of Sicily, and Emperor Frederick II in southern Italy with his *augustales* in 1232 also initiated two-metal systems, although more for the prestige than anything else. The economic importance of these coinages was very weak. The large merchant cities of Italy were a different case. A number of them made a smashing and durable entry into the use of gold coinage for large-scale international commerce: Lucca a little before 1246, Genoa in 1252 with the *genovino,* Florence in 1253 with the *florin,* and Venice with the *ducat* beginning in 1284. Some western monarchies also introduced gold coinage for the collection of public taxes. The two largest of these monarchies, England and France, sought to enter this group of banking and commercial powers primarily for reasons of political prestige. In 1257, Henry III struck a "gold penny," but it was a failure. Its mint and circulation ended some time around 1270, and England had to wait until 1344 before it had a new gold coin, the florin. Saint Louis created the golden ecu in 1266, but this was not a success either. At the end of the century, the ecu gave way to a variety of gold pieces that met with only mediocre success before taking off again in 1330.

The *denier parisis* and the gold ecu were therefore failures, and the very small number of these surviving coins is evidence of this. On the other hand, the big *tournois* was a great success not only in France but also on the international market. Its long-lasting success continued well into the fourteenth century, even through that century's great monetary crisis. It fell right into a productive monetary niche that corresponded to important needs.

It is also clear that Saint Louis' monetary policy responded to political objectives in ways closely tied to economic and financial goals. What people have sometimes referred to—in disregard of a more complex reality—as the state monarchy's struggle against feudalism finds a privileged field of application here. Saint Louis adopted the traditional idea of money as a kingly instrument and as an object of state monopoly. In opposition to the barons and the Church, he had to be happy to proclaim the superiority of royal money over seigniorial moneys, paving the way for their demise. He took a decisive step in this direction. The monarchy's monetary monopoly began to take shape. Once again, the monarchical state in the process of forming benefited from three important trends: the formation of canonical law that was underway, the renaissance of Roman law that was closely tied to it, and the emergence of an opinion—whose existence in the preceding period Thomas Bisson has demonstrated so well—that wanted political powers to guarantee the stability and the quality of money that a growing number of people were using more and more often. The "conservation" of money (*conservatio monetae*) was becoming a more strident demand. As in the case of justice, wherever the king was strong or getting stronger, he could only be the main beneficiary of this development. This was even more true in the sense that monetary power was evolving toward this supreme image of power, the majesty or *majestas* with which royalty identified itself more and more closely, especially in France. The counterfeit of royal coins soon joined the list of crimes of lese-majesty, and counterfeiters appeared again among the first rank of criminals just as in ancient times.

Royal policy in monetary matters arose from its duty with regard to justice. Royal monetary action lined up on the battlefield on the side of "good" money against "bad" money, for "pure" deniers, as the edicts of Saint Louis called them, against deniers that were "bare," worn down, counterfeited, or of dubious quality. Saint Louis and his advisors understood perfectly well that the fight for "good" money, as they would say in the fourteenth century, comprised a key element in the formation of prices, prices the ideology of the time wanted to keep "just." The "just price," the "just wage," and the "good coin" were three sides of the same moral concept of socio-economic life. The canonists and theologians of Saint Louis' time made themselves the theorists of this concept. Monetary measures like those taken by Saint Louis can thus be situated in the context of what people had for quite some time already been calling the *renovatio monetae*. For these men of the Middle Ages, marked by Roman and Carolingian ideology, this renovation had a holy, religious, quasi-eschatological connotation. Monetary reform was a pious work; it was even a holy work in the proper sense. The minters of coins and especially of gold coins understood this when they placed the figure of Saint John, the patron saint of the city, on the Florentine florin, or when they put Christ in his glory on the Venetian ducat with the image of Saint Mark passing the standard to the kneeling doge on the other side of the coin.

Saint Louis understood this, too. He placed a cross and his royal name (*Ludovicus rex*) on the large *tournois,* along with the legend, "Holy be the name of God, Jesus Christ our Lord" (*Benedictus sit nomen Domini nostri Dei Jesu Christi*). The ecu especially proclaimed the glory of Christ and king. The obverse side showed the Capetian symbol of the shield with a fleur-de-lis and the legend, "Louis, by the grace of God, king of France" (*Ludovicus Dei gracia Francorum rex*), and on the reverse side a cross boxed between four fleur-de-lis and the solemn proclamation, "Christ triumphs, Christ rules, Christ dominates" (*Christus vincit, Christus regnat, Christus imperat*).

An unexpected document sheds fascinating light on Louis IX's monetary policy. We like to imagine that the University theologians of the Middle Ages spent their time discussing abstract, eternal problems. However, on

Easter 1265, the famous Parisian master Gérard d'Abbeville had to answer a question asked by the members of the faculty of theology in the *quodlibet* debate, an exercise administered to the masters of the University twice a year at Christmas and Easter. The question they asked him: in his recent edict did the king have the right to impose an oath on his subjects, who were also the subjects of bishops and other churchmen, to no longer use the English sterling in their transactions? Wasn't the king violating their rights by imposing this obligation on them?[72] At the same time, the question was being dealt with in a trial before the pope.

By means of this formulation that placed the problem under the authority of the faculty, this hotly debated question became an invitation to test the king's rights in monetary matters. Master Gérard answered that coining was definitely a royal prerogative and he based his claim on a three-fold authority: first of all on the authority of the Bible in Jesus' words about the silver piece with the image of the imperial effigy "Render unto Caesar that which is Caesar's" (Matthew 22:21), and those of Saint Paul commanding that "each person be subject to the highest authorities" (Romans 13:1); second, on the authority of Aristotle on the subject of the common good of which the king is the supreme guardian; and finally on the authority of canon law as it adopted the notion of "public utility" (*utilitas publica*) from Roman law as it had been formulated in Gratian's *Decree* of 1140 (C.7, q.1, c.35) and expressed in the bull *Per venerabilem* of Innocent III (1203). This bull established the claim that the king of France knew no temporal superior, and was also included in the letter sent by the same Innocent III to the king of Aragon, recognizing his right and duty to assure that money be "healthy and loyal," a principle inserted in the collection of *Décrétales* inscribed in the code of canon law. It did not particularly matter that Gérard followed this up by stressing "the return to sterling is useful for everyone, and that therefore to abandon the measures that have been adopted would be useful and should take place at the proper time." The essential thing was that he corroborated the rights of royalty in monetary affairs. Moreover, it seems that Louis IX suppressed his order for an oath to boycott the sterling when faced with the hostility of the clerics and the intellectuals, while enforcing the prohibition of their use in the kingdom at the same time. Pierre Michaud-Quantin leaves us with this interesting observation on the affair in light of Gérard's argument: "the university clerics, the professor's immediate audience, and the professor himself all seem completely deprived of the intellectual tools needed to conceive of a political policy to deal with the reality of money." Contrary to the claims of certain historians, at least in the thirteenth century the scholars remained incapable of developing economic theories adapted to the realities and problems of the time.

Did the king and the clerics of his entourage therefore have advisors for economic and, notably, monetary matters? Yes. Their advisors were the bourgeois and particularly the important merchants in their ranks who were used to handling money. In 1254 and 1259, Louis IX had already established councils for the seneschalcies of the Midi. They were set up to instruct the seneschals about the prohibitions against grain imports and other commodities in case of widespread shortages in the region. These advisory groups were made up of prelates, barons, knights, and bourgeois from the *bonnes villes*. The edict of 1265 issued at Chartres on the status of coins was written up after a consultation the king had with the bourgeois of Paris, Orléans, Sens, and Laon. They were sworn in, and their names appear in the text of the edict.[73] Economic and especially monetary problems led to assemblies of the three social orders. Money thus introduced the bourgeoisie into the state apparatus. The bourgeoisie became the representation of the third Indo-European social function.[74]

THE PEACEMAKER

Two important responsibilities faced the Christian king, two ideals whose realization was supposed to assure the eternal salvation of the king and his subjects. These two responsibilities were peace and justice.[75] Louis IX's actions here were twofold. On the one hand, he worked to establish peace in all matters involving his authority. He had to set an example and give his preference to solutions to the great centuries-old conflicts he had inherited. He tried to eliminate the causes of the conflicts and establish peace, if not forever, for as long as possible. Between eternity and the present time, he worked for the future as well. On the other hand, his prestige led his opponents to approach him as recourse for a procedure that was highly valued by the men of the Middle Ages—arbitration. Louis' actions and their renown spread beyond the borders of the kingdom. He was the arbitrator and the peacemaker of the Christian world. What follows is an account of the most important and the most spectacular arbitrations he made and peace treaties he sealed.

THE FLEMISH INHERITANCE

Flanders was one of the largest and probably the richest fief of the kingdom. According to a feudal custom that was different from the royal Capetian traditions of exclusively male inheritance, a woman there could inherit the county if birthright played in her favor. However, for nearly thirty years there had been an ongoing conflict arising from the matrimonial situation of the countess Marguerite. The situation persisted both in favor and in spite of a number of twists and turns. I will discuss this imbroglio only to the extent that it will allow us to understand Louis IX's intervention.[76]

The countess Jeanne was the widow of Ferrand de Portugal who had been defeated at Bouvines. She died in 1244 and, having no children, left the county to her younger sister Marguerite. Marguerite had wed Bouchard d'Avesnes, the bailiff of Hainaut, in her first marriage. However, this marriage was not valid because Bouchard had been designated to join the Church and was already ordained as subdeacon. Jeanne obtained an annulment of her sister's marriage at the court of Rome in 1216. Marguerite and Bouchard d'Avesnes did not immediately split and had two sons together. In 1223, Marguerite remarried with Guillaume de Dampierre and had three sons with him. Thus began the struggle between the Avesnes, who insisted on their inheritance rights as a matter of birthright, and the Dampierres, who received their mother's support and who denied their half-brothers' inheritance rights on the grounds that they were illegitimate children.

Louis IX was called upon a number of times to intervene in this affair, either at the behest of one of the two parties or by his own decision as a suzerain concerned about one of his most important fiefs. In 1235, he secured an agreement between Jeanne and Marguerite that called for an unequal division of the inheritance that granted two-sevenths of it to the Avesnes and five-sevenths to the Dampierres. The whole matter was complicated by the fact that the inheritance was partially situated in the Kingdom of France (the county of Flanders) and partly in the Empire (the duchy of Flanders). To make matters even more complicated, the marquisate of Namur was added to this in 1245 when Frederick II conferred it upon Countess Marguerite, although the king of France held it as a gage for the considerable loan he had made to the Latin emperor of Constantinople, Baudouin II of Flanders. The lack of an emperor after Frederick II's death in 1250 left the king of France more freedom to maneuver. He was, moreover, cautious to remain impartial toward the various pretenders to the throne who benefited from only limited authority even though they were recognized as the kings of the Romans, albeit without ever having been crowned as emperors.

In 1246, in the framework of the attempts at pacification on the eve of the crusade, Louis IX and the pontifical legate, Eudes de Châteauroux, arranged an agreement on the basis of giving Hainaut to the Avesnes and Flanders to the Dampierres. Marguerite accepted the title of count of Flanders for her son, Guillaume de Dampierre, who left with Louis IX on the crusade and came back with the most important barons in 1250. He died in an accident the following year. Marguerite recognized his younger brother, Guy, as his successor for the county of Flanders. While Saint Louis was still in the Holy Land, absent from his kingdom, Guy went to Paris to swear allegiance to Blanche of Castile in February 1252. However, the court of Rome had finally recognized the Avesnes as the legitimate successors in 1249.

Countess Marguerite refused to grant the title of count of Hainaut to Jean d'Avesnes, leaving him only the marquisate of Namur, whose homage she had surrendered to him in 1249. Moreover, she urged her Dampierre sons, the count of Flanders and his brother, and a number of French barons to seize the islands of Zeeland that she claimed for the county of Flanders. Their descent upon Walcheren was a disaster, and in July 1253 the count of Holland, a brother of the king of the Romans, took the Dampierres and several French barons prisoner. Countess Marguerite then appealed to Louis IX's younger brother, Charles d'Anjou. She promised him the Hainaut in return for his assistance. Charles accepted and came to occupy Valenciennes and Mons, although his advisors managed to convince him to avoid an armed conflict with the king of the Romans who had excellent relations with the king of France.

After his return from the crusade, Louis IX decided to intervene. He had three good reasons for choosing this course of action. His vassals, the count of Flanders and his brother, were being held prisoner. (The count of Holland had released the other French barons.) His own brother was mixed up in the conflict. In addition, he wanted to reimpose the agreement of 1246. Quite upset with his brother's careless initiatives, he began by recalling Charles d'Anjou to Paris.

Proceeding with caution, he first went to Gand to find Countess Marguerite as a show of support and to explain his plans to her. As the countess and her Avesnes sons had already accepted the previous arbitration, Louis IX reinstated most of the treaty of 1246 with the "declaration of Péronne" [*le dit de Péronne*] (September 24, 1256), which granted the Hainaut to the Avesnes and Flanders to the Dampierres. However, Marguerite had already given Hainaut to the king's brother. The king of France gave it all back while allowing his brother to save face at the same time: Countess Marguerite bought the Hainaut back from him at a very high price. She also had to pay a large ransom to the count of Holland in order to free the Dampierres. Shortly thereafter, her surviving Avesnes son, Baudouin, the count of Hainaut, reconciled with her, and peace was restored along the northeastern border of the Kingdom of France.

Saint Louis' attitude in this affair was typical of him. He wanted to reconcile peace and justice with the interests of the kingdom and the familial relations that were so important to him. In the text called the "declaration of Péronne," he stated that he did not want to favor either party, the Avesnes or the Dampierres, to the detriment of the other, because they were all relatives of the same blood [*consanguinei nostri*]. He expressed the same balanced sense of justice and familial duty in his attitude toward his brother. Finally, he also refused to intervene in Namur and favored the definitive solution that called for the surrender of the marquisate to the county of Flanders (1263). The peace was certainly worth abandoning the lands held as collateral. Public opinion in Flanders nevertheless remained hostile to the king of France; the bourgeois frequently blamed him for the heavy taxes that were imposed on them. He was heckled when he visited Gand in 1255. The king's prestige could not outweigh the population's long-standing opposition.

Peace with Aragon: The Treaty of Corbeil (1258)

The Pyrenees did not extend along the northeastern border of the Kingdom of Aragon and Catalonia to separate France and Spain. Theoretically, the Capetians had inherited the old Carolingian march of Spain, although Hugh Capet had been unable to answer the calls for help from the Christians of this region against the Muslims at the end of the tenth century. The council of Tarragon subsequently decided to date its acts in the years of the Christian calendar and not in the years of the rule of French kings.

The counties of Barcelona, Roussillon, Cerdagne, Conflent, Besalù, Ampur-
dàn, Urgel, Gerone, and Osona followed suit, and this contributed to the
distancing and disappearance of ties between the two regions. When the
counts of Barcelona became kings of Aragon in 1162, they stopped swearing allegiance to the king of France. Furthermore, both before and after
their promotion as kings of Aragon, the counts of Barcelona had gradually
expanded into the French Midi.

Although it was part of the Capetian kingdom, the Midi sometimes
seemed ready to break apart from it in order to form an independent state
set up around the three political centers predominant there: Poitiers led
by the dukes of Aquitaine, Toulouse and its counts, and Barcelona with
its counts and, later on, its kings. However, the formation of a southern
state had failed to occur throughout the Pyrenees. The counts of Barcelona,
however, still claimed suzerainty over the viscounty of Carcassonne, as the
Trencavel had sworn allegiance to them, and over all the domains of the
counts of Toulouse of the house of Saint-Gilles. In addition, for the period
lasting until the end of the twelfth century during which the kings of Aragon had also been the counts of Provence, they pursued their claim to the
succession of Douce de Sarlat, the wife of Raimond Bérenger III. These
territories included part of the Massif Central including Gévaudan, Sarlat,
and Millau. The crusade against the Albigenses put an end to the Aragonese
expansion, without, however, getting them to abandon all their claims in
the region. Simon de Montfort, who had at first recognized the suzerainty
of Pierre II of Aragon over Carcassonne, concluded that the king of Aragon had lost all his rights and domains in the Kingdom of France after the
French victory of Muret in 1213. The conflict between the two kingdoms
had arisen around three towns: Millau, Carcassonne, and Montpellier.
Millau had been occupied by Aragonese forces for a short time in 1237
and nearly set off a war between the Aragonese and the French in 1234 and
again between 1240 and 1242. In order to protect Carcassonne, Louis IX
built massive fortifications, surrounding the city with a crown of royal keeps
(Peyrepertuse and Quéribus) occupied by a royal garrison with the permission of the local lords. Montpellier presented a more delicate situation.
The last heiress had brought its seigniory to her husband, the king of Aragon, at the end of the twelfth century, but it was also a fief of the bishop of
Maguelonne, who claimed the suzerainty of the king of France in 1252 in
order to protect himself from the Aragonese.

Tensions rose again when the king of Aragon, Jaime I, reasserted his claims to Millau, the county of Foix, Gévaudan, and Fenouilledès. The princes of Aragon led incursions into the region of Carcassonne, and troubadors in the service of Jaime I led the call to war against the king of France. In response, the seneschal of Beaucaire placed an embargo on foodstuffs destined for Montpellier and other Aragonese lands.

In the end, the two kings' interest to put an end to these old quarrels carried the day. Louis did this out of respect for his ideals and also to better establish his power over a Midi that was still poorly integrated into his kingdom. Jaime I was interested in expansion elsewhere, toward the south and the Reconquest against the Muslims and to the west for domination of the western Mediterranean. Jaime I the Conqueror had captured the Balaeres between 1229 and 1235, Valencia in 1238, followed by Alcira and Jativa. In 1255, the two kings selected two ecclesiastical arbitrators, one French and one Catalan, and accepted their peace proposals. Jaime I's envoys came to sign the treaty of Corbeil on May 11, 1258. It was ratified in Barcelona on July 16. The king of France renounced his claims to the Spanish march, and the king of Aragon renounced his claims to the lands of Carcassonne, Peyrepertuse, Lauragais, Razès, the Minervois, Gévaudan, Millau, and Grizes, and also to the counties of Toulouse and Saint-Gilles. During the passage of the treaty, he added a renunciation of his claims to the Agenais and the Comtat Venaissin. The king of France received Fenouilledès in exchange for Roussillon and Besalú. The treaty did not resolve the status of Montpellier, and Louis IX used force to reassert his claim to the town in 1264. Roussillon remained a source of conflict between France and Spain until Louis XIV secured it through the Treaty of the Pyrenees in 1659.

THE FRANCO-ENGLISH PEACE: THE TREATY OF PARIS (1259)

Louis IX's greatest achievement to establish peace for the Kingdom of France was the resolution of the age-old conflict with England. The English possessions in France and Gascogny were the most serious threats to the unity and independence of the French kingdom. An enormous mass of territory—much larger than the Capetian royal domain—fell under English rule in France through the ascension of Henry Plantagenet, the count of Anjou, to the throne of England in 1154. Duke of Normandy in 1150, count

of Anjou, Maine, and Touraine in 1151, Henry II married the famous Eleanor of Aquitaine in 1152. She had previously been the somewhat freewheeling and divorced spouse of Louis VII, and in marriage brought Henry II all
of Aquitaine (Poitou, Limousin, Périgord, Quercy, Saintonge, Guyenne[77])
and Gascogny, which, despite any Capetian pretensions, remained independent from the Kingdom of France. In 1202, Philip Augustus used the
French court's condemnation of the English king, John Lackland, for for-
feiture as a pretext for declaring all bonds of vassalage broken between the
king of France and the king of England. In 1204–1205, Philip Augustus
conquered Anjou, Maine, Touraine, and Normandy and reunited them with
the royal domain, although Normandy received special privileges. During
the dubbing of his younger brother Charles in 1246, Louis IX granted him
full possession of Anjou and Maine in the place of an older brother for
whom Louis VIII had originally designated this holding and who had died
young. We have already seen how, in 1242, King Henry III of England's attempt to reclaim the lands to which he still held rights in western France led
to his defeat. The truce agreed to by the two kings on March 12, 1243, left
matters where they stood for five years. The crusade prolonged the conditions of the truce.

In 1253 and 1254, Henry III came to Bordeaux to put down a revolt
by the Gascon barons. With this business taken care of, he wanted to return
to England by way of the Kingdom of France in order to visit the abbey of
Fontevrault in Anjou that held the necropolis of his ancestors, the abbey
of Pontigny that contained the relics of Saint Edmond Rich, the archbishop
of Canterbury with whom he had a disagreement and who had died in exile,
and the cathedral of Chartres, a Marian sanctuary. Louis IX was happy to
grant Henry III authorization for his passage through France and invited
him to Paris. They celebrated Christmas together there in 1254 along with
the four sisters, the daughters of the deceased count of Provence: Marguerite, the queen of France, Éléonore, the queen of England, Sanchie, the wife
of Richard of Cornwall who was Henry III's brother, and Beatrice, the wife
of Charles d'Anjou who was Louis IX's brother. A warm friendship developed between the two kings. Louis' constant desire to respect family ties in
his political relations was strengthened. He accompanied his brother-in-law
all the way to Boulogne, where the English king boarded his ships. Shortly
thereafter, he also gave him an elephant that he had received as a gift from
the sultan of Egypt.[78]

Later that year, Henry III requested a renewal of their truces, which Louis IX granted willingly. In 1257, Louis gave only halfhearted support to King Alphonse of Castile, Richard of Cornwall's rival for the throne of the Empire. Henry III's brother was elected king of the Romans and crowned with Sanchie at Aix-la-Chapelle on May 17, 1257. However, he never wore the imperial crown, and the long interregnum continued.

In 1257, Henry III sent the bishop of Winchester to Louis IX. His mission was to convey the dual intention of reassuring the king of France about the English policy toward the Empire and to propose an actual treaty to replace the truces that kept a precarious peace between the two kingdoms. Although Louis IX specialized in making peace, he did not have a monopoly on it, and Henry III was trying to solidify his image as a Christian king alongside him. However, he had not renounced his claims to the lands his ancestors had held in France, insisting that the heirs of his father, John Lackland, were not responsible for the mistakes of their ancestor. The two kings clearly had the intention of making peace, but Henry III was also still at odds with the English barons who imposed new limits on his powers with the "Oxford provisions" in 1258. The negotiations were long and laborious.[79] The treaty was finally concluded in Paris on May 28, 1258. It was sworn according to custom on the Holy Gospels by the procurators of the king of England and the king of France in the presence of the latter and his two oldest sons, Louis and Philip, who were respectively fourteen and thirteen years old at the time.

The king of England definitively renounced his claims to Normandy, Anjou, Touraine, Maine, and Poitou, but retained his rights to Agenais and Quercy. He also had to secure a renunciation from his brother, Richard of Cornwall, and his sister, Eleanor, countess of Leicester, of all their claims in the Kingdom of France. From the king of France, who was easily capable of paying generous sums provided by the docile and prosperous cities of the kingdom, the king of England, who was short of money, was to receive the amount necessary for the upkeep of five hundred knights for two years. He was also to receive the revenue from the Agenais each year until the status of this land could be resolved. In addition, the king of France would give the king of England his domains in the dioceses of Limoges, Cahors, and Périgueux, with the exception of the lands held by the bishops of these towns and the fiefs that he had conferred on his brothers Alphonse de Poitiers and Charles d'Anjou. He promised to give the king of

England the part of Saintonge located south of the Charente after the death of Alphonse de Poitiers. However, the king of France held on to his seneschal in Périgord and kept the right to build new towns there across from the walled English enclaves. Above all, Bordeaux, Bayonne, and Gascogny returned to the French sphere of influence as the king of England recognized that he held them as fiefs from the king of France and in this respect became a peer of France with the obligation of swearing homage as vassal to the Capetian.

Richard of Cornwall and his son ratified the treaty on February 10, 1259. It was ratified on February 17 in the name of the king of England by his procurators. It took them a long time to persuade the count and countess of Leicester, Simon de Montfort and his wife Eleanor, to agree to the treaty. They only ratified it *in extremis* on December 4, 1259. Invited by Louis IX, Henry III set foot on the continent on November 14 accompanied by his wife, his second son Edmond, and a large and magnificent escort. On November 25, Louis IX went to greet him at Saint-Denis and housed him in Paris in his own Palais de la Cité. On December 4, 1259, the king of England swore homage to the king of France in the palace garden. Here, in front of a large number of prelates, English and French barons, and a crowd of commoners, Henry III knelt and placed his hands in the hands of Louis IX. This ceremony had been preceded by a solemn reading of the treaty by the chancellor of France, the Franciscan Eudes Rigaud, the archbishop of Rouen.

The treaty gave rise to heated debate among the advisors of the two kings. Joinville offers reliable testimony about what was said on the French side:

> It happened that the holy king negotiated when the king of England, his wife, and children came to France to arrange the peace between him and them. The people on his council were strongly opposed to this peace, and thus told him: "Sire, we are quite astounded that you would want this and that you would want to give the king of England such a large part of your land, which you and your forbearers took from him by your conquest and his forfeiture. For this reason, it seems to us that if you believe you have no right to these lands, your restitution to the king of England is insufficient as long as you don't give him back everything that you and your ancestors

have conquered from him, but if you believe you have a right to these lands, it seems to us that you are losing everything that you are giving back to him."

The holy king answered them in the following way: "Lords, I am certain that the ancestors of the king of England have fairly and squarely lost the conquests that I hold, and that I am not giving him the land I am giving him as something I owe to him or his heirs, but as something that will bring love between my children and his, who are first cousins. It also seems to me that I am making good use of what I am giving him because he was never my man before, and by this gift he is entering into my homage."[80]

Joinville approves of the king's conduct, and concludes with the following observation:

> He was the one man who worked more than any other to establish peace among his subjects, and especially between our rich neighbors and the princes of the kingdom.[81]

Joinville then gives numerous examples of conflicts that Saint Louis resolved both inside and outside of the Kingdom of France. He ends this passage on the peace-making king with some of his interesting proposals.

> On the subject of these foreigners that the king had reconciled, some of the men on his council told him he was not doing a good thing by not letting them continue to fight, for if he let them impoverish themselves, they would not come running up against him as quickly as they would if they were rich. To this the king answered and said that they were not speaking well: "Because if our neighboring rulers saw that I let them continue with their wars, they would conspire amongst themselves and say: 'It is by sheer malice that the king allows us to go on battling.' Then, due to the hatred they would hold against me, they would join forces and attack me, and I could very well lose, not to mention that I would earn the hatred of God who says, 'Blessed are all peaceful men'."

> From all of this, it came to pass that the Burgundians and the Lorrainians whom he had pacified loved him and obeyed him so much that I saw them come to plead their cases before the king at

his courts in Reims, Paris, and Orléans for the trials that they had amongst themselves.

Nothing explains Saint Louis' motives for establishing peace and the general principles behind his policies as well as these two pages from Joinville and the king's declarations they contain. An inseparable union between the interests of the kingdom and the accomplishments of the ideal Christian formed the basis of his politics. He returned certain lands to the king of England but made a vassal of him in exchange. In this period, homage was no trifling matter to be broken with impunity. In 1274, Primat of Saint-Denis stressed the importance of this allegiance for Gascogny in his French version of the *Roman des rois,* translated at Saint Louis' request before his death, and which became *Les Grandes Chroniques de France.* Modern historians confirm his assessment: "Before 1259, as Primat says, 'Gascogny was neither part of the French kingdom, nor within the sphere of influence of the kings of France,' and, therefore, Henry III was not 'the man' of the king of France any more in law than in reality. By swearing homage to Louis IX for Gascogny on December 4, 1259—something none of his predecessors had ever done—Henry III transformed a land that had been independent to this point as part of his own royal domain into a fief. Instead of ending at its border with Gascogny, the Kingdom of France now extended all the way to the Pyrenees."[82]

Another of Saint Louis' motives we have already come across was familial sentiment. Here, we must ask ourselves again whether the argument served a political program with other purposes, or whether the politics themselves were determined by the familial imperative? We must answer that it was both, without really being able to distinguish the affective impulses of political realism in Saint Louis' character, as is usually the case for him.

Was it the hatred of his enemies Saint Louis feared out of a sense of political realism, or the hatred of God he feared due to his religious faith? We can discern the religious faith behind his political realism, making any choice between these two impossible to maintain. The Christian's duties duplicated and served the interests of the king.

Did the treaty of Paris of 1259 really put an end to the Franco-English conflict on the continent? In 1271, Alphonse de Poitiers and his wife Jeanne died childless, a scenario covered by the treaty of 1259. Nevertheless, the king of France was in no hurry to return the Agenais and the south of Saintonge to the king of England. When this restitution finally took place in

1286, it reintroduced a number of unresolved questions about the actual borders and the rights of the two sovereigns there. Two incidents provided Philip the Fair in 1294 and Charles IV the Fair in 1324 with pretexts for military intervention in Guyenne, allowing them to proclaim their right to confiscate the fief. In both cases, pontifical mediation easily resulted in the king of France's return of the duchy to the king of England (in 1297 and again in 1325). However, the ease with which the French had occupied it gave them the impression that an eventual reconquest of the English possessions in France would be a cakewalk. And this was not even the most dangerous problem confronting them here. Henry III's successors swore homage to the king of France with increasingly less good grace. Edward I did it in 1274 and 1286, Edward II did it first in his father's name in 1304 and again in 1308 after becoming king of England, Edward III did it for his father in 1325 and again in his own name in 1329. This last act of homage took place under different circumstances. In effect, the king of France was no longer a direct descendant of the Capetian line, but the Valois Philip VI, who was from a younger branch of the family. The French nobility had accepted him specifically in preference to the young king of England who was the grandson of Philip the Fair through a wife, his mother Isabelle, who was the widow of Edward II. Isabelle continued to claim the crown of France for her son. Capetian tradition reserved it exclusively for male heirs of the masculine line, and Isabelle's claims were made in vain. The young Edward came to Amiens in 1329 to swear homage to Philip VI only because his position was too weak to refuse. From this point on, the king of England's recognition of his vassalage to the king of France became highly problematic for at least three reasons. First, although it had been presented as a "final peace," the territorial and juridical status of Guyenne had not been definitively decided by the agreement of March 31, 1327 between Edward III and Charles IV the Fair. Second, the dynastic change in France created a new relationship between the two kings with the English king as a pretender to the French crown. Finally, perhaps because of the evolution of the French and English monarchies into "modern" and "national" states, the subordination of one king to the other in terms of feudal relations was becoming more fragile and more contestable. The condition that Louis IX had imposed to resolve the problem of the English presence in France once and for all henceforth became the main obstacle to a Franco-English peace. If I have mentioned this series of events that extends far beyond Saint

Louis' reign, it has been to allow us to survey Saint Louis' ideas and his influence on the development of French political problems and the course
of the following events. The treaty of 1259 had actually been a success for
Saint Louis in his dual and complementary intentions of achieving peace
between England and France through the strongest existing tie at the time,
vassalage, which, in addition, established the preeminence of the French
king. The subsequent evolution of structures and events had been hard to
predict and eventually transformed the Treaty of Paris into a justification
for war. This war was the Hundred Years' War, but the saintly king was no
prophet or fortuneteller.

The "Mise" [Judgment] of Amiens

Among the various arbitrations that he conducted, I will only deal with one,
which has had a particularly strong effect upon historians: the one Saint
Louis negotiated between the king of England, Henry III, and his barons. In
England, the entire thirteenth century had been marked by the aristocracy's
attempts to limit and control royal power. Their efforts led to the granting
of the Magna Carta (1215) and the Oxford provisions (1258). Henry III's
own brother-in-law, Simon de Montfort, the count of Leicester, led the opposition. The king managed to have his oath to observe the Oxford provisions dissolved by two popes, Alexander IV (1254–1261) and his successor,
Urban IV, but the barons refused to accept the pontifical decision. In December 1263, Henry III and his barons appealed to Louis IX as an arbiter,
agreeing to accept his "mise," his arbitrational decision.

He made his ruling in Amiens in January 1264. For the most part, it
was favorable to the English king. First of all, he ratified the pontifical bull
that did away with the Oxford provisions. He then declared that the king
should exercise the full power and unrestricted sovereignty he had in the
past. He added, however, that they all had to respect "the royal privileges,
charters, freedoms, institutions, and good customs of the Kingdom of
England as they had existed before these provisions."

Some have tried to prove that the "mise" of Amiens was not a real arbitration but a judgment made by the king of France as the lord of the king
of England and, therefore, as the suzerain of the English barons considered as his rear vassals. The ruling of Amiens should be interpreted in a

purely feudal framework, and not in the context of a modern conception of monarchy.[83] According to other historians at the opposite end of the spectrum, Louis IX refused to grant the barons the right to limit the king's powers because he considered the king as the source of all power. I believe that Louis IX made his ruling in accordance with two convergent principles. One of these principles was his respect for the function of the king, which should only be limited by respect for justice. When the king of France stated through his investigating officers [*enquêteurs*] that agents acting in his name had committed an injustice, the offense had to be corrected. In this case, though, Henry III could not be blamed for committing any injustice. The other principle was that the king did not have to observe "bad customs." A feudal king, Louis IX combined the new spirit of royal sovereignty inspired by Roman canonical law with customary law. It was with a traditional attitude that he associated the Oxford provisions with "bad customs," reminding everyone on the other hand that the king of England was supposed to respect the good ones. As for the authority on which his decision was based, it was not his authority as the king of France nor as lord and suzerain of the king of England and his barons. Instead, he exercised the authority the two parties had placed in him by approaching him as a mediator and by agreeing to accept his ruling. As a just and peace-making king, Louis IX relied on all the juridical practices available to him, including arbitration, in order to impose his authority. At the same time, he gave these practices the religious and moral ideal of the Christian king as their common basis and foundation.

Of course, the circumstances made things easier for him. After the death of Frederick II (1250), there was a long interregnum when there was no emperor. During the same period, the king of England faced opposition within his own kingdom, and the Spanish kings were wrapped up in the Reconquista against the Muslims. Louis IX's material power was augmented by his moral prestige. He was the one ruler the Mongol khan Hülegü considered "the most eminent of the Christian kings of the West."[84] He was not only "the greatest king of the West," he was the true moral leader of this erratic Christendom to which he briefly gave the illusory impression of actually existing, because he was respected everywhere within it and because he embodied its ideals in government.

The peace-making king wanted to go even further and tried to exercise strict control over war and peace within his kingdom. One mandate

given at Saint-Germain-en-Laye in January 1258 declared that, in deliberation with his council, the king banned all war within the kingdom, all arson,
and any attacks on plows, threatening to send his officers out against any
offenders.[85] Some have disputed the importance of this text and refused to
give it the same status as an edict, which it had traditionally been granted.[86]
It was addressed to the bishop of Puy, Guy Foulcois, a member of the king's
inner circle, and was probably made at the request of this jurist-prelate.[87]
Some historians therefore conclude that the mandate was only a temporary measure granted to reinforce the bishop's authority and to help him
keep the peace on his land. Certainly, it is obvious that Louis IX and his
successors had to make sustained and repeated efforts to stamp out private
wars in the Kingdom of France. Nevertheless, this text still holds a special
interest. It shows how the king of France "patched together" the construction of monarchical power. It reveals the French monarchy's dream
of having a king who would be in charge in war and peace. Louis IX conceived of the king's role as that of a peaceful king with the function of deciding whether a war was just or not. His jurist advisors conceived a royal
power that would completely fulfill one of the most important attributes
of sovereignty: the right to decide to make war and peace. The two dreams
became one.

   Louis IX also attempted to determine what cases constituted infrac-
tions of the peace. The text of this mandate has been lost. There is one
reference to it in an edict made by Philip III in 1275.[88] Louis IX tried hard
to secure *assensements* instead of truces, in other words, to obtain oaths from
opposing parties never to use violence against a designated individual or
group. Once this oath was taken, no one could retract it. Truces, then, were
provisional, while *assensements* were perpetual at least in theory. The Parlement guaranteed more and more of the *assensements*.

Louis IX and the Future of the Capetian Dynasty and the Royal Family

During the last phase of his reign, Louis IX's eschatological desire drove
him to carry out what would be any ruler's duty with the most possible zeal.
This duty was to achieve his own salvation and that of his kingdom, first of
all by assuring the future of his dynasty and his family.

Births and Deaths

We must first give an account of his extensive bereavement. When Louis IX returned to France in 1254, two deaths had submerged him in the throes of mourning. There was the death of his second-born brother, Robert d'Artois, who died on the crusade in 1250. Then, there was the death of his mother in France in December 1252.

Robert d'Artois had been the victim of his own hotheaded chivalry and carelessness. He was killed at the battle of Mansourah on February 9, 1250. Louis, who felt special affection for his entire group of brothers, was strongly affected by his death. Fortunately, there were no problems with Robert's succession. He left a young son, also named Robert, who succeeded him.[89] Louis IX knighted him in 1267. Louis tried to have his brother recognized as a martyr for having died on the crusade, but the papacy turned a deaf ear to this request, as it would later do for Louis himself whom it recognized as a saint but never as a martyr. In the eyes of the papacy, crusading opened the door to salvation but not to martyrdom; moreover, the Church wanted to avoid creating any impression that saintliness was inherent within a dynasty.

The death of Blanche of Castile afflicted Louis IX with incredible pain. Joinville and many of his contemporaries blamed the king for the excessive nature of his emotional reaction. Saint Louis bore the brunt of two great losses in his life: his mother and Jerusalem. The memory of Blanche, however, was all in the past and, as the king wished, she had been sent to await the Resurrection outside of the royal necropolises of Saint-Denis and Royaumont to the Cistercian abbey of Maubuisson that she had founded and which was her Royaumont.

Another unexpected death dealt a cruel blow to Louis IX, a death with the most serious implications. This was the death of his oldest son, Louis, who was prince and heir to the throne. He died unexpectedly in January 1260. The king suffered deeply from this death and announced it himself with incredible emotion according to his main advisor, the chancellor and archbishop of Rouen, Eudes Rigaud, who made note of it in his journal. The king of England and the young English prince who had just spent Christmas in Paris with the royal family doubled back on their journey home in order to attend the funeral ceremony. The young prince was buried at Royaumont because the king decided that Saint-Denis would be reserved exclusively for the kings and queens of France who had actually worn the crown. Royaumont became the necropolis for the children of the royal family who never ruled. His death hit the family even harder since it seems that he had already come close to assuming royal power. In addition to his status as heir to the throne, he had already exercised a theoretical and specific kind of lieutenantship to the king in governing the kingdom with the title of "first-born" (*primogenitus*) during the last stage of his father's time in the Holy Land. Moreover, the chroniclers all agree in describing him as a man who was already full of brilliant virtues and royal capacities, the worthy son of his father. The problem of a king's successors held an important place in the Mirrors of the Princes of the time. The ultimate reward that God granted good kings was to give them a good successor. Saint Louis must have felt that this death was a divine warning. He must not yet have earned salvation for himself and his subjects. He concluded that he had to intensify the moral reform of the kingdom once again, which, as we have seen, was exactly what he would do.

Young Louis' death appeared as such a painful event for the king that he received extraordinary messages of sympathy and consolation. Pope Alexander IV sent him a letter. The most important intellectual in his entourage, the Dominican Vincent de Beauvais, composed an "epistle of consolation" for him that historians of the "Christian consolation" rate as the medieval masterpiece in this genre alongside Saint Bernard's consolation sermon on the death of his own brother.[90] Of course, Louis IX still had other sons. Philip, the second-born, was only one year younger than his dead brother. On certain occasions such as the swearing of the Treaty of Paris the king had already associated him with his oldest son. The dynastic succession did not seem to be threatened by the young prince's death. Vincent de Beauvais emphasized this by reminding the king that this situation had already arisen in the history of the Capetian dynasty without ever leading to any harmful results.

Louis and Queen Marguerite had succeeded in producing abundant progeny following the Christian monarchical tradition in which God ideally grants the royal partners the grace of being naturally fecund. The royal couple had eleven children. Their first daughter, Blanche, was born in 1240 and died in 1243. She was followed by Isabelle (born in 1242), Louis (born in 1244 and deceased in 1260), Philip (born in 1245), another son who died shortly after his birth, Jean (born in 1248), and three children born during the crusade and the stay in the Holy Land: Jean-Tristan who was born in April 1250 during his father's captivity and whose name recalled the sadness of those circumstances, Pierre who was born in 1251, and another

Blanche born at the beginning of 1253. There were also three children born
after their return to France: Marguerite (born in late 1254 or early 1255),
Robert (born in 1256), and Agnès (born in 1260). The large number of
descendants was a source of prestige and power, all the more insofar as
Louis IX, unlike his father Louis VIII, did not give any important lands
to his younger sons. When he made his inheritance in 1269 on the eve of
his departure for Tunis, he only granted them small dukedoms but married them to women who were the heiresses of extensive lands.[91] Through
the intermediary of his sons, Louis IX became the ancestor of all of the
subsequent kings of France. They would all be able to call themselves the
"sons of Saint Louis," and the priest in attendance said the same thing to
Louis XVI on the scaffold.

The younger sons made good marriages, as did the older sons and
daughters, all according to the customs of the time: they were engaged at a
very young age and married at a young age to partners selected in harmony
with royal politics.[92]

In the thirteenth century, a young noble only became a man when he
became a knight. In a royal family where the king, his brothers, and sons
had to be knighted in order to attain their full status and assume their functions, the dubbing of young men took on special significance. The normally
austere Louis IX made an exception for the brilliance of these formal ceremonies. Philip's was the most brilliant of these dubbing ceremonies. He
was the future Philip III, henceforth heir to the throne. His dubbing took
place on June 5, 1267, which was also Pentecost, the day that Christian feudalism had made into the great festival day of the monarchy and the aristocracy as it replaced the traditional festival of spring. The celebration took
place in the palace garden in Paris in the midst of a great throng of nobles
and commoners at the same time as the dubbing of a great number of other
young nobles. By vowing to take up the cross for a second time, Louis IX
had recently made such a strong impression that many people predicted that
his poor health would prevent him from surviving the crusade. The new
knight was not just the heir to the throne, but nearly a king.

His Sister and Brothers

Following the typical example of the important noble families, Louis IX
wanted some of his children to join the Church. He would have been happy

to have seen Jean-Tristan become a Dominican, Pierre a Franciscan, and Blanche a Cistercian at Maubuisson, her grandmother's monastery. The three children successfully resisted this pressure from their authoritarian father. The most resistant was undoubtedly Blanche, who offered a model of behavior very different from the usual one in the great royal, seigniorial, and even bourgeois Christian families. Typically, daughters revolted in order to join a convent against their parents' will and especially against fathers who were hostile to a vocation that deprived them of the advantages of matrimonial alliances to be made through their daughters. Blanche even asked Pope Urban IV for the privilege of being released from her vows if she were ever to give in to her father's will. The pope granted her wish before she had even reached the age of eleven, although we do not know who her intermediary was. Even a pope could sometimes find Saint Louis' religious zeal excessive. Nevertheless, the king did not force his desires upon his children.

On the other hand, he was certainly happy with the conduct of his sister Isabelle. Born in 1225, she led a life comparable to his, independently of their different genders and functions. She took a vow of chastity and, notably, refused to marry the son of Emperor Frederick II, Conrad de Hohenstaufen, after having been promised to the oldest son of the count of the March. She lived at the court, dressed modestly, and practiced exercises of remarkable piety. She founded the convent of the Clares of Longchamp to which she retired in 1263. She died there in 1270 shortly before Louis IX's departure on the crusade. The king devoutly attended his sister's funeral rites, and the Church beatified her although not until 1521. The convent of Longchamp seems to have been the center of an attempt to create a monastic cult based on Isabelle's character. For example, Philip V the Tall came there to die in 1322; however, quite different from the way things happened in Central Europe, the Church seems to have blocked the development of a royal cult dedicated to princesses who were recognized as saintly or blessed.[93] According to Joinville, Blanche of Castile had developed a particular devotion for Saint Elisabeth of Hungary (of Thuringia) whose son had served her during the great feast given by Louis IX in Saumur in 1241 for the dubbing of his brother Alphonse.[94] As the story goes, Blanche kissed the young man on his forehead, in the same place where she thought his sainted mother had kissed him. Isabelle had to wait until the sixteenth century for her exceptional piety to be recognized by the Church.

Of Louis' two brothers who survived the crusade, Alphonse, the eldest, became count of Toulouse in 1249 as stipulated by the treaty of Paris of 1229 that had put an end to the crusade against the Albigenses. Louis IX had already given him possession of Poitou and part of Saintonge and Auvergne in 1241 as called for in the will of their father, Louis VIII. A large part of the inheritance of his wife, Jeanne, the daughter of Raimond VII the count of Toulouse, also fell under his control. Although his health was fragile, he was very close to his royal brother and followed him on both of the crusades. He rarely resided on his own lands, usually staying in Île-de-France or in Paris itself where he had a palace built for himself near the Louvre. He nevertheless administered his vast domains with remarkable skill. They stretched from the south of France into the west, and he governed them according to the model of the royal domain with the help of good bailiffs and seneschals. He may have even provided the royal administration with certain models. The ties between the two brothers reinforced the similarities between their two governments. This goes a long way to explain why, after the deaths of Alphonse and Jeanne, who were childless, in 1271, when Alphonse's domains reverted to the royal domain in conformity with the rules of succession for the royal territories, their integration was remarkably peaceful.[95]

Louis' second brother was the family's *enfant terrible*.[96] He assumed control of his territory of Anjou-Maine-Touraine in 1246. From his wife, Beatrice, he received the county of Provence, which they inherited from her father, Raimond Bérenger who died in 1245, although Marguerite, the queen of France, Raimond Bérenger's oldest daughter, maintained her claims to Provence. Charles's lands, then, were not only divided in two separate parts but one of them was in the Kingdom of France and the other in the Empire. This situation fed his ambitions and careless tendencies. He had major disputes with his Provencal subjects, notably with the towns, and especially with Marseilles, which considered him a foreigner. Louis IX retained his brother's services for a long time. We have seen the role he played in the Hainaut affair; Charles threw himself into it when his brother was still in the Holy Land. Acting on the papacy's request, Louis finally accepted Frederick II's Italian inheritance for his brother. It included southern Italy and Sicily. Charles conquered his kingdom with the victories of Benevento (February 1266) and Tagliacozzo (August). Thus the Capetian dynasty came to rule in the Italian Mezzogiorno, independent of Louis IX's Kingdom of France though still with a fraternal bond.

Michael VIII Palaeologus and the Greeks had dispossessed the Latin emperor of Constantinople. Beginning in 1261, he had tried to secure Charles of Anjou's support for the reconquest of Constantinople. After numerous reversals, Charles accepted and concluded a treaty at Viterbo on May 27, 1267 under the auspices of Clement IV. He received suzerainty over Morea, the islands of the Aegean Sea, Epirus, and Corfu in addition to a third of the lands to be reconquered in common. At the beginning of 1270, Charles sent some of his troops to Morea. Louis IX disapproved of his brother's new enterprise. At this point, he had only a single goal: his new crusade. He thought that the conflict over Constantinople could be resolved by a peaceful compromise. Michael Palaeologus cleverly requested his mediation, hinting at an end to the schism between Greek and Latin Christians. Charles d'Anjou had no other choice than to first participate in his brother's crusade. He admired his brother and respected his authority.

Thus Louis IX settled his family affairs by applying his principles and by following the interests of the Kingdom of France and Christendom. These matters did not concern only the living. They required peace, order, and solidarity with the dead. Georges Duby has brilliantly shown how lineage is a site of memory, and how genealogical passion demands the attention of dynastic memory.[97] The meeting of the living and the dead of the great families of the time took place in the necropolises.

SAINT LOUIS AND THE ROYAL BODIES

Toward the end of his rule, probably in 1263–1264, Saint Louis had the tombs of the royal necropolis of Saint-Denis reorganized and carried out the largest funerary project of the Middle Ages: sixteen tombs for the dead queens and kings from the seventh to the twelfth century represented by as many recumbent statues aligned together alongside the tombs of his grandfather Philip Augustus (who died in 1223) and his father Louis VIII (dead in 1226). At the same time, he arranged to have the sepulcher of Saint-Denis reserved exclusively from this point on for the persons of the royal family, for the men and women who actually wore the crown.

This ambitious and impressive program not only raised the question of the Capetians' funerary politics. It can only be understood in terms of a long-term change in Christianity's prevalent attitude toward the dead and the profound transformation in this attitude that took place between the eleventh and thirteenth centuries. The new artistic theme of the recumbent statue bears witness to this transformation. A phenomenon of primary importance can be glimpsed behind this development: the placement of the body in medieval Christian ideology or, rather, the placement of a particular body, the body of the king.

From its origins, Christianity bore the seeds of the peculiar paradox of the ambiguous status of the body.[98] On the one hand, the body was condemned as the evil part of man: "For if ye live after the flesh, ye shall die; but if ye through the Spirit do mortify the deeds of the body, ye shall live" (Romans 8:13). In the barbaric manicheanization of the High Middle Ages, the body became "the abominable clothing of the soul" (Gregory the Great). However, resurrection was promised to the body and eternal life to the saints and the people who would join them after their purification in the fires of Purgatory. Again, it was Saint Paul who asserted: "For our conversation is in heaven; from whence also we look for the Savior, the Lord Jesus Christ: Who shall change our vile body, that it may be fashioned like unto his glorious body" (Philippians 3:20–21). Dead or alive, the Christian's body awaited the body of glory it would assume if it did not sink into the body of misery. All Christian funerary ideology played out between this body of misery and this body of glory, and it organized itself around this tug-of-war between the two.

The funerary ideology of the Ancients was entirely oriented toward the memory of the dead.[99] Of course, this was clearest in the case of the most important dead figures. In Mesopotamia, dead royalty assured the order and prosperity of their society and its harmony with the heavens through the intermediary of their vertically standing statues. They assured its harmony with the earth through the mediation of their horizontally buried bones.[100] In Greece, the glorious dead were heroes whose commemoration reminded people of their "unique personal fates," the cohesion of a military group like the army in the epic age or even the city itself in the civic period.[101] Then, there were the accomplished dead [*évergètes*] whose funerary munificence was rather meant to quell "the torment of the afterlife" and to perpetuate their "ostentation."[102] This ostentation was intended to perpetuate the power of their social category of notables through their memory.[103] Finally, in the case of royal statues it is important to note that in ancient Mesopotamia, because the king was "the mediator for the heavens, instead of laying his corpse out at the bottom of the tomb, they raise him upright after his death in the form of a statue erected in the palace or the temples," and this statue was "the dead man himself made into a statue."[104]

In the Hellenistic period, the king became a cultural object and his tomb a *hierothesion,* a sanctuary tomb.[105] At the same time, however, and this ambiguity exists in most ancient societies and especially in Greco-Roman societies, the cadaver was an abominable object.[106] It was excluded from civic space and confined to the outer edges of the city, although tombs, or at least the tombs of important families, were freely placed alongside suburban roads or in other commonly visited places so as to better perpetuate the memory and the worship of the dead.

Christianity changed all of this. Although the dialectic between the body of misery and the body of glory seems essential to Christian conduct toward the dead, in practice, the Christian revolution in funerary ideology resulted from one of Christianity's great novelties—the cult of the saints.[107] This cult was primarily based on the worship of the dead. It was the only form of worship of the dead that survived in the Christian world, although it initiated a rupture with the practices of pagan Antiquity. The tombs of the saints became main attractions for Christian communities. For the Church, the remains of saints established their power to intercede at God's side, while the mass endowed them with a positive, immediate, magical force. Just as the tombs of saints were ideal places for miraculous healing, sepulchers *ad sanctos*—"near the tombs of saints"—benefited those who could derive some kind of reassurance from them about their salvation in the future life. During the Resurrection, these privileged individuals would be well positioned to receive the help of these special beings. As Peter Brown explains, the saint's tomb was "the place where heaven and earth touch and come together," whereas for the Ancients and especially the Greeks death was the great line separating men and gods: when a man was about to die, the gods had to move away from him.[108]

One important change in Christian funerary ideology tied to the attraction of the saints' tombs was the urbanization (the Italians call it the *inurbamento*) of the dead, their reinsertion into the space of the living, the installation of cemeteries in cities near holy bodies whenever possible or at least near churches.[109]

A second change in Christian funerary ideology occurred with the disappearance of the commemorative character of the tomb and its personalization. Erwin Panofsky has stressed that Christian funerary art excluded the "retrospective" or "commemorative" principle and was dominated by the "eschatological" principle: the tomb should announce the Resurrection and call out for eternal life.[110] Philippe Ariès has insisted that from around the beginning of the fifth century the Christian tomb became anonymous. It no longer bore any inscription or portrait. Still, we must not exaggerate the extent of the rupture with ancient funerary ideology. The Christian sepulcher still upheld an idea of remembrance. The monument or the part of the monument where the body of a saint was placed was generally called the *memoria,* yet it is also true that the Christian funerary monument had the special function of reminding the living that the body is dust and must return to dust. The memory it incited was oriented toward the final end of man rather than toward his past and what he was on earth.

Among the illustrious dead that required special treatment, though inferior to and different from that reserved for the bodies of saints, were the people who held power and, foremost among these *potentes,* those who had been distinct from others since the dawn of Antiquity: dead royalty.[111] They managed to slip into the ecclesial space defined by the division between the clerics and the laity. Buried *in sacrario,* in other words in the choir or an adjacent sanctuary, beginning in the High Middle Ages kings had a tendency to consider a specific church as their own necropolis, as the "pantheon" of their dynasty.

In Gaul, the tendency to select royal funerary churches became established around the beginning of the Merovingian dynasty.[112] Before their conversion to Christianity, the Franks followed funeral customs for their leaders that were very similar to those of the Romans. Thus Childeric I, Clovis's father, was interred under a burial mound at the side of an ancient road near Tournai. It was a solitary tomb situated outside of any urban space and, of course, it bore no resemblance to any monument of Christian worship. Clovis brutally changed this custom. From that point on all Merovingian kings were interred in Christian basilicas, although they were suburban basilicas *extra muros.* Is there any more or less latent connection in this choice (that can be found later—and for centuries—at Saint-Denis) between the king and the space, a consequence of the absence of any real capital city and the attraction of the suburban monasteries?[113]

Clovis chose to be buried in the Church of the Saints-Apôtres that he had built on a hill above Paris on the left bank of the Seine to house the relics of Saint Geneviève, who probably died shortly after 500. The queen Clothilde joined him there upon her death in 544, but the son of Clovis who had acquired Paris for his kingdom, Childebert, decided to be buried in a different suburban monastery in 558, Saint-Vincent-Sainte-Croix. He had established this monastery himself to hold the relics that he brought back from Spain, especially the tunic of Saint Vincent, and probably also to serve as a necropolis for himself and his family. The bishop of Paris, Saint Germain, was also buried there in 576. He later gave his name to this church when it was rebaptised Saint-Germain-des-Près. Most of the Merovingian rulers of Paris, their wives, and their children were actually buried in Saint-Vincent-Sainte-Croix, although this church had no more of a monopoly on royal tombs than Saints-Apôtres (which later became Sainte-Geneviève). There was no single and definitive royal necropolis for the Merovingian kings.

The selection of an original sepulcher for one of the Merovingian kings ended up having important future consequences. Since the end of the fifth century, a church and a monastery that interested Saint Geneviève existed at Saint-Denis. Denis, the first bishop of Paris who had been martyred in 250 and the martyrs Rustique and Éleuthère were said to have been buried on this site. The Merovingian kings of Paris gradually established close ties with this abbey, and between 565 and 570 Queen Arnegonde, the widow of Clotaire I, was buried there. Although magnificent jewels were recently discovered in it, her tomb was placed anonymously among others, so Saint-Denis did not seem a likely choice for a royal necropolis. Everything changed when Dagobert I had the church rebuilt and was buried there in 639. In the throes of fatal illness, he had himself carried there, which indicated that it was the site he had chosen for his tomb.

Under the Carolingians, Saint-Denis seems to become the necropolis of the new dynasty. Charles Martel, who founded the dynasty although he never had the title of king, chose Saint-Denis to house his sepulcher and was buried there in 741. His choice seems to result from his particular devotion to the saint, although it also probably related the political objective of establishing a close rapport with one of the abbeys previously devoted to the Merovingians, which he had not been able to do in Paris with Saint Vincent. He wanted to be interred alongside the kings of the dynasty he ended in favor of his own descendants. Thus the choice of a necropolis was politicized even more. The interment site was a claim to legitimacy and continuity for the dynasty. In effect, Charles Martel's son, Pepin the Short first chose Saint-Denis as the site for his coronation by Pope Stephen II in 755 and then as his burial site in 768. His widow joined him there in 783, re-uniting the royal couple in death, just like the former couples of Clovis and Clothilde and Dagobert and Nanthilde. Pepin's son, however, broke the royal funerary succession of Saint-Denis. Charlemagne, who made an empire of the Merovingian kingdom unified by his father and grandfather, chose Aix-la-Chapelle as his new capital. This attempt to forge a new tradition had no future. Most of Charlemagne's descendants chose to be buried in other churches. A return to the traditional sepulcher of Saint-Denis took place under Charles the Bald who had very close ties to the abbey, so close that it practically considered him its second founder after Dagobert. He was buried there seven years after his death in 884.

It was under a new dynasty, the Capetians, that Saint-Denis definitively became the "cemetery of the kings." Once again, the ambitions of achieving dynastic substitution and continuity expressed themselves early on through the choice of a funerary site. Eudes, the king of the Franks, took the abbey under his wing and was buried there in 888. His nephew, Hugues I the Great, was also buried there in 956. It was under Hugues I's son, Hugues II, known as Hugh Capet, who changed the Robertians into the Capetians who would be the kings of the Franks and then the kings of France for centuries to come, that Saint-Denis definitively became the royal necropolis. Down through Louis XI at the end of the fifteenth century, there are only two kings who did come to lie at Saint-Denis: Philip I who was buried at the monastery of Fleury (Saint-Benoît-sur-Loire) in 1108 and Louis VII who was buried in 1180 in the Cistercian abbey of Barbeau that he founded near Melun.

This long digression can help us to understand how royal funerary politics emerged through a large number of hesitations and the extent to which the choice of a "cemetery of the kings" had been slow to develop as it passed through a number of incarnations. The political and ideological tool that the royal necropolis held out to the French monarchy was fully utilized by Saint Louis. With him, Saint-Denis became a site of monarchical immortality.

There are two texts that inform us about Saint Louis' funerary politics at Saint-Denis. The first can be found in the official chronicle the abbey kept for itself, the *Annales de Saint-Denis*: "1263. This year on the day of Saint Gregory, they carried out the transfer of the kings Eudes, Hugh Capet, Robert, his wife Constance, Henry, Louis the Fat, Philip the son of Louis the

Fat, and Queen Constance who came from Spain. 1264. They transferred King Louis the son of Dagobert, the king Charles Martel, Queen Bertha the wife of Pepin, King Pepin, Queen Ermentrude the wife of Charles the Bald, King Carloman the son of Pepin, King Carloman the son of Louis the Stammerer, and King Louis the son of Louis the Stammerer into the right side of the choir." In his own *Chronique* written immediately after 1300, for the year 1267 Guillaume de Nangis notes: "At Saint-Denis in France the holy king of France Louis and the abbot Mathieu carried out the simultaneous transfer of the kings of the Franks who were lying in different places in the monastery; the kings and queens descended from the race of Charlemagne were raised two-and-a-half feet above the ground and placed on the right side of the monastery along with their sculpted images, and the ones descended from the race of Hugh Capet were placed on the left side." The difference between the reported dates matters little for our purposes. The dates of 1263–1264 given in the *Annales de Saint-Denis* seem to me to be more accurate than that of 1267 indicated by Guillaume de Nangis. Only Guillaume de Nangis mentions the eminent role Saint Louis played in this operation along with Abbot Mathieu de Vendôme. The abbot's agreement was obviously necessary for the transfer to take place. He and the king got along very well, although I do not doubt that this was Saint Louis' own idea and his own desired action.

It was a political decision of a dual nature. First of all, the royal necropolis of Saint-Denis had to express the continuity between the two lines of kings who ruled in France since the beginnings of the Frankish monarchy. The only distinction made was the division between Carolingians and Capetians. This not only served to respect the right-left symmetry that divided the kings and queens between two dynasties but also to efface the biological discontinuity between Merovingians and Carolingians, whether intentionally or due to indifference to that change. Besides, the Merovingian presence at Saint-Denis was very weak. From the moment Dagobert and Nanthilde were set apart, as we shall soon see, the only Merovingian to be found in Saint-Denis was Dagobert's son, Clovis II, whom the *Annales* errantly name Louis. It was probably also, at least in part, the weak Merovingian representation that allowed Charles Martel to be identified as a king by encouraging a certain ignorance of the rupture between Merovingians and Carolingians.[114] In any case, the essential thing for Louis IX was to affirm the continuity between Carolingians and Capetians. Here we find the most important articulation of the French monarchy in its ambition to affiliate itself with the most imposing figure of medieval, monarchical ideology—Charlemagne. The goal was to establish the legitimacy of the Capetian dynasty, which had long been vilified in the figure of its founder Hugh Capet whom Dante alluded to with scorn. The goal, in other words, was to establish what Bernard Guenée has called "the pride of being Capetian."[115]

Louis IX's second important decision was to make Saint-Denis into a royal necropolis in the strict sense according to which only people who have ruled—or rather who have been crowned or who are imagined to have been crowned—only kings and queens in other words, would have the right to be interred there. This was the case for sixteen of the deceased who were kept there under Saint Louis' program.

Proceeding on the right from west to east, from the nave to the choir, we find Charles Martel (d. 741) transformed into a king, and Clovis II (under the attributed name of Louis) who became king in 635 (in Burgundy and Neustria) and king of the Franks in 657, the year of his death; then, Pepin the Short, king from 751 to 768, and his wife Bertha (d. 783); Ermentrude the wife of Charles the Bald, and Carloman (who was actually buried at Saint-Rémi in Reims), Charlemagne's brother, king of Alemania, Burgundy, and Provence from 768 to 771; Louis III, king from 879 to 882, and his brother Carloman III, co-king from 879 to 882 and sole king of the Franks from 882 to 884.

On the left, there is Eudes, king from 888 to 898, and his grand-nephew (Hugh Capet) who was king from 987 to 996; Robert the Pious, co-king with his father Hugh Capet and then sole king from 996 to 1031, and his third wife, Constance d'Arles who died in 1032; Henri I, co-king from 1027 and sole king from 1031 to 1060, and his grandson Louis VI, co-king from 1108 to 1137; Philip, the son of Louis VI, co-king from 1129 to 1131, and Constance de Castille, the second wife of Louis VII, who died in 1160.

The provisions Saint Louis made for the sepulcher of Royaumont confirmed his will to reserve the necropolis of Saint-Denis exclusively for kings and queens. He had founded Royaumont with his mother Blanche of Castile, and it was consecrated in 1235. The evidence indicates it was his preferred religious domain, and he also turned it into the necropolis for children of the royal family. Even before the consecration of the church, he had already transported the body of his younger brother Philippe Dagobert there after his death in 1233 or 1234. He later interred his daughter Blanche (1240–1243) there, his son Jean (1247–1248), and his eldest son Louis who died at the age of sixteen in 1260. The most surprising thing was that upon learning of the death of his much loved son Jean-Tristan, count of Nevers, born twenty years earlier at Damietta during his father's first crusade, who died from a case of dysentery to which his father too would soon succumb, Saint Louis commanded that he be buried at Royaumont, thus excluding him from Saint-Denis.[116]

What is even more striking is that Saint Louis articulated a specific and grandiose funerary plan. What it affirmed was neither the king himself, nor the royal family, but the dynasty or rather the fiction of dynastic continuity, the monarchical state, and the crown. The queen was closely associated with the monarchical state here, as the arrangement expressed the triumph of the Church's model of monogamous marriage.[117] Whenever possible, Saint Louis' edict for the tombs at Saint-Denis stressed the significance of the royal couples such as Pepin and Bertha, and Robert and Constance. Acquiring new force under Saint Louis, the monarchical ideology went on display and became ostentatious whether in its theoretical expressions or, especially, in its ceremonial of crowning. This ceremonial was minutely regulated by new *ordines*[118] and paralleled the new ceremony of Corpus Christi instituted by Urban IV in 1264 as well as the ceremonial rites for funerals and mortuary ostentation. God had more than ever become the great model for the king. Dead kings henceforth displayed the perpetuity of the monarchy's existence. They had been enrolled for eternity in the ideology of the monarchy and the nation, a nation that still knew how to assert itself only through the *regnum,* the kingdom.

What was particularly new was that Saint Louis was not content simply to regroup the royal bodies; he had to display them and celebrate them. He had them exhumed from the basilica and "elevated" in tombs two-and-a-half feet above the ground. Better still, he presented them to viewers' eyes in the form of sculpted statues placed upon their tombs. An artistic program expressed and reinforced the ideological program.

This program was first of all expressed in its own particular space. Originally, as was usually the case for the sepulchers of great figures in churches, the kings of Saint-Denis were buried in the choir close to the great altar (the altar of the Holy Trinity) and the altar of the relics (of Saint Denis, Rustique, and Éleuthère) in the back of the choir. When Suger had

the choir rebuilt between 1140 and 1144, he clearly had the altar of the
Trinity moved without disturbing the royal sepulchers because, as he wrote
in his *Vie de Louis VI,* when they had to bury the king in 1137, they first
thought they would have to move Emperor Charles the Bald's tomb,[119]
which shocked Suger as "neither right nor custom allow anyone to exhume
kings."[120] A century later the attitude toward the royal bodies had changed.
The idea of monarchical power henceforth took precedence over respect
for royal cadavers. Under Saint Louis the choir was reconfigured, and a new
exceptionally large transept was built as well. Specialists often discuss the
date of this transept. In any case, it seems very likely to me that it was constructed to house the royal tombs.[121]

It was already quite an impressive feat to arrange the bodies of sixteen
kings and queens belonging to three successive dynasties in a designated
place and according to a rational organization that stressed their continuity.
The program reached extraordinary proportions when Saint Louis completed it with the execution of sixteen recumbent statues placed on the already glorious tombs. We must therefore examine the place of this great
figure of the recumbent statue in royal funerary ideology.[122] First, however,
we must return to the origins of the tradition.

Philippe Ariès has brilliantly analyzed the evolution of tombs from
Antiquity to medieval Christendom. For wealthy families (in the Middle
Ages as in ancient times these funerary programs only existed among the
higher social classes) the tomb was a monument, a memorial that included
a portrait of the deceased and an inscription and, for the richest families,
sculptures. After the advent of Christianity, the tomb became anonymous;
the portraits, inscriptions, and sculptures disappeared. Coffins of lead and
later of wood gradually replaced the sarcophagus. The tomb was dug into
the surface of the earth, so the typical Christian funerary monument became the tombstone. Beginning at the end of the eleventh century, there
was a return to the commemorative tomb and a renewed concern for the
identity of the deceased. This change was one aspect of the great expansion of western Christendom that lasted from the eleventh to the middle
of the thirteenth century. For the clerics, the apparent rebirth of an ancient
custom was only a means for capturing the forceful innovation of this development. One of its most important aspects was the return to the use of
a visible tomb, which, as Philippe Ariès tells us, was "often dissociated from
the body." Christianity effectively maintained an ambiguous attitude toward
the body that shifted between polite reverence and indifference. The body

was only a pretext for a more important lesson that was separable from its perishable origin. At the same time, however, the men of expanding Christendom were investing more and more in their own worldly existence that they were in the process of transforming. The *contemptus mundi,* the "scorn for the world," the great slogan of the monastic spirit, was retreating before worldly values. Sculpture rediscovered the methods of figuration and three-dimensional representation in this revival of earthly existence. Statuary art exploded. It was applied to the living as well as the dead. Upright, living statues became detached from columns, and statues of laid out dead figures emerged from the flatness of their tombstones.

Here, we must note the variety of artistic methods and solutions. Although the dead person seated or standing had little chance of coming back to life, the walled vertical tomb and the great monument rediscovered verticality in funerary commemoration. The use of stone underwent a fabulous transformation in England. Enamel plaques decorated the tombs of Geoffrey Plantagenet in England in the second half of the twelfth century and of Saint Louis' children Jean and Blanche at Royaumont.[123]

The most original creation was the recumbent statue. Here, with Erwin Panofsky, we must stress one of the great cultural and ideological breaks in the medieval West. In southern Christendom, in Italy and Spain, the solution of the vertical tomb[124] and the great monument carried the day, especially when the recumbent figures were dead individuals: the drapings of their clothing were wrinkles in their shrouds, they did not express the attributes of power placed beside them, they made no gestures, and their eyes were shut or half-closed. On the other hand, in the Nordic version of gothic art, although the recumbent figure was not quite portrayed as living, it at least appeared in the scenario of an eschatological vision: its eyes were open to eternal light. Erwin Panofsky has done a fine job evaluating the balance that exists in these recumbent figures between the desire to express the power of worldly values, the glorification of the memory of these powerful figures, and the desire to represent them in the eschatological perspective in which they were meant to be seen: "The funerary sculpture of the northern Middle Ages, while essentially 'prospective' or *anticipatory* in its intentions, differs from that of early Christianity in that terrestrial values are no longer ignored in it."[125]

Beginning in the eleventh century, the theme of the recumbent statue expanded in a way that favored two well-known figures of power in the Middle Ages: bishops and kings. The oldest surviving recumbent statue in northern France is of Childebert. It was completed shortly before 1163 for Saint-Germain-des-Prés. The first funerary arrangement of recumbent statues carried out in the medieval Western world seems to be the one that represented the Plantagenet kings at Fontevrault in the first years of the thirteenth century. Despite the close relations binding Henry III and Saint Louis, the French and English monarchies were locked in ongoing competition throughout the Middle Ages. They struggled over political power but also competed for its symbols and instruments.[126] It is not impossible that the example of Fontevrault could have inspired the royal funerary arrangement at Saint-Denis, although the French achievement was on an entirely different scale.

Philippe Ariès has explored the question of the relation between the sculptural theme of the recumbent figure and the ritual of exposing the deceased between their death and their funeral rites. In order to stress the element of ideological innovation, he has claimed that the recumbent statue was not a copy of the exposed figure but instead the display of the dead person was based on the model of the recumbent statue. I would more cautiously venture that between the middle of the twelfth and thirteenth centuries a habit formed for the ceremonial of funerals of important people, for the description of the deaths of heroes in literary works, and for the representation of recumbent figures in art, which involved showing the illustrious dead in new and identical poses, laid out with their heads on cushions and their feet resting on symbolic objects, holding the distinguished signs of the power they had when they were still alive. His documents inform us that Philip Augustus was the first king of France whose body was displayed with scepter and crown from his death at Mantes on July 14, 1223 to his burial the next day at Saint-Denis.[127]

What place do the recumbent statues of the royal tombs at Saint-Denis have among all the other "real" and literary dead figures of the time?

First, the recumbent statue remained a Christian figure, a creation that was merely a creature, however glorious one may have been. As Willibald Saurländer has explained so well, in contrast to the ancient statue, whether standing or lying the medieval statue "is not prayed to or venerated. It is not the object of any cult. It is never anything but a representation, the reflection of a figure from the history of salvation, an image (*imago*) and not a statue (*statua*)." An image, a double, an archetype, an *imago* in the psychoanalytic sense, almost a complex, an imaginary schema establishing relations between the person represented and the one who viewed him. Since they were not supposed to appeal to the realm of domination by the sacred, these relations evoked the realm of domination by power. The recumbent figure also recaptured an old aspiration of Christians facing death that was very common in funerary inscriptions and death liturgies from the first centuries of Christianity. The recumbent statue was a *requiem* in stone. The sculptor only represented the idea that contemporaries had about the transfer of bodies. We have already seen Guillaume de Nangis speaking of a "translation of the kings of France who lay [*reposaient*] in different places in this monastery." Far from the dead who were set upon by demons, or better yet like Dagobert on the monument of the choir of the abbey church, the sixteen kings in the royal necropolis calmly lived out the time that separated them from the Resurrection. The bodies of the kings and queens were shielded from the danger of hell.

The recumbent figures were represented in their age of strength and maturity. Funerary sculptures of the time ignored the age at which the deceased passed away. On their tombstones at Royaumont, Saint Louis' children, Blanche and Jean, are represented as fully grown children, almost adolescents, although they died at the respective ages of one and three. Because old age was excluded from these idealized representations, there were only two abstract categories for it: youth approaching adulthood and adults at full maturity, the only age that the Middle Ages really recognized as positive. Perhaps the sculptors were inspired by the idea that the dead would resuscitate with their thirty- or thirty-three-year-old bodies, the age of Christ at his death. I believe, however, that the ideal of mature age suffices to explain the depiction of individuals in recumbent statues in the thirteenth century.

Like Gothic statues representing positive characters (God, the Virgin Mary, angels, the virtues, biblical kings and queens), the royal recumbent figures were all peaceful and beautiful even though they could be distinguished according to the stylistic variations in the work of three different artists. It is therefore pointless to look for any realist intention in the faces of these figures that would have reproduced their physical individuality. They were already long dead by the end of Saint-Louis' reign. Along with Alain Erlande-Brandenburg, I do believe that the artists who could have known him or who could have questioned people who knew him did not represent Saint Louis with his actual physical characteristics. Certainly, the recumbent figures reveal Saint-Denis' program's attempt to restore the individuality of their human faces, but this was not yet any form of realism. The recumbent statues were a product of royal ideology, not of any quest for the unique individual semblance of kings.

Finally, and not least of all, the recumbent figures at Saint-Denis have their eyes open, open to all eternity. While describing Louis VI's funeral rites, Suger already evoked their anticipation of the Resurrection although he also stressed the importance of Saint-Denis and the proximity of the king's body to the saint's relics: "It is there [between the altar of the Holy Trinity and the altar of the relics] that he awaits the moment to play a part in the future Resurrection, all the closer in spirit to the assembly of the holy spirits for having his body interred closer to the holy martyrs in order to benefit from their help." The scholarly abbot quotes Lucain for support (*Pharsalus* 4.393), although he alters and modifies the quotation:

> *Felix qui potuit, mundi mutante ruina,*
> *Quo jaceat preacisse loco.*

> [Happy he who could know in advance
> When the world threatens ruin
> The place where he will be lying!]

Saint Louis' funerary plan for Saint-Denis definitively assured that the monarchy and the Capetian dynasty would have absolute power over time. From the Merovingians to the age of Louis IX, the continuity it affirmed handed the reins of the past to the monarchy. For as long as kings of the Franks existed, power belonged to them. The simultaneous arrangement of all these kings and queens whose lives extended over six centuries, each of whom never knew most of the others, put them all together in an eternal present from that time forth.

With open eyes expressing hope and anticipation for the Resurrection, the extended horizontal positions of these figures at rest[128] tied them to the future and the hereafter. It would be a peaceful future in the time that would expire between their deaths and the Last Judgment, which people believed was drawing nigh,[129] and, finally, the eternity that they tried to glimpse with empty pupils and open eyes. These living dead lay ready to convert their ever-present worldly glory into the celestial glory of eternal life.[130]

LOUIS IX CRUSADING FOR THE SECOND TIME

In 1267, Louis IX decided to leave on a new crusade. He announced this to an assembly of barons and prelates on Annunciation Day, March 25, 1267. During a new assembly on February 9, 1268, he added that he would leave in May 1270. His decision was made in the summer of 1266 because he secretly informed the pope of it in October of that year. Jean Richard has effectively shown how developments in the military and political situation in the eastern Mediterranean explain this decision. He calls this "the return toward the Mediterranean and the Orient."

First, there was the establishment of his brother, Charles d'Anjou, in Sicily and southern Italy. Sicily was capable of being used as a more secure base of operations than it had been under the whimsical Frederick II and his heirs. It was also closer than Cyprus.[131]

Then, there was also the definitive renunciation of any attempt to make an alliance with the Mongols, although a letter written in 1262 from the khan Hülegü to Saint Louis offered a clearly defined alliance against the Muslims and promised to give the Christians Jerusalem and the holy sites. However, the Mongols' recent conquest of Syria from the Muslims cast serious doubt on their intentions in the Holy Land. The repetition in Hülegü's letter of the condition that the Christians recognize Mongol suzerainty provided them with a reason or a pretext to reject his offer.[132]

Third, there was the military and political situation. The Greeks had reconquered Constantinople in 1261 and put an end to the Latin Empire in Byzantium. The land route and the northern shores of the eastern Mediterranean were under their control. Access to them had become risky.

Last and not least, the Mameluke sultan Baybars' victories in Palestine and the Latin reconquest of a part of the coastal region of the Holy Land signaled an exacerbation and an acceleration of the Muslim threat against the holy sites.

How should we understand Saint Louis' choice of Tunis as his first destination for the crusade? Historians have often pointed to pressure placed on him by his brother, Charles d'Anjou, who had become king of Sicily and who was anxious to control the two shores of the Straits of Sicily which were the main passage between the eastern and western Mediterranean. My impression is that it was rather the convenience of using Sicily as a base that influenced Saint Louis' choice, and not any direct pressure from Charles who was above all interested in the Byzantine Empire. In my hypothesis that the crusade was supposed to be more one of expiation and conversion than of conquest, the sultan of Tunis probably appeared as a favorable religious target because their illusions of converting a great Muslim leader seem to have shifted from the sultans and emirs of the Orient to the chief of Tunis at some time in the 1260s. Finally, the ignorance of geography Saint Louis and the French shared with all of their contemporaries may have played a role as well: they may have believed that Tunis was much closer to Egypt than it actually was and therefore that they could have used it as a good land base for a subsequent attack against the sultan.[133]

FINAL PURIFICATIONS BEFORE THE CRUSADE

With the approach of the departure date in 1270, new calls for acts of purification multiplied. An edict of 1268 or 1269 again forbade and repressed "villainous swearing," blasphemy in other words. It represented an act of divine lese-majesty to which the king was particularly sensitive because of the importance that he, like his century, gave to the more and more widespread expression and idea of lese-majesty for the construction of the monarchical state. The king specified that the edict must be observed "on the king's lands, on the lands of his lords, and in the cities of the commons," in other words throughout the entire kingdom.[134]

In 1269, another edict obligated Jews to attend the sermons of converting preachers and to wear strips of felt or scarlet cloth. This degrading mark was the forerunner of the yellow star. It corresponded to other medieval practices that applied signs of infamy and characterized a society steeped in symbolic denunciation. Louis IX was obeying a call from the papacy asking Christian rulers to apply this measure that had been adopted by the Fourth Lateran Council (1215) at the behest of a Dominican who was probably a converted Jew.[135]

Finally, one week before setting sail, Louis sent a letter from Aigues-Mortes dated June 25, 1270 to his "lieutenants," the abbot of Saint-Denis Mathieu de Vendôme and Simon de Nesle. In the letter, he advised them to deal harshly with the "polluters" of the kingdom, which included blasphemers, prostitutes, criminals, and other villains.

The campaign for preaching the crusade was also very active.[136] Additional encouragement was probably needed insofar as feelings of hostility toward the crusades were growing.[137] Joinville himself refused to take part. He alleged that during the crusade in Egypt sergeants of the king of France and the king of Navarre, who was also the count of Champagne, "destroyed and impoverished his people," and that if he were to crusade again, he would be opposing God's will, because God had given him the responsibility of protecting and "saving his own people."[138]

Thus Christendom turned inward upon itself. Serving God no longer meant going overseas but working inside of Christian Europe. The Holy Land lay beyond the borders of Christendom, and rare were those like Saint Louis who viewed the Mediterranean as a sea that lay within the Christian world. The poet Rutebeuf, a partisan of the crusades, praised Saint Louis' attitude, although elsewhere he attacked his devotion for the Mendicant friars. His poems, particularly "*La disputaison du croisé et du décroisé*," clearly express the debate that was stirring throughout the Christian world.[139]

The material preparations for the crusade were as rigorous as for the previous one. The financial preparations again depended on the raising of urban "*tailles*" and ecclesiastical tithes. The king also relied on loans made through the intermediary of the Templars. His brothers and in particular, Alphonse de Poitiers, also made intensive preparations.[140]

Their diplomatic preparations were less successful than they had been for the Egyptian crusade. After Pope Clement IV's death on November 29, 1268, the vacancy on the pontifical throne lasted until 1271. On the eve of the crusade of Tunis, Christendom had no pope. King Jaime I of Aragon wanted to be the first to leave in 1269, but for Acre. His flotilla was caught in a storm and he abandoned the project. Only the eldest son of the king of England took up the cross, but he left from Aigues-Mortes three months after Saint Louis.

The crusade of Tunis was nonetheless an event marked by significant innovations. Annoyed with the conditions that the Venetians wanted to impose, Saint Louis relied mainly on the Genoese for building his fleet. Instead of renting the ships as he had previously done, he had them build boats that he would own himself. Instead of giving the command of the fleet to two Genoese as he had done in 1248, he named a Frenchman admiral for the first time in French history. His admiral was the Picardian lord Florent de Verennes, although it was not until the rule of Philip the Fair that the French military navy was born on the northern seas in service against the English and the Flemish.

The crusade of Tunis also introduced an attempt to better organize royal administration in the king's absence. They created a special royal seal: *Si(gillum) Ludovici Dei G(ratia) Francor(um) reg(is) in partibus trans-marinis agentis* (Seal of Louis, king of the French by the grace of God on an expedition overseas). The reverse side had an image of the crown whose newly acquired symbolic relevance was aptly emphasized: "The adopted design [for the seal] says a lot about the meaning that the symbol of the crown had assumed thanks to the work of the jurists in the royal entourage."[141] Again, Louis wanted to put as many things as possible in order before his departure. He made his will and testament at the beginning of 1270. It was basically a list of bequests to religious houses. He drew up his list of advice (*Enseignements*) for his son Philip and his daughter Isabelle at an unknown date. In the previous year he had taken a tour of the royal domain just as he had done before the crusade of 1248: he thus obtained the favor of prayers in exchange for the gift of relics, for instance to the bishop of Clermont, the Dominicans of Rouen, and a convent in Dijon. He sought out opportunities to repair injustices in places that he had rarely visited like Ham in Picardy, Meaux, Vendôme, and Tours. In March, he made arrangements for the government of the kingdom in his absence. With his royal seal, he entrusted "the upkeep, the defense, and the administration of the kingdom" to the abbot of Saint-Denis Mathieu de Vendôme and Simon de Nesle, his oldest and closest advisor. Although it is surprising that there was no mention of Queen Marguerite and the highest-ranking prelates in this document, I think we must draw the same conclusion as Jean Richard that "the king of France was bent on confiding government leadership to the people who were the most closely involved in exercising it in order to assure the continuity of its actions; this is probably a sign of the importance that the State had assumed in Saint Louis' time."[142] To the recently appointed bishop of Paris, Étienne Tempier, he entrusted the right of granting ecclesiastical honors, prebends, and benefices. These were all at the king's disposal upon the advice of the chancellor of the church of Paris, the prior of the Dominicans, and the guardian of the Franciscans of Paris — the chapter of Notre Dame, the Preaching Friars, and the Minors. Together they formed Saint Louis' trio in charge of religious affairs in Paris.

His departure repeated the one he made in 1248. On March 14, 1270, the king went to Saint-Denis to take the banner and the pilgrim's staff. Their raising signified the royal army's departure on a campaign. On March 15, he marched barefoot to the Palais de la Cité at Notre-Dame-de-Paris. He bade Queen Marguerite adieu at the castle of Vincennes and left from there. The stages of the voyage were punctuated by stops at important sanctuaries including Villeneuve-Saint-Georges, Melun, Sens, Auxerre, Vézelay, Cluny, Mâcon, Vienne, and Beaucaire. The other crusaders joined the king and his three sons at Aigues-Mortes. With them was his powerful son-in-law, Thibaud de Navarre. While waiting for the ships, a battle broke out between the Catalans and Provençals on one side and the French on the other. There were a hundred casualties. Louis had the individuals found responsible for the fracas hung. He finally set sail on the *Montjoie* on July 1, 1270.

As we already know, the "passage to Tunis" was Saint Louis' last march with the cross. The nightmare of Egypt happened all over again, but this time it was worse. After a brief stop in Sardinia, instead of Sicily as originally planned (it was a secret they kept until the last minute[143]), the king landed at La Goulette near Tunis on July 17. The landing was a success,[144] but any hope of converting the Muslim emir was very quickly wiped out for everyone but Louis who refused to give up hope. Once more, an outbreak of dysentery or typhus, the Mediterranean scourge, spread among the army of crusaders. Following the death of his son, Jean-Tristan, on August 3, Saint Louis died in turn on August 25.

There are many more or less official accounts of his death. I refer you to the one given by his confessor, Geoffroy de Beaulieu, who was an eyewitness:

> Shortly after [the death of his son Jean-Tristan on August 3, which everyone tried to conceal from him, but which he learned of with great sadness[145]], God's will that wanted his tribulations to end happily and to give him the glorious fruit of those good tribulations felled him under the stroke of continuous fever, and, as the illness grew worse, he received the final sacraments of the Church very Christianly and very devoutly in full consciousness and of sane mind. When we showed him the sacrament of the last unction while reciting the seven psalms with a litany, he recited the verses of the psalms himself and named the saints in the litany, very devoutly invoking their aid. While the outer signs indicated that he was reaching the end, he had no concerns other than the affairs of God and the exaltation of the Christian faith. As he had trouble speaking and could

only speak to us in a hushed voice as we stood around him with ears turned to hear his words, this truly Catholic man full of God said: "Let us try, for the love of God, to preach and implant the Catholic faith in Tunis. Oh! What skilled preacher could we send there!" Then, he named a Preaching Friar who had gone there under somewhat different circumstances and who was known to the king of Tunis. This is how this truly faithful man of God, this steady and enthusiastic practitioner of the Christian faith finished his holy life in confession of the true faith. As the strength of his body and voice gradually faded, he still did not stop asking for the support of the saints to whom he was especially devoted for as long as his strength allowed him to speak and especially for Saint-Denis, the patron saint of his kingdom. In this condition, we heard him repeat the prayer for Saint-Denis several times in a soft murmur: "We pray to you Lord, for your love, and to give us the grace needed to reject earthly prosperity and to not fear adversity." He repeated these words several times. He also repeated the beginning of the apostle Saint James's prayer several times: "Be, O Lord, the sanctifier and the guardian of your people,"[146] and he devoutly recalled the memory of other saints. This servant of God, laid out on a bed of ashes spread out in the form of the cross rendered his last joyful breath to the Creator, and it was at the exact time that the Son of God expired while dying on the cross for the world's salvation.[147]

Thus the Christ-king died in the eternal present of Jesus' salvational death. According to one tradition, the night before his death he murmured: "We will go unto Jerusalem."

Toward Sainthood

From Death to Canonization

(1270–1297)

There was King Louis IX, dead in the land of the infidels. There was no question of leaving his remains on these hostile grounds outside of Christendom and far from his Kingdom of France. They had to repatriate his cadaver. To do this they used a procedure employed since the time of Charles the Bald in the ninth century whenever a ruler died far from the royal necropolis and either they could not or did not want to bury him near the place where he died. They preserved his body. Because they had not yet mastered embalming techniques, they boiled the body in wine mixed with water so that the flesh came off the bones, which were the most precious parts of the body to be saved.

The technical problem in this case was accompanied by an even more serious political problem. Charles d'Anjou, the king of Sicily, arrived with his fleet and army shortly after his brother's death. (One legendary story has it that he set sail at the very moment of the king's death.) He tried to impose himself as leader of the army in opposition to his younger inexperienced nephew Philip III. Spurred on no doubt by his father's advisors who were there, the young king did not hesitate to assert his own authority. Just as they could not bury his father quickly at Saint-Denis, it would be months before the young king could be crowned at Reims. He therefore made the barons and other military leaders around him swear an oath of loyalty on August 27. On September 12, he sent two messengers to Mathieu de Vendôme and Simon de Nesle to confirm the powers his father had entrusted to him. He also sent them Louis IX's testament and authorized them to continue using the seal the dead king left them but to replace his father's name in the inscription with his own. In fact, people began to date the acts of his rule starting from the date of his father's death on August 25, 1270. Thus they resolved the delicate problem of the interregnum by following Louis IX's provisions and the established means of assuring the continuity of the French monarchy that had already been worked out.

The fate of the royal cadaver then became a political stake between Charles d'Anjou and his young nephew Philip III. Each first proposed his own solution to the problem, and each solution corresponded to a different but reasonable point of view. Philip wanted his father's remains to be repatriated to France as quickly as possible. However, the voyage of such an important "cadaver" could not be taken lightly. Charles proposed that they send his brother's remains to be kept in his Kingdom of Sicily. The argument seemed practical. The island was nearby, and the voyage would be quick. He and his successors could watch over the king's remains. Of course, there was also a certain political calculation behind this commonsensical argument. Political rumors had it that Louis IX had a good chance of becoming an official saint. It would be an incredible source of prestige and material gain for the Angevin dynasty in Sicily to have these relics on its soil. The chroniclers inform us that the two kings, the uncle and his nephew, finally worked out a more sensible ["*sage,*" "*saine,*" "*sanior*"] solution. First, the two monarchs agreed to a compromise: the king's flesh and entrails would be given to the king of Sicily, while his bones would go to the royal necropolis in Saint-Denis. No doubt supported by the prelates and important French leaders, the young king put up a good fight. He won the most important prize, the bones that were likely to become relics in and of themselves, the hard part of the cadaver in opposition to the soft flesh and guts in this corporal dialectic of the hard and the soft, which symbolically reprersented a dialectic of power. There was still a question about the heart. According to certain witnesses like Geoffroy de Beaulieu, Philip III would have been happy to let his uncle take it to Monreale along with the entrails. According to other more credible testimony, he brought it along with the bones to Saint-Denis. We actually do know that the monks of Saint-Denis believed that kings' hearts were supposed to stay together with their skeletal remains,[1] and a seventeenth-century inscription on Saint-Denis' tomb attests to the presence of his heart inside. According to Louis Carolus-Barré, who interprets the texts in a way that I think is a bit forced, "the army demanded that his 'heart' remain in Africa among the combatants, and we do not really know what became of it."[2] Another highly questionable hypothesis claims that the sainted king's heart was deposited in the Sainte-Chapelle.[3]

Philip also rallied behind the idea that they should not send his father's cadaver ahead and risk exposing it to all kinds of dangers. He wanted to wait until he, the new king, was able to accompany it himself in a military convoy, with an army of men who already felt that it was "holy" ["*saint*," saintly], and that it would be a form of protection and, if I dare say, a good luck charm.

They then proceeded to dismember the royal cadaver. The various testimonies converge at this point, although some of them differ in their details. According to Geoffroy de Beaulieu: "The fleshy parts of his body were boiled and separated from his bones."[4] According to Primat: "The king's valets and all his servants [*ministres*] and those whose job it was to carry out this task took the king's body and cut it apart member by member and cooked it in wine and water so long that the bones came out all white and clean of flesh so that they could be taken apart cleanly without using any force."[5]

After several military skirmishes and diplomatic exchanges, the Christians signed an accord with the emir of Tunis on October 30. The emir received a guarantee that the crusaders would leave his territory and give back the lands they occupied in exchange for a war indemnity, the freedom of Christian merchants to trade in Tunisia, and the right of Christian priests to preach and pray in the churches there.

THE RETURN TO FRANCE

On November 11, the Christian army re-embarked, and the fleet dropped anchor in the port of Trapani in Sicily on the fourteenth. The king and queen of France set sail on the fifteenth with a large number of other passengers on board. Then, on the night of the November 15 or 16 a terrible storm broke and destroyed most of the fleet. The return trip was made under the protection of the skeletal remains of Louis IX and his son Jean-Tristan whose body had been boiled in the same way. Their bones were placed in small coffins. Louis IX's was transported on two bars suspended between the backs of two horses. A third coffin contained the body of the deceased king's chaplain, Pierre de Villebéon. New grief descended upon the royal family at Trapani. Louis IX's son-in-law, Thibaud de Champagne, king of Navarre, died in turn. The cortege grew by one more coffin. They soon made a fifth coffin for the new queen of France. The young Isabelle of Aragon, Philip III's wife, fell off her horse on January 11, 1271 while crossing a flooded river in Calabria. She prematurely gave birth that day to a stillborn child and died on January 30.

The young king and his army slowly rode up the Italian peninsula with their coffins, passing through Rome, Viterbo where the cardinals had not managed to elect a new pope, Montefiascone, Orvieto, Florence, Bologna, Modena, Parma, Cremona, Milan, and Vercelli. They crossed the Alps near Mount-Cenis at the feet of the Susa. They ascended the valley of Maurienne and then passed through Lyon, Mâcon, Cluny, Châlons, and Troyes before finally arriving in Paris on May 21, 1271. The new king left two more coffins behind him. They were those of his uncle Alphonse de Poitiers and his wife Jeanne who died a day apart in Italy. They were buried in the cathedral of Savona. They put Louis IX's coffin on display at Notre-Dame-de-Paris and the funeral ceremony took place at Saint-Denis on May 22, almost nine months after the king's death and at a time of disturbing conflicts between the Parisian clergy and the monks of Saint-Denis.

TOWARD CANONIZATION

A new period commenced in the saga of the dead and buried king's existence. His body had already accomplished miracles. His entrails had also accomplished numerous miracles in devout Sicily, a land rich in popular miracles. The Church recognized two of them. It accepted two others that occurred during the coffin's passage through northern Italy in Parma and at Reggio d'Emilie, along with a third that took place at Bonneuil-sur-

Marne on the outskirts of Paris. Other miracles proliferated at Saint-Denis
following the traditional occurrence of miracles accomplished at the tombs
of saints.

For almost a century, however, renown alone was not enough to earn
saints lasting recognition in Christendom. The Roman curia reserved for
itself the right to make saints. In the words of Jean-Claude Schmitt, it became a "saint-making factory." It made them (or refused to make them) in
the course of a long process, the canonization proceeding. This was a procedure of juridical inquiry that often took on a political character because
the Roman curia was a political force whose decision to canonize an individual was an instrument of power. In order to open and close a canonization proceeding it was necessary to have solid lobbying groups in addition
to a good record. Three factors acted in support of Louis IX's canonization: his fame (*bona fama, vox populi*), the Capetian house, and the Church
of France. To these we must add the religious orders he had supported
and with whom he had maintained close relations: the Cistercians, the Dominicans, and the Franciscans. This was a lot of support, and yet Louis IX
had to wait twenty-seven years after his death until he was canonized. The
waiting period was extended by the deaths of a number of popes, none of
whom stayed long on the pontifical throne. After the death of each pope,
they had to start the proceeding anew from its earliest phases. The length
of time also grew longer as a result of the switch between pontiffs who
were favorable and others who were less receptive and moved slowly on
the record.[6]

The first move to canonize Louis IX fell upon Gregory X, who was
elected on September 1, 1271, after the office had been unoccupied for quite
some time. Theobaldo Visconti de Plaisance was not a cardinal. He was in
the Holy Land at the time. After his arrival at Viterbo, his first pontifical act
was to write to the Dominican, Geoffroy de Beaulieu, Louis IX's confessor,
on March 4, 1272. He wrote to ask him to provide as much information as
possible about his royal penitent whom he admired intensely and considered
a "true model for all Christian rulers." A pontiff obsessed with the crusades,
Gregory X was fascinated by the royal crusade. In several weeks or months,
Geoffroy de Beaulieu wrote up a report that had fifty-two chapters on Louis'
life and conduct. He concluded that in his opinion the deceased king was
worthy of being officially recognized as a saint.[7] Gregory X undoubtedly
also spoke with Philip III about his father's proceeding that he wanted to

open soon when the king came to visit him at Lyon in March 1274 before the opening of the Second Ecumenical Council of Lyon (May 7–July 17, 1274). For the time being, however, the Council occupied all of the pope's attention. Pressure groups became more active in the following year. We possess three texts sent to the pope to ask him to hasten the opening of Louis IX's canonization process. One was from the archbishop of Reims and his suffragan bishops (June 1275). Another came from the archbishop of Sens and his suffragans (July 1275). The last was from the prior of the Dominicans of the "province" of France (September 1275). The whole affair took on a "national" dimension that became more and more acute. Gregory next asked his cardinal-legate in France, Simon de Brie, Louis IX's former advisor and chancellor, to open up a *secret* inquiry on the deceased king. Simon de Brie proceeded quickly, too quickly, because he would be blamed for botching the affair, which required a minute examination. Then, Gregory X died on January 10, 1276.

Three different popes succeeded him on the pontifical throne in less than a year-and-a-half. At the end of 1277, Nicolas III asked for the records on the miracles. When Philip III sent him an urgent embassy on the matter, he responded that he needed more detailed documentation, however persuaded he may already have been about Louis' sainthood. He ordered Simon de Brie to conduct a new supplementary investigation, which would be *public* this time. Simon de Brie recruited the help of two priors, one a Franciscan, the other a Dominican, the prior of Saint-Denis, and two other religious. They sent the results to the pope who confided the examination to two cardinals. However, the new pope died in turn on August 22, 1280. Simon de Brie succeeded him as Pope Martin IV. He decisively injected the proceeding with new life. A new assembly of the Church of France sent him an urgent supplication. He answered by assuring the prelates of his good intentions and reminding them of the importance of proceeding by the rules in an orderly fashion. Then Louis IX's sainthood could be established all the more firmly. On December 23, 1281, Martin IV entrusted the final [*solenelle*] investigation into Louis' life, manners [*conversatio*], and miracles to the archbishop of Rouen and the bishops of Auxerre and Spoleto. He asked them to go on location to Saint-Denis to investigate the miracles people said had been taking place at Louis' tomb and he sent them the outline for a questionnaire to use in interrogating the witnesses. The interviews lasted from May 1282 until March 1283. The investigators would hear testimony about the miracles from 330 witnesses, most of whom were poor folk. They heard testimony from thirty-eight people about his life, and these witnesses were powerful figures, starting with his brother King Charles of Anjou (whose deposition was taken at Naples), his two sons King Philip III and Count Pierre d'Alençon, Mathieu de Vendôme and Simon de Nesle the kingdom's two regents during the crusade of Tunis, a number of knights including the king's friend and future biographer Joinville, religious, and even three Hospitaler nuns.

The records were all sent to Rome, but the affair took another turn when Martin IV died on March 28, 1285. His successor, Honorius IV, read and discussed some of the miracles in his consistory, but he passed away on April 3, 1287. Nicolas IV (1288–1292), a Franciscan, nominated a new commission of three cardinals (the ones on the former commission had all died) to undertake a minute examination of the miracles, but the examination did not conclude before his death. The pontifical throne stayed empty for more than a year-and-a-half when the Benedictine Celestin V was elected due to an inadvertence. He soon realized he was not cut out for the job, resigned, and returned to his hermitage after several months in 1294. This unique situation that Dante called "the great refusal" tacked on several more lost months.

The situation changed for good with the election of Cardinal Benoît Caetani on December 24, 1294. He took the name of Boniface VIII. He decided to bring the proceeding to a close. As a cardinal, he had taken the deposition from King Charles d'Anjou and had been a part of the commission that examined the miracles. He seems to have sincerely believed in Louis' sainthood, but the main motive for his decision was political. He wanted to establish good relations with Louis IX's grandson, King Philip IV the Fair of France, who became his worst enemy several years later.

On August 4, 1297, at Orvieto, which was one of the pope's residences as it had been for his predecessors, fearing the rivalries between the great families and the outbursts of the populace in Rome, Boniface VIII announced his decision to canonize the king. He dedicated a second sermon to Louis IX on August 11, and the papal bull, *Gloria, laus,* pronounced the official canonization. It fixed Saint Louis' celebration day on the anniversary of his death, August 25. Now all the individual efforts in the king's life and all the hopes upheld by the Capetian dynasty for more than two centuries were finally crowned with success. The Kingdom of France had a sainted king.

Born during a period of mourning, dead in a foreign land of infidels, the king had full glory at last. On August 25, 1298, an official ceremony was held at Saint-Denis in the presence of the king, the new saint's grandson, Philip IV the Fair, many of the people who testified in the canonization proceeding including Joinville, and as many prelates, barons, clerics, knights, bourgeois, and common people as the basilica could hold. During the ceremony, Saint Louis' bones were "elevated" and placed in a shrine behind the altar.

THE HISTORY OF THE RELICS

I have no intention of recounting the fate of Saint Louis' memory and image from 1297 to the present day. That is a vast and beautiful subject that may explain the history of another memory, the active memory of the French nation.[8] However, I would like to discuss the curious and dramatic fate of Saint Louis' bodily remains.

The sainted king's bones were deposited in the shrine behind the main altar at Saint-Denis on August 25, 1298. Following a custom of the time, the kings of France who succeeded Saint Louis made gifts of these relics by offering one of their ancestor's bones to various churches or important persons. Philip the Fair pursued this political use of the relics in an almost maniacal way. Saint Louis' grandson wanted to have his grandfather's relics transferred from Saint-Denis to the Sainte-Chapelle so that he could enjoy them more in his royal palace, which he was putting through a magnificent expansion.

The relics of saints were objects of impassioned worship in the Middle Ages.[9] While a critique of "false" relics had been developing in the Church for a long time, at least since the end of the eleventh century, belief in the virtues of "true" relics remained fervent and widespread regardless of one's social class or education. They healed people. They achieved their effects when people touched the tomb or the shrine that contained them. When he was alive, Saint Louis only healed the scrofulous by touching them. Touching the relics could heal anything, at least in theory. Their power was not simply thaumaturgical; it was miraculous. The prestige of Saint-Denis grew considerably as a result of being the site for this royal miracle renewed, extended, and perpetuated. Philip the Fair, however, wanted to confiscate these extraordinary relics for his own private chapel and personal gain. From the origins of its march toward absolutism, the French monarchy wanted to keep the people away from the virtues of Saint Louis' relics. Pope Boniface VIII always tried to maintain good relations with the king of France. He authorized the king to go ahead with this transfer, specifying that he leave an arm or a tibia behind for the monks of Saint-Denis. The monks, however, would not be had. Philip the Fair had to renounce his project, although he did get a part of what he wanted. After the violent conflict with Boniface VIII, relations improved between the king of France and the new pope, Clement V, the Frenchman Bertrand de Got. Philip attended Clement's coronation ceremony in Lyon in November 1305 and got him to agree to approve the transfer of Saint Louis' head to the Sainte-Chapelle, minus his chin, teeth, and lower jaw, which were left to the monks of Saint-Denis as a consolation prize. The heart may have been transferred to the Sainte-Chapelle as well.

Elizabeth Brown has judiciously remarked that numerous peoples considered the head as the most important part of a person's body and the center of one's strength and identity. For many of the same peoples, the lower jaw was often considered the second most important part of the human body. From the fourteenth century on, a macabre pun justified the transfer by claiming that it was a good and legitimate thing for the sainted king's head to have been transported to a place (the holy chapel of the royal palace) that was itself considered to be "the head of the kingdom" (*caput regni*). Betraying his unflinching intention, in 1299 Philip the Fair ordered a magnificent shrine from a reputed Parisian goldsmith, Guillaume Julien, to hold the skull in the Sainte-Chapelle. The ceremonial transfer from Saint-Denis to Paris took place on May 17, 1306. Notre-Dame-de-Paris also had its consolation prize, receiving one of the holy king's ribs.

The monks of Saint-Denis received certain forms of compensation. In 1300, Boniface VIII allowed them to celebrate the anniversary of the saint's death on August 25 with a ceremonial festival each year. Philip the Fair tried to attend on a regular basis. After the skull's transfer to the Sainte-Chapelle in 1306, the one person that the monks reviled as the king's damned soul in this affair, the bishop of Auxerre Pierre de Monay, suddenly died on May 29. In the meantime, Philip the Fair was unable to attend the ceremony of August 25 due to a leg wound he received while hunting. The Dionysians interpreted this as a sign of divine punishment. They had a superb reliquary constructed for the parts of Saint Louis' head that were still in their possession, and it was formally inaugurated on August 25, 1307 in the presence of Philip the Fair and a crowd of prelates and barons.

Despite all this, the division of Saint Louis' skeleton had not ended. Philip the Fair and his successors gave parts of his finger bones to Haakon Magnusson, the king of Norway, for the church dedicated to the sanctified king that he had built on the isle of Tysoen near Bergen. Among the first beneficiaries were the canons of Notre-Dame-de-Paris, the Dominicans of Paris and Reims, and the abbeys of Royaumont and Pontoise. The queen of Sweden received a reliquary containing several fragments bound for the monastery of Sainte-Brigitte in Vadstena during a visit to Paris made between 1330 and 1340. During his voyage to Paris in 1378, Emperor Charles IV received several other pieces that he sent to the cathedral of Prague. In 1392, they placed Saint Louis' remaining bones in a new shrine. On this occasion, Charles VI gave a rib to Master Pierre d'Ailly to take to the pope, two ribs for the dukes of Berry and Burgundy, and one bone for the prelates who attended the ceremony to share among themselves. Around 1430, Louis VII, the duke of Bavaria, received some of the remains for the church in his capital, Ingolstadt. In 1568, all of the remaining bones were brought together in Paris for a formal procession against the Protestants. In September 1610, Marie de Medici was given one bone, but remorse plagued her and she gave it back during Louis XIII's coronation ceremony. Anne of Austria only received a small piece of a rib in 1616. She complained and was given an entire rib the following year. She later solicited Cardinal de Guise in order to obtain another rib and an arm bone for the Jesuits of Paris and Rome. During the exhumations of the royal cadavers at Saint-Denis and the destruction of their remains, people found that Saint Louis' tomb was empty, obviously because his bones had already been moved to the shrine in 1298.[10] This shrine must have been destroyed and whatever was left of the bones dispersed or obliterated.

What is left of Saint Louis' relics? Only a small enamel fragment still remains from the shrine that held Saint Louis' head in the Sainte-Chapelle. It is preserved in the cabinet of Medals in the National Library in Paris. The lower jaw and the rib kept at Notre-Dame-de-Paris did not escape the fragmentation of the relics. In 1926, the archbishop of Paris offered another piece of the rib to the Church of Saint-Louis-de-France in Montreal. The basilica at Saint-Denis displays one of Saint Louis' bones in the apsidal chapel of the Virgin. The date and conditions of its acquisition are unknown. In 1941, the Memorial Society for Saint-Denis ordered a new reliquary to house it, and the relic's transfer in its new shrine was occasion for another formal ceremony in 1956.[11]

The fate of Saint Louis' heart has been of interest to scholars since the nineteenth century. During work on the Sainte-Chapelle in 1843, pieces of a heart were found near the altar. Some came out with the hypothesis that these were fragments of the sainted king's heart, and a sharp polemic on the subject divided the main scholars of the time.[12] I have adopted Alain Erlande-Brandenburg's opinion on this matter: "The lack of any inscription, the fact that none of the chronicles ever mentioned this burial, the complete forgetfulness in which this precious relic would have to have fallen, all justify our rejection of this identification."[13] He adds that there is no reason to doubt the inscription that could still be read on Saint Louis' tomb at Saint-Denis in the seventeenth century: "Enclosed here are the viscera of Saint Louis, king of France."[14] Moreover, as the entrails had been sent to Monreale in Sicily, this inscription can only refer to the heart, which, as we have already seen, Philip III had decided to send to Saint-Denis with the bones when he was in Tunisia. Because it had not been transferred with the bones in the shrine in 1298, it must have fallen apart in the tomb before the Revolution when any remaining fragments might have escaped the attention of Dom Perrier and the destroyers of 1793.

Finally, the fate of the entrails is rather surprising. They had remained at Monreale in Sicily until 1860. Then they were taken away into exile by François II, the last Bourbon king of Sicily, when he was thrown out by Garibaldi's Thousand. He took the precious entrails to Gaeta where he retired, and then to Rome. When he had to leave Rome for Paris, stopping in the castle that Emperor Franz-Joseph of Austria let him use, he deposited the relics in this castle's chapel. In his testament written in 1894, he bequeathed the reliquary with the entrails to Cardinal Lavigerie and the Dominican fathers for their cathedral in Carthage. Thus Saint Louis' entrails made their way back to the site of the saint king's death.[15]

The partition of Saint Louis' cadaver took place in 1270. With the bull *Detestandae feritatis,* Pope Boniface VIII forbade such practices in the future, describing them as barbarous and monstrous.[16] A new feeling of respect for the integrity of the human body, even reduced to a cadaver, began to appear, although in France, notably, it conflicted with another growing sentiment concerning the bodies of kings and important figures: the desire for multiple sepulchers (a tomb for the body, a tomb for the heart, a tomb for the entrails) in different locations that would multiply the presence of their physical memory. The desire for prestige in Old Regime society, fed by a taste for the macabre and an excessive funerary art that prolonged pagan traditions, prevailed for a long time over a concept of respect for the human body that the Church failed to impose on the upper echelon of the social ladder. This monarchical custom favored the distribution of Saint Louis' bones once they became relics.

The Production of
Royal Memory:
Did Saint Louis Exist?

INTRODUCTION

Now that we have seen Saint Louis live and die, we have reached the point where we have to ask ourselves whether we can go any further and try to know who he was. I have told the story of his life as the historian must do, solely with the help of the only existing original documents of the time. Still, the memories of witnesses offer varying degrees of uncertainty, shaped as they are by individual and collective interests. Although it was still full of banter in the eighteenth century, even history that tries to be truthful or "scientific" voluntarily or involuntarily depends on the situation and objectives of the people who write it. History is still dependent on the people who produce and construct it in order to write it and on their act of writing it. Because this is the history of a king and, moreover, the history of a saint— of a king whom many people wanted to have recognized as a saint—the force and extent of their manipulations must have been considerable. To be sure that we have some hope of reaching an adequate understanding of the individual (saint) Louis IX, we have to conduct a careful study of how and why his memory was produced.

The project that I am proposing to my readers extends beyond what professional historians traditionally call "criticism of sources." The goal is to determine whether we can know anything more than the expressions of the interests of the different individuals and milieus who produced historical memory in thirteenth-century Christendom and the means of its production at that time. We can only attempt to learn this by means of documents, the only authentic material available in the historian's work. Is it really Saint Louis that we understand as an outcome of this research, or can we learn only about how the people who had the reasons and the material and intellectual resources to bequeath him to our memory had neither the desire nor the ability to allow us to know Saint Louis as an individual person, the person whom today we have a legitimate desire to know and understand? Did they just construct a model of a king, an ideal type of saint, or this specific king and this specific saint, a person who actually existed? Therefore, in order to continue our quest for Saint Louis, we have to radically question our endeavor. Did the Saint Louis of our documents exist? Did Saint Louis exist at all if the Saint Louis of the records is the only one we have?

However I try to explain Saint Louis and reach an adequate understanding of him, whatever my efforts to approach him as a historian—and as a historian who benefits from the significant progress that this profession has made since the Middle Ages—I cannot pretend that this Saint Louis from the sources is not also "my" Saint Louis. Not that the purpose of this work is to propose a subjective image of Saint Louis. I will not discuss the problem of historical truth here. However, I do believe that the historian's profession is a profession that deals with truth and that utilizes "scientific" methods, in other words methods that are demonstrable and verifiable. Still, I am neither so naïve or vain as to believe that "my" Saint Louis is the "real" Saint Louis. Without wanting to bore my readers with this implicit self-criticism, throughout this book from beginning to end I have striven to account for my own situation, my own professional formation, and my own personal tendencies in the production of "my Saint Louis."

In the second part of this book I also implicitly apply one of Marc Bloch's statements to myself in this work: "The historian is nothing like a free man" (*l'historien n'a rien d'un homme libre*).[1]

We have to try to answer a series of questions now. What documents involuntarily provide us with information about Saint Louis? Which documents result instead from a desire to convey a certain image or a certain idea of him to posterity? What did his contemporaries consider "memorable" about him? What information about him did they think was worthy of entering our collective memory? What were the main centers involved in the production of royal memory? What were their conscious and unconscious interests? What networks of tradition relayed Saint Louis' memory? And what do these documents fail to mention that we would want to know? This last question appears today on any typical questionnaire about important people or even any typical individuals. What is the particular formation of the propaganda and omissions in which the memory of Saint Louis that has been handed down to us has been embedded?

The King from
the Official Documents

HISTORY HAS RELEGATED THE USE OF ADMINISTRATIVE SOURCES TO approach rulers and governments to the background for a long time, limiting it to the secondary role of history's so-called "auxiliary" sciences along with chronology, diplomatic history, and sigillography. Without meaning to make a bad pun, however, it constitutes a royal path to understanding the realities of power through its routine practices. The relationships that kings had with writing, with the customs of the chancery, with the rules for establishing and using expressions for their will and sovereignty, with the conservation of archival records that provided one of the major foundations for their power, are part and parcel of their personalities and biographies. Saint Louis' person expressed itself through this administrative activity. He existed through it and it is at least in part thanks to it that he continues to exist for us. Through all these witnesses he does not appear as the same king as his grandfather Philip Augustus or his grandson Philip the Fair.[1]

The first category of information about Saint Louis is made up of the official documents that bear his mark or name. Today, rulers write or at least sign some of the important official acts of government and delegate their signatures for the less important documents. In the thirteenth century, people did not sign documents. A king had no signature, but a seal carried out the signature's function.[2] Just as the king was the only sovereign, the great royal seal was the only one that could confer full authority upon the acts that it sealed. There was only one in existence at any given time. Even if they used the matrix from the seal of the preceding king, the inscription with the sovereign's name appeared on it as soon as the new king assumed power and only stopped being used when he died, unless for some exceptional reason the king decided to change seals in the middle of his reign. The fabrication of the matrix for a royal seal was a "long, costly, and delicate labor" (M. Pastoureau). A great seal is also called a "seal of majesty" [*sceau de majesté*] because the king appears on it seated in a pose that art historians have identified with majesty—the supreme and mysterious power of the king alone. When a great seal was no longer used, normally after the ruler's death, they destroyed it. Saint Louis was the first king to have a seal made for his absence from the kingdom, which was used while he was on the crusade. The seal of the distant king manifested the continuity of his power which could only be used by those to whom he had delegated that power. The seal remained in the chancellor's possession as he was normally the one who accompanied the king in all his travels through his kingdom. Another subaltern yet important officer, the *chauffe-cire* (wax-warmer), always followed the king, the chancellor, and the great seal during the ruler's travels.

The multiplication of the chancery's acts and the need to speed up the bureaucratic process led to new administrative practices. This happened specifically under Saint Louis around 1250. A hierarchy for the acts of the royal chancery took shape; it rated their importance by the way they were sealed. The charters or patent letters in the form of charters were acts sealed in green wax on a pattern of red and green silk.[3] Less official were the patent letters sealed in yellow wax on a double stem. Around 1250, patent letters sealed more easily in yellow wax on a single stem were usually called "*mandements*" from the word *mandamus,* which marked the royal decision in the initial pronouncement of the act. They constituted a diplomatic category of acts.[4] Finally, at the very end of the reign, they began to feel the need to add mentions of service that were noted "*hors de sceau*" (*sic signatum extra sigillum* [outside the seal]), and that diplomats called "*mentions hors de la teneur*" (outside the terms, i.e., off the record). The oldest existing example dates from December 30, 1269. It is a letter sealed with a single stem that Saint Louis used to announce a shipment of relics to the bishop of Clermont transported "by Friar Guillaume de Chartres." This last indication appears "*hors de la teneur.*"[5]

It is obviously very difficult to determine whether the production of royal acts resulted from the simple functioning of institutions or from a declared decision that was the sovereign's personal action. At best, we can determine that Louis IX was actually present in the places where the royal acts were dated, which would no longer be the case under Philip the Fair.[6] From this we can deduce that the king in all probability was at least aware of the content of these acts, and that they in turn allow us to follow the king's movements and visits.

One thing is certain here. The royal bureaucracy underwent a new phase of growth under Saint Louis. Saint Louis was a king of the written word. This increase was not only tied to the development of royal institutions, it also expressed Saint Louis' conception of his function, his duty to intervene in the kingdom's affairs, and his confidence in the efficiency of written acts as evidence of the official royal will.[7]

A quantitative leap marked the qualitative progress in royal administration under Philip Augustus. We can see this as a result of the better preservation of the royal archives brought on by the disastrous battle of Fréteval in 1194 when the records of the king of France fell into the hands of Richard the Lion-Hearted. It was probably also an effect of the increase in the number of acts due to the growth of the royal domain. We currently possess 701 of Philip Augustus's original acts that have been preserved (from his rule lasting forty-three years) compared to 96 for his grandfather Louis VI (who ruled for twenty-nine years), and 197 from the forty-three year reign of his father Louis VII. We have roughly 1,900 acts of all kinds from the reign of Philip Augustus, nearly double the number left by Louis VII. We should also remember that the number of preserved acts is only a fraction of those produced overall. In this respect, the French monarchy still lagged behind the pontifical monarchy, the most important and most precocious producer of written acts. They also trailed the English monarchy, which did a better job of preserving its records, although they continued to use the impractical roll for writing them down. The French had to wait for Philip the Fair to catch up with these others. Saint Louis' reign can be placed in the middle of this period during which the French were closing the gap.

Catalogs of the records of the acts of Henri I and Louis have been published in an unsystematic fashion; the records of the acts of Philip Augustus and Philip the Fair have been published in an exhaustive form. Unfortunately, the periods of Saint Louis and his son, Philip III, form a gap. In any case, it is not my intention to study these documents that teach us more about the institutions than about the king, but it will still prove useful to examine these official acts issued in his name and marked with his official seal. They yield valuable information about Saint Louis.

A majority of the acts of the chancery can be found in a record book called the *registrum Guarini* after the name of the chancellor Guérin, Philip Augustus's main advisor who died at the beginning of Saint Louis' reign. In 1220, Guérin decided to create this record book in order to combine and complete the two preceding ones.[8]

The acts transcribed into a registry form a chronological sequence. They situate the activities of the institution or individual figure, the royal chancery in this case, in time. Divided into seventeen chapters with blank folios for subsequent additions (which proves that the royal administration had a sense of the future), the Guérin registry was used until 1276. It thus covered all of Saint Louis' reign. We can sense the close personal tie between the king and this book of royal administrative memory when the sovereign took the record book with him on his crusade but only after wisely having a copy of it made, which was completed in May 1247 more than a year before his departure. As a symbol of his desire for governmental continuity (which also called for certain nuances in the depiction of the distant king), he had the acts of all the decisions he made between 1248 and 1255 in Egypt, the Holy Land, and the first months after his return to France copied down into it. Gérard de Sivery has suggested that Saint Louis brought it with him on his second crusade to Tunis because it contains acts dated in 1270.[9] Sivery recovered the evidence from this "patchwork" that represented royal pragmatism for a long time. By examining the registry he detected "additions, corrections, and innovations," but, most of all, roughly sketched out attempts to adapt royal politics to the evolution of socioeconomic structures, which can be seen for example in the attempts to substitute an assessment of fiefs' revenues in monetary terms for the simple enumeration of feudal charges. Saint Louis was king of the ineluctable emergence of a monetary economy. The unfinished condition of their attempts to enumerate royal resources is another sign of these failed efforts. The lists were left unfinished and they had to use the old lists.[10] The king was running behind and could not slow time's acceleration of this process.

Along with the record books, where Saint Louis basically continued the practices of Philip Augustus despite any vague attempts at innovation, there were also the chests called *layettes* that held the charters. The entire group of charters formed what people in the thirteenth century began to call the "Treasury" of the charters [*Trésor des chartes*]. The name is not lacking in significance. Saint Louis carried out an important accomplishment in this domain. After Fréteval, Philip Augustus decided to house the royal archives in a fixed location. Saint Louis gave them a sacred residence in the Sainte-Chapelle of his palace just above the treasury of the sacristy. The authentic written act became a precious object in the fashion of gold and gems.

The *layettes* contained the records of the king's relations with foreign rulers, important feudal lords of the kingdom, and other vassals in the form of treaties, declarations of allegiance, promises, and lists of food supplies [*cantines*], in other words all the titles that classify and authenticate the holdings of the crown, the king's active and passive correspondence—letters sent and received, copies, the reintegrated acts sent back from the Treasury under the name of *litterae redditae* or *recuperatae,* acts related to the great political affairs like Saint Louis' canonization, and records of the king's acquisitions.[11]

It seems difficult to draw information about Saint Louis' person from these documents, although it is still possible to note the classification of acts concerning a particular problem.[12] This suggests that the documents were grouped together in files, or at least that a special effort was made to archive materials that were of particular interest to Saint Louis or on topics that we could even call his obsessions. For instance, we find documents about the Holy Land and the preparations for his second crusade grouped together as this was a privileged subject. Documents pertaining to the king's arbitrations, especially to his mediation between the king of England and his barons and between the barons of his own kingdom, appear together, expressing the peace-making king's concern for explaining and supporting his decisions. Finally, the groupings express the king's interest in his family, which held such an important place among his preoccupations as a man and as a sovereign, despite the various oddities in his behavior. This was almost an echo of some premonition on the eve of his new absence and death. He particularly wanted to deal with the problem of the entitlements of his last children in a way that would set up a stable balance between their interests and those of the kingdom. In this period dominated by morality and eschatology, we find something like a bureaucracy of dynastic and monarchical scruples in him.

The reign's most important innovation in matters of preserving royal acts was the constitution of the acts of the Parlement of Paris starting in 1254. The record books containing these acts were given the name "*olim*" (yore) in the fourteenth century, because one of the registries began with the words, "*Olim homines de Baiona* . . ." (in days of yore, the men of Bayonne . . .), and the word was subsequently applied to seven of the oldest record books. The date of the beginning of these records is significant: 1254, the year of Saint Louis' return from the Holy Land, his meeting with the Franciscan Hugh of Digne who focused the king's attention on his duty toward justice, and the year of the Great Edict of 1254, which inaugurated the period of moral order. This period has also been called "the opening of an age of improvement in the activities of the Parlement." During this period, the Parlement definitively distinguished itself from the royal curia (*Curia regis*) by specializing in judicial affairs.

Of course, the Parlement functioned more or less independently of the king. The king, however, almost always attended the three or four annual general meetings, which he presided over on the day after or the eighth day after Pentecost, All Saints' Day or Saint Martin's Day on November 11, Candlemas, and the Nativity of the Virgin. The appearance of these records corresponded to Saint Louis' strong desire and to the unyielding inflexibility in his behavior and politics after his return from the crusade. It constituted an affirmation of the primacy of royal justice over seigniorial justice and other forms of justice (urban, for example) through the procedure of appeal to the Parlement (a court of appeals), in other words, by appeals to royal justice. This was also a period of decisive advances in recourse to written procedure. The *olim* form the bureaucratic face of Saint Louis the dispenser of justice.[13] The record inscribed the king's will and presence in writing, in recorded memory, this new cog in the machinery of the monarchical state. In order to fulfill his function, he needed to establish continuity. The first titled recorder of the *olim* that some have seen as a "*greffier*" of the Parlement, Jean de Montluçon, exercised his duties from 1257 to 1273.

We can guess that the king intervened in some particular way whenever the mention "*de mandato regis*" (on orders of the king) appears in the record. Although the royal officers and especially the bailiffs were capable of making decisions in the king's name most of the time, we sometimes find a distinction between *quantum ad consilium* (in that which concerns the council) and *quantum ad regem* (in that which concerns the king). For example, there is an act relative to the investigation carried out in 1260 on the subject of a palfrey the royal chamberlains requested from the abbot of Colombe when he entered into service. In this act, they note that the investigatory expedition had been made in this Parlement *quantum ad concilium,* but not *quantum ad regem,* because someone still had "to speak" with the king about it.[14] The particular interest that Saint Louis had in these archives can be seen in 1260 when he ordered the original pieces to be deposited in the Sainte-Chapelle. Here again, we can observe the formation of records on subjects that attracted the king's interest at one time or another. Thus, although Saint Louis sometimes seems interested in the affairs of Languedoc and sometimes indifferent to the south of France, in 1269 he flooded the parliamentary archives with documents related to the conquest of Languedoc and, in particular, with letters and sealed acts concerning the former fiefs and rights of Simon de Montfort.

Beginning around the end of Saint Louis' reign, the archives of Parlement were inundated with documents. The clutter did not facilitate the maintenance of political order, which the nascent royal bureaucracy was only establishing in fits and starts. For example, there was no clear division between the archives of the Parlement and the *Trésor des chartes.* Records of parliamentary investigations were all mixed up with the acts of the *Trésor.* Saint Louis' image fades amid the documents of the archives.

The one significant gap that Saint Louis' royal documents share with those of the other kings of France arose from the loss of the books and accounting records destroyed in the fire at the Chamber of Accounts in Paris in 1737. The only records from Saint Louis' reign that survived were several "important" tomes, the accounts of the hotel, in other words the record of all the sovereign's domestic services preserved on wax tablets, for example the tablets on which the hotel accountant, Jean Sarrasin, noted the daily expenses for the hotel for 638 days from Candlemas 1256 to All Saints' Day of 1257.[15] The accounts for the years 1231, 1234, 1238, 1248, and 1267 were also saved. Earlier, we saw the recorded figures for the expenses for Saint Louis' wedding in 1234 and the listing of expenses for the crusade.[16] Certain sums for servicing the army have also been preserved,[17] and the records of the investigators, especially for the investigations of 1247.[18] The archives thus convey the image of a Saint Louis who wrote a lot (in other words, who made others write), who recorded more and more, but who counted little. He was not surrounded by numbers. This is probably a result of the lost records of the royal accountancy because the monarchy was counting everything more and more in the thirteenth century, which some have described as a century of arithmetic and calculus.[19]

The edicts are of the utmost importance when it comes to the investigations. I remind my readers that this term [*ordonnance,* edict] only appeared after the Middle Ages and that the denomination of this type of act and the diplomatic form resulting from its juridical nature were still not set under Saint Louis. We are talking about acts of legislative and regulatory import that the king alone had the right to decree. Sometimes they were called "*établissements*" (*stabilimenta*), sometimes "*statuts*" (statutes, *statuta*), "*défenses*" (interdictions, *inhibitiones*), or for coinage, "*attirement,*" "*ordonnement,*" and "*établissement.*" These were important texts that generally applied to everyone, valid in the royal domain or in only a part of the kingdom. Under Saint Louis, they applied more and more often to the entire kingdom.[20] The first *ordonnance* that applied to the entire kingdom was decreed during Saint Louis' minority.[21]

In the absence of any suitable edition of the edicts of the kings of France, we have to stick with the undoubtedly correct impression that an approximate list can give us.[22] For the six edicts of Philip Augustus we can identify twenty-five for Louis IX, without counting eight regulations that were associated with the edicts. These acts of sovereign authority concerned both essential domains of expanding royal power and certain questions that obsessed Saint Louis: Languedoc, coinages, and cities in the case of the first, the Jews and usurers and the reform of manners in the case of the second, as well as private wars and God's judgments, which also pertained to royal authority.

Whatever uncertainties surround these acts, we can see that in the midst of a certain confusion but with a will that became clearer and clearer, Saint Louis' reign was characterized by a new (or at least rediscovered since the Carolingians) assertion of the king's "legislative power." To a certain extent, Saint Louis was and wanted to be the first law-making Capetian king.

Finally, time has preserved several of Saint Louis' letters for us, whether printed in editions of scholarly publications of the *Ancien Régime* or in foreign collections. This is the case for the letter sent to his subjects from the Holy Land in 1250 after his capture[23] and for the letter sent from Carthage to the Church of France after his landing.[24] The Office of Public Records in London possesses thirteen of Saint Louis' letters addressed to Henry III.[25]

Despite a few personal touches, the official royal acts of Saint Louis originate primarily in the collective monarchical memory. They are relatively "objective," usually lack any personal character, and offer us an image of a king that is abstract, although they show that he was more and more present in his kingdom and in history.

The King of the Mendicant
Hagiographers

A Saint King of Resurgent Christendom

SAINT LOUIS' LIFE WAS INTIMATELY RELATED TO A NEW CHURCH
institution in the first half of the century: the Mendicant orders. Since the
middle of the eleventh century the Church had attempted to react to profound changes in Western society. The most remarkable of these changes
was prodigious economic expansion, which culminated in the spread of
coinage in which Saint Louis played an important role. The king also played
a significant role in the impressive urban growth of this period by controlling the governments of the "good" towns and increasing the extent to
which Paris played a leading role in this movement. There was also the fabulous flowering of Romanesque and Gothic art, which, from the Sainte-
Chapelle to Notre-Dame-de-Paris to the cathedral of Amiens, provided
Saint Louis with his sites of worship. Finally, there were changes in mentalities and practices that inaugurated a new alignment in values that favored,
for example, a stronger attraction to the things of this world alongside the
ever-present fear of the afterlife, the new lure of material gain and the re-

newed call for a spirit of poverty, and the emergence of the individual within a reorganization of community structures. The Church responded to these challenges with an initial reform movement between the middle of the eleventh and twelfth centuries. This was the so-called Gregorian reform of Pope Gregory VII (1073–1085). This reform created a stricter separation between clerics and laymen around the widening moat of sexuality with virginity, chastity, and celibacy emphasized on one side of the divide, monogamous and indissoluble marriage on the other. It also defined a new relationship between the spiritual and the temporal. A second reform movement began around the beginning of the thirteenth century. The Church was spurred into action by heretical movements, which questioned it as an institution and criticized its growing wealth, its increasing distance from simple laypeople, the distance it maintained between worshippers and the Gospel, and its inability to formulate a discourse that was accessible to the mass of Christian believers. Clerics and laypersons reacted to these conditions by trying to return to the spirit and the letter of the Gospel, by practicing and setting an example of humility and poverty, and by preaching the word of God.

THE MENDICANT ORDERS

In 1215, the Fourth Lateran Council forbade the creation of new orders outside of the already existing rules. The two main orders that already existed were the Order of Saint Benedict and the Order of Saint Augustine. In response to the influence of two outstanding personalities — the regular Spanish canon Domingo de Guzman and the Italian layman Francis of Assisi — the Church accepted the establishment of the Preaching Friars, whose name indicated the importance they attributed to predication, and the Friars Minor who took this name for the emphasis they placed on humility. The Preaching Friars were called "Jacobins" in France at the time, after the name of their Parisian convent under the patronage of Saint Jacques. They were also called Dominicans after the name of their founder. They adopted a rule of regular canons similar to the rule of the Premonstrants, with specific constitutions drafted in 1216 and 1220 that were codified as a "rule" in 1226. The Minorites were called "Cordeliers" due to the knotted cords they wore as belts. They were also called Franciscans after the name of their founder. The pope granted them a special authorization to obey a new rule that Saint Francis drew up in 1221 despite his reservations about transforming his community into an order. It was accepted by the pontifical curia only in a corrected form in 1223. Rejecting all property and income from property, the two orders lived on the income from their collections and donations, and for this reason they were called the Mendicant orders. Francis of Assisi died in 1226, the same year Saint Louis became king. He was canonized in 1228. Dominic died in 1221 and was canonized in 1233. Under pressure from the papacy, other religious, the Carmelites, joined the Mendicants in several stages, first in 1229, then later in 1247 and 1250. In 1256, the pope united several anchorite congregations to form a fourth Mendicant order, the Hermits of Saint Augustine.[1]

The Mendicant orders founded their convents in cities amid other men rather than amid solitude. Their members were friars, not monks. They were joined by a second order (of sisters or nuns) and a third order (of laymen). Their reach thus extended to all segments of society. They were instruments of the Church deployed to christianize the new society emerging from the prosperity that was spreading from the eleventh to the thirteenth century. Some of the orders united around the reaction of the spirit of poverty confronted with economic growth, the spread of money, and the development of a desire for profit. In reaction to these phenomena, they invented ethical and religious solutions—though not free of paradox—that justified the merchants. By validating certain financial operations, they effectively facilitated the development of capitalism. In the thirteenth century, it was under their influence that the great debate on money and religion that Max Weber[2] associated with Protestantism took place—in theory and practice. What the Mendicants proposed and partially managed to impose was a moralization of economic life and especially of money.[3] As Saint Louis' main advisors who depended on his influence and who benefited from his support, they left their mark on French attitudes with their disdainful, moralist validation of money and business that still characterizes French society today. This is the common mark that Saint Louis and the Mendicants left upon the economic behavior of a majority of the French people and especially on their most impressive leaders in the twentieth century from De Gaulle to Mitterand.[4]

The success of the Mendicant orders and above all of the two most important orders, the Dominicans and the Franciscans, was brilliant. France was one of the countries where they established themselves very early. The

Franciscans' first establishments date from 1217 at Vézelay and Auxerre and from 1219 in Paris. The Dominicans moved in earlier with the female monastery of Prouille in 1206, the convent of Toulouse in 1215, and their establishment in Paris in 1217. The great period for the foundation of convents of Preachers and Minorites in France lasted from 1230 to 1260. This almost precisely corresponded to the period of Saint Louis' reign.[5] At the time of Saint Louis' death, there were nearly 200 Franciscan convents and almost 100 Dominican convents in France. The Preachers usually set themselves up in larger cities than the Minorites.

Saint Louis was surrounded by Mendicant friars from very early on in life. The first friar he met was most certainly Jourdain de Saxe, Saint Dominic's successor as master general of the Preachers from 1222 to 1237. During his stays in Paris, he seems to have cemented close relations with Blanche of Castile. After the death of Saint Francis in 1226, the Minorite friars were said to have sent the pillow that he used all his life to the young king and the Queen Mother.[6] If the report is authentic, the child king had to have kept a strong memory of this gift as he later became a great collector of relics.

He signaled his predilection for the Mendicants well before his departure on his first crusade. He confided two enterprises that he held most dear almost exclusively to them. First, he entrusted them with the Sainte-Chapelle and the worship of the exceptional relics that he deposited there and the three special services dedicated to them every year, one led by the Dominican convent of Paris, the second in the charge of the Franciscan convent, while a third was conducted by the other Parisian religious orders.[7] For the most part, he also entrusted them with the investigations conducted throughout the kingdom in preparation for the crusade in 1247. The Franciscan convents in Paris, Rouen, Jaffa, and Compiègne, and the Dominican convents in Rouen, Mâcon, Jaffa, Compiègne, Béziers, Carcassonne, and Caen were all built thanks to the king's generosity. Royal donations also paid for the expansion of the convent of Saint-Jacques in Paris and the convent of the Dominicans in Rouen. After the king's return from the Holy Land in 1254, the Franciscan Eudes Rigaud, the archbishop of Rouen, was his closest friend and advisor.

Contrary to what Geoffroy de Beaulieu, his Dominican confessor, claimed, I do not believe that Saint Louis ever seriously considered becoming a Mendicant friar himself. According to Geoffroy, his inability to choose between the Dominicans and the Franciscans was the only thing that kept him from making his desire a reality. He was really much too strongly imbued with his sense of duty as a king and his vocation as a pious layman to desert the position in which God had placed him, even if it were for a more honorable one that involved less responsibility. On the other hand, it is credible that he wanted his second and third sons to take up the robe, one for the Dominicans and the other for the Franciscans.

Saint Louis and the Mendicants basically had the same objectives, and they often employed the same methods of using power for society's religious and moral reform. Most of the time, these efforts assumed the aspect of what we would now call political reform. Saint Louis used the Mendicants for his investigations, and sometimes the Mendicants directly took on a political role—in the Italian cities, for example, where there was no strong central power as in a monarchy and where the reform of the cities' statutes was what they tried to undertake,[8] investing royal power so as to inspire its action and reforms.

Finally, the Mendicants formulated a new model of sainthood.[9] They had become the papacy's most zealous agents, and thus it was perfectly normal for the papacy to entrust them with a major role in Saint Louis' canonization. Both before and after his canonization, the memory of the king was first and foremost the one provided by the Mendicants on the scene. Whether he was already a saint or had not yet become one, in their writings about Saint Louis the Mendicants were not satisfied with simply expressing their gratitude toward their benefactor. Instead, they seized on the occasion to assert the ideals of their orders through his memory. The saint they described was a Mendicant friar who happened to be a king. Three Mendicants had exceptional importance for Saint Louis' memory. Two of them are important for having written biographies of Saint Louis before his canonization. They wrote with the specific intention of having him recognized as a saint. The third is important for having written his *Life*, which in some ways is his official biography, using the records from the canonization inquiry which have since been lost.

GEOFFROY DE BEAULIEU

The first of these important Mendicants was Geoffroy de Beaulieu. He was the king's confessor, in his own words, for "almost the last twenty years of his life." He accompanied him to Tunis and attended to him in his last moments of life. Even before his consecration on March 27, 1272, the pope-elect Gregory X asked him to "inform them as quickly as possible about the king's conduct in each and every one of his actions and practices in matters of religion."[10] What Geoffroy wrote up and sent to the pope, probably near the end of 1272 or the beginning of 1273, was an exposé (*libellus*) of fifty-two chapters entitled *Vita et sancta*[11] *conversatio piae memoriae Ludovici quondam Regis Francorum* (The Life and Holy Conduct of Louis of Pious Memory, Formerly King of France).[12] This was actually a succinct hagiography as it was intended to set the whole canonization process in motion. Geoffroy recounted exactly what God deigned "to inspire with his memory." He related everything memorable that he could recall about the deceased king. He was not only acting on the pope's orders but out of obedience to his superiors—no doubt his superiors in the Dominican order, including its leader. The whole enterprise therefore began with the pope and the Order of the Preachers.

The praise (there was almost never anything but praise for the king) developed in a somewhat disorganized way in which we can nevertheless recognize certain general tendencies. Louis is compared to Josiah in chapters 1 to 4, which also allowed the author to slip strong praise for Blanche of Castile into chapter 4 in the form of a mention of Josiah's mother in the Old Testament. Praise for Louis' virtues and piety fill most of the treatise (chapters 5 to 24), including two chapters (12 and 14) on his desire to abdicate and become a Mendicant friar, his wish to see two of his sons become Mendicants, and for his daughter Blanche to join a convent of nuns. The fifteenth chapter essentially repeats his *Enseignements* (Instructions) to his son and heir presented as his "testament." Another chapter recounts his pilgrimage to Nazareth. A generally chronological section next evokes his first crusade, chapters 25 to 28, which includes a long description of his mourning upon learning of his mother's death. Geoffroy would have had to insert the chapter on the pilgrimage to Nazareth into this section in order to maintain the story's chronological order. This is followed by his return to France (chapters 31 to 36), his preparations for the second crusade (42 to 50), and two concluding chapters. The conclusion brings us back to the point of departure with a comparison to Josiah and the direct, conclusive statement: "He is worthy of being listed among the saints."[13]

Following the custom of Lives of saints, the text was not dated. Geoffroy juxtaposed a thematic section with an essentially chronological section that corresponded, on the one hand, to the period during which he was the king's confessor and, on the other, to the part of Saint Louis' life and reign after his first crusade and visit to the Holy Land. That moment represented a turning point for almost all his biographers. This division also seemed to justify as fitting for a canonization proceeding the comparison with Josiah whose rule, according to the Old Testament, also knew two contrasting periods.[14] Overall, Geoffroy's text was a testimonial intended to help Louis IX enter the category of saints, and it therefore depicted him in conformity with the models that defined the saints.

There is only one short chapter several lines long on Saint Louis' actions as a king. This is chapter 6 on his conduct in governing his subjects.[15] We can summarize Geoffroy's *libellus* with these words: "He had the pious manners of a very devout layman who very much loved the Mendicant orders and his mother and who went on the crusades two times, where he was taken prisoner the first time and where the second time he died a very Christian death."

GUILLAUME DE CHARTRES

As far as we can tell, Saint Louis' second biographer and hagiographer duplicated and continued the work of the first. Guillaume de Chartres was a Dominican, too. He was Saint Louis' chaplain during his first crusade. They were captured and imprisoned together, and during that time Guillaume comforted Louis with religious services authorized by their Muslim captors. Five-and-a-half years after their return to France, in 1259 or 1260, he joined the Dominican order, although he was still part of the royal entourage. During the crusade of Tunis, he was present when Saint Louis died and accompanied his remains on the cortege through Italy and France to Saint-Denis. He wanted to write a complement to Geoffroy de Beaulieu's treatise after Geoffroy died, but he himself must have died shortly thereafter because he did not testify for the inquiry for Saint Louis' canonization in 1282. Otherwise, we would expect to find his name there as his presence alongside the king in so many special circumstances would have made him an important witness.

His rather short *libellus* was composed in two parts like the other typical hagiographies of the thirteenth century.[16] The first part was called the *Life* (*Vita*), although it usually dealt with the saint's virtues rather than his biography. The second part covered the saint's miracles. Having actually lived a little longer than Geoffroy de Beaulieu, Guillaume de Chartres had more miracles to report, particularly the ones that occurred at the king's tomb at Saint-Denis and in a few other places. He also wanted to fill in some of Geoffroy's omissions.

As a former chaplain, he mentioned the construction of the Sainte-Chapelle and Saint Louis' practices of worship. He recalled certain memories from the crusade to Egypt and the Holy Land and reported meaningful anecdotes about the king's virtues. He spoke much more than Geoffroy de Beaulieu about the kingdom's government viewed as a body reinforcing royal authority with the king cast in the specific role of serving the Church, justice, and peace. We find this in his emphasis on the king's respect for the Church, his support for the inquisitors, his abolition of "bad" customs, his punishment of dishonest officers, his measures against the Jews and usurers, his struggle to suppress private wars, and his replacement of judicial procedures "*par gages de bataille*" (by battle wagers) with the procedure "*par témoins*" (by witnesses) and "*par arguments*" (by arguments), *per testes* and *per rationes*. He insisted every bit as much as Geoffroy on the king's humility, charity, practice of "works of mercy," frugality, and asceticism. His *libellus* resembles a Mirror of Princes.[17]

As a Dominican like Geoffroy, he too stressed Louis' predilection for the friars of the Mendicant orders and the generous donations he made to their convents. One of his rare personal contributions to the story was the way he narrated the king's death, which he viewed. He described it at great length and with certain details that do not exist in the other accounts.

When the king died, he praised him as an ideal Christian king, a king to uphold as a model for other kings, a sun-king for the world.[18]

The originality of Guillaume's account primarily consists in his nearly five-page (36–41) report of detailed miracles, seventeen of them in all, duly verified and authenticated. These miracles took place from 1271 to 1272. They are all dated. They were, in fact, the only events on which Louis IX's sainthood could be established. His life became worthy of sainthood only through virtues whose value arose through their habitual exercise; the king's sainthood did not depend on any human chronology.

GUILLAUME DE SAINT-PATHUS

Saint Louis' third important hagiographer was a Franciscan, Guillaume de Saint-Pathus. He was Queen Marguerite's confessor from 1277 to some time around her death in 1297. After that he was confessor to her daughter Blanche, the widow of the infante Ferdinand of Castile. He a priori seems to be the least reliable, if not the least interesting, of the three Mendicant hagiographers. He wrote after Saint Louis' canonization, probably in 1303, more than thirty years after his death. Obviously, he never knew him. However, he was probably the one author who provided us with the best information about the image that Saint Louis' contemporaries had of his saint-hood and on what actually made the king memorable for them. He seems to have used and closely followed the records from Louis IX's canonization proceeding, a document that has not survived for us except in several fragments that allow us to appreciate exactly how faithful Guillaume was to this essential record.[19] Guillaume thus gave us an image of Saint Louis that was more in the process of being developed than one that had come to him already made. Following the thirteenth-century custom, Guillaume de Saint-Pathus composed Saint Louis' *Life* alongside the completely indispensable catalog of the official miracles that had been confirmed by the canonization commission.[20]

In fact, the Franciscan could not have used the complete text of the depositions of the 330 witnesses. He used a summary that comprised the official *Life* approved by the curia (*Vita per curiam approbata*) which has been lost. The queen's confessor then arranged this official summary in rather short sections, and an unknown translator translated the original Latin text into French. The same was done for the *Miracles*. It is this translation that we now possess.[21] The *Miracles* thus form a separate collection and are sixty-five in number. This indicates that Saint Louis' hagiography had struck a balance at this point between his life and his miracles. According to the evidence, Saint Louis did not accomplish any miracles before his death; this complied with what the Church expected since the papacy of Innocent III. This led to an imbalance in favor of the *Life* (in other words, the account of his virtues and piety) in the earlier testimonials for the canonization process. In any case, we can observe that the canonization made Saint Louis' image shift from one of spiritual and moral prestige toward thaumaturgical accomplishments. And yet, the Mendicants who wrote down Saint Louis' *Life* were very sensitive to miracles, and the pontifical curia held this *Life* in the highest esteem. The "life supplement" added between 1270 and 1297 privileged the image of Saint Louis as a maker of miracles.

We still have to take another look at the witnesses for the proceeding because Guillaume de Saint-Pathus transmitted their image of Saint Louis even more clearly than any image of Saint Louis he could have formed on his own by reading them or by hearing other testimonies. Guillaume de Saint-Pathus's Saint Louis was the collective creation of the witnesses for the proceeding. His work obviously contained only the witnesses' ideas about Saint Louis' life, all thirty-eight of them.[22]

The hierarchical order in which Guillaume cited them is of particular interest. He began with the two kings who were closest to the saint — his son and successor Philip III and his brother Charles d'Anjou, the king of Sicily. Next, he gave the testimony of two bishops, the bishop of Évreux and the bishop of Senlis. Then came the three abbots of the saint's favorite abbeys: the abbot of Saint-Denis — a Benedictine who was the kingdom's regent during the crusade of Tunis — and the two Cistercian abbots of Royaumont and Chaalis. After them came the accounts of nine barons beginning with the saint's son Pierre d'Alençon, the son of the king of Jerusalem Jean d'Acre, the saint's cousin and master cupbearer of France Simon de Nesle who was the other regent during the crusade of Tunis, Philip III's constable Pierre de Chambly, and Jean de Joinville, the seneschal of Champagne and a close friend of the saint whose famous life he would end up writing. These were followed by two of the king's clerics, five Benedictine friars, a Cistercian, seven of the saint's servants including two of his cooks, three bourgeois, three monachal sisters, and the king's surgeon. Although they were all close to the saint, we can classify twenty-four of the laymen into three main groups — the king's relatives, the barons, and the servants along with several bourgeois. There are fourteen clerics for the twenty-nine laymen, including two prelates, three abbots, two clerics of the royal curia, five Dominican friars, as well as three nuns.

This saint was a secular saint and a king, so the number of laymen and people close to the king was preponderant here, although we must add that we know about the mentality and piety of these laymen, which was very close to the spirituality and devotional practice of the clerics with whom they lived. We can also observe that this saint was presented as a saint by a disproportionately large number of Dominicans. They numbered a third of all the ecclesiastical witnesses along with the Franciscan author of the *Life*. In addition, although Louis benefited from the testimony of three nuns, no women from his family were called upon to testify.

It is also interesting to observe where the witnesses came from and where they lived, as this also reveals where the king lived. Although many of the figures on the list are there because they accompanied the king on his two crusades, if we exclude his family members, we find that the others came from the dioceses of Évreux, Senlis, Beauvais, Noyon, Paris, Châlons, Sens, Rouen, Reims, Soissons, Compiègne, and Chartres. Two of the valets were Britons from the diocese of Nantes. To sum things up, this was a saint of the Île-de-France, its neighboring regions, and the crusade.

Guillaume de Saint-Pathus carefully organized the information drawn from the canonization record.[23] The *Life* is framed by three truly biographical chapters in chronological order. The first two present the saint's childhood and adolescence. They do not offer any great details, emphasizing the influence of his mother and the decisively inseparable pair of Louis and Blanche. These chapters also stress his good education. The final chapter recounts his death and accredits the version of it that has the dying king exclaim, "Oh, Jerusalem! Oh, Jerusalem!"

Eighteen chapters focus on Saint Louis' exercise of the three theological virtues (faith, hope, and charity, which is love), the triple form of his piety (worship, study of Scripture, and prayer), the two ways he took care of his fellow man (love and compassion), his practice of works of mercy (pity); the five main virtues in his conduct (humility, patience, penitence, self-control, and "beauty of conscience"), his three great virtues as a king (justice, honesty, and clemency), and his most consistent personal character trait—his "long" perseverance. The eighteenth chapter leads into the story of the saint's death.

The most important element of what the hagiographers called his Life was therefore his habitual practice of worship and the virtues. This concept of the Life, which was actually a literary genre, is very different from our own conception of biography. Although it contained events in the life of a saint, they did not form any chronological sequence. In each chapter the hagiographer gave specific information about the saint's habitual conduct and only more rarely would he use an anecdote to illustrate his points. Thus in chapter 8, when he speaks again of the king's habits of praying, Guillaume de Saint-Pathus tells us:

. . . and in addition to his other prayers, the saint king knelt fifty
times each evening and each time he would stand up again and kneel
back down and then he would very slowly say an Ave Maria, and
after that he did not drink at all[24] but would go straight to bed.[25]

Here is another story of the king's habitual actions that had the Cistercian abbey of Chaalis for their backdrop:

And the holy king held the saints in such great reverence that once
when he was in the church of Chaalis, which is of the order of the Cistercians in the diocese of Senlis, he heard someone say that the bodies of the monks who died there would be washed on a stone that was
there. And the saint king kissed this stone, exclaiming, "Oh, God! So
many saintly men have been washed here!"[26]

Of course, the Franciscan highlighted the special affection the saint
had for the Mendicant orders. He reminded his readers that each time the
king visited a town that had Mendicant convents he had some food and
alms passed out to the friars.[27] His generosity toward them was often experienced in Paris where the king often stayed and where the Mendicant friars lived in large numbers. This generosity even extended to the friars of
the lesser Mendicant orders, to those "who had no possessions."

We must add another closely related document to this record of Saint
Louis, the saint of the Mendicants.[28] This is a sermon composed by Guillaume de Saint-Pathus. It was written after his *Vie de Saint Louis* and his *Miracles* of Saint Louis some time after 1303 and after the lost *Vita approbata*,
the official summary of the canonization proceeding. After having served
as Queen Marguerite's confessor until her death in 1295, Guillaume became her daughter Blanche's confessor. She was the widow of the infante
Ferdinand de Castile. Guillaume was still her confessor in 1314–1315, and
Blanche finally died in 1323. Guillaume's sermon was a panegyric to Saint
Louis. It corresponds perfectly to the genre of the scholastic sermon as it
was defined and practiced at the end of the thirteenth and the beginning of
the fourteenth centuries. The text seemed "insipid" even to its scholarly editor, the same one who edited Guillaume de Saint-Pathus's *Vie de Saint Louis,*
Henri-François Delaborde.[29] He only published what he called its "historical passages," along with "the beginning and the peroration." This gives a

false impression of Guillaume de Saint-Pathus's sermon, which was poorly edited as a selection appearing as a group of texts. The author was not trying to respond to the interests of people of the nineteenth and twentieth centuries. He composed a hagiographical sermon based on a theme. According to the rules of the time, this theme was necessarily drawn from the Bible and chosen for its relevance to the sermon's purpose. The sermon's objective was to praise Saint Louis, and the theme was an expression from the first book of Maccabees (2:17): "*Princeps clarissimus et magnus es*" (You are a very great and illustrious ruler). From this point it was clear that the preacher's work consisted in placing Saint Louis in the framework of the scholastic development of this theme, and not the other way around. The definition of Saint Louis as "*generosus, famosus, virtuosus*" (of noble origin, of good renown, of great virtue) produced a series of scholastic subdivisions applied to Saint Louis' virtues and grouped around the "dignity of his royal preeminence" and the "sublimity of his fundamental perfection." This justified the application of the three words—*princeps, clarissimus, and magnus*—that were used to characterize him.

Then, each of the saint's qualities was subdivided in turn into a group of others defined either by the "authorities" (other biblical verses) or by "reasons" (rational arguments). For example, "the dignity of his royal preeminence" broke down into four virtues: the "splendor of his wisdom" illustrated by the verse from Kings, "*David sedeus in cathedra sapientissimus princeps*" (David seated on the throne, the very wise prince); the "sweetness of his compassion" illustrated by the verse from Ezekiel, "*Servus meus David erit princeps in medio eram*" (My servant David will be their prince); the "brilliance of his countenance" and the "fervor of his devotion," which were demonstrated with proofs instead of authorities.

In fact, this sermon was a real Mirror of the Prince in the form of a homily. Guillaume de Saint-Pathus had a model of the ideal ruler in mind and he adjusted Saint Louis' Life (in other words the habitual exercise of his virtues) to fit this model more than he made the model correspond to the Life.[30] The genre of the sermon came together here with the genre of the Mirror of the Prince in Saint Louis' case because what interested the thirteenth-century "memorialists" was first of all to impose a model of the ideal Christian ruler and, second of all, to show us that Saint Louis' life corresponded to this model. In Saint Louis, it was not the man but the model that interested them. The larger part of the record of Saint Louis' contemporaries' memories of him form an organized group of texts that refer to one another because they were produced by the same manufacturers of memory: clerics working in the same production centers (abbeys, convents), and with the same genres that were replicated over time: "lives," "mirrors," "sermons," etc. Thus we are taken within a mass of memory inside of which an image takes shape for us, a largely stereotyped image, of Saint Louis.

The sermon referred to anecdotal events from Saint Louis' life that amount to little in the end. They were general episodes that already appeared in the *Life* and the *Miracles*. There were only four passages in the sermon that had no equivalent in the *Life*.[31]

Guillaume mentioned Queen Marguerite herself as the source of the first episode that did not appear in the *Life*. It showed Saint Louis in an intimate scene with his family, his wife, and children.[32] The second, also conveyed by Marguerite, told how the queen threw a piece of cloth over her husband's shoulders when he got up at night to pray. A third anecdote related that Saint Louis continued to pray after matins for a period of time as long as the service. The fourth passage described the punishments that he inflicted on himself and that he liked to offer to God; it does not actually appear in Guillaume de Saint-Pathus's *Life* but corresponds to a passage in the *Life* by Geoffroy de Beaulieu.[33]

Guillaume applied the etymology for the word 'king' to Saint Louis: "*rex a recte regendo*" (king comes from governing rightly). He also applied the etymology for 'prince': "*princeps qui primus capiat*" (he who takes the first).[34] He "took the first because he reached the dignity of royal majesty due to primogeniture."

The sermon is plainly a Mirror of the Prince adapted to Saint Louis and the French monarchy. Although the sermon followed scholastic methods in its form, its content was not influenced by them. The Mendicants of the royal entourage were not familiar with the great scholarly Mendicants like Alexandre de Halès, Saint Bonaventure, Saint Albert the Great, and Saint Thomas Aquinas. Saint Louis was the saint of devotion, but not of Mendicant theology. He was a pre-scholastic saint.[35]

The King of Saint-Denis

A Dynastic and "National" Saint King

THE ROYAL IMAGE THE CLERICS APPLIED TO SAINT LOUIS HAD TWO
sides: the one fashioned by the friars of the Mendicant orders that presented
the saint as a top model, and the one shaped by the Benedictine monks of
Saint-Denis that focused on the king himself. For the first group, the king
was primarily treated as a saint king, and Guillaume de Saint-Pathus made
this the theme of his sermon. For the second group, the king was a saint king
whose sainthood enhanced his royal image. Although the pressure group of
the Mendicants represented a new force born around the same time as Saint
Louis, as a site of memory Saint-Denis' origins extended almost as far back
as the French monarchy. Their patron saint was Denis, the first bishop of
Paris who was martyred in the third century. A tradition spread by Abbot
Hilduin in the ninth century confused him with Denys the Areopagite, the
Athenian who was converted by Saint Paul. Saint-Denis originated with
a church constructed on the site where people in the Middle Ages thought
that Saint Denis had been buried. In a number of convincing arguments,
Anne Lombard-Jourdan has demonstrated that the place had a very long tra-
dition. According to her, it was a major site where the Gauls gathered for re-

266

ligious rites their tribes held in common. It was situated on an important trade route for tin in the Middle Ages that ran from the British Isles to Italy, and it was associated very early on with the Gallo-Roman city of Lutèce that later became Paris. Saint-Denis formed a pair with this city, and together they were destined to become the inseparable twin capitals of France.[1]

There were three men who made Saint-Denis' glory and built up its role as a site of "national" memory that its subsequent history would continue, confirm, and enrich.[2] The first was the Merovingian Dagobert who transformed the church into a Benedictine abbey in the seventh century. He rebuilt it and was buried there, initiating what would become the "cemetery of the kings" under the Capetians after serving only intermittently in a funerary role. The second was the Carolingian Charles the Bald. He reestablished the traditions of his ancestors Charles Martel and Pepin the Short, refurbishing the abbey in magnificent fashion. In accordance with his will, he was buried there in 884, seven years after his death in the Alps. The third was Suger, the abbot of Saint-Denis from 1122 to 1151. He introduced Gothic art when he rebuilt the church. He also definitively associated the abbey with the Capetian dynasty. He became the main advisor to the kings Louis VI and Louis VII and made the royal army's oriflamme the standard of the abbey. Suger also revised *Histoire de Charlemagne,* which became "one of the most frequently read books in the West" (Colette Beaune). He brought together a library that allowed Saint-Denis to recapture its role as France's historical center from Fleury (Saint-Benoît-sur-Loire), which had become the site of the Capetian monarchy's historical memory in the eleventh century.[3] Saint-Denis usurped this role in the twelfth century, succeeded it, and fulfilled this role in its entirety.[4]

Saint-Denis' function as a site of royal memory was strengthened under the reign of Philip Augustus (1179–1223). He officially entrusted the abbey with the royal insignia used for the coronation in Reims. He was also the hero of a Life written by the monk Rigord who was the author of a short chronicle of the kings of France that later became a guide for visitors to the abbey. In his *Gesta Philippi Augusti,* Rigord enfolded the ruler in a miraculous aura that the royal entourage later used in an attempt to support their project of having Philip Augustus recognized as a saint after his death. Their project, however, came up against the negative image that the Church had spread of a bigamist king who challenged pontifical authority by refusing to honor his marriage to Ingeburg of Denmark.[5]

We have seen how Saint Louis took great care to maintain close ties
with the abbey, especially toward the end of his reign at the time Mathieu de
Vendôme was the abbot. He made him one of the kingdom's two regents
before leaving for Tunis. We have also seen how he redesigned the royal necropolis in a way that displayed the Capetian dynasty's great project, which
had been completed under his father, Louis VIII. This great project that
Saint-Denis served so brilliantly was to impose the idea of a dynastic continuity running from the Merovingians through the Carolingians to the Capetians, while above all claiming that the Capetians represented a return to the
"race" of Charlemagne (*reditus ad stirpem Karoli*), the prestigious dominating
figure that the French monarchy disputed with the German Empire.

PRIMAT

Saint Louis' reign saw the continuation of the *Gesta Francorum usque 1180*
(History of the Franks up to 1180) beyond 1180 in the form of various
Latin chronicles. King Louis took the main initiative by asking Saint-Denis
to write a chronicle of the kings of France in French using the previously
existing chronicles in Latin. This decision was influential for two reasons.
First, it marked a decisive step toward the composition of a quasi-official
history of France, regrouping and reorganizing the earlier chronicles in
a single body. Second, it marked the emergence of historical memory in
French, extending beyond the milieu of the clerics and accessible to at least
a minority of educated laymen who were interested in the history of kings,
which represented "national" history in its embryonic form.

The abbot of Saint-Denis entrusted this work to the monk Primat,
who completed the work only in 1274. He ceremoniously handed the book
over to Philip III, Saint Louis' son, and this scene was immortalized in a
miniature.

The *Roman aux rois* (Story of the Kings)[6] stopped before Saint Louis'
reign. However, it conveyed a very strong impression of the king who commissioned it. It gave the French royal tradition that produced Saint Louis
such a grand and long-lasting expression that we have to give Primat full
credit here.

Bernard Guenée has reminded us that modern scholarship initially believed that Primat was only the copyist for the manuscript given to Philip III
in 1274 because he was also a modest translator of Latin Christian works.

Today, along with Bernard Guenée, we have finally recognized him as one of the best historians of the great Dionysian school of historiography,[7] a truly "great historian."[8] Of course he was a historian in the fashion of the Middle Ages, in other words a compiler who tried to integrate everything that seemed important to him in the sources that he used while respecting these materials as the literal truth. A "serious" historian, Primat used a large number of different sources including all of those he thought were likely to contribute to the image of the history of France that he wanted to produce. His main themes were the dynastic continuity running from Clovis's baptism to the reign of Philip Augustus, the Carolingian glory that continued to shine on all of the subsequent rulers in the French monarchy, and the favor that God had always shown toward France—for instance with the "miraculous" birth of Philip Augustus, who was born to Louis VII very late in life after all his various wives had given birth only to girls. France appeared alongside the kings as a "lady renowned above all other nations." She was heir not only to the Catholic faith, which first came to her with Clovis, but also to ancient culture, because "clergy [knowledge] and chivalry came to France from Greece and Rome." Primat also adopted and spread the legend of the French monarchy's origins in ancient Troy. After 1196, Primat was hardly bothered by Philip Augustus's matrimonial conduct. As the creator of an image of Saint Louis, Primat gave *Roman aux rois* the coherence and patriotic tone of a history of France. Primat's history of France laid the groundwork for the French grandeur in which Saint Louis appeared as the crowning achievement. French history seemed to be waiting just for him.[9]

GUILLAUME DE NANGIS AND THE *LIFE OF SAINT LOUIS*

The main Dionysian source for our knowledge of Saint Louis was the work of the great historian, the monk Guillaume de Nangis.[10] Some scholars have showered him with ambiguous praise. On the one hand, they have recognized his "irreproachable objectivity," pointing out how he abstained from making judgments of praise or blame. On the other hand, they have insisted that it is impossible to find in his work "any general idea other than that of submission to civil and ecclesiastical powers" and that he reported "the greatest faults of the kings of France without comment."[11] I think that we have to make a distinction here between Guillaume de Nangis the biographer of Saint Louis and Philip III the Bold, and Guillaume de Nangis the author of a universal chronicle in which Saint Louis' reign occupied an important place. The disparity results mainly from the difference between these literary genres, which were governed by strict rules in the Middle Ages.

Born around 1250 and having joined Saint-Denis at a young age, Guillaume began to work as Saint-Denis' archivist at an unknown date. He wrote his *Life* of Louis IX there, probably after 1285, and completed it before Louis' canonization in 1297. He also wrote a *Life* of Philip III and the *Universal Chronicle* in which he continued the work of the early twelfth-century chronicler Sigebert de Gembloux. The chronicle has no originality up to 1113 and becomes more personal after this date. The *Saint Louis* offers second-hand information, but Guillaume was the primary and original source for Philip III and for the first years of the reign of Philip IV the Fair.[12] He probably died in 1300.

GUILLAUME DE NANGIS'S *UNIVERSAL CHRONICLE*

The *Chronicle* is actually "objective." It is presented in the traditional form of "Annals," presenting main events year by year in a dry manner. Narrative developments, general ideas, judgments, and events considered secondary were excluded from the narration. Thus, for the year 1231, the episode of the loss of the Holy Nail disappeared completely from the *Chronicle*. The *Chronicle* did follow the *Life* but only by reducing it to its basic sequence of events. Guillaume had covered this episode in great detail in his *Life* of Saint Louis, where he also made a number of interesting remarks about the young king's piety and the way his expressions of piety were received by his entourage.[13] Saint Louis still held an important place in the universal chronicle, although other states and important persons appeared in it too. A specific idea of history appears in the structure of the *Chronicle*. Guillaume de Nangis was especially interested in men and most of all in the great men who shaped history. Although they did not make history because God was the only true maker [*môteur*], they were at least the heroes of this human history. These men, however, could also act collectively. Sometimes Guillaume also stressed the locations of events because he had a sense of the "places" where history was made and where memory was constructed.

Here are two significant examples of this conception of the history as chronicle and the place that Saint Louis occupied in it.

There are four events mentioned for the year 1229, and Guillaume committed four paragraphs to them.[14]

The first episode is the count of Brittany's revolt and its suppression by the young Louis IX. It begins with the words, "The count of Brittany" (*Comes Britanniae*) and passes directly to the king of France's intervention: "The count of Brittany, upset by his loss of the castle of Bellène [Bellême], began to invade Louis the king of France's lands again." The king immediately grabs center stage from the count of Brittany who started the war. "Refusing to tolerate this attitude, the king reassembled a new army. . . ." The paragraph then concludes with the victorious king of France: "and for four years and even longer the king of France governed his kingdom in peace" (*Ludovicus Franciae rex regnum gubernavit*). The allegedly "objective" Guillaume who "abstains from judgment" actually condemned the count of Brittany simply with the way he organized the story and with his choice of words. To express the fact that the count had invaded royal lands he used the word *infestare*. The most common meaning of this word, "to infest," was extremely pejorative. The count was the bad guy and he was punished not only by being defeated but also by being "*humilié*" (humiliated, humbled)— "*Et sic, Petro Britanniae comite humiliato*" (And thus Pierre the count of Brittany was humbled). The count's rebellion against the king was very harshly condemned. In addition to the vassal's revolt against his lord that occurred here, it was the insult to the king that was condemned.[15]

Writing at the beginning of the reign of Philip the Fair roughly twenty years after Saint Louis' death, Guillaume de Nangis tended to make the king of France appear even more powerful than he actually was: "The king's presence there was stronger than ever."[16] Guillaume de Nangis's Louis IX was a precocious Philip the Fair—not in character (Philip the Fair was already an enigma for the chroniclers of his time), but through the depiction of the power that he exercised. Thus, if I dare say, after Primat, Guillaume de Nangis made the Saint Louis of Saint-Denis into an even more royal king.

The second paragraph for the year 1229, less than half as long as the preceding entry, is about the king of Aragon, Jaime I the Conqueror. A mention of the king begins the paragraph: "The king of Aragon. . . ." Guillaume recalled his conquests against the Saracens: the Baleares and Valencia, the site of Saint Vincent's martyrdom. He increased the size of Christendom. Guillaume's story was a chronicle of Christendom, and Saint Louis' predominant place in it was exactly what made him the most powerful ruler in Christendom.

The third paragraph—three lines long—is dedicated to two other important figures in Christendom whose renown for saintliness emerged in that year: Saint Elizabeth, "the daughter of the king of Hungary and wife of the Landgrave of Thuringia," and Saint Anthony of Padua "of the order of the Minorite friars." Guillaume thus situated his reader within an atmosphere of saintliness.

The last paragraph (of fourteen lines) is about the important event in Christendom in which Saint Louis played an important part later on, the crusades. The first hero of the crusades was collective, the entire mass of crusaders. Guillaume also had a sense of the role of the masses in history, describing "a great crowd of crusaders" (*multitudine magna peregrinorum crusesignatorum*). Next came Christendom's two "official" main characters, the pope and the emperor. The emperor did not come off so favorably. After the departure for the crusade, Frederick II secretly ("*en cachette,*" furtive) abandoned the crusaders and returned to Brindisi. The pope excommunicated him. One last important figure that appeared here was the Muslim sultan. Guillaume was very attentive to events in the Orient and still shared the traditional conception of Christendom as one that encompassed Latin European Christendom and the Holy Land. He thus took an interest in mentioning the sultan's death.

The following year, 1230, is even more interesting from the point of view of writings about Saint Louis.

The year begins with a mention of the king: "*Ludovicus rex Franciae.*" He founded the abbey of Royaumont in the bishopric of Beauvais near Beaumont-sur-Oise. Guillaume thus showed him in one of his most memorable activities, as the founder and benefactor of churches, abbeys, and convents. And, as we now know, Royaumont was the abbey dearest to the king's heart, his favorite place.

The second paragraph of three lines reintroduces the emperor, whose image continued to deteriorate. "The Roman emperor Frederick sent ambassadors to the sultan of Baghdad and, according to what people say, made a pact of friendship with him, which seems suspect to Christendom."[17] This is followed by a long development (thirty-seven lines, twenty of them added later by Guillaume) that is of the greatest interest for Saint Louis' memory.

Guillaume began with a place, but it was not just any place. The section begins with the image of the young king's capital. The actors in the event were the two groups that dominated Paris: the bourgeois and the clerics of the young university.

In Paris a large quarrel broke out between the schoolmen [*schol-ares* refers to both masters and students] and the bourgeois. In effect, the bourgeois had killed some of the clerics, and, for this, the clerics left Paris and spread out through all the regions of the world.[18]

The young king soon appeared; he was sixteen years old:

When he saw that the study of letters and philosophy by which one acquires the treasure of knowledge that prevails over all others[19] had left Paris [a treasure that first came from Athens to Rome and then from Rome to Gaul under the name of chivalry after the time of Denis the Areopagite] the king was profoundly upset by this. And fearing that such a good and important treasure would leave his king-dom, because knowledge and wisdom are the riches of salvation,[20] and because he did not want God to be able to say to him some day, "As you have rejected science, I will reject you,"[21] the very pious king ordered the clerics to return to Paris, greeted them with great clem-ency upon their return, and had them quickly compensated by the bourgeois who had committed offenses against them.

The text that follows is an addition that did not appear in the oldest existing manuscript of the *Chronicle*. The scholarly editor could not decide whether it was written by Guillaume de Nangis or a continuator. In either case, it is useful for our understanding of the image of Saint Louis that was cultivated in the milieu of Saint-Denis.

In effect, if the precious treasure of the knowledge that saves had been taken away from the Kingdom of France, the emblem of the fleur-de-lis of the kings of France would have been strangely ru-ined. For, as God and our Lord Jesus Christ wanted to decorate the Kingdom of France more distinctly than the other kingdoms with faith, wisdom, and chivalry, the kings of France have traditionally painted their arms and their flags with a three-leaved lily as though they wanted to tell the whole universe that faith, knowledge, and chivalric prowess serve our kingdom more than any of the others by providence and the grace of God. These two identical leaves actu-ally signify the knowledge and the chivalry that protect and defend the third leaf placed higher up between them that signifies faith. For faith is ruled and governed by knowledge and defended by chivalry. For as long as these three virtues are held together [*sibi invicem cohaerentia*] in the Kingdom of France by peace, force, and order [*pacifice, fortiter et ordinatim*], the kingdom will solidly hold up [*stabit*]. If they are ever separated or torn from it, the entire kingdom divided against itself will be made desolate and collapse.[22]

With extraordinary depth, this text summed up the philosophy of the "national" history that gradually emerged in France from the beginning of the twelfth century. Three essential themes came together here. The first was the theme of the *translatio studii,* the transfer of science and knowledge from Athens to Rome and from Rome to France. Just as Germany had been the benefactor of a *translatio imperii,* a transfer of power, France received the heritage of knowledge. In France, Christianity inseparably united the prestige of the scholar with the glory of the warrior. Already in the twelfth century, the pairing of the clergy and the knighthood that was blessed by the Church expressed the kingdom's high position in Christendom. In his courtly novels, Chrétien de Troyes praised this prestigious pair as more brilliant in France than anywhere else. In the thirteenth century, a third power, university education, asserted itself in Paris, which became the center of the highest knowledge, theology. This third power arrived on the scene, reinforcing the secular power embodied in the monarchy and the spiritual power represented by the priests. A new three-functioned triad— *sacerdotium, regnum, studium*—expressed this new figure of power.[23] It was under Saint Louis that this new system of values found its highest incarnation in France. Louis IX favored a rise in the power of the priests, the king, and men of science. While his mother was insensitive to this new power represented by the intellectuals and had no idea how to control the masters and students in Paris, a youthful intuition enabled Saint Louis to end the strike and the secession that could have killed the institution. By bringing stability to the University of Paris, Saint Louis assured the preeminence of the Kingdom of France. Because he was also the one ruler who raised the fleur-de-lis to its highest level of prestige as an emblem of the French monarchy, it was possible to use the allegorical method of interpretation that was fashionable at the time to interpret the three leaves of the fleur-de-lis as the symbol of these three powers. Faith was anchored within it in wisdom and knowledge. This corresponded to the great intellectual movement of the age that sought to make things intelligible—from Saint Anselm to Thomas Aquinas, from the centers of monastic learning to the urban center of Paris—the foundry of scholastic science: *fides quaerens intellectum.* A political and ideological triad corresponded to this social-ethical three-some: the unity of peace, force, and order that Saint Louis embodied. This was the image that Saint-Denis gave of Saint Louis on the threshold between the thirteenth and fourteenth centuries. Whether this development in the chronicle was the work of Guillaume de Nangis or of another Dionysian continuator matters little.[24] Louis was the king of the fleur-de-lis whose particular merit consisted in the fact that the two leaves of the clergy and the knighthood, of faith and force, had not had the third leaf torn away from them. The third leaf provided the whole with its coherence: knowledge. Louis IX was king of the knowledge that structured the social and political system.[25]

The essential role that Saint-Denis played can be found at the origins of France's great rise to power because it was thanks to Saint-Denis that wisdom and chivalry came from Greece to France. Now, we can better understand the outrage of the Dionysian monks against Abelard in the preceding century. Abelard confronted the abbey with intellectual criticism in his search for historical and scientific truth. He wanted and was able to prove that the patron saint of the abbey had never been the Areopagite, while the great abbey was helping the French monarchy set up a different system of knowledge, a system of stable power anchored in traditional history and the symbolic imaginary.[26] Abelard probably did not understand that his obstinacy in seeking out the historical truth as we understand it today undermined the foundations of this system. Thus we end up with peace, force, and order. If there is a relevant application for the Gramscian notion of the "organic intellectual," it may very well be in thirteenth-century Christendom among these monks of Saint-Denis, these great ideologues, who made Saint Louis the king of the French monarchical state.

Beyond this reminder of Saint-Denis' historical role, as a member of the Dionysian lobby Guillaume de Nangis never failed to emphasize the privileged ties that Saint Louis maintained with the abbey, just as all of his Mendicant hagiographers highlighted his preferential treatment of the friars. For the year 1231, Guillaume de Nangis noted that "upon the advice of Louis the king of France and the religious, the church of Saint-Denis in France[27] is renovated under the abbot Eudes Clément; none of the monks had dared to do this before because of the sacred [*mysterium*] character of the dedication that this church received from God, which is well known."[28] Let us note in passing that Guillaume took advantage of the situation by mentioning that God did not accomplish miracles solely in favor of the rival abbey of Saint-Rémi de Reims, which he did not mention by name, but also in favor of Saint-Denis. Although Guillaume has been accused of lacking any original conception of history, we should appreciate the remarkable dialectic that he set up between tradition and renewal, and, even more, his sense of the historicity of the sacred that grew richer with time.

Now we can observe how the Saint Louis of Saint-Denis made use of the Saint Louis of the Mendicants. The Saint Louis of Guillaume de Nangis's *Chronicle* was the king of a preeminent France. He was immersed in universal history, as the genre required. The *Chronicle* often followed the *Life* word for word, although it eliminated many details that would be important in an individual biography but that were superfluous in a universal chronicle that aimed for a more general perspective. On the other hand, it related facts in ways that the monk omitted from the *Life*. It included notations on unusual climatic disturbances, symbolic signs, omens, and marvels. For instance, here is the first noted event for the year 1235: "A famine of great magnitude [*fames valde magna*] struck in France, especially in Aquitaine. It struck so hard that men ate grass from the fields like animals. A sester [*setier*] of wheat actually cost one hundred pence in Poitou, and many people in this region died of hunger and suffered from convulsions" (187). Similarly, for the year 1266 he wrote, "In the Kingdom of France, in August, just before dawn, a comet [*cometes horribilis*] appeared and directed its rays toward the East" (230). These two events that affected the Kingdom of France did not appear in the *Life* of Saint Louis under whose reign they took place. Guillaume de Nangis separated Saint Louis from the realm of the marvelous. He bathed him in the light of the religious but distanced him from the fantastic.

Guillaume de Saint-Pathus's *Life* of Saint Louis

Vita et Gesta would be a better title for the *Vie* of Saint Louis, which was written before his canonization. The first term generally applied to the Lives of saints and was later used for people who were similar to them due to the fact that their functions had a certain sacred character—kings, for example, especially if they had been officially sainted but also if they had only a reputation for saintliness. The particular uniqueness of this *Life* consists in the fact that it was written before the canonization but without its author ever having personally known the king. He mentions that he merely attended the arrival and the burial of Saint Louis' bones at Saint-Denis. He had to have been a very young monk at that time. The term *Gesta* referred to the "deeds and actions" [*faits et gestes*] of its hero. It was a history. Guillaume presented himself as a simple monk lacking in any literary culture, a claim that resounds with excessive humility. He acknowledged that he had copied much of his work from other sources. Some critics have observed that he never claimed to have been an eyewitness of the events he narrated, which ran contrary to most of the biographers of his time. He did not pretend and say "*vidi*" (I have seen). One reason for this was that he obviously never knew Saint Louis, but there was also the fact that he considered himself a "historian" and not a "chronicler" [*mémorialiste*]. He compiled information, arranged it, and tried to explain it. He used two primary sources for his work: the *Life* by Geoffroy de Beaulieu and another *Life* of Louis IX by Gilon de Reims that has been lost. Because we can measure Guillaume de Nangis's fidelity to the first of these sources, we can guess that he also used the second one in the same way and thus probably saved the essential information that it contained. However, as Bernard Guenée has astutely pointed out, a compiler in the Middle Ages was still an author as a result of the way he arranged his sources and the interpretations he suggested.

Guillaume distinguished the major events in the *Vie* and *Histoire of Saint Louis* that formed the sequence of the plot from the secondary events that were only indirectly related to it. He called these secondary events "*incidentia*" (digressions).

His Saint Louis was a warrior, and the military was one of the major forces in the kingdom. He called attention to the fact that even the Tartars had heard that "the French were incredibly tough fighters." His text abounds in details about the unrest during Louis' minority, military operations, and the births of the sons of the king who were likely to assure his succession. He also understood the logic behind their first names: the first-born took the name of his father, and the second-born took the name of his grandfather, which gave us "Louis" for his first-born who died in 1260, and Philip for his second-born who became King Philip III. The text is also rich in details about the crusades, particularly the crusade of Tunis that was more recent. He also brought remarkable attention to bear on Charles d'Anjou, first as count of Provence and then especially as king of Naples and Sicily. This was because one of his main motives as a historian was to sing the praise of the French. As a result of his brilliant political and military career, Charles deserved a good spot in the story alongside his brother. Guillaume even had him proclaim an appeal to French pride before the battle of Tagliacozzo (1268): "Chivalrous lords born in France, renowned for your strength and prowess. . . ."[29]

God, of course, was the master of history. The barons who revolted against the young Louis renounced their rebellion once they perceived that the "hand of God" was on his side. In 1239, the king saw that the Lord had finally shielded him from his enemies' machinations. However, when Guillaume was astonished by the ease with which Louis bought his freedom from the Muslims for a modest ransom soon after they took him prisoner, he divided the responsibility for the event between God who made a "miracle" and the "good king" whose qualities enabled it to occur. In this history where conflicts and wars held such important place, the psychology of great men was the main cause of events. It was almost always the pride (*superbia*) of one great man or another that disrupted the state of peace and tranquility.[30] Of all expressions of this pride or "presumption," the worst was the one that turned against the king. The count of Brittany and the count of the March, the most treacherous of the king's great vassals, were respectively "proud and haughty" and "full of vanity and odious presumption." Guillaume stuck with reasons of character because he had trouble discerning that these intrigues needed to be judged in relation to the code that governed relations between a king and his vassals. He was not comfortable with juridical vocabulary, and this was a time when concepts of public law were rapidly evolving, especially the ones that applied to royal power. He did not seem to make a clear distinction between royal *majestas,* that supreme and mysterious sacred character, and *potestas,* which was sovereignty. He also judged Saint Louis in psychological terms and had trouble distinguishing between the role that feelings played in his behavior and conduct related to institutional politics. Like others, he noted that Saint Louis returned from his first crusade a changed man. He saw that the king was full of remorse and bad conscience and that he began to lead a more repentant, more ascetic life, while also applying his power more harshly. He did not seem to notice that the king's real remorse drove him to assert his power for political reasons. Guillaume gave a version of the Great Edict of 1254, which instituted the reign of moral order: "The barons and knights and all the others, great and small, who saw and heard and knew the divine wisdom that existed and ruled in King Louis' acts and measures when he issued righteous justice, honored and feared him more and more with each passing day because they saw and knew that he was a holy man and a gentleman; there was no one left who would dare oppose him in his kingdom, and if anyone rebelled, he was immediately put down" (401). This was the period of Louis the peacemaker. God made the peace that he imposed in France and abroad last through the reign of his son Philip III as a reward for his father's merits. "In comparison with the other kingdoms, the throne of France shone in the time of King Louis like the sun that casts its rays of light everywhere" (ibid).[31]

So, here was the Saint Louis of Saint-Denis, a sun-king, or rather this sun was the throne that diffused its rays and benefits. The king had been absorbed within the royal insignia, by the crown on the seal and the throne in historiography. Saint Louis' metamorphosis after his return from the Holy Land also provided Guillaume de Nangis with an opportunity to insert most of Geoffroy de Beaulieu's treatise into his *Gesta* for the reason that it contained proof of his sainthood. A Mendicant king now appeared in the sun-king's shadow, as Guillaume made his contribution to the approaching canonization of his hero. He sang his praise and told of his first miracles. In order to promote France through its kings, Saint-Denis used any materials at its disposal.

In Saint Louis we find a saint who was capable of destabilizing Christian society in the same way as the Mendicants by extolling poverty, humility, and a peace that represented eschatological justice. According to the vision of Saint-Denis, there was also a Christian king in him who helped stabilize Christendom through the cohesiveness of faith, force, and order. He was a saint king with two faces. By striking a balance between these two tendencies, the Mendicants of the university saved Saint Louis' image from a certain schizophrenia. The monks of Saint-Denis anchored the Mendicant king's image firmly within the channels of royal power and national sentiment.

Guillaume de Nangis synthesized an idea of Christian monarchy with his portrayal of Louis IX. He integrated other images of the king that had appeared during the early period of his rule with the image of the Sun-King at its end. At the end of the thirteenth century, the king was not an absolute monarch. Among the reciprocal obligations between vassal and lord in feudalism, he upheld his duty to protect his subjects in return for their loyalty. From the earliest period of his reign, Saint Louis "thought in his heart that the loyalty that subjects owe their lord calls for comparable assistance from the lord for his subjects."[32] (Guillaume combined the vocabulary of sovereignty that spoke of "subjects" with that of feudalism that spoke of "lords.") At this early stage he was already the same "very good and very noble" king and led a "saintly life," which explained why God granted "prosperity" to him and his kingdom. He stood out against the model of bad rulers like the barons who rebelled against him or even Emperor Frederick II who was "suspect" without necessarily being bad. There was also the opposing model of the ruler inspired by "the devil, who is always jealous of good men" (325).

In his *Life* as in his *Chronicle,* Guillaume was very interested in the Orient, an essential space in Saint Louis' life and preoccupations that we cannot forget. It was in the Orient that Guillaume discovered the anti–good king and the anti–Saint Louis. The anti–Saint Louis was not a Muslim, a Saracen, or a Turk. He was the Old Man of the Mountain, the king of an extremist Shiite sect, the Assassins. Saint Louis came into contact with him in the Holy Land. This "very bad and very mean" king who was counseled by the devil actually became good through God's intervention.[33] Maybe this was Guillaume de Nangis's way of justifying Saint Louis' diplomatic relations with infidel rulers. If this was his intention, he joined the Mendicants again insofar as they were the king's privileged intermediaries in the Orient. Both historians, the Mendicant and the Dionysian, highlighted Saint Louis' oriental horizon.

The King of the *Exempla*

IN THIS PERIOD HISTORY DID NOT YET ISOLATE EVENTS VERY CLEARLY in the form of human time, as a literary genre, or even less as a discipline of knowledge. For want of history, the thirteenth century was fond of stories and anecdotes.[1] People at that time were also eager to learn. The Church knew this and its didactic efforts were intensive. It furnished its main pedagogues, the preachers, with anecdotes. These edifying little stories with which the preachers peppered their sermons were known as *exempla*.

The medieval *exemplum* was "a short story given as true and meant to be inserted within a speech (usually a sermon) in order to persuade the audience with a salutary lesson."[2] This kind of narrative also attempted to captivate its audience with its pleasing or striking character. It was a rhetorical device, an anecdote intended to convey some lesson. As the lessons of the *exempla* were meant to assure the listener's salvation, some writers have called the medieval *exemplum* "an eschatological gadget."[3] "The *exemplum* introduces the pleasing and realistic quality of a story that breaks the sermon's general mode of enunciation and seems to establish a furtive complicity between the preacher and his audience. But, we should not be fooled. Far from being an isolated unit or foreign body in the sermon, the *exemplum* is tied in with all of the other arguments, and the momentary interruption

281

that it introduces into the sermon reinforces its ideological function as the speech of authority."[4] It often resembled the popular tale, which was one of its sources or one of the forms to which it referred. The *exemplum* also showed a hero, which could be an animal as in the fable. The ancient *exemplum* frequently drew its seductive power from the fact that the subject in its story was often a hero who was himself a living example whose words and actions had exemplary value. When Christians took to the *exemplum* along with most of the other forms of ancient culture, they tended to link it to the great Christian models of sacred history, to Jesus, who was the model par excellence, the Virgin Mary, and other characters from the Old Testament. This type of *exemplum* was not revived in the Middle Ages, which separated literature from sacred history and kept holy and biblical figures out of these little tales.

The medieval *exemplum* was not usually suited to include historical characters. First of all, because it was addressed to all Christians it tended to use the "common" man for its stories, the type who did not surpass the ordinary in his usual acts and accomplishments. Some have said that the collections of *exempla* made up the "bible of daily life." In addition, because the *exemplum* tended to objectify the anecdote, in other words, to withdraw the hero's status as a subject in order to make an object out of him, a simple tool of the lesson that the story presented, the lesson itself became the story's subject. The historical character in a medieval *exemplum* was often nothing more than a front and a borrowed name. He became stuck within the "sermon's ideological function," absorbed by the use that it made of him.

However, as the Lives of saints and important figures were often written up in the form of a string of edifying anecdotes and, more particularly, miracles, the preachers and compilers of *exempla* sometimes slipped a fragment from a Life into a sermon and passed it off as an *exemplum*. (Miracles comprised a genre that was entirely separate and distinct from the *exempla*.) The temptation to do this may have been even greater if the hero of the *vita* was a prestigious person. In this case, the status of the genre shifted from the *exemplum* that used an average or anonymous Christian as its main character to a heroic or personal *exemplum*. Some people have even thought that it is possible to identify a "biographical" *exemplum* that originated from a *vita* and "based its structure on the original form of the *vita*," although the anecdote was supposed to have been taken from the biography of a historical figure.[5]

We should also note that the *exemplum* usually relied on negative examples to deter Christians from sin. The historical figures best suited for *exempla* were the bad ones. Their best heroes were the bad kings Theodoric and Charles Martel (identified as a king) who persecuted Catholics and the Church and who, according to legend, had been thrown down into hell. In the thirteenth century, however, the kings of France sometimes appeared as the heroes of anecdotal tales that circulated and sometimes ended up in collections of *exempla*. It was the ambivalent character of King Philip Augustus who seems to have been the first of these and who seems to have inspired more of them than any other king.[6]

Although Saint Louis was a potential source of *exempla* because of his virtues and the edifying anecdotes that people told about him, he paradoxically ended up being suspected, and then officially sanctioned, as a bad hero for *exempla* because of his holiness. Judged a saint, he exhibited none of the condemnable behaviors that could be given as negative "examples." Once he became a saint, he escaped this genre and was relegated to the Lives and the Miracles.

THE LIMITED TESTIMONY OF THE *EXEMPLA*

We do, however, know of several *exempla* that had Saint Louis as their hero. They are very few in number if we exclude, as we should, the anecdotes in which he was only mentioned in order to date one of these little stories "from the times of King Louis" or in order to give it an additional stamp of authority. In general, they explain a lot about Saint Louis' image and the processes of memory that dealt with him.

Here are two of them taken from a treatise written for preachers by the Dominican Étienne de Bourbon. His life and activities were centered at the Preaching Friars' convent in Lyon after he finished his studies in Paris. The treatise was composed sometime around 1250, and he died in 1261.[7] His work and his death predating Saint Louis' testify to the rapid transformation of anecdotes circulating as *exempla*, even while their protagonists were still alive. In this work dealing with the *Dons du Saint-Esprit* (Gifts of the Holy Spirit), the first anecdote about Saint Louis was used to illustrate the "third title" of the fifth section on the gift of advice (*donum consilii*). The section explained the strength (*de fortitudine*) that supported the gift of good judgment by means of which man could choose the virtues that lead him to salvation. Charity was one of this strength's supporting elements as it was given through the love of God (*elemosina data pro Deo*). The youthful Saint Louis was the hero of this "positive" *exemplum*.

> One day, King Louis of France, the same who is still ruling now, made an excellent statement that was reported by a religious who was there at the time and who heard it straight from his mouth. One morning, when this prince was still very young, a group of poor people gathered in the court of his palace and waited for alms. Taking advantage of the early hour when everyone was still asleep, he left his room by himself and went down with a servant carrying a large sack full of deniers under his squire's outfit. He next began to pass them all out with his own hands, giving more generously to the ones who seemed to be the poorest. When this was done, he was returning to his quarters when a religious who had witnessed this scene from a window's embrasure where he had been talking with the king's mother went up to him and said: "Lord, I had a perfect view of your misdeeds." "My very dear brother," answered the embarrassed prince, "those people are in my pay; they fight for me against my enemies and keep the peace in the kingdom. I still have not yet paid them the amount that is their due."[8]

This *exemplum* illustrated the importance of charity. It exploited Saint Louis' reputation—already well established in his lifetime—as a generous giver of alms. The story also echoed the legendary image of the precociousness of the king's virtues and charitable practices. The *exemplum*'s lesson was both moral maxim and witty remark, but it was placed in the young king's mouth, which was not very realistic. Saint Louis was used to stage a *topos,* a commonplace idea. The *exemplum* used an image of the king and reinforced it with an anecdote that was destined to succeed. It thus helped to credit the memory of an exceptionally pious ruler. It also helped counter the image of a weak child king and in order to build up the memory of an outstanding man it relied on a customary strategy of the hagiographers by demonstrating that even as children saints and exceptional men had the mentality and behavior of adults. Saint Louis had no childhood; he was an *enfant prodige* who resembled an adult very early in life.[9]

Étienne de Bourbon's second *exemplum* refers to the episode of the king's serious illness in 1244 and his subsequent vow to crusade:

> The king of France was sick, near death, and beyond the help of any doctors. He lay down on the ashes and called everyone there around him and told them: "Look! I who was the wealthiest and most noble lord in the universe, I who was more powerful than any other man, who presided over them by my rank, my fortune, and the number of my friends, I cannot even snatch the shortest delay from death nor a single hour of rest from sickness! So what are all of these things worth?" When they heard him speaking like this, all the people there began to sob. Yet against all expectations, the Lord healed him at the very moment that everyone thought he was dead. He got up from his bed and gave thanks to God, and it was after this that he took up the cross.[10]

This *exemplum* illustrated the seventh "title" of the first book, *Du don de crainte* (*De dono timoris*, Of the Gift of Fear). More specifically, it appeared in the section on the ninth reason for a Christian to fear death, which was that one can fall prey to serious illness.

Departing from the real historical facts about Saint Louis' illness and vow to crusade, the author of the example exploited it for the purpose of introducing another commonplace, the *topos* of the impotence of the rich and powerful in facing death. The speech and the specific detail that Saint Louis had been placed on a bed of ashes cannot be found in any other testimony about this episode. Lecoy de la Marche sees "new details" in it that had been "reported first-hand," which is not impossible. I think it is probably more of an invention forged or simply collected by the author who exploited it—within the logic of the ideology of the *exemplum* and outside any considerations of historical authenticity—in order to introduce the allusion to a habitual practice among important persons: the act of laying the body *in articulo mortis* upon a bed of ashes as a form of penitence *in extremis* that adopted a traditional *topos* of Antiquity. As for the historical veracity of Saint Louis' speech, my skepticism not only arises from the banality of this commonplace, but also because the idea and its formulation seem very different from what we know about the king's vocabulary and way of thinking. The flamboyant allusion to his power and wealth, the personification of death, and the lack of any Christian reference all lead me to consider the speech apocryphal. Once again, a known fact, in this case Saint Louis' sickness and taking up the cross, worked to confer a false semblance of authenticity on the simple historical staging of a common lesson. Étienne de Bourbon did not care about what Saint Louis "really said." He cared about whatever he could have said that corresponded to the Dominican's classical culture and didactic purpose. Saint Louis is no more present in this *exemplum* than in the last one we examined. These anecdotes were only byproducts of the precociously stereotypical image of the future saint king.

The king is even less conspicuous in a thirteenth-century manuscript from Tours[11] that contains *exempla* involving Gregory of Tours, among others. He was the bishop of Paris from 1228 to 1248, and one of the king's close advisors. It also contains one *exemplum* presenting Saint Louis. The scene took place during the birth of the king's first child. This must have been Blanche who was born in 1241 and who died at a very young age.

> Marguerite, the queen of France and King Louis' wife, first had a girl, and no one dared to announce it to the king. They summoned the bishop Guillaume to break the news to him. He went to the king and announced the news to him in these terms: "Sire, rejoice, for I will bring you young cattle, as today the crown of France has gained a king; in effect, you have a daughter whose marriage will bring you another kingdom, whereas, if you had had a son, you would have had to have given him a large county." This is the way he made him happy.[12]

Let's skip over the dubious elegance with which the bishop mentioned the king's daughter alongside his heifers and the inaccuracy with which he stated that the king would have to give a son a large fief when, in fact, the son in question[13] would have been the oldest and therefore would have received the royal crown after his father's death and not a large fief, which was what the sons born after received. As we know, Louis VII suffered the misfortune of having only daughters for a very long time, and the late birth of Philip Augustus had been heralded as a miracle. However, even if Saint Louis was concerned about having male heirs (he later had six sons), he is presented here as someone capable of reacting poorly to the news of his daughter's birth, so poorly that his entourage had to call on a venerable spokesman to announce it, who, in turn, had to manufacture a witticism just to pacify the king. It is clear that this story was an invention that allowed the preacher to slip a joke into his sermon. It recalled the way that daughters were scorned in a traditional society more than the hereditary customs of the French monarchy. Here, Saint Louis was merely a name borrowed for the purposes of the *exemplum*.

Another *exemplum,* which I find more interesting, could appear in our chapter on Saint Louis' system of justice:[14]

> The king Saint Louis had taken to reading the entire prayer book from beginning to end in the evening each year on Good Friday. One year, a certain person who belonged to a noble family was imprisoned in the Châtelet for the many offenses he had committed. When Good Friday came, the king withdrew to his chapel and became absorbed in his pious exercise. However, accompanied by the king's own son and his brothers the princes, the family and friends of the prisoner came all the way into the sanctuary to pester him. When he saw them, he placed his finger on the verse where he had stopped reading so that he would be able to resume his interrupted reading in the same spot. One of the lords who had been nominated to speak for the group approached him and said, "Very illustrious sire, today is a day of mercy and thanks. It was on a day like this that our Lord redeemed us and pardoned the thief from high on the cross; he died while praying for his tormentors. So, all of us present here, we throw ourselves at your feet, most illustrious sire, and humbly beg you to follow Christ's example by having pity on the noble captive who is pining away in the dungeons of the Châtelet." The pious king heard them with goodness; he was ready to exercise his clemency when, while lifting the finger that he held pressed in the prayer book, he read the verse that goes: "Happy are those who uphold justice and render their judgments each day of their lives." He thought for a moment and, then, his only response was to tell the supplicants to bring the provost of Paris and returned to his reading. The group thought that they were going to get their pardon for the guilty party and rushed off to send for the provost. The magistrate soon arrived before his lord. Louis requested him to read off the crimes committed by the prisoner, if he knew about them. With this demand, the provost, not

daring to hide the truth, obeyed the order and rattled off a long list of crimes horrendous enough to make one shudder. After hearing him, the king ordered him to let justice take its course and to lead the criminal to the gallows on that very day with no regard for the occasion they were celebrating.[15]

Again in this case, nothing guarantees the authenticity of the anecdote as the genre of the *exemplum* for the most part arose either from hearsay, meting out both true and false, or from pure and simple invention. Still, the little story effectively illustrated things that we can assess through other sources such as the struggle in Saint Louis between harshness and forgiveness. This struggle was closely related to the royal ideology of the Mirrors of Princes, which advocated a balance between those two attitudes, and which also seemed to have divided Saint Louis' entourage and the opinions of the time between a camp that favored indulgence and another that favored severity. The anti-leniency movement could very well have produced this *exemplum*. The king's tendency to have a violent temper could turn into repression; his mercy resulted from his desire to create a milder Christianity. This was basically the same goal of the Mendicants' spirituality, although it did not prevent them from acting as pitiless judges throughout the Inquisition. The *exemplum* also illustrated the disposition of the king's conscience when facing situations of potential non-respect for the letter of ecclesiastical prescriptions. Saint Louis did not consider these prescriptions sacred. Moral urgency could justify the transgression of religious taboos. A death sentence could be handed down on Good Friday just as fasting on Friday could be suspended for the banquet with Henry III.[16]

There are two other *exempla* that seem to me to illustrate the use that the great ideological currents of the thirteenth century made of Saint Louis by exploiting events from his life in a plausible fashion. The first places Saint Louis in a situation involving the promotion of laymen in religious matters:[17]

A learned cleric was preaching before King Louis and in his sermon he had the opportunity to pronounce these words: "During the Passion, all the apostles abandoned Christ, and their faith faded from their hearts. The Virgin Mary alone preserved him from the day of the Passion to the Resurrection. In memory of this, at matins during the week of penitence, we put out all the lights one after another, all but one that is used to relight them at Easter." Upon hearing this, another cleric of a higher rank got up to correct the speaker: "I hold you," he said, "to affirming only what is written; the apostles actually did abandon Jesus Christ in body, but not in heart." The misfortunate fellow was about to be forced to retract his words right on the pulpit, but at this point the king stood up and intervened: "The proposition that has been advanced is not false at all," he said. "It can be found well and true in the writings of the Fathers. Bring me the book of Saint Augustine." Some people hurried off to obey his command. They returned with the book, and to the embarrassment of the unfortunate interrupter, the king showed anyone who wanted to see it a text of the *Commentary on the Gospel of Saint John* by the illustrious scholar that went as follows, "*Fugerunt, relicto eo corde e corpore.* They fled, abandoning him in heart and body."[18]

An initial reading brings out Saint Louis' penchant for intervening in matters of faith, his patristic culture, and knowledge of scripture.[19] As he respected the separation between the functions and capacities of clerics and laymen, Saint Louis did not hesitate to step into the religious domain as far as any layman was allowed to tread. Granted, he was an exceptional layman, but a layman all the same. In the thirteenth century, preaching was separate from the liturgy of the mass. This development authorized the king to intervene in the middle of a sermon. Thus the anecdote is not improbable, although there is no guarantee of its authenticity. The *exemplum* was above all meant to underscore the king's patristic erudition.

The second *exemplum* seems to have originated in Italy.[20]

One day the king Louis asked the friar Bonaventure the following question: "What should man find preferable, if he had the choice, either not to exist at all, or to be condemned to eternal torments?" Bonaventure answered him: "My lord, this question assumes two things: on the one hand, the perpetual offense of God without which the supreme Judge would not inflict eternal punishment, and, on the other, an endless suffering. As no one would know how to accept remaining in a state of perpetual hostility with God, I think that it would be better to choose not to exist at all." Then this very pious worshiper of the divine Majesty and very Christian ruler turned toward those present and added, "I am sticking with my brother Bonaventure's decision, and I swear to you that I would a thousand times rather be reduced to nothingness than to live eternally in this world and even in full possession of my royal omnipotence while offending my Creator."

This anecdote emerged from the Franciscan milieus. It was above all intended to highlight Saint Bonaventure's prestige and developed in the same sense as the ideas and behavior of Saint Louis as we know them through more reliable sources. It demonstrated the high esteem in which the king held the Mendicant friars and more specifically the influence that Bonaventure exerted on him as a theologian and as a preacher. The term "decision" evoked the authority of a university master. The famous Franciscan was one of the great theologians of the University of Paris. He was elected general minister of his order in 1256. He preached before Louis and the royal family several times.[21] Examining the content, we find the conviction that Saint Louis expressed several times—notably in Joinville[22]—that death was preferable to living in mortal sin.

Finally, I have selected two *exempla* taken from a collection that falls a little bit outside the chronological timeframe that I set for this book. Compiled by a Dominican, it was part of a group of treatises for use by preachers. The treatises were collected in a manuscript composed in Bologna in 1326.[23]

The first one, the fifty-ninth in the collection, is entitled "A Thoughtless Oath" (*De iuramento improviso*).

In the happy times of Louis, the king of France, a great bishop came from Germany to Paris to visit the king. He brought two young people with him to assist him, and they were sons of his brother. One day when the bishop was busy with his affairs, these youths played at hunting birds for sport and entered the orchard of an important noble. When this man saw them from his palace, he asked who they were and, as no one could tell him this, he had them hung from the trees. The bishop told the king about this matter. Being with the bishop, the king was forthwith very shocked and swore on the holy Gospels that he would have the nobleman hung. He brought the affair before his council and most of them dissuaded him from carrying out his oath, arguing that it would cause great dissension in the kingdom. The king summoned a large number of religious scholars and asked them if he could be dispensed from carrying out his oath. They answered that this renunciation would be a good thing in consideration of the common good of the entire kingdom, claiming that Herod was not held to his oath to decapitate John the Baptist because the young girl's [Salomé's] demand was unreasonable and iniquitous. They added that although this bishop had justifiably asked for justice for the death of his nephews, because a great disturbance in the kingdom would result from this, the king was not obligated to carry out the oath that he had made without thinking about it. Even though he was not able to carry out his intention, he still carried out his oath in the spirit of the letter. He had the nobleman suspended alive and naked in a sack for several hours on the gibbet, and when they brought him down he made him pay his weight in florins as compensation. But, so that no one could accuse him of having acted out of greed, he divided the money in three parts and gave one part to the Dominicans, which we used to build a dormitory and a refectory, and the two others to the Franciscans and the monks of Saint-Germain [des Près], which they used to build churches.[24]

This story is an odd recollection of the affair of the lord of Coucy and his hanging of the three young Flemish nobles who had been hunting in his forest.[25] We find the same image of Saint Louis' severity toward the arbitrary justice of the nobles in it, the same hostile reaction from a segment of the kingdom—the nobles mainly—and the same obligation for the king to reverse the machine of justice and accept a compromise based on monetary compensation. To this political lesson, the *exemplum* added a case for jurisprudence in the non-execution of an oath. (Saint Louis actually detested oaths, so at least on this point the *exemplum* departed from what would have been realistic.) The account is interesting for two reasons. First, it illustrates the importance of the development of casuistry that was taking place in Saint Louis' time under the influence of the scholastics. As in the Good Friday affair, it involved the acceptance of the non-observance of a traditional and apparently sacred rule, in this case an oath sworn on the Gospels. The most interesting element is probably that the word for political order, which was becoming more prevalent under Saint Louis, is "the common good" [*le bien commun*]. Finally, there is the testimony to the privileged though not exclusive interest that Saint Louis took in the friars, which was emphasized here by the Mendicant pressure group. Saint Louis not only appeared here as a king whose powers were limited by reasons of state and opinion, but also, once more, as the king of the Mendicants.

The last *exemplum* is simply titled, "Of Saint Louis" (*De beato Ludovico*). And yet . . .

> They say that one day when Saint Louis was eating in Paris with the masters and friars in the house of the hosts [of our convent of Preachers], he sent a page up to the high end of the table to see what the friars were doing in the refectory. When he returned, he said, "They are behaving well. Each of them is paying attention to his reading and what he has before him." The king replied: "They are not behaving well." An hour later, he sent the page back, and when he returned he told the king, "They are behaving worse than before because they are not murmuring amongst themselves and are not listening to the reader with the same attention as before." The king responded: "They are behaving better." He sent him around a third time, and when he came back he answered that they were behaving as poorly as possible because they were screaming so much that no one could hear the reader. The king replied: "Now they are behaving perfectly. When the friars eat well, they are happy, but when they eat poorly, there are scarcely any of them who open their mouths to sing, as we can see on Good Friday."[26]

Barring his familiarity with the Mendicant friars, Saint Louis' conduct in this anecdote is entirely unlikely. The pious king, an adept of frugality, would never have accepted this "good story of the friars" that resembled the "good words of the monks" of the High Middle Ages and our own "stories [jokes] about priests." The genre of the *exemplum* only asked its heroes for their names to hang a story on. Here we have an extreme case that falls in the category of the exact opposite of what an accurate biographical *exemplum* would be. As we have just seen, several of the anecdotes come close to such accuracy.

Still, the *exempla* more or less functioned to circulate information about the stereotyped image of Saint Louis as it existed at the time, although this was certainly not their purpose. At times they exaggerated some of his traits and qualities, shifting between what was historically authentic and the commonplace idea. They offered a simplified, manipulated image in order to follow the rules of a short narrative genre with the purposes of edifying its listeners and of responding to the generally ordinary, far from demanding needs of preachers and perhaps of their audience as well. This was a result of the poverty of communications media in the thirteenth century. Through the *exempla,* Saint Louis' very memory created commonplaces rooted in the mental and ideological realities of the thirteenth century. The king and his time reflected one another's image in this hall of mirrors produced by the *exempla.*

THE STORIES OF THE MINSTREL OF REIMS

I am following up these true *exempla* with a number of stories from an anonymous thirteenth-century author whose works do not seem to have been very well known in the Middle Ages: the Minstrel of Reims. The interest of his work lies in its nature and in the nature of the audience that it addressed. It is a repertoire of stories annotated by one of the traveling comedians who went from castle to castle entertaining audiences. These audiences were usually made up of nobles, although they were also sometimes bourgeois in the towns like the people of Reims whom the Minstrel defends when he mentions their conflict with Archbishop Henri de Braine who died in 1240. All we know about him is that he was a native of Reims and that he wrote some time around 1260. His book is a universal history beginning around 1150. It is made up mainly of anecdotes and little stories that some have compared to the *exempla,* but the only thing that the two have in common is that they are short narratives. The Minstrel pursued the two-sided goal of instructing and amusing his readers at the same time. His real talent was limited, although he was probably better as a storyteller. For the most part, his stories follow a chronological order and he crammed them full of legends and apologues. Most of the stories he collected were gossip and rumors. He tried to be satirical and sometimes went so far as to be a little saucy, and his text is full of all kinds of errors, particularly chronological errors.[27] He was interested most in the history of France and the crusades. His only interest for us is from the perspective of mentalities and cultural consumption. Whereas the authors and compilers of *exempla* usually transcribed them in Latin, the Minstrel of Reims' little histories were told and written in the vernacular, which was much closer to Saint Louis' usual language. The Minstrel's work allows us to revisit several episodes from Saint Louis' life, not as I have presented them here in the first part of the book, not as critical history allows us verify them and situate them in historical perspective today, but as a "communicator" of the time presented them to different contemporary publics along with all the errors and prejudices meant to flatter public tastes.

For example, it was not enough for the Minstrel to just collect the calumnies circulating about intimate relations between Blanche of Castile and the cardinal legate Romain de Saint-Ange, but he had to add that after the bishop of Beauvais accused her of being pregnant with the prelate's child, she allegedly came naked covered only in a robe before an assembly of barons and bishops including the bishop of Beauvais and stood up on a table and disrobed, saying, "All of you look at me, so that none of you can say that I am pregnant with child." Then, the Minstrel added that she showed herself entirely, "front and back," so that it was perfectly clear that "she had no child in her belly."[28] The Minstrel or his source embellished on the malicious gossip about Blanche of Castile spread by the baronial milieu that had risen up against "the foreigner" and her royal child.[29] He did this by molding the gossip into a well-known type of story of the time that can be found, for instance, in Gautier de Coincy's *Miracles de Notre-Dame,* a bestseller of the time. The story goes like this: a nun, usually an abbess, was accused of being pregnant, and she disrobed in front of the entire chapter in order to prove her innocence. The Minstrel fabricated this story on the basis of rumors, and, although it asserts Blanche of Castile's purity, he circulated it in a milieu that was well disposed to receive it. He flattered this audience by offering it this spicy scene. At the same time, the story also testifies to the troubled atmosphere surrounding Louis IX's minority with a child king and a foreign queen. The king spent his youth in a male-dominated seigniorial milieu that was misogynous and xenophobic.

The Minstrel rambled on about the unrest during the king's minority and pretended to take pity on the "child." He always called him this, although he informs us that Louis was fourteen years old when his father died. Albeit ill defined, this was the traditional age of majority in most of the large fiefs and in the royal family. The Minstrel showed the king at his coronation and in the wars of his youth but he never represented him in any worthwhile detail. Later, at the moment of Louis' wedding, he slipped in two descriptions of the royal family—the queen's family and the royal couple—to inform his audience.

> We can tell you that here the king of France was twenty years old. The queen decided to marry him off, and he took the daughter of the count of Provence. He had four daughters, and she was the oldest one. King Henry of England took the second one, and Count Richard his brother who is now king of Germany took the third. The count of Anjou, the brother of the king of France took the last one and the county of Provence along with her, because it is the custom of the country that the last child receives everything if there is no male heir. . . .[30] And know that this lady that the king of France took for wife had the name of Marguerite, and that she is a very wise and very good lady. She had eight children from the king, five sons and three daughters. The oldest of the sons was named Louis,[31] the second was Philip, the third was Pierre, the fourth was Jean, and the fifth was Robert. The oldest of the girls is named Isabeau and is married to the king of Navarre, and the second is named Marguerite and is given to the son of the duke of Brabant, and the third is named Blanche.[32]

For an audience hungry for information about the great families, this was one way of situating Saint Louis and the queen within a tight familial network. The Minstrel either did not know about the children who died young or passed over them in silence: the elder Blanche (1240–1244), Jean who died shortly after his birth and before Louis and Marguerite's departure for the crusade in 1248, and Agnès who was born in 1260. He switched the order of the births of the third and fourth sons; Jean-Tristan was born at Damietta in 1250 during his father's captivity and Pierre was born in the Holy Land in 1251, the following year. Generally lacking precision with the dates, the Minstrel naturally paid more attention to the chronology of the royal family. In the thirteenth century, people began to keep better track of birthdates and this habit obviously began for the children of important figures.

When he got to the conflict between the count of the March and the king of England—a good subject for an audience that craved feats of war—the Minstrel presented Louis as decisive but cautious. Thus, when Louis learned of Henry's arrival at Bordeaux, "he was not alarmed, but went out to confront them." He did not back down and made such careful preparations that the count of the March saw that the king "was wise."

The third episode from Louis' life that provided fodder for the Minstrel's narrative was the crusade. A series of short, rapid scenes relate it. First, we have the vow to crusade: "Then there came a time when a very terrible illness afflicted him, and he was sick almost to the point of dying, and at this moment he took up the cross to go overseas and recovered and prepared for his voyage and had everyone preach the crusade. And many men of high standing took up the cross." This is followed by a list of the prominent crusaders. Their more or less famous names were meant to inform and delight the audience: ". . . and so many other great lords that France was emptied of them, and their absence can still be felt to this day."[33] The Minstrel echoed a certain hostility toward the crusades that was particularly strong in the noble milieu that was bled dry and impoverished by them.

The criticism became even more direct when combined with that of the English Benedictine Matthew Paris on the financing of the crusade, but from a different point of view:

> But the king did one thing from which no good would come, because he accepted the three-year delay that the knights requested from the legate for a moratorium guaranteed by the legate on the debts that they owed the bourgeois. This granted, they left for overseas. But this is not what Godefroy de Bouillon did. He sold his dukedom once and for all and went overseas with only his own remaining property and brought no one else's goods or money with him. Thus did he, and the Scripture says that God never wants to have anything to do with plundering.[34]

Again, we come across a large problem for the men of the thirteenth century and most of all for kings. It was a problem that Saint Louis resolved, but not without provoking a certain amount of criticism and not without allowing people to perceive that, whenever war and major undertakings were concerned, the question of finances raised a nearly unsolvable problem for the noble class and especially for the monarchy which could no longer simply rely on revenues from their domains and payments from their vassals.

Saint Louis was the first king of debt in an obvious way. How times had changed since the first crusade when a Godefroy de Bouillon would leave for the Holy Land without any hope of ever returning and sufficiently in love with the land overseas to invest himself in it entirely! Just as Joinville did not want to turn back to look at his castle as he left on the crusade for fear that his resolve would melt away, yet who still turned back in his heart,[35] the crusading knights departed with their minds turned toward what they were leaving behind: their families, their castles, their country, and their interests. They imagined their eventual return with great anxiety. Saint Louis was the crusading king of this nostalgia.

Next comes a scene with a crowd and a great spectacle: "When the king had prepared for his voyage, he took the scarf and his pilgrim's staff to Notre-Dame in Paris, and the bishops sang the mass. Then he left Notre-Dame with the queen and his brothers and all their wives unshod and barefoot, and all the congregations and the people of Paris accompanied them all the way to Saint-Denis in cries and tears. And there, the king left them and sent them back to Paris and he cried many tears on their departure."[36] Here we have all the emotion of the departure for the crusade, the great collective turmoil of the military pilgrimage to Jerusalem. However, although the king and his retinue left, the people stayed behind. For them, his voyage was reduced to participation in a ceremony and a procession. The ones who were leaving departed in a flood of tears. The Middle Ages belonged to men, but they were always crying. Saint Louis, a king of tears, was also a king of grief beyond tears, as we shall see.[37]

In the Minstrel's text, the scene implies that emotion had even become individualized, as in the face-to face dialogue between mother and son:

> But his mother the queen stayed with him and accompanied him for three days despite his will. And then he said to her: "Sweet beautiful mother, by this faith that you owe me, please go back now. I am leaving you my three children, Louis, Philip, and Isabelle to keep, and leave you to govern the Kingdom of France and I know that the children will be well kept and the kingdom well governed." Then the queen answered him, crying, "Very sweet handsome son, how will my heart be able to suffer our separation? It will be harder than stone if it doesn't split in two halves because you have been a better son to me than any mother has ever had." With these words she fainted and fell to the ground. The king lifted her up, kissed her,

and took leave of her, crying. And the queen fainted again and when she came to she said: "Handsome, tender son, my heart tells me that I will never see you again." And she was speaking the truth for she died before he could return.[38]

It is not possible to reproduce all the anecdotal episodes from this *Histoire de Saint Louis* here. I am therefore skipping over the abridged versions of the voyage to Aigues-Mortes, the voyage by sea, and the stay in Cyprus. However, there is one interesting episode that seems authentic after a certain amount of crosschecking, and it is an episode that is mentioned only in the Minstrel's text.[39] It was in the spring of 1249 on the eve of the departure from Cyprus to Egypt. "And then the king wanted them to enter all the ships, and this was done when he commanded it. And he sent the commander of each ship sealed letters, and he forbade them from reading them before leaving the port. And when they left, they each broke the seals off their letters from the king and they saw that the king commanded them all to sail to Damietta, and so each of them ordered his sailors to steer for it."[40]

This episode gives us some familiarity with the secrets henceforth necessitated by strategy. Saint Louis replayed this game of secret destinations in 1270. In 1249, they may have hesitated between two directions: Egypt or Palestine. In 1270 the suspense was even greater. They planned to sail to the east and chose Carthage and Tunis. We get the impression that when Saint Louis was in the Mediterranean he was moving through a world of spies, and that generally, whether at peace or war, secrecy became a weapon in the arsenals of leaders, although this was certainly not an invention of the thirteenth century.

The following scene describes their landing. Joinville had already described it, and the Minstrel was well informed about it. Their parallel accounts follow, with Joinville's lived testimony and the Minstrel's transformation of a serious report into a historical tale.

The Minstrel states that the approach to Damietta was difficult, and that the Muslims shot so many arrows at the approaching Christian ships that "the Christians took a break."

And when the king saw that the Christians were stopping, he entered a state of violent anger. He put his feet together and leapt into the sea entirely armed, his shield around his neck and sword in fist; and the sea came all the way up to his waist and he made it to the shore, thanks be to God. And he leapt amongst the Saracens and battled against them marvelously. And everyone was amazed at the sight. And when the Christians saw the king do all this, they leapt into the sea in droves and took the land and shouted out Montjoie and fought and killed so many [enemies] that one could hardly count them all, and they kept on ceaselessly jumping from the ships.[41]

Joinville narrates the same scene but with much more talent.

When the king heard people saying that the banner of Saint Denis had fallen, he crossed his ship in leaps and bounds, and despite the fact that the legate was with him and that he had never wanted to abandon him, he leapt into the sea where he was in the water up to his armpits. And he moved forward with his shield on his neck and his helm on his head and his lance in his hand, all the way to his people who were on the seashore. When he came aground and saw the Saracens, he asked several people who they were, and they told him that they were Saracens and he placed his lance under his shoulder and his shield in front of him and he would have run and thrown himself upon them if the brave men with him had allowed it to happen.[42]

An eyewitness, Joinville brings more details and greater accuracy, while the Minstrel keeps the information from the episode that seemed essential to him. Through these secular artisans of Saint Louis' memory, we can plainly see the knight king emerge.[43]

This episode is followed by the capture of Damietta and the major episodes of the Egyptian campaign, according to a model that was also used by Matthew Paris: alongside the wise king (despite his outburst during the landing), there was also the mean crazed character among the crusaders, his brother Count Robert d'Artois. As a result of his errors, they suffered defeat, the king's capture and imprisonment—which the Minstrel did not dwell on and which he shortened by ten days. He also reduced the stay in the Holy Land, Blanche de Castile's sickness and death, and the king's return to France to almost nothing. Like Matthew Paris, he dwelt on the conflicts in Flanders and, especially, the reconciliation between the English and the French. It is at this point that he underscored one of Saint Louis' character traits that struck many of his contemporaries and that played an important role in the king's political conduct. This is Saint Louis' "conscience."[44] To describe Louis, he relied on a label that Louis had taken for his own: *le prud'homme*" (the man of probity):[45] "We will now speak about Saint Louis, the *prud'homme* who currently reigns; his conscience was troubled about the land of Normandy that King Philip had conquered from King John of England, the bad king. . . ."[46] The Minstrel then combined two separate events, Henry III's visit to Paris in 1254[47] and the Franco-English treaty of 1259. He placed the conclusion of the treaty in 1254 and stated that Saint Louis was in "doubt" about his rights[48] and was freed from this doubt by the treaty and the reestablishment of the "friendship" with his brother-in-law Henry III: "and the conscience of the king of France was relieved." Likewise, the Minstrel confused the king of England's two visits to Paris in 1254 and 1259 and combined them into one. It was not in 1254 but in 1259 that "the English king swore homage in Paris, in the house [of the king of France], in the presence of the people."[49] Confirming Saint Louis' opinion that granted enormous importance to this homage from the king of England, the Minstrel highlighted the event and described the agreement as "good."[50]

The Minstrel is interesting at this point, because in speaking of the king's "conscience" he highlighted not only an important psychological trait of the scrupulous Saint Louis, but he opened up his repertoire and its usually superficial concerns to a very important change in thirteenth-century values. Father Chenu has written about the "birth of conscience" that took place in the twelfth and thirteenth centuries as individuals opened up to internal questioning of their intentions, introspection, and the internalization of moral life.[51] This internalization was definitively encouraged by the obligation to confess at least once a year, which was prescribed for all Christians by the Fourth Lateran Council in 1215. Confession was supposed to be preceded by an examination of conscience. The Mendicant friars specialized in the examination of conscience and utilized it to indoctrinate their members. The awakening of conscience did not just change behaviors and attitudes, but became a political factor, as we have seen with Saint Louis and the Franco-English treaty of 1259. The Minstrel of Reims's last anecdote about Saint Louis involves the death of his oldest son Louis in 1260. He was a young man sixteen years old. People said he was "marvelously wise and gracious." The king's grief was just like the pain he expressed when he learned of his mother's death: "He fell into such grief that no one could calm him . . . thus the king went on mourning for his son whom he loved so much and he was so sad that no one could tear a word from him."[52] The archbishop of Reims, Eudes Rigaud, a Franciscan friend and advisor to the king, came "to see him and comfort him": "He recited many of the good words of Scripture for him and reminded him of Saint Job's patience." Here we encounter the theme of Saint Louis' patience. Matthew Paris gave this association of Saint Louis with Job its full force and significance.[53] To console the king, the archbishop "recited an example [*exemplum*] for him, the example of the titmouse that was caught in the titmouse net in a peasant's garden; when the peasant caught him, he told him that he was going to eat him."[54]

It is now worthwhile to recapitulate the story that the Minstrel tells in great detail, delighted as he was with the opportunity to entertain his audience. The titmouse answered the peasant, telling him that if he were to eat him, he would not really be satisfied because he was so small. On the other hand, if he let him fly away, he would give him three pieces of advice that would prove very useful. The peasant was convinced, let him go, and received the following three pieces of advice: "What you hold in your hands, don't cast it down at your feet. Don't believe everything that you hear. Do not grieve too much for what you cannot have and cannot recover." The peasant's lesson was clear. The titmouse was mocking his naivety and gullibility. What the archbishop was showcasing for Saint Louis' attention is obviously the third piece of advice: "Sire," said the archbishop, "you can very well see that you cannot recover your son, and you have to believe that he is in heaven, and you should console yourself with this." Next, we hear that Saint Louis saw that the archbishop was telling the truth, that he took consolation "and forgot his grieving."[55] Once again, Saint Louis and his son's death were only pretexts allowing the speaker to slip an amusing and edifying story into his discourse, while the story was actually poorly adapted to the character and the situation.

This last example reminds us that Saint Louis lived at a time when folklore still permeated the culture of society's upper crust, when what was good for a peasant could still be good for a king, and when birds were not simply content to listen to Saint Francis but spoke among themselves and were even capable of reciting lessons for rulers. The Middle Ages were rural, noble and peasant. Saint Louis was capable of lending his ear to a titmouse.

The Minstrel of Reims thus gives us one last testimonial of Saint Louis' memory. We have seen him tell the same anecdotes about the king as the English Benedictine Matthew Paris and, later, the lord Joinville of Champagne. As we are examining the production of Saint Louis' memory, it would be pointless to look for the connections between the sources for these three witnesses. Joinville accompanied the king; he saw him and directly heard him speak, but he included gossip in his story, too. Saint Louis existed at the heart of a huge network of information, stories, and rumors that circulated through this vast cultural apparatus that Christendom comprised in the thirteenth century. His image was also formed and deformed in this hall of multiple mirrors. The Minstrel was one of those mirrors.

Prefigurations of Saint Louis in the Old Testament

THE SOURCE USED FOR FORMING A TYPICAL IMAGE OF SAINT LOUIS that we will now examine carried even more weight than the ones we have just discussed.

When Western Christendom was born from the dissolution of the Roman Empire in the beginning of the fifth century under the influence of the "barbarian" invasions, it was split into a number of territorial groupings. A leader who held the title of king headed each of these groups.[1] The medieval monarchical regime resulted from a historical condition that combined several ancient traditions of royalty. However, from an ideological perspective, the predominant tradition came from the Bible, especially after Pepin the Short received the royal unction in 752 in the same manner as Saul and David. The monarchical ideal drew its main inspiration from the Old Testament. The Christian ideologues of the Middle Ages adopted individual models of royalty and a theory of "the good king" from the Old Testament.

The only true king was Yahweh. The earthly king was chosen by him, had to be faithful to him, serve him, and embody his image insofar as possible. The unction was what made a king legitimate, sanctifying his function and power. Among his duties, in addition to serving God, the king had responsibilities toward his subjects: he had to enforce the laws, protect his subjects, and, above all, instill a reign of peace and justice. Among all kings, there would eventually be a single one who governed the entire world, a king who would be the messiah.

These are the characteristics that the Old Testament bequeathed upon the kings of the Western Middle Ages. Of course, there were also good kings and bad kings. In the Bible, the bad kings were obviously foreign kings, idolaters, and persecutors of the Jews. The two most famous were the Egyptian Pharaoh, who was given no individual name, and Nebuchadnezzar the Babylonian, but there were also good and bad kings among the Jewish kings of the Old Testament. David was the model of the good king who was always faithful to Yahweh, although he was not perfect either. Solomon presented an ambiguous case. The Old Testament presents him in a generally favorable light, but the reader can also sense that there was already some hostility toward him.[2] In the Middle Ages, "King Solomon was chosen as the prototype of the evil monarch."[3] The legend that subsumed him associated him with Alexander the Great and transformed the wise king who built the Temple into a luxurious, idolatrous monarch who practiced sorcery. As a victim of carnal concupiscence, Solomon ended up in the control of demons that he had first subjugated in order to get them to build the Temple. Following a Talmudic tradition, one of these demons, Asmodeus, mocked Solomon without relent. As he shifted back and forth between white magic and black magic, Solomon wound up becoming the devil's henchman. He was the Faust of the Middle Ages.[4]

In the medieval Mirrors of the Princes and in official royal ceremonies, David was the model that was usually evoked. This occurred first in the Orient when the emperor Marcian was acclaimed in 451 at the Council of Chalcedon with the title of a *novus David*, a "new David." The title was not used in the West until 626–627 when it was applied to Clothaire II.[5] However, it was especially with the Carolingians that the actual genre of the Mirror of the Prince got started.[6] The reference to David as either an ideal or inspirational model for a real monarch presented as a "new David" was by far the most important.[7] It is well known that Charlemagne benefited from this tradition and that members of his entourage often called him David.[8] The custom seems to have spread considerably beginning with Louis the Pious. During the anointing at coronation ceremonies, the title evoked the idea that the sovereign was being reborn or that he was undergoing a second baptism. This association forged between David and the monarch should be generally situated within the context of the wide use that medieval political ideology made of the Bible and especially the Old Testament.[9] We find this tendency prevalent in the High Middle Ages and more particularly during the Carolingian period. We shall soon see how this tradition was maintained and that it was still quite alive in the thirteenth century. There can be no doubt that David was the most successful of all the biblical kings. In the *Via Regia* (The Royal Path) written between 819 and 830, one of the most important Carolingian Mirrors of the Princes, Smaragde singled out Josiah, David, Hezekiah, Solomon, and Josiah, among others, as models for Christian rulers.[10] In these biblical kings, Smaragde saw most of the virtues required of a king: *timor domine, sapientia, prudentia, simplicitas, patientia, iustitia, iudicium, misericordia, humilitas, zelum rectitudinis, clementia,* and *consilium.*[11]

In some cases, the Old Testament model for the ideal medieval monarch was not a king but a patriarch or a prophet. One German chronicle describes Frederick Barbarossa as *"quasi alter Moyses"* (like another Moses) as he departed for the crusades.[12] Guillaume de Chartres similarly compared Saint Louis to Moses: "And just as the Lord said to Moses, 'Act in accordance with the design that was revealed to you on the mountain,' it was shown and revealed to each of us what we had to do on that high mountain, in other words, we were shown the excellence of the dignity and nobility of this illustrious king, the evidence of his goodness and the eminence of his life."[13]

It is with Abraham that Geoffroy de Beaulieu compared Louis. He did so in order to place him above the patriarch: "And if people praised Abraham for his justice because he once wanted to sacrifice his only son at the command of his Lord, would the Lord not consider this royal worshipper even more worthy of eternal justice and final recompense, he who, not just once but twice, very piously exposed himself to death, himself and his brothers and the flower of the army of his entire kingdom, in order to serve our Savior. Especially in this last and unfortunate crusade of Tunis where with his own sons and his entire army, for the zeal and the exaltation of the Christian faith, he proved worthy of becoming a sacrificial victim [*hostie,* host] for Christ, and where, as a martyr and an indefatigable champion of the Lord, he reached the happy end of his life in our Lord."[14]

Geoffroy made Louis into a "super Abraham," going so far as to mention martyrdom and the sacrificial host. Boniface VIII rejected these outrageous claims, but he too made Louis into a kind of "superman" [*surhomme*] anyway.[15] In the sermon he delivered on the day of Saint Louis' canonization, Sunday, August 11, 1297, Pope Boniface VIII compared the saint king to Samuel whose name means *obediens Deo,* "obedient to God," for Louis "obeyed God unto death."[16]

DAVID AND SOLOMON

The most important models for an ideal or idealized king were still the biblical kings. In his *Vie de Robert le Pieux,* which was probably written between 1031 and 1033 immediately after the king's death, the Benedictine Helgaud de Fleury mentioned David eight times. At the very beginning of his work he claimed that no king had displayed as many virtues and accomplished as many good works since "the holy king and prophet David."[17] He then repeated the entire claim at the end of the work. The twelfth century saw a resurgence in comparisons between biblical kings and contemporary kings. This was in fact a way of grounding monarchy in sacred history as its powers continued to expand in England, Spain, and even more in France. The new Gothic art, a royal art, introduced and developed two important iconographical themes that glorified royalty: the royal gates and the Tree of Jesse. Suger, the great ideologue and minister of Gothic French royalty, displayed these two themes—that were but two different expressions of the same monarchical ideology—in sculpture and stained glass. A typological symbolism made each character or event from the New Testament or the contemporary world correspond to the model of a character or event in the Old Testament. This symbolism promoted the ideological program. The biblical kings and queens evinced the kings and queens of the day. The filiations leading from Jesse to David and then to Mary and Jesus provided the monarchy with a sacred genealogy at a time when the values and ways of thinking of genealogical culture were being established with little resistance.[18] Finally, the king was not only chosen by God and anointed by God, but he was also God's image. *Rex imago Dei:* "the king image of God." The king was God on earth.[19]

Within this ideological promotion of the king, the ambiguous model of Solomon's fate appeared in a number of contradictory forms.

In the twelfth century, Thomas Becket, the famous archbishop of Canterbury, professed an "ideal of biblical royalty," as we have seen.[20] Becket was in the middle of the conflict between the Church and King Henry II of England. It is impossible to compare Henry to David, because, although in addition to his outstanding merits David sinned heavily in his private life, committing adultery and murder, he did not cling stubbornly to his sins and humbled himself before the prophet Nathan. After putting the child of David and Bathsheba to death, Yahweh forgave David and allowed him to have a second child with Bathsheba. Their child was Solomon (2 Samuel 12). On the other hand, Becket saw the malicious Solomon as prefiguring Henry II. Unlike David, the luxurious and idolatrous Solomon never repented either, and Yahweh punished him by splitting the Kingdom of Israel into two parts after his death (1 Kings 11). Henry II of England's struggles with his Church and the eventual murder of Thomas Becket led the English clerics to demonize the entire Plantagenet family, whom they claimed were descended from some satanic Jezebel. In one Mirror of the Prince, the *De principis instructione* (For the Instruction of the Prince), written sometime between 1190 and 1217, Giraud de Galles, one of Henry II's advisors, painted a very dark portrait of the deceased king. Giraud avoided comparing him to David and Augustus, comparing him instead with Herod and Nero.[21] Carried away by his hostility toward the English dynasty, he sang resounding praise for the French monarchy, its reigning king Philip Augustus and his son and heir Louis, the future Louis VIII. The murder of Thomas Becket was widely exploited by the Roman Church. Becket's cadaver transformed the dismal relations between the English royalty and the Church of England into long-lasting hatred, to the great benefit of the French monarchy. What the king of England lost in prestige based on the Old Testament monarchy, the king of France gained by obeying God and the Church. In the thirteenth century, the king of France became the great beneficiary of the typological symbolism inherited from the Bible. This movement was facilitated by the artistic propaganda proliferating in the figures and statues of the kings and queens of Israel and Judah around the entrances to churches, in their stained glass windows, and in shining paintings of the Tree of Jesse. The French sovereign thus benefited from a dual promotion in the field of monarchical ideology based on the Old Testament. The first promotion was for the model of Solomon. Until then, David's son had been stuck with a contradictory reputation. On the one hand, his figure was subjected to an increasing demonization stirred up by these events; at the same time, he was still the builder of the Temple and the model example of royal wealth and wisdom. This second aspect of his image became more and more prominent for the rulers of the time due to the influence of *Policraticus sive de nugis curialium* (*Policraticus,* or On the Futilities of Courtiers). This was a Mirror of Princes that presented a new monarchical ideal. John of Salisbury proposed a new image of the good king in it. His king was at least well educated, if not a great intellect.[22] Here, the wise (*sapiens*) king of the Old Testament was Solomon. He therefore benefited from a revalorization of his model that paralleled and contradicted his demonization.

Josiah was the second figure to be promoted. Among all the biblical monarchs, Josiah does not appear to have been used very often as a model of reference for the kings of the medieval West,[23] but he was the one that seemed to be the preferred model of comparison for Saint Louis.

Of course, David, the biblical king par excellence, also evoked comparisons with Saint Louis among his contemporaries. This occurred in a sermon given by Guillaume de Saint-Pathus.[24] Of the four main virtues (*splendor sapientie, dulcor compassionis, nitor continientie, fervor devotionis*[25]) that he identified with Saint Louis, two of them refer to the biblical king: "*David sedens in cathedra sapientissimus princeps*"[26] (2 Samuel 23:8), and, "*Servus meus David erit princeps in medio eorum*"[27] (Ezekiel 34:24). The parallel with David can finally be found in the fourth liturgical service for the festival of Saint Louis on August 25. The service seems to be the work of the Benedictines and appeared for the first time in a manuscript from Saint-Germain-des-Près shortly after the canonization of 1297.[28] The theme of Guillaume de Saint-Pathus's sermon on Saint Louis suggested a comparison with Mattathias, the father of the Maccabees, since it contained the words addressed by the envoys that Antiochus sent to this prince: "*Princeps clarissimus et magnus es*" (Maccabees 2:17).[29] However, the appearance of the model of Solomon alongside that of David in an *ordo* for the anointment and coronation of the kings of France that almost certainly dates from the reign of Louis IX is even more significant.[30] Marc Bloch observed that the "examples of David and Solomon allowed them to restore the sacred character of kings in a Christian manner."[31] The two names also came up regularly in the *ordines* for the royal coronation. In the *ordo* that we just mentioned, after the king swore his oath for the second time, one of the bishops present prays and calls on God to visit him in the forms of Moses, Josiah, Gideon, and Samuel, and to sprinkle him with the same dew of wisdom that he had poured down on the fortunate king David and his son Solomon. Then, as the archbishop of Reims continues to anoint the king's hands, he evokes David's anointment by Samuel. Finally, in the preface to the prayer spoken after the king's anointment, there is an allusion to David's elevation to supreme royal power and to the gift of wisdom and peace that God conferred upon Solomon. They pray to God to endow the king with the same faith as Abraham, the same courage as Samuel, the same humility as David, and the same wisdom as Solomon.

Finally, in his sermon for Saint Louis' canonization on August 11, 1297, Boniface VIII took the theme: *"Magnificatus est ergo rex Salomon, super omnes reges terrae, divitiis et sapientia"* (1 Kings 10:23). Without mentioning Solomon's name and without citing his power, wealth, and wisdom as they are praised in the Holy Book, he modified the quotation by introducing an epithet that suited the new saint better than the biblical monarch—*pacificus* (*"Rex pacificus magnificatus est"*).[32]

Louis and Josiah

Josiah only appeared fleetingly in a Mirror of the Princes from Saint Louis' time. He figured in *De eruditione filiorum nobilium* (On the Education of Noble Children) written by the Dominican Vincent de Beauvais for a cleric named Simon who was the schoolmaster to the king's son, Philip, the future Philip III the Bold.[33] The Preaching Friar wrote a sustained praise of childhood, and this was precisely at a time when children seem to be more and more highly valued by a society that had not paid much attention to them until then. He claimed that thanks to divine election, the "first and best" kings of Israel had been children.[34] He gave David as an example (*"iunior inter fratres suos"*), and Josiah who was eight years old when he began his reign (2 Kings 221).[35] Vincent de Beauvais undoubtedly invited his readers to note the resemblance with Louis IX who was crowned king at the age of twelve. However, he was not thinking about the Capetian policy of succession by primogeniture because this dynastic policy turned out more masculine in reality than in theory.

Josiah appears again in the liturgical services for the canonized Saint Louis. In the third one (the first response to the third nocturn), the theme of childhood comes up again: "Beginning in childhood, Saint Louis sought

God with all his heart like King Josiah."[36] At another point (in the hymn of *Laudes* in the second service), it is said that Saint Louis, like Josiah, "rendered attentive worship to God in words and deeds."[37] Once again, what Saint Louis' hagiographers tell us about his actual worship coincides with what the Old Testament says about Josiah:[38] "And like unto him was there no king before him, that turned to the Lord with all his heart, and with all his soul, and with all his might" (2 Kings 23:25).

The comparison between Louis IX and Josiah seems to have been a discovery of his first biographer, his confessor for the last twenty years of his life, the Dominican Geoffroy de Beaulieu. He wrote his *Life* of Saint Louis at the request of Pope Gregory X who was already thinking of the recently deceased French king's canonization between 1273 and 1275.[39] Geoffroy announces from the start that in order to praise Louis IX, he will use the praise for King Josiah in the Bible. He employs three passages from the Old Testament including one from Ecclesiastes (chapter 49), one from the second book of Kings (chapter 22), and one from the second book of Chronicles (*Paralipomenon,* chapter 34). Chapter 49 from Ecclesiastes states:

> The memory of Josiah is a mixture of incense prepared
>   with the perfume maker's care,
> It is like honey, sweet to every mouth, like the music in
>   the midst of a banquet,
> He took the good path, the path of converting the people.
> He cut out the abominable impiety,
> He directed his heart toward the Lord
> And in impious times he made piety prevail.

Geoffroy de Beaulieu gives the following summary of the story of Josiah as it exists in very similar terms in chapter 22 of the second book of Kings and in chapter 34 of the second book of Chronicles: "When Josiah was still a child he began to look for the Lord and he did what was right and pleasing in the eyes of the Lord and he walked in all the paths of David his father.[40] He did not leave the path, neither to the right nor to the left. His mother's name was Ydida. He restored the temple and the house of the Lord. There had been no king like him before who could give himself to the Lord the way he did with all his heart, his soul, and his might, and after him, there was no other king like him. He actually held a Passover the likes of which had never been seen before, and which no king ever since has ever matched." And Geoffroy adds: "All of this applies perfectly to our glorious king, as I will show."

He explicitly retained three of these homologies: the *name* of Josiah suited Saint Louis, both of them were exemplary Christians in their conduct, and both led pure and holy lives.

We know the importance that a name held in the Middle Ages. It was the truth and essence of the person who bore it. The game of falsely constructed, scholarly etymologies allowed people to uncover the deeper meaning of a name. The name 'Josiah' can be interpreted in four different ways, all of which were appropriate for Saint Louis. In effect, the name can mean *Salus Dominis, Elevatio Domini, Incensum Domini,* and *Sacrificium.* So, who more than Saint Louis worked for the salvation of Christendom, the elevation and exaltation of the Christian faith, the practice of worship born in childhood, and, finally, the sacrifice of his own life on the crusade? A royal host, as Joinville would say, Saint Louis died in Tunis just like Christ at three o'clock in the afternoon.

Next, Louis like Josiah was innocent and fair. Like Josiah, he followed his father's example in this. For Josiah, this father was David, whom Geoffroy de Beaulieu identified as his father, taking the term of *pater* as literally as possible, rather than as his grandfather, which would be more accurate. For Louis IX, this was his real father, Louis VIII who proved his faith and rectitude by leading the crusade against the Albigenses and who also, or rather already, had died on his return from the crusades. Thus, by stretching out the two similar sequences in time, Geoffroy associated the two pairs of fathers and sons, David and Josiah, Louis VIII and Louis IX. Or better still, Louis IX had two fathers, an earthly father who was also a model, and a symbolic father who was himself the son of a model father in former time. Moreover, by reusing the expression, *"non declinavit ad dexteram neque ad sinistram"* (he strayed neither to the left nor to the right), he also unveiled the definition of the king given by Isidore de Séville: *rex a recte regendo.*

Finally, the most remarkable thing here may be that Geoffroy de Beaulieu gave posterity the phrase from the second book of Kings that names Josiah's mother, Ydida. He used this as an opportunity to praise Louis' mother, Blanche of Castile, thus suggesting the idea of a royal Holy Family that included the father Louis VIII, the mother Blanche, and the son Louis IX who only came off more strongly as an *imago* of Jesus.

The rest of the *Vita* develops according to the customs of the hagiography of the period, cleverly combining historical sequences (Geoffroy slipped in his own testimony once in a while) and passages on the king's virtues. The model of Josiah always lies just beneath the surface although it rarely appears. The biblical king's name resurfaces in passages on repentance and confession and especially in the sections about religious laws, the measures taken against people who swear and blaspheme, and Louis' efforts to restore religious observance throughout his kingdom. He fully deserved the name of Josiah because, like him, "*tulit abominationes impietatis, et gubernavit ad Dominium cor suum et in diebus peccatorum corroboravit pietatem in cultum divinum.*"[41]

Being the good preacher and literary scholar that he was, Geoffroy de Beaulieu ended his *Vita* by coming back to Josiah and his first biblical quotation: "What else are we left with, if not the eternally perfumed memory, so sweet like honey, so melodious in the Church of God, of *our Josiah?*" Louis IX was not simply a "second" Josiah or an "other" Josiah; he was *our* Josiah. Can this mean anything other than that Louis IX was not only the Josiah of our time, but that he was our own Josiah, the one who allowed us to relive "holy history"?

Geoffroy de Beaulieu's continuator, Guillaume de Chartres, was also a Dominican. He had been the king's chaplain, although he wrote after the king's canonization, after 1297. He, last of all, though more briefly, took up the parallel with Josiah. He retained the biblical text on the *memoria Josiae* and the allusion to Josiah's name but condensed them. His memory faded quickly into perfume and music. Josiah was no more than an "aromatic memory."[42]

The strong impetus behind the comparison between Saint Louis and Josiah appears to me to ultimately reside in the passage we examined above in which Geoffroy de Beaulieu likened the final years of Saint Louis' reign to those of Josiah's. Saint Louis' biographers and hagiographers all agree in identifying two important phases in his life and reign. The division occurs before and after the crusade of 1248. Certainly, as early as childhood the king was virtuous and pious, but in an ordinary way, with the possible exception of his enthusiasm for the outmoded adventure of the crusade. He dressed and ate in a manner corresponding to his rank. He often joked. He was bent on establishing justice in his kingdom and appointed the royal investigators, although he seldom made new laws. After 1254, he led an asce-

tic life and tried to impose laws for moral and religious order on his subjects. These laws were against gaming, prostitution, and blasphemy. He encouraged his investigating officers in an almost unhealthy way to act as actual inquisitors for the agents of the crown. In his person and in the body
of his subjects, he wanted to extirpate the sin that caused the failure of the
crusade in Egypt. He had to restore religious faith and practice in order to
become worthy of victory on a second crusade, or at least to be worthy of
becoming a martyr in the process.

So what does the Bible tell us about Josiah (2 Kings 22–23)? During
the first eighteen years of his reign, "he did that which was right in the sight
of the Lord, and walked in all the way of David his father, and turned not
aside to the right hand or to the left." About these first eighteen years we
are told nothing more. Then, in the eighteenth year of his reign, he restored
the Temple and found the book of Laws inside it, in other words, the book
of Deuteronomy. Josiah and his people marched in a solemn procession to
the Temple of Yahweh. Josiah renewed the pact and destroyed all the remaining traces of paganism in the Kingdom of Judah, including the lodgings of the holy prostitutes in Yahweh's Temple. Then, after leading this religious reform, he celebrated an extraordinary Passover to honor Yahweh in
Jerusalem. He later died at Meggido in a battle against the Pharaoh who was
making preparations to invade his kingdom. His body was brought back to
Jerusalem.

Who could fail to perceive the similarities between the two kings and
their two reigns? Our examination sheds new light on this traditional comparison between the kings of medieval Christendom and the kings of the
Old Testament. In the thirteenth century they needed more than just abstract comparisons situated within a purely ideological dimension between
two kings who had nothing more in common than having or wanting to
embody the model of a ruler who pleases God. From this time on, a certain *historical resemblance* was also required. Henceforward, instead of simply
recruiting the best royal model from the Old Testament, David, the hagiographers and biographers thought that it was better to associate Saint Louis
with a king who was a good king, of course, but above all a king whose reign
in some way prefigured the reign of the king of France.

Thus the two kings were related to the point of coming together on
three similar paths in time: the symbolic time of history in which contemporary history was only an image of the time of the great biblical past; an

eschatological time in which each ruler strove to draw his people closer to God for their eternal salvation; and, finally, a historical time in which certain sequences of events recurred but in which kings and their reigns were no longer interchangeable. They had to resemble one another in the same way that art was paired with the world and the portrait with the individual because what Saint Louis paradoxically tried to borrow from Josiah, though with perhaps only limited success, was a particular historical originality and an individual identity. Now, we must stop at this border where the pairing of Saint Louis and Josiah seems to shift from its non-temporal symbolism into history. With Josiah, the producers of memory had not yet torn Saint Louis away from typological abstractions. He was only another Josiah here, or one of Josiah's avatars.

The King of the Mirrors
of the Princes

THE HISTORIAN CAN OFTEN IDENTIFY A HIERARCHICAL FORM THAT
eventually produced a single leader in the organization of most ancient societies. We call societies like this monarchical and their leaders "kings."
Originally, this chief-king not only had a sacred character but embodied all
kinds of supernatural powers in his person. No sooner had this type of
leader appeared than people tried to limit the extent of his authority. These
people were those who held military or economic power—which usually
went hand in hand in these societies. They were warriors and wealthy land-
owners who tried to seize or share the powers of the king. At a very early
stage the Romans abolished their monarchy and replaced it with an oligarchy
that they called a "republic." For a long time, they hated even the very name
of "king."

It also seems that the birth of monarchy in these ancient societies
marked the passage from a simple form of memory sustained by scattered
documents (inscriptions, tablets, etc.), myths (the myth of Gilgamesh, the
king of Uruk, for example), or monuments to the construction of a true
history, often legendary in its traditional origins but capable of forming a
continuous, coherent framework around the king. This framework favored

315

a system that submitted everything to the monarch and the succession of kings, which was often reinforced by a dynastic principle. Monarchy offered society an explanation and a narrative at the same time, the two complementary faces of history. Pierre Gibert has given us a subtle demonstration of this twin birth of monarchy and history, using the example of ancient Israel and the first kings—Saul, David, and Solomon.[1]

On the other hand, other people worked even more fervently to limit royal prerogatives in the religious domain. This was the concern of the priests. At the beginning of the seventh century, the archbishop and encyclopedist, Isidore of Seville, went back to Latin etymology [*rex, "roi"* (king); *regere, "diriger"* (to rule); *recte, "droit"* (right, rightly)] to claim that a king must govern "*droit*" (right, rightly, fairly) and make his nobles, administrators, and subjects act "*droit.*" We have already seen this definition applied to Saint Louis. The king was not satisfied just with embodying all power in his person; he was also supposed to embody all virtues. There were a number of particular specialized works dedicated to this model from the ninth to the thirteenth century, the Mirrors of the Princes.[2]

The first objective of the clerics who wrote these treatises was to avoid having the "sacred" character of kings lead to a divine or sacerdotal character for the royal function. The king was only supposed to be the elect chosen by God, the man who received the unction of coronation in the Judeo-Christian tradition. The septenary of the sacraments drawn up in the twelfth century in the West excluded the royal coronation from the list of sacraments. The attempt by certain clerics to make the king into the "image of God" in the twelfth and thirteenth centuries met with only limited success. The attempt to make the king into a "priest king" (*rex et sacerdos*) based on the biblical model of Melchizedek, the "king of Salem" and "the priest of the most high God" (Genesis 14:18), never had long-lasting success in the Bible, nor in Christianity, nor in the Christian ideology of the medieval West, despite the efforts of certain clerics in the service of the emperors.

In the priests' desire to separate the king from any sacerdotal function, it seems that both the ancient Jewish clergy and the medieval Western Church insisted on obtaining the king's solemn commitment to profess and defend the orthodox faith and, more specifically, to put his powers in the service of the Church. This was the main purpose of the promises and, later, the oaths that Western kings had to pronounce beginning in the Carolingian period. Finally, the limitations placed on the king's powers were supposed to prevent him from becoming a tyrant and crossing over to the side of evil and the devil. The kings therefore had duties too, first of all toward God, then toward the priests and the Church, and then toward their subjects and their people.

Since the earliest times of the oriental monarchies, the writings in which clerics spelled out the duties of kings concentrated either on their respect for certain rituals (in the law of Moses, for example) or, more and more over time, on the exercise of personal and public virtues. To cite only the Bible, the obligatory ideological reference in the medieval West, I point to the short treatise on royal ethics inserted into Deuteronomy (17:14–20). We can still observe the influence of this text in the age of Saint Louis. Despite a number of interdictions applicable to kings, it presents a positive image of royalty and the royal figure. On the other hand, at the moment royalty was established, when Yahweh responded "to the people who asked him for a king," the Old Testament gives a rather pessimistic image of royalty. It presents the king as an eventual tyrant who would turn the Hebrews into "his slaves" (1 Samuel 8:10–18). Thus, as is often the case, the Bible offers some arguments in favor of royalty and others against it. However, it also defined one of the criteria for royalty: royalty was only worth as much as the king himself. The task of instructing the king and presenting him with a system of royal ethics was therefore one of the priesthood's most important functions.

When the ruler converted to Christianity in the fourth century, a doctrine had to be worked out. Augustine did this, particularly in chapter 24 of the fifth book of *The City of God*. H. H. Anton calls it "the first Christian mirror of the princes." The archbishop of Hippo insisted on "Peace, Order, and Justice" (*Pax, Ordo, Justicia*) as the foundations of monarchy. He defined the virtues that made the Christian ruler a good ruler according to the Roman tradition of the "happy emperor" (*imperator felix*). Later, at the turn of the sixth and seventh centuries, Pope Gregory the Great also became preoccupied with the problem of royalty and the king. He above all emphasized the importance of justice as an ideal for the monarchy and as the virtue required of the king.

Carolingian Mirrors

In the Carolingian period opuscules appeared that were intended solely to remind kings of the virtues inherent to their "function" (*officium*) or their "mission" (*ministère, ministerium*). They reminded kings of the virtues that were especially necessary to justify their elevation to the throne or, rather, to remind them of the religious ceremony that henceforth legitimated the choice that God had bestowed on their persons. If God's choice normally corresponded to the choice that men made within royal families, it could also confirm a shift of power from one family to another—like the replacement of the Merovingians by the Carolingians in the middle of the eighth century. However, in France for example, a hereditary right favoring the oldest or second closest male heir of the deceased king was gradually set in place. In Reims, the two separate ceremonies of the anointment and the coronation were combined for the coronation of Louis the Pious in 816. In addition, we can consider the texts utilized for the coronations of Christian kings in the Middle Ages as a specific category of the Mirrors of the Princes. These texts were called *ordines* and were actually liturgical texts or records, memory aids intended to facilitate the execution of the ceremony.

The cultural semiotics of the Middle Ages relied heavily on the image of the mirror (*speculum*). Rather than using it to express the theory of the sign or the reflection in which each earthly reality was the more or less successful replication of its ideal type, it was a matter of showing instead that the image seen in the mirror was in fact the *ideal* image of an earthly reality. Every mirror was an instrument of *truth* and therefore led to the deepest levels of the medieval imagination. However, more often than not, the mirror renounced its theological, metaphysical function in order to become a normative genre bound up in the process of *moralization* or ethical illustration that began to take shape in the twelfth century and that became more popular in the late Middle Ages from the thirteenth century on. Every Mirror became *exemplary*.

The authors of the ninth-century Carolingian Mirrors of the Princes were Church dignitaries. They offered the kings of their time the model of certain kings from the Old Testament: David, Solomon, Hezekiah, Josiah, etc. They focused mainly on the virtues that were specifically appropriate for kings—*justice* first and foremost, but also *wisdom, prudence, patience, mercy, humility, zeal for righteousness* [droiture], *clemency, piety,* and so forth. Finally, they stressed the king's urgent duty to protect the churches and the clerics. Thus the Church asserted its growing political and ideological role in the Carolingian period. However, with the possible exception of Hincmar's, all these Mirrors are not political treatises.[3]

JOHN OF SALISBURY'S *POLICRATICUS*

A turning point comes in the middle of the twelfth century with John of Salisbury's *Policraticus*. In 1159, this was the first great treatise on political science of the Middle Ages. It was written in England by a cleric of very high intellectual standing who was educated in the schools of Paris. A high-ranking ecclesiastical official in the pontifical curia, then secretary to Theobald the archbishop of Canterbury, John of Salisbury was a friend of Thomas Becket. He took refuge in Reims for a period of time as the guest of his close friend, the Benedictine Pierre de Celle, the abbot of the famous abbey of Saint-Rémi where they kept the Holy Ampulla used in the coronation ceremonies for the kings of France. He ended his career as bishop of Chartres from 1176 to his death in 1180.

The *Policraticus* made a significant contribution to the royal ideology of the Middle Ages. John of Salisbury based his work on an opuscule that was falsely attributed to Plutarch, the *Institutio Traiani,* which was probably forged in Rome around 400. This pseudo-manual for Trajan's education is actually a Mirror of the Princes. Notably, it contains the first use in the Christian West (of the twelfth century) of the organic metaphor of the human body for political society with the king as its head. The *Policraticus* goes beyond the *Institutio Traiani* by launching the concept of the learned, intellectual ruler, "*rex illiteratus quasi asinus coronatus*" (an illiterate king is but a crowned ass). It especially gave monarchical ideology (which John had seen at work in the nascent bureaucracy of the English and pontifical courts) a very solid foundation. John of Salisbury was one of the most cultivated men of his time. He may be the best representative of the humanist renaissance of the twelfth century. Marked by the "naturalism" that characterized the schools of Paris and Chartres, he conceived of society—with the king at its head—as an organized whole. He also introduced the theme of tyranicide into the theological and philosophical discussions of the period. This theme would come to play a great role in the political science (and in the political realities) of the end of the Middle Ages and of modern times. Finally, the court was in the process of taking shape, destined as it was to undergo such an important development from the twelfth to the eighteenth century, and he analyzed this phenomenon with a very critical eye. The subtitle of the *Policraticus* is "*sive de nugis curialium*" (or on the futility of courtiers).[4]

Mirrors of the Thirteenth Century

Renewed by the model of the *Policraticus* and the rapid evolution of monarchies toward the form of the state, a new blossoming of the Mirrors of the Princes occurred in the thirteenth century.[5] Certainly, no one experienced this flourishing more strongly than Louis IX, the king of France. He indirectly gave rise to and directly favored the composition of several of these texts along with manuals for the coronation (*ordines*) that were supposed to help carry out this impassioned task.

Some have therefore spoken of a "political academy" of Saint Louis whose center was the convent of the Jacobins, the famous convent of Saint-Jacques of the Parisian Dominicans. We thus find the Mendicant and more specifically Dominican lobby here, which we have already seen at work in the production of Saint Louis' hagiographical record. At the request of Humbert de Romans, the master general of the order from 1254 to 1263, solicited by Saint Louis, the convent of the Jacobins supposedly entrusted the composition of a Mirror of the Princes, or what was rather to be a vast political treatise, to a team of monks. The treatise *De eruditione filiorum regalium* (or *nobilium*), "Of the Education of Royal (or Noble) Children," was supposed to be a part of this collection. It was written by the Dominican Vincent de Beauvais—then a lecturer at the Cistercian abbey of Royaumont and already in contact with the king—who offered it to Queen Marguerite in a first edition for the education of the young Philip, the future Philip III who was then the royal couple's second oldest son.[6] Another part of this treatise would be the *De morali principis institutione*, "Of the Moral Education of the Prince." It was written between 1260 and 1263, also by Vincent de Beauvais. He had left Royaumont by this time and conjointly dedicated the work to Louis IX and his son-in-law, Thibaud, the king of Navarre and count of Champagne. Finally, a third section was to have been comprised by the *De eruditione principum*, "Of the Education of Princes," which was later falsely attributed to Thomas Aquinas (hence the name of Pseudo-Thomas given to the author in the modern edition). It may have been written by Vincent de Beauvais or by another well-known Dominican, Guillaume Peyraut.[7]

To these three Dominican treatises, we must add the *Morale somnium Pharaonis sive de regia disciplina*, the "Moralized Dream of Pharaoh or Of Royal Science," probably written by the Cistercian Jean de Limoges for

Thibaud de Navarre between 1255 and 1260. The Mirror that interests me even more here is the *Eruditio regum et principum,* "Education of Kings and Princes" by the Franciscan Gilbert de Tournai. It was written for Saint Louis in 1259. Finally, we must examine the *Enseignements* composed by Saint Louis at the end of his life for his son Philip, the future Philip III the Bold. It is a veritable Mirror of the Princes written by the king himself.

THE *ERUDITIO REGUM ET PRINCIPUM* BY GILBERT DE TOURNAI

We know practically nothing about Gilbert (or Guibert) de Tournai. He was a student and a master at the University of Paris. In his day, he was considered one of the intellectual glories of his order. Along with his various treatises on education and morality, he wrote sermons and, notably, sermons addressed to the crusaders. He probably took part in Saint Louis' crusade in Egypt and the Holy Land (1248–1254). The *Eruditio* may have been born of the friendship that developed between them on the crusade.

The *Eruditio regum et principum*[8] is made up of three letters addressed to Saint Louis. The last letter indicates that it was completed in Paris on the day of the octave of the festival of Saint Francis, in other words, on October 11, 1259. The three letters treat four principles that were "necessary for rulers," according to the *Institutio Traiani*: reverence for God (*reverentia Dei*), self-discipline (*diligentia sui*), discipline toward officers and powerful members of society (*disciplina potestatum et officialium*), and affection and protection for one's subjects (*affectus et protectio subditorum*).

The first letter is made up of two parts. The first part, four chapters in length, is dedicated to the reverence owed to God. It highlighted the cultural and intellectual formations of the clerics of the first part of the thirteenth century. Gilbert relied on reasoning through opposition. The demonstration first takes the form of a positive argument, the *reverentia Dei*. He relied just as much on a dual system of cultural references, Christian (especially from the Old Testament) and pagan. His method was traditional. It consisted in cumulatively listing *authorities* in favor of the argument he wanted to support. In this case, the references borrowed from pagan literature are almost as numerous as the ones drawn from the Bible and the writings of the Church Fathers.[9] The renaissance of the twelfth century was not far off.

The author first recalled "through examples from the New and Old Testaments, that irreverence toward God among rulers ruins reigns and principalities." Next, he demonstrated "the same thing with the help of histories of pagan kings." However, let us note this opposition: the biblical examples were evidence of eternal truths; the pagan examples constituted only "historical" evidence. History was the domain of the uncertain and the adaptable. Its symbol was the wheel of fortune. The third chapter refers to Saul who died ignominiously with his sons, the kings Ela, Zimri, Nadab, Joas, Jeroboam, and all the other kings who died violent deaths. On the other hand, the Christian emperors Constantine and Theodosius showed reverence to God, the first by refusing to occupy the seat of honor at the Council of Nicea, the second by expiating his crime through the patient and public execution of the penitence ordered by Saint Ambrose. The author finally mentions the murder of Caesar the usurper of the Empire, the poisonings of Tiberius and Claudius, the murder of Caligula, the violent deaths of Vitellius, Galba, and Otho, and above all the miserable fates of the emperors who had persecuted Christians since Nero. So, the Roman Empire was but a long succession of violent deaths, divine punishments of unworthy emperors, a long but inevitable march to ruin, and the disappearance or, rather, the transfer of its power to other forces.

The twelve chapters of the second part of the first letter on the king's discipline in relation to himself form a Mirror of the Prince inserted inside the entire treatise. This section is more personal and focuses more directly on the royal person. The development of the theme of *diligentia sui,* of the king's personal duties, is presented as a commentary of the Mirror of the Princes in chapter 17 of Deuteronomy. Following the customs of medieval biblical exegesis, Gilbert de Tournai wrote an interpretation devoid of any historical and scientific exegetical bases. He simply interpreted the biblical citations in whatever sense he pleased. They have "a nose of wax" in the words of Alain de Lille at the very end of the twelfth century.

There are twelve stipulations: "The king shall not multiply his horses," "he shall not bring his people back to Egypt," "he shall not have several (or many) wives," "he shall not keep great treasures of silver and gold," "once mounted on the throne, he shall read and meditate on Deuteronomy," "he shall receive the text of the law from the priests," "he shall learn to fear the Lord his God," "he shall respect the terms of the Law," "his heart shall not swell with pride above and beyond his brothers," "he shall not stray either to the right or left," "that he may live a long life," and, finally, "that he desire eternal life." These were all pretexts for so many rhetorical developments in which either the commonplaces of Christian thought or contemporary concerns appeared.

"The king shall not multiply his horses." This recommendation was transformed into a diatribe against hunting. It is an astonishing text that begins with prior condemnations of hunting that had been addressed to bishops and clerics and scant allusions to the uselessness or harmfulness of hunting done by kings. (Such allusions can be found in Jonas d'Orléans in the ninth century and in John of Salisbury, Gilbert de Tournai's source, in the twelfth.) The text here turns into a kind of royal anthropology in which hunting figures as a game too puerile for a king. Moreover, the traditional condemnation of games of chance that follows (of dice and other games) appeals less to religious and moral arguments and more to a social system of values. Anything puerile, anything that could make the king look childish, must be avoided. We should add that this diatribe runs entirely contrary to the practice of hunting in the Middle Ages. The kings tried to make hunting into their own monopolistic activity. They formed vast hunting preserves when they created the juridical-geographical notion of "the forest," and threw themselves into this sport with a passion, thinking of it as the royal sport par excellence. Curiously, Saint Louis is the only king of France for whom there is no surviving record proving that he ever practiced hunting.[10] And we know how he hated games of chance, how he would sometimes become enraged against gamblers, and that he made laws to abolish these activities after his return from the Holy Land.

"The king shall not have several wives." Though he did not make any recent or contemporary allusions, we get the impression that Gilbert de Tournai was taking aim at the Capetian kings who, up until Philip Augustus, had all had very stormy love lives and married lives. They came into conflict with the Church over issues of divorce, concubinage, and incest (at least in the sense of ecclesiastical prohibitions against marriage between family members related in the fourth or even the seventh degree, and perhaps also in the actual sense in the dated case of Charlemagne). Indeed, it was polygamy that was the issue here, and Georges Duby has shown how it was only in the twelfth century that the Church began to make its model of monogamous and indissoluble marriage prevail over the aristocratic model of polygamous marriage that could be revoked by the spouse.[11]

"He shall not keep great treasures of silver and gold." The commentary broached the subject that we would now call "the economic domain." Monetary economy and its practices—from the classifications to the manipulations of coinages—formed one of the paths to a growing awareness of a specific domain of power and government: money. Although there was no direct tie, in 1259 Saint Louis' monetary decisions followed closely with the minting of large silver pieces, the reinvention of the gold mint, and his struggle against the barons' rights to strike coins.[12]

"Once mounted on the throne, he shall read and meditate on Deuteronomy." Gilbert de Tournai adopted and developed John of Salisbury's adage here: "An illiterate king is but a crowned ass." In Saint Louis' France and in the Europe of the university scholars, it was no longer enough for a king just to be wise; he had to be "cultivated." It was preferable if he were an intellectual, too.

"He shall receive the text of the laws from the priests." The king must honor, protect, and listen to the Church. The oath that he took for his coronation was first of all intended to satisfy the bishops and priests. The logic of the growth of royal power ended up reducing the Church's influence. In France in 1259, it was thus the right time to seek out some balance between the king and the Church. The king was the secular arm of God and the Church. He protected the faith and he was himself a very Christian king but he could not allow himself to take orders from the Church, particularly in temporal matters. For Gilbert de Tournai, in these high spheres of power the number one mortal sin was still *superbia* or pride. *Avaritia,* avarice, the cupidity that tended to supplant it in the hierarchy of vices, did not threaten the king as much as pride, despite the lesson on contempt for treasure.[13] The onus of royal finances had not yet become unbearable.

Finally, there were three concerns that should dominate the mind and the actions of the king: (1) he should walk straight without deviating and go forward on the paths of righteousness; (2) he should be worthy of having an heir and of living a long life—having heirs and leading a long life guarantee the stability needed for good government; (3) the king should not be simply contented with his divine election confirmed by his holy anointment. He should think of his fate as much as his origins and act to assure his own salvation and the salvation of his people. Heaven was the monarchy's horizon. A true king must be an eschatological king. Saint Louis was haunted more and more by this royal vocation.

The second letter of the opuscule dealt with the discipline of officers and powerful figures (the royal administrators and the members of the king's entourage). This letter is also based on an opposition. The letter opposes the negative discipline that the ruler must impose on the people who serve him and the positive discipline of duty for those who act in the king's name. First of all, kings have to punish others. They have to fulfill their duty to act as the secular arm. The ruler also has be a model for the people who depend on him. Gilbert de Tournai reintroduced John of Salisbury's organic metaphor here. The king should act as the head in relation to all of the body's other members. The positive signals [*ondes*] that go out through the monarchy's entire body should emanate from him. But, he should also know how to reflect within himself in order to contemplate the spectacle of society "in the mirror of his mind." He would discover the depths of evil there. In effect, Gilbert attached great importance to the exposure of what was hidden, and this applied particularly to evil. The king was supposed to investigate evil and wrongdoing; he should be an inquisitor.

Among the wrongs to be detected and corrected, there were first of all the evils of urban life and the offenses of the people. During this period that saw the results of a great wave of urbanization, cities were generally praised and admired. Gilbert, however, was pessimistic when it came to the urban phenomenon. In a city, sins were worse than anywhere else. Saint Bonaventure, the minister general of his order, forcefully said the same thing and drew the conclusion that the Franciscans should set themselves up in the places that had the most serious evils to combat. The ruler also had to reform the laws. There were good ones and bad ones. Gilbert de Tournai set rulers on the path to a *topos* that flourished in the fourteenth century and especially in Italy. This was the topos of the Good and Bad Governments that Ambrogio Lorenzetti painted as a fresco on the walls of the communal palace of Siena.

The last eleven chapters of this first part deal with the most despicable characters in the royal entourage, the *curiales,* the men of the *curia,* the court. Here, we should not take the word "court" in the seigniorial and ceremonial sense that it later acquired beginning in the sixteenth century. The *curia* was the site of the administrative and governmental apparatus of a feudal king. It was in the process of developing the idea and the organs of a centralized, bureaucratic state. In his critical description of the *curiales,* Gilbert de Tournai sometimes had recourse to one of the great thirteenth-century rhetorical procedures of moralization: comparisons with animals. Here, alongside the Bible, the Church Fathers, and the ancient pagan authors, we find a fourth field of reference: nature. Its beasts, plants, flowers, and stones symbolized and prefigured human virtues and vices. At the top of the list were flattery and hypocrisy represented by the chameleon, the millipede, snakes, other venomous creatures, and the leopard.

The second part of this second letter treats the discipline of officers and powerful men in a positive light. First, it had its source in good reputation (*bona fama*), a very important idea in the Middle Ages, especially in the juridical domain. The desire for a good reputation gave rise to justice and discipline in the ruler. Justice was the main subject here. Gilbert de Tournai reminds his reader that it should be the same for everyone. The judge's sword was meant to serve justice. The just ruler had to ban illicit oaths and repress the injustices of citizens and bourgeois against the clerics and the weak (this was one of the key policies of French kings toward the cities in the thirteenth century). Whenever necessary, he must supervise and punish his "prefects" and bailiffs. (This was the meaning of the many investigations ordered by Saint Louis to repair the wrongs committed by his representatives.) Finally, the prince had to restrain himself and avoid abusing royal justice against the poor; he should uphold justice for the poor without letting sentencing drag out for years and years.

The third letter in Gilbert de Tournai's treatise comprises only seven chapters. It is about the king's conduct in relation to his subjects. He owed them his affection and protection. The Franciscan demonstrated this first with examples taken from nature such as reptiles, winged creatures (bees mainly), and marine creatures (dolphins and seals). Last but not least, the hen was a model mother who sacrificed herself for her chicks. The king must be able to exercise clemency toward his subjects as clemency does not weaken justice. (The commonplaces of moderation and forgiveness figured at the center of the thirteenth-century princely ethic.) He should also be harder on injustices committed against others than on wrongs done to himself. On the contrary, the king had nothing to lose by trying to be good to his people. The best defense that kings had was the love of their people. This love did more than anything else to assure the highest political goal of peace.

The cultural and historical materials that formed the base of the larger part of the material for Gilbert de Tournai's treatise are obvious: the Bible, and above all, the Old Testament whose stories were very present and very much alive in the thirteenth century; the tradition of the Mirrors of the Princes as it was renewed by John of Salisbury and the *Institutiio Traiani*; and a certain folkloric culture that was accepted by the Christian culture of the day and profoundly enriched by the "twelfth-century Renaissance." The ideological foundation of the treatise, however, lay in the hierarchical theology of the Pseudo-Dionysius. The writings of this Greek theologian date from the late fourth or early fifth century and were later translated into Latin in the ninth century.

After deeply penetrating the political, cultural, and theological thought of the High Middle Ages, they still exerted a powerful influence in the thirteenth century. They were read and commented at the University of Paris. This body of thought that presented the celestial hierarchy as the model of the terrestrial hierarchy was seized upon by the political-theological reflection on monarchy. With its final references to the Seraphs and the Dominations, Gilbert de Tournai's treatise is one of the best testimonies to the influence of this system of thought.

Finally, through its examples and authorities the *Eruditio regum et principum* provided an outline of a history of royalty. Two series of historical models established the positive and negative traits of medieval monarchy. There was the biblical series and the ancient series of sources and examples, then the Christian series in its earliest beginnings. There is only one example cited from the Middle Ages that predates Saint Louis. This is in chapter 5 of the second part of the first letter in the commentary on the passage from Deuteronomy about "literate" kings. After citing David, Hezekiah, and Josiah on the one hand, and Constantine, Theodosius, Justinian, and Leo on the other, Gilbert de Tournai wrote: "We must add the pious and ever august very Christian ruler and invincible Charlemagne, your predecessor of blessed memory." What a fabulous testimony to the power of Charlemagne's image and to the importance of the Capetian campaign to claim their uninterrupted descent from the great emperor to Louis! Charlemagne was then the tie between antiquity and the present day. But did this present exist anywhere in the treatise aside from its dedication and some implicit references to contemporary situations? In general, the Mirrors of the Princes formed a genre whose matter lay outside of history. If Giraud de Galles had vilified King Henry II of England in his *De principum institutione* at the beginning of the thirteenth century, this was because his treatise was more of a polemical work against the Plantagenets than a true Mirror of the Princes.

Gilbert de Tournai's treatise contains one amazing chapter without parallel in any other Mirror of the Princes. This is the second chapter of the second part of the first letter. The phrase from Deuteronomy 17, "And he [the king] shall not cause the people to return to Egypt," is commented entirely through the lens of Saint Louis' captivity in Egypt. This event occurred only ten years before the treatise's composition, so it was a *contemporary* event. The content of the chapter is not the most interesting thing about it. Despite the reference, the king was still actually praised for his religious zeal, although the crusade's failure was blamed on the vices of the people and the French army in particular. As a new Moses, like him a victim of his own people, Louis never entered the Promised Land. When Christ wants to free the Holy Land, he will do it himself. This text sounds like an adieu to the crusades. Saint Louis would never hear it, happy as he was to replace Egypt with Tunisia. However, in my eyes, the most important thing here is this entry of contemporary history into the field of the examples. In the collections of *exempla* from the thirteenth century, one can observe the same tendency to grant more and more importance to what happened *nostris temporibus,* "in our time." From this point on, the prince could see himself in the mirror.

THE CORONATION: A MIRROR OF THE PRINCE

In its own way, the coronation ceremony of kings constituted a Mirror of the Princes in words, gestures, and actions. I will come back to the topic of Saint Louis' royal sacred status later in order to deal with it in greater detail.[14] The coronation followed a ritual intended to reconnect royal power with its divine origin during each regime change. It was meant to guarantee the continuity of God's protection for the monarchy. Functioning as both an explicit and a symbolic contract, it was also meant to secure the support of the Church in exchange for privileged status from the clergy and to replicate the preceding reigns in order to reinforce the kingdom's stability for all its members from the highest to the lowest levels of the social hierarchy. To be effective, the coronation had to be a profoundly conservative ceremony; its archaic nature guaranteed its validity. There could only be rare innovations, and they had to reinforce the original rites by carrying them even farther in the same direction.[15]

We only possess one very succinct description of a coronation ceremony that predates Charles V's coronation in the fourteenth century (1364). This is a description of Philip I's coronation in 1059. The *ordines* are not descriptions properly speaking, but models or instructions for coronations that had not yet taken place. They are usually hard to date, and it is hard to know whether they were actually used and for which coronations because there was a collection of *ordines* in Reims that the clergy and the new king's entourage chose from. We do not know which *ordo* was used for Louis' coronation, although it is fairly certain that three new *ordines* entered the collection during his reign. There is one from the beginning of his reign called the "*ordo* of Reims," another from the end of the reign called the "last Capetian *ordo*" because there were no new *ordines* before the accession of the Valois (1328), and then there is the "*ordo* of 1250" that I will discuss later in this work.[16] There is nothing surprising about any of this if we think, on the one hand, of the increased symbolic prestige that French royalty acquired under Louis IX and, on the other, of the acute interest that he himself had in this ceremony as he advised his son and successor to be "worthy of receiving the unction with which the kings of France are crowned."[17] The most interesting of the three is the *ordo* of 1250. It was most certainly composed during Saint Louis' reign, and a new royal emblem appears within it, the hand of justice, held in the left hand. It would remain an exclusive sign of the French monarchy. Justice was not only the main royal function in monarchical ideology or even in Christian monarchical ideology, it was a function that was foundationally anchored in the sacred. Along with peace, it was the one virtue most strongly associated with Saint Louis' image in thought and action. One might consider whether this sign was directly or indirectly his own personal contribution to the royal imagery, expressed and diffused through the coronation (and his seal) and noted in the *ordo* for the coronation as though in a program from a Mirror of the Princes. One might also conclude that during his reign the *ordines* for the coronation of the king of France reflected the essential characteristics of the French monarchy more fully than before and testified to the fact that the formation of royal religion had nearly reached its highest point with him.[18]

If the record of the Mirrors of the Princes that involved Saint Louis however tightly or loosely ended there, the saint king would more or less completely disappear behind their generalizations.

The *Enseignements* for His Son and Daughter

It is an exceptional fact that Saint Louis himself composed a Mirror of the Princes,[19] the *Enseignements* that he drew up for his son Philip, the future Philip III who succeeded him at Tunis after his death. Legends and obscurities surround this text, or perhaps we should say these texts, because Louis doubled his *Instructions* with others written for his daughter Isabelle, queen of Navarre. Some have romantically pretended that the king had them dictated in Carthage on his deathbed. On the contrary, the date of their composition was earlier: the composition dates from as early as 1267 on the eve of his decision to leave on the crusade. It would be more realistic to date them from 1270, just before the departure for Tunisia. On the other hand, some writers have advanced the idea that Saint Louis did not dictate them to a scribe and that, in light of their intimate nature, he wrote them himself. This would have gone against the habits of laymen of the time, including and even more specifically important laymen. However, as there is no doubt that Saint Louis knew how to write and because of the very personal nature of the texts (Saint Louis asked Isabelle never to show the *Enseignements* that he composed for her to anyone but her brother Philip without his permission), it is quite plausible when he tells his daughter that he "wrote these instructions with my own hand." We can guess that he did the same for the ones addressed to his son, even though he never asked him to keep them secret. The future king was a public person, whereas the queen of Navarre was still a private person. There is also the problem of the manuscripts that have preserved these texts for us. They have not been signed and do not date from any time close to the period in which they were composed. Someone added these texts to the end of the *Lives* of Saint Louis by Guillaume de Chartres, Guillaume de Saint-Pathus, Guillaume de Nangis, and Joinville. No doubt, the *Enseignements* were therefore reproduced as pieces of the record for the canonization proceeding. The version given by Joinville had been considered the best, until the American medievalist David O'Connell reconstructed the original text on the basis of Latin translations.[20] Of course, this is the version that must be accepted as authentic, most directly expressing Saint Louis' ideas. We still need a rigorous study of the manuscripts that have conveyed these manipulated texts to us. Nonetheless, it is still reasonable to think that the different versions and especially the additions represent the points of view of people who knew

Saint Louis or who gathered his statements from viable sources. Alongside the modifications meant to advance the interests of one milieu or another—an ecclesiastical milieu more often than not—it is reasonable to believe that the text is also a veritable "*enseignement*" of Saint Louis that was added to the work, for instance, in the case of his recommendation to take care of the "good towns."[21]

First of all, Saint Louis expressed his affection for his family and underscored the emotional ties that were supposed to exist between parents and children. This theme recurs throughout the text. He stated his "friendship as a father" (paragraph 1), desired "with all his heart" for his son to be "well instructed" (22), and also called on him to "love and honor" his mother and to follow her "good instructions" and her "good advice" (21). He gave him all the blessings that a father can and should give his son (31). The first instruction thus stressed the primordial family unit founded on affection and respect for the family defined in the limited sense as parents and their children. But, these instructions were practically self-evident. The real lesson lay elsewhere. No earthly affection should be placed before one's love of good and sense of duty: "Be careful lest for love of whomever it may be, you abstain from doing good or do things that you should not do." Saint Louis no doubt recalled Blanche of Castile's declarations asserting that she would prefer to see her son dead than in a state of mortal sin. He also repeated the words that, according to Joinville, he had himself spoken to his older son Louis during a serious illness: "Handsome son, I pray that you make yourself loved by the people of your kingdom, for truly I would rather see a Scotsman come from Scotland and govern the people loyally and well than for you to govern them poorly for all to see."[22]

Any earthly attachment therefore had to fade before the love of God and the values that come from him.

We can feel how sensitive Louis was to the esteem and confidence that his son placed in him. He was finally persuaded to write this text for his son because "I heard you say several times that you would retain more from me than from any other person." His charisma comes through first in his words, and because he liked to "teach," and because being taught well as he was himself was essential, especially for a future king, teaching his son and natural successor after the death of his oldest son was an incomparable pleasure. Philip was a privileged disciple, but nothing was valid without the essential virtue of faith: "Love God with all your heart and all your power."

The corollary principle was the hatred of sin, which was first and foremost a personal offense against God. In this feudal world where personal relations held the most importance, to sin was "to displease" God. For Louis and his mother, conscious mortal sin was so horrendous that its mere mention set off the most excessive imaginings: "You must have this desire that before knowingly committing any mortal sin, you would rather have your legs and arms cut off and your life taken through the cruelest suffering." He had already said this to Joinville:

> "Let me ask you, then, whether you would rather be leprous or have committed a mortal sin." And I, who never lied to him, I answered that I would rather have committed thirty of them than be a leper. When the friars had left, he took me aside and sat me down at his feet and told me: "How could you have told me that yesterday?" And I told him that I would still say the same thing today. And he told me: "You were speaking like a fool and a babbling idiot, because you should know as well as I that there is no leprosy as ugly as living in mortal sin, because the soul that is in mortal sin is like the devil, and that is why there can be no leprosy as ugly.
>
> "And it is perfectly true that when a man dies, he is healed of the leprosy of the body, but when a man who has committed mortal sin dies, he cannot know or be certain whether he repented enough in his lifetime for God to have forgiven him. This is why he always has to be afraid that this leprosy may last for as long as God will be in heaven. And I beg you," said he, "as much as I can for God's love and mine, to put your heart in the habit of preferring any evil that could happen to your body through leprosy or any other sickness to mortal sin entering your soul."

As faith consisted in one's personal fidelity toward God, it was always proper to thank him, even when he sent tests like "persecution, sickness, or any other form of suffering," "because you should always understand that he did this for your own good." People were also supposed to reflect on the fact that they deserved these punishments, because their cause lay in "having little loved and little served" God and in having done "many things against his will." Once again, Louis was thinking about himself and his trials on the crusade. The suffering king had meditated on the causes of these misfortunes and had found their causes in his shortcomings and had thus attempted to change his ways. This was all the more reason to express one's gratitude to God for the good things he had given ("prosperity, bodily health, or anything else"), and in order to avoid misfortune one had to avoid wrongdoing and especially to avoid the feudal sin par excellence for any Christian, but especially for a king, which was "pride." Of all the unjust wars, the most harmful was the one that involved fighting the gifts of God, "battling our Lord for his gifts."

Now we come to the instructions for devout worship. The first is the frequent practice of confession (which did not lead to a frequent practice of communion). Since the Fourth Lateran Council (1215), confession based on admission had been at the center of Christian worship. It reinforced the Church's control over Christian society. The choice of a confessor was therefore essential—especially for a king.[23] It was through this process that the royal confessors, those characters who later took on such great importance, appeared. During the absolutist period, as long as they had the courage, they represented one of the few powers to offset the ruler's omnipotence. Believing in the necessity and the benefits of instruction, Saint Louis advised his son to choose confessors "who are not just pious, but who are also sufficiently educated." Any powerful Christian, and the king more than anyone else, must allow his confessor not to spare him any reproof. This would make the confessor effective, and the king should expect the same thing from his friends. "Spare the rod and spoil the child"— Christianity adopted the ancient adage. A confessor who was a fearful courtier would be a disaster for his penitent. Beyond his official religious function, the confessor should also be a friend and like any "loyal" and "faithful" friend, he should be able to calm his penitent's soul by listening to him when he "feels bad" [*a malaise de coeur*]. A virtually sacred conception of speech is revealed here.[24] One could confide a "secret" to a confessor and a loyal friend. The intensification of confession and admission created or at least deepened a space for the avowed secret, although it could not pry open the fortress of the unspeakable:[25] "provided that this is, of course, something of which you are capable of speaking." Thus, a space of secrecy that led to a dialectic between ineffability and admission took shape in the hearts of thirteenth-century Christians.

Attendance at mass and prayers comes after confession in a descending order of importance. It was good to hear mass as often as possible.

Saint Louis discovered an impressive competitor in this form of worship; during the negotiations for the treaty of Paris in 1259, King Henry III of England often arrived late for the meetings because he would stop in all the churches on his path to listen to mass.[26] He managed to annoy Saint Louis by doing this. In the thirteenth century, the church building was a social gathering place where the fervent reception of the mass was often disrupted by numerous distractions. Louis advised his son to avoid these distractions: "When you are in church, make sure that you do not waste your time and that you do not speak any vain words." Whether thought to oneself or spoken aloud, prayer should be very meditative. The practice of silent reading seems to have begun in the thirteenth century, and it gradually supplanted the traditional custom of reading aloud.[27] Prayer settled into the silence even more, occupying the internal space of the individual.[28] There was still one moment when the Christian's inner tension during the mass rose to an extreme. This took place during the consecration and the elevation of the host: "and be especially more meditative and more attentive to the prayer while the body of Our Lord Jesus Christ is present during the mass and also for a little time before." People paid close attention to their bodies and to the promotion of the body during the thirteenth century. The first body to be promoted is that of Christ embodied in the host.[29] In this Eucharistic period, the liturgy and gestures of the mass changed to accommodate the Holy Communion, the present and visible Eucharist.[30]

Works of mercy round out the trilogy of worship made up of confession, mass, and prayer. Philip should be charitable. The suffering king was supposed to help "all of those whom he would consider to be suffering," whether their suffering was corporal or spiritual [*de coeur ou de corps*]. The support itself may be moral or material given in alms. The king should be an almsgiver, like Louis was and as he would soon be again in the testament that he was about to dictate. The poor made up the first rank of suffering people to assist. In this century in which poverty was queen, with Saint Francis, the *Poverello,* the little poor guy, and the Mendicant friars who surrounded Louis, the king had to be a king of mendicants, like Louis. He should be a king not simply for those who were symbolically and voluntarily poor, but for actual poor people who were in duress.

After asking his son to seek out the company of good people and to flee the company of bad people and to love good and hate evil—which corresponded to the basically Manichean mentality of the Middle Ages—the king came back to one of his obsessions, speech,[31] and the need to struggle against "bad speech." By "bad speech," he meant speech that tempted people to sin, malicious gossip, and especially blasphemy. Saint Louis became stirred up with such excitement here that he advised his son to refer any case in which the crime fell outside royal jurisdiction to the ecclesiastical or seigniorial authority responsible for administering justice. He also defined the sacred persons who could be blasphemed against when someone applied bad speech to them. They were God, of course, and the Virgin Mary, which was not surprising either, because ever since the eleventh century the rapid spread of the cult of Mary practically made the Virgin into a fourth figure of the Holy Trinity. However, he also designated the saints here, which was a bit surprising. Here, as in other areas, Saint Louis was a maximalist. He was an extremist when it came to certain forms of worship and, in the present case, a champion of moral repression.

The following articles addressed the future king more directly. They make up a small Mirror of the Princes inside the larger body of the *Instructions*.

The first precept was to be worthy of God's gift, the divine election that the royal function represented even more strongly in France because of the coronation anointment that was carried out with the miraculous oil.[32] It was not enough for the "goodness in all things" that came from it to be real for the king; this goodness had to be shown and made "evident." Saint Louis' royal morality wanted appearance to figure on the same level as existence. The king should be a living symbol, manifest and visible to his subjects. Sometimes sacred royalty was expressed in the realm of secrets and hidden designs, through absence, the empty throne, or the curtain before the throne. However, in compliance with the new theories and political manners, Louis' royalty was above all a royalty that showed itself and that even put itself on display.[33]

Justice was the king's primary virtue. Louis insisted upon this point and highlighted the case in which the king was responsible for judging a political opponent. In this case, he should not attempt to influence the council whose verdict should be based on the truth alone. Once again, ideals and values took precedence over any individual human being, however loved or powerful he or she may be (paragraph 17). Saint Louis worked to strengthen royal power, but he maintained it in a condition that was far from the absolutism into which the kings of France eventually fell.[34]

Not only were the truth and the law that was meant to uphold it above him, but the king also had to respect the decisions of organizations that he established for the purpose of pronouncing justice—these "members of [his] council" who made up the Parlement that he had just put in place.

We encounter another of Saint Louis' obsessions here, one that first appeared especially strong around 1247: political remorse. Politics was a matter of morality. The king should redress any wrong that he had done to his subjects, particularly any unjust appropriation "of lands or deniers." This had been the object of the investigations that he so diligently undertook. In the thirteenth century, the Church had a strong interest in limiting and restoring illicit benefices like the prohibited collection of interest by merchants and moneylenders or their heirs. There were numerous manuals from the period that explained these restitutions, as there were also testaments that made provisions for restitutions and expressed the remorse of those who benefited from abusive acquisitions. It was far less common and far more difficult to obtain restitution for the one essential thing of value: land. Saint Louis knew perfectly well that this word "*rendre*" (render, return) that he recommended to his son was hard to pronounce because it referred to an action that was even harder to accomplish. He sometimes confided as much to his close friends, like Joinville who once heard him say this.[35] He went on to define the attitude that the ruler should have toward the Church, the clerics, and the religious.

We might ask whether there isn't a touch of irony here. Through Joinville we know that Louis was quite capable of it, for instance in the advice that he issued on the members of the Holy Church while referring to some words uttered by his grandfather Philip Augustus. When members of his council pointed out to him "that the clerics were committing great wrongs against him, and they asked with astonishment how he put up with it," Philip Augustus had answered that he knew all about it but that out of respect for Our Lord, he did not want any "scandal to come between me and the Holy Church." Louis probably had another of Philip Augustus's remarks in mind, one that he gave as an instruction to his own son, Louis' father. His advice was that it was in his interest always to remain on good terms with the people of the Church.[36] Among the latter, one must always love the religious—the monks and friars—more than the others, in other words more than the secular members of the Church, because the religious were "the ones who honor and serve Our Lord the most." One must therefore "help them willingly" with their needs.

Finally, the king should be cautious in exercising the rights he held in ecclesiastical matters, specifically in conferring certain benefices. (He had been very cautious in delegating these rights during his crusades.) He should confer them only to "good people," and privilege those clerics who had no prebends instead of allowing them to accumulate in the same hands. This advice was dictated by his sense of justice and concern for the poor. Because these issues were always very "thorny," Louis directed his son to take advice from his council in these matters. Here is another essential theme of the Christian Mirrors of the Princes. The king should always choose good advisors, consult with them, and listen to them.

This whole group of recommendations was crowned with the instruction to be "devoted to the Church of Rome and our holy father the pope," to whom he must "show the respect and honor that you owe your spiritual father." In practice, we have already seen how this was meant to be taken and we will see it again later on.[37]

The section on war and peace is one of the most original parts of these instructions. It is a veritable small treatise on just and unjust wars. It also happened to be one of the obsessions of the Christian world in the twelfth and thirteenth centuries,[38] not to mention a personal obsession of Saint Louis. War was fundamentally wrong because "sins" were fatally committed in war and "poor people" were almost inevitably victimized by it. Louis also recommended the tactic of forcing the enemy's hand, although he never spoke of "enemies" and only used the word "*malfaiteur*" (wrongdoer) since war for him could only be a work of justice. The enemy should not be reined in by laying waste to his lands as was the custom of the time. This mainly afflicts the "poor people." It should be done instead "by taking his possessions and his towns or his castles by siege." One had to be careful to spare churches and the poor. A large number of precautions needed to be taken before declaring war. The ruler had to be sure that he was receiving good advice about whether to make war or not. He had to be sure that "the reason for it was entirely justified," that he had exhausted all possibilities of convincing the "wrongdoer," that he had "given him ample warning," and, finally, that he "had waited long enough." War should only be a king's last resort.

This moralization of war is complemented by a second section expressing Louis' passion for peace and the resolution of existing conflicts, especially when they involved people "from the land" of the king or any of his vassals, any of "his men." The king, who had just presented an *exemplum* about his grandfather, presents another one here from the life of Saint Martin. "At the moment Our Lord let him know that he was about to die, he went to make peace between the clerics of his archbishopric, and in doing so he had the impression that he was putting the end of his life to good purpose."[39] Louis emphasized that this was "a very important example."

These acts of justice should not only be pursued against war and in wartime, but also in so-called times "of peace." This demanded specific precautions such as the surveillance of royal officers, the eradication of the kingdom's sins, and fair and economical management of the Royal Treasury.

The king was responsible for the men he had appointed as his servants and representatives. He had to make sure that he had good officers [*prévôts*] and good members of his "hotel," his household in other words. They had been called upon to establish the rule of justice so they had to be just men themselves. The purging of the kingdom's sins primarily targeted the ones he came down on after his return from the Holy Land: "villainous oaths and everything that is done or said against God or Our Lady or the saints: sins of the flesh, dice games, taverns, or other sins." All of these had to be "struck down." As for the "heretics and other bad people on your land"— he was definitely thinking of the Cahorsin, Lombard, and Jewish usurers— they all had to be purged as well, not by destroying them but by chasing them out of the kingdom. The essential thing here was this notion of purging and purification, not the physical repression. As we have seen, even the blasphemers were harshly punished. Finally, this king who had been accused of ruining the treasury filled by his grandfather in order to pay for his crusades—and who is still accused of this today—advised his son to spend his deniers only "for good use" and "to collect them fairly." He even asked Philip to cultivate a "sense" of economy, to avoid "outrageous expenses" and "unjust perceptions [of taxes]," and "to collect the royal money fairly and to put it to good use."

A single phrase sums up this moral and political program: "Advance the good with all your power." This had always been Saint Louis' program for governing and even more so after 1254.

Several concepts and obsessions also sum up Saint Louis' vision of the structures and people needed for a man and more specifically for a king to act. First of all, there was the complementary opposition between *the body* and *the heart*. This can be found in several places, and it is dually interesting because it unified an attention to the body, which men in the Middle Ages often only regarded with scorn, and a tendency to situate the spiritual in the *heart,* that great figure promoted at the end of the Middle Ages. This opposition also expressed a new fascination with blood and the idea that spirituality could be invaded by affectivity.

Next, there was the traditional opposition between clerics and laymen. Here, however, it took on two original characteristics related to new trends that developed in the thirteenth century. One of these characteristics was the preference for the religious among all clerics, a preference that was even greater for the new Mendicant friars than for the monks, although there were also frequent comparisons to laymen. Although some said he was exclusively in the hand of the Dominicans and Franciscans, the king counseled his son to take advice from "good" laymen as much as from "good" religious.

This advice articulated the pairing of "mouth" and "thought," which underscored the importance of speech in this century of "new speech." It also recalled the necessary relation between what was said and what was thought. Speech was not supposed to have any autonomy; it should be submitted to thought. What people say should come from the heart and from reason and should translate them faithfully.[40]

The pairing of attending sermons and accomplishing pious deeds "in private" expressed the complementary nature of public, oral worship and private, silent piety. The expression confirmed both the spread of preaching and the construction of a private sphere, both of which characterized the thirteenth century.

Finally, among all the people who were supposed to hold the future king's attention, in addition to the churchmen and the religious, on one side there were the poor, those suffering brothers of the Christian man, and on the other, ancestors. Saint Louis was particularly sensitive to thoughts about dead family members, and his manner of thinking in this domain was based on aristocracy and lineage, royalty and dynasty.

Saint Louis' instructions for his daughter Isabelle basically repeated the ones he left for his son, sometimes word for word. Of course, the section that contained an actual Mirror of the Princes on the ruler and government had been left out, but this version still presented all the passages on faith, the hatred of mortal sin, the importance of confession, mass, and prayer, the patience needed to face suffering, rejection, and pride, the pity one should have for the poor and the misfortunate, and the choice of a "good" entourage. Certain instructions had been adapted to the feminine condition. In step with his time, Louis believed in the importance of instructing girls as well as boys, women as well as men. While he advised his son to save his deniers, he extolled modesty in dress and finery to his daughter: "Do not have too many dresses or jewels at the same time," "never dedicate too much time or too much study to your dress and adornment," "do not go to any extremes in your finery and always be inclined to wear less rather than more." Still, woman was created to obey man: "Humbly obey your husband and your father and your mother according to God's commandments; you should do this willingly for the love that you have for them and especially for the love of Our Lord who commanded it thus as it should be." However, just as for Philip, he instructed her that no earthly attachment should take precedence over actions of justice and the duty desired by God: "You should obey no one against God." The daughter's submission to her parents and the wife's subjection to her husband had their limits in her obedience to God and the values that he gave to men.

Finally, feminine devotion to God should have something more extreme and more absolute than a man's devotion. In order "to please our Lord," "have a desire in yourself that never leaves you." When he wrote for Isabelle, Louis said more about loving God than he had confided in Philip: "The measure according to which we must love him is to love him without measure."

The King of the
Foreign Chroniclers

THIRTEENTH-CENTURY FRENCH CULTURE WAS FIRST AND FOREMOST
Christian and European. The collective consciousness, the sentiment of
Western identity, was based on belonging to Christendom. This feeling
was even stronger for individuals who participated in the common culture
and its institutions. The clerics thought within the general terms of Christendom, which formed the horizon of their thoughts and lives. When they
wrote history, they wrote universal chronicles more often than not.[1] Saint
Louis appeared vital to them in at least two ways, first of all because he occupied such an important position in the Christian world, and also because
his image as a king of remarkable piety had spread very quickly. The two
most important foreign chroniclers who were practically contemporaries
of Saint Louis spoke about him, but each one's testimony was very different
from the other's. In the Benedictine Englishman Matthew Paris's *Chronicle*
(*Chronica majora*), when the king appeared at the forefront as one of the major
figures, he occupied the position that he held in history. The author was actually writing a chronicle of Christendom, and Louis figured within it as
a king like all the others but only as one who was more pious. Although

341

Matthew had heard a lot about Louis from people who knew him in varying degrees, he does not seem to have ever met him himself. The atmosphere in Matthew's chronicle was one of traditional Christendom in which the pope, the emperor, the kings, and other powerful figures, the feudal society of Northern Europe occupied center stage. Salimbene of Parma's chronicle was extremely different. It was the work of a Franciscan who was familiar with the new forms of Christian religiosity and who divided his time between stays in urban convents and living as an itinerant. More often than not, he was interested in telling what he had seen or heard instead of narrating the general history of Christendom. His chronicle resembles a personal journal or a collection of memoirs. He was a man who basked in Southern culture, which, in his case, was primarily urban and Italian. He spoke little of Saint Louis, but he actually met him once and from this brief meeting was able to draw out the most moving vision of the saint king that the thirteenth century has given us.

THE ENGLISH BENEDICTINE, MATTHEW PARIS

Matthew Paris spent almost all his life in the south of England in the aristocratic monastery of Saint Albans, which was founded by the king of Mercia, Offa II, in the second half of the eighth century.[2] He took the monastic habit in 1217. As a general rule, one never became a Benedictine novice before the age of fifteen, so he was probably born around 1200. Aside from a number of moves in England, particularly while accompanying King Henry III to London where he stayed in the abbey of Westminster, he seems to have carried out only a single mission to a foreign land. In 1247, the king of Norway, Haakon IV, obtained a papal bull calling on Matthew to reform the abbey of Saint-Benet Holm on the island of Nidarholm near Bergen. The abbey had serious problems with Cahorsin financiers (usurers). Matthew also carried a message from Louis IX to Haakon, which asked him to crusade with him. We do not know how or why the king of France entrusted this mission to the English Benedictine. This was the only contact that we know the two individuals ever had, and it was probably very indirect. Having arrived in Bergen in June 1248, Matthew probably returned from Norway the following year. After going back to Saint Albans, he was definitely there in 1259.

The *Chronica majora* (the "Grand Chronicle," usually simply referred to as the *Chronicle*) constitutes the most important body of his works from the perspective of modern historiography. However, people in the Middle Ages were more interested in his collection of historical anecdotes, the *Flores historiarum* (Flowers of History), and his biographical and hagiographical works: the *Life of the Two Kings Named Offa*, and, in Anglo-Saxon verse, the four lives of the great "English" saints, Saint Alban, Saint Edward the Confessor, Saint Thomas Becket, and Saint Edmond Rich, like Becket the archbishop of Canterbury. They were also interested in his "History of the English" (*Historia Anglorum*) and his works dedicated to his monastery, though to a lesser degree. Several qualities of Matthew Paris's works and their tradition gave them an original character; a few of them have been preserved in autograph manuscript form, and certain ones were decorated with drawings in his own hand.[3] To avoid any doubts about his name, we should underscore that Matthew Paris was an Englishman. The name "Paris" was a fairly common patronymic in thirteenth-century England that implied neither any French origin nor any frequentation of the University of Paris. Besides, Matthew had no university education whatsoever.

The *Chronica majora* in which Saint Louis appears was a continuation of the chronicle of Matthew's predecessor at Saint Albans, Roger Wendover. His chronicle copied Wendover's very closely up until 1236, and after that date it contained Matthew's original work.[4] Although the chronicle is universal, it centered on the monastery of Saint Albans, a center for information on Christendom and, especially, on France, England, the papacy, and the Empire above all. Furthermore, Matthew did not submit the information he received to any verification or critical examination. He made frequent errors. For example, he called King Ferdinand III, about whom he says many good things, Alphonse, which was a common given name for the kings of Castile. His chronology has to be looked on with caution. For the most part, he was a collector and circulator of rumors and gossip. He should not be read for the truth about facts, events, and people. Instead, we have to read him for the echo of stories that were commonly told in the Christian world.

Matthew identified himself as an Englishman, but he did not care for King Henry III of England, even though he seems to have been on familiar terms with him. (He cared even less for his father, the much maligned John Lackland.) He always refers to him as "the king of England" (*rex Angliae*), whereas he almost never mentions Louis IX's name without appending some laudatory epithet. He was aware of the clerics' superiority, but was still a monk in the old style. He did not like the Mendicant friars and their innovations. He actually detested any innovation and, notably, any new forms of taxation. He thus reserved his most scathing hostility for the papacy whose fiscal greed never seemed to stop growing. He was very pessimistic about the contemporary world and its evolution. At the end of each year, he noted that year's significant events just as certain newspapers still do today. However, these events were mainly heavenly signs like comets, the appearance of monsters, droughts, floods, and bad harvests. He had no specific conception of history as anything other than the affirmation of God's will, particularly as it acted to punish the vices of men. Certain characters nonetheless influenced him, like Emperor Frederick II whose personality fascinated him even though he viewed him as a tyrant. Seduced by powerful figures, he was easily impressed with one oriental ruler or another, whether Muslim or not. He had an interesting way of viewing the opposition between Westerners and Easterners (these were the terms he used to designate them): thanks to a certain relative impartiality, he was capable of recognizing the positive qualities of a Muslim sultan and could even identify certain virtues in the oriental rulers as superior to those of the Western Christians. He resembled Saint Louis in this regard, as he also sometimes paid homage to his oriental enemies with the exception of their worship of the horrible Mohammed. Matthew knew how to observe and narrate. He also knew how to draw, which was even more exceptional. He was an engaged witness of the past, though lacking any critical spirit or dignified perspective. Still, he related and reflected the reverberating sounds and images of Christendom with talent.

He seems to have changed his opinion about Saint Louis and his mother Blanche who was associated with him very often, since he perceived the pair formed by them as governing France until her death at the end of 1252. When Saint Louis' mother died, Matthew used this as an occasion to pay her a strong homage. He praised her pious death in a nun's robe at Maubuisson. He depicts her in these laudatory terms: "Blanche was magnanimous, a woman by her sex but masculine in character, a new Semiramis, a blessing for her century, and she left the Kingdom of France inconsolable."[5] Her life had amassed sadness upon sadness from the premature death of her husband Louis VIII to her son's unhealthy condition, to his departure on the crusade, his captivity, her second son Robert d'Artois' shameful death on the crusade after fleeing the Muslims before being killed in battle, the incurable illness of her third son Alphonse who became paralyzed, to the rumor that her oldest son Louis wanted to spend the rest of his days in the Holy Land and die there to exchange his earthly kingdom for the Kingdom of Heaven. This is a typical device that Matthew Paris used, alternating praise with scrutiny while underscoring weaknesses and misfortunes, albeit without denigrating anyone. Still, one sometimes senses that he may have done this with a certain perversity, as though he wanted to imply that these may have been punishments for hidden sins. He gives Saint Louis similar treatment.

Matthew Paris was interested in the king of France before his first crusade. This interest applied mainly to three areas: the political and military strife of his youth, his manifestations of piety in the acquisition of distinguished relics, and his relations with the king of England. With respect to the testimony of his French contemporaries, Matthew's choices were unoriginal. The young Louis IX appeared to him as a physically fragile being of weak health and wan complexion. For the year 1242, when Louis was twenty-eight years old and an epidemic struck the French army after its victory at Taillebourg, he noted the fears to which this fragility gave rise: "In effect, the king was young, tender, and fragile."[6] He thus allowed us to glimpse the image that people had of Louis throughout the Christian world. We often find this recurring fear about kings who were still children.[7] Louis had barely grown past childhood; he was *iuvenis*. His father Louis VIII's premature death at thirty-nine years of age also weighed on him: "The French are terribly afraid of losing their king, just as they unexpectedly lost his father Louis before the walls of Avignon."[8] We can observe that the principle of heredity was particularly strong among kings, like father, like son, for their fates and all the rest. God and the nature that he created team up in this sense. Matthew Paris, a continuator of Roger Wendover, saw Louis as ruling under his mother's control until 1246. He displayed little sympathy for Blanche of Castile. He willingly echoed the calumnies that the French barons spread about Blanche who, he claimed, thus weakened the fragile royal minority even more through her conduct:

The barons accused the count[9] of treason and lese-majesty for having killed his Royal Highness Louis at the siege of Avignon by poisoning him for the love of Blanche, according to what they said. And, as these lords had tried to embroil the count several times in a judiciary duel,[10] the queen, who took over all the kingdom's affairs because of the immaturity and the age of the child king, refused to listen to them. Then, they renounced their loyalty to the king and the queen and began to ravage the Kingdom of the Franks with war. They were enraged, in fact, that they had for lady and lord a woman whom they claimed had been stained with the sperm of both the count and the legate and who transgressed the limits of modesty and widowhood.[11]

Here we have what appeared to the monastic couple of Roger Wendover and Matthew Paris as a serious explanation of the strife that marked Saint Louis' minority.

In explaining the affairs in Brittany, he accused the young king of denying the truth about the rights of the king of England, stating that he "followed the advice of a woman [Blanche of Castile] more than the law of justice."[12] In 1236, the two English chroniclers mentioned the new unrest and a new insurrection by the French barony: "They were upset that the kingdom of kingdoms, France,[13] was governed through the counsel of a woman."[14] During a meeting of Christian rulers convoked by Emperor Frederick II at Vaucouleurs, Matthew still maintained that the king of France "set a bad example that was pernicious and terrifying for everyone else by arriving with an army at a meeting in times of peace." At the same time, the king of England was merely happy to send excuses for his absence along with his brother Richard of Cornwall and several lords under the direction of the archbishop of York and the bishop of Ely in an attempt to pacify the rest of the assembly.[15] The tone began to change in 1239–1240[16] with the acquisition of the relics of the Passion and the construction of the Sainte-Chapelle to house them, an eminently praiseworthy action. Matthew also admired the king's reply to his mother[17] on the subject of the Tartars[18] and praised the "noble and praiseworthy words that strengthened the courage of the French nobility and the people who live on the frontiers."[19]

During the Franco-English war of 1242, Matthew maintained a fairly equal balance between the two kings. In 1241, however, when Louis invested his brother Alphonse with the county of Poitiers that their father Louis VIII had assigned to him in apanage, he sharply protested against the injustice that the French king committed against the king of England's brother, Richard of Cornwall. According to the English version of events, the county actually belonged to him and had been unjustly seized from them, first by Philip Augustus and the French peers and again by Louis VIII. He reported that people were saying that the king of France "was following the advice of the people who hated the Kingdom of England."[20] When war broke out between Saint Louis and Henry III who came to support his vassals, Hugh of the March and Raimond de Toulouse, who had revolted against the French throne, Matthew was upset by Louis' decision to arrest English merchants on French soil and to seize their merchandise. Through this act of brigandage, "he did great harm to the ancient dignity of France; this country traditionally offered safe shelter and protection to all refugees and exiles and especially to people who came in peace and welcoming them into its bosom to defend them, hence the origin of the name of France in the native language."[21] The English monk was well aware that England was already a country of commerce where merchants count.

What nevertheless completed what we might call Matthew Paris's conversion to Saint Louis was that even before the opening of hostilities, the French king recognized the king of England's rights to his former possessions in France and, according to his sources, announced his intention to return Poitou and a large part of Normandy to him.[22] This claim then began to figure as a leitmotif in Matthew Paris's *Chronicle* as Louis became "he who wants to render and restore." Is this true? Nothing leads us to believe it at this date, and it is fairly certain that the king of France never thought of returning Normandy, which was conquered by his grandfather Philip Augustus, to the king of England. It seems that when, according to Matthew Paris, Louis realized his barons' insurmountable hostility to this restitution, it was more of a pretext, a certain shrewdness that he wielded, rather than any real conviction. He was thoroughly capable of this. However, it is still bothersome to note that this was exactly what he did in the treaty of 1259, not for Normandy and Poitou but for the other territories in the west and the southwest of France despite the opposition declared by a number of his barons and part of his entourage.[23] We can conclude that Matthew not only took his desires for realities but that news of Saint Louis' conciliatory position on the former English possessions in France had been circulating well before 1259. Here, we must also add the reference to Louis' familial ties with the king of England whom he calls *consanguineus,* although they were only brothers-in-law who had married two sisters. These relations proved so important to him, as we have seen. Matthew Paris redoubled his praise when on the eve of his departure for the crusade in 1247 Louis appointed investigators to pursue eventual restitutions for unfair royal taxation and appropriations. In the case of territorial restitutions, Matthew's "patriotism" as an Englishman was delighted. In the case of the investigations, it was his hostility to any taxation, especially royal (feudal or "public") taxation and to the extension of the authority of royal officials within a kingdom.

The chronicler was definitively won over by Saint Louis when he decided to take the cross. Thoroughly imbued with traditional feudal spirit, even though he had no illusions about the flaws of the powerful, Matthew Paris was a great fan of the crusades. He only deplored that Saint Louis obtained the right from the pope to impose a heavy tax that mainly affected the clergy. He gave the opposing example of an English lord who sold his lands and goods so he could afford to leave on the crusade. Moreover, he saw this extortion of funds to support the crusade as the cause and explanation of its failure: "The king of France set a pernicious example by extracting an infinite amount of money from his kingdom. Due to God's punishment, this money was of no help for the crusade. We shall see the benefits he reaped from it later."[24] On the other hand, he showered Saint Louis with praise for his decision to reintroduce the "good money" into his kingdom before his departure. The king of England also carefully tried to apprehend the counterfeiters [*faux-monnayeurs, falsarii*] who scratched all the way into the insides of coins, erasing or ruining their outer circle with new inscriptions. He had decreed that only pieces with the proper legal weight [*pondus legitimum*] and a perfectly circular form would be considered authentic. He also punished the Jews, Cahorsins, and several Flemish merchants who were guilty of these crimes. Louis followed his example with even greater severity: "His Royal Highness the king of France also ordered people to seek out these criminals in his kingdom and to have them hung in the wind on gibbets."[25]

We do not know the exact measures of 1248 that Matthew Paris refers to, but they correspond to Louis' conduct during the final years of his reign including his efforts to clean up the monetary situation and measures against usurers and manipulators of coins. Again, we have a lasting idea of Saint Louis and his reign based on an image that was formed early on: money was a matter of morality; the king was responsible for assuring the circulation of "good" money, and the people who dealt with money—mainly Jews and usurers—were despicable.

Matthew Paris also praised the king of France for his actions in a curious event that occurred during his voyage from Paris to Aigues-Mortes on his departure for the crusade in 1248. Louis visited the Cistercian abbey at Pontigny-en-Bourgogne to honor the body of Saint Edmond Rich (or Abingdon), the former archbishop of Canterbury who was canonized in 1246. Matthew gives the strange report that in order to please the king and to reduce the crowd of pilgrims who bothered them, or perhaps out of greed, the Cistercians cut off one of the saint's arms and tried to give it to the king as a gift. As a black monk, a Benedictine, Matthew Paris used the event as an occasion to speak ill of his competitors, the white monks:

> Thus the shame of the monks of Pontigny was multiplied. What am I saying? I mean the shame of all the Cistercians, for many people lamented that such a venerable body lay in one of the Cistercians' churches, while the bodies of other saints are preserved so piously in the churches of the monks of the Black Order. O rash presumption! Men dare to mutilate[26] what God had preserved intact and uncorrupted.[27] On his way to the crusade, the pious king of France to whom they offered this body part, responded: "Thank God that for my sake no one will hack off what God preserved as beautiful and uncorrupted." O, lack of faith! What the Lord preserved as beautiful and uncorrupted, the monks themselves try to embalm, and they try to improve the state of this body with this unction, and so the color of the flesh becomes earthly again. It would be just if from now on our angry God only rarely accomplished the miracles that used to flourish in this place. Then, the venerable order of the Cistercians would decline in the eyes of the barons, the prelates, and the clerics. And, in addition to the order's reputation, their behavior would be a sad omen for all Christendom.

This passage is surprising when we think about what happened to Saint Louis' body and to his skeleton after his canonization and the use that was made of them.[28] The text is a precursor to the respect that cadavers and the treatment of the human body begin to increasingly inspire toward the end of the thirteenth century. It is also remarkable for the light it sheds on the Benedictine mentality, always in search of historical omens, as it managed to predict the future failure of the crusade while vilifying the Cistercians and glorifying Saint Louis at the same time.

Louis subsequently received two tributes from the English Benedictine that came in the form of epithets. The first is *christianissimus,* "very Christian." He was the most Christian of the Christian kings. Matthew recognized the preeminence of the French monarchy that arose from the anointment in the coronation at Reims and carried out with the miraculous oil from the baptism of Clovis, the first Catholic king. He already recognized this preeminence with expressions like *regnum regnorum,* "the kingdom of kingdoms," that he used to refer to France.[29] There is also his acknowledgment of Saint Denis' superiority in Christendom. During the difficult election of the pope in 1243, the French pressured the cardinals to elect a pontiff as quickly as possible. Matthew Paris justified their attitude, attributing it to "their ancient privilege that Saint Clement granted Saint Denis giving Denis the apostolate over all Westerners."[30] On his way to the crusade, Louis met with Pope Innocent IV in Lyon. He criticized the pope's intransigence toward Frederick II because it was putting the success of the crusade at risk. Narrating this with obvious approval, Matthew has the king say: "France, France,[31] guard it like the pupil of your eye, because your prosperity and the prosperity of all Christendom depend on its condition."[32]

At another point, Matthew called Louis *rex magnanimus.*[33] Reminding his readers again of his preeminence over all earthly kings, he also called him, "the successor of the invincible Charlemagne," perhaps insinuating with his usual perversity that there was a contrast between the victorious ancestor and the vanquished descendant.[34] At the same time, he was acknowledging the pretense assumed by the kings of France since the time of Louis VIII of claiming descent from Charlemagne.[35] As a supreme homage, Matthew placed the most magnificent praise for Saint Louis in the mouth of a sultan. To the Muslims who reproached him for his willingness to release the king in exchange for his ransom instead of killing him, the sultan was said to have answered, "Friends, remember that of all Christians, this one is the most noble. . . . I wouldn't dare use poison to kill such a dignified person."[36] Louis ranked first among Christians because he combined the preeminent position of the king of France in Christendom with his own exceptional personal qualities.

However the crusade confirmed the definitive rise of the French king's image in Matthew Paris's eyes, his already negative opinion of the French only became worse. Their great flaw was pride, conceit, the *superbia* that was expressed rudely and indecently. The reality of the crusade had just cruelly exposed this braggart's conceit.[37]

Saint Louis' oldest brother, Robert, count of Artois, was the embodiment of the despicable Frenchman who piled dishonor on distasteful boasting for he was the one who disobeyed his brother and thoughtlessly threw himself into his attack on the Saracens and, then, failing, fled and brought on the failure of the crusade. Matthew described him, "bragging and swearing indecently in the manner of the French."[38] This was not the worst of it. According to Matthew, the faith of many French crusaders foundered in contact with the Muslims. Matthew Paris complained about the numerous defections of crusaders to the enemy, pointing out how their treason was facilitated by the Muslims' tolerance, a quality he inadvertently praised.

> In this moment of such great misfortune, a number of Christians [the context makes clear that they are mainly Frenchmen] clandestinely left the camps and the city and went to fill the enemy ranks due to the gentleness of the conditions that the Saracens imposed. They fought efficiently against our people. The Saracens greeted them and congratulated these famished men by feeding them. And it is true that many of the Christians were able to keep their religion thanks to the Saracens' "tolerance."[39]

Many of the crusaders ostensibly said, "What good is our devotion, the prayers of the religious, and the alms of our friends? Isn't the law of Mohammed better than the law of Christ?"[40]

Highlighting what he presented as an obvious comparison with the misfortunes that occurred on the crusade, Matthew Paris noted that at almost the same time in 1251 a similar disaffection arose in France. Under the impetus of the shepherds' movement [*le movement des pastoureaux*] that he treated in attentive detail,[41] Matthew Paris stated that the French, beginning with Blanche of Castile, were traumatized and lost faith:

> Serious men and men of quality and some prelates of great intelligence were saying that never since the time of Mohammed had

such a dangerous plague descended on the Church of Christ, and it appeared at the very moment when the faith in the Kingdom of France was beginning to falter due to the misfortune that had struck the king of France.[42]

This is Matthew Paris speaking, with his usual tendency to blow hot and cold air in quick succession. At the same time that the crusading king grew in his esteem and admiration, he underscored the king's humiliation with a hypocritical complacency that all too poorly concealed his own tacit satisfaction.

> There is no other historical account but this one in which people can find that the king of France could have been taken prisoner and conquered by the infidels, but that only if he had been saved from death and dishonor, even alone, and even if all the others had perished, the Christians would have had at least some reason to breath easily and avoid the shame. This is the reason why in *Psalms* David prays specifically for the royal personage to be saved, because the salvation of the entire army depends on him. He says: "God save the king" [*Domine, salvum fac regem*].[43]

All of the royal person's symbolic value is highlighted here. Vanquished and taken prisoner, Louis lost his symbolic aura. He thus became *rex ingloriosus*, a "king without glory."[44] His bad fortune discredited France in turn: "So, the name of the king of France began to be greatly reviled in the Kingdom of France among the nobles just as much as among the people, and this was first of all because he had been so shamefully defeated by the Infidels in Egypt...."[45] As in other passages, we can measure Matthew Paris's seriousness here by his juxtaposition of this discussion of the failed crusade with his mention of the supposed fact that the vanquished Louis offered to restore Normandy and his former possessions on the continent to the king of England. The Benedictine was conjuring fantasies, and his *Chronicle* tended to circulate these fantasies more than any serious information. What he wrote about the conquered king was not only riddled with hypocrisy but he also never managed to resolve this obvious contradiction: although Louis was dishonored by his defeat, it also earned him an incredible amount of prestige. In order to get out of this bind, Matthew Paris presented what he took for a fact (although it is likely that Saint Louis experienced this humiliation and remorse for some time) and then had to balance out his denigration of the French king with an adequate amount of praise. Matthew never managed to grasp and explain this ambiguity of the image of a Saint Louis vanquished and yet still crowned with the halo of his defeat. The monk lived by the feudal idea of the shame of being defeated and could not imagine the new virtue present in the imitation of the Christ of the Passion.

The *rex ingloriosus* was henceforth *rex tristis,* the sad king. After his capture, people feared that he might die from this sadness.[46] Once he was freed, his sadness continued at Acre: "The king stayed in Acre, sad and inglorious, swearing in his heart with extreme bitterness that he would never be able to return to sweet France in this downtrodden state."[47] The reason for this was that his personal humiliation was the shame of all Christendom. Louis supposedly responded to a bishop who tried to console him by saying, "If it were I alone who suffered from this shame and adversity, and if my sins did not fall upon the universal Church, I could tolerate them with a balanced soul. But alas! It is all Christendom that I have plunged into disarray."[48] He was a sad king for the rest of his life, the sad king for eternity, as though he were already facing his death: "And falling prey to a premature grief, miserably anticipating the moment of his death, he could no longer be humored nor accept the consolation of breathing freely again."[49] From this point on, his only virtue was patience (*patientia*), the power to "suffer adversity in silence."[50] Here, we may recall the astonishing portrait of the saddened king, sobbing and crying on the road back from Hyéres to Paris.[51]

We know with certainty that Saint Louis strengthened his penitential practices after this point, and that this was one of the major traits of his life, which the crusade divided into two periods. On the other hand, Louis' definitive renunciation of any joy was one of Matthew Paris's fantasies that all of the sources refute—not only Joinville, but Matthew Paris himself when he dealt with the period between 1254 and 1259.

For the monks of Saint-Denis and the Mendicant friars, men who lived through the turn of the twelfth and thirteenth centuries, Saint Louis' image vacillated between typological symbolism, an Old Testament adaptation of a new Josiah and a successful modern imitation of the Christ of the Passion. For the traditional English Benedictine, the king was a new incarnation of the High Middle Ages' model of the man who was entirely faithful to God and yet still crushed by him, Job: "One could truly take him for a second Job."[52]

Matthew finally drew one last advantage from this image of Saint Louis, prostrate and humiliated. He saw it as an opportunity to give a supplementary lesson to his own king, Henry III. He put up with Henry III and even courted him. He had to accept him as his king and as the king of the English with whom he identified, but he was also a king he scorned. He too was a defeated king, and defeated precisely by Saint Louis, not on the crusade but in an ill-fated war to win back his English possessions in France. He was a king who had neither the courage nor the piety to leave on the crusades. Through his methods of governing and raising taxes, Henry III tyrannized his subjects, his clerics, and his nobles nonetheless. He was an anti–Saint Louis in every respect that Saint Louis was a model to admire and imitate with the exception of his financial cupidity that stained the dignity of the crusade: "The example of the king of France that God has given you as a mirror should terrify you. By extorting money from his kingdom, he enriched his enemies the Saracens, and his defeat sanctioned by this greed cast indelible shame upon Christians everywhere."[53]

After his return from the crusade, Louis captured Matthew Paris's interest in only three areas: the affairs in Flanders, the problems with the University of Paris, and above all the improvement in Franco-English relations.

Matthew Paris made no mention of the policies for moral order instituted by the king starting in 1254, with the possible exception of the measures taken against the Jews. On the other hand, since the English had an interest in them, he expatiated on the incidents in Flanders and saw them as a serious threat to the French monarchy[54] and the main reason for Louis' return from the Holy Land. If this point of view was not wrong, it was at least very reductive as it was the news of his mother's death and the lack of any strong personalities to govern the kingdom during his son's minority that convinced Louis to return to France. Questioning Countess Marguerite's authority, Matthew gave free rein to his misogyny: "The crown of France is tottering because of a woman's pride, the countess of Flanders."[55]

In the quarrel between the ordinary masters and the Mendicant monastic masters at the University of Paris in 1255 in which Saint Louis took the side of the Mendicants and accepted serving as the secular arm of the papacy against the leader of the ordinary masters, Guillaume de Saint-Amour,[56] the English chronicler instead attributed the desire to support the ordinary masters and the autonomy (the "freedom") of the University to Saint Louis, so great was the extent to which he despised the Dominicans, the Franciscans, and the pope who supported them: "Although the king of France had hoped to preserve the freedom of the masters and students of the University just as he had done for the citizens of Paris," the Preaching Friars made a better move by making themselves the servants of the pope.[57]

The thing that mattered most of all to Matthew Paris was the improvement in relations between the kings of France and England.[58] This development went through a first phase in 1254 that was primarily sentimental and symbolic. Henry III came to France to transfer his mother's body to the Plantagenet's royal necropolis at the abbey of Fontrevault in Anjou and to meditate before the body of Saint Edmond Rich in Pontigny. On this occasion, the saint seems to have exercised his miraculous powers of intervention and healed the king of England who was sick. Then, when Henry wanted to return to England by way of France proper, Louis was delighted to grant his permission. Underscoring their family ties, he invited Henry to be his guest in Paris and to participate in a family reunion for the four sisters of Provence: their wives Marguerite the queen of France, Éléonore the queen of England, and their sisters, Sanchie the wife of count Richard of Cornwall, Henry's brother, and Beatrice the wife of Saint Louis' brother Count Charles d'Anjou. To make the party complete, Saint Louis even invited his mother-in-law, the mother of the four princesses, the dowager countess of Provence. He went forth to meet Henry at Chartres and when he saw him he rushed up to embrace him [*ruit in oscula*]. There were only "embraces and mutual salutations and affable conversations between them."

Once they arrived in Paris, the two kings visited the town and took in the crowds that flooded their path. "Compact crowds gathered in long lines, rushing and fighting to see the king of England in Paris."[59] In the middle of the thirteenth century, monarchy willingly put itself on display.

Louis gave Henry the choice of staying either in his own royal palace in the heart of the city or outside Philip Augustus's city walls in the vast center of the Templars. Accompanied by a large retinue and a troop of horses, the king of England chose the old Temple. He visited Paris as a tourist in the company of his host, admiring the Sainte-Chapelle, the quarter of the Strand, the bridges, and especially the well-constructed houses of Paris made of gypsum with three rooms and up to four or more apartments. A multitude of men and women watched from their windows, full of curiosity.[60]

Henry spent eight days in Paris. One evening, he gave the most splendid banquet of the likes never seen before in the courts of Ahasuerus, Arthur, or Charlemagne.[61] Etiquette was strictly observed among so many illustrious tablemates. There were dukes, bishops, barons, and eighteen countesses along with the queen sisters. Louis tried to give Henry the seat of honor, but the king of England insisted: "No, my lord king, you should be more decently and honorably seated in the middle; you are and will be my Lord." Louis gave in, and Matthew Paris approved of this hierarchy: "There was His Royal Highness the king of France in the center, as he is the king of earthly kings because of his heavenly unction, his power, and his superiority in arms; on his right, His Royal Highness the king of England, and on his left His Royal Highness the king of Navarre."[62]

At the end of the meal, Louis invited the English king to come spend the night in his palace. The king of France, who seems to have forgotten his sadness, joked [*jocose dicens*] by parodying the Gospel of Matthew: "Suffer it be so now, for thus it becometh us to fulfill [*facetie, facetiam*] all righteousness [*iustitia*]."[63] Then, he added laughing, "I am lord and king in my kingdom. I want everyone to obey me." And the king of England acquiesced.[64]

The kings took advantage of their meeting by engaging in close discussions. Saint Louis restated his intense desire to return the king of England's French territories, including Normandy, but he also mentioned his barons' absolute opposition to this. He confided in his new friend that he came away from his failure on the crusade with great bitterness, but that he had recovered from it now that he had "gone back into his heart" and "rejoices in the sufferings—*patientia*—that the grace of God has sent him as though the whole world were at his command."[65]

The dialogue gained serious momentum in 1258. Saint Louis seemed decisive about imposing his will on his barons and returning the lands taken from the king of England. Now, however, obstacles were thrown down on the other side. When Matthew Paris recorded the last state of the Franco-English negotiations in 1259, probably shortly before he died, it was the countess of Leicester, Simon de Montfort's wife, who opposed the signing of the peace treaty.[66] Matthew plainly never learned about the signing of the peace treaty and never had the satisfaction of knowing that certain lands in France were to be returned to the king of England. Nor would he know the disappointment of learning that Louis kept Normandy for France. At the center of all this, however powerful the impression that Louis IX made on him, Matthew Paris always looked for an example to propose to the king of England. (The examples were usually positive, although there was also the important negative example of taxation.) In this selective soap opera on Saint Louis' life, the choice of the episodes, the interpretation of his character, and the lessons drawn from anecdotes all expressed the English Benedictine's ideas more than the efforts of an impartial historian. When he spoke about Saint Louis, he seemed to be thinking even more of Henry III.

SALIMBENE OF PARMA, AN ITALIAN FRANCISCAN

The Franciscan Fra Salimbene of Parma was the author of a chronicle in Latin. The part of it that has been preserved goes from 1168 to 1287 shortly before his death, which probably came in 1288. It belongs to the genre of the universal chronicle, but beginning in 1229 it mainly narrates events contemporary with Salimbene's life. These were events he witnessed and others he collected as hearsay from a well-informed source. His field of interest particularly covered the regions that he lived in or visited: northern and central urban Italy and France, which he visited twice. He generally presented the perspective of the Franciscan order to which he belonged.[67]

He was born on October 9, 1221 to a family of rich bourgeois in Parma. In his youth, he was deeply impressed with the movement for political-religious reform in the communes of northern Italy and the *Alleluia* that stirred up the urban crowds at the call of certain Dominicans and Franciscans in 1233, a kind of medieval May '68.[68] At the age of sixteen, he decided to enter the Order of the Minorites. Despite his father Guido de Adam's violent opposition, he entered the Franciscan convent of Parma on February 4, 1238, reenacting the rupture between Saint Francis of Assisi and his own father. He was one of those friars of the first half-century of the order who never stayed in the same place and moved around from one convent to another. He did his novitiate at Fano, spent two years in Lucca, two more in Siena, and four in Pisa before receiving authorization to preach and being ordained as a priest in Genoa in 1249. He made two long journeys in France, first in 1247–1248, then again in 1249. He then passed through the convents of Genoa, Bologna, Ferrara, and Reggio, and said he also spent five years in Faenza, five more in Imola, and five more in Ravenna. He probably died at the convent of Montefalcone in Emilia in 1286.

The editor of his works, Giuseppe Scalia, states that he was "aware of his worth, inspired by the Guelphs and with aristocratic tendencies." He interests us for two reasons. First of all, for a long time he was a follower of the Joachimite ideas. He tells us that he followed them until 1260, up to the movement of the Flagellants in which he took part, but which troubled him and led him to break with the disciples of the Calabrian abbot who were numerous in the Franciscan order at the time. His work also gives us a better understanding of Saint Louis' attraction to these ideas and their influence on him.[69] He had close ties with the Joachimite Minorite Hugh of Digne, whom the king met at Hyères in 1254 on his return from the crusade. Saint Louis tried in vain to persuade Hugh to come with him to his court in Paris. Salimbene of Parma also had long discussions in Provins in 1248 and in Mantua in 1253 with another Joachimite, Gerardo da Borgo san Donnino, who published his *Introduction à l'Évangile eternel de Joachim de Flore* in Paris in 1254. It was sold on the square in front of Notre-Dame-de-Paris but was banned by the papacy and the Franciscan order, while Gerard was imprisoned for the rest of his life, deprived of his books, his friends, and the sacraments.

The second reason for our interest is that Friar Salimbene found himself in the king's presence on two occasions, first, when Louis was still alive in 1248 at the general chapter of the Franciscans in Sens when the king was leaving on his first crusade. The second time was when the king was dead, in 1271, when the coffin containing his remains passed through Reggio d'Emilia where the dead Saint Louis accomplished his first official miracle. The description of their meeting in 1248 is an extraordinary document, and the other brief mentions of Saint Louis in the *Cronica* give us an image of the king as seen through the eyes of a religious who was very different from Matthew Paris. In addition, the testimony comes from someone whose life's chronology did not entirely overlap with the king's. Matthew was Saint Louis' senior by fifteen to twenty years and he died eleven years before him. Salimbene was seven years younger and he died eighteen years after Saint Louis.

Matthew was a Benedictine, Salimbene a Franciscan. One was English, the other Italian. The first never met Saint Louis; the second saw him in the flesh. Matthew wrote in a traditional convent and he lived in a traditional feudal society. Salimbene came out of the teeming communal world, moving from one convent to another. Matthew wrote his chronicle outside of any intellectual context, despite several allusions to the University of Paris; Salimbene participated in the great disputes surrounding Joachimism. This was the very stuff of his chronicle, and Louis also lived out these debates to a certain extent.

Salimbene almost always calls the king of France "saint" Louis, although he died ten years before his canonization. William Jordan has pertinently observed that we should not forget that in the thirteenth century "saint" (*sanctus*) was not exclusively reserved for officially recognized saints who were objects of worship for the Church but was applied to figures who enjoyed a reputation for saintliness. He adds that Salimbene also used this qualifier out of anticipation, being well aware of the development of the inquiry into his canonization.[70] In an equally habitual manner, Salimbene gave him the epithet "of good memory," an expression that commonly referred to a person who left a good memory that others liked to recall. It was a topical formula that had the advantage of evoking the role played by these recipes for remembrance used in the production of the historical image of an important figure.

Louis IX first appears in the *Cronica* with his crusade. With his Guelph tendencies that favored the imperial party over the pontifical party, Salimbene emphasized the king of France's resistance to Pope Innocent IV who, obsessed by his conflict with the emperor, wanted Louis to delay his departure for the crusade so that he could help him keep Frederick II at bay. After their conversation at Cluny in 1245,[71] Louis refused to push back the date of his departure any further for the sake of the pope's conflict with Frederick II. Our Franciscan author highlighted his commitment and his refusal to budge on this matter: "Louis the king of France thus insisted on carrying out his irrevocable project and readied himself with resolution and devotion to push his project forward to its end and to bring assistance to the Holy Land as quickly as possible."[72]

This brings us to the famous story of the king of France's arrival and stay at Sens during his voyage to Aigues-Mortes as a penitential crusader. During his visit to Sens, he attended the meeting of the general chapter of the Franciscans.

Salimbene was there at the same time. He had been in France for several months and had been traveling in the region of Auxerre the preceding year with a fellow friar who was preaching the king's crusade. He was an eyewitness who knew how to observe and recount what he had seen.

The king of France had left Paris and was coming to visit the chapter. When he approached the convent, all the Minorite friars went out to meet him to greet him honorably. Friar Rigaud[73] of the order of the Minorites who held a magistrate's chair in Paris and was archbishop of Rouen left the convent dressed in his pontifical garb and rushed to meet the king, asking and saying, "Where is the king? Where is the king?" As for myself, I followed him, because he went out absentminded and alone with his miter on his head and the pastoral staff in his hand. He had actually been delayed by preparing so well that the other friars had already left and were waiting in spots along the route with their faces turned in the direction from which the king was supposed to be coming, hoping to see him as he arrived. . . .[74]

And now, the king appears:

The king was slender and graceful [*subtilis et gracilis*], tall, and harmoniously thin [*macilentus convenienter et longus*]. His face was angelic and his traits were graceful. And, he came up to the church of the Minorite friars not with all the royal pomp but with the usual trappings of a pilgrim with the beggar's pouch and the pilgrim's staff around his neck, the perfect ornaments for his royal shoulders. And he did not come on horseback but on foot, and his brothers, the three counts . . . followed him with the same humility and the same appearance. . . . And the king did not bother with having a following of nobles in train, but he preferred to be accompanied by the prayers and acclaims of the poor. . . . And, honestly, one could say he looked more like a monk, with devotion in his heart, than a knight armed for war. When he entered the church of the friars, he very piously kneeled before the altar and began to pray. When he left the church and stopped in the doorway, I was standing next to him. Someone presented him with a large pike on behalf of the treasurer of the church of Sens. They showed it to him live where they kept it in a basin of water made of pine, for in France the pike is a precious and valuable fish. The natives of Tuscany call this basin a "*bigonca*," and they are made for washing and bathing babies from their cradles. The king thanked the messenger along with the giver. He then said in a loud voice that no one should enter the chapter house if he was

not a noble, with the exception of the friars with whom he wanted
to speak.

When we were all together inside the chapter, the king began to
speak of the undertakings that commended him, his brothers, the
queen madam, his mother, and his entire entourage, and, very piously
kneeling, he asked for the friars' prayers and approval. Some of the
friars from France who sat next to me began crying out of piety and
devotion as though they were inconsolable. . . .[75]

The cardinal legate, Eudes de Châteauroux who was accompanying the
king on the crusade, spoke next. He was followed by John of Parma, the general minister of the Franciscans. He praised the king, stating that through
his humility and generosity he was both "the king [*noster rex*], lord, father,
and benefactor" of the friars to whom he had spoken so well. He had not
come to ask for silver and gold ("for, thanks to God, his coffers were full
of them"—an interesting testimonial to the reputed wealth of the king of
France), but to solicit their prayers and spiritual support for the crusade.
He praised the crusade and the spirit of crusading, which the French Franciscans expressed more than the friars from any other provinces, and he
asked all the friar priests to give four masses for the king and his entourage.
And if the king were to die [on the crusade], the friars should increase the
number of these masses. If the king should find these deeds inadequate, he
had only to give the order, and the friars would obey. Louis was delighted,
thanked the general minister, and asked that John of Parma's words be
written down, stamped with the seal of the order, and given to him, which
was promptly done. Louis was a man who liked to keep records [*un homme
d'archives*] for whom the official written document complemented and acted
as the necessary completion of a speech act.[76]

In order to celebrate the event, the king, despite his humility, offered
the friars a meal in the refectory. He shared the meal with them. Cherries
and very white bread were on the menu, and the French washed the meal
down with lots of wine as was their custom, forcing the hesitant friars to
drink with them. This was followed by fresh beans cooked in milk, fish and
crayfish, eel pies, rice with almond milk and cinnamon powder, roasted eels
with an excellent seasoning, torts, cheeses, and fruits in abundance. And all
of it was served with attentive courtesy.[77] They abstained from eating meat,
but it was still an incredible feast. It was a regal meal, despite everything.

Louis' devotion and humility were generally contagious and inspired emulation. We have already seen this when he was with Henry III in Paris. In Sens, it was the general minister of the Franciscans, John of Parma, who distanced himself from the royal guest. He deserted the royal table, fleeing this group of nobles and dignitaries. Three counts, a cardinal, and an archbishop ate at another table with the more humble guests.[78] Similarly, Salimbene also looked on with admiration when the king's younger brother, Charles, the count of Provence, lingered in the church to pray as the king patiently waited for him outside the door.[79]

Salimbene's wanderlust led him to obtain permission to follow the king of France all the way to the Midi. He thus witnessed more examples of the king's devoutness. "He repeatedly turned off the main road [*strata publica*] to visit the hermitages of the Minorite friars and of other religious, going off to the right and to the left to request their prayers for him."[80] In Auxerre, the Franciscans offered him and his retinue seats and stumps of wood to sit on, but even though the church had no flooring he chose to sit on the ground in the dust. He then had all of his brothers and the religious sit on the ground too, grouped in a circle around him, and asked them to listen to him.[81]

Salimbene took leave of the king in Lyon. He descended the Rhone all the way to Arles, and then went on to Marseille by sea before continuing on to Hyères to meet the famous Franciscan Joachimite Hugh of Digne. Hugh, a little dark-haired man, was "one of the greatest clerics in the world," a great preacher with a booming voice who spoke beautifully of heaven and frighteningly of hell, making his listeners tremble like reeds. It was this same Hugh of Digne whom Saint Louis went to see six years later on his return from the crusade, vainly attempting to get him to join his following.[82]

Salimbene reported the main events of the crusade and the anecdotes that went on to build the history and legend of Saint Louis. He reported the same events as the other chroniclers because his sources were the same. His narrative included the capture of Damietta, the death of Robert d'Artois, and the defeat caused by both the sins of the French and Saint Louis' brother's tactical error, which made him the chroniclers' whipping boy. He wrote of the king's captivity and the death of a large part of the army under the Saracens' blows, the epidemic, and the famine. Once he was freed, Louis had to return Damietta to the enemy. He then left to fortify the sites in the

Holy Land. Here, the *Cronica* contains an episode that also made a strong impression on Joinville. After the Saracens surprised a group of unarmed Frenchmen working on the fortifications of Caesaria and killed them, Saint Louis dug a common ditch and buried them with his own hands, fearing neither the stench nor his own fatigue.[83]

However much Salimbene admired Saint Louis in defeat and captivity, his judgment of the crusade was more subtly nuanced. He highlighted the fact that it was not unanimously approved. He tells how in 1248, when he was residing in Provins, he met two "extremist Joachimite" [*totaliter Ioachimite*] Franciscans, one of whom was Gerardo da Borgo san Donnino, who soon gained a reputation. They mocked and sneered at the king of France as he was preparing to leave for the crusade, predicting that things would go wrong for him on this adventure. They also quoted one of Joachim de Fiore's prophecies in his commentary on Jeremiah, proclaiming that "the king of France would be captured, the French conquered, and [that] an epidemic would kill many of them."[84]

Like Matthew Paris, Salimbene attributed great importance to the shepherds' movement. He too had an apocalyptic vision of it.[85] He was extremely hostile to them because the cleric that he was could only feel fear, scorn, and hatred for these rustic wild men. However, he did stress their desire to go to avenge the king of France against the Saracens. They won many French people over to their ideas in what was a revolt against the Mendicant friars who were guilty of having preached this disastrous crusade and who were therefore responsible for the fact that many people lost faith.[86] This was a new kind of testimony on the appearance of a form of religious disbelief in Saint Louis' France. One can sense an entire patch of irreligion beneath the mantle of piety with which the saint king covers France and Christendom. The social and economic crisis that began toward the end of his reign may also signal a religious crisis that ran deeper than the traditional rejections of heresy or hostility toward the papacy. The Psalmist's famous phrase—"the foolish man says in his heart that there is no God"— may actually correspond to a new reality.[87] In this case, Saint Louis was even more a king of defeat. Still, the times of disbelief and atheism had not yet arrived.

Salimbene opposed the impatience of the shepherds to Saint Louis' patience.[88] Although the king emerged all the stronger from this trial, the crusade remained a defeat in a world where victory was a sign of divine approval. One of Louis' brothers, Robert d'Artois, was partly responsible for the failure of the crusade and the shame that resulted from it for the French.

Later, another brother Charles, the king of Naples and Sicily, erased this stained memory with his victories over the descendants of Frederick II. After he died in 1285, Salimbene says that he would never call him anything but "the brother of the king of France" or "king Louis' brother": "he was an excellent fighter and he erased the shame that the French had incurred in their crusade under Saint Louis."[89]

Salimbene returned to Italy and said almost nothing about the second part of Saint Louis' reign after his return from the crusade. However, at two points[90] he did mention the ordinary Parisian master Guillaume de Saint-Amour's expulsion from France by Saint Louis, carried out at the pope's request.[91] Guillaume de Saint-Amour had violently attacked the Mendicant orders "whom he wanted to expel from the University."

The king did a good thing to avenge the friars by expelling this hothead. Salimbene then went on to relate the crusade of Tunis and the king's death in a single page. Like Matthew Paris, he referred to him here as "very Christian" (*christianissimus*). He also offered an explanation for the choice of Tunis as the objective of the first stage of the crusade: "In order to reconquer the Holy Land more easily, Louis and the leaders of the crusade had the idea of submitting the Kingdom of Tunis to the Christians first. Tunis is located at the half-way point to the Holy Land and represents a considerable obstacle for the crusaders."[92] This judgment seems to justify the hypothesis that the choice of Tunis resulted from the Christians' ignorance of geography and their errors about the actual distances between Tunisia, Egypt, and Palestine.

Finally, Friar Salimbene was privileged to have one final meeting with Saint Louis as a witness to an important event in the posthumous life of the king. In April 1271, Philip, the new king, brought his father's body back to France, "embalmed with incense in a coffin."[93] They passed through the cities of Reggio d'Emilia and Parma, Salimbene's hometown. Then, suddenly, in each of these cities, the king's remains produced a miracle, the first in a long series of miracles that unfolded primarily around Saint Louis' tomb at Saint-Denis. At Reggio he healed the lame leg of a town notable; in Parma he healed a young girl who had had an ulcer on her arm for several years.[94] As an obedient son of the Church, Saint Louis wisely waited to be dead before performing his miracles as Pope Innocent III called for at the beginning of the century. And Salimbene was there as an outstanding witness. He later took an interest in the canonization inquiry for the man whose piety and humility he had long admired before confirming his miraculous powers. He never learned the outcome, which was only reached ten years after his death.

He did, however, note that at Reggio upon returning from France where he was officially investigating the miracles of the deceased king, the future pope Martin IV confided to him that God had carried out seventy-four miracles for his love of Saint Louis, all duly recorded and verified. He thus wanted the king to be canonized, but, as Salimbene pointed out with discernible regret, because he died in 1285, he was never able to see his wish come true. The chronicler left Saint Louis on a note of hope that was no longer haphazard: "Perhaps this canonization is meant to take place under another pontifical sovereign."[95] It was—and it did, under Boniface VIII in 1297.

The King of
Commonplace Ideas

Did Saint Louis Exist?

WE KNOW THE EVENTS, THE NAMES OF THE PEOPLE, AND THE PLACES
in his life, but Louis IX's personality still seems to escape us. The producers of his memory dissolved it in commonplace ideas that they needed to
make their points. They made the king into a model, a model of sainthood
and more specifically of royal sainthood. Some contemporary historians
have tried to find an explanation for our limited knowledge of Saint Louis'
inner self within his own personality: he must have felt it was repugnant to
express himself, he concealed his personality out of modesty and discretion. Étienne Delaruelle thus writes: "We can only regret the reserved nature that the king always displays; although he is not entirely unknowable
for us, he still too often escapes the scrutiny of the historian who tries
to grasp his intimate thoughts and the development of his personality."[1]
Edmond-René Labande stresses that "this term, 'reserved,' seems to me to
be an essential one for defining the man whose memory the French celebrated in 1970; it obviously corresponds to what his temperament was."[2]

And Jacques Madaule adds: "His greatest and most difficult deeds were accomplished *in secret* because he had to constantly make sure that his taste for humility did not contradict his royal majesty. His secret cannot be revealed. We can only be resigned to not knowing a whole lot about Saint Louis' inner life."[3]

We should, however, maintain a guarded stance when it comes to these loose psychological interpretations. Before attempting to define the individual temperament or character of a historical figure, we must first examine what contemporaries tell us about his behavior while using the ethical categories of his time and the conceptual arsenal of the authors of literary portraits from the period.

Instead of speaking of "reserve" in this case, it makes more sense to talk about self-control and temperance in the terms of the ethical code elaborated in the twelfth century against the excesses of warlike behavior and "furor." This chivalric ideal developed to tame the warrior's mentality and gave the ancient morality of Cicero and Seneca a Christian form. It was made fashionable by the twelfth-century "Renaissance." This self-control was exercised through control of the body and especially through control of one's gestures. For instance, in the first half of the twelfth century Hugh of Saint Victor defined these gestures for monastic novices, and it did not take long for these definitions to be applied by laymen.[4] More than anything else, Louis wants to be a *prud'homme*.[5] A list of surnames from the early fourteenth century attests to this, enumerating the nicknames of the last three kings of France as Philip the Bold [*le Hardi*], Louis the *Prud'homme,* and Philip the Fair [*le Bel*].[6]

Far from escaping us, the intimate thoughts, inner life, and personality development of Louis IX are revealed to us by his confessor, his biographers, and his hagiographers. They tell us about his search for humility, justice, and renunciation, which corresponded to the ideal preached by the Mendicant friars. They emphasize the important break that occurred in his thought and conduct and even identify this as the cause of the division of his reign into two parts—before and after the crusade. The first was a period of simple piety and typically Christian government; then came a period of penitence and moral order. This is underscored by their tendency to compare him with Josiah both before and after the discovery of the Pentateuch.[7] In all of this, Louis was only acting in conformity with the ideals of his century. However, Jacques Madaule has quite accurately pointed out the fundamental conflict in the king's life between the Christian ideal of the Mendicants and a monarchical code of conduct worked out according to royal traditions independent of the Christian religion and even predating it.[8] At this point, we may return to William Jordan's subtle and intelligent hypothesis about the discomfort Saint Louis felt in facing criticism provoked by his devout and moralist conduct on the one hand, and the conflict between his Christian ideal and his function as a king on the other.[9] He seems to have internalized this conflict without surmounting it.

The American historian is certainly right to react against the absence of any critical spirit on the part of most of Saint Louis' modern biographers, which led them to accept the idealized, intrepid image constructed by the hagiographers. I am attempting to take this construction apart here. I will expose the cracks revealed by our sources in the edification of this beautiful statue. However, I would first like to point out that the contradictions that William Jordan has accurately perceived here themselves belong to the commonplace ideas of the time and are not testimonials on Saint Louis' individual character. Jordan, moreover, suspects as much himself when he makes the following remark on the king's sensitivity to criticisms: "We may regard these [anecdotes] as pleasant little *topoi,* again almost deliberately articulated for us in order to create an image of a saintly king" (215).

That a ruler would be exposed to criticism was actually a part of his traditional image, regardless of whether or not he was a saint. Likewise, the *secret* that Louis supposedly kept about his good actions, according to Jacques Madaule, originated in a commonplace idea that had taken on a particular importance in this period. For instance, it was at this time that the character type of the shameful poor man appeared. Keeping quiet about one's poverty or charity does not translate as an individual character type, but instead refers to a common social and ethical code. We find a similar attempt to conceal his stigmata in the case of Saint Francis of Assisi and a similar practice of praying in secret with Saint Dominic.

The excessive outbursts of grieving for the death of one's loved ones and all the abundant tears whose relevance William Jordan has pointed out are also part and parcel of the commonplace ideas that people of the time had about great figures. These signs demonstrated their humanity and sense of lineage or, in Saint Louis' case, family. Although this image is not a stereotyped formula in the style of the chroniclers and biographers, the abundant tears and loud mourning are the ritualized expressions of the great sadness of powerful persons. Although they expressed a plausible sincerity, it was difficult to detect any truly personal disturbance behind these expressions. This is the reason why we cannot look at Saint Louis' intense mourning and determine the extent to which it expressed anything more than an externalization of feelings that was customary for the rulers of the time. If we consider Charlemagne in *The Song of Roland,* we might wonder whether he was not the model for these tearful sovereigns.

After learning of his mother's death in 1252 while he was in the Holy Land, Saint Louis displayed exaggerated grief in the eyes of Joinville and his entourage. This, then, was a true sign of the exceptional emotional ties that bound the son to his mother.[10] When his oldest son and heir died in 1260 at the age of sixteen, this plunged the king into such great despair that Vincent de Beauvais reproached him in his poem of consolation.[11] More than a king's ritual lamentations for an heir who died before him, we tend to view this as the great pain of a father and a king for whom this death may be the sign of divine anger. People had also reproached Louis VI for his excessive grieving in 1131 after the accidental death of his oldest son Philip who had already been crowned king.[12] Similarly, Pierre de Blois reprimanded King Henry II of England when he abandoned himself to grieving and tears after the death of the crown prince.[13] What should we think of the extreme grief that Saint Louis displayed after the death of his oldest brother Robert d'Artois on the battlefield in Egypt in 1250? And how should we view his final mourning for a family member after the passing of his sister Isabelle in February 1270? (This does not count the last-minute news of the death of his son Jean-Tristan announced to him several days before his own death in Tunis.) Before her corpse dressed in a nun's robe and laid out on the bed of straw where she died, the king, overcome with emotion, collapsed to his knees.[14] Should we see this as an early example of the macabre sensitivity to cadavers that marked the end of the Middle Ages?

We have two crying kings in Saint Louis and Henry II. They were kings of ostentatious mourning. But then, we also find Louis' brother Charles d'Anjou in the same position, although the count of Provence and king of Naples and Sicily from 1266 on was not particularly known for being a sensitive soul according to the chroniclers. Moreover, his relations with Louis were usually tempestuous. When the king made the decision to stay in the Holy Land and to send his brothers Alphonse de Poitiers and Charles d'Anjou immediately home to France to help their mother govern the kingdom, Joinville reports that "when the count of Anjou saw that he had to embark on the ship, he began grieving so hard that everyone was amazed by it; and he still went back to France."[15] During the fatal crusade of 1270, Charles d'Anjou, now king of Sicily, arrived late to Tunis. Louis had just expired. When Charles found his brother's corpse beneath the royal tent, he threw himself at his feet crying. We are clearly dealing with a model of conduct that transcends the individual person.

The attitudes that the historical myth of Louis presents as most characteristic of his personal saintliness can also very often be found in his contemporaries and predecessors.

King Henry III of England's devoutness does not appear to have been any less intense than Louis', even though it was sometimes expressed differently. Louis was a fanatic for sermons; Henry loved mass.[16] Before their spectacular reconciliation in the 1250s, a veritable emulation or even a rivalry seems to have existed between the two rulers in matters of piety alongside their conflicts in politics and war. This competition seems to have outlasted their reconciliation. In 1250, when Henry III came to negotiate the peace in Paris, Louis could not conceal his irritation at having to wait for the Englishman for their meetings in his palace. Lodged in the Île de la Cité, Henry stopped in all the churches on his route to listen to all the masses he could hear. In 1271, when they interred the king of France's remains at Saint-Denis, the funeral cortege passed announcing that the deceased king was a saint and an Englishman protested that his own king was no less of one.

His letter to his subjects on his defeat and captivity in Egypt appears as the new initiative of a sovereign who did not want to hide any of his misfortunes from his people in his quest for truth and confession. This act seems to inaugurate an incredible new relation between the ruler and his people that was full of trust and confidence. However, did it never occur to him that Richard the Lion-Hearted had also addressed a similar letter to his subjects to announce his victory at Gisors over Philip Augustus in 1198?[17]

We have to look for Saint Louis' antecedents in the French Capetian tradition. The first and best outline of a model that Saint Louis perfectly embodied was Robert the Pious as depicted by the monk Helgaud. Helgaud belonged to the Benedictine abbey of Fleury (Benoît-sur-Loire), which tried to serve the first Capetians as a historiographical and ideological center and promotional agent. It attempted to play the role that Saint-Denis would take on beginning in the twelfth century. Helgaud wrote his *Vie de Robert le*

Pieux (Life of Robert the Pious)[18] between the king's death in 1031 and 1041. It is a panegyric, a "quasi-hagiographical" work, to use Robert-Henri Bautier's expression. Its author hoped that it would help to get Hugh Capet's son and heir recognized as a saint. Opening with an invocation of God and Saint Aignan, this *Life* presents itself as a glorification of "works of charity, humility, and mercy, without which no one would be able to reach the realms of the heavens." It was in this realm that "the very gentle and very pious Robert, king of the Francs . . . shone with a brilliance that no one has equaled since the very saintly king and prophet David." Helgaud then wrote Robert's physical and moral portrait, detailing his mercy, his humility, his piety, his respect for relics, and his love of prayer. He went on to enumerate the foundations of monasteries and donations to churches made by the king and his family, and then listed Robert's miracles. He ultimately presented him as a new David.

If we leave out the portrait of the king and set aside the considerably larger number of miracles verified by the canonization inquiry, and if we replace David with Josiah, we can recognize the basic structure of the *Lives* of Saint Louis written by Geoffroy de Beaulieu and Guillaume de Saint-Pathus. Only the habit of the Mendicants in which they dressed up Saint Louis distinguished him from the Benedictine semblance that Helgaud gave to Robert.

Here is the most significant passage from this *Life* of Robert the Pious by the eleventh-century monk of Fleury:

> As this land possessed many sick people and especially many lepers, this man of God did not turn away in horror for he had read in the Holy Scripture that Christ our Lord in his human form had very often accepted the hospitality of lepers. He approached them anxiously, his soul full of desire, and entered their homes and gave them a certain amount of deniers from his own hand and he pressed their hands with kisses from his own mouth, praising God in all things and recalling the words of the Lord who said, "Remember that you are dust and that you will return to dust." He sent help to others with piety for the love of all-powerful God who accomplishes many things wherever He is found. Better still, the divine virtue gave this perfect man such grace to heal bodies, so that when he touched the wounds of the sick with his very pious hand and marked them

with the sign of the Holy Cross, he delivered them from all the pain of their illness.[19]

Who reading this text today would not intuitively perceive the resemblance to Saint Louis? Except for this oldest known attempt, the general power of healing by touch attributed to the kings of France developed between the eleventh and thirteenth centuries and was limited to laying on hands for the scrofulous.[20]

Doesn't this other passage from Helgaud's *Vie de Robert le Pieux* make us think of Saint Louis again today as long as we replace David with Josiah?

> [F]or certainly there has been no king on earth since the saint king David, not a one who could compare with him in his saintly virtues, his humility, his mercy, his piety, and his charity—this virtue that is above all others and without which no one could see God, because he was always attached to the Lord and, in the perfection of his heart, he never strayed from his precepts.[21]

After this first abortive construction of a Capetian saint king attempted by Helgaud de Fleury for Robert the Pious, we find another antecedent for Saint Louis in Louis VII, his great grandfather. This was a century after Robert the Pious and a century before Louis IX. Certain sources that seem more reliable than Helgaud's testimony for Robert present us first of all with a man who was exceptionally devout and, notably, with a piety that was not that of a layman but that of a religious. His wife, Eleanor of Aquitaine, complained about this: "This is not a man, it is a monk that I have married." Before Saint Louis, Louis VII was also taken as an arbiter on two occasions by the king of England, his contemporary Henry II. This happened the first time in his conflict with his sons and the archbishop of Canterbury, Thomas Becket. It happened a second time during Henry's increasingly aggravated struggles with the prelate. Their efforts to reach an arbitrational solution failed, but this was clearly not the reason why Louis VII's political prestige could not be transformed into a reputation for moral saintliness. He lacked convincing biographers and the support of any group that could have persuaded the Church to place him on the altars. His piety did not seem sufficiently brilliant, and this was in part the cause of the breakup of his marriage with Eleanor, who later married Henry II. His political arbitrations for the English were explained away as political maneuvers motivated by the rivalry between the kings of France and England arising from Eleanor's remarriage.

We may certainly be more surprised to find a second forerunner of Saint Louis in the figure of his grandfather, Philip Augustus. A warrior king, he was not known as Philip Augustus but as Philip the Conqueror in the thirteenth century.[22] He had a penchant for wine, women, and food, and, in the eyes of the Church, was identified for a long time as a bigamist. He was excommunicated for refusing to carry out his conjugal duty with his second legitimate wife, Ingeburg of Denmark. He was also known for his fits of furious rage. Nevertheless, after his death an actual "record of sainthood" existed for Philip Augustus, which his entourage hoped they would be able to exploit.[23] Set up like this, everything in his life exuded the sweet smell of miracles. He was born in 1165, sired by his forty-five-year-old father Louis VII who was considered an old man at the time and who had had only girls from his first two wives as from his third wife after five years of marriage. During the queen's pregnancy, Louis VII saw a male heir in a dream giving his barons human blood to drink from a golden chalice—a pelican king, a Christ king giving his own blood to his important vassals. His first biographer, Rigord, attributes three miracles to Philip executed during his military expeditions: he pushed back the time of the harvests, made miraculous water surge forth in the middle of a drought, and found an equally miraculous ford in the Loire with his lance. According to his second biographer, Guillaume le Breton, he was favored with two visions. While attending mass he alone of everyone present saw the Christ child in all his splendor at the moment the priest was holding up the host. This vision cemented his reputation for "mystical virtue." In August 1190, when the boat that brought him to the crusade with his army was trapped in a violent storm between Genoa and Sicily, Philip saw God descend from the skies to visit and reassure his companions. They also made Bouvines into a sacred victory in which the king supposedly carried himself like Christ. Finally, on the eve of his death in 1223, a comet announced that his end was near, and Saint Denis also warned an Italian knight about it at the same time that he healed him. The knight reported this news to the pope.

Of course we know that Philip Augustus never became a saint. His sexual conduct and the disputes it incited with the Church closed the path to canonization for him. In addition, his supporters made the obvious mistake of insisting that he had accomplished miracles that seemed suspicious in the eyes of the Church, which hardly appreciated thaumaturgical laymen. Starting around this time, the holiness of one's life and manners would carry more weight than miracles, which were only the seal—required, it is true—that gave a final stamp of approval to one's moral and religious perfection. His biographers did not neglect this aspect of his personality, and it was on this point that Philip Augustus remarkably bridged the lives of Robert the Pious and Saint Louis. He did not participate in hunts and tournaments, he "tamed the proud [*les superbes*], defended the Church, and fed the poor." He gave clothes to the poor, created a chaplaincy in the king's palace,[24] and transformed the royal chapel into a major institution fit for a sovereign's worship. As in 1195, he played an active part in combating the effects of floods and famines, followed expiatory processions, and distributed wine. He entrusted missions of justice to the bailiffs whose positions he created and named investigators who were responsible for supervising them. He hated swearing [*les jurons*] and repressed it. Does Saint Louis now not seem like the result of the enduring patience that the Capetians applied in the process of trying to make the king of France into the embodiment of the ideal Christian king, a saintly king? Isn't Saint Louis another Robert the Pious, a Philip Augustus who succeeded where the others failed?

Does he not reincarnate even older models? In this age when the Capetian dynasty managed to realize its connection with the Carolingians, the *reditus ad stirpem Karoli* (the "return to the race of Charles,") isn't Saint Louis a new Charlemagne? Doesn't the Mirror of the Princes that Gilles de Paris offered to his father Louis in 1201 as a young heir to the throne, a work that presented Charlemagne—the *Karolinus*—as a model, doesn't it establish a direct tie between Saint Louis and the great emperor?[25] On a more specific and exemplary point, don't Saint Louis' eating habits and table manners also liken him to the great eater and drinker Charlemagne?[26]

Is he not also "a new Constantine," as one text calls him, anchored even more profoundly in Christian time? Is he not the Josiah of the new law, as his hagiographers claimed, and as Pope Boniface VIII called him in his bull for the canonization following the typological symbolism that made characters from history and the New Testament into doubles of Old Testament models?[27] As Caroline Bynum has said, personality had existed since the twelfth century only by molding itself within a repertoire of "types" and by defining itself according to the rule of resemblance.[28]

An individual only existed and realized itself at this time through a "collective identification," a category. Saint Louis was "the Christian king."[29] A character was only characterized by its resemblance to a model. To be a saint was to be "like God." If, according to Genesis, man was made in the image of God, man in the fallen state can become an "image of God" only in becoming a saint by imitating God, or by achieving the perfection of royalty as it was the king's vocation to be an *imago Dei,* an image of God, here on earth.[30]

As for the miracles God accomplished through the intermediary of the dead king's skeletal remains, whether during the funerary cortege or through contact with his tomb at Saint-Denis, these were all banal, traditional miracles. Saint Louis healed people in exactly the same way as any other saint of his time.[31]

Thus we have to ask whether the figure of Saint Louis produced by his biographers and hagiographers is anything more than an ideal image, an automated portrait of an otherworldly model. Did Saint Louis exist?

The "Real" Louis IX
of Joinville

ONCE IT SEEMED LIKE EVERYTHING NEEDED FOR THE PRODUCTION of Saint Louis' memory had been completed, once he had been canonized, and once Boniface VIII had drawn up his official image as it was meant to exist for all time in his bull and two sermons, once the hagiographers who knew him or who collected the testimony from people who were close to him wrote down the saint king's life and authentic miracles, as Guillaume de Saint-Pathus also did using the witnesses' depositions from the canonization proceeding, an eighty-year-old man began to dictate "a book about the saintly words and good deeds of our king Saint Louis." And, although it does not change everything, this book profoundly alters the means available to us for dealing with Saint Louis' "real" personality.

The queen Jeanne de Navarre, the wife of Philip the Fair, Louis IX's grandson, had solicited Jean, lord of Joinville, seneschal of Champagne, of his own admission. She asked him to write his book shortly before her death on April 2, 1305. He completed it in 1309 and dedicated it to Jeanne's son Louis, king of Navarre, count of Champagne and Brie, and future king of France as Louis X (1314–1316). Born ten years after Saint Louis in 1224, Joinville was an octogenarian when he composed this work.

An Exceptional Witness

Two things make Joinville an exceptional witness. First of all, he knew the king well. He had been one of Saint Louis' closest friends, especially during the first part of the crusade in Egypt, but he was also close to the king for various stretches of time that he spent living in the royal palace in Paris. In addition, he was able to ask witnesses who had been well placed for information on other events in Saint Louis' life. For example, for the crusade of Tunis and the king's death, he was able to collect information from Louis' son Pierre, count of Alençon, who was present when his father died. Joinville was one of the witnesses questioned for the inquiry on the king's canonization in 1282 and was the major source of information on one of Louis' traits of moral sanctity that most astonished his contemporaries: the saint king's great dislike of lies. During his captivity he actually refused to fail to keep his word to the Saracens at a time when tricking an infidel was not considered a sin, if not an act of virtue. Boniface VIII recognized this extreme moral sensitivity during the canonization, and it was also mentioned by the Dominican friar who delivered the sermon at Saint-Denis on August 25, 1298 for the raising of the new saint's body in the presence of King Philip the Fair. Joinville was there too, and the preacher pointed him out to the audience when he cited him. This was sweet revenge for Joinville, whom Saint Louis' son and grandson, the kings Philip III the Bold and Philip IV the Fair held in no particular regard.

The second original thing about Joinville is that he was a layman, a pious layman no doubt, but a layman all the same. He therefore did not limit himself to showing the king's religious devotion like the Mendicant hagiographers. He also showed us the warrior, the knight king that Louis IX had been, and this is a side of him that we would never have known without Joinville. He even dedicated one of the two sections of his book to these aspects of Saint Louis' life and character: "the second part of this book discusses his great prowess and his great feats at arms." We see him at Taillebourg marching against the English in 1242. When the battle started, Louis did not hold back but "threw himself in harm's way with the others." We see him most of all in Egypt in 1249–1250. It was here that Joinville laid eyes on the most "handsome knight" he had ever seen.[1]

Joinville also emphasized the exceptional fact that the king had been canonized and that, despite being a layman, he had still been a secular saint: "There has never been any layman in our time who lived in such a saintly

way for his entire life from the beginning of his reign to the end of his life."
The thirteenth century, which saw the promotion of laymen, was more worthy than any other for raising laity to the recognition of a sanctity that was
usually only reserved for clerics and religious.[2]

Everything in Joinville's testimony is exceptional. This was the first time
that a layman wrote the life of a saint. This exception, however, is not inex-
plicable. Certain members of the nobility had attained a level of instruction
that allowed them to produce literary works. Joinville was definitely an especially cultivated layman. Michel Zink has perspicaciously observed that in
the background of the passage where Joinville shows Louis IX mourning
the death of his brother Robert d'Artois, we can find the same rhetoric of
grief that Saint Bernard used to mourn his brother a century earlier.[3] Joinville, however, did not comply with the genre's conventional outline that
placed the saint's miracles after the account of his life.

This very pious layman had little to say about miracles that he had not
seen and was satisfied to mention them in a single sentence: "And his remains were kept in a coffer and brought to Saint-Denis in France and interred there in the place he had chosen for his sepulture in which they were
buried; for his merits, God made many a beautiful miracle for him there
since then." Even when he relied on the testimony of others, whenever it
seemed necessary, Joinville gave his own testimony first. Although he completed his recollections with the story of the king's death, where he was not
present, this was because death was the crowning moment of a Christian's
life, the moment when he definitively won or lost eternal life and revealed
himself in the final act of the earthly role he played. In Louis' case, this death
had the additional importance of confirming the omen of his birth, as
we have seen.[4] The king's death therefore completed his destiny. It also
expressed the definitive success of his imitation of Jesus: "He imitated the
act of our Lord on the cross, for just as God died on the cross, so did he, for
he was a crusader [*croisé,* "crossed"] when he died in Tunis" at three in the
afternoon, "at this same hour that the Son of God died on the cross for
the world's salvation."

A CREDIBLE WITNESS

Joinville's book is such a unique work that we have to ask several questions about it before using it as a means of accessing Saint Louis. First, we

have to ask about the credibility of written memories that relate the essential part about the crusade more than a half-century later. First of all, we should remember that writing was rare in medieval society, and that it was a society in which memory was stronger, longer, and more precise than in a literate society like our own. It is also possible that Joinville wrote his memoirs at some earlier point, perhaps immediately after the king's death when his memory became the center of his being and his life. Philological and linguistic studies like those carried out by Jacques Monfrin and Michèle Perret may actually prove this. In any case, during the canonization proceedings in 1282, the seneschal evoked some of Saint Louis' qualities as proof of his sainthood, and they were taken down for the inquiry. These memories then paved the way for the *Life*.[5] Finally, the very vividness of the king's memory within him must have kept his recollections alive. As Michel Zink has noted so well, Joinville possessed an affective memory that preserved his recollection of moving images and the feelings related to them. This memory flowed directly from the king's person, even though it seemed to take shape with the young Joinville's first meeting with Louis in 1241 during the grand banquet given by the king at Saumur when the plenary court was reunited for the occasion of his brother Alphonse's knighting. Joinville was seventeen at the time. Joinville kept a bright memory of this episode and relates it in a remarkable description.[6] However, this memory of the king focused on the crusade, the great moment in Joinville's life, because this experience represented a remarkable time for most of the crusaders and because it enabled the seneschal to become friends with the king. It also caused a great disruption in Joinville's life; his heart was torn between God and the king on one side and his family, his land, and his castle on the other. The entire dramatic contradiction of the feudal mentality lies here. "The day that I left Joinville. . . ." The story is famous:

> The abbot of Cheminon gave me my scarf and my pilgrim's staff, and then I left Joinville without ever going back to the castle until my return. I left on foot, with no hose, and wearing my shirt, and I went like this to Blécourt and Saint-Urbain and to see the other relics that are there. And as I went to Blécourt and Saint-Urbain, I didn't ever want to look back toward Joinville for fear that my heart would soften at the sight of the beautiful castle and the two children I was leaving behind.[7]

Joinville's memory was rich in vivid visual and auditory signs. He recalled the image of Saint Louis' fleet setting sail from Cyprus for Egypt:

> On Saturday the king set sail with all the other ships, which was
> a very beautiful sight to see, for it seemed that the entire sea was cov-
> ered with the canvas of the ships' sails for as far as the eye could see,
> and they counted eighteen hundred ships, both big and small.[8]

He remembered the Greek fire that the Muslims fired at the crusading army:

> The Greek fire worked in such a way that it came with its front
> as big as a barrel of verjuice, and the tail of the fire that came out of
> it was as big as a large lance. It made such a noise when it came that it
> seemed like lightning from the sky; it was like a dragon flying through
> the air. It burned so brightly that people in the camp could see as
> clearly as though it were day from the great abundance of fire that
> gave off this incredible brightness.[9]

He remembered Saint Louis battling the Saracens in Egypt, "the most
handsome knight" he had ever seen.[10]

Joinville was particularly sensitive to clothing and colors. He brings
Saint Louis to life for us in precise detail with all his colorful dress. Already,
during their first meeting in Saumur, we read: "The king was wearing a blue
satin tunic and an overcoat and a cloak of vermilion satin trimmed with ermine, and on his head a cotton hat that suited him poorly because he was
still a young man."[11] Then, after their return from the lost crusade, there was
the phase of penitential dress.[12] And, finally, when Joinville saw the king in
the first of two dreams he had about Saint Louis, he saw the king in bright
colors as he prepared for his second crusade: "And I was given a vision in
which several prelates in church clothes were dressing him in a vermillion
chasuble made of serge from Reims." The color is profoundly symbolic here
as it was in Louis VII's dream of blood and gold about his soon to be born
son, Philip Augustus:

> After I had this vision I called Monsignor Guillaume, my priest,
> who was very knowledgeable, and I told him the vision. And he said

to me: "Sire, you will see the king take the cross tomorrow." And I asked him why he thought this, and he told me that he thought this because of the dream that I had dreamt, because the chasuble of vermillion serge signified the cross, which was red with the blood God had spilled from his side and his hands and feet. "As for the chasuble made of serge of Reims, that means that the crusade will bring little gain, as you shall see if God gives you life."[13]

Biography or Autobiography?

In reading Joinville, we still have to ask what his object was, whether he was aware of it or not. Was his object the king or himself? Is his work a biography or an autobiography? If Joinville had previously written some type of memoirs, even if it had only been mainly to evoke Louis' memory, his hesitancy about their hero can be explained. The new composition, written at the request of the queen Jeanne, would not have completely erased what had probably been the autobiographical character of the earlier version. However, to this day there has been no decisive argument to support this hypothesis. We still have to explain the abnormally emphatic presence of Joinville within a work that bore a title responding to Jeanne's request, "the saintly words and good deeds of our king Saint Louis," even though this work was largely based on the seneschal's personal testimony. Michèle Perret has calculated that "Joinville intervenes directly in seventy-three percent of the paragraphs in his text as divided by modern editors," showing "that he privileged the relationship between himself and the king so much and at the same time establishes his presence at the center of his story with so much force that the king's figure is sometimes obscured; this occurs to such an extent that sometimes we cannot be sure whether he was actually present for certain events, nor exactly how he is placed in relation to a 'we' that either includes the king or that is situated in relation to him."[14]

In contrast to the cleric biographers, Joinville wrote in French and had the king speak in the language that he actually used to express himself. Thus, whether Joinville faithfully retained his actual words or whether he placed the words that he thought he heard—or wanted to hear—in the king's mouth, it is only in Joinville's work that we hear what sounds like the king's "real" speech. His *Enseignements* comprise the only exception as this is a normative text in which Saint Louis speaks personally to his son and daughter.

The confusion over whether the work is "auto- or exo- biographical," a problem that has been very subtly analyzed by Michel Zink, arises first of all from the fact that Joinville "is the first person to write in the French language speaking about himself in the first person."[15] This is a sign of the times as the thirteenth century was a period marked by "the transition from lyrical poetry to personal poetry." In this *Life,* autobiography and the biography of "the other" are inextricably combined. Saint Louis seemed to lend himself in a very strange way to the formation of "Siamese" twins: in one case, he was joined with his mother; in this case, it was Joinville who tried to merge with him.

From the start of his book, Joinville seems to let this new style of writing that proclaimed the unity of the "I" and the "we" go to his head:

> In the name of God Almighty, *I,* Jehan, lord of Joinville, seneschal of Champagne, am having the life of our saint king Louis written,[16] what *I* saw and heard over the space of six years when *I* was in his company on the pilgrimage overseas and was with him after *we* returned. And before *I* tell you of his great feats and acts of prowess, *I* will tell you what *I* saw and heard of his holy words and his good instructions. . . .[17]

Since we are searching for Saint Louis in this great hall of mirrors, isn't the one imagined by the seneschal the most disturbing, the most subtly produced in order to engender an illusion that Joinville wanted to make into a reality for himself and his readers?

> Joinville combines autobiographical testimony, his own retrospective view of the saint king, and his own retrospective view of himself. . . . Joinville leads one to suspect that the image he gives us of the king, a product of his own emotion, refers to his own image, and that his text functions like those numerous passages within it where the king's personality is revealed explicitly at the same time as his own through the familiar conversation of the two men who shed light on each other's personalities.[18]

Does this symbiosis lead us to another, to a new illusion engendered by subjectivity and literary affectivity? Isn't Joinville's Saint Louis just a phantom created by the seneschal's emotions, even at those moments when along with Joinville and thanks to Joinville he seems so close to us that we think we can see him and hear him and touch him? There can be no doubt that "Joinville loved the king," and the "real" details of his narrative depicted the king, although they depicted Joinville's love for him even more. He thus set up a barrier between the king and what we know about him.

Joinville's Concrete Saint Louis

Nevertheless, the text still introduces us into the heart of an authentic relationship. It introduces us to a "real" Saint Louis whom Joinville knew and not an ideal model transmitted by culture. However they were altered or lightened at times, the concrete details that the seneschal's loving memory drew from were "real" details.

Joinville did not just see and hear Louis; he touched him, and it appears that this need for closeness and physical contact corresponded to a need that the king also felt. Of course, we could see another imitation of Christ in this attitude, a Christ who assembled his disciples around him and who kept them close to him. But before we accept this conclusion, we should reread all these scenes that were not borrowed from any Mirror of the Princes, nor from any literary code or manual of gestures, nor even from the New Testament. Although the Jesus of the Gospels may have been a conscious or unconscious model for Louis, they were not a model for Joinville. What he wanted to say came from his experience and his memory of experience. If he had wanted to rediscover his friend in his book and have recourse to lies, even prettified literary lies, this would have ruined his project. The seneschal's modernity resides in the fact that he was not writing for other people, nor was he writing for the deceased queen or her son. He was writing for himself.

Who then was the Saint Louis that he gave us? First of all, he was a Saint Louis that he had seen and touched and been close with. The first one of these scenes involving "touch" took place in the palace in Paris. The actors who appear in it are the king, his son the future Philip III, his son-in-law Thibaud de Champagne the king of Navarre, and Joinville:

After this, His Royal Highness the king summoned His Highness Philip his son—the father of the current king—and King Thibaud. He sat down at the entrance to his oratory, put his hand on the ground, and said: "Sit down here right close to me, so that no one will hear us." "Ah! Sire," they said, "we wouldn't dare sit so close to you." And to me he said, "Seneschal, sit down right here." And that is exactly what I did, so close to him that my robe was touching his.[19]

A second scene like this takes place in Acre on the day the king assembled a council to ask his entourage whether he should stay in the Holy Land or return to France. The gravity of the situation gives this scene an even greater effect. Joinville was practically the only man to advise the king to stay, and during the following meal, Louis did not speak to him at all. He thought that the king was angry with him.

While the king was listening to grace, I went up to a barred window in a recess in the wall near the head of the king's bed; I was holding my arms through the bars on the window. . . . As I was standing there, the king came and leaned on my shoulders with his two hands on my head. At first I thought it was Lord Philippe de Nemours who had given me a lot of grief that day because of the advice I had given the king, and I said: "Leave me be, Lord Philippe." By an unfortunate accident, as I turned my head I made the king's hand fall into the middle of my face, and I recognized that it was the king from an emerald that he had on his finger.[20]

Michel Zink has elaborated a seductive Freudian hypothesis about these moments of physical contact. The happiness that Joinville expresses about having "touched" the king on several occasions was both an aspect and evidence of his strong love for Saint Louis.[21]

It is hard to decide whether this need for physical contact that Louis seemed to share with Joinville was a personal trait or part of a more general code of gestures in which touching had a particular function. We can guess that the example of Jesus when he had Thomas touch the wounds at his side after the Passion and the Resurrection made a strong impression on the men and women of the Middle Ages, especially since this was a period when Christ's passion was an almost obsessive representation. More generally, it is plausible that touching had a special value in a society where people searched for material evidence of internal feelings and their visible, tangible signs and in which they expected the supernatural to be expressed in visions. Miracles and especially miracles of healing by touch were numerous and pleasing. In his own lifetime, Saint Louis healed the scrofulous by touching them. Soon after his death, the coffin filled with his remains passing through Italy healed people. Then, after his burial at Saint-Denis, his tomb healed the sick and injured people who touched it. Without needing to make any other hypotheses, I think we can conclude that Joinville sought out physical contact with the king because he had a clear premonition of the saint he would become. The body that he touched was already a living relic. In any case, he knew the king was a saint when he composed his *Life,* and his memory was enriched by the factual confirmation of this, benefiting from the time that had passed between the lived event and its written recording.

One anecdote that occurred in the Holy Land plainly reveals the seneschal's secret thoughts about this matter. The anecdote appears in a humorous mode, which was a modest form of avowal. One day Louis was camping near Acre. A troop of Christian Armenian pilgrims passed by on their way to Jerusalem, and, as they passed, they paid a tribute to a group of Saracens who had them surrounded:

> I was going to see the king where he was seated in a pavilion, leaning against the tent pole, and he was sitting on the sand with no carpet or anything else beneath him. I said to him: "Sire, there is a large crowd outside from Grand Armenia on their way to Jerusalem. They are asking me, sire, to let them in to see the saint king, but I am not yet ready to kiss your bones."[22]

Here is an example of something that Joinville alone can tell us about the king, one of his habits and customary attitudes, which were usually neglected by the hagiographers, and which, however, evoke Saint Louis' concrete personality as closely as possible: his preference for sitting on the ground.

We have already seen one example of this.[23] And there are others. Louis normally let his advisors deal with the problems of complainants and applicants who addressed their requests more and more frequently to the royal judicial system. However, he also liked to "deliver" them from the onslaught of these solicitors, coming to their assistance by receiving some of these people himself and either dividing their cases among his assistants or deciding their cases himself.

> And when he came back from Church he would summon us, and, sitting at the foot of his bed, he would have us all sit down around him and ask us whether we had any cases to handle that could not be handled without him; and we would name them for him, and he would order them to be summoned. . . .[24]

The famous scene of the oak tree at Vincennes follows:

> It happened many times that in the summer after his mass he would go to sit in the woods of Vincennes and lean against an oak tree and have us sit down around him. And all of the people who had some matter to address would come talk to him without having to go through any bailiff or any other people. . . .[25]

What became a legendary occurrence at Vincennes also took place in the garden of the royal palace in Paris, and Joinville found one of his other favorite themes here: the king's clothing.

> Sometimes in the summer I would see him go into the garden in Paris to dispatch his people. He was dressed in a tunic of camlet and a sleeveless woolen overcoat with a cloak of black taffeta around his neck, and his hair was neatly combed without any headdress but a hat of white peacock feathers on his head. And he had carpets rolled out for us to sit on around him, and all the people who had affairs to discuss stood around him. And then he would expedite their affairs in the same way I just told you about in the woods of Vincennes.[26]

This characteristic humility was also and may primarily be a physical preference for a certain body position: seated on the ground with a group assembled around him. Joinville was the only witness to furnish this information. And in the end, after exercising all his critical skills, the historian has the rare and no doubt misleading feeling (isn't this one of Christ's positions among the apostles?) that he is reduced to trusting in order to judge the authenticity of a source, that he is now in front of the "real" Saint Louis. He is tempted to admit to himself that "Joinville could not have invented this. This seems like the truth and this must have been the way Saint Louis really was." Joinville's reader often experiences this impression. One feels it all the more strongly as the seneschal passionately strives to find Saint Louis in his memory as he truly knew him, without any lies or embellishments, going easy neither on himself nor the king.

He often presented himself as being rebuffed or teased by Louis (what a pleasure for him!), who liked to teach lessons and more or less gently poke fun at the naïve seneschal, terrified of displeasing the king, not out of interest but for fear of damaging his attachment to him. According to his recollections, Joinville formed a picturesque couple with another of the king's friends, the canon Robert de Sorbon, the founder of the college for poor Parisian theology students that later became the Sorbonne. This pair of inseparable friends was united in their passionate, affectionate admiration for the king but they were also rivals who competed for his love, keeping a jealous eye out for any sign of friendship or esteem that was granted to one instead of the other. It seems that Louis took malicious pleasure in toying with their jealousy and stirring up the rivalry of the two courtiers as an amusement for the court.

The relations between Saint Louis and Joinville sometimes took the form of sophisticated banter in which the naïve seneschal, smitten with love, did not always seem to grasp the irony that the holy king directed at him. However, this may also be Joinville's tendency to use subtle self-irony that pretended to take certain exchanges literally when their literalism gratified him. The seneschal shows us an ironic, malicious king who toyed with him in a kind of comedic scholastic dispute that he agreed to arbitrate. Joinville was just as quick to jump for joy when the king confided to him that he really shared his opinion as he was to sink into despair when Louis publicly favored Master Robert's opinion over his own. And he seems delighted to believe the king when he told him with ironic flattery: "I do not dare talk to you, as subtle as you are, about matters concerning God. . . ."[27]

In Saint Louis, Joinville thus shows us the king of a court where prelates and barons, the traditional members and elect advisors of a feudal king, mixed with more modest characters who were the favorite pets of his good will or chosen after his heart. These confidants and advisors foreshadowed the favorites of following ages in the course of which the king assumed more distance from the actual feudal hierarchy that emerged from the traditional politics of the Capetian kings. Louis advanced their domestication through the use of irony and humor.

Joinville thus also shows us a king who to a certain extent illustrated the new manners of the court, a king who was supposed to amuse his entourage and make them laugh with his jokes, *rex facetus*.[28] But he was also a king who knew how to get away from the devout sobriety in which his hagiographers immersed him. We see a king who had worldly attachments and who said as much when he did not hesitate to brave dangers in refusing to abandon his people. When people tried to persuade him to leave his ship when it was in danger of sinking off the coast of Cyprus, did he not admit: "Is there anyone who loves his life as much as I love mine?"[29]

He did not hesitate to say out loud what many thirteenth-century Christians often quietly thought to themselves. This was common in a period when, without ever ceasing to be good Christians, people insisted that values descended from the heavens to the earth, decided that life on earth was worth living, and that preparations for eternal salvation began here on earth not only negatively—with penitence and disdain for the world—but also with a measured joy for this earthly life.[30]

The King Who Laughs

Thanks to Joinville we get to see the king laughing, sometimes to the point of splitting his seams.[31] When Joinville placed the clever word that I quoted above about the relics of the king's bones that he did not want to kiss yet, the king burst out laughing: "And he laughed very clearly" (*Et il rit moult clairement*).[32]

Joinville lost everything he had with him when he was taken prisoner with the king. When Saint Louis decided to stay in the Holy Land as Joinville advised, his seneschal asked him for two thousand pounds so that he could stay and support himself and three knights until Easter 1251. The king gave them to him. As Easter drew near, Joinville relied on a ruse, knowing that the king did not like to be solicited:

> While the king was fortifying Caesaria, I went to his pavilion to see him. As soon as he saw me enter his room where he was speaking

with a legate, he got up and drew me aside and told me, "You know," said the king, "I am only retaining you until Easter, so I pray you tell me what I will give you to stay with me for another year." And I told him that I did not want him to give me any more of the deniers he had given me, but that I wanted to make another deal with him.

"Because you get angry" I said, "when people ask you for things, I want you to agree with me that if I ask you for anything during this entire year, you won't get angry, and if you refuse me, I won't get angry either." When he heard that, he burst out laughing and he told me that he would retain me on that condition and he took me by the hand and led me to the legate and his council and repeated to them the deal that we had made, and they were very happy because I was the richest man in the whole camp.[33]

And the king burst into laughter again: "When he heard that, he began to laugh out loud" (*Quand il ouït cela, il se mit à rire moult clairement*).[34] One day, when he was angered at hearing one of Joinville's requests, Joinville reminded him about their contract, and he started laughing again.[35] On another occasion, during a meeting of the Parlement, the prelates asked the king to come speak with them alone. Again he found their demands unreasonable and rejected them.

> When he came back from speaking with the prelates, he came to us where we were waiting for him in the trial chamber and laughing told us about the torturous time he had with the prelates. And he recounted his dialogue with the archbishop of Reims, the bishop of Chartres, and the bishop of Châlons, impersonating them and making fun of them throughout.[36]

One part of Joinville's testimony confirmed what the hagiographers said about the king. For the most part, we find the same man in each type of life story. We find the same horror for sin ("there is no leprosy uglier than mortal sin"), the same love of the poor—he even asked Joinville to wash their feet on Holy Thursday just as he did himself. He urged Joinville to remain firm in his faith and to keep himself from the temptations of the devil, whose name he did not even want people to utter in his kingdom, just as he succeeded in doing himself.[37] He wanted to uphold justice all the time. He held out on the bishops and refused to have his officers confiscate the goods of people who had been excommunicated when the reasons for their condemnation appeared unjust to him. During his captivity, he maintained his dignity and kept his word, even with the Muslims. He was a great lover of peace: "This was the one man in the world who worked the most to maintain peace between his subjects," but between foreigners as well, for example, between the Burgundians and Lorrainians who loved him and brought their complaints to his court. His charity was universal.

> The king was such a great giver of alms that everywhere he went in his kingdom he would give to the poor churches, the lazar houses, the hospices, the hospitals, and to poor men and women. Every day, he would give food to the poor in abundance, without counting the people who ate in his chamber; and many times I saw that he would cut their bread and give them to drink himself.[38]

Joinville also reported the great care he took to conduct investigations throughout his kingdom in order to redress the wrongs committed by his bailiffs and seneschals and to oversee them, although these were borrowings from a chronicle Joinville used and not events that he witnessed himself. Likewise, he mentioned the reform of the provost's position in Paris. Finally, Louis favored the religious orders and particularly the Mendicant orders.

The King's Flaws

But there is more. In addition to the lively, concrete notations that he was the only one to report, Joinville is a unique source on the king's flaws. His openness arose from two of the deeper intentions that crop up in his Memoirs. The first of these was his absolute desire to speak "true." He wrote of his relations with the king with pride: "I who never lied to him." He did not want to start lying to him after his death. The second of these intentions arose from the fact that his work says as much about himself as about the king, as we have seen. It was a book about both of them, a book about their exceptional friendship, but which consisted in their lucidity and mutual openness. Joinville did not have an idealized, hygienic concept of sainthood. Even a great saint was not a perfect man.

So, with what did he reproach Louis? First of all, he criticized him for failing to maintain the moderation required of the *prud'homme* that the king flattered himself to think he tried to be. Confronted with the braggart warrior who cannot control his rage, the king-*prud'homme* had to keep his head, even in battle operations. But what did he do upon landing in Egypt? He impulsively threw himself into the water and, seeing the Saracens, wanted to attack them without thinking.[39]

Joinville does not explicitly blame the king here, but it is clear that his silence conveyed reproach for this tempestuous, raging temperament. The seneschal was content with simply showing the king in his moment of anger, but the narrative was an implicit criticism.

During the crossing from Egypt to Acre after his liberation, the king confided in Joinville.

> He complained to me about the count of Anjou too, who was on his ship, saying that he never kept him company. One day, he asked what the count of Anjou was doing, and they told him that he was playing backgammon with Lord Gautier de Nemours. And he went off staggering from the weakness caused by his sickness, and he took the dice and the boards and threw them into the sea, and he was enraged with his brother for taking so easily to playing dice games.[40]

This was clearly a pious anger born of the king's laudable horror for games of chance and the forgetfulness of penitence, but which also showed a lack of self-control and a tendency to exaggerate.

Joinville disapproved even more of Saint Louis' excessive displays of mourning after learning of his mother's death. We have already seen that it was normal in the Middle Ages for a man, a warrior, or a king to cry publicly in certain circumstances, but he was not supposed to overdo it.[41]

Sometimes the king's hatred of certain sins led him to commit acts of justice so outrageous that justice itself became unjust. A maniacal and pathological judge, he exhibited harshness and even cruelty, particularly in punishing blasphemers, although it is true that he imagined himself being subjected to the same kind of treatment: "I would willingly be branded with a hot iron if all the villainous swearing were banished from my kingdom." It is hard not to label this declaration hypocritical. Louis knew perfectly well that a situation like this was never likely to arise.[42]

Joinville witnessed yet another of the king's merciless qualities during the voyage by sea on the return from the crusade.

We saw a large island in the sea that was named *Pantennelée*. It was peopled with Saracens who were subjects of the king of Sicily and the king of Tunis. The queen asked the king to send three galleys to pick up some fruit there for her children, and the king granted her request. He ordered the commanders of the galleys to be ready to come to him when his ship passed in front of the island. The galleys approached the island through a port that was there, but then when the king's ship passed in front of the port, we did not hear any signal from our galleys.

The sailors began to mutter amongst themselves. The king summoned them and asked them what they thought about this adventure, and they told them they were under the impression that the Saracens had captured his people and the galleys. "But we offer you the opinion and advice not to wait for them, Sire, because you are between the Kingdom of Sicily and the Kingdom of Tunis, and neither of them like us very much, and, if you let us sail on, we will have you out of harm's way by nightfall, because we will have cleared these straits." "Really," said the king, "I cannot believe that you would tell me to leave my people in the hands of the Saracens without me at least doing everything in my power to free them. So, now I command you to turn your sails so that we can go attack them." And when the queen heard that she began to grieve deeply, saying: "Alas! I am the one who caused all this to happen." As they were turning the sails of the king's ship and all the others, we saw the galleys leaving the island. When they approached the king, the king asked the sailors why they had done that, and they answered that they couldn't have done otherwise, and that the ones who did this were the sons of some Parisian bourgeois, six of whom lingered to eat fruits from the gardens. This was the reason why the sailors couldn't come out to meet them, for they didn't want to leave these others behind. Then, the king ordered the ones who stayed behind to be placed in the launch [in tow behind the ship], and they started to scream and bray: "Sire, for God's sake, ransom us for everything that we own as long as you don't put us out there where they put thieves and murderers, because people will hold this against us forever." The queen and the rest of us tried our best to get the king to back down, but the king never wanted to listen to anyone. They were placed in the launch and stayed out there until we landed. They were in so much danger there that when the sea began to swell, the waves crashed above their heads, and they had to stay seated for fear the wind would blow them into the sea.

Nevertheless, the seneschal, who in spite of everything still had trouble blaming his royal friend, concludes:

> And this was done with good reason, for their gluttony hurt us so badly that we were delayed by eight full days, because the king had them turn all the ships entirely around.[43]

Sometimes the king seemed to forget the incorruptible nature that he had taken as a rule for himself and his agents. After his disembarkation in Provence, he waited in Hyères for people to bring him the horses he needed for his return trip to France. The abbot of Cluny came to give him two strong palfreys, one for himself and one for the queen. The very next day he returned to present the king with a number of requests, and the king "listened to him very attentively and for a very long time." Joinville then told the king, "I wanted to ask you, if you please, whether you listened more kindly to the abbot of Cluny because he gave you those two palfreys yesterday." The king thought about it and admitted that, yes, he had. Joinville then lectured the king for a change.

> "Sire, I advise and counsel you to forbid all your sworn advisors from taking anything from people who have business to settle with you when you return to France. For you can be certain that if they accept them [any gift], they will listen to those who gave them more willingly and attentively, just as you did for the abbot of Cluny." Then the king summoned all his council and immediately related what I had told him, and they said that I had given him a good piece of advice.[44]

Without being invented, the story had probably been touched up by good old Joinville, ever happy to demonstrate that the friendship that existed between him and the king sometimes authorized him to teach the king a moral lesson now and then, and thereby also allowing him to sing his own praise at the same time as the king's. This was a good occasion to highlight the fact that no one was perfect and, for us, to evaluate this relationship with a Saint Louis who had his own weaknesses: the portrait thus seems more likely to be "true." Joinville's advice was echoed in the Great Edict of 1254, which was issued only several weeks later. If we wanted to be hypercritical, we could ask whether it was not the Edict that retrospectively inspired Joinville with this anecdote that presented him in such an honorable light. I am under the impression that a lie like this would ruin Joinville's project. He may have cleaned certain things up a bit and sometimes turned things to his own advantage but he did not just make things up.

A more serious defect in the seneschal's eyes was the king's indifference to his own wife. Joinville had almost as much admiration and affection for Queen Marguerite as he had for the king. On the other hand, he did not seem to have any soft spot in his heart for the Queen Mother. He shows her odious behavior toward her daughter-in-law.[45] He was also visibly hostile to the king's excessive obedience toward Blanche of Castile. He would have wanted the king to be as firm in confronting his mother as he was with the other members of his family, his entourage, and some of the prelates and barons. He was probably jealous of the king's affection for his mother, but his jealousy allowed him to see things clearly.

The queen, whom he held in high regard, displayed the most admirable conduct during one of the worst moments of the crusade when she gave birth to Jean-Tristan. Full of heroism, she had made preparations for a loyal knight to cut off her head if she were ever in danger of falling into the Saracens' hands.[46] She exhibited the generosity and grandeur of her soul with the grief she felt on hearing the news of her terrible and despicable mother-in-law's death.[47] She explained to Joinville that she was not crying for the dead queen but for the king's anguish. Nor did the pious Queen Marguerite forget to thank God for saving the royal fleet from destruction in the tempest that hit them on the trip home. At Joinville's suggestion, in Paris she had a silver ship made in the form of an offering that the good seneschal must have carried to Saint-Nicolas-du-Port, the important church for this saint's pilgrimage, the protector of those who traveled by sea.[48]

The queen gave birth for the third time in the Holy Land in 1253. She brought a daughter into the world who received the given name of her paternal grandmother, Blanche. They had already given this name to their first child, a daughter born in 1240, but she died at a young age. Some time after the delivery, Marguerite went to find the king in Sayette (Sidon). Joinville went out to meet her.

> And when I came back to the king in his chapel, he asked me whether the queen and the children were doing well, and I told him, yes. And he said to me: "When you got up to go out before me, I knew you were going out to greet the queen, and that is why I have waited for you to come back before hearing the sermon." I am telling you these things because I had already been at the king's side for five years, and, as far as I know, never had he yet spoken of the queen or his children either to me or to anyone else, and it seems to me that this was not a good manner of conduct to be such a stranger to his wife and children.[49]

Joinville could not keep silent this time when he was confronted with this attitude. Expressing his disapproval, he did not try to find any excuses for the king. He went five years without saying a word to his entourage about the queen, the queen who collected all the money for his ransom, his children's ransom, and the ransom of the entire army when she was pregnant, and who bore him three children in these foreign lands! What a strange man! What a bizarre saint!

Moreover, this was exactly what the queen thought about it. She felt uncomfortable in the presence of her royal spouse. Without any doubt, this is the most worrisome and disturbing thing that Joinville divulged about Saint Louis.

During the same storm, the queen entered the king's chamber on their ship but she was forced to leave because it was in danger of being engulfed by the sea, and the constable Gilles le Brun and Joinville were there in bed alone. Joinville asked the queen what brought her there. She replied "that she came to speak with the king to get him to promise God or the saints to go on some pilgrimage so that God would deliver them from the peril we were in." It was at that moment that Joinville advised her to promise to go on a pilgrimage to Saint-Nicolas-de-Varangéville (Saint-Nicolas-du-Port). The queen, however, did not want to make this commitment: "Seneschal, truly I would do it willingly, but the king is so *divers* that if he knew I made this promise without him, he would never allow me to go."[50] *Divers*: what does this mean? The word is not easy to understand. Natalis de Wailly has translated it with the word *bizarre*. At the time, people might say of a child that he was *divers*, unstable or unpredictable. The *Roman de la rose* states that woman is *diverse* and *muable* (*donna mobile!*). We have to try to figure out this epithet that came from a reliable source: the queen, relayed by Joinville, plainly revealing a Saint Louis who was odd.[51]

JOINVILLE'S DREAM

The relations between Saint Louis and Joinville ended with an astonishing episode in the seneschal's testimony, the sublimation of a dream.

This was the second dream in which Louis appeared to the seneschal. The first had been that dream of blood on the eve of Saint Louis' decision to crusade for a second time.[52]

> I was on my way to Paris. When I arrived on the evening of the vigil of Notre-Dame in March, I could not find anyone, neither the queen nor anyone else who could tell me why the king had summoned me. And so it happened just as God willed it that I went to sleep at the matins. And as I slept I had a vision that I saw the king on his knees before an altar. And I was given a vision in which several prelates in church clothes were dressing him in a vermillion chasuble made of serge from Reims.

The second dream occurs at the end of the story. Saint Louis was dead. He had officially become a saint. Joinville had already given his deposition for the canonization inquiry. His testimony was retained, and the preacher at the official ceremony at Saint-Denis in 1298 had pointed out the seventy-four-year-old fellow to King Philip the Fair and the entire assembly.

Joinville, however, was unhappy. First of all, he still had a bad conscience. He did not follow the king to Tunis. He refused—even vehemently—to accompany him. He replied to him that during his first crusade when he was with him overseas, the sergeants of the king of France and the king of Navarre "had destroyed and impoverished his people," and that this time he wanted to stay "to help and defend his people." If he were to crusade, he

would anger God "who placed his body on this earth to save his people."
This was therefore an indirect albeit clear and harsh criticism of the king
who for his part was not afraid to abandon his people "to harm and evil."
Now though, Joinville felt remorse for his decision. Wasn't the holy king
upset with him for this desertion and disloyalty? Didn't he die after retract-
ing his friendship for Joinville? What did Joinville have left when his life, if
it had any meaning, was this friendship with the holy king? If he had lost
this friendship forever, what would become of him?

Joinville was also unhappy because the current king, Louis' grandson,
had just carried out a large-scale distribution of the relic remains of his
holy grandfather. The king did not like Joinville, had no consideration for
him, forgot him, and gave him nothing. Was the relic in his heart enough
for him? In this period, in the eyes of Christians, the supernatural required
a material support. Joinville needed a tangible souvenir of his holy friend.

Then, the great messenger from heaven suddenly appeared, the inform-
ant from beyond, the dream.

> Hereafter, I still want to tell our saint king some things that will
> honor him and that I saw of him when I was sleeping. What I want
> to say is that it appeared to me in my dream that I saw him stand-
> ing in my chapel at Joinville, and he was exactly as he always seemed
> to me, marvelously joyful and lighthearted. And I myself was pleased
> because I was seeing him in my castle and I told him: "Sire, when you
> leave here, I will lodge you in a house of mine in a town of mine
> called Chevillon." And he answered me laughing and told me: "Sire
> of Joinville, on the faith that I owe you, I do not wish to leave here
> so soon."
>
> When I woke up, I started to think. And I had the impression
> that it pleased God and him that I was lodging him in my chapel just
> as I did, so I set up an altar in God's honor and his, and there is a
> donation established in perpetuity for this. And I told these things
> to my lord King Louis who has inherited his name. And it seems to
> me that he would be doing God's will and the will of our saint king
> Louis if he procured some of the relics of his true holy body and
> sent them to the said chapel of Saint-Laurent in Joinville so that all
> the people who come to his altar would have even greater religious
> devotion there.[53]

Joinville was still holding out hope that the new king, Louis X, would give him some of the true relics. The important thing, however, had been obtained. By appearing joyous to Joinville at his home, in his castle, and by telling him, "I do not wish to leave here so soon," Saint Louis had reassured him that their friendship had not died, and that if he had been upset with him, he had now forgiven him, and that the pair of friends that they had been was now reunited.

By setting up this altar, it was in his home and his chapel that Joinville had the saint king, and he had him entirely to himself, forever, since he had set up a donation in perpetuity for his worship. And it was in this castle, the symbolic place representing Joinville's person, that Saint Louis would live forever. What the seneschal did not mention was that in the absence of any relic, he completed this eternal representation of the holy king by having a statue of him set up on his altar or next to it. The image of the king was his incarnation, his double, possessed for all time.[54] Joinville's testimony ended as an imaginary monument to the king.

Saint Louis

Between the Model and the Individual

IF WE WANT TO UNDERSTAND SAINT LOUIS AS AN INDIVIDUAL, THE production of his memory then condemns us to put aside the record of hagiographical commonplace ideas and information manipulated by the sovereign's clerical and official entourage. Must we then privilege the exceptional testimony that reveals at least certain aspects of the "real" Saint Louis, Joinville's testimony?

This matter is not that simple. In effect, we must ask whether the society that the saint king belonged to, the mental tools of the biographers and witnesses for the canonization inquiry, and the sensibility of the period and its modes of memorization were different for the individual, including the one who was placed at society's highest point, or whether, instead, considerations of individual personality were one of their modes of perceiving, defining, and explaining the self and the other, and, in particular, whether this applied to the heroes of the biographies, the *Vitae*.

History and the Individual

Historians often have the irritating habit of seeing the emergence or the affirmation of the individual in many different periods of history. This repetitive assertion ends up discrediting the search for the appearance of the individual in history. This matter, however, is a very real problem that requires a great deal of specific and sensitive research. Let us be satisfied, first of all, with two or three propositions based on experience and good sense.

Like many historical phenomena that take place over an extended duration, the affirmation of the individual does not follow a single, constant line of development. What corresponds to our idea of the individual is different within a given period and a specific society.[1] The Socratic individual imagined by ancient Greek philosophy, the Christian endowed with an individual soul, the Renaissance man animated by his *virtù,* the hero of Rousseau or Romanticism, to remain within the boundaries of Western culture, are not only distinct types of individuals but also do not respond to the same type of concept of the individual and do not have the same relations with the society to which they belong. There is a model of the individual in the ancient city, in the Augustinian City of God, in Rabelais' abbey of Thélème, in Thomas More's utopia, in Calvin's Geneva, in Port-Royal or the Society of Jesus. I am only mentioning real or imaginary societies here. Each time, there is a specific model that differs from the others.

In addition, one can truly speak of the individual and individualism in Western society only in the contemporary period, and to situate this phenomenon at a definite time, although it emerges through a long, varied, and often underground development, we can say that it is only realized openly with the American Constitution and the French Revolution. Nevertheless, it undoubtedly existed since the beginnings of history, taking shape around different notions of the individual in phases of individualism of varying duration, varying strength, and varying influence followed by low points and retreats. If any history is discontinuous and multi-formed, it has to be the history of the notion and status of the individual.

However, we can identify certain kinds of historical production intended specifically to fix the memory of the individual. They indubitably mark a more particular interest in and a clearer affirmation of the individual: this is the case for autobiography and the portrait. Several historians, and not the least important among them, have recently advanced the argument that the period preceding or even including Saint Louis' life constituted one of these moments in the rise of the individual.

In his work *The Individual and Society in the Middle Ages,* the Englishman Walter Ullmann, a historian of law and ecclesiastical institutions, ventures that the medieval notion of the individual as a subject began to evolve toward the notion of the individual as citizen around the heart of the Middle Ages, although it still did not attain its full realization until the end of the eighteenth century. In medieval Christian society, the individual could not be represented due to the limitations imposed by two fundamental representations: the superiority of the law and the superiority of society perceived as an organic body. The first of these representations presupposed the image of a hierarchical society of inequalities in which the individual was an inferior who had to obey a superior responsible for enforcing the law. There was no existing rule of a majority that gave equal value to each individual; instead, there was the *sanior pars,* the most "healthy" minority and a group of "the best" that imposed itself on the less "good." The individual was only a subject (*subjectus,* subjected, submitted). Walter Ullmann stresses that one result of this among others was what appears to us as the impersonal character of medieval historiography.[2]

Between the Twelfth and Thirteenth Centuries

The other predominant representation dissolved the individual within the communities to which it belonged: the social state or order (*status, ordo*), the parish, the corporation, and, eventually, the emergent state. This representation originated in Saint Paul and was revived by John of Salisbury with his organic conception of society resembling a human being in which the members were supposed to obey the head (or the heart).

According to Walter Ullmann, however, it was the very supremacy of law that favored the transformation of the subject-individual into a citizen-individual by combining with other developing elements. For him, the essence of the feudal system lay in "the individual and personal contract between lord and vassal."[3] He finds the most remarkable expression of this trend that would unite the primacy of the law with consideration for the individual in article 39 of the Great Charter (1215) that the barons imposed on the king of England: "No free man will be arrested or imprisoned or

seized or outlawed or exiled or condemned in any way, except by a judgment of his peers [*judicium parium suorum*] according to the law of the land
[*per legem terrae*]." This interpretation seems debatable to me. We have to observe, for instance, that the long, slow march of Western countries toward
democracy followed two main routes. The English path was based on the
guarantee of individual rights by the laws of the country and the judgment
of peers; the French path developed through the affirmation that the law of
the state was equal for all citizens, and its formulation and application were
assured by the king in the time of the monarchical state. This is exactly
what Saint Louis did in the case of the lord of Coucy.[4] The feudal system
can thus be considered as a stimulus for the protection of the individual
(the English case) or as an obstacle to this protection that favored a hierarchical system in which equality only existed in the heart of the privileged
upper echelon of society (the French case). Each system could be perverted,
and this is exactly what began to happen in the Middle Ages. In one case,
we find the domination of the privileged; in another, the tyranny of the state,
which was what happened in France under Philip the Fair and perhaps already under Philip III, and which at least a segment of the nobility already
saw in certain acts of Louis IX.

Let us take another look at Walter Ullmann's conception of this. He
identifies a third path through which the notion of the individual made its
appearance in the medieval West. He calls it "humanist." It resulted from
the convergence of developments in very different but important fields of
thought, mentalities, and human behavior. In this regard, he also mentions
how philosophical and theological Aristotelianism paved the way for literature in vernacular languages, the development of "naturalism" in the visual
arts, the political philosophy of Marsile of Padua, and the juridical thought
of Bartole de Sassoferrato. These considerations lead us beyond the age
of Saint Louis. On the other hand, his reign was in the middle of the period
in which Ullmann situates the decisive thrust in the transformation of the
subject-individual into a citizen-individual. "Historical scholarship has come
to recognize that in the West the turn of the twelfth and thirteenth centuries formed the period in which the seeds for the future constitutional
development as well as for the standing of the individual in society were
sown."[5] As vernacular literature expresses it best, this was a fundamental reversal in mentalities and sensibilities from which the individual emerged:
"While in the High Middle Ages it was the *Memento mori* [Remember that

you will die] that set the tone in literature, from the late twelfth century on it was the *Memento vivere* [Remember to live]. The earlier tone of resignation and flight from the world into eternity was replaced by a joie de vivre, by optimism and the appeal to man's own capacities to bring his life on earth to full fruition."[6] Here, we might recall Saint Louis' surprising statement that "there is no one who loves his life as much as I love mine."[7] He too was touched by this "descent of heavenly values to the earth."[8] Saint Louis navigated between this individualized and newly valued terrestrial existence and the collective heaven of the communion of the saints.

Another British historian, Colin Morris, goes even further. While he still identifies Greco-Roman antiquity as one of the probable sources of the concept of the individual and highlights the Christian origins of the notion, following the title of his book, he reserves the honor of the veritable "discovery of the individual" for the Middle Ages.[9] His second original point is that he moves the beginning of this phenomenon up to the middle of the eleventh century, the chronological summit of his study that extends from 1050 to 1200. However, for him, the decisive period is the twelfth century. Although he points out that there was no term for the individual at this time, as the words *individuum, individualis,* and *singularis* were strictly limited to the technical language of logic, he insists on "the search for the self," which has also been called Christian Socratism. Saint Bernard's friend, the Benedictine Guillaume de Saint-Thierry (1085–1148) provided a dual source of this transformation in his treatise "On the Nature of the Body and the Soul" (*De natura corporis et animae*): "Apollo of Delphi's response was famous among the Greeks: Man, know thyself." And Solomon, or rather Christ, said the same thing in the Song of Songs (1:7): "If thou know not, go thy way" (*Si te ignoras . . . egredere*). This Christian Socratism inspired a diverse number of other thinkers from Abelard to Saint Bernard. The search for the self was pursued in the increased emphasis on private, auricular confession in which people tried to discern the sinner's intentions instead of simply punishing the actual wrongdoing. Autobiography inspired by Saint Augustine's *Confessions* was reinvented by the monk of Ratisbonne, Otloh de Saint-Emmeran (who died around 1070), and the Benedictine of northern France, Guibert de Nogent (who died around 1123). Otloh seeks "the inner man," and Guibert meets with "the internal mystery."[10]

This self [*ce moi*] seeks out other "selves" [*d'autres 'moi'*]. The twelfth century was a century of praise for friendship. The English Cistercian

Aelred de Rievaulx discovered Cicero's treatise on friendship (*De amicitia*) and produced the crowning achievement of his career with his book on *L'Amitié spirituelle* (Spiritual Friendship), written between 1150 and 1165. He claimed that "God is friendship," and also that friendship was true love. There was sacred love and there was profane love, with all the ambiguities contained in the most commented biblical book of the twelfth century, the Song of Songs. Saint Bernard and Guillaume de Saint-Thierry were eulogists of God's love. As Guillaume put it, if the friend you are seeking is in your love, he is in you, and he does not only want to see God. He wants "to touch" him too and even to "enter into him entirely all the way to his heart."[11] Saint Bernard, as we have seen, mourned for his brother with the same intensity that Saint Louis mourned for his mother, his son, his brother, and his sister. In the midst of Saint Louis' devoutness, intense love and friendship existed between him and Joinville, and this kind of loving friendship between individuals culminated in the sixteenth-century model of Montaigne and La Boétie with its characteristic statement, "because it was him, because it was me," which exhibited the same fascination with the "inner man."

Finally, the new individual explored new religious paths: the cult of Christ's Passion, eschatology, and mystical theology. The Passion of Christ, the new Jerusalem, the search for God in friendship and love, these were all part of Saint Louis' religion.

The Russian medievalist Aaron J. Gourevitch is another supporter of the argument that the individual emerged in the course of the thirteenth century. He emphasizes how much the individual in the Middle Ages was absorbed within the collectivities he belonged to and the extent to which what counted most in this age when people would say *individuum est ineffabile* (the individual cannot be expressed) was not the part but the whole, the *universitas*. He concludes his important book on the categories of medieval culture with an essay entitled, "À la recherche de la personnalité" (In Search of the Personality).[12]

For him, it is more a case of "personality" rather than "individuality" that began to assert itself in the Middle Ages. The notion of *persona* primarily referred to the theater mask in the Roman world; it was transformed into the concept of personhood in the field of law. However, the feudal system prevented the individual from becoming an independent entity for a long time. In medieval thought, the individual was still encompassed within the universal and the type, and in social reality he was subordinated to the community to which he belonged. Ultimately, the thirteenth century marked a turning point at which "symptoms [appeared that] testify to the human person's growing pretensions to be recognized."[13]

Gourevitch then proceeds even further, dating not only the birth of the moral person from the Middle Ages but also the individual proper. He uses narratives of other-worldly travel to support the argument that the image of an individual biography conceived as "the fate of a soul" and the notion of a human personality completely formed at the moment of death in an individual judgment made at the dying person's side appeared in Christianity as early as the eighth century.[14]

THE "SELF"

These ideas have been the object of nuanced criticisms. First of all, the American historian Caroline Bynum has suggested that we need to make an initial distinction between the individual—for which the Middle Ages had no specific word—and the self which would correspond to the terms "soul" (*anima*), "oneself" (*seipsum*), and "inner man" (*homo interior*).[15] According to her, even after the twelfth century the Middle Ages did not identify the individual as unique and separable from any group. What the twelfth and thirteenth centuries found or recovered was an awareness of the inner man, the self, but this self could not exist outside the groups it was a part of. The novelty of these centuries was to replace or double the old unitary, binary, or ternary conceptions of society with a concept of society as formed of multiple groups. New social and socio-professional typologies arose both inside the Church—with monks, canons, ordinaries, and orders of all kinds[16]—and among laymen classed by their "states" (*status*). These new categories arose alongside those of the Church, Christendom, the mystical body of Christ, the pairing of clerics and laymen, the powerful and the poor, even fat people and thin people (*peuple gras* and *peuple menu, popolo grasso* and *popolo minuto*), and more recent ternary systems like the three orders (of clerics, warriors, and workers—*oratores, bellatores, laboratores*), or the powerful, the middle class, and the "little" people (*maiores, mediocres, minores*).[17] For example, thirteenth-century preachers would compose sermons adapted to people with specific professions or to their place in society—widows, married people, young people, judges, merchants, artisans, peasants, the poor, lepers, pilgrims, etc. These various statuses were then defined according to models or types that evolved along with society. Whether it was a false work or an authentic work, the thirteenth-century autobiography attributed to Abelard, the *Story of My Misfortunes* (*Historia calamitatum*), is actually "the story of the rise and fall of a type: 'the philosopher'." Francis of Assisi, whom people looked on as "an individual in revolt against the world," became "a model for the world."

Finally, we have to ask ourselves what awareness Saint Louis could have had of his "self." The distinction established by Marcel Mauss between the "sense of the self" [*sens du moi*] and the concept of the individual is relevant here.

Did Saint Louis actually have a "sense of self"? Did he think of himself as an "individual"? Nothing is less certain.[18]

Caroline Bynum does not discuss Saint Louis' case. To search for the individual Saint Louis without any complete concept of the individual would be an illusion. The only Saint Louis that we can know would be either the Church's model of the saint king at the end of the thirteenth century or the model of the king according to the Mendicants, Saint-Denis, or a pious knight.

Jean-Claude Schmitt's judgment is even more nuanced. He goes back to the sources of what he calls the historiographical "fiction" of the "discovery of the individual," which he attributes to the rise of the German tradition led by Jacob Burckhardt and Otto von Gierke at the end of the nineteenth century. He denies the existence of any notion of the individual in the Middle Ages, at least in the contemporary sense of this term, which is already fairly ambiguous. He recognizes only a late appearance of a concept of the person, which was itself caught up in contradictory pressures, because "far from first of all exalting individual consciousness, it tended to obliterate the subject within the divinity that it serves as an image and within humanity whose fate it shares." However, in the tradition of Saint Augustine, starting in the eleventh century, clerics of the Middle Ages experienced an unexpected return of this contradiction affecting the Christian person. "The abolition of the self paradoxically presupposes a deepening of individual consciousness."

It seems to me that this idea explains the internal tension that William Jordan thought he was able to discern in Saint Louis, which, in my opinion, was harmoniously surmounted rather than dolefully suffered by the king. Through his faith in God, Saint Louis transformed his individual weaknesses into personal power and managed to unite morality and politics in his behavior. He shaped his personality by modeling his individual self on what he thought was divine will.

Finally, Jean-Claude Schmitt thinks that we need to pursue further research on the things that correspond to the process underlying the individual's development in the thirteenth century, not only from the perspective of a history of spirituality, as Caroline Bynum has done, but also by retracing the converging paths of the rise of autobiography, the internalization of moral life, the transformations of intellectual techniques that pushed away the "authorities" in favor of "reasons," and the mutations in affectivity and spirituality that were particularly evident in the domains of love and death.[19]

THE CASE OF SAINT LOUIS

The slow progression that I have followed in recapitulating the arguments of these historians will now allow me to approach the individual Saint Louis as I believe he emerges from the sources that were made to immerse him within models and commonplace ideas. An autobiography of the king himself emerges from the works of his biographers, a person from his inner life, from his words an individual who articulated his own personal reasons for acting as he did, and from his affective reactions and attitudes faced with death, a unique Christian king whom I believe that I am capable of approaching, not in any fiction or illusion but in historical reality.

However, although the notion of the individual was different in the thirteenth century from the one that subsequently developed after the French Revolution, although what emerged from the twelfth century on was the self assimilated to the inner man brought to life by the search for the sinner's intentions and the practice of individual confession, and, although the individual did not exist outside the community that included him or, rather, lived within a constantly evolving dialectic relation between the self and the group, it is no less true that this self spoke more and more loudly and that individuals in the thirteenth century appear as combinations of the self, the inner man, and the individual in the more modern sense.

Saint Louis was a more "personal" holy king than his predecessors.[20] In the Mirror of the Princes that he dedicated to him, the Franciscan Gilbert de Tournai inserted a personal chapter on Louis' captivity in Egypt into his impersonal portrait of the ideal king inspired by Deuteronomy. This chapter is historical in the factual sense. The *exemplum,* an anecdote slipped into a sermon, was immensely popular in the thirteenth century. Saint Louis enjoyed them himself. In this literary genre, there was a tendency to privilege contemporary facts that happened "in our time" (*nostris temporibus*) and that were "true" and not reduced to models and commonplace ideas. In speaking of these facts, the preacher or his source could say "I have seen" (*vidi*) and "I have heard people say" (*audivi*) instead of "I have read" (*legi*).[21] This was exactly how Joinville treated and spoke of Saint Louis. He also recognized information that he owed to other sources, to Robert de Clermont, for example, who told him about his father's death, which Joinville himself could not have experienced, or to a work in French that he found and of which we know nothing today.

> I am letting everyone know that I am including a large number of acts here that our saint king is supposed to have done or said, which I have seen or heard about, and that a large number of his acts that I have found are in a work in French which I have taken down in this book. I am reminding you of these things so that people who listen to this book may believe firmly in what the book says that I actually saw and heard myself, while I cannot vouch for the veracity of the other things that I have written here, because I neither saw them nor heard them myself.[22]

He proceeded with Saint Louis just as some authors did with another great contemporary saint[23] whom we can sense that he closely resembled, although he was so different by virtue of his personality, his status, and his life.

We can observe the struggle between the individual and the model for Saint Francis of Assisi. We have already seen how these authors began with rather spontaneous testimonials and ended up with a portrait drawn up shortly after the end of his life that resisted uniqueness and that sought to establish a resemblance with models.[24] We can see this by comparing the Life that Thomas de Celano dedicated to the saint (the *Vita prima*), written in 1229 three years after Francis's death, and the second Life that he wrote in 1246 (*Vita secunda*) to expose the evolution of the order and to show a Francis who corresponded to the models. The *Vita prima* presented him as "a man unlike all others" (*vir dissimilens omnibus*: I.57.19). The *Vita secunda* described him as "avoiding uniqueness in everything" (*singularitatem in omnibus fugiens*: II.14.4). The Church had been leaning on the order more and more and made it restore Francis's obedience to traditional models. The same pressure was exerted in Louis' case, although thanks especially to Joinville, it is sometimes exposed as being in error: the individual's actions break the harmony of the model of the ideal king in which he had been confined. This could occur because the period allowed these movements and first words of the individual in the modern sense.

Certain kinds of documents and certain modes of expression allow me to nuance the arguments of the historians who deny our ability to perceive the individual in the thirteenth century. For instance, some of these documents are literary sources written in the vernacular in which we can see the appearance not of the self but of the "I" in the blossoming of a literary subjectivity, which was a sign of a more widespread subjectivity. Joinville and his Saint Louis figure in the tradition of this set of texts.[25] There were also the new judiciary practices. Under Saint Louis' reign the new interrogational procedure in which a competent ecclesiastical or secular judge looked for the means to validly accuse a suspect began to replace the older accusatory procedure in which a guilty party was indicted only if there was an accuser. The best proof that a judge could find would henceforth be the admission [*l'aveu*] of guilt, to be obtained by torture if necessary. The Church's inquisitional obsession favored the treatment of the suspect and the accused as individual cases. This resulted from their insistence on apprehending every heretic and letting none escape but also on condemning only those who were guilty and distinguishing heresy from what it was not. These legal concepts tended to separate the public from the private more and more. There is a fundamental distinction here that has to be applied to the king, as Guibert de Tournai shows in his *Miroir des princes* dedicated to Saint Louis. The private was situated on the side of the particular and became an attribute of the individual or at least of certain individuals, the most powerful ones.[26] We can add the rediscovery of testaments here as they individualized each testator.

The reshaping of the geography of the afterlife and the resulting modification of beliefs and practices tied to death especially favored the affirmation of the individual in the clearest way. At the very moment of death God would decide whether the deceased would have to undergo a passage through Purgatory. This was a new place for the afterlife that people henceforth identified as a separate territory because Purgatory would exist only until the end of time. God no longer had to wait for the day of the Last Judgment to send the deceased to Heaven or Hell but instead had to choose an eventually temporary destination for his soul. The decisive moment of eternal salvation or damnation was the moment of death, an individual's death.[27] However, I cannot go so far as to accept Aaron Gourevitch's conclusion that the belief in Purgatory detached the individual from all community.[28] The shortening of one's stay in Purgatory depended on the approval that living people who knew the dead person procured for him in the form of prayers, masses, and alms. New ties were thereby forged between the living and the dead, while alongside the carnal family the importance of spiritual or artificial families was reinforced. These spiritual or artificial families were the religious orders, the brotherhoods, etc. A new balance was struck between the individual and the groups with which he had ties. It was in this balance that Saint Louis lived.

CONSCIENCE

The best word for this dual awakening of the self and the subject [*du moi et du je*] is *conscience*.[29] The examination of conscience and cases of conscience became pregnant realities in the thirteenth century. We have already stressed how much the French kings of the thirteenth and fourteenth centuries listened to their conscience and tried to be at peace with it in governing by appointing and sending out investigators. Their conscience here was supposed to assure their personal salvation and the salvation of their people. This was a new form of contact between the individual and the community. Of all these kings, Saint Louis was the one with the highest degree of conscience.

The hagiographers who sometimes gave in to it also felt this pressure that the individual exerted on the model whether they actually knew the king or had merely heard about him from members of his entourage. In his work on Francis of Assisi, Thomas de Celano calls the model the *forma* or the "mold." In the first group, we find the king's confessor Geoffroy de Beaulieu who knew him both as a close friend and as the confidant of the "inner man." Guillaume de Saint-Pathus is an example of the second category. He was the queen's confessor and had access to the canonization records and the testimonies that it contained.

Even for them, Saint Louis sometimes diverged from the model. The first reason for this is that a saint also has to struggle against himself and the devil, and no one, not even a saint, is perfect in this world and therefore should not always be idealized. The main reason, however, is that these witnesses could not avoid the direct knowledge that they had of their hero's personality. They were limited by their concrete experience and they sometimes had to depict the real king and not the typical ideal king.

Here is one of Saint Louis' personal character traits credited to his ability to resist temptation. Louis scrupulously observed the Church's interdictions in matters of conjugal sexual relations. However, he sometimes had to struggle with these rules. It is a commonplace representation for hagiography to show the saint in the act of overcoming the temptations of the flesh. Since Gregory the Great's *Life of Saint Benet,* the stereotypical representation of this victory was the purging of carnal flames in the material flames of thorns that the saint would go roll upon. Geoffroy de Beaulieu, however, substituted a realistic reaction for the commonplace idea. "If, on these days of continence, he happened to visit his wife the queen for whatever reason and to stay with her and sometimes through contact with her to feel the turmoil of the flesh caused by human weakness, he would pace back and forth through the room [*per cameram deambulans*] until the rebellion of the flesh was quieted."[30] It is hard to doubt the reality of this image of Louis marching to and fro through the conjugal chamber.

Sometimes the hagiographer confessor expressed blame provoked by his excessive piety. Louis had developed the habit of worshipping at night in the monastic fashion. He would get up in the middle of the night to go hear the matins and then pray for a moment at the foot of his bed, a good example of individual private prayer. However, he would get up at the earliest possible moment of the day. "As these awakenings could greatly weaken and affect his body and particularly his head, he ended up accepting the advice and insistence of several discreet persons [in his entourage] and began to wake up for matins at one o'clock [a later time], which allowed him to hear the masses and the hours that followed almost immediately after the first hour of the day."[31]

We find a similar remark made about the hair shirt that he would wear during the Advent and Lent and the four vigils of the Virgin: "His confessor [in other words, the narrator himself, Geoffroy de Beaulieu] had nonetheless told him that this was not appropriate for his rank [*status*] and that he should instead give large alms to the poor and obtain quicker [*festinata*] justice for his subjects."[32] Geoffroy made a similar remark about his fasting when he wanted to add an additional Monday fast to the complete fasts on Fridays and the partial fasts of Wednesdays that forbade meats and fats: "but because of his physical weakness he renounced this project on the advice of several discreet persons [in his entourage]."[33]

Instead of surfacing through some divergence from the model, the reality effect can also arise from a concrete detail that does not seem like it could have been invented or taken from any source other than direct experience.

Sometimes the hagiographer confessor slips in some detail that was known by him alone. This concretely evokes the king's very personal behavior, although it was done to add something to the very praiseworthy image of the king that he was trying to convey: "He always treated his confessors with great respect, so much so in fact that sometimes when he was already sitting down in front of the confessor in order to confess, if the confessor wanted to open or close a door or a window, he would rush to get up to do it himself and would humbly go to close [it]. . . ."[34]

Guillaume de Saint-Pathus reports his habit of using the formal "*vous*" to address everyone, including his domestic servants.[35] His renunciation of the traditional and familiar "*tu*," which would identify anyone he spoke to as part of the herd, denoted his attentiveness to individual dignity, which was better observed with the polite "*vous*."

A French-Speaking King

What enhances our impression of being able to approach and even to hear the "real" Saint Louis is the fact that a number of the biographical sources have him speak in French.

In effect, the French language made decisive progress in its evolution under Louis IX. The number of charters written in French increased dramatically. When Louis launched his investigations in 1247, the first petitions addressed to the king were still written up in Latin. By the end of his reign, they were written in French. When the king wrote his *Instructions* to his oldest son and daughter in his own hand, he wrote in French, as Guillaume de Nangis observed.[36] It was also a French version of the *Chronicles of Saint-Denis* that he requested from the monk Primat. Although he fell into Latin, the language of the priests, on his deathbed, he promoted French, the maternal language,[37] throughout his life. He also accomplished a linguistic miracle from his tomb at Saint-Denis, making the receiver of one of his miracles speak in the French of Île-de-France, even though he was a Burgundian.[38] The first king that we can hear speaking expressed himself in French.[39]

THE PORTRAIT OF THE KING

The history of portraiture provides us with decisive evidence that allows us to track the emergence of this new attention to the individual. Saint Louis belongs only to its prehistory.[40]

Roland Recht has recently reminded us that realism is a code.[41] The term that seems best suited to him for defining this interest in the world and "real" beings is the "reality principle." He defines it as "the taking into account of the real world through the world of art." He quite accurately determines that this principle "is necessarily a principle of individuation," and he traces it to sculpture "beginning around 1300." Funerary sculpture is a privileged domain for observing this principle. Beginning around 1320–1330, the "temptation of portraiture" appeared as the culminating point of thirteenth-century research, notably in the field of physiognomy. These preoccupations were inspired by one of Aristotle's treatises and by a work of one of the scholars at the court of Frederick II von Hohenstaufen. His name was Michael Scot, and his work focused on astrology, although it also included a section on physiognomy presented as the study of the physiognomy of individuals. This interest grew with the spread of scholasticism in the second half of the thirteenth century. Some examples are the *De animalibus* (On Animals) by Albert the Great and the *De physiognomonia* attributed to Saint Thomas Aquinas. Funerary sculpture, however, stayed at the level of idealized portraits as we can see by looking at the recumbent statues at Saint-Denis produced for the reorganization of the royal tombs in 1263–1264 on the orders of Saint Louis and his close advisor, Mathieu de Vendôme.[42]

Do the reputedly old, in other words contemporary, images of Saint Louis enable us to see his real face? My study of the iconographic research on Saint Louis has led me to the same conclusion as Alain Erlande-Brandenburg: "We do not know of any real portrait of Saint Louis." A miniature from a moralized Bible painted in Paris at a date that the specialists place around 1235—in other words at the time Louis IX was roughly twenty years old—represents the king seated with a conventional face. The document is interesting because it presents Louis IX and Blanche of Castile on the same level in two symmetrical frames. To me, this image seems to define the odd royal couple that they actually formed.[43] Both of them are sitting, crowned on a throne, and at first sight this gives their image an impression of equality as the idea of their shared rule emerges from the image. However, a more attentive examination can make out that Saint Louis is seated on a real throne, while his mother is sitting on some kind of curule chair, the type of chair that people called a "throne of Dagobert" at the time. If we compare these thrones to the ones that appear on the seals of the kings of France, we notice that Blanche's resembles the ones that the kings of France sit upon in their seals of majesty, whereas Louis' resembles a more "modern" throne. This observation is reinforced by the fact that the Queen Mother's feet are concealed beneath the folds of her long dress, while Louis' feet are visible and rest upon a small red carpet, a symbol of royal power. Although Blanche is wearing a coat trimmed with ermine, she holds nothing in her hands, while Louis is holding the insignia of royal power with the scepter decorated with a fleur-de-lis in his right hand—a distinctive sign of the kings of France—and a small globe in his left hand. The globe confers symbolic power of the imperial kind, signifying supreme nature though in a reduced format.[44] The image conveys precisely the relation that existed between Louis and his mother, the extraordinary case of the royal couple of mother and son. Behind the façade of equality lies a fundamental inequality favoring the young king who had always been the only one to possess all the attributes of supreme royal power. There was never any diarchy at the head of the Kingdom of France. Although there is a certain realism in this image, it is institutional in nature. The image represents the royal function and the relations that actually existed between the king and his mother.

We have another image of a totally different nature. It is a drawing in ink on parchment probably executed in the seventeenth century by a Parisian copyist for the scholar Fabri de Peiresc. It represents a fragment from one of the paintings from the beginning of the fourteenth century in the Sainte-Chapelle in Paris. Those paintings had in all likelihood been inspired by another cycle of frescoes on Saint Louis' life, executed between 1304 and 1320 in the church of the lady Cordeliers (the Clares) of Lourcine and commissioned by Blanche, Louis' daughter.[45] This was the same daughter who asked Guillaume de Saint-Pathus to write her father's life. The original document presented Saint Louis' head in the scene where he is washing the feet of the poor. This image, executed for the Mendicant nuns and commissioned by a daughter who was attached to the image of her father whom she knew and at a time when the first realistic portraits of great figures were beginning to appear, undoubtedly comes close to presenting Saint Louis' real traits, showing the bearded penitent in a posture of humility upon returning from his first crusade.

I believe that these two old images clearly define Saint Louis' place in the tradition that led to the individual portrait properly speaking. Peiresc's drawing evokes this "temptation of the portrait" identified by Roland Recht as existing around the beginning of the fourteenth century. The moralized Bible miniature keeps the king's portrait within the tradition of the idealized, symbolic, and stereotypical portrait, although it has been adapted to a position of power that was unique and real.[46]

Since the end of the Middle Ages, people have tried to identify Louis as the model for a statue in the church of Mainneville in Eure dating from the early fourteenth century.[47] Today we have confirmed that this is not a statue of Saint Louis but of his grandson Philip the Fair. There is really nothing surprising about this in the church of a fief of Enguerran de Marigny, Philip the Fair's powerful advisor. The confusion nonetheless attests to the very early impression that Saint Louis had lived around the time that individualized portraits began to appear. It can also be explained by the fact that Saint Louis, like Philip the Fair, had a reputation for good looks that was handed down to the last direct descendants of the Capetian line. This quality probably facilitated the transition from the idealized statue to the realist statue. The statue of Saint Louis that was placed on his tomb in Saint-Denis at the beginning of the fourteenth century was symbolic: the beardless king wears a coat ornamented with fleurs-de-lis and holds the three nails of the Passion and a double-barred crucifix, which had to have been the image of the reliquary of the true cross in the Sainte-Chapelle. The image unites the symbolism of the French monarchy with the symbols of the worship of Christ's Passion, the cross and the relics.[48]

Alain Erlande-Brandenburg has observed that just as we do not know any real portrait of Saint Louis, "no chronicler has gone to the trouble of describing his physical traits for us." One Life of the saint king written shortly after his canonization and generally addressed to preachers and readers in convents does give us an interesting sketch of the king's physique.[49]

> His stature surpassed everyone else's by the shoulder's height and up. The beauty of his body resulted from its harmonious proportions, and his head was round as is appropriate for the seat of wisdom. His placid, serene face had something outwardly angelic about it. His dove-like eyes emitted graceful rays, and his face was white and shiny. The precocious whiteness of his hair (and his beard) presaged his inner maturity and even the venerable wisdom of old age. It may be superfluous to praise all of this because it is only the ornamentation of the outer man. The internal qualities come from sanctity and these are the ones that we must try to venerate. This is something that led people to love the king even more, and they were inwardly moved to joy by his outward appearance alone.

This is the image of the king that had been fixed in people's minds very soon after his death and canonization. It is an idealized image based on the traditional harmony (since the eleventh century) between the internal and the external man. At the same time, however, it is partly corroborated by the live impressions reported by Joinville about his stature and by Salimbene of Parma on his soft eyes like a dove's. The white hair of his later years clearly belonged to the penitential king of the second half of his reign. One last trait is especially in step with the time—the reference to the joy that radiated from the king's face. He was evidently a Franciscan king with a laughing face who conveyed a message of joy instead of sorrow.

Obviously, the model and the reality are confused in Louis, and his physique is the first evidence of this. Let us sum things up. What actually allows us to claim that it is possible to get close to the "real" Saint Louis is first of all the desire he expressed very early on to realize and embody the ideal Christian king and his undeniable success in this enterprise. This intention was initially expressed by his mother and his educators and then on

his own with the assistance of the religious figures in his entourage and reinforced by the image of himself that his contemporaries projected back
onto him. The ideal king described by his hagiographers is actually him. In
a slightly different sense from the one proposed by Louis Marin for the absolute monarch of the seventeenth century, "the portrait of the king is the
king." Far from obliterating Louis' personality with the commonplace ideas
of monarchy, the Mirrors of the Princes and the royal hagiographers depict
a Saint Louis who wanted to be the living embodiment of the commonplace ideas. Here lies Saint Louis' profound originality and, therefore, the
originality of his life story. This is a rare case among the great figures of history, including the saints. From the first centuries of the Middle Ages to the
twelfth century, the personalities of history's protagonists elude us, and this
is due to either the silences that conceal their individuality or the absorption
of their individuality within the model that was imposed on it. The *Histoire
de Saint Louis* by Joinville, his familiar friend, adds anecdotal detail to these
objective but specific structures defining the king's personality, and this re-
stores a part of his personality that is irreducible to any other. Moreover,
our documents, the hagiographical ones as well as those that are "realistic," tell us enough to allow us to feel and even to know the specific ways in
which he was distinct from his model, whether through his excesses, moral
zeal, or temperament. They do this either out of admiration or in expressing critical reservations. Whether through their closeness to him or simply
through his renown, the familiarity that some of his contemporaries had
with his flaws and the criticism to which this sometimes gave rise during his
lifetime allow us to add a third dimension to our perception of Saint Louis.
In his own life and times he had been a controversial personality and his
memory drew a more "real" human dimension from this fact. Saint Louis
existed, and we can get to know him through the documents. What finally
gives his image its own unique reality is that he lived at a time when a general interest in the individual as such was beginning to take shape. In compliance with the old Christian attempt to reach and shape "the inner man"
and to make people's external expressions conform with their internal being
through the mediation of words and gestures[50] and attitudes toward the
movements of the heart and the soul, people came to consider appearance
more and more as an expression of being. Knowledge of individuals had
been based for a long time on consideration of their familial predecessors
and their social and professional status, but at the time this knowledge was

being reoriented toward the analysis of individual external signs. The proper name had already been adopted as a means of identification. The "realist" portrait would soon appear. Saint Louis was the first king of France whose individual traits people imagined they could represent visually from the Middle Ages and beyond, and of whom people attempted to produce "lifelike" portraits. It was still a time in which the insignia of power and symbolic instruments like seals identified the royal person. We have to wait until the fourteenth century to find autographs, signatures, and realistic portraits of the kings of France. However, the uniqueness of the king tended to take on external forms beginning in the age of Saint Louis. Two contradictory movements seem to act at cross-purposes here. The image of an exceptional king that rapidly spread far and wide accelerated the rising interest in his personality, but, on the other hand, the development of the state and a political system that tended to privilege the crown at the expense of the person who wore it delayed the appearance of any individual representation of the king. To use Kantorowicz's terms, the tension between the political body and the natural body of the king allowed his unique traits to appear but did not allow them to be fully established.[51]

Saint Louis,
the Unique and Ideal King

We now have to reconstitute the elements that make Saint Louis both unique and exemplary, relating him to the ideal historical portrait of a Christian king and explaining the Saint Louis who existed in relation to his model. In order to accomplish this, we will sometimes have to examine texts we have already used, though in this new perspective.

From the Outside to the Inside

Now that I have a clear idea of the extent to which we can trust the sources, I will try to approach Saint Louis through his life and his actions in his relations with the world and the society in which he lived.

I will first consider him in his relations with space and time. These are lived and objective elements that he experienced and that were effected by his choices and actions. I will examine his relations with space and time within the networks of material realities and the social and cultural organization of his actions and his dreams. Then, I will consider him within the sensory, signifying environment of the works and images and texts he looked at or may have thought about, whether or not he inspired or helped produce them. After this, I will put his own figure into play as he expressed himself in words and gestures, with spontaneous or premeditated actions, in his use of the codes of communication of his time, in his spoken language, body language, and dietary habits. In one of the middle chapters here, I will define him in relation to his tripartite royal function: his sacred and therefore judicial function, his war-making function, and his function as a benefactor, which was thus his economic function. I will consider these functions in terms of their intellectual, social, and political organization, which were different from our own.

After that, I will attempt to formulate a number of synthetic propositions that respond to the interests of historians and readers who would like to situate Saint Louis within the lines of development to which some people still tend too forcefully to reduce the thirteenth century. I am talking about the transformation of a monarchy deemed "feudal" into the so-called "modern" monarchical state.

After this, I will resume my search for the inner man, following the predominant moral and intellectual movement of his time. This movement increasingly favored being over appearances, or rather strove to subordinate appearances to being and to make them the external expression of internal truth. This section therefore deals with Saint Louis' religion as it was expressed in his faith and works and attitude toward people who rejected this faith: heretics, Jews, and Muslims.

Next, we will have to examine the man in his physical family, considering his relationships with his family members in reference to the existing model of the Christian family, granted that we are dealing with the royal family here. I will discuss his wife, his children, his brothers and sisters, the dynasty that he belonged to, and the privileged dead who were his ancestors. This will bring us to the questions of what led Louis to sainthood and of what led to the recognition and proclamation of his sainthood. At this point, I will identify the personal style that allowed him to embody collective though independently existing character types: the sacred king, the religious king, the thaumaturgical king, and this other figure who owes his title solely to his individual virtues and works—the saint king.

I will conclude by summing up the things that lead to the heart of his character and to the image of himself that he gave to his contemporaries and bequeathed to posterity: this is the image of a king who suffered in his body and in his heart and who, though he failed to become a martyr, still succeeded in becoming a Christlike king.

Saint Louis in Space and Time

Saint Louis' World

A Christian's salvation plays out first of all in his management of space and time. *Homo viator,* the "man of the road": did he know how to carry out his pilgrimage on earth by following material and spiritual paths appropriate to his vocation and by choosing the right places to stop and stay along the way? As the king of a kingdom that is a territory, did Saint Louis know how to make good use of the space that comprised *his land?*

Saint Louis and Space

Let us begin with space as it existed for Saint Louis in the thirteenth century. In this mixture of material and ideological realities and experiences and representations, let's try to identify the things we can use to connect Saint Louis to the space he lived in beyond the Christian concept of the *homo viator.* What led him to think and act in relation to space as an individual

423

and as king: his homes, his "land," the royal domain, the kingdom, his kingdom, the whole of which he was a part, Christendom and the world beyond it. Within Christendom's borders, his greatest concern was defending his land. This involved his rights more than a single territorial entity. He had to extract all of the legal and necessary benefits available from his lands, instill a reign of justice and peace over them, and distribute the advantages of his rule throughout. This explains the increasing attention paid to borders in his time; they marked the limits of those rights.[1] Louis' movements can usually be placed within these borders, though often near them. For example, we find him at Cluny for his meeting with the pope and at Clermont for the marriage of his son Philip in 1262. Within these borders, he usually moved along land routes or river routes and only rarely by sea despite the considerable length of his kingdom's coasts. He had various reasons for crossing this space. Sometimes he was moving from one residence to another. Other times, he was going on a pilgrimage. Other times, he was going to meet some important person. For instance, he met with Innocent IV again in 1248 in Lyon while he was en route to the crusade. He met with the king of England three times—at Chartres in 1254, at Abbeville in 1259, and at Boulogne-sur-Mer in 1269. The planned meeting with Jaime I of Aragon at Puy in July 1243 probably never took place. Saint Louis went to Sens for the most important meetings of his life. He met his wife Marguerite de Provence there in 1234. He also went there in 1239 for the arrival of Christ's Crown of Thorns. He traveled a number of times to dub men who were close to him. He made the journey to Compiègne to dub his brother Robert in 1237, to Melun in 1239 to dub the Latin emperor of Constantinople, Baudouin II de Courtenay, to Saumur in 1241 to dub his brother Alphonse, and again to Melun in 1246 to dub his brother Charles.[2] He traveled to Péronne in 1256 and to Amiens in 1264 to make arbitrations. He less frequently traveled on military expeditions—in the west of France during the first half of his reign—and he also made journeys to take care of certain matters that had to be handled on location, for example, when he went to Gand in November 1255 to deal with the conflict between Flanders and Hainaut.

Sometimes Saint Louis took long tours through Île-de-France or the neighboring provinces (Normandy, Berry). One purpose of these tours was to redress wrongs that had been done. On these journeys, Saint Louis presented himself as a super-investigator, the master of all the investigators that he sent out through the kingdom and the royal domain beginning in 1247. These were also tours for charity marked by the distribution of alms. They simultaneously served the purpose of what we might call "publicity," mutatis mutandis. The king put himself on display. Royalty appears here at the crossroads between greater ostentation and greater secrecy.[3] These are the two poles of the expression of power—the ostentatious public tourney and the hidden retreat. The oriental emperors of ancient times would hide behind a curtain during ceremonies. The Roman and Byzantine emperors of the late Empire did the same, although they also practiced ostentatious display at the games. With Saint Louis, the king put himself on display with growing frequency, but the state remained concealed. On the one hand, we encounter the shining power of royalty (Saint Louis was a sun-king), and a mysterious power on the other. Under Louis XIV, these two forces came together. As the king became the state, the Sun King showed himself and concealed himself at the same time. That was the setting at Versailles; the sun only revealed itself in court. Saint Louis liked to put himself on display for purposes of personalizing power and justice. He opened the doors to the palace gardens in Paris and the woods of Vincennes with this same combination of charity, humility, and political stagecraft. However, he also tended to slip away into his palace for moral cleansing,[4] and the other side of his humility also led him to carry out acts of charity *in secret*.[5]

When he left the frontiers of Christendom to go crusading—whether in reality, in his thoughts, or in his dreams—he was often really escaping into an imaginary space. The Orient was the land of the medieval imagination par excellence,[6] and the Holy Land was the site of Christian imagination par excellence because Western Christians had only the most tentative knowledge of these regions.

How did Saint Louis know about space? He was a king without a map. It is highly unlikely that he ever saw any of the maps produced during or before his time. They were of little material value during this period. The map that he may have used on his boat to go to Tunis in 1270 must have been fairly crude.[7] His learned knowledge of space came from the Bible and what he picked up from the clerics in his entourage, in particular from the Dominican encyclopedist Vincent de Beauvais.[8]

As far as his kingdom was concerned,[9] he benefited from the knowledge assembled around him on the spot by the clerics of his bureaus and chancery and by the ecclesiastics and religious who formed networks of travelers. The laymen of his council and his home base were also well informed about the various places within the kingdom and the domain. And, of course, he got around a lot on his own.

Let us start by looking at a map in order to single out Saint Louis' places of residence and follow his movements throughout the land.

PARIS, HIS CAPITAL

Since the eleventh century and especially since the thirteenth century under Saint Louis, Paris was the customary residence of the king and therefore also of his council, the Curia, which was gradually transformed from an itinerant feudal court into a government agency encouraging stability. Paris became the *caput regni,* the capital of the kingdom.[10] Saint-Denis, however, was also called the *caput regni.*[11] It was the place where the king took up the oriflamme before leaving to go to war, where he paid an annual tribute of four gold bezants that he carefully placed on the altar each year, where the emblems of royal power were kept between coronation ceremonies, and where his predecessors lay waiting for the Resurrection.

The Kingdom of France had a two-headed capital, Paris and Saint-Denis. Strewn with "*montjoies,*" the road between them was the veritable royal path.[12] The sacred triangle of monarchical space was formed by Reims where the king received royal power in the cathedral of the coronation, Paris where he usually exercised power from his palace, and Saint-Denis where he relinquished power for the "national" abbey's "cemetery of the kings."

The king's customary residence in Paris was the palace of the Cité (on the current site of the Palais de la justice). It had been a count's manor in the Carolingian period. Robert the Pious took it over at the beginning of the eleventh century. He restored it and built a chapel dedicated to Saint Nicolas there.[13] A century later, Louis VI reinforced it with a tower, so the palace was transformed into a formidable fortress. In the thirteenth century this spared the kings the trouble of having to leave to take refuge in the fortress of the Louvre that Philip Augustus had built at the beginning of the century just before his wall around the city. Of course, the city was never really threatened in this period. The palace included a garden around which Philip Augustus had also built a wall. During Saint Louis' reign, several important ceremonies took place in this garden including the king of England

Henry III's swearing of homage on December 4, 1259, and the dubbing of the future Philip III the Bold on June 5, 1267, the day of Pentecost. Saint Louis only made one innovation, but it was an important one. He erected the Sainte-Chapelle on the site of the chapel of Saint Nicolas in order to house the relics of Christ's Passion that he had purchased.[14] Their miraculous power provided protection for the king, his family, and the kingdom, and they were an object of the sovereign's frequent personal worship and piety.

Just next to the Sainte-Chapelle, Saint Louis built a smaller three-storied edifice with a first floor the same height as the church's first floor but whose two upper floors were still lower than the high chapel of the Sainte-Chapelle. The first and second floors of this building served as sacristies for the Sainte-Chapelle's upper and lower chapels. The third floor of this building housed the royal archives, which were named the "*Trésor des chartes*" (Treasury of the Charters) due to the almost sacred character that was attributed to them. The name has stuck in scholarly terminology to this day and was extended to the entire building at that time. The only access to the archives was through a special spiral staircase built against one of the Sainte-Chapelle's buttresses. This special access route reserved the exclusive use of the archives for the king. This layout simultaneously represented the sanctification and the permanent localization of the kingdom's legal and administrative memory as they directly related to the sovereign's sacred person. They set up the Royal Library alongside the charters. Most of the collection was formed after the Egyptian crusade. During his captivity Saint Louis had been allowed to see the emir's religious library, which made a very strong impression on him. Saint Louis' was also a religious library, and sometimes he lent works to his associates. The collection was dispersed after his death either in keeping with the instructions in his last will and testament or through gifts given by his successors.

Despite all this, Louis was still an itinerant king with multiple residences. He had three kinds of residences: the royal "palaces," the "royal" abbeys, and the churches where he had specific lodging rights.[15]

SAINT LOUIS' RESIDENCES AND ITINERARIES

How do we know where Saint Louis resided and when? The information I am using here was all assembled in the nineteenth century. The data is subject to caution, first of all because medieval documents were not systematically organized. This is also because the historian did not possess the information that allowed him to criticize these sources. It still seems to be a given that under Saint Louis' reign the stamp of the royal seal and any mention of royal decisions on a given day and in a specific place mentioned in the act imply the actual presence of the king on that day and in that place. This was an archaic aspect of the administration that still clung to the personal character of royal power under Saint Louis, but it is useful for anyone who is interested in the king's person. In the absence of any recent scholarly publication of Saint Louis' acts,[16] we must rely on the documents that were published by nineteenth-century scholars in the *Recueil des historiens des Gaules et de la France.*[17]

One fairly approximate result of this is that the king's most frequent stays were in the Île-de-France. In addition to the palace of the Cité in Paris, three places received the most visits from the king. They were Vincennes to the east of Paris, which is mentioned sixty times;[18] Saint-Germain-en-Laye to the west of Paris, which is mentioned fifty times; and Pontoise to the northwest, which is mentioned forty-eight times. Although the king seems to have a preference for Vincennes, it only offered him a modest manor at this time. He apparently sometimes stayed with the Grandomontine monks who had a priory in the woods. The place was generally referred to as the "woods of Vincennes." Although he apparently never hunted there (no more here than anywhere else[19]), Saint Louis loved to come here. He must have appreciated Vincennes' short distance from Paris and the modest condition of the buildings. Thanks to its proximity to a major river route it was also a convenient point for arrivals and departures for his travels throughout the kingdom. Vincennes was his second to last stop before Paris on his return trip from the reception of the Crown of Thorns in Sens in 1239. He also departed from Vincennes for his second crusade and final voyage in 1270. He took leave of Queen Marguerite there with an adieu that would end up being the last.[20]

Saint-Germain-en-Laye had a larger "palace," and Saint Louis had a holy chapel built there in 1238 that was larger and more beautiful than the one Philip Augustus had erected on the site.[21] The same architect who renovated Saint-Denis at the same time probably built it. As it was near the Seine, it played the same role to the west of Paris that Vincennes had to the south and the southeast.

The royal "palace" of Pontoise held a special allure for Saint Louis because it was close to the Cistercian abbey of Maubuisson that he founded at his mother's request in 1236. Like his mother, he liked to stay there, too. She withdrew to this site to die in 1252. Like the other two sites, Pontoise was easily accessible by water.

Saint Louis visited his residences in Île-de-France as often as possible by boat. The itineraries often specify this. For example, we can read, "by boat from Melun to Paris" for May 15, 1239, "by boat from Pontoise to Mantes" for June 30, 1239, "by boat from Vernon to Rueil" for July 5, 1239, etc. Of course the king of the road was often a "horseback rider," but he traveled by boat whenever possible and Île-de-France had a fabulous network of navigable rivers for small craft. This also simplified things when it came to praying.

Here is a list of his less frequent stays along the river routes. First, there is the group of places he visited on the Seine upstream from Paris. Vincennes is probably the bridgehead for this group, which includes stops at the royal residences in Corbeil (nineteen listed), Melun (thirty-five), and Fontainebleau (twenty-two). Downstream from Paris on the Seine, there were landings at Autueil (nine) and Neuilly (seven), and at the residences at Mantes (four) and Vernon (sixteen). The most important river route may have been the Oise, which identifies Saint Louis as a continuator of an old Merovingian and Carolingian tradition. He traveled along the Oise to the two Cistercian monasteries he built near Asnières-sur-Oise: Maubuisson and Royaumont. He built these monasteries for his own enjoyment and the enjoyment of his family, and as a sepulture for his children. If we follow the Oise upstream, his stays began at Conflans at the confluence with the Seine (eight recorded visits), with Pontoise (forty-eight) and Maubuisson as relay points, Beaumont-sur-Oise (seven), Asnières-sur-Oise (twenty-nine), Royaumont (eighteen), Senlis (eleven) — which was a little further east of the Oise on the Nonette, a royal residence since the age of Clovis and the site where Hugh Capet was elected king in 987, and, finally, Compiègne (twenty-three). Compiègne attracted Saint Louis' interest not only for its "palace" that had been handed down to him from the Merovingians and Carolingians, but also for the Dominican convent there that he financed. He liked to go there to hear the mass and the sermons. He founded a hospital in Compiègne, and others in Pontoise and Vernon. Finally, standing alone at the end of the short "royal way"[22] that connected it with Paris, there was Saint-Denis (listed eleven times).

THE KING OF ÎLE-DE-FRANCE

Under Saint Louis' rule the meaning of *Francia* came to refer to the entire Kingdom of France instead of just Île-de-France.[23] Despite this development, Saint Louis was first and foremost a king of Île-de-France. In Saint Louis' Île-de-France, we can also observe the decline of the grand old Capetian route from Paris to Orléans. Saint Louis only rarely went to Orléans and Fleury (Saint-Benoît-sur-Loire), although his presence is recorded eight times at Étampes, the royal castle where his ancestor Louis VII learned of the birth of his son Philip (Augustus), "the child of the miracle," in 1165. Saint Louis still made a number of journeys outside Île-de-France to display his royalty, to conduct his investigations, and to carry out works of charity. He traveled in Gâtinais (Montargis and Lorris), in Berry (Bourges), and, particularly, in Normandy — a beautiful province with special rights that had to be ceaselessly defended from the English — both militarily and psychologically — ever since Philip Augustus won it back for the French. This was what Guillaume de Saint-Pathus called visiting "several parts of his kingdom."[24]

VISITING THE KINGDOM

Upon returning from the crusade, Saint Louis got the urge to "visit his kingdom."[25] He had been gone a long time. As we know, he was disturbed by the memory of his defeat in the Orient. Goaded by this memory, he feverishly threw himself into action in the second half of 1254. After lingering in his seneschalcies in Languedoc, he returned to Paris in September only to leave again on a tour of the northeast of the kingdom. We know that he stopped in Soissons where he had a joyous reunion with Joinville, and he may have pushed on as far as Tournai and Vervins. He was in Orléans in November and greeted the king of England there on the road to Fontevrault where Henry III stopped to contemplate the Plantagenets' dynastic royal necropolis. After this Henry went on to the Cistercian abbey of Pontigny-en-Bourgogne where he prayed over the body of Saint Edmond Rich whom he had forced into exile and who had just been canonized. Saint Louis returned to Paris where he convened the Parlement to deal with affairs pertaining to the succession of Navarre after the death of Thibaud IV of

Champagne, the king of Navarre who died at Pamplona in 1253. It was probably around this time that he promulgated the famous "Great Edict" dated in December 1254. He then left for Chartres to meet Henry III whom he escorted back to Paris where the two kings spent Christmas together with their families.

ARRIVALS AND DEPARTURES FOR THE CRUSADE

The roads leading to and from the ports of embarkation and disembarkation for the crusade were marked by frequent detours away from the normal route. These excursions usually allowed the king to visit different pilgrimage sites.

As a pilgrim on the crusade, Louis carried out the ritual gestures prescribed by the authorities for the crusades. He was at Saint-Denis on June 12, 1248. There the legate Eudes de Châteauroux handed him the pilgrim's staff and scarf. He raised the oriflamme, which signaled the departure of the royal army.[26] Then he returned to Paris and heard the mass in Notre-Dame before walking barefoot in pilgrim's dress on a procession to the abbey of Saint-Antoine to pray. He then stopped at the castle of Corbeil to take leave of his mother.

He stopped in Sens to meet with the general chapter of the Franciscans. Friar Salimbene of Parma saw him there. Then there were a number of churches that he visited to the east and west of his route. He made a special stop in Vézelay to pray to Saint Mary Magdalene. He met Pope Innocent IV in Lyon before traveling down the Rhone in a boat. The river route formed the border between the kingdom and the empire. He ran into some resistance at the castle of Roche-de-Glun; as a pilgrim, he refused to pay the toll to the lord of the castle. Instead, he captured the castle and razed it. He ran into more trouble in Avignon; according to Matthew Paris, the town's inhabitants attacked the pilgrims. When he finally reached Aigues-Mortes, he received his vassal, Count Raimond VII of Toulouse, and set sail on August 25.

When he returned from the crusade, Louis wanted to travel exclusively through his own lands and to land in his own port of Aigues-Mortes, which he built for this specific purpose. He only reluctantly accepted the idea of putting in on his brother Charles the count of Provence's lands, which lay within the empire. After landing at Salins d'Hyères on July 3, he visited with the famous monk Hugh of Digne at the Franciscan convent of Hyères, and then he reentered his kingdom in Beaucaire.[27] On the road through Beaucaire, he made the pilgrimage to Sainte-Baume, one of the two sites for the veneration of Mary Magdalene, the other being Vézelay. Joinville accompanied the king and he was particularly impressed with this site: "The king passed through the county of Provence and came to a city called Aix-en-Provence where people say that the body of Mary Magdalene lies. We were under a very high arch of rock where they say that the Magdalene had lived as a hermit for seventeen years."[28] After gathering information on the intrigues of his agents in the seneschalcies in the Midi, he went back through Auvergne to visit the important pilgrimage sanctuaries of Puy (dedicated to the Virgin Mary) and Brioude (Saint Julien). Then he passed through Issoire, Clermont, Saint-Pourçain, and Saint-Benoît-sur-Loire before finally arriving at Vincennes on September 5. One final detour took him to Saint-Denis to return the oriflamme. He made it back to Paris on September 7.

In 1270, the ritual started all over again with a visit to Saint-Denis on March 14, a barefoot procession from the palace of the Cité to Notre-Dame on June 15, his departure for Vincennes to bid his adieus to Queen Marguerite, and a second journey along the road through Sens, Vézelay, Cluny, Lyon, and down the Rhone. While waiting to leave from Aigues-Mortes, he made a pilgrimage to Saint-Gilles on Pentecost, which was his last.

Saint Louis seldom visited the Midi and, despite his tours in Normandy and Berry and his stop in the seneschalcies of Languedoc in 1254, he did not really practice the grand tours of inspection and display that became more common at the end of the Middle Ages and in the Renaissance. He did not undertake any special voyages in the south of France. The political travels of the king of the modern state only truly began with Philip the Fair's grand tour in 1303–1304.[29]

The Pilgrim King

Saint Louis took advantage of his travels to worship at various pilgrimage centers, although sometimes pilgrimage was the sole purpose of his journeys.[30] He felt a special devotion for the Virgin, who had become the object of a rapidly expanding cult in the thirteenth century. The king's worship of the Virgin was all the more fervent because she was the supreme mediator with her son Jesus, and thus the best possible auxiliary for his kingdom, his subjects, and himself.[31] Saint Louis went to pray several times at Notre-Dame de Chartres, Notre-Dame de Sées, and Notre-Dame de la Couture in Bernay.

Saint Louis' most remarkable pilgrimage to a Marian sanctuary was undoubtedly the one he made on May 2, 1244 to Rocamadour with his mother and his three brothers.[32] This was clearly a familial pilgrimage carried out in Saint Louis' grand style, and it was also a royal pilgrimage because Henry II of England initiated the pilgrimage to Rocamadour by visiting it twice, once after the discovery of Saint Amadur's body there. Blanche of Castile's father, King Alphonso VIII (1158–1214), had gone there as well. As Alphonse Dupront insightfully puts it, "in addition to the thaumaturgical aura that follows the king of France's person when he goes out to meet with the crowds, the royal pilgrim confers a special distinction on the pilgrimage sites that he visits."[33] The pilgrimage was a quest for propitiation made to obtain Mary's protection. It was a pilgrimage of thanks for the king's recovery after the battle of Taillebourg and for the birth of his first son. Alphonse Dupront has also argued that like any other pilgrim Saint Louis had to have been sensitive to the symbolic spirituality of vertical space (as he was later at the cavern of Sainte-Baume) suggested by the rock. As Dupront indicates, he also had to have been sensitive to the image of maternal refuge within the rock that sheltered a virgin mother, a black virgin whose image evoked the Orient as well. Finally, it was a political pilgrimage that this one rare time expressed the king of France's intention to strike "a balance between north and south."

Louis went to Mont Saint-Michel in March 1256. This was a pilgrimage honoring the archangel who dwelled in high places. Saint Michael had not yet become the protector of the kings and the Kingdom of France, although he still rose up—not only against the dangers of the sea but also against the English who had not yet made peace with the French. We encounter the sacredness of another vertical figure here; it signified the predominance of the high over the low, which was so commonly proclaimed throughout the Christian world. Saint Louis corrected this notion with his own version of sacredness, his sacredness in humility that lay close to the ground.

With the exception of his travels to the Orient for the crusades, Saint Louis never left the Kingdom of France to visit any other Christian country. He only made war when others brought it to his own lands as his important vassals and the king of England did in his youth. He made France more and more independent from the empire. His grandfather Philip Augustus had begun this process in a decisive way, although Saint Louis tried to avoid getting mixed up in the empire's affairs. The empire's affairs became foreign affairs to him.

There were three great pilgrimages for a thirteenth-century Christian, and two of them lay within Christendom: Rome and Saint-Jacques-de-Compostelle. Louis never went on either of these and apparently never even thought about going. Of course, the pilgrimage to Rome did not seem like it would be a peaceful journey when the papacy was in conflict first with Frederick II and then with Manfred in southern Italy. Still, there were deeper reasons for Louis' lack of interest in making the pilgrimage to the tomb of the apostles. Rome was a destination *ad limina* for Church people. Louis was a layman. He venerated the Holy Church and the "apostle of Rome," but he would rather leave them be. At the same time, Rome was the emperor's city. Although the king of France respected the emperor, he did not owe him any homage. By leaving Rome to him alone among all secular rulers, Louis expressed his respect for him without having to grant him any hierarchical recognition.

His indifference to Compostelle is more astonishing. His friend Joinville went there and was happy and proud about it. Although certain texts claim that Saint Louis mentioned him on his deathbed, Saint Jacques apparently was never one of his favorite saints.

The grand trilogy of figures he worshiped was the saint of his kingdom and dynasty, Saint Denis, whose site was only a short ride from his palace in Paris; the Virgin who was present in so many places including some of the most important ones that were in his kingdom; and first and foremost, Christ whose pilgrimage site was Jerusalem, the site of Saint Louis' great sadness and desire. He came so close to this holy place, but proved powerless to deliver it. He followed the advice of his barons who told him it was impossible for the very Christian king to be satisfied with seeing Jerusalem as long as the infidel ruled over it. He could not ask for a pass of safe-conduct. Although Frederick II felt free to buy the Holy City from the Muslims, unable to conquer it and embrace it Saint Louis never saw it.

But which Jerusalem was it that he invoked before dying? The terrestrial Jerusalem or the celestial Jerusalem? The crusade was born of this great confusion.

For Saint Louis, the space of Christendom comprised Latin European Christendom and the Holy Land. The crusade was not conceived as a conquest but as a reconquest. In this geographically challenged spiritual space, whatever geographically separated the original heart of Christendom in the Orient from its Western body mattered little. Christendom and the Holy Land were one. Saint Louis' mission was to reestablish this unity. However, in the middle of this divided Christendom lay a vast space of trials and hardships: the sea.

SAINT LOUIS AND THE SEA

Between 1248 and 1254 the sea was an almost daily presence in Saint Louis' thoughts and life.[34] He spent several weeks at sea, made a number of important decisions there, and died by the sea in 1270 after another maritime voyage. Of course, we are talking about the Mediterranean Sea.

We have seen that Saint Louis experienced his share of storms and "adventures at sea."[35] His contemporaries were the ones who called them "sea adventures," whereas we might have a tendency to say "fortunes at sea," to use an expression that soon became more popular. The transition between these two expressions probably articulates the difference between the mentality of men imbued with the spirit of chivalry as they went to sea and that of men who were more familiar with the benefits of maritime commerce and how it could be threatened by what they referred to as fortune.

Maritime tribulations offered a trial that characterized the passion for the saints of the men of the Middle Ages. The hagiographical *topos* or commonplace idea of the perils of the sea applied directly to the crusaders, these penitential heroes who undertook the most dangerous of pilgrimages—the one that required a maritime "passage" leading to the region defined so well by the term "overseas" [*outre-mer, partes ultramarinae*]. In the sermon he pronounced at Orvieto on August 6, 1297 for Saint Louis' canonization, Pope Boniface VIII mentioned his manner of confronting the sea on the crusade as a proof of his sainthood: "He exposed his body and his life for Christ by crossing the sea."[36]

For Saint Louis, the sea was another site of personal and collective experiences. He too was a seafaring nomad with all of the disturbances this introduced into the life of a highly disciplined Christian. He tried to compensate for these disturbances as much as possible. He persuaded the Church to let him set up an altar with hosts aboard his ship. They were able to say mass and take communion there. The times for prayer were generally observed aboard the ships. As usual, priests and religious in addition to secular lords like Joinville surrounded the king. The sailors were another source of trouble for the king; they were a gang of wild and sinful men. The vast majority of men of the Middle Ages lived exclusively on land. The sailors' world was unfamiliar to them. It was a disturbing world of seafaring nomads who sometimes settled temporarily as poorly mannered foreigners in their ports of call. Geoffroy de Beaulieu tells us that when Saint Louis first boarded his ship he was saddened and surprised by the sailors' impious behavior.[37] He insisted that they attend the services and prayers that henceforth measured the time of their voyage. Naturally, these half-savages were hardly delighted with this demand. Saint Louis' reaction to them arose not only from surprise and inexperience but also from the Church's negative image of this marginalized group. Jacques de Vitry was a famous preacher who went to the Holy Land. He had been one of Saint Louis' companions in his youth. One of his sermons, or rather one of his outlines for an unpublished sermon, is addressed *ad marinarios* (to sailors and seamen).[38] It took on the theme of Psalm 16, which speaks of the marvels and perils of the sea. He referred to the sea as the sea of this "century," in other words as the sea of human society and the terrestrial world. The sea was *tenebrosa* and *lubrica*, shadowy and sinful. It was ever changing, multi-formed, and multi-layered (*multiplex*).[39]

Jacques de Vitry was familiar with the sailors' language and used terms from their common language. He listed the sins and vices of sailors and seamen. Exaggeration often typifies these sermons, but the image here was exceptionally dark. This was the kind of literature that fed Saint Louis' perceptions.

What did the sailors do? Sometimes they abandoned pilgrims on islands where they robbed them or let them die of hunger. Or worse, sometimes they sold them as slaves to the Saracens. Sometimes they took advantage of their lack of experience at sea and sank their ships with pilgrims and merchants aboard before escaping on rowboats or fishing boats loaded with their treasure or merchandise. The examples of these sailors who robbed their passengers and sank their ships alluded to the real, near-legendary episode in medieval Christendom of Saint Paul's shipwreck. The sailors' vices in ports of call were also disturbing; they frequented taverns and brothels where they spent their ill-gotten gains on dubious pleasures. On the high seas, the king ran up against moral and physical dangers.

The sea was ultimately a religious and symbolic space for Saint Louis. The sea is a fairly common image throughout the Bible, and it is a terrible image, emerging as it does from the chaotic abyss at the beginning of time. When God created the world in Genesis, the sea appeared as a world of chaos, the dwelling place of demoniacal powers, monsters, and dead things that would be unleashed against God and men. Land became civilized; the sea stayed wild. In a different version of Genesis presented in the book of Job, there is another mention of the monsters that dwelled in the sea. Sometimes they left it, to the great horror of men. This is the specific case of Leviathan, where monstrous beasts and sea beasts confronted Daniel. These monsters returned to play a major role in the Apocalypse: "And I saw a beast rise up out of the sea, having seven heads and ten horns, and upon his horns ten crowns, and upon his heads the name of blasphemy" (Revelation 13:1). There is another threatening image of the sea in the New Testament: the Lake of Tiberias is identified with the sea. It was a storm-filled lake that physically and symbolically represented the sea.[40]

Fear of the sea, the ubiquitous storms and shipwrecks—Saint Louis could find them all in the Lives of the saints that he had heard about or read for himself. One particular example was the famous collection of the *Légende dorée,* a nearly contemporary book written and compiled by the Genoese Jacopo da Varazze (Jacques de Voragine). Mary Magdalene, Saint Maurice, and Saint Clement, among others, were the saints who typically protected or saved people from shipwrecks.

Although the sea was a world of fear, in the Middle Ages it was even more a world of fluctuation. The Church appeared within this world in the iconographical form of Saint Peter's boat. Powerful men were battered by the sea, if they were not swept away by the Wheel of Fortune. Saint Louis' actual boat was another incarnation of this same symbol, subject to the whims of the waves and adventures.

It was also a world where Jesus mastered the unfurled waves and walked on the water, while Saint Peter was in danger of drowning for his lack of faith. Ultimately, they need not fear the sea because God would destroy it at the end of the world, bringing peace and tranquility before Judgment and eternity. "And there was no more sea" (Revelation 21:1). "And there shall be no more death" (Revelation 21:4). The sea was death, as the formula implies. Isaiah had already said this: "In that day . . . he [Yahweh] shall slay the dragon that is in the sea" (Isaiah 27:1).

Yet the sea was also the space that led to the crusade, a space of trials and penitence but also of hope and desire, the hope of finding the Muslim rulers ready to convert at the end of the water route. This was Saint Louis' constant desire. The mirage of conversion influenced him in both Egypt and Tunis.

Saint Louis was also familiar with other more positive images of the sea transmitted in the biblical and Christian traditions. The first of these images presented the sea as a world of marvels. It was prevalent in the form of islands, islets of paradise, precious ruins of the golden age, and islands of good fortune. Christianity adopted this tradition from the ancient world and adapted it just as easily to the islands of the northern seas that Saint Brendan navigated as to the islands of the Atlantic that were beginning to arouse some interest, and the islands of the Mediterranean. Joinville's work presents two marvelous insular episodes that took place in the course of Saint Louis' maritime travels.[41] The first involved a stop on an island that was unnecessarily prolonged by a group of youths from one of the ships who lingered to gather fruit and failed to return to the ship. The second more important episode showed Saint Louis, Joinville, and several other lords when they disembarked on an island where they discovered flowers, grass, trees, and a very old hermitage holding human remains. Being Christians, this scene did not evoke the idea of the pagan golden age for them but an image of the primitive Church and the first Christian hermits who withdrew to live in nature and the marvelous solitude of an island. The sea was also a space of miracles, and Joinville tells us about the miracle that saved one of Saint Louis' companions when he fell into the sea.[42]

The sea, however, was first and foremost the path he chose and tried to master in order to reach the Orient.

THE ORIENT FOR SAINT LOUIS

The real Orient for Saint Louis began in Cyprus, that amazing platform for Latin Christendom in the heart of the Muslim and Byzantine eastern Mediterranean.[43] Cyprus was a hub for commerce with the Levant and an ad-

vanced base for Christian merchants and crusaders. After a period of political instability, the island came to be governed by the French family of
the Lusignan whom the pope released from its vassalage to the emperor in
1247. There were many noble families of French origin who had gone to
live there. Saint Louis discovered a little piece of France there, proving that
Christendom could be at home in the East.

What did the king know about the Orient as he stood on the verge
of landing in Egypt? The mainly oral accounts of the former crusaders
who had returned to the West marked the transition from "holy geography"
to "palestinography," to use Aryeh Grabois' wonderful expression.[44] However, this transition from biblical, paleo-Christian knowledge to a more
contemporary understanding of geography only applied to Christian Palestine. Although the descriptions became more precise, they continued to
focus primarily on Christian sites and monuments. Despite this limitation, Westerners acquired a better understanding of the Muslim population
thanks to the work of the Mendicant orders. For the most part they collected this knowledge in view of converting the native population to Christianity. Dominicans and Franciscans learned "Saracenish," in other words
Arabic. (Saint Louis once relied on the services of an Arabic-speaking Dominican.) Although the idea and the reality of crusading were changing rapidly in the thirteenth century, we can observe their evolution toward a
pacifist form inspired by Saint Francis after his voyage to the Holy Land.
Sometimes this was called the "spiritual crusade."[45] Saint Louis appeared at
the juncture between the traditional military crusade and the new spiritual
crusade.[46]

In matters of geographical knowledge, the ignorance of the king and
his entourage was still extensive. We have already seen this in our discussion
of the crusade of Tunis. Writing on the crusade of 1270, Mohamed Talbi
has stated, "The direction that Saint Louis chose for the crusade resulted
from a series of geographical (a false calculation of distances), strategic, eco-
logical, political, diplomatic, and human errors."[47]

SARACENS, BEDOUINS, AND ASSASSINS

One thing that thirteenth-century Christian Islamology learned was the
recently acquired distinction between "Saracens," the sole generic term
used up to this point, "Bedouins," and "Assassins." In Palestine, Saint Louis

learned how to identify the actual differences between these groups. Joinville provides us with valuable information about this experience.

For Saint Louis and Joinville, on the one hand the Saracens (whom Joinville also refers to as Turks) were the entire group of Muslims who followed Mohammed's law; they were nonetheless still identified as "pagans." On the other hand, this term also applied to the subjects of the rulers of the organized states they were confronting; in other words, the term also referred to Sunni Muslims.[48] Sunnism's return to prominence in the Middle East began under the Kurd Saladin when he overthrew the Fatimid Shiite dynasty of Cairo in 1171.

In 1250, Saint Louis and Joinville became better acquainted with the Bedouins in Egypt after a battle between Christians and Saracens. After the battle, Bedouins arrived on the scene to pillage the Saracen camp. Joinville was certainly more curious about this episode than Saint Louis. In seeking out information about the Bedouins, his intention was also to inform the king. He wrote a long digression about these looters who were different from the Saracens and less refined than them.

These pillagers were nomadic shepherds armed only with swords. They only attacked weaker parties and were not true warriors. They were fatalists who had no fear of death, believing that it came at a set time that did not even depend on God's will. They looked down on the Franks and their armor. When they scolded their children, they told them: "Curse you, like the Franks who arm themselves out of fear of death." Their faith made them formidable opponents; they followed the faith of Ali instead of Mohammed—which made them Shiites—and believed in metempsychosis like other barbarians. Joinville and the king could only react to this negatively. These Bedouins with their black beards and black hair and heads wrapped in some kind of towel [*touaille*] were "ugly and hideous." They were even more dangerous because they followed the Old Man of the Mountain [*le Vieux de la Montagne*], the leader of the Assassins.[49]

The Christian's experience of this diversity existing among peoples that they had been in the habit of lumping together as "Saracens" culminated in a number of contacts with the Assassins who followed the Old Man of the Mountain.[50]

The Assassins emerged from a group of Muslim partisans of Ali in the second half of the seventh century. This group had formed the sect of Ishmaelites, which had existed in secrecy for a long time. They awaited the return of the true imam and believed he existed anonymously in hiding. The Ishmaelite doctrine contained beliefs that strongly resembled certain millenarian Christian tendencies. In 909, the imam emerged from hiding and proclaimed himself caliph of North Africa under the title "al-Mahdi." He established the new dynasty of the Fatimids who ruled from Cairo in Egypt. As the Fatimid dynasty was falling into a period of decline in the eleventh century, the empire of the Seljuk Turks restored Sunnism to prominence. The Seljuk Empire's numerous malcontents rallied behind Ishmaelism, which was reorganized by a "revolutionary of genius," Hasan-i-Sabbàh. He was a native of Qum, one of the great Shiite centers in Iran, and set up operations in the Elbourz mountains in the fortress of Alamût in 1090. He stayed there until his death in 1124.[51]

There he founded an order of *fidâ'i* (the "devoted ones"), and they vowed to execute the imam's orders without hesitation. The imam was committed to establishing justice and the reign of Allah by assassinating anyone who represented a threat or an insult to his power.

The Ishmaelites in Syria formed an organized group and had varying relations with the Latin Christian principalities. The two groups sometimes formed alliances, but some Christian leaders also fell victim to the Ishmaelites. Their most remarkable Christian victim was Marquis Conrad Montferrat, the king of Jerusalem. They assassinated him at Tyre on April 28, 1192. Their greatest enemy was Saladin, and he escaped their attacks, although after 1176 he elected to live in a specially designed wooden tower protected by guards who refused to let any unknown person go anywhere near him.

Some people credited the Assassins with murders committed beyond the oriental outpost in Christendom. A paranoid fear of assassination swept through the West. Some people spread the rumor that Richard the Lion-Hearted had armed Conrad de Montferrat's assassins because his protégé Henri de Champagne coveted the throne and actually received it after Conrad's murder. Others claimed that the Assassins had secretly come into the West to kill Richard himself. People said the same thing about Philip Augustus several years later, and some said the same thing about Saint Louis. For the year 1236 in his *Life,* Guillaume de Nangis writes: "The devil, that shady despicable plotter whose nature is always to envy the best men, seeing King Louis' saintliness and success in governing his kingdom, began to prepare an unheard of and almost unavoidable threat to harm the king." Passed over for the devil, the Old Man of the Mountain began to plot the death of the king of France.

This vicious and evil king lived in nearly impregnable mountaintop fortresses inside the borders of Antioch and Damascus. Both the Saracens and Christians of the outlying regions and beyond feared him as his envoys had indiscriminately killed their leaders many times. He actually raised adolescents from the country in his palace to learn all languages and to swear him obedience unto death, which was supposed to guarantee them the pleasures of Paradise. He thus sent his emissaries to France with the order to kill Louis the king of France any way they could.

> Fortunately, God knows how to make his own plans prevail over those of human rulers, and changed the minds of the old king and his subjects, transforming his plans to kill into plans for peace. The old King sent other emissaries who were supposed to arrive before the first ones and warn the king.

This was what happened. The second group of envoys stopped the first and turned them over to the king of France. Delighted, Louis was said to have showered them all with gifts and sent royal presents to the Old Man of the Mountain as a sign of peace and friendship.[52]

This legend reveals the extent to which the image of the Assassins was present in the West at the end of the thirteenth and beginning of the fourteenth century.[53] It obviously originated as a prettified version of the episode of Saint Louis' real reception of an embassy from the Old Man of the Mountain, the leader of the Syrian Ishmaelites, at Acre.

Joinville's version of these meetings is worth reproducing here in its basic parts.

> When the king was staying in Acre, messengers from the Old Man of the Mountain came to see him. When the king returned from his mass, he summoned them to come before him. He seated them in the following way: there was an emir in front who was well dressed and well equipped, behind the emir was a bachelor who was also well armed with three knives in his hand and each one's blade slid into the sleeve of the next, because if the emir had been refused, he would have presented these three knives to the king as a challenge. Behind

the man who was holding the three knives, there was another who held a *bougran*[54] twisted around his arm, and he would have presented this to the king as well in an attempt to wrap him up in it if he had refused the Old Man of the Mountain's request.[55]

The emir presented the king with letters of credit and asked him to pay an annual tribute to the Old Man of the Mountain just as the emperor of Germany, the king of Hungary, and the sultan of Babylon had done so that he would let them live. To these veiled death threats they added that Louis must discontinue the tribute the Old Man of the Mountain had to pay to the Templars and the Hospitalers because he knew that if he were to assassinate their masters, they would be replaced with others who would be equally demanding. The king had the emir repeat this message in "Saracenish" in the presence of the two masters who summoned the emir to come see them the next day. When he returned, they told him that if the king's honor were not at stake—because they were official messengers—they would have him thrown into the sea. They added that he should come back in fifteen days with gifts for the king from the Old Man of the Mountain to help the king forget about the insulting threats they had made against him.

The messengers from the Old Man of the Mountain came back in two weeks. They brought the king a shirt from the Old Man of the Mountain. On his behalf, they told the king that because the shirt is closer to the body than any other article of clothing, this meant that the Old Man wanted to hold the king closer in his love than any other king. And he sent him his ring, which was made of very fine gold with his name written inside it. And he commanded that with this ring he was marrying the king, because from this point on he wanted them to be as one.

Among the other precious jewels he sent the king, he sent him an elephant made of very finely made crystal and a beast called a giraffe that was in crystal too. He sent apples made of various kinds of crystal and table games and chess sets. All of these things were ornamented with amber flowers, and the amber was attached to the crystal with beautiful images of good fine gold. And you should know that when the messengers opened the boxes that held these things, the whole room seemed to light up, as they glistened so well.

The king sent his messengers to the Old Man and sent him a multitude of jewels, scarlet cloths, golden cups, and silver bits, and he sent Friar Yves le Breton with the messengers because he knew how to speak Saracenish.[56]

Joinville then gives the details about the Old Man of the Mountain that Brother Yves reported to Louis, who was not entirely convinced of their truth.[57] Thus the knowledge that Saint Louis and his companions had about the diversity of the Muslim world in the Middle East grew more specific. They reacted in a manner that was typical of Christians, split between feelings of horror and admiration. Although their mission was horrifying, these terrorists who remained faithful to the death to the Old Man of the Mountain were still heroes who represented the sentiment that feudal Christians valued more than any other: faith and fidelity. The Orient seemed simultaneously marvelous and despicable to them.

The Mongol Illusion

During his stay in Palestine Saint Louis received another Asiatic embassy at Caesaria. This embassy came from much further away; it was a "Tartar" embassy, in other words an embassy from the Mongols. Was this the fulfillment of the king and all Christendom's hope to see the Great Khan convert to Christianity or at least to make an alliance with them against the Muslims? Until now, all hopes had been dashed.[58]

The papacy had been the first group in Christendom to express an interest in the Mongols. In 1245, Innocent IV sent three diplomatic missions in search of the Great Khan. Two Dominicans, André de Longjumeau—who would later become part of Saint Louis' inner circle—and Ascelin de Crémone, the aide to the French Dominican Simon de Saint-Quentin, left from the Holy Land. A Franciscan, Jean de Piano di Carpino (Plancarpin) left with Benoît de Pologne and set out across Bohemia, Poland, Kiev, and the lower Volga.[59]

Plancarpin managed to reach the Great Khan and actually attended Guyuk's enthronement. The others reached the courts of other important leaders. They all reported receiving the same reply, which, in Plancarpin's version goes: "You, at the head of all the kings together, come in person to offer your service and homage."

Saint Louis learned of these replies from the friars who also reported to him on their travels. He received Plancarpin in 1248. In his *Speculum historiale,* Vincent de Beauvais transcribed long passages from the travel narratives of Plancarpin and Simon de Saint-Quentin.

During his stay in Cyprus, Saint Louis was surprised to receive messengers from the "great king of the Tartars." His message contained "many good and honest words." The Mongol king also told him "that he was ready to help him conquer the Holy Land and deliver Jerusalem from the hands of the Saracens."[60] Saint Louis was delighted and immediately dispatched two Arabic-speaking preachers to Guyuk. (They imagined that the Mongols would be more familiar with Arabic than with Latin.) His messengers carried an immensely valuable scarlet tent shaped like a chapel with "images" inside that were supposed to illustrate the basic tenets of the Christian faith.

André de Longjumeau returned to Saint Louis' side in Caesaria in 1251. Mongol messengers came with him, but they always brought the same reply.

> And we order this thing from you in order to warn you: you can have no peace if you don't have it with us. And Preacher John rose up against us, and one king after another (and they proceeded to name a long list of them) and we put them all to the sword. Therefore, we order you to send us so much of your gold and silver every year in order to retain us as your friend. And if you do not do this, we will destroy you and your people just as we have done to all the people we have just named.

Saint Louis drew the sad conclusion from this exchange: "And know that the king strongly repented for ever having sent anyone to them."[61]

Saint Louis was not yet through with the Mongols. News reached him in 1249 that an important khan, Sartaq, one of Genghis Khan's descendants, had converted to Christianity and been baptized. Saint Louis sent another messenger, the Flemish Franciscan Guillaume de Rubrouck who was one of his subjects living in the Holy Land. He was not a titular ambassador because Saint Louis wanted to avoid any future rebuffs. However, he did carry a letter of congratulations from the king of France, which placed the Franciscan at his service. Rubrouck met with Sartaq who merely bore a seemingly Christian name. Sartaq sent Rubrouck to Möngke, the new Khan of khans in Karakorum, his capital in the heart of Mongolia. Rubrouck returned after encountering no more success than his predecessors. When he returned to Cyprus in 1255, Saint Louis had already gone back to France. Rubrouck sent him the account of his voyage, the most beautiful of all these travel narratives, a veritable chef-d'oeuvre.[62]

A potential turning point in Christian-Mongol relations finally came at the beginning of the 1260s. Harried more and more by the Muslims, the Christians of Acre sent an embassy to the new Great Khan Hülegü in 1260 and asked him to bring them peace and aid. Hülegü liberated Christian captives and promised to leave the Christians in peace and to restore the Kingdom of Jerusalem to them.

Saint Louis did not know anything about this when he received a letter that Hülegü wrote to him and translated into Latin in Maragha near the Lake of Ourmiah on April 10 in the year of the dog (1262). Hülegü's Hungarian ambassador carried the letter "to King Louis and all the rulers, dukes, counts, barons, knights, and other subjects of the Kingdom of France."[63]

After the reminder of the Great Khan's sovereignty over the entire world and the victories that he and his ancestors won over all the peoples who resisted them, Hülegü decorated himself with the title of "destroyer of the perfidious Saracen nations and benevolent champion of the Christian faith." He emphasized his good will toward the Christians in his empire and the regions where he had made war and announced the liberation of all Christians taken prisoner or held as slaves in the countries he had conquered. The beautiful scarlet tent brought by André de Longjumeau had been received in Karakorum with great satisfaction. However, the Mongols did not yet understand the hierarchy among the leaders in the Christian world. They still thought the pope was the single supreme leader. They only later learned that he was a spiritual leader and that the most powerful Christian king was the king of France, a friend. After capturing Aleppo and Damascus from the Mamelukes, Hülegü wanted to attack and destroy them in Egypt. He needed ships to do this, and he did not have any. He asked the king of France to provide them, the king who had to have learned by now of his promise to restore the Kingdom of Jerusalem to the Christians.

Louis and his council could only think about the letter's preamble and its mention of the Khan's suzerainty. Troubled by these claims, even if they were only theoretical, the king of France could not accept this offer. Saint Louis thanked the embassy and directed them to Rome where the papacy carried on negotiations with them for several years. These negotiations failed to produce an agreement.

Saint Louis let this opportunity slip away. Mongol space closed up for him.

THE MARVELOUS AND IMAGINARY ORIENT

Whatever valid objective knowledge Saint Louis acquired in Egypt and Palestine, he still did not give up his mythical, imaginary ideas about geography. This mythical geography lay at the center of the idea that Christians had about the Orient. Nothing demonstrates the persistence of the idea of a fabled Orient in their mind better than what Joinville writes about the Nile.

Here is the real Nile as Saint Louis and Joinville saw it, after the Greeks and Romans of the ancient world and after the Byzantines. It is presented as they saw it and heard about it from eyewitnesses in Lower Egypt:

> First of all, we have to talk about the river that flows through Egypt and the earthly Paradise. This river is different from all other rivers, because the more one moves upstream on other rivers, the more small rivers and streams enter into them, but on this river there are no other rivers that enter it upstream. Instead, it flows through a single channel all through Egypt until it divides into seven branches that spread out across Egypt.
>
> And around Saint Rémi's Day, the seven rivers flood the country and cover the plains, and when they retreat, all of the laborers go to work their lands with ploughs that have no wheels that they use to turn over the earth and sow wheat, barley, cumin, and rice, and this system works so well that no one would ever change it. And no one knows where these floodwaters come from other than God's will, and if this didn't happen, the country would have no goods at all because of the great heat that would burn everything because it never rains in this country. The river is always murky, and the people of the country who want to drink from it draw water from it in the evening and put four crushed almonds or beans in it, and the next day it is perfectly good for drinking.[64]

Then, as the description moves upriver, their geographical knowledge swerves wildly into the imaginary:

> Before the river enters Egypt, the people who are accustomed to doing so throw their nets into the river in the evening. When they come back in the morning, they find in their nets those goods people bring into the country to sell by the pound: ginger, rhubarb, aloe, and cinnamon. And people say that these things come from the earthly Paradise, because the wind batters the trees in Paradise just as it buffets the hardwood trees in the forests in these countries, and the merchants in this country sell us what falls from the trees into the river. The river's water is of such a nature that when we hang it up (in pots of white clay that they make in the country) on the cords of our pavilions, in the heat of the day it becomes as cold as water from a fountain.
>
> In the country they say that the sultan of Babylon tried many times to learn where the river came from, and he sent out people who took a kind of bread with them that they call biscuits because they are cooked twice, and they lived off this bread until they came back to the sultan. They reported that they had gone up the river and that they came to a large mound of pointed rocks that no one could climb. The river fell out of this hillside, and they had the impression that there was an abundance of trees on the mountain above them, and they said they had found marvels like many wild beasts and multi-formed beasts and lions and serpents and elephants that came to the top of the riverbank to look at them as they were going up the river.[65]

It is not hard to see the articulation of mythical thought in this amazing text. The mythology was bound up with the belief in the rivers of Paradise, biblical geography, rational doubts about traditional rumors, experimentation (the water suspended in special pots), and scientific exploration—a common preoccupation among the leaders of Muslim and Christian states. The sultan of Babylon sent explorers to carry out his experimental, scientific research on the sources of the river. Once again, we see how Saint Louis lived on the historical threshold between a form of knowledge rooted in myth and a desire for experimental knowledge. However, their attitude about the Nile was still characteristic of this science of marvels that saw no contradiction or separation between nature and myth or Egypt and Paradise. People could simply move from one to the other by going up the river. There may only be one place or natural phenomenon that acted as a border or dividing line between the two worlds, and this was the cataract, "this large mound of pointed rocks" from which the river fell.[66]

The Holy Land was the best place for a Christian to learn geography in the middle of the thirteenth century because it was the meeting place for Christians who came from all over the world.

Saint Louis received a Norwegian lord in Caesaria, and his horizon suddenly expanded to the lands of "white nights."

> So, let's get back to our subject and thus mention that while the king was fortifying Caesaria, Sir Alernard de Senaingnan arrived in the camp. He told us he had built his ship in the Kingdom of Norway, which is at the end of the world in the direction of the West, and that in the voyage he made to join the king he passed all the way around Spain and then had to pass through the straits of Morocco. He passed through many great perils before he could reach us. The king retained him, he, the tenth of knights [a leader in command of nine knights under him—Trans.]. And he told us that in the land of Norway the nights were so short in the summer that there were no nights when one couldn't see the light of the day that is ending at the same time as the light of the next day as it begins.

A certain Philippe de Toucy also arrived at Caesaria. He was related to and in the service of the Latin emperor of Constantinople who made an alliance with the Cumanians, a pagan Turkic people who were threatening Hungary.[67] This alliance was against the Orthodox Greek emperor who had fled to Nicea. Philippe de Toucy told Saint Louis about the Cumanians' barbarous customs including vows of fraternity sealed with blood and the butchering of a dog, and the burial of a dead rich knight in a ditch along with a living horse, a live servant, and a fortune in silver and gold.

Thus Saint Louis extended and peopled space with ideas that were always divided between fear and amazement. Giving thanks to God for this great diversity on earth that he desired or at least accepted, he learned to understand it in the only perspective he could call his own: the conversion of peoples to Christianity. His space was a world of conversion.

At the end of his life, he also wanted to go back to a continent he had neglected, Africa, in other words, North Africa.

As Guillaume de Chartres effectively put it: "He pushed his people to strive to think about propagating and multiplying the faith in these African regions."[68] Expanding the space of the Christian faith to Africa and mistaking the distance from Tunis to Egypt—there was the crusade to Tunis in a nutshell.

Saint Louis' space was partial and fragmented, but it was also unified by a sense of Christianity's universality and of the universality of the sovereignty of its God who was supposed to act in all places. This captivation by faith was even stronger in Saint Louis' experience of time.

SAINT LOUIS' EXPERIENCES OF TIME

In Louis' day and age, the measurement of time was still vague because the experience of duration was multiple and fragmented. The first mechanical clocks did not appear until the end of the thirteenth century. We seldom know people's dates of birth or even the birthdates of important figures; hence, we do not know their exact age either. The numbering of kings, princes, and members of other important families was still seldom used, and this leaves us with a fair number of uncertain identifications. Saint Louis was not called Louis IX in his own lifetime. It is only in Primat's chronicle—which he commissioned and which was finished shortly after his death in 1275—that the numbering of the kings of France was used for the first time in a systematic way. Days were still more clearly identified by the festival of the saint associated with each of them than by the number of the month. Saint Louis lived within a multiplicity of indefinite forms of time.

THE GOOD USE OF TIME

King Louis knew how to make good use of his land and of his kingdom. As a Christian and a king did he know how to make the best use of time? Time had many overlapping forms in the thirteenth century. It existed as the duration of a life or a reign, as the quotidian time of the irregular alternation of days and nights, or in the rhythm of clocks that attempted to impose a Christian order on time that lasted into the heart of night. There was the circular time of the liturgical year split up by a calendar that allowed Christians to relive the time of their Savior from Christmas to Easter and from Ascension Day to Pentecost, prolonged to the point when people awaited the return of the Advent. There was the linear time of the years of a life, a short segment on the path from the Creation to the creation of man to the incarnation of Jesus, inexorably leading to the end of time as it passed through the ultimate sieve of the Last Judgment to end in an infernal or heavenly eternity. There was the eschatological time of fear and waiting, hope and horror. This form of time was even more frightening for a king who was not only supposed to present himself as personally worthy of divine grace but who was also supposed to place the greatest number of his subjects in a position to be saved. There were the multiple times of an age and a society that had not yet unified time or its measurement in a single form. (Saint Louis' grandson, Philip the Fair, and the following kings gradually made more systematic use of the mechanical clock as an instrument permitting a better mastery of time, which they strove to place under the control of the monarchical state after the example of money. They imposed the time on the palace clock as a main point of reference in the new system for measuring time.) There was the natural time of work in the fields, which was essential in both the rural world and the urban world where communes and merchants set up clocks to regulate the time of work, the times for military expeditions in the warmer seasons or the semi-annual crusades, the times for the system of royal justice, the times for prayer and calling upon God, the times for eating, leisure, and chatting with family members or friends. There were also the long and radically varying times that it took for news to reach a king. In the Holy Land, Saint Louis only learned of his mother's death several months later.

Candles of varying or equal height were used to measure units of time. Clocks were used to divide the time in a Christian's day. Time was read on sundials in monasteries and castles. Like that of his contemporaries, Saint Louis' time was closely linked to nature and the daily experience of duration. The king thus learned to exercise patience in dealing with duration. There was the long time spent on paths on horseback that was subject to the roads, which were usually in poor condition. There was the immobilization of seafaring ships caused by long winters and capricious winds in which sailors still did not know how to navigate. There were long waits and great delays in transmitting news.

In retrospect, the one period of time that clearly seems to have been the most painfully long for Saint Louis was the time it took for the announcement of his mother's death to reach him.

The length of certain events in his own life surprised his contemporaries. First, there was the length of his reign, which lasted nearly forty-four years. Guillaume de Saint-Pathus highlights this fact at the beginning of his *Vie*: "The serene Saint Louis governed his Kingdom of France for a long space of time [*par l'espace de long temps*]." He benefited all the more for living so long without sin. His saintliness was saintliness over the long run. The other long stretch of time in his reign was the period he spent in the Orient. Joinville knew its duration all too well as a result of living through it with the king: "For a time as long as the space of six years I stayed in the Holy Land. . . ."[69]

CIRCULAR AND LITURGICAL TIME

Saint Louis' habitual time was the time of the liturgical calendar. It combined a daily cycle and an annual cycle. Guillaume de Saint-Pathus provides us with essential information about it in his chapter on the king's "fervent devotion."

> The saint king would very devoutly say his canonical hours with one of his chaplains at the desired times or he would say them a little before the hour but only a little [out of monastic respect for liturgical time]. And he would still have all the canonical hours ceremoniously sung at the designated times without having the hour moved up or only advancing it as little as possible by his chaplains and clerics, and he would listen to them very devoutly. . . . The saint king's custom toward the service of God was the following: the saint king would get out of bed at midnight and summon the clerics and chaplains, and then they would go into the chapel in the king's presence each night; and then they would sing the matins of the day aloud with accompaniment and then they would sing the matins of Notre-Dame, and during this time the saint king would say both matins in a low voice with one of his chaplains in this same chapel, and once they finished the matins, the chaplains would go back to

bed if they wanted to. A short time later, and sometimes it was so short that they did not have time to fall asleep before returning, he would call them to say the prime, and they would sing the prime out loud with an accompaniment in the chapel and the prime of Notre-Dame, the saint king saying both with one of his chaplains. In winter, however, prime was said before the break of day; after Easter, they would say matins before the break of day or shortly after. . . . And when prime was sung, the saint king would hear a first one every day for the dead, which was usually said without music, but for birthdays or if someone in his household had died, he would sing the mass with accompaniment. Every Monday the king would have the mass of the Angels sung aloud with accompaniment; each Tuesday it was the mass of the holy Virgin Mary, on Thursdays there was the mass for the Holy Spirit, every Friday the mass of the Cross, and each Saturday they sang the mass for Notre-Dame again. And in addition to these masses, he had the mass of the day sung aloud every day with accompaniment. During Lent he would hear three masses a day including one at noon or around noon. . . . At the dinner hour, before eating he would go into his chapel and the chaplains would say the terce and mid-day hours with music and the hours of Notre-Dame, but he would say these same hours softly with one of his chaplains. . . . . He would listen to vespers every day with music and would say them in a soft voice with a chaplain. After supper, the chaplains would enter his chapel and sing the compline out loud with the music of the day and the music of Notre-Dame. And when he was in his oratory the saint king would often kneel while someone sang the compline and he would spend this entire time in prayer. Every day when the compline of the mother of God was said, the chaplains would sing one of the antiphonies of Notre-Dame very solemnly in this same place to music. Sometimes they would sing the "*Salve regina*," and sometimes one of the others. After the saint went back to his room, then one of the priests would come to bring the holy water with which he would sprinkle the room while saying, "*Asperges me*," and the prayer that is supposed to follow it. And when the time came for the saint king to get into bed, he would say both complines with the chaplain.[70]

This was a program of monastic worship that advanced two particular forms of piety: piety for the dead and piety for the Virgin. His schedule was as well ordered as any monk's, although it was frequently disturbed or rearranged. There were four particular types of circumstances that introduced changes into this schedule, although Saint Louis struggled to limit them as much as possible.

The first of these situations, which arose quite often, was travel on horseback. The biographers, Guillaume de Saint-Pathus in particular, carefully noted the time spent riding and they must have been quite surprised by it. During these times, the king would cut back on his chapel and the number of masses he heard; however, several clerics from his chapel would accompany him and sing around him on horseback, while he said the chants and prayers in a soft voice with his chaplain or another priest.

Sickness was the second cause of disturbances in the order of worship. When he was sick Saint Louis followed the prayers and services from his bed and participated in the measure his condition allowed.

Another kind of disturbance in the schedule would occur when no chapel existed in the place the king was staying. In that case, his room was used instead, but this situation was rare because "there was a chapel in every place in the kingdom."

Last of all, there was the month he spent as a prisoner of the Muslims in Egypt with his Christian cook as the only companion from his entourage. He did what he could, and his jailers were so impressed with his devotion that they gave him a breviary they had found on the battlefield.

The king granted immense importance to times for exceptions that were marked by sadness and cutbacks in the schedule or by incredible joy. There were times for penitence and times for festivities. This was obviously the case for Lent.

> He would fast on Fridays for the entire year and abstained from eating meat and fat on Wednesdays. He wanted to do this on Mondays too, but they dissuaded him from it. He would fast on bread and water on the eve of the four great festivals of the Virgin, and also on Good Friday, on the eve of All Saints' Day, and for certain solemn days of the year. On the Fridays during Lent and Advent he would abstain from eating fish and fruit. Sometimes, however, with his confessor's permission he would eat only one kind of fish and one kind of fruit on those days.[71]

Similarly, we also know that he abstained from any carnal relations with his wife during Advent and all of Lent, on certain days of each week, on the eves and days of important festivals, and for several days preceding the days he was supposed to receive communion.

Mendicant piety was strongly influenced by theological and canonical casuistry. It deliberately prescribed a discipline of conduct based on the calendar. Thus Louis, who sought to reconcile his naturally joyful temperament with the old Christian taboo against laughter tempered with more liberal new attitudes,[72] was advised by his confessor to relieve his conscience by abstaining from laughter on Fridays.

Instead, he preferred the important festival days to be marked with a great liturgical solemnity made up of ornaments, candles, chants, the presence of bishops, all packed into an extremely long service that drew hushed murmurs from the crowd.[73]

He instituted ceremonious festivals in honor of the sacred relics in the Sainte-Chapelle. August 11 was the date of the festival for the Crown of Thorns, and September 30 was the festival date for the other relics. The precious shrines and reliquaries were carried in a procession for these occasions. A crowd of churchmen in silk copes sang in loud voices with the king himself, the magnates, and a crowd of people. Saint Louis wanted to be the stage director of a festive religious time. Easter was a similar occasion for great festivities.[74]

Guillaume de Saint-Pathus tells of the great solemnity with which he celebrated Saint Michael's Day on September 29. He reports how he went to celebrate it at Royaumont. He also celebrated the festival of Saint Denis there, the patron saint of the French royal dynasty, on October 19. On that day, accompanied by his oldest son, he placed the four gold bezants he owed in dues to the lord saint of the kingdom on the altar.

Holy Thursday was his day for washing the feet of the poor. Saint Louis held fast to this ritual of humility, and it also reinforced his Christlike image.[75]

Likewise, he attentively celebrated the great profane festivals that existed in the shadow of the religious festivals, though sanctioned by royal and aristocratic tradition. These festivities continued pagan traditions, readapted in christianized forms by the warrior class not entirely detached from its primitive savagery. The meeting with the king and queen of England, between sisters and brothers-in-law in 1254, took place at the time of the Christmas festivals. The dubbing of Louis' brothers Robert and Charles, of his son and successor Philip, and wedding of Philip and Isabelle of Aragon took place on Pentecost. Alphonse's wedding was held on Saint John's Day, June 24, a day with a rich history of folkloric traditions. Saint Louis accessed all the wealth of the inexhaustible Christian calendar.

However, with the exception of the great festivals and the modifications necessitated by travel or illness, Louis' daily schedule was usually regulated according to a rhythm that combined religious and bodily rhythms.

> The government of his land was arranged in such a way that he was able to hear his hours with accompanying chants every day and a mass of the Requiem without song, and, if there was a place for it, the mass of the day of the saint with song. He would rest in his bed every day after eating and when he had slept and rested, he would say the service for the dead on his own in his room with one of his chaplains before hearing vespers. In the evenings, he would listen to complines. . . .[76]

Saint Louis does not seem to have observed the kind of schedule typically reserved for the day of a king. The royal profession did not fix its temporal order until a regular court existed around the monarch and not until the execution of equally regular royal tasks absorbed the sovereign in their twofold system. Christine de Pisan described a typical royal day for the first time in the second half of the fourteenth century when she detailed the life of Charles V. While Saint Louis' religious biographers certainly had to highlight his quasi-monastic use of time, secular tasks intervened in this schedule. Thus, the duty of rendering justice, a sacred duty, found a regular place in the days of the king and his entourage.

We have seen how Hugh of Digne bolstered Louis in his daily responsibility toward justice.[77] However, Saint Louis was also preoccupied with the time of the long duration of history.

SAINT LOUIS AND HISTORICAL TIME

Saint Louis played a key role in two of the most important historical projects of the thirteenth century. He commissioned the Dominican Vincent de Beauvais[78] to write a historical encyclopedia, the *Speculum historiale* (Historical Mirror), and he entrusted Primat, the monk of Saint-Denis, with the French composition of the history of the kings of France based on the historical chronicles in Latin that were written or preserved at Saint-Denis and that made up the "*Roman aux rois.*"[79] He never saw this work completed after his death. Primat offered it to his son Philip III in 1275.

Primat ended his history at the death of Philip Augustus in 1223. Other chroniclers continued his "*roman*" afterward, whether at Saint-Denis or other locations. The section on Saint Louis was added after his canonization and was based on other sources, mainly Guillaume de Nangis. It does not teach us anything new about the saint king.

Primat's chronicle, however, written at Saint Louis' request, does reflect a conception of historical time that is largely the same as the one the king had during his life and reign.[80]

The chronicle's primary characteristic is that it is historical in the proper modern sense of the term. First of all, it relied on research dealing with sources. Primat writes: "This history shall be described according to the letter and the ordinance for the chronicles of the abbey of Saint-Denis in France, where the histories and facts of all the kings are written down, because we should look for and take the original history here, and if anything worthwhile for this work can be found in the chronicles of other churches, it can very well be added according to the pure truth of the letter." According to Bernard Guenée, in this research for a more "scientific" history, Primat did not directly appeal to Providence or the supernatural. Like the previous chroniclers, he certainly believed that "divine protection had never failed the kings of France." However, "he was bothered by the emphasis Suger and Rigord had constantly placed on the influence of God and the Devil." When Primat translated them, he omitted expressions like "the hand of God was with him," "the devil favoring him," "at the Devil's instigation," etc. Nevertheless, Primat did believe that history was first and foremost "a long lesson in morality" (Bernard Guenée), and when the opportunity arose he stressed the idea that "every ruler should adopt the example" of one historical figure or another. When it was documented and truthful, historical time was thus an instructive, exemplary time. This was what Saint Louis liked about it. Like the sermon or the Mirrors of the Princes, historiography was a genre that proved useful for the ruler. It made use of times past for the instruction and actions of the king.

Primat's *Histoire,* on the other hand, was royal and, more specifically, dynastic. He was the one who began to divide the periods of the history of the kings of France into three dynasties or "races," or, as he says, "generations." According to this statement, his history was also a "genealogy" of the kings of France. The French monarchy was clearly the Tree of Jesse that Suger had first represented in the famous stained-glass window at the royal abbey of Saint-Denis. It was a Tree of Jesse with three levels: the Merovingian, the Carolingian, and the Capetian. There had been a certain mishap in its growth. Hugh Capet was a "usurper." A new tree had to be grafted on to the one before it because in this French royal tree Charlemagne had been the major founder. Philip Augustus's marriage with one of Charlemagne's authentic descendants achieved the "return to the race of Charles," which definitively established the legitimacy of the Capetians as the continuing line of the French monarchy. Ever attentive to his position in this royal dynastic age, Saint Louis lived in this specific and essential historical time, and Primat revealed its construction.

Finally, as it developed through the working rhythm of Saint-Denis' historiographical action and the invention of a royal, dynastic time, the *"Roman des rois"* ended up producing a new kind of time forged by the abbey and the monarchy in their close alliance: the time of France. Arriving on the scene just after the time covered by Primat's *Histoire,* Saint Louis was the first king to be immersed within a national time. And, as he requested Primat to do when he commissioned the book, this national time was written in French.

Vincent de Beauvais' *Speculum historiale* was a universal chronicle that began with the Creation and biblical history. It then followed the succession of empires and emperors. It only really began to take an interest in the history of France with Louis VII and Philip Augustus, mentioning the restoration of the Capetian dynasty's direct tie to Charlemagne (*reditus regni ad stirpem Karoli*). It only began to give very specific information after 1244. Vincent de Beauvais mainly saw Saint Louis as a wise and sacred king who resembled David, the anointed king, and Solomon, the wise king. He presented him as the culminating point in the transfer of knowledge (*translatio studii*) that brought the sciences and the "arts" from Athens to Rome and from Rome to Paris. For him, Saint Louis embodied the form of "chivalry" that favored the "clergy," which Chrétien de Troyes had already presented as a social and ethical ideal more than a half-century earlier.

Serge Lusignan has made the pertinent observation that Saint Louis united two different forms of historical time in the texts of his hagiographers.[81] He embodied the time of two different lineages: the "human lineage" that he belonged to and that had existed since Adam and Eve, and the lineage of the *Franci* that was in his hands and the hands of his successors. The lineage of the *Franci* originated in Troy. Just as Saint Louis was born with his baptism at Poissy, this lineage was truly born out of Clovis's baptism. This logic extended even further in the sense that Saint Louis thought that as a very Christian king, *christianissimus,* the king of France not only had a special responsibility toward his French lineage but also toward the human lineage. This human lineage was supposed to be identified with the Christian lineage at the end of time, and the vocation of the Christian lineage was to unite all men and women who had existed since Adam and Eve.

From another point of view, the king of France was supposed to make his imprint on terrestrial time and on eschatological time in a responsible way.

Human beings master time on earth by dividing it into past, present, and future. This requires memory, attention, and foresight. This was what Vincent de Beauvais wrote in his role of pedagogue in the Mirror of the Princes addressed to Louis' son Philip, the *De eruditione filiorum nobilium.*[82] In particular, the king had to sustain the memory of the past and support the writing of history. He had to act in the present and predict and prepare for the future. This was the same program Saint Louis presented to his son in his *Enseignements.*

This earthly time, however, was itself placed inside a history that began and ended in God. Evicted from Paradise, man was supposed to occupy his present time with efforts to deserve returning there. Time on this earth was a time of penitence, trial, and patience; people needed to transform it into a time of salvation. The king of France had a specific duty in utilizing this time. Destined to occupy an eminent position by his Trojan origins in history, by his spiritual birth, and by the unction of his coronation, the king of France had acquired the ability to save others beginning with his own subjects—"may you be worthy of receiving the unction with which the kings of France are crowned." His eschatological mission was to lead his people to salvation, which explains his duty to abolish all impurities—"take great care to see that sins are repressed in your land: this includes villainous swearing, sins of the body, dice games, taverns, and other sins." This eschatological policy can also be read in the context of his reign's duration: the great turning point took shape after his return from the Orient when he definitively bound the present time at his disposal to a future oriented toward the time of joyful eternity, eternal salvation, and Paradise regained— "so that after this mortal life we may be able to come to Him for eternal life in the place where we will be able to see Him and endlessly love Him and praise Him." This was the horizon defined by the "Great Edict" of December 1254.

Claude Kappler has come forward with the hypothesis that Vincent de Beauvais may have seen Saint Louis as this king of the end of time. He bases this on the fact that Vincent de Beauvais followed a tradition extending back to the Merovingians that bestowed an eschatological mission upon the kings of France, a tradition that was expressed in its most profound sense by the epithet *christianissimus*. Could Louis IX have been the one king who was capable of synthesizing times and spaces, including the East and the West? And by virtue of this, could he have been the king who was likely to open the final phase of History and bring it to completion? I would not dare go so far. In any case, for Saint Louis himself, I have the impression that within his own personal time on earth he wanted to anchor the time of history on earth within the divine time that extended from the Creation to the Last Judgment and eternity, although without dissolving earthly time in celestial time before the right moment.[83] The scholarly historiography of Saint-Denis and the convent libraries was intended to preserve and develop the memory of this time on earth.

2

Words and Images

WORDS AND IMAGES WERE HIGHLY SIGNIFICANT IN A THIRTEENTH-century king's environment. Words were still almost always oral and spoken. We will listen to Saint Louis speak later on, but thanks to the considerable progress made by writing in this century we will naturally pay close attention to texts.

This was France's first "Great Century." The realm of art and images underwent an incredible flourishing throughout Christendom and especially in France under Saint Louis, as did literature, philosophy, and theology. This was the great period of the construction of the Gothic cathedrals with their stained-glass windows, of miniatures in the new style, scholastic theology at the University of Paris, the Arthurian novel in prose, the "High Writing of the Holy Grail" around 1240 (Saint Louis was twenty-six years old), the *Roman de Renart* and the *Roman de la Rose,* and the first great French lyrical poet, Rutebeuf, who mentioned the king (whom he disliked) in his poems.[1] What kind of relations did Saint Louis entertain with all these works and movements of ideas? There is a great temptation to associate this important time for culture and creativity in France with the most important king of medieval France who was their contemporary, as some historians have already done.

A king in the Middle Ages was supposed to please God and express his prestige by favoring and financing artistic and intellectual activity. Although man and society valued what was in the head and the heart and the soul more and more, appearances were just as important in the system of feudal values as in forming the modern monarchical state. In this society that engendered a world ordered by symbols, monuments and other artistic works were privileged signs. Did Saint Louis want to organize or submit to the expression and the meaning of these signs?

A King in Music

I would like to immediately express my regrets for the near total absence of music in this chapter due to my ignorance and the lack of in-depth synthetic and analytical studies on the subject.[2] Still, no civilization has ever existed without music, and the thirteenth century was an important one for music. Notre-Dame's important school of polyphony was born with the construction of the Gothic cathedral in 1165 and was honored by the illustrious name of Léonin. They carried on their tradition, especially in Paris. Léonin's most highly reputed disciple, Pérotin, was probably still alive under Saint Louis. Significantly, Île-de-France became a great musical center at the turn between the twelfth and thirteenth centuries[3]—at the same time Gothic art was born and at the same time Paris was becoming the capital of the Capetian kings. So, in a certain way, we can say that music was a royal art. Pérotin was an organist and composer of processional *conduits* (or *chants de conduite*) for several voices. This musical form broke with the "Gregorian" tradition. People call this polyphonic phase *ars antica* in opposition to the *ars nova* of the fourteenth century, but it was still fully innovative.

Saint Louis participated directly in this musical environment. Though modest, his relationship to music was no less real, close, and profound.

The king had mass and the canonical hours sung every day by his chaplains and clerics. The royal chapel that he had turned into a key institution[4] surrounded him with song day and night even when he was traveling:

> The saint king would get up at midnight and summon the priests and chaplains and then they would enter the chapel in the king's presence each night, and then they would sing the daily matins aloud and with music and then the matins of Notre-Dame . . . and even

when he was out riding he would have the canonical hours sung aloud and to music by his chaplains on horseback.[5]

The Sainte-Chapelle provided the environment of musical sacredness that the prestige of a medieval king required. More than any other monarch or ruler, Louis had a heart made for basking in this musical aura. His personal and royal life unfolded to music, a music he considered as a prayer and homage to God and also as an instrument for his individual pleasure and as an accompaniment transfiguring his royal function. He listened to the music but did not sing along with his chaplains, choosing instead to pray in spoken words.

On the other hand, the king did not really appreciate profane songs and did not like to hear them sung in his presence. In order to encourage his entourage to sing only religious songs, he sometimes sang them with them.[6]

> He would not sing worldly songs and could not stand to have the people of his household sing them. He once ordered one of his squires who would sing such songs in his youth to abstain from singing them and taught him the antiphonies of Notre-Dame and the hymn "*Ave Maria Stella*" because this was a very good thing to learn. And sometimes the saint king would himself sing these [religious songs] with this squire.[7]

Louis does not seem to have regularly kept minstrels around him. However, he sometimes felt obliged to make concessions for this profane music, especially when nobles had it played for him. Minstrels show up in a fragment of the royal accounts from 1234, recruited for the entertainment at the king's wedding in Sens. The king accepted listening to them on other less ceremonious occasions: "When the minstrels of wealthy men would come in with their lutes after meals, he would wait for the minstrel to finish his song before going to hear his blessings; then he would get up. . . ."[8]

ARCHITECTURE: A COURT STYLE?

A king of music, Saint Louis was also a king surrounded by monuments and images. It is too tempting and too easy to give in to flights of lyricism about Saint Louis and Gothic art. It is true that Saint Louis lived and acted when the great cathedrals were under construction, barely completed, not yet completed, or in phases of intensive rebuilding.

The cathedral of Chartres where he went to meet Henry III of England in 1254 was finally consecrated only in 1260. The cathedral of Amiens where he pronounced his famous "mise d'Amiens" was still uncompleted on its upper levels and in the canopy over the choir. Notre-Dame in Paris was basically finished in 1245, but had the two arms of its transept significantly lengthened with work that began around 1250. The inside of the abbey church at Saint-Denis is a masterpiece of early Gothic art of the previous century; it underwent significant modifications that began in 1231 and lasted until the reorganization of the royal necropolis at the center of the transept in 1262–1263. Saint Louis played a role in this restructuring. As for Reims, the cathedral used for the coronation ceremony, its construction began shortly before Saint Louis' accession to the throne and was completed only shortly after his death. Its construction unfolded over the king's entire reign.

Saint Louis financed and even ordered the construction of a large number of churches, but we cannot know if he played any role in designing them. We know nothing about his aesthetic tastes. He did not inspire any style or ideas in architecture as Suger, the abbot of Saint-Denis and all-powerful advisor to Louis VI and the young Louis VII had done in the first part of the twelfth century. Can we trust the later and, in my view, artificial testimony of Gilles Collona, the archbishop of Bourges, who states that when Saint Louis wanted to construct a building, he began by consulting with his friends, advisors, and officers who were supposed to discuss the project with him and help him to formulate it in a more precise way? He claims that these men would in turn communicate the plan to others including the architect who designed the work, the project's auxiliaries, and the people who acquired the land and took care of financing the construction.[9]

Joinville offered vague but admiring praise when he wrote: "Just as the writer who writes his book and has it illuminated with azure and gold, the king illuminated his kingdom with the beautiful abbeys he made and the large number of hospitals and convents for the Preachers and the Cordeliers and other religious orders."[10] However, in a "passionately partisan" book,[11] the outstanding art historian Robert Branner has argued that during Saint Louis' reign architecture in Paris "became a sophisticated art" that bore the mark of the king and his entourage. He characterizes this architecture as the "Court Style." This art developed after Saint Louis' return from the crusade in 1254, but it had taken shape before the crusade with a group of buildings in Île-de-France where the king had a regular presence. These buildings were the Cistercian abbey of Royaumont, the monastery of Saint-Denis, and, above all, the Sainte-Chapelle. This art expressed the wealth and prestige of the Kingdom of France and its ruler. The Englishman Matthew Paris was a witness to this when he saw Saint Louis as "the king of earthly kings, both because of his heavenly anointment and because of his military power and superiority."[12] Paris became an artistic capital at this time with the construction site of Notre-Dame and its artisans' workshops that produced luxury goods like illuminated manuscripts, ivories, embroidery, tapestries, liturgical jewelry and objects, cameos, and precious stones in the ancient style.

The king favored three other genres in addition to civil architecture: the military architecture at Aigues-Mortes and Jaffa, for example; the domestic architecture that appeared with the royal castle in Tours (which we only know through certain texts); and religious architecture. There does not seem to have been any master in charge of royal works. Louis used a number of different architects. In all likelihood, he usually financed the building's construction, which was then carried out by the beneficiary like the Cistercian abbot of Royaumont or the Benedictine abbot of Saint-Denis. However, as Louis was at home at Royaumont, he went with his brothers and oldest sons to help the monks transport the stones. Their assistance was at least symbolic. Saint-Denis was the royal abbey par excellence, and the Sainte-Chapelle was not just his private chapel but it was also the shrine for his most precious acquisition, the relics of Christ's Passion. It was the materialization of one of the more ardent places, the most ardent even, the place for his deepest worship. Although the king did not direct the architects himself, he certainly must have imparted to them that he wanted this place to be a marvel—and from its completion in 1248 to the eve of his departure on the crusade it seemed like a marvel to him, too.[13] During his visit to Paris in 1254, a somewhat special tourist named Henry III of England made it the main artistic attraction of his visit.[14]

Whatever Louis' part may have been in developing this architectural style, it formed a framework in which his personal image evolved in harmonious complicity. It was an art of "elegance and taste," as Robert Branner so effectively defines it. It was also an ascetic art: "Light and thin in the extreme, they mark the absolute victory of void over solid. Structurally each one is a spare skeleton from which the unnecessary parts have been removed. . . . And each is a speculation upon the nature of plane geometry, using the straight line, the circle, the arc, and the square. The Court Style did not innovate in the composition of ground plans or of volumes. In fact, it hardly innovated at all, but developed to an unusually high degree certain tendencies already latent in the architecture of the early thirteenth century. The most apparent are the co-ordination of surface effects and the dissolution of masses. The surface patterns seem to originate in the window tracery and to flow freely across triforium and dado, pier, portal and gable. . . . But for all their fineness of detail, the buildings are not devoid of monumentality."[15] This was like the appearance of Saint Louis himself with his "measured elegance." The name that art historians have given to this art, the radiant Gothic, is very much in harmony with the saint king's personality.

LESSONS IN IMAGES

I have finally given in to the temptation of discussing Saint Louis' relations with Gothic art in terms of a moral and aesthetic complicity. Can this be avoided when our search for a deeper relation between collective creations and an individual sensibility is limited to forms and appearances? Can we go beyond this notion of the existing environment without using texts?

Donna L. Sadler has tried to explain some of the iconographical programs that may have had Saint Louis as their author rather than their subject. She cannot prove that the king actually defined these programs personally and she is well aware of the fact that when she imagines Saint Louis walking around arm in arm with the architect Pierre de Montreuil discussing the aesthetic virtues of the façade of the transept of Notre-Dame-de-Paris just as Alexander the Great had done with Apelles or as Philip IV of Spain would later do with Velázquez, this is only a fantasy.[16] However, since she has uncovered the principles that inspired Saint Louis' conduct and politics in this iconography, and as she knows that like the clerics and other rulers of his time Saint Louis thought that images were programs for religious education and sometimes political manifestoes too, she has used these images to look for the different ways Saint Louis placed art in the service of politics. In effect, the works she examines are Mirrors of the Princes in the form of images.

This historian has already given us an interesting interpretation of the reverse side of the western façade of the cathedral of Reims, which was executed between roughly 1244 and 1250: "Christ's baptism appears here as an allusion to the baptism of Clovis and the royal unction. It contains a lesson for kings about the 'royal path' (*via regia*), which can be good or bad. Herod is representative of the bad king in this image, deaf to the warnings of John the Baptist and seduced by the diabolical Hérodias. David on one side and Melchizedek and Abraham on the other express what the relations between royalty and the Church are supposed to be. The knight's communion incarnates religion's investment in the warrior within the heart of a chivalry inspired by the Church and with the king at its head."[17]

She returns to this work to stress the importance Saint Louis attached to royal lineage.[18] Christ's lineage from David to the Virgin Mary was already presented on the portal. It represented the theme of the Tree of Jesse, which Suger had produced at Saint-Denis. Christ had said, "If you are the children of Abraham, go and carry out Abraham's works." This explains the vertical juxtaposition of Abraham's communion carried out by Melchizedek with Abraham's descendant Herod who, on the other hand, embodied the bad line of these kings.

Here is another example. Since the times of Louis VII, the king of France was identified as "the monarch at the end of time," and his coronation inaugurated his co-royalty with Christ that was supposed to culminate in the Last Judgment. The portal of the north transept of Reims is decorated with "an unusual Last Judgment [in which] the separation of the Elect and the Damned presents a king enthroned in the heavens and his royal alter ego leading the procession of the damned to the cauldron of Hell."

The representation of scenes of psychic and spiritual healing on the inside of the north portal, which gave access to the chapel where they brought the Holy Ampulla and through which Louis IX passed to go "touch" the scrofulous, may very well be an allusion to the fact that the king's healing power resulted from his anointment.

As for the stained-glass windows of the Sainte-Chapelle, they expose the king of France's role in the ongoing process of Redemption that extended from Genesis to the Apocalypse through Job, Christ, and Saint Louis, the king who acquired the relics of Christ's Passion. In these stained-glass windows, David was supposed to evoke Louis, and Esther's figure alluded to Blanche of Castile.[19]

Finally, the dynastic program articulated by the reorganization of the royal necropolis of Saint-Denis in 1262–1263 is interpreted as "the crowning achievement of Louis IX's desire to evoke the Christian kingdom on earth through the Capetian dynasty as the legitimate successor to the Merovingian and Carolingian dynasties."[20] These are all likely and ingenious hypotheses, although there are no texts to support them.

BOOKS OF IMAGES

The study of Saint Louis' relations to painting, in other words with illuminated manuscripts, is even more delicate. It is not simply a matter of being able to say whether Saint Louis commissioned these works, nor whether the existing miniatures correspond to the king's directions or intentions, but also of being able to determine whether they teach us anything about him. It is even impossible for us to respond to the basic question of whether the notion of the iconic environment in this case corresponded to the mere possession of the illuminated works, or whether the king looked at them regularly, or even whether or not he had ever seen them. We will have to accept the hypothesis that Saint Louis actually had looked at the works I am now going to discuss.

We have not yet reached the time when kings possessed a library that was not just personal but dynastic and that they passed on to their heirs. This monarchical state institution did not take shape until the time of Charles V, a descendant of Saint Louis whose tastes corresponded to it. Nevertheless, Louis IX did own books and we have seen how much he was impressed by the Muslim emir's library, which inspired him to form a library of his own. His library was made up of the fundamental Christian religious works, notably the works of the Church Fathers. He honored visitors or members of his entourage by lending his books to them and he also lent books to people he thought were in need of a more solid religious formation.[21] These works did not contain any images though.

The king also possessed luxurious illuminated manuscripts as powerful laymen had for a long time, though now more frequently. Precious books were written on high-quality parchment in beautiful handwriting. They were magnificently bound and richly illuminated with rubrics, in other words with titles in red, with colored or historiated initials, or, even better, with miniatures. A French king in the thirteenth century would have been extremely sensitive to the importance of possessing these immensely prestigious books because their exceptional quality imparted an imperial character. In a century when the kings of France from Philip Augustus to Philip the Fair claimed to have the status of emperor,[22] the possession of these magnificently illuminated books fell within the nexus between art and politics.

Of all the available works that appealed to laymen, the most important one was the Psalter, the book of Psalms from the Old Testament. It was even more sought after than the Bible. This was the text that school-children and the children of noble families used to learn how to read. As adults, the richest and most powerful individuals possessed their own personal Psalter that they could use as a kind of breviary and that they read more or less regularly depending on the intensity of their devotion. High-ranking secular women sometimes commissioned and possessed Psalters, too. This was the case for one woman of illustrious rank who has since been identified as Blanche of Castile. It was also the case for Philip Augustus's second wife, Ingeburg of Denmark, who had been cast aside and confined to a monastery by Louis' grandfather on the day after her wedding ceremony.[23] In the course of the thirteenth century, women of this class gradually replaced the Psalter with the Book of Hours as the book of worship to keep at their bedsides. This occurred under the influence of the spread of the Marian cult. One of the first richly illuminated Books of Hours was made for Saint Louis' daughter Isabelle. It was probably made for her wedding with Thibaud, count of Champagne and king of Navarre, in 1258.[24]

We do know that Saint Louis possessed a Psalter said to have belonged to his mother, and that he had at least two Psalters produced for his personal use.

Ingeburg's Psalter had been made in a monastic workshop in the north of France. By the time Blanche of Castile ordered hers, their production had become centered in the Parisian workshops. During Louis' reign, Paris became the European capital for illuminated manuscripts.[25] Blanche of Castile's Psalter contains a calendar with twenty-four medallions that represent the positions of the months and the signs of the zodiac.[26] The decoration is made up of twenty-two full-length miniatures on gold backgrounds, seventeen of which are shaped as two superimposed round medallions with thirty-nine small paintings in all.[27] The rather remarkable first miniature represents an astronomer holding an astrolabe in his hand as he stands between a copyist and a counter. The corpus of the other miniatures extends from the fall of the rebel angels to the creation of Eve, and from the original Fall to the Resurrection and the Last Judgment. It is an outstanding representation of Christian historical time in its thought, program, and materialization.[28] Finally, there are ten historiated initials on a golden background that decorate the text of the Psalms. Most of them represent David, a royal theme par excellence.

Louis did not collect manuscripts. He did not have any preferred artist or workshop.[29] The earliest Psalter to bear his name was the one he used to learn how to read.[30] A note dating from the fourteenth century confirms this: "This Psalter belonged to His Royal Highness Saint Louis who was king of France, and he learned in it when he was a child." It was made in England at the beginning of the thirteenth century and was acquired by Saint Louis' father, the future Louis VIII. In addition to a calendar, it contains twenty-three full-page miniatures representing the Creation and the Fall, the sacrifice of Abel and Cain, the murder of Abel, Noah's ark, the stories of Abraham and Samson, and the life of Christ from the Annunciation to Pentecost. In relation to Blanche of Castile's Psalter, it presents no eschatological perspective, omitting the fall of the rebellious angels, the Antichrist, and the Last Judgment.

The second more famous Psalter contains a note from the fourteenth century. "This Psalter belonged to Saint Louis." The calendar gives the anniversaries of the deaths of Philip Augustus (July 14, 1223), Louis VIII (November 8, 1226), Robert d'Artois (February 9, 1250), and Blanche of Castile (November 27, 1252).[31] The rest of the manuscript includes seventy-eight full-page miniatures that are together considered the masterwork of thirteenth-century Parisian illumination. They also contain an explanatory legend. The architectural components of the miniatures "faithfully reproduce the arcatures, the curves, and the roses of the Sainte-Chapelle. It seems certain that we can recognize the directives of Saint Louis' architect here, Pierre de Montreuil, and perhaps even the king's personal action."[32] The book was made for use in the Sainte-Chapelle.

The scenes in this Psalter were all taken from the Old Testament from the sacrifice of Abel and Cain to Saul's anointment. The idea of the providential mission confided to royalty through the anointment of the coronation is predominant here.

A significant number of military scenes also appear in this manuscript. Harvey Stahl has already highlighted their importance in his study of the miniatures in another illuminated manuscript of the Old Testament preserved at the Pierpont Morgan Library in New York (M 638) dating from the 1240s, probably just before Saint Louis' departure for his first crusade. Stahl demonstrates that the illustrations in this manuscript "mark an important change in the history of the illustration of the Old Testament." Before the thirteenth century, its illustration was done "in relation to the biblical texts and typological programs that made the Old and New Testaments respond to one another." With this manuscript, the Old Testament becomes a "history"—"in other words a long, continuous narrative chronicle rich in picturesque details, showing continuous action, and with no apparent Christological or typological significations."[33]

This iconological turning point was part of an essential mental and cultural development that took place in the thirteenth century, and Saint Louis played a role in it. I am talking about the triumph and promotion of narrative. Based on the model of the characters from the Old Testament and the life of Christ, individual lives assumed a primordial historical form in history and artistic and literary creation. For instance, Gérard de Frachet wrote his lives of the Dominicans to execute the decision of the general chapter of the order of Paris in 1256.[34] The Mendicants were in the vanguard here again. Beyond the traditional model for the lives of saints from hagiography, the idea of a life as a chronicle continued to spread among the people of the time. Saint Louis thought of his existence as a life history, and his contemporaries saw him from this point of view. This blossoming of a new conception of biography also offered the most profound justification for writing Saint Louis' biography.

On the other hand, the importance granted to battle scenes and the realistic depiction of the armaments (weapons, armor, war machines) found in Saint Louis' Psalter look like updated versions of Old Testament battles. This development must have taken place due to the interest people had in the struggle between Christians and Saracens as they imagined it existed even before Saint Louis' crusade. The crusade probably benefited from this interest; it was more popular than the growing but still minor opposition might lead us to believe. Here, we find ourselves in the midst of an environment forged by icons.

Another manuscript puts us in this same position, although we know for certain that the king did not commission it and almost certainly never even saw it. I am talking about the liturgical text for the coronations of the kings of France produced around 1250 and therefore known as the *ordo* of 1250. Its outstanding characteristics come from its illustrations: it contains eighteen miniatures that form a kind of film of the coronation ceremony. This document was probably written for the bishop of Châlons-sur-Marne, the suffragant to the archbishop of Reims and the main ecclesiastical figure presiding over the coronation.[35]

This illustrated account of the ceremony emphasizes the importance of the Holy Ampulla, thereby stressing the unique and marvelous character of the anointment of the king of France. It also highlights the presence of the royal emblems, the irreplaceable quality of this ceremony as a rite of passage for the king of France, the honorific role of the peers of France, and the subtle balance between the Church and royalty that characterized Saint Louis' politics as well as the relations between sacerdotal power and royal power in the middle of the thirteenth century.[36]

These miniatures do not describe a specific coronation, and there are no names to place with the characters, beginning with the anonymous king that appears in them. However, even if only in a very limited way, they do reinforce and diffuse the image Saint Louis wanted to give of the king of France, the image of a sacred king. These scenes from the coronation had never been put into images before, and they would not be again until the *ordo* of Charles V in 1364, which represents the identity of this descendant of Saint Louis in a realistic portrait. These miniatures illustrate the relations between art and politics in a new way. More specifically, they show how much Saint Louis strengthened the sacred character of the French monarchy and its expression, if not the "royal religion" itself.[37]

The King and His Intellectuals

Saint Louis also lived in an outstanding intellectual environment. The thirteenth century was a period of burgeoning growth for the faculties of art and theology at the University of Paris. It was also the time of the great intellectual renewal sparked by the new Mendicant orders and especially the two most important. The Dominicans were called "Jacobins" in Paris because of the site of their convent on the pilgrim's road to Compostelle. Their program for study was developed by their founder Saint Dominic who died in 1221. The Franciscans or Cordeliers finally found their niche in the advanced study of theology, a discipline their founder Saint Francis of Assisi (who died in 1226, the year of Louis' accession to the throne) had disdained for almost all his life.

If we want to get beyond the legends and hollow formulas about the "century of Saint Louis" and the purely rhetorical associations made between the saint king, the prestigious University of Paris, and the great intellectuals who taught there, we must first recognize that Saint Louis frequented only two of the reputed masters of his time. They were not even masters of the highest order. These two men were the Parisian canon Robert de Sorbon and the Dominican Vincent de Beauvais.

Robert de Sorbon was born in the Ardennes in 1201 and died in Paris in 1274. His work has never been published in its entirety and has not yet been thoroughly studied.[38] It is obvious that his sermons made up the bulk of his work, which must have pleased this impassioned fan of preaching known as Saint Louis. We are familiar with the canon and have a fairly strong impression of his character because Joinville spoke about him with his usual vivacity in several passages of his *Histoire de Saint Louis*. Both of them had close contact with the king, often at the same time. As they appear in Joinville's work, they seem to have been a classic example of one of those inseparable pairs of very different friends—the old cleric and the young knight—always at loggerheads and always envious of one another in their desire to be their saintly royal companion's preferred friend yet still closely bound by mutual esteem and affection. Saint Louis found amusement (in a nice way?) in provoking their squabbles and doubts as to which of them he truly preferred as a friend.

As a knight, a noble, and a seneschal, Joinville was not afraid to remind Robert de Sorbon of his modest peasant origins. He referred to them openly in front of the king: "You, who are the son of a peasant [*vilain*] and a peasant's wife [*vilaine*]." He also upbraided him for dressing too elegantly in relation to his obscure birth. Robert de Sorbon was an example of the social climbing that a high level of study made possible. The new university created fortune and fame for those who figured out how to take advantage of the clerical status of the scholars and come away with a few good prebends. A preacher in Robert's region probably noticed him and provided assistance to help him continue with his studies. After that, he probably received some kind of fellowship or stipend to attend the University of Paris. He never forgot his difficult youth and his social advancement, which was rather exceptional and lucky in spite of everything. He founded a college for poor masters of the arts who were students in theology. Because his college took his name, which wound up designating the entire faculty of theology and the whole university, Robert has become nearly as well known in history as his royal friend. He was the founder of the Sorbonne. However, he was only able to do this thanks to his friend's support because Saint Louis had in fact been the co-founder of the Sorbonne along with him. They were an amazing pair.

After receiving his *maîtrise ès arts* and then his masters in theology in Paris, Robert became canon of Cambrai and then canon of Paris in 1258. He was especially known as a great master of theology holding school in Paris. One rather generous source indicates that he was considered one of the most illustrious masters at the University along with Thomas Aquinas, Bonaventure, and Gérard d'Abbeville. Posterity has knocked him down a few notches from this prestigious position, but may have taken him down too far. Since that time, he has been completely overshadowed by the institution he founded as it became more and more famous.

According to some, he was one of the king's confessors, and this would explain his familiarity with the king and probable influence on him. He was a man of conscience, like Saint Louis.[39] Among his short treatises are some manuals that are "models for the examination of conscience," according to Nicole Bériou. Here is a man who was useful to Saint Louis, a man who could help him prepare his salvation, which was much more important to the king than any scholarly high theology. Moreover, the good canon "was enraged by the infatuation certain clerics had with the study of the stars and metaphysics or the subtleties of speculative theology." He was interested in Aristotle, the fashionable favorite of masters and students, but he quoted him much less often than Seneca or Cato. He was a late product and disciple of the twelfth-century Renaissance. He had a great love for the pastorals and an even greater love of charity. Although he belonged to the ordinary clergy, he had a fair amount of sympathy for the Mendicant friars and their spirit of penitence and humility. For instance, he admired them for walking barefoot all the time.

There is nothing surprising about the fact that Saint Louis liked him, although, as he did with Joinville, he kept a certain distance from him that was sustained by humor without being haughty.[40]

Nevertheless, the "intellectual" who was closest to Saint Louis, the one who undertook an intellectual, scientific work through dialogue with him, a work that was probably carried out at his request, was the Dominican Vincent de Beauvais.[41] Born in Beauvais in 1190, Vincent studied in Paris toward the end of the reign of Philip Augustus. He most certainly joined the Dominicans shortly after their move to the convent of Saint-Jacques in 1218. He probably took part in the foundation of a convent of the Preachers at Beauvais in 1225, and became the sub-prior there. Radulfus was probably one of the first abbots of the new Cistercian abbey of Royaumont in the diocese of Beauvais, which Saint Louis founded and often visited. It was through his intermediary that Vincent met Saint Louis at some time between 1243 and 1245. Then Vincent was summoned to Royaumont to be a *lecteur* (instructor) in 1246.

An Encyclopedist in the Service of the King: Vincent de Beauvais

The king commissioned an encyclopedia from him or took an interest in the encyclopedia he had already begun writing. This is exactly the kind of work that Saint Louis would fall in love with—a summary of the knowledge that a *prud'homme* required, not a work of high theology like the surveys of the great contemporary university scholars, Alexandre de Halès, Guillaume d'Auvergne, the bishop of Paris from 1228 to 1249, who had nevertheless been his friend and advisor, or Thomas Aquinas. The thirteenth century was not only the great century of theology but it was also a century of intellectual innovation. It was also a great century of encyclopedic knowledge[42] as it took stock of the enormous mass of facts and ideas produced during the two previous centuries and especially by the creative and turbulent twelfth century.[43] After its own spirit, its desire was to catalog, order, and classify this new knowledge. The thirteenth century was a century of categorization and classifications in every field of knowledge—scientific and technological, intellectual, social, political, and religious. It was a century of organizing and organizations involving the universities, the corporations, the legal codes, council proceedings, the *ordonnances* (edicts)—the word itself is revealing in its dual sense of "ordering" [*ordonner*]—encyclopedias, and surveys. Louis was a man of his own time in this domain too because he was profoundly imbued with the importance of order. Justice and peace were principles and virtues of order.[44] Furthermore, according to what he saw and by virtue of his own experience, he observed that Christians often ran into difficulties in the field of knowledge when they were debated and contradicted by heretics, Muslims, and Jews. Vincent's encyclopedia was to be an arsenal of knowledge, ideas, and debating weapons for Christians and the king.

Vincent de Beauvais was only a middling intellectual. There were not only "great intellectuals" among the thirteenth-century Dominicans. He was also strongly influenced by the Cistercians, especially in the field of history where Hélinand de Froidmont's chronicle served him as a model and a source. Vincent composed his encyclopedia, the *Speculum maius* (Great Mirror[45]), by following at least two successive outlines. He divided the work into three main parts: the *Mirror of Nature* (*Speculum naturale*), the *Mirror of Sciences* (*Speculum doctrinale*), and the *Mirror of History* (*Speculum historiale*). The work was a compilation recording vast materials and areas of knowledge. In fact, the work was so extensive that Vincent had to be helped by two teams of workers, one composed of Cistercians at Royaumont and the other of Dominicans at the convent of Saint-Jacques in Paris. Saint Louis actually helped him assemble a library for all of the documentation.[46]

The Great Mirror was retouched by Vincent de Beauvais several times, and historians suppose that several of these revisions in the *Speculum historiale* were inspired or even requested by Saint Louis because the king was extremely interested in history and wanted the history of the Capetian dynasty to appear in a more favorable light.

Saint Louis may have been an occasional student of Vincent de Beauvais' at Royaumont. At the beginning of the *Liber consolatorius*, composed for the king on the occasion of the death of his oldest son in 1260, Vincent writes: "When I was living in the monastery of Royaumont exercising the function of reader [*lecteur*], you humbly listened to the words from my mouth with respect for God and divine speech."[47] Guillaume de Saint-Pathus also writes, "When a master of divinity [theology] was reading the Psalter in the abbey of Royaumont when the king was there, when he heard the bell that they would ring when the monks had to gather to go to their schools [to go listen to their lessons], sometimes he would go into the school and sit down among the monks, like a monk at the feet of the master who was reading [who was giving the lesson], and he would listen attentively, and the saint king acted this way several times."[48]

Vincent de Beauvais possessed the culture of a twelfth-century cleric. He was a tributary of the twelfth-century Renaissance, like Saint Louis himself. Serge Lusignan has demonstrated this for the field of logic,[49] and Jacqueline Hamesse has shown it in philosophy.[50] In the conclusion to her minute study of the *Speculum doctrinale,* Hamesse concludes that in the field of ethics, the first section of practical philosophy, Aristotle "is only one source among others, and we can see that he is one of the least cited authors." Like Saint Louis, Vincent belonged to the pre-Aristotelean phase of the thirteenth century. Even more specifically: "From a philosophical point of view, Vincent de Beauvais cannot at all be situated in the scholastic line of his period. For him, morality does not comprise a philosophical discipline but rather one of the arts, a component of the knowledge of the twelfth century. . . . Vincent is much more of a disciple of the twelfth-century school than a product of the thirteenth-century University."[51] Moreover, again like Saint Louis, his imperviousness to contemporary intellectual history is astonishing, and yet his history is brilliant and moving: "There is no discernible philosophical evolution through the different sections of the *Speculum.* Despite the impassioned current affairs at the University of Paris, Vincent de Beauvais does not revise his manuscript in response to any events."[52]

Vincent de Beauvais also published several treatises and a few short works including several dedicated to Saint Louis or his entourage. Following the tradition of the genre, he wrote a consolatory epistle for him when his oldest son died in 1260, the *Liber consolatorius pro morte amici.*[53] I have already discussed the *De morali principis institutione* dedicated to the king and his son-in-law Thibaud de Navarre and the *De eruditione filiorum nobilium* offered to Queen Marguerite.[54] I remind my readers that certain historians think that these two Mirrors of the Princes were pieces he intended to insert later into a more complete work that would have formed a kind of "Political Mirror" as a follow-up to the *Speculum maius;* they think it was meant to be an *Opus universale de statu principis* (Universal Treatise on the Royal State) that would have comprised a great Mirror of the French Princes of the thirteenth century. Vincent supposedly announced his never-completed project in his prologue to the *De eruditione filiorum nobilium* when he declared that for the love of "his most illustrious Royal Highness our king," he wanted to compose "an *Opus universale* on the state of the prince and all the court or royal family, on the public administration, and the government of the entire kingdom."

Did Saint Louis actually commission or inspire this grandiose project? We really do not know. However, Vincent de Beauvais does not seem to have been up to such a lofty task.[55]

Vincent left Royaumont shortly before 1259 and returned to the convent of Saint-Jacques in Paris, which allowed him to continue his relations with the king. He died there in 1264.

THE NEW SOLOMON

Just like Vincent de Beauvais, Saint Louis knew nothing about the "impassioned current affairs at the University of Paris" in the thirteenth century.[56] The story that claims he invited Thomas Aquinas to his dinner table sounds like it almost certainly has to be a legend.[57] And, although he invited Saint Bonaventure to his court, it was to preach pastoral sermons.[58] Of course, we have to mention another great thirteenth-century cleric here: Eudes de Châteauroux, the former chancellor of the Church of Paris and master in theology who was made a cardinal by Innocent IV in 1244. As the pontifical legate for the preparations for his crusade, Eudes was in close contact with the king, accompanied him to Egypt, and wrote up a report on the crusade for the pope. Eudes' works are still not very well known, but they are now the objects of some important studies. He seems to have been a very famous preacher, so we are still dealing with sermons, the genre that interested Saint Louis the most.

I have presented the argument that one of the young king's first acts had been to push for the reconciliation between the monarchy and the University of Paris during the great strike of 1229–1231, and this despite the initial resistance of his mother.[59] If this were actually the case, it was because he understood the advantages for a Christian sovereign to have this source of knowledge and prestige in his capital. His two major interventions in the history of the University of Paris exhibited concerns that filled out this political vision.

As we have seen, the first intervention dealt with the quarrel between the ordinary masters and the Mendicant masters. Although the king carried out the measures demanded by Pope Alexander IV, he did this out of sympathy for the Mendicants and mainly because this was a church matter in which he only intervened as the secular arm of the Church. Guillaume de Saint-Amour was not his subject; he was the leader of the ordinary masters in the Empire, so the king also acted here because Saint-Amour's exile would restore peace to the University that Saint Louis held in the highest regard. By exiling Saint-Amour, he attracted the ire of other masters like Gérard d'Abbeville, one of the most famous theologians of the University in the final phase of his reign, and the hostility of other disciples or supporters of Saint-Amour, like the poet Rutebeuf.[60]

The second event that required Saint Louis' intervention was the foundation of a college by his friend Robert de Sorbon. He donated several houses in the Latin Quarter that belonged to him, in particular on the rue Coupe-Gueule. He also guaranteed support for several students. This gesture certainly proves the interest Saint Louis had in the study of theology, the crown jewel of the University of Paris, but it was primarily an act of charity, a gift made for good works, and an act of generosity for a friend.[61]

His intellectuals were these two mid-level talents, Robert de Sorbon and Vincent de Beauvais. He was not interested in high philosophical and theological speculation. The knowledge he wanted to acquire and see diffused was useful knowledge, knowledge useful for salvation. This preference privileged three genres: the sermon, the spiritual treatise, and the pedagogical treatise. In intellectual and literary terms, they were minor genres, although they did hold considerable importance in the medieval culture and mentality. Moreover, the clerics did not recognize him for any superior intellectual activity derived from reason, which they reserved for themselves.[62] Solomon was a wise man, but not an intellectual. Such was Saint Louis, the new Solomon.

Words and Gestures

The Prud'homme

The thirteenth century was a period when institutions, collective groups, and even individuals granted more and more importance to writing and when memory based on oral transmission retreated before the document fixed in writing.[1] Writing in particular became more and more of a tool of government. Since the reign of Philip Augustus, the monarchy carefully kept its archives, which never stopped growing through the course of the century.[2] With this new power, the knowledge embodied by the *studium* (the university) also continued to produce more writing. Students took notes and university scribes and booksellers reproduced courses and manuals through the system of the *pecia*.[3] Merchants began to rely more on written records.[4] After the examples of Roman law and canonical law, customary law was put in writing.[5]

Despite these advances in writing, the century also saw an important renewal of spoken language, a new form of speech.[6] A renewal of divine speech took place through the new spread of preaching honored by the

Mendicant orders.[7] There was a diffusion of the whispered speech of auricular confession imposed by the Fourth Lateran Council (1215), of prayer, and of reading that had not yet become completely silent.[8] Spaces for speaking were spreading with the churches of the Mendicants in the towns, the Parlement, and the nascent theater. The literary space of the period was ultimately a space of speech. Paul Zumthor sees the thirteenth century as the period of "the triumph of the spoken language."[9] He defines the "*dit*" in relation to the "*chant*" as "a lyricism of persuasion" in relation to the "lyricism of celebration." It arose "from demonstrative or deliberative discourse."

ROYAL SPEECH

Royal speech also took shape within this "general movement of speech."[10] In the two main traditions inherited by the medieval Christian king, spoken action comprised a characteristic or, better, a duty of the royal function. In the Indo-European system, the king's authority articulated by the Greek verb *krainein,* "to execute" (from *kara,* "head," "head signal") "is derived from the gesture with which the god gives existence to what would otherwise only be speech."[11] Royal authority "allows speech to become action."[12] In the Bible, Lemuel the king of Massa confirmed the effectiveness and responsibility embodied in the king's speech with unusual clarity when he repeated what his mother taught him: "Open thy mouth for the dumb in the cause of all such as are appointed to destruction. Open thy mouth, judge righteously, and plead the cause of the poor and needy" (Proverbs 31:8–9).

The Capetian kings more specifically inherited the idealized portraits of the Roman emperors as they were handed down by Suetonius and Aurelius Victor, the fourth-century author of *Liber de Caesaribus,* from which he drew the *Epitome of Caesaribus* that was well known and utilized in the Middle Ages. In his portrait of Robert the Pious written around 1033,[13] Helgaud de Fleury adopted this characteristic granted by speech with its conviviality and variations as an expression and bonding force of the royal group. He lifted it directly from Aurelius Victor's portrait of Pertinax who was described as very sociable and engaging his entourage in relations based on conversation, meals, and walks together [*communi se affatu, convivio, incessu predebat*]. Drawing an even more stereotyped portrait of Philip Augustus in his *Gesta Philippi Augusti* at the very end of the twelfth century, Rigord de Saint-Denis called him "*in sermone subtilis*" (subtle in conversation).[14] We can identify a traditional model here, and it is one Saint Louis carried out to near perfection.

SAINT LOUIS SPEAKS

Saint Louis was actually the first king to speak in the history of France. Of course, the idea here is not to "reassemble the fragments of what was spoken in the days of old, of this voice that has been silenced and whose echoes we cannot hear, only having access to the representation."[15] Nevertheless, Saint Louis' speech held an incredible fascination for his biographers and hagiographers. The words attributed to him obviously corresponded to the traditional code for the speech of saints. However, since sainthood was exposed to the strong influence of a highly personalized saint, Francis of Assisi, at the end of the thirteenth century the canonization inquiries also attempted to get close to the real saint,[16] the "true saint," in the chapters on his life and not the ones on miracles.[17] Joinville, the layman, had his work taken down in French, the language of the king, and tried so hard to stay close to the king in his own lifetime. In his narrative, Joinville reminds us better than anyone that we can be sure he "drank in" the king's words, all of them apparently taken down shortly after Louis' death and well before the composition of the fourteenth-century *Life*. They were recorded so well that we can often find the king's own *spoken* words here.[18] Joinville defined Queen Jean of Navarre's commission for the work as follows: "make a book of the saintly words and good deeds of our king Saint Louis." Following an old idea presented by Charles-Victor Langlois, we have thus been able to collect "Saint Louis' sayings" by determining that a corpus of texts from the thirteenth century (or the beginning of the fourteenth century) "brings us closer . . . to the never extinguished voice of Saint Louis [which] largely reflects the way he spoke."[19] Elsewhere, David O'Connell, the author of this collection, has been able to reconstitute the authentic, original version of Saint Louis' *Enseignements* for his son and daughter.[20]

Saint Louis' royal speech had its place within a tradition, and he notably reported some of the sayings of his grandfather, Philip Augustus. However, his speech was marked most of all by the characteristics of the thirteenth century, thus confirming Marc Bloch's statement that men resemble their own times more than their own fathers.

Saint Louis' speech was moral and instructive in the midst of this didactic and moralizing century. It was preachy in this age of predication and in the mouth of a king surrounded by preachers, mostly Dominicans and Franciscans. His speech preached by example at a time that the *exempla,* anecdotes inserted into sermons, were proliferating. It was devout after the new fashion, expressing itself in prayer and even more in confession. It dispensed justice as the king executed the highest royal duty — rendering justice through speech or delegating it to well-instructed and supervised representatives. Alongside justice, peace was the other great royal ideal and the king's speech was also pacifying, expressing itself in arbitrations and treaties. It was measured speech, moderate as befitting a king who valued self-control and who sought to replace the ideal of the valorous knight's excesses with that of the *prud'homme*'s moderation. At the same time, his speech enacted the repression of bad speech, of swearing and blasphemy.

Familiar Speech

Royal speech in its direct state was addressed mainly to a small group of familiar characters, the king's usual interlocutors invited by him to respond to him, although in the heart of this group Louis held the prerogative of speaking when he wanted. Royal conversation was the center, the place, and the function of this group, and it played a role in government that has been overlooked by historians. This group was different from the curia, the feudal body of the sovereign's advisors. It existed halfway between the king's intimate personal space and his public space. We are familiar with it mainly thanks to Joinville, and it was fairly heterogeneous in its make-up. We can identify three key moments of its existence in reading Joinville: the times when the biographer was with the king, the period between the two crusades, and the other times between 1254 and 1270. In this group, we find the pair formed by Joinville and Robert de Sorbon, the inseparable companions. There was Thibaud II, the young king of Navarre who was Saint Louis' son-in-law, and in the later years there was Philip, Saint Louis' son, the future Philip III. The group was also joined by a number of Mendicant friars, Saint Louis' religious favorites. When he mentions this group, Joinville writes "we" in referring to it, as he does in this example:

When we were there inside [in his court] in private, he would sit down at the foot of his bed, and when the Preachers and the Cordeliers who were there with him reminded him about a book he normally would have been happy to hear, he would tell them: "You won't read to me now, because there is no book good enough to serve as jest [*quolibet*] after dinner."[21]

The *quolibet* was a discussion *ad libitum,* a random conversation. The king actually meant: "Everyone here should feel free to say what he pleases."

Guillaume de Saint-Pathus defined this group of intimates as "honorable persons of worthy faith who conversed with him for long periods of time."[22] There was an intimacy [*conversatio*] here that was best expressed in conversation, in the modern sense of the word. Joinville was never so happy as when he reported royal speech that appeared to be addressed exclusively to him in a kind of aside.

He called on me once and told me: "I don't dare speak with you, as subtle as you are, about matters concerning God, and for this reason I have summoned these two friars here, because I want to ask you something." Here was his question: "Seneschal," he said, "what is God?" And I said to him: "Sire, it is a thing so good that there can be nothing better." "Truly," he said, "you have answered well, because the answer you have given is written down in this book that I am holding in my hand.

"So, I ask you," he said, "which would you like better, to be leprous or to have committed a mortal sin?" And I, who never lied to him, I replied that I would rather have committed thirty of them than be a leper. When the friars were gone, he called me aside and sat me down at his feet and said to me: "How could you have told me that yesterday?" And I answered that I would still say the same thing today. And he told me: "You were speaking like a fool who talks without thinking. . . ."[23]

The king's children formed a group for whom speech became even more intimate: "Before he would lay down in his bed, he would call his children in before him and tell them about the actions of good kings and emperors and would tell them that they should follow the examples of people like this."[24]

INSTRUCTIVE SPEECH

Enseigner (to teach, to instruct) or *enseignement* (teaching, instruction) was the word that popped into Joinville's head to refer to this didactic and moral speech. The king's speech closely resembled that of the Mendicant friars he surrounded himself with in that it was instructive and predicative.[25] Despite what his confessor Geoffroy de Beaulieu said about it, I do not believe he ever seriously considered becoming a Dominican or a Franciscan. However, he did make as much progress as a layman could in the kind of speech rendered simpler and more intimate by the Mendicant friars. He took advantage of his unique status as the exceptional layman that the king was in order to make royal speech more closely resemble the language of these new preachers who used speech to instruct others.

"I will tell you," Joinville says, "what I saw and heard of his saintly words and his good teachings."[26] Here was the preacher king who took bold steps into the realm of doctrine and even of theology: "The saint king tried with all his might using his words to get me to believe firmly in the Christian law that God gave us. . . ."[27] His passion for instructive speech never left him when he was traveling at sea, during the "passage," on the crusade, and on the return trip: "Next you will hear a lesson that he gave me at sea, when we were returning from overseas."[28]

He was able to give full rein to his propensity for instruction at the end of his life when he dictated or wrote down his *Enseignements* for his son Philip and his daughter Isabelle: "Dear son, I teach you. . . ." This expression recurs ten times in the text written for Philip. "Dear daughter, I teach you. . ." occurs less frequently in the text for Isabelle because the king was both more courteous—he used "*vous*" to address her[29]—and more direct in relation to his daughter. He commanded her to do things using the imperative: hear, listen, love, take care, obey, etc.[30]

A king during the age of the triumph of scholasticism at the University of Paris, he adopted a number of new methods from the university milieu, as many as someone who was not a clergy member and who had an intellectual level free of pretensions.[31] We have seen him encourage the free speech of the *quolibet*, no doubt in reference to the university *quodlibet*. He liked to organize "disputes" (*disputatio,* debates) between Joinville and Robert de Sorbon, based on the model of the university exercise with himself presiding as a "master" who would pronounce his conclusion:

"After we had argued for a long time, then he would render his sentence and say. . . ."[32]

Of all the new techniques for preaching, there was one Saint Louis practiced with a particular pleasure, the *exemplum*.[33] Saint Louis ornamented his conversation with *exempla*. Sometimes it was a recollection of his grandfather, Philip Augustus. In these cases, royal speech became a form of dynastic memory: "King Philip, my ancestor, told me that a king should compensate the members of his household by giving more to some and less to others, according to the value of their service; and he also said that no one could govern his land well if he did not also know how to harshly and boldly refuse what he was able to give." And then he draws the moral conclusion: "And these things . . . I am teaching you about them because our age is so avid when it comes to asking for things that there are few people who look to the salvation of their souls and the honor of their bodies as long as they can attract someone else's wealth to themselves, whether wrongly or rightly."[34]

THE GOVERNMENT OF SPEECH

A king of speech, a king who governed through speech, Saint Louis used speech to exercise two of the highest royal functions exalted by the Mirrors of the Princes: justice and peacemaking.

The king who dispensed justice questioned and rendered his own sentences in his famous "*plaids de la porte*" (door trials) in the palace, which were later called "*requêtes*" (petitions), as Joinville observes. Then there were the even more famous "*parties*" he had judged in his presence, seated against an oak tree in the woods of Vincennes: "And then he would ask them from his own mouth. . . . And then he would say to them. . . ."[35] Whenever necessary, his own speech intervened in place of the speech of those he had appointed to speak in his place: "And when he saw something that had to be changed in the speech of the people who were speaking for him or anyone else, he would amend it himself from his own mouth."[36]

The peace-making king rendered arbitrations in his own words. His speech reestablished peace not just in his kingdom but also in other parts of Christendom. When his advisors reproached him for failing to let foreigners go on fighting among themselves in order to weaken them to his own advantage, he reminded them of God's words, "Blessed are all those who make peace."[37]

WORDS OF FAITH

Saint Louis was also the king of the new form of devoutness, and the Mendicant friars were its propagandists. He was a king of both silent and spoken prayer, "from the mouth or in thought."[38] He never forgot this speech of prayer, whether set in one place or moving along the roads: "Even when he was riding, he would have his canonical hours said aloud with his chaplains singing on horseback."[39] He recommended the same spoken prayer to his son: "Say your prayers in a meditative state of mind, whether with your own mouth or in thought."[40] This recommendation preceded those he gave for other speech practices like conversation with small groups of friends: "Dear son, always seek out the company of good people, whether religious or laymen. . . . Speak freely with good people." He also recommended listening to preaching in public and private: "and gladly listen when they speak of Our Lord in sermons or in private."[41]

There was the speech of confession, this speech that departs from the mouth to alight in the preacher's ear. The Fourth Lateran Council in 1215 had made it obligatory for everyone at least once a year. Saint Louis practiced confession piously and assiduously, and his confessor Geoffroy de Beaulieu praised him for this. Saint Louis actively recommended confession to his son and daughter: "If you are troubled in your heart, tell it to your confessor or to someone else whom you can depend upon as a loyal man who can keep your secret, for thus you will have greater peace of mind, provided of course that it is something you can talk about."[42]

His speech was essentially truthful because he hated lies so much that he even refused to lie to the Saracens when he was their prisoner. He was praised for this during his canonization inquiry and in the pontifical bull for his canonization.

His intense love of truthful speech also made him hate bad speech and led him to severely repress "sins of language" after his return from the Holy Land.[43] He always avoided swearing, blasphemy, and any speech that referred to the devil. "I never heard him name the devil," Joinville declared, adding, "whose name is widespread throughout the kingdom, which, I believe, does not please God."[44] Saint Louis used violence to fight blasphemy:

The king loved God and his sweet Mother so much that he would severely punish anyone he could find who engaged in dishonest or villainous swearing against God or his Mother. Thus in Caesaria I once saw him put a jeweler [who had blasphemed] on top of a ladder in his shirt and undergarments with the guts and innards of a pig hung around his neck in such abundance that they came all the way up to his nose. Since I came back from overseas I also heard that he had had the nose and inner lip of a bourgeois of Paris burned for this [blasphemy], although I did not see it myself. And I remember that the saint king would say: "I would willingly be branded with a hot iron if all villainous swearing were removed from my kingdom."[45]

Toward the end of his life, Louis' aversion to "bad language" became even more intense. Pope Clement IV approved of this but attempted to moderate it—the punishment should not go so far as mutilation or the death penalty. One year before Louis' death, the edict of 1269 ordered for blasphemers to be punished with fines or the stocks or the whip.[46]

There is at least one other passage that mentioned Saint Louis' voice.[47] It is Joinville again who lets us hear it: "He used to say it was a bad thing to take someone else's property, 'because returning it was so difficult that merely pronouncing the words *to give back* [*rendre*] could burn one's throat with the two rr [*erres*] that are in the word and that signify the devil's rakes that always pull back anyone who wants to return someone else's goods'."[48] This text reminds us of the most important characteristic of Saint Louis' speech. He was the first king of France whose speech has been passed down to us, whom we can hear speaking in the vernacular language, in the French that he actually spoke.

We still have to discuss two characteristics of this royal speech. The first one bears the stamp of modernity. In contrast, the second expresses a certain affiliation between Saint Louis' speech and great medieval tradition.

The new characteristic is that this speech avoided the usual rhetoric of mentions of royal speech in the High Middle Ages. Saint Louis strove to keep his speech simple, and his biographers and hagiographers attempted to translate this simplicity derived from Mendicant spirituality and the ideal of self-control inherited from the humanism of the twelfth century. Joinville found the perfect word to describe it: "In his speech, he was *attrempez*," in other words, "a moderate one."[49]

LAST WORDS

At the very end of his life, however, traditional royal speech returned. This was what his hagiographers give us. They made Saint Louis say a variety of different things as he was dying. What Guillaume de Saint-Pathus reported about it corresponds to the basic details given by all the reports of Saint Louis' agony and death.

First of all, the king lost his ability to speak as death approached: "At the very end, he went for four days without speaking." He only used signs to express himself. This was the devil's final assault as he attempted to prevent the dying king's final confession, although he could do nothing against his internal resolve. Then, on the day before his death, he found the words to say: "O Jerusalem! O Jerusalem," returning to the eschatological speech of the crusaders. Finally, on the day of his death, he first pronounced the traditional words of a Christian king, recommending his people to God, words adapted to his army's situation on Saracen land: "Your magnificent Highness God, have mercy on these people who are here and lead them back to their country; do not let them fall into enemy hands and do not let them be forced to deny your Holy name."

And his last words were: "Father, I entrust my spirit to your protection," but "the holy king said these words in Latin."[50] At death's door, Louis abandoned his mother tongue in favor of the holy language, the language of the Fathers.

WELL-TEMPERED GESTURES

We know that actions and gestures form a kind of language in any society. Like all languages, gestures are codified and controlled by ideological and political authorities. At this stage in our inquiry, we have the impression that the Christian Church tried especially hard to do away with the pagan systems of gestures, especially in an area that was particularly odious to Christianity—the theater. The Church also tried to hold the most frightening expression of gesticulations in check—those of diabolical possession. Gestures were paganism's and Satan's privileged means of expression as they were always near the point of crossing the line to the side of evil and too closely tied to the body. Like dreams, this "abominable cloak of the soul" seemed suspicious and dangerous in the eyes of the Church during the first centuries of the Middle Ages. The words *gestus* that had been so common in ancient texts and *gesticulatio* disappear around this time. Either they were censored or else they took on partially new technical meanings, particularly in the field of music where Christianity utilized the body in order to submit it to the soul and forge the new man.[51] Starting with the fifth-century Christian rhetorician Martianus Capella, gestures were only considered "harmonious" and permissible when they were an integral part of the liturgy.

Beginning some time in the twelfth century, this repression gradually gave way before the notion of self-control, which first appeared in monastic regulations. Gestures had been absent from the monastic rules and customs of the High Middle Ages. However, they assumed an important position in one of the first texts of its genre, the *De institutione novitiorum* written by Hugh of Saint Victor in the first half of the twelfth century. They were part of the *disciplina* imposed on the novices and, with appropriate modifications, on clerics and laymen as a model for human society beyond the monastic milieu.[52]

Between the mid-twelfth and mid-thirteenth centuries, the normativity of gestures and the dividing line between licit and illicit gestures were defined by codes that regulated the new society. These codes had been emerging from the expansion and transformation of the Christian West since the year 1000. They consisted in ecclesiastical regulations perfected by the new orders and canonical law, monarchical legislation that applied to society in its entirety, and the codes of courtesy and gallantry that took shape among the secular elite. Even though there had always been censorship of gestures and disdain for the body, the Christian humanism that took shape mainly in the twelfth century henceforth demanded that Christians pursue their destiny in their earthly existence and in view of their eternal salvation with both "body and soul." The gestural code therefore not only had an ethical dimension but an eschatological dimension as well.

Saint Louis existed at the very heart and center of the network of these regulations in the thirteenth century. Along the path opened up by Hugh of Saint Victor, the new Mendicant orders defined the system of proper gestures. This notably occurred with Saint Bonaventure's *Regula novitiorum*, Humbert de Romans' *De officiis ordonis*, and Gilbert de Tournai's *Sermones ad status*.[53] The king took his own model from the monastic clergy, basing his own gestures on theirs. As we shall see, his hagiographers were never so precise in describing his gestures as when they show him in his practices of worship. Guillaume de Chartres, his Dominican chaplain, stressed that his conduct in his manners, actions, and *gestures* was not only that of a king but also that of the monastic clergy: "*Mores enim ejus, actus, et gestus, non solum regales, sed etiam regulares.*"[54]

Saint Louis' gestures, the gestures of a king, can be placed in the tradition of the Mirrors of the Princes and culminated in the gestures of the coronation and the healings carried out by the thaumaturgical kings. The two essential terms in this context are *signer* (to sign) because of the sign of the cross that the king made on the sick people and *toucher* (to touch) since the healing act required physical contact.[55]

Finally, these were the gestures of one of the most powerful laymen. Saint Louis became the model for the form that courtesy assumed in the thirteenth century. The valorous warrior became a *prud'homme*.

Where Should We Look for Saint Louis' Gestures?

Let us for just one moment consider the question of the possibility of attaining Saint Louis' reality. Some have doubted our ability to uncover the reality of gestures before the age of photography and cinema. These people forget that art and simple figuration obey specific codes and that the code called realism appeared only toward the end of the Middle Ages. Moreover, when it is a question of the gestures of a historical figure like Saint Louis, we have to remember that there are no existing contemporary images of the king. The frescoes of the Clares on the rue de Lourcine and the ones in the Sainte-Chapelle that were executed in the early years of the fourteenth century and are said to have preserved something of the original traits and appearance of the king have disappeared.[56] We are therefore reduced to seeking out the king's gestures as they are represented in works of art from Saint Louis' time—in miniatures in particular. Once upon a time, this concern sparked Henri Martin's interest in the "royal pose" in medieval miniatures and more specifically in a certain gesture that appears to have characterized royal gestures in the Middle Ages: the seated position with the legs crossed, a gesture expressing the sovereign's anger and superiority. This pose notably appears in a schematic fashion in a document of incalculable value from Saint Louis' time—Villard de Honnecourt's album. Another exceptional document that shows us gestures that were probably "real" is made up of the miniatures, which, as we have seen,[57] illustrate the *ordo* of Reims. The document had to have been written and illuminated shortly before 1250. It does not show Saint Louis' gestures as he was crowned in 1226, but the ones Philip III would use during his coronation in 1271, and it represents them in accordance with the models perfected during Saint Louis' reign. Nonetheless, the king executed these gestures only a single time during his coronation. They are representative of a royal ceremony that was of the utmost importance but nevertheless unique.[58]

Aside from these few examples, we must resign ourselves to having to look for Saint Louis' gestures mainly in texts. The problem here involves the gestures his biographers chose and their specific manners of evoking them, which run the gamut from simple allusions to highly detailed descriptions of just one gesture or of an entire series of gestures. Two preliminary remarks are in order here.

Our first observation is that Saint Louis' biographers were all not only panegyrists in varying degrees, but, more specifically, they were all hagiographers. They not only presented Saint Louis' code of gestures as fundamentally exemplary and as existing in conformity with the highest Christian models, but they skewed their presentation in favor of his religious gestures. However, this hagiographical concern sometimes allowed them to stress certain tensions expressed in terms of gestures split between the models Saint Louis embodied—between the layman he was and the cleric or monastic cleric he may have wanted to be, between the king he had to be and the king he wanted to be, between his function's tendency toward pride, *la superbia,* or at least to more or less often display himself "in his majesty," and the saint he wanted to be, a saint strongly imbued with the thirteenth-century ideals of sainthood and most of all with humility. There is one passage in Geoffroy de Beaulieu's text that shows how Saint Louis' humility sometimes led him to make gestures incompatible with royal dignity.

One Saturday when he was at the Cistercian abbey of Clairvaux, the king "wanted to attend the washing of feet . . . out of humility, several times he wanted to take off his coat and get down on his knees and touch the feet of God's servants with his hands to humbly wash them, but there were several powerful figures [*magnates*] there who were not part of his inner circle, and on their advice, he abstained from carrying out this humble duty."[59]

As a layman, Joinville had the advantage of not letting himself get too wrapped up in an ecclesiastical vision of his hero. He also wrote his personal memoirs, which he had to have dictated shortly after the king's death and well before his canonization. This offered him the advantage of not being limited to describing the saint, allowing him to present the other facets of Saint Louis that he knew: the king, the feudal king with his essential functions as a knight, a lord, and a sovereign deliberating with his council, rendering justice, and establishing peace, and also the friend. Joinville witnessed the tension between two gestural codes, between the gestures of the knight, the valorous warrior, the man of impetuosity and violence, and the *prud'homme,* the man of reflection and moderation. Thus, when Saint Louis landed in Egypt he gave in to the temptation to engage in prowess, forgetting his wisdom. As we have seen, the "*prud'hommes*" who were with him disapproved of his gesture.[60]

My second observation involves the divisions that need to be drawn within the field of gestures in function of the nature of the sources and the normative codes of the time. This has led me to distinguish between three types of gestures whose definition as gestures — and as Saint Louis' gestures — was not entirely obvious in the first place.

The first type is made up of *implicit* gestures, those contained in actions that were not explicitly described by his biographers. For example, eating, sleeping, giving orders, and horseback riding belong in this group. The gestural categories associated with these actions are important nonetheless. First of all, the fact that the biographers often mention them proves that they comprised a class of gestures that was quantitatively and qualitatively meaningful in its non-descript entirety. In effect, all of these acts posed problems for Saint Louis due to the gestures they required, that his royal function imposed, or that his religious ideal demanded. Eating and sleeping presupposed a discipline of the body in which his ascetic ideal often came into conflict with the dietary luxury attached to his status and the normal sleeping habits of a layman, let alone a layman who wore the crown.[61] Giving orders became a particularly sensitive issue when the receivers of those orders were churchmen whom Saint Louis regarded with special reverence.[62] Horseback riding interrupted the king's normal schedule for worship dictated by his religious practices that seemed to require the regularity and sedentary nature of convent life.[63] In contrast to William Jordan, I think that Saint Louis easily resolved the difficulties, although these tensions clearly existed.

The second type is made up of *passive* gestures. In a strongly hierarchical world like the medieval West, the balance between gestures that expressed and imposed one's will and gestures to which one submitted identified a person's social position and ethical quality.[64] Therefore, if I dare say, Saint Louis was positively passive in two aspects of his life. First of all, in his youth, in conformity with the image of the child as it existed in the system of values in the Middle Ages in which the child was a kind of nonentity who only became someone by emerging from childhood as quickly as possible, he only existed through his submission and obedience. At this time, he excelled in letting himself be shaped by his mother and his master, even though the first was not particularly affectionate[65] and the second did not hesitate to punish him physically.[66] In his worshipping practices and admiration of martyrdom, however, his character was also shaped by God.[67]

The third category of gestures that I believe useful to identify for Saint Louis is comprised of what I call *negative* gestures. The thirteenth century was an oasis on the path between the Christianity of the High Middle Ages with its contempt for the world and the Christianity of the last medieval centuries, a Christianity steeped in fear. A Christian in the Middle Ages — even in this thirteenth century that seemed more willing to allow men to flourish — earned his salvation as much by what he abstained from, what he did not do, by his active or even passive resistance to Satan, as by his positive actions and gestures. A number of the gestures that Saint Louis' biographers mentioned were the ones he did not make. For example, Guillaume de Saint-Pathus observes: "He avoided all improper games and kept himself from committing any ugly or dishonest actions, nor did he insult anyone in words or deeds, nor did he disdain or blame anyone in any way but instead would very gently reprove those who sometimes did something that could have angered him. . . . He did not sing any worldly songs either, and he would not put up with anyone in his household singing them either. . . ."[68]

Of all the biographies, the ones that contain the richest corpus of Saint Louis' gestures are Joinville's *History* and the *Life* by Guillaume de Saint-Pathus.[69] The latter lacks the concrete images and memories that can be found in the works of the other biographers who were close to the king and who were his close friends and associates to varying degrees. However, on the basis of the information provided by members of Saint Louis' entourage on the one hand and its use of the record of the canonization proceedings on the other, this work is also the most complete normative text, the best "Mirror of the holy king."

A Saint King's Gestures

In his introduction, Queen Marguerite's confessor announces that he did not follow the order of the depositions of the witnesses for the inquiry, "the ordinance of time," chronological order in other words, in his work. Instead, he followed the "ordinance of the dignity" of the reported facts, "the ordinance of the most appropriate succession." In other words, after two chapters on Saint Louis' "childhood" and "growth"—weak phases in life whose only value was to prepare the individual for adult life—he gave an exposé of Saint Louis' virtues presented in a hierarchical thematic order. Here we can identify the gestures of a saint king, from the most important to the most obvious ones. First of all, there were the gestures related to the theological virtues (chapters 3 to 5): "firm belief," "righteous hope," and "ardent love," which defined the gestures of faith, hope, and charity. Next, there were the king's pious practices: "fervent worship," "study of holy scripture," and "devout prayer to God" (chapters 6 to 8), which created a place to mention gestures of worship, biblical reading, and prayer. Then came specific virtues: "fervent love of the people who were close to him"—which in Saint Louis' case, apart from his attachment to his mother Blanche of Castile and the little interest other than procreative that he seems to have felt for his wife Marguerite de Provence, signified his gestures as a father and older brother—"compassion," "works of pity" (in other words charity), "profound humility," "vigorous patience," "unflinching penitence," "beauty of conscience," and "saintly self-control" (chapters 9 to 16). These were followed by the royal virtues: "upstanding justice," "simple honesty," and "graceful clemency" (chapters 17 to 19). Finally, this leads us to the term for the greatest value in his life and its continuity with sainthood, its culminating point, his death on the crusade understood as a form of martyrdom: "his long perseverance and his blessed demise."

The Apotheosis: The Gestures of Saintly Death

In his twentieth and final chapter, Guillaume de Saint-Pathus describes the gestures of Saint Louis' royal Christian death before the walls of Tunis. It is a veritable apotheosis of gestures.

He was sick for three weeks or thereabouts, and, at the onset of his illness although he was in a very serious condition, he would say his matins and all the other hours in his bed with one of his chaplains. And, in addition to this, the mass and all the other canonical hours were sung aloud in his tent, and a mass was also said in his presence in a low voice each day. The cross was placed in front of his bed where he could see it, and it was put there on the orders of the saint king himself when he began to feel sick, and he would look at it very often and would cast his gaze upon it and pray to it with his hands joined and would have it brought to him in the morning when he was fasting and he would kiss it with great devotion and great reverence and embrace it. He would often give thanks to God, his Creator, and during his illness would very often say and repeat the *Pater Noster,* the *Miserere,* and the *Credo.* Since the saint king began to be sick and bedridden because of the sickness he died from, he would speak as though he were always talking to himself and seemed to be saying Psalms and prayers, and he would often rub his eyes and often praise and bless God. During his illness, he often confessed to Friar Geoffroy de Beaulieu of the Order of the Preachers. Moreover, during his sickness, the saint king asked for the body of Jesus Christ and had it and received it several times. One time when he was going to receive the body of Christ and it was brought to him, when the person who was carrying it came into his chamber, although he was sick and weak, the saint king threw himself off his bed to the ground, but the members of his entourage immediately threw his coat on him. The saint king remained bent on the ground for a long time before receiving the body of Jesus Christ and then he received it kneeling on the ground in great devotion. He could not get back into bed on his own, so the attendants put him back in the bed. The saint king requested the Extreme Unction and he was anointed just before he lost his ability to speak.

In the end, he did not speak for four days, but he still had a good memory and would raise his joined hands to the sky and would sometimes beat his chest and recognize people, and he would make signs when he wanted to eat and drink, albeit little, and he would signal with his hands as people usually do to either refuse something or ask for something.

His condition grew worse, and he would speak very softly, but when the others said Psalms, the good king would move his lips.

On the Sunday before he died, Friar Geoffroy de Beaulieu brought him the body of Christ, and as he entered the room where the king was in bed, he found him outside the bed, kneeling on the ground with his hands joined [in prayer] at his bedside. . . .[70]

The gestures of a sick man praying and taking communion replaced the gestures made with facial signs, eyes, and hands. We see the gestures of a bedridden Christian who, despite his extreme weakness, leaves his bed in the presence of the body of his Lord. We see the gestures of a dying man who can no longer speak and who replaces words with signs. In the throes of death, Louis expressed his faith with all of the gestural resources that were still available to him.

GESTURES OF RELIGIOUS DEVOTION

In the Christian system, gestures were supposed to be the expression and continuation of the movements of the heart and man's internal virtues. Saint Louis could not keep his own devotion "pent up in his heart"; instead, he "showed it through several kinds of signs."[71] Gestures were signs. In other words, they were symbols in the Augustinian sense of the term *signum*. They therefore have to be understood as an essential element in the great medieval symbolic system.

They were defined first of all in relation to the space that the king moved through. Here, as we have seen, there were two important categories divided by the distinction between the times the king was in his palace or at some other stopping place "*en ostel*" (in a lodging) or when he was on the road out "riding." In the first situation, Louis modeled his pious practices after those of the monastic clergy and his movements led him back and forth between his room and his chapel or his oratory for the singing of the hours ("he would return to his room"; "when the time came, the holy king would go back to bed"). In moments of worship, his most meaningful gesture was kneeling ("he would kneel quite frequently"), but an even more significant fact is that he never sat during these exercises unless it was to sit on the ground—"when he was in the church or the chapel he was always standing, upright on his feet or kneeling on the ground or the floor or leaning on the side of a bench in front of him, or he would sit on the ground without any cushion but with only a carpet spread out on the ground beneath him." In these circumstances when the gesture also depended on the environment, interlocutors, and spectators—the king was never alone. His chaplains surrounded him and stood "before him," and in his worship he was always accompanied by a kind of ecclesiastical double—he carried out each of his acts of worship "with one of his chaplains." When horseback riding, he even tried to re-create the sedentary position that afforded him the best opportunity to accomplish the gestures of religious devotion.

We must add a third category to these two important types of gestures. Louis IX had fragile health and his ascetic practices endangered his physical condition. On days when "the king was sick" and "lying in bed," his room was transformed into a chapel. His gestures were reduced to speaking, and "when he was so weak that he could not speak," his ecclesiastical double executed these gestures in his place: "He had another cleric with him who would say the Psalms for him."[72]

His other religious practices involved listening to preaching, communion, his worship of the cross and relics, and his marks of respect for clerics. His love of listening to sermons led him to make two kinds of gestures: "sitting on the ground" in order to listen to them in a position of humility and, in this same spirit of humility, "sometimes he would walk twice a day on foot for a quarter league to hear a sermon."[73] His gestures for receiving communion (which occurred infrequently for a king who normally only took communion six times a year at Easter, Pentecost, the Assumption of the Virgin, All Saints' Day, Christmas, and the Purification of the Virgin) were all of "very great devoutness": "He would wash his hands and his mouth beforehand and remove his head covering and his headdress." Then, when he reached the church choir, "he would not walk to the altar on his feet, but would go up to it on his knees." Then, when he reached the altar, "he would say his *Confiteor* on his own with many sighs and moans and with his hands clasped together."[74]

Especially on Good Friday, he expressed his devotion for the cross by visiting churches "near the place where he was." He would show up there and listen to the mass "barefoot," and then, in order to worship the cross, he would remove his cope and his headdress and go bareheaded on his knees up to the cross, which he "would kiss," and then finally he would "lean on the ground in the shape of a cross the entire time that he was kissing it, and some people think he would shed tears as he was doing this."[75]

Other gestures appeared with his devotion for the relics. There was his role in the processions and the act of carrying relics on his shoulders: "And in this procession, the holy king carried the aforementioned relics on his own shoulders with the bishops." On these occasions, the king did not express his religious devotion in front of his chaplains or several clerics alone but before "the clergy of Paris and the people."[76] These were gestures of public religious devotion. Finally, facing the clerics and particularly in front of groups of monks, these gestures highlighted certain values that were articulated through his conduct: the hierarchy as it existed in relation to the situation and the space in which it took place, admiring observation, and imitation.

The king would have his chaplains eat at a table that was "higher than the holy king's table or at least of equal height," and "the saint king would rise" in the presence of the "*prud'hommes*."[77] Louis "visited churches and religious sites [in other words, convents and monasteries] very often and was very familiar with them." He would passionately observe the actions and gestures of monks, notably those of the Cistercians of Chaalis. During the feet-washing ceremony on Saturday after vespers, he "would watch what the monks were doing with great devotion."[78] He would accompany the abbot to the dormitory door in order to see him give the holy water to each of the monks before they went to bed: "he watched with great devotion what was being done." He would imitate the monks' gestures "and received the holy water from the aforementioned abbot just like one of the monks with his head bowed, and leave the cloister and go to his lodging."[79]

The wealth of gestural details that Guillaume de Saint-Pathus gives here was meant to show Saint Louis as a man who came very close, as close as a layman could come, to embodying the conduct of the monks and monastic clergy. Gestures formed the code of reference for the state, the status, and the value of the Christian. Just as the heretic[80] or the pious layman could be recognized by their gestures, the saint was identified through his gestures, too.

Models and Personality

In the thirteenth century were gestures allowed to express a personality at the same time that they articulated a model? Do the gestures that the biographers report to us only inform us about a model of royalty and sainthood or do they give us access to the individuality of Saint Louis, the man?

It is clear that Saint Louis' biographers complied with certain models in representing him, but there is more to it. In the words of Boniface VIII, which may not be as outstanding as people say but which were still amazing in spite of everything, Saint Louis' contemporaries appeared to have seen more than a man in him. They seem to have looked on him as a kind of superman.[81] Doesn't this mean that his personality escaped them? According to Guillaume de Saint-Pathus, Joinville expressed the same idea in a more traditional fashion: "He had never seen a man who looked more harmonious [*atempré*] nor with greater perfection in everything that can be seen in a man."[82]

First of all, my impression is that when the biographers show us Saint Louis with the poor, his gestures seem to be placed at their level and appear more "real." Thus, when he gave out food to the blind:

> If there were any blind or poorly sighted person among these poor people, the holy king would give him a morsel from the platter and teach him how to place his hand in the platter. And again, if there were any poorly sighted or weak person when he had fish in front of him, the holy king would take a piece of fish and carefully remove the bones with his own hands, dip it in the sauce, and then place it in the sick person's mouth.[83]

I especially believe that the gestures mentioned or described by his biographers allow us to approach Saint Louis not only as an exemplary figure in conformity with the models but also to grasp his historical personality. There are at least three reasons that authorize me to reassert my conviction about these gestures — that they allow us to access the "real" Saint Louis.

The first of these reasons is that the biographers who knew him and were close to him sought to persuade the listeners and readers of their works that they really were the familiar associates and sometimes even the friends of this great king, this extraordinary man, this saint. They also tried to justify the pride or happiness—or both the pride and happiness—that this privilege procured for them by appealing to their lived experience. This was the proof that people wanted in the late thirteenth century when "realism" was spreading through the arts and the portrait was on the verge of being born. Joinville especially had this ambition. Joinville describes Saint Louis approaching him from behind, leaning on his shoulders, and placing his hands over his head when he was at a window in the royal ship. Thinking that it was Philippe de Nemours, Joinville cried out: "Leave me alone, my lord Philippe." Then, when the king's hand slipped across his face, he recognized the man behind this familiar gesture from an emerald that he saw on his hand. In this anecdote, it is clearly Louis who has been rendered for us in all the simplicity and familiarity of his gestures.[84]

When his biographers depict the king for us so often seated on the ground to converse with his close associates at the foot of his bed, to preside over judicial cases in the palace garden in Paris or at Vincennes, to listen to a sermon, we are not only allowed to grasp the gestures that correspond to the norms of humility as Boniface VIII highlighted them,[85] but also the preference that the man Saint Louis had for a specific bodily position.

Last and most important of all, doesn't Saint Louis' personality express itself directly in his will to make all his gestures comply with the Christian model? In Egypt, in Palestine, and everywhere else, he proclaimed it was necessary to teach by example. Doesn't the adaptation of Saint Louis' gestures as reported by his biographers to the model of idealized Christian gestures translate the fact that Saint Louis fully identified with the attempt to translate his ideals into gestures? Aren't the king and the portrait of the king historically combined?

THE *PRUD'HOMME*

In both his words and gestures, Saint Louis tried to realize what seemed like the highest human ideal to him. In the thirteenth century this ideal tended to replace the ideals of the valorous or courteous knight [*le preux* or *le courtois*] by taming them and combining them. This was the ideal of the *prud'homme*.

In the Middle Ages, people loved to give surnames to important figures and especially to kings. This was at the time that the system for giving them a number in the dynastic order had not yet been established. In a chronicle composed between 1293 and 1297 by the minstrel of the count of Poitiers that included a genealogy of the kings of France, Louis (IX), his son Philip (III), and his grandson Philip (IV) were designated as Louis "*le prud'homme,*" Philip the Bold, and Philip the Fair.[86]

The *prud'homme* was defined by his prudence, his wisdom, and his moderation. Joinville presented the duke Hugues de Bourgogne as an example of a knight who was valorous but not a *prud'homme*.[87] He attributed the following judgment of Hugues to Philip Augustus: "for there is a great difference between *preuhomme* [*preux,* a valorous man] and *preudhomme* [man of probity]."

At Lyon in 1244, Emperor Frederick II proposed Saint Louis' arbitration to Pope Innocent IV on the grounds of his *prud'homie*: "And he was prepared to accept the judgment of the king of France, who was a *prud'homme*."[88] The king also claimed this characteristic for himself. According to Joinville, Louis confided the following statement to Robert de Sorbon: "Master Robert, I would quite like to have the name of *prud'homme,* provided that I am one, and I will leave all the rest to you because a *prud'homme* is such a great and good thing that the word fills one's mouth simply by pronouncing it."[89]

The *prud'homme* united "chivalry" and "clergy" in a continuation of Chrétien de Troye's ideal; he combined *fortitudo* and *sapientia,* power and wisdom. The notion of the *prud'homme* articulated the evolution of moral values at the turn of the twelfth and thirteenth centuries. The term described a man "who had moral authority," who was "full of merit," and, according to Charles Brucker, it could be translated as "man of worth" [*homme de valeur*] or "man of good" [*homme de bien*]. In some ways, it is the medieval equivalent of the "*honnête homme*" (honest man) of the classical period. It referred to a man who acted in accordance with "moral values with religious connotations." Better yet, it was the "just" that was comparable to the qualities of the Old Testament characters whom Jesus freed when he descended into Limbo.[90]

If on the side of the warriors the *prud'homme* was distinguished from the "*preux*" (valorous) by tempering valor with wisdom and piety, on the side of the clerics, he was distinguished from the "*béguin,*" the affected devout man. Although Joinville called him a "*prud'homme,*" Robert de Sorbon defended the *béguin* against Joinville when the king called upon them to debate the topic: "Seneschal, tell us the reasons why the *prud'homme* is better than the *béguin*."[91] And Saint Louis ended his life with a *prud'homme*'s profession of faith. Thus the *roi prud'homme* (king of probity) situated himself between bellicosity and sanctimoniousness. *Prud'homie,* however, was not warmth; it was combat and wisdom, too.

It was therefore a secular ideal that Saint Louis valued above all else. We know that he did not always manage to be faithful to this ideal. Either he forgot all prudence when he was seized by chivalric "fury" as he did during the landing in Egypt, or he got carried away in irritation against his entourage or his interlocutors. He was aware of this. But despite several impulsive eruptions, Saint Louis generally succeeded in maintaining this self-control, this middle ground that appeared to him as a rule for good conduct. He translated this possibility in a significant way in his style of dress.

During one of those friendly quarrels that took place before the king between the canon and the seneschal, the two of them debated clothing, and the king rendered his judgment: "For, thus as the seneschal says, you should dress yourself well and proper because our women will love you all the better for it, and your people will value you for it more. Because, as the wise man says, one should adorn oneself in clothes and armor in such a way that the *prud'hommes* of this century do not say you are overdoing it, and so that the young people do not say you are not doing it enough."[92] What became of this moderation and this *prud'homie* when the king was at the supper table? His biographers and chroniclers gave prolix details about the king's table manners, and these scenes offer a good place to observe his behavior.

Saint Louis at the Table: Between Royal Conviviality and Dietary Humility

Saint Louis also expressed his desire for moderation against the temptation of excess in an exemplary fashion at the dinner table.[93] The meals of a thirteenth-century Christian king followed several rituals. There are basically two that concern us here. The first is one that was imposed on all Christians. It was made up of a dietary code that basically consisted in fasting or abstaining from eating meat or other foods on certain days and during certain periods. These days were essentially Fridays and the period of Lent. The second ritual was one that was imposed on powerful figures. Just like dress, food was a sign of status and social rank, and the powerful were supposed to show their rank by indulging in a certain dietary luxury. As we are concerned with a king here, the realm of food represented this status either by certain taboos on the consumption of dishes limited or forbidden for the king (this was not the case for Christian kings) or by certain ceremonial rites. There are examples of monarchical societies where the king was supposed to eat alone—this was the case in absolutist Europe and for the pope—and, on the other hand, there are other more numerous ones in which the king was supposed to signal his status either through a particular prandial ceremonial rite that placed him above and in some ways beyond the other guests through his place, his seat, his table setting, or the presentation of the dishes, or through an obligation to eat in numerous or select company, or both. Some of these obligations arose from a ritualized and obligatory etiquette and others, which were more numerous, arose from simple custom, fame (*fama*), and reputation.

In the two rituals, both the religious and the secular, certain occasions imposed a new upsurge in dietary splendor: the important religious festivals, the great chivalric festivals such as the dubbing ceremonies, the feasts for important feudal assemblies (notably the ones held on Pentecost), and the banquets held in honor of powerful figures.

However, in Saint Louis' case there were other rituals that can be added to these general rites. Especially in the monastic milieu and, to a certain degree, in the convent milieu of the Mendicant friars, clerics who followed monastic traditions with less austerity observed dietary customs of a regulatory nature prescribed by their "customs" [*consuetudines*], which were more rigorous than any of those followed by laymen. Saint Louis strove to emulate the conduct of the monks and friars and tried to adopt dietary customs and table manners that resembled theirs. In addition, in a spirit of penance, he had taken it upon himself to exceed the restrictions prescribed to simple laymen. We have already seen how he did the same thing in abstaining from conjugal relations.

On the other hand though, Louis wanted to comply with the rules of *prud'homie,* a model of conduct for laymen that he praised in passionate terms. *Prud'homie* entailed a discipline of moderation, temperance, wisdom, and self-control in all things. The king took care to respect what I would call a dietary *prud'homie* that cannot be confused with religious or monastic discretion.

Finally, here as in other realms—and this attitude became more pronounced after his return from the crusade and with age—Saint Louis strove to imitate Christ. He became even more preoccupied with serving the poor, the sick, and the leprous from his table, and, remarkably, before meals he practiced the ritual washing of the feet of the poor or monks or friars in his desire to reenact the Last Supper.

It is obvious that if these models of dietary conduct could coexist for the same person while they were hierarchically ordered and spread out following their special moments and occasions, certain conflicts appear inevitable. What did the king choose: royal conviviality or dietary humility?

I will now regroup the corpus of contemporary texts that present us with the saint king at his table. I will examine them in an ascending order of likelihood, moving from the hagiographers to the chroniclers.

MODERATION

My first source is Geoffroy de Beaulieu, the king's confessor "for roughly twenty years of his life." His text is the *Vita,* which was probably written in 1272–1273. It is a treatise on Louis' manners composed from Geoffroy's personal memories according to the hagiographical model of the time. It bears the strong mark of Mendicant religious devotion and was written in view of an eventual canonization of the sovereign.

> During the whole year, he had the habit of fasting on Fridays and abstaining from eating meat and fat on Wednesdays. Sometimes he would also abstain from eating meat on Mondays, but because of his body's weakness he gave up this day on the advice of his friends. In addition, he would fast on bread and water for the four vigils of the main festival days for the Holy Virgin. Similarly, he wanted to fast on bread and water on Good Friday and sometimes on the eve of All Saints' Day and for certain other ceremonious fasts during the year. During Lent and Advent, he would abstain from eating fish and fruit on Fridays. However, with his confessor's permission, on that day he would eat only a single kind of fish and a single kind of fruit. He had heard of a religious who would completely abstain from eating any kind of fruit, except that when people offered him a perfectly ripe fruit for the first time in the year, he would taste it once as an act of thanks and then would abstain from eating that kind of fruit for the

entire remainder of the year. The saint king reported this fact to his confessor, disappointed that he did not have the audacity to attain this kind of perfection, but he thought of the idea of at least doing the inverse, in other words, when anyone offered him a fruit that had just come into season, he would not eat it that time and would sacrifice the new fruits of the season to the Lord. After that, he would eat that kind of fruit without any bad conscience. I believe that he observed this suggestion afterward. I cannot recall ever having seen anyone — or almost anyone — who cut his wine with as much water as he did.[94]

Here we find an entire casuistry of fasting and abstinence. The full fast was only observed on Fridays; a less severe fast on bread and water was observed on the vigils of the four great festivals of the Virgin as a sign of his Marian devotion, on Good Friday, and on the eve of All Saints' Day and for several other ceremonious fasts. There was also his act of abstaining from certain other quality foods — meat and fat on Wednesday and fish and fruit on the Fridays of Lent and Advent. Another form of casuistry presupposed a dietary asceticism concerning the regularity of fasts and periods of abstinence: sometimes there were no tolerable exceptions to the rule, and other times the rules were only "sometimes" enacted. Saint Louis' ideal of dietary asceticism, which he intended to make very rigorous, underwent certain attenuations such as his renunciation of abstaining from meat on Mondays or his replacement of completely abstaining from fish and fruit with the consumption of only a single kind of fish and a single kind of fruit on the Fridays of Lent and Advent.

Three factors came into play in this (relative) moderation in dietary asceticism: Saint Louis' poor health (the "weakness of his body," *debilitas corporis*), the moderating influence of his confessor and his entourage, and his own desire for moderation that we can sense was inspired by a concern to avoid the pride of an excessive asceticism. He did not wish to rival the religious who abstained from eating fruit but made the concession of doing this once a year. He also wanted to observe the *prud'homme*'s moderation in his dietary asceticism and, of course, ended up making certain concessions to his tastes. The anecdote about his consumption of fruit every day of the year but one, inverting the rule of the exemplary religious, which may not be exempt from a certain irony, explains the king's conduct in relation to his pronounced taste for fruit that was noted by his biographers and even his hagiographers. The Saint Louis they show us is no doubt, in accordance with their wishes, a man who had penchants for certain pleasures or even passions (in addition to fruit he was crazy about good fish like pike) and who therefore had more merit in controlling them. The saint was an athlete who wrestled with these things. In the example of the proportion of water he mixed with his wine, Louis was presented as a true champion. The dietary model that inspired him was clearly monastic. Beyond the concern for his health, in the plentiful advice to use moderation that he received we can see his confessor's and his entourage's concern to see him maintain the dignity of his rank within his eating habits. The royal and aristocratic model was clearly opposed to the monastic model here.

Finally, through Saint Louis, Geoffroy de Beaulieu's text allows us to identify the foods around which the opposition between a rich dietary model and a poor one were constructed: meats and fatty foods, fish, fruit, and wine. Just above the zero degree of the fast, bread and water defined the voluntary poverty of dietary consumption.

HUMILITY AND ASCETICISM

My second source is Guillaume de Saint-Pathus. He was Queen Marguerite's Franciscan confessor and was commissioned to write an official life, a *Vita* or a hagiography to use the proper term, after the canonization took place in 1297. We only possess the French translation of this life that dates from the final years of the thirteenth century.[95]

Guillaume reports that Louis liked to have "persons of reverence" at his table. These were religious with whom he could "talk about God" in place of the lesson that was read in the convents "during meals." Guillaume points out that when the king came to the hospital in Vernon he served the poor with his own hands "in the presence of his sons" whom he wanted to "form and instruct in works of pity." And, he had "dishes of meat or fish appropriate for their illnesses" prepared so that he could serve them to them.[96]

The table then cannot be reduced to dietary matters. It was also a place and an occasion for him to prepare his salvation. It was a place where people expressed concern for their bodies (nourishing them, nourishing themselves) and for their pleasures (the pleasures of and related to food like conversation and entertainment) but which were susceptible to degrade into vicious behavior like excessive indulgence in food and drink, indigestion and drunkenness, exaggerated or obscene remarks, and luxurious actions in mixed company (here, we find the pairing of *gula* and *luxuria*). The table could and should be an instrument for perfection and edification through edifying conversation and serving the poor. Saint Louis appears here as the nourishing king, the king of Dumézil's third function.

This concern is spread throughout chapter 11 on works of "pity" (*miséricorde*). Here we find an entire calendar for the king's table service for feeding the poor:

> [First, on each day] Wednesdays, Fridays, and Saturdays during Lent and Advent, he personally served thirteen poor people that he would have eat in his room or his wardrobe and he would minister to them [the food] by putting porridge and two pairs of platters of fish or some other food before them. And, he would cut two loaves of bread himself, and he would put [the pieces] before each of them, and the king's valets would cut as many of the other loaves of bread as they needed and put them before the aforementioned poor people. Moreover, the holy king would put two more loaves of bread before the aforementioned poor people for them to take away with them.

It is at this point that we find the episode of the poor blind man.[97] The king paired his gesture with a charitable gift:

> And before they ate, he would give each of them twelve deniers of Paris and he would give even more to the people he saw who were in greater need, and whenever there was a woman who had a small child with her, he would increase his gift.[98]

> ... The holy king would usually have three platters of porridge brought out, and he would add pieces of bread he had in front of him himself, and he would make soups in these bowls and place the bowls of soup before the aforementioned poor people. And he would call the most deplorable poor people that could be found to this service and he would serve poor people like this more happily and more often than others. Each of these ten poor would receive twelve deniers of Paris in alms from the saintly king.[99]

This scene took place in a spot he often visited: the Cistercian abbey of Royaumont. Sometimes he ate in the refectory at the abbot's table. He took his seat at the same table with the monks who served all the others. They numbered roughly one hundred in all, in addition to about forty laymen:

> He would come to the kitchen window and take platters full of food ["meat"] and carry them and put them down in front of the monks who were seated at the table. . . . And when the platters were too hot, sometimes he would wrap his hands in his cope because of the heat of the food and the platters and sometimes he would spill food on his cope. The abbot would tell him that he was getting his cope dirty, and the holy king would answer: "It isn't important at all; I have others." Sometimes he would go by himself among the tables pouring wine into the monks' steins, and he would praise the wine when it was good, and when it was bitter or if it smelled like the barrel, he would order someone to bring some good wine. . . .[100]

At Vernon one nun even refused to eat food from anyone's hands but the king's. Saint Louis "went to her bedside and put the pieces of food in her mouth with his own hands."[101]

The table reappears in chapter 12, the one that deals with the king's "high humility." We can find other examples of the king's table service for the poor and the sick there. Louis ate with his own hands from the same platters as the poor[102] and, remarkably, the leprous. He cut a pear and, kneeling before him, placed it in the mouth of a leper who had blood and pus running from his nostrils that soiled the king's hands.[103]

At Chaalis, where they gave him better food than they fed the monks, he had his silver platter brought to a monk and traded it for his wooden platter with less appetizing food.[104]

Finally, the king's humility increased after his return from the crusade.[105] This increased humility was marked by his greater modesty in what he wore to meals. The coat he usually wore was inconvenient for eating so he would switch it with a surcoat. We have already seen that after 1254 he no longer wore any clothing trimmed with fur of vair or gray [*petit-gris*— Siberian blue squirrel], but only with rabbit or sheepskin, although he would sometimes wear a white lambskin surcoat as a kind of partial luxury.[106]

Chapter 14 largely emphasizes the "rigorous penitence" [*raideur de pénitence*] that became so strong after his return from the Holy Land:

Although the holy king would happily eat large fish, he would often put the big ones that were brought to him [aside] and have small ones brought for his mouth and he would eat those. Sometimes, he would have the large fish that were brought to him cut into pieces so that people would think he had eaten some of them, but he did not eat these large fish or any others, but would simply be satisfied with just his porridge, and would give out these large fish as alms [he would save them for the serving of alms]. And people thought that he did this out of abstinence. Although he really loved large pikes and other fish, and they were purchased and brought to his table, after his return from overseas he would not eat them but would have them distributed for alms, and he would eat other smaller fish. And it often happened that people would bring him roasted meats or other dishes and delicious sauces, and he would add water to the seasoning to destroy the quality of the sauce. And when the person who was serving before him would say to him: "Sire, you are ruining your flavoring," he would reply, "Don't you worry about that. I like it better this way." And people think he did this to rein in his own appetite. He often ate bad-tasting porridge that was "poorly flavored" and that no one else wanted to eat because it wasn't flavorful. The holy king also ate crude dishes such as peas and the like. And when someone would bring him a delicious gruel or some other [delicious] dish, he would mix cold water with it to take away the delight of the flavor of this dish. When people brought the first lampreys to Paris and someone brought them to the table before the blessed king and the others there, he would not eat them but would give them to the poor or send them out for the communal charities. . . . So, these dishes became so degraded that they were no longer worth more than five sous or something like that, whereas in the beginning they were worth forty sous or four pounds. And he would do the same thing with fresh fruit, although he was still happy to eat them. And he would do the same with many other things that were set before him in their freshness. And he would do this only out of abstinence, as people truly believe, in order to rein in the appetite he naturally had for these things.

His dietary *prud'homie* that limited him to a veritable culinary asceticism was even displayed in his use of bread and wine around 1254:

His custom was to never indulge in any excesses [*outrages*] in drinking and eating, and he would slice his bread at the table in such a way that when he was in good health he did not cut any larger slices than on the days he was not. He would have a golden cup[107] and a glass in front of him, and on the glass there was a mark [*une verge*] up to which he would fill the glass with wine and he would add water beyond this mark in such great quantity that only a quarter of the glass was wine and the other three quarters were water. And yet he never used any strong wine, but only very weak wine. And after he drank from the glass or after the drink had been measured out like this, sometimes he would put it in the golden cup and drink from the cup. And then he would dilute his wine with so much water that it had barely any taste of wine left.

This dietary abstinence reached its culminating point with his practice of fasting.

He would fast each year for the entire duration of Lent. He would fast once more during Advent, forty days before Christmas, eating only Lenten dishes. And he would fast on the vigils for which the Church ordered fasting and for the four Ember Weeks and the other fasts of the Holy Church, in other words for the four vigils for the festivals of Our Lady, on Good Friday, and on the vigil for the Nativity of Our Lord he would fast on only bread and water. But on the days when he fasted on bread and water, he would set his high table as on any other days, and if any of his knights wanted to fast on bread and water with him they would eat with him at his table. On Fridays during Lent, he would not eat fish, and on other Fridays the blessed king would abstain quite often from eating fish, and on the Fridays of Advent he would not eat any fish. Furthermore, on Fridays throughout the whole year he would not eat any fruit although he very much enjoyed eating it. On Mondays and Wednesdays during Lent he would eat much less than people considered appropriate. On Fridays, he would dilute his wine with so much water that it seemed like it was just water. And, although the blessed king did not like beer [*cervoise*], which showed up on his face whenever he drank it, he still drank enough of it during Lent to rein in his appetite. Once more, before going across the sea and after his return the blessed king would always fast on Fridays during the whole year except when Christmas Day fell on a Friday because then he would eat meat because of the grandeur [*hautesse*] of the festival. Once again, he would fast each week on Monday, Wednesday, and Saturday. When the holy king was overseas during the time of his first crusade [*passage*], he would start to fast fifteen days before the festival of Pentecost and he would continue to observe this fast up to his death. Once more, he would not eat all the dishes people placed before him, and people believe he did this out of abstinence and for God.[108]

Louis thus perfected an entire form of asceticism applied to food. His dietary system consisted in eating what was less good (for example, the small fish instead of the big ones), in devaluing what was good (for instance, by putting cold water in his sauces, soups, and wine), in abstaining from fine foods (like lampreys and fresh fruit), in eating and drinking moderately, in always eating and drinking the same measured quantity (his bread and wine), and in frequent fasting. He corrected the royal quality of the tableware—his golden cup for example—with the mediocrity of the food or drink that it contained. He applied this asceticism in order to renounce the culinary pleasures to which he was naturally inclined and, inversely, he forced himself to consume things he did not like—beer for example. His behavior here was the same as when he confronted danger despite the fact that he "loved life," or as in his practice of sexuality where his ultra-scrupulous observation of ecclesiastical regulations for conjugal sexuality reined in a temperament that seems quite passionate.

Caught between his desire for moderation and his passion for devout moral excellence, Saint Louis wanted to be the champion of a dietary asceticism although he accepted his own temperaments for reasons having to do with his physical condition, his ideal of the *prud'homme*'s moderation, and his will to hold his own rank despite all else.

JOINVILLE: SELF-CONTROL

My third source is Joinville. He wanted to show us a Saint Louis who confirmed the thirteenth-century ideal of sainthood, but he was by far the most sincere and the most authentic, the closest and the most affectionately admiring of all the biographers. He also did not get as caught up as the clerics in the commonplace ideas about pious conduct.

Beginning with his introduction, among all the king's virtues Joinville notes his sobriety:

> He was so sober of mouth that never in my life did I ever hear him order any dish, as many rich men often do, but he would happily eat whatever his cook prepared for him and put before him. . . . He would dilute his wine with a certain measure according to what he saw the wine could hold. In Cyprus once he asked me why I didn't put water in my wine, and I told him it was because the doctors had told me that I had a large head and a cold stomach, and that I could not get drunk. And he told me they were deceiving me, because if I had not learned how to dilute my wine in my youth and only wanted to do it in my old age, gout and other stomach illnesses would afflict me so much that I would never recover my health, and that if I drank pure wine in my old age, I would become intoxicated every night, and it was an ugly thing for a good man to get drunk.[109]

Three traits appear here: Saint Louis' moderate approach to food and even his attempted indifference to eating and drinking, which formed a kind of dietary ataraxia; his practice of diluting his wine with water and his condemnation of drunkenness; and his dietary considerations about drinking.[110]

We have already seen that the first time Joinville met Louis was at the table on an occasion that was very memorable for him. This was the great banquet given by the king when he was twenty-seven years old during the plenary court held in Saumur in 1241 after the knighting of his brother Alphonse de Poitiers. Joinville took part in the festivities as a young squire responsible for slicing the meat.[111]

We have no details about whatever Saint Louis ate, but, on this occasion, everything leads us to believe that the food had to be up to par with the splendor of such an exceptional royal banquet.

Later on, however, Joinville also provides testimony about Saint Louis' charitable use of food: "Every day he would feed a great multitude of poor people, without counting the ones who would eat in his room, and many times I saw that he would slice their bread and give them to drink on his own."[112]

He in turn emphasized the king's dietary moderation, which underwent a change around 1254, becoming a veritable program of penitential table manners.[113] The king, however, still did not forget his rank and his duties. We have seen that he tolerated listening to the minstrels of "wealthy men" and fulfilled his duties of hospitality: "When certain wealthy foreign men ate with him, he would keep them good company."[114]

This testimony is of precious value, for, although Louis became an ascetic, he continued to uphold his rank for those aspects of table manners that did not concern food itself, listening to music after meals and taking part in the sociability centered around the table.

The King's Duties

There are still several sources we have not yet examined—not the testimonies of the biographer-hagiographers but that of two chroniclers. They are both foreigners and religious.

The younger one is the Italian Franciscan Fra Salimbene of Parma. We have seen him awaiting the king's arrival at Sens en route to the crusade. The general chapter of the Franciscans was held there in June 1248.[115] Salimbene highlighted the episode of the presentation of a large pike to the king.[116]

It was only a gift, and we do not get to see the king eating it, but we do know that he was a pike aficionado, and the episode does introduce a gastronomic note into the scene of the king's devout arrival. The king could not escape without taking part in a culinary feast. In the honor of the king and his companions, the good Franciscan friends of joy did not hesitate to place small dishes inside of large ones:

> On that day, the king covered all the expenses and he ate with the friars, and the king's three brothers ate there too along with the cardinal of the Roman court, the general minister, Friar Rigaud the archbishop of Rouen, the provincial minister of France, the custodes, definitors, and discreets, everyone who belonged to the chapter and all the other friars who lodged there whom we call *forains*. Seeing that the king had noble and honorable company with him, the general minister . . . did not want to act with any ostentation . . . although he

had been invited to sit by the king's side, and preferred to exhibit what the Lord taught through words and showed by example, in other words courtesy [*curialitas*] and humility.... Friar John [of Parma] then chose to sit down at the table of the humble which was ennobled by his presence and where he set a good example for many....[117]

So, here Saint Louis was not the one to give an example of humility at the table but instead it was the general minister John of Parma who set one; he was a Joachimite, a "leftist" after all. And here is their menu:

> First we had cherries, then very white bread, and wine which was worthy of the royal munificence, rich and excellent. And after the habit of the French, there were many who invited people to drink with them who did not want to drink at all, and they would force them into it. Then, there were fresh beans in almond milk and cinnamon powder, roasted eels with a wonderful seasoning, pies and cheeses [in small wicker baskets], and fruits in abundance. And it was all served courteously and with care.[118]

The menu reconciled the abundance of the feast and the quality of the dishes with a Franciscan retinue — no meat was served. Did Saint Louis eat some of everything? Did he eat a lot? Fra Salimbene does not tell us. In his account, however, Saint Louis was more closely associated with the splendor of the royal table than with any dietary abstinence.

At last, here is my final source, the English Benedictine chronicler Matthew Paris. He had been informed about Henry III the king of England's stay in Paris in 1254, invited by the king of France. The high point was the banquet Saint Louis held in the honor of his royal guest:

> On the same day, his Royal Highness the king of France, as he had promised, dined with his Royal Highness the king of England in the grand royal hall of the so-called Old Temple with the numerous entourages [*familia*] of the two kings. And all of the rooms were full of guests. There were no porters or clerks at the main door, nor at any of the entrances. The access was generally open to everyone, and they received a sumptuous meal. The only possible source of disgust could have come from the overabundance of dishes.... No

one had ever seen such a noble, brilliant, and well-attended banquet in the past, neither in the times of Ahasuerus, Arthur, or Charlemagne. The endless variety of the dishes was magnificent, the abundance of the drinks delicious, the quality of the service pleasing, the order of the guests well controlled, the largesse of the gifts overabundant. . . . They ate in the following arrangement: His Royal Highness the king of France who is the king of kings of the world was placed in the center in the highest seat, with His Royal Highness the king of England to his right and his Royal Highness the king of Navarre on his left. . . . Then, the dukes were seated according to their dignity and their ranks, and twenty-five people sat on higher seats among the dukes. There were twelve bishops, whom some people place higher than dukes, but they were seated among the barons. As for the number of illustrious knights who were there, no one could have counted them all. There were eighteen countesses, of whom three were the sisters of the queens I have mentioned, to be more precise—the countess of Cornwall and the countess of Anjou and Provence with their mother the countess Beatrice, who were comparable to queens. After the sumptuous and splendid meal, even though it was supposed to be a day for fish,[119] the king of England spent the night in the main palace of His Royal Highness the king of France, which is at the center of Paris.[120]

Here it was November 1254, a date when, according to the other biographers, the king was stricken with sadness due to the crusade's failure. This was also around the time he began the dietary asceticism that he would take more and more seriously. So, what did he do? He held a great banquet where people ate meat on a day that they were supposed to go meatless. Royal splendor was in full effect, even in the toasts that had political characteristics. And even though he had been a moderate guest in the past (Matthew Paris does not say anything about this), the king came away from it laughing and joking.

Louis respected his standing at the table when he needed to and even knew how to make sacrifices for the sake of royal table manners, including culinary splendor and princely gastronomy.

Once more, I am adding several nuances to the opinion of William Jordan who depicts Saint Louis as still suffering from the conflict between his tendencies toward asceticism and the splendorous obligations of his function, torn between the monastic convent model that he preferred and the super-aristocratic royal model that tradition and public opinion tried to impose on him. In Jordan's view, there had to be a conflict here between the two external models that he was supposed to have internalized and that he had trouble living with. Although he did bring masochistic tendencies to the table, I do not believe Saint Louis ever had any schizophrenic behavior. Just as he harmoniously united within himself the knight and the peacemaker, war and peace, respect for the Church, the religious and the clerics with resistance to the bishops and the papacy, the inquiries into the abuses of royal officers and the pursuit of the construction of the centralized monarchical state, ethics and politics, he balanced his dietary morality and the execution of his royal duties at the table both within his conduct and his conscience. On the other hand, some of his contemporaries and subjects were able to see a form of hypocrisy in this that they identified with the model of the Mendicant friars, his advisors and models, and they blamed him for it.

A ROYAL MODEL

No sooner do we get the impression that the record assembled here allows us to come close to the personal truth about Saint Louis' eating habits than at least one text throws us back into the realm of the collective, the normative, and the commonplace.

The *Carolinum* is a Mirror of the Princes written in verse by Gilles de Paris. He offered it to the prince Louis, the oldest son and future heir of Philip Augustus, Saint Louis' own father, in 1200. Gilles proposed Charlemagne as a model for the young prince, and this is how he describes the emperor at his table:

> Feeling no burning sensation in his gullet,
> Nor shiver in his open throat, nor urgency in his stomach,
> But in a way adept at living moderately, except when it was appropriate
> For the royal palace to shine with luxurious abundance, he was only
> Rarely a good dinner companion, allowing no more than four dishes
> At the table, with a preference for roasted meats

Which he said were his favorite food,
Asking them to skewer choice morsels of game,
And consuming even those moderately
And far from reaching full satiety,
And never drinking wine more than four times during his meals.[121]

It is obvious that behind these lines lies Eginhard's ninth-century *Vita Caroli,* the *Life of Charlemagne.*

> In eating and drinking he was moderate [*temperans*] but he was even more moderate in his drinking because he hated drunkenness not just in his home and among his own people but in any place at all. He had more trouble abstaining from food and would often complain that fasts were harmful to his body. He only rarely took part in banquets and only on the great festival days, but then it would be in the midst of a crowd of people. For lunch he usually only had four dishes with the exception of the roasted meat that the hunters would usually prepare on brochettes, which was his favorite food. While eating, he would happily listen to a singer or someone reading. . . . He was so modest in his consumption of wine or any other drink that he only rarely drank more than three times in the course of a meal. In the summer, after the noon meal, he would eat a fruit and would only drink once, then, undressing as if it were nighttime, he would nap for two or three hours.[122]

If we replace the roasts with fish, slip some water into the wine, and get rid of the siesta, Charlemagne at the table is transformed into Saint Louis at the table. It was at the beginning of the thirteenth century that the Capetians realized their dream of making real and manifest the idea that they descended from Charlemagne—the *reditus ad stirpem Karoli*—and that they behaved like he did. With only a little exaggeration, Saint Louis at his table was only a Capetian imitating Charlemagne at his table. When we are tracking the individual and think we can surprise him with his specific qualities, it is obviously quite difficult to get away from the collective, the models, and the commonplace ideas. Did Saint Louis even eat?

The King's Three Functions

Roughly thirty years ago, some medievalists came to recognize that George Dumézil's hypotheses about the existence of a general organizing principle of thought in Indo-European societies according to three basic functions could be applied to medieval Western society.[1] From the tenth century on (and already in the ninth century with the Anglo-Saxon king Alfred's translation of Boethius's *Consolation of Philosophy*), this tri-functional ideology began to show up in Latin Christian thought in conditions and along paths of transmission that are still unclear. Ireland may have played an important role in this process, although it has not been proven that these ideas were disseminated from this source. The ideology showed up in a formula that occurred in the famous poem that Bishop Adalbéron of Laon addressed to the Capetian king Robert the Pious around 1027. According to this formula, society was made up of three orders: the order of those who pray (*oratores*), the order of those who fight (*bellatores*), and the order of those who work (*laboratores*).[2]

Georges Duby demonstrated that this organizing principle could be found in a large number of the intellectual and institutional structures of

Western society in the eleventh and twelfth centuries. He also showed that it was still very much alive up through the seventeenth century, for example in the works of the political theorist Loyseau. It remained influential up to the beginning of the French Revolution, which, in a certain way, represented its triumph and its end.[3]

THE CHRISTIAN KING, A KING WITH THREE FUNCTIONS

This model seems helpful to me for understanding the nature and image of royalty embodied in Saint Louis. Let us first recall that the most important characteristic of medieval Christian thought's application of the tri-functional ideology to royalty was that each king united all three functions within himself.[4] In contrast to the situation in ancient India and early Rome, kings were not thought to characterize one or another of the three functions after the examples of the gods, essentially appearing as either a legislator or a warrior or protector of the land's prosperity.

Finally, without going into the details of the complex problems regarding the tri-functional ideology's dissemination, we should emphasize one thing: that its influence and applications in the medieval West were limited. This was due to the existence of other competing schemas that were first and foremost binary (clerics and laymen, the powerful and the poor), but also ternary (virgins, abstinent men, married men, or, for women, virgins, abstinent women, wives), and, finally, multiple (with the different "states" in the world, the play of socio-professional categories in vogue in the thirteenth century, and the king and the bishop at the head of the chain of states after the emperor and the pope). As George Dumézil has shown, this limited influence was also due to the fact that tri-functional thought was foreign to Christianity's main text of reference — the Bible. Clerics in the Middle Ages attempted to introduce tri-functionalism into the Bible through a slow process that in the twelfth century, for example, ended up identifying Noah's three sons Shem, Japheth, and Ham with the three functions or social groups of clerics, warriors, and serfs and with the third group subordinated to the first two.

The schema of the three social orders still more or less explicitly and more or less clearly existed at the end of the thirteenth century in the way the clerics viewed the society of their time. Pope Boniface VIII referred to the system in his bull for Saint Louis' canonization in 1297. As he wished to associate all Frenchmen with the joy of canonizing "a ruler of such quality and grandeur" who came out of "the illustrious house of France," he called on them all to rejoice, naming the three "states" in order, including and beginning with the mass of workers who made up the third function, "the very devout people of France."[5] He then named "the prelates and the clergy" who represented the first function, followed by "the powerful, the magnates, the nobles, and the knights," who were all men of the second function. The pope did not follow the schema's usual order and he expanded the third function to include the entire people, but it was clearly the same model of classification.

THE FIRST FUNCTION: THE SACRED KING AS DISPENSER OF PEACE AND JUSTICE

A sacred king, Saint Louis practiced and embodied the values and roles that defined the king's first function in a Christian society to the utmost degree.[6]

The king's first sacred attribute was justice.[7]

In the preamble to his biography, Guillaume de Saint-Pathus states that the king "did neither harm nor violence to anyone and upheld justice with supreme power [*souverainement*]." The expression was more than appropriate. His justice was "supreme" (*souveraine*) due to both the moral perfection and the judicial authority of the man who rendered it.

Boniface VIII said the same thing in one of his sermons from Orvieto: "His justice was so great that it appeared manifest not only through examples but [through the fact that] people could reach out and touch him [as he rendered it.] He would actually almost constantly sit on a carpet on the ground in order to hear judicial cases, especially those of orphans and the poor, and he would render justice for them completely."[8] In the first sentences of the bull for his canonization he also praised Saint Louis as "a fair judge and a praiseworthy distributor of rewards."[9] In this function of rewarding others, the king proved himself the image of God on earth who was the giver of rewards par excellence and for all eternity.

This judgment is also confirmed by contemporary sources. At Hyères, during the return from the crusade of 1254, the Joachimite Franciscan Hugh of Digne who made such a strong impression on Saint Louis,[10] "taught the king in his sermon how he should conduct himself according to the will of his people. At the end of his sermon, he thus said . . . that in the book of the faithful nor in the books of the infidels, he had never seen any kingdom or any domain that was ever lost or passed from one seigniory to another or from one king to another except by a failure of justice. 'So', he said, 'since he is returning to France, the king must take care to execute justice well enough for his people to keep the love of God and in such a way that God will not take the Kingdom of France away from him with his life'."[11]

The king was not only a dispenser of justice in France, Paris, or Vincennes, but he also exercised justice overseas. Joinville mentions a number of "condemnations and judgments" pronounced at Caesaria in Palestine "when the king was staying there."[12]

In following God's example, Louis was capable of clemency as well. On one day of deliberations, a woman who was standing at the bottom of the palace stairs insulted the king and told him: "It is a terrible shame that you are the king of France and it is amazing that no one has booted you out of the kingdom." The royal sergeants wanted to chase her down and give her a beating, but Louis ordered them not to chase her and not to touch her. Then, after carefully listening to her, he answered: "Certainly you are telling the truth. I am not worthy of being king. And, if it had pleased Our Lord, it would have been better for another man to have been king in my place if he could have known how to govern the kingdom any better." And then he ordered one of his chamberlains to give her money, "forty sous, they say."[13]

Guillaume de Saint-Pathus also tells the story of several people who were stealing silver platters and other objects from the king's hall. Louis put up with this and even gave the thieves some money before sending them across the sea.[14] Clemency and deportation: these were two sides of Saint Louis' royal justice.

Of course, he was also capable of being very harsh and even cruel in his judgments. He was pitiless in punishing blasphemers. In Caesaria he once had a blaspheming jeweler stripped and put in the stocks. In Paris, "he had the nose and the lip of a bourgeois burnt" for the same crime.[15] However, the one case of judicial severity for which he was blamed the most was the famous affair of Enguerran the lord of Coucy who without any trial had hung three young nobles who got lost in some woods on his land. He accused them of coming to hunt on his lands although they did not even have any arms or dogs with them. We should recall Louis' reaction and conduct in this affair. He had Enguerran, his knights, and the sergeants who were his advisors arrested. He also refused his request for a judicial "combat" (a duel). The barons on his council asked him to free Enguerran. He curtly refused and got up, leaving the barons "astonished and confused." He finally freed him "on the counsel of his advisors," but only after condemning him to pay a heavy penalty: Enguerran had to pay a fine of 12,000 pounds *parisis* that would be sent to Acre for the defense of the Holy Land; Louis confiscated the forest where he hung the youths, sentenced him to build three chapels to pray for their souls, and stripped him of his rights and privileges over his woods and ponds.

Saint Louis' severity here cannot be explained solely by the fact that the uncle of one of these boys who was the plaintiff in this affair was an abbot, or by the king's desire to see law replace "combat" in judicial affairs. For him, it was mainly a matter of showing that justice was the same for everyone, and that even the most powerful lords were not exempt from its rule. And, as royal justice alone was capable of enforcing this principle, he strengthened it by taking these actions when confronted with opposition from the barons and nobles. In his counsel he vigorously "squelched" ["*moucha,*" i.e., put in his place] the count of Brittany, Jean I the Red when he denied the king's right to lead investigations against the barons in matters touching upon "their persons, their inheritances, and their honors." The nobles were not mistaken. Saint Louis' royal justice was no longer a justice apportioned according to rank. The affair stirred up a lot of people despite the king's partial retreat from his original position.[16]

It would still be inaccurate and anachronistic to attribute some project or desire for social equality to Saint Louis. He clearly had the hierarchical spirit of the men of the Middle Ages. And yet, all men were equal facing sin. In effect, justice always presented him with an eschatological horizon. It prefigured the equality of the elect and the damned in eternity.[17] In this respect, Saint Louis was well disposed for hearing the Joachimite Hugh of Digne's message. He may have even been exposed to more radical views. In the Middle Ages and even after them, millenarianism fed the most "revolutionary" impulses and ideas.[18] Although Saint Louis' spirit looked toward eternity, he still kept his feet on the ground.

PEACE

With justice comes the second important royal function exercised by Saint Louis—peace.[19]

Peace and justice were bound together in the oath sworn by Louis IX for his coronation.[20] Justice had to establish peace, and the desire for peace should inspire justice. Boniface VIII made the same declaration: "Justice and peace go together, and he governed so well with justice that his kingdom was able to enjoy lasting peace."[21]

In this bellicose medieval world, Louis dreaded war because it inevitably existed as a source of sin and injustice. In his *Enseignements* for his son he wrote:

> Dear Son, I teach you that you are to prevent yourself, as much as possible, from having war with any Christian; and, if anyone does you any wrong, try different ways to find out if you cannot find some means to recover your rights before making war, and take care to remember that this is in order to avoid the sins committed in war. . . . And be sure you know that you are well advised before declaring war, and that you have given ample warning to the offender, and that you have listened enough, as you should.[22]

He was the great "peacemaker" of his time, and he first exercised this function at home, in his own kingdom. In his advice to his son, he continued on this topic:

> Dear Son, I teach you that the wars and struggles that will take place on your land or between your own men should occupy all your efforts, as much as possible, to put them to rest, because this is a thing that pleases Our Lord very much.[23]

But he was also a peacemaker outside the kingdom, especially at its borders, as if to create a zone of peace along the French borders. Guillaume de Saint-Pathus alludes to this at the end of his chapter on the king's love for his neighbors, evoking the instable and bellicose eastern frontier:

> When he heard the news that there was war between the noblemen beyond his kingdom, he sent them official messengers to pacify them, and not without significant expense. This is what he did when the count of Bar and His Grace Henry count of Luxembourg made war on one another. He also did this when hostilities broke out be-

tween the duke of Lorraine and this same count of Bar, and for many others. And so it appears that not only did he know how to form his neighbor in goodness but also how to reform him in goodness.[24]

As we have seen, Joinville also goes over the defining episodes of Louis' peace-making political role. The term recurs obsessively throughout these pages.[25]

We know that this policy was not pursued with unanimity among the king's advisors. They opposed his idealism with the cynicism of a feudal tradition that, far from putting out the fires of war, fanned them in order to profit from them. Joinville, however, was in agreement with the king here, stressing how he also benefited from his peace-making politics.[26] As was almost always the case, he drew a double reward for this—a reward in heaven for pleasing God and a reward on earth for having put one or several leaders in his debt. This was his way of contributing to this "descent of the values of heaven to earth," which, in my view, characterized the turn of the twelfth and thirteenth centuries.[27]

Saint Louis put his politics for peace to work most frequently when the Kingdom of France and his own royal function were at risk. It was especially at those moments that he showed how peace concessions could simultaneously function as pious acts and skillful political maneuvers. This was what occurred with the peace treaty with Aragon in 1258 and especially with the treaty with England in 1259.[28]

It is easy to see the collision between the two systems of values here, one of them inspired by the new religiosity that had deep and far-reaching roots in Christianity, the other inherited from feudal tradition. Louis combined them, making this a practically unique moment in the history of medieval France.

For the Kingdom of France, the result was the exceptional benefit of a long period of peace. In his *Gesta,* Guillaume de Nangis dedicates a long paragraph to this subject, making his peace-making ability one of the saint king's main merits after the example of "Solomon, the peace-loving king." According to him, God granted Saint Louis the condition that peace would rule throughout the Kingdom of France from his return from the Holy Land in 1254 to his death in 1270. He even prolonged this favor to the benefit of his son and heir Philip III, or at least "as long as he ruled in accordance with the saint king's merits"—in other words, until his war against Aragon (1284–1285).[29] The papacy hypocritically dubbed this war a "crusade," as they had previously done for their war against Frederick II.

Returning to the theme in his second sermon of Orvieto dated August 11, 1297, Boniface VIII gave the terms *pax* and *rex pacificus* their fully charged eschatological meanings. He calls Solomon *rex pacificus* and applies the same term to Saint Louis; this was his sermon's theme drawn from the Old Testament: "*Magnificatus est Solomon*" (1 Kings 10:23)."

> When they call him [Saint Louis] "peaceable" [*pacifique*] and "peacemaking" [*pacem faciens*], by this gift and this virtue they designate all gifts and all virtues. He was peaceable within himself and in relation to everyone else, not just his subjects but foreigners as well. He was, in himself, peaceable. In effect, he had peace in this world, the peace of the heart, and so he attained the peace of eternity. All his contemporaries saw how he upheld the peace in his kingdom. This peace cannot exist without justice. And it is because he was just in respect to himself, in respect to God, and in respect to his neighbor that he had peace.[30]

It was not just a matter of an absence of war or worldly tranquility here, but an essential eschatological peace that outlined the peace of Heaven and eternity in this world. As with justice, it is clear that we are dealing with a function of the sacred.

Louis' prestige and renown as a peacemaker were already so great at the time of the Council of Lyon in 1244–1245 that Frederick II, already at daggers drawn with Pope Innocent IV, proposed the arbitration of the king of France "who was a *prud'homme*," swearing that he would do everything he commanded.[31] Saint Louis was already viewed as an arbiter for Christendom.

However, he did not always succeed. When he was asked to arbitrate the conflict between the king of England and his barons in revolt, he was partial to the king and ruled in his favor. His familial ties with the sovereign, his lack of knowledge about England's history and social and political structures, and his steadfast belief in the eminent superiority of the royal function all led him to a ruling that pacified no one and that, for once, led him to be condemned for being biased.[32]

The Second Function: A Warrior King

Saint Louis dreaded war and its injustices. It was a source of sin, but not always, not against the infidel, hence the crusade. Nor was it a source of sin when it was a matter of pushing back attacking Christian rulers who violated their oaths of fidelity or who unjustly engaged in uprisings—hence the war against his revolting vassals early in his reign, the expedition of 1242 against the king of England and his French allies, and the repression of the Occitan aftereffects of the war against the Albigensian heretics and their protectors that had been gloriously executed by his father Louis VIII. When he engaged in a war he believed was just, Louis did so without any misgivings. And like his ancestors, he participated in combat and fought well. He was a good knight, a king who fulfilled his second function.

The chronicles inform us about the king's wars, but tell us little about the king at war. The biographers and hagiographers who were clerics and, for the most part, Mendicants, passed over this aspect of the king's life in silence. They were much more interested in peace than in war.

Because he was a layman and a knight himself and because he was at the king's side on the crusade and in the Holy Land, only Joinville strongly emphasized this aspect of the warrior king. He mentions the king's "great acts of prowess" and "great daring." The battle between the French and English at Taillebourg[33] began "great and strong," and "when the king saw this he threw himself in harm's way with the others."[34] And at the battle of Mansourah, when the disaster had not yet played out, Joinville gives us an exemplary, emblematic visual image of Saint Louis the knight king.[35]

Louis carried out his royal military duty. And we can guess that he even fought with the enthusiasm of the feudal warrior, joyless perhaps, but not without a certain virile abandon.

He took on his royal war-making function in all the dimensions that war assumed at its highest level in the thirteenth century.[36] He very carefully prepared the material logistics for his expeditions, especially for his crusades. He brought an important stockpile of siege engines with him to Egypt, particularly the *chats-châteaux*.[37] Whenever there was a war or the danger of war, he took care to maintain, repair, or construct fortified castles and fortifications. This was the main objective of his stay in the Holy Land where he fortified or reinforced the fortifications of Sayette (Sidon), Sur (Tyre), Acre, Châtel-Pèlerin, Caesaria, and Jaffa among others. Even in France he was preparing for war at the same time that he was trying to make peace. Matthew Paris twice tells how he was still conducting a campaign building fortifications in Normandy in 1257.[38]

He had been knighted at the age of twelve in December 1229 at Soissons while en route to his coronation in Reims. He held great ceremonious celebrations for the young men of the royal family when they entered the knighthood. The dubbing of his younger brother took place on June 7, 1237, the day of Pentecost. On this day important festivals of the nobility were also held alongside the other traditional festivals of the religious calendar. His dubbing took place in the palace in Compiègne during a large ceremony in which Louis was said to have dubbed many other young nobles in the presence of two thousand knights. On Saint John's Day, June 24, 1241, the day of a sacred pagan festival that had been appropriated by the Christian nobility, the no less ceremonious dubbing of his second brother Alphonse de Poitiers was held in Saumur.[39] In 1246, again on Pentecost, his third and youngest brother Charles d'Anjou was dubbed in Melun. The brothers became knights when they reached the age of their majority at twenty. The king then placed them in possession of the apanages bequeathed to them by their father, Louis VIII, and they pledged liege homage to their royal brother. Finally, there was the ceremonial dubbing of Louis' son and from this point future heir Philip on Pentecost, June 5, 1267 in the garden of the royal palace of the Cité in Paris along with a large number of other young nobles. Saint Louis clearly appeared as the knight king presiding over a family of knights, the warrior king of a family of warriors.

Saint Louis and the Third Function

The third function is the trickiest to define, as Georges Dumézil himself has stressed. It was a Protean function with numerous and sometimes disconcerting features. It was as a king of the third function, the function of the "production of material goods," that Saint Louis is the hardest to grasp. This is all the more true insofar as this function seems particularly well concealed in the Christian medieval West—outside those cases where it applied to magic objects bordering on the marvelous, or, more clearly, when it referred to the specific, though dominated, producers of these goods such as peasants or artisans and laborers, "manual workers"—the *laboratores* in Aldabéron of Laon's schema.

Royalty was experiencing declining efficiency in its ability to carry out its third function at this time. Despite the appeal to God to assure *abundantia* for the new king during the coronation ceremony, we can observe a weakening and a virtual disappearance of the king's magical powers in economic matters. Charlemagne was called *summus agricola*, the agricultural producer par excellence. Dagobert made the crops grow as he passed. According to the record assembled just after Philip Augustus's death in the attempt to have him sainted, he was said to have accomplished three miracles in the early years of his reign, all of which related to the third function.[40]

We can find nothing like this for Saint Louis. Among the sixty officially recognized miracles he accomplished, we can only find one that even modestly relates to the third function: the king miraculously dried three flooded cellars belonging to the widow of one of his squires, who recognized his power over nature in this. Of course, many people underscored his physical beauty, which was one facet of the third function. His contemporaries praised his beauty in terms that evoked the rhetorical commonplace ideas on the human physique, although we can glimpse a reflection of reality in them.[41] We have seen the almost "raw" shock that the sight of the royal visage struck in the heart of the Franciscan Salimbene of Parma at Sens in 1248.[42] What people insisted on above all here was the fact that the beauty of his face and body expressed the beauty of his heart and spirit in accordance with the medieval Christian concept of external appearance as the image of internal being. Boniface VIII did not fail to allude to this: "The saintliness of his life was manifest to everyone who looked upon his face: 'He was full of grace' [Esther 15]."[43] We have also seen how one of the *Lives*, destined for liturgical use and probably written shortly after his canonization, detailed his physical beauty.[44]

More importantly, Saint Louis took the material benefits already attributed to his predecessors and other Christian rulers to new heights. He was an incredible almsgiver, generously providing the poor with food and other charitable gifts either directly or through the intermediary of the clergy and religious orders. He fed monks, friars, the sick, and the poor himself. He was a king who nursed his subjects to health and who always seemed to be expending his wealth for them, without even counting the bequests of his will and testament. He combined three important characteristics of the third function within his life: the largesse that characterized princely and aristocratic morality, the charity that played a central role in the system of works of mercy that took shape in the thirteenth century, the munificence involved in constructing important buildings, especially religious buildings, which proliferated in this century of burgeoning Gothic art.[45]

The alms-giving king particularly impressed his contemporaries in this century when charity in the form of money was nevertheless largely exercised by rulers and nobles—and by bourgeois as well who were already entering high society more easily. These gifts were made through the new "works of mercy" advocated by the Mendicants and encouraged by the spreading use of currency.

"As for the works," says Boniface VIII in his sermon of Orvieto dated August 6, 1297, "the saintliness of his life was above all expressed in his alms for the poor, his construction of hospices and churches, and all his other works of mercy that form a list too long to mention here."[46] And the pope added that if anyone wanted to guess the amount of his alms, they could consider the single example of one of the new charitable measures he took: his decision that for each of his "entrances" into Paris, additional alms would be given to the religious and especially to the Mendicant friars.[47] Guillaume de Saint-Pathus dedicated a long chapter to his "works of piety," emphasizing—as we already know—that Louis' voyages through his kingdom were above all campaigns for the distribution of alms.[48] Joinville highlighted this as well: "The king was such a great giver of alms that everywhere he went in his kingdom, he would give to the poor, the churches, the lazar houses, the hospices, the hospitals, and poor noblemen and noble women."[49] Joinville also committed an entire chapter to the king's "large and generous almsgiving" for the construction of hospices—including the house of Quatre-Vingts in Paris built for three hundred blind people, and the building of churches and convents.[50] Saint Louis was not just satisfied with considerably increasing the amount given for royal alms. He organized them by granting a certificate in 1260 that created a position and a leader, the *aumônier,* who was responsible for repairing the measures taken by his grandfather Philip Augustus around 1190, imitating an action that had already been taken by the king of England. Louis thus institutionalized the alms distributed by his predecessors, estimated at around 2,119 livres *parisis,* 63 *muids* of wheat (one *muid* was the equivalent of roughly 1,500 Parisian liters), and 68,000 herrings that the *aumônier* and the bailiffs had to distribute. A copy of this certificate was deposited in the hospice as a testimony for posterity and future reference. This text lists the details of royal charity "in such minute detail that all by itself it is enough to give us a clear sense of Louis' spirit that was as generous as it was scrupulous if not downright fastidious."[51] Finally, under Saint Louis, almsgiving was integrated into the handling of affairs at the king's *hôtel*. This united the first administrative and sacred function with the third function, which was economic, financial, and charitable.[52]

He set down the important principles of his largesse and charity in his testament drawn up in February 1270. He allotted all his moveable goods and the revenue from the woods of the royal domains to three kinds of legatees: victims of royal exactions who deserved some restitution, a number of his officers whom it was appropriate to reward, and a long list of hospitals and religious orders with the Mendicants—who used these alms to care for the poor and build churches—topping off the list. In return, his beneficiaries were supposed to pray for him, his family, and the kingdom. If any money was left after these restitutions had been made, his successor was supposed to use it "for the honor of God and the benefit of the kingdom."[53]

Still, Saint Louis was not as freewheeling with his spending as some say. On this point, he shared the new values of economic conduct and savings just as he tempered the ferocity of the valorous knight with the wisdom of the *prud'homme*. He partook of this new tendency to more accurately and more moderately keep track of his funds. Alexander Murray has demonstrated that this was a new characteristic of a society that was beginning to calculate in the dual sense of *ratio*, of "calculation and reason" in its public and private acts.[54] In his *Enseignements* for his son, Saint Louis declared:

> Dear Son, I teach you to have the solid intention that the *deniers* that you spend be spent for good use and that they be raised justly. And, this is a sense that I would like you to have—what I mean is that you prevent yourself from making any frivolous expenses and unjust collections and that your *deniers* be raised justly and well employed. . . .

However, what led the way in Saint Louis' exercise of the third royal function was his application of miraculous therapy. The king of France made up for everything he had abandoned of his function as a magical force in agriculture with his acquisition of the prestige of one who could touch and heal the scrofulous.[55]

My impression is that this miraculous gift for healing that originally belonged to the first function of the king's sacredness evolved toward the third function through the dimension of health, healing, and charity that it fundamentally assumed with Saint Louis. The king as benefactor eclipsed the thaumaturgical king in the eyes of his contemporaries. Healing was a work of mercy. In the thirteenth century there was no difference between the sick and poor, and Saint Louis made no distinction between them.

I suspect that the theme of the sun-king, which only appeared briefly in the works of Saint Louis' hagiographers and which undoubtedly came from a Hellenistic and imperial Roman tradition, tended to slip from the function of the sacred to the function of charity from the point of view that fixated on the idea of the perfect Western Christian king.

The rays of Saint Louis' royal sun lit the way for his subjects and kept them warm.[56]

From our own modern perspective, what most characterizes the third function, defined by its ties to prosperity and the material reproduction of society, is the economic domain. Now, we have to examine Saint Louis' role in the economy. His conduct is not entirely clear.

Saint Louis and the Economy

How did a king of thirteenth-century France see and conceive of the economy? What interest did he take in it? What was his influence over it? What access to our knowledge and understanding of the king can it offer? This investigation is a difficult undertaking, especially since there are no precedents to help us here, to the best of my knowledge. It is even more difficult for another fundamental reason: what we call the economy today did not constitute any specific domain perceived as such nor any particular mental category in the thirteenth century. This is an important problem for the study of the economies of the past and it is a problem economists and historians have only rarely dealt with. Among all these, only Karl Polanyi has been of any assistance here with his notion of an embedded economy[57]—in other words an economy that did not appear as such in any specific way, but which was always caught up within a social whole, contained within the society without any autonomous nature or representation— without any proper name, and which did not confer any primary or principle characteristics to this whole.

I will nevertheless attempt to outline the relations that existed between Saint Louis and the economy. First, I will attempt this by trying to understand how he perceived what we call the economy today. (He usually perceived it in a fragmentary way.) Then I will attempt to explain the ideological tools and non-economic concepts that mediated his understanding, the grids for reading and frameworks for action that defined his behavior in the economic domain. In the first case, the economy was embedded within the royal administration and its finances; in the second case, it was embedded in religion, morality, and political theory.

ECONOMY AND ADMINISTRATION

Saint Louis was not aware of the existence of economics or political economy, nor did he engage in any self-conscious economic behavior. How could he have had any education in this matter? Contrary to the arguments of some historians, I do not believe that any economic doctrine existed in the thirteenth-century Church. There were simply certain scholastic masters and friars inspired by them who in their writings and teachings on commerce and usury liked to recall several moral or theological principles that had consequences we would identify today as belonging to the field of economics. Thomas Aquinas was one of the major figures to adopt this position, which typically appeared in treatises on the "restitutions" (*De restitutionibus*) demanded by usurers. The king, however, encountered economic forces in several important sectors of the royal administration and dealt with them according to non-economic criteria. Without going into too many details, which would lead us too far from the subject of the king, I will go over five royal administrative activities that had economic and financial components: the management of the domain, the king's attitude toward the cities and notably Paris, the financing of war and the crusades, the struggle against usury, and monetary problems.

In the thirteenth century, revenue from the royal domain still made up the largest part of the king's resources. He "lived off his own." These revenues were primarily derived from agriculture. Louis was a king of land. Most of this revenue came from land and forest, as the surviving accounts from 1234, 1238, and 1248 show that the king's forests brought him one-fourth of the income from his domains.[58] The royal domain had quadrupled in size under Philip Augustus. This made Louis a wealthy heir. There was no definite system for the economic management of the domain. The bailiffs and seneschals, and the officers [*prévôts*] beneath them had judicial, financial, and military responsibilities at the same time. They did not have any particular specialized function. They were jacks-of-all-trades for the royal government.

Of course, a certain administrative, financial order came into being through the continuity established with the projects undertaken by Philip Augustus.[59] In 1238, a new system for classifying expenses was put into place. They henceforth distinguished between expenses of a "feudal" nature, those pertaining to the king's public authority, and the earnings of the royal officers. The first were called "fiefs and alms" [*feoda et elemoysynae*]. The word *feodum* here was used in the sense of *beneficium,* "benefice" [*bienfait*], and, in addition to a fief represented by a certain land, it may also be a fief represented by a sum of money, a kind of allowance called a *"fief de bourse."* The latter were starting to become more common as the king did not want to diminish his land holdings and the circulation of money was on the rise, so these payments met the growing needs of the nobles at a time when Louis was rich in cash. Joinville was a beneficiary of one of these *fiefs de bourse* when he was in the Holy Land. The purchases of new fiefs that increased the royal domain also fell into this category. One example was the purchase of the Mâconnais in 1240. Expenses of the second type were called *"oeuvres"* (*opera,* works), and included payments for the construction and upkeep of buildings, the maintenance and development of roadways and related infrastructure—the *"grand-route"* depended on public authority—and, more generally, what we today would call "facilities" or "public works." Finally, the royal agents' salaries appeared under the category called "liberalities" [*liberationes*].

The record of expenses for the officers and bailiffs dating from Ascension 1248 were considered a masterwork of presentation and served as a model for a long time to come. Louis IX's agents also began to exercise a more thorough surveillance of the Royal Treasury kept in the Temple whose role was now reduced to keeping track of accounts.

Although expenses became the object of just a few new arrangements, records of revenue offer even fewer examples of change.

Royal serfs could buy their freedom, individually or collectively. This was an additional resource for the monarchy, a testimony to the growing wealth of certain rural milieus, and a phenomenon that expressed the overall decline in social and moral servitude. Historians have often determined that Saint Louis' reign was a period of improving conditions for the French peasantry.[60] The king freed his serfs at Villeneuve-le-Roi in 1246, as he would later free those at Thiais, Val d'Arcueil, Grauchet, Orly, Paray, Issy, Meudon, Fleury, Villeneuve-Saint-Georges, and Valenton in 1263. Did the royal domain serve as an example for the freeing of serfs in the fiefdoms? The actions of a number of lords lead us to think that it did.[61]

Some historians have asserted that "the attention that Saint Louis brings to bear on the kingdom's economy is above all fiscal."[62] Without denying the importance of the king's concerns about fiscal matters, we must nevertheless stress that in the king's mind, financial problems were first of all problems of morality and justice more than problems of recordkeeping. Louis had no doubts about the king's right to raise taxes, which was contested by certain thirteenth-century commentators of the Bible, but he thought that he was justified in raising taxes only if he did it in a just and moderate way.[63]

The mission confided to the royal investigators in 1247 on the eve of the crusade was the crowning achievement of this general action of setting the kingdom's affairs in order. However, the purpose of this operation was not economic. Its objective was the reestablishment of order and justice, the restitution of illegitimate exactions, and the punishment of corrupt royal officers, along with a certain will to put everything in order before the departure for the crusade. Yet, in this characteristic mixture of morality and the pursuit of his material interests, the king lost nothing by taking these measures. What he lost through restitutions, he more than made up in increased revenue and prestige. He garnered both moral and material benefits from these actions at the same time.

Generally speaking, in the domain, the fiefs, and the kingdom, Louis sought to take the best possible advantage of his feudal and royal revenues, although without innovating in any particular way. He continued in the tradition of his grandfather Philip Augustus here—whom Thomas Bisson has identified as the first truly feudal king of France because he took advantage of his increased royal power in order to better exercise his feudal prerogatives.[64] Thus Louis rigorously applied his "*droit de gîte*," the right to be lodged by certain vassals; he minutely concentrated on raising "assistance" [*aide*] in the form of taxes his vassals owed for the knighthood of his two brothers; he consistently exercised his rights to exact revenue from the circulation of merchandise such as tolls and transport fees. However, it was still respect for his political authority that he sought more than the profit of economic power. Some historians have noted that in Flanders and some of his other large fiefs, "the king did not lay hold of economic power when he was in the process of reassuming control over non-economic factors that had been monopolized by the feudal lords there for such a long time."[65]

More generally still, although he was attentive to the kingdom's material interests in the name of moral and religious principles; in the name of the same principles, he was even more hostile to the Church's increasing temporal wealth. In this Louis was heir to a burgeoning thirteenth-century tradition fostered by the Mendicant orders whose members were numerous in his entourage. He was a real stickler when it came to royal rights in episcopal lands as he showed very early in his conflict with the bishop of Beauvais and the archbishop of Reims in the 1230s.[66] This motivating factor combined with his condemnation of ecclesiastical greed. This was even truer in his dealings with the Roman curia; Louis became enflamed as he did in his "Protest" of 1247 addressed to the Holy See.[67]

THE KING AND HIS "GOOD TOWNS"

Cities were an ever growing force in thirteenth-century France. This was true from an economic point of view with the intensification of commerce, the growth of markets, the development of skilled labor, and the growing role of money. It was true from a social point of view with the increasing influence of the "bourgeois." It was true from a political angle with the development of city councils. It was also true in the cultural domain in which, for example, the copying and illustration of manuscripts shifted from the rural monastic scriptoria to urban workshops, and in which poetry and theater were being reborn through the impetus of social movements that included clerics and bourgeois. Finally, this was even true in the military domain where contingents of urban militias could play an important role as they did at Bouvines.

The monarchy under Saint Louis pursued a nuanced policy toward the cities.[68] Royal interventions in the affairs of the towns became more frequent. A number of edicts defined a framework for actions that could be taken by urban authorities.[69] The general trend was to place the towns under royal control. As William Jordan puts it so well, royal government expressed "evidence of continued vigorous moral concern with communal administration."[70] Once again, the essential motives were ethical and religious. It was a matter of making order and justice prevail in the towns. Louis and his advisors were scandalized by the way the wealthy individuals who governed the cities financially managed them for their own personal gain by exploiting the poor. In a text that has become a classic, the bailiff Philippe de Beaumanoir denounced the inequalities and injustices that the rich imposed on the urban lower classes.[71] However, once again, royal interest was associated with moral imperatives.

There were two important changes concerning royal control over the cities that occurred under Saint Louis.

The first of these changes concerned Paris. Paris became a demographic monster peopled by perhaps as many as 200,000 inhabitants at a time when no other city in Christendom exceeded a population of 100,000. At the very moment that Paris was in the process of becoming the capital of the monarchy, the numerous peasants who had recently emigrated to the city, the students who set a bad example for the town's youth (in the view of the monarchy)—an example of violence, gambling, and whoring—the beggars and other marginal groups, all increased those two intolerable evils for Saint Louis: disorder and sin.[72]

Louis granted Paris a special status that has survived in varying forms to this day. In 1261, the king proceeded with a reform of the provostship that granted the provost virtually unlimited powers for maintaining order—a very extensive notion—in the town. The provost became what we would now call a "police prefect" (or commissioner). Louis entrusted this office to Étienne Boileau, a firm-handed man who inspired confidence. The action imparted to him focused on three objectives: to assure respect for social order, to favor the development of prosperity, and to fill the Royal Treasury with financial contributions derived from the increasing wealth of the city and its well-off inhabitants. This action therefore possessed a truly "economic" aspect under the mantle of a policy for finance and policing.

One particularly important aspect of Parisian life—and therefore subject to the provost's function—was the activity of the tradesmen grouped into corporations. One year before the king's death in 1269, Étienne Boileau composed a book in order to document and explain his actions. Known as the *Livre des métiers* (Book of Trades), it was named after the content of its first section.[73] He began by reassembling all the texts of the statutes of the 101 registered Parisian corporations. This undertaking perfectly illustrates that although these regulations were made by the trades people for themselves, the royal government presented itself as the supreme protector of this professional order and assumed the means of intervening in its affairs with full knowledge of the fact should the need arise. This text, which is our main source of information on thirteenth-century economic life in Paris, was, in fact, a police document and cannot be generalized and extended to apply to all the towns of the kingdom.

The second part of Beaumanoir's work, which historians discuss little, is a list of the levies imposed by the royal power in Paris. Under the title *"Droitures et coutumes"* (Rights and Customs), it compiled an inventory of the tolls and levies forming two sorts of royal taxes—the civil contributions collected from everyone including the taille, tolls, and fees for passage [*conduits*], and the contributions levied specifically on commercial activities like the *hautban,* the *tonlieu* [a tax on transported merchandise or fee merchants paid to display their wares in the fairs and markets—Trans.], etc. This section that deals with commerce was the follow-up to the first part of the *Livre des métiers* for the skilled tradesmen.

Paris, however, was not the monarchy's only concern. Under Saint Louis the monarchy encouraged the formation of an urban network made up of those cities that were more important than the others. They called these cities the "good towns," and in times of need they were capable of serving as centers of refuge and resistance to enemy attacks thanks to the strength of their walls. They also formed centers of prosperity thanks to their economic activity. "Good" must be understood here in the sense of "strong and rich." For the king, these towns were reservoirs of wealth in the service of the monarchy. In his *Enseignements* for his son, he reminds him: "In case of need, you will be able to defend yourself with force and the wealth of your good towns."[74]

In the urban history of France, the age of Saint Louis appeared "to shape up as a veritable turning point."[75] Saint Louis involved representatives from the towns in important decisions alongside the barons who had been the only ones consulted in the feudal council to this point.[76]

Louis' attitude toward the cities allows us to posit a certain perception of economic factors on his part. The towns became an incarnation of the third function.

Financing War and the Crusade

Saint Louis' rule was a fairly peaceful reign for the Middle Ages, and Pope Boniface VIII pointed this out in his bull for the king's canonization. The only military operations were the "feudal" expeditions during the early years of the reign—the campaign against the English in 1241–1242, the expeditions in Languedoc in 1240 and 1242, and the two crusades, especially the crusade of 1248–1254. The Kingdom of France was at peace from 1254 to 1270.

Until 1253 when the weakening of royal power between the death of Blanche de Castile and the return of Louis IX provoked difficulties in keeping Saint Louis and his army in the Holy Land supplied with money, the crusade, the regime's one enormous expense, did not place any excessive burden on royal finances. The cities and especially the clergy provided most of the financing for the crusade, and the transfer of money from Paris through the control of the Temple and the royal curia to Egypt and Palestine was carried out regularly and without difficulty.

Surprisingly, the crusade, a religious act par excellence, was probably the one phenomenon more than any other that led Saint Louis and the royal government to perfect their financial techniques, although we should be careful not to exaggerate this point.[77]

Usury

The struggle against usury[78] (or "usuries" as people would say in the thirteenth century) was closely tied to the measures taken against the Jews. From 1230 (with the edict of Melun) to 1269, an entire series of measures against Jewish usurers were taken by Saint Louis or in his name.[79] Saint Louis' antiusurious legislation can be explained in light of the abundance of texts and treatises in which it appeared.

This was a period during which, on one hand, the basic attitudes against usury and usurers were set up on the grounds of the very ancient condemnations of usury. It was also the time when the most efficient practical and theoretical texts against luxury were written. These were the texts of the consular canons, the Third Lateran Council in 1179, the Fourth Lateran Council in 1215 that ordered restitutions, and the Second Council of Lyon

in 1274; the pontifical decretals from Urban III's decretal *Consuluit* (1187) to
the title *De usuris* and its twenty-nine chapters in the decretals of Gregory IX;
theological treatises like Robert de Courson's treatise *De Usura* from the
early years of the thirteenth century, Guillaume d'Auxerre's exposé (Treatise 26 in the book) in his *Summa* (*Summa in IV libros sententiarium*), Thomas
Aquinas's treatise in his *Summa theologica* (IIa-IIae, q. 78), Vincent de Beauvais'
treatise in Book 10 of his *Speculum doctrinale,* and, finally, after Saint Louis'
death, the most complete treatise against usury by Gilles de Lessine, a disciple of Thomas Aquinas from 1276 to 1285, the *De usura.* A large number
of *exempla* also showed usurers who were typically condemned to hell and, in
certain significant exceptions, to Purgatory. At the same time, the canonists
developed the "excuses" that authorized charging interest on a growing
number of financial operations and tended to recommend limiting usurious
interest rates instead of eliminating "moderate" usury.

Only Christian usurers brought down the wrath of the ecclesiastical
tribunals, while Jewish and foreign (Italian, Lombard, Cahorsin) moneylenders were the targets of repressive secular monarchical laws. While the
important phenomenon in the thirteenth century was the rapid increase in
the number of Christian usurers, public monarchical repression (e.g., Saint
Louis' edicts) only struck the Jews and the foreigners who were not subject
to the justice of the Church. This repression was much more than an economic measure. It included the king's confiscation of the property of Jews
who were moneylenders and the cancellation of debts that were owed to
them: it was a component of the general indictment leveled against all Jews.
In a preamble to the edict of 1258, Saint Louis said that the Jews' usurious
practices "impoverish our kingdom." This was the economic component
of an essentially religious, ideological, and political program of exclusion.[80]
While usury was tolerated among both Christians and Jews when practiced
among the foreign community, under Saint Louis there was a reversal in
practice, if not in doctrine, in the tendency to tolerate usury more easily
when it was practiced in the framework of the "fraternal" community. In
fact, these measures protected Christians at the expense of Jews. One piece
of evidence that indicates that the economic motive was relatively secondary here is the fact that usury was designated and condemned as a vice but
not as a crime or offense.

In 1247, people advised Saint Louis to confiscate the usurious profits
of the Jews in order to use them for financing the crusade. He refused to
use goods that had been acquired so shamefully for such a sacred cause.

CURRENCY

We know that at the end of his reign, from 1262 to 1270, Saint Louis issued a series of edicts on currency.[81] Let us now go back over the essential information about the measures that were taken. They were interdictions placed on the circulation of English sterling in the kingdom, the condemnation of the counterfeiting of royal currencies, the establishment of a monopoly on circulation throughout the kingdom reserved for royal coinages, an interdiction forbidding the coinages of feudal lords from circulating outside their own lands, the resumption of the minting of a gold coin, the *écu*—only a very small quantity of which were produced before the fourteenth century—and the striking of a *gros d'argent* (large silver coin), the *gros tournois*. These measures were taken to meet obvious political and economic goals. They contributed to the struggle against inflation and assured a constant supply of money for exchanges within the kingdom; they facilitated the development of long-distance trade in higher quantities and values of merchandise. (This applies to the *gros d'argent,* which was well adapted to France's position in this market, but not to gold coinage which was better suited for the large Italian merchant cities.) Finally, these measures allowed the king to take control of a regal monopoly on currency in the framework of the construction of the monarchical state.

However, there were also moral and religious reasons for these measures because they were decisions about justice, "in Saint Louis' eyes, a strong currency guarantees justice in commercial exchanges."[82] We must not forget Isidore de Séville's ubiquitous definition of money: *moneta* comes from *monere,* "to warn," "because it puts us on our guard against all kinds of fraud in metal and weight." We have a struggle against bad coinage here, against *falsa* or *defraudata* (fraudulent) currency, and an effort to establish *good* currency, or "healthy and loyal" coinage.

Saint Louis' policy created disturbances in seigniorial and ecclesiastical milieus. In 1265 at the faculty of theology of the University of Paris, the master Gérard d'Abbeville had to answer the question: "in his recent edict did the king have the right to impose an oath on his subjects, who are also the subjects of bishops and other Churchmen, to no longer use the English sterling in their transactions?" The question introduced a pretext for discussing monetary problems and for examining the notion of public utility (*utilitas publica*), but the debate was aborted for lack of adequate intellectual means of discussing the topic.[83] If the theologians lacked these means, imagine how poorly the king was prepared to deal with this topic! Being aware of this, he relied on practitioners. He convoked assemblies and councils that called on the expertise of the bourgeois to resolve these issues. The monarchy's incompetence in monetary matters made economics a stepping-stone in the political rise of the bourgeoisie and its entry into royal politics. We still must note the symbolic aspects of currency that existed alongside its moral aspects. These aspects were caught up in the *conservatio monetae,* "the preservation of money," whose fetishistic character has been described by Thomas Bisson, and in the *renovatio monetae* that arose under the sign of Christ. On Saint Louis' ecu, we can see the fleur-de-lis on the right accompanied by the legend: *Ludovicus Dieigracia Francorum rex* (Louis by the grace of God king of the Franks). On the reverse side there is a cross with the proclamation: *Christus vivat, Christus regnat, Christus imperat* (Long live Christ, Christ's reign, and Christ's sovereign command).[84]

SALVATION AND NECESSITY

The third function's conceptual and ideological frameworks are hard to identify because the documents directly pertaining to power and royal government rarely articulated them.

The presentation of the motives behind the charters and public acts were virtually non-existent or at the very least extremely understated in Saint Louis' edicts. They usually explained a lot, even though we still have to decipher their terms in many cases. I have been able to find only two expressions that summed up their motives: *"anime nostri cupientes providere saluti"* (wishing to provide for the salvation of our soul), which not only marked the primacy of the religious in the royal administration, but also the way in which the king's personal salvation was at stake. (During his coronation, before God, the clergy, and his people, the king took on the engagement to govern "righteously," which placed his personal salvation at stake in his governing acts.) The other expression I have come across is *"pro communi utilitate"* (for the common utility), which I will comment upon later. We have to examine certain juridical texts, administrative acts, and moral writings in order to track down the notions that seemed to inspire royal conduct in matters involving economic thought and activities. Some of the royal decisions in this realm arose from the supreme nature of the king's power, from the higher principles that founded it, and from what was truly kingly.

For example, what allowed Saint Louis to make laws on money was not just his *potestas* (supreme power) or *auctoritas* (the right of legitimation and decision-making power), but the indescribable *majestas* that expressed the ruler's sacred quality. People did not address Saint Louis as "His Majesty" or "Your Majesty" orally but only in writing.

We have also seen that along with peace and justice this was one of the two great virtues and one of the two important royal functions that justified his actions.

Still, the measures effecting economic matters cannot be dissociated from other purposes. The ones that applied to the cities, the management of the domain, the king's right to lodging, the fight against usury as well as those favoring the "good" money all arose from less eminent principles situated at a lower level. Three notions emerged from this development: *utilitas, necessitas,*[85] and *commoditas.* All three were marked with the stamp of man's servitude in relation to the body and physical matter.

These notions no doubt all concerned a form of good for the people who were the king's subjects: *necessitas populi,* as Innocent III had already said to King Peter of Aragon in 1199 on the topic of "bad currency." Here, however, it was not a question of the goodness of one's soul but of material subsistence within the kingdom. This watchword was imposed in the regulations for cities in the course of the fourteenth century and first appeared in the works of thirteenth-century jurists who worked out the theory of royal legislative power, and in the works of biblical exegetes.[86] Urban power should always be exercised *pro communi utilitate, pro commodo et utilitate communi, pro necessitate et utilitate,* in other words, "for the common advantage." It was applied in situations that involved material interests.

More often than not, the authors specified that this was a matter of the *necessitas corporis* or *necessitates corporales* ("bodily necessity" or "bodily necessities"), or the *bonum corporis* ("the good of the body"—with the biblical reference, *"nemo carnem suam odio habuit"* [no one has despised his own flesh]). They were dealing with matters concerning *res corporales* ("bodily things"), a term that designated the products of the technical arts beginning with agriculture and vital natural demands.

These goods were caught up in the very low regard in which people held matters related to the body, if not in downright disdain for the body itself. In addition, these natural goods were more or less threatened by the *fragilitas carnis,* "the weakness of the flesh." This was especially true of money. However, wherever economic factors were concerned, there was also a great danger that the king and his subjects might fall into two enormous sins: cupidity and treachery, *avaritia* and *fraus*. In any case, it does not seem that in Saint Louis' eyes these goods arose from what Thomas Aquinas in imitation of Aristotle called the "common good," which was situated on a higher plane. This Aristotelian concept did not enter into the workings of the French monarchy until after Gilles de Rome's *De regimine principum* dedicated to the future Philip the Fair in 1280. Louis did not hold the body in contempt but considered it subaltern, and for him, what we would call the realm of economics was tied to and situated within an inferior state of being that was particularly threatened by sin.

Saint Louis, then, did not have any conscious ties to the economy and seems to have been a non-interventionist, whether personally or through the people who governed in his name. However, in the seneschalcies of Beaucaire and Carcassonne and Nîmes in July and August 1254, two edicts established veritable councils that worked with the seneschal in order to deliberate on eventual bans on the exportation of grains and other materials should any shortages strike the region. In 1259, the seneschal of Beaucaire and Nîmes organized a meeting for the purpose of discussing other possible bans on the export of grains to Aragon. These economic measures had an important social and political aspect. The counsels and representatives of the good towns were fairly well represented at these meetings alongside the barons, prelates, judges, vicars, and bailiffs. The bourgeois definitively appeared as men of the third function alongside the royal officers. In this function they found their way into the assemblies of the royal administration. They soon made up the elite of the Third Estate, a position they occupied until 1789.

We still have to situate Louis' behavior within the economic development we have glimpsed through the entire group of documents on France and thirteenth-century Christendom. All the evidence leads us to think that this reign was situated at the end of the great economic expansion that lasted from the tenth to the thirteenth century, and that the beginnings of the reversal of this trend referred to as the crisis of the fourteenth century can be placed at the end of his reign around the year 1260.[87] Saint Louis' final measures (particularly in the field of monetary policy) partially reflect the beginning of this crisis. However, Saint Louis and his contemporaries were still not aware of the oncoming crisis.

Although in light of the long-term economic circumstances, the essential phenomenon seems to be Saint Louis' position between the height of the great economic expansion running from the tenth to the thirteenth century and the beginning of a major crisis, there was another phenomenon that seems very important to me. This phenomenon consisted in the advances of a market economy that the Mendicant orders, Saint Louis' important friends and advisors, were happy to moralize vaguely and contain with what was really a justification for the autonomous functioning of the market in the guise of religious and moral principles.[88]

We must take note of this weakening of the third royal function (outside of the king's acts of charity). The abundance of cash that Saint Louis drew from the kingdom's pluri-secular prosperity by tapping the wealth of the cities and the clergy in the tradition of Philip Augustus, the king's indifference to an entire category of material realities for which he shared the ideological contempt of the greater segment of the nobility and clergy ("economic" forms of labor including the mechanical arts were "servile" and held down to an inferior status), the rebirth of Roman law, and the theological thought of a Thomas Aquinas all accentuated this disparagement. The devaluation of the economic realm was due in part to the absence of any conceptual tools adequate for dealing with it. All of this contributed to the fact that, beyond several interventions that were marginal in the overall scheme of things and that took place in cases where the prestige and morality of royalty could have suffered serious setbacks, Saint Louis mainly practiced a kind of laissez-faire economics.

Saint Louis' encounter with the economy never took place.[89] He did not personally participate in any of the great debates of his time that were charged with economic implications. We cannot find any trace in his mind or actions of these contemporary controversies that took place at the University of Paris, in the confessors' manuals, or in the religious orders, particularly among the Franciscans. The two great debates were about the value of labor and the justification of commerce and merchants. Likewise, he stayed outside the great thirteenth-century debate on money. It was considered diabolical by Saint Francis of Assisi. The scholastics believed it was appreciable according to one's intentions in acquiring or using it. How can money be tamed and moralized? This problem does not appear to have interested the king.[90] Louis made no fuss about complying with the imperceptible mechanisms that benefited his apparently prosperous kingdom and his royal administration that was well supplied with cash. His conscience was not bothered by any of this. The satisfaction he got out of his charitable actions for the poor and his repression of Jewish usury kept him from asking any more disturbing questions. He appears here once again as the disciple of those Mendicant friars who in both theory and practice elaborated the compromise that would later facilitate the birth of capitalism.[91]

I think that we have to conclude with a paradox. The king who had wagered everything on immaterial values left the French imagination with a memory of the kingdom's material prosperity in his time that was stronger than the memory of his virtues and miracles. People began to attribute this accomplishment to him after his death as this memory took hold at the end of the thirteenth century. This was the meaning of the phrase invoked so often with regret—"the good age of His Royal Highness Saint Louis" (*le bon temps Monseigneur Saint Louis*). The period was a time free of monetary fluctuations, widespread famines, and high rises in prices. The Saint Louis of nostalgia and collective memory was a Saint Louis of economic prosperity. To a significant extent, this was an imaginary recollection of the king.

Saint Louis

Feudal King or Modern King?

I HAVE DISCUSSED THE TYPE OF KING SAINT LOUIS WAS IN RELATION to the evolution of the medieval French monarchy several times now in this book. What voluntary or involuntary mark did he make on this road that split up into so many diverging paths whose overall coherence is only discovered by the historian long after the fact? I am distancing myself a little here from the king's person, body and soul, which lie at the heart of my approach to the subject. Saint Louis, however, was such a personal king that fortunately I could never manage to get away from him. Readers who are at least a little familiar with French history cannot keep themselves from thinking at the same time about two ideas that have been presented to them since they were in school: on the one hand, feudalism was the essential crux of the Middle Ages—and the thirteenth century was right in the middle of them. Therefore, Saint Louis had to be a feudal king. However, the thirteenth century also saw the birth of the modern state. Saint Louis' grandfather Philip Augustus was already virtually a monarch with a system of state control, and Louis' grandson Philip the Fair would be the same in an even more overt fashion. So, was Saint Louis a modern king? Certain historians have emphasized the first aspect of his reign, considering the thirteenth-century monarchy as truly feudal when all is said and done.[1] Others have paid particularly close attention to the process that formed the modern state. The outstanding body of research on the birth of the modern European state that has been carried out for some time now in Europe and North America gets a little carried away with the cogs of history.[2] Some of these researchers tend to lump Saint Louis together with Philip the Fair. I will now try to reassemble certain observations scattered throughout this book in an attempt to define Saint Louis' political environment. Of course, the movement he lived through and contributed to is not linear and was never dictated by any rational or providential finality. Some people like to frequently repeat it as a kind of truism, but it is still worth reminding oneself here that the reality was actually far more complex than this problematic schema of the feudal and the modern. Philosophers, sociologists, and political scientists have had the immense honor, among others, of forcing historians *to think* history. At the same time, however, they too often induce them to betray history's factual and structural complexity in favor of simplifying or simplistic programs. Certainly, historical science proceeds just like the others by making abstractions. But the abstractions of history are dense and wavering, just like the ones Saint Louis was absorbed in and helped feed. At the end of this book in the final steps on my winding path to the heart of Saint Louis and the royalty he embodied, I will discuss what constitutes the very foundation of this type of royalty—the sacredness to which Saint Louis contributed his own saintliness.

Feudalism and the Modern State

Saint Louis' reign occupied a unique place in thirteenth-century France and in medieval French historiography. People generally recognize the apogee of medieval France in his reign, but they rarely situate it in relation to the two processes I have just mentioned that characterize the medieval West to the greatest extent: the establishment of feudalism and the origins of the modern state.

The king's personality, the religious atmosphere surrounding his reign, and the brilliance of civilization in his time all veil the infrastructures of this half-century of French history. More recently, the image of prosperity that surrounded him like a blinding halo has just barely begun to fade with studies on economic fields, social classes, and intellectual life beginning around 1260 that have detected the symptoms that announced the great crisis of the fourteenth century.[3] Yet modern historians still share the early fourteenth-century French nostalgia for "the good age of His Royal Highness Saint Louis."

In order to be able to define the type of monarchy embodied by Saint Louis, I must therefore first amend the question I asked at the beginning of this chapter as I situated myself in relation to other historical works on this topic. There was no clear historical opposition between a feudal king and a modern king. The evolution leading from feudalism to the modern state passed through an essential, intermediary phase of "feudal monarchy" in the thirteenth century, and Saint Louis occupied a central position in this development.

Even though they respond in theory to two distinct types of logic, the feudal system and the monarchical system were not opposed but actually joined in historical reality. The decrease in the number of serfs and the expansion of the monetary economy that took place under Saint Louis did not weaken the feudal system. They strengthened it. The cities that became his "good towns" were integral components of this feudal system—and Saint Louis was the one French king who best represented this original integration of the cities into the kingdom.[4]

Under his rule, the feudal monarchy decisively pursued its own transformation into a modern monarchical state.[5]

On the Royal Use of the Feudal System

Under Saint Louis the prerogatives of suzerainty attributed to the king as the head of the feudal pyramid of fiefs and homages came closest to what modern historians and the jurists of the time who practiced Roman law call sovereignty. The king multiplied the number of lords directly bound to him by liege homage. Thus, during the crusade, when Joinville received a regular stipend (a *fief-rente* or *fief de bourse*) from the king after losing everything he had, he became his liegeman. Before this point, Joinville had only been a rear vassal to the king. The king alone could be a vassal to no one. Around 1260, the chapter entitled "*De l'office de roi*" in the *Livre de justice et de plet* asserted that "the king should not depend on anyone" (*Le roi ne doit tenir de nul*). The use of the expression *souverain fieffeux* (fiefly sovereign) as a synonym of "suzerain" in Saint Louis' time attested to this convergence of the notions and realities of suzerainty and sovereignty. Dual nomenclature attested to this amalgam of the feudal and monarchical systems. On the one hand, the king was "*sire*," "*messire*," "*monseigneur*," and "*dominus*," while on the other hand, when people addressed him in Latin he was *Vestra Serenitas,* "Your Highness"; *Votre Majesté,* "Your Majesty"; and, already, *Vestra Majestas. Majestas* was the term that best expressed sovereignty.

Although the use and prestige of writing were on the rise, in this society where the impact of speech and gestures and the value of the symbolic still carried considerable weight, the king appropriated the words and rites of feudalism for his own use. Just before leaving on the crusade, Louis IX summoned all his barons to Paris and, according to Joinville, made them swear an oath that "they would uphold their faith and loyalty for his children should anything happen to him on his voyage." Oaths, faith, loyalty—along with the fief, these were the very bases of feudal relations.

The *ordines* composed under his rule that described or regulated the ritual of the royal coronation integrated the rituals of the dubbing ceremony— the essential rites marking the young man's entry into the feudal order— into the conferment of the *regalia* and the crowning that marked the heir's accession to royalty.

Outside the revenues from his domain, Louis could still only rely on feudal funds.[6] He tried to get as much of them as he could, but still came up against rules and attitudes that were still very much alive. However, he did fairly frequently obtain the authorization from his vassals, whom he pressured heavily, to claim funds from their vassals, in other words from his rear vassals [*arriere-vassaux*] from whom he was not allowed to ask anything in principle. He had to respect the custom, although each time he found himself in a situation covered by the custom he demanded feudal assistance in a very rigorous way. He limited privileges for exemptions as much as possible and chipped away at those granted by his predecessors. He was particularly demanding of the towns, the majority of which were within his vassalage. Although, as the bailiff Philippe de Beaumanoir stated in his *Coutumes de Beauvaisis,*[7] by virtue of his regal power in a growing number of cases he was able to take "measures for the common good" [*établissements pour le commun profit*] applicable to his vassals and rear vassals for feudal assistance—a decisive source of his finances—he still had trouble getting around feudal constraints. Finally, he was powerless to do anything to speed up the slow rate of incoming feudal revenue. At his accession to the throne in 1270 his son Philip III not only had to ask for assistance for his own knighting in 1267 but also for his sister Isabelle's marriage in 1255.

On the other hand, in his actions as a peacemaker, Louis made dexterous use of the vassalage obtained from a powerful lord or even from another king, which represented an effective instrument for domination. This was one of the advantages he sought from the king of England in the treaty of Paris of 1259. It was also the thinking behind his arbitration between Henry and his barons in the "*mise*" of Amiens in 1260. Charles T. Wood has seen this perfectly: "the result was a precedent that demonstrated to all his ambitious successors how vassalage could provide a vehicle for an incredible growth in the scope of royal judicial competence."[8] As we have seen, it was in this realm that royal justice made decisive progress under Saint Louis' reign as the procedure of the appeal multiplied cases in which people had direct recourse to the king.

More generally, the meetings of royal advisors necessitated by the swelling volume of "cases and affairs" that reached all the way to the king began to proliferate at some point in the 1250s.[9] These "*parlements*" could not be held in the absence of the king and his advisors. The sessions grew longer, the bureaucratic nature of their organization became more accentuated, and their members soon split up into sections. At the end of Saint Louis' reign, these *parlements* dealt primarily with city affairs and monetary problems. Saint Louis reorganized the functioning of the "good towns" in 1262. Annual elections of new mayors were to be held on October 29 and November 18, selecting three elected officials from whom the king would choose the next mayor. The treasurers of the cities had to come to the "*parlement*" in Paris with the exiting mayors at this time. The kingdom's centralization was progressing.

The important decisions were always made, or at least announced, in the meetings of the royal court. The court was for the most part made up of prelates and powerful laymen, some of whom more regularly and more specifically served as the king's advisors. These meetings could also take on the name of "*parlements*." More specialized decisions were made in these "*parlements*" of a more or less new kind.

As we have seen, the affair of Enguerran de Coucy was brought before a *parlement*: "The personal impact of Saint Louis in cases like these can hardly be exaggerated."[10]

In this transitional period, Louis once more combined the evolution of the bodies of government, which more or less surpassed his control, with his own personal ideas.

Finally, Louis liked to surround himself with a limited circle of familiar figures from a composite of social backgrounds. The group included a prince like Thibaud, count of Champagne and king of Navarre, his son-in-law, just as well as the canon Robert de Sorbon. This was the group that Joinville simply referred to as "we who were around him."[11] This was his "entourage" proper, a group with whom Louis liked to hold open-ended discussions and tell jokes. He was also particularly bent on imparting his moral and religious message to them, and, finally, it was with them that he tested out the decisions that he was thinking of making. They were a personal version of the *familia*, the feudal household [*mesnie*].[12]

However, Saint Louis' monopolization of the feudal system was only possible because he was a very powerful king, even more than his grandfather Philip Augustus. He was such a powerful king due to the characteristics and prerogatives of the monarchy, his wealth, and his military might—and also thanks to his close alliance with the Church.

The Great Alliance of the Altar and the Throne

Although he sometimes rejected some of the excesses of the Church and the papacy—notably in matters of excommunication and finances—through his piety and conduct Saint Louis brought the alliance between the Church and the monarchy to its highest point. This was one of the strengths of the Capetian monarchy from its beginnings and over the long run. He did this out of conviction and also by political design.

Saint Louis had been told that when his grandfather Philip Augustus was on his deathbed he supposedly said to his son the future Louis VIII: "I ask you to honor God and the Holy Church, as I have done. I have drawn great usefulness from this, and you will obtain just as much." In his *Instructions* for his son, he reminds him that according to what was reported to him by a member of his council, Philip Augustus one day said: "I prefer by far to take my losses than to do anything that would create a scandal between me and the Holy Church."[13] After this, Louis adds of his own account: "I remind you of this so you will not be predisposed to believe anyone else in opposition to the people of the Holy Church. You must therefore honor them and protect them so that they will be able to carry out the service of Our Lord in peace."

The Church was the cornerstone of the feudal system not only because it was one of the major beneficiaries of the feudal order through its social status and its riches—even after the Gregorian reform and its liberation from the ascendancy of the secular aristocracy, but especially because it provided the feudal order with its ideological justifications.

Even if the twelve-year-old child did not completely understand the words of the oaths he pronounced during his coronation ceremony,[14] the adult Louis IX considered himself bound by those engagements even though he did not particularly care for oaths. The mutual assistance exchanged between the monarchy and the Church served as the basis for this alliance. Each of them represented God in its own way. The king held his function from his birth and directly from God. He was God's lieutenant in his own kingdom. He was God's "image," but he only assumed possession of this grace through the intermediary of the Church represented by the prelate who anointed and crowned him. The Church definitively made him a king, and he committed himself to protecting it. He benefited from its sanctifying power and was its secular arm. Saint Louis possessed a sharp awareness of this alliance between the altar and the throne, and it was the cornerstone of the French monarchy over the long term, ever since Clovis's baptism.

This alliance and his respect for the Church did not prevent the king from fighting the pretensions of the bishops in temporal and judicial matters. We have seen how this was true even in his youth.[15] Nor did it prevent him from vigorously protesting the papacy's conduct in respect to the Church of France.[16] He would not serve as the righteous arm of the Church for causes that he deemed unjust.[17] He rigorously exercised his royal prerogatives in ecclesiastical affairs, and in conferring the ecclesiastical benefices that fell to him he applied the same moral principles that he accused the papacy of sometimes failing to respect.

Louis paid careful attention to these prerogatives. In his *Enseignements,* he gave the following recommendation to his son:

> Dear Son, on the benefices of the Holy Church that you will have to give out, I teach you that you should give them to good people

through the great counsel of *prud'hommes;* and it seems to me that it would be better to give them to those who have no prebends than to those who already have some, because if you search for them well, you will find enough men who have nothing and who will put the gift to good use.[18]

Geoffroy de Beaulieu similarly praised Saint Louis' conduct in conferring ecclesiastical benefices. He praised his choice of people who had an excellent reputation, his reliance on the advice of the *prud'hommes* like the chancellor of the Church of Paris and the Mendicant friars, his concern that the benefices did not accumulate in the same hands, and his policy of conferring benefices only when it was certain that there was a vacancy for the benefices to confer.[19]

LOCAL GOVERNMENT AND LEGISLATIVE POWER

Philip Augustus had been the great "aggrandizer"[20] of the royal domain, which he had quadrupled in size. He had also put a better administration into place for the domain, notably a better financial administration. Following the king's example, most of his vassals in the thirteenth century also sought to improve the yields from their feudal or rather seigniorial administrations by employing better financial methods and by improving the functioning of banal lordship.[21] This was characteristic of what Marc Bloch has called the second age of feudalism.[22] Saint Louis was the one who profited the most from the exploitation and administration of the kingdom. The naming of *enquêteurs* charged with the tasks of keeping the king informed about the management conducted by his representatives, bailiffs, and seneschals, and of redressing any wrongs they might have committed had the purpose and consequence of assuring a better functioning royal administration that was more efficient and more widely accepted. Some have quite accurately remarked that "the skill with which the rulers managed to respect local customs and win over [regional] notables explains the success of the royal agents."[23] This was especially true of Louis IX. However, the measures that the king alone was entitled to take were presented in the form of special texts.

They called these texts that expressed royal decisions made for reasons deriving from the king's sovereignty *ordonnances* (edicts). Other terms were also used to designate them, *établissements* (establishments) in particular, and sometimes they were simply referred to as letters [*lettres*]. These are all expressions of what we would call the king's "legislative power." Louis IX's predecessors rarely issued *ordonnances*. Their legislative power hardly ever exceeded the borders of the royal domain. Their numbers increased for the first time under Louis IX. We can count twenty-five of them issued by Saint Louis, as opposed to six for Philip Augustus, to which we have to add eight regulations "that no one dared count among his *ordonnances*," according to their eighteenth-century publisher, Eusèbe de Laurière.

The edicts, however, sometimes only had a limited nature in either the areas to which they applied or the actual persons to whom they applied. Their limited application to certain areas can be explained by the privileges possessed by certain regions that had only recently been submitted to royal sovereignty. This was especially the case for Normandy, which Philip Augustus had retaken from the English. An edict issued from Orléans dated May 1246 dealt with the problems of collecting rent and dues [*le bail et le rachat*] for land in the customs of Anjou and Maine at the very moment when Charles d'Anjou was about to take possession of his apanage. We can see that a certain number of these texts created legislation in the properly "feudal" domain of customs, but the king was respectful of this traditional framework even when he intervened in it. Thus an edict of May 1235 regulated the "exploitation [*relief*] and redemption of fiefs," fixing the portion of the "fruits" to be collected by the lord (every year for arable lands and vines, every five years for ponds and warrens, every seven years for woods). Some of these regulations did away with "bad customs"—this was an essential thing demanded by local populations who were submitted to the "feudal" regime. Saint Louis continued to respect the rights of eminent lords within their own fiefs. As the customary law of Touraine-Anjou states, "Baron a toutes justices" (the Baron has all the rights). In other words, the baron had all public power: "on his land, the king can place no ban on a baron's land without his consent."

The edicts that applied to a single category of people dealt primarily with the Jews.[24] The edict of Melun from December 1230 readopted the measures decreed by Philip Augustus against the Jews and their practices of usury. It was the first edict that applied to the entire kingdom (*in toto regno nostro*). This marked an important date in the history of royal power. In addition to the edicts that targeted the Jews, the edicts presented Louis' other obsessive concerns, the ones that seemed to him to most particularly require the intervention of royal power in his time and that were matters to be dealt with by him alone.

The first of these was the realm of war and peace. The king alone was the master who unleashed or put a stop to war and who allowed it to break out only after exhausting all other peace efforts. This was the subject of the edicts of 1245, 1247, and 1260, which instituted the "king's fortieth," a truce of forty days imposed on the "carnal friends" of enemies at the beginning of an armed conflict. These edicts also forbade private wars and "judgments of God," challenges or "battle wages," and called for "judicial duels" to be replaced by "proofs by witnesses."

The second realm reserved for the king's legal authority was coinage (with the edicts of 1262 and 1265). For the cause of justice, it had to be "good" and "strong." These edicts also stipulated that the king alone possessed a monopoly on the circulation of royal currency, and that it was the only coinage to be used throughout the entire kingdom.[25]

The edicts that held the most importance in Saint Louis' view were the ones with moral objectives (against prostitution, blasphemy, malfeasance, and wickedness) and the ones that instituted justice (against exactions and the injustices and abuses of power committed by agents of royal power and leaders of the good towns). The edicts that fell within this category were the Great Edict of 1254, the edict "for the utility of the kingdom" of 1256, and the letter addressed from Aigues-Mortes on June 25, 1270 to the abbot of Saint-Denis Mathieu de Vendôme and Simon de Nesle, the kingdom's regents in the absence of the king during his departure on the crusade to Tunis.

In this group, there is one text of special interest. It was considered an edict at the time. These are the letters dated June 1248 from Corbeil. Saint Louis entrusted the kingdom's government or the regency, as we would say, to his mother with these letters. They defined the nature and the content of the royal power entrusted to her.

The letters first granted her the full power to handle the kingdom's affairs, whether they were presented to her or whether she decided on her own to take them on:

> To our very dear Lady and mother the queen we grant and wish that in our absence on the crusade she have full power to deal with and take on our kingdom's affairs as she pleases and according to what seems good to her to take on.[26]

He also granted her the power to "abolish whatever seems to her like it needs to be abolished according to what seems good to her."[27] Blanche of Castile thus had full power to deal with all of the kingdom's affairs including the ones she seized upon herself, in legal terms the ones to which she could apply the *saisine*. She also had full powers of abolition. This was a particularly important aspect of power, not only because this power had to be specifically mentioned, but also because the medieval mentality considered any abolition of laws or customs as an especially grave and objectionable matter. The existing ones were made to last. This complete royal power bordered on allowing the sovereign to do as he or she pleased; nevertheless, it had to be subordinated to the good, a good that was no doubt left to the king's judgment but that still had to respond to objective criteria. These criteria were those of the "common good" as defined by ancient Greek thought and redefined in Christian doctrine.

As readers have often remarked, although Louis IX seems to grant supreme power (*plena potestas*) to his mother, the regent, by allowing her to deal with all affairs that seemed "good" for her to take up (he did this with the formula "*quos sibi placuerit*" [whatever pleases her], a phrase that typified complete power), he amended this delegation of power by adding, "according to what seems good" (*secundum quod ipsi videbetur bonum esse*). What he conferred to her then was not so much the exercise of a personal power as the recognition of a system of government and administration dominated by the notion of the common good or common utility. This notion was derived from the confluence of a reinterpreted customary law, an adaptation of Roman law, and an ancient ethical and political concept that had been reworked by the scholastic theologians of the period. Saint Louis liked this notion for its moral and religious connotations.[28]

The power entrusted to the regent also included control over everyone who administered the kingdom in the service of the king, but also for the service of the kingdom itself—or, as we would say, the state. Again, this was a matter of naming people to various positions, moving them, or stripping them of their posts:

> That she have the power to appoint bailiffs, to name or dismiss chatelains, foresters, and anyone else in our service and in the service of the kingdom, in accordance with what seems to her to be the good thing to do.[29]

Last of all, he entrusted her with the power to intervene in the ecclesiastical affairs that fell under the jurisdiction of the king of France:

> That she also have the power to confer vacant ecclesiastical honors and benefices, to receive the loyalty of the bishops and abbots, and restore the *régale* to them [the king collected the ecclesiastical revenues during vacancies of bishoprics and abbots' posts], and to give the authorization to elect [bishops and abbots] to the chapters and convents in our place.[30]

We can see how Saint Louis defined and practiced royal power. It was a power of absolute discretion, but which was still subordinated to the good. It was particularly attentive to the quality of the persons belonging to two networks that depended on the king. The first of these networks was the new body of officers who extended the exercise of royal power to the entire kingdom. They were the king's direct representatives. The second was the traditional body of ecclesiastical office-holders over whom he cautiously exercised sovereign rights in accordance with moral criteria.

Measures taken by many of the important feudal lords and particularly by the king's brothers in their apanages imitated the measures taken by the king in the royal domain. In certain cases, the king's measures may have followed the ones taken by other lords. They led to an introduction of uniformity in the feudal structures of power and administration in the kingdom. In fact, under Saint Louis' reign the royal domain became the definitive mold into which the entire kingdom was cast.

SAINT LOUIS AND THE LAW

The spread of Roman law was not the great juridical event of Saint Louis' reign. Its practice was largely limited to southern France, the France of the *langue d'oc,* where it actually favored the inroads of royal power. It was in the South that jurists began to receive their training, and notably in the new university in Toulouse—which failed in its struggle against the heretics but succeeded in becoming a center for legal instruction. The University of Toulouse took on this role before the University of Orléans. The jurists trained there became important men in the royal government under Philip the Fair. In northern France, the University of Orléans still had a modest program. Roman law was not taught at the University of Paris. According to some, this was due to Philip Augustus's request to Pope Honorius III to prevent a form of law that was still basically considered imperial law in the thirteenth century from taking root in his capital. This was at a time when the king of France was still trying to emerge from the emperor's shadow. Others believe it was the papacy that wanted to assure the primacy of theology in Paris without any competition from the study of law.[31]

As we have seen, the important event of the reign in juridical matters was the phenomenon of writing down most of the regional customary laws. These included the *Grand coutumier* of Normandy, the *Conseil à un ami* by Pierre de Fontaines who was the bailiff of Vermandois, the *Livre de justice et de plet* for the Orléanais, the *Établissements de Saint Louis* in Touraine and Anjou, and—composed shortly after Saint Louis' death—the famous *Coutumes de Beauvaisis* by Philippe de Beaumanoir. As typical of feudal law, customary law passed from oral language into written language, although it was still no less a kind of feudal law, reinforced by its written composition.

As for Saint Louis' investigators, one of their primary missions was to reform or suppress "bad customs" in the purest feudal tradition.

Sometimes the king himself rendered judgment in symbolic and spectacular fashion under the famous oak tree at Vincennes, or, more often, he had cases judged by his advisors. The increasingly frequent appeals to the king contributed to the growth of royal power and the unification of the kingdom's judicial system. Still, this was not a matter of substituting another order of justice for seigniorial judicial institutions. It was rather one of imposing the superiority of the justice of the suzerain-sovereign over that of his vassals. As Philip III's lawyers said after Saint Louis' death to those of Louis' brother Charles d'Anjou, who commanded the respect dictated by custom, it was a matter of having the superiority of the "custom of the kingdom" recognized over the customs of the fiefs, the feudal principalities. This had not yet been entirely achieved.

A jurist who was strongly marked by Roman law like Jacques de Révigny, a famous master at the University of Orléans and a strong supporter of royal power,[32] could still assert that he had to prefer "his own country," in other words the seigniory where he lived, to "the common country," the kingdom in other words.

A Feudal and Bourgeois Society

In Saint Louis' time, the Kingdom of France was still founded on land and the rural economy. Peasants still comprised at least 90 percent of the kingdom's population. Of course, Saint Louis greatly increased the number of emancipations and instructed his agents to prefer the interests of the weak to those of the powerful, admonishing them to protect the peasants. However, he did not change anything in the economic system of production that rested on the exploitation of the peasant and did nothing to modify the peasant's position in the social hierarchy. Economic development and the spread of the monetary economy and of the nobility's methods of exploitation transformed the nature of the peasants' payments. Monetary exactions in the form of rent henceforth prevailed over *corvées* and dues in the form of goods. The sources of feudal revenues changed, but, although money's place in them increased certain social differences in the peasant mass, globally it only reinforced the seigniorial system. In fact, this system was at its zenith.

If we look at this issue from the side of the nobles, we are certainly struck by the cases where royal justice sanctioned nobles and even barons. The case of Enguerran de Coucy became famous in Saint Louis' time and caused a stir in the heart of the barony. However, we must take note of the fact that all these affairs opposed nobles to other nobles, or knights to barons at the very least. There were no bourgeois in Saint Louis' entourage. Although it contained modest clerics like Robert de Sorbon, the son of a peasant, and knights of middling rank like Joinville, these exceptions fell under an old Capetian tradition that still failed to mask the majority presence of prelates and barons closest to the monarch. Saint Louis remained bound to the nobility and even to the aristocracy, as the French monarchy continued to be until 1789. He took particular care to assist poor nobles, nobles who had been ruined by the crusade or the expansion of the monetary economy and who were a part of these "shameful poor." This category was particularly touching for the royal disciple of the Mendicant friars. He gave them aid, either by making them his vassals and giving them a pension in the form of a "*fief de bourse*," or by hiring them to work in the expanding royal administration. According to Guy Fourquin, under his rule they made "a massive entry" into the royal administration. However, I hesitate to agree with him in seeing a "nobility of the state" engendered by the crusade in this phenomenon.[33] We must not pull Saint Louis and French society under his reign too far behind or too far in advance. The ideal of the secular *prud'homme* that the king opposed to the *preux* was still a thoroughly noble ideal. And the *prud'homme* was opposed to both the bourgeois and the *vilain* [a peasant and, yes, the etymological source of the English "villain"—Trans.].

Saint Louis was not a king of the bourgeois. Moreover, the cities were not the anti-feudal organisms imagined by a certain brand of historiography. As we have seen, the urban economy was situated inside the feudal system of production. In addition, as some have quite accurately stated, the towns saw themselves and behaved like "collective seigniories." There is no justification for speaking of pre-capitalism in this case. Even artisan's fiefs were not uncommon in Saint Louis' France. Certainly, some developments show up that cannot be ignored: a spirit of profit and expansion was asserted, merchants began to sell time through usury, and the university members sold knowledge, both of which previously only belonged to God. Saint Louis, however, detested usurers, whether they were Christians or Jews, and no matter what anyone else has said about it, he also held intellectuals in contempt. Like Jose Luis Romero, I prefer to speak of a feudal-bourgeois society in observing the urban and commercial economy and society of Saint Louis' time.[34]

A suffering king, a humble king, a friend to the poor, a king of the Mendicant friars, Saint Louis was only a new kind of king in the same measure that God, the Christ of the thirteenth century, himself became a crucified king, a God-King of the Passion.[35] But, if the Lord made himself humble, he did not make himself a commoner. Loving the poor and the weak [*chétifs*[36]] was more a work of mercy than of justice for Louis.

Saint Louis was not a revolutionary king. He was not even a reformist king in the modern sense of this term. He thoroughly complied with the Mirrors of the Princes that had appeared since the Carolingian period and that were modified by the twelfth-century Renaissance and the spirit of the Mendicant orders born in the thirteenth century. He was still, or, rather, he became a feudal king, drawing all the advantages he could from the feudal system. On the other hand, he was also a utopian king. He was a *rex pacificus,* as Pope Boniface VIII called him in the papal bull for his canonization. In other words, he was a king of the last time on earth who wanted to lead his people to their salvation in heaven, not to worldly happiness—an idea that

did not yet exist in the thirteenth century, although the following generations did imagine his reign as a time of peace and prosperity on earth. Of
course, the great movement of the descent of heavenly values to the earth
sped up under his rule, but they were still religious values.[37] Although the
feudal model that ruled the heavens of the Pseudo-Dionysus with its hierarchy of a celestial society of angels and archangels descended to the earth,
it was to become even more firmly rooted within it.

Saint Louis Does Not Hunt

Hunting was an activity that all French kings from Clovis to Louis XVI
practiced more or less passionately. The royal hunt led to the creation of a
large number of royal forests and the construction of numerous residences
in the heart of these forests or in immediate proximity to them. These residences were first and foremost residences of France. The Île-de-France
was one of the first vast hunting areas for the kings. Philip Augustus had
wanted to turn the "woods of Vincennes" into a hunting ground, whereas
it was basically a place for relaxation and justice for Saint Louis. A king
could never assert his image and privileges any better than by hunting.[38]

Despite all this, there are no texts or documents that give us a glimpse
of Saint Louis hunting. It is likely that he never hunted.[39]

Doing this, or rather not doing this, he also confirmed his exceptional
status among laymen. His abstention from hunting also enhanced his resemblance to the bishops. Beginning with the fourth council, the oldest
Church councils forbade bishops from engaging in this activity, labeling it
a diversion that was primarily a sign of nobility, of secular nobility. Furthermore, there was a tradition that assigned a negative connotation to hunters and particularly to rulers who hunt. Wasn't Nimrod, the tyrant king who
defied Yahweh by building the Tower of Babel, a great hunter too? In the
Bible, the rulers of peoples [*principes gentium*] "who play with the birds of
the sky [*qui in avibus celi ludunt*] were all exterminated and sent down to hell"
(Baruch 3:16–17, 19). A text attributed to Saint Jerome states: "I have never
seen a hunter who was a saint."[40] In one of his treatises, Bishop Jonas
d'Orléans, the author of one of the most important Carolingian Mirrors of
the Princes of the ninth century, dedicated a chapter (*De institutione laicali,*
Book II, chapter 23) to "those who for the hunt and their love of dogs ne-

glect the cause of the poor." This seems like it could have been written with Saint Louis, the servant of the poor, in mind.[41]

At the beginning of the twelfth century, the great canonist Yves de Chartres assembled an impressive dossier against hunting in his *Décret*. This text includes no fewer than seven titles against hunting. It contains patristic texts that condemn hunters of any kind alongside the council canons that forbid hunting to the bishops, priests, and deacons. Saint Augustine declared that giving something to a hunter was as bad as giving to an actor or a prostitute: "Anyone who gives something to a hunter is not giving to the man but to a very bad activity, for if the hunter were only a man, no one would give him anything, and, therefore, people are rewarding his vice and not his nature." This same Augustine also stated, "Misfortune to those who take pleasure in the sight of a hunter! They should repent. Should they fail to repent, when they see the Savior [on Judgment Day], they will be plunged in sadness." Saint Jerome reminded us that Esau was a hunter because he was a sinner [*pécheur*], a man of sin, and that "we can find no saintly hunter in Scripture, the only saints there are fishermen [*pécheurs*]." Responding to Jesus' call, Saint Peter and his companions became fishers and not hunters of men. Finally, Saint Ambrose condemned the man who did not get up at dawn to pray but to gather his servants, prepare his nets, bring out his dogs, and scamper through the bushes and forests.[42]

THE ROYAL SYSTEM

We can trace the elements of a political theory that defined Saint Louis' royalty from two texts that were directly tied to him. The first one is a letter Pope Gregory IX addressed to Louis IX and Blanche of Castile on November 26, 1229.[43] In this letter, the pope stressed that between the king's two main attributes, the *potentia* or "power" that carried the power to punish others, and the *benignitas* or "goodness" that gave rise to the power of mercy and forgiveness, the king had to possess the *sapientia* or "wisdom" that kept *potentia* from becoming arrogance and *benignitas* from degenerating into "laxity" [*dissolutio*]. We have seen that *sapientia* was a virtue for which Saint Louis, the new Solomon, was frequently praised. This triad of attributes allows us to categorize other royal faculties that were also qualities of the Christ-king: *potestas,* which marked the entry of terminology from

Roman law into the system; *majestas,* also an old Roman concept that the Christian king was in the process of appropriating in the thirteenth century within the framework of Christian theology;[44] and *timor,* a positive form of fear that was different from negative fear. Thus, a theory of the Christian king's sovereignty was elaborated here. *Sapientia* the "wisdom" that implied *veritas* in Christ was the mediating figure. The Christian king who was an image of God and Christ therefore had the potential of thinking and acting according to the truth. Just as *timor* corresponded to *potentia, sapientia* responded to *honor,* a term with complex connotations in the feudal-Christian system. Finally, the king's *benignitas* was the *bonitas* of Christ. It was the basis of Christ's sanctity (*sanctitas*). However, this function of sanctity (or saintliness) was different from what became Saint Louis' personal sanctity [*sainteté*].[45] Finally, *amor* joined with *bonitas* to form the *compassion* and *pity* that Saint Louis manifested for others. He loved his subjects, and the monarchical propaganda that has him as its first important model strove to win the reciprocal love of his subjects both during his life and after his death.

The second text I mentioned here is Vincent de Beauvais' *De morali principis institutione.* This text combines elements of a Mirror of the Prince and a treatise of political science conceived at Saint Louis' behest.[46] The theme of the king as an image of God assumed a very interesting form here in light of the success of the ternary schemas like the one that presented the king as an "image of the Trinity" (*rex imago trinitatis*). The first aspect of this was the *potentia regalis.* This *potentia* or royal power was licit as long as the king avoided "the love of domination" (*amor dominandi*) and tyranny, and as long as he remembered Saint Augustine's words: "Great empires are great bands of thieves."[47] And, of course, royal power was also licit as long as it was rendered legitimate by the king's birth. Vincent also reminded his readers that Louis IX was a descendant of Charlemagne,[48] and that the long duration of the Capetian dynasty (236 years from the accession of Hugh Capet to the accession of Saint Louis' father Louis VIII) was proof of providential favor. The second aspect of the king as an image of Christ was the ruler's wisdom (*sapientia principis*). It consisted in mastery of character and conduct, in good government of the entire social body that was submitted to him, in his aptitude for giving and receiving advice and council, in his personal administration of justice, in the establishment of laws and rules, in the choice of good friends, advisors, and agents, in the good financial administration of his house and the kingdom, in reliance on reflection before going to war, and in the instruction acquired from the study of sacred and profane literature. Here, we can identify the theme launched by John of Salisbury a century earlier: "An ignorant king is but a crowned ass" (*rex illiteratus quasi asinus coronatus*). The theme appeared in the key position that Gregory IX reserved for wisdom (*sapientia*) in his letter, and in Saint Louis' common practices as they were described and praised by his biographers. Finally, Vincent described the third component of the royal trinity—goodness (*bonitas*). He emphasized the king's need to defend goodness against flattery and malicious gossip, an important theme of political morality in monarchical systems.

Alongside the Romanist jurists, we have to take account of the canonists in the thirteenth century. A concept from the ecclesiastical world tended to sum up the nature of the royal function: *dignitas*. It originally designated ecclesiastical offices whose "dignity" was independent of the person who held them and came to be applied to various secular offices. The term held great importance for the Capetians because it implied the function's perpetuity across the appointments of its successive titleholders. It responded to the major concern of rulers and their entourages for reducing the period of any vacancy of power between two reigns as much as possible. The legal adage about this stated that, "dignity never dies" (*dignitas nunquam moritur*). However, dynastic practice under Saint Louis tended to empty the concept of *dignitas* of its utility and to replace it with the *maiestas* that better expressed the plenitude of sovereignty.

LIMITS OF ROYAL POWER

Other formulae playing in favor of the sovereignty of the king of France were spreading at this time. First of all, there was the concession Pope Innocent III made to the king of France in his bull *Per venerabilem* in 1205. In his bull, the pope admitted that "the king does not answer to [*reconnaît*] any superior in temporal matters." According to certain historians of law and political theory,[49] in a general way, theorists of canon law helped establish this affirmation of royal sovereignty more than any theorists of Roman law. Its most typical formulae were well known: "The ruler is not submitted to the laws" (*princeps legibus solutus est* [*Digeste* I, 3, 31]); and "What pleases the ruler has the force of law" (*quod principi placuit legis habet vigorem* [*Digeste,* I, 4, 1 and *Institutes,* I, 2, 6]).[50]

However, as others have shown, the formula *quod principi placuit* as it applied to the king in the thirteenth century in no case gave him the ability to act according to his will alone. Instead, the formula was inscribed within a framework of strict legality. We have seen that when Saint Louis applied the formula in his mother's favor to establish her second regency, he subordinated the exercise of this power to do as one pleased to the principle of the common good.[51] This is a specific example of one of the virtues of the ruler's wisdom, which consisted in knowing how to surround himself with good advisors and in obeying enlightened principles that prevented him from making use of his good pleasure in an arbitrary manner.[52]

Similarly, the king was not really "not bound by the laws" because he was both "above the law" and "beneath the law" [*supra et infra legem*], "being the son and the father of the law at the same time, he finds himself in a position that bars him from violating it."[53]

Jacques de Révigny was a professor of law at Orléans at the end of Louis' reign. Although he was a supporter of royal power, he imposed two basic limitations on it. Outside the kingdom, royal power was still submitted at least to the Empire, if not to the emperor, which was scarcely any different: "Some say that France benefits from an exemption in relation to the Empire; this is impossible according to the law, whence it results that France is submitted to the Empire."[54] Inside of France, "while some say that just as Rome is the common country [*patrie*], the royal crown is the common country because it is its head." As we have seen, however, Révigny also reckoned that "a vassal's duty is to defend his own country [*patrie*]— in other words the barony to which he owes his allegiance rather than the common country, in other words, the king."[55] One of the king's most faithful men, Joinville did not say anything different when he refused to follow Saint Louis on the crusade to Tunis, opting instead to take care of his primordial duty, the good of his seigniory in Champagne that had suffered tremendously from his absence.

Thus, the formulae "*quod principi placuit*" and "*princeps legibus*" appear to have had only a limited influence in thirteenth-century France. They were known and received, but always in an extremely formal manner."[56] Saint Louis was far from having been an absolutist king. Three obligations prevented this from happening. The first was the demand for his obedience to God, which took precedence over everything else. Beaumanoir articulated this perfectly when he stated that each person, the king just as well as his subjects, "must do what belongs to Our Lord's commandment above all else."[57] Like Charles Petit-Dutaillis, I believe that for Saint Louis, "the essential obligation . . . was to guide his subjects toward heaven and to assure the salvation of their souls."[58] However, along with Rigaudière, I also think that Petit-Dutaillis exaggerates when he reduces a second obligation to this first duty. The second duty here is the king's obligation to the common good. For Saint Louis, "the common advantage [*profit*] could only be the abolition of sin, the expulsion of the devil." For the saintly king, the common advantage [*profit*] could not be exhausted in this eschatological design, even though the eschatological program was the essential thing for him. The "common profit" was also the principle that inspired a good government here below. This was occurring in increasingly technical fields in which new forms of royal action tied to the construction of the modern monarchical state had to be exercised. These fields of action were first of all justice, finance, and currency. At this point, none of them had yet been freed from a religious and moral vision that took the Augustinian *City of God* as its ultimate point of reference. The men of the Middle Ages thought of these things in terms of places and a logic of relations situated between heaven and the earth, where we only see fundamental incompatibilities and a need for separation. The tempting idea of a "secularization" or "laicization" of politics here seems somewhat anachronous to me.[59]

On the other hand, I agree with Strayer and his disciples like Elizabeth Brown when they stress the importance of an attitude that formed the third limitation on the Christian king's absolute power beginning with Saint Louis and continuing with his successors.[60] This third limitation was *conscience*.[61] It took shape in the examination of conscience tied to the new practice of confession, mediating between God's will and the exercise of royal sovereignty. Especially in matters of finance and money, it partly explains the hesitations and tentative steps involving apparent contradictions between the king of France's actions and legislation. As he interrogated his conscience, Saint Louis was held back from the path to absolutism that became a reality later on.[62]

SAINT LOUIS ON DISPLAY FOR HIS SUBJECTS

Between the mysterious veiling of the sacred royal person and regal ostentation—I am tempted to say "*ostension*"—we have seen how Saint Louis chose the second position.[63] Saint Louis made use of this "display" of the royal person more than his predecessors, but he shrouded this royal ostentation in the humility of processions and tours to give alms to the poor. In Salimbene of Parma's work, we saw him arrive at the general chapter of the Franciscans in Sens in 1248 on his way to the crusade, walking barefoot and treading through the dust on the road. This appearance of penitential humility only made the royal person shine all the more brightly.[64]

Two of Guillaume de Saint-Pathus's texts effectively illustrate this habit that Saint Louis had of basking in a crowd in an atmosphere of humble devotion that was never lacking in ostentation.

The first example recounts the organized public procession for the transfer of the twenty-four bodies of the martyred saints of the legion of Saint Maurice in 1262 to Senlis where he had built a church for them. He had acquired them at the abbey of Saint-Maurice d'Agaune. He had them transported in several reliquaries covered in silk cloth. The procession in-cluded several bishops and abbots and took place in the presence of a large number of barons and a "great multitude of people." "He had all the clergy of the city of Senlis carry out a procession in good order" and brought the reliquaries holding the relics "in a grand procession through the city," all the way to the chapel of the royal palace where they were laid and would wait for the completion of the construction of the church of Saint-Maurice. "The saint king carried the last reliquary on his own shoul-ders along with his son-in-law Thibaud the king of Navarre, and the other reliquaries were carried before him by other barons and knights. . . . When the bodies of the saints were in the church, the saint king had a solemn mass sung there and he had a sermon made to the people who were as-sembled there."[65] Louis publicly humbled himself before the relics, al-though in doing so he imposed an image on the clergy, the nobles, and the people who were there. It was the image of a king who was a dispenser of relics, which guaranteed a protection from which he would be the first to benefit.

The second text shows the king on horseback distributing alms to the poor: "When the saint king rode through the kingdom, the poor would come to him, and he would give them each a denier, and when he saw people who were even more indigent, he would give five sous to one, ten sous to another, and as much as twenty sous to another. . . ."[66]

Upon returning from the Holy Land, "when he visited his land, he would serve two poor people every day from his own hands, giving each of them

two loaves of bread and twelve deniers *parisis*." He also distributed money
and food when there were shortages of basic staples or during periods of
excessively high prices, thus fulfilling his role as a king, a king who nour-
ished his people. "And sometimes he would say: 'Let's go visit the poor
people in such-and-such a country and feed them.'"[67]

Good Friday was the day for the almsgiving king's great "ostension":

> And as the saint king went through the churches on the day of
> Good Friday, giving deniers to the poor who would come up to him,
> he would forbid his sergeants to prevent the poor from approach-
> ing him. Doing this, the poor people would jostle the saint king so
> much that they nearly made him fall. And he took all of this in stride
> [*patience*] because although he was harried by the poor who would
> follow him to receive alms and who sometimes were so many that
> they stood right on his feet, he would still not allow the officers and
> others who stood around him to push the poor away. . . .[68]

These tours for charity were also tours for the royal person's ostentatious display. In his royal palaces, and especially at Vincennes and the Palais
de la Cité in Paris, he employed a strategy that combined concealment and
exhibition. His "hôtel," as we shall see, tended to become a "sacred home"
for him and his household.[69] His Sainte-Chapelle became his private shrine
for the relics of the Passion. He had put them on display after their arrival
in Paris only to shut them up afterward in his private chapel for his own
use. The relics were still taken out for exceptional occasions and carried in
processions for the people to see. The palace garden was open to people
who came to solicit the king's personal judgment and for the important
royal festivals.

WAS SAINT LOUIS A CALCULATING KING?

The Capetian kings advanced the agenda of the monarchical state under the
cover of feudalism and religion. This was particularly true of Saint Louis.
Under his reign, the state advanced disguised beneath the mask of holiness.
Is this a sign of the times or a case of the sovereign's Machiavellianism before the existence of this term?[70]

There is an outstanding trait in Saint Louis' behavior that is so astonishing that we might ask if it wasn't a "secret" of his? By adhering to religious and moral imperatives and claiming to put nothing above the interests of God and religion, he continually served the interests of France and royal power at the same time. Voltaire understood this perfectly well.[71] So did Fustel de Coulanges, who wrote, "His skill lies in being just."[72]

By embodying the model of the "very Christian" (*christianissimus*) king better than any of his predecessors had done, he more solidly established the epithet as a natural attribute of the king of France, elevating him above the other Christian kings. He justified the Englishman Matthew Paris's act of referring to the king of France as "the highest and most dignified of the worldly kings."[73]

When Louis got the king of England to swear homage to him in the Palais de la Cité on December 4, 1259, how can we distinguish this immensely successful political achievement from the expression of a very Christian reconciliation?

When Louis appointed the investigators in 1247 to gather complaints against the abuses and denials of justice committed by royal officers, there was also the idea of royal justice that was asserted and imposed. When the royal bailiffs denounced the fiscal policies of the bourgeois who governed the towns and passed most of the burden of taxes off on the people, when they accused these "rich men" of injustice, this was an instance of royal power insinuating itself into the government of the "good towns."

His manner of rendering justice or establishing peace for explicit moral and religious reasons in particular advanced the sovereign's power and prestige and strengthened the newly forming state at the same time.

Let's reread Joinville's famous passage and its recollection of Saint Louis rendering justice under the oak tree in the royal woods of Vincennes:

> It happened many times that in the summer after his mass he would go sit in the woods of Vincennes and lean against an oak tree and have us sit down around him. And all of the people who had some matter to address would come talk to him without having to go through any bailiff or any other people. Then, he would ask them from his own mouth: "Is there anyone here who has his case?" And the people who had their case ready would stand. And then he would say: "Be quiet, all of you, and we will expedite you one after another."

And then he would call His Lordship Pierre de Fontaines and His Lordship Geoffroi de Villette and say to one of them: "Expedite this case for me."[74]

He did the same in the garden of the royal palace in Paris:

And he would spread carpets out on the ground so that we could sit down around him; and all the people who had some affair to take up before him would stand all around him. And then he would expedite them in the same way I just told you about for the woods of Vincennes.[75]

Joinville was writing roughly forty years after the fact and did not care for the reigning king Philip the Fair (who was two years old when his grand-father died) any more than for his government dominated by jurists and auxiliaries whom we would call bureaucrats. He was happy to emphasize the easy access that plaintiffs had to the king and his direct, personal manner of rendering justice.[76] However, although Saint Louis allowed the plaintiffs to appear before him, and although he listened to them, for judgment and a ruling he sent them to the specialists in his company: Pierre de Fontaines who was a famous jurist and Geoffroi de Villette, a well-known bailiff. In fact, Saint Louis fixed royal justice in place here in the guise of this personal justice. He was actually putting his reign's great political and administrative act of progress into place — the development of a system of appeals to the king. In other words, this was a form of royal justice that short-circuited the private, local, subaltern systems of seigniorial justice. Montesquieu noted this when he wrote: "Saint Louis introduced the custom of redress without combat [*fausser sans combattre*]: a change that was a kind of revolution in it-self."[77] The resulting increase in the number of trials to be judged required more judicial specialists; for the most important cases, the appeal was in-creasingly made at the royal court in *parlement*. Saint Louis was still an itiner-ant king, but his system of justice became fixed in a single place.[78]

Two historians have written: "the influx of trials brought to the king's court is due to Saint Louis' moral influence."[79] We have to clarify things here. No two distinct movements existed in this situation — one that was an in-stitutional development of royal justice and another that responded to Saint Louis' moral concerns. There was no cleverness on Saint Louis' part here either because, if it existed, his capacity for political calculation was inseparable from his religious motives. Saint Louis was both a Christian judge and the founder of a system of royal justice at the same time as royal justice for him was only an instrument for his moral action. This was undoubtedly Saint Louis' "secret" to avoid separating politics and ethics.

This was his great strength. Although he prolonged the crusade beyond its historical moment, it was still prestigious at that moment when it was beginning to seem like an anachronism. Although it led him to a twofold disaster, even the crusade enriched his image and enhanced the prestige of the Kingdom of France. It was still a heroic event at that time before it became a mere utopian fantasy. Just as the Arthurian adventure could only end with Arthur's death when the spirit of the times had moved beyond it, when the crusades faded from the common thoughts of the age, they could only end with a heroic death, the death of Saint Louis.

Saint Louis and His Family

MEN—AND ESPECIALLY THE MEN OF THE MIDDLE AGES—DID NOT live alone. Familial and kinship networks bound men together even tighter at the summit of the social pyramid than at its base. Their carnal family, the blood family, was also a family of alliances in which the powerful more than any others had to assure reproduction, guarantee mutual assistance, and do everything possible to maintain their rank and multiply their lineage. This human network and the duties attached to it were stronger and more binding if the leader had to protect the "royal state" through his lineage first of all. His lineage was superior to all others, and it was different from them. It was a dynasty, a "race" as people used to say, a sacred line. The love that Saint Louis was supposed to express toward members of his family exuded the aura of these sacred ties.[1]

HIS FATHER

Love runs upstream toward one's parents in the beginning. We do not know of anything Saint Louis said about his father. In the edict of Melun issued in 1230 against the usurious Jews, we find a stereotypical statement:

573

"in the memory of our father the illustrious king Louis and our ancestors." This mention came from the royal chancellery and not from the young king. Louis IX's later edicts only mentioned "our ancestors." It is true that Louis VIII ruled for only three years, and the royal edicts whose numbers did not pile up until the reign of Saint Louis did not have enough time to exist in any quantity. The Church especially celebrated his father's memory, grateful for his military engagement against the Albigenses; they may also have celebrated his memory as a discreet reproach to his son for not showing an equally active zeal against the heretics.

Numerous texts from the end of the thirteenth century were content to reiterate the commonplace statement—"like father, like son"—and the political ideology of the time applied the adage to kings in particular. So Louis was praised as the "inheritor of his father's merits" and of " his piety and his faith."[2] It is clear that he never knew his father very well; he died when Louis was twelve years old. A noble child usually lived with the women until the age of seven, and the men he saw were mostly churchmen. In addition, Louis VIII was often absent and off at war. He had been a warrior more than anything else and although Saint Louis bravely fulfilled his role as a knight and a military leader, it was not the valorous men but the *prud'-hommes* whose company he liked to keep.

His Grandfather

On the other hand, he preserved a bright admiring memory of his grandfather Philip Augustus who died when Louis was nine years old. Saint Louis was the first king of France to have known his grandfather. He knew him when he was at the height of his glory, after Bouvines where the forty-nine-year-old king inspired universal admiration for throwing himself into the heat of the battle and was lucky to escape death. In the Middle Ages, a man was old at the age of fifty. Philip Augustus still went hunting but no longer took part in war; he passed this duty on to his heir. He reconciled with the Church after the death of Agnès de Méran in 1201, and in 1213 he released his second legitimate spouse, Ingeburg of Denmark, from her confinement in a convent.

Pope Innocent III legitimated the children Philip Augustus had with Agnès de Méran. Among those children was a son, Philip Hurepel, to whom he gave the county of Boulogne after the battle of Bouvines. Blanche of Castile (and Louis) had to handle Philip Hurepel with caution so that he would not join the powerful vassals who revolted during Louis IX's minority.[3]

Philip Augustus had committed no lapses in conduct since the birth of an illegitimate son in 1209. With a particularly remarkable flare for audacity, he favored this bastard son with the given name of Pierre Charlot, a thoroughly honorific diminutive that finally appropriated the name of Charlemagne for the first time for a son of a Capetian king. By his first marriage with Isabelle de Hainaut, Philip Augustus was able to have a son, the future Louis VIII, who would truly be the first Capetian directly descended from the great emperor, though through the female line. Saint Louis thus knew his aging grandfather in his state of semi-retirement. He enjoyed speaking with his grandson who became a future king of France at the age of nine upon the death of his older brother Philip.

Despite this familiarity, can we imagine two men who could be any more different than Philip Augustus and the future Saint Louis? One was a conquering warrior, a hunter, a bon vivant, a lover of women, and prone to anger. The other was peaceable though he fought well when he had to, abstaining from the hunt and indulgence in good food and women (except his own wife), in control of his impulses, devout, and ascetic. The child, however, no doubt proud of the attention he received from his grandfather the king, impressed with his prestige and his imperious manner of embodying royal dignity, drank in his words and remembered them until the end of his life. During his own reign, people told anecdotes about Philip Augustus,[4] and he related a few of them himself. They most often repeated his grandfather's words and sayings, things he had said to his friends and even to his servants, and Louis felt that his sayings were exemplary.[5]

Philip Augustus was also a point of reference for him, an authority with which he sometimes shielded himself.

In the Enguerran de Coucy affair, he reminded his audience that his grandfather had once confiscated the lands of a nobleman who had committed murder and thrown him in the prison of the Louvre.[6] Philip Augustus was the only person he quoted in his *Enseignements* for his son. When Louis advised Philip to respect the Church even when the people of the Church have done him some wrong, he reminded him that Philip Augustus had said that for the graces he received from God he preferred to accept any harm the Church could do him "rather than create dissension between me and the Holy Church."[7] In both cases, Louis was trying to win acceptance for contested aspects of his own politics: his strictness in justice and his limited tolerance toward the Church.

For Saint Louis, Philip Augustus was a living model for the king of France as a governor of his kingdom. Did he see him in all the glory of a dead king when he was transported on a litter from Paris to Saint-Denis, his body wrapped in a gold sheet with his scepter in his hand and his crown on his head?[8] It is not very likely. However, the image he kept of him was that of a prestigious king. What he owed to the fact of having seen, heard, and touched his grandfather was a concrete, physical perception of the dynastic continuity he inherited. This was an essential political phenomenon in the thirteenth century and one of the most pressing concerns for Louis' own political conduct. His familial sentiments were always intermingled with his political sensibility.

His Mother

Since the age of Charlemagne, it was customary to identify the kings of France with the kings of Israel and Judah in compliance with typological correspondences with the Old and New Testaments. According to this custom, for his educated contemporaries Saint Louis was a new David, a new Solomon, and, most of all, a new Josiah.[9] In his *Vie de Saint Louis* written shortly after his death, Geoffroy de Beaulieu spoke of Blanche of Castile on the basis of this identification.[10] One of the similarities between Louis and Josiah was that both of them had a remarkable mother.

> What's more, we must not pass the name of Josiah's mother over in silence. She was named Ydida, which means "Beloved of the Lord" or "who pleases the Lord," which perfectly matches our king's very illustrious mother, Her Lady Queen Blanche, who was truly loved by the Lord and pleasing to the Lord and useful and pleasing to men.[11]

For Saint Louis' biographers, the king owed a large number of his virtues to his mother. His person, his life, and his reign would not have been what they were without her. We would expect to hear Blanche praised for the woman that she was. However, most of her praiseworthy qualities were attributed to her resemblance to a man and her ability to raise a man, her son. In the Middle Ages, women and children were only valued for their ability to act like adult men. These were the "male" Middle Ages.[12]

> Under the saintly tutelage and salutary instruction of such a pious mother, through his child's nature our Louis began to show handsome dispositions and great promise and from day to day he grew up and became an accomplished man, seeking out the Lord, doing what was right and pleasing in the eyes of the Lord, and truly turned to the Lord with all his heart, all his soul, and all his strength, like the good fruit from a good tree.[13]

Here is a list of all the conditions required for a child to become a good Christian. He needed to have a good natural disposition, as gifts of nature were indispensable, and he had to benefit from a good education. There could be no good results without this combination of the innate and the acquired. This was the doctrine of the Mirrors of the Princes as presented by John of Salisbury in the *Policraticus*—the great inspirational work for the clerics in Louis' entourage—and by Vincent de Beauvais in his *De eruditione filiorum nobilium* dedicated to Saint Louis' wife.

Blanche of Castile nevertheless exhibited other virtues when her son became a king at the age of twelve.

> When he began to rule when he was only about twelve years old, the people who were members of the king's entourage at the time can attest to the strength, the zeal, the rectitude, and the power with which his mother administered, upheld, and defended the rights of the kingdom. However, at this time the king had many powerful enemies at the beginning of his reign. Yet, thanks to the merits of his innocence and his mother's excellent foresight (she proved herself as a perfect *virago*[14] and naturally brought a man's heart[15] to her woman's sex and mind), the rabble-rousers in the kingdom were overcome. They gave up, and the king's justice triumphed.

An anecdote illustrates the love of a Christian mother in Blanche's love for her son. Blanche also spoke through the intermediary of her son, whereas history has left us with a Louis VIII who was silent.

We must not silently pass over the story of a religious who on the faith of false testimony claimed he had heard people say that before his marriage His Royal Highness the king had concubines with whom he sometimes sinned, and that his mother knew about it and pretended she was not aware of it. This religious was very surprised, and reproached Her Lady the queen for this. She humbly established her innocence of this lie, both hers and her son's, and she added a word worthy of praise. If the king, her son, whom she loved more than any other mortal creature, was sick and in danger of dying and someone told him he would be healed by sinning a single time with a woman other than his wife, she would rather see him die than offend the Creator by sinning mortally even one single time.[16]

Boniface VIII echoed this testimony on Blanche's role as an outstanding mother and educator in his bull for Saint Louis' canonization, and so did Guillaume de Saint-Pathus in his *Life* based on the record of the canonization inquiry. The pope declared:

> When he was twelve years old, he was deprived of his father's support and remained under the protection and direction of his mother Blanche the queen of France of illustrious memory. She was ever fervently concerned with the duties we owe to God, and committed herself to guiding him with wisdom and instructing him with diligence so that he would be able to prove himself worthy, suitable, and proper for governing the kingdom that demanded the foresight of his guidance as she had taught him.[17]

This was Blanche's fundamental lesson for her son. It was a lesson he never forgot and that he brilliantly put to work: he must not separate God's worship from the government of his kingdom. Obedience to God and the interest of the kingdom were one and the same duty. They went together. They had to go together. Devotion and political skill was one and the same thing.[18]

Guillaume de Saint-Pathus evoked the same idea:

> For mother he had the honorable queen Blanche who, after her lord's death, religiously raised her son who began to rule at the age

of twelve; she took on the bravery of a man in a woman's heart and vigorously, wisely, mightily, and righteously administered and upheld the rights of the kingdom and defended it against several enemies with her good foresight.[19]

Her devout son often recalled her memory. Guillaume de Saint-Pathus repeated Saint Louis' own words that tell of the time his mother said she would rather he died than commit a mortal sin.

Blanche was born in 1188. She was the daughter of King Alphonso VIII of Castile and Eleanor of England. She married Louis when she was twelve years old in 1200. He was the oldest son and heir of Philip Augustus. The marriage was arranged with the hope that it would seal the peace between the king of France and the king of England, which did not happen. She gave him eleven or twelve children, and three or four of them died at a young age — the oldest son Philip who died at the age of nine in 1218, Jean who died at thirteen in 1232, and Philippe Dagobert who died at seven, also in 1232. After Louis, the children who reached adulthood were Robert, Alphonse, Isabelle, and Charles.

These given names corresponded to dynastic politics in this matter. Philip, the eldest, received the name of his grandfather. Louis was given the name of his father. "Robert" came from the line of the Robertans, the ancestors of the Capetians and Robert the Pious, the second Capetian king. Alphonse was named in honor of his Spanish grandfather. Philippe Dagobert's name united his grandfather's name with the name of the old Merovingian king (for whom Saint Louis built a new tomb in Saint-Denis). "Charles" definitively introduced the given name of Charlemagne into the Capetian family. The only surviving daughter, Isabelle, received the name of her grandmother, Isabelle de Hainaut, the first wife of her grandfather Philip Augustus and mother of her father Louis VIII.

With her husband Louis VIII's premature death, Blanche became the guardian of her twelve-year-old son, the future Saint Louis. She also became the regent of the kingdom, certainly not through the will of Louis VIII on his deathbed as people claimed at the time, but, as we have guessed, because her husband's advisors chose her, the former advisors to Philip Augustus, who were present at Louis VIII's bedside at the time of his death. They selected her as regent whether or not they had already detected the great qualities she soon showed.[20]

She inherited a difficult situation. Her son, a minor, was threatened by a revolt that was brewing among several of their powerful vassals. She was probably pregnant with their last child, Charles. She was a foreigner. In the Middle Ages and particularly in France, it was not considered a good thing for a queen to be a foreigner. Already in the eleventh century, Constance d'Arles (or de Provence), the daughter of the count of Toulouse and third wife of Robert the Pious, had to put up with the hostility of the court of the Île-de-France, center of the *langue d'oui,* toward a southern princess who spoke the *langue d'oc.* Blanche was Castilian by birth and in appearance. In fact, the only thing we know about her physical appearance is that people described it as "Castilian," meaning that her hair was very black.[21] She probably also possessed a penchant for ardent, spectacular worship that she passed on to her son, although this was also a Capetian tradition of worship, particularly for their very pious ancestor Louis VII. Her nephew, the king of Castile Ferdinand III also worshipped in this manner, although his reputation for being a saint was not sanctioned by the Church with a canonization until the seventeenth century.

She not only had the difficult task of making her son into as perfect a king as possible (she did program him to become an ideal Christian king, if not a saint),[22] but also the more troublesome task of heading off the revolt of their powerful vassals and confronting the English who were anxious to recover the possessions they had lost to Philip Augustus. She had to govern the Kingdom of France without the help of Philip Augustus's now deceased advisors, and she was also a target of the vilest calumnies. People accused her of being the mistress of Count Thibaud IV of Champagne and, more commonly, of the pontifical legate, Cardinal Romain de Saint-Ange (Romain Frangipani).

Strong, courageous, and authoritarian, she held her own and triumphed over this adversity. She may have even been a bit too authoritarian at times; for instance, she nearly lost the University for Paris during the strike of 1229–1231. After putting up a long fight, she finally gave in to the pleas of the legate and perhaps also the insistence of her son, the young king.

During these difficult years, mother and son forged an intimate bond. On the very day after Louis VIII's death, she took her child in a cart on the risky and painstaking journey to be crowned at Reims. An early fourteenth-century miniature leaves us an image of this event.[23] Louis always kept the memory of his mother and himself, terrified as they were, holed up in the castle of Monthlhéry until the armed Parisians came to find them and accompany them safely back to the capital in the midst of the cheers of the people who lined their path.[24] Memories like this create unbreakable ties. They reinforced the assiduous education Blanche gave to her son and made it easier for their vassals to accept the practice of confiding the kingdom's government to the royal mother who was in agreement with her son.

Thus began a special story, unique in the annals of France, of the great love that existed between a king and his mother. This love was equally powerful for his mother even after her son reached adulthood. I have characterized this exceptional situation as a form of co-royalty.[25] No doubt after his twentieth year and his marriage in 1234 Louis governed France and fully assumed his functions as king, but his mother's name continued to appear alongside his on many of the official acts. Between 1226 and 1252, we find "the king Louis and the queen Blanche" at the head of France. Once again, I believe that Louis had no difficulty reconciling this situation with his desire to perfectly execute his duties as king and to fulfill his royal function. He was not just imbued with a sense of duty, he was also authoritarian despite the love and respect he had for his mother whom he accepted in this role of co-sovereign. The two characters in this couple were equally strong, the two leaders equally passionate about the good of the kingdom. Louis, however, sufficiently loved his mother and fully respected the importance of her advice and he was sufficiently grateful to her for what she had done for him and the kingdom to accept this type of co-government without any trouble. At the same time, she sufficiently loved her son and had enough confidence in him and admiration for him and well enough understood that the king was the monarch, the head, not to abuse or take advantage of the appearance and reality of the power he left her. This is an idealized image of an astonishing pair. It is remarkable that we have no evidence of any disagreement between them. Blanche may have been a little more indulgent than Louis toward the unreliable count of Toulouse, Raimond VII. Even this is not certain though.

A terrible confrontation arose between them on only one occasion, and it was Blanche who gave in. This happened in 1244 when Louis decided to leave on the crusade.[26] The king was at death's door and nearly ready for his final sacraments. He had lost his ability to speak. Suddenly, one day, he resuscitated and almost immediately after this made his vow to crusade. Someone came to announce the news to Blanche.

When the queen his mother heard the news that his speech had been restored to him, she showed as much joy as she could. And when she learned that he had decided to take the cross, as he told it to her himself, she expressed as much grief as though she had seen him dead.[27]

Why did she express such tremendous and spectacular grief? Two very powerful anxieties were united within her here. One was quite simply her maternal love for her son, as she admitted. Would she ever see her beloved son again? She actually never did see him again. This was a normal reaction, especially for a fifty-six-year-old woman who was approaching the age of death. The king himself was sick, a suffering man, prone to illness.[28] Would he be able to stand the trials of a crusade? As always, political calculation was mingled with their feelings. Was the great distance of a crusade compatible with "the duties of a sovereign and his obligations for the kingdom's safety"? It was not just the memory of the "feudal" difficulties of Louis' youth that troubled her. More than this, it was the feeling that the growing complexity of the royal administration and the priority given to the kingdom's internal peace and prosperity over conquests and military expeditions that characterized this phase in the formation of the monarchical state demanded the king's presence within his kingdom. Out of instinct and understanding acquired through her experience of government, Blanche understood the evolution of the political structures of her time better than Louis.

Louis had decided to crusade and became entrenched in this position. Nothing could be done about it. We can see that when he truly took something to heart, he was the one who made the decisions. He even found a reason to appease his conscience as a king: Blanche herself was his reason. She had already shown that she possessed the energy and savoir-faire needed to rule. She had never really given up her role in political affairs. She would be regent again, and he found this reassuring.

It was at this moment that the royal pair's ceremony par excellence took place. On Sunday April 26, 1248, the Sunday of Quasimodo, on the eve of the crusade, Saint Louis inaugurated the Sainte-Chapelle—with his mother. This was the first and last time they would take part in a ceremony together in the Sainte-Chapelle.

In the spring of 1253 while Saint Louis was in Sidon he learned of his mother's death several months after it occurred on November 27, 1252.

Louis was thrust into a period of mourning of astonishing intensity and theatricality, which everyone admired, although it drew reproof from some due to its excessive nature. This was Joinville's reaction; Louis' grief made him forget his admiration and respect for the king. He had never seen the king so far from the moderation and self-control he had always tried to maintain. The following scene struck many of their contemporaries and its account was widely diffused. Joinville's version of it that I am presenting here is the liveliest.

> The news reached the king in Sayette that his mother was dead. He was so grief-stricken that no one could even talk to him. Afterwards, he sent me to find a valet for him. When I came before him in his chamber where he was alone, and he saw me, he threw out his arms[29] and told me: "Ah! Seneschal, I have lost my mother!" "Sire," I said, "I am not surprised by this, because she had to die, but I am surprised that you, who are a wise man, have shown such great grief, for you know that the wise man says that whatever trouble a man has in his heart, none of it should show on his face, because the man who shows it rejoices his enemies and worries his friends." He had many beautiful services held for her overseas and later he sent a ledger to France that was full of letters with prayers for the churches so that they would pray for her.[30]

If Joinville had never written down his memories of Saint Louis, we would have still had an image of Blanche of Castile as a strong and pious woman who very much loved her husband, her children, and especially her son the king. We would have held an image of a woman who always sought the good and who always did good, as reported by Saint Louis' biographers whom I have just quoted. But Joinville was there and he told a different story.

> The hardships that Queen Blanche imposed on Queen Marguerite were such that Queen Blanche would not even suffer her son to be in the company of his wife unless it was to go to bed with her at night. The manor that the king and queen liked to stay in the most was Pontoise, because the king's chamber there was upstairs and the queen's just below. . . . And they arranged things in such a way that they could speak together on a spiral staircase that descended from

one room to the next. And they arranged their affairs so that when the servants saw the queen coming to enter the chamber of the king her son, they would strike the door with their sticks, and the king would come running into his chamber so that his mother would find him there. The ushers for Queen Marguerite's chamber would do the same thing in turn if Queen Blanche was coming so that she would find Queen Marguerite there.[31]

Here we see the typical relationship between a mother-in-law who was a possessive mother and her daughter-in-law pushed to the point of hysteria. Joinville was scandalized by what he had just told, but, consciously or unconsciously, there was still some humor in this tragicomic story. On the other hand, there was nothing the least bit funny about the following story:

Once the king was at the side of the queen his wife, and she was in great danger of dying because she was wounded from a child she had just had. Queen Blanche came in and took her son by the hand and said: "Come away now; you have nothing to do here." When Queen Marguerite saw that the king's mother was taking him away she cried out: "Alas! You won't let me see my lord whether I am alive or dead." And then she fainted, and they thought she was dead, and the king thought that she was dying and returned; and it was with great difficulty that they restored her to health.[32]

Saint Louis did no better here than sons who hide to avoid having to obey a terrible mother. Fortunately, in this painful scene of his wife's labor, Saint Louis recovered, although it was a bit too late and only once his mother had already left. As for Blanche, she was aggressive and insufferable in the preceding anecdote, mean spirited and, frankly, odious. Saint Louis was not perfect. Blanche of Castile was even less so.

His Brothers and Sisters

After considering his ascendants, the lineage does not lead us directly to his descendants, to his children, but to those particular collateral members of the family who, in Saint Louis' case, are primarily his brothers and sisters.

We do not know whether Saint Louis was affected by the disappearance of his siblings who died at a young or very young age. They left no other mark upon history aside from the fact that they left Louis the top position as heir, thereby enriching or modifying the inheritances.

This leaves us with the siblings who survived. There were three brothers; later the number was reduced to two. First, there was Robert, the oldest after Louis. He was born in 1216 and was killed in Egypt at the battle of Mansourah in 1250. Then, there was Alphonse. He was born in 1220 and died in Italy on his return from the crusade to Tunis in 1271. Finally, there was Charles who was born in 1226 (or more likely in 1227). He became king of Naples and Sicily in 1266 and died in 1285 after losing Sicily in 1282 during the uprising of the Sicilian Vespers, which benefited the Aragonese.

We have to look at these brothers together, first of all, because they formed the group of princely sons of the king who received a special seigniory, an apanage, taken from the royal domain by virtue of their father's decision.[33] Saint Louis respected his father's will, but he executed it as though it were his own decision. When his brothers successively reached the age of twenty, he dubbed them and placed them in possession of their apanages. "The apanages appear to be a familial institution and not a royal institution."[34] However, it is useful to immediately qualify this statement with the following: "but whose family leader does not forget that he is king." He made a very strict adjustment to the conditions of possession for the apanages; notably, the apanage had to revert to the royal domain in the case that its holder died without a direct heir. This actually was the case for Alphonse.[35]

We should recall that when the policy of giving apanages was systematized by Louis VIII it was not the instrument for dismembering the state that it later became at the end of the fourteenth century when the greed of Charles VI's uncles nearly did permanent damage to the monarchical state despite the fact that it was more advanced at that time. Instead, it was a well-adapted means for avoiding the kinds of conflicts between brothers or between fathers and sons that had torn England apart. It articulated the still living tradition of treating the royal domain as the *land* of the royal family of which each of the king's sons inherited a portion when his father died. However, a prudent implementation of the policy matched with restrictive clauses prevented the kingdom from being fragmented and preserved the rights and the authority of the king.[36] The apanages provided the material and psychological bases for the entente between Saint Louis and his brothers. As always, clever and good at the same time, Louis was able to do the rest himself.

The group of brothers was not split with the king on one side and the brothers on the other. The king was a part of the group, even though he maintained his preeminence. He was both equal and unequal at the same time, and this was a fundamental structure in medieval feudal society.[37] The reality of this group's cohesiveness was articulated on several important occasions. The treaty of 1259 specified that Louis' brothers would not have to render homage to the king of England for the lands they held from him. After the Egyptian disaster, when Alphonse and Charles returned to France while Louis stayed behind in the Holy Land, they officially guaranteed their responsibility for taking over and leading the regency: "This is the first time in the history of the Capetian family that this role was entrusted to cadets" (A. Lewis). Philip III followed this example after his father's death. When they were at Carthage, surrounded by cadavers including the corpse of his father and his brother Jean-Tristan, Philip designated his nineteen-year-old brother Pierre as regent in the case he were to die before his own son and heir reached the age of his majority. Simple external regalia individualized the group of brothers. The younger brothers often wore crowns and diadems that resembled the royal crown, and they all adapted the fleur-de-lis as their dynastic symbol after the example of Philip Hurepel.

Their wives benefited from this advancement as well, as Louis tended to enjoy gathering and exhibiting the entire royal family around him on certain occasions. His feelings encouraged these displays combining lineage, the family of the blood, and the family of power.

He thus treated the crusades as familial expeditions. In 1248, he left with his three brothers and the queen. The queen's presence on the journey can be explained by the facts that the king was young—thirty-four years old at the time—and that he needed his wife with him because the dynastic continuity had not yet been assured. Marguerite had three children during the six years they spent in the Orient: Jean-Tristan (1250), Pierre (1251), and Blanche (1253).

In 1270, Alphonse, his wife, and his three oldest surviving sons including his heir Philip, Jean-Tristan, and Pierre all accompanied him on the crusade. His brother, Charles d'Anjou the king of Naples would join them later. In the letter he sent from Carthage to France one month before his death on July 25, 1270, he underscored the presence of his daughter-in-law, the wife of "our first-born son Philip" (*primogeniti nostri Philippi*) in the crusaders' camp.[38]

He was all the more attentive to the brilliance of the festivals marking the dubbing of his brothers as these ceremonies preceded the great change in his conduct that took place after the crusade. The dubbing ceremony also marked their attainment of the age of majority (at twenty) and the moment they assumed possession of their apanages.

Louis' brothers also began to lay claim to a condition that later became a title: "*fils de roi*" (sons of the king) and later, more specifically, "*fils de roi de France*" (sons of the king of France), which was sometimes shortened to "*fils de France*" (sons of France). Only the children of a king could call themselves "*de France*" in the fourteenth century,[39] although I do not think that the institution of the "*princes du sang*" (princes of the blood) had already appeared under Saint Louis. Nonetheless, "*fils de roi de France*" was one important sign of the simultaneous reinforcement of the ideas of the dynasty and the "nation." This idea even took the form of the expression, "*frère du roi de France*" (brother of the king of France). The king himself manipulated this title with impressive political skill. We saw how he threw it in the face of the pope in order to reject his proposal of offering the imperial crown to his brother Robert.[40]

Louis added the bond of fraternal love to this dynastic and lineal solidarity between the brothers. It seems this love was usually lively and reciprocal. In his deposition for the inquiry into his brother's canonization, Charles d'Anjou expanded the tree of brothers (although it is also true that he was speaking in his own interest here): "The holy root produced saintly branches, not just the saint king, but also the count of Artois who was a glorious martyr and the count of Poitiers, a martyr by intention."[41]

Strictly educated by a mother for whom sex outside of marriage was the worst of mortal sins, the four brothers had a reputation for absolute chastity in marriage. Charles d'Anjou swore that to the best of his knowledge neither Robert nor Alphonse had ever committed mortal sin, and that he benefited from this same reputation.[42]

The four brothers were still very different from each other as were the relations that bound them to Louis.

Robert was the brother he cherished above all. Only two years set them apart in age, and they were raised together. He was the king's companion.

Robert was also a brilliant knight. Perhaps he bedazzled Saint Louis with his chivalric conduct. Saint Louis had both reservations and fascination about this form of behavior as it was not based on reason and in some ways seemed to belong to another time. Robert was a powerful ruler. His father had bequeathed Artois to him as his apanage, and Saint Louis granted it to him at his dubbing ceremony, which was also a celebration of Robert's marriage to Mathilde de Brabant. This marriage made him a cousin of Emperor Frederick II and brother-in-law to the future duke of Brabant, the landgrave of Thuringia, and the duke of Bavaria. He thus became "a figure who was well introduced into the lands of the Empire."[43] Saint Louis added to his lands with the gifts of Hesdin, Lens, and Bapaume, which he exchanged for other lands held by their mother. In addition, he gave him the manor of Poissy, the place of his birth. Despite his brother's new interests, Louis did not want any military or political conflicts with the Empire. As we have seen, he had his eyes on England to the west and the Mediterranean to the south. During his life, Robert did not always have a good reputation. Matthew Paris, who showed great consideration for Saint Louis, was hard on his brother. He accused him of poor conduct on the crusade, of treating the other crusading knights and the English in particular with condescension [*superbia*], and of acting like a coward on the battlefield where he was not killed fighting but fleeing the enemy.[44]

In any case, due to his lack of discipline and lack of reflection, Robert seems to have been the cause of the disaster by having rashly and prematurely charged the Muslims.

Louis would hear nothing of it. Until the day he died, he continued to consider Robert a martyr (along with their brother Charles, as we have seen) and repeatedly asked the papacy to recognize his martyrdom, in vain.

Alphonse was the second brother. He took the nicest inheritance. With the execution of Louis VIII's decision, during his dubbing ceremony in 1241 he received two regions taken on the Albigensian crusade, Poitou and Auvergne. He was engaged to Jeanne de Toulouse, the daughter of Count Raimond VII, in 1229. When Raimond died in 1249, and Alphonse was on the crusade, Blanche of Castile and Alphonse's representatives easily seized many of his former father-in-law's extensive domains in Languedoc for him. He thus became "the most powerful of the kingdom's feudal lords."[45] Saint Louis insisted on having him freed as quickly as possible from his captivity with the Muslims, and once the ransom was paid, they released him shortly after his brother. He returned home in 1251 to help govern the kingdom and his lands, but shortly after his return he was struck with paralysis. He was cared for as well as one could have been at that time and, in particular, benefited from the care of a famous Jewish doctor. He recovered some of his faculties but stayed sick for the rest of his life, which he spent mainly in Paris and the environs. He had a palace built for himself near the Louvre, and it became known as the "*hôtel d'Autriche*" (hotel of Austria or "*de l'Autriche*"), which was a corrupted form of "*de l'hôte riche*" (of the rich host). Despite his condition, he governed his lands remarkably, usually from afar. Some have seen him as a progressive administrator that the king himself imitated in ruling his domain and the kingdom. This impression, however, may result from the fact that there was a wealth of administrative documentation from Alphonse's domain, which can be explained by the stronger written traditions in southern France and the near total loss of any comparable royal documentation in a fire that occurred in the eighteenth century. These archives show us Alphonse at the head of a large number of apparently competent officials who oversaw the minting and circulation of coins, the effective management of finances, the fair execution of justice, the maintenance of his authority in relations with the "three orders" without any major conflicts, and manners of favoring economic development and the spread of Roman law, which was already well rooted in the Midi. Alphonse was a loyal brother who did not rock the boat. He advanced France's insertion into the south of the Kingdom without commotion and accomplished this by charting a development that paralleled the rest of the kingdom rather than through any attempts to assimilate the new lands.[46] Rutebeuf wrote a poem in praise of Alphonse de Poitiers, "*La Complainte du comte de Poitiers.*" The poem relies on a single model that applied to all the brothers to such an extent that we might think we were listening to a story about Saint Louis.[47] "He upheld the peace in his land . . . he loves God perfectly and honors the Holy Church . . . he loves the religious orders, he was a mirror of chivalry . . . he loved the poor, gave generously . . . a strict judge . . . he had only suffering and sickness in life, but the health of his soul was strengthened by this." In addition, the poem associates him with his brother more than once in this litany of commonplace ideas in the tradition of funerary elegy that still seems to offer a good reflection of Alphonse's image.

Despite his poor health (his sister-in-law Queen Marguerite asked about his health each time she wrote to him), he still left on the crusade to

Tunis with Saint Louis. He had great personal enthusiasm for the crusade for a long period of time and, after his return to Italy, he started to organize one of his own by buying boats from the Genoese. When he was at Savona in Liguria, he fell sick and died one year after his brother on August 21, 1271. His wife died the very next day. They did not have any children. Their lands reverted directly to the crown as a result of both the rule established for the apanages and the conditions of the treaty of Paris of 1229. Thanks in part to his brother Alphonse, Saint Louis was able to welcome southern France into the Kingdom of France.

We do not know anything about Saint Louis' feelings with respect to the Midi. As we have seen, he took great care in governing the seneschalcies of Beaucaire and Béziers that fell under his direct rule. He also built and developed the port of Aigues-Mortes, the only French port on the Mediterranean shore. He followed the advice of his southern jurists who were steeped in both Roman law and customary law, and he sought out their advice before consulting the jurists formed at the University of Orléans. He harshly put down the revolts there, like the one led by Raimond Trencavel in 1240. He also put an end to the machinations of Raimond VII, the count of Toulouse, who often favored the English and the Cathars. He allowed his brother Alphonse to govern the Midi not so much by following the example of the North, but by implementing an administrative model that was simultaneously developing in both regions. He never attempted to destroy Occitan culture, which never had any real political dimension and which was already fading on its own. The most brutal phases of the repression took place under his grandfather and particularly under his father, who had accepted his role as the secular arm of the Church in a crusade that he had wanted, directed, and opened up to an army of rabble from the North. The final episode of the war was the capture of Montségur. It was led by a royal bailiff and ended in the burning at the stake of Cathars (1244). This cruel operation did not target Occitans; it targeted rebels and heretics.

Under other conditions, we certainly should examine this record with as much serenity and detachment as possible, putting aside both the Occitanist myths that often present an anachronistic historical perspective and the Jacobin passions that insist that unification and centralization excuse all the crimes that were committed here.

Although Saint Louis was no benefactor to southern France, he was neither consciously or unconsciously its torturer either.[48]

The youngest brother Charles was twelve or thirteen years younger than Louis. He was the most unruly of the three brothers, although he was not lacking in talent. He holds a more important place in the history of Italy than in the history of France. In his *Vie de Saint Louis,* Guillaume de Nangis dedicated many long pages to the man who became king of Sicily in 1264. I will not pursue this angle here.

Charles was born just before or probably shortly after their father's death. Louis reacted to him with a mixture of indulgence and annoyance that was probably inspired as much by his place at the end of the chain of sons as by his conduct. I am not hazarding these "psychological" hypotheses only because they are implied in the documents but also because human relations and dynastic strategies were bound together very tightly in a thirteenth-century royal family. When Charles was nineteen years old in 1245, the Aragonese invaded Provence. The count of Provence had just died, and the king of Aragon coveted the hand of his youngest daughter for his son. Charles was sent to meet with the archbishop of Lyon, Philippe de Savoie, whom Saint Louis had probably just met when he visited the pope in Lyon for the council that was held there. Alongside the archbishop who was the brother-in-law of the count of Provence who was Saint Louis' own father-in-law, Charles led a small army with the mission of repulsing the Aragonese. The Aragonese withdrew, and Charles won the hand of the count of Provence's youngest daughter Beatrice, a princess who had been highly sought after in marriage. He wed her in 1246. She was the sister of Queen Marguerite, the wife of his brother King Louis. Alongside his apanage of Anjou and Maine that he received the same year, he acquired extensive new lands by becoming count of Provence.

If Alphonse easily took control of his father-in-law's inheritance, this was not the case for Charles d'Anjou. He had to confront an uprising of lords and towns, which flared up again during his absence on the crusade with his brother. Upon his return, he had a lot of trouble bringing his rebellious subjects back into line. He imposed a county provost on Arles and Avignon in 1251, on Tarascon in 1256, and on Marseille—which revolted again—in 1257.

Frederick II was the emperor of Germany and the king of Naples and Sicily. After his death, the history of southern Italy became very complicated.[49] The successive popes believed that they had an eminent right to the Kingdom of Sicily. They attempted to establish a Christian ruler of their choosing there in order to replace Manfred, Frederick II's illegitimate son who had taken control of his father's Italian possessions. Charles d'Anjou was one of the potential candidates. Louis had retained his brother to this point, but in May 1263, he decided to accept the pope's new proposal to make Charles a king. Charles had waited on his brother's decision for both moral and political reasons but now conveyed his acceptance to the pope.

The new pope elected in 1264 was Guy Foulcois, Saint Louis' former advisor. He rushed the issue. The king handled the entire affair for his brother, and on June 28, 1265, the pope gave Charles the crown of Sicily in Rome.

Louis attempted to unite all the necessary conditions for engaging in one of those wars whose malfeasance he denounced because they were a source of sins. He put off the onset of the war by attempting to exhaust all of the existing avenues for peace. He emphasized that the pope's decision complied with feudal law because the pope was the suzerain of the Kingdom of Sicily. More than his attacks against the Holy See, Manfred's alliance with the Muslims further justified the crusade-like character of the war they were declaring on him. They made one final appeal to Manfred: he could still save himself if he agreed to campaign with the Latin emperor, who had been driven out of Constantinople against the Byzantine emperor who had retaken his capital. Louis was clearly thinking of the interest of having Sicily allied with the rest of Christendom as a base for operations to Constantinople or the Holy Land. Manfred refused.

Louis gave his brother the green light at this point. Charles d'Anjou conquered his kingdom in a single battle, the battle of Benevento on February 26, 1266. Manfred was killed there. Conradin, the fifteen-year-old son of Conrad and grandson of Frederick II, descended into Italy from Germany. He attacked Charles at Tagliacozzo on August 22, 1268 and was crushed. This was the beginning of the French Angevin dynasty of Naples.

Charles rushed to his brother's side during the fatal crusade of Tunis in 1270.[50] Some historians have conjectured that it was Charles who, as master of Sicily, had pressed his brother to debark in Tunisia. I do not think this was the case because Charles had always had imperial dreams and it seems he was thinking mainly of reconquering Constantinople after the Greeks had taken it back from the Latins. I wonder if it was not Louis instead who finally thrust his brother into the conquest of the Kingdom of Naples and Sicily in order to make it a base and point of departure for the new crusade he was planning.

Of course, Charles took up the cross out of a sense of solidarity with his brother. He arrived just at the moment Louis had expired. He threw himself in tears at the feet of his corpse. Then he pulled himself together, took control of the army, decided on withdrawing, and negotiated an honorable retreat with the Muslims. He tried to obtain his brother's remains, the future relics, from his nephew Philip III, the new king of France, but received only the entrails, which he took back to his church of Monreale near Palermo.

Because we are following Saint Louis' life here, Charles does not reappear in our story until 1282 when he gave his deposition in support of his brother's sainthood at the canonization proceedings.

There were times that he irritated Louis. After they were freed in Egypt, during the six-day journey by sail to Acre, Louis complained about his brother to Joinville and, as we saw, became enraged with him for playing dice games almost immediately after his liberation.[51] Charles was also the one who angered the saint king during the important and mixed-up affair of the succession of Flanders.[52]

He was obviously quite a troublesome brother.

His Sister

The conduct of his only surviving sister, Isabelle, was nothing like that. She was born in 1223. According to the rule for the apanages, royal daughters received money instead of lands. This was the case for Isabelle. At the court she had everything she needed to live—humbly and modestly. She loved her brother and lived like him, away from the royal pomp. She got along well with the queen, her sister-in-law. They tried to place her in the diplomatic and political menagerie of marriage for the daughter of a king. As a child she was "fiancéed" to the son of Hugh the Brown of Lusignan, the count of the March, the main conspirator against the young Saint Louis. The project eventually died out. At twenty, she was presented with a good match. Emperor Frederick II wanted her for his son Conrad. As an adult, she refused. She did not want to marry. Saint Louis did not force her. She wanted to live her life as a virgin, among her own people no doubt, but in worship and asceticism. Her royal brother loved and admired her. In 1245, she accompanied him with their mother Blanche of Castile and their brother Robert on a voyage to Cluny to meet Pope Innocent IV. She did not refuse to take part in these family voyages Louis liked so much, especially when she had a chance to visit such a holy place and to meet such an important religious figure. It was a brilliant place, and the pope was a very prestigious figure, but she respected the splendor of the Holy Church, even though she thought it was not for her. Saint Louis' biographers mention her along with his brothers in this group of children to whom Blanche of Castile had been so attentive to give a good religious education. She figured among this fraternal group of princely adults whose last surviving member, Charles d'Anjou, the king of Sicily, affirmed in 1282 that they were all saints, his sister included. She played a role in her royal brother's program for building churches and convents and had him build a convent for the Clares (who were called the Ladies of Saint Damien at the time) at Longchamp. It was completed in 1259. She withdrew there in 1263, but without taking the religious habit. She belonged to that group of pious women who remained laywomen as they led a life like that of nuns, often in the shadow of the Mendicant orders. This was a characteristic form of feminine devotion in the thirteenth century, as they existed in the world and outside it at the same time.[53] She died at Longchamp in 1269, just before Saint Louis' departure on his second crusade. This was one of the king's last great causes for sadness. The Church made her a "*bienheureuse*," but not until the sixteenth century.[54] In death she thus managed to modestly remain at her brother's side. We should not separate them.

In this nearly idyllic image of a royal family, there may be a black sheep, but no one was out of place or out of step.

His Wife

We know that Louis married Marguerite de Provence in 1234, and that her youngest sister Beatrice married Charles d'Anjou in 1246. Actually, she was one of four sisters who were the daughters of Raimond Bérenger V, the count of Provence. They had no brothers. They were all queens, though not at the same time. Marguerite was the oldest. She was born in 1221. She wed the king of France in 1234 and died twenty-five years after him in 1295. Éléonore, the second daughter, was born in 1223. She married the king of England, Henry III, in 1236, and died in 1291. The third daughter, Sanchie, was born in 1228. She married Henry III's brother, Richard of Cornwall, in 1243. He became "king of the Romans" in 1257 in a contested election that ultimately did not give him the imperial crown. Sanchie died in 1261. Last, as we remember, was the youngest daughter named Beatrice like her mother. She was born in 1231 and in 1246 married Saint Louis' brother Charles d'Anjou, wrapping up what Gérard Sivery calls "one of the master works of great medieval matrimonial strategy." She too died young, in 1267.

Matthew Paris in awe described the extraordinary dinner one evening at the Temple in 1257 that reunited the four sisters and their mother Beatrice de Savoie the dowager countess of Provence for the occasion of Henry III of England's official visit to Paris. Beatrice de Savoie was the mother-in-law of all Christendom. Some say that she was still as beautiful as her daughters. Sanchie, however, had not yet become "queen of the Romans," and Beatrice had not yet become queen of Sicily, a title she held for only a short time. Saint Louis was delighted with this dinner. He was ravished to see the four sisters of Provence and their mother reunited before his eyes, and his pleasure was doubled because they formed the counterpart to the group he formed with his three brothers. This parallelism was simultaneously doubled in an astonishing way by the parallel between the French and English royal families in each of which the king and his brother had married two of the four sisters.

This masterpiece of alliance making pleased Saint Louis all the more because he attached great importance to kinship relations established by alliance. He saw it as one of the things that guaranteed the solidarity between the great families of Christendom, and especially between royal families, and as a necessary factor for internal peace and unity against the pagan or infidel. Despite their serious differences, he was happy to see the friendship that was supposed to exist between him and the king of England solidified by the fact that they were brothers-in-law. In 1259 after the signing of the treaty of Paris that reconciled France and England, he emphasized that one of the best results of this treaty was that it restored peace and friendship between him and Henry III as relatives, "because we have two sisters for wives and our children are first cousins, and this is why it is important for peace to exist between them."[55]

As for Marguerite, the queen of France, Saint Louis' wife, she was an essential link in the chain that united the people of England, France, and Provence at the highest level. She seems perfectly integrated into this company, happy to be with her mother and sisters, especially Éléonore, the queen of England with whom she frequently corresponded, and also happy to be with her husband the king of France. She had a powerful reason to be so joyful. Since her return from the Orient two years earlier, she had been rid of her nightmare, her mother-in-law Blanche of Castile. Not only was the Queen Mother no longer around, waiting to take the king away from her, but now Marguerite could also finally and fully be the only queen of France. Before, there had always been the other, the "Castilian" queen of France. Although previously Marguerite had never held the harmonious place at the court that her position, her education, her character, and her capacities warranted, this was mainly due to her terrible mother-in-law.[56]

Saint Louis' attitude toward his wife is disconcerting. We cannot put our finger on it by ourselves. Joinville tells us about it. Joinville admired the king; even more, he loved the king.[57] But like Saint Louis, and sometimes more than Saint Louis, he too hated what was unjust, and Saint Louis was unjust in his treatment of the queen. We saw this in two episodes narrated by Joinville; they took place on the crusade and at sea on their return from the crusade and described Louis' attitude toward Marguerite.[58]

The story in which Marguerite told Joinville about her royal spouse gives us two pieces of information about Saint Louis' disposition toward his wife.[59] First of all, she called him "*divers.*" The translator has rendered this correctly as "bizarre." It was an epithet usually reserved for children and meant "unstable, someone who cannot be trusted." I would gladly interpret it to mean: "the king is an unpredictable lunatic." The rest of what the queen said offers some additional information: she told Joinville that if she took the initiative to go on a pilgrimage without talking about it with the king, he would refuse to let her go. Another facet of the king's character in relation to his wife appears here—he was tyrannical and subject to wild mood swings. To sum things up, he was a hard man to live with and his behavior vacillated between indifference and tempestuous authoritarian control.

How can we explain this attitude and how can we reconcile it with the mass of testimony on the king's goodness? Let us first of all note that what the queen confided to Joinville in no way prevented her from otherwise sincerely stating that her spouse was a good man. We certainly have to conclude that for the men and women of the thirteenth century saintliness did not concern daily domestic life but particular conduct in worship and charity, along with hatred of lying, chastity, and abstention from blasphemy and certain oaths.

This explanation is not really satisfying. It seems to me that on the king's part we can detect some indifference toward two categories of people that figured in these anecdotes: babies and wives.

Louis did not seem to have any interest in very young children, although by contrast he was very interested in his own children when they were grown. This statement applies only to the three babies born to him in the Holy Land between 1250 and 1253. He was probably waiting for them to be older before expressing any interest in them. The worship of the infant Jesus had not yet spread. He had to feel Joinville's reproachful gaze fixed upon him in order to ask for news about his wife and children's health though without even going to see them.

As for the queen, she did not worry for herself; although his daily behavior toward her was sometimes tyrannical, it was not because she was a woman. As much as Louis belonged to the "male Middle Ages," he was not particularly contemptuous of women. If he acted like this, it was not because his wife did not please him either; on the contrary, we have seen that he was attracted to her, and, although he had eleven children with her, it does not seem like it was uniquely to assure the dynasty's survival or to satisfy a purely physical need. Marguerite had a good education and she was as pious as anyone could want a queen to be, even in a family that was rather extreme in this regard. She was not a spendthrift, with the possible exception of her gifts for her family in Savoie, although the king authorized all these. Louis seemed to like the fact that she did a good job fulfilling her duties as a wife and queen, especially since his mother was no longer around. There is still something else here though, and here is my own hypothesis about it.

Saint Louis was a fervent—we could even say a fanatical—supporter of his lineage. Certainly, the queen made an indispensable contribution to perpetuating his lineage and she did so generously. Still, she did not belong to this lineage. It was within his own line that Louis felt most capable of developing feelings of love, and as he never really knew his father, this love was expressed for his mother, his sister, and brothers. A wife did not normally arouse an interest and feelings of the same intensity.

However, Saint Louis also expressed a marked attentiveness for the queen. The king usually got up every night to say prime, but he refrained from doing this on the days and nights "when he was with his wife."[60] In his *Enseignements* for his son, in a special chapter he gave him the following advice: "Dear son, I instruct you to love and honor your mother, and to happily keep her with you, and to observe her good teachings and to be inclined to believe her good advice."[61] When Joinville made his observation, Louis may have been entirely absorbed by his concerns about the crusade and his ruminations about the defeat. But isn't a spouse a source of comfort and support in circumstances like this—which was what Marguerite was and tried to be—and didn't Saint Louis fail to recognize this?

Of course, there are some "affairs" that have been dissected by certain historians that cast a few shadows on the life of the royal couple. I doubt their seriousness. First of all, it was highly unlikely that Marguerite, in her warm affection for her sister Éléonore, ever led an "English" party at the court unless Blanche of Castile cooked up this horrid story to turn her son against his wife.

There is one strange story that was discovered in the Vatican archives at a much later date. On June 6, 1263, at the king's request Pope Urban IV dissolved an oath that his son and heir Philip had made to his mother. He had promised Queen Marguerite to remain under her tutelage until he reached the age of thirty, to never take on any advisor who was hostile to her, to never contract any alliance with Charles d'Anjou, to inform her of any rumors circulating against her, and to keep silent about all these promises.[62]

The act seems to be authentic. What could have pushed Marguerite to demand this commitment from her son? Did Philip seem like a weak spirit in his mother's eyes, a son in need of strict guidance? His father may not have been very far from thinking the same thing when he assigned him a preceptor, Pierre de la Brosse, in 1268, which turned out not to have been such a good idea. Did she finally want to play the political role her husband had denied her? Or, worse, did she dream of imitating her hideous mother-in-law by turning her son into her docile servant as her mother-in-law had tried to do with her own son?

In any case, the affair probably figured in one of Saint Louis' surprising decisions. Before departing for the crusade, he refused to give the regency to Queen Marguerite. Like Jean Richard, I believe that the main reason for this decision is that "the meaning of the State had taken on a new dimension" in Saint Louis' time, and that the king wanted to leave the protection and administration of the kingdom to two people who were more closely involved in his government and who could better assure its continuity: Mathieu de Vendôme the abbot of Saint-Denis and Simon de Clermont the lord of Nesle.

I would like to take leave of Marguerite on another note—with Join-ville's beautiful anecdote that shows her love for her husband.

When Joinville went to look for Marguerite after the announcement of Blanche of Castile's death, he found her in tears. He was amazed "because it was the woman you hated the most who has died, and you are in such a state of mourning?" Marguerite replied "that it was not for the queen that she was crying but for the pain that the king had from the grief he was showing."[63]

THE CHILDREN

People did not marry for the sole purpose of having children, but it was im-portant for a king to have them and of the utmost importance to have male children. No doubt Saint Louis enjoyed the sexual act with his wife. The an-ecdote about Blanche of Castile's rage when Louis went to join his wife in her room during the day should make this clear enough. The information Guillaume de Nangis gives us makes it even clearer. He reminds us of what we already know from other sources: in carnal matters Saint Louis, with Queen Marguerite's consent, respected what the Church in his time desig-nated as "the time for embracing" (*le temps d'embrasser*).[64] These times were Advent and all of Lent, certain days of the week, the eves and days of the important festivals, and several days before and after the day of communion for anyone who is supposed to take communion. This was a way of obeying the Church and practicing a certain form of birth control at the same time. Civilization always requires a certain control over the birthrate. However, the king's flesh, more or less like the flesh of all men, more in his case, was weak. As we have seen, he was subject to nocturnal temptations.

> If during these days of continence he happened to visit his wife the queen for whatever reason and to stay with her, and if sometimes her closeness would make him feel the turmoil of the flesh caused by human weakness, he would get up from the bed and pace back and forth through the room until the rebellion of the flesh was quieted.[65]

Eleven children were the result of this combined passion and discipline. Louis VIII and Blanche of Castile had nine children who are known to us, but we also know that early in their marriage they lost several, probably three, to stillbirth or illnesses in infancy. In Saint Louis' time, the births of royal children were recorded with greater precision, even for those who died at birth or at a very tender age. By Louis' time, there had been advances in medicine and notably in obstetrics and pediatrics; the royal family called on the best doctors. The survival of Louis and Marguerite's children was better assured than those of Louis VIII and Blanche of Castile.

Louis and Marguerite were married in 1234. Marguerite was only thirteen years old. The couple's first known child, Blanche, was born six years later in 1240. Did the queen have any stillborn children or miscarriages prior to this? It is possible, but not likely because we know that some people in the royal entourage were beginning to worry about her fertility.

Quoting a *Vie de Saint Thibaud* published by Duchesne, Le Nain de Tillemont writes:

> People were already talking about a divorce, which would have been shameful and pernicious for the whole kingdom. In this situation, they called on various persons of great piety so that they would implore divine mercy and, among others, they called on Saint Thibaud. . . . He had entered the abbey of Vaux de Cernay or the order of the Cistercians . . . and was the abbot at the time. This saintly man, particularly touched by the queen's affliction, said that they still had to wait a little while, and that he hoped God would grant the grace they were imploring. He began to pray and his prayers were finally answered. The queen became pregnant and happily gave birth on July 11 of this same year [1240], which was a great relief for the entire kingdom. . . . They note that this queen and Philip the Bold her son had great devotion for Saint Thibaud and came to visit his tomb.[66]

None of the biographers confirm this story, but the "miraculous" birth of the first child of a French king was a commonplace of the time.

Another anecdote is placed here and it shows us the king's sadness and irritation upon learning that the queen has given birth to a girl instead of a boy. According to the story, the bishop of Paris, Guillaume d'Auxerre, consoled the king with a clever phrase.[67]

If this anecdote is true, we must not see any particular "anti-feminism" in it on Saint Louis' part. In a dynasty where a tradition of succession by male primogeniture existed (which was officially established by an edict only a century later by Charles V), the wait for a son provoked incredible anxiety. The chroniclers tell us how much Louis' birth, the "long awaited" son, in 1244, gave rise to joy and relief.

Marguerite definitively won the admiration of her contemporaries for her fecundity: "we owe the treasure of the kingdom to Queen Marguerite."

The children were born during the three periods of Saint Louis' reign that we have identified: before, during, and after the crusade. The work of childbearing never stopped during the central period of the queen's fertility from nineteen to thirty-nine years of age, from 1240 to 1260. The repartition between the two sexes was more balanced for Saint Louis' offspring with five girls and six boys.

Their first names were given in compliance with dynastic tradition. A majority of their names were Capetian, and a minority of them originated in families they were allied with, although in this case there were more names taken from the grandmother's family than from the mother's. Thus an image of dynastic continuity was pursued through their given names. The oldest son received the name of his grandfather, Louis. The second son was given the name of their great-grandfather, Philip. The next two sons were given the name of Castilian origin, Jean, and, for the second of them, it was appended with the name Tristan in reference to the sadness of the child's birth in a besieged city on the verge of being abandoned after a military disaster while his father was a prisoner in enemy hands. The dynastic memory was long. There had been a Pierre among the many sons of Louis VI, Pierre de Courtenay, and, as we have seen, the bastard son of Philip Augustus bore the remarkable double first name Pierre Charlot. The name Agnès alludes to a distant Castilian ancestor. The name Blanche was reintroduced after having been lost and obviously came from their grandmother, while Marguerite, born after Blanche of Castile's death, received her own mother's name. Finally, we get Robert, and there was no more Capetian name than that.

We have seen Saint Louis' royal, paternal sadness upon the death of his oldest son Louis at the age of sixteen.[68] We know that two other children, a son and a daughter, died at a very young age.[69] What worldly destiny did Saint Louis assure for his surviving children? It was dictated by service for the dynasty and the kingdom. The three means of assuring their future were lands, marriages, and money.

In 1269 on the eve of his departure for the crusade of Tunis, Louis endowed his sons with their apanages.[70] Louis did better than his father in assuring the rights and powers of the crown; of course, he had more options than his father had. To begin with, he only gave them comparatively small counties. Jean-Tristan received the Valois. Pierre got Alençon and the Perche. Robert got Clermont-en-Beauvaisis. On the other hand, he married them to rich heiresses who brought Nevers for Jean-Tristan, Blois for Pierre, and the seigniory of Bourbon for Robert. The weddings of Pierre and Robert took place only in 1272, two years after Louis' death. With the exception of Pierre, their wives' lands were not contiguous with their own, which prevented any one of them from forming an excessively powerful single territorial possession. Louis died before he could be married. As a provision of the treaty of Corbeil that put an end to the conflict between Aragon and France in 1258, Philip was promised the hand of Isabelle, the daughter of the king of Aragon. This highly political marriage was not celebrated until 1262 on Easter Day at Clermont-en-Auvergne. Saint Louis took advantage of the occasion by getting Jaime I of Aragon to promise not to support the people of Marseille in their latest revolt against his brother Charles d'Anjou the count of Provence.

On the other hand, the daughters who received money for their apanages in the form of their dowries were richly married. Isabelle wed Thibaud V, count of Champagne and king of Navarre, in 1255. He was a familiar friend, an admirer, and an imitator of Saint Louis who loved him like a son. Rutebeuf wrote "*La Complainte du roi de Navarre*" for him.[71] Isabelle and Thibaud died in 1271 upon returning from the crusade of Tunis. Blanche married the infante Ferdinand of Castile, the son of King Alphonse X the Wise, in 1269. He died in 1275. Marguerite married Jean I the duke of Brabant in 1270, and Agnès married Robert II the duke of Burgundy in 1279. Louis experienced one final bout of sadness on earth before dying. His son Jean-Tristan, the child of the sadness of the first crusade, was among the first victims of typhoid in the Christian camp at Carthage. He was only twenty years old. They tried to conceal the news from the sick king, but he learned about it anyway. He seems to have been especially fond of this son born of sadness. Geoffroy de Beaulieu simply notes: "Upon hearing the news of his death, his pious father's guts were not softly shaken."[72]

The king's greatest concern was to assure a good moral and religious education for his children. He would have liked to see some of them join the orders. He wanted Jean-Tristan and Pierre to become Mendicants, one of them a Dominican and the other a Franciscan, but neither of them wanted to, so he did not insist. Even among the religious, people were suspicious of Saint Louis' irresolute proselytism toward his children. At some time between 1261 and 1264, Pope Urban IV granted Blanche the privilege of not having to remain a nun for life if her father forced her to take the vows.[73] This was probably done on the initiative of her confessor.

As for the rest, most of Saint Louis' biographers inform us about how the king imposed religious exercises on his children. Here is what Guillaume de Nangis says about this:

> By the grace of God, the holy couple had abundant progeny. Their pious father conducted himself very Christianly in the instruction and government of his children. As his children neared adulthood,[74] he not only wanted them to hear the mass every day but also wanted them to hear matins and the singing of the canonical hours and to go with him to listen to sermons. He wanted each one of them to be instructed in singing the hours of the Holy Virgin and always to participate with him in the complines he would ceremoniously sing every day in church after his dinner. Then, at the end of the day they would always sing a special song out loud to the Holy Virgin. After complines, he would go back to his room with his children, and after a priest sprinkled holy water around the bed and the room, the children would sit all around him and before they left he would tell them some edifying words for their instruction.

Joinville also gives us some details about their instruction:

> Before going to bed, he would assemble all his children before him and remind them of the deeds of good kings and good emperors and then he would tell them to follow the example of people like this. He would also tell them about the acts of bad rulers who had lost their kingdoms due to their taste for luxury, their plundering, and greed. Then, he would tell them: "I am reminding you about these things so that you can keep yourselves from doing them so that God will not be angered against you."[75] He wanted them to wear crowns of roses and other flowers on Good Friday in memory of the holy

Crown of Thorns that had atrociously crowned the Savior's head on that day, the crown with which the King of kings Our Lord Jesus Christ had magnificently decorated his kingdom.[76]

Once more, we can see the pleasure Saint Louis took in the company of these assembled familial groups. At the end of this life, each year he associated his son Philip, who had become his "first-born" and successor, with the act of swearing vassalage to Saint-Denis as the protector of the dynasty and the kingdom. This act consisted in placing four gold bezants on the sainted martyr's altar on his festival day (October 9).

Saint Louis' *Enseignements* for his oldest son Philip and the ones addressed to his daughter Isabelle queen of Navarre show both his love and his conscience as a father. His contemporaries highlighted the exceptional fact that he supposedly wrote them in his own hand instead of having them dictated. This shows how much importance he attached to them as well as their confidential nature. In fact, this was really an affectionate gesture for his son and daughter, whom he addressed in stereotyped terms through which we can sense a genuine love.

"To his dear son Philip, a father's greetings and love." Seventeen of the thirty-four paragraphs of the text begin with the words: "Dear son." Another word appears repeatedly, "heart" (*coeur*): "I desire *with all my heart*," "that you have *the heart* to be compassionate to the poor," "if your *heart* is troubled." The epistle includes one part addressed to the individual and another addressed to the future king. In the first part, he mentions faith, patience, frequent confession, piety toward the Church, charity for the poor and suffering, keeping the company of good people, listening to sermons, and the rejection of bad speech. In the second he asks him to be worthy of the holy anointment, rendering justice, pacifying quarrels, honoring the people of the Church, avoiding war, having good officers, repressing sins of the mouth and the body and gambling, getting rid of heretics, and being economical.

"Dear son, I give you all the blessings a father can and should give his son." Then, he prays to God for him. The letter articulates two kinds of wishes. The first kind relates to the cohesiveness and mutual love in the heart of the royal family. We have already seen how he advised him to love and honor his mother and follow her advice. Likewise, Louis entrusted the oldest with the responsibility of taking care of his younger brothers: "Love your brothers, and always wish for their own good and advancement, and act as a father to them in order to instruct them in all things good. . . ." Thirteenth-century Christianity and the Franciscan version in particular mixed paternal, maternal, and fraternal roles in carnal and spiritual families. Saint Francis of Assisi thus distinguished a mother and a son among a group of friars [*frères,* brothers] who are going to live in pairs in hermitages.[77]

The other type of wish related to prayers for the dead. In his profound dynastic sentiment, the king embraced the present but also the future and the past. Children represented the future, and it was necessary to assure a good future for the lineage through them. Emotionally, however, for him the dynasty was especially comprised of the dead.

Act in such a way, he asks his son, that "your soul and the soul of your ancestors may rest in peace, and if you ever hear people say that your ancestors made restitution, always take the trouble to learn whether there is still something to render, and if you find that there is, render it immediately for the salvation of your soul and the souls of your ancestors." And he recommends himself to his son as the first dead person, the first future ancestor, for whom he should pray: "Dear son, I beg you that if it please Our Lord that I pass from this life before you, that you help me with masses and other oraisons and that you ask the religious orders of the Kingdom of France to say prayers for my soul." The dead, the ancestors—they were the most important members of the lineage because they were the fathers, the bearers of origin and continuity—who placed salvation, which was supposed to be collective, the most at risk because the dead could no longer acquire any merits. Their salvation now depended on the memory and the zeal of their descendants. The dead were the ones they had to love the most. This explains the importance of Saint Louis' action of repositioning the royal tombs at Saint-Denis.

His letter to Isabelle begins with a declaration that expresses the warmth of the particular mutual affection that united the king and his oldest daughter:

> To his very dear and much loved daughter Isabelle, queen of Navarre, greetings and paternal friendship.
>
> Dear daughter, because I believe you will learn more from me than from some others because you love me, I thought that I would make several instructions for you written in my own hand.[78]

The content of this text mostly resembles the individual section of the instructions for Philip in a shorter form and with adaptations appropriate for the addressee's gender. She should have only perfectly honest women in her service; she should obey her husband and his father and mother, and avoid any luxury in dress. And, of course, she should pray for his soul.

In this world of ancestors and predecessors, the birthdays of the dead were of the utmost importance. On the days of the most solemn festivals, Louis placed twelve candles on the altar of his chapel, "and also on the birth dates of his father and mother and of all the kings whose birth dates he recognized."[79] In addition to these exceptional dead figures, there was the mass for all the other dead for whom "he would say the service of the dead each day with one of his chaplains according to the custom of the Church of Paris."[80] Saint Louis was truly a king of the dead.

Shortly after his own disappearance, his *Enseignements* became words that were no longer the words of a living person but of a dead man, and they acted on the son for whom they were written.

In the letter that Philip—now Philip III—had carried to all the members of the Church of France by the Dominicans Geoffroy de Beaulieu and Guillaume de Chartres and the Franciscan Jean de Mons to announce the death of his father, among all the obligatory but emphatic formulas we find a more personal passage in which we can feel how much he missed the imposing but reassuring presence of this father, not just for his moral and political advice but also emotionally: "It is no doubt a great glory to have had such a father, but it is also an irreparable pain to have lost such sweet and great consolation of [having] a father like this, his conversation that was so delightful, his advice that was so effective, and such great help." This may be a conventional string of phrases dictated by an advisor, but it perfectly translates the impression Saint Louis left his son.[81]

His Household [*Mesnie*] and Entourage

Saint Louis' family then was first of all his lineage, the dynastic lineage, and then the family more narrowly defined. However, he also possessed a larger carnal family. Matthew Paris notes that he had "habitual considerations for [people of] his flesh and his blood."[82]

The king ultimately had a larger and more loosely defined family around him. This larger family housed near his "*hôtel*"[83] included noble and non-noble familiar figures that assured all of the services required for his material existence and that of his family. This was his *mesnie.* This old group of free men who used to live in the home of a powerful figure, his clientele, was in the process of simply becoming his household. Guillaume de Saint-Pathus directly mentions them: "Often when he [Louis] was in his room with his *mesnie,* he would say simple and discreet things and would tell beautiful stories for the edification of the people who were around him, words that were good and saintly." They were good servants and *prud'hommes.*[84] Guillaume continues in this sense:

> The saint king Louis was very happy to have good, just, and honest men in his company, and very gladly avoided the company and conversation of bad men and those whom he knew to be in sin. And the wrongdoers and people who spoke nastily displeased him more than anything. He wanted his household to be of such great purity that if anyone from his household vilely swore against God or the blessed Virgin, he would immediately kick him out of his *hôtel.* . . . And if he learned that anyone in his *hôtel* had committed a mortal sin, he would kick him out of his court and his household. . . .[85]

We find all of Saint Louis' ambiguity here. On the one hand, his *mesnie* was a circle of very moral people bound to the king's person. On the other, it was the remnant of a surviving archaic institution in the process of becoming a group of familiar figures attached to the house of the king. The king always had his council for important political affairs, and it was in the process of becoming the *parlement* for judicial affairs. He did not hesitate to ask one group for things that fell under the other's authority. In the guise of edifying conversations, he gathered advice from the household friends whom he had chosen among men he liked, more or less counterbalancing the council, which was a feudal institution in the midst of becoming a body of the forming state and in which he did not have the same freedom to make his own choices and decisions and to say what he wanted.

Better still, for explicitly religious and moral reasons, he banned all those who might compromise the purity of these two circles whose members directly affected him. Thus, a sacred, purified space was created around the king. The space of the sacred state with the king, its sun, at its center came together along these indirect paths. The king and his men formed a sacred family in a sacred manor. An archaic institution and a modern state converged through a ruse of history and the king. Moreover, from another perspective concerning the king, Joinville sometimes used the following formula when speaking of the king's familiar circle: "we who were around him."[86] This was a borrowing of the expression from the Gospels that designated the group of Jesus' apostles, which had also recently been adopted by some of the early companions of the Christ-like saint[87] Francis of Assisi in the thirteenth century. Before dying in Carthage at three in the afternoon, Saint Louis was already a Christ-King. This was one of the greatest "mysteries of state."[88]

Saint Louis' Religion

SAINT LOUIS' RELIGION CONSISTED FIRST OF ALL IN HIS PRACTICE of worship. It was expressed through gestures and rituals that were regularly and frequently repeated throughout the day and even at night. His religion, however, was also a faith, a piety in harmony with the evolving religious practice of his time that always strove to reach the inner man and, in return, to make him the force of his spiritual life.[1]

We are well informed about Saint Louis' worship thanks to his many biographers, although we must not forget that they were also hagiographers. Some of them, actually the majority of them, wrote after his canonization in 1297. Others wrote about the king with the goal of having him canonized. Even though they did this with some emphasis, their intentions in any case led them to privilege this theme. Moreover, they were writing at a time when the Church and what we would call public opinion attached increasing importance to the exercise of virtues and one's conduct in life (*vita* in its precise, limited sense, or *conversatio*),[2] even though miracles remained the primary criteria for sainthood. The devotion they described for Saint Louis was not just the worship of a saint but of a particular saint: he was a layman (at a time when monks, bishops, and clerics had a quasi-monopoly on sainthood) and a king. His devotion was that of a layman who to a great extent tried to achieve his personal salvation through the exercise of his royal function. Louis IX had a strict notion of what distinguished a layman from a cleric, but he tried to exploit his eminent position in the secular hierarchy in order to come as close as possible to having the piety of clerics. Above all, he thought his highest duty was to pray even more for the salvation of his subjects than for his own salvation, or, rather, to make the two almost completely coincide. He prayed like a royal orant.

Saint Louis' worship encompassed all the existing forms of devotion: services, confession, communion, the cult of the relics, respect for the Church (limited in the temporal realm), and penitential, charitable, and ascetic practices.

The Cistercian Model and the Mendicant Model

We must not neglect the attraction that monastic spirituality held for Saint Louis, especially that of the Cistercians who were the most important representatives of twelfth-century reformed monasticism. Their traditions were still very much alive in the thirteenth century and formed a link between the world of the monks prior to the thirteenth century and the Mendicant friars. This link was stronger than some historians have claimed. Louis frequented the Cistercians and the Mendicants with equal fervor. The first attracted him in their monastic solitude; the second in their urban sociability. These complementary natures allowed him to entirely realize his potential. His favorite place, however, the place where his heart and soul could flourish, was in the midst of nature among the Cistercians at Royaumont.

Some have nevertheless insisted on the closeness of his relations with the Mendicants, and it is true that they had a decisive influence on his public actions and his "politics."[3]

The two important Mendicant orders, the Minorites or Franciscans and the Preachers or Dominicans, were as old as Saint Louis. They established the essential part of their networks of convents before 1250. The Dominican convents were concentrated in the "large" cities, and the Franciscan convents in small towns. Louis favored and ushered in a new trend by supporting them and visiting them as he did. These new kinds of religious encountered extraordinary success throughout all Christendom. In contrast to the monks, they lived among men in the towns and mixed closely with laymen. They were great disseminators of religious practices, which they renewed profoundly with confession, the belief in Purgatory, and preaching. They entered people's homes and minds, getting to know individuals and entire families. They practiced the fundamental virtues of primitive Christianity in the midst of a new society: poverty, charity, and humility.

They had no property of their own and became adept at taking collections. Thanks to the help of wealthy laymen like Louis, they built increasingly impressive convents, which went against the desires of their founders — the Spaniard Saint Dominic and the Italian Saint Francis. These apostles of poverty thus became specialists in monetary matters, one of the great problems of the century. They strove to moralize the new commercial and banking practices without condemning the most important ones, paving the way for a pre-capitalist society. They advocated methods of persuasion based on speech and example in order to assure the salvation of men and women. However, they depended directly on the papacy and not on any episcopal authority, so when the pope entrusted them with running the inquisitional tribunals for the repression of heresy in the 1230s, they carried out this task with more or less severity and usually with great zeal, although they did not all attain the same level of cruelty as the Dominican Robert who was nicknamed "le Bougre," in other words, "the Bulgar." This was one of the names for heretics, which points to the Oriental origins of certain heresies. A "Bougre" himself, Robert had converted and become a Preaching friar. With the fury typical of converts, he cruelly dealt with the heretics in the Kingdom of France in the late 1230s, especially in Flanders, a region whose economic prosperity encouraged the development of commercial practices quickly labeled usurious by our inquisitor. He covered Flanders with the fires of his victims burning at the stake. He soon became drunk with power and his appetite for these life-devouring flames. He burnt good people along with the bad, condemning innocent and simple-minded folk to death. In Matthew Paris's words, he had become *formidabilis,* a terror. The pope was warned about his conduct, stripped him of his powers, and condemned him to life in prison. However, during his murderous reign of terror, Saint Louis gave him all the help he wanted, exhibiting just as much zeal for carrying out his duties as the secular arm of the Church. The English Benedictine communicated these facts to posterity.[4]

Finally, despite Saint Francis's reservations, the Mendicant friars determined that the apostolate should be sustained with knowledge. This led to the creation of the Mendicant schools for secondary and higher learning — the *studia*.[5] It also led them to study at the universities. Some of them even became university masters, which was a source of strident conflict as some viewed their presence there as an intrusion, although in general their innovative instruction was a success with the students. (This was the case for Thomas Aquinas in Paris.) This also explains the strong attraction that Paris held for them as the great center for the study of theology in thirteenth-century Christendom. Saint Louis thus had the intellectual elite of the friars at his disposal, although, as we have seen, it was their piety, their knowledge of social problems, and their eloquence as preachers that interested him the most.

All of his confessors seem to have been Mendicant friars. The most well known is the Dominican Geoffroy de Beaulieu, who wrote an invaluable Life of the king shortly after his death. His only other confessor whose name is known to us today was Jean de Mons.[6] Because he always wanted to have a confessor available, he appointed two of them after his return from the Holy Land. One was a Dominican, and the other a Franciscan.

The Mendicants also played an important role in running his chapel. His chaplain Guillaume de Chartres accompanied him to Tunis like Geoffroy de Beaulieu. He too was a Dominican. Dominican friars also went to Constantinople to negotiate the purchase of the relics of the Passion, and they were the ones who brought them back to Paris. Saint Louis instituted three services to be held annually in their honor, one entrusted to the Dominicans of Paris, another for the Franciscans, and a third to be shared on a rotating basis among the other religious orders that had convents in the capital.

A great lover of sermons, Louis usually called on the Mendicants to preach privately to him, his family, and familiar circle in the Sainte-Chapelle. Although he failed to persuade the Franciscan Hugh of Digne to leave his convent of Hyères, he did succeed in getting one of the greatest preachers of the time to come there to preach to them. This was the Franciscan Saint Bonaventure who was master at the University of Paris since 1257 and general minister of his order. Of the 113 sermons that Bonaventure gave in Paris between 1257 and 1269, nineteen of them were preached before the king.[7]

The friar who probably had the closest ties with Saint Louis was the Franciscan master of theology in Paris, Eudes Rigaud. In 1248, he became archbishop of Rouen, the center of Normandy that had an important, special status in the kingdom. He remained a Mendicant on the episcopal throne. There is a unique document that has been passed down to us; it is the record of this conscientious prelate's parish visits, which provides essential knowledge about the rural clergy and religious life in the middle of the thirteenth century.[8] Louis was not satisfied with simply asking him to provide ecclesiastical assistance; for example, he also invited him to preach in the Sainte-Chapelle for Pentecost in 1261. He even presided over the mass at Royaumont when the king was there for Assumption Day in 1262. In 1255, he presided over the marriage between the king's daughter Isabelle and Thibaud de Champagne, the king of Navarre. On November 8, 1258, he presided over the anniversary mass for the death of the king's father, Louis VIII, at Saint-Denis. In 1259, he visited the sick king at Fontainebleau, although he was recovering from an illness himself. In January 1260, he came to console the king after the death of his son Louis. The king also entrusted him with political missions. As early as 1258, Eudes Rigaud often sat at the royal court and in the parlements held in the palace in Paris. He also negotiated for the king during the treaty of Paris with England in 1259.

Beginning in 1247, when Saint Louis sent investigators throughout the kingdom in order to reform the royal administration and make reparations for injustices that had been committed, many of these investigators were Mendicant friars. Among the thirty-eight known investigators, eight were Dominicans and seven were Franciscans.

The manuals written for Saint Louis were also primarily the work of the Mendicant friars, from the encyclopedia by the Dominican Vincent de Beauvais to the Mirror of the Princes by the Franciscan Gilbert de Tournai.

When the liveliest episode in the quarrel between the ordinary and Mendicant masters at the University of Paris broke out between 1254 and 1257, the king supported pontifical decisions that favored the Mendicants. Again, when Pope Alexander IV condemned the leader of the ordinary masters, Guillaume de Saint-Amour, stripping him of all his charges and benefices, forbidding him from teaching and preaching, and exiling him from the Kingdom of France, Saint Louis rigorously executed the part of the sentence that depended on his role as the secular arm of the Church.

Finally, there was the malicious gossip that circulated stating that Saint Louis wanted to abdicate in order to become a Mendicant friar and that he renounced this project less due to the protests of Queen Marguerite and more out of the impossibility of choosing between the Dominicans and the Franciscans. All of this smacks of an invented anecdote.[9] On the other hand, he did want his younger sons to enter each of the two orders, although he did not insist when they refused.

One thing that is definitely true is that in certain milieus and perhaps generally throughout much of the kingdom, people had the image of a king who was not only manipulated by the Mendicants[10] but who himself acted like a religious upon the throne. One dubious anecdote that still expressed the actual prevalence of this opinion has him respond to a knight who blamed him for letting people say he behaved more like a religious than a king:

> Pay no heed to what those imbeciles say. I am going to tell you about what sometimes happens when I am alone in my private chambers. I hear the cries of "friar Louis" and the insults uttered against me when people think I cannot hear them. At those times, I go inside myself and ask myself if I shouldn't repress the people who say these things, but then I realize that it is to my advantage to put up with them for the love of God. And to speak frankly, I do not regret that this occurs.[11]

SAINT LOUIS' FAITH

Faith was the basis for Saint Louis' religion, an unshakeable faith that consisted first of all in the love of God. He said this to his son Philip in his *Enseignements*: "Dear son, I instruct you first to love God with all your heart and all your power, for without that no one can be worth a thing."[12]

The God to love and believe in without the least doubt was the Son above all—the center of Saint Louis' religion. His faith was "the faith of Jesus Christ."[13] It was also the faith of the traditions and teachings of the Church:

> The saint king struggled with all his might to strengthen himself in the Christian law through his words. He used to say that we should believe the articles of faith so firmly that whatever happens—death or physical calamity—we would have no desire to renounce our faith through words or deeds.[14]

And again:

> The king used to say that faith consisted in believing, even though our certainty is based only on words [*sur un dire*]. On this point, he asked me my father's name. I told him that his name was Simon. He

asked me how I knew this, and I answered that I firmly believed it and held it for certain because my mother had told me this. "So," he said to me, "you must firmly believe all the articles of faith on the testimony of the apostles as you hear it sung in the *Credo* on Sundays."[15]

This faith had to be defended against the doubt and temptation sent by the Enemy, the devil. It also had to be reinforced with the yearning for Heaven. The devil's assault was particularly aggressive and dangerous at the moment of death. Saint Louis took part in this religious movement that focused more and more on agony and that led to the worship of the *Artes moriendi,* the "Arts of dying," in the fourteenth and fifteenth centuries.[16]

> He would say: "The demon is so subtle that at the moment of agony he works as hard as he can to make us die in doubt and failure in some point of faith, because he sees that he cannot take the good works that a man has accomplished away from him and, at the same time, that the person who dies in confessing the true religion is lost to him."[17]

He continues:

> This is why we must defend and protect ourselves from this trap in such a way as to say to the Enemy when he sends us a temptation like this: "Be gone. You will not tempt me to the point of preventing me from firmly believing in all the articles of faith. Even if you were to cut off all my members, I would still live and die in this state of mind." Whoever speaks like this vanquishes the Enemy with the same staff and sword that the Enemy wanted to use to slay him.[18]

Louis tells Joinville what Simon de Montfort had said to him about his faith, and he had clearly made this faith his own.

> The saint king told me that some Albigenses had come to see the count of Montfort who was occupying the lands of the Albigenses in the king's name at that time. They invited him to come see the host that had transformed itself into flesh and blood under the hands of the priest. And he answered them: "Go see it for yourselves, you who

don't believe in it. As for me, I firmly believe in the real presence [in it], as the Holy Church teaches us. And do you know what I gain by believing in it in this mortal life, as the Holy Church teaches us? I will have a crown in the heavens more beautiful than any of the crowns of the angels who see God face to face and who earn nothing by believing in him."[19]

This is what he again defined as a faith that guaranteed "being honored in the century and gaining Heaven at death."[20]

Saint Louis had never affirmed his faith as firmly and courageously as when he was held prisoner by the Saracens and called upon either to swear an oath that was incompatible with the Christian faith or be condemned to torture. He told them: "You can very well kill my body, but you will never have my soul." In effect, for him, "there was nothing worse than being outside the faith of Jesus Christ."[21]

Military, physical, and psychological misfortunes were generally interpreted as trials that God sends us to punish us for our sins and to give us the chance to correct ourselves. Louis fully adhered to the Christian doctrine of evil as God's punishment for the good of those men who knew how to understand it.

After they narrowly avoided a shipwreck, he told Joinville that great tribulations and great illnesses in particular were threats sent to us to make us think of our salvation: "He [God] wakes us with his threats so that we can clearly see our faults and rid ourselves of what displeases him." This was his definitive explanation for the failure of his crusade.

The God of his faith was a lord, and he was his vassal. His faith also lay in the fidelity of the homage sworn to God during the coronation, and this homage was not expressed with hand gestures but through the soul. It made the king a unique vassal of his kind, a minister and image of God in his own kingdom. "Beautiful Sire God, I will raise my soul toward you and I will entrust myself to you."

Finally, his faith was confident. Although fear of God [*timor*] and fear of the devil were indispensable for one's salvation, Saint Louis' God was not a God of wrath and anger. His religion was not a religion of fear. He took the words of Guillaume d'Auvergne (d. 1248), the bishop of Paris and advisor and friend in his youth, made them his own, and cited them in Joinville's presence: "No one can sin so much that God would not be able to forgive him."[22]

HIS RELIGIOUS KNOWLEDGE

Louis was neither an intellectual nor a theologian, but he was concerned with instructing himself in matters of religion. He read the Bible and the Church Fathers, discussed religion with his entourage, and, notably, questioned the learned clerics he met. To sum this up perfectly: "Saint Louis is a great cleric according to the cultural categories of the thirteenth century. This is not in the sense of the great clerics of our churches, but on the level of culture . . . a cleric with a solid culture that was closer to that of the rather traditional culture of the French Dominicans than that of the great foreign intellectuals like Albert the Great and Thomas Aquinas."[23]

His appetite for religious knowledge struck his contemporaries. Guillaume de Saint-Pathus dedicated an entire chapter, the seventh chapter of his *Life,* to the theme of "Studying Holy Scripture":

> Judging that people should not waste their time on trifling things or strange demands of this world, and that people should spend their time on better and more weighty things, the holy king Louis worked on reading Holy Scripture, for he had a glossed Bible and the original writings of Saint Augustine and of other saints and other books of Holy Scripture which he often read and had read before him between dinner and bedtime. . . . On the days he would take a nap, if he did not have any important affairs to attend to, between his nap and vespers, he would summon religious or other honest people with whom he would speak about God, his saints, and their acts, stories from the Holy Scripture, and the lives of the Fathers. After complines were said by his chaplains in his chapel, he would go into his room, light a candle that was about three feet high, and for the entire time it burnt he would read in the Bible or some other holy book. . . . And when he was able to have people of reverence with him at his table, he would gladly invite them, whether they were men of religion or even laymen, and he would talk to them about God at his table in imitation of the lesson they read in the convents when the friars are gathered round the table.[24]

Sometimes he went to Royaumont to sit down with the monks at the times when they held school. And

like a monk he would sit down at the feet of the master who was giving the lesson and diligently listen to him. Several times he went to the
school of the Preaching Friars in Compiègne, and he would sit down
on a block on the ground in front of the master who was reading
from the pulpit and he would listen to him with diligence. The friars
who were seated on chairs above the ground wanted to go down and
sit on the ground with him, but he would never let them. In the refectory of the Preachers of Compiègne he would go up to the lectern
and stand next to the friar who was reading the lesson there.[25]

We find the same theme along with other details in Geoffroy de Beaulieu: when he was overseas, the faithful king heard of a powerful Saracen
sultan who looked for books of all kinds that could be of use to the Saracen philosophers, and he had them copied at his own expense and kept
them in his library. This way, the people who could read were able to use
the books they needed.

> The pious king decided that the sons of darkness were wiser
> than the sons of light, and that they were more zealous for their
> error than the sons of the Church were for their true Christian faith.
> He conceived the plan to have all the useful and authentic books of
> holy Scripture transcribed at his own expense when he returned to
> France, so that people would be able to find them in the libraries of
> the various abbeys, and so that he and other literate men would be
> able to study them for their own benefit and the benefit of their as-
> sociates. After his return, he realized his plan and had an appropri-
> ate and well-defended place built to this effect. This was the room of
> the treasury of the Sainte-Chapelle, in which he collected most of the
> original writings of Augustine, Ambrose, Jerome, Gregory, and the
> books of other orthodox scholars. When he had free time, he liked to
> study there and gladly allowed others to study there too. . . . He pre-
> ferred to have new copies of these books made instead of buying old
> ones because this way the number and use of these holy books was
> increased.[26]

In his testament, he bequeathed a part of these books in his library in
Paris to the Minorite Friars [of Paris], one "part to the Preaching Friars [of
Paris], and the rest to the Cistercian monks of the abbey of Royaumont

that he had founded."[27] We have to wait for Charles V to see the establishment of a royal library handed down from king to king and that would become a national library after the fall of the monarchy. It is true Saint Louis set aside his luxurious illuminated manuscripts that were obviously few in number.[28] Here is one last bit of information in which we can find the king of the French language:

> When he was studying in these books in the presence of some of friends who did not know Latin, as he read the text and understood it, he would translate it into French for them with excellent precision.[29]

His readings were still all closely related to his faith: "He did not like to read the writings of the [university] masters, but the books of the authentic and confirmed saints."

This explains Saint Louis' desire to be instructed in Christian doctrine from the important clerics. Here, he took advantage of a conversation with Saint Bonaventure who came to preach before him:

> Friar Bonaventure, the general minister, reports that His Royal Highness Louis, the king of France, asked him this question: could a man prefer not to exist at all to always suffering torments as in hell, for example? He answered him: "Sire, this is a twofold question. First of all, it implies a perpetual offense against God, for God who is a just judge would not inflict a perpetual punishment for any other reason; and, on the other hand, there is the interminable suffering of the punishment, and no one should choose to remain in a state of perpetual offense in relation to God. Therefore, one would have to prefer not to exist rather than being God's perpetual enemy." The very pious and very Christian king faithful to God added: "I adhere to Friar Bonaventure's opinion and I can assure you," he said to the people in attendance, "that I would rather not exist at all and be reduced to nothingness than live eternally in this world and always rule as I rule now in a state of perpetual offense against my Creator."[30]

Finally, there he was again, with a holy book in his hand, asking a question about religion and not the least important one he could ask, as he liked to do unexpectedly. He asked one of his close associates, Joinville to be specific: "Seneschal, what is God?"—"Sire, it is a thing so good that there can be nothing better." We know that Joinville's answer made Louis happy.[31]

Worship and Asceticism

As a convinced disciple of the holy books he read and teachings of the Church that he listened to, along with the love of God, Louis based his worship on the meaning of sin and its consequences and the will to repent. He had an almost physical horror of mortal sin, which was all the stronger since his own mother inculcated it in him. Here is another question he tossed Joinville: "So, I ask you which would you like better, to be leprous or to have committed a mortal sin?" Joinville's reply: "I would rather have committed thirty of them than be a leper." Saint Louis did not respond to this immediately because there were witnesses present, but the next day he let him have it: "You were speaking like an idiot and a fool [*hâtif musard*] who talks without thinking, because the soul that is in mortal sin is like the devil."[32]

Under the risk of death, drastic remedies were called for. This was the source of the king's "stiff penitence," this penitential rigor that was the subject of the fourteenth chapter in Guillaume de Saint-Pathus's *Life*. Penitence was first of all the rejection of pleasure, hence the king's abstinence at the dinner table and in bed.[33] His confessor Geoffroy de Beaulieu testified to the purity of his manners and his chastity in two chapters of his biography, the fifth chapter "On the Purity and Innocence of His Life," and the eleventh chapter "On His Chastity and Continence in Marriage." His preferred form of penitence was fasting, which was both the most physical and the most spiritual act of repentance as it gave to the soul what it withheld from the body. He had such an excessive desire to fast that according to his confessor people had to prevent him from fasting on Mondays in addition to the other days of fasting as he wished to do. "He gave in to the advice of his entourage."[34]

This was not the only penitential excess he committed and that his religious advisors failed to persuade him to give up. They were torn between admiration and serious reservations about a layman, a king, moreover a sickly king, who behaved like a monastic ascetic. At the very most, they managed

to persuade him to mitigate these mortifications of his body. They had
the same discussions over his self-flagellation and practice of wearing a
hair shirt.

His age experienced great penitential disturbances. Epidemics of public, collective flagellation erupted throughout Christendom from time to
time. This was the case in 1260, a year that the Joachimite millenarians
expected to usher in the end of the world.[35] Saint Louis was more discreet.
His flagellation took the form of private penitence. After each confession,
he received discipline from the hand of his confessor in the form of five
small pliable iron chains kept in the bottom of a small ivory box. He always wore this pyxis hanging from his belt like a purse, although he kept it
out of sight. He had more than one of them, and sometimes he offered
them as gifts to his children and close friends as a means of encouraging
them to do penance. The vigor of this form of penance depended on his
confessors' temperament. Geoffroy de Beaulieu happened to know that
one of them would strike with excessive force, seriously wounding the king's
flesh, which was soft. If any confessor tried to spare him any pain, the
king would ask him to strike harder and signaled when the desired intensity had been attained.[36] (Geoffroy was probably alluding to his own experience here.)

Louis also wanted to wear a hair shirt right on his skin for Advent, Lent,
and every Friday. His confessor (Geoffroy de Beaulieu) had to tell him several times that this kind of penance was not appropriate for a king, and that
he should replace it with alms for the poor and greater expediency in his administration of justice. Saint Louis ended up giving in to his pleas. However,
for Lent he continued to wear a section of a hair shirt that formed a large
belt around his waist. Every Friday during Advent and Lent, he secretly had
his confessor give out forty sous *parisis* to the poor. This was a substitutive
form of penance that the Church began to increase. Saint Louis engaged
in this ecclesiastical accounting for spiritual life[37] that benefited from the
spread of the monetary economy, which counted for more than a little in the
revolt of someone like Luther and the outburst of the Reformation. Not
that these acts of penance were easy for him. They actually represented a
struggle and a renunciation for him. This was also what set the price to be
paid. Louis was hot-blooded, he had carnal needs, he was a gourmand, he
loved life, and he liked to joke and laugh. Hence, his decision not to laugh
on Fridays, to abstain from laughing as well: "The saint king abstained from

laughing as much as he could on Fridays, and, if sometimes he started to laugh unexpectedly, he would stop himself immediately."[38]

We should not limit Saint Louis' forms of worship to his gestures alone. His biographers underscored his habit of constantly listening to his conscience and the quality and the sensitivity of his conscience.[39] Guillaume de Saint-Pathus's fifteenth chapter treats the subject of "what beauty of conscience is" "because more than any of the other good qualities of the soul, pure conscience delights the watchful eyes of God, and the blessed king Saint Louis was of such great purity that he was able to delight God's watchful eyes."[40]

On the other hand, Saint Louis was disheartened that the grace of the gift of tears, a sign of God's acceptance of the sinner's contrition and an expression of contrition in the traditional spirituality marked with the monastic seal of approval, had been refused him. This was "the gift of tears refused to Saint Louis," which struck Michelet when he read the thirteenth-century biographies. However, "although the Lord sometimes granted him several tears while he was praying, when he felt them softly run down his cheeks into his mouth, he would savor them very sweetly not only in his heart but also on his tongue."[41] Louis needed these physical pleasures in his devotion, especially when they came from inside him.

His Conscience

Saint Louis' religious devotion can be situated on the threshold between two distinct styles of spirituality. The first of these was traditional and monastic; it emerged in bursts of contrition and tears. The second was associated with a new conception of sin as something judged according to the sinner's intentions and centered on conscience and the examination of conscience. Saint Louis' refusal to cry was no doubt related to his individual sensibility, but it was also a part of this change in spirituality. Conscience tended to dry up all tears.

This conscience fed into a group of Saint Louis' virtues. First of all, it nurtured one of his fundamental virtues, his quasi-Franciscan humility. We have already examined so many of the signs of this virtue within him, and he was often astonished when he found it lacking in certain churchmen. This occurred, for instance, after his meeting with Pope Innocent IV in

Cluny in 1246 when he failed to convince the pontiff to reconcile with Frederick II in order to unify Christendom in view of the upcoming crusade.

> When His Lordship the Pope had proudly and haughtily refused, His Royal Highness the king of France went away angry and indignant that he had not been able to find the least sign of humility in the man who bore the title of the servant of the servants of God.[42]

Conscience also fostered Saint Louis' patience, another essential virtue for this man-king who was always turning to the man-Christ. He was a suffering king who viewed himself as an image of Jesus in his suffering, who wished to be the Christ of the Passion.[43] His biographers and hagiographers made a great deal of this virtue of patience.[44] Let's listen to the testimony of one of the more independent chroniclers, the Englishman Matthew Paris: "The very Christian king stayed in Acre, silently and patiently putting up with this adversity."[45] Louis confided to the king of England in a friendly conversation: "Getting back to myself, and getting back to my heart and looking inside it, I am more overjoyed with the patience the Lord has granted me through his grace than I would be if I ruled the entire world."[46]

His contemporaries frequently related his loyalty and his passion for truth to his conscience. One of Joinville's anecdotes illustrates this:

> People have pointed out Saint Louis' loyalty in his reception of Sir Renaud de Trie who brought him a letter containing the donation of the county of Dammartin-en-Gohelle to the heirs of the countess of Boulogne who had recently died. The letter's seal had been broken, showing only half of the king's legs in the image and the cushion on which he rests his feet. The king showed it to us and asked for our advice.
>
> Without a single exception we all agreed that he was in no way bound to execute the letter. He then ordered his chamberlain John Sarrasin to show him the letter. As he held it in his hands, he said, "Lords, this is the seal I used before going overseas, and anyone can plainly see that the imprint of the broken part of the seal is connected to the whole seal. Because of this then, I could not dare keep this county with a good conscience." Then, he summoned Sir Renaud de Trie and told him: "I am giving you the county back."[47]

There is no better example of Saint Louis' loyalty than the demonstration he gave by observing it in his relations with the Muslims. His contemporaries were so used to considering that the moral rules Christians were normally supposed to respect were suspended in their dealings with the Muslims that this incident made a powerful impression on them. Boniface VIII mentioned it in his canonization sermon of August 6, 1297.[48] Joinville witnessed this episode and narrates it in his *Histoire de Saint Louis,*[49] but he had already mentioned it in his deposition for the canonization proceedings, so Guillaume de Saint-Pathus was able to include it in his *Life* because he had access to the record of the proceedings. I am relying on his version of these events here. After paying 30,000 of the 200,000 pounds demanded by the Muslims for the ransom of the king and the other French prisoners, the Saracens released the king on the condition that he promised to stay on his ship off the coast of Damietta until the entire sum was paid. Saint Louis gave his promise orally and not in writing. The barons who were with him advised him to take advantage of the situation and set sail. He answered that there was no question of his not keeping his promise, even if the Saracens broke their promise by massacring the Christian prisoners in Damietta. Some time later, they informed the king that the entire ransom had been paid.

But His Lordship Philippe de Nemours, the holy king's knight, told him: "The sum of money has been paid in full, but we cheated the Saracens out of 10,000 pounds." When the saint king heard these words he became very angry and said: "Know that I want the 200,000 pounds to be paid in full, because I promised them and I don't want a single pound to be missing." At that moment, the seneschal of Champagne[50] interrupted His Lordship Philippe, winked at him, and told the king: "Sire, do you believe what His Lordship Philippe says? He is only joking." And when His Lordship Philippe heard the seneschal's voice, he remembered the saint king's incredibly great desire for truth, and then continued and said: "Sire, His Lordship the seneschal is telling the truth. I only spoke like that to sport and joke and to hear what you would say." The saint king replied: "Do not expect any congratulations for this game and this test, but see to it that the sum of money is paid in its entirety."[51]

SACRAMENTAL PRACTICE

Saint Louis attached great importance to the rites and necessary mediation of the Church and the priests in the religious life of laymen, including the king's. Since the twelfth century, the theology of the sacraments was regularized within the framework of a sacramental septenary. In particular, this had been the case since the appearance of Hugh of Saint Victor's *De sacramentis*. Louis believed that the Church was never more indispensable than in its role of dispensing the sacraments.[52]

Saint Louis' attitude typified what Father Gy says about sacramental practices in the thirteenth century: "There are two sacraments that are indispensable for everyone: one is baptism, and the other is confession for anyone who has committed a mortal sin."[53] We have seen the importance Saint Louis attached to his own baptism and his zeal for baptizing non-Christians. Baptism marked one's entry into the Christian community as one's true birth, one's spiritual birth, and the basic necessary condition that allowed someone to hope for salvation and to go to Heaven. The site of one's baptism, which was often one's birthplace, was always considered one's true birthplace. This explains Louis' insistence on being called Louis de Poissy after the place he was baptized.

Confession was of great concern to Saint Louis because it was the one sacrament that erased mortal sins, recreating the conditions of purity of baptism. The thirteenth century was the century of confession. In 1215, the year after Saint Louis' birth, the Fourth Lateran Council instituted obligatory annual confession for all Christians. Annual confession was not enough for Saint Louis. It left too many long intervals in which the power of mortal sin was too great and too dangerous. Weekly confession provided a safer regimen, and the ideal day of the week was the one that had been specifically designated for penance: Friday. The king, however, was afraid of committing a sin that might be mortal between any two Fridays, especially at night—this time for temptations, the devil's favorite time for mounting his assaults. So, the king felt it was necessary to keep a daytime confessor and a nighttime confessor near his room and had the two trade off to hear his confessions.

Some may be surprised to see eucharistic practice lag behind these two others in the order of Louis' sacramental activity. However, in the thirteenth century more emphasis was placed on the conditions that were supposed to make the sinner worthy of receiving the Eucharist—confession and penance: "Before taking communion, it is necessary to test one's conscience."[54]

Thus Louis did not frequently take part in communion. Guillaume de Saint-Pathus explains this in more detail:

> The blessed king had such fervent devotion when he took the sacrament of the true body [the body of Our Lord], because he would stay to take communion six times each year at the very least. This was on Easter, Pentecost, the Ascension Day of the Blessed Virgin Mary, All Saints' Day, Christmas, and for the purification of Notre-Dame.[55]

This text also informs us about the hierarchy ordering his worship: worship for Christ (three communions), for the Virgin (two communions), and for the saints (one communion).

Louis, however, surrounded these communions with recommended "conditions of dignity" and humility. He honored Christ's body by surrounding his communions with fasts, periods of continence, and prayer—in addition to preliminary confession. He had an impressive array of gestures he employed in the very act of communing.

> And he would go to receive his savior with such great devotion that he would wash his hands and mouth and remove his hood and headdress beforehand. Once he had entered the church choir he would not walk on his feet to the altar, but he would walk up to it on his knees. And when he was before the altar, he would say his *Confiteor.*[56]

The thirteenth century was also a period of expansion for the eucharistic cult. In 1264, Pope Urban IV instituted the Festival of Corpus Christi in which the host was carried in a procession under the dais. This action launched the tradition of the sanctifying object that soon spread to princely secular ceremonies.[57] Eucharistic miracles occurred more frequently in the thirteenth century as well.

As for the other sacraments, of course Louis had received the sacrament of marriage.[58] He celebrated his own as devoutly as possible for the time, incorporating a mass into the wedding ceremony and observing the "three nights of Tobias," although the marriage liturgy in the Middle Ages did not have "the importance that it would acquire later on."[59]

This was also the case for the Extreme Unction. If the dying person was still conscious, it was confession that counted the most, as well as prayer, gestures of humility like lifting the dying person from his bed and laying him on a sheet or even on the ground, or dressing the body in a monastic habit, although royal dignity undoubtedly forbade this in Saint Louis' case. Blanche of Castile died at Maubuisson in a Cistercian robe. Saint Louis' biographers, however, insisted on pointing out that he received the Extreme Unction while he was still conscious on his deathbed in Carthage.[60]

SAINT LOUIS AND PRAYER

Prayer seems to lie at the heart of Saint Louis' worship.[61] It consisted in love and established a direct relationship between God and the person who prayed through traditional texts taught by the Church and the clerics. This connection was all the more important when the praying man was a king and the leader of his people.

Descriptions of Saint Louis praying are most common in the *Lives* of his confessor Geoffroy de Beaulieu and Guillaume de Saint-Pathus. On the other hand, we find little information on his praying in the works of the other biographers and particularly in Joinville, the bull for his canonization, and the two sermons given for the occasion by Boniface VIII. Only two allusions to Saint Louis' prayer can be found in the canonization bull. Boniface VIII emphasized that the king's piety became stronger after his return from the first crusade. During Lent, Advent, the days before the festival days and the Ember Weeks, "he would commit himself to fasting and prayer" (*in jejuniis et orationibus existebat*).[62] The pope stressed the length of his prayers and his way of settling into prayer, although this was not the most important thing that made a saint from the perspective of the curia. Boniface also recalled the prayers the king said on his deathbed. They allowed him to die the *good* death: "By recommending his soul to God with devout prayers and by pronouncing the following words to the letter— 'Father, I am putting my spirit in your hands,' he happily passed on to Christ" (*suam Domino* devotis precibus *animam recommendans, ac literaliter exprimens verba sequentia, videlicet*—Pater, in manus tuus commendo spiritum meum, *feliciter migravit ad Christum*).[63] Louis relied on prayers and customary formulae, but he did not repeat them mechanically; he gave the words their profound true meaning—*literaliter exprimens.*

We can compare this mention of the praying king with the recommendations for his son written in his *Enseignements.* At church during mass, one must express oneself "with one's mouth and in thought." It was necessary to meditate on a prayer's words at the same time one uttered them.[64] Prayer should become more meditative as one proceeded from the consecration to the communion. In Joinville's version, he gave his son the following advice: "Pray to God with your heart and your mouth especially during the mass [while] the consecration is being made," and, further on, he advised him again: "and willingly engage in prayers [*proieres*] and pardons [*indulgences*]." The king's devoutness moved along the overlapping border between heartfelt enthusiasm and objectively predetermined rites.

Joinville mentioned the king's prayers on only two occasions. The first occurred after his mother's death, which Saint Louis only learned about several months afterward. We know that this one time his grief made him lose his sense of moderation. Among his reactions, there was his act of sending "a ledger [to France] full of letters for prayers to the churches so that they would pray for her."[65]

Joinville reintroduces the subject of Saint Louis' prayers when he narrates his death as an eyewitness, Pierre the count d'Alençon, the king's son reported it to him.

> When he was getting close to death, he called on the saints to assist him and help him, especially on His Grace Saint Jacques, as he said his oraison that begins with the words *Esto, Domine,* in other words, "God, be the sanctifier and guardian of your people." He then called on the assistance of His Grace Saint Denis of France by saying his prayer that goes: "Lord, God, grant us the power to scorn the wealth of this world in such manner that we have no adversity to fear."[66]

The vocabulary for "prayer" was rather simple: in Latin it was *orare, oratio,* and only rarely *preces;* in French it was *"oraison"* or, more rarely, *"orer"* and, less frequently *"prier"* or *"prières (proieres)."* Nevertheless, Saint Louis' biographers, and Geoffroy de Beaulieu and Guillaume de Saint-Pathus in particular, described all of his manners of praying.

When dealing with his devoutness in attending mass and sermons, Geoffroy described his manner of praying in detail.[67]

The prayer services that he listened to daily were the canonical hours and the hours of the Virgin, and he always wanted to hear them accompanied by song. When he was traveling he also wanted to hear them and said them in a soft voice with his chaplain. He said the service for the dead accompanied by nine *lectiones* every day with his chaplain, even on the days of the ceremonial festivals. The *lectiones* were passages selected from Scripture or the writings of the Church Fathers and integrated into a service. He listened to two masses almost every day and he even frequently heard three or four of them. When he heard that some of the nobles were muttering things against the amount of time he spent attending so many masses and sermons, he replied that no one would say anything if he spent twice as much time playing dice games and running through the forests hunting.[68]

It was his custom to get out of bed around midnight to sing matins with his chaplains and clerics in the royal chapel. Upon returning from matins, he took a break to rest [*quietum spatium*] and prayed at the foot of his bed. If the Lord had inspired him to worship, he had no fear of being interrupted by any intruders in these moments. He wanted to continue praying for as long as matins lasted in the church. However, as he did not want to get up too early for prime in case any urgent affairs arose, and because staying up weakened his body and head and placed a serious burden on them, on the advice and insistence of his friends he ended up waking for matins at one o'clock, which allowed him to hear prime, the masses, and the other canonical hours in a row with only a short pause in between. He did not want to be distracted by any conversations when they were singing the hours, except in the case of an emergency, and even in that case he only briefly stopped praying. He did the same thing whether he was staying in a royal castle or in a monastery or convent as he often did.

He paid close attention to the celebrations of the important festivals and was very visible when they took place. He loved the songs sung during the services and as he increased the number of clerics in his chapel, he also increased the number of singers there. He was particularly fond of the "Good Children" (*les Bons-Enfants*), in other words the children who sang in the choir who were usually poor students who ended up forming a veritable choir school.

For Saint Louis, prayer was a sensual experience, and he hoped that it would move him to the point where he had tears running down his cheeks into his mouth.

When he visited a house of congregation, he immediately asked the religious to pray for him and his people, both the living and the dead. When he made this request on his knees in the chapter houses, the humility of his pose often brought them to tears. In his quest for suffrages (prayers and masses) for his associates, servants, and deceased friends in addition to himself and his family members, he showed the same loyalty and solidarity for this "artificial" family formed by his entourage as for his natural family. Prayer expressed blood ties and ties of the heart.

According to Guillaume de Saint-Pathus in his chapter "On Devoutly Praying to God," prayers and works formed an inseparable pair in Saint Louis' devotional practice. To pray meant "to put one's spirit present before God," it was "having God's contemplation, consolation, and assistance in order to accomplish a good work."

When he was not sick, the king prayed every evening after complines with a chaplain in his chapel or in his dressing room. After the chaplain left, he kept praying whether he was in the chapel, his dressing room, or at the side of his bed. He prayed leaning toward the ground with his elbows on a bench. He usually prayed for such a long time that the people in his service [*la maisnie de sa chambre*] grew impatient waiting outside. Fifty times each night, he knelt down, stood back up, and knelt down again as he slowly said an *Ave Maria*. Instead of drinking a glass of wine each night before bed as was the custom of many of his contemporaries, he did not take any "bedtime wine." Before his first crusade, he always went to bed after matins, even in winter. After his return from the crusade, he rose after matins but well before daybreak, reciting matins a little later and then saying a solitary prayer before the altar or at his bedside. He prayed hunched over with his head bowed so low toward the ground that his eyesight and his mind were weakened by it and he could not get back into bed on his own.

Guillaume de Saint-Pathus highlighted his numerous requests for prayers from others. When he visited a convent or a monastery, Louis knelt before the religious whom he asked for prayers. He sent an annual letter to the Cistercians that solicited their prayers. Each monk had to say three masses for him every year: one mass of the Holy Spirit, one mass of the Holy Cross, and one mass of Notre-Dame. He wrote to his daughter Blanche to ask her to pray for him after his death. He put the same request down in his own hand in his *Enseignements* for his son and daughter. Before leaving for Tunis, he visited the Parisian convents and knelt before the friars as he asked them to pray for him in front of his household, knights, and everyone else in attendance.

Guillaume cited other exceptional examples of his prayers and requests for prayers. At the very moment of his liberation in Egypt, people heard an uproar in the Muslim camp: the king was making his people say the service of the Holy Cross, the service of the day, the service of the Holy Spirit, the service of the dead, "and all the other good prayers he knew." At Sidon, he had the patriarch give a sermon and made the Christian populace attend it "barefoot and in rags [woolen shirts]" so that they could pray to God for a sign indicating whether it was better for Louis to stay in the Holy Land or to return to France. Finally, when he had a difficult problem to resolve with his council, he often asked the convents of religious to beseech God in their prayers to inspire the king with the right solution. Thus, even before making his most important decisions, Saint Louis surrounded himself with an army of praying men charged with the task of drawing the secrets for success from God.

He combined individual and collective prayer, praying aloud and praying quietly ("with the mouth or in thought"). However, praying aloud was what predominated in his practice even when he was alone. We should remember that "silent reading" was only slowly beginning in this period.[69] Saint Louis tried to strike a balance between individual and collective prayer. He often prayed with his chaplain or the clerics of his chapel, but he also liked to pray alone.

His prayer was also a royal prayer in its form. He carried it out either with his chapel, which was a royal chapel more numerous and more brilliant than all those belonging to any other nobles and powerful men in the kingdom, or alone. When he engaged in private prayer, it was not just an individual's prayer that this expressed in the thirteenth century,[70] but also the prayer of the solitary leader.

Collective prayer was for important occasions, the festival ceremonies where he played his role as king. In these ceremonies, he was particularly attentive to what seemed to him like a natural continuation of prayer, its mystical envelope — song.

Louis' practice of prayer tended to become ubiquitous; he prayed everywhere and at almost any time — on land and at sea, on horseback and in fixed domiciles, in private and in public, day and night. He still had to accept the interruptions in its exercise. During the day, he reserved two necessary moments for it in the morning and the evening. However, the disruptions also arose from the exceptional moments of the great festivals and great dangers. Prayer shaped Saint Louis' exceptional experience as much as his daily experience, his ceremonious experience as much as his habitual experience. The general trend, however, resided in his daily, frequent, and lengthy practice. His hagiographers underscored the impatience of his entourage when they were confronted with the length of his prayers, and they did this to show how much the king was different from and superior to others and distinct from them on the basis of the extent of his praying. His prayer was the prayer of a saint.

The hagiographers and notably Guillaume de Saint-Pathus noted Saint Louis' gestures in prayer. In this age of renewed attention to gestures that the Church attempted to codify, this man of moderation and the happy medium was prone to excess. His frequent worship, all his kneeling and other tiring gestures, his exaggerated bowing toward the ground that warped his senses, all of this far exceeded the normal practice of prayer.[71] However, no saints existed without excesses like these.

Even though the king took part in the joyous prayers for the great festivals (Easter, notably), even though he was sensitive to songs of rejoicing, prayer was still primarily a form of penance for him.

To whom did he address his prayers? He addressed them to God— seen mainly with the traits of Christ the Son, to the Holy Spirit, and to the Virgin Mary—who virtually became a fourth figure in the Trinity in the thirteenth century.

When he came back from the crusade in 1254 grief-stricken with remorse over his defeat as it sent tremors through all Christendom, "they sang a mass in the honor of the Holy Spirit so that the king would receive consolation from He who is above all else." As for the Virgin Mary, we have seen her appear as an important mediator on men's behalf with her son Jesus. This therefore generally made her a special object for the worship of rulers who commended themselves to her with their subjects. She was especially venerated by Saint Louis who often prayed to her in the Marian sanctuaries and who had the service for the Virgin said every day. In his *Enseignements* for his son, he asked him to repress "everything that is done or said against God or Our Lady," and advised him to pray to God to protect him "through his great mercy and through the prayers and merits of his blessed mother, the Virgin Mary."[72]

For whom did he pray? He prayed for himself. Prayer was first of all the means of attaining personal salvation. However, he also prayed for others. As a king devoted to his lineage, he prayed for the memory of his ancestors, for his father, and perhaps even more for his grandfather Philip Augustus, for his mother whom he cherished more than anyone else, for his brothers and sisters, and for his children (the queen belonged to a different lineage). Saint Louis practiced a dynastic form of prayer.

As a king who valued friendship, full of recognition for his servants and his entourage, Saint Louis was also the center of an "artificial" family held together by prayer within a religious and eschatological perspective. The king was aware of his duties to his people ("*sa gent*," as he says of his soldiers on the crusade and his subjects in general); he made his royal prayer for the kingdom and its inhabitants into one of the most demanding responsibilities of his function. A good Christian king was a king who prayed for his people.

Perhaps above all else, Saint Louis prayed and had others pray for the dead. As the king of a dynastic kingdom with very great funerary ambitions,[73] as a contemporary of the spread of the belief in Purgatory that required suffrages from the living for the dead,[74] and as the heir to an important monastic and aristocratic tradition of worshipping the dead[75] for whom the orders endowed with a clientele of deceased figures prayed since the foundation of Cluny, he accorded a disproportionate importance to services for the dead, although in this he followed meticulously the practice of his time.[76] He was a king of the dead just as much as a king of the living.[77]

No doubt people prayed in order to assure their own personal salvation and the salvation of others in this form of penitence and humility, but people also used prayer to accompany good works. However, at the end of prayer worship, there was direct contact with God, the contemplation of God, and the direct appeal for help for oneself and for others that the person who prays addressed to God. By praying, the king fulfilled the mission explicitly confided to him by the clerics on the day of his coronation and crowning, the mission for him to serve as the intermediary between God and his subjects.

Another characteristic of the period led Louis to practice individual prayer. This was the trend of seeking to worship and practice charity in secrecy. Hidden charity was a response to the shameful poverty that was increasing among certain types of the people.

Following one of the attitudes advocated by the rules of piety in his time and in particular by Mendicant devotion for humility, he hid his actions in order to do good. He tried to conceal his dietary rigor with pious ruses, but at the same time did not entirely manage to rein in the exhibitionism particular to asceticism. If we were to try to situate him within the evolutionary development of medieval worship, we would have to simplify things by saying that although he partook of a certain "Gothic" love of life, he also articulated the beginnings of a certain "flamboyant" asceticism.

Louis assiduously frequented the Cistercians and the Mendicant friars, who often continued the Cistercian practices and spirit of devotion into the thirteenth century. Finally we must not forget that Louis viewed prayer as a means for a layman to come as close as possible to having the same conduct, the same status, and the same chances of pleasing God as the religious. His praying may above all have been a monastic form of prayer. This was compatible with the global image of the king that a number of his contemporaries had, particularly those like Geoffroy de Beaulieu who thought he had seriously entertained the idea of joining a Mendicant order. One of his other biographers, Guillaume de Chartres, wrote that "his manners, his actions, and his gestures were not just those of a king but those of a religious."[78]

HIS WORSHIP OF THE SAINTS

Although the Virgin was the privileged intermediary between God and men, the saints represented another group of mediators for the king. He imagined them existing as part of a heavenly government functioning on the model of a feudal monarchical regime. He also saw them as auxiliaries for realizing his project of melding religion and politics together—to succeed on earth *and* in heaven, or, rather, in heaven as on earth. Other wealthy and powerful individuals in the thirteenth century shared this personal vision of Saint Louis. The relation between heaven and earth had somehow been inverted in relation to the Augustinian model in which the earthly city has to strive to imitate the heavenly city. A significant parallelism still existed here, but it had been reversed. It was no longer "on earth as it is in heaven," but "in heaven as it is on earth." The merchant wanted to possess both money in this life and eternal life in the beyond.[79] The powerful man should have "honor" on this earth and "glory" in heaven.

Louis exposed his plan for realizing this project to an astonished Join-ville: "Would you like to learn how you can have honor and please men in this world and have God's grace and glory in the time to come?" The means for achieving this relied on the saints:

> The saint king told the knight to attend Church during the ceremonious festivals for the saints and to honor the saints, and he said that the saints in Heaven are like the king's advisors on earth, because whoever has business with an earthly king, he asks who has good relations with him, who can ask him for something he will be sure to obtain, and to whom does the king listen? And when he knows who this person is, he goes to find him, and asks him to ask the king on his behalf. This is how things work with the saints in heaven who are the intimate friends [*privés*] of Our Lord, and his familiar circle and who can ask him without hesitation, because he listens to them. So, you should go to church on their festival days, honor them, and pray to them so that they can pray Our Lord for you.[80]

Did Louis ever dream that in becoming a saint he would be able to play this same role in Heaven as a mediator at God's side that he played on earth as king between God and his subjects? Isn't the fate of a good king to be-come a saint who can exercise his function in perpetuity?

SAINT LOUIS' DEVOTIONAL OBSESSIONS

Furthermore, I can identify four types of worship in which he invested a virtually obsessive commitment: listening to sermons, the cult of the relics, acts of charity, and the construction of religious buildings.

I have already discussed Saint Louis' love of sermons at length (and didn't he also often act like an amateur preacher?), so I will content myself with presenting an anecdote that conveys a sense of the quasi-magical char-acter of this passion of his:

> He very frequently wanted to listen to sermons, and, when he liked them, he would retain them very well and was able to repeat them to others with great success. During his return voyage from

the crusade, which lasted six weeks, he ordered them to give three sermons a week on his ship. When the seas were calm and the ship did not need the sailors to work on it, the pious king wanted these sailors to hear a special sermon on a theme that was of particular concern to them such as the articles of faith, manners, and sins, in light of the fact that these types of men very rarely heard the word of God. . . .[81]

Louis also had a quasi-fetishistic attraction for relics. He no doubt considered his acquisition of the relics of the Passion as the greatest accomplishment of his reign. He had the Sainte-Chapelle built for them and created three annual services for them. He also acquired the relics of Saint Maurice and built a church in Senlis to house them, organizing a grand procession of the saints' bodies for the occasion.

His third great obsession was charity, and we have already seen many examples of this in two basic forms: serving the poor at the supper table, caring for the sick, and, above all, distributing alms either secretly or publicly, and sometimes even in an ostentatious way. This occurred on his journeys throughout the kingdom, his almsgiving tours where he was assailed by legions of poor people.[82] For Saint Louis, faith and devoutness could not exist without works. According to Guillaume de Saint-Pathus, "These two things agree with one another in the eyes of Our Lord almighty— that works should be backed up with prayer and prayer with works."[83] And the thirteenth century was a time when works of charity were strongly advocated by the Mendicant friars and became an essential element of piety, especially for wealthy and powerful laymen. This was the theme of Guillaume de Saint-Pathus's eleventh chapter, "Works of Charity." Louis' acts of providing aid for the sick, particularly for the "ill-sighted" and the blind for whom Louis built the hospice of the Quinze-Vingts in Paris that was intended to house three hundred blind persons, dressing people who had no clothes, giving food to people who were starving, giving alms to the poor, lodging the homeless, providing for the needs of the widows of crusaders who died across the sea, delivering prisoners from the infidels, taking care of lepers, burying the dead properly as he did in the Holy Land, staying at the bedside of people who were dying as he did in the hospital of Compiègne and at the Cistercian abbey of Chaalis are all so many illustrations.

Joinville was a witness to it all.

> The king was such a generous almsgiver that everywhere he went in his kingdom, he would give to the poor churches, the lazar houses, the hospitals, the hospices, and to poor noblemen and noble women. Every day, he would feed a multitude of poor people, without counting the ones who ate in his chamber, and many times I saw that he would slice their bread and give them to drink with his own hands.[84]

To these good works we must add his construction of religious buildings. Saint Louis practiced this passion of kings (and of certain leaders of republican states to this day) to the utmost degree. He had a passion for building monuments and leaving them as signs of memory. He only constructed a few non-religious buildings, palaces or strongholds, but he endowed some of them with holy chapels, notably at Saint-Germain-en-Laye and the Palais de la Cité in Paris. With combined admiration and reproof for the excess of his expenses, his biographers smugly wrote up the list of the religious buildings he had built in his lifetime as well as those built after he died thanks to his gifts that made up the largest part of his testament.[85] Joinville gives a detailed list that includes the Cistercian abbey of Royaumont, the monastic Cistercian abbeys of Lys and Maubuisson built at his mother's request, the convent of Saint-Antoine near Paris (in the current *faubourg* of Saint-Antoine), several convents of the Preachers and the Cordeliers, the hospitals of Pontoise and Vernon, the house for the blind in Paris, and the abbey of the Lady Cordeliers of Saint-Cloud at the request of his sister Isabelle. In order to satisfy these pious obsessions, the king of probity forgot his desire to respect moderation and to be economical. He claimed that he preferred the *prud'homme* to the *béguin,* the devout man without openness or moderation, but he still often behaved like a layman of excessive piety in all of this, like a king who had everything but the religious habit.

His Religious Devotion on the Crusade

At this point, we must briefly return to the topic of Saint Louis on the crusade. Even though I do not give the crusade as central and far-reaching a place in Saint Louis' life and reign as Jean Richard and William Jordan, the crusade was still his most important religious experience, and it was still the one great adventure of religious devotion for Christians in the middle of the thirteenth century. Because everything about Saint Louis seems to target Christian perfection, some have asked whether he was the "ideal crusader."[86]

If we refer to the concept of the "ideal crusader," we can see that Saint Louis was one of the best incarnations of this imaginary character in the eyes of his contemporaries, posterity, and modern historians.

He was an "ideal crusader" first of all because he carried out his preparations for the "pilgrimage overseas" better than most of the leaders of the other crusades, and he also made more preparations for his crusade. Like the chivalric adventure, the crusade was a religious expedition that required a moral preparation including various rites of purification.[87] Saint Louis' biographers noted the change in his attitude after the first expedition: he renounced luxury in dress and ostentation in his eating habits. They dated this change from his return from the Holy Land and observed that it lasted until his second crusade and his death. His life would henceforth be a long act of penance and a slow preparation for his new and final "passage." However, this transformation really dated from the day he took the cross as noted in the legislation for the crusade decreed by the pontifical bulls.

His grand *tournées* (tours) through the heart of the kingdom, in Île-de-France, from the Orléans region to Vexin, undertaken in 1248 and again in 1269–1270 were important preparatory actions. And, as Louis IX never separated his concern for his worldly kingdom from his religious aims, he launched the important campaign that sent his investigators throughout the kingdom in 1247, and later dispatched a new wave of them after issuing the edict of 1254. He launched these campaigns with the intention of putting an end to the abuses committed by royal officers.

The crusade can also be associated with his preparations in terms of his devout worship of the Christ of the Passion, the historical (and divine) Jesus of the Holy Land, through the relics of the Passion, their reception at Villeneuve-l'Archevêque, the barefoot procession that escorted them from Sens to Vincennes after their ceremonious arrival, their transfer to the royal palace, and the construction of the Sainte-Chapelle, which was inaugurated on April 25, 1248 just before the departure for the crusade.[88] Once again, the fact that Louis' preparations consisted in acts of religious devotion is essential.

Louis IX may also be considered an ideal crusader for having united the proper motives of a crusader in the thirteenth century; these were the motives of conquest, mission, and penitence. When he left in 1248, he had rejected the diplomatic path opened by Frederick II and the new missionary plan for the crusade that Innocent IX had just defined—"he is a crusader in the old-fashioned mode."[89] He was the valiant soldier of the crusade that Joinville laid eyes upon one day in Egypt, armed for battle and resplendent: "the most beautiful knight he had ever seen." However, he was also an impassioned partisan of conversion that took the salvation of the souls of the sultan of Egypt in 1248 and of the sultan to Tunis in 1270 as its supreme objective.

Paradoxically, however, he was also an "ideal crusader" because he failed, and because his crusades were almost anachronous. Saint Louis came up against the two great misfortunes any crusader could meet with: captivity and death. In a society where the model of Christ presented the Passion as a supreme victory over the world, these two failures gave Saint Louis a halo purer than any that victory could have conferred upon him. Even though the Church refused to recognize him as a martyr of the crusade, in the eyes of his contemporaries like Joinville his trials and tribulations earned him this honor. According to his confessor Geoffroy de Beaulieu, this characteristic that he had as an expiatory victim and host made him resemble Christ. Nevertheless, it seems to me that this "popular" aura was more commonly attributed to him as a king of suffering than as a crusading martyr.

For posterity, he was still the last great crusader. After him, the adventure of the crusades was over. His expeditions were to the crusades what "the death of King Arthur" was to the great epic courtly romance—a twilight of the heroes, a funerary and quasi-suicidal apotheosis. Saint Louis possessed the dual grandeur of having been an anachronistic crusader who closed the book on a heroic adventure and who simultaneously paved the way for a nostalgic utopia—at the turning point between a real but dead history and an imaginary history to come.

Conflicts and Criticisms

FOR SAINT LOUIS, THE UNIVERSE OF RELIGION WAS NOT LIMITED TO worship. He had the Church before him first of all. He respected it and acted as its servant and supporter in the realm of faith, although he quite often came into conflict with it over the temporal chapter, the jurisdiction, and the pretensions of the Roman curia. He was also engaged in conflicts against the enemies of the Christian faith: against heretics, who were numerous and active within his kingdom, against the Muslims whom he came up against directly in his crusades, and against the Jews who also had a strong presence in France and whom he treated with an attitude that vacillated between protection and persecution. Finally, the pious king was the target of a certain number of criticisms—if not actual opposition—and his devout conduct played an essential role in relation to those criticisms.

SAINT LOUIS AND THE CHURCH

A specific commitment and a penchant bordering on obsession tightly bound Saint Louis to the Church.[1]

This commitment was the one the king made during his coronation when he promised to support and protect the Church and carry out the or-

640

ders that it issued and could not execute on its own, which implied the use of force and the execution of death sentences. This was royalty's function as the "secular arm" of the Church. The essential part of his duty and promise consisted in the vow "to honor and protect." He insisted on this in his *Instructions* for his son: "Be very diligent about protecting all types of people in your domains, especially the people of the Holy Church; prevent anyone from doing any wrong or harm to their persons or their property. . . . You must honor them and protect them so that they can carry out the service of Our Lord in peace."[2]

However, he also felt a great fascination for the clerics and especially for the monks and friars—the "religious." Joinville clearly stated this: "The king loved all people who placed themselves in the service of God and put on the habits of the religious."[3] He favored the new orders and particularly the small Mendicant orders whose anti-establishment appearance (dressed in habits of poor quality with disheveled hair) and marginalized forms of worship (excessive affectations of poverty and humility, millenarian influences) worried the Church. Four years after the king's death, at the Second Council of Lyon in 1274, the Church repressed smaller orders like the Friars of the Sack, the Order of the Servites, and the Order of the Holy Cross. The more orthodox Order of the Carmelites survived. Louis had a house built for them on the banks of the Seine near Charenton. The Friars of Saint Augustine also survived this purge; Louis had bought a bourgeois' farm and its dependencies for them located just outside the gate of Montmartre.

Despite his loyalty, Louis did not submit to the Church in all of its actions and decisions. The way he quoted his grandfather Philip Augustus when he told his son why he had to take care of the Church implies that he had a clear understanding of the Church's desire for power and that he adopted a realistic stance in dealing with it.[4] He did not tolerate any clerics who impinged upon the legitimate power of the king or the state. When he was a young king he demonstrated this in his dealings with several abusive bishops.[5] He did not hesitate to warn the Church against the errors it made that compromised its own efficiency, for example in the case of its abuse of excommunication that ran the risk of devaluing the punishment to the point that it would no longer have any effect on anyone. Joinville reported a heated exchange between the king and a number of bishops during a parlement where they were discussing certain conflicts between secular lords and bishops and, notably, between Joinville himself and the bishop of Châlons. After the plenary meeting, they asked the king to come to talk with them alone. After their interview, Saint Louis reported on it to Joinville and his entourage ("we who were waiting for him in the court chamber [*chambre aux plaids*]"). The bishops sharply reproached him for failing in his function as "secular arm" to help them carry out excommunication sentences they had issued against certain secular lords. Laughing through the whole story, the king told them how he refused to cede them anything in this matter. He was making fun of them. As much as he venerated churchmen who behaved virtuously and who stayed within the limits of their own realm, he just as much condemned the ones who stepped beyond their spiritual power and acted like they were starved for glory and temporal power. He shared the opinion of the many people both inside and outside the Church who criticized its increasing wealth and appetite for earthly goods and vanities. We have already seen how on two occasions he officially asked the pope to choose good cardinals and truly religious prelates.

The pope and the pontifical court were not exempt from his criticism and resistance. On the contrary, he was very demanding toward the head of the Church. The pope was supposed to provide an example of mercy and humility, but he often exhibited excessive pride, a desire for domination, and intransigence. This was notably the case with Innocent IV, particularly in his struggles against Frederick II. Here, we may recall the king's stormy interview with the pontiff at Cluny in 1246.[6] In agreement on this point with the French prelates, Louis' hostility reached its boiling point in 1247 with the dispatch of a letter protesting the papacy's attitude in its relations with the Church of France.[7] The king addressed two main complaints in very sharp terms. The first denounced the papacy's financial exactions that drained the resources of the Church of France. He complained that the imposition of tithes and taxes on the French clergy exhibited an un-Christian cupidity. The second complaint related to the conferment of benefices. The pope reserved the right to confer most of them for himself, impinging upon the well-established rights of the king, the nobles, and the bishops to confer them. The king made a point of mentioning foreigners who did not reside in their churches as well as their failure to respect measures for providing pecuniary aid for the survival of the poor that had been established by the founders of these benefices and dues owed to the king in times of need.

Several eminent historians have viewed Saint Louis' attitude as one that helped bring about the development of the "process through which a laical order of social life began to take shape."[8] I think that this term of lai-cization is inappropriate here; instead, I see this phenomenon as a transfer of the sacredness operating within the Church to the state and as an appro-priation of part of the Church's temporal power by the monarchical state in the name of the royal government. Just as he claimed a kind of imperial power within his kingdom, in temporal matters the sovereign laid claim to a power independent from the churches for himself and his clergy. I think it would be more appropriate to speak of Gallicanism here. It was an error that forged the legend of a "pragmatic sanction" decreed by Saint Louis that supposedly formed a "national" Church, although Saint Louis still seems to have at least flirted with the idea of autonomy for the Church of France to be achieved through an agreement between the king and kingdom's clergy on the temporal plane.

Saint Louis and the Heretics

Saint Louis' conception of royalty as the defender of faith and the secular arm of the Church led him to intervene against the enemies of this faith, just as his predecessors had done. There were basically three types of enemies—heretics, infidels, and Jews.

Although the Albigensian crusade struck a major blow against the here-tics in the Midi, the Cathars and their followers were still very numerous and active, especially in Languedoc, Provence, and Lombardy. They nonetheless became less numerous and less visible after 1230 under the combined effect of the Inquisition, the nobility's and the bourgeoisie's growing disaffection with Catharism, and a general exhaustion of the heretics' doctrine, practice, and organization.

For Saint Louis, just as for the Church, heretics were the worst enemies of the true Christian faith because they once knew and practiced this faith only to deny it. They were apostates, traitors, and felons in relation to God.

In his *Chronicle,* Primat clearly described the priority Saint Louis granted to the fight against the heretics: "And when any negotiation of the faith [the *negotium fidei* is the hunt for heretics or the letter or document order-ing it] was brought to him by the prelates or the inquisitors of the buggers [the "*bougres,*" Bulgars, heretics], putting all things aside, he would immedi-ately rush to have it executed."[9]

Furthermore, in compliance with a canon of the Fourth Lateran Council of 1215 that had been incorporated into the *ordo* for the coronation of the kings of France, Louis had promised to hunt down heretics and to act against them as the secular arm of the Church. He gave the following recommendation in his *Enseignements* for his son: "Hunt down heretics and bad people in your land as much as you can, and in order to purge your land of them, solicit the wise advice of good people whenever necessary."[10] Guillaume de Saint-Pathus gave a slightly different version of this advice: "Chase the buggers and other bad people out of your kingdom as much as your power allows, so that your land may be purged of them, and take the advice of the good people who tell you that this has to be done."[11]

This text provides the historian with several important pieces of information and leaves us with a question. The most important thing in this text is the affirmation of Saint Louis' desire to purify his kingdom by ridding it of heretics. Saint Louis was entirely in step with his century on this point, but he obviously abhorred impurity more strongly than many of his contemporaries. Christendom wanted to protect its gains, uphold the identity it had acquired, and defend its purity as it harvested the benefits of the great expansion of the eleventh and twelfth centuries. It experienced any dissent as a threat and labeled anything that disturbed its unity and harmony as an impurity. Robert I. Moore has effectively described this birth of dissent in the context of a newly forming persecutory society that marginalized, excluded, and eliminated everything that diverged from the existing orthodoxy.[12]

Boniface VIII clearly articulated this conception of heresy as an impurity and a contagious disease in his bull for Saint Louis' canonization:

> He abhorred those who were infected with the macula of perversion. So that they would not infect the adepts of the Christian faith with the rot of this contagious disease, he hunted it out with efficient efforts beyond the borders of his kingdom, and by exercising his attentive, preventative concerns for the condition of his kingdom, he cast these ferments out of it and allowed the true faith to shine there in its authentic state.[13]

The second important statement in this text resides in Saint Louis' claim that the king somehow needed to take expert advice in order to identify heretics and select the measures to adopt in dealing with them. These experts were obviously the inquisitors first of all—particularly the Mendicant friars who were inquisitors—and also converted heretics whom Louis especially trusted due to their personal knowledge of heresy and its adepts. This undoubtedly explains why he gave such strong support to the despicable Robert le Bougre (Matthew Paris blamed him for this) before anyone figured out what a monster he was.[14]

Another question arises around what Saint Louis called "bad people." Who were these people? What type of disgraceful and dangerous persons was he associating with heretics in this formula: "the buggers and the bad people"? Is he thinking of the Jews and usurers here or, from a different perspective, prostitutes or criminals? We are reduced to observing that he did not consider heretics as a completely separate category of people.

The most remarkable thing here is no doubt Saint Louis' desire to purge the kingdom of heretics—not by fire, although he did execute the inquisitors' sentences that condemned people to be burned at the stake—but through expulsion.[15]

Can we identify any connection between this type of punishment and the famous declaration that Louis reportedly made to Joinville about a "great debate" between Christian clerics and Jews held at the abbey of Cluny and that ended with his extended condemnation of all people who "speak ill of the Christian law"?

> The king adds: "I can also tell you that no one should debate with them [the Jews] if he is a very good cleric. But, when any layman hears anyone maligning the Christian law, he should only defend it with his sword and he should thrust it into his enemy's stomach as far as it can go."[16]

Perhaps we shouldn't try to find any coherent position here since it is possible that none existed. Louis may have had contradictory reactions like any other man. Maybe we have to distinguish between the case of a heretic to be driven out and one who openly attacks the Christian law. Or perhaps Joinville, who was more of a warrior than his king, placed his own feelings in the king's mouth.

Whatever the case may be, Saint Louis' attitude toward heretics reveals three principles to us here that he enacted against all people he considered enemies of the Christian faith: they polluted the Kingdom of France that had to be cleansed of them; at least theoretically, faced with "bad people," the only choice was between conversion and expulsion; and orthodox non-Christians were formidable opponents who were better debaters than Christians or at least better debaters than Christian laymen: discussions with them should be avoided.

SAINT LOUIS AND THE MUSLIMS

In relation to the Muslims, his position was clear in principle, but his actual behavior was more complex. Louis dealt with Muslims in Egypt, Palestine, and Tunisia. He usually called them Saracens, an ethnic term with religious implications. The only religious term that he used for them in the texts that have survived for us is "infidels."[17] The Christian West generally considered Muslims as pagans, but we only hear Louis speak of them after he first encountered them in Egypt. At this time, he seemed to understand that they had a religion, which prevented them from being assimilated to pagans, although they were still very close to pagans in his eyes. What he knew about Mohammed and the Koran seems to fall mainly within the realm of impiety and sorcery. In a conversation with the sultan, he mentioned Mohammed as a "magician [*illicebrosus*] who prescribes and allows so many dishonest things."[18] He claimed that he had "looked at and examined" his Koran [*Al-choran*], which he described as "full of filth" [*spurcissimus*]. Due to all this, the attitude to adopt toward the Muslims was simple. War against them was not just allowed, it was recommended, whereas it was supposed to be avoided among Christians. This was the crusade as defined and preached by the Church. Furthermore, the crusade was not a war of aggression. It was not a war of conquest. It was a means for allowing Christendom to retake possession of a land that belonged to it. It was a reconquest. Just as the Christians in Spain were recovering the lands that the Saracens illicitly seized from them, the crusaders wanted to seize the Holy Land from the Saracens in the East, and the Holy Land belonged to them because it was the cradle of Christianity, the site of Christ's worldly existence, and the place where his human body lay from his death on the cross in the afternoon on Holy Friday to his resurrection on Easter morning.

However, his expedition in Egypt had another objective, which he explained to the sultan in a discussion that they had during his captivity. Let's read Matthew Paris's version of this astounding conversation.

On one of those days after the confirmation of the truce when the lord of France and the sultan of Babylon enjoyed holding a long-awaited meeting and informed one another of their respective wishes through a faithful interpreter, with a serene face and a joyous tone the sultan said to the king: "How are you doing, lord king?"

The king answered him in a sad downtrodden tone: "I'm doing the best I can."

"Why don't you answer that you are well," said the sultan. "What is the cause of your sadness?"

And the king replied: "It is because I have not won the thing I wanted to win the most, the thing for which I left the sweet Kingdom of France and my dear mother who was crying as I left, the thing for which I exposed myself to the perils of the sea and war."

The sultan was very surprised and wanted to know what this thing was that he so much desired, and said to him: "And what is it then, O lord king, that you so ardently desire?"

"It is your soul," said the king, "which the devil is promising to throw down into the abyss. But thanks to Jesus Christ who wants all souls to be saved, Satan will never be able to glorify himself with such a handsome prey. The Most High who knows everything knows this; if this entire visible world belonged to me, I would give it all in exchange for the salvation of [your] souls."

The sultan responded: "What! Good king, this was the purpose of your immensely difficult pilgrimage! Here in the Orient we all thought that all you Christians ardently aspired to our submission and that you wanted to triumph over us and conquer our lands out of greed, not out of any desire to save our souls."

"I take the Almighty as my witness," said the king; "I have no concern about ever returning to my Kingdom of France as long as I can win your soul and the souls of other infidels for God, so that they can be glorified."

When he heard this, the sultan said: "In following the law of the most blessed Mohammed we hope to one day come to enjoy the greatest pleasures in the afterlife."

The king immediately replied: "That is why I can only be thoroughly astonished that you men who are discreet and circumspect give your faith to that sorcerer Mohammed who commands and allows so many dishonest things. I have actually looked at and examined his Koran, and I have only seen filth and impurities in it, whereas honesty is the supreme good in this life according to the ancient wise men, the pagans."[19]

Matthew Paris ended up painting an idyllic picture of this scene. The sultan was so moved by Louis' words that he began sobbing, and Louis, caught up in these emotions and feeling that the sultan was near the point of converting, declared that he would never return to France but would stay in the Holy Land for the rest of his life in order to fight to win souls for God, leaving the Kingdom of France under his mother's leadership. The sultan, however, was assassinated several days later, and Divine Providence wiped out this beautiful dream.

What should we think about this obviously staged and embellished version of the event? Were these just the words of a prisoner who wanted to win over his captor? Of course they were, but Saint Louis was not just clever; he was always sincere, and his words here correspond to his obsessive desire for conversion. In addition, this motive did not contradict the enterprise's military character that was meant to initiate relations that led to the conversion of the infidels with the possible intention of establishing communities in the coastal region of Egypt. (This would explain the agricultural implements brought by the king according to one text. The occupation of these territories had the exclusive purpose of assuring the security of a Christian Holy Land. The second crusade to Tunis was probably meant to accomplish the same goal, as Saint Louis' ignorance of geography may have led him to think that Tunisia was another gate to the Holy Land.) Above all, we know rumors that the sultan of Tunis was favorably disposed to the idea of converting to the Christian faith had been a major factor in Saint Louis' decision to undertake the crusade of Tunis.

Matthew Paris's unrealistic text is rooted in a very real and very lively imaginary force that did not exist just for Saint Louis but was shared by many thirteenth-century Christians. That force was the illusion of conversions that gave birth to a passion to convert.[20] Another illusion lay behind this first one. It was Saint Louis' grand illusion and another great illusion of the thirteenth century, the illusion of universal peace. Of course, this peace was supposed to cover a Christian world that extended to all lands and all nations. The king paradoxically appeared here at the heart of this crusade of war as the *rex pacificus,* the artisan of peace on earth, an eschato-logical peace that prefigured the eternal peace to come. It was a millenarian century, and, shorn of its heretical perversion, the wing of millenarianism brushed against Saint Louis who passionately listened to the Joachimite Franciscan Hugh of Digne.

The very Christian king's vision of the Saracens evolved during his stay in Egypt and the Holy Land. What he saw, what others reported to him, and the conversations he had during his captivity and in the course of his follow-ing stay in Palestine all tended to dispel his idea of the Muslims as pagans who had no religion. Although he did not change his opinion about Mo-hammed, the Koran, and the Muslim faith, he did recognize a true religious zeal among at least some of his adversaries. He even learned a few things from them as we saw with his creation of a religious library in the Sainte-Chapelle. For his part, he impressed some of the Muslim leaders who met him or heard about him. Matthew Paris's highly embellished speeches at-tributed to the sultan undoubtedly echo true feelings of admiration. When Matthew Paris put the words "discreet and circumspect" (*discretos et circum-spectos*) in Saint Louis' mouth, this definitely translated the respect that the king of France had conceived for his interlocutors who were also his jailers. This esteem made him all the more regret that they were under the sway of a false, ignoble doctrine that was created and spread by a magician. More-over, we also know that twelfth-century Muslims and Christians in Syria and Palestine sometimes expressed mutual esteem for each other as knights, war-riors, and hunters.[21] For several brief moments in Egypt in 1250, a Christian king and a Muslim sultan were able to express their mutual respect for one another as believers and as men. Why shouldn't we believe this?

Let us go back one more time to look at the texts and more definite re-alities. Two texts attest to Saint Louis' moderation and confirm his politics of conversion in terms of facts and not just in dreams. The first text is by Guillaume de Saint-Pathus.

> The blessed Saint Louis was so incredibly debonair [*fut de si grande débonnaireté*] that when he was overseas he commanded and conveyed the order to all his people not to kill Saracen women and children but to take them alive and bring them in to be baptized. At the same time, he ordered his people to avoid killing the Saracens as much as possible and to capture them and hold them as prisoners.[22]

Our own age quite justifiably cannot accept the idea of these forced conversions. But, at a time when the other more frequent alternative was murder, we can understand how the Franciscan biographer was able to speak of Saint Louis' "*débonnaireté*" in this situation.

The second text is from Geoffroy de Beaulieu.

> While he was residing in the Holy Land, many Saracens sought him out to receive the Christian faith. He received them joyously and had them baptized and instructed them in the faith of Christ. He also took care of all their living expenses. He brought them back to France with him and guaranteed them, their wives, and their children means to live on for their entire lives. He also brought the freedom of many slaves who were Saracens or pagans and had them baptized and provided them with means for survival.[23]

The history of these *harkis* is an interesting episode in the thirteenth century. We must add that there were also many cases of Syrian and Palestinian Christians who converted to Islam, and that the history of the crusades is much more complex than a simple religious and military confrontation between Christians and Muslims.

Saint Louis and the Jews

The Jews probably caused delicate problems for Saint Louis.[24] The first was their number. Jews were numerous in France under Saint Louis. One attentive study by Gérard Nahon leads to the hypothesis that contrary to the received opinion since the thirteenth century that has been adopted by modern historians, Jews in France were more widely dispersed and more numerous than the Jews in Spain whose populations were concentrated in large communities. The numbers in Spain are estimated at roughly 50,000, while there seem to have been between 50,000 and 100,000 Jews in France spread out through the entire kingdom. During the investigations, there were 156 localities "where complaints are leveled against Jews or come from Jews." A precise study shows that the Jewish presence in France was widely dispersed throughout the kingdom. It was strongest in the cities, but was not entirely absent in villages and towns.[25]

There was an important Jewish community in Paris. Out of a population that probably numbered around 150,000 inhabitants (by far the largest city in Christendom), according to serious estimates 3 to 5 percent were Jews, in other words between 4,500 and 7,500 persons.[26] There was a large concentration in the Île de la Cité, probably 20 percent of the island's population. From his palace, the king may therefore have had the impression that there was a strong Jewish infiltration of his capital, if not of his kingdom.

An important development took shape during his reign; to a great extent it was caused by the king's administrative politics. In Gérard Nahon's estimation, we have to envisage the existence of "a veritable geography of Jewish attitudes in thirteenth-century France." Especially at the beginning of Saint Louis' reign, there was an important historical division between the Jews in the North and the Jews in the Midi, although it tended to fade over time.[27]

Saint Louis also knew that the case of the Hebrew religion was different from the Christian heresy or the religion of the Muslims. Jews and Christians had the Old Testament in common. Judaism was a real religion, if not a true religion. Christianity emerged from Judaism, even though the Jews committed the great sin of failing to recognize Jesus, thereby remaining under the old law after it was replaced with the new law of the Gospel. The Jews thus formed the most hated example of those categories of people who embarrassed the Christians of the Middle Ages so much: people who existed both inside and outside of Christendom at the same time. They figured within it due to both their geographical location inside of Christendom spread throughout the Kingdom of France and their partially shared historical religious community. They fell outside of Christendom because their religion did not recognize the true faith, their unified organization in specific separate communities (even though these communities were not as organized in France as they were in Spain), their particular religious customs, a different liturgical calendar, the rite of male circumcision, dietary restrictions, their special religious and educational establishments, and the existence of a type of clergy—the rabbis. In a symbolic order that was both full of imagery and highly internalized, the Synagogue was opposed to the Church just as Error was opposed to Truth.

Finally, a third source of embarrassment was that the king—like all spiritual and temporal leaders in Christendom—had a dual and fundamentally contradictory responsibility toward them. He had a duty to repress the perverse conduct that resulted from their erroneous religion but he also had a duty to protect them akin to his responsibility for protecting widows, minors, and foreigners. According to Guillaume de Chartres, Louis declared that "as a Catholic," in other words as a ruler responsible for all his subjects, "the bishops may do what they are supposed to do for the Christians who depend on them. As for me, I want to do what I am responsible for doing when it comes to the Jews."[28] As we shall see, by this he basically meant that he was responsible for punishing their bad actions just as bishops punished the sins of Christians. He was supposed to act as a kind of "external bishop" for the Jews.

On an even deeper level, Saint Louis' attitude toward the Jews was part and parcel of Christianity's political program for purification that sought to purge Christendom of its impurities in the thirteenth century—a century of political persecution and exclusion.[29] This policy applied directly to the Jews, and the Christians even turned the Jewish dietary taboo against pork against them by insinuating that there was a likeness between Jews and pigs.[30] Saint Louis was very susceptible to this type of accusation, obsessed as he was with his desire for purity and purification.

More generally, certain accusations, old and new, built up a fantasy of sacrilege and anti-Christian criminality around the Jews. The primary accusation was that the Jews murdered Jesus, that they were guilty of deicide. As an impassioned worshipper of Christ, obsessed with his passion, Saint Louis shared this abomination for the Jews in whom the medieval mentality that abolished historical time and believed in collective guilt saw the murderers of Jesus.[31] Then there were the accusations of ritualistic murder that began to appear in the twelfth century and that identified Jews as murderers of Christian children.[32] Finally, there were the accusations that grew louder in the course of the thirteenth century, the century of Eucharistic devotion, that the Jews profaned the sacred host, which represented a real deicide for the Christians who believed in transubstantiation and Christ's real presence within the Eucharist.

In his attitude toward the Jews, Louis also inherited the attitudes of the Church and his predecessors. Canons 67, 68, and 69 of the Fourth Lateran Council, "wanting to prevent Christians from being treated inhumanely by Jews," demanded that the Jews make restitution for interest that was considered usurious (*graves et immoderatas,* in other words excessive) on loans granted to Christians. In the case that they failed to make restitution, Christians were to be banned from doing business with these Jews. The Council also ordered Jews to wear special clothing, notably a round yellow or red mark, the "*rouelle*," on their chests and backs. It also banned them from going outside on the anniversary of Christ's Passion and from exercising any public work. Finally, it declared that the Jews were to be treated as "perpetual serfs." These measures were only partially applied by lords and rulers. Around 1210, Philip Augustus had limited the interest rate that Jews were allowed to raise on loans to Christians in the royal domain, but he had also thereby legalized Jewish lending in a certain way. The legal rate for this "usury" was set at two deniers per pound per week, which amounted to about 43.3 percent. This legislation was extended to the Jews in Normandy in 1218. At the beginning of his reign, Louis VIII decreed a return of interest paid to Jewish creditors and that the reimbursement of borrowed sums was to take place within a period of three years.[33] Jews were thus despoiled of any profits, even legal profits, according to the church legislation. This legislation ran contrary to the interests of the economic development underway because it wound up chasing the Jews out of the "noble" lending market. This market was based on the use of property as collateral (*mortgage*) in order to provide liquidity to landed property holders. Some religious establishments also used this practice, and it has been called a kind of "credit union [*crédit agricole*] before its time." In effect, the constant rise in prices and the immutability of seigniorial revenue from landed property in the thirteenth century led to a strong demand for credit on the part of the lords.[34] However, one reason for this offensive against Jewish credit to borrowers for purposes of economic investment or to maintain a higher standard of living (Jews practiced neither banking for deposit nor transfers of funds) may have originated in the growing demand of Christian merchants who seem to have been entering this type of financial market in force. When the Fourth Lateran Council declared that it wanted to protect Christians from the "perfidy of Jews who exhaust the wealth of Christians in short time," isn't this also, if not primarily, a way of protecting Christian merchants from their competitors? This protection was probably already harmful enough to the economy in terms of the availability of credit during the period of economic growth, but it became even more unfavorable when this expansion petered out in the second part of Saint Louis' reign.

Pushed out of this higher level of lending, the Jews were reduced to practicing credit for consumption involving much smaller sums of money.

According to the *Enquêtes* (Investigations), in 69 percent of quantifiable loans, the capital lent was less than five pounds or one hundred *sous* at a time when ten *sous* represented one or two months of income for the majority of the population in thirteenth-century France. These small sums were often borrowed by using clothing or livestock as collateral. This "legal decline" of Jewish credit (B. Blumenkranz) limited the majority of Jewish lenders to being "small lenders," who "did business mainly with people from modest backgrounds." Thus they became a "lightning rod for popular hatred" due to "their contacts with the mass of little people, as the popular mentality exaggerated their role and described them as 'usurers par excellence'."[35]

However, in relation to the Jews, the French monarchy (like others) practiced a policy that seemed to contradict the restrictions imposed on Jewish lending. It sought to take advantage of Jewish credit for its own financial ends, levying a tax on Jewish "usuries" and arbitrarily imposing taxes on their financial operations or simply and purely confiscating portions of their property like their houses, for example. This kind of taxation was called a *captio,* a "seizure." Philip Augustus carried some of these out in 1210, and Louis VIII executed them in 1224, 1225, and 1226.[36] By stifling Jewish lending, the Capetian monarchy dried up one of its financial resources.

However, in more or less applying the recommendations of the Church, through their attitude toward Jewish "usuries" the Capetians practiced a very incoherent policy from an economic point of view—and Louis aggravated the situation by following in the path of his father and grandfather. As Gérard Nahon effectively puts it: "Jewish credit accompanied the expansion; its decline went hand in hand with the recession already being felt at the end of the thirteenth century. The ecclesiastical doctrine of the Church manages to become part of French law at the very moment when the opposite pressure tied to the economic expansion is weakening."[37]

Describing Saint Louis' feelings and conduct toward the Jews, Guillaume de Chartres made the following statement:

> As for the Jews who are odious to God and men, he held them in such abomination that he could not bear to see them and that he could not stand to have any of their goods turned to his own profit, declaring that he did not want to hold on to any of their venom, nor to allow them to take usuries, but that they would have to make their living from legal trades or businesses, as was the practice in other

countries. Some of his advisors tried to persuade him of the contrary, pretending that the people would not be able to live without loans, and that the lands could not be cultivated without them, and that trades and businesses could not be practiced without them. And they would say that it was preferable and more acceptable for the Jews, who are already damned, to practice the service of this damnation instead of certain Christians who would take advantage of the situation and oppress the people with even greater usuries. He responded to this as a Catholic should: "On the subject of Christians who practice lending and other usuries, this seems to be a matter for the prelates of their churches to deal with. On the other hand, as for the Jews, this is a matter I have to deal with: they are submitted to me by the yoke of servitude. They must not oppress Christians and they must not be allowed to take and infect my land with their venom when they are in the shadow of my protection. Let the prelates do what they have to do in matters concerning the Christians who depend on them. As for me, I want to do what I am supposed to do on the subject of the Jews. They should either give up their usuries or leave my land entirely so that it may no longer be sullied by their filthy actions."[38]

This text contains the previously quoted sentence that Saint Louis used to declare that he was responsible for the Jews.[39] However, as one can see, he basically understood his duty to protect them as a right to suppress them. As for the claim that he did not want to keep any of their property, the documents refute this. In any case, even if this had been his intention—which would have once more put him at odds with his more realistic advisors—his agents acted otherwise. He ended up letting his repugnance for the impurity of Jewish practices explode: they were filth [*ordures, sordes*] that sullied [*inquinare*] "his" land. It was clearly a program for purification and exclusion that is exposed here. And who employed the symbol for the Jewish people in medieval Christendom? The scorpion did, because it was the scorpion that gave off the "venom" that Saint Louis attributed to the Jews two times in this text—that venom that infected "his" land.[40]

The Fourth Lateran Council of 1215 defined the legal status of Jews in Christendom and more specifically in the kingdom: they were "perpetual serfs." This status did not enter into the framework of the monarchical state but into that of the feudal monarchy. Thus Louis acted as he usually did in this case: he recognized the rights of feudal lords that seemed legitimate to him or that he was obligated to respect, and he transgressed them by supplanting them with royal authority whenever he could. He even took advantage of the ecclesiastical legislation in order to lay claim to this authority over the Jews. The edict of 1230 (an edict that is obviously an action taken by his mother and her advisors as he was only sixteen at the time and had not yet taken the reins of power) was the first that applied to the entire kingdom. Furthermore, it articulated a compromise between the king and those lords who held large fiefs because its second article stipulated "that no one in our entire kingdom may hold a Jew from another domain, and in whatever place anyone finds 'his' Jew, he may take him as his own serf for whatever length of time this Jew is found to have stayed in another domain or even in another kingdom." Article 5 also skillfully combined the measure's claim to royal authority throughout the kingdom with the appeal to the feudal assistance of the barons in order to enforce it: "And if any barons do not want to uphold this edict [*établissement*], we will force them to, and all of our other barons will be obligated to help us do this with all their power and good faith." This royal edict of Melun from 1230 was also part of the policy of pacifying the kingdom during the king's long minority, and it was countersigned by the count of the March, the count of Montfort, the constable of France, the count of Saint-Paul, the viscount of Limoges, the duke of Burgundy, the cupbearer of France, the count of Bar-le-Duc, the count of Auge, the count of Châlons, Enguerran de Coucy, Archambaud de Bourbon, Guy de Dampierre, Jean de Nesle, and Guillaume de Vergy. Philip Augustus had also employed this policy. At the beginning of the thirteenth century, "at least in the spirit of the people, the equation serf = Jew tends to spread."[41] In this framework, Philip Augustus worked out agreements after 1200 between the king and various lords like Gaucher de Châtillon in 1210[42] and Count Thibaud de Champagne[43] for the reciprocal return of Jews living on their lands. Nevertheless, it was the Fourth Lateran Council that made this action into a measure to be applied systematically by supporting it with ecclesiastical legislation. In 1218, Philip Augustus instituted a regulation *de judaeis potestatis suae,* "for Jews in dependence on his power."[44]

Louis continued to pass agreements with various powerful lords that provided for the return of Jews considered as serfs.[45]

As William Jordan has clearly demonstrated, the expression *tanquam proprium servum* ("like his own serf") that was used in the edict of Melun of 1230 established an analogy with the fugitive serf. The analogy, however, stops there: the serf could buy his freedom or be considered free after residing in another seigniory for a certain period of time. The Jew could and must be recaptured and returned without delay. A Jew was a *perpetual serf,* just as the Fourth Lateran Council decreed. This legalized his victimization by taxation and confiscation, the *captiones* carried out by the king according to his whims. The Jew could obviously be "exploited at will."[46]

Once again, legislation on the Jews ran counter to the social and economic evolution in progress. In Christendom and particularly in France, the thirteenth century was the time of a significant acceleration in the freeing of serfs. On the other hand, the servitude of the Jews only grew stronger. Jews were increasingly becoming pariahs or outcasts in French society. They were already living in a legal ghetto.

The influence and pressure applied by certain people in his entourage reinforced these precedents and this general context in shaping Saint Louis' attitude. The evidence indicates that Blanche of Castile was very hostile to the Jews as were many Mendicant friars. Finally, converted Jews—often those who had become Dominicans—pressed Saint Louis to brutally crack down on the members of their former religion, much like Robert le Bougre had done against the heretics.

This explains the king's extreme aggression. At the beginning of the text quoted above, Guillaume de Chartres stated: "As for the Jews, odious to God and men, he held them in such abomination that he could not bear to see them." Louis continued and increased the anti-Jewish legislation begun by his father and grandfather. A significant number of the edicts he proclaimed deal with the Jews.[47]

The first, which we already know about, was the famous decree of Melun of 1230. In addition to the two articles from it that we have already examined, there are three others. One forbade the Jews from borrowing, another decreed that their debtors should pay them back in three terms on the three coming festivals of All Saints' Day, and another established that the Jews could not take any interest [*usure*] for the loans that they had made. Usury was defined here as "any sum beyond the principal."

The edict of 1234 obligated Jewish lenders to return one-third of any Christian's debt, forbade debtors from being seized for non-payment of their debts, and outlawed Jews from receiving any collateral that was not declared before credible witnesses under penalty of losing their capital and being tried in a court of royal justice. The royal bailiffs were responsible for executing these measures.

The great reform edict of December 1254 includes two articles on the Jews. Article 32 stipulated that they had to stop "their usuries, sortileges, and characters,"[48] and that the Talmud and "other books in which blasphemies are discovered" were to be burned.[49] People who failed to observe these measures were to be expelled from the kingdom. All Jews had to live "off the labors of their own hands or other work without lending at term or with interest [*à usures*]." Article 33 forbade barons and royal agents from helping them recover their debts; it also repeated the obligation imposed on the barons to not keep Jews from other seigniories on their lands and to prevent them from "taking usuries." It also reiterated the definition of usury as "what exceeds the principal."

In matters of usury, these edicts were not very strictly applied at first. Some barons were afraid to dry up Jewish credit on their lands. Furthermore, certain bailiffs and seneschals exhibited little zeal for applying the royal rulings against the "usuries of Jews." The reiteration and stiffening of these measures in 1254 were accompanied by a much stricter application. A third phase in the French royalty's actions against Jewish credit has been dated to the edict of 1254. After encouraging large-scale credit based on landed property, then limiting Jewish banking activities to lending on short-term collateral (in particular beginning with the edict of Melun in 1230), this final phase deprived Jewish lending practices of any legal existence whatsoever.[50] William Jordan's detailed study has shown that the fight against Jewish usury in Picardy was won by the royalty,[51] and he thinks the same thing may have more or less transpired throughout all of northern France.[52] In the French Midi, Alphonse de Poitiers adopted measures against Jewish usury that were just as strict as his brother's, although we do not know how they were applied.[53] On the other hand, the well-organized Jewish communities in the Narbonnais put up a better resistance.[54]

The royal power added a new assault against the Jews to its fight against usury: the burning of the Talmud. The idea that the sacred book of the Jews was no longer the Bible or the Old Testament but the Talmud appeared in the first half of the thirteenth century. The Talmud, the "oral" Law, was a compilation of commentaries on the Bible, the "written" Law. They were written down between the first and the sixth century A.D. The Talmud of Babylon, a work of the Jewish diaspora in Babylonia, had been composed starting around the end of the fifth century.[55] This new hostility seems to take shape in response to the diffusion of new versions of the Talmud or, in any case, in response to information provided by Mendicant friars, Dominicans in particular, about the content of certain Talmuds and especially the Talmud of Babylon.[56]

A Jewish convert, Nicolas de Donin de la Rochelle, played a key role in instigating this new hostility. Addressing himself directly to Pope Gregory IX, he requested that he no longer treat the Talmud with the same guilty tolerance of his predecessors who had judged that it figured among the sacred books that the Jews could use legitimately. Donin repeated the accusations that were beginning to circulate among certain religious Christians, blaming the Talmud for having replaced the Bible and for being full of blasphemies and insanities directed primarily against Jesus and his mother. Louis could only have been sensitive to these arguments that passed as well founded.[57]

In 1239, Gregory IX addressed a circular letter to all Christian rulers asking them to search their domains and seize all copies of the Talmud "that has anchored the Jews in their perfidy." Blanche of Castile and Louis IX rushed to obey. Copies of the Talmud were seized on March 3, 1240. On June 12 of the same year, an event took place that some called a "debate" (*controverse*) on the Talmud between Jews and Christians, while others called it a "judgment" of the Talmud, and others an "inquisitional trial" of the Talmud. It does not seem very likely that Blanche of Castile, Saint Louis, their religious advisors, and Nicolas Donin would have accepted a contradictory debate with Jews. The inquisitional procedure instituted by the pope in 1233 had probably not yet been perfected; it was more likely a trial with inquisitional trappings that Jewish scholars participated in as mediators between the accused and their accusers. The most well-known scholar in this group was Rabbi Yehiel of Paris. Nicolas Donin was in charge of the prosecution. On the topic of blasphemies against Jesus, Yehiel responded that the Jesus mentioned in the Talmud was not the same Jesus in the New Testament. He observed that many named Jesus existed at that time, just as there were many named Louis in contemporary France who were not kings of France. This remark was all the more ironic in the sense that the given name of Louis was very rare in France outside of the Capetian dynasty at that time, and that most of the others were usually converted Jews that the king had brought to the baptismal fonts, giving them his own first name as their godfather, which was the custom then. As for attacks against the Christians, Yehiel answered that the word "Christians" did not appear a single time in the incriminated texts, which only took issue with the pagans. The outcome of this "judgment" was that the Talmud was condemned to be burned. Gautier Cornut the archbishop of Sens, who assisted the king and the Queen Mother and contested this sentence, unexpectedly died the following year in 1241. The anti-Jewish Christians saw his death as a punishment from God. The king then proceeded to conduct a public cremation of twenty-two cartloads full of manuscripts of the Talmud. Pope Innocent IV who succeeded Gregory IX was even more hostile to the Jews. On May 9, 1244, he sent Louis a letter written in a threatening tone that congratulated him for the burning of 1242, but that urged him to burn any surviving copies. Thus, there was a second public cremation in Paris in 1244, and other auto-da-fés in the following years.

However, in 1247 Innocent IV ordered Saint Louis and his legate for the preparations for the crusade, Eudes de Châteauroux, to return all of the surviving Talmuds to the Jews because they were necessary for their religious practice. This probably occurred in response to various interventions and also resulted from the popes' usual policy of alternating instigations to persecute the Jews with appeals for their protection. Eudes de Châteauroux, however, urged the pope to let them destroy the remaining copies, and on May 15, 1248, under the probable influence of the Dominican Henri de Cologne, Guillaume d'Auvergne the bishop of Paris pronounced a public condemnation of the Talmud.[58]

Several eminent university masters of the time like Albert the Great approved of these measures. The idea of tolerance did not exist. Only a few relatively liberal practices sometimes appeared, and they were usually inspired by opportunism. As we already know, Louis renewed the call for the Talmud's destruction in the Great Edict of 1254.

Once more, we can conclude that the combined zeal of royal agents, a large part of the Mendicant religious, and the Church proved very efficient because there is only a single surviving medieval copy of the Talmud in France. One unexpected result of these actions was the departure of rabbis for Palestine where they founded a Talmudic school in Acre.[59]

Following or innovating upon the acts of his predecessors, Louis adopted other measures against the Jews.

Before his departure, he decreed a *captio* of Jewish properties that was meant to help finance the crusade. He engaged in his policy of expulsion and the spirit of exclusion with greater consistency. He sent an order from the Holy Land in 1253 to have all Jews expelled from the kingdom and reiterated this decision in the form of a threat in the Great Edict of 1254. A new order for their expulsion was issued in 1256. This threat was not definitively executed in France until the fourteenth century, but Saint Louis had done everything to pave the way for its completion.[60]

Finally, Louis ordered the execution of a recommendation of the Fourth Lateran Council. This was a recommendation that Philip Augustus, Louis VIII, and Louis himself for almost his entire reign had not wanted to apply. He did this under pressure—or even blackmail apparently—from a Dominican, the converted Jew Paul Chrétien. In an edict of 1269 he ordered all Jews to wear the distinguishing mark of the *rouelle*. It was not yellow, but scarlet. Here is this shameful text:

> Louis, King of France, to the bailiffs, counts, seneschals, provosts, and all others who hold power from us, salutations. Due to the fact that we want the Jews to be able to be identified and recognized by Christians, we order you—on the request presented to us by our brother in Christ Paul Chrétien of the order of the Preaching Friars—that you impose the wearing of insignia on each and every Jew of both sexes. This sign is to be a wheel of felt or scarlet cloth woven into the upper part of the garment on the chest and on the back that makes them known [i.e., identifiable]. The width of the wheel shall be four fingers in circumference so that the entire circle will contain a palm. Should any Jew henceforth be found without this sign, his upper garment will become the property of his denouncer. Moreover, the Jew who is found without this sign is to be fined up to a sum of ten pounds; however, his penalty must not exceed the aforementioned sum. The fine in this sum must be recorded in the accounts, by us, or upon our order converted to pious use.[61]

The king believed that it was his duty to oppose all these persecutions with another measure that he viewed as positive: the conversion of Jews. He tried to achieve this through actions carried out in the guise of persuasion that were actually forced conversions. For example, he forced

Jews to attend sermons given by Christian preachers. His biographers insisted upon his zeal and the success of these attempts at conversion. In order to show how much importance he attached to it, he often accepted serving as a godfather for converted Jews. Here is an example of this taken from Guillaume de Saint-Pathus.

> The holy king brought a Jewish woman and her three sons and one of her daughters to the baptism at Beaumont-sur-Oise and had them baptized, and the saint king, his mother, and his brothers lifted the Jewish woman and her children from the baptismal fonts at the time of their baptism.[62]

This baptism took place in 1243. The Jewish woman took the name of Blanche from Blanche of Castile, and one of her sons took the name of Louis from the name of the king. In order to entice these highly coveted candidates for conversion, they were guaranteed a pension. We can find traces of this practice in the surviving fragments of the royal accountancy. Thus, for May 18, 1239, we find: "For a converted woman who was Jewish, lodged in the hospice of Paris, 40 sous, witness: the almsgiver. For a recent convert in Gonesse: 40 sous, witness: Thibaud de Saint-Denis."

The Jewish Blanche of Beaumont-sur-Oise would later have a lot of trouble getting the archbishop of Rouen Eudes Rigaud to give her the pension the pope had ordered him to pay her in order to provide for her needs.

The number of these converts was undoubtedly relatively significant. An edict of 1260 granted the mayors of the "good cities" the task of administering justice for the converted Jews.[63] According to Gérard Nahon, "the erosion of Jewish positions" under Saint Louis "is not only economic but religious as well, even before the great policy of converting Jews was undertaken around 1253. . . . The economic rewards of conversion cannot be overlooked. . . . The greater importance of the North and the West in the chapter of conversions is still quite remarkable."[64]

How did the Jews react to all of these persecutions? The most complete text on this that we possess is the protest and complaint sent to Saint Louis by Rabbi Meir ben Simeon of Narbonne between 1245 and 1260.

After attempting to demonstrate the utility of Jewish credit for the king and his Christian subjects, he listed seven iniquitous laws the king had made against the Jews.

Now it so happens that our lord the king has changed and decreed for members of our people who are under his government [laws] and sentences that are unjust according to the Law and the Prophets. The first of these that he has established as a law over the members of our people is that a Jew cannot leave the domain of one lord for the domain of another lord. The second is that he has confiscated our loans and our money with the result that we cannot even feed ourselves or our children, so that a good number of our people have died of starvation. The third is that he has left the levying of taxes [from us] in place and has not abolished it: he should have decreed that no one could demand any taxes from any Jews in his kingdom because he has already taken all their money. . . . The question here is that he ordered his barons—even though it did not please them, and he even decreed the same thing to his bailiffs—not to reimburse the Israelites for the credit they had lent to Gentiles—both for the capital and the interest. The fifth is that of forcing the Israelite to pay back the money that he owes to a Gentile, when an Israelite owes money to a Gentile. The sixth is that we should no longer lend on interest at all, even within the limits allowed us by the Torah according to the opinion of the Ancients, thereby tearing away the subsistence of the poor and miserable among our people who can no longer find work among you. The seventh is that he has confiscated the large homes that the wealthy among our people in his domain possessed, saying: "Let them be satisfied with small houses that are worth between forty and fifty pounds." But, if a man has two or three heirs, this house will not be enough for them, nor for the progeny they engender. The Creator—blessed be His Name—did He not create the world for Adam and Eve so they could give birth to multiple generations?

He then went on to draw up a list of thirty-five painful results of these laws, from the sins and legal violations thus committed by the king to the physical and moral abuses to which the Jews had been subjected. I will take only two of them from this list: "The twenty-fifth is the result that the mean-spirited among his people harass the Jews in every possible way; the twenty-sixth is that people spit at them and upon them." He stressed the resulting poverty for Jewish families, the troubles they had in raising a lot of children, and the economic necessity for young people to marry later in life.

This was a clever address. It expressed everything that should touch the king and lead him to renounce these "laws": his own interest, his piety, his desire for justice and peace, his fear of sin and hell—"Take care for your person and your soul, so that in this world and the other you will not be struck with all the heavy pains that these laws merit because of all the grave sins that they contain."[65]

We do not know if this text ever reached Saint Louis. In any case, near the end of his life on the eve of his second crusade—for which the kingdom's purification appeared to him as a condition for success—he had a tendency to make his anti-Jewish measures even stronger.

What final assessment can we give of Saint Louis' attitude toward the Jews? Touching attempts have been made to deny his cruelty toward the Jews, but they all presuppose a tolerance and an ecumenicalism that were nonexistent in the thirteenth century. Did his only excuse lie in the habitual concepts and conducts of the men of his century, aggravated by his royal responsibilities? It appears undeniable to me that he was more anti-Jewish than a number of the popes, prelates, rulers, and lords of his time. For all that, was there no attenuating circumstance for his behavior?

We know that people who were even more hostile to the Jews than he was spurred him on: certain popes, a large segment of the Mendicant friars in his entourage, the attitude of the Parisian intellectuals, and the hysteria of certain converted Jews. Do we really need to go any further and ask whether his biographers, who were more anti-Jewish than he was, did not exaggerate the expression of his hostile feelings for the Jews? This is true in at least one case. We do know that in his *Instructions* for his son he had written: "Work to remove sins and likewise villainous sins and villainous oaths and destroy and put down heresies whenever you can." His confessor Geoffroy de Beaulieu modified this sentence, and the modified version was added to the pieces for the canonization proceedings. In place of the phrase, "and destroy and put down heresies whenever you can" (*et fais détruire et abaisser à ton pouvoir hérésies*), the confessor substituted, "and above all hold the Jews in great revulsion, and all manners of people who oppose the faith" (*et spécialement tiens en grand vilté juifs et toutes manières de gens qui sont contre la foi*).[66]

Similarly, Aryeh Grabois thinks that the famous passage in Joinville where Louis invited Christians "to thrust their swords into the bellies of Jews,"[67] was probably hardened by the seneschal who was composing his

Histoire de Saint Louis at the time of the great expulsion of the Jews ordered by Philip the Fair in 1306. Even though Joinville may have given an extra thrust to Saint Louis' feelings about the Jews, my impression is that he truly despised them anyway. Besides, Joinville did not particularly care for Philip the Fair and would have been all too happy to expose any of the grandson's contradictions with his sainted grandfather.[68]

I do not believe, as Gérard Nahon does, that we should explain Saint Louis' attitude only in reference to the sentiments of his time: "Through his Jewish policy," he writes, "Saint Louis was fully a saint for the Christian people. It is the very notion of sainthood according to the norms accepted by the Church that is in question here."[69] If this is true, then how is it possible that in his bull and his two sermons for Saint Louis' canonization Boniface VIII did not say a thing about Saint Louis' attitude toward the Jews? Although Saint Louis' attitude toward the Jews obviously did not prevent anyone from proclaiming him a saint, this had not, however, been any argument in favor of his sainthood.

In general, Saint Louis did not have any qualms about making his faith coincide with his politics. With his lone fear of committing sins and not being a good enough Christian, he had doubts when he was faced with the Jews. There were reasons for this that I pointed out when I began this study. The Jewish religion was a true religion so he had to be persuaded that the Talmud was a perverted substitute for the Bible. Although he felt it was his duty to repress Jewish outrages, he also felt responsible for protecting the Jews as they did not fall under the authority of the Christian Church, which, in relation to Christians, could exercise only the dual responsibility of punishment and protection. Hence, his indecisiveness, wavering, and half-hearted regrets. The fact that the measures were issued repeatedly not only shows the difficulty of applying them, but also a certain reticence on the king's part about pushing their execution too far and too fast. We can see he had doubts about the definition of usury that were identical to those of the Church itself.[70] Besides, the Jews were not the only ones implicated in the question of usury and the question of defending the Christian faith. Although Louis spared his Christian subjects who practiced usury, he ended up condemning the usury of the Lombards (Italians) and Cahorsins who were also affected by the kingdom's purification because they were foreigners. Between September 1268 and 1269, the king decided to expel them from the kingdom, and their debtors had to reimburse them for their loans with the exception of usury, in other words, with the exception of the interest they owed.[71] The harshness of the announced measures was probably intended in part to frighten the Jews and lead them to convert. It was supposed to lead to that hypocritically forced conversion that the people of the time considered a form of leniency toward the Jews. Louis took until the end of his reign to give in to the pressure that led him to impose the *rouelle* on them.

In 1257, Saint Louis took a few actions to correct the plundering of the Jews that these measures had engendered. He designated three churchmen he trusted—the bishop of Orléans, Abbot Bonneval, and the archdeacon of Poissy—to correct the abuses committed during the *captio* before the crusade and in the course of the expulsions of 1253–1254. Although they were still charged with overseeing the refund of Jewish "usuries," these commissioners were also responsible for enforcing the return of property seized from the Jews wherever this had not already been done. We may remember that the king had assured that "he had no intention of keeping them [i.e., Jewish goods and property]." Although he granted these commissioners "full power to sell the houses, rental properties, and all other immovable goods of Jews" that had been legally confiscated, he "nonetheless wants the former synagogues with the implements without which they cannot properly worship in their synagogues to be returned to these Jews."[72] We can determine that these *old* synagogues must be the ones that existed before the canonical interdiction against building new synagogues that was imposed on the Jews under Philip Augustus at the beginning of the thirteenth century, and that, therefore, there could not have been very many of them. However, this order for restitution shows that Saint Louis meant to respect the Christian tradition of tolerance for the Jews' religious practices. The Jewish religion had always been recognized in contrast to heresy and the Muslim religion.

Similarly, in the case of the only pogrom known to have taken place in France under his reign, Saint Louis had the guilty parties arrested when they were found. We only know about this massacre from a letter that Pope Gregory IX sent to the king of France on September 5, 1236 that asked him to protect the Jews. This pogrom in Anjou and Poitou was the act of members of the lower classes who believed it was preparation for a crusade. The bailiffs looked for the Christians who had participated in the "slaughter of Jews" and imposed fines on the would-be "crusaders" they were able to arrest.[73]

Finally, we do not know of any case of accusations of ritual murder made against the Jews during his reign.

How should we characterize Saint Louis' politics and attitude toward the Jews? We have two terms available to us today: anti-Judaism and anti-Semitism. The first term exclusively applies to religion, and, whatever the importance of religion in Jewish society and Saint Louis' behavior toward it, the term is still inadequate. The group of programs effected by this behavior surpasses the limited framework of religion and brings feelings of hatred and a will for exclusion into play, and these feelings exceed mere hostility to the Jewish religion. Anti-Semitism, however, is inadequate and anachronistic.[74] There was no racial component in Saint Louis' attitude and ideas. We have to wait until the nineteenth century to see pseudo-scientific racial theories that feed racist and anti-Semitic mentalities and sensibilities. In my view, we can only use the term "anti-Jewish" to characterize Saint Louis' conduct, although his anti-Jewish concepts, practice, and politics paved the way for future anti-Semitism. Saint Louis was a signpost on the road of French, Western, and Christian anti-Semitism.

CRITICISMS AND RESISTANCE

Although the documents stressed the veneration and admiration that Saint Louis' entourage, subjects, all of Christendom, and even his Muslim enemies felt for him, they did not conceal a certain number of criticisms and resistances that were expressed against him. Some of these came from his entourage itself, others from various social milieus, from men and women in the kingdom, and foreigners. Some of them targeted his personal conduct; others focused on aspects of his politics. However, the majority of the criticism revolved around religion. They targeted his devoutness and his practice of peace and justice.

First, we have to make a special place for the reproach that he was indifferent to the queen and his children. We can only find this reproach in Joinville, but he was an eyewitness and, as we know, very favorable to the king overall.[75]

His entourage (clerics, servants, familiar friends) became irritated with his practices of worship that they considered excessive and that sometimes made the king unbearable to them. For example, he got out of bed very early in the morning without a sound in order to go to church, which caused chaos among his guards who woke up too late to get dressed in time to follow him to the church:

> And sometimes he would get up so quietly from his bed and get dressed and shod in order to go into the church so early that the others who were still in bed in his chamber did not even have time to put their shoes on and had to run after him barefoot.[76]

When he went to Royaumont to help the monks transport the stones for the abbey's construction, he forced his brothers to do the same. They balked at this hard labor.[77]

When he forced the sailors of his ship to listen to the religious services, when he obliged his entourage to listen to interminable sermons, when he made the members of his household sit down around him to listen to him preach to them, we do not possess any testimony about the reactions they had to all this forced devoutness, but we can bet that they did not simply feel gratitude for the king who tried to assure their salvation despite themselves.

For example, what did his bodyguards think when they could no longer eat in taverns and were forced to listen to sermons as they ate?

> And so that the sergeants in arms would be more willing to attend sermons, he ordered them to eat in the palace, whereas these sergeants were not in the habit of eating there, but received wages for their expenses to eat outside. The saint continued to give them the same wages but they were henceforth fed at the court.[78]

Their worship was forced but paid. Before the sermon, a group of men left the church of Compiègne where the king was listening to mass to go to the tavern across the way. What did they think when Saint Louis ordered his sergeants to forcefully bring them back into the church?

In the thirteenth century, taverns were starting to become important spaces for male entertainment, sociability, and communication. Saint Louis opposed them almost as much as brothels. When he tried to completely outlaw brothels and prostitution, his advisors—who were mostly religious— dissuaded him from engaging in this pointless battle because the Church knew the flesh was weak and that original sin made lapses inevitable.

The religious in his entourage also combated his excesses in worship and personal asceticism. The fasts, the flagellations, the exaggerated attendance of countless services even at night, all these typical practices of the monks of the High Middle Ages, hermits, and the religious of the most ascetic orders were no longer appropriate for Christians whose religion was in the process of becoming less excessive. All these practices were especially inappropriate for laymen.

They were inappropriate for a layman and they were even less appropriate for a king. Saint Louis took Christ as his obsessive model. Prevented from carrying out the gestures reserved for the divine person or the priests, there was one act of Christ-like humility for which he developed a liking—washing the feet of the poor or monks, especially during the holy week, as we have seen.[79] On Good Friday, when they wanted to shoo away the poor people who assailed him, "he would say that instead they should leave them, because Christ suffered more for us on this day than I am suffering today for Him." Saint Louis' deepest aspiration is revealed here: to imitate Christ in suffering.[80]

When he asked Joinville if he too washed the feet of the poor on Ascension Day, the seneschal cried out, God forbid! The king was quite disappointed with his faithful companion. On Saturdays, whenever he could, he got down on his knees and washed the feet of three old poor men. He did this in secret out of his excessive humility but also to avoid any reproaches for it. When he finished washing their feet, he kissed them, and then he washed their hands and kissed them too. Sometimes he gave them money and served them something to eat at his table.[81]

He also wanted to wash the feet of certain monks. That would round out his practices of humility—washing the feet of men who were vowed to poverty as well as the feet of men who were poor despite themselves.

Both Geoffroy de Beaulieu and Guillaume de Saint-Pathus reported this anecdote, although two things differ between their two versions. They both agree that it took place in a Cistercian abbey in the context of the custom that the Cistercian monks had of washing one another's feet on Saturdays. Geoffroy placed the scene in Clairvaux. Saint Louis was present at the abbey one Saturday, and wanted to take part in the rite and wash the monks' feet. But, certain important laymen [*magnats*] who were with him and who were not part of his usual company—which suggests that they were even more shocked—let him know that an act of humility like this was not appropriate for him. Louis gave in to their advice.[82] According to Guillaume,

the scene took place at Royaumont, and it was the abbot himself who dissuaded the king: "He said to the abbot: 'It would be a good thing if I could
wash the monks' feet.' And the abbot answered him: 'Renounce suffering
this action!' And the holy king asked him: 'Why?' And the abbot answered:
'People will talk about it [*jaseraient*].' And the saint king answered and said:
'What would they say?' And the abbot replied that some people would say
good things and others would say bad things, and so the king gave up this
desire, because the abbot dissuaded him, as this man believes."[83]

Whatever the truth may be, we can see that the tradition retained the
opposition of both the powerful laymen and the churchmen to the king's
acts of self-humiliation. The reasons for their opposition were complex.
The king was not at home in a Cistercian abbey, but, more than this, the
gesture was incompatible with what the royal *dignitas* had become. In his
idea of the "king as an image of God," Saint Louis had a tendency to mold
himself after the image of Christ, the Christ of the Passion, but for his
subjects he was also and increasingly the image of the God of *majesty*. This
was the *majestas* of God the Father and of Christ as it appears in sculpture
on the gates of the cathedrals throughout his kingdom. Louis was torn between the majesty of God and the humility of Christ. Once more, he took
on both images.

In the critique of royal conduct, the excess of his charitable expenses
shows up alongside these excessive acts of humility. People blamed him
for giving away too much in alms and for spending too much on the construction of religious edifices. He rejected these reproaches, justified his
actions, and refused to change. Here is the testimony of Guillaume de
Nangis:

> Realizing that some members of his familiar circle were com-
> plaining about the largesse of his almsgiving, he told them that when
> it came to occasional excesses of liberality, he preferred that these
> excesses were committed in the form of alms given for the love of
> God instead of in worldly frivolities. The excess he committed in
> spiritual actions excused and redeemed the excess that he too often
> had to engage in by spending on worldly things.

Guillaume then added something that showed how Saint Louis' politics
struck a balance between Christian charity and royal dignity.

But, in effect, in the royal ceremonies and the daily expenses of his house as well as in the *parlements* and meetings of the knights and barons, he carried himself with a liberality and generosity appropriate for royal dignity; and he was served in his house as fitting for a court, more than was done at the courts of the kings who were his predecessors for a very long time.[84]

People also reproached him for his excessive harshness in dealing with actions and habits he detested. For example, people blamed him for his cruel ways of punishing blasphemers.[85]

When people close to him blamed him for his excessive spending for the construction of Franciscan and Dominican convents in Paris, he cried out:

> My God! I believe that this money is well spent on all those eminent friars who converge on these Parisian convents from all over the world in order to study the sacred science, and who, once they have drawn from it, go back out through the entire world to spread it for the love of God and the salvation of souls![86]

On other occasions, he justified the excessive liberality toward the religious and the poor that people reproached him with by mentioning his function as a minister of God charged with dispensing generous gifts:

> And when some of his advisors upbraided him for his large spending for the houses of the religious and the large amount of alms he would give to them, the saint king replied: "Be quiet. God gave me everything I have. What I spend like this could not be any better spent."[87]

POLITICAL CRITICISMS

With these last quotes we have passed from an essentially private and personal terrain into the public, political realm.

We have seen that the English Benedictine Matthew Paris did not have an exclusively favorable image of Saint Louis, although he admired the French king in many ways.[88] It is interesting that some of his criticisms undoubtedly circulated in other milieus outside of the English abbey of Saint Albans and even in France.

Matthew's first criticism was leveled against the act of abandoning power to a woman. For the year 1235, Matthew condemned the young king when he refused to recognize English rights over the territories in western France. Blanche of Castile was singled out as the guilty party here, and Louis IX's mistake lay in obeying his mother instead of justice: "All these rights [of the king of England], the king of France pretends to ignore them, preferring to follow the advice of a woman more than the rule of justice, forgetting fear of the God of vengeance."[89] Matthew also approved of the revolt of the great French feudal lords in 1236: "They were indignant that the kingdom of kingdoms, in other words France [la Gaule-Gallia] was governed by a woman."[90] In 1242, when the rupture broke out between Henry III and Louis IX, Matthew was infuriated with a measure taken by the king of France that heralded the economic aspects of the wars that the monarchical states would wage in the future.

> In the most improper fashion, the king of France savagely had the persons and goods of the English merchants doing business in his kingdom seized, thereby doing enormous harm to the ancient dignity of France [*Gaule*]. In effect, this country had a tradition of offering shelter and safety to all fugitives and exiles and manifestly came to their defense; hence the name of France had been given to it in its own language.[91]

In the meantime, Matthew Paris became one of Blanche of Castile's admirers. In 1241 during the Mongol invasion he called her, "the queen Blanche, the mother of the king of France, and venerable matron beloved by God." He exploded against Saint Louis for the last time at the moment of the crusade, violently blaming him for having it financed by the Church, which was crushed by the burden of the financial contribution demanded by the king of France with the pope's authorization. Matthew was an embittered religious.

Inside the Kingdom of France, there were three main criticisms voiced against the king's politics.

The first was usually formulated by some of his advisors; it targeted his politics of appeasement. They had trouble accepting his reign insofar as it represented a peaceable interlude between endemic feudal wars and threatening "national" wars. They were especially critical of the treaty of Paris with England. As the victor on the battlefield, the king could have dictated his conditions, so, for them, the compromise he offered to the king of England was a sign of weakness.[92]

The second criticism coming out of the seigniorial milieu concerned the restrictions imposed on the powers of nobles and the loss of their independence and full and complete authority within their fiefs. We saw how this took place in the Enguerran de Coucy affair.[93] One song expressed the rancor of a man who wanted to "stay master of my fief."[94] Its scholarly editor dates it from the end of the reign.

> People of France, now you are quite stunned! I tell all the people who are born in the fiefs: By God, you are no longer free [*franc*]; they have taken you far away from your freedoms [*franchises*], because now you are judged by investigation. They have cruelly tricked and betrayed you all, since no defense can help you now. Sweet France! We need not call you this anymore, but we now have to call you a country of slaves, a land of cowards, a kingdom of the miserable poor, exposed to endless violence.
>
> What I know in truth is that servitude like this does not come from God! As exploited as he may be. Alas! Loyalty, poor astounded thing, you won't find anyone to take pity on you. You may have might and power and be strong on your feet, because you are the friend of our king, but your partisans are spread out too thinly around him. I only know of a single one of them, after the king, but he is held down so firmly by the hands of the clergy that he cannot come to your assistance. They have ground up charity and sin and mixed them all together.
>
> And don't let anyone think that I am saying this to attack my lord; Heaven forbid. But I am afraid that his soul might be lost for this, and then I am glad to still be the master of my fief. When he knows that, he will do swift justice; his noble heart would not stand to have things any differently. This is why I want him to be well warned and instructed about it. This way that enemy devil who is lying in wait for him won't have any power over him. I would have failed my faith if I had left my lord ill advised like that.

This text contains all the commonplaces of remonstrances addressed to a ruler. The king was not the guilty party. It was all the fault of his advisors. The author of the song perfidiously turned the king's personal ethic against him. The king who was so concerned about his soul's salvation, who was so preoccupied with justice, and who called on the advice of good people, he was poised to flout justice, to listen to bad advice, and to fall prey to the devil. Could anyone say anything worse to Saint Louis?

Finally, there was this outrageous attack that showed that by replacing the old procedures that respected feudal freedoms with the investigative procedure, Saint Louis had hit the nail on the head. The song's author did not hesitate to speak of betrayal and the *laudator temporis acti,* the good old days of feudalism, when he blew up: "Sweet France! We need not call you this anymore, but we now have to call you a country of slaves, a land of cowards, a kingdom of the miserable poor, exposed to endless violence."

It is interesting to observe that this violent pamphlet assumed the form of a song. This means that the people who held this point of view did not have the direct means to oppose these decisions militarily or legally. However, as the thirteenth century was the time when the political song was developed, they seized upon one of the instruments for forming public opinion, which appeared in full force in France under Philip the Fair. In the meantime, in a more punctual and more quotidian form, the grievances formulated here against the actions of the king's agents revealed the discontentment provoked by the centralization of the kingdom.[95]

One third and final criticism here seems like it was fairly widespread, notably in milieus that can be described as "popular." It denounced Louis' habit of surrounding himself with religious and identified them as the people who primarily inspired not only his personal conduct but his politics as well. Opinion toward these religious was still very divided, particularly when it came to the friars of the Mendicant orders, the Dominicans and Franciscans.[96] Many people were violently hostile to these explorers of conscience, these excavators of private life who invaded houses and families, these hijackers of testaments, these zealots of poverty who became great specialists in matters of money. The image of the Mendicant friar was an image of the hypocrite, the "*faux-semblant*" (false pretense) character in the *Roman de la Rose.* Jean de Meung and Rutebeuf directly implicated Saint Louis for his privileged relations with the Mendicants although they represented a more or less limited intellectual milieu.[97] However, there is another text that reveals this hostility to us as it spilled beyond this milieu and sometimes took on very violent expressions.

"You Are Only the King of the Friars"

We have already seen this episode reported by Guillaume de Saint-Pathus.[98] A woman named Sarrete insulted the king at the foot of the stairs in the palace one day when parlement was in session. She was surprised that no one had chased him off his throne. What did she rebuke him for then? "You are only the king of the Minor friars and the Preaching friars, of priests and clerics!"[99]

If the Franciscan recorded this anecdote for posterity, it was because he wanted to turn it to Saint Louis' advantage. The king prevented his sergeants from kicking Sarrete out and even from touching her. He told the woman that she was right, that he was not worthy of being king, that someone else could govern the kingdom better. Then, he had his chamberlains give her some money.

But the damage was done. Thus, we learn that there was at least one anti-clerical woman in Saint Louis' time, and that everyone was not gaping in admiration before the saint king, and that not everyone was favorably impressed by his devoutness.

Another anecdote was not satisfied with simply criticizing the king but attempted to ridicule him with a physical caricature of a sanctimonious, "stuttering" [béguin] king. Its social framework was the milieu of the high nobility. The count of Gueldre Otton II (1229–1271) had married a French woman, Philippa the daughter of Simon de Dammartin the count of Ponthieu. He sent a messenger to Paris, perhaps for some legal affair. After he returned, Otton de Gueldre asked him about the king of France. The messenger related that a secular preacher had accused the Preaching friars "who advise so much humility to the king" of committing mortal sins. Then, "twisting his neck" in derision, he told the count: "I saw him. I saw that miserable holier-than-thou king with a hood hanging behind him for a hat." The story was narrated by the Dominican Thomas de Cantimpré who used it to praise the king of France's conduct and avenge him with a miracle that was supposed to have taken place while the king was still alive. The insulting messenger who had imitated the pious king and made fun of his silhouette became stuck in this "counterfeit" posture for the rest of his life.[100]

There were more profound changes in mentalities and sensibilities at work behind these differences between Saint Louis and his contemporaries, although they may often seem like they are simply anecdotal. We are faced with a kind of revolving dance [*chasse-croisé*]. As much as Saint Louis respected the essential practices of "feudal" society, he referred to values of justice and peace that demolished feudal customs and that moved the royal function closer to the modern state. Likewise, his way of using feudal concepts in order to advance the monarchical state was not understood. When he behaved like a monk-king and appeared to give up some of his power to the religious, public opinion (or its forming skeleton) did not follow. The crown was actually in the process of becoming a sacred secular object.

Public opinion on the crusade was more divided. It still shared Saint Louis' nostalgia for Jerusalem, a Jerusalem that still needed to be regained by methods that were not limited only to military means. Saint Francis went that route. Joinville, however, was certainly not the only one in the Kingdom of France to look more toward his Champagne than to the Holy Land. With this shifting glance that was tied to a change in political representations (European Christendom or Oriental-European?), we are not far from our old study question: was Saint Louis feudal or modern? We have managed to ask this question in different terms: if we want to use these concepts, the crusade is plainly the supreme stage of feudalism. But, by failing resoundingly in his crusades, without knowing this and without ever having wished for it, Saint Louis struck a fatal blow to classical feudalism.

9

Saint Louis, Sacred King, Thaumaturge, and Saint

SAINT LOUIS WAS A CHARISMATIC PERSON.[1] FOR THOSE WHO HAD been around the king, insofar as it could be defined this charisma had its source in the aura that surrounded his person. For those who knew him only through hearsay, it originated in the extraordinary character of the image of him that had been transmitted to them. To describe this image, his contemporaries only had the term "saint" at their disposal, but we are talking about an exceptional saint here. What Saint Francis had been as a religious, Louis was as a layman and a king. In his canonization bull, Boniface VIII attempted to express this with the term *superhomo,* "*surhomme*," superman.

His charisma was not just an instinctive, irrational given. It included specific dynastic and categorical traits, the qualities of a sacred and thaumaturgical king as well as the individual merits of sainthood sanctioned by an official canonization.

It is important to make a clear distinction between the traits held in common by the kings of France and the ones that belonged to Saint Louis himself.

THE SACRED STATUSES OF THE KING OF FRANCE

This is the right point to shed a little light on a realm often approached in ways that can cause some confusion; we can start by distinguishing between several different concepts: the sacred, the religious, the sacerdotal, and the thaumaturgical. Taken together, these different elements formed a coherent system that characterized royal power and its representations in medieval France. This system was built up through the various failures and successes of the Capetian monarchy in its attempts to extend the reality and the image of its power from the accession of Hugh Capet in 987 to the canonization of Saint Louis in 1297.[2]

THE VALUES OF THE CORONATION

The fundamental sacred and religious traits of a Capetian king were expressed in the coronation liturgy. Another important source is made up of the royal chronicles and biographies, and the specific examples are the *Vie de Robert le Pieux* written by the monk Helgaud de Fleury, Suger's *Vie de Louis VI,* the works of Rigord de Saint-Denis and Guillaume le Breton that had Philip Augustus as their hero, and the biographies, hagiographies, and collections of miracles about Saint Louis. The thirteenth-century Mirrors of the Princes actually contributed very little to the image of the sacred Capetian king. However, the coronation ceremony can itself be read as a Mirror of the Princes that was acted out and that existed in a condensed form. We possess few accounts of coronations of Capetian kings. The main example is from the coronation of Philip I in 1059, and the account is rather brief because its goal was to justify the exclusive rights of the church of Reims to hold the anointment and crowning of the kings of the Western Franks.

There are three royal *ordines* that quite probably date from Saint Louis' reign. One is from the beginning of his reign and is called the *ordo* of Reims. One is from the end of his reign and is known as the "last Capetian *ordo.*" Another falls between these two. I refer to it as the *ordo* of 1250, and it includes the invaluable eighteen miniatures that present us with the structure, the process, and the key moments of the coronation.[3]

The consecration was a kind of sanctification. The *sacred*[4] was what expressed and usually created a tie with supernatural powers, the ability to play a part in exercising these powers, and, in a Christian society, a direct relationship with God. More than just a delegation of power (although this was there too, represented by the crowning: *rex a Deo coronatus,* a "king crowned by God"), the coronation assured the insufflation of the supernatural forces through the unction and the manifestation of the bestowal of some of these forces through the conferral of the symbolic emblems of power.

The *religious* is harder to define in a society that had scarcely any notion of the *civil,* and that distinguished between the temporal and the spiritual. It was basically everything that involved the regular functioning of the sacred here on earth as essentially assured by the Church. The religious function of the monarchy thus consisted in allowing, aiding, and favoring the Church's role and action. During the coronation, this was expressed most of all in the responsibilities that the king took on in his oath. These responsibilities can be summed up in the notion of his role as the "secular arm" of the Church.

The *sacerdotal* designated everything that conferred any of the characters or functions of a man of the Church upon the king. The coronation ritual evoked a certain characteristic of the sovereign that was simultaneously episcopal, sacerdotal, and diaconal. However, there were strict limitations that prevented the king from being and appearing as a *rex sacerdos,* a "priest king."

Finally, the *thaumaturgical* was close to the magical and evoked the king of France's recognized supernatural power to heal others in well-defined and more or less ceremonious circumstances—on festival days, in sacred places like a cloister. He exercised this healing power through his touch, accompanied by the sign of the cross, which was a christianized form of a magical ritual gesture. The sick people he healed all suffered from a particular disease—scrofula or adenoid tuberculosis, the *morbus regius,* the royal disease, in other words the disease that could be healed by the king.[5] Contemporaries attributed the pious addition of the sign of the cross in the healing gesture to Saint Louis, although earlier kings are known to have used it too.[6]

THE ROYAL CORONATION

The coronation was closely tied to the anointment. The archbishop of Reims anointed the king on his head, his chest, between his shoulders, on his shoulders, on the joints of his arms, and, finally, shortly thereafter, on his hands. All the meaningful parts of the king's body, all the centers of his strength, were endowed with the holy chrism, the oil that the Holy Spirit miraculously brought to Rémi the bishop of Reims for Clovis's baptism. Each time, the archbishop took it out of the Holy Ampulla where the miraculous oil was stored. The Ampulla was kept in the monastery of Saint-Rémi, and the abbot of Saint-Rémi came to the cathedral to bring it for the coronation.

Endowed with this supernatural power, the king was henceforth the sacred intermediary between God and his people. Divine protection and divine inspiration passed through him and his anointed body. He was the link between God and his people, and, until his death, he assured divine assistance for his kingdom and his people, not only for their safety here on earth, but especially for their salvation in the afterlife.

The sacred was also transmitted to the king through the intermediary of the royal emblems he received in the course of the ceremony.

The first phase preceding the unction was the royal dubbing.[7] At this point, the king began to receive some of the objects that had been placed on the altar by the abbot of Saint-Denis who brought them. These objects invested the king with a sacred status increased by their contact with the most sacred part of the church—the altar. The king completed the rite of *separation* that comprised the initial phase of the rite of passage that transformed him from a king by heredity into a king by religious consecration. He brought the rite of separation to a close by shedding his old outer garments. He then received slippers decorated with fleurs-de-lis from his grand chamberlain, golden spurs from the duke of Burgundy, sword and scabbard from the archbishop, all given in the course of a complex ritual in which they were placed upon and withdrawn from the altar. The sword made the king the secular arm of the Church, and the seneschal of France would now begin to wear it unsheathed.[8]

The coronation's second phase after the anointment was the conferment of the royal insignia proper.[9] The chamberlain gave the king the hyacinth tunic. This was the color of the robes of the great Israelite priest, and it became the adopted color of the French kings who identified blue as the color of power and the sacred. (It was also the color of the Virgin, which became the fashionable color of the time thanks to the intensive use of pastel.) The tunic was dotted with golden fleurs-de-lis and had a cope or covering that went over it. Then the archbishop gave the king the ring, the sign of royal dignity and the catholic faith, and perhaps also of the marriage that God was contracting with his people. He placed the scepter, the symbol of sacred power, in Louis' right hand and a hand of justice in his left hand, which appeared for the first time in Louis' coronation, replacing the wand that had been used in the past.

We must highlight the appearance here of the clothing decorated with golden fleurs-de-lis. The fleur-de-lis was in the process of becoming the most sacred symbol of the royal insignia. According to one recent study, it was a solar symbol.[10] Saint Louis and probably Philip Augustus and Louis VIII before him were already sun-kings.

The third and final phase was the crowning. It was marked by two episodes: first, there was the placing of the crown, a "barbarian" variation on the old diadem of sacred imperial Hellenistic royalty; then, there was the installment on the raised throne, symbolizing the primordial mountain as a cosmic seat of power.

The placing of the crown by the archbishop played on the idea of the collaboration of the twelve peers from the legend of Charlemagne in the royal sanctification by calling upon six bishops and six powerful secular lords to take part in the royal ritual. This gesture integrated the ecclesiastical and laical aristocracies.

The religious was especially evident in the oaths the king pronounced during the coronation. According to the *ordines* of Reims and 1250, the king pronounced four series of oaths:

(1) First, he promised the Church to protect it, both its persons and its property.

(2) Next, he promised to uphold the rule of peace and justice — values that had strong religious and even eschatological connotations — and to engage in acts of mercy after God's example (a supplementary oath introduced into the ceremony after the Fourth Lateran Council of 1215 established the king's commitment to fighting heretics).

(3) He promised to defend the holy Catholic faith, to be the protector and defender of the churches and their ministers, to rule and defend the kingdom that God had given him in accordance with the tradition of justice of his forefathers.

(4) Finally, after the crowning and enthronement, the king made one last comprehensive promise, *coram Deo, clero et populo* (before God, the clergy, and the people).

In fact, and in a general way, in these oaths taken during the coronation a pact was concluded between the king and the Church. The Church spoke for itself here, and for the people for whom it presented itself as the representative. The miniatures from the manuscript of the *ordo* of 1250 clearly show their concern for respecting an initial inequality between the clergy and the king with the consecrator presented as superior to the consecrated. The ceremony ended with the king presented as having a certain superiority over the clergy. The kiss of peace (and of homage) that the archbishop gave the crowned king on his throne may be the symbol of this promotion of the crowned and anointed king, the "sanctified" king.

As for the sacerdotal aspect of the ceremony, we have to make note of the important fact that the Capetian king did not attain and undoubtedly did not seek to attain the status of a *rex sacerdos,* of a "priest king." He was still a layman both during and after the coronation. However, just as the coronation and interment of kings were carried out in a part of the church adjacent to the choir reserved for the clergy and that was even just before this choir, the Capetian king did receive several secondary elements of ecclesiastical dignity.

In the course of the coronation ritual, the king resembled a deacon at times, a priest at others (his cope was raised upon his left arm like a sacerdotal chasuble), and sometimes he even looked like a bishop:[11] like the bishop and the bishop alone he received an unction upon his forehead.[12] During the mass that followed the ceremony, the king took communion under two species after the example of the preachers, although this was a unique moment that would never occur again in his life.

Finally, he held the *thaumaturgical* power, the power to heal the sick, although it was limited to healing a single disease: scrofula. It is hard to determine how and when the ancient belief in kings' ability to cure disease changed in content. For Isidore de Séville in the seventh century, jaundice was the *morbus regius.* Before this, Saint Jerome thought it was leprosy. For the Capetian kings, it is scrofula. Marc Bloch no doubt overestimated the meaning of certain texts in which he detected the practice of the royal miracle of touching the scrofulous. He probably also dates the Capetians' regular institutional exercise of the royal miracle to too early a time. Philip I touched the scrofulous and then lost his thaumaturgical powers because of his sins. Louis VI laid hands on the scrofulous, but we do not know how many times. There are no texts that allow us to conclude that Louis VII,

Philip Augustus, and Louis VIII exercised this power. It seems prudent to date the regular practice of the royal laying-on-hands as beginning only with Saint Louis.[13] From Saint Louis to Louis XIV, this first use of the royal touch was exercised exclusively in the nearby sanctuary of Saint-Marcoul in Corbeny.[14]

THE CORONATION SYSTEM

At the end of Saint Louis' reign the ceremonies that established the sacredness of royal power formed a system.

The description of the king as he awakened in the morning in the room where two bishops had come for him completed the initiation rite at its inception. This rite transformed the king, designated as king by the custom of the hereditary transmission of power by primogeniture along the male line, into a king sanctified by the divine unction dispensed by the Church in exchange for royal promises sworn as oaths. The Rhemish liturgy tied together the oaths, the anointment, the bestowal of the royal insignia in two distinct phases, the crowning, and the enthronement.[15] At the end, it was completed by the first exercise of the royal laying-on-hands by virtue of the thaumaturgical power acquired through the unction made of an oil that was miraculous and generative in itself. Because it had touched him, this miraculous liquid gave the king the power to touch and miraculously heal people suffering from scrofula.

Moreover, through the presence and participation of their religious leaders, the ceremony of Reims united the three sanctuaries that were the centers of the royal religion: Saint-Rémi of Reims represented by its abbot who was the keeper of the Holy Ampulla, the cathedral of Reims, the site of the coronation represented by its archbishop,[16] and Saint-Denis represented by its abbot who kept the royal insignia. It was at Saint-Denis that the exercise of the sacred and religious power that each king held since his coronation came to rest in the sanctity of a royal sepulcher.

With Saint Louis, the construction of the "royal religion" had almost reached its high point.

The new *ordines* separated the royal French coronation from the common European custom it had originally been a part of and, in particular, since the *ordo* of Fulrad at the end of the tenth century. Although we find a passage borrowed from the imperial *ordo* in one of the oaths taken by the king of France, an oath that could only validly be pronounced by the emperor, I do not think that this was because someone forgot to remove it as Schramm has suggested, but because the king of France found the means to assert himself—not as *imperator in regno suo* (an emperor in his kingdom), but as Innocent III had allowed for Philip Augustus, as "recognizing no superior in his kingdom."[17]

The new *ordines* placed the liturgy of the Holy Ampulla at the center of the consecration ceremony and thus proclaimed the king of France's superiority over all other Christian kings because he alone was anointed with the miraculous oil contained in a relic: he was a *rex christianissimus.* This better allowed him to legitimate his thaumaturgical power of touching the scrofulous, which he was undoubtedly the first king to have exercised in a regular and institutional way.

The new *ordines* also introduced a new object among the royal insignia, the hand of justice. In monarchical ideology and especially in Christian monarchical ideology, justice, along with peace, was the principal royal function, a function that was fundamentally grounded in the sacred.[18]

We should not forget that Saint Louis was the king who reorganized the royal necropolis of Saint-Denis as an echo to this system for the coronation that was affirmed with him. He did this in such a fashion as to make it the sacred necropolis par excellence for the Capetian dynasty, or better, the French monarchy. It was a necropolis reserved for the kings and queens who had been sanctified and crowned, a necropolis that confirmed the sacred continuity between the three races that extended all the way back to and beyond the *reditus ad stirpem Karoli* to the Merovingian dynasty. Through the arrangement of the tombs and the representations of the recumbent royal figures, the French monarchy affirmed its sacred ties with the past in continuity with this lineage of kings and queens, with the present as it synchronically united the remains and images of rulers who succeeded each other in reality, and with the future upon which the open eyes of these royal figures gazed.

Saint Louis' Sainthood

Even though Saint Louis' sainthood can be connected to various prior or contemporary models of sainthood, it was highly original. It combined different models of sainthood and figured in the transformation of the medieval concept of sainthood.[19] It was both the synthesis and the highest expression of different components of sainthood in the thirteenth century.

Its originality came from the corpus first of all. Saint Louis' royal function allows us to examine his eventual sainthood through involuntary sources produced in his lifetime before the emergence of any eventual sainthood for him. The chronicles of Matthew Paris and Salimbene of Parma recounted his actions and highlighted traits that were already characteristics of a certain kind of saint well before his canonization. For example, the first praised his *puritas conscientiae* both in the missions he entrusted to his investigators and in his conduct toward the king of England. The second drew an unforgettable portrait of the king moving forward on his path as a pilgrim and a penitent. The royal acts issued by him convey the preoccupations and decisions of a ruler who wanted to be a Christian king above all else. A close study of the reign's edicts, their content, and their explicit motives, not only the great edict for "moral order" of 1254 but the entire group of the king's general edicts, allows us, as we have seen, to apprehend the mental structures of a king whose spirituality and actions made a saint in his practice of a political power that bound the construction of a French monarchical state to the realization of a Christian politics in an inseparable way.

The texts of a hagiographical nature that dealt with him and that date from the transitional period between his death (1270) and his canonization (1297) show us with exceptional richness and precision how and why the canonization of a medieval figure was prepared. They offer us the chronicle of a canonization in the works. This is particularly the case for the *Vita* of Geoffroy de Beaulieu, the king's Dominican confessor. He constructed the image of a saint king that complied with the impressions of his entourage, the dynastic motives of the royal family, the religious ideas of the Mendicant orders, and, of course, the hagiographical politics of Gregory X, a pope who was haunted by the idea of the crusade. This is also the case for the letter sent in 1275 from the prelates of the ecclesiastical province of Sens to the college of the cardinals. It lobbied for the canonization of the deceased king and comprised a veritable program for royal sainthood elaborated by an especially representative section of the Church of France. This had already been the case with the letter addressed to all the French clergy from the new king Philip III, Louis IX's son and successor. This is an exceptional document written in the name of a king who was assuming his functions. It outlined the model of a king who not only realized the ideal for a Christian king, but who, his successor claimed, had already been transported *ad aeternum regnum, et gloriam sine fine,* "to the eternal Kingdom and glory without end."

As we have also seen, with the exception of several fragments, the pieces from Saint Louis' canonization proceedings are lost, although the Franciscan Guillaume de Saint-Pathus, Queen Marguerite's confessor, had these documents in hand when he wrote his *Vita* and his *Miracula.* These texts represented several stages in the process of gathering testimonies. They allow us to follow the way the image of Saint Louis' sainthood was distilled from the period immediately following his death and how it was stripped of exact references to the events of the saint king's life so that it could be idealized in an essentially spiritual vision that was virtually detached from history. On the other hand, they offer the second panel in the diptych of sainthood, the history of his miracles, which was very different from the "biographical" segment.

On the other hand, the canonization bull and the sermons Boniface VIII pronounced for the occasion — texts too often neglected by the historiography on Saint Louis — transmitted the vision the pope and the curia had of him. It is sometimes different, if not distanced, from the image the other documents bring us, and from the image of him circulated by modern historians who have not always entirely freed themselves from certain anachronisms. For example, the pontifical texts silently reject the idea that Louis had been a martyr because he died on the crusade. The French promoters of his canonization had advanced this idea (Joinville adopted it), and Louis himself had presented it in favor of his brother Robert d'Artois and his companions who were killed in 1250 at the battle of Mansourah. It is also necessary to consider the liturgical texts that appeared shortly after his canonization, as we have done. For instance, one of these defined Saint Louis as *norma sanctitatis regibus* (the norm of sainthood for kings). This confirms our observation that the historian must situate him within a typology of saint kings. The current study of this could be extended and developed in greater depth.[20]

The record should also include a text composed by Saint Louis, his *Enseignements* for his son and the ones for his daughter. This is a royal mirror he held out to his successor, but also and first of all for himself. The text sketches a self-portrait of a saint king. Robert Folz has shown how his originality shines in comparison with the *Libellus de insitutione morum* attributed to Saint Stephen of Hungary for the edification of his son. This comparative study allows us to measure the distance covered between a Christian saint king of the eleventh century who was a recent convert in a peripheral Christian state and another Christian saint from the thirteenth century who was *christianissimus,* the heir of a long dynastic tradition of piety in the heart of Christendom. More than this, we need to resituate these texts in relation to all of Saint Louis' discourse. In Saint Louis, in the century of a "new speech," we get the words of a saint king.

The dossier is finally completed by an extraordinary document, a work with an ambiguous pseudo-biographical status written by a layman, Joinville's *Vie de Saint Louis.*

A SECULAR SAINT

If we now try to define Saint Louis' sainthood, we have to stress that what his contemporaries strongly felt was its most original quality was that he was a secular saint. This was a rare category in the Middle Ages.[21] Saint Louis was a laical saint who came after the Gregorian reform, which made a sharp distinction between clerics and laypersons. As thoroughly secular as they were, the saint kings of the preceding centuries were laymen mixed with sacerdotal sanctity. Although a king of France in the thirteenth century preserved and, as we have just seen, even enhanced a certain sacred character that was recognized by the Church, though not without some reticence, and in any case by what we can call public opinion, he was no longer this *rex sacerdos* that the emperors and the kings who emulated them had been previously. A man like Joinville, who was a layman himself, took care to highlight Louis' exceptional character as a secular saint.

This saint manifested his secularity in three specific domains: sexuality, war, and politics.

Sexuality fundamentally defined the division between clerics and laymen since the Gregorian reform. Saint Louis' hagiographers and his confessors in particular therefore stressed Saint Louis' perfection in matters of conjugal sexuality as it defined the very condition of the laity. For the Church, marriage and the sexual practice resulting from it were based on the mutual consent of husband and wife. Saint Louis and Queen Marguerite not only respected the periods during which normally licit sexual relations between spouses, the "time for embracing,"[22] were forbidden, but they added supplementary periods of abstinence to this. Louis was a hero and champion of conjugal sexuality. This was one aspect of his sainthood. In this respect, he recalled the sainthood of the German emperor Henry II. It has been shown that Henry II, who died in 1024, "fully corresponds to the image of the sacred king prior to the Gregorian reform," and that, a century after his death, his canonization seemed like it should have been impossible "because he absolutely did not correspond to the type of king who was a servant of spiritual power as defined by the Gregorian reform, which had rejected the tradition of sacred royalty." More than a century later, the clergy of Bamberg had to dream up the legend of Henry II's virginal marriage with Cunégonde of Luxembourg in order for Pope Eugene III to proclaim the emperor's sainthood in 1146, basing it in large part on the fact that he "maintained the most absolute chastity until the end of his life." The spirit of reform had finally remade Henry II's biography, but his supposed chastity differed from the sexual observance of Louis IX.[23] Only the latter matched the model of the just—or even more than just—secular conjugality that had to be compatible with the royal, dynastic duty of procreation for a king in the thirteenth century.

Louis was also a knight saint, a warrior saint. We would hardly know anything about this aspect of his personality and his life if we possessed only the hagiographies written by the people of the Church. Joinville was the one who emphasized it. The king applied two important rules of Christian warfare—war should be just, and war should be licit. Confronted with the infidels, this was the model for holy war. Despite the Church's official refusal to make him a martyred saint, he was one of the few saints of the crusades. Jean Richard and William Jordan, who have studied Louis' fascination with the crusades so closely, have perhaps not sufficiently viewed Louis IX as a crusading saint.[24] In conflicts with Christian princes, the rule was to never be the aggressor and to seek out a just peace. Once again, Louis was a model in this as well. He was a peacemaker, even at the risk of being blamed by his entourage for what seemed like weakness in his conflicts with the king of Aragon and especially with the king of England. Nonetheless, he also knew how to be a saint for peace, for instance, as he himself pointed out, by binding the king of England to the king of France through the oath of homage.

In politics he wanted to be an ideal Christian king. For understanding his sainthood from an ideological point of view, this explains the importance not only of his *Enseignements* but also of the five Mirrors of the Princes composed during his reign either at his own request, for his gratification, or by members of his entourage. This is especially true of the Franciscan Gilbert de Tournai's *Eruditio regum et principum* (1259).[25] In this respect, it would be interesting to compare these Mirrors of the Princes with the contemporary Norwegian *Speculum regale* (ca. 1260) that has recently been placed in the category of the Mirrors of the Princes.[26] Although I follow Einar Mar Jonsson in the majority of his remarkable analyses, I do not agree with his idea that "the Fürstenspiegel do not develop over time," and that "in their variety they possess a unity that has existed since they first appeared and that we can therefore situate in the long-term development of historical time." For my part, I identify a decisive change in the notion of the ideal ruler that arose between the Carolingian Mirrors of the Prince and those of the period running from around 1160 to 1260. These are rough dates, although they bear the mark of John of Salisbury's *Policraticus* (1159) and the *Institutio Trajani,* which falls within them, although it was falsely attributed to Plutarch and supposedly composed in Rome around 400 and may have actually been forged by John of Salisbury himself. Another mutation in the tradition occurred after 1260 with Thomas Aquinas and Gilles de Rome, but their Mirrors of the Princes, marked by Aristotelian influence, came after the political ideology that inspired Louis and his entourage. To the extent that the king's political sainthood in governing his kingdom and the king's attitude toward his subjects was influenced by the Mirrors of the Princes, Louis' sainthood bore the mark of the twelfth-century Renaissance, including the organic theory of society that saw the king as the head of a body, a political body.

As for the grand *opus politicum,* the great political treatise for which Vincent is said to have written only the *De morali principis institutione* and the *De eruditione filiorum nobilium,* it was meant to define the conduct of the ruler, his advisors, and his officers with regard to "honesty in life and the salvation of the soul."[27]

Here, perhaps more than in the other Mirrors of the Princes, we enter a realm that the ideal king and the saint king in the thirteenth-century sense had in common, although Vincent de Beauvais also referred to Carolingian authors of Mirrors of the Princes, to John of Salisbury's *Policraticus,* and to the *De constituendo rege* (Of the Royal Institution) by the Cistercian Hélinand de Froidmont, which he also included in his chronicle (*Chronicon,* Book XI).[28] He also presented Charlemagne as an example for the king, and this treatise thus integrated itself into the great Capetian movement of the *reditus ad stirpem Karoli.* We have already seen the importance this movement held for Philip Augustus, Louis VIII, and Louis IX himself.[29]

The pertinent theme here seems to me to be that of the *rex imago Trinitatis* (the king [as an] image of the Trinity). This was a variant on the theme of the king as an "image of God." It deployed the tri-functional structure, which was different from the traditional Indo-European tri-functionality, though not without ties to it.[30]

Vincent attributed a virtue, *virtus,* to the king that was manifested in three attributes: power, wisdom, and goodness. Vincent defined power (*potentia*) according to the pessimist theory of the origin of royal power as a usurpation originating in the lineage of Cain and Nimrod, which was also Jean de Meung's thesis in the *Roman de la Rose.* He legitimated it, however, by reference to the need to repress the evil introduced into society through the "corruption of nature," the original sin. The king who used his power "righteously" (*droitement*) could and should control it through the second attribute of "wisdom" (*sapientia*), which kept him from transforming his power into tyranny. This wisdom included the good use of war, the ability to choose his friends, advisors, and officers well, and being well instructed in sacred and profane literature. The third attribute of "goodness" (*bonitas*) crowned this trinity of royal virtue, for the king had to "surpass in goodness all those he must govern." He could achieve this by avoiding envy, flattery, and adulation. This threefold virtue brought the "good" king closer to sainthood.

In Saint Louis' case, the individual and his ideal models were historically unified. Thus, as we have seen, studying Saint Louis' models of sainthood amounts to studying the "real" Saint Louis.

Saint Louis' Models of Sainthood

The first model was biblical. We already saw that Saint Louis was a new Josiah.[31] Like Josiah, "there had been no other king before him who could compare with him in his ability to give himself to the Lord with all his heart, all his soul, and all his strength; and no other king like him appeared after him" (Geoffroy de Beaulieu). Like Josiah, Louis had been pious in the first part of his reign, but in the second, after the crusade, he had undergone a veritable conversion. In effect, in restoring the Temple Josiah had found the Book of Laws, Deuteronomy, and on this basis he renewed the covenant with God, which was celebrated in an extraordinary Passover held in Yahweh's honor in Jerusalem. He died at Meggido in a battle against the Pharaoh. According to the Bible, this was how a king passed from devoutness to sainthood.

The second model was Capetian. Helgaud de Fleury had already tried to make Robert the Pious a saint in the eleventh century by emphasizing certain aspects of the conduct of Hugh Capet's son. The resemblance between this model and Saint Louis' devoutness is striking.[32] In a way that seems even more astonishing to us, Philip Augustus's entourage also attempted to make him a saint after his death. Once again, they based their claims on traits of charity that were mentioned with more likelihood and more testimony in favor of Saint Louis.[33] The Capetian attempts at sainthood that proved abortive for Robert the Pious and Philip Augustus succeeded for Saint Louis. He was a dynastic saint, and his canonization had undeniable political elements; in 1297 Boniface VIII was still under the illusion that he could seduce Saint Louis' grandson Philip the Fair, who was later his implacable foe.

Finally, Saint Louis' sainthood corresponded to a royal model, the model of saint kings.[34] However, there is more separation than continuity between Saint Louis and the bleeding heart kings of the High Middle Ages or the confessor kings of the eleventh and twelfth centuries who were associated with the conversion of peoples, monastic models, and an ideology of sacred royalty. We have to resist the false idea that the concept of royal sainthood remained unchanged over a long period of time. Louis' sainthood was different.

Notably, it was marked by a dual model characteristic of the thirteenth century. Louis was a saint of the Mendicant orders that surrounded, inspired, and shaped him to the point that his hagiographers and his opponents evoked the temptation he had to become a friar. It was a useless argument as these orders admitted a tertiary order of laymen and, even in this context, the royal function and majesty were incompatible with

belonging to an order. Alain Boureau has appropriately seen "a public figure of private worship" in Saint Louis' sainthood shaped by the influence
of the Mendicant orders.[35]

The second contemporary model was that of *prud'homie,* this mixture
of courtesy and reason, prowess and moderation that could reach religious
heights. Saint Louis was a saint-*prud'homme,* a courtly hero seized by devoutness, a medieval Polyeucte.[36]

It is necessary to explain Louis' sainthood through the two complementary inquiries that I have previously indicated. The first applies to the
nature and functions of a French king in the thirteenth century. We have to
make a distinction between the individual saint king and the functional collective Christian king in Louis IX. Saint Louis' sainthood was individual,
not automatically tied to the royal function, and dependent on a single pontifical decision.

We also have to analyze the nature, the composition, and the action of
the lobbies that produced and constructed Saint Louis' sainthood and won
its recognition: the late partisans of the crusade, beginning with Gregory X;
the Capetian dynasty, especially his grandson Philip the Fair; the Church of
France, notably as it expressed itself in the petition to the cardinals from
the prelates of the province of Sens and the French party at the Roman
court; the Mendicant orders, assuredly; and also the *vox populi.* Saint Louis
was a French saint, a saint of the Mendicants, a "popular" saint, and spontaneously recognized by common opinion as well.

Our second inquiry involves the miracles.

SAINT LOUIS' MIRACLES

A study of Saint Louis' miracles gives us a much more traditional image
of his sainthood. They were all essentially miracles of healing or of the
body. However, this thaumaturgical sainthood only manifested itself after
the king's death. This was in compliance with Innocent III's prescriptions,
which only recognized miracles accomplished after a saint's death as valid
as a means of avoiding claims of illusory pseudo-miracles carried out by
false saints during their own lifetime.[37] Once more, Louis proved to be a
very orthodox saint in this regard, in conformity with the prescriptions of
the Church. We still need to examine these miracles more closely.[38]

A Christian saint was defined by the qualities of his life and miracles. By examining the miracles of Saint Louis reported during the years preceding and following his canonization and at the time of his canonization, we should be able to answer a twofold question. What importance did these miracles have for Saint Louis' canonization? What was the balance between his life and virtues on the one hand and his miraculous actions on the other? Was Saint Louis original in his miracles?

The sixty-five miracles in the official corpus allow us to determine the times and places that they occurred, the persons who benefited from them, and their nature.

The first essential fact then is that all of Saint Louis' miracles took place after his death. The biographers often emphasized this. Geoffroy de Beaulieu had already indicated that the miracles followed the burial of the king's bones at Saint-Denis: "*Sepultis igitur ossibus sacrosanctis divina non defuere magnalia; sed mox mirificavit Dominus sanctum suum. . . .*"[39] Guillaume de Chartres, who compared the deceased king to the sun—"a new sun rising in the West" (*sol novus ortus in partibus Occidentis*), claimed that "after his laying to rest," he "continued to shine thanks to the light of his miracles" (*post occasum etiam lucere non desinens miraculorum evidentium claritate*).[40] In the canonization bull of August 11, 1297, Boniface VIII emphasized that after his death, Christ wanted the saint king "to shine through the multitude of his miracles as he had shone [during his life] by the multitude of his merits."[41]

Saint Louis' sainthood thus respected the guidelines established a century earlier by Innocent III. It was useful for them to distinguish between the two types of manifestations of sainthood: the virtues expressed during the saint's life and the miracles that could only be accomplished after the saint's death. Up until this point the Church had more or less accepted that public opinion would attribute miracles accomplished in their own lifetime to individuals whom it spontaneously recognized as saints. However, the pope and the curia had henceforth taken control over the recognition of sainthood by instituting the canonization procedure. It was important to give the saint a fully orthodox image in conformity with the general evolution of the Church that was in the process of purging itself of "popular" religion as much as possible. To this point, it had only tolerated popular religion when it had not been able to integrate it, cautiously attempting to avoid situations in which saints could be confused with magicians while they were still alive.[42] This policy that put miracles off until after a saint's death had the result that more miracles took place beside the tombs of the saints in accordance with the ancient Christian tradition.

Only one miracle is mentioned that occurred during Saint Louis' lifetime, and he was not its author (or rather its divine instrument) but its beneficiary. Boniface VIII wanted to build up an atmosphere of saintliness and miracles that existed during the king's life and particularly for the period that seemed to warrant it the most in his eyes, the time of Louis' captivity in Egypt. The pope thus reported one of the miracles that took place at this time. One day the king was praying in an isolated room and complained that he did not have his breviary which he needed in order to say his canonical hours. A religious who was with the king consoled him, but suddenly the king discovered his breviary right next to him, miraculously brought to him by God.[43]

With this sole exception, the miracles began after the king's death, although at that moment they began to occur in droves. They began on the return trip of the king's remains from Tunis to Paris and Saint-Denis. As we have seen, Jean de Vignay even mentioned two miracles that took place in Sicily during Charles d'Anjou's transfer of his brother's heart and entrails to his monastery in Monreale. The official list indicated two other miracles that took place on the passage of the king's remains through northern Italy, at Parma and Reggio d'Emilia. (These are miracles 64 and 65 in Guillaume de Saint-Pathus's work.) Another miracle occurred as the king's remains were entering Paris (miracle 66). Guillaume de Saint-Pathus gave a very vivid account of it:

> When they announced King Philip III's imminent arrival in Paris with his father's remains in the spring of 1271, the bourgeois of Paris went out to meet the cortege. Heading up the group were the fullers [more than 300 of them according to Guillaume de Saint-Pathus] who wanted to present the new king with a complaint about some wrong that had been done to them with regard to a worksite near the Baudroyer gate. They went to wait for the cortege at the elm of Bonnel [Bonnueil-sur-Marne] just past Cristeu [Créteil]. They met a woman there who said that she had come from Burgundy with her son, a child who was about eight years old, who was afflicted with a swelling the size of a goose's egg under his left ear. The numerous

saints of the sanctuaries she had visited in pilgrimage (Saint-Éloi-de-Ferrière in particular) and a great many doctors had been powerless to help. When the cortege arrived, the woman asked the people who were leading the two horses that were carrying the reliquary with Saint Louis' bones, before which everyone was kneeling, to stop so that the child could touch the reliquary with the sick part of his body. One of the drivers gently lifted the child up and let him touch the reliquary with his bump. The swelling immediately burst, and a lot of "filth" came out and ran down the child's chest and clothes, and he showed no signs of pain. All those present cried out in praise of the miracle and the merits of the blessed Saint Louis. A bishop who was there stated that this was not the first miracle that the blessed Saint Louis had made on his voyage.[44]

Of course, the vast majority of the miracles take place next to the tomb at Saint-Denis. Saint Louis was a saint of Saint-Denis.

The mention of the legions of the sick and infirm, the crippled and maimed, and beggars who pressed up against the tomb to touch it and who lay down upon it is poignant. (They had not yet sculpted the "royal image" for it.) The mention of people who scratched the stone and swallowed the powder reminds us that little had changed in beliefs and practices since Gregory of Tours and Merovingian times.

Of the sixty-four individuals graced with the miracles recorded by Guillaume de Saint-Pathus, fifty-three were healed at Saint-Denis. Five of them suffered from conditions that prevented them from traveling to Saint-Denis but promised to make the journey there if Saint Louis healed them, and they kept their promise. In two cases, the miracles took place at Chaalis and Paris through the intermediary of one of Saint Louis' relics — a coat and a hat the king had worn. A dead child was brought back to life (miracle 19) with the offering of a candle before the king's tomb. In another case, a simple invocation of Saint Louis was enough to produce a miracle (miracle 62): this was the miracle carried out for the chatelain of Aigues-Mortes who nearly drowned in the Saône on his return from Saint-Denis. To all these, we must add the two miracles done in Italy and the one that took place at the gates of Paris.

Despite this overwhelming concentration of Saint Louis' miracles at Saint-Denis (more than four-fifths of them overall), most of Saint Louis' biographers indicated that his miracles took place at Saint-Denis or *elsewhere*.[45] They did this no doubt to uphold the tendency to delocalize miracles, which was a sensitive issue in the thirteenth century.[46] As for the places of residence of those blessed with the miracles, with the exception of the two Italians (miracles 64 and 65), the chatelain of Aigues-Mortes (miracles 61 and 62), the child from Burgundy who came to the gates of Paris for the arrival of the king's remains (miracle 56), and a young valet from the Jura who followed the royal funeral cortege all the way from Lyon (miracle 15), the miracles break down into the three categories of Saint-Denis, Paris, and the Île-de-France all the way to its borders with Normandy and Artois.[47]

With the exception of a single miracle (miracle 46, the drying of the three Parisian cellars), all the miracles involved people who were healed of illnesses or deformities or saved from situations where they were in danger of dying. They affected men and women in almost equal proportions— twenty-three men and twenty women. Likewise, among the twenty children and adolescents blessed with them, eleven were male, and nine were female. So, with regard to both sex and age, there was a fairly equal balance among the people cured or saved by the miracles: there were twenty-three men and twenty women, eleven male and nine female children and adolescents. A large majority of those healed or saved, fifty out of sixty-three individuals were either poor or from modest backgrounds. The rest of the group breaks down into seven churchpeople (a canon, two priests, a Cistercian monk, two nuns from the house of the Daughters of God in Paris, one female lay religious), three bourgeois, and five nobles (a chatelain, three knights, and a lady). Many have often stressed that these were mainly people who had to work with their hands or who were stuck in poverty or even mendicancy. Observers have also pointed out that their healing sometimes allowed them to escape destitute lives.[48]

We can clearly perceive the miracle's social function here. It worked to sustain the hope of the least privileged members of society and occupied the place that the welfare system and the lottery have in our own time. As I have already said, nearly all the miracles involved the physical condition of their beneficiaries.

Do we have to make a separate place for the healing of scrofula (adenoid tuberculosis) that the kings of France were reputed for being able to heal *ex officio,* whether they were saints or not, while they were still alive? Yes and no. No, because the thaumaturgical power of the kings of France existed independently of their spiritual qualities and the Christian value of their lives. It was considered apart from their personal qualities. Geoffroy de Beaulieu dedicated a short chapter to Saint Louis' healing of the scrofulous, and the other biographers did not discuss it at all or only alluded to it in passing.[49] And yet, there seems to have been a connection between the specialized thaumaturgical power Saint Louis exercised in his own lifetime as a king of France and his miraculous powers as a would-be saint after his death. In effect, a woman who played an important role in one of the miracles retained for the official record (the sixtieth), Emmeline de Melun, the widow of a man who had been employed in the king's storeroom, "said under oath that when the bones of the blessed Saint Louis were brought to France on their return from overseas, they cured many people with scrofula who kissed the reliquary that held his bones, and on the roads and in the towns where it stopped, these people commonly said that they were immediately healed."[50] We can thus infer that the living king's reputation as a healer of scrofula attracted sick people along the route where his remains were carried. The shift in his thaumaturgical power from the time he was alive to the period that immediately followed his death played a certain role in shaping the belief in his miraculous powers after death and therefore in his sainthood, even though, as we have seen, other kinds of miracles were requested and obtained from God along the route followed by his remains, which thus proved to be relics. The healing of the scrofulous affected a transition between Louis IX the thaumaturge and Saint Louis.

What the king's biographers emphasized, however, was that the miracles accomplished through Saint Louis' mediation after his death had not only been great and numerous, but varied in nature. In his canonization bull, Boniface VIII mentioned the saint king's *diversitas miraculorum*.[51] In effect, to the extent that Louis IX had been endowed with a narrowly specialized thaumaturgical power in his own lifetime, the ability to heal a single disease — scrofula — Saint Louis became recognized very early on as one of those great saints whose power was not limited to one kind of miracle achieved in a particular sanctuary but one that applied to any illnesses for which people could request his intervention with God. This power was not just manifest at the tomb at Saint-Denis but also "elsewhere." Thus the list of miracles retained by the Roman curia is a veritable inventory of the kinds of miracles considered "great" at the end of the thirteenth century.

Guillaume de Saint-Pathus gave two lists of them, one in a sermon and the other in the *De miraculis* section of his *Life*.

In the sermon he lists sixty of the people who were healed by Saint Louis' miracles, classified in the following way:

Mentally ill (*alienati mente*)	III
Afflicted with a drying up of the members (*aridi membris*)	II
Saved from drowning (*ab acque inundanti periculo*)	II
Afflicted with deformities (*contracti curati*)	VI
Hunchbacks straightened (*curvi erecti*)	II
Lame made to walk again (*claudi recuperaverunt gressum*)	V
Blind made to see again (*ceci visum*)	III
Afflicted with incurable fever (*febricitantes continua sanati*)	III
Sick with quartan fever (*a febre quartana*)	III
Afflicted with fistula (*fistulati*)	III
Sick with cataracts (?) (*a gutta forma*)[52]	I
Mute made to speak again (*muti recuperaverunt verbum*)	II
Paralytics (*paralitici curati*)	XVI
Afflicted with scrofulous swelling on the eye or throat (*a struma super oculum et in gutture*)	II
Scrofulous (*a scrofulis*)	I
Deaf made to hear again (*surdus recepit auditum*)	I
Afflicted with a tumor (*a tumore sil et dolore*)[53]	III
Dead brought back to life (*mortuis suscitati sunt*)	II

This list differs little from the one that can be drawn up from the *Miracles,* which mentioned sixty-five instead of sixty of them.[54] Guillaume summarized this other list of them in the following way:

He cured those who suffered from deformities [*contrez*] and stretched out their members again, the people who were hunched nearly touched the ground with their faces, and he cured them and restored them to full health and straightened them out so that their faces were held high again. He healed the hunchbacked and the gouty and people who were suffering from a powerful and unpredictable sickness called fistula [*flestre*], people who had dried up members, people who had lost their memory [insane or amnesiac], people who had constant and quartan fevers . . . several people who were paralytic and he cured others who were afflicted with different types of wasting diseases and restored them to full health. He restored the sight of the blind, the hearing of the deaf, the movement of the lame, and the dead to life. . . .[55]

Although the proportion of the "deformed" [*contractés*] among those who were miraculously cured decreased in the thirteenth century according to certain historians,[56] if we add together the deformed, the hunchbacked, the lame, and people designated as paralytic (whose numbers also seem to include several epileptics—epilepsy was called the "*mal Saint-Leu*"—and people afflicted with Parkinson's disease), in other words all those who have some problem of movement, this is still the largest category of people who were officially healed by Saint Louis. The model individual he healed seems to be a man or woman who braved great difficulties to arrive at Saint-Denis "*à potence*" (with support), in other words on crutches, because he or she "had lost" the use of his or her thighs or a leg or a foot, and who then returned home without the help of crutches. An infirmity like this severely diminished the individual's capacities and sentenced him or her to live at the mercy of others like family members, a hospital, or alms-givers. The objectively verifiable, spectacular healing restored their human nature and potential in the form of their ability to move around, to stand upright, to be independent, and to work. The miracles represented the restitution of human dignity even more than the disappearance of pain and suffering.

There is another important category to take into account: all the people who were healed of a disease that made them ugly and dirty, full of pus and "filth": fistula, bumps, swollen glands, wounds, etc., all these fetid, purulent, swelling, and bleeding people whose tragic bands in sixteenth- to eighteenth-century Italy have been brilliantly described by Piero Camporesi.[57] The miracle restored the integrity if not the beauty of their bodies too, their cleanliness if not a certain radiance, and the ability to have normal relations with their entourages.

There is ultimately nothing exceptional about Saint Louis' miracles. He accomplished the miracles that people expected from an important saint at the end of the thirteenth century, whether the saint was a layman or a churchman, a king or a monk. As some have noted in the case of his nephew Saint Louis of Toulouse, through his miracles Saint Louis was a saint like any other.[58]

His Miracles and His Life

I will not go on too long about the pilgrimage to Saint Louis' tomb at Saint-Denis. I will mention that the miracle often occurred in the course and as the outcome of a novena, a continuation of old practices carried out at saint's tombs that were developed during the High Middle Ages. The miracle was typically the outcome of a series of fruitless pilgrimages to the sanctuaries of impotent saints whom Saint Louis outclassed with his superior powers. In one case, the miracle only took place as the result of a second pilgrimage to Saint-Denis (miracle 39). The second pilgrimage succeeded because the postulant for the miracle preceded it with a confession of his sins. This introduced the problem of the place of novelty and tradition in Saint Louis' miracles. They did seem to be submerged in an atmosphere of old "superstitious" practices. First, there were the two miracles that did not take place at the tomb but through the intermediary of the object-relics that belonged to Saint Louis. A Cistercian of Chaalis was cured of a pain running from his head down his back to his kidneys when he slipped on a coat that Saint Louis had given to the abbey (miracle 12). Three flooded cellars in Paris were miraculously dried because someone dipped a hat in the water, a hat with peacock feathers that Saint Louis had worn and given to one of his squires whose widow was the owner of the cellars (miracle 46). Several pilgrims brought a candle of their own height to Saint Louis' tomb at Saint-Denis. This was a magical substitute object. One of the women who were miraculously healed presented a wax leg as a thanks offering to the basilica of Saint-Denis in order to heal her own leg (miracle 55).

Several pilgrimages and miracles were set in motion by a vision of the saint that appeared to living people who knew him.[59] For example, Saint Louis appeared to Master Dudes, a canon and "physician" from Paris who had accompanied the king and served as his doctor on the crusade to Tunis (miracle 38). He also appeared to Friar Jehan de Lagny, a curate of Thorigny. Saint Louis appeared to him wearing the clothes Jehan had often seen him wear (miracle 50). For his part, Guillaume de Chartres told the story of how a Parisian matron whose husband knew the king saw him in a dream accompanied by another figure who was shining with amazing brilliance as he seemed to be making an offering on the altar of his royal chapel in Paris. This was a classical vision that announced the saint's death before the news of the deaths of Louis IX and his son Jean-Tristan the count of Nevers reached Paris.

Facing this traditional symbolic imaginary of sainthood and miracles, I note that on the other hand we have the indication that in certain cases (like that of the healed woman who was on her second pilgrimage to Saint-Denis) a sincere confession of one's sins was a necessary precondition for obtaining a miracle and should be made before making the voyage to Saint-Denis. This attested to an "advance" in spiritual life, a pious and personal preparation for a miracle, and the growing importance of confession in thirteenth-century Christian life.

More generally, if we examine the entire corpus of Saint Louis' biographies that were written between 1270 and the beginning of the fourteenth century, we get the impression that what counted the most in their eyes was his life more than his miracles.[60] They went on at length about the king's life and the virtues and merits that first and foremost made him a saint. In his sermon of August 6, 1297, Boniface VIII recalled that his predecessor Nicolas III (1277–1280) had declared "that the life of this saint was so well known to him that two or three miracles would be enough to canonize him," "but his death prevented it from happening."[61] Certainly, his life included some of the traditional characteristics of a saint—sometimes some of them were even overdeveloped as in the case of the cult of relics, or outmoded like his ardent zeal for the crusades. However, I would like to remind my readers that for the most part his life was marked by the new piety of the thirteenth century. This was the piety of a time when the memory of a Saint Bernard or the even closer memory of a Saint Francis of Assisi, not to mention the deep trends that they shaped and represented, upheld a new spirit and new practices of piety including profound humility, worship of the Eucharist, laymen who imitated the piety of the religious, and the practice of works of charity (*miséricorde*).

Is it necessary, then, to divide Saint Louis' sainthood into two parts? Do we have to divide his sainthood between his life, which would be its modern part, and his miracles, which would represent its traditional component? Are his personality, his originality, and his message for history only expressed within his life? In his miracles, does he disappear behind the models, the commonplace ideas, and the "deep" structures of the thirteenth century? Was his life marked by the "scholarly" and "progressive" mentality of the clerics, and his miracles dictated by the "popular" and "traditional" mentality of the age?

We should be cautious here. Saint Louis was a man, a king, and a saint who was both new and traditional at the same time. Like his life, his miracles were part of a long tradition and expressed new attitudes as well. As for the clerics, they believed in miracles like everyone else. This belief was part of the common mentality at the end of the thirteenth century.[62] Even Pope Nicolas III did not believe that sainthood could exist without miracles.

THE RELICS

A study of Saint Louis' relics has to be added to the study of his miracles. This is the classic story of the divided royal bodies and the bodily relics split up between the tomb for his entrails at Monreale in Sicily built on the orders of his brother Charles, the king of Naples, and the tomb for his remains at Saint-Denis built on the orders of his son Philip III in compliance with dynastic tradition of the French monarchy. It is also the classic story of the dismembering of the royal skeleton into a large number of relic remains that disseminated the proof of Louis' sainthood. This is also a unique story, because the transport of the relic-cadaver took months to make the journey from Tunisia to Saint-Denis, and a long line of miracles immediately occurred in support of the popular belief in the deceased king's sainthood. Finally, it is a unique history due to the fate of the entrails kept at Monreale, which then followed the Bourbons of Naples into their Austrian exile in the nineteenth century and were bequeathed to the French White Fathers of Carthage, thus returning to the site of the saint king's death.[63]

THE LAST OF THE SAINT KINGS

Saint Louis was ultimately a saint situated between tradition and modernity. His sainthood became distinct from the royal sainthood of the High Middle Ages without entirely swinging toward the mystical, charitable individual sainthood of the twilight of the Middle Ages. With the exception of Ferdinand III of Castile who was nearly his contemporary but not canonized until 1671, he was the last of the saint kings. He was also the only saint king of the thirteenth century and the new society that emerged from Christendom's great period of growth whose beginnings date from the start of the eleventh century. After him, the absolutist Aristotelian kings escaped the individual sainthood that was henceforth incompatible with the sanctification of the state. The only monarchs who could be canonized would now be popes.

The Suffering King, the Christ King

CERTAINLY, MORE THAN SHAKESPEARE'S RICHARD II, LOUIS WAS A "king of sorrows" in the medieval context. However, his image as a suffering king presented his contemporaries with large and difficult problems. Was suffering a kind of value? Could it have a positive image? Could it help people attain salvation like work which was given by God to Adam as a punishment for his sin and as it evolved from a concept of work as penance to a concept of work as merit between the eleventh and thirteenth centuries? The concept of Purgatory was born at the end of the twelfth century and it is true that in Purgatory the suffering of souls held in bodies made them evolve from a situation of punishment to a state of purification. But could a king suffer like this too? Saint Louis was very different from those Anglo-Saxon kings of the High Middle Ages that Robert Folz, translating a Russian expression (*strastoterptis*) has called "passion-suffering [*souffre-passion*] kings," and who had become somewhat well known in Slavic and especially Russian hagiography with its Byzantine backgrounds.[1] These martyr kings accepted their tragic fates, and their suffering only figured posthumously in the appraisal of their images. Saint Louis suffered on a daily basis. His suffering was structural and involuntary because he was sickly, and it was voluntary because he practiced asceticism. His halo of suffering was gradually acquired over the course of his life, and his death as a martyr for the crusade only affixed the stamp of tradition on a new kind of suffering king because, apart from martyrdom, suffering had become a value in the West and even came to place value on kings. It did not purely depend on the grace of God, but existed at the point where divine grace met with human effort. However, because the king was still a superior figure, the suffering king was a great sufferer and a great king.

Joinville presented the mournful, tragic opening of Saint Louis' life and placed it on the same prophetic day of his birth. A few essential themes in Saint Louis' relations to suffering were expressed there.[2]

It was an individual form of suffering first of all. It was the suffering of the cross, of pilgrimages, and the crusade—the great road of pain and sadness on which man followed and rejoined the crucified Christ. It was also a collective suffering: a sharing of suffering and death between the king and a multitude of his subjects and companions. Finally, it was a valorization of this suffering, since human pain here on earth led to eternal joy in heaven. The past time of earthly history in which pain occurred and the already present time of eternity held suffering that transformed into happiness.

THE VALUES OF THE BODY

Saint Louis maintained complex relations with his body. He combined the Christian doctrine on the body with his personal health problems, his obsessions, and his own sensibility. The Christianity of his age simultaneously taught contempt for the body as it opposed the flourishing of the soul, the noble and divine principle of man, and a certain respect for the body that would be revived for the Last Judgment. He was prone to experience an obvious physical and mental pleasure in the mortification of his body. He both felt and wanted to come close to the rigors of monastic asceticism with the painful positions he adopted while praying, his fasts, his practice of wearing the hair shirt, and flagellation. Beyond his desire for humility and penitence, he liked to sit on the ground and to lie in uncomfortable positions. He liked to touch people. His moral and psychological life was lived through his body. He found the word *prud'homme,* which defined his ideal as a man, delightful to pronounce. On the other hand, the word *rendre* (to render) scratched his throat, obsessed as he was with the duty of making restitutions.³ The two "*r*'s" in this word were "the devil's rakes." We may also recall the sensual joy he experienced when God gave him the gift of a tear that he joyfully felt running down his cheek. As it reached the corner of his mouth, he tasted it and swallowed it.⁴

In his *Enseignements* for his son and daughter, he stressed the importance of the divine gift of "bodily health," the patience needed for dealing with illness, and the charity to be expressed toward "sufferers of bodily ills" [*souffrants de corps*]. He also warned Philip that he should avoid "sins of the body."⁵

Louis was chaste and continent, despised prostitution, but carried out his conjugal duty without displeasure. In the only anecdote we possess in which we see him confronted by a woman who tried to tempt him, he gave her a moral lesson in front of other witnesses: she was beautiful, but the body's beauty passes away like a flower's, and when old age sets in, no artifice could restore this useless beauty; the beauty of the soul, on the other hand, pleased God and assured eternal salvation.⁶

In the case of an adulterous woman who had her lover kill her husband, he showed no mercy. She recognized the facts and repented. The queen, a number of other powerful ladies, and even some of the Mendicant friars asked for Louis' mercy. The king consulted with his faithful advisor Simon de Nesle who shared his sense of the demands of royal and public justice. The king followed his advice and had the woman publicly burned in Pontoise.⁷

A Case of Rape

Similarly, when a woman in Melun came to the king to complain about a man who forced his way into her house and raped her, he referred the case to Simon de Nesle and other members of his council. The accused admitted that he had sexual relations with the woman, but declared that she was a "*folle femme*," a prostitute. Several members of the court asked Louis to spare the man from hanging after he was found guilty by the judges appointed by the king. They reasoned on the grounds that the accused belonged to the king's retinue. However, the king ordered Simon de Nesle to execute the guilty man's sentence, and he was hanged.⁸

At the opposite pole of this chain of bodies, far from the guilty bodies of these men and women who proved incapable of redeeming their bodies from the corruption of original sin, Louis venerated the immaculate body that held the key to redemption and salvation, the body of Christ.

In his *Enseignements,* he named the supreme body, "the body of Our Lord Jesus Christ," the host, which Philip should worship with special attention, "while [it] is present in the mass and then also for a short time before this."[9]

Louis, however, did not shield his own body from human care. Saint Louis' body was subjected to harsh acts of physical penance, but when he was sick he offered it for examination by doctors. A king should have doctors, and a Christian was supposed to take care of his own body and avoid any behavior that could equate with suicide.

We know the names of a certain number of Saint Louis' doctors. Two of them appear in specific acts. One of them was a woman. The royal act was issued at Acre in August 1250, shortly after the king was liberated and left Egypt for the Holy Land. It stipulated that the provost of Sens had to guarantee a pension of twelve Parisian deniers per day for the rest of her life to a certain Hersende who did a good job caring for the king when he was sick. She must have had some university titles because the act referred to her as *magistra,* the feminine form of master. As she was supposed to collect this pension after she returned to France from overseas, she probably healed the king on the crusade in Egypt and was preparing to return to Sens or the surrounding region with a group of Frenchmen including her brothers who were not able to stay on with Saint Louis in the Holy Land.[10]

The other doctor was an Italian. He was probably a native of Cremona, "the doctor of His Royal Highness the king." His name was Pierre Lombard, and he died in 1247. The cartulary of the Cistercian abbey of Froidmont recorded the bequests presented in his testament. He had purchased houses and bequeathed some of them to the abbeys of Sainte-Geneviève and Saint-Victor. Pierre Lombard was also a canon of Chartres and he was buried there in the cathedral.[11]

Another of Louis IX's doctor clerics was Master Robert de Douai, cannon of Senlis and Saint-Quentin. When he died in 1258, he bequeathed 1,500 pounds for the foundation of the college planned by Robert de Sorbon. In exchange, his birthday was to be celebrated in various Parisian institutions including the Sorbonne.

Louis expressed an extreme prudery toward his body; he was disturbed to see it even partially exposed. Guillaume de Saint-Pathus testified to this.

> All the honesty that ever existed in a married man existed in him. His Lordship Pierre de Laon who was his knight spent a lot of time with him over the course of roughly thirty-eight years and served as his chamberlain. He slept at the foot of his bed, unshod him, and helped him get into bed just like the sergeants of noble lords do. For about fifteen years, he was never able to see the saint king's flesh [skin] except for his feet and his hands, and his arms and sometimes the fat of his leg when he would wash his feet, and his arms when he was being bled, and his legs when he was sick. No one ever helped the saint king when he got out of bed, but he would dress and put on his shoes or boots all by himself. His chamberlains would ready his clothing and footwear next to his bed, and he would take them and dress on his own.[12]

Saint Louis understood that in order to have salvation in the afterlife, he could only prepare for it here on earth in both body and soul. He understood this even better because he was a sick king.

THE SICK KING

As a suffering king, Saint Louis suffered first of all in his own body.[13] He was often sick, either from chronic diseases like a recurring erysipelas in his right leg and malaria or "*fièvre tierçaine*" or from sporadic illnesses like the dysentery he suffered after the campaign against the English in 1242 and in Egypt, scorbut—the "sickness of the army"—on his first crusade, and the typhus that killed him on his second crusade.[14]

The king was sick when he returned from the campaign against the English and their allies in Poitou and Saintonge in 1242. He had a serious relapse when he was in Pontoise in 1244, and one day they even thought he had died. It was at that moment that he promised to crusade if he were cured.

Boniface VIII alluded to this in his bull for Saint Louis' canonization: "In his thirtieth year of life, he was stricken with a disease that he survived" (*In anno tricesimo constitutus, et quadam sibi aegritudine superveniente gravatus*).[15]

Guillaume de Saint-Pathus and Joinville also mentioned this illness, which was probably malaria. Guillaume de Saint-Pathus indicated that "once he was gravely ill at Pontoise,"[16] and specified: "And when the aforementioned blessed king was once sick in Pontoise with the *tierçaine double* [paludism?], he was so sick he thought he would die of this illness . . . he was so gravely ill that people despaired for his life."[17] Joinville mistook the place as he was not present there either, but wrote: "After God's will, it happened that a great sickness took hold of the king in Paris, and he was in such a sad state that people thought he was dead."[18]

These same authors bore witness to his physical sufferings on the crusade in Egypt. Guillaume writes:

> And when the blessed king was held prisoner by the Saracens after his first passage [crusade], he was so sick that his teeth chattered and his flesh was discolored and pale, and he had very serious nausea [*flux de ventre*] and he was so thin that the bones of his spine in his back seemed sharp, and he was so weak that a man of his house had to carry him around for all his necessities. . . .

For his part, Joinville added a very realistic stroke.

> This advice [to go from Mansourah to Damietta by boat] was given to him due to the weak state of his body that resulted from several illnesses, because he had the *double tierceinne* [malaria?] and a very bad case of dysentery and the disease of the army in his mouth and legs [scorbut] so badly that they had to cut out the bottom of his britches, and the strength of the army's disease made him faint in the evening a number of times. . . .[19]

Guillaume de Saint-Pathus informs us about the illness he sporadically suffered in his right leg:

> The blessed king had an illness that would grip him each year, two or three or four times a year, and sometimes it would more or less torment him. When this illness seized the blessed king, he could not understand things very clearly and had trouble understanding for as long as the malady had him in its grasp, and he could neither

eat nor sleep. . . . This illness would afflict him for three days, sometimes less, until he could get out of bed on his own strength. And
when this illness became less painful, his right leg became red like
blood from his calf to his ankle, and it was swollen in this spot. The
redness and swelling would last for an entire day until the evening.
And afterward, this redness and swelling gradually subsided enough
so that on the third or fourth day the leg became just like his other
leg, and the blessed king was completely healed.[20]

He behaved like any man would when he was suffering like this: "He
would moan and complain." Between 1254 and 1260, Louis fell into "a very
serious illness" at Fontainebleau in 1259. Joinville mentioned this,[21] and
Boniface VIII alluded to it as well. The king thought he was near death and
summoned the archbishop of Rouen, Eudes Rigaud, to his bedside.[22]

Finally, on the eve of his second crusade, Louis was so weak that Joinville grew indignant with his entourage for letting him leave on the crusade.
When he went to say goodbye to him in Paris, he had to carry the king in
his arms.

> The people who let him go did a great sin, considering the great
> weakness his body was in, because he could tolerate neither riding in
> a cart nor riding on horseback. His weakness was so great that he al-
> lowed me to carry him in my arms from the manor of the count of
> Auxerre to the Cordeliers.[23]

This recollection would remain strongly imprinted in Joinville's memory.
With it, he presented one of the oldest images of the Pietà, which soon became a successful iconographic theme. The image of a Christ king inspired
this scene that also translated Joinville's maternal fantasy.

THE PATIENT KING

Patience was what allowed Saint Louis to convert his bouts of suffering
into merits. When he was held prisoner by the Saracens, suffering terribly
from the "disease of the army," he responded to his suffering with patience
and prayer. Only one of his servants was allowed to stay with him because

all the others were sick. This was the cook Ysembart, whose testimony was relayed by Guillaume de Saint-Pathus:

> He never saw that blessed king become irritated or revolted because of his condition, nor did he mutter against anything, but he tolerated and sustained all these maladies and the great adversity in which his people found themselves with great patience and good nature, and he was always praying.[24]

Boniface VIII echoed this patience in his canonization bull, although the Latin word *patiens* is more ambiguous, meaning both "who tolerates with patience," but also "who suffers from": "The king was suffering patiently [?] at this time from nausea and other illnesses" (*eodem rege tunc temporis fluxum ventris et aegritudines alias patiente*).[25]

Louis was not merely satisfied with accepting his suffering; he had to sublimate it:

> Thus as a man entirely anchored in faith, and entirely absorbed in spirit, the more he was crushed by these hammers of adversity and disease, the more he showed fervor and the more the perfecting of faith declared itself within him.[26]

In his *Enseignements,* he placed persecution, illness, and suffering on the same level. He not only advised his son and daughter to put up with them patiently; he also told them to be grateful for the merits they might acquire from them.[27] In these texts, Saint Louis also used a very typical expression of his conception of emotional life: he spoke of "malaise de coeur" (illness of the heart, heartache), which implied the parallel with "malaise de corps" (illness of the body), because for him the heart and the body formed the essential pair, rather than those of mind and body or body and soul. With this marked preference for the heart, we encounter a turning point in sensibilities and vocabulary that took shape here.[28]

Finally, the only time Louis said anything about Purgatory in our documentation was to tell a leper whom he was visiting at Royaumont that his disease was "his Purgatory in this world."[29] A conservative on this point, Saint Louis adhered to the old doctrine of Gregory the Great (although Saint Thomas Aquinas himself remained open to this possibility), according to whom people could suffer "purgatory punishment" here on earth. It is especially here that Saint Louis revealed his basic concept of disease: it was an opportunity to pass from purgation to purification, from penitential punishment to salvation, through a merit that could only be obtained here on earth and not in the afterlife.[30]

A sickly king, a patient king, a king who transformed his physical suffering into merit, Saint Louis was not a "sad" king despite all this. Joinville tells us quite clearly that outside certain periods—like Fridays, for example—when the king banned all external signs of happiness for religious reasons, the king's natural temperament was to be joyous: "When the king was full of joy."[31] This may also be a characteristic of his Franciscan spirituality.

VOLUNTARY SUFFERING: THE ASCETIC AND PENITENT KING

The king was marked by the monastic tradition through the influence of the Cistercians of Royaumont as much as through the new Mendicant spirituality. Saint Louis did not fail to observe traditional practices of asceticism and mortification. This attitude undoubtedly came to him through a certain slightly masochistic personal tendency and through the penitential practices of the times, which were sometimes taken to an outrageous point by certain laymen.[32]

The king, as we may recall, had his confessor administer his discipline, and he also administered it to himself. He often wore a hair shirt, slept on a cotton mattress without any straw or silk, and fasted more than the Church required. His excessive penance was most strongly expressed after the failure of his first crusade.

Guillaume de Saint-Pathus detailed these ascetic practices.

> Since his return from overseas at the time of his first passage, he never slept on a bed of straw or feathers, but his bed was made of wood and they carried it with him everywhere he went, and they would put a mattress of cotton on it with a cover of wool and not of silk, and he would lie there without any other padding. . . . On each Good Friday and every Lent since his return from overseas, and on every Monday, Wednesday, and Friday, he would wear the hair shirt directly on his body.[33] He would carry out these acts of

penance as secretly as possible and would hide them from his chamberlains so well that with one single exception none of them ever knew the harshness of the penances he did. He had three small cords joined together that measured about a foot-and-a-half in length, and each of these cords had four or five knots in them, and on every Friday during the entire year and on Lent and on Mondays, Wednesdays, and Fridays, he would check all the corners of his room to make sure no one was there, close the door, and shut himself up in the room with Friar Geoffroy de Beaulieu of the Order of the Preachers, where they would stay for a long time together. The chamberlains locked outside the room would say that the blessed king was confessing to the friar, while, in fact, the friar was disciplining him with the cords I just described.[34]

His confessor Geoffroy de Beaulieu was thus well informed about these practices, which he confirmed, although he claimed that he attempted to limit them.

Of all these practices, Boniface VIII mentioned the hair shirt, the fasts, and the portable wooden bed without straw in his bull for the canonization.[35]

The Deaths of Family Members and Friends: Familial and Dynastic Pain

Mourning was another one of those trials in which a man of "heart" experienced suffering and learned to transcend it. Family, or rather his royal line, was what counted for Louis more than anything else, his mother—especially his mother—his brothers, and his children. We have seen Joinville reproach him for the fact that he seemed to feel less affection for his wife, Queen Marguerite de Provence, a spouse and mother weighed down by one pregnancy after another. According to his confessor, Louis was never unfaithful to her. He suffered through the deaths of several of his loved ones: his brother Robert d'Artois who was killed in Egypt in 1250, his mother Blanche of Castile who died in 1252 when he was still in Palestine, the kingdom's heir Louis who was struck down in 1260 at the age of sixteen, and another son, Jean-Tristan, who was born in Damietta just after the defeat at

Mansourah during Louis' captivity. He was named Tristan after the sad situation of that time and died several days before his father in front of the walls of Tunis. Let's reread these texts that show us Louis' pain after these familial deaths.

After the death of Robert d'Artois, Joinville showed us Saint Louis' "patience" when he was overcome with suffering: "The king responded that God had to be thanked for all that he had given him, and then very large tears fell from his eyes."[36] In his letter from Acre in August 1250, the king announced his brother's death to his subjects with the same mixture of suffering and submission to God, with joy surging forth from the king's hope that Robert was in heaven as a martyr for the crusade.[37]

When he learned of his mother Blanche of Castile's death several months later, Saint Louis was plunged in sadness, displaying such strong emotion that Joinville felt obligated to reprimand him.[38]

Geoffroy de Beaulieu who was with the king at the time in his function as his confessor underscored his submission to God's will in a more discreet and less exhibitionistic manner, although he did not hide Louis' sobs, tears, sighs, and loud complaints. He mentioned that he was unable to pray appropriately and spoke of his "immoderate sadness."[39]

When Saint Louis learned of his son Jean-Tristan's death as he lay on his own deathbed, a death his entourage had concealed from him for several days, "this good father's guts were strongly stirred."

THE PAIN BORN FROM THE FAILURE OF THE CRUSADE

Saint Louis also suffered for his army, whom he referred to as "my people," for the people of his kingdom, and for Christendom. The misfortunes that took place on his crusade in Egypt and its failure affected them in a way that made them a source of additional grief for him.

Joinville witnessed the king's pain when he heard the Saracens' Greek fire falling on his army in the night from his tent. He cried and prayed: "Every time the saint king heard that they were shooting the Greek fire at us, he rose up on his bed and held his hands out to Our Lord and said crying: 'Beautiful Lord God, protect my people for me.'"[40]

After his return to France, he mentioned his sufferings overseas to Henry III of England in 1254: "My friend dear king, it is not easy to show you what great and painful bitterness I experienced in body and soul for the love of Christ on my pilgrimage."[41] Matthew Paris also recounted the sadness and actual "depression" that struck Saint Louis on his return to France in 1254.

> The face and heart of the king of France were troubled, and he did not want to receive any consoling, and musical instruments, humorous words, and consoling speeches had no power to make him laugh or distract him. His passage through his native country, through his own kingdom, the respectful greetings from the people who gathered along his path and who recognized their legitimate sovereign with gift offerings, nothing could stop him from keeping his eyes fixed on the ground in profound sadness and from sighing deeply as he thought that his capture had resulted in general embarrassment for Christendom.

When a bishop tried to console him, the king replied:

> "If I were the only one to have to put up with the shame and adversity, and if my sins did not fall upon the universal Church, I would bear them more serenely. But, unfortunately for me, it is all Christendom that has been exposed to the embarrassment because of me." They sang a mass in honor of the Holy Spirit so that he might receive its consoling, which is stronger than anything. And, henceforth, through the grace of God, he accepted the salutary council of consolation.[42]

Louis recovered later on and rediscovered his duties and activities as a king who drew inspiration from his defeat and sadness for a penitential politics that pursued his task of edification as a Christian monarch in new forms. He bounced back stronger and more resolute than ever.

His Suffering as a Prisoner

Saint Louis knew the three greatest forms of pain a man of his age could experience, especially if he was a warrior and a leader: defeat, imprisonment, and death. They all happened to him in the course of a military expedition but not on the battlefield. Since the imprisonment of the first martyrs, Christianity always considered captivity as a major trial. A military order, the Order of Mercy, the *Mercédaires,* had been created at the beginning of the thirteenth century with the mission of buying back prisoners who had been captured by the Muslims. However, in this humbling adventure Saint Louis still found an opportunity for growth and for making the royal function grow with him along with his people and Christendom.

When he remembered the story of these misfortunes (defeat and captivity), Joinville adopted a tone of lament: "But you have already heard about the great persecutions we suffered with the king in Egypt."[43]

In his letter to his subjects in 1250, the king very simply stated his grief in having been taken prisoner along with the majority of his army, whereas they came to deliver Christian prisoners themselves: "We who had come to its [the Holy Land's] aid, bemoaning the captivity and pains of our prisoners."[44]

In the same letter, he justified the truce made with the Saracens in reference to the dangers of imprisonment:

> . . . we decided that it would be better for Christendom if we and the other prisoners were freed by the means of a truce rather than to keep this city [Damietta] with the rest of the Christians who were there, while remaining, we and the other prisoners, exposed to all the dangers of captivity. . . .[45]

The religious appropriation of this trial changed the prisoner's suffering into virtue and prestige. For Guillaume de Saint-Pathus, it was through mercy and the desire for "marvels," if not miracles, that God delivered Saint Louis into the hands of the infidels: "and then the Father of mercy, who wanted to be revealed in his marvelous saint, turned the blessed king Saint Louis over into the hands of the felonious Saracens. . . ."[46]

The king could exhibit his "patience" best in prison. Thus, for Guillaume de Chartres: "I cannot pass over in silence the time he was held prisoner by the infidels in Egypt. For the entire time he was held in prison he did not stop his practices of worship and his praise for God." The witness detailed the services he recited according to the custom of Paris with a Dominican priest who knew Arabic and Guillaume de Chartres himself, thanks to the breviary from his chapel and the missal that the Saracens gave him as a gift.[47]

In his sermon of August 6, 1297 Boniface VIII echoed this episode that contributed to Louis' reputation for sainthood. Saint Louis pushed his religious zeal "to the point of combating the enemies of Christ's cross and the Christian faith, to the point of the captivity and imprisonment of his own body, his wife, and his brothers." In his bull for the canonization, the pope recalled that in prison Saint Louis "humbly and patiently tolerated the many disgraces and insults whose humiliating character was augmented by the miserable condition of the people who inflicted them on him."[48]

THE SUFFERING OF TEARS DENIED

Among all the signs of religion in the etymological sense of the word, all the expressions that God's grace gave to the human sinner, there was one that Saint Louis cherished more than any others: tears. Tears expressed the idea that God had recognized the potential of the sinner's penitence. He made purifying water spring forth from him. Saint Louis cried through the entire length of his biographies.

However, he often failed to cry. His heart remained "hard and dry." In the account of his confessor, Geoffroy de Beaulieu, we can feel the king's private suffering when he was deprived of tears. That great intuitive master of French history — he too had read the texts — Michelet understood the drama of the "gift of tears denied to Saint Louis."[49] Michelet was a Romantic in an age that rediscovered the secret source of tears flowing from the depths of being after the virtuous tears of the late eighteenth century, a source of the creation of man's artistic productions, and tears mixed with suffering and joy. In an Old French version of the text that dates from after the canonization, he gives the confessor's text that I have modernized here: "The blessed king so marvelously desired the grace of tears that he complained to his confessor that he could not cry tears, and he humbly, softly, and privately said to him that when they said these words in the litany, 'Beautiful Lord God, we pray that you give us a fountain of tears,' the saint king would devoutly say: "But Lord God, I do not dare ask you for a fountain of tears; small teardrops would be enough for me to water the dryness of my heart.' And sometimes he admitted to his confessor in private that the Lord sometimes granted him a few tears in his prayers, and that when he felt them softly flowing down his cheeks into his mouth, he would very sweetly savor them not only in his heart but also on his tongue."[50]

When he put together a number of quotes from Joinville, Michelet thought that Saint Louis might have even suffered doubts about his faith.[51] Instead, I think these signs that Michelet identifies as "light" after all involved Saint Louis' fears about his salvation but not his faith.

THE SUFFERING OF OTHERS: THE WORKS OF MERCY

The meaning of suffering for Saint Louis gave rise to his complete devotion to it. Beyond his individual existence, this devotion was exercised in relation to others. This produced his service for the sick, the poor, the leprous, and his construction of hospitals. As he experienced it, there was no separation of the body's suffering from the suffering of the heart or the soul.

Guillaume de Saint-Pathus showed the extent to which the king practiced the code of charity that took on a new systematic form in the thirteenth century, the system of "works of mercy" (oeuvres de miséricorde).

> He had charity for his fellow men and virtuous methodical compassion, and he did the works of mercy by housing, feeding, giving drink to, clothing, visiting, and comforting the sick and the poor, assisting them directly by supporting them and serving them in person, and by paying the ransoms of captured prisoners, burying the dead, and helping everyone virtuously and generously.[52]

This practice of charity could not be kept secret and it made a powerful impression on his contemporaries. There is no shortage of documentation for it. Guillaume de Saint-Pathus reported that every time he went to Royaumont, depending on the days, he would distribute meat or fish to all the sick people in the abbey whether they were monks or laypersons and was especially attentive to feeding all the sick foreigners in the abbey who were staying in its hospital at the time.[53] His works of mercy extended to that unpopular figure, the foreigner.

At the hospital of Vernon, which was built with royal funds, he also gave "beds and other necessities for the poor and the sick." For the inauguration of this hospital, he and his close son-in-law King Thibaud of Navarre carried out a kind of enthronement or "coronation" for the first sick person to be admitted:

And when the hospital of Compiègne was built, the saint king on the one hand and His Royal Highness Thibaud who was king of Navarre, his son-in-law, who helped him on the other, carried and put [into his bed] the first ever poor sick man to be placed in the newly built hospital.[54]

Guillaume de Saint-Pathus[55] and Geoffroy de Beaulieu[56] both also recalled his founding of the house of the Quinze-Vingts in Paris. For his part, Guillaume de Chartres stressed the assistance the king gave to sick people who were dying and possibly contagious.

> The king was so full of the spirit of charity [*pietatis*] that he would be happy to make visits of charity [*causa charitative visitationes*] to sick people who were still suffering in agony [*in extremis etiam laborantes*], although many of his people tried to discourage him from doing so because of the danger, and he would give them words of pious consolation and salvation and very necessary pieces of advice.[57]

At the end of his life, in his *Enseignements* he advised his children to feel compassion for all people who are suffering in their hearts or bodies. To his son, he wrote: "Dear son, I instruct you to have a compassionate heart toward the poor and all those whom you would consider to be suffering in their hearts or their bodies."[58] To his daughter, he wrote: "Have a heart full of pity for all people you know have some misfortune of the body or the heart."[59]

Guillaume de Saint-Pathus assembled the most extensive record on this topic in his *Vie de Saint Louis*.[60] I will recall only a few examples from it. In general, the "blessed king Saint Louis had marvelous tender compassion for people who were in a bad way [*dans le mésaise*]." In particular, Guillaume showed him during his first crusade when there were "many poor and others sick with various diseases of the kidneys, the teeth, and other infirmities in his army." In order to protect them from the Saracens, the king emptied the boats of any supplies that were not indispensable and filled them "with the poor and sick in the hundreds." When he in turn became sick with several illnesses, "he wanted to share the misfortunes and the dangers his people were in," "out of love and charity he wanted to expose his body to all misfortunes in order to protect the people who were with him," and "he had such great compassion that he never wanted to go into the boats without the others."[61]

The most famous of these passages from Guillaume de Saint-Pathus described Saint Louis' visit to the sick in the abbey of Royaumont. The hagiographer stressed how the king sought out physical contact with the sick, his doctor-like attitude, and his act of feeding the ones who were in the most dismal condition, and, more specifically, his charity for a leprous monk.

> He went into the abbey's infirmary and visited with the sick friars, comforted them, and asked each one of them what disease he was suffering from and for certain ones took their pulse and touched their temples even if they were sweating. He would call on the doctors [*physiciens*] who were with him and have them examine the urine of the sick people in his presence. . . . He would have food that was appropriate for them brought from his kitchen.
>
> He would more eagerly and more attentively visit those who were the sickest, and he would even touch their hands and the places where they were ailing, and the more the disease was serious—whether an abscess or something else like that—the happier the king would be to touch the sick person.
>
> There was one monk who was named Léger. He was leprous [*mesel*] and lived in a house apart from the others. He was in such a miserable [*despis*] abominable condition because of his disease that his eyes were so ruined that he could hardly see. He had lost his nose, and his lips were split and swollen, and the holes of his eyes were all red and hideous "to see."

The king knelt down before him, sliced some meat for him, and put the pieces in his mouth. He asked him if he would enjoy eating some chickens and partridges, and when Léger answered that he would, Louis had some brought from his kitchen. When the leper said he wished the dishes were salted, Louis salted the meat for him, but the salt got into the poor man's split lips and made "poison" come out of them, which started to pour down his chin. The leper complained, so the king dipped the pieces of meat in the salt to flavor them and wiped off the grains of salt before feeding them to him. The king often went to visit this leper and said to his knights: "Let's go visit our sick man," but they would let him go in to visit him alone with the abbot or the prior.[62]

In a hospital, Louis carried out all the acts of service and charity toward the suffering people who were housed there. However, on these occasions he also wanted to set a humble but public example of paying homage to people who suffered in their hearts and human dignity. The king was also putting himself on display, a gesture that was equally political and religious.

On one Good Friday when Saint Louis was staying at his castle in Compiègne and going around barefoot to visit the churches of the town, he met a leper in the street. As he crossed the street, he stepped into a puddle of cold, muddy water in the middle of the street, and when he reached the leper [*mesel*], he gave him alms and kissed his hand. The people who saw this crossed themselves and told each other: "Look what the king has done: he has kissed the leper's hand."[63]

It is not the least bit surprising that this behavior showed up again in Boniface VIII's sermon of August 6, 1297, and then again in the bull for Louis' canonization. The pope recalled the same scene in his sermon:

> The king was a pious doctor to this leper. He visited him often and humbly served him, attentively wiping the pus from his ulcers and giving him to eat and drink from his own hands. He regularly accomplished these actions and others in the hospitals and leper-houses.[64]

In his bull, Boniface cited "the visits that the king personally made to the sick and infirm in different monasteries and hospitals," the leper of Royaumont "whom leprosy had attacked to such extent that he had become abominable and profoundly rejected, living apart [*segregatus*] from others," as well as a man suffering from Saint Éloi's disease (ulcers) whom the king would visit in Compiègne.[65]

The Leprosy of Sin

The profound cause of the pain that constantly dwelt inside Saint Louis was the meaning of sin, this sin that was a kind of leprosy to which physical death should be preferred. Voluntary suffering offered redemption from sin.

Blanche of Castile inculcated this horror of mortal sin in her son. Confusing her strict morality as a Christian woman with her passion as a jealous possessive mother, she loudly and forcefully proclaimed that she would rather see her son die than sin with a woman other than his own.[66]

He never forgot this lesson: "He remembered that his mother had repeatedly made him understand that she would rather he died than commit a mortal sin."[67]

Saint Louis put the question to Joinville in another form. Would he rather commit a mortal sin or be a leper? The seneschal was a man and a pious but normal Christian. He answered that he would rather commit thirty mortal sins than be leprous. To this, the king replied:

> You should know that there is no leprosy as ugly as existing in mortal sin. . . . When a man dies, he is healed of the leprosy of the body, but when a man who has committed a mortal sin dies, he does not know and cannot know for certain that he repented enough in his lifetime for God to have pardoned him. Thus, he has to be extremely afraid that this leprosy may last for him for as long as God will be in heaven. So, I pray that you would rather any misfortunes happen to your body, whether leprosy or any other disease, than mortal sin arise within your soul. . . .[68]

And Louis handed down the same lesson to his son:

> You must be resolved not to commit any mortal sin no matter what happens, and that you would suffer having your arms and legs chopped off and have your life taken away in the cruelest martyrdom before ever knowingly committing a mortal sin.[69]

Louis was a key link in this chain of moral inculpation that used the leper's suffering body as a symbolic image for the leprosy of the soul.

THE MODEL OF THE CRUCIFIED CHRIST

This suffering utilized to confront sin engendered a particular devotion to Christ who through his passion allowed man to achieve salvation despite the original sin. It also produced a special devotion for the Cross, which served as the instrument of this passion and redemption

Saint Louis' great model then was the suffering Christ, the Christ of the Passion, and the Christ of the Cross.[70] The thirteenth-century king was a crucified Christ who wore the crown. This was the new image of monarchy par excellence.

Saint Louis evoked the crucified Christ on ceremonious occasions. At Cluny in 1246, he told Pope Innocent IV: "Don't we read that Christ humbled himself to the point of suffering the ignominy of the Cross?"[71] In his letter from Acre in August 1250, he asked his subjects: "We invite you all to serve the man who served you on the cross by spilling his own blood for your salvation. . . ."[72] By acquiring the distinguished relic of the Crown of Thorns and by building the shrine of the Saint-Chapelle to house it, Saint Louis wanted to dedicate the chapel of his royal palace to divine suffering.

Paradoxically, Joinville entrusted an infidel with the care of ironically telling Saint Louis what Christ suffered for them. During the captivity in Egypt, an old Muslim told the Christian prisoners: "You should not complain about having been captured for him, beaten for him, and wounded [*navrés*] for him, since he did the same for you. . . ."[73]

Martyrdom: Agony and Death

As we already saw in the case of his brother Robert d'Artois, Louis always considered death on the crusades as a form of martyrdom. As early as 1241, speaking about the Tartars who were invading Christendom, he told his mother: "Either we will push them back, or, if it happens that we are conquered, we will go away toward God like martyrs or Christ's confessors."[74]

During his stay in the Holy Land between 1250 and 1254, when he went to look for the corpses of the Christians who were killed by Saracens before Sidon in order to bury them, he declared to his companions:

> Let us go forth and bury these martyrs. . . . They have suffered death, so we can certainly suffer this [the stench of the cadavers and the work of burying them]. Do not hold these bodies in abomination because they are martyrs and in Heaven.[75]

From the very onset of his biography written shortly after Louis' death, Geoffroy de Beaulieu presented the king as a willing victim.

> He who, in addition to the sacrifice of bodily penance that he made to God every day according to the condition and weakness of

his own body, in his second passage overseas finally offered himself as a perfect sacrifice [*quasi holocaustum integrum*] to the Lord with an air of sweetness . . . and who was worthy of becoming Christ's *host* there [in Tunisia] and gladly consumed the end of his life in the Lord like a martyr and a tireless champion of the Lord.[76]

Beginning with the first biographies, the account of his illness, his agony, and his death before Tunis became an obligatory theme, a piece of inevitable bravura in which most of the commonplaces about a good Christian's death, the good death, poured out. Geoffroy de Beaulieu insisted upon this grace of God that imposed a happy ending on the king's trials (*qui labores ipsius voluit feliciter consummare*). As his condition worsened, he piously received the final sacraments, "sane of mind and in full possession of consciousness" (*sana mente et integro intellectu*). As the end drew near, he only thought of God and the exaltation of the Christian faith. He even thought about sending a Dominican preacher to the king of Tunis. As his strength and his voice gradually began to fade, he never stopped requesting the suffrages of the saints to whom he was especially devoted: Saint Denis the "special patron of his kingdom," Saint Jacques, and many others. "When he reached his final hour, he had himself lain out with his *arms in the form of the cross* on a bed of ashes and he rendered his soul to the Creator. *It was at the very same hour that the Son of God expired as he was dying on the cross for the world's salvation.*"[77] We can find other allusions to this good death in Boniface VIII's canonization bull ("he happily passed on to Christ" [*faciliter migravit ad Christum*]), but any christological references (to his death with his arms in the form of the cross or the fact that he died at three in the afternoon) were struck from it.[78]

In contrast, Joinville, who was not present at Tunis when the king died and who suffered some remorse for this, subscribed to the tradition that placed Saint Louis' death "at that same hour when the Son of God died on the cross for the world's salvation."[79]

He objected most of all to the fact that the canonization did not make Saint Louis a martyred saint. They did not do Saint Louis justice, not even in sainthood.

> And it seems to me that they did not do enough for him when they did not place him in the number of the martyrs for the great pains he suffered on the pilgrimage of the Cross, and also because he followed Our Lord in the high act of the Cross. Because, if God

died on the cross, he did the same because he was crossed when he died in Tunis.[80]

The importance and the forms of suffering in Saint Louis' life and personality summed up the evolution of Latin Christianity in the thirteenth century. This development consisted in the growing importance given to the body and physical pain, the codified introduction of "works of mercy" into the heart of the religious system, the charity expressed for "suffering hearts and bodies," the valorization of pain for sin, the omnipresence of tears beyond traditional contrition, the worship of the suffering Christ and the Cross of the Passion, and the stress placed on the agony of the dying. All this painful glorification of suffering led to an image close to the Man of Sorrow, the *Ecce homo* of whom Saint Louis was one of the precursors.

However, he represents even more in the history of the valorization of suffering. As a saint, he was a saint of suffering that was accepted and desired—in his charity for the poor and sick and in his imitative love for the crucified Christ. He was a saint of penitence and self-immolation, the dual layman of Francis of Assisi. While Saint Francis saw his vocation for suffering crowned with stigmata, Saint Louis reached the end of his path of pain at the tragic and glorious hour of Jesus' death.

Worship of the crucified Christ and the Cross led Saint Louis down the same path of sacrifice as a penitent for this penitence that was superior to all others, the crusade; tormented by disease, defeat, and imprisonment, he reached martyrdom on his second crusade. He was a self-sacrificing king, and this has been one of the aspects of sacred royalty in various societies.[81] A host-king, at the end of his long agony he attained the grace of dying in the image of Christ.

This saint was thus ultimately a model king through suffering. Thanks to it, he was able to raise the image of royalty above and beyond any of its other incarnations. More than all his riches and victories, for his contemporaries his glory consisted in his behavior in sickness, prison, failure, and mourning. He was a Christ-King, and this extraordinary memory combined political meaning and religious sentiment in an inseparable unity, making suffering into an instrument for both personal salvation and political success. An eschatological king, a king of psychodrama, it was on pain—and physical pain most of all—that he founded a political practice and ideology.

Conclusion

IN A WORK BUILT AROUND A GREAT HISTORICAL FIGURE, IT IS FIRST of all hard to escape making some kind of confidence to one's readers. At different more or less lengthy moments over the course of the last ten years or more in Saint Louis' company, what were my relations with him and how did they evolve? I certainly do not have the presumptuousness to write up an essay on "Me and Saint Louis." I do believe that the historian has the right, and perhaps also the duty, to implicate himself in his subject matter, even when this subject is a historical figure. However, like any man of science—and even if it is a science as particular and conjectural as history— he has to stay outside of what is really more of an object for him, his object of study. The historian is not a judge. Nonetheless, one of the charms and major risks of historical biography is that a certain bond forms and develops between the historian and his character. It is not up to me to say what predisposed me to attempt to become a historian of Saint Louis, nor whatever inside me could have influenced my way of seeing him, showing him, and explaining him. If they think it is useful, others may try to answer this question. However, I do owe it to my readers to let them know what I felt in my contact with this figure. The historian does not have the same kind of relationship with the subject of a biography that he has with other historical problems. It was a problem more than a man that I took as my point of departure: how and why can a historical biography be written? I have already explained this, along with my professional reasons for choosing Saint Louis. However, one does not just take more than ten years of life with a single character lightly, even one that died seven centuries ago, especially if one believes that controlled and enlightened imagination is necessary to the historian's work. Thus the perhaps illusory feeling came to me that I was getting to know Louis better and better, that I could see him, that I could hear him, and that, while keeping my distance and staying in the background, I was becoming a new Robert de Sorbon or another Joinville. This displacement was part of my project after all; it was inscribed in the very heart of my problematic: could one approach Saint Louis as an individual? And the positive response that my inquiry brought me little by little reinforced a more subjective, more intimate feeling in me.

At first, I felt very distant from him. This was the distance of time and social status. Even with the historian's privileges, how can one approach a king and a saint? Then, through the documents and my analysis of their production, I felt him getting closer and closer. I did not see him in my dreams, but I think that, like Joinville, I could have done it. And what I felt more and more is the attraction and the fascination of the character. I think I understood how many people had a desire to see him, to hear him, and to touch him. A personal charisma was added to the prestige of his function, which his Capetian predecessors had carefully constructed. This was the charisma of a king who did not need to wear the crown and the emblems of power to impress anyone, the charisma of a tall, thin, handsome king with the eyes of a dove whom Salimbene of Parma had seen coming barefoot through the dust on the path to Sens. He was an impressive character regardless of his appearance, one of the most striking illustrations of Weber's theory of charisma, one of the most remarkable incarnations of a type and a category of power. He had the will to become a type of ideal ruler and a talent for being profoundly idealistic and considerably realistic at the same time. He had grandeur in victory and defeat. He embodied a harmony—contradictory in appearance—between politics and religion. He was a pacifist warrior and a builder of the state who was always concerned about the behavior of his representatives. He indulged his fascination with poverty while still upholding his rank; he had a passion for justice while still respecting a profoundly non-egalitarian order. He united will and grace, logic and chance, without which no destiny exists.

Then he became more familiar to me. I heard him laughing, joking, teasing his friends, and making simple gestures, like sitting down on the ground, with a minimal amount of affectation. I thought I understood what it cost him to rein in his natural tendencies, his hot-blooded nature in love, his anger and physical exuberance, his love of good food, big fish, and fresh fruit, his need to laugh, and the pleasure of chatting, even if it were Friday. There was just a man behind the "superman" drawn up in the bull for his canonization. And I began to conceive a mixture of friendship and admiration for him, as the historian's impertinence and distance in time allowed him to forget his position. Without ever trying to figure out if he would accept me, he became one of my familiar friends. I finally began to have the kind of feelings for him that we have for our intimate friends and family members. And I hated him as much as I loved him. Of course, this feeling came mainly from my feelings as a man of the twentieth century. I felt raw hostility toward his ascetic ideal bound up with external penitential practices especially flagellation, his intolerance that arose from his literal respect for the rigors of religion, his fanaticism toward the Jews, his attempts to impose his own practices of worship upon his entourage, his irresistible march toward a blinder and stricter moral order (did Joinville resist seeing the king on a daily basis after his return from the crusade?), his increasingly narrow-minded morality, his incessant sermonizing speeches, and his increasingly inhuman love of pain. Then, there was the indifference to others that often took hold of him and that Joinville stigmatized when it affected his wife and children, the indifference into which he was drawn by his penchant for religious rumination and preference for the pursuit of the ideal over worldly attachments, which still sometimes held him in its sway. And then, he could still cry.

However, I have to admit that the fascination remains.

I think that I also have to attempt to answer two traditional questions. There is the question about the role of great men in history and the question of the hero's status between tradition and modernity. I will leave others the task of studying Saint Louis in the perspective of a theory of the great man or of a comparative history of great men. I am satisfied to point out certain general conditions and circumstances that allowed Saint Louis to come to the fore in his time and as an exceptional figure over the long run. He benefited from his position at the summit of two important hierarchies, the temporal hierarchy of royalty and the spiritual hierarchy of sainthood. In the first case, it was enough for him to be an heir, although he took full advantage of his dynastic prestige.[1] As expressed in the rearrangement of the royal necropolis of Saint-Denis and his encouragement for the composition of a "*Roman des rois*" in French, the nucleus of the *Grandes Chroniques de France,* Louis relied on the prestige of the legendary continuity between the three dynasties and the emblematic figures of the first two, Clovis and Charlemagne. Stressing the heritage of his "predecessors" and ancestors, he multiplied references to the most illustrious of his close ascendants, his grandfather Philip Augustus. He also benefited from the image of a father who was strangely more distant and ephemeral in the royal function but still decorated with the victor's halo as the conqueror of the most formidable heretics, the Cathars.

He knew how to take advantage of three outstanding heritages. The first one was political: belonging to a sacred dynasty, sanctified by an exceptional gesture, the anointment carried out with a miraculous oil that made him the "very Christian king" above all the other monarchs in Christendom. The anointment haloed him with a thaumaturgical power.

The second heritage was economic. He had extraordinary revenues at his disposal due to the accumulation of riches in the Royal Treasury achieved by his grandfather Philip Augustus and to the considerable prosperity of the Kingdom of France as a whole and the royal domain in particular. Île-de-France, Picardy, Normandy, and Languedoc were regions that especially benefited during the economic expansion.

The third heritage was "national." The Midi had been directly and indirectly welded to the north of the kingdom since 1229, while the monarchy's presence there had only been distant and theoretical to this point. For the first time in history, Louis was the acting king of the entire kingdom. He hardly seems to have been concerned with the Midi before the crusade of 1248 except to reinforce its position in the kingdom: he put down Raymond Trencavel's revolt in 1240 and defeated him, and the seneschalcies of Beaucaire and Carcassonne were stabilized. The defeat of Raimond VII who was allied with the English followed their failure in 1242, and the peace of Lorris normalized the king's suzerainty over the lands of the count of Toulouse (although he seems to have been dealt with rather gently thanks to Blanche of Castile's protection). Although it was mainly due to the Church, the Inquisition, and the erosion of the heresy itself, the end of active Catharism reinforced the return to peace. It is clear that the second quarter of the thirteenth century marked the failure of the south of France confronted with the north on both political and cultural grounds. Whatever we may think about the brutality of the "French of the north" who were the aggressors in this affair, we must not dismiss the southerners' inability to create an Occitan state before the Albigensian Crusade and the internal exhaustion of Occitan culture at the end of the thirteenth and beginning of the fourteenth century after the high point in the civilization of the troubadours which had been closely tied to the military aristocracy. It is certainly legitimate for the Occitan renewal of the nineteenth and twentieth centuries to have been marked by nostalgia about these failures and hostility toward the brutal way that the northern crusaders and the Capetian monarchy took advantage of this. However, a sensible and serene approach to the relations between the north and south of France in the Middle Ages stands out more than excessively partial, anachronistic extravagances.[2]

Even more than his royalty, the sainthood he attained through his merits and the zeal of certain supporters placed Louis above the mass of great historical figures. We have seen what was new about this sainthood in the hagiographical landscape of the Middle Ages, strongly influenced by Mendicant devoutness, even though some of its aspects were more traditional. In the very exclusive company of saint kings that became an even more restrictive group after the Gregorian reform, Louis marked a clear break with the earlier models of sainthood, and, as he was the first and last in this series, he constituted a unique model. This helped advance his image too, and continues to do so.

His sainthood gave him an additional advantage: Louis became the hero of a body of literature that strove to represent him as he truly existed, while still highlighting his good qualities and virtues and repressing his weaknesses. Although he had not been the first Capetian king to serve as the object of quasi-official and necessarily laudatory biographies — as had been the case of Robert the Pious, Louis VI, and his grandfather Philip Augustus — Saint Louis was the first beneficiary of a biography written by a layman who knew him well. Without Joinville, Saint Louis would not be what he has been since the fourteenth century — a living image. Saint Louis was Joinville's creation, perhaps even more than Charlemagne was for Éginard, Louis VI for Suger, and Napoleon for Las Cases. However, at the end of his inquiry, the historian tends to think that the model resembled the hero in the book.

One final stroke of luck is that Joinville did not write in Latin but in French. Since he drank in the words of the king, his idol and his friend, he often presents him speaking in the first person. In this age when the writer is just beginning to say "I," Saint Louis was one of the first in dignity and authority to speak like this in the first person.[3] If we disregard the stereotyped speeches placed in the mouths of the great figures of Antiquity and the High Middle Ages since the very ancient days of rulers whose words were set down on inscription stones and fixed in an official formalized language, Saint Louis was the first great man of the West to appear to us using daily speech.

Over the long course of history, Louis benefited from having been contemporary with a great moment of civilization that was particularly brilliant in his kingdom, although his own actions never had much of an impact on it. I am referring to the great flourishing of Gothic art, the glorious establishment of the University of Paris, and the newly established prestige of the French language. It is true, however, that his memory is associated with a dazzling monument that is, like him, both modest and brilliant, the Sainte-Chapelle.

The good fortune of his historical legacy has endured. The saint king has been fortunate enough to weather the different avatars of historical memory across changes in regimes, societies, and mentalities without sustaining any significant damage. From his death to the Revolution, he embodied the unequaled essence of the French monarchy. Whether they ruled or not, whether they descended from him through primogeniture, through his second-born sons, or even through women, whether they were Capetians, Valois, or Bourbons, thanks to the powerful ideology of *the blood,* as long as they had a drop of his blood in their veins (and the blood of this virtuous king who had no bastard children was necessarily *pure*), they all belonged to this elite that was superior to any other, the elite of princes and princesses issued from Saint Louis. The priest who accompanied Louis XVI on the scaffold told him—or someone else appropriately had him say at the ultimate moment: "Son of Saint Louis, rise to the heavens!" The very-Christian king was especially venerated after the Revolution and the Empire in catholic and conservative, if not counter-revolutionary, milieus. He held up quite well against the establishment of the Republic and the progress of secular ideas because he had also embodied the ideals professed by these new milieus— moderation, and, above all, peace and justice. It was even the Third Republic that promoted a short passage from Joinville to the status of a mythological image through Lavisse's *Histoire de France* and various school manuals. This is the image of Saint Louis administering justice beneath the oak tree at Vincennes. Today, his profound identification with Christendom may earn him the respect of the supporters of European unity.

The revisions that periodically result from advances in historical research and new historiographical orientations have spared him. No one has ever discovered or documented an underside of Saint Louis' century, even though we know with even greater certainty that the beacons of the thirteenth century left large patches of darkness over the lives of the men and women of this time. Famines had more or less ceased, and works of charity clearly progressed. The accusation that he abandoned and weakened France with his crusades and his long stay in the Holy Land does not hold up under careful examination, and I hope that I have shown this here.

Even his failures enhanced his image. They made him more human. They also placed him in the line of a national history made up of an alternation between periods of good fortune and hardship that allowed the collective consciousness to integrate misfortunes into the historical identity.

For a Frenchman at the end of the twentieth century, there are still some dark zones in this history. There is the support Louis gave to the Inquisition, his attitude toward the Jews, his role in the crusades and in relations between Christians and Muslims. All these domains arose from the same obsession that took shape in the course of the twelfth century and that was institutionalized in the thirteenth century: the desire to consolidate all Christendom in a single body, a simultaneously natural and mystical body that would exclude all those who could pollute it, corrupt it, weaken it, dissolve it. This vision was leveled against heretics, Jews, homosexuals to a lesser degree, lepers in an ambiguous way, and Muslims in a problematic manner, since Islam no longer existed inside of Christendom after the Spanish Reconquista. But, didn't Jerusalem and the Holy Land belong to Christendom, and weren't they even its very center and heart? Saint Louis was a product of this society that feared impurity, but contrary to appearances he only played a moderated role in it that was submitted to other trends like moderating scholastic casuistry and the Mendicant pedagogy that supported moderation in speech, for example.

Nevertheless, because I place myself here in the perspective of long historical time, I reject the argument according to which Saint Louis only acted in these realms as a man of his time. First of all, personal engagement in one past mode of action or another may have been more or less involved; moreover, it is normal to assess the weight of the past in phenomena of long historical duration.

As for the Inquisition, we have seen that he did not think of opposing the papacy's request that he act as the secular arm of the Church any more than almost all the rulers of the age. Nor did he ever consider not executing the measures resulting from the condemnations of the ecclesiastical tribunals of the Inquisition. However, as Jean Richard has very aptly remarked, none of his hagiographers ever indicated that he displayed a particular zeal in repressing heresy—which they no doubt would have liked to have been able to do. Saint Louis was deceived by Robert le Bougre at the beginning of his anti-heretical fury. Saint Louis attempted to limit the extent of the repression. His goal was conversion, the return of the stray sheep to the fold of orthodoxy, the reconciliation of all Christians.

This was also his objective in his dealings with the Jews. The baptism of a Jew was one of his most joyful experiences, and in several cases he became a godfather to converted Jews. His hostility toward them was of a religious nature. Not only had he never been afflicted with the virus of racism—the idea of race was not a medieval concept—he did not classify the Jews among the "nations," the term that more or less corresponded to that of ethnicity today. Still, it is true that he viewed the Jews as foreigners of a particularly perfidious and despicable nature, and in dealing with them he hesitated between repression and protection.

Finally, with his engagement in the crusades, he participated in an aggression of Western Christendom against Islam, which would have a long-lasting legacy. However, the failure of his crusades makes him more of a pitiful hero of what people have called Western pre-colonialism than a triumphant enemy of the Muslims. Once again, in this case he also clung to his illusions of conversion.

In both his successes and failures, Louis did not make any significant innovations. He continued the important historical movements that were born before him and tried to carry them further. These movements included the aspiration to justice and peace, the advances in the institutions and practices that favored royal power and the unification of the state, while reinforcing a change in mentality that tried to limit violence and displace the central focus of religious worship. As it continued to base itself on the cult of the relics and ascetic practices, religious worship also came to emphasize humility, the imitation of Christ, the practice of works of mercy, and a "mendicant" piety that had not yet become "modern worship" (*devotio moderna*), but was a response to the challenge of Christendom's great expansion that lasted from the tenth to the thirteenth century. Saint Louis also made advances in techniques for social control and contributed to the profound transformation in the relations that people had "with authority, truth, and belief" that took place between the Middle Ages and the Renaissance.[4]

He was the type of great man that we can consider as a "great man of a historical high point," who brought the material, spiritual, and political advances of a long self-sustained period of growth to completion. Louis could be the emblematic figure of a "century" comparable to the ones into which the Enlightenment liked to divide the past: the century of Pericles, the century of Augustus, or the century of Louis XIV. Besides, some people have already dubbed it "the century of Saint Louis." He may be a figure that is more emblematic than creative. His contemporaries had the impression that he dominated the age, and history cannot refute them if one considers all of the symbolism that came together in his life and character.

Even though he was marked by the evolution of the values and political structures of his time, the ideal he embodied was oriented more toward the past than toward the future. Saint Louis was the ideal king of Christendom as defined by Roman Catholic Europe and the Holy Land, the Old Testament, and the twelfth-century Renaissance. After him, there were no more kings of the crusade, no more saint kings, no more kings without faces. Another age was fast approaching, the time of the kings of the law, politics, and economy, the kings of the jurists, Aristotle, and the crisis. Saint Louis was the king of a political ideal that came to die on the shore of this other age.

As a sacred symbol of Christendom, Saint Louis was unrivalled in his time. Only the nineteenth and twentieth centuries—especially the twentieth century—raised up another great thirteenth-century figure alongside him: Emperor Frederick II. For better or worse, historians have viewed the emperor as the first modern ruler for whom justice was only a means in the service of the veritable end, reason, the reason of state, instead of an end in itself. In upholding this view, they have overlooked a much more complex historical reality. According to this view, the emperor attempted to form a "closed commercial state" based on state monopolies and a perfected customs system in Sicily. He supposedly practiced tolerance toward the Muslims and the Jews, prefiguring a pluri-religious, pluri-cultural, pluri-ethnic state. He might have been one of the first "scientific" intellectuals and a possible unbeliever, a combination of a tyrant and an enlightened despot. Ernst Kantorowicz had a better approach to Frederick II, despite the anachronisms of his pre-Nazi German ideology. He sees him instead as a ruler oriented in his ancient dreams toward an imperial past, who saw himself as the last chance to reincarnate this ancient glory, although this earned him his reputation as the Antichrist in his own time: "Frederick II was the last emperor to experience deification and find his place among the stars."[5] In the eyes of today's historian, regardless of whatever movements they anticipated in other domains, the extraordinary couple formed by the last emperor to be deified and the last saint king is a pair turned toward the past in a dream of universality, the dream of the ancient universal Empire for Frederick and of Saint Augustine's universal Christendom for Louis. They brought a close to these great dreams that collapsed around them in an apotheosis. Even though some of their ideas or actions may have heralded it, the future only really began after them.

The modernity to come would first of all be manifested in the crisis that affected the old values and that undermined this accomplishment that Christendom and France had achieved under Saint Louis' reign. The beginning of a social and economic crisis surfaced with the first labor conflicts and the first monetary manipulations at the end of the reign. These were a prelude to the crisis that had other warning signs[6] including: attacks against the scholastic balancing of faith and reason, attacks made, for example, by the aggressive naturalism of Jean de Meung's *Roman de la Rose*; fierce criticism of the Mendicant orders presented by individuals like Rutebeuf; and, finally, the failure of the crusade. Contemporaries at the end of Saint Louis' reign were not aware of this turning point, this conclusion to a long ascendant period. When they finally perceived the evidence and the deepening of the crisis at the very end of the thirteenth and beginning of the fourteenth century, Saint Louis' person and reign only appeared more brilliant and beneficial to them, and more worthy of their regret. The myth of a golden age that had existed under Saint Louis and thanks to Saint Louis took shape; it partly corresponded to the reality and was partly born of the embellishment of memory. The harsh realities of the present time would find their counterpoint in the recollection of the "[good old] days of his Royal Highness Saint Louis" ([*bon*] *temps monseigneur Saint Louis*). Saint Louis' final chance to make his mark as a great man would be as a king of nostalgia, but nostalgia for a monarch of the past decked out with all the honors refused in his present time, isn't this another *topos,* another commonplace idea of historical sentiment? In the end, did Saint Louis exist?

Appendix 1

Saint Louis' "Somatic Formula"
According to Dr. Auguste Brachet (1894)

AUGUSTE BRACHET WAS A REMARKABLE CHARACTER. HE HAD TO LIVE off modest occupations including a subordinate position in the catalogue office of the Bibliothèque nationale (at that time, the Bibliothèque impériale) and as a tutor to Empress Eugénie. He was born in Tours in 1844 and died of tuberculosis in 1898. He was partly formed as an autodidact (he studied for only a short time at the École des Chartes) and became a specialist in Romance Philology. He published a French grammar "based on the history of the language," and it went through numerous reprints beginning in 1867. He was a disciple of the great Littré, scholarly editor of Hippocrates, and positivist philologist. Thanks to his knowledge of medicine, philology, and history, in 1880 he undertook a "Mental Pathology of the Kings of France," which he was only able to complete through the end of the Middle Ages. The first edition of 1896 was not released. The edition that was used was posthumous and published in 1903 by his widow, Anna Brachet, née Korf.

Obsessed with the theory of heredity, Auguste Brachet tried to situate Saint Louis in the Capetian chain leading from Charles VI, an insane king, to Louis XI, an epileptic. A positivist doctor, he still did not try to reduce Saint Louis' behavior to physiology. For example, he writes that "for Louis IX, the generative functions are normal. The king's continence . . . results from his religious scruples and not any physiological causes." What is astonishing, though explained by the scholarly methods of this quasi-Chartist, is that he managed to assemble the exhaustive record of everything concerning Saint Louis' body and health in the sources from the time.

On the king's nervous system, Brachet states that he suffered from "olfactory anesthesia" because he could not smell the stench of the cadavers on the battlefield at Sidon. But if the king didn't stuff his nose, wasn't this out of respect for the dead?

Brachet speaks of the "clouding" [*obnubilation*] of his vision when after a bedside prayer he asks his entourage: "Where am I?" However, this seems more like Guillaume de Saint-Pathus's attempt to achieve a rhetorical effect that highlights the intensity of the saint's praying.

Is the pain accompanied by redness that Louis periodically felt in his right leg that Brachet diagnoses as recurring erysipelas of an infectious nature really a symptom of malaria as the doctor hypothesizes? He claims that Louis must have contracted it during the campaign against the English in Poitou and Saintonge. This would also be the source of the famous coma into which the king fell before pronouncing his vow to crusade. Is it necessary, though, to rely on the scholarly terms employed by the pedant Brachet who describes this as "a mixed typho-paludal form, a symptom [*allure*] often taken on by the comatose (*febris intermittens comitata*)"?

The king's illnesses during the crusade in Egypt, illnesses that also affected the majority of his army, were nothing extraordinary: "recurrence of malaria and dysentery, scorbut."

After the return from the crusade, the king suffered from diseases that Brachet cannot identify because of the lack of details in the sources. More generally, he suffered from a "cachectic state coinciding with the infectious diseases contracted in Palestine." At the time of his departure on the crusade of Tunis, Louis could no longer mount a horse, as Joinville testifies.

He died from "dysentery, pernicious fever, and the typhus of the camps."

Dr. Brachet's final effort to attribute an abnormal pathology to Saint Louis is articulated in his commentary on the loss of speech that affected the king shortly before his death: "Was this a morbid mutism produced under the blow of the emotion caused by the extreme unction and disappearing under the influence of the emotion due to the presentation of the Holy Sacrament?"

Thus, despite Brachet's desire to demonstrate the burden of heredity that affected Louis XI, the honest and positivist doctor fails to make Louis an important link in the pathological chain tying the Capetians to the Valois. Nevertheless, the scholar assembled a fabulous record of the texts on the king's natural, physical body.

Appendix 2

Louis IX's Letter to His Subjects from the Holy Land (1250)

(From the French translation
in D. O'Connell,
Les Propos de Saint Louis, 163–72)

LOUIS, BY THE GRACE OF GOD, KING OF THE FRENCH, TO HIS DEAR and faithful prelates, barons, warriors, citizens, bourgeois, and all other inhabitants of his kingdom that these present letters reach, salute:

For the honor and the glory of God's name, desiring with all our soul to continue the enterprise of the crusade, we have deemed it appropriate to inform you that after the capture of Damietta (which Our Lord Jesus Christ, by his ineffable mercy, had delivered over to the power of the Christians as if by miracle, as you have no doubt already learned from the news of our council), we left this city on the twentieth of the month of last November. Our armies of land and sea united, we marched against the army of the Saracens that was assembled and camped in a place named Massoure in the vulgar language. During our march, we sustained the enemy's attacks, and they constantly experienced quite considerable losses. On one of these days, several men of the Egyptian army came to attack our people and were all killed. On our route, we learned that the sultan of Cairo had just put an end to his unhappy life, and that before he died he had sent for his son who was still in the eastern provinces and had all the leading officers of his army swear an oath of fidelity in favor of this prince, and that he had left the command of all these troops to one of his emirs, Facreddin. Upon arriving at the place we just named, we learned that this news was true. It was on Tuesday before the festival of Christmas that we arrived there, but we could not get near the Saracens because of the waters flowing between the two armies that are called the river Thanis, a current that breaks off from the great river Nile in this spot. We struck our camp between these two rivers, spreading out between the large one and the small one. We had several engagements with the Saracens there who had several of their men killed by our men's swords, but the larger number of them were drowned in the waters. Since the Thanis was not fordable because of the depth of its waters and the height of its banks, we began to build a causeway to open a passage for the Christian army; we worked on it for several days with great difficulties, dangers, and endless expenses. The Saracens opposed our works with all their efforts. They raised up war engines against our war engines; they burned the wooden towers we raised on the causeway with their Greek fire and broke them with stones. We had almost lost all hope of passing on this causeway when a Saracen renegade showed us a ford over which the Christian army could cross the river. Having assembled our barons and the main officers in our army on the Monday before Cendres, it was agreed that on the next day, in other words on the day of Shrovetide, we would go in the morning to the place pointed out to us to cross the river, and that we would leave a small part of the army behind to guard the camp. The next day, we arranged our troops in battle order, went to the ford, and crossed the river, although not without exposing ourselves to great dangers, because the ford was deeper and more perilous than we had been told. Our horses had to cross by swimming, and it was not easy to get out of the river due to the height of the bank, which was silt-laden. When we had crossed the river, we came to the place where the Saracens' war engines were raised in front of our causeway. Having attacked the enemy, our vanguard killed many and spared neither sex nor age.

In the number, the Saracens lost a chief and several emirs. Our troops split up next, and some of our soldiers crossed the enemy camp and came to the village called Massoure, killing all the enemies they met on their way, but the Saracens, noticing the imprudence of our troops, regained their courage and fell upon them. They surrounded them on all sides and struck them down. A great carnage was made there of our barons and our warriors and religious and others, whose loss we had good reason to deplore and still deplore. There, we also lost our brave and illustrious brother the count of Artois, worthy of eternal memory. It is with bitterness in our heart that we recall this painful loss, although we should rejoice for it instead, for we believe and hope that having received the martyr's crown, he has gone to the heavenly country and that he is enjoying the recompense awarded to the martyr saints there. On that day, the Saracens fell upon us from all sides, and as they struck us with showers of arrows, we sustained their rude assaults until the ninth hour when the support of our missiles completely gave out. Finally, after having had a large number of our warriors and horses wounded or killed, with the help of Our Lord we held our position there, rallied ourselves, and went on the same day to strike our camp right next to the Saracens' machines. We stayed there with a small number of our men, and we built a bridge with our boats there so that the men who were on the other side of the river could come join us. On the next day, several of them came over and camped next to us. So, the Saracens' war engines were destroyed, and our soldiers could come and go freely and safely from one army to the other by crossing the bridge of boats. On the following Friday, the children of damnation, having reassembled their forces from all over with the intention of exterminating the Christian army, came to attack our lines with much audacity and in infinite numbers. The shock was so terrible all over the place that people said that nothing like this had ever been seen on these shores. With the help of God, we resisted on all sides. We pushed back the enemies and we made a large number of them fall under our blows. After several days, the sultan's son arrived at Massoure from the eastern provinces. The Egyptians greeted him as their master and in transports of delight. His arrival doubled their courage, but from this moment, and we do not know by what judgment of God, everything on our side went against our desires. A contagious disease broke out in our army and took so many of our men and animals that there were not many left to mourn their companions or heal the sick. The Christian army was

severely diminished in little time. There was such scarcity that several died
of need and hunger because the boats from Damietta could not bring the
army the provisions that had been sent by river because enemy ships and
pirates blocked their passage. They even captured some of our boats and
two successive caravans that were bringing us supplies and provisions,
and they killed a large number of the sailors and others who were there.
The absolute dearth of supplies and foodstuffs struck fear and despair into
the army and, along with the losses we had just incurred, forced us to leave
our position and return to Damietta. Such was God's will. But, because
the paths of man do not lie in himself but in He who guides his steps and
arranges everything according to his will, while we were on the road, it was
the fifth of the month of April, the Saracens had gathered all their forces
and attacked the Christian army and, with God's permission, because of
our sins, we fell into the enemy's hands. We and our dear brothers the
counts of Poitiers and Anjou and the others who were returning with us by
land were all taken prisoner, though not without great carnage and a great
outpouring of Christian blood. Most of the men who were returning on
the river were also taken prisoner or killed. Most of the ships that carried
them were burned with the sick people left on board. Several days after our
capture, the sultan proposed us a truce. He asked in earnest but also with
threats for us to return Damietta and everything we found in it without
delay, and for us to compensate him for all the losses and expenses that
he had incurred to that day since the moment the Christians had entered
Damietta. After several conferences, we concluded a ten-year truce with the
following conditions:

The sultan would free us from prison and all those who had been captured by the Saracens since our arrival in Egypt, and all the other Christians
no matter what country they were from who had been taken prisoner since
the sultan Kamel, the current sultan's predecessor, had concluded a truce
with the emperor, and would let us all go wherever we wanted. The Christians would keep the peace in all the lands they possessed in the Kingdom
of Jerusalem at the time of our arrival. For our part, we were obligated
to return Damietta and to pay eight hundred thousand Saracen bezants for
the liberation of the prisoners and the losses and expenses that we just
mentioned (we have already paid four hundred of them), and to free all the
Saracen prisoners that we had taken in Egypt since we had been there and
all those who had been captured in the Kingdom of Jerusalem since the

truce concluded between the emperor and the last sultan. All our moveable goods and those of all the others who were in Damietta would be under the sultan's guard and defense and transported to our Christian countries when the occasion arose. Any Christians who were sick and those who would stay behind in Damietta to sell what they possessed would have the same security and could leave by sea or by land whenever they would like without any obstacles or contradictions. The sultan was held to giving safe-passage to Christian countries to all those who would like to leave by land.

This truce concluded with the sultan had just been sworn on both sides, and the sultan had already begun to march to Damietta with his army to fulfill the conditions that had been stipulated, when, by God's judgment, some Saracen warriors no doubt in connivance with the majority of the army fell upon the sultan as he was rising from his table and cruelly wounded him. Despite this, the sultan left his tent in the hope that he would be able to escape, but he was killed under the blows of their swords in the presence of almost all the emirs and a multitude of other Saracens. After that, several Saracens in the onset of their fury came armed into our tent as if they wanted (several of us feared it) to cut our throats and kill us and the other Christians, but divine clemency calmed their fury, and they hurried to execute the conditions of the truce. Still their words and actions were mixed with terrible threats. Finally, by the will of God who is the father of mercies, the consoler of the grief-stricken who listens to the sobs of his servants, reinforced our position with a new swearing of the truce that we had just made with the sultan. From all of them and each one individually we received an identical oath taken in accordance with their law to observe the conditions of the truce. We fixed the time when we would turn over the prisoners and the town of Damietta. It was not without difficulty that we reached an agreement with the sultan for the surrender of this place; and it was not without difficulty that again we reached the same agreement with the emirs. As we had no hope of keeping it according to what we were told by the people who came back from Damietta and who knew the actual state of affairs there, on the opinion of the barons of France and several others, we decided that it would be better for Christendom if we and the other prisoners were freed by means of a truce than to keep this city with the rest of the Christians who were there, while remaining, we and the other prisoners, exposed to all the dangers of captivity like this: that is why the emirs received the town of Damietta on the appointed day, after which they freed us and our brothers, and the counts of Flanders, Brittany, and Soissons, Guillaume de Dampierre, Pierre Mauclerc, and Jean de Nesle, and several other barons and warriors of the Kingdoms of France, Jerusalem, and Cyprus. We had the firm hope then that they would render and deliver all the other Christians and that they would keep their oath following the tenor of the treaty.

When this was done, we left Egypt after leaving behind people responsible for receiving the prisoners from the hands of the Saracens and keeping the things that we could not take with us for lack of enough transport ships. When we arrived here, we sent boats and commissioners to Egypt to bring back the prisoners (because the deliverance of these prisoners makes all our solicitude) and the other things we had left behind like the war engines, weapons, tents, and a certain number of horses and other objects, but the emirs retained these commissioners in Cairo for a long time, and in the end they only gave them four hundred of the twelve thousand prisoners held in Egypt. Some of them still only got out of prison by paying money. As for the other items, the emirs did not want to give anything back, but the most despicable thing after the truce that was concluded and sworn is that according to the report of our commissioners and other captives worthy of faith who came back from this country, from among their prisoners they chose young people whom they forced with swords hanging over their heads to abjure the Catholic faith and to embrace the law of Mohammed, which several of them were weak enough to do. But, the others, like courageous athletes, rooted in their faith and constantly persisting in their firm resolution, could not be shaken by the enemies threats and blows and they received the martyr's crown. We have no doubt that their blood cries out to the Lord for the Christian people; they will be more useful in that country than if we had kept them on earth. The Muslims also slaughtered a number of Christians who had stayed behind sick in Damietta. Although we had observed the conditions of the treaty we had made with them and were always ready to continue observing them, we had nothing definite to make them deliver the Christian prisoners or restore what belonged to us. After the truce was concluded and our deliverance, we were quite confident that the country overseas occupied by the Christians would remain in a state of peace until the treaty expired, and it had been our project and intention to return to France at that point. We were already making preparations for our passage, but when we saw clearly from what we just told that the emirs were openly violating the truce in disregard of their oath and that they had no fear of playing tricks on us and Christendom, we assembled the barons of France, the knights of the Temple, the Hospital, and the Teutonic Order, and the barons of the Kingdom of Jerusalem, and we consulted with them about what was to be done. The larger number judged that if we withdrew at this time and abandoned this country that we were on the point of losing, it would be entirely exposed to the Saracens, especially in the state of poverty and weakness to which it had been reduced, and that we could consider the Christian prisoners in the enemy's hands as lost and with no hope of deliverance. On the contrary, if we stayed, we had the hope that time would bring something good, the deliverance of the captives, the preservation of the castles and fortresses of the Kingdom of Jerusalem, and other advantages for Christendom, especially since a conflict had broken out between the sultan of Aleppo and the people who were governing in Cairo. People said that he had to go to Egypt to avenge the death of the sultan whom the emirs had killed, to take it over, and if he could, the entire country with it. After these considerations, and sympathizing with the miseries and torments of the Holy Land, we who had come to its aid, bemoaning the captivity and pains of our prisoners, although several tried to dissuade us from staying any longer overseas, we decided better to defer our passage and to stay on for some time in Syria instead of entirely abandoning the cause of Christ and leaving our prisoners exposed to such great dangers. However, we decided to send our dear brothers the counts of Poitiers and Anjou back to France to console our very dear lady and mother and the entire kingdom. And all those known as Christians should be full of zeal for the enterprise we have undertaken, and you in particular who descend from the blood of those whom the Lord chose as a privileged people for the conquest of the Holy Land, which you should look upon as your property, we invite you all to serve He who served you on the cross by spilling his blood for your salvation, because this criminal nation, aside from the blasphemies it vomits against the Creator in the presence of the Christian people, beat the cross with sticks, spat on it, and trampled it underfoot in hatred of the Christian faith. Have courage then, soldiers of Christ! Arm yourselves and be ready to avenge these outrages and affronts. Take the example of your predecessors who distinguished themselves among the other nations by their beautiful actions. We have gone before you in the service of God; come and join us. Although you may arrive later, the Lord will grant you the reward that the father of the family of the Gospel grants without distinction to the workers who come to work on his vines at the end of the day as to the workers who came at its start. Those who come or who send help while we are here will obtain God's favor and the favor of men in addition to the indulgences promised to crusaders. So, make your preparations, and may those who are inspired by the virtue of the Almighty to come or send help be ready by the month of next April or May. As for those who cannot be ready for this first passage, may they at least be ready for the one that will take place on Saint John's Day. The nature of the enterprise demands one act quickly, and any delay could prove deadly. For you, prelates and faithful servants of Christ, help us before the Almighty through the fervor of your prayers; ordain that this be done in all the places under your control, so that they obtain the goods of divine clemency for us, goods we are unworthy of because of our sins.

Done at Acre in the month of August in the year 1250 of the Lord.

Chronology

1231–1232	Disappearance and reappearance of the Holy Nail.
1233	First inquisitors in France named by the papacy.
1234	April 25. Louis reaches the age of his majority.
1234	May 27. Louis weds Marguerite de Provence in Sens.
1235	October 19. Consecration of the Cistercian abbey of Royaumont. Louis is present.
1237	June 7. He knights his brother Robert d'Artois in Compiègne.
1239	August 11–18. Louis obtains the relics of Christ's Passion.
	Louis acquires the county of Mâcon, which he joins to the royal domain.
	Death of Philip Hurepel, Louis' uncle.
1240–1241	Revolt and defeat of Raymond Trencavel, viscount of Béziers.
1240	Debate with Jewish scholars over the Talmud held before Louis and Blanche of Castile.
1241	March-April. The Mongols ravage Central Europe.
	Saint John's Day: Louis holds large festivals in Saumur for the knighting of his brother Alphonse de Poitiers.
1242	Burning of the Talmud.
1242	July 21–22. Louis defeats King Henry III of England at Taillebourg and Saintes.
1242–1243	Uprising and defeat of Raimond VII de Toulouse and other lords of the South; consolidation of the royal seneschalcies of Nîmes-Beaucaire and Béziers-Carcassonne.
1244	New burnings of the Talmud
	Fall of Montségur. Spread of the Inquisition in France.
1244	August 23. The Muslims capture Jerusalem.
1244	October 17. The Christians of Palestine experience a disastrous defeat at the hands of the Muslims at La Forbie near Gaza.
1244	December. Louis' illness and vow to crusade.
1245	November. Louis meets with Pope Innocent IV at Cluny.

1246	May 27. Louis' youngest brother Charles d'Anjou is knighted.
1247	Louis appoints investigators to reform royal abuses throughout the kingdom.
1248	April 26. Consecration of the Sainte-Chapelle of the royal palace.
1248	June 12. Louis leaves Paris to depart on the crusade.
1248	August 28. Louis leaves Aigues-Mortes to cross the sea.
1248	September 18. The crusading force lands at Cyprus.
1248	December. Louis meets the Dominican André de Longjumeau in Nicosia after his return from a trip to Central Asia. He also receives two Mongol envoys.
1249	January. André de Longjumeau leaves Cyprus with an embassy from Louis to the great Mongol khan with a valuable gift.
1249	May. Louis arrives in Egypt and would remain there until May 8, 1250. The army of crusaders takes Damietta in June.
1250	April 5. Defeat of the crusading army at Mansourah. Death of Robert d'Artois. Louis is captured by the Muslims.
1250	May 6. His ransom is paid, and Louis is freed.
	Beginning of labor unrest among Parisian tradesmen.
1250–1251	Louis is in Acre from May to March.
1251	The Shepherd's Movement in France.
1251–1252	Louis is in Caesaria from May 1251 to May 1252.
1251	Spring. André de Longjumeau returns to Caesaria.
1252–1253	Louis is in Jaffa from May 1252 to June 1253.
1252	November. Blanche of Castile dies.
1253	Late winter. The Franciscan Guillaume de Rubrouck leaves the Holy Land with a letter of recommendation from Louis to the Mongol prince Sartaq.
1253–1254	Louis is in Sidon from June to February.
	Winter: Guillaume de Rubrouck stays at the great khan Möngke's court in Karakorum.

1254	April 25. Louis re-embarks from Acre.
1254	July 17. Louis lands at Salins d'Hyères. He meets with the Franciscan Hugh of Digne.
1254	September 7. Louis returns to Paris.
1254	December. The "Great Edict" for the kingdom's reform from 1254 until 1270 is issued. This is the great "moral order."
	First records of the Parlements of Paris, the *Olim*.
1255	Louis' daughter Isabelle marries Thibaud V, count of Champagne and king of Navarre.
1255	June 29. Guillaume de Rubrouck returns to Nicosia.
1255	September 24. Louis resolves the succession of Flanders with the "*Dit de Péronne*."
1257	The canon Robert de Sorbon, Louis' friend, founds a college for twelve poor students in theology at the University of Paris.
1258	Étienne Boileau is named provost in order to restore order to Paris. He composes his *Livre des métiers*.
1258	May 11. Treaty of Corbeil passed with the king of Aragon.
1258	May 28. The treaty of Paris is sworn at the Temple between Louis and Henry III of England and ratified in December 1259.
1259	The trial of Enguerran de Coucy.
	The Franciscan Guibert de Tournai dedicates a Mirror of the Princes to Louis.
1260	January. Louis IX's oldest son and heir, Louis, dies.
1262	Philip, the kingdom's new heir, marries Isabelle of Aragon at Clermont.
1263–1266	Monetary decrees.
1264	January 24. The "*dit d'Amiens*," Louis' arbitration rendered for the king of England and his barons fails.
	The Dominican encyclopedist and preceptor to Louis' children, Vincent de Beauvais dies.

1265	February 27. The sultan Baybars captures Caesaria.
	Charles d'Anjou becomes king of Naples and Sicily.
1267	March 24. Louis decides to take up the cross for the second time.
1267	Pentecost. Festivities at the royal palace in Paris are held for the knighting of Philip, Louis' son and heir.
1268	March 7. The sultan Baybars captures Jaffa.
1269	Louis issues an edict against blasphemy, which also requires Jews in the kingdom to wear the *rouelle*.
1270	February 23. Louis' sister Isabelle dies.
1270	July 1. Louis embarks at Aigues-Mortes
1270	August 25. Louis dies outside the walls of Tunis. His body is dismembered, boiled in wine, and the flesh is separated from the bones.
1271	May 22. Louis IX's remains are buried at Saint-Denis.
1272–1273	Geoffroy de Beaulieu writes a Life of Louis.
1273, 1278, 1282	Pontifical proceedings are held on Louis IX's canonization.
1285	Reading of the report from the proceedings to Pope Honorius IV.
1297	August 6. The bull for Louis IX's canonization is promulgated by Boniface VIII at Orvieto.
1298	August 25. Saint Louis tomb is exhumed and "elevated." Friar Jean de Samois delivers his sermon before Philip the Fair and numerous other prelates and lords for this "elevation" ceremony. Joinville is also present, a witness to the inquiry of 1282.
1302–1303	Guillaume de Saint-Pathus writes an official Life of Saint Louis.
1308	May 17. Philip the Fair splits up Saint Louis' remains. He gives most of them as relics to powerful persons and churches.
1309	Joinville presents his *Histoire de Saint Louis* to the future Louis X.

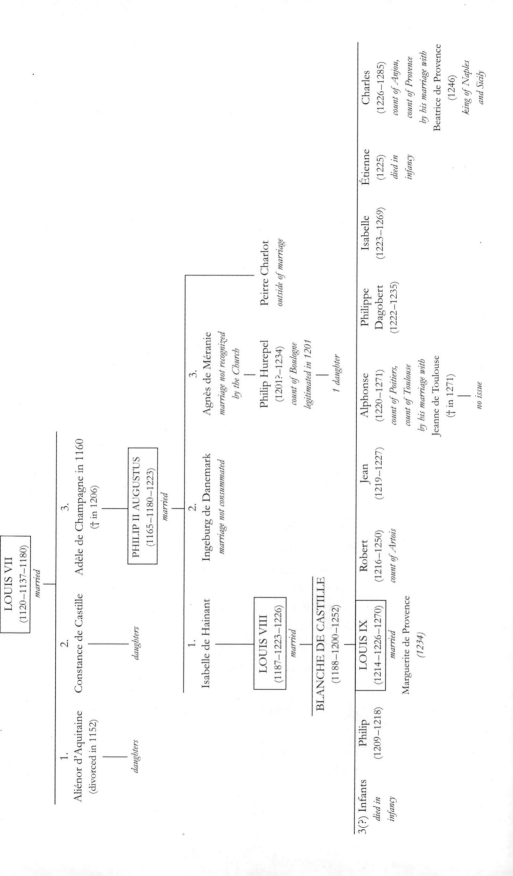

LOUIS VII
(1120–1137–1180)

married

1.
Aliénor d'Aquitaine
(divorced in 1152)

daughters

2.
Constance de Castille

daughters

3.
Adèle de Champagne in 1160
(† in 1206)

PHILIP II AUGUSTUS
(1165–1180–1223)

married

1.
Isabelle de Hainant

LOUIS VIII
(1187–1223–1226)

married

2.
Ingeburg de Danemark
marriage not consummated

3.
Agnès de Méranie
marriage not recognized by the Church

Philip Hurepel
(1201?–1234)
*count of Boulogne
legitimated in 1201*

Peirre Charlot
outside of marriage

1 daughter

BLANCHE DE CASTILLE
(1188–1200–1252)

Philip
(1209–1218)

Robert
(1216–1250)
count of Artois

LOUIS IX
(1214–1226–1270)

married
Marguerite de Provence
(1234)

Jean
(1219–1227)

Alphonse
(1220–1271)
*count of Poitiers,
count of Toulouse
by his marriage with
Jeanne de Toulouse
(† in 1271)*

no issue

Philippe
Dagobert
(1222–1235)

Isabelle
(1223–1269)

Étienne
(1225)
*died in
infancy*

Charles
(1226–1285)
*count of Anjou,
count of Provence
by his marriage with
Beatrice de Provence
(1246)
king of Naples
and Sicily*

3(?) Infants
*died in
infancy*

LOUIS IX
(1214–1226–1270)

married

Marguerite de Provence
(1221–1234–1295)

Blanche
(1240–1243)

Isabelle
(1242–1271)
married
(1255)
Thibald V
count of
Champagne,
king of Navarre

Louis
(1244–1260)
fiancé of
Bérangère
de Castille

Philip III
(1245–1270–1285)
married
(1262)
Isabelle
d'Aragon
(†1271)

Jean
(1247–1248)

Jean Tristan
(1250 in
Damiette
1270)
count of Nevers,
married
(1266)
Yolande
de Bourgogne

Pierre
(1251 in
Châtel-Pèlerin
1284)
count of
Perche
and Alençon

Blanche
(1253 in
Jaffa
1323)
married
(1269)
Ferdinand
de Castille

Marguerite
(1254–1271)
married
(1270)
Jean I
duke of
Brabant

Robert
(1256–1318)
count
of Clermont
married
(1272)
Beatrice
de Bourbon

House of Bourbon

Agnès
(1260–1327)
married
(1279)
Robert II
duke
of Bourgogne

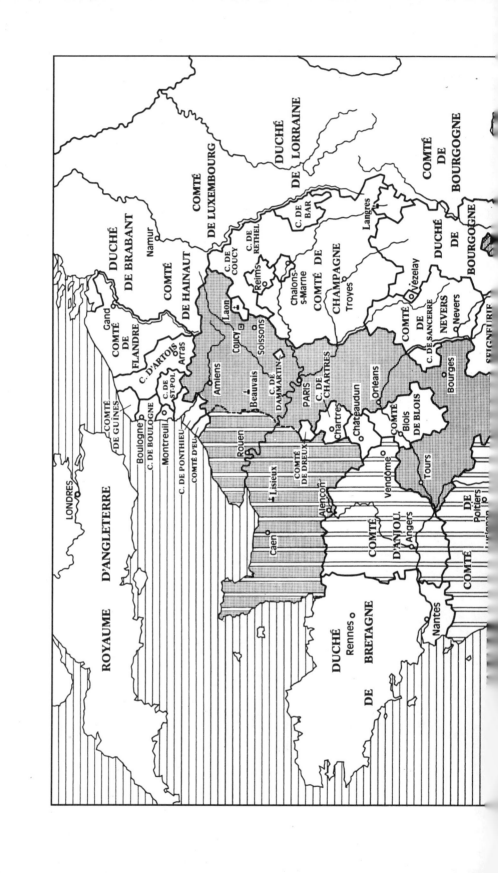

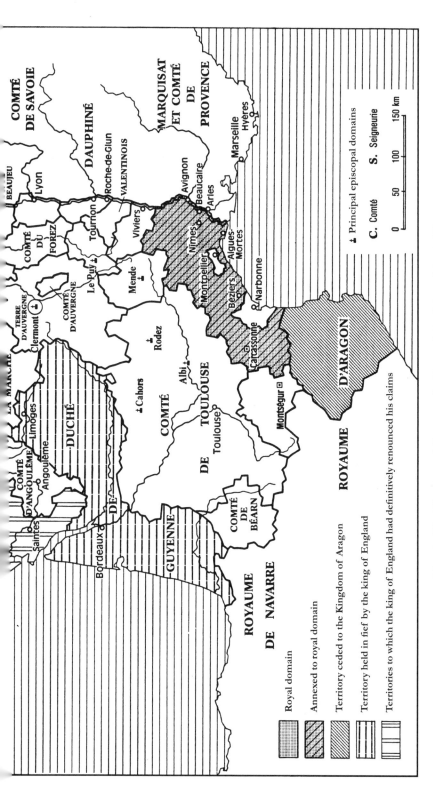

Map 1. The Kingdom of France at the Close of the Reign of Louis IX

COMTÉ DE SAVOIE

DAUPHINÉ

MARQUISAT ET COMTÉ DE PROVENCE

BEAUJEU

Lyon

Roche-de-Glun
VALENTINOIS

Avignon
Beaucaire
Arles

Marseille
Hyères

Tournon

Viviers

Le Puy ‡

Mende ‡

Nîmes
Montpellier
Aigues-Mortes
Béziers
Narbonne
Carcassonne

COMTÉ DU FOREZ

TERRE D'AUVERGNE
Clermont ‡

COMTÉ D'AUVERGNE

Rodez ‡

Albi ‡

LA MARCHE

COMTÉ D'ANGOULÊME
Angoulême
Limoges

DUCHÉ DE

Saintes

Bordeaux

GUYENNE

COMTÉ DE BÉARN

‡ Cahors

COMTÉ DE TOULOUSE
Toulouse

Montségur

ROYAUME D'ARAGON

ROYAUME

ROYAUME DE NAVARRE

‡ Principal episcopal domains

C. Comté   S. Seigneurie

0   50   100   150 km

Royal domain

Annexed to royal domain

Territory ceded to the Kingdom of Aragon

Territory held in fief by the king of England

Territories to which the king of England had definitively renounced his claims

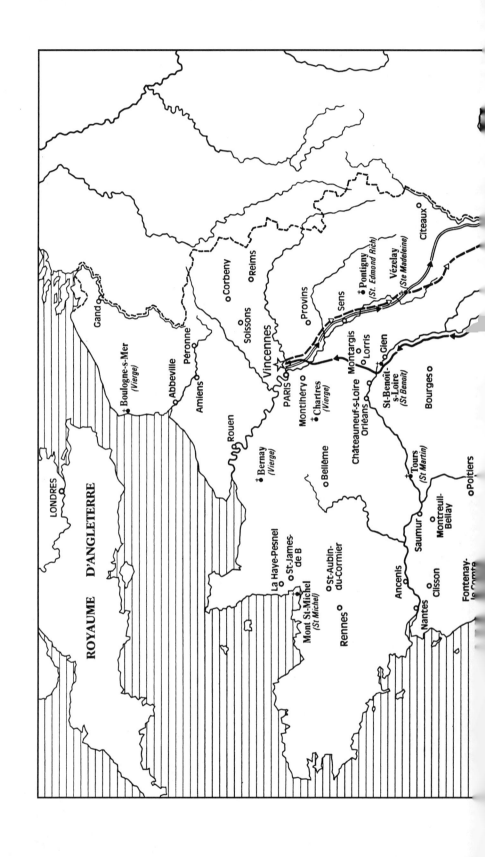

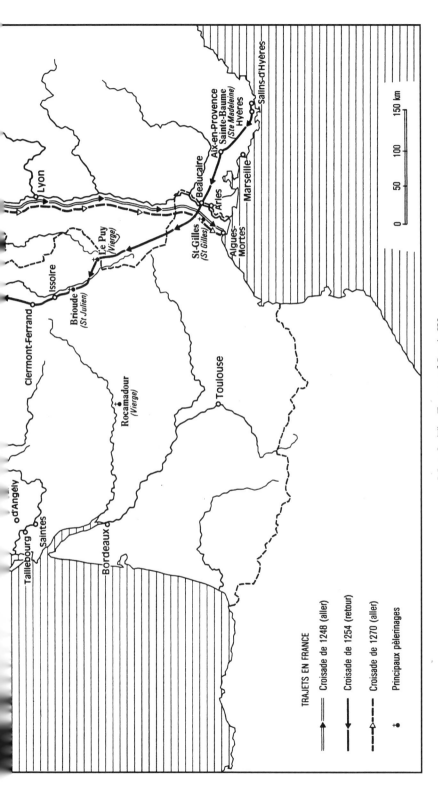

TRAJETS EN FRANCE

→ Croisade de 1248 (aller)

→ Croisade de 1254 (retour)

⇢ Croisade de 1270 (aller)

✝ Principaux pèlerinages

Taillebourg
Saintes
d'Angély
Bordeaux
Clermont-Ferrand
Issoire
Brioude
(St Julien)
Le Puy
(Vierge)
Rocamadour
(Vierge)
Toulouse
Lyon
Beaucaire
Arles
St-Gilles
(St Gilles)
Aigues-
Mortes
Marseille
Aix-en-Provence
Sainte-Baume
(Ste Madeleine)
Hyères
Salins-d'Hyères

0   50   100   150 km

Map 2. The France of Louis IX

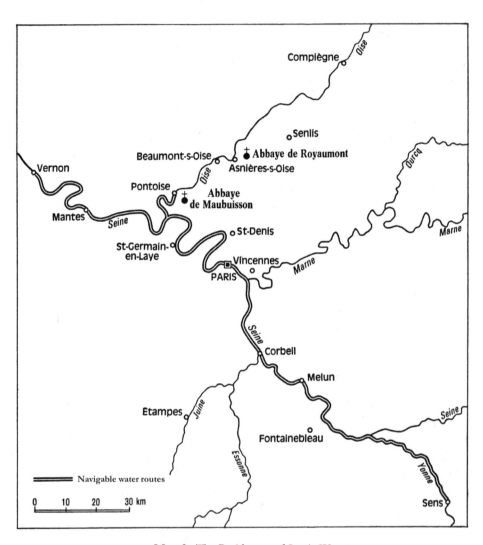

Map 3. The Residences of Louis IX

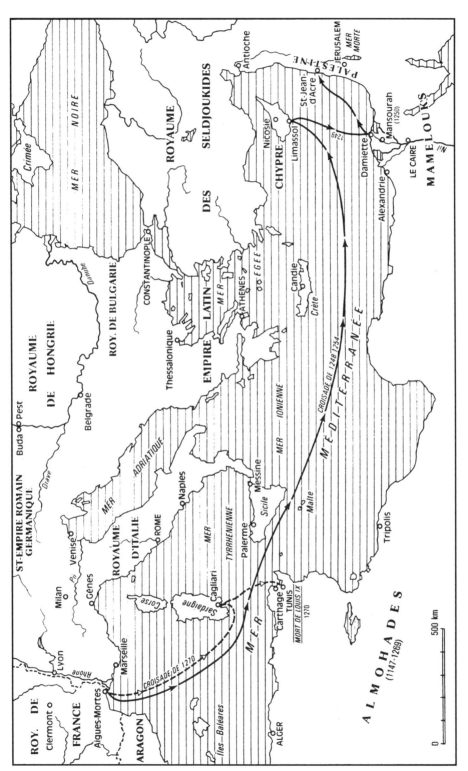

Map 4. The Mediterranean of Louis IX

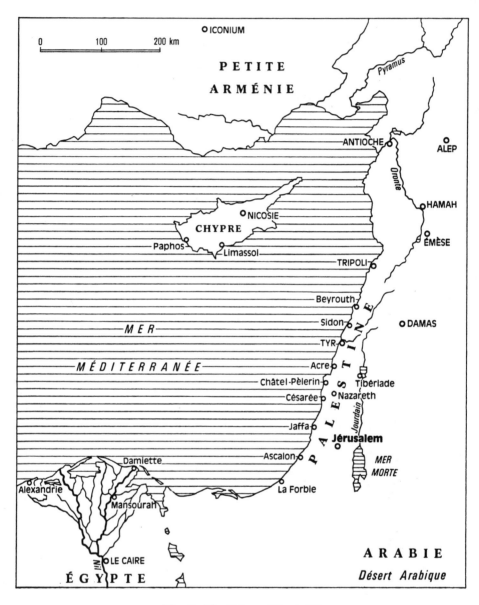

Map 5. The Orient of Louis IX

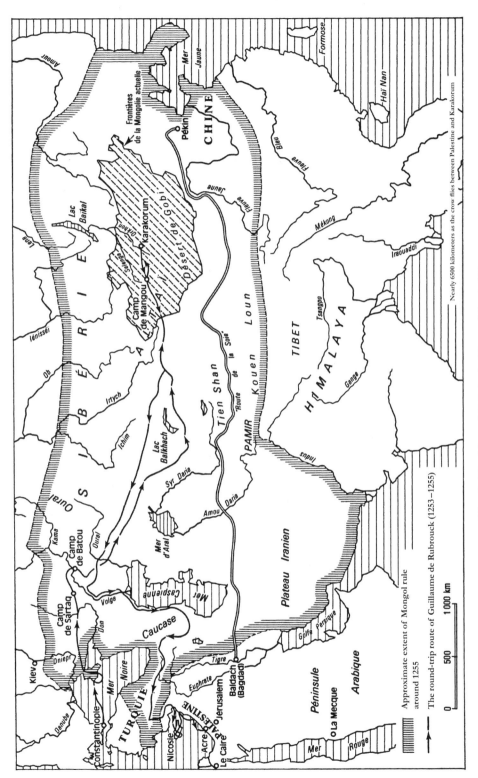

Map 6. The Mongol Rule in the Time of Louis IX

Nearly 6500 kilometers as the crow flies between Palestine and Karakorum

Approximate extent of Mongol rule around 1255

The round-trip route of Guillaume de Rubrouck (1253–1255)

0   500   1000 km

Notes

Note to the Introduction

1. The recently renewed fashionability of historical biography has inspired numerous colloquia and articles. The articles that have proven most useful to my reflections and the problems dealt with in this book were the historian Giovanni Levi's "Les usages de la biographie," *Annales, E.S.C.* (1989): 1325–36, and by two sociologists, Jean-Claude Chamboredon, "Le temps de la biographie et les temps de l'histoire," in *Quotidienneté et histoire,* colloquium of the École normale supérieure, Lyon, May 1982, 17–29, and Jean-Claude Passeron, "Le scénario et le corpus. Biographies, flux, itinéraires, trajectoires," in *Le Raisonnement sociologique* (Paris, 1991), 185–206. In addition to these, there is, of course, the classic article by Pierre Bourdieu, "L'illusion biographique," *Actes de la recherche en sciences sociales* 62–63 (January 1986): 69–72. See also the remarks of Bernard Guenée in the Introduction to *Entre l'Église et l'Etat. Quatre vies de prélats français à la fin du Moyen Âge* (Paris, 1987), 7–16.

Other works:

G. Klingenstein, ed., *Biographie und Geschichtswissenschaft* (Vienna, 1979).

E. Engelberg and H. Schleser, "Zu Geschichte und Theorie der historischen Biographie. Theorie verständnisbiographische Totalität—Darstellungstypen und Formen," *Zeitschrift für Geschichtswissenschaft* 30 (1990).

Problèmes et méthodes de la biographie, colloquium proceedings of the Sorbonne, May 1989.

Sources, travaux historiques (Paris: Publications de la Sorbonne, 1985).

Colloquium "Biographie et cycle de vie," Marseille, 1988.

Enquête. Cahiers du Cercom, Association internationale de sociologie, no. 51 (March 1989).

While I was preparing this work, I presented a few of its problems in two articles: "Comment écrire une biographie historique aujourd'hui?" *Le Débat,* no. 54 (March-April 1989): 48–53; "Whys and Ways of Writing a Biography: The Case of Saint Louis," *Exemplaria* 1, no. 1 (March 1989): 207–25.

The question that I attempted to answer, with Pierre Toubert, is given here in the title of an article we published together: "Une histoire totale du Moyen Âge est-elle possible?" *Actes du 100è congrès national des sociétés savantes* (Paris, 1977), 31–44.

Marc Bloch's reflection is taken from *Apologie pour l'histoire ou métier d'historien,* 1st ed. (1949), with a new critical edition prepared by Étienne Bloch, with a preface by J. Le Goff (Paris, 1993).

The expression "*démontage*" applied not to a character but to a "social structure" can be found in an unpublished manuscript by Marc Bloch that is a part of his archives that were stolen by the Germans and recently discovered in Moscow. Étienne Bloch—to whose amicability I owe this information, will publish it in the *Cahiers Marc Bloch.*

Pierre Bourdieu's pronouncement on "the entirely scientifically absurd opposition between the individual and society" can be found in "Fieldwork in Philosophy," *Choses dites* (Paris, 1987), 43. Marcel Mauss presented the distinction between "*sens du moi*" (sense of the self) and "*concept d'individu*" (concept of the individual) in "Une catégorie de l'esprit humain: la notion de personne, celle de 'moi'," in *Sociologie et anthropologie,* 8th ed. (Paris, 1983), 335. On the "society in man," see Norbert Elias, *La Société des individus* (French translation: Paris, 1991).

Part I
Notes to Chapter 1

1. The numbering of great persons with identical names began only in the thirteenth century, the century of Saint Louis. The first person to number the kings of France was Vincent de Beauvais, who was very close to the king. At Saint-Denis, Primat wrote a chronicle of the kings of France at Saint Louis' behest. This delicate task, which required solid documentation and demanded political choices (did such-and-such a figure deserve to appear on a list with emperors, popes, and kings?) was only more or less complete at the end of the fifteenth century. See Bernard Guenée, *Histoire et culture historique dans l'Occident médiéval* (Paris, 1980), 162–63.

2. The exclusion of women and their descendants from succession to the French throne became official with Charles V's decree of August 1374. Under his rule people began to appeal to Salic law. Institutional history occurs slowly, and the law often legitimates something only after the fact, finding the authorities called upon to justify it after long practice. See the genealogical table in the back of the book.

3. On Bouvines, it is imperative to read Georges Duby's important book, *Le Dimanche de Bouvines* (Paris, 1973).

4. Joinville, *Histoire de Saint Louis,* 40–41.

5. Le Nain de Tillemont, *Vie de Saint Louis,* 1:419–20.

6. *Rex illiteratus quasi asinus coronatus.*

7. Alain Erlande-Brandenburg, *Le Roi est mort. Étude sur les funérailles, les sépultures et les tombeaux des rois de France jusqu'à la fin du XIIIᵉ siècle* (Geneva, 1975), 18–19.

8. As a widower, Philip Augustus had remarried with the Danish princess Ingeburg, toward whom he formed a strong aversion on their wedding night and with whom he could never fulfill his conjugal duties. He repudiated her and confined her to forced residence in various monasteries. He remarried again with Agnès de Méran. The papacy did not recognize this marriage and considered him a bigamist.

9. Innocent III thus returned to the primitive conception of the saints in the Christianity of the ancient world: saints were exceptional beings in death.

10. See André Vauchez, *La Sainteté en Occident aux derniers siècles du Moyen Âge* (Rome, 1981). On the attempt to canonize Philip Augustus, see Jacques Le Goff, "Le dossier de sainteté de Phillipe Auguste," *L'Histoire,* no. 100 (May 1987): 22–29. In one anecdote, an *exemplum* addressed to the preachers, Saint Denis frees Philip Augustus from Purgatory because he had honored the saints, respected their holy days, and defended churches and holy and religious places. This became a new commonplace on the afterlife at the beginning of the thirteenth century. See Jacques Le Goff, "Philippe Auguste dans les *exempla,*" in *La France de Philippe Auguste. Le temps des mutations,* ed. Robert-Henri Bautier (Paris, 1982), 150–51, and Jacques Le Goff, *La Naissance du Purgatoire* (Paris, 1981). See Part 3, ch. 9

11. Guillaume de Saint-Pathus, *Vie de Saint Louis,* 117.

12. Joinville, *Histoire de Saint Louis,* 363–65.

13. David O'Connell, *The Teachings of Saint Louis* (Chapel Hill, 1972), 57.

14. F. Aubin, "Mongolie (Histoire)," in *Encyclopaedia Universalis,* vol. 11 (Paris, 1971), 241.

15. David Bigalli, *I Tartari e l'Apocalisse. Ricerche sull'escatologia in Adamo Marsh e Ruggero Bacone* (Florence, 1971).

16. Raoul Manselli, "I popoli immaginarie: Gog e Magog," in *Popoli e Paesi nella cultura alto medievale,* Settimane di Studio del Centro Italiano di Studi sull'Alto Medioevo (Spolete, 1981), vol. 3 (Spolete, 1983), 487 ff.

17. D. Bigalli, *I Tartari e l'Apocalisse,* 163.

18. Quoted by F. Alessio, *Introduzione a Ruggero Bacone* (Rome and Bari, 1985), 112.

19. Matthew Paris, *Chronica majora,* 4:76.

20. "Infernal."

21. Matthew Paris, *Chronica majora,* 4:111–12.

22. Ibid., 112. Everywhere they went the Mongols did in fact terrify people with their cruelty, leaving behind the cadavers of entire cities and populations that resisted them. However, this cruelty had a purpose: the complete submission of peoples and states. Once this was attained, the Mongols became urban dwellers, liv-

ing in cities, though without forgetting their tents. They created administrations, developed economic relations, and sponsored literature and the sciences. Thanks to them, previously tenuous commercial paths were reunited into a single route running from China to the Black Sea. This was the famous Silk Road. It worked successfully thanks to the *pax mongolica,* the Mongol Peace, which ruled Asia as the *pax romana,* the Roman Peace, had ruled in the West a little over a millenium before.

23. The Nestorians were Christian disciples of the patriarch Nestorius of Constantinople, who was condemned in 431 by the Council of Ephesus. They professed that there were not only two natures in Christ, but also that there were two people in him. The Nestorian Church, whose leader or *catholikos* resided in Baghdad since the Arab conquest, spread throughout Asia and into China. It fell into decline after the conversion of the Mongol khan of Persia to Islam at the end of the thirteenth century and died out after the end of the Mongol Empire (1368). See Jean Richard, *La Papauté et les missions d'Orient au Moyen Âge (XIIIᵉ–XVᵉ siècles)* (Rome, 1977).

24. Guillaume de Rubrouck, envoy of Saint Louis, *Voyage dans l'Empire mongol,* trans. Claude and René Kappler, who have re-edited this translation with their commentaries in a superb illustrated book (Paris, 1985; repr. 1993); Jean Richard, "Sur les pas de Plancarpin et de Rubrouck. La lettre de Saint Louis à Sartaq," *Journal des savants* (Paris, 1977).

25. P. Meyvaert, "An Unknown Letter of Hulagu il Khan of Persia, to King Louis IX of France," *Viator* 11 (1980): 245–49. Jean Richard, "Une ambassade mongole à Paris en 1262," *Journal des savants* (Paris, 1979).

26. For an overview, see Jacques Le Goff, *L'Apogée de la Chrétienté (v. 1180–v. 1330)* (Paris, 1982), based on the German text of 1965. See also, among others, Léopold Génicot, *Le XIIIᵉ Siècle européen* (Paris, 1968), and John H. Mundy, *Europe in the High Middle Ages (1150–1309)* (London, 1973).

27. Joinville, *Histoire de Saint Louis,* 369. Here, the term may have the limited meaning of "ecclesiastical jurisdiction." B. Landry (*L'Idée de chrétienté chez les scolastiques du XIIIᵉ siècle* [Paris, 1929]) does not deal with the question of vocabulary. In his excellent synthesis, *Le XIIIᵉ Siècle européen,* L. Génicot stresses the ambiguities of this expression in the thirteenth century (386–87).

28. *Insolentia Saracenorum, schisma Graecorum, sevitia Tartarorum,* in *Brevis nota (Monumenta Germaniae Historica, Legum sectio IV, Constitutiones et acta publica,* III, no. 401), quoted by L. Génicot, *Le XIIIᵉ Siècle européen,* 288.

29. Oscar Halecki, "Diplomatie pontificale et activité missionnaire en Asie aux XIIIᵉ–XIVᵉ siècles," *XIIᵉ Congrès international des sciences historiques* (Vienna, 1965), report 2, *Histoire des continents,* 5–32.

30. *Stadtluft macht frei* (City air makes you free).

31. Jacques Verger, *Les Universités du Moyen Âge* (Paris, 1973) and "Des écoles à l'Université. La mutation institutionnelle," in *La France de Philippe Auguste* (Paris, 1982).

32. Jacques Le Goff, *Les Intellectuels au Moyen Âge* (Paris, 1957; repr. 1984) and "Quelle conscience l'Université médiévale a-t-elle eue d'elle-même?" in *Pour un autre Moyen Âge* (Paris, 1977; repr. 1994), 181–97.

33. Jean Gaudemet, "Les ordalies au Moyen Âge: doctrine, législation et pratique canoniques," *Recueils de la société Jean Bodin* 17, no. 2, *La preuve* (1965); Dominique Barthélemey, "Moyen Âge: le jugement de Dieu," *L'Histoire,* no. 99 (April 1987): 33–36; John Baldwin, "The Intellectual Preparation for the Canon of 1215 against Ordeals," *Speculum* 36 (1961): 613–36.

34. Thibaud V, count of Champagne, king of Navarre under the name Thibaud II, was the son-in-law of Saint Louis and was very attached to him.

35. Joinville, *Histoire de Saint Louis,* 399–401.

36. Ibid., 69.

37. Ibid., 407.

38. On the religious movement from the eleventh to the thirteenth centuries, see Jacques Le Goff and René Rémond, eds., *Histoire de la France religieuse,* vol. 1 (Paris, 1988).

39. Cf. Olga Dobriache-Rojdesventsky, *La Poésie des Goliards* (Paris, 1981).

40. On heresies, see Jacques Le Goff, ed., *Hérésies et sociétés dans l'Europe préindustrielle, XIᵉ–XVIIIᵉ siècles* (Paris and the Hague, 1968); Malcolm Lambert, *Medieval Heresy,* 2nd ed. (Oxford, 1992); Robert I. Moore, *The Formation of a Persecuting Society* (Oxford, 1987).

41. See below, "The Meeting with Hugh of Digne," in Part I, ch. 4.

42. On Catharism: Arno Borst, *Les Cathares* (1953); Raoul Manselli, *L'Eresia del male* (Naples, 1963); René Nelli, *Le Phénomène cathare* (Toulouse, 1976), vol. 2, *L'Histoire des cathares* (1980). For a different view, see Jean Biget, "Les Cathares: mise à mort d'une légende," *L'Histoire,* no. 94 (November 1986): 10–21. The most vivid presentation of the lives of a group of Cathars is Emmanuel Le Roy Ladurie, *Montaillou, village occitan de 1294 à 1324* (Paris, 1975), although it covers a later period than that of Saint Louis.

43. Monique Zerner-Chardavoine, *La Croisade albigeoise* (Paris, 1979).

44. *L'Aveu. Antiquité et Moyen Âge,* Actes du colloque de Rome, 1984 (Rome, 1986).

45. In fact, recourse to the secular arm had already occurred in France before Saint Louis' reign. In 1210, an ecclesiastical synod in Paris presided over by Pierre de Corbeil, archbishop of Sens, condemned the members of a little known sect whose spiritual leaders were the university professors Amaury de Bène (d. ca. 1205) and David de Dinant. They handed them over to the secular arm. One tradition represented by a miniature that regularly appeared in the iconography of the *Grandes Chroniques de France* at the end of the Middle Ages shows Philip Augustus watching heretics being burned at the stake. See Marie-Thérèse d'Alverny, "Un fragment du procès des Amauriciens," *Archives d'histoire doctrinale et littéraire du Moyen Âge* 25–26 (1950–1951); G. C. Capelle, *Autour du décret de 1210. III. Amaury de Bène: étude sur son panthéisme formel* (Paris, 1932).

46. Pierre Marie Gy, "Les définitions de la confession après le quatrième concile du Latran," in *L'Aveu,* 283–96; R. Rusconi, "Ordinate confiteri. La confessione dei peccati nelle 'summae de casibus' e nei manuale per i confessori (metà XII–in-

izio XIV secolo)," ibid., 297–313; Pierre Michaud-Quantin, *Sommes de casuistique et manuels de confession au Moyen Âge (XIIe–XVIe siècles),* Analecta mediaevelia Namurcensia 13 (Louvain, Lille, and Montreal, 1962); Nicole Bériou, "Autour de Latran IV (1215). La naissance de la confession moderne et sa diffusion," in *Pratiques de la confession: des Pères au désert à Vatican II. Quinze études d'histoire* (Paris, 1983).

47. Jacques Le Goff and Jean-Claude Schmitt, "Au XIIIe siècle: une parole nouvelle," in *Histoire vécue du peuple chrétien,* vol. 1, ed. Jean Delumeau (Toulouse, 1979); David L. d'Avray, *The Preaching of the Friars. Sermons Diffused from Paris before 1300* (Oxford, 1985); Nicole Bériou, "La prédication au béguinage de Paris pendant l'année liturgique 1272–1273," *Recherches augustiniennes* 13 (1978): 105–229; idem, *La Prédication du Ranulphe de la Houblonnière. Sermons aux clercs et aux simples gens à Paris au XIIIe siècle,* 2 vols. (Paris, 1987); Jean Longère, *La Prédication médiévale* (Paris, 1975).

48. J. Le Goff, *La Naissance du Purgatoire.*

49. In thirteenth-century France some people also referred to the Dominicans as Jacobins after the name of their convent in Paris. Likewise, they called the Franciscans "Cordeliers" because of the thick, knotted cords that they used as belts.

50. See Lester K. Little, "Saint Louis' Involvement with the Friars," *Church History* 33, no. 2 (1964): 1–24.

51. See André Vauchez, *Les Laïcs au Moyen Âge. Pratiques et expériences religieuses,* 2nd ed. (Paris, 1987); Guy Lobrichon, *La Religion des laïcs en Occident, XIe–XVe siècles* (Paris, 1994).

52. G. G. Meersseman, *Ordo fraternitatis. Confraternite e pietà dei laici nel Medioevo* in *Italia sacra,* vols. 24–26 (1977); *Le Mouvement confraternel au Moyen Âge: France, Italie, Suisse* (Rome, 1987).

53. On the Beguines of Paris at the end of the reign of Saint Louis, see Bériou, "La prédication au béguinage de Paris."

54. On medieval millenarianism, its important trends, and the essential bibliography, see Jacques Le Goff, "Millénarisme" in the *Encyclopaedia Universalis.* For a considerable bibliography on Joachim de Fiore and Joachimism, see Henri Mottu, *La Manifestation de l'Esprit selon Joachim de Fiore* (Neuchâtel, Paris, 1977); Marjorie Reeves, *The Influence of Prophecy in the Later Middle Ages. A Study in Joachimism* (Oxford, 1969); idem, "The Originality and Influence of Joachim of Fiore," *Traditio* (1980).

55. *Il movimento dei Disciplinati nel settimo centenario del suo inizio* (Perugia, 1960; Pérouse, 1962).

56. See the important book by André Vauchez, *La Sainteté en Occident.*

57. Jean Delumeau, *La Peur en Occident (XIVe–XVIIIe siècles)* (Paris, 1978); idem, *Le Péché et la Peur. La culpabilisation en Occident (XIIIe–XVIIIe siècles)* (Paris, 1983).

58. Jacques-Guy Bougerol, *La Théologie de l'espérance aux XIIe et XIIIe siècles,* 2 vols. (Paris, 1985).

59. On Frederick II, Ernst H. Kantorowicz's masterpiece published in 1927 during the troubled years of the Weimar Republic has been translated into French as *L'Empereur Frédéric II* (Paris, 1987). It contains a remarkable portrait of Saint Louis, 514–15.

60. Around 1270, at the end of Saint Louis' reign, chess was the subject of a treatise written by the Dominican Jacques de Cessoles. He treated it as a symbolic explanation of the workings of Christian society. Chess was a monarchical game dominated by a king and a queen. The queen in the game was an invention of the West. On this *Liber de moribus hominum ac officiis nobilium super ludum scaccorum* (Book of Human Manners and the Positions of Nobles according to the Game of Chess), see Jean-Michel Mehl, "L'*exemplum* chez Jacques de Cessoles," in *Le Moyen Âge* (1978): 227–46.

61. See the excellent study of John W. Baldwin, *The Government of Philip Augustus: Foundations of French Royal Power in the Middle Ages* (Berkeley: University of California Press, 1986).

62. In addition to J.W. Baldwin, see Thomas N. Bisson, "The Problem of Feudal Monarchy: Aragon, Catalonia, and France," *Speculum* (1978): 460–78. Charles Petit-Dutaillis, *La Monarchie féodale en France et en Angleterre* (Paris, 1933; repr. 1971) is still interesting. The intelligent synthesis of Joseph R. Strayer, *The Medieval Origins of the Modern State* (1970) introduces reflections on the antagonism between the edification of the state and religious, local, and familial structures.

63. J. C. Holt, *Magna Carta* (Cambridge, 1965); *Magna Carta and Medieval Government* (London, 1985).

64. To his contemporaries Frederick II's government in Sicily looked more like a form of tyrannical rule (the worst kind in the eyes of the Christian political theorists of the thirteenth century who fed on ancient political theories christianized by John of Salisbury in the twelfth century) than an authentic and legitimate monarchical power.

65. André Vauchez, "Une campagne de pacification en Lombardie autour de 1233. L'action politique des ordres Mendiants d'après la réforme des statuts communaux et les accords de paix," *Mélanges d'histoire et d'archéologie publiés par l'École française de Rome* 78 (1966): 503–49.

66. He was canonized too, but only in 1671, so he is not exactly a medieval saint.

67. Regis Boyer, "Introduction" to the edition of the French translation of the *Sagas islandaises* (Paris, 1987), xxxii.

68. Karol Gorski, *L'ordine teutonico. Alle origini dello stato prussiano,* translated from Polish (Turin, 1971).

69. This is the subject of Eisenstein's famous film, *Alexander Nevsky* (1938).

70. A good survey of France in the thirteenth century is Marie-Thérèse Lorcin, *La France au XIIIᵉ siècle* (Paris, 1975). On the development of the French monarchical state, consult the recent syntheses of Jean Favier, *Histoire de France,* vol. 2, *Le Temps des principautés* (Paris, 1984); Georges Duby, *Histoire de France,* vol. 1, *Le Moyen Âge de Hugues Capet à Jeanne d'Arc (987–1460)* (Paris, 1987); Jacques Le Goff, "La genèse de l'État français au Moyen Âge" in *Histoire de la France,* edited by André Burguière and Jacques Revel, vol. 2, *L'État des pouvoirs* (Paris, 1989), 19–180.

71. These figures are drawn from R. Fossier, "Les campagnes au temps de Philippe Auguste: développement démographique et transformations sociales dans le monde rural," in *La France de Philippe Auguste. Le temps des mutations* (Paris, 1982), 628; and L. Génicot, *Le XIIIᵉ Siècle européen,* 52.

72. This is the estimate of Philippe Wolff, quoted in John H. Mundy, *Liberty and Political Power in Toulouse (1050–1230)* (New York, 1954), 225.

73. "In 1200 . . . the number of Reims's inhabitants definitely exceeds 10,000. This is the threshold that is usually used to designate a *grande ville* for the Middle Ages" (P. Desportes, *Reims et les Rémois aux XIIIe et XIVe siècles* [Paris, 1979], 93).

74. Henri Dubois, "Le commerce et les foires au temps de Philippe Auguste," in *La France de Philippe Auguste,* 701.

75. The illumination of manuscripts underwent an equally important expansion under Philip Augustus. Paradoxically, it was for the king's repudiated, encloistered wife, the Danish queen Ingeburg that the first masterwork of this kind had been executed. The Psalter's success represented the laymen's progress in matters of piety. Probably dating from the first years of the thirteenth century, Ingeburg's Psalter led to the production of other royal Psalters including Blanche of Castile's, inherited by Louis after her death, and Saint Louis' own Psalter. An important change took place over this time. At the end of the twelfth and at the beginning of the thirteenth century, the monastic workshops that produced the Psalters were all located in England and northeastern France. Beginning between 1220 and 1230, most of the production took place in the Parisian workshops. See Louis Grodecki, "Le psautier de la reine Ingeburg et ses problèmes," in *Le Moyen Âge retrouvé* (Paris, 1986); Robert Branner, *Manuscript Painting in Paris during the Reign of Saint Louis. A Study of Styles* (Berkeley: University of California Press, 1977).

76. Robert-Henri Bautier, "Le règne de Philippe Auguste dans l'histoire de France," in *La France de Philippe Auguste,* 17.

77. J.W. Baldwin, *Philippe Auguste,* 42 n. 59.

78. R.-H. Bautier, "Le règne de Philippe Auguste," 22–23.

79. A. G. Poulain, *Les Séjours du roi Saint Louis en Normandie et particulièrement à Vernon-sur-Seine* (Rouen, 1957).

80. This expression may be an exaggeration. Although the king, the royal family, and royalty were haloed with a certain religious prestige, there was no "royal religion" properly speaking. See Part III, ch. 9, "Saint Louis, Sacred King, Thaumaturge, and Saint."

81. "Li rois ne tient de nului, fors de Dieu et de lui" (*Établissements de Saint Louis,* vol. 2, 135).

82. Ibid., 262.

83. Charles Petit-Dutaillis, *Étude sur la vie et le règne de Louis VIII (1187–1226),* (Paris, 1894).

[84. The French "*comté*" is derived from the Latin word "*comitatus.*" In the medieval context, it referred to a district or territory over which the authority of a feudal lord extended. By this time in French history, it had become synonymous with the actual territory, or any of several, held by a count [*comte*] or, in many cases, by a feudal lord with a different title. The English equivalent was the earldom, as the French referred to the English earls as *comtes.* Unlike the *comtés,* earldoms were not independent principalities ruled and administered by their lords; I have therefore decided to follow most contemporary historians in opting for the more literal rendering as "county."—Trans.]

85. Here I am following the beautiful book of Andrew W. Lewis, *Royal Succession in Capetian France: Studies on Familial Order and the State* (Cambridge, MA, 1981), 209. The text of the testament can be found in the *Layettes du Trésor des chartes,* vol. 2, no. 1710. It was a part of the royal archives, which had both a "private" (familial) and a "public" (properly public and almost stately) character.

86. The royal jewels were related to the existence of each king and left the Royal Treasury upon his death, especially the numerous crowns in his possession.

87. We should recall that the main part of the Treasury belonging to the kingdom and not the family was kept in the tower of the Temple. Philip the Fair transferred it to the Louvre in 1295 before the suppression of the Order of the Templars. It was in this tower of the Louvre that the count of Flanders, Ferrand, was imprisoned after Bouvines (1214). He was freed shortly after Saint Louis' coronation.

88. Charles T. Wood, *The French Apanages and the Capetian Monarchy, 1224–1328* (Cambridge, MA, 1966); A. W. Lewis, *Royal Succession in Capetian France*; J. Le Goff, "Apanage," article in the *Encyclopaedia Universalis,* vol. 2 (Paris, 1970), 1322–24.

89. It would be nice to see another study on the legend of Charlemagne in medieval France conducted after the beautiful example of Robert Folz's *Le Souvenir et la légende de Charlemagne dans l'Empire germanique médiéval* (Paris, 1950).

90. Bernard Guenée, "Les généalogies entre l'histoire et la politique: la fierté d'être Capétien en France, au Moyen Âge," *Annales, E.S.C.* (1978): 450–77, reprinted in *Politique et Histoire au Moyen Âge* (Paris, 1981), 341–68. See also Karl Ferdinand Werner, "Die Legitimität der Kapetinger und die Entstehung des '*Reditus regni Francorum ad Stirpem Karoli*'," in *Die Welt als Geschichte* (1952): 203–25; Gabrielle M. Spiegel, "The *Reditus Regni ad Stirpem Karoli Magni*: A New Look," *French Historical Studies* (1972): 145–74.

91. Ferdinand Lot, "Quelques mots sur l'origine des pairs de France," *Revue historique* 54 (1894): 34–37.

92. Elizabeth A. R. Brown, "La notion de la légitimité et la prophétie à la cour de Philippe Auguste," in *La France de Philippe Auguste,* 77–111.

93. With the exception of the Russian princess Anne of Kiev, the wife of Henri I, all of the wives of the Capetian kings were of Carolingian descent.

94. Karl Ferdinand Werner, "Andrew von Marchiennes und die Geschichtsschreibung von Audouin und marchiennes am Ende des 12. Jahrhunderts," *Deutsches Archiv* (1952): 402–63.

95. See below, "Saint Louis and the Royal Bodies," in Part I, ch. 4.

96. We may observe that this Carolingian ancestry was transmitted through the women. As long as no one invoked the Salic law to exclude women and their progeny from inheriting the French throne, which happened at the end of the fourteenth century, this genealogy that ran contrary to the Capetian practice of succession did not seem to cause any problems. Later, a prudent silence surrounded this contradiction.

97. The castle of Montpensier whose site currently lies in Puy-de-Dôme was razed on the orders of Richelieu in the seventeenth century.

98. Chronicles from the end of the Middle Ages state that "Louis left the government of the kingdom to his wife" (Le Nain de Tillemont, *Vie de Saint Louis,* 1:395). They do not present any serious proof of this and are contradicted by the following events.

99. A. Teulet, *Layettes du Trésor des chartes,* vol. 2, no. 1811.

100. Philippe Mouskès, *Chronique rimée,* vol. 2, ed. F. de Reiffenberg (Brussels, 1838), vv. 27251–58.

101. François Olivier-Martin, *Études sur les régences,* vol. 1, *Les Régences et la majorité des rois sur les Capétiens directs et les premiers Valois (1060–1375)* (Paris, 1931). An excellent study, even though it exaggerates the importance of the problem of the regency—which only concerned the powerful—and underestimates the importance of the child king, which had much greater symbolic resonance.

102. We know that he was born in 1052, but we do not know the day or the month of his birth. Henri I died on August 4, 1060.

103. Jean-François Lemarignier, *Le Gouvernement royal aux premiers temps capétiens (987–1108)* (Paris, 1965), 152.

104. "*ad etatem legitimam*" (quoted from A. Teulet, *Layettes du Trésor des chartes,* vol. 2, no. 1828).

105. "*voluit et disposuit.*"

106. "*in bona deliberatione.*"

107. "*Et sana mente.*" This "attestation" of the three prelates gave the will that the dying king was supposed to have dictated to them a form that was very close to that of a testament with the mention of a deliberation, the affirmation of his mental stability, and the presence of three witnesses. A papal decree of Alexander III (1159–1181) determined that in canon law a testament was valid if it had been made in the presence of two or three witnesses.

108. Minstrel of Reims, 176; on Hugues de la Ferté-Bernard, see F. Olivier-Martin, *Études sur les régences,* 60.

109. This expression is taken from Gérard Sivery, "L'équipe gouvernementale, Blanche de Castille et la succession de Louis VIII en 1226," *L'Information historique* (1979): 203–11. It is G. Sivery who has better than anyone formulated the hypothesis that I am advancing here.

110. Yves Sassier used the verse from Ecclesiastes, "Misfortune to the land whose ruler is a child" in his excellent *Louis VII* (Paris, 1991), 85. However, when Louis VII became king in 1137, he was seventeen years old and governed on his own as soon as he pushed his mother aside with Suger's help.

111. "There is no need to commend children much [to parents], because not one [of them] detests his flesh [*nemo carnem suam odio habuerit*]," writes John of Salisbury in his *Policraticus* (1159), ed. C. Webb, 289–90.

112. Philippe Ariès, *L'Enfant et la vie familiale sous l'Ancien Régime* (Paris, 1960; repr. 1973); Jacques Le Goff, "Images de l'enfant léguées par le Moyen Âge," *Les*

Cahiers franco-polonais (1979): 139–55; idem, "Le roi enfant dans l'idéologie monarchique de l'Occident médiéval," in *Historicité de l'enfance et de la jeunesse* (Athens, 1986), 231–50. See also, *L'Enfant au Moyen Âge,* colloquium at C.U.E.R.M.A., *Senefiance,* no. 9 (Aix-en-Provence, 1980); *Enfants et Sociétés,* special issue of *Annales de démographie historique* (1973). B. Vadin, "L'absence de représentation de l'enfant et/ou du sentiment de l'enfance dans la littérature médiévale," in *Exclus et systèmes d'exclusion dans la littérature et la civilisation médiévale,* C.U.E.R.M.A., *Senefiance,* no. 2 (Aix-en-Provence, 1978), 363–84; Roger Colliot, "Perspectives sur la condition familiale de l'enfant dans la littérature française du Moyen Âge," in *Morale, pratique et vie quotidienne dans la littérature française de Moyen Âge, Senefiance,* no. 1 (Aix-en-Provence, 1976); Silvana Vecchio, "L'imagine del puer nella letteratura esegatica del Medioevo," in *Kind und Gesellschaft in Mittelalter und Renaissance, Beiträge und Texte zur Geschichte der Kindheit,* ed. K. Arnold (Munich and Paderborn, 1980), errs in its lack of critical spirit. An interesting psychoanalytic approach appears in *Hönt ihr die Kinder weinen. Eine psychogenetische Geschichte der Kindheit,* ed. L. de Mause (Frankfurt-am-Main, 1977). Explaining the medical literature, see S. Nagel, "Puer e puerita nella letteratura medica del XIII secolo. Per una storia del costume educativo (Età classica e Medio Evo)," in *Quaderni della Fondazione G. G. Feltrinelli,* no. 23 (1993): 87–108. On the iconography, Danièle Alexandre-Bidon and M. Classon, *L'Enfant à l'ombre des cathédrales* (Lyon, 1985). For a different explanation, see Pierre Riché, "L'enfant au Moyen Âge," in *L'Histoire* (1994). This conception that valued children and childhood in the Middle Ages has been developed by Pierre Riché and Danièle Alexandre-Bodin in a beautiful book, *L'Enfance au Moyen Âge* (Paris, 1994), written for an exposition at the *Bibliothèque nationale* (Paris, October 1994–January 1995). The bibliography on the child in history is extensive. Many other titles on this subject can be found in the works cited here.

113. Ernst Robert Curtius, "L'enfant et le vieillard," in *La Littérature européenne et le Moyen Âge latin* (French translation: Paris, 1956), 122–25.

114. Gregory the Great, *Dialogi,* Book II: "*Fuit vir vitae venerabilis . . . ab ipso suae pueritiae tempore cor gerens senile*"; Geoffroy de Beaulieu, *Vita,* ch. 4 (*Receuil des historiens des Gaules et de la France,* 20:4): "*de die in diem in virum perfectum crescere.*"

115. Henri-Irène Marrou, *Histoire de l'éducation dans l'Antiquité* (Paris, 1948; repr. 1965), 325.

116. On John of Salisbury, see *The World of John of Salisbury,* ed. M. Wilks (Oxford, 1984); B. Munk-Olsen, "L'humanisme de Jean de Salisbury, un cicéronien au XIIᵉ siècle," in *Entretiens sur la Renaissance du XIIᵉ siècle,* ed. M. de Gandillac and E. Jeauneau (Paris and the Hague, 1968), 53–83; H. Liebeschütz, *Medieval Humanism in the Life and Writings of John of Salisbury* (London, 1950); Robert W. Southern, "Humanism and the School of Chartres," in *Medieval Humanism and Other Studies* (Oxford, 1970).

117. From the vast bibliography on the twelfth-century Renaissance, I would like to single out *Entretiens* cited in the preceding note. See also, Marshall Clagett, Gaines Post, and R. Reynolds, eds., *Twelfth Century Europe and the Foundations of Modern Society* (Madison: University of Wisconsin Press, 1961); R. L. Benson and Giles

Constable, eds., *Renaissance and Renewal in the Twelfth Century* (Cambridge, MA, 1992); Marie-Dominique Chenu, *La Théologie du XIIe siècle* (Paris, 1957).

118. John of Salisbury, *Policraticus,* IV, 11 and 12 (Webb edition, 269 [533b], 276 [537a, b, c]).

119. *Vae, terra, cujus rex puer est.* The Bible of Jerusalem repeats, somewhat uselessly: "Woe to thee, O land, whose king is a child." We might think of other works like Montherlant's play, *La Ville dont le prince est un enfant* (1952).

120. *Policraticus,* IV, ch. 7.

121. See below, "Louis and Josiah," in Part II, ch. 5.

122. This was the subject of the first ordinance of 1374. See Raymond Cazelles, *Société politique, noblesse et couronne sous Jean le Bon et Charles V* (Geneva, 1982), 579–80.

123. René Metz, "L'enfant dans le droit canonique médiéval," *Recueils de la société Jean Bodin,* vol. 36, 2, *L'Enfant* (Brussels, 1976), 9–96.

124. F. Olivier-Martin, *Études sur la régence,* n. 30, 77 ff., for my inspiration here. See also A. Wolf, "Königtum Minderjährigkeit und die Institution der Regentschaft," *Receuils de la société Jean Bodin,* 97–106. On the slightly earlier minority of Henry III of England, made king ten years before Louis in 1216, see D. A. Carpenter, *The Minority of Henry III* (London, 1990).

125. Blanche of Castile was pregnant with her last child at the time, a posthumously born son of Louis VIII who was born at the beginning of 1227 and became Charles d'Anjou, king of Naples and Sicily.

126. This miniature can be found in the folio 97 of the manuscript of Nouvelles Acquisitions latines 3145 at the Bibliothèque nationale in Paris. It has been reproduced on page 216 of the article by Marcel Thomas, "L'iconographie de Saint Louis dans les *Heures de Jeanne de Navarre,*" in *Septième centenaire de la mort de Saint Louis . . .* (1970) (Paris, 1976), illustration 9.

127. Jean Richard, "L'adoubement de Saint Louis," *Journal des savants* (1988): 208–17.

128. Matthew Paris, *Chronica majora,* 3:118.

129. In 1316, at the age of two, the young Jeanne, the eldest daughter of Louis X "le Hutin," embodied two misfortunate conditions that excluded her from the throne: her feminine sex and the suspicion that she was a bastard (arising from the affair of the tower of Nesle). In order to distinguish itself from the other important aristocratic families, the Capetians seem to have excluded bastards as well as women from the royal succession. At the beginning of the fifteenth century, this would play against the future Charles VII.

130. Joinville, *Histoire de Saint Louis,* 42–43.

131. Ibid., 44.

132. This is a topos of feminine hagiography. Abbesses and cloistered women unjustly accused of indecent conduct undressed themselves in order to show that they were not pregnant. The Minstrel of Reims maliciously transposed this common image to the attacks against the Queen Mother. This evidence also points to her innocence, if any additional proof is required.

133. The new pope, Gregory IX, had already granted the dispensations allowing this marriage to take place as the future spouses were cousins in the third and fourth degree.

134. J. Verger has indicated that the masters formed at the University of Paris under Philip Augustus between roughly 1200 and 1220 only rose into the high clergy and other offices under Saint Louis. See Verger, "Des écoles à l'Université," 842.

135. This is an adaptation of the version in Old French in the *Vie de Saint Louis* by Guillaume de Nangis, in *Receuil des historiens des Gaules et de la France*, 20:519–21.

136. This is the subject of an interesting article by Odette Pontal, "Le différend entre Louis IX et les évêques de Beauvais et ses incidences sur les conciles (1232–1248)," *Bibliothèque de l'École des Chartes* 123 (Paris, 1965), 7–34.

137. An agreement between the king of France and the bishop of Beauvais resolving the royal right of residence was reached only in June 1248 on the eve of the king's departure for the crusade.

138. According to Joinville, the king soon after showed his resolve in an assembly of the bishops of the kingdom. Contrary to what we may be inclined to think in the twentieth century, there was no contradiction between Saint Louis' desire to maintain great respect for the Church in all spiritual matters and his unflinching attitude in temporal affairs.

139. This was translated into modern French by Natalis de Wailly in the 1874 edition. The original manuscript reads: "dès qu'il se sut apercevoir" for "dès qu'il sut se faire *connaître*," in other words roughly "as soon as he knew what he wanted to do" ("*aperçu*" means "wise, prudent, well instructed"). This is an interesting expression for the historian of Saint Louis, the man. The manuscript still speaks not of churches and religious houses but of "moustiers et maisons de religion," in other words of monasteries and religious convents. Among church people, Saint Louis was more attracted by the ones who followed a regimen than by the ordinary clergy who were attached to the things of the time, even if they were ecclesiastical things. Finally, Joinville spoke of the "honor and highness" of the abbey of Royaumont. The aesthetic vocabulary was not yet separated from other values and a vocabulary in which artistic notions were mixed with ethical ideas.

140. Guillaume de Saint-Pathus, *Vie de Saint Louis*, 71. They carried stones on a stretcher. The wheelbarrow, an invention of the thirteenth century, appeared only a little later on the building sites of the cathedrals.

141. These brothers cannot be Jean and Philippe Dagobert. They were probably dead at that time as this scene must have occurred between 1232 and 1234. In 1233, Louis was nineteen years old. Robert was seventeen, Alphonse thirteen, and Charles six.

142. No doubt so that the chore would end more quickly.

143. Guillaume de Nangis, *Vie de Saint Louis*, 320–26. On the Holy Nail of Saint-Denis, see the remarkable study of Anne Lombard-Jourdan.

144. See below, "Guillaume de Saint-Pathus" in Part II, ch. 2.

PART I
Notes to Chapter 2

1. See below "The Portrait of the King " in Part II, ch. 10, and "His Mother," in Part III, ch. 6.

2. Gérard Sivery presents the hypothesis that Saint Louis may have sought out information about the young girl because the chronicler Guillaume de Puylaurens mentioned that during the preceding year, Louis IX had asked Gilles de Flagy, his envoy in Languedoc, to make a stop in Provence in order to meet the count and his daughter.

3. Guillaume de Nangis, *Vie de Saint Louuis,* 323.

4. On the countal family of Provence, consult Gérard Sivery, *Marguerite de Provence. Une reine au temps des cathédrales* (Paris, 1987).

5. According to Sivery, this was "a masterpiece of medieval marriage strategy."

6. With the extinction of the House of Anjou and Sicily in 1481, Provence returned to the Kingdom of France.

7. The larger part of Marguerite's dowry would never be paid.

8. The record of this event can be found in the catalogue, *Le Mariage de Saint Louis à Sens in 1234,* the catalogue of the exhibit organized in Sens in 1984.

9. See Jean-Baptiste Molin and Pierre Mutembe, *Le Rituel du mariage en France, du XIIᵉ au XVIᵉ siècle* (Paris, 1974); Jean-Baptiste Molin, "La liturgie du mariage dans l'ancien diocèse de Sens," *Bulletin de la Société d'histoire et d'art du diocèse de Meaux* (1968): 9–32; and idem, "L'iconographie des rites nuptiaux," in *102ᵉ Congrès national des sociétés savantes* (Limoges, 1977), 353–66.

10. This was the situation up to the point when Marie de Médicis managed with great difficulty to be crowned *in extremis* the night before Ravaillac's assassination attempt, which cost her husband Henri IV his life in 1610.

11. The feast and the dubbings appear in the royal accounts. Le Nain de Tillemont, who does not mention any sources for this information, may have invented the laying on hands for the scrofulous.

12. The genette is a small carnivorous mammal in the family of *Viverridae,* which includes the civet and the mongoose.

13. This error probably resulted from a poor translation of the expressions *in nova militia sua* in the royal accounts of the ceremonies at Sens that dealt with Gautier de Ligne, and *pro factione robarum regis et fratrum et novarum militium* (which was probably a misreading of *novorum militum*) "and for the creation of the robes of the king, his brothers, and the new knights." These new knights were the ones who had just been dubbed and who received several rewards for this occasion. In the first half of the thirteenth century, the expression *nova militia* had only two possible meanings: (1) dubbing; (2) the metaphor employed by Saint Bernard in the previous century in a famous treatise where he used it to describe the new military orders of the Templars, the Hospitalers, etc. In this case, we would have to read *militiarum.*

14. These accounts have been published in the *Recueil des historiens des Gaules et de la France*, vol. 21 (1855), 226–51. They have been commented on and analyzed by Régine Pernoud in *La Reine Blanche* (Paris, 1972).

15. On furs in the Middle Ages, see Robert Delort, *Le Commerce des fourrures en Occident à la fin du Moyen Âge (vers 1300–vers 1450)*, 2 vols. (Rome, 1978). This important book also contains information on the previous period.

16. The rituals of royal "joyous entries" were established in the fourteenth century.

17. Joinville, *Histoire de Saint Louis*, 55–57.

18. Baudouin's mother, Yolande, was the sister of Isabelle, Philip Augustus's first wife and Louis IX's grandmother.

19. Gautier Cornut, *Historia susceptionis coronae spineae Iesu Christi*, in *Historiae Francorum Scriptores*, 5:407–14.

20. Ibid., 409.

21. Some modern historians have falsely seen a forerunner of modern critical spirit in Guibert de Nogent. However, this treatise proves that on very different grounds (which admitted the authenticity of many relics) intellectuals in the Middle Ages, far from lacking any critical spirit, developed techniques for identifying fakes, which forces us not only to modify the reproach of "gullibility" that Moderns have leveled against the men of the Middle Ages, but, especially, to revise traditional commonplaces about medieval mentalities. The medieval critique of fakes comfortably coexisted with belief structures that were very different from our own criteria of judgment. The truth of the Incarnation and its earthly traces, the truth of the existence of the supernatural and miraculous things on earth produced very specific techniques for detecting fakes, although it did not suppress them. On the contrary, because individual and collective salvation might depend on it, the stakes were so great that distrust of cruel tricks and the superstitious beliefs of peasants and idiots arose. Cf. Klaus Schreiner, " 'Discrimen veri ac falsi.' Ansätze und Formen der Kritik in der Heiligen- und Reliquienverehrung des Mittelalters," *Archiv für Kulturgeschichte* 48 (1966): 1–53.

22. Gautier Cornut, *Historia susceptionis*, 410. The archbishop was an eyewitness to the scene.

23. P. Rousset, "La conception de l'histoire à l'époque féodale," in *Mélanges d'histoire du Moyen Âge dédiés à la mémoire de Louis Halphen* (Paris, 1951), 623–33.

24. Jean-Michel Leniaud and Françoise Perrot, *La Sainte-Chapelle* (Paris, 1991).

25. Matthew Paris, *Chronica majora*, 4:92.

26. Henri Focillon, *The Art of the West*, vol. 2, *Gothic Art*, trans. Donald King (London: Phaidon, 1963), 42.

27. On May 19, 1940, people marched in a procession carrying the Holy Crown of Thorns during a religious ceremony at Notre-Dame de Paris in the presence of the French government and the diplomatic corps in order to protect Paris and France from the lighting fast advance of the German army. Cf. Jean-Pierre Azéma, "1939–1940. L'année terrible," *Le Monde* 6 (July 25, 1989): 2.

28. J.-M. Leniaud and F. Perrot, *La Sainte-Chapelle.*

29. See above, "The Oriental Horizon," in ch. 1.

30. Isabelle, Henry III's sister and the wife of Frederick II, died in December 1241.

31. Matthew Paris, *Chronica majora,* 3:626–27.

32. The ailing Celestin IV only lasted as pope from October 25 to November 10.

33. I am following the study of Charles Bemont, "La campagne de Poitou 1242–1243, Taillebourg et Saintes," *Annales du Midi* (1893): 289–314.

34. Jean Richard (*Saint Louis* [Paris, 1983], 116) mentions Montreuil-en-Gâtine, Fontenay-le-Comte, Moncontour, Vouvant, and Frontenay. The list that I give here comes from Guillaume de Nangis's *Vie de Saint Louis,* 335–38, which maintains the spelling in the French edition from the end of the thirteenth century, *Receuil des historiens des Gaules et de la France,* vol. 20 (1940).

35. Jean Richard gives the respective dates of May 10 and May 15.

36. Guillaume de Nangis, *Vie de Saint Louis,* 339.

37. See below "The Sick King" in Part III, ch. 10.

38. Joinville, *Histoire de Saint Louis,* 61–63. See also Matthew Paris's drawing that represents the sick king.

39. The bibliography on the crusades is immense. Two bibliographical guides are A. S. Atiya, *The Crusades: Historiography and Bibliography* (Bloomington, 1962) and H. E. Meyer, "Literaturbericht über die Geschichte der Kreuzzüge," in *Historische Zeitschrift,* Sonderheft 3 (Munich, 1969), 642–736. The annual record of the latest published works is in the *Bulletin of the Society for the Study of the Crusades and the Latin East.* The synthetic works of René Grousset (*Histoire des croisades et du royaume franc de Jérusalem,* 3 vols. (Paris, 1933–1936; repr. 1975) and of Steven Runciman, 3 vols. (1951–1954) are dated. The monumental collective synthesis directed by K. M. Setton, *A History of the Crusades,* 5 vols. (Philadelphia: Pennsylvania University Press, 1955–1985) is a good reference. Less complete but better done are Michel Balard, *Les Croisades* (Paris, 1988); Cécile Morrisson, *Les Croisades* (Paris, 1969); James A. Brundage, ed., *The Crusades: Motives and Achievements* (Boston, 1964); Hans Eberhard Mayer, *The Crusades,* 2nd ed. (Oxford, 1988). For a collection of brief and uneven but often stimulating essays, see "Les croisades," *L'Histoire,* special issue with an introduction by Robert Delort (Paris, 1988); F. Cardini, *Le crociate tra i mito e la storia* (Rome, 1971). On the laws and ideology of the crusades, see L. and J. Riley-Smith, *The Crusades: Idea and Reality 1095–1274* (London, 1981); Paul Alphandéry and Alphonse Dupront, *La Chrétienté et l'idée de croisade,* 2 vols. (Paris, 1995); James A. Brundage, *Medieval Canon Law and the Crusader* (Madison, Milwaukee, 1969); Jean Richard, *L'Esprit de la croisade* (Paris, 1969); Paul Rousset, *Histoire d'une idéologie de la croisade* (Lausanne, 1983); Benjamin Z. Kedar, *Crusade and Mission: European Approaches toward the Muslims* (Princeton, 1984). On the historical environment of the crusades, see Claude Cahen, *Orient et Occident au temps des croisades* (Paris, 1983); P. M. Holt, *The Age of the Crusades* (London, 1986).

40. On medieval criticism of the crusades, see P. A. Throop, *Criticism of the Crusade* (Amsterdam, 1940); E. Siberry, *Criticism of Crusading, 1095–1274* (Oxford, 1985).

41. This is a fragment of an extract quoted by J. Richard, *Saint Louis,* 173. The original text of the poem has been published by W. Meyer, "Wie Ludwig IX der Heilige das Kreuz nahm," *Nachrichten der königlichen Gesellschaft der Wissenschaften zu Göttingen* (1907): 246–57.

42. On Saint Louis' millenarianism, see "The Meeting with Hugh of Digne," in Part I, ch. 4. This section recounts Louis IX's meeting with the Franciscan Joachimite Hugh of Digne of the convent of the Minors of Hyères after his return from his first crusade.

43. See M. Balard, *Les Croisades,* 84–85.

44. Steven Runciman, "The Decline of the Crusading Idea," in *Relazioni del X congresso internazionale di scienze storiche,* vol. 3 (Florence, 1955), 637–52; E. Siberry, "Missionaries and Crusaders, 1095–1274: Opponents or Allies?" in *Studies in Church History* 20 (1978): 103–10; Franco Cardini, "Nella presenza del Soldan superbo: Bernardo, Fransesco, Bonaventura e il superamento dell'idea di Crociata," *Studi Francescani* 71 (1974): 199–250; B. Z. Kedar, *Crusade and Mission.*

45. Jacques Le Goff, "Saint Louis, croisé idéal?" in *Notre histoire,* no. 20 (February 1986): 42 ff.

46. The epic poem [*chanson de geste*] *Le Pèlerinage de Charlemagne* established and spread this legend. It dates from around 1150 (the ending of the *Chanson de Roland* hints at a possible expedition to the Holy Land by Charlemagne). Cf. Jules Horrent, "La chanson du Pèlerinage de Charlemagne et la réalité historique contemporaine," *Mélanges Frappier* 1 (1970): 411–17.

47. Sidney Painter, "The Crusade of Theobold of Champagne and Richard of Cornwall, 1239–1241," in *A History of the Crusades,* ed. K. M. Setton, 2:463–86.

48. I will discuss the opinions of W. C. Jordan and J. Richard about the importance of the crusades in the thought and the rule of Saint Louis at the beginning of the next chapter.

49. Based on the conflict between Frederick II and the papacy and Saint Louis' conduct in this affair, Ernst Kantorowicz painted a brilliant portrait of the king of France as standing out in relation to other European rulers. He concluded that "placed side by side with Louis IX, the other kings do not measure up" (Ernst Kantorowicz, *L'Empereur Frédéric II,* 514–15).

50. I have modernized the original text in Old French from Guillaume de Nangis's *Vie de Saint Louis,* remaining as faithful as possible to the original.

51. The chronicler's text corresponds to the original documents. Both Frederick's and Louis' letters have been published in reverse chronological order in the *Chronique des ducs de Brabant (Collection de chroniques belges),* 2:171–72. See the commentary written by Carlrichard Brühl, *Naissance de deux peuples: Français et Allemands (IXᵉ–XIᵉ siècle)* (Paris, 1995), 305.

52. According to Matthew Paris, the French warned the cardinals to elect a pope who would serve all Christendom, who would serve Christendom north of

the Alps (*citra montes*) by virtue of a supposed privilege granted by Saint Clement to Saint Denis. We can see here the extent to which what was later called 'Gallicanism' had old roots, although most specialists do not accept this letter's authenticity. Because the document is located in the archives of Frederick II, we have to wonder if it is not a fake designed by the imperial chancery to compromise Louis IX with the papacy by attributing the emperor's position to him. The question still merits consideration. The letter is published in Jean Huillard-Brétolles, *Historia Diplomatica Frederici secundi,* vol. 6, book 1 (Paris, 1852–1861), 68.

53. My account of this affair follows Élie Berger, *Saint Louis et Innocent IV. Étude sur le rapport de la France et du Saint Siège* (Paris, 1893). Although it is old, this study is still worth reading today.

54. During the voyage, Louis IX negotiated the purchase of Mâconnais from Countess Alix at Mâcon. After the sale of her lands, she withdrew to the abbey of Maubuisson near Pontoise, which had been founded by Blanche of Castile.

55. Louis had been shocked by the pope's arrogance. See below, "His Conscience," in Part III, ch. 7.

56. Louis sent two successive embassies to the pope. In the highly detailed record of proposals conveyed by the second embassy, the royal agent declared, "My master, the king, has with great difficulty put up for a long time with the wrong done to the Church of France and therefore himself and his kingdom," document published by Matthew Paris in annex to his chronicle (Matthew Paris, *Chronica majora,* 6:99–112). Cf. Gerard J. Campbell, "The Protest of Saint Louis," *Traditio* 15 (1959): 405–18. Campbell believes that this statement expressed Louis' ideas, but that the envoy composed the text and gave them an abrupt and aggressive form that did not correspond to the king's intentions. See below, "Saint Louis and the Church" in Part III, ch. 8.

57. Jean Richard, "La politique orientale de Saint Louis: la croisade 1248," in *Septième centenaire de la mort de Saint Louis (1970)* (Paris, 1976), 197–207; Jacques Le Goff, "Saint Louis and the Mediterranean," *Mediterranean Historical Review* 5 (1990): 21–43; see also Pierre Chaunu's essential remarks in *L'Expansion européenne du XIIIe au XVe siècle* (Paris, 1969), Part II, ch. 1, "La Méditerranée," 61–64.

58. P. Alphandéry and A. Dupront, *La Chrétienté et l'idée de croisade,* 1:133.

59. Jean Richard, *Le Royaume latin de Jérusalem* (Paris, 1953), 120–21.

60. E. C. Furber, "The Kingdom of Cyprus, 1191–1291," in *A History of the Crusades,* ed. K. M. Setton, 2:599–629.

61. Josuah Prawer, *The World of the Crusaders* (London and Jerusalem, 1972), 83.

62. Idem, *Histoire du royaume latin de Jérusalem,* 2 vols. (Paris, 1969–1970); J. Richard, *Le Royaume latin de Jérusalem.*

63. See above, "The Oriental Horizon," in ch. 1.

64. Frederick C. Lane, "The Economic Meaning of the Invention of the Compass," *American Historical Review* 68 (1863): 605–17.

65. Joinville, *Histoire de Saint Louis,* 70–71.

66. Jean-Claude Hocquet, *Le Sel et la Fortune de Venise,* vol. 2, *Voiliers et commerce en Méditerranée, 1200–1650* (Lille, 1959), 102.

67. On Mediterranean ships, in addition to J.-C. Hocquet (preceding note) see R. Bastard de Père, "Navires méditerranéens au temps de Saint Louis," *Revue d'histoire économique et sociale* 50 (1972): 327–56; Michel Mollat, ed., *Le Navire et l'économie maritime du Moyen Âge au XIIIe siècle, principalement en Méditerranée,* Acts of the Second International Colloquium on Maritime History, 1957 (Paris, 1958); Eugene H. Byrne, *Genoese Shipping in the XIIth and XIIIth Centuries* (Cambridge, MA, 1930); Ugo Tucci, "La navigazione veneziana nel Duecento e nel primo Trecento e la sua evoluzione tecnia," in *Venezia e il Levante,* Actes du congrès tenu à la Fondazione Cini, 1968, 2 vols. (Florence, 1973).

68. According to Patrick Gautier-Dalché, a historian of space in the Middle Ages, cartography provided little useful information.

69. When the French fleet returned to Sicily on the night of November 15–16, 1270 after Saint Louis' death outside Tunis, a violent storm destroyed most of the ships. The destruction of the ships made any rapid resumption of the crusade impossible, assuming anyone actually wanted to pursue this course of action.

70. Joinville, *Histoire de Saint Louis,* 72–73.

71. Jacques Monprin, "Joinville et la mer" in *Études offertes à Félix Lecoy* (Paris, 1973), 445–68.

72. Jean Delumeau, *La Peur en Occident (XIVe–XVIIe siècles),* esp. "La Peur de la mer," 31 ff. See below, "Saint Louis and the Sea," in Part III, ch. 1

73. J. Richard, *Saint Louis,* 100, 200.

74. P. Alphandéry and A. Dupront, *La Chrétienté et l'idée de croisade.*

75. B. Z. Kedar, *Crusade and Mission*; E. Siberry, "Missionaries and Crusaders."

76. John Moorman, *A History of the Franciscan Order* (Oxford, 1968), 46 and 226 ff.; M. Roncaglia, *Saint Francis of Assisi and the Middle East* (Cairo, 1957); F. Van Ortroy, "Saint François d'Assise et son voyage en Orient," *Analecta Bollandiana* 31 (1912): 451–62.

77. In Majorca, notably, a *studium* for teaching the Arabic language was established at the request of Pope John XXI in 1276. See J. Moorman, *A History of the Franciscan Order.*

78. Louis IX's interest in the Byzantines surfaced especially toward the end of his reign. In 1269 and 1270, from his camp outside of Tunis he exchanged embassies with the Emperor Michael VII Palaeologus who carried out the Greek reconquest of what was left of the Latin Empire of Constantinople in 1261. In contrast to his brother Charles d'Anjou, Louis showed again that he put the union of Christian peoples (the Greeks being called upon to "convert") before the selfish interests of the Latins. See M. Dabrowska, "L'attitude pro-byzantine de Saint Louis," *Byzantinoslavia* 50 (1989): 11–23.

79. J. Morize, "Aigues-Mortes au XIIIe siècle," *Annales du Midi* 26 (1914): 313–48; Jean Combes, "Origine et passé d'Aigues-Mortes. Saint Louis et le problème de la fondation d'Aigues-Mortes," in *Hommages à André Dupont* (Montpellier, 1974), 255–65; W. C. Jordan, "Supplying Aigues-Mortes for the Crusade of 1248: The Problem of Restructuring Trade," in *Order and Innovation (Mélanges J. Strayer)* (Princeton, 1976).

80. For information about the rental contracts for the ships, see L. T. Belgrano, *Documenti inediti riguardanti le due crociate di San Ludovico* (Genoa, 1959).

81. Joinville, *Histoire de Saint Louis,* 72–75, 80–81.

82. See W. C. Jordan, *Louis IX and the Challenge of the Crusade: A Study in Rulership* (Princeton, 1979), ch. 4, "War Finance: Men, Material, and Money."

83. Idem, "Supplying Aigues-Mortes."

84. André Sayous, "Les mandats de Saint Louis sur son Trésor pendant la septième croisade," *Revue historique* 167 (1931).

85. W. C. Jordan, *Louis IX and the Challenge of the Crusade.*

86. See below, "The Crusade, Louis IX, and the West," in Part I, ch. 3.

87. As a preacher and a statesman, Eudes de Châteauroux does not seem to deserve the scorn of Barthélemy Hauréau (*Notices et extraits des manuscrits de la Bibliothèque nationale,* 24:2.2 [Paris, 1876], 204–35). See the unpublished thesis for the D.E.A. by A. Charansonnet—whom I thank—"Études de quelques sermons d'Eudes de Châteauroux (1190?–1274) sur la croisade et la croix," Université de Paris I, directed by Bernard Guenée.

88. Jacques Le Goff, "Réalités sociales et codes idéologiques au début du XIIIᵉ siècle: un *exemplum* de Jacques de Vitry sur les tournois," in *L'Imaginaire médiéval* (Paris, 1985), 238–61.

89. See the detailed list of articles passed in support of the crusade in É. Berger, *Saint Louis et Innocent IV,* 134–37.

90. See below, "Saint Louis and the Jews," Part III, ch. 8, and M. W. Labarge, "Saint Louis et les Juifs," in *Le Siècle de Saint Louis,* ed. R. Pernoud (Paris, 1970), 267–73. I deal with Saint Louis' general attitude toward the Jews in Part III, ch. 8.

91. Claude Cahen, "Saint Louis et l'Islam," *Journal asiatique* 258 (1970): 3–12; Marie-Thérèse d'Alverny, "La connaissance de l'Islam au temps de Saint Louis," in *Septième centenaire de la mort de Saint Louis,* 235–46; Aryeh Grabois, "Islam and Muslims as seen by Christian Pilgrims in Palestine in the XIIIth Century," *Asian and African Studies. Journal of the Israel Oriental Society* 20 (1986): 309–27.

PART I
Notes to Chapter 3

1. W. C. Jordan, *Louis IX and the Challenge of the Crusade* (Princeton, 1979).

2. P. Alphandéry and A. Dupront, *La Chrétienté et l'idée de croisade,* 2:201.

3. On Saint Louis and the crusade, see below, Part III, ch. 7, and J. Le Goff, "Saint Louis, croisé idéal?"

4. This is "pivotal Egypt," to use an expression of Pierre Chaunu.

5. See J. Prawer, *Histoire du royaume latin de Jérusalem,* 2:326 n. 14 and J. Richard, "La politique orientale de Saint Louis: la croisade de 1248."

6. Jean Richard, "La fondation d'une église latine en Orient par Saint Louis: Damiette," *Bibliothèque de l'École des chartes* 120 (1962): 44–73.

7. J. Richard, "La politique orientale de Saint Louis," 205–7.

8. See above, in ch. 2, "The King's Illness and His Vow to Crusade."

9. P. Alphandéry and A. Dupront, *La Chrétienté et l'idée de croisade,* 1:18.

10. For example, in 1217 on the occasion of the capture of Damietta by Jean de Brienne, which was well known to the young Louis IX at the French court.

11. Le Nain de Tillemont, *Vie de Saint Louis,* 3:180–81. The terms "regency" and "regent" did not exist in the thirteenth century. Blanche received the "guardianship" (*custodia*) of the kingdom and apparently continued to carry the title of "queen." In 1251, Matthew Paris (*Chronica majora,* 5:248) called her *moderatrix et regina,* "moderator and queen" (although *moderare* already meant "to rule, to govern" in Classical Latin).

12. See below, "Local Government and Legislative Power," in Part III, ch. 5.

13. We must not forget that blue was the color of the French monarchy. As he often did, Saint Louis combined a religious attitude with an expression of political publicity.

14. Beginning in the thirteenth century, camlet designated an imitation of high-value fabric and a local imitation, which would lead one to think that the original camlet must have belonged to the family of serge or rep. The basic material for camlet was originally wool: mohair or cashmere? Camel wool? However, the word's etymology comes from the Arabic "*Khamlat*" (smooth surface) and not from "camel" (Françoise Piponnier, "À propos de textiles anciens principalement médiévaux," *Annales, E.S.C.* [1967] 864–90).

15. Le Nain de Tillemont, *Vie de Saint Louis,* 3:177–78.

16. See Part II, ch. 7.

17. See Part III, ch. 6.

18. He arrived too late to leave before winter and had to wait for the spring of 1249 to put to sea.

19. See above, "Saint Louis and the Mediterranean," in ch. 2.

20. On Joinville's style of narrating the crusade, cf. Jacques Monfrin, "Joinville et la prise de Damiette, 1249," *Compte rendu de l'Académie des inscriptions et belles-lettres* (1976): 268–85.

21. Jean-Noël Biraben and Jacques Le Goff, "La peste du haut Moyen Âge," *Annales, E.S.C.* (1969): 1484–1510.

22. The Muslims seized the secret of Greek fire from the Byzantines, who invented it in the second half of the seventh century. It had helped them win many a maritime battle against their Muslim and Russian enemies, and its success lasted at least until the eleventh century. Emperor Constantine VII (d. 959) instituted this *palladium* as a sacred talisman of the Empire. People have debated its qualities and manner of use for a long time. After eliminating saltpeter as a possible ingredient—its existence was unknown in the Middle Ages—today people think it was a mixture of naptha (raw petroleum) and chalk placed in contact with water; the heating of the chalk created naptha vapors that exploded when they reached a certain temperature and mixed with air. Transformed into self-igniting torches, these balls of fire were projected by flamethrowers or primitive canons (a "stoning" or "crossbow tower"). This secret weapon of Greek fire was a forerunner of modern missiles. See, J. F. Partington, "A History of the Problem of Greek Fire," *Byzantinische Zeitschrift* (1970):

91–99; J. R. Ellis Davidson, "The Secret Weapon of Byzantium," ibid. (1973): 71–74; E. Gabriel, "Griechlisches Feuer," in *Lexikon des Mittelalters* 4, no. 8 (1989): 1711–12.

23. The *chat* ["cat" or "Welsh cat" in English] was "a rolling war machine in the form of a covered gallery that protected the sappers and miners inside when it was pushed up against a fortification's walls. The *chat-château* was a *chat* outfitted with belfries to protect and defend the people working in the gallery" (Algirdas-Julien Greimas, *Dictionnaire de l'ancien français jusqu'au mileu du XIVe siècle* [Paris, 1968], 108).

24. This drove up the price of wood to an extreme.

25. Joinville, *Histoire de Saint Louis,* 113–15.

26. Ibid., 125–27. See Part III, ch. 4.

27. Joinville, *Histoire de Saint Louis,* 124–27.

28. Ibid., 118–21. Aside from a passionate outburst during the landing, according to Joinville, Saint Louis always recommended caution. For example: "On the day of Saint-Nicolas, the king ordered everyone to prepare their mounts for battle, and forbade anyone to be so bold as to try any individual strike against the Saracens that had come" (103).

29. Ibid., 408–9. See below, "Toward Canonization," in ch. 5.

30. See Part III, ch. 7.

31. Richard the Lion-Hearted had also sent a letter to his subjects after his victory over Philip Augustus at Gisors in 1198. His letter is quoted by Georges Duby in *Histoire de France,* vol. 1, *Le Moyen Âge de Hugues Capet à Jeanne d'Arc, 987–1460,* 260. See Appendix 2 below.

32. The original Latin text of the letter has been published by Duchesne, *Historiae Francorum Scriptores,* vol. 5 (Paris, 1649), 428. There is also a French translation in David O'Connell, *Les Propos de Saint Louis* (Paris, 1974), 163–72. This is a new initiative for a French king.

33. Joinville, *Histoire de Saint Louis,* 239.

34. From the record whose references can be found in N. Cohn, I have retained the two most detailed accounts: Guillaume de Nangis, *Chronicon,* 553–54; Matthew Paris, *Chronica majora,* 5:246 ff. This astonishing and revealing episode has not yet found its modern historian, although there is an outline of a study in Norman Cohn, *The Pursuit of Millenium,* French translation *Les Fanatiques de l'Apocalypse* (1983), 97 ("Dans le ressac des croisades: le Pseudo-Baudouin et le Maître de Hongrie"); G. Gourquin, *Les Soulèvements populaires au Moyen Âge* (Paris, 1972).

35. Donning a miter, the Master of Hungary had preached violently against the clergy at Saint-Eustache.

36. As we reflect on this slightly obscure episode from the history of medieval France, it would not be a bad idea to note that the Latin word employed here, *dux,* gave the twentieth century the words *duce, Führer, caudillo, conducator,* etc., mutatis mutandis.

37. He was an apostate monk who claimed to be a native of Hungary.

38. Gérard Sivery, *Saint Louis et son siècle* (Paris, 1983), 438.

39. Louis Carolus-Barré, "Le prince héritier Louis (1244–1260) et l'intérim du pouvoir royal de la mort de Blanche (nov. 1252) au retour du roi (julliet 1254)," *Comptes rendus de l'Académie des inscriptions et belles-lettres* (1970): 588–96.

40. See above in ch. 1, "The Oriental Horizon: Byzantium, Islam, and the Mongol Empire."

41. Some readers may object that there were many similar projects following the crusades, particularly in the fourteenth and fifteenth centuries. As for these projects, I do not doubt the sincerity of their leaders, but I consider them mere fantasies. See Alphonse Dupront's important book on the crusades over the long term.

42. Paul Deschamps, *Les Châteaux des croisés en Terre sainte,* 2 vols. (Paris, 1934–1939); Henri-Paul Eydoux, *Les Châteaux du soleil. Forteresses et guerres des croisés* (Paris, 1982); Michel Balard, "Des châteaux forts en Palestine" in *Les Croisades,* 167–83.

43. This figure, found in vol. 21 (513 ff.) of the *Recueil des historiens des Gaules et de la France* should be taken with a grain of salt: Gérard Sivery, *Saint Louis et son siècle,* 466–67. The figure had already been given by Le Nain de Tillemont, *Vie de Saint Louis,* 4:45.

44. Joinville, *Histoire de Saint Louis,* 233.

45. Ibid., 241.

46. Ibid., 275.

47. See Part III, ch. 4.

48. Bernard Lewis, *The Muslim Discovery of Europe* (New York, 1982), 24–25.

49. Among other works, see André Miquel's delightful presentation of a Muslim noble of twelfth-century Syria, *Ousâma, un prince syrien face aux croisés* (Paris, 1986). We might also recall Jean Renoir's film, *La Grande Illusion.*

50. Jacques Le Goff, *La Civilisation de l'Occident médiéval* (Paris, 1964; repr. 1984), 85.

51. "While Christians forgot the Crusade, Muslims remembered the jihad and once again launched a holy war for the faith, first to restore and defend what had been lost to Christian invaders and then, in the flood of victory, to bring the message and the power of Islam to new lands and new peoples that had never known them before" (B. Lewis, *The Muslim Discovery of Europe* [New York, 1982], 24). See Emmanuel Sivan, *L'Islam et la Croisade. Idéologie et propagande dans les réactions musulmanes aux croisades* (Paris, 1968); N. Daniel, *Islam and the West: The Making of an Image* (Edinburgh, 1960); idem, *The Arabs and Medieval Europe* (London, 1975); Amin Maalouf, *Les Croisades vues par les Arabes* (Paris, 1983); E. Weber and G. Reynaud, *Croisade d'hier et djihad d'aujourd'hui* (Paris, 1990); Franco Cardini, *Noi et Islam. Un incontro possibile?* (Rome, 1994).

52. S. Runciman, *A History of the Crusades,* 480, reprinted in *The Crusades: Motives and Achievements,* ed. J. A. Brundage, 81. See above in ch. 2, "The King's Illness and His Vow to Crusade."

53. Joshua Prawer, *The Latin Kingdom of Jerusalem: European Colonization in the Middle Ages* (London, 1972).

54. Joinville, *Histoire de Saint Louis,* 237.

55. See below "His Mother," in Part III, ch. 6.

Part I
Notes to Chapter 4

1. Joinville, *Histoire de Saint Louis,* 351–53. On a similar adventure, see below, "The King Who Laughs," in Part II, ch. 9.

2. Joinville, *Histoire de Saint Louis,* 359.

3. A. Sisto, *Figure del primo Francescanesimo in Provenza: Ugo e Douceline di Digne* (Florence, 1971); P. Peano, in *Archivum Franciscanum Historicum* 79 (1986): 14–19.

4. For a French translation of her life written in Provençal around 1300, see R. Gout, *La Vie de sainte Douceline* (Paris, 1927); Claude Carozzi, "Une béguine joachimite, Douceline soeur d'Hugues de Digne," *Cahiers de Fanjeaux* 10 (1975): 169–201, and "Douceline et les autres," *Cahiers de Fanjeaux* 11 (1976): 251–67.

5. Salimbene de Adam, *Cronica,* in *Monumenta Germaniae Historica, Scriptores,* vol. 32, ed. O. Holder-Egger (Hanover, 1905–1913), see especially 226–54; see the new edition by Giuseppe Scalia (Bari, 1966); a partial French translation of it appears in Marie-Thérèse Laureilhe, *Sur les routes d'Europe au XIIIᵉ siècle* (Paris, 1954).

6. Joinville, *Histoire de Saint Louis,* 361.

7. Ibid., 363.

8. Michel-Marie Dufeil, *Guillaume de Saint-Amour et la polémique universitaire parisienne, 1250–1259* (Paris, 1972).

9. Matthew Paris, *Chronica majora,* 5:465–66. The translation is my own. See D. O'Connell's translation below in "The Pain Born from the Failure of the Crusade," in Part III, ch. 10 where I use part of the text in a different perspective.

10. Joinville, *Histoire de Saint Louis,* 367–69.

11. Geoffroy de Beaulieu, *Vita* in *Recueil des historiens des Gaules et de la France,* 20:18–19.

12. Normandy held special privileges since its reconquest from the English by Philip Augustus. See Joseph R. Strayer, *The Administration of Normandy under Saint Louis* (Cambridge, MA, 1972) and Lucien Musset, "Saint Louis et la Normandie," *Annales de Basse-Normandie* (1972): 8–18.

13. Louis Carolus-Barré, "La grande ordonnance de 1254 sur la réforme de l'administration et la police du royaume," in *Septième centenaire de la mort de Saint Louis,* 85–96.

14. Charles Petit-Dutaillis, "L'essor des États d'Occident," in *Histoire générale* (founded by Gustav Glotz), vol. 4, *Histoire du Moyen Âge* (Paris, 1937), 273.

15. Edgar Boutaric, *Saint Louis et Alphonse de Poitiers. Étude sur la réunion des provinces du Midi et de l'Ouest à la couronne et sur les origines de la centralisation administrative* (Paris, 1870), 150.

16. L. Carolus-Barré, "La grande ordonnance de 1254."

17. While the original text from the thirteenth century speaks of "brothels" (*bordeaux*), the summary of the royal edicts in E. de Laurière's 1723 edition bashfully mentions "bad places" (*mauvais lieux*). In the Middle Ages even the governments were not afraid of words.

18. The original text states "folles femmes et ribaudes communes" (wild women and common bawds), while the seventeenth-century summary waters this down by speaking of "public women."

19. The Third Republic outlawed drinking establishments near schools. The nature of public vices and sacred places has evolved over time.

20. See below "Saint Louis and the Jews," in Part III, ch. 8.

21. On Joinville, see Part II, ch. 9.

22. Today we have the record of his pastoral visits, which provides the most concrete description of the life of a diocese in the thirteenth century: P. Andrieu-Guitran-Court, *L'Archevêque Eudes Rigaud et la vie de l'église au XIIIᵉ siècle* (Paris, 1938). On Saint Louis and Eudes Rigaud, see below, "The Cistercian Model and the Mendicant Model," in Part III, ch. 7.

23. Q. Griffiths, "New Men among the Lay Counselors of Saint Louis' Parliament," *Medieval Studies* 32–33 (1970–1971): 234–72; Fred Cheyette, "Custom, Case Law and Medieval Constitutionalism," *Political Science Quarterly* 78 (1963): 362–90.

24. Marguerite Boulet-Sautel, "Le concept de souveraineté chez Jacques de Révigny," in *Actes du Congrès sur l'ancienne université d'Orléans* (Orléans: 1962), 22 ff. Moreover, Jacques de Révigny was an academician who stuck to the texts and kept his distance from realities whether they were legal or, even more so, political. On the relations between the king of France and the emperor he writes: "Some say France is independent from the Empire, but this is a legal impossibility. Get it into your head that France is under the authority of the Empire," and he adds, "If the king of France does not want to recognize this, I can only laugh" (*de hoc non curo*: in other words, "that's not my problem").

25. Ed. A. Marnier, *Le Conseil de Pierre de Fontaines* (Paris, 1846); Q. Griffiths, "Les origines et la carrière de Pierre de Fontaines," *Revue historique de droit français et étranger* (1970); Pierre Petot, "Pierre de Fontaines et le droit romain," in *Études d'histoire du droit. Mélanges Gabriel Le Bras,* vol. 2 (Paris, 1965), 955–64.

26. Roland Fietier, "Le choix des baillis et sénéchaux aux XIIIᵉ et XIVᵉ siècles (1230–1350)," *Mémoires de la Société pour l'histoire du droit et des institutions des anciens pays bourguignons, comtois et romands* 29 (1968–1969): 255–74.

27. This text was composed in Latin, since, although it excluded any use of the *langue d'oc* which was probably known only poorly by the royal chancery and the royal agents, the royal government did not want to impose the *langue d'oïl* on the people of the Midi.

28. Joseph R. Strayer, "La conscience du roi: les enquêtes de 1258–1262 dans la sénéchaussée de Carcasonne-Béziers," in *Mélanges Roger Aubenas* (Montpellier, 1974), 725–36.

29. *Layettes du Trésor des chartes,* 4207, 4269, 4272, 4320, 4367; *Recueil des historiens des Gaules et de la France,* 24:530–41; R. Michel, *L'Administration royale dans la sénéchaussée de Beaucaire au temps de Saint Louis* (Paris, 1910).

30. *Recueil des historiens des Gaules et de la France,* 24:619–21.

31. He thus adopted a "liberal" stance on individual justice in one of the great debates of the thirteenth century, which arose mainly around the question of whether

or not the wives of condemned usurers should have to pay the restitutions imposed on their husbands during their lives or after their deaths.

32. See below, "Saint Louis and the Church," in Part III, ch. 8.

33. On this movement as a whole, see Jacques Le Goff, "La monarchie et les villes," in *Histoire de la France urbaine,* ed. Georges Duby, vol. 2, *La Ville médiévale* (Paris, 1980), 303–10. On the changes under Louis IX, see Jean Schneider, "Les villes du royaume de France au temps de Saint Louis," *Comptes rendus de l'Académie des inscriptions et belles-lettres* (1981); William C. Jordan, "Communal Administration in France, 1257–1270: Problems Discovered and Solutions Imposed," *Revue belge de philologie et d'histoire* 59 (1971): 292–313.

34. Bernard Chevalier, *Les Bonnes Villes de France du XIV*^e *au XV*^e *siècle* (Paris, 1982); G. Mauduech, "La 'bonne' ville: origine et sens de l'expression," *Annales, E.S.C.* (1972): 1441–1448; M. François, "Les bonnes villes," *Comptes rendus de l'Académie des inscriptions et belles-lettres* (1975); Albert Rigaudière, "Qu'est-ce qu'une bonne ville dans la France du Moyen Âge?" in *La Charte de Beaumont et les franchises municipales entre Loire et Rhin,* colloquium (Nancy, 1988), 59–105.

35. The original version has been found and restored by D. O'Connell, *The Teachings of Saint Louis* (French translation, *Les Propos de Saint Louis,* 183–91). The two passages quoted here and previously quoted by A. Rigaudière are taken from the version that was retouched by Geoffroy de Beaulieu that Joinville inserted in his *Histoire de Saint Louis,* 52.

36. See above, "A Difficult Minority," in Part I, ch. 1.

37. See below, "The Franco-English Peace."

38. These documents have been published in the *Layettes du Trésor des chartes,* vols. 2, 3, and 4.

39. These edicts were published by Eusèbe de Laurière, *Ordonnances des rois de France,* vol. 1 (1723), 82–83; Augustin Thierry, *Recueil des monuments inédits de l'histoire du tiers état,* vol. 1 (1850), 219; Arthur Giry, ed., *Documents sur les relations de la royauté avec les villes en France* (Paris, 1885), 85, 88; and in the appendix to W. C. Jordan, "Communal Administration in France," 312–13.

40. J. Le Goff, "La monarchie et les villes," in *Histoire de la France urbaine,* vol. 2, 308. Philippe de Beaumanoir's text can be found in vol. 2, paragraphs 1516 and 1520 of the A. Salmon edition of the *Coutumes de Beauvaisis* (1970).

41. Jean Richard, "Une consultation donnée par la commune de Soissons à celle de Beaune (1264)," *Annales de Bourgogne* 21 (1949).

42. Albert Rigaudière, "Réglementation urbaine et 'législation d'État' dans les villes du Midi français aux XIIIe et XIVe siècles," in *La Ville, la bourgeoisie et la genèse de l'État moderne (XIIe–XVIIIe siècles)* (Paris, 1988), 35–70; André Gouron, *La Science du droit dans le Midi de la France au Moyen Âge* (London, 1984).

43. On Paris's status as an "uncompleted capital" until the Revolution, see Jacques Le Goff, "La genèse de l'État français au Moyen Âge"; Raymond Cazelles, "Paris de la fin du règne de Philippe Auguste à la mort de Charles V," in *Nouvelle Histoire de Paris,* vol. 3 (1972); Robert-Henri Bautier, "Quand et comment Paris devient capitale," *Bulletin de la Société historique de Paris et de l'Île-de-France* 105 (1978): 17–46;

Anne Lombard-Johnson, *Paris, genèse de la ville. La rive droite de la Seine des origines à 1223* (Paris, 1976); "Montjoie et Saint-Denis!" *Le Centre de la Gaule aux origines de Paris et de Saint-Denis* (Paris, 1989).

44. Arié Serper, "L'administration royale de Paris au temps de Louis IX," *Francia* 7 (1979): 124.

45. This is an exceptional figure in Christendom. After Paris, the largest cities were Milan and Florence whose populations did not exceed 100,000. A city was considered "*grosse*" (large) once it had roughly 20,000 inhabitants.

46. *Recueil des historiens des Gaules et de la France,* 21:117–18.

47. Joinville, *Histoire de Saint Louis,* 390–93.

48. In an important work appearing at the end of the nineteenth century, the scholar Borelli de Serres presented a rigorous critique of the gilded legend of Saint Louis' "Parisian reform" as related by Joinville and Guillaume de Nangis. I will not enter into the somewhat cumbersome details of this polemic, which would take us away from our considerations of Saint Louis' person and character: Borelli de Serres, *Recherches sur divers services publics du XIIIe au XVIIe siècle,* vol. 1 (Paris, 1895). See also, Part III, ch. 4.

49. A foreign merchant was obligated to enter into a partnership with a Parisian merchant in order to conduct business in Paris.

50. The office of mayor has only existed in Paris since 1977.

51. On Saint Louis and blasphemy, see the following section and "The First Function: The Sacred King as Dispenser of Peace and Justice" in Part III, ch. 4.

52. Matthew 5:11.

53. Guillaume de Nangis, *Vie de Saint Louis,* 399.

54. This affair took place in 1259.

55. The apogee of French as an international language of culture alongside Latin took place in the age of Saint Louis. It was "the most delectable in the world," according to the Florentine Brunetto Latini, Dante's master.

56. Gilles le Brun, the lord of Trazegnies in Hainaut, was not French. Louis IX made him constable of France because of his piety and bravery. This was probably just after Louis' return from the crusade. France was not yet a nation. The important offices in government could be given to foreigners who were bound by loyalty to the king. Gilles le Brun played an important role in the conquest of the Kingdom of Naples by Louis IX's brother, Charles d'Anjou.

57. The French version of the text has been corrupted in this passage, so I have restored it by referring to the Latin version (398–400) and to the version of the story in Le Nain de Tillemont (*Vie de Saint Louis,* 4:188–92), which relied upon different sources. Enguerran de Coucy bought out his vow to crusade for 12,000 pounds in 1261. See D. Barthélemy, *Les Deux Âges de la seigneurie banale. Coucy (XIe–XIIe siècle)* (Paris, 1984).

58. Guillaume de Nangis, *Vie de Saint Louis,* 399–401.

59. This is exactly what Jacques Chiffoleau and Yann Thomas will show in their important study on the crime of lèse-majesty.

60. This term used, for example, by J. Richard (*Saint Louis,* 310) stresses how the number of new juridical principles and practices in the thirteenth century derived from confusions between the newly rediscovered Roman law and canonical (ecclesiastical) law, which rapidly developed after Gratian's decree (Bologna, 1140), the first component of the code of canonical law that continued to take shape up to the fourteenth century.

61. On ordeals, see J.W. Baldwin, "The Intellectual Preparation for the Canon of 1215 against Ordeals"; Dominique Barthélemy, "Présence de l'aveu dans le déroulement des ordalies (IXᵉ–XIIIᵉ siécles)," in *L'Aveu,*191–214; Robert Bartlett, *Trial by Fire and Water: The Medieval Judicial Ordeal* (Oxford, 1986); Jean Gaudemet, "Les ordalies au Moyen Âge: doctrine, législation et pratique canonique," in *La Preuve* (*Recueils de la Société Jean Bodin*) 17, no. 2 (Brussels, 1965): 99–135; Charles Radding, "Superstition to Science: Nature, Fortune and the Passing of the Medieval Ordeal," *American Historical Review* 84 (1979): 945–69.

62. P. Guilhiermoz, "Saint Louis, les gages de bataille et la procédure civile," *Bibliothèque de l'École des chartes* 48 (1887): 11–120. The text of this anonymous chronicler can be found in *Recueil des historiens des Gaules et de la France,* vol. 21 (1855), 84.

63. *Ordonnances des rois de France,* 1:85.

64. People generally trace this term to the town of Cahors, which was thought of as a great center for businessmen. Cahors was an episcopal seigniory (see above, "Religious Anxieties," in ch. 1). Still, I do not understand the identification of the inhabitants of Cahors as foreigners, which is undeniably stated in the edict of 1268. See Philippe Wolff, "Le problème des Cahorsins," *Annales du Midi* (1950): 229–38; Yves Renouard, "Les Cahorsins, hommes d'affaires français du XIIIᵉ siècle," *Transactions of the Royal Historical Society* 11 (1961): 43–67.

65. *Ordonnances des rois de France,* 1:96.

66. This attitude can be explained by the juridical value attached to *fama* or "reputation" at this time.

67. See below, "Saint Louis and the Economy," in Part III, ch. 4.

68. Some have even spoken of "*the* monetary reform of the king." Although these measures comprise a unified policy, they do not constitute "a" single coherent reform or a systematic monetary program.

69. L. Blanchard, "La réforme monétaire de Saint Louis," *Mémoires de l'Académie des sciences, lettres et arts de Marseille* (1833); Jean Lafaurie, *Les Monnaies des rois de France. De Hugues Capet à Louis XII* (Paris, Bale, 1951); E. Fournial, *Histoire monétaire de l'Occident médiéval* (Paris, 1970); Marc Bloch, *Esquisse d'une histoire monétaire de l'Europe* (Paris, 1954) (posthumous).

70. On inflation, see Thomas N. Bisson, *Conservation of Coinage. Monetary Exploitation and Its Restraint in France, Catalonia and Aragon (ca. 1000–1225 A.D.)* (Oxford, 1979).

71. Jean Favier, "Les finances de Saint Louis," *Septième centenaire,* 135.

72. Pierre Michaud-Quantin, "La politique monétaire royale à la Faculté de théologie de Paris en 1265," *Le Moyen Âge* 17 (1962): 137–51.

73. *Ordonnances des rois de France,* 1:94.

74. See below, "Salvation and Necessity," in Part III, ch. 4.

75. See below, "Peace," in Part III, ch. 4.

76. An excellent account of this affair can be found in J. Richard, *Saint Louis,* 329–37.

77. Beginning in the thirteenth century, the term "Guyenne" designated the entire group of English possessions on the continent including Gascogny.

78. According to Matthew Paris, whose contemporary manuscript displays a drawing of the elephant with the elephant driver holding a ladder for mounting the animal, this was the first elephant ever seen in England.

79. M. Gavrilovitch, *Étude sur le traité de Paris de 1259 entre Louis IX, roi de France, et Henri III, roi d'Angleterre* (Paris, 1899).

80. Joinville, *Histoire de Saint Louis,* 375. See below, "Political Criticisms," in Part III, ch. 8.

81. Ibid.

82. Pierre Chaplais, "Le traité de Paris de 1259," *Le Moyen Âge* (1955): 121–37.

83. Charles T. Wood, "The Mise of Amiens and Saint Louis' Theory of Kingship," *French Historical Studies* 6 (1969–1970): 300–10.

84. See later in this chapter, "Louis IX Crusading for the Second Time," and "The Mongol Illusion," in Part III, ch. 1.

85. *Ordonnances des rois de France,* 1:84.

86. Raymond Cazelles, "La guerre privée de Saint Louis à Charles V," *Revue historique de droit français et étranger* (1960): 530–48.

87. Ferdinand Lot and Robert Fawtier, *Histoire des institutions françaises au Moyen Âge,* vol. 2, *Les Institutions royales* (Paris, 1958), 425–26.

88. *Ordonnances des rois de France,* 1:344; F. Lot and R. Fawtier, *Histoire des institutions françaises,* 426.

89. He also left a daughter, Blanche, who married Henry, the son of Thibaud V of Champagne and Isabelle, the daughter of Louis IX in 1259. This marriage strengthened the ties between the royal family and the family of the counts of Champagne.

90. Peter van Moos, "Die Trostschrift des Vincenz von Beauvais für Ludwig IX. Vorstudie zur Motiv uund Gattungsgeschichte der *consolatio,*" *Mittellateinisches Jahrbuch* 4 (1967): 173–219.

91. See below, "The Children," in Part III, ch. 6.

92. Ibid.

93. See below, "His Sister," in Part III, ch. 6.

94. Joinville, *Histoire de Saint Louis,* 57.

95. E. Boutaric, *Saint Louis et Alphonse de Poitiers.*

96. See below, "His Brothers and Sisters," in Part III, ch.6.

97. Georges Duby, "Le lignage" in *Les Lieux de mémoire,* ed. P. Nora, vol. 2, *La Nation* (Paris, 1986), 1:31–56.

98. See the first issue of the review *Dialogus. I discorsi dei corpi* (1993) and the magnificent book by Agostino Paravicini Bagliani, *Il corpo del Papa* (Turin, 1994). See also, S. Bertelli, *Il corpo del re* (Florence, 1990); M.-C. Pouchelle, *Corps et chirurgie*

à l'apogée du Moyen Âge (Paris, 1983); and Peter Brown, *Le Renoncement à la chair. Virginité, célibat et continence dans le christianisme primitif* (French translation, Paris, 1995).

99. *La Mort, les morts dans les sociétés anciennes,* ed. G. Gnoli and J.-P. Vernant (Cambridge and Paris, 1982).

100. Jean-Pierre Vernant, "Introduction" in *La Mort, les morts,* 10; Elena Cassin, "La mort: valeur et représentation en Mésopotamie ancienne," in ibid., 366.

101. J.-P. Vernant, "Introduction," 5–15; idem, "La belle mort et le cadavre outragé," in *La Mort, les morts,* 45–76; see especially Nicole Loraux, "Mourir devant Troie, tomber pour Athènes: de la gloire du héros à l'idée de la cité," in ibid., 2–43, and *L'Invention d'Athènes. Histoire de l'oraison funèbre dans la cité classique* (Paris and the Hague, 1981; repr. Paris, 1994).

102. Paul Veyne, *Le Pain et le cirque* (Paris, 1976), esp. 245–51.

103. Pauline Schmitt-Pantel, "Évergétisme et mémoire du mort" in *La Mort, les morts,* 177–88.

104. E. Cassin, "Le mort; valeur et représentation en Mésopotamie ancienne," 366.

105. Erwin Panofsky (*Tomb Sculpture. Its Changing Aspects from Ancient Egypt to Bernini* [London, 1964], 45) reminds us that Artemis leaves Hippolytus to die, that Apollo departs from Admetus's home before Alcestus dies, and that all the tombs were emptied and transported to another island when the island of Delos was dedicated to Apollo.

106. J.-P. Vernant, "Introduction," 10.

107. Peter Brown, *The Cult of the Saints: Its Rise and Function in Latin Christianity* (Chicago: University of Chicago Press, 1981).

108. Ibid., 3.

109. "The lifting of the religious ban on the sepulcher *intra muros,* which was a millenium old . . . is the sign of a real historical mutation" (Jean Guyon, "La vente des tombes à travers l'épigraphie de la Rome chrétienne," *Mélanges d'archéologie et d'histoire: Antiquité* 86 [1974]: 594).

110. E. Panofsky, *Tomb Sculpture.*

111. On another case involving exceptional dead individuals who had benefited since the High Middle Ages from special conditions for the place of their sepulchers and funerary monuments — the popes; see Jean-Charles Picard, "Étude sur l'emplacement des tombes des papes du IIIᵉ au Xᵉ siècle," *Mélanges d'archéologie et d'histoire* 81 (1969): 735–82. In his study, "Sacred Corpse: Profane Carrion: Social Ideas and Death Rituals in the Later Middle Ages" (in *Mirrors of Morality: Studies in the Social History of Death,* ed. Joachim Whaley [London, 1981], 40–60), Ronald C. Finucane studies medieval attitudes toward four classes of dead people: kings, criminals and traitors, saints, heretics and stillborn children.

112. Here, I am following Alain Erlande-Brandenburg, *Le Roi est mort,* to whom this development in my argument owes quite a bit.

113. François Hartog relates the interment of the Scythian kings at the distant borders of their territory to nomadic traditions in *Le Miroir d'Hérodote* (Paris, 1980). Part I, ch. 4, "Le corps du roi: espace et pouvoir," is especially interesting.

114. The list of the *Annales de Saint-Denis* (in the *Monumenta Germaniae Historica, Scriptores,* 14) contains three errors: Dagobert's son was not named Louis but Clovis II; Charles Martel was not a king; Carloman, son of Pepin the Short and brother to Charlemagne, was not buried at Saint-Denis but at Saint-Rémi in Reims. With the exception of the mistake about Charles Martel, which may have been intentional, these errors can be explained by the difficulty involved in recognizing the tombs and the bodies and by the limits of historical memory that the monks of Saint-Denis were facing even though they were specialists in it.

115. B. Guenée, "Les généaologies entre l'histoire et la politique."

116. This information comes from the letter of a witness, Pierre de Condé, in Luc d'Achery, *Spicilegium sive collectio veterum aliquot scriptorum,* vol. 3, new edition (Paris, 1723), 667.

117. See Georges Duby, *Le Chevalier, la femme et le prêtre. Le mariage dans la France féodale* (Paris, 1981).

118. On the *ordines,* liturgical manuals for the kings of France composed at the time of Saint Louis, see Richard A. Jackson, "Les manuscrits des *ordines* de couronnement de la bibliothèque de Charles V, roi de France," *Le Moyen Âge* (1976): 67–88. See especially p. 73, which corrects Percy Ernst Schramm, "Ordines-Studien II: Die Krönung bei den Westfranken und den Franzosen," *Archiv für Urkundenforschung* 15 (1938). An *ordo* from around 1250 found in the Latin MS. 1246 of the Bibliothèque nationale in Paris is of particular interest due to the series of miniatures that it contains.

119. Charles the Bald's exclusion from the bodies in Saint Louis' plan is surprising.

120. *"Quia nec fas nec consuetudo permittit reges exhospitari"* (Suger, *Vie de Louis VI le Gros,* ed. H. Waquet, 285).

121. See a summary of this discussion in A. Erlande-Brandenburg, *Le Roi est mort,* 81. The *Annales de Saint-Denis* (721) indicate that in 1259, four years before the transfer of the royal bodies, the bodies of seven abbots of Saint-Denis were transferred into the southern arm of the transept.

122. On the ideology of the recumbent figure, see Philippe Ariès, *L'Homme devant la mort* (Paris, 1977); for an iconographical study, see E. Panofsky, *Tomb Sculpture*; Willibald Sauerländer, *Gotische Skulptur in Frankreich, 1140–1270* (Munich, 1970), French translation, *La Sculpture gothique en France* (Paris, 1977), 18–20; A. Erlande-Brandenburg, *Le Roi est mort,* 109–17.

123. Jean, who died at a young age, is represented somewhat enigmatically with a scepter in his left hand.

124. Of course, it is the Italian context that explains the originality of the tomb of the *"chairs"* (flesh, entrails) of Queen Isabella of Aragon, the first wife of Philip III, in the cathedral of Cosenza in Calabria. Saint Louis' daughter-in-law died in an accident in January 1271 on the return from the crusade of Tunis. The monument's interpretation is hard to understand. It represents Isabelle and Philip kneeling in different places before the standing Virgin. This is undoubtably the work of a French

artist. Cf. Émile Bertaux, "Le tombeau d'une reine de France à Cosenza en Calabre," *Gazette des beaux-arts* (1898): 265–76, 369–78; G. Martelli, "Il monumento funerario della regina Isabella nella cattedrale di Cosenza," *Calabria nobilissima* (1950): 9–22; A. Erlande-Brandenburg, "Le tombeau de Saint Louis," *Bulletin monumental* 126 (1968): 16–17.

125. E. Panofsky, *Tomb Sculpture*, 62.

126. See Marc Bloch's famous book, *Les Rois thaumaturges* (Paris, 1924; 3rd ed., 1983).

127. A. Erlande-Brandenburg, *Le Roi est mort*, 15. See Ralph E. Giesey's marvelous book that also deals with the Middle Ages, *Le Roi ne meurt jamais. Les obsèques royales dans la France de la Renaissance* (1960; French translation, Paris, 1987). For the entire background of this ideology, see the classical work by Ernst Kantorowicz, *The King's Two Bodies* (Princeton, 1957).

128. Using different iconographic examples, Jean-Claude Schmitt has stressed that only the vertical positioning of the body permitted entry into Hell (Jean-Claude Schmitt, "Le suicide au Moyen Âge," *Annales, E.S.C.* [1975]: 13).

129. See J. Le Goff, *La Naissance du Purgatoire*, 311.

130. See Elizabeth A. Brown, "Burying and Unburying the Kings of France" in *Persons in Groups: Social Behavior as Identity Formation in Medieval and Renaissance Europe*, ed. Richard C. Trexler (Binghamton, 1985), 241–66.

131. J. Richard, *Saint Louis*, 455 ff.

132. J. Richard, "Une ambassade Mongole à Paris en 1262," and P. Meyvaert, "An Unknown Letter of Hulagu, il-Khan of Persia to King Louis IX of France." See above, The Oriental Horizon," in ch. 1.

133. Michel Mollat, "Le 'passage' de Saint Louis à Tunis. Sa place dans l'histoire des croisades," *Revue d'histoire économique et sociale* 50 (1972): 289–303.

134. *Ordonnances des rois de France*, 1:99–102.

135. See below, "Saint Louis and the Jews," in Part III, ch. 8.

136. Franco Cardini, "Gilberto di Tournai: un francescano predicatore della crociata," *Studi francescani* 72 (1975): 31–48.

137. See ch. 2 above.

138. Joinville, *Histoire de Saint Louis*, 397–98.

139. Julia Bastin and Edmond Faral, *Onze poèmes de Rutebeuf concernant la croisade* (Paris, 1946); Jean Dufournet, *Rutebeuf. Poèmes de l'infortune et poèmes de la croisade* (Paris, 1979).

140. Yves Dossat, "Alphonse de Poitiers et la préparation financière de la croisade de Tunis: les ventes des forêts (1268–1270)," in *Septième centenaire*, 121–32.

141. J. Richard, *Saint Louis*, 554.

142. Ibid., 553.

143. During the last put-in at Cagliari, Louis dictated a codicile to his testament. He asked for his older son Philip to act "like a father" to his two younger sons Jean-Tristan and Pierre. He also increased the sum of money designated for Pierre and asked Philip to retain his servants.

144. Louis IX sent a letter from Carthage to France that described the landing and the taking of Carthage. He also indicated that his son and heir, Philip, and his wife were also present (*primogeniti nostri Philippi*). After Louis' death, Philip became the "first-born," a title equivalent to the official heir. See L. d'Achery, *Spicilegium,* 2:4, *Miscellanea, Epistularum,* 549.

145. "*Super cuius morte pii patris viscera non modicum sunt commota*" (by this death his dear loving fatherly guts were not little stirred).

146. According to Guillaume de Nangis, he also repeated, "I will go into your house, I will go to worship you in your holy temple, and I will confess myself to you, O Lord."

147. This is translated from Geoffroy de Beaulieu's text in the *Recueil des historiens des Gaules et de la France,* 20:23. A translation of the letter that Philip III sent to the French clergy after his father's death is included in its appendix.

PART I
Notes to Chapter 5

1. A. Erlande-Brandenbug, *Le Roi est mort,* 96.

2. Louis Carolus-Barré, "Les enquêtes pour la canonisation de Saint Louis, de Grégoire X à Boniface VIII, et la bulle *Gloria, laus* du 11 août 1287," *Revue d'histoire de l'Église de France* 57 (1971): 20.

3. See below the end of the section, "The History of the Relics."

4. Geoffroy de Beaulieu, *Vita,* 24.

5. Primat, in *Recueil des historiens des Gaules et de la France,* 23:87–88.

6. We now possess the excellent work by Louis Carolus-Barré, *Le Procès de canonisation de Saint Louis (1272–1297). Essai de reconstitution* (Rome, 1995). This work has collected everything that allows the lost record of the proceeding to be reconstructed. Although the texts have been edited, their publication together, their translation, and their presentation will be of great service. This text can be supplemented with a reading of the original text recently published by Peter Lineham and Francisco J. Hernandez, "*Animadverto*: A Recently Discovered *Consilium* Concerning the Sanctity of King Louis IX," *Revue Mabillon* 66, n.s. 5 (1994): 83–105.

7. This is the *Vita et sancta conversatio et miracula sancti Ludovici quondam regis Francorum,* 3–27. See below, "Geoffroy de Beaulieu," in Part II, ch. 2.

8. This subject has hardly been touched upon. The sources that exist to the best of my knowledge are: Colette Beaune, *Naissance de la nation France* (Paris, 1985), 125–84; Alain Boureau, "Les enseignements absolutistes de Saint Louis, 1610–1630," in *La Monarchie absolutiste et l'histoire en France,* Acts of the Colloquium (Paris, 1986), 79–97; Christian Amalvi, *De l'art et la maniére d'accommoder les héros de l'histoire de France. De Vercingétorix à la Révolution. Essais de mythologie nationale* (Paris, 1988); J. Buisson, "La Représentation de Saint Louis dans les manuels d'histoire des écoles élémentaires (du XVIe siècle à nos jours)," unpublished thesis for E.H.E.S.S., directed by M. Ferro, 1990.

9. Patrick J. Geary, *Furta Sacra: Thefts of Relics in the Central Middle Ages* (Princeton: Princeton University Press, 1978).

10. The Benedictine friar, Dom Poirier, was an official witness of this event for the *Commission des monuments de la Convention*. He wrote up a rather dry report: "On Saturday, October 19, 1793. . . . As they continued to dig in the choir, they found the tomb that Saint Louis had been placed in after his death in 1270. It was next to Louis VIII's tomb. It was shorter and less wide than the others, and the bones had been removed during his canonization in 1297. Nota. According to the historians, the reason why his coffin is less wide and less long than the others is that his flesh had been taken to Sicily and only the bones were brought to Saint-Denis, which is why they only needed a narrower coffin for the whole body," in Alain Boureau, *Le Simple Corps du roi* (Paris, 1988), 86.

11. Elizabeth A. R. Brown, "Phillipe le Bel and the Remains of Saint Louis," *Gazette des beaux-arts* (1980–1981): 175–82; *Acta Sanctorum*, vol. 5 (August), 536–37; Robert Folz, *Les Saints Rois du Moyen Âge en Occident (VIe–XIIIe siècles)* (Brussels, 1984), 179–80.

12. See Auguste Molinier, *Les Sources de l'histoire de France des origines aux guerres d'Italie (1494)*, vol. 2, *Les Capétiens (1180–1328)* (Paris, 1903), n. 2542.

13. A. Erlande–Brandenburg, *Le Roi est mort*, 96.

14. Ibid., n. 103.

15. On the development of a curious Tunisian legend about Saint Louis, see A. Demeerseman, *La légende tunisienne de Saint Louis* (Tunis, 1986). In 1990, we saw a tomb containing what were Saint Louis' remains according to an inscription in the now defunct cathedral of Carthage.

16. A. Erlande-Brandenburg, *Le Roi est mort*, 30; Elizabeth A. R. Brown, "Death and Human Body in the Later Middle Ages: The Legislation of Boniface VIII on the Division of the Corpse," *Viator* 12 (1981): 221–70; A. Paravicini Bagliani, *Il corpo del Papa*.

PART II

1. Marc Bloch, La Société féodale, new edition (Paris, 1968), 16.

Notes to Chapter 1

1. French historiography has made significant progress in this regard thanks to Jean-François Lemarignier and his students. See especially, Lemarignier, *Le Gouvernement royal aux premiers temps capétiens* (Paris, 1965); idem, *La France médiévale. Institutions et société* (Paris, 1970); E. Bournazel, *Le Gouvernement capétien au XIIe siècle, 1108–1180. Structures sociales et mutations institutionnelles* (Paris, 1975). On the contribution made by the "prosopographical" method, see *Genèse de l'État moderne: prosopographie et histoire de l'État*, a round table discussion, Paris, 1984 (Paris, 1986).

2. Michel Pastoureau, *Les Sceaux* (Turnhout, 1981); Brigitte Bedos Rezak, "Signes et insignes du pouvoir royal et seigneurial au Moyen Âge: le témoignage des sceaux" in *Actes du 105ᵉ Congrès national des sociétés savantes* (Caen, 1980), *Comité des travaux historiques, Philologie et histoire* 1 (1984): 47–82.

3. Gaston Tessier, *La Diplomatique royale française* (Paris, 1962), 237 ff.

4. Ibid., 244–46.

5. Ibid., 246–47.

6. Natalis de Wailly, *Recueil des historiens des Gaules et de la France,* xxviii–xliv and 407–512 (*regum mansiones et itinera*); G. Tessier, *La Diplomatique royale française,* 293.

7. The case of the English monarchy has been studied in remarkable detail by M. Clanchy, *From Memory to Written Record, England, 1066–1307,* new edition (London, 1993).

8. This record has been preserved in the Archives nationales under the call number TJ 26. Georges Tessier has defined a record book as "a manuscript book in which a physical or moral person transcribes or has others transcribe the acts that it transmits, that it receives, or that are communicated to it through their expedition, reception, or communication." Transcription here is synonymous with recording.

9. G. Tessier, *La Diplomatique.*

10. G. Sivery, *Saint Louis et son siècle.*

11. *Layettes du Trésor des chartes,* ed. A. Teulet (Paris, 1863), 1:vi.

12. See especially, Robert-Henri Bautier, "Critique diplomatique, commandement des actes et psychologie des souverains du Moyen Âge," *Comptes rendus de l'Académie des inscriptions et belles-lettres* (1978): 8–26; Élie Berger led the inquiry into "Saint Louis' final years according to the *layettes* of the *Trésor des chartes*" (*Layettes du Trésor des chartes,* vol. 4 [Paris, 1902]). With this title we were hoping for a study on the contribution of the royal archives to our knowledge of the person who put them together during the last decade of his life (1261–1270). Unfortunately, despite certain references to the documents in the *layettes,* Berger used these documents as a pretext for a general outline of royal politics during the last ten years of the reign with a particular focus on what he somewhat anachronistically calls Saint Louis' "foreign policy," and with a desire to judge this policy that is characteristic of the positivist historiography of the late nineteenth century.

13. *Olim ou registres des arrêts rendus par la cour du roi sous les règnes de Saint Louis, Philippe le Hardi, etc.,* ed. Arthur Beugnot, vol. 1, *1254–1273* (Paris, 1839); Edgar Boutaric, *Actes du Parlement de Paris,* vol. 1, *1254–1299* (Paris, 1863), lxiv–lxvi.

14. *Olim,* 1:131 n. 75.

15. *Recueil des historiens des Gaules et de la France,* 21:284–392. The surviving traces of royal accounting have been published by Natalis de Wailly in volumes 21 and 22 of this collection in 1855 and 1865. On the hotel, see F. Lot and R. Fawtier, *Histoire des institutions françaises du Moyen Âge,* vol. 2, *Les Institutions royales,* "L'Hôtel du roi," 66 ff.

16. See above, in Part I, chs. 2 and 3.

17. *Recueil des historiens des Gaules et de la France,* vol. 23.

18. Saint Louis' investigations have been published by Léopold Delisle, ibid., vol. 24 (1904).

19. On the advances in calculus made in the thirteenth century, see the wonderful book by Alexander Murray, *Reason and Society in the Middle Ages* (Oxford, 1978).

20. On the edicts, see below, "Local Government and Legislative Power," in Part III, ch. 5.

21. See above, "A Difficult Minority," in Part I, ch.1.

22. Upon the request of Louis XV, in other words of the regent, Eusèbe de Laurière published the *Ordonnances des rois de France* in 1723 in a very faulty edition that should be replaced (reprint by Farnborough, 1967). Gérard Giordanengo has defended this edition along with the *Recueil général des anciennes lois françaises depuis 420 jusqu'à la Révolution de 1789* (Paris, 1822–1833) for the reason "that a vision . . . closer [than that of current medievalists] of medieval reality presided over this compilation" ("Le pouvoir législatif du roi de France, XIᵉ–XIIIᵉ siècles: travaux récents et hypothèses de recherche," *Bibliothèque de l'École des chartes* 147 [1989]: 285–86). I have the impression that a truly "scientific" edition would give better versions of the edicts, which would allow today's historians to use them, while respecting medieval administrative practices and mentalities at the same time. On the evolution of Saint Louis' legislative power, see Albert Rigaudière, "Législation royale et construction de l'État dans la France du XIIIᵉ siècle" in *Renaissance du pouvoir législatif et genèse de l'État,* ed. André Goudron and Albert Rigaudière (Montpellier, 1988).

23. See above, "The Distant King," in Part I, ch. 3.

24. See above, "Final Purifications before the Crusade," in Part I, ch. 4.

25. G. Tessier, *La Diplomatique royale française.*

PART II
Notes to Chapter 2

1. In 1274, the Second Council of Lyon suppressed several smaller Mendicant orders and one larger one, the *Sachets* or Friars of the Sack. The Council allowed only the four larger Mendicant orders to exist: the Dominicans, the Franciscans, the Carmelites, and the Augustinians.

2. I am referring here to my preface to the new edition of Max Weber, *L'Éthique protestante et l'esprit du capitalisme* (Paris, 1990), 7–24.

3. Lester K. Little, *Religious Poverty and the Profit Economy in Medieval Europe* (London, 1978).

4. Jean Daniel, *Les Religions d'un Président: regards sur les aventures du mitterandisme* (Paris, 1988).

5. Richard W. Emery, *The Friars in Medieval France: A Catalogue of French Mendicant Convents (1200–1550)* (New York and London, 1962); Jacques Le Goff, "Ordres mendiants et urbanisation dans la France médiévale," *Annales, E.S.C.* (1970): 924–43.

6. L. Wadding, *Annales Minorum,* vol. 2, 3rd ed. (Karachi, 1931), 182.

7. See Part III, ch. 7. Colette Beaune has presented the very likely hypothesis that "the closeness of the relations between Saint Louis and the Franciscans is a legend [I would qualify this as an exaggeration] born at the Angevin court at Naples in the second half of the thirteenth century." The purported purpose of this legend was to bring Saint Louis closer to his grandnephew, Louis, the bishop of Toulouse, a Franciscan who was canonized in 1317. Around 1330, Giotto, who was close to the Angevin court, represented Saint Louis with his grandnephew in the chapel of Bardi in the Church of Santa Croce in Florence. He is wearing the robe and the cord of the tertiary Franciscans. In 1547, a papal bull issued by Paul IV officially recognized Saint Louis as a tertiary Franciscan, and around 1550 their office stated that "Louis associated himself with Saint Francis so that he could direct his steps under the rule of penitence" (C. Beaune, *Naissance de la nation France,* 138–39).

8. A. Vauchez, "Une campagne de pacification en Lombardie autour de 1233."

9. See below, "Saint Louis' Sainthood" and, particularly, "Saint Louis' Models of Sainthood," in Part III, ch. 9.

10. L. Carolus-Barré, *Le Procès de canonisation de Saint Louis.*

11. *Sancta* here does not mean "saint" or "saintly" in the official juridical sense of the word; instead, it means "very pious." Today, people still say *"une sainte femme"* or *"un saint homme"* to refer to people who have not been canonized.

12. *Recueil des historiens des Gaules et de la France,* 20:3–27. Readers can find a translation of Geoffroy de Beaulieu's text in L. Carolus-Barré, *Le Procès de canonisation de Saint Louis.*

13. The edition of volume 20 of the *Recueil des historiens des Gaules et de la France* ends with a French version of Saint Louis' *Enseignements* for his son.

14. See below, "David and Solomon," and "Louis and Josiah," in Part II, ch. 5.

15. *"De statu ejus, quantum ad regimen subditorum."*

16. This comprises thirteen pages in volume 20 of the *Recueil des historiens des Gaules et de la France* (2–41), compared with twenty-three in Geoffroy de Beaulieu.

17. See below, "Conscience," in Part II, ch. 10.

18. *"Sol et decus regum ac principum orbis terrae"* (*Recueil des historiens des Gaules et de la France,* 37).

19. There are only a few rare surviving traces of the original pieces from the proceedings at the Archives of the Vatican. They have been published by Henri-François Delaborde, "Fragments de l'enquête faite à Saint-Denis en 1282 en vue de la canonisation de Saint Louis," *Mémoires de la Société de l'histoire de Paris et de l'Île-de-France* 23 (1896): 1–71, and Louis Carolus-Barré, "Consultation du cardinal Pietro Colonna sur le deuxième miracle de Saint Louis," *Bibliothèque de l'École des chartes* 118 (1959): 57–72. A copy of Charles d'Anjou's deposition that has been discovered was published by Count P. E. Riant, "1282: deposition de Charles d'Anjou pour la canonisation de Saint Louis" in *Notices et documents publiés pour la Société de l'histoire de France à l'occasion de son cinquantième anniversaire* (Paris, 1884), 155–76.

20. For an account of the *Miracles,* see "Saint Louis' Miracles," in Part III, ch. 9.

21. Guillaume de Saint-Pathus, *Vie de Saint Louis* (Paris, 1899). I am following Delaborde's point of view on this. In his *Essai de reconstitution du procès,* L. Carolus-

Barré believes that he is capable of giving each of the witnesses for the proceeding his proper due. Despite the ingenuity, erudition, and interest of this attempt, I am not always persuaded by his deconstruction of Guillaume de Saint-Pathus's *Life,* and regret that it does not actually constitute as coherent a text as the work of its Franciscan author, even if it can also be read as "the collective creation of the witnesses for the proceeding."

22. Guillaume de Saint-Pathus, *Vie de Saint Louis,* 7–11.

23. We can find the outline of his work, which fills 155 pages, in the Delaborde edition, xxix–xxxii. Here are the titles of the twenty-one chapters as they are given in the manuscript. Guillaume probably titled them himself: "The first chapter is on his holy nourishment in childhood; the second on his marvelous conversation during his youth; the third on his firm belief; the fourth on his unswerving hope; the fifth on his ardent love; the sixth on his fervent worship; the seventh on his studies of the Holy Scripture; the eighth on devoutly praying to God; the ninth on his fervent love for the people around him; the tenth on his attentive [*decorant*] compassion for them; the eleventh on his works of pity; the twelfth on his profound humility; the thirteenth on the strength of his patience; the fourteenth on his unflinching penitence; the fifteenth on his beauty of conscience; the sixteenth on the sanctity of his continence; the seventeenth on his unwavering justice; the eighteenth on his simple honesty; the nineteenth on his debonair clemency; the twentieth on his long perseverance, / And on his fortunate decease / Whence he passed from here to the heavens."

24. Among the upper echelons of society, it was customary to have a drink of what people called "*le vin du coucher*" (bedtime wine, a nightcap) before going to bed.

25. Guillaume de Saint-Pathus, *Vie de Saint Louis,* 54–55.

26. Ibid., 50.

27. Ibid., 83. In the third part of this book, I give more details about his generous gifts.

28. I will later show the influence that the Mendicants and their ideal had upon Saint Louis' sainthood (Part III, ch. 9).

29. Henri-François Delaborde, "Une oeuvre nouvelle de Guillaume de Saint-Pathus," *Bibliothèque de l'École des chartes* 63 (1902): 267–88.

30. I am insisting on this problem of the literary genres through which the clerics of the Middle Ages forged the memory of the saints and illustrious men whom they considered memorable and passed down to us because these forms teach us about the mechanisms used to produce this memory.

31. H.-F. Delaborde, "Une oeuvre nouvelle de Guillaume de Saint-Pathus," 268.

32. The queen told a confessor that if the king took a break from his affairs to see his wife and children when he was in a period of sexual continence, he would avoid looking at the queen out of a sense of chastity.

33. See below, "Worship and Asceticism," in Part III, ch. 7.

34. See Part II, ch. 6.

35. To these three Mendicant legatees of Saint Louis' memory, we can add the Dominican Thomas de Cantimpré who probably entered the convent of the Preachers of Louvain in 1232 and who died around the same time as Saint Louis,

between 1270 and 1272. His *Bonum universale de apibus* (The Universal Good Drawn from the Bees) was composed some time between 1256 and 1263, with subsequent additions. It was "a kind of treatise on moral practice in the guise of an allegorical development on bees." In it, Thomas several times evoked his contemporary Louis, the king of France, in order to illustrate one virtue or another after his example. He was usually hard on lords and princes but expressed his admiration for Saint Louis in these terms: "Give thanks to the Lord of the heavens, give thanks to Christ, the prince of salvation, oh Church; give thanks to every preacher and Minorite; let us render all the solemn acts of thanks to God who gave us such a king in these times, a king who holds his kingdom with a strong hand and yet who provides everyone with examples of peace, charity, and humility" (Thomas de Cantimpré, *Bonum universale de apibus,* ed. G. Colvenere [Douai, 1617], 588–90, trans. L. Carolus-Barré in *Le Procès de canonisation,* 247–48).

PART II
Notes to Chapter 3

1. The words *caput regni* designated Saint-Denis as well as Paris. See Anne Lombard-Jourdan, "Montjoie et Saint-Denis."

2. See above, "France," in Part I, ch. 1, and "Saint Louis and the Royal Bodies," in Part I, ch. 4.

3. Bernard Guenée, "Chancelleries et monastères. La mémoire de la France au Moyen Âge," in *Les Lieux de mémoire,* ed. P. Nora, vol. 2, *La Nation* (Paris, 1986), 1:15–21; Alexandre Verdier, *L'Historiographie à Saint-Benoît-sur-Loire et les miracles de saint Benoît* (Paris, 1965).

4. Colette Beaune, "Les sanctuaires royaux," in *Les Lieux de mémoire,* ed. P. Nora, vol. 2, *La Nation* (Paris, 1986), 1:58; Gabrielle M. Spiegel, *The Chronicle Tradition of Saint-Denis* (Brookline, MA, and Leyden, 1978). The summary of her argument does not fully explain the complex problems presented by the historical manuscripts of Saint-Denis.

5. J. Le Goff, "Le dossier de sainteté de Philippe Auguste."

6. I remind my readers that "*roman*" here means a work written in French.

7. Bernard Guenée, "Histoire d'un succès," in F. Avril, M.-T. Gousset, and B. Guenée, *Les Grandes Chroniques de France* (Paris, 1987), 93.

8. B. Guenée, "Chancelleries et monastères. La mémoire de la France au Moyen Âge," 25.

9. Some scholars have attributed a Latin chronicle running from 1250 to 1285 to Primat, of which we only possess a fourteenth-century French translation by Jean de Vignay. I am under the impression that this attribution still needs to be proven. Cf. G. Spiegel, *The Chronicle Tradition of Saint-Denis,* 89–92.

10. J.-B. La Curne de Sainte-Palaye, "Mémoire sur la vie et les ouvrages de Guillaume de Nangis et de ses continuateurs," *Mémoires de l'Académie royale des inscrip-*

tions et belles-lettres 8 (1733): 560–79; H. Géraud, "De Guillaume de Nangis et de ses continuateurs," *Bibliothèque de l'École des chartes* 3 (1841): 17–46; Léopold Delisle, "Mémoire sur les ouvrages de Guillaume de Nangis," *Mémoires de l'Académie des inscriptions et belles-lettres* 27, part 2 (1873): 287–372; H.-F. Delaborde, "Notes sur Guillaume de Nangis," *Bibliothèque de l'École des chartes* 44 (1883): 192–201; G. M. Spiegel, *The Chronicle Tradition of Saint-Denis,* 98–108.

11. See H. Géraud, "De Guillaume de Nangis et de ses continuateurs," and above, "The Oriental Horizon," in Part I, ch. 1. Also quoted in G. M. Spiegel, *The Chronicle Tradition of Saint-Denis,* 101.

12. The *Vie* of Saint Louis and the *Vie* of Philip III were published by M. Daunou in the *Recueil des historiens des Gaules et de la France,* 20:310–465 (Latin text with the French translation from the end of the thirteenth century). The Latin *Chronicle* was also published in volume 20 (554) and by H. Géraud in his *Continuations de la Chronique,* 2 vols. (Paris, 1843). Guillaume de Nangis also wrote a *Chronique abrégée* that was published by M. Daunou in the *Recueil des historiens des Gaules et de la France,* 20: 645–53.

13. See above, "The Devout King and the Loss of the Holy Nail," in Part I, ch. 1.

14. Guillaume de Nangis's Latin *Chronicle, Recueil des historiens des Gaules et de la France,* 20:545–46 (in M. Daunou's edition, 180–81).

15. As Bernard Guenée has already quite correctly noted.

16. B. Guenée, "Chancelleries et monastères," 25.

17. *Fredericus imperator Romanus misit nuntios ad soldanum Babyloniae et contrapit cum eo, ut dicitur, amicitias Christianiati suspectas* (ibid, 181).

18. I remind my readers that this was the earliest known strike in European history.

19. *Studium litterarum et philosophiae, per quod thesaurus scientiae qui cunctis aliis praeminet et praevalet acquisitur* (182).

20. "*Divitiae salutes sapientia et scientia*" (Isaiah 33:6).

21. "*Quia repulisti scientiam, repellam te*" (Hosea 4:6).

22. *Si autem de eodem separata fuerint vel aversa, omne regnum in seipsum divisum desolabitur atque cadet* (183).

23. H. Grundmann, "*Sacerdotium-Regnum-Studium.* Zur Wertung der Wissenschaft im 13. Jahrhundert," *Archiv für Kulturgeschichte* 34 (1951).

24. I tend to think that it was written by Guillaume de Nangis because the same basic development can be found in the *Vie,* and it was published based on a manuscript that is supposed to have included Guillaume's text (318–20).

25. This is the result of the new conception of the king that John of Salisbury disseminated in the middle of the twelfth century, as we have seen: "An illiterate king is but a crowned ass" (*Rex illiteratus quasi asinus coronatus*).

26. See J. Le Goff, "La France monarchique. I. Le Moyen Âge" in *Histoire de la France,* ed. A. Burguière and J. Revel, 2:83–85.

27. *Francia* here has the limited meaning of the Île-de-France.

28. *Recueil des historiens des Gaules et de la France,* 20:183.

29. Ibid., 433.

30. Ibid., 343.

31. The solar metaphor does not seem to belong to the tradition of the royal symbolism of Latin Christianity. The topic warrants further research. See below in Part III, "Saint Louis and Space" in ch. 1, and "Saint Louis and the Third Function" in ch. 4, and above, "Guillaume de Chartres," in Part II, ch. 2.

32. *Recueil des historiens des Gaules et de la France,* 20:315–17.

33. See the account of this episode in "Saracens, Bedouins, and Assassins," in Part III, ch. 1, and Bernard Lewis, *The Assassins: A Radical Sect in Islam* (New York, 1968). This work points out that Saint Louis did have contact with the Assassins during his stay in the Holy Land (120–21), although it is not documented. An envoy from Frederick Barbarossa gave its etymology in 1175 as *Heyssessini,* in other words as the "lord of the mountain" (ibid., 2).

PART II
Notes to Chapter 4

1. The nineteenth-century scholar Albert Lecoy de la Marche entitled a collection of medieval *exempla* that he published *Anecdotes historiques.*

2. C. Brémond, J. Le Goff, J.-C. Schmitt, *L'"Exemplum"* (Turnhout, 1982); J.-T. Welter, *L'Exemplum dans la littérature religieuse et didactique du Moyen Âge* (Toulouse, 1927); Jacques Berlioz and Marie-Anne Polo de Beaulieu, *Les Exempla médiévaux. Introduction à la recherche* followed by the Tables of the *Index exemplorum* by F. C. Tubach (Carcassonne, 1992); C. Delcorno, "Nuovi, studi sull'"exemplum.' Rassegna," *Lettere italiane* (1994): 459–97. A colloquium on "Les *exempla* médiévaux: nouvelles perspectives" was held at Saint-Cloud in fall 1994 under the direction of M. Brossard, J. Berlioz, and M. A. Polo de Beaulieu.

3. C. Brémond, J. Le Goff, J.-C. Schmitt, *L'"Exemplum,"* 37.

4. Ibid., 164.

5. Marie-Anne Polo de Beaulieu, "L'anecdote historique dans les *exempla* médiévaux," *Sources. Travaux historiques,* no. 3–4, *La Biographie* (1985): 13–22.

6. J. Le Goff, "Philippe Auguste dans les *exempla,*" 145–54.

7. For more information on Étienne de Bourbon, consult the introduction to Jacques Berlioz's edition of the *Tractatus de diversis materiis praedicabilibus.*

8. Étienne de Bourbon, *Anecdotes historiques (Tractatus de diversis materiis praedicabilibus),* ed. A. Lecoy de la Marche (Paris, 1877), 443, trans. A. Lecoy de la Marche in *L'Esprit de nos aïeux. Anecdotes et bons mots tirés des manuscrits du XIIIᵉ siècle* (Paris, 1888), 95–96.

9. See above "A Plague on the Land Whose Ruler Is a Child," in Part I, ch.1.

10. This is from the Latin text in the edition of segments of the *Tractatus* published by Lecoy de la Marche referenced above, 63; for Lecoy de la Marche's translation, *L'Esprit de nos Aïeux,* 97.

11. Tours, Bibliothèque municipale, MS 205.

12. A. Lecoy de la Marche, *Anecdotes historiques,* 388 n. 1.

13. It is not explicitly stated here, but if this could not have been the oldest son, then the *exemplum* would not make any sense.

14. See below "The First Function," in Part III, ch. 4.

15. A. Lecoy de la Marche, *L'Esprit de nos aïeux,* 98–100.

16. See below "The King's Duties," in Part III, ch. 3.

17. A. Vauchez, *Les Laïcs au Moyen Âge*; G. Lobrichon, *La Religion des laics en Occident.*

18. A. Lecoy de la Marche, *L'Esprit de nos aïeux,* 100–101.

19. See below, "His Religious Knowledge," in Part III, ch. 7.

20. A. Lecoy de la Marche translated this passage and presents it in the following way: "This dialogue between Saint Louis and Saint Bonaventure, which was reported by Saint Bonventure himself, has been taken from a manuscript that was recently discovered in Italy by Father Fedele da Fanna who quotes it in the introduction that he wrote for the new edition of the works of the Seraphic doctor" (*L'Esprit de nos aïeux,* 102–3).

21. See below, "The Cistercian Model and the Mendicant Model" and "His Religious Knowledge," in Part III, ch. 7.

22. See below, "His Religious Knowledge."

23. *Tractatus de diversis historiis Romanorum et quibsdam aliis verfangt in Bologna im Jahre 1326,* ed. S. Herzstein, Erlanger Beiträge, Helft, 14 (1893). See also, J.-T. Welter, in *L'Exemplum,* 358 n. 54.

24. *Tractatus de diversis historiis Romanorum,* 29–30.

25. See above, "The Uncompromising Dispenser of Justice," in Part I, ch. 4, and below in Part III, "Words of Faith," in ch. 3, and "The First Function," in ch. 4.

26. *Tractatus de diversis historiis Romanorum,* 27.

27. The Minstrel's scholarly editor Natalis de Wailly in the nineteenth century elaborated a "summary critique of the work" that lists its main errors and measures several pages in length.

28. Ibid., 98.

29. As the Minstrel of Reims states it, "The queen Blanche was in great mourning . . . her child was young, and she was a woman alone in a foreign country" (174). "The barons thought great ill of the queen of France. They met together often and said there was no one in France who could govern them. They saw that the king and his brothers were young and they had little appreciation for their mother" (176).

30. Ibid., 182–83.

31. It therefore seems that Louis was already dead, and that the Minstrel must have written this passage after 1260.

32. This allows us to date the text from 1261 or from the end of 1260.

33. Minstrel of Reims, 189–90, *"et encore i pert."*

34. Ibid., 190. On Matthew Paris, see below, Part II, ch. 7.

35. Joinville, *Histoire de Saint Louis,* 69. A traditional noble, Joinville tried to emulate the model of Geoffroy de Bouillon, even though he very well hoped to return

home. He mortgaged his lands so as to avoid taking on debt in money. "Because I did not want to take any deniers wrongly, I went to Metz in Lorraine and pawned off a large part of my land. And know that on the day that I left our country to go to the Holy Land, I did not even have a thousand pounds of income in lands, because Madame, my mother was still alive, and yet I still went leader of ten knights and third of the bannerets" (ibid., 65).

36. Minstrel of Reims, 190–91.

37. See below, "Worship and Asceticism," in Part III, ch. 7, and Michelet's important text.

38. Minstrel of Reims, 191–92.

39. I did not give an account of this in Part I, as the Minstrel's testimony is subject to caution. However, he is an interesting source for the behaviors, mentalities, and interests of the men of the thirteenth century.

40. Minstrel of Reims, 192–93.

41. Ibid., 193–94.

42. Joinville, *Histoire de Saint Louis,* 89–91.

43. See below, "The Second Function," in Part III, ch. 4.

44. See "The King and the Investigations in Languedoc," Part I, ch. 4; "The Limits of Royal Power," in Part III, ch. 5, and "His Conscience," in Part III, ch.7.

45. See "The *Prud'homme*" in Part III, ch. 3, and "Saint Louis' Models of Sainthood," in Part III, ch. 9.

46. Minstrel of Reims, 234–35. The "bad king John" is John Lackland.

47. On this, see Matthew Paris, 448 ff.

48. The Minstrel of Reims, 235.

49. Ibid., 236.

50. Ibid., 235.

51. Marie-Dominique Chenu, *L'Éveil de la conscience dans la civilization médiévale* (Montreal and Paris, 1969).

52. Minstrel of Reims, 237. On young Louis' death and Saint Louis' mourning, see above, "Births and Deaths," in Part I, ch. 4, and below, "The Children," in Part III, ch. 6.

53. See below, Part II, ch. 7.

54. Minstrel of Reims, 237 ff.

55. Ibid., 239.

PART II
Notes to Chapter 5

1. Marc Reydellet, *La Royauté dans la littératute latine, de Sidoine Apollinaire à Isidore de Seville* (Rome, 1981). On the Bible as a Mirror of the Prince, see the following chapter.

2. F. Langlamet, "Pour ou contre Salomon? La rédaction pro-salomonienne de I Rois I–II," *Revue biblique* 83 (1976): 321–79, 481–528.

3. Aryeh Grabois, "L'idéal de la royauté biblique dans la pensée de Thomas Becket," in *Thomas Becket,* Acts from the International Colloquium of Sédières, August 19–24, 1973, published by R. Foreville (Paris, 1975), 107.

4. Alexandre Cisek, "La rencontre de deux 'sages': Salomon le 'Pacifique' et Alexandre le Grand dans la légende héllenistique médiévale," in *Images et signes de l'Orient dans l'Occident médiéval, Senefiance,* no. 11 (1982): 75–100. Cf. Marc Bloch, "La vie d'outre-tombe du roi Salomon," *Revue belge de philosophie et d'histoire* 4 (1925), reprinted in *Mélanges historiques,* vol. 2 (Paris, 1963), 920–38. There was a rehabilitation of Solomon as a model of the wise king in the thirteenth century. See Philippe Buc, *L'Ambiguïté du livre. Prince, pouvoir et peuple dans les commentaires de la Bible au Moyen Âge* (Paris, 1994), 28–29.

5. Eugen Ewig, "Zum christlichen Königsgedanken im Frühmittelalter," in *Das Königstum. Seine geistigen und rechtlichen Grundlagen,* Mainauvorträge, 1954, *Vorträge und Forschungen,* ed. T. Mayer, vol. 3 (Constance, 1956), 11, 21; Frantisek Graus, *Volk, Herrscher und Heiliger im Reich der Merowinger* (Prague, 1965), 344 n. 223.

6. L. K. Born, "The *Specula Principis* of the Carolingian Renaissance," *Revue belge de philosophie et d'histoire* 12 (1933): 583–612; H. H. Anton, *Fürstenspiegel und Herrscherethos in der Karolingerzeit* (Bonn, 1969); Walter Ullmann, *The Carolingian Renaissance and the Idea of Kingship* (London, 1969). See the following chapter as well.

7. H. Steger, *David rex propheta. König David als vorbidliche Verkörperung des Herrschers und Dichters im Mittelalter* (Nuremberg, 1961).

8. Ernst H. Kantorowicz, *Laudes regiae. A Study in Liturgical Acclamations and Mediaeval Ruler Worship* (Berkeley and Los Angeles, 1946), 53–54; Robert Folz, *Le Couronnement impérial de Charlemagne* (Paris, 1964), 97–98, 118–20.

9. Percy Ernst Schramm, "Das Alte und das Neue Testament in der Staatslehre und der Staatssymbolik des Mittelalters" in *Settimane di studio del Centro italiano di studi sull'Alto Medioevo* 10 (Spoleto, 1963): 229–55.

10. *Patrologie latine,* vol. 102, col. 934 ff.

11. "Fear of God, wisdom, prudence, simplicity, patience, justice, [fair] judgment, mercy, humility, zeal for righteousness, clemency, [good] counsel."

12. *Gesta Treverorum Continuatio,* in *Monumenta Germaniae Historica. Scriptores,* vol. 24 (Leipzig, 1879), 388–89. Also quoted by E. A. R. Brown, "La notion de la légitimité et la prophétie à la cour de Philippe Auguste," 87.

13. Guillaume de Chartres, *De Vita et de Miraculis,* 30.

14. Geoffroy de Beaulieu, *Vita,* 3–4.

15. See below, Part III, ch. 9.

16. *Recueil des historiens des Gaules et de la France,* 23:153.

17. Helgaud de Fleury, *Vie de Robert le Pieux,* text edited, translated, and annotated by R.-H. Bautier and G. Labory (Paris, 1965), 58, 138.

18. G. Duby, "Le lignage," 31–56.

19. Wilhelm Berges, *Die Fürstenspiegel des hohen und späten Mittelalters* (Leipzig, 1938), 24 ff.

20. A. Grabois, "L'idéal de la royauté biblique dans la pensée de Thomas Becket."

21. Robert Bartlett, *Gerald of Wales, 1146–1223* (Oxford, 1982), 712.

22. See below, "John of Salisbury's *Policraticus*," in Part II, ch. 6.

23. "In the preface of the *Admonitio generalis* of 787, Charlemagne is compared to King Josiah who attempted to bring the kingdom that God gave him back to the true worship of God" (Pierre Riché, *Les Carolingiens* [Paris, 1983], 123). I hope to see a forthcoming publication of Dominique Alibert's doctoral thesis, "Les Carolingiens et leurs images. Iconographie et idéologie," Université de Paris IV, 1994. Here I am repeating the basic information from my study, "Royauté biblique et idéal monarchique médiéval: Saint Louis et Josias," in *Les Juifs au regard de l'histoire. Mélanges Bernhard Blumenkranz* (Paris, 1985), 157–68.

24. See above, "Guillaume de Saint-Pathus," in Part II, ch. 2. It is hard to tell if this sermon was written before or after the composition of the *Life*. It does contain some details that were almost certainly taken from the lost *Vita* drafted by the Roman Curia. The outline for the sermon that has been published by H.-F. Delaborde allows us to note that Guillaume de Saint-Pathus at least twice presented David as a model for Saint Louis.

25. "Splendor of wisdom, sweetness of compassion, purity of continence, fervor of devotion."

26. "David seated at the pulpit, a very wise ruler."

27. "My servant David will be the ruler in the midst of you."

28. Robert Folz, "La sainteté de Louis IX d'après les textes liturgiques de sa fête," *Revue d'histoire de l'Église de France* 57 (1971): 36.

29. "You are a very great and illustrious ruler."

30. Théodore and Denis Godefroy, *Le Cérémonial français,* vol. 1 (Paris, 1649), 17. An *ordo* is a liturgical manual for the consecration of a sacred person, a bishop or a king for instance.

31. M. Bloch, *Les Rois thaumaturges,* 68.

32. *Recueil des historiens des Gaules et de la France,* 23:152. "The peaceful king was raised over all the kings of the land by his riches and his wisdom."

33. Vincent de Beauvais, *De eruditione filiorum nobilium,* ed. A. Steiner (Cambridge, MA, 1938; repr. New York, 1970).

34. See above, "A Plague on the Land Whose Ruler Is a Child," in Part I, ch. 1, on the child king. On the value of childhood, see the somewhat overoptimistic P. Riché and D. Alexandre-Bidon, *L'Enfance au Moyen Âge.*

35. Vincent de Beauvais, *De eruditione filiorum nobilium,* 87.

36. R. Folz, "La sainteté de Louis IX," 34 n. 22: *Toto corde cum rege Josia quaesivit Deum ab infantia.*

37. Ibid., 38: *culta colebat sedula Deum verbis et actibus.*

38. *Similis illi non fuit ante eum rex, qui reverteretur ad Dominum in omni corde suo, et in tota anima sua, et in universa virtute sua.*

39. Geoffroy de Beaulieu, *Vita,* 3–26.

40. David was actually just his ancestor.

41. He got rid of the abominations of impiety and ruled his own heart by guiding it toward the Lord, and, in a time of sin, he strengthened his piety for the worship of God.

42. Guillaume de Chartres, *De Vita et de Miraculis,* 29. These aromatic metaphors are more important than one would imagine. Jean-Pierre Albert has shown that they were a part of royal ideology and the Christlike model, *Odeurs de sainteté. La mythologie chrétienne des aromates* (Paris, 1990).

PART II
Notes to Chapter 6

1. Pierre Gibert, *La Bible à la naissance de l'histoire* (Paris, 1979).

2. On the forerunners of the "Mirrors of the Princes," see Pierre Hadot, s. v. "Fürstenspiegel," in *Reallexikon für Antike und Christentum,* vol. 8 (1972), col. 555–632.

3. H. H. Anton, *Fürstenspiegel und Herrscherethos in der Karolingerzeit.* Michel Roche has recently asked whether these "Mirrors" did not primarily reflect the backgrounds and opinions of their ecclesiastical authors: "Miroirs des princes ou miroir du clergé?" in *Committenti e produzione artistico-letteraria nell' alto medioevo occidentale,* Centro italiano di studi sull'Alto Medioevo (Spoleto, 1992), 341–67. This is one aspect of the problem that I deal with here.

4. J. Dickinson, "The Medieval Conception of Kingship and Some of Its Limitations as Developed in the "Policraticus" of John of Salisbury," *Speculum* (1926): 308–37. See above, "David and Solomon," in the preceding chapter.

5. L. K. Born, "The Perfect Prince: A Study in a 13th and 14th Century Ideal," *Speculum* (1928): 470–504. For the preceding period, see Georges Duby, "L'image des princes en France au début du XIᵉ siècle," *Cahiers d'histoire* (1982): 211–16. For an overview, D. M. Bell, *L'Idéal éthique de la monarchie en France d'après quelques moralistes de ce temps* (Paris and Geneva, 1962).

6. In the *De eruditione filiorum regalium,* Vincent de Beauvais repeats John of Salisbury's ideas about the appropriate education for children, but he displays what is clearly a more positive concept of the child.

7. On Vincent de Beauvais and this project, see below, "An Encyclopedist in the Service of the King: Vincent de Beauvais," in Part III, ch. 2, and "A Secular Saint," in Part III, ch. 9. Vincent J. Schneider has just published the *De morali principis institutione,* Corpus Christianorum, Continuatio Mediaevalis, vol. 137 (Turnhout, 1995).

8. *Éducation des rois et des princes,* ed. A. de Porter in *Les Philosophes belges,* vol. 9 (Louvain, 1914).

9. If we count them, we find that there are respectively forty-five (46 percent), forty-one (42 percent), and twelve (12 percent).

10. On Saint Louis and hunting, see below, "Saint Louis Does Not Hunt," in Part III, ch. 5.

11. G. Duby, *Le Chevalier, la Femme et le Prêtre.*

12. See above, "The 'Good' Money," in Part I, ch. 4, and below, "Currency," in Part III, ch. 4.

13. Lester K. Little, "Pride Goes before Avarice: Social Change and the Vices in Latin Christendom," *American Historical Review* 76 (1971).

14. See below, "The Royal Coronation," in Part III, ch. 9.

15. Richard A. Jackson has focused on the innovations introduced into the coronation for the entire series of French kings in his remarkable work: *Vivat rex. Histoire des sacres et couronnements en France, 1634–1825* (Strasbourg, 1984). I have insisted all the more on this conservatism in my study, "Reims, ville du sacre," in *Les Lieux de mémoire,* ed. P. Nora, vol. 2, *La Nation,* 1:89–184. In this work, I stress the forces of resistance to innovation confronting the pressures of the Enlightenment and the Revolution at the time of the coronations of Louis XVI (1775), Charles X (1825), and the planned but failed coronation of Louis XVIII (1815–1824).

16. See below, "Books of Images," in Part III, ch. 2.

17. D. O'Connell, *Les Propos de Saint Louis,* 187.

18. See below, "The Coronation System," in Part III, ch. 9.

19. Robert Folz has made the germane comparison of Saint Louis' *Enseignements* with their only precedent, those of Saint Stephen, the first Christian king of Hungary in the first years of the eleventh century.

20. D. O'Connell, *The Teachings of Saint Louis*; French translation in D. O'Connell, *Les Propos de Saint Louis,* 29–55.

21. See below, "The King and His 'Good Towns'," in Part III, ch. 4.

22. Joinville, *Histoire de Saint Louis,* 11–13.

23. Groupe de la Bussière, *Pratiques de la confession* (Paris, 1983).

24. Carla Casagrande and Silvana Vecchio, *Les Péchés de la langue. Discipline et éthique de la parole dans la culture médiévale* (Paris, 1991).

25. Jacques Chiffoleau, "Dire l'indicible. Remarques sur la catégorie du *nefandum* du XIIe au XVe siècle," *Annales, E.S.C.* (1990): 289–324.

26. This path went from the hotel where he was staying to the south point of the Cité to the royal palace. It may seem short to us today, but churches were very numerous on the Île de la Cité in the thirteenth century.

27. P. Saenger, "Silent Reading: Its Impact on Late Medieval Script and Society," *Viator* 13 (1982): 367–414; idem, "Prier de bouche et prier de coeur," in *Les Usages de l'imprimé,* ed. Roger Chartier (Paris, 1987), 191–227.

28. See Nicole Bériou, Jacques Berlioz, and Jean Longère, eds., *Prier au Moyen Âge* (Turnhout, 1991); C.U.E.R.M.A., *La Prière au Moyen Âge, Senefiance,* no. 10 (Aix-en-Provence, 1991).

29. A. Paravicini-Bagliani, *Il corpo del Papa.*

30. Jean-Claude Schmitt, "Entre le texte et l'image: les gestes de la prière de Saint Dominique," in *Persons in Group:. Behaviour as Identity Formation in Medieval and Renaissance Europe* (New York, 1985), 195–214; idem, *La Raison des gestes dans l'Occident médiéval* (Paris, 1990); Miri Rubin, *Corpus Christi: The Eucharist in Late Medieval Culture* (Cambridge, 1991); Pierre Marie Gy, *La Liturgie dans l'histoire* (Paris, 1990), see especially the section on the *Fête-Dieu.*

31. Jacques Le Goff, "Saint Louis et la parole royale," in *Le Nombre du temps. En hommage à Paul Zumthor* (Paris, 1988), 127–36. See also below, "The King's Speech," in Part III, ch. 3.

32. Although Saint Louis did not actually say this, it is clear that when he was speaking about "the unction with which the kings of France are crowned," he was thinking of the Holy Ampulla of Reims that holds the oil from Clovis's baptism that was miraculously produced by the Holy Spirit. It was under Saint Louis that the Holy Ampulla definitively took on its essential role in the first part of the coronation ceremony. See "The Coronation System," in Part III, ch. 9.

33. See below, "Saint Louis on Display for His Subjects," in Part III, ch. 5.

34. Jacques Krynen argues that the medieval French monarchy evolved toward absolutism along a direct, if not always deliberate, line. See his wonderful book, *L'Empire du roi. Idées et croyances politiques en France, XIIIe–XVe siècles* (Paris, 1993).

35. Joinville, *Vie de Saint Louis,* 18–19. Also see below, "The Values of the Body," in Part III, ch. 10.

36. See below in Part III, "The Great Alliance of the Altar and the Throne," in ch. 5, and "His Grandfather," in ch. 6.

37. See above, "Conflicts with the Bishops," in Part I, ch. 1, and below, Part III, ch. 8.

38. Philippe Contamine, *La Guerre au Moyen Âge,* 3rd ed. (Paris, 1992), ch. 10, "La guerre: aspects juridiques, éthiques et religieux," 419–77; F. H. Russell, *The Just War in the Middle Ages* (Cambridge, 1975).

39. Sulpice Sévère, *Vie de saint Martin,* 11:2, ed. and trans. Jacques Fontaine, vol. 1 (Paris, 1967), 336–39.

40. J. Le Goff and J.-C. Schmitt, "Au XIIIe siècle: une parole nouvelle," 257–80.

PART II
Notes to Chapter 7

1. B. Guenée, *Histoire et culture historique dans l'Occident medieval,* 20–22.

2. On Matthew Paris, see R. Vaughan, *Matthew Paris,* 3rd ed. (Cambridge, 1979).

3. M. R. James, "The Drawings of Matthew Paris," *Walpole Society* 14 (1925–1926).

4. Roger Wendover's chronicle is entitled, *Flores historiarum,* not to be confused with Matthew Paris's work of the same title.

5. Matthew Paris, *Chronica majora,* 5:354.

6. Ibid., 4:225: "*Erat namque rex juvenis, tener et delicatus.*"

7. See above, "A Plague on the Land Whose Ruler Is a Child," in Part I, ch. 1.

8. This is one of Matthew Paris's many errors. We have already seen that Louis VIII died at Monpensier in Auvergne and not at the siege of Avignon. The error is all the more astonishing when we consider that the careless Benedictine also forgot that he thought that Louis VIII had been poisoned by the count of Champagne. This type of death can hardly be hereditary.

9. They were presenting Thibaud de Champagne as her lover.

10. The "judgment of God."

11. Matthew Paris, *Chronica majora,* 2:196.

12. Ibid., 325.

13. The Latin text states, "*regnum regnorum, scilicet Gallia,*" which shows France's prestige throughout Christendom, *Gallia* being used to designate France, and *Francia* usually being used at the time to refer to the heart of France that was called "Île-de-France" by the end of the Middle Ages.

14. Matthew Paris, *Chronica majora,* 2:366.

15. Ibid., 393.

16. This is also the point at which his chronicle stops reproducing Roger Wendover's.

17. In 1241 Blanche of Castile became "*venerabilis ac Deo dilecta matrona*" (a venerable matron beloved by God).

18. See above, "An Eschatological King," in Part I, ch. 2.

19. Matthew Paris, *Chronica majora,* 4:112.

20. Ibid., 137.

21. Ibid., 198. *Francus,* "frank," "free."

22. Ibid., 203–4.

23. See above, "The Franco-English Peace: The Treaty of Paris (1259)," in Part I, ch. 4, and below, "Political Criticisms," in Part III, ch. 8.

24. Matthew Paris, *Chronica majora,* 5:102. For a list of Saint Louis' extractions in France for the crusade: ibid., 5:171–72.

25. Ibid., 16.

26. In 1297, the year of Saint Louis' canonization, Pope Boniface VIII forbade the dismembering of cadavers in the bull *Detestande feritatis.* See E. A. R. Brown, "Death and the Human Body in the Later Middle Ages"; A. Paravicini-Bagliani, *Il corpo del Papa.*

27. We know that the men of the Middle Ages believed in the incorruptible nature of the bodies of the saints and in the good "odor of sainthood" that was supposed to emanate from their bodies. This was even one of the official criteria for the recognition of sainthood.

28. See above, "The Tribulations of the Royal Body," in Part I, ch. 5.

29. See above, this chapter.

30. Matthew Paris, *Chronica majora,* 4:249: "*apostolatum super gentem Occidentalem.*"

31. The text states *Francia*: little by little the word came to replace *Gallia* in referring to the whole of France.

32. Matthew Paris, *Chronica majora,* 5:23.

33. Ibid., 5:239.

34. Ibid., 5:307.

35. See above, "The Brief Reign of the Father," in Part I, ch. 1.

36. Matthew Paris, *Chronica majora,* 5:202.

37. Ibid., 5:247: "in effect, the military braggadocio of the French displeased God" (*non enim complacuit Deo Francorum superbia militaris*).

38. Ibid., 5:151: "*more Gallico reboans et indecenter inhians.*"

39. Ibid., 5:106–7. The written expression is "*ex Sarracenorum tolerantia.*"

40. Ibid., 5:108.

41. See above, "The Affair of the Shepherds," in Part I, ch. 3.

42. Matthew Paris, *Chronica majora,* 5:254.

43. Ibid., 5:158.

44. Ibid., 5:385: "*dominus rex Francorum tempore tribulationis in Terra Sancta inglorios.*"

45. Ibid., 5:280.

46. Ibid., 5:160: "*ne forte rex moreretur prae tristitia.*" We might also recall that the son born to him during his short captivity was named Jean-Tristan. He died beneath the walls of Tunis several days before his father.

47. Ibid., 5:175.

48. Ibid., 5:466.

49. Ibid., 5:312.

50. Ibid., 5:203.

51. See above, "The Return of a Grief-Stricken Crusader," in Part I, ch. 4.

52. Matthew Paris, *Chronica majora,* 5:331.

53. Ibid., 5:239; this statement was made about an incident in which he displayed his acceptance of God's punishments: "*ut secundus Job vere posset censeri.*" The bishop who tried to console Louis after his return from the crusade (see above, "The Return of a Grief-Stricken Crusader") also offered him the example of Job, which did not console the king at all because his sense of spirituality was different and more modern.

54. See above, "The Flemish Inheritance," in Part I, ch. 4.

55. Matthew Paris, *Chronica majora,* 5:433: "*per superbiam muliebrem.*"

56. See below, "The New Solomon," in Part III, ch. 2.

57. Matthew Paris, *Chronica majora,* 5:506–7.

58. See above, "The Franco-English Peace," in Part I, ch. 4.

59. Matthew Paris, *Chronica majora,* 5:481.

60. Ibid., 5:478–79.

61. Ibid., 5:479.

62. Ibid., 5:480–81.

63. The text from the Gospel is Jesus' response to John the Baptist when he said that he wanted to be baptized by Jesus and not the other way around: "*sine modo, sic enim dicet omnem adimplere justitiam*" (Matthew 3:15)." As a *rex facetus,* Louis inserted *facetiam,* which particularly in this context gave a humorous and parodied turn to the very serious phrase of Jesus.

64. Matthew Paris, *Chronica majora,* 5:481. I treat this banquet in greater detail in the third part of my book. Another banquet was organized by the University where there were many English students and masters. They suspended their courses to participate in processions in festival costumes, singing, carrying branches and flowers, wearing crowns, and playing various musical instruments. The festival lasted for two days and one night throughout Paris, and the city was splendidly decorated and illuminated. It was the most beautiful festival that anyone had ever heard of in France (ibid., 5:477).

65. Ibid., 5:482.

66. Ibid., 5:745.

67. Salimbene de Adam, *Cronica,* ed. G. Scalia.

68. See the account in the *Cronica,* 1:99. Also, see the excellent study by A. Vauchez, "Une campagne de pacification en Lombardie autour de 1233."

69. See above, "The Meeting with Hugh of Digne," in Part I, ch. 4. On Joachim's ideas, see H. Mottu, *La Manifestation de l'Esprit selon Joachim de Fiore*; D.C. West, ed., *Joachim of Fiore in Christian Thought* (New York, 1975). On movements of prophecy in the thirteenth century, see Marjorie Reeves, *The Influence of Prophecy in the Later Middle Ages. A Study in Joachimism* (Oxford, 1969); on Millenarianism, Bernhard Töpfer, *Das Kommende Reich des Friedens* (Berlin, 1964); Ernst Benz, *Ecclesia Spiritualis. Kirchenidee und Geschichtstheologie der Franziskanischen Reformation* (Stuttgart, 1934); J. Le Goff, s. v., "Millénarisme."

70. W.C. Jordan, *Louis IX and the Challenge of the Crusade,* 182.

71. Salimbene, *Cronica,* 1:256.

72. Ibid., 304.

73. This is Eudes Rigaud, about whom I have spoken several times. He was a friend and advisor to Saint Louis.

74. Salimbene, *Cronica,* 318.

75. Ibid., 319–20.

76. Ibid., 320–21.

77. Ibid., 322. I deal with the "gastronomical" part of Louis' stay in Sens in greater detail in "The King's Duties," in Part III, ch. 3.

78. Salimbene, *Cronica,* 21–22.

79. Ibid., 323.

80. Ibid., 322–23.

81. Ibid., 323.

82. See above, "The Meeting with Hugh of Digne," in Part I, ch. 4.

83. Salimbene, *Cronica,* 486. See below, "Martyrdom: Agony and Death," in Part III, ch. 10, and Appendix 2.

84. Salimbene, *Cronica,* 340.

85. See above, "The Affair of the Shepherds," in Part I, ch. 3.

86. Salimbene, *Cronica,* 645–46.

87. This argument supports R.E. Lerner's thesis about the existence of forms of unbelief in the thirteenth century, although I think that his idea that the Capetian monarchy afforded protection to heretics and unbelievers seems unfounded: see his "The Uses of Heterodoxy: The French Monarchy and Unbelief in the XIIIth Century," *French Historical Studies* 4 (1965). See below, "Saint Louis and the Church," in Part III, ch. 8.

88. Salimbene, *Cronica,* 646.

89. Ibid., 821.

90. Ibid., 438 and 659.

91. Pope Alexander IV (1255–1261).

92. Salimbene, *Cronica,* 702–3.

93. Actually, the coffin contained only the remains of the deceased. See above, Part I, ch. 5.

94. Salimbene, *Cronica,* 707.

95. Ibid., 865.

PART II
Notes to Chapter 8

1. Étienne Delaruelle, "L'idée de croisade chez Saint Louis," *Bulletin de littérature ecclésiastique* (1960): 242.

2. Edmond-René Labande, "Saint Louis pèlerin," *Revue d'histoire de l'Église de France* 57 (1971): 5–17.

3. Jacques Madaule, *Saint Louis, roi de France* (Paris, 1943), 23.

4. See J.-C. Schmitt, *La Raison des gestes.*

5. See below, "The *Prud'homme,*" in Part III, ch. 3.

6. This is from a genealogy of the kings of France extracted from a chronicle by the minstrel of the count of Poitiers written between 1293 and 1297; the dates and ages are approximate: "Louis the *Prudhomme* was crowned at the age of thirteen and seven months. . . . He died in Carthage after ruling for forty-three years, and he was at the age of fifty-eight. There was peace in the kingdom in his time, he loved God and the Holy Church, and people say he is a Saint" (*Receuil des historiens des Gaules et de la France,* 23:146). Written before the canonization, this text is interesting for what it says and for what it omits (any mention of the defeat and imprisonment in Egypt), and also for its information about the methods that clerics used in the Middle Ages to keep track of chronology: the ages of people and the durations of reigns and prison terms and not dates.

7. See above, "Louis and Josiah," in Part II, ch. 5.

8. We will later see how Louis worked out a compromise between these two codes that he applied at the dinner table; see below, "Saint Louis at the Table," in Part III, ch. 3.

9. William C. Jordan, "*Persona et gesta*: The Image and Deeds of the Thirteenth-Century Capetians. The Case of Saint Louis," *Viator* 19, no. 2 (1988): 209–18, esp. 215.

10. See below, "His Mother," in Part III, ch. 6.

11. See above, "Births and Deaths," in Part I, ch. 4.

12. Suger, *Vie de Louis VI le Gros,* 267. At the age of fifteen, the royal adolescent took a mortal spill from his horse which was upset by a pig running through the streets in a neighborhood of Paris.

13. Pierre de Blois, *Epistola 2,* in *Patrologie latine,* vol. 207.

14. See Le Nain de Tillemont, *Vie de Saint Louis,* 5:117. On the brother-sister couple of Louis and Isabelle, see W. C. Jordan, *Louis IX and the Challenge of the Crusade,* 9–12.

15. Joinville, *Histoire de Saint Louis,* 243.

16. L. K. Little, "Saint Louis' Involvement with the Friars," 5.

17. Quoted by G. Duby in *Le Moyen Âge, de Hugues Capet à Jeanne d'Arc,* 260.

18. Helgaud de Fleury, *Vie de Robert le Pieux*.

19. Ibid., 127–29.

20. M. Bloch, *Les Rois thaumaturges*; Jacques Le Goff, "Le miracle royal" in *Actes du colloque de Paris pour le centenaire de la naissance de Marc Bloch* (Paris, 1986).

21. Helgaud de Fleury, *Vie de Robert le Pieux*, 138–39.

22. The surname "Augustus" was given to Philip II very early on for having "increased" the royal domain, but disappeared in the course of the thirteenth century in favor of the name "Conqueror." "Augustus" only came back into use for him in the fourteenth century.

23. J. Le Goff, "Le dossier de sainteté de Philippe Auguste."

24. Robert-Henri Bautier, "Les aumônes du roi aux maladreries, maisons-Dieu et pauvres établissements du royaume. Contribution à l'étude du réseau hospitalier . . . de Philippe Auguste à Charles VII," in *Actes du 97ᵉ congrès national des sociétés savantes* (Nantes, 1972), printed in the *Bulletin philologique et historique* (Paris, 1979), 37–105.

25. M. M. Coker, ed., "The *Karolinus of Egidius Parisiensis*," *Traditio* 34 (1973): 99–325. Cf. Andrew W. Lewis, "Dynastic Structures and Capetian Throne-Right: One View of Giles of Paris," *Traditio* 33 (1977).

26. See below, "A Royal Model," in Part III, ch. 3.

27. See above, "Louis and Josiah," in Part II, ch. 5.

28. Caroline Bynum, "Did the Twelfth Century Discover the Individual?" *Journal of Ecclesiastical History* 31 (1980), reprinted in *Jesus as Mother: Studies in the Spirituality of the High Middle Ages* (Berkeley, 1982), 82–109. On the individual in the thirteenth century, see below, Part II, ch. 10.

29. On the model of the Christian king, see the preceding chapter on the Mirrors of the Princes above, and Part III.

30. Cf. W. Berges, *Die Fürstenspiegel des hohen und späten Mittelalters*.

31. See below, "Saint Louis' Miracles," in Part III, ch. 9.

Part II
Notes to Chapter 9

1. See above, "The Voyage and the Campaign in Egypt," in Part I, ch. 3.

2. A. Vauchez, *Les Laïcs au Moyen Âge*; G. Lobrichon, *La Religion des laïcs en Occident*.

3. M. Zink, "Joinville ne pleure pas mais il rêve," *Poétique* 33 (1978): 34.

4. See above, the first section of Part I, ch. 1.

5. Louis Carolus-Barré quotes extracts from Guillaume de Saint-Pathus's *Life of Saint Louis*, which, according to him, transcribed Joinville's declaration for the inquiry. He then compares them with the corresponding passages from Joinville's own work (L. Carolus-Barré, *Le Procès de canonisation*, 78–87); see also the presentation of the witness Jean de Joinville, whose birth he places in 1225 and not 1224, without this being a case of a transcription in modern chronological years, adding a year to the medieval dating system for the months of January and February with the year beginning in March, as he gives May 1 as Joinville's hypothetical birth date (152–58).

6. *Histoire de Saint Louis,* 69. See above, "The 'Chivalry' of Brothers," in Part I, ch. 2.

7. *Histoire de Saint Louis,* 54–57.

8. Ibid., 82–83.

9. Ibid., 112–13.

10. Ibid., 124–27.

11. Ibid., 54–55. See above, "The 'Chivalry' of Brothers," in Part I, ch. 2.

12. See above, "The Return of a Grief-Stricken Crusader," in Part I, ch. 4.

13. *Histoire de Saint Louis,* 396–99.

14. Michèle Perret, "À la fin de sa vie ne fuz je mie," *Revue des sciences humaines* 183 (1981–1983): 17–37. For their valuable analyses presented at my seminar at the École des hautes etudes en sciences sociales, I would like to thank Michèle Perret ("Le statut du narrateur dans l'*Histoire de Saint Louis de Joinville*") and Christiane Marchello-Nizia ("Formes verbales et stratégie discursive dans l'*Histoire de Saint Louis de Joinville*").

15. Michel Zink, *La Subjectivité littéraire. Autour du siècle de Saint Louis* (Paris, 1985), 219. See also the remarkable article already cited, "Joinville ne pleure pas."

16. "Dictated," in other words, as was done by most of the "authors" of the time, including the clerics.

17. *Histoire de Saint Louis,* 10–11.

18. M. Zink, "La Subjectivité littéraire," 220, 226.

19. *Histoire de Saint Louis,* 20–21.

20. Ibid., 234–37.

21. M. Zink, "Joinville ne pleure pas," 42–44.

22. *Histoire de Saint Louis,* 308–11.

23. See above, "Salimbene of Parma, an Italian Franciscan," in Part II, ch. 7.

24. *Histoire de Saint Louis,* 35.

25. Ibid., 34–35. The scene was plainly meant to stress the opposition between the free access to the king's personal execution of justice and the barriers that existed between complainants and the judiciary apparatus that was already becoming more and more cumbersome under Louis IX. It became much more cumbersome in the reign of Philip the Fair, at the time Joinville was composing his *Life.* This passage presents the idealized model of the direct, personal monarchical government that Joinville was familiar with as a young man. Joinville opposed it to the contemporary model of a bureaucratic monarchy whose workings he disparaged in his old age and nostalgia, viewing them as an obstacle for the king to hide behind.

26. Ibid., 34–35.

27. Ibid., 14–15.

28. J. S. P. Tatlock, "Medieval Laughter," *Speculum* 21 (1946): 290–94. Henry II of England (1154–1189) was called a *rex facetus.*

29. *Histoire de Saint Louis,* 8–9, 344–45.

30. See Jacques Le Goff, "Du ciel sur la terre: la mutation des valeurs du XIIe au XIIIe siècle dans l'Occident Chrétien," in *Odysseus. Man in History. Anthropology History Today* (Moscow, 1991), 25–47 (in Russian).

31. This has been noted by Edmond-René Labande, "Quelques traits de carac-tère du roi Saint Louis," *Revue d'histoire de la spiritualité* 50 (1974): 143–46. Also, see above, "The Crusade, Louis IX, and the West," in Part I, ch. 3.

32. *Histoire de Saint Louis,* 310.

33. Ibid., 275.

34. Ibid., 274–75.

35. Ibid., 278–79.

36. Ibid., 370–73.

37. "Never once did I hear him name the devil, unless it was in some book that it was appropriate to speak about or in the lives of saints that the book discussed" (ibid., 378–79).

38. Ibid., 380–81.

39. Ibid., 89–91. See above, "The Stories of the Minstrel of Reims," in Part II, ch. 4.

40. *Histoire de Saint Louis,* 220–21.

41. Ibid, 331. See below, "His Mother," in Part III, ch. 6.

42. Although he too hated blasphemy, Joinville was more moderate: "Anyone who says a word like that in the manor of Joinville gets a slap [*bafe*] or a good knock [*paumelle*]."

43. *Histoire de Saint Louis,* 353–55.

44. Ibid., 358–61.

45. See below, Part III, ch. 6, for a more in-depth treatment of Saint Louis' rela-tions with his family considered from his own point of view.

46. *Histoire de Saint Louis,* 216–19.

47. Ibid., 330–33.

48. Ibid., 347.

49. Ibid., 326–27.

50. Ibid., 346–47.

51. See below, "His Wife," in Part III, ch. 6.

52. *Histoire de Saint Louis,* 397–99.

53. Ibid., 411–13.

54. On the meaning of images for the men of the Middle Ages, see J. Wirth, *L'Image médiévale. Naissance et développement (VIᵉ–XVᵉ siècles)* (Paris, 1989), and Jean-Claude Schmitt, "L'historien et les images aujourd'hui," *Xoana* 1 (1993): 131–37.

PART II
Notes to Chapter 10

1. In *La Personne humaine au XIIIᵉ siècle* (Paris, 1991), E. H. Weber also dis-cusses "history shaken by the notion of the 'person'." I have decided not to deal with this notion because it seems to me to be confined to the domains of philoso-phy and theology in the Middle Ages. We should resist the temptation to extend

concepts that were limited to the world of theologians to the common mentality of the time. I believe that in a general way the twelfth-century world of scholastic theology did not explain the mental concepts of the great majority of laymen and even clerics of the time. Clearly, only the political thought of Thomas Aquinas was more widely diffused (after Saint Louis), along with certain forms of "rational" thought.

2. Walter Ullmann, *The Individual and Society in the Middle Ages* (Baltimore, 1966), 45.

3. Ibid., 73.

4. See above, "The Uncompromising Dispenser of Justice," in Part I, ch. 4, and below, in Part III, ch. 4, "The First Function."

5. W. Ullmann, *The Individual and Society,* 69.

6. Ibid., 109.

7. See above, "Joinville's Concrete Saint Louis," in Part II, ch. 9.

8. See W. Ullmann, *The Individual and Society.*

9. Colin Morris, *The Discovery of the Individual, 1050–1200* (London, 1972). Morris complements the argument of his book in his article: "Individualism in XIIth-Century Religion: Some Further Reflections," *Journal of Ecclesiastical History* 31 (1980): 195–206. See also, Aaron Gourevitch, *La Naissance de l'individu au Moyen Âge* (Paris, 1995).

10. Georg Misch, *Geschichte der Autobiographie,* 2nd ed., 4 vols. (Frankfurt, 1949–1969); K. J. Weintraub, *The Value of the Individual. Self and Circumstance in Autobiography* (Chicago, 1978, repr. 1982); Sverre Bagge, "The Autobiography of Abelard and Medieval Individualism," *Journal of Medieval History* 19 (1993): 327–50. Bagge has undertaken a study on "the individual in European culture."

11. Claudio Leonardi, Introduction to the edition with the Italian translation of Guillaume de Saint-Thierry, *La lettere d'Oro* (Florence, 1983), 25.

12. 1972; French translation, Paris, 1983.

13. See the end of the preceding section for my thoughts about this notion of the "person."

14. Aaron J. Gurevič, "Conscience individuelle et image de l'au-delà au Moyen Âge," *Annales, E.S.C.* (1982): 255–75, reprinted under the title, "Perceptions of the Individual and the Hereafter in the Middle Ages," in *Historical Anthropology of the Middle Ages* (Polity Press, 1992), 65–89. I will discuss this argument in the next section.

15. C. Bynum, "Did the XIIth Century Discover the Individual?" On the theme of the emergence of the individual in the twelfth and thirteenth centuries, see also, John Benton, *Self and Society in Medieval France. The Memoirs of Abbot Guibert of Nogent* (New York, 1970); "Individualism and Conformity in Mediaeval Western Europe," in *Individualism and Conformity in Classical Islam,* ed. A. Banani and S. Vryonis, Jr. (Wiesbaden, 1977), 148–58; and "Consciousness of Self and Perceptions of 'Personality'," in *Culture, Power and Personality in Medieval France,* ed. T. N. Bisson (London, 1991), 327–56. See also the very suggestive article by Peter Brown, "Society and the Supernatural: A Medieval Change," *Daedalus* 104 (1975) and two studies of literary history: Peter Dronke, *Poetic Individuality in the Middle Ages* (Oxford,

1970), and R. W. Hanning, *The Individual in Twelfth-Century Romance* (New Haven, 1977). A colloquium on the theme *Individuum und Individualität im Mittelalter* was held at the Thomas-Institut of the University of Cologne in September 1994.

16. There is an eleventh-century anonymous treatise on this, *Libellus de diversis ordinibus quae sunt in ecclesia* (Book of the Different Orders that Exist in the Church).

17. Jacques Le Goff, "Le vocabulaire des catégories sociales chez saint François d'Assise et ses biographes au XIIIᵉ siècle," in *Ordres et classes.* Colloque d'histoire sociale at Saint-Cloud, 1967 (Paris and the Hague, 1973), 93–123.

18. See my Introduction.

19. Jean-Claude Schmitt, "La 'découverte de l'individu': une fiction historiographique?" in *La Fabrique, la figure et la feinte. Fictions et statut des fictions en psychologie*, ed. P. Mengal and F. Parot (Paris, 1984), 213–36. J.-C. Schmitt refers notably to Jacob Burckhardt's *La Civilisation en Italie au temps de la Renaissance* (Paris, 1885), and its second part, "Development and the Individual"; Otto von Gierke, *Deutsches Genossenschaftrecht* (1891), partially translated into French as *Les Théories politiques au Moyen Âge* (Paris, 1914); Louis Dumont, *Essais sur l'individualisme. Une perspective anthropologique sur l'idéologie moderne* (Paris, 1983); Charles M. Radding, *A World Made by Men: Cognition and Society. 400–1200* (Chapel Hill, 1985).

20. See below, "Saint Louis' Sainthood," in Part III, ch. 9. Robert Folz has effectively analyzed the differences between Saint Louis' *Enseignements* and the manual written by the saint king Stephen of Hungary in the eleventh century for his son. This is in his marvelous book *Les Saints Rois du Moyen Âge*.

21. C. Brémont, J. Le Goff, and J.-C. Schmitt, *L'Exemplum*. See above, Part II, ch. 4.

22. *Histoire de Saint Louis,* 413.

23. Francis of Assisi died in 1226, the same year the child Louis became king. He was canonized in 1228, sixty-nine years before Saint Louis.

24. Francis de Beer, *La Conversion de saint François selon Thomas de Celano* (Paris, 1963), 240–43.

25. M. Zink, *La Subjectivité littéraire.*

26. Paul Ourliac and Jean-Louis Gazzaniga, *Histoire du droit privé français de l'an mil au Code civil* (Paris, 1985).

27. J. Le Goff, *La Naissance du Purgatoire.*

28. A. Gourevic, "Conscience individuelle et image de l'au-delà au Moyen Âge." I proposed making this argument more nuanced in the same issue of the *Annales.*

29. M.-D. Chenu, *L'Éveil de la conscience dans la civilisation médiévale*; Joseph R. Strayer, "La conscience du roi," *Mélanges R. Aubenas* (Montpellier, 1974); Elizabeth A. R. Brown, "Taxation and Morality in the XIIIth and XIVth Centuries: Conscience and Political Power and the Kings of France," *French Historical Studies* 8 (1973): 1–28.

30. Geoffroy de Beaulieu, *Vita,* 7.

31. Ibid., 13.

32. Ibid., 10.

33. Ibid.

34. Ibid., 6.

35. Guillaume de Saint-Pathus, *Vie,* 19.

36. Guillaume de Nangis, *Vie de Saint Louis,* 456: "*manu sua in gallico scripserat.*"

37. Jean Batany, "L'amère maternité du français mediéval," *Langue française,* no. 54 (May 1982), 37.

38. Queen Marguerite similarly wrote her letters before 1270 in Latin and after 1270 in French (G. Sivery, *Marguerite de Provence*).

39. D. O'Connell, *Les Propos de Saint Louis.*

40. Here are the sources that I have consulted on the saint's iconography: Gaston Le Breton, *Essai iconographique sur Saint Louis* (Paris, 1880); Auguste Longnon, *Documents parisiens sur l'iconographie de Saint Louis* (Paris, 1882); Émile Mâle, "La vie de Saint Louis dans l'art français au commencement du XIVe siècle," in *Mélanges Bertaux* (Paris, 1924), 193–204; Émile van Moe, *Un vrai portrait de Saint Louis* (Paris, 1940); P. M. Auzas, "Essai d'un repertoire iconographique de Saint Louis," in *Septième centenaire de la mort de Saint Louis,* 3–56. The two most interesting studies that I have found are those of Meredith Parsons Lilich, "An Early Image of Saint Louis," *Gazette des beaux-arts* (1970–1971): 251–56, and, above all, A. Erlande-Brandenburg, "Le tombeau de Saint Louis."

41. Roland Recht, "Le portrait et le principe de réalité dans la sculpture: Philippe le Bel et l'image royale," in *Europäische Kunst um 1300,* for the 25th Annual Congress on Art History (Vienna, 1984), 189–201. Readers may also want to consult other articles on the theme of the portrait. R. Recht relies on the dated but outstanding work of F. Siebert, *Der Mensch um Dreizehnhundert im Spiegel deutscher Quellen. Studien über Geisteshaltung und Geistesentwicklung,* in *Historische Studien* 206 (Berlin, 1931). This is an important study for the emergence of the individual in the thirteenth century. On the beginnings of the history of the portrait, see Pierre and Galienne Francastel, *Le Portrait. Cinquante siècles d'humanisme en peinture* (Paris, 1969) and Enrico Castelnuovo, *Portrait et société dans la peinture italienne* (Paris, 1993); Jean-Baptiste Giard, "L'illusion du portrait," *Bulletin de la Bibliothèque nationale* (1978): 29–34; Percy Ernst Schramm, *Die deutschen Kaiser und Könige in Bildern ihrer Zeit* (Leipzig and Berlin, 1928), 2:751–1152; Gerhard B. Ladner, *Papstbildnisse des Altertums und des Mittelalters* vol. 2, *Von Innocenz II zu Benedikt XI* (Vatican City, 1970); Jean-Claude Bonne, "L'image de soi au Moyen Âge (IXe–XIIe siècle): Raban Maur and Godefroy de Saint-Victor," in *Il ritratto e la memoria,* ed. B. Gentili, P. Morel, and C. Cieri Via (1993), 37–60.

42. See above, "Saint Louis and the Royal Bodies," in Part I, ch. 4.

43. See above, Part I, ch. 2.

44. This miniature currently exists in folio 8, MS 240 of the Pierpont Morgan Library in New York.

45. Catalogue for the exposition, "Saint Louis," organized at the Sainte-Chapelle May-August 1960 by the Direction générale des Archives de France, no. 117. Giles Constable has studied the symbolism of beards in the Middle Ages in his long

introduction to the edition of Burchard de Bellevaux's *Apologia de barbis,* ed. R. B. C. Huygens, *Corpus Christianorum, Continuatio Mediaevalis* 62 (Turnhout, 1985) and in his article "Beards in History: Symbols, Modes, Perceptions" (in Russian), *Ulysse. Revue de l'Académie russe des sciences* (1994): 165–81.

46. Roland Recht has given a satisfying definition of the portrait's status around 1300: "There are two distinct conceptions of the royal effigy present: one embodies a general principle of idealization—this is the retrospective portrait, the other tends to integrate observation *ad vivum*" ("Le Portrait et le principe de réalité dans la sculpture," 190).

47. Paul Deschamps, "A propos de la statue de Saint Louis à Mainneville (Eure)," *Bulletin monumental* (1969): 35–40.

48. Georgia Sommers Wright, "The Tomb of Saint Louis," *Journal of the Warburg and Courtauld Institute* 34 (1971): 65–82.

49. *Beati Ludovici vita, partim ad lectiones, partim ad sacrum sermonem parata,* in *Recueil des historiens des Gaules det de la France,* 23:167–76.

50. J.-C. Schmitt, *La Raison des gestes dans l'Occident medieval.*

51. E. H. Kantorowicz, *The King's Two Bodies.*

PART III
Notes to Chapter 1

1. *Histoire de la France,* ed. A. Burguière and J. Revel, vol. 1, *L'Espace français* (Paris, 1989). See P. Gautier-Dalché's interesting remarks on this in "Un problème d'histoire culturelle: perception et représentation de l'espace au Moyen Âge," *Médiévales,* special issue entitled *Espaces du Moyen Âge,* no. 18 (1990): 7. See also, Charles Higounet, "À propos de la perception de l'espace au Moyen Âge," in *Media in Francia. Mélanges Karl Ferdinand Werner* (1988).

2. He dubbed his son and heir in the garden of the royal palace in Paris in 1267.

3. See below, "Saint Louis on Display for His Subjects" in Part III, ch. 5.

4. See below, "His Household and His Entourage" in Part III, ch. 6.

5. J. Madaule, *Saint Louis de France,* 23.

6. Jacques Le Goff, "L'Occident médiéval et l'océan Indien: un horizon onirique," in *Mediterraneo e Oceano Indiano* (Florence, 1970): 243–63, reprinted in *Pour un autre Moyen Âge,* 280–98.

7. See P. Gautier-Dalché, in *L'Uomo e il mare nella civiltà occidentale.*

8. See below, "The King and His Intellectuals" in Part III, ch. 2,

9. Robert Fawtier, "Comment le roi de France, au début du XIVe siècle, pouvait-il se représenter son royaume?" in *Mélanges P. E. Martin* (Geneva, 1961), 65–77.

10. On Paris's transformation into a capital, see the work of A. Lombard-Jourdan, "Montjoie et Saint-Denis!"; R.-H. Bautier, "Quand et comment Paris devint capitale."

11. On the pairing of Saint-Denis and Paris, see A. Lombard-Jourdan, "Montjoie et Saint-Denis!"

12. See Anne Lombard-Jourdan, "Montjoies et Montjoie dans la plaine Saint-Denis," *Paris et Île-de-France* 25 (1974): 141–81. This article is preferable to Robert Branner's, "The Montjoies of Saint Louis," in *Essays Presented to Rudolf Wittkower,* vol. 1 (Oxford, 1967), 13–16. The first "*montjoie,*" in the sense of a talisman protecting the country, was the tumulus said to contain the remains of a deified patriarchal ancestor that was transformed by Christianity into the tomb of the tutelary Saint Denis. The "*montjoies*" were small monuments with a pedestal, a high cross in the form of a fleur-de-lis, and three large statues of kings that bordered the road from Paris to Saint-Denis. They were built in the thirteenth century. The war cry "*Montjoie et Saint-Denis!*" was adopted by French knights in the twelfth century.

13. Jean Guérout, "Le palais de la Cité, à Paris, des origines à 1417," *Fédération des sociétés historiques et archéologiques de Paris et de l'Île-de-France. Mémoires* 1, 2, and 3 (1949, 1950, and 1951).

14. See above, "The Sainte-Chapelle," in Part I, ch. 2, and below, "Architecture: A Court Style?" in Part III, ch. 2.

15. Carlrichard Brühl, *Fodrum, Gistum, Servitiuum Regis,* 2 vols. (Cologne and Graz, 1968).

16. There is a gap in the publication of the royal acts from the Middle Ages that extends from the death of Philip Augustus in 1223 to the accession of Philip the Fair in 1285.

17. In Book 21 of the *Recueil des historiens des Gaules et de la France,* we find: (1) the "Séjours et itinéraires de Louis IX" (Stays and Itineraries of Louis IX) (*Ludovici Noni Mansiones et Itinera*) in the "Séjours et itinéraires des rois" (*Regum mansiones et Itinera*), 408–23; (2) most of the "Compléments aux séjours et itinéraires des rois" (*Addenda mansionibus et itineribus regum*), 488–99 concerning Louis IX; (3) another "Complément aux séjours et itinéraires des rois" (*Additum regum mansionibus et iteneribus alterum supplementum*), pp. l–li, which concerns Louis IX for the most part; and (4) the "Gîtes pris par Louis IX de 1254 à 1269 (*Gista quae Ludovicus IX cepit ab anno MCCLIIII ad annum MCCLXIX*), 397–403. Book 22 (pp. xxv–xxxvi) contains the "Extraits de comptes concernant les séjours et itinéraires des rois" (*Excerpta e rationibus ad mansioines et itinera regum spectantia*) for the months of February to May 1234 and from May to October 1239, which partially repeat some of the information contained in the aforementioned lists from Book 21.

18. Starting with Philip Augustus, a tie was established here that resulted from both the growth of the royal bureaucracy and Saint Louis' greater preference for Vincennes. According to the records that still exist, Philip Augustus only sealed six acts at Vincennes.

19. See below, "Saint Louis Does Not Hunt" in Part III, ch. 5.

20. See Jean Chapelot, *Le Château de Vincennes* (Paris, 1994). J. Chapelot is directing a number of interesting archeological digs at the site and, along with Élizabeth Lalou, he organized a colloquium on Vincennes (1994).

21. Robert Branner sees this as a decisive point in the formation of the court style promoted by Philip Augustus. See below, "Architecture: A Court Style?" in Part III, ch. 2.

22. A. Lombard-Jourdan, "Montjoie et Saint-Denis."

23. The actual term 'Île-de-France' only appeared in the fifteenth century and became an administrative entity at the beginning of the sixteenth century.

24. Guillaume de Saint-Pathus, *Vie de Saint Louis,* 90.

25. See above, "The King as Investigator" in Part I, ch. 4.

26. Philippe Contamine, "L'oriflamme de Saint-Denis aux XIV⁰ et XV⁰ siècles. Études de symbolique religieuse et royale," *Annales de l'Est* (1973): 179–244.

27. See above, "From Paris to Aigues-Mortes" in Part I, ch. 3.

28. Joinville, *Histoire de Saint Louis,* 365.

29. Jean Favier, *Philippe le Bel* (Paris, 1978), 335.

30. See E.-R. Labande's interesting article, "Saint Louis pèlerin."

31. Saint Louis' contemporary, the king of Castile Alphonse X the Wise, presented himself as an intimate worshipper of the Virgin for whom he composed his *Cantigas de Santa Maria.*

32. I would like to thank Marie-Claire Gasnault here for the information on this pilgrimage that she collected for me. See Jacques Juillet, "Saint Louis à Rocamadour," *Bulletin de la Société des études littéraires, scientifiques et artistiques du Lot* 92 (1971): 19–30.

33. Alphonse Dupront, *Du sacré. Croisades et pèlerinages. Images et langages* (Paris, 1987), 317–18.

34. See Jacques Le Goff, "Saint Louis et la mer," in *L'Uomo e il mare nella civiltà occidentale: da Ulisse a Cristoforo Colombo* (Genoa, 1992), 13–24. See also, "Saint Louis and the Mediterranean" in Part I, ch. 2.

35. See above, "Saint Louis and the Mediterranean" in Part I, ch. 2.

36. *"Corpus suum et vitam suam exposuit pro Christo, mare transfretando."*

37. *Recueil des historiens des Gaules et de la France,* 20:14–15.

38. I would like to thank Marie-Claire Gasnault for her transcription of this sermon from the Latin MS 17 509 in the Bibliothèque nationale in Paris.

39. They made a distinction between the upper sea and the lower sea and the inner sea and the outer sea. The inner sea is in hell and it is very bitter—*amarissimum.* The upper sea is in this world; like a prostitute, it is full of sins and perils. The sermon contains a fascinating description that lists the different dangers of the sea and how they are stirred up by different winds. Jacques de Vitry also insists on the importance of straits or *Bitalassum,* the very dangerous spot where two seas meet, and the inverse danger of the *bonatium* or *"bonasse,"* the lack of wind that immobilizes boats.

40. This is the well-known story of the storm that rose up to threaten the boat of Peter and his seafaring companions when Christ was sleeping. Peter and his companions were frightened and screamed, "Lord, save us; we perish," and Jesus calmed the storm just as Yahweh had calmed the storm in the Old Testament.

41. See above, "Fortunes at Sea" in Part I, ch. 4, and "The King's Flaws" in Part II, ch. 9.

42. Joinville, *Histoire de Saint Louis,* 357.

43. In Part I, ch. 1, I discussed the world and the Orient as they existed around Saint Louis. Here, I am examining the Orient as he knew it in real and imaginary terms at the same time.

44. Aryeh Grabois, "From 'Holy Geography' to 'Palestinography'," in Hebrew, *Cathedra* 31 (1984): 43–66; "Islams and Muslims as Seen by Christian Pilgrims in Palestine in the XIIIth Century." The most useful work is still the classic study by J. K. Wright, *Geographical Lore in the Times of the Crusades* (New York, 1925). On the image that Christians had of Islam in the Middle Ages, Robert W. Southern, *Western Views of Islam in the Middle Ages* (Cambridge, MA, 1962); Claude Cahen, "Saint Louis et l'Islam."

45. F. van Ortroy, "Saint François d'Assise et son voyage en Orient."

46. See below, "His Religious Devotion on the Crusade," in Part III, ch. 7.

47. Mohamed Talbi, "Saint Louis à Tunis," in *Les Croisades,* a collective work published by the review *Histoire* (Paris, 1988).

48. On the origins of the important division of Muslims into Sunnis and Shiites, see Hichem Djaït, *La Grande Discorde. Religion et politique dans l'Islam des origines* (Paris, 1989).

49. Joinville, *Histoire de Saint Louis,* 136–41.

50. B. Lewis, *The Assassins.*

51. Ibid., 63.

52. Guillaume de Nangis, *Gesta Ludovici IX,* 324.

53. Guillaume of Tyre mentions them, and he died in 1185. They also appear in the narrative of the voyage of the Dominican Guillaume de Rubrouck who was Saint Louis' envoy to Asia. People really began to talk about them around 1300 when Guillaume de Nangis and Joinville were writing. Marco Polo mentions them, and in 1332 the German priest Brocardus wrote a treatise on the Assassins to be used by Philippe de Valois who was thinking of starting a new crusade. Brocardus's treatise was meant to prepare him for dealing with them. Matthew Paris accused the "Saracens" in general, and not the Assassins, of attempting a mass poisoning of Christians in the West by sending poisoned shipments of pepper. After a few poisoning incidents, people noticed and warned others by having public heralds cry out the news in large cities. There was no shortage of pepper, however, because Christian merchants had stocked large supplies of good pepper that they released (4:490). In Canto XIX of the *Inferno,* Dante makes a brief allusion to "the perfidious assassin" [*lo perfido assissin*]. Beginning in Saint Louis' times, the word "assassin" began to spread throughout Europe with its current meaning of "professional killer."

54. The "*bougran*" (also the name of the city of Bukhara) was a large piece of strong, sticky cloth.

55. Joinville, *Histoire de Saint Louis,* 247.

56. Ibid., 251.

57. These details can be found in Joinville's *Histoire de Saint Louis,* 251–55.

58. On the Mongols and Christendom, see above, "The Oriental Horizon," in Part I, ch. 1.

59. J. Richard, *La Papauté et les missions d'Orient au Moyen Âge, XIIIᵉ–XVᵉ siècles.*

60. Joinville, *Histoire de Saint Louis,* 75.

61. Ibid., 259–71. André de Longumeau, however, reported very interesting new information that Joinville partially mentions. We can see how the Mongols themselves established their glory through an imaginary history. They glorified themselves for having conquered and killed the legendary Prester John and emperor of Persia.

62. See the superb edition by Claude and René Kappler.

63. J. Richard, *Saint Louis,* 509. This letter has been discovered and published by P. Meyvaert, "An Unknown Letter of Hulagu, il-Khan of Persia to King Louis IX of France."

64. Joinville, *Histoire de Saint Louis,* 103–5.

65. Ibid., 105.

66. J. Le Goff, "Le merveilleux scientifique au Moyen Âge," in *Zwischen Wahn Glaube und Wissenschaft,* ed. J.-F. Bergier (Zurich, 1988), 87–113.

67. The Arabic and oriental sources call them "Qiptchaqs." The Russians call them "Polovtsy." There are Polovtsian dances in Borodin's *Prince Igor.* See Joinville, *Histoire de Saint Louis,* 273.

68. Guillaume de Chartres, *De Vita et de Miraculis,* 36.

69. Joinville, *Histoire de Saint Louis,* 65.

70. Guillaume de Saint-Pathus, *Vie de Saint Louis,* 33–35.

71. Geoffroy de Beaulieu, *Vita,* 10–11. Saint Louis loved big fish and fresh fruit. See the anecdote given below, "Humility and Asceticism," in Part III, ch. 3.

72. J. Le Goff, "Rire au Moyen Âge," *Cahiers du Centre de recherches historiques,* no. 3 (April 1989): 1–14.

73. Guillaume de Saint-Pathus, *Vie de Saint Louis*: "He bothered everyone else with the length of the service" (37).

74. Guillaume de Chartres, *De Vita et de Miraculis,* 24.

75. Guillaume de Saint-Pathus, *Vie de Saint Louis,* 42–44.

76. Joinville, *Histoire de Saint Louis,* 33.

77. See above, "The Meeting with Hugh of Digne," in Part I, ch. 4.

78. See below, "The King and His Intellectuals," in Part III, ch. 2.

79. "*Roman*" means "work written in the Romance language," in other words in French.

80. B. Guenée, *Histoire et culture historique dans l'Occident médiéval*; "Les Grandes Chroniques de France. Le Roman aux roys (1274–1518)," in *Les Lieux de mémoire,* ed. P. Nora, vol. 2, *La Nation* (Paris, 1986), 1:189–214; G. M. Spiegel, *The Chronicle Tradition of Saint Denis.* On Primat, also see above, "Primat," in Part II, ch. 3.

81. Serge Lusignan, "Le temps de l'homme au temps de monseigneur Saint Louis: le *Speculum historiale* et les *Grandes Chroniques de France,*" in *Vincent de Beauvais. Intentions et receptions d'une oeuvre encyclopédique au Moyen Âge,* ed. Serge Lusignan, Monique Paulmier-Foucart, and Alain Nadeau (Saint Laurent and Paris, 1990), 495–505.

82. "*Quod vir praeterita debet recolere et presentia attendere,*" ch. 40; "*Quodliter eciam futura debet providere,*" ch. 41 (*De eruditione,* ed. A. Steiner, 159–66, 166–72).

83. C. Kappler, *Vincent de Beauvais,* 238.

PART III
Notes to Chapter 2

1. See later in this chapter, "The New Solomon," and in Part III, ch. 8, "Political Criticisms."

2. Several groups of musicians and scholars have made outstanding progress in advancing our knowledge of musical manuscripts of the Middle Ages and their interpretation. I can cite the group Organum under the leadership of Marcel Perès at the center in Royaumont, a place imbued with Saint Louis' memory. See Mark Everist, *Polyphonic Music in XIIIth-Century France. Aspects of Sources and Distribution* (New York and London, 1989).

3. Jacques Chailley, *Histoire musicale du Moyen Âge,* 3rd ed. (1984); see esp. ch. 12, "Le primat de l'Île-de-France: fin XIIe–début XIIIe siècle" and ch. 13, "Le Grand Siècle: siècle de Saint Louis."

4. Claudine Billot, "Les saintes chapelles de Saint Louis," in *Les Capétiens et Vincennes au Moyen Âge,* colloquium, 1994, acts forthcoming.

5. Guillaume de Saint-Pathus, *Vie de Saint Louis,* 33.

6. Robert Branner, "The Sainte-Chapelle and the *Capella Regis* in the XIIIth Century," *Gesta* 10, no. 1 (1971): 19–22.

7. Guillaume de Saint-Pathus, *Vie de Saint Louis,* 19.

8. Joinville, *Histoire de Saint Louis,* 369.

9. R. Branner, "The Sainte-Chapelle and the *Capella Regis.*"

10. Joinville, *Histoire de Saint Louis,* 407.

11. Robert Branner, *Saint Louis and the Court Style in Gothic Architecture* (London, 1965), xv.

12. Matthew Paris, *Chronica,* 480.

13. See above, "The Sainte-Chapelle," in Part I, ch. 2.

14. See above, "The Franco-English Peace," in Part I, ch. 4, and "Matthew Paris," in Part II, ch. 7.

15. R. Branner, *Saint Louis and the Court Style in Gothic Architecture,* 12.

16. Donna L. Sadler, "The King as Subject, the King as Author. Art and Politics of Louis IX" (1990). I thank Donna Sadler for sharing this text with me. She has just published another study on the relations between the king and the sculptures of Notre-Dame of Villeneuve-l'Archevêque where Saint Louis went to receive the relics of the Passion, "Courting Louis IX in the Sculptural Program of Villeneuve-l'Archevêque," *Majestas* 2 (1994): 3–16.

17. J. Le Goff, "Reims, ville du sacre," 127, taken from D. Sadler's paper presented at the Toronto colloquium on royal crowning ceremonies in the Middle Ages

and the Renaissance, which was not published in the Acts of the Congress, *Coronations, Medieval and Early Modern Monarchic Ritual,* ed. Janos M. Bak (Berkeley: University of California Press, 1990).

18. See below, "The Children," in Part III, ch. 6.

19. Françoise Perrot has given this interpretation new meaning by finding a royal program in the stained-glass works of the Sainte-Chapelle in J.-M. Leniaud and Fr. Perrot, *La Sainte-Chapelle.*

20. See above, "Saint Louis and the Royal Bodies," in Part I, ch. 4.

21. See below, "His Religious Knowledge," in Part III, ch. 7; Günter Haseloff, "Die Psalterillustration," in *13.Jahrhundert. Studien zur Geschichte der Buchmalerei in England, Frankreich und den Niederlanden* (Florence, 1938); Victor Leroquais, *Les Psautiers manuscrits latins des bibliothèques publiques de France,* in 2 vols., with one album (Mâcon, 1940–1941).

22. See J. Krynen, *L'Empire du roi.*

23. Florens Deuchler, *Der Ingeborg Psalter* (Berlin, 1967); François Avril, "Der Ingeborg Psalter," *Bulletin monumental* (1969): 58–60; Louis Grodecki, "Le psautier de la reine Ingeburg et ses problèmes."

24. This manuscript is preserved at Cambridge (Fitzwilliam 300) and is usually designated by the name "Isabelle's Psalter" [*le Psautier d'Isabelle*] because it is not exactly a Book of Hours.

25. R. Branner, *Manuscript Painting in Paris during the Reign of Saint Louis.*

26. Paris, Bibliothèque de l'Arsenal, MS 1186.

27. V. Leroquais, *Les Psautiers manuscrits latins,* 2:16.

28. See above, "The Good Use of Time," in Part II, ch. 1.

29. Robert Branner, "Saint Louis et l'enluminure parisienne au XIIIᵉ siècle," in *Septième centenaire de la mort de Saint Louis,* Acts of the colloquium of Royaumont and Paris, May 1970 (Paris, 1976), 69–84.

30. Leyden University Library, MS BPL (76A).

31. Here we find the close attention Saint Louis paid to dynastic anniversaries. See below, "His Household and Entourage," in Part III, ch. 6.

32. Catalogue for the exposition "Saint Louis" at the Sainte-Chapelle (May-August 1960), 95. Harvey Stahl's book that will include an exhaustive study of this Psalter is still forthcoming at this moment, and promises to be of great interest. In the meantime, see Arthur Haselhoff, "Les Psautiers de Saint Louis," *Mémoires de la Société des antiquaires de France,* vol. 59, bk. 1 (1898): 18–42; H. Omont, *Le Psautier de Saint Louis* (Graz, 1972); William C. Jordan, "The Psalter of Saint Louis. The Program of the 78 full-page Illustrations," *Acta. The High Middle Ages* 7 (1980): 65–91. A facsimile of Saint Louis' Psalter (Paris, Bibliothèque nationale, MS Latin 10525) has been published by the Akademische Druk und Verlagsanstalt (Graz, 1972).

33. Harvey Stahl, "Old Testament Illustration during the Reign of Saint Louis: The Morgan Picture Book and the New Biblical Cycle," in *Il Medio oriente e l'Occidente nell'Arte del XIII secolo,* ed. Hans Belting, Atti del XXIV Congresso Internazionale di storia dell'Arte, 1979 (Bologna, 1982), 85–86.

34. Gérard de Frachet, *Vitae Fratrum ordinis Praedicatorum necnon Cronica ordonis ab anno MCCIII usque ad MCCLIV* (Louvain, 1896).

35. Jean-Claude Bonne and I presented and commented on these miniatures at the colloquium on coronations in Toronto in 1985. The proceedings of this colloquium have been published by Janos M. Bak in *Coronations*: J. Le Goff, "A Coronation Program for the Age of Saint Louis," 46–57; J.-C. Bonne, "The Manuscript of the *Ordo* of 1250 and its Illuminations," 58–71. We plan to publish this manuscript in its entirety with its illustrations and commentary and in collaboration with Eric Palazzo for the liturgical section.

36. This is also the context that Philippe Buc identifies with a "moralized Bible," in other words a Bible loaded with commentaries and glosses that was produced in the second quarter of the thirteenth century and offered to Saint Louis. Today it is kept in three parts in Paris (Bibliothèque nationale, MS 11560), Oxford (Bodleian 270 B), and London (British Museum, Harley 1526 and 1527). Some of these miniatures presented Saint Louis with images of biblical royalty based on the interpretations of the thirteenth-century glossators. See Philippe Buc, *L'Ambiguïté du livre,* 189.

37. Cf. below, "The Coronation System," in Part III, ch. 9.

38. Palémon Glorieux, *Aux origines de la Sorbonne,* vol. 1, *Robert de Sorbon* (Paris, 1966); Nicole Bériou, "Robert de Sorbon," in the *Dictionnaire de spiritualité* 13 (Paris, 1988), 816–24; "Robert de Sorbon. Le prud'homme et le béguin," *Comptes rendus de l'Académie des inscriptions et belles-lettres* (April-June 1994): 469–510; A.L. Gabriel, "Robert de Sorbon at the University of Paris," *The American Ecclesiastical Review* 134 (1956): 73–86.

39. See above, "The Stories of the Minstrel of Reims," in Part II, ch. 4, and "The Limits of Royal Power," in Part III, ch. 5.

40. The good canon was not always very gentle with his religion. Here is the summary of Robert's short treatise on conscience (*De conscientia*) as given by his scholarly editor, Félix Chambon (who was a librarian at the Sorbonne), in 1902: "The subject of this treatise is the Last Judgment, which the author compares to the examination for *la licence* [a university degree]; the chancellor is God, the angels are his assessors, but the heavenly examination is more detailed than the university exam because if anyone fails to answer a question on the celestial exam, even a single one, he is immediately rejected and condemned to hell, not for one year like the people who fail the scholarly exams, but for all eternity. It is therefore of the utmost importance to know the book on which we will be examined, the book of conscience." Robert had no knowledge of Purgatory, whereas Saint Louis believed in it. See Robert de Sorbon, *De conscientia,* ed. F. Chambon (Paris, 1902).

41. Serge Lusignan, *Préface au "Speculum maius" de Vincent de Beauvais, refraction et diffraction* (Montreal and Paris, 1979); *Vincent de Beauvais.* The workshop on Vincent de Beauvais organized by M. Paulmier-Foucart under the leadership of J. Schneider in Nancy is pursuing important research and publishing the specialized journal, *Spicae.* The research workshop on medieval texts in Nancy, the Royaumont foundation, and

the University of Montreal organized a round table on "Vincent de Beauvais, frère Prêcheur: un dominicain et son milieu intellectuel" in June 1995.

42. J. Le Goff, "Pourquoi le XIIIᵉ siècle est-il un grand siècle encyclopédique?" in *L'enciclopedismo medievale,* ed. M. Picone (Ravenna, 1994), 23–40.

43. From the abundant bibliography on the twelfth century and what is often referred to as the twelfth-century Renaissance, I refer my readers to the important book by Père Chenu, *La Théologie du XIIᵉ siècle.* This is a work that exceeds its title, or, rather, that explores all of its possible dimensions with profound historical intelligence.

44. Cf. below, Part III, ch. 4.

45. On the meaning of the "mirror" or "*speculum,*" see Einar Mar Jonsson, "Le sens du titre *Speculum* aux XIIᵉ et XIIIᵉ siècles et son utilisation par Vincent de Beauvais," in *Vincent de Beauvais,* 11–32.

46. On the collective works that were carried out by the thirteenth-century Dominicans in particular, see Yves Congar, "*In dulcedine societatis quarere veritatem.* Notes sur le travail en équipe chez S. Albert et chez les Prêcheurs au XIIIᵉ siècle," in *Albertus Magnus Doctor Universalis* 1280–1980, ed. G. Mayer and A. Zimmerman (Mainz, 1980).

47. S. Lusignan, *Préface au "Speculum maius,"* 57.

48. Guillaume de Saint-Pathus, *Vie de Saint Louis,* 79.

49. *Le "Speculum doctrinal," livre III. Études de la logique dans le Miroir des sciences de Vincent de Beauvais,* Doctoral thesis, University of Montreal, 1971.

50. J. Hamesse, "Le dossier Aristote dans l'oeuvre de Vincent de Beauvais. À propos de l'*Éthique,*" in *Vincent de Beauvais,* 197–218.

51. Ibid., 213–15.

52. Ibid., 216.

53. See above, "Births and Deaths," in Part I, ch. 4, and Peter von Moos, "Die Trotschrift des Vincenz von Beauvais für Ludwig IX."

54. See above, "John of Salisbury's *Policraticus,*" in Part II, ch. 6.

55. Robert J. Schneider has conducted remarkable research on this document. In his estimation, this would not have been a true synthesis of political doctrine, but a group of four juxtaposed treatises of which Vincent was only able to write the first two aforementioned Mirrors. According to Schneider, this work and these treatises were not supposed to compose a survey and were to remain faithful to the principle of compilation, and yet Vincent was planning to complete a personal work and would have used it to reach "his maturity as a scholar and a thinker." In my opinion, Schneider only embellishes a little on reality. Vincent de Beauvais would have remained faithful to the Cistercian Hélinand de Froidmont whose *De constituendo rege* he had already inserted into his *Speculum historiale* under the title *De bono regimine principis.* The part of the work that was completed leads us to this conclusion. *L'Opus universale* would have already been an outmoded work in its own time, falling between the two great innovative political treatises of the central Middle Ages: John of Salisbury's *Policraticus* (1159) written in Chartres, and Gille de Rome's *De regimine principum* written in 1280

for the future Philip the Fair. See Robert J. Schneider, "Vincent of Beauvais, *Opus universale de statu principis*: A Reconstruction of its History and Contents," in *Vincent de Beauvais*, 285–99. Michel Senellart (*Les Arts de gouverner. Du regimen médiéval au concept de gouvernement* [Paris, 1995], 147) has adopted my hypothesis about Saint Louis' project "of founding an academy with the mission of formulating a vast political survey" ("Portrait du roi idéal," *L'Histoire*, no. 81 [September 1985]: 72–73).

56. Marie-Christine Duchenne, "Autour de 1254, une révision capétienne du *Speculum historiale*," in *Vincent de Beauvais*, 141–66.

57. Le Nain de Tillemont (5:337), incapable of citing any written source, is reduced to declaring, "I have heard it said that Saint Thomas, while eating once at Saint Louis' table, sat for some time without speaking and then suddenly cried out, 'I have convinced the Manicheans,' which Saint Louis enjoyed very much."

58. The publication and study of sermons have been the object of some excellent works. For the thirteenth century I only mention the works of Nicole Bériou, *La Prédication de Ranulphe de la Houblonnière*, and David d'Avray, *The Preaching of the Friars*.

59. See above, "The English Benedictine, Matthew Paris," in Part II, ch. 7.

60. *Le Dit de Maître Guillaume de Saint-Amour* and *La Complainte de Maître Guillaume*, in Rutebeuf, *Oeuvres complètes*, ed. M. Zink (Paris, 1989), 1:137–57.

61. P. Glorieux, *Aux origines de la Sorbonne*, vol. 2, *Le cartulaire* (Paris, 1965).

62. See P. Buc, *L'Ambiguïté du livre*, 176.

PART III
Notes to Chapter 3

1. Michael T. Clanchy, *From Memory to Written Record*. On the advances and results of cultural practices tied to writing, see Brian Stock, *The Implications of Literacy: Written Language and Models of Interpretation in the XIth and XIIth Centuries* (Princeton, 1983).

2. J.W. Baldwin, *Philippe Auguste*.

3. Jean Destrez, *La Pecia dans les manuscrits universitaires des XIIIᵉ et XIVᵉ siècles* (Paris, 1935). This is an old but groundbreaking work.

4. I refer my readers to the classic articles of Henri Pirenne, "L'instruction des marchands au Moyen Âge," *Annales d'histoire économique et sociale* 1 (1929): 13–28, and Armando Sapori, "La cultura del mercante medievale italiano," *Rivista di storia economica* 2 (1937): 89–125, reprinted in *Studi di storia economica, sec. XIII–XV*, vol. 1 (Florence, 1985), 53–93.

5. Four important works of customary law were written in thirteenth-century France: *Le Conseil à un ami* by the bailiff of Vermandois, Pierre de Fontaines (written prior to 1258); *Jostice et Plait* (written between 1255 and 1260); the *Établissements de Saint Louis* (written at some time shortly before 1273); and the *Coutumes de Beauvaisis* by Philippe de Beaumanoir (1283). Cf. P. Ourliac and J.-L. Gazzaniga, *Histoire du droit privé*, 99.

6. J. Le Goff and J.-C. Schmitt, "Au XIIIe siècle: une parole nouvelle." For a philosophical and linguistic perspective, see Irène Rosier, *La Parole comme acte. Sur la grammaire et la sémantique au XIIIe siècle* (Paris, 1994).

7. D. L. D'Avray, *The Preaching of the Friars.*

8. P. Saenger, "Silent Reading."

9. Paul Zumthor presented another trailblazing work with his *Essai de poétique médiévale* (Paris, 1972), 405–28. Here he explains how this new discourse arose within "a universe of speech, often tongue-tied in an incoherent knot around several types of clerical origin, and which discovers a principle of organization in the 'lyrical' *dit* that takes shape around and about a "me" and a "you" that are fictitiously identified with the poet and his public." [The "dit" is a dialogical genre of French medieval lyric poetry.—Trans.]

10. Ibid., 419; J. Le Goff, "Saint Louis et la parole royale."

11. Émile Benveniste, *Le Vocabulaire des institutions indo-européennes,* vol. 2 (Paris, 1969), 42.

12. Ibid., 35.

13. Helgaud de Fleury, *Vie de Robert le Pieux,* 60.

14. Henry-François Delaborde, ed., *Oeuvres de Rigord et de Guillaume le Breton, historiens de Philippe Auguste,* vol. 1 (Paris, 1882), 31.

15. B. Cerquiglini, *La Parole médiévale. Discours, syntaxe, texte* (Paris, 1981), 247. On the importance of the fact that the sources present us with a French-speaking Saint Louis, see above, Part II, ch. 10. For an in-depth study of the relations between a thirteenth-century saint and the languages he spoke, see I. Baldelli, "La 'Parola' di Francesco e le nuove lingue d'Europa," in *Francesco, il francescanesimo e la cultura della nuova Europa,* ed. I. Baldelli and A. M. Romanini (Rome, 1986), 13–35.

16. On the evolution of the concept of sainthood in the thirteenth century, see A. Vauchez, *La Sainteté en Occident.* On the formation of a "reality principle" at the end of the thirteenth century, see Roland Recht, "Le portrait et le principe de réalité dans la sculpture."

17. The miracles attributed to Saint Louis are all posthumous and are all traditional, "ordinary" miracles: Sarah Chennaf and Odile Redon, "Les miracles de Saint Louis" in *Les Miracles, miroirs des corps,* ed. Jacques Gelis and Odile Redon (Paris, 1983), 53–85; Jacques Le Goff, "Saint de l'Église et saint du peuple: les miracles officiels de Saint Louis entre sa mort et sa canonization," in *Histoire sociale, sensibilités collectives et mentalités,* Mélanges R. Mandrou (Paris, 1985), 169–80. Also, see below, Part III, ch. 9.

18. On the relations between Joinville and Saint Louis, Michel Zink, "Joinville ne pleure pas," and *La Subjectivité littéraire,* 219–39.

19. D. O'Connell, *Les Propos de Saint Louis,* 30.

20. Idem, *The Teachings of Saint Louis.*

21. Joinville, *Histoire de Saint Louis,* 3468–69. See below, "His Household and Entourage," in Part III, ch. 6.

22. Guillaume de Saint-Pathus, *Vie de Saint Louis,* 123.

23. Joinville, *Histoire de Saint Louis,* 14–15.

24. Ibid., 380–81.

25. L. K. Little, "Saint Louis' Involvement with the Friars."

26. Joinville, *Histoire de Saint Louis,* 10–11.

27. Ibid., 24–25.

28. Ibid., 22–23.

29. Guillaume de Saint-Pathus noted Saint Louis' habitual use of the *"vous"* form: "and he always spoke to each person in the plural" (*Vie de Saint Louis,* 19).

30. I refer readers to the translation of the "original" text discovered by David O'Connell in the French manuscripts 12814 and 25462 of the Bibliothèque nationale in Paris (*Les Propos de Saint Louis,* 183–94).

31. See the preceding chapter.

32. Joinville, *Histoire de Saint Louis,* 16–19.

33. C. Brémont, J. Le Goff, and J.-C. Schmitt, *L'"Exemplum"*; "Prêcher d'exemples. Récits de prédicateurs du Moyen Âge," presented by Jean-Claude Schmitt, Paris, 1984. See above, Part II, ch. 4.

34. Joinville, *Histoire de Saint Louis,* 364–65.

35. Ibid., 34–35.

36. Ibid.

37. Ibid., 376–77.

38. On the devotional prayer of Saint Louis, see below, "Saint Louis and Prayer," in Part III, ch. 7.

39. Joinville, *Histoire de Saint Louis,* 33.

40. D. O'Connell, *Les Propos de Saint Louis,* 186.

41. Ibid., 187.

42. Ibid., 187, 193.

43. C. Casagrande and S. Vecchio, *Les Péchés de la langue.*

44. Joinville, *Histoire de Saint Louis,* 12–13, 378–79.

45. Ibid., 378–79. Joinville also notes: "I had been in his company for twenty-two years without ever hearing him swear in the name of God, his Mother, or the saints; and when he wanted to exclaim something, he would say, 'truly, it was so,' or, 'truly it is so.'" On the Parisian bourgeois' punishment for blaspheming, see above, "The Uncompromising Dispenser of Justice," in Part I, ch. 4. On the story of the jeweler who was punished in Caesaria, see below, "The First Function," in Part III, ch. 4.

46. J. Richard, *Saint Louis,* 286–87.

47. On "speech" [*parole*]" and "voice" [*voix*], see the two fabulous books by Paul Zumthor, *Introduction à la poésie orale* (Paris, 1983), and *La Poésie et la Voix dans la civilisation médiévale* (Paris, 1984).

48. Joinville, *Histoire de Saint Louis,* 18–19. See above, "The *Enseignements* for His Son and Daughter," Part II, ch. 6, and below, "The Values of the Body," in Part III, ch. 10.

49. Joinville, *Histoire de Saint Louis,* 12–13.

50. Guillaume de Saint-Pathus, *Vie de Saint Louis,* 154–55.

51. On the role of gestures in the feudal system, see J.-C. Schmitt, *La Raison des gestes dans l'Occident médiéval*; Jacques Le Goff, "Le rituel symbolique de la vassalité," (Spoleto, 1976), reprinted in *Pour un autre Moyen Âge*, 349–420.

52. Hugh of Saint Victor, *De institutione novitiorum* in *Patrologie latine,* vol. 176, col. 925–52, ch. 12: "*De disciplina servanda in gestu*"; ch. 18: "*De disciplina in mensa et primo in habitu et gestu.*"

53. Bonaventure, *Regula nov itiorum,* in *Opera omnia,* vol. 12 (Paris, 1968), 313–25; Humbert de Romans, *De officiis ordonis,* cf. 5: "De officio magistri noviciorum," in B. Humbert de Romans, *Opera,* ed. J. Berthier (Rome, 1888), 2:213; Guibert de Tournai, *Sermones ad status* (Lyon, 1511): "*Ad virgines et puellas sermo primus,*" fol. cxlvi.

54. "*De vita et actibus . . . regis Francorum Ludovici auctore fratre Gullelmo Carnotensi,*" in *Recueil des historiens des Gaules et de la France* 20:29. See below, ch. 6.

55. On the gestures that the kings of France used to heal the scrofulous, cf. M. Bloch, *Les Rois thaumaturges,* passim and 90 ff. See also, the Geoffroy de Beaulieu's testimony in ch. 35 of his *Vita*: "*quod in tangendo infirmos signum sanctae crucis super addidit,*" 20. In fact, Robert the Pious already used the sign of the cross. Cf. Guillaume de Saint-Pathus, *Vie de Saint Louis*: "*il fesoit apeler ses malades ses escroeles et les touchoit*" (he would call his sick people scrofulous and touch them), 99, and, "*il avoit touché ses malades du mal des escroeles*" (he had touched his sick people who were suffering from the disease of the scrofulous), 142.

56. This is Henri Martin's idea. Henri Martin, "Les enseignements des miniatures. Attitude royale," *Gazette des beaux-arts* (March 1913): 174. This was an outstanding, groundbreaking article for its time.

57. See above, "Books of Images," in Part III, ch. 2.

58. See below, "The Royal Coronation," in Part III, ch. 9.

59. Geoffroy de Beaulieu, *Vita,* 6.

60. Joinville, *Histoire de Saint Louis,* 89–91. See above, "The Stories of the Minstrel of Reims," in Part II, ch. 4.

61. On Saint Louis' eating habits and the tensions revealed by them, see the following section in this chapter, "Saint Louis at the Table."

62. On the signs of respect Saint Louis expressed for the clerics, see Guillaume de Saint-Pathus, *Vie de Saint Louis,* 50–51, 53–54.

63. On the disturbances caused by horseback riding in Saint Louis' devotional practices, see ibid., 34–35, and above, "The Good Use of Time,"in Part III, ch. 1, and below, "The Gestures of Religious Devotion," Part III, ch. 3, and "Saint Louis and Prayer," in Part III, ch. 7.

64. On the extreme case of the deceased souls in Purgatory who cannot acquire any more merits and who are therefore exposed to purifying and expiatory punishments and whose gestures are passive, see J. Le Goff, "Les gestes du Purgatoire," in *Mélanges offerts à Maurice de Gandillac* (Paris, 1985), 457–64.

65. The biographers repeatedly relate the episode when Blanche of Castile reportedly told her son that she would rather see him dead than guilty of a mortal sin

(Guillaume de Saint-Pathus, *Vie de Saint Louis,* 13) or that she would rather see the Kingdom of France governed by a Scotsman than her son turn out to be a bad king (Joinville, *Histoire de Saint Louis,* ed. Corbett, 86–87.)

66. "The aforesaid master would sometimes beat him for disciplinary reasons" (Guillaume de Saint-Pathus, *Vie de Saint Louis,* 18).

67. For example, "of his devotion to the body of Our Lord he received" (ibid., 39). Joinville thought that Saint Louis' conduct on his first crusade was already a case worthy of martyrdom—"and I think that they did not do him justice when they failed to place him in the ranks of the martyrs for the great pains he suffered on the pilgrimage of the crusade during the six years that I was in his company" (ed. Corbett, 84. Guillaume de Chartres writes, "After the end of the battle, the running of the race, the glorious leadership of the government, the King had to go to the heavenly kingdom to receive the prize for all his pains, the martyr's unrivaled crown" (*De Vita et de Miraculis,* 36).

68. Guillaume de Saint-Pathus, *Vie de Saint Louis,* 18–19.

69. I have studied the image of Saint Louis that Joinville conveys in Part II, ch. 9. Cf. Maureen Durlay Slattery, "Joinville's Portrait of a King," Doctoral thesis at the Institute for Medieval Studies, University of Montreal, 1971.

70. Guillaume de Saint-Pathus, *Vie de Saint Louis,* 153–55.

71. Here I am only dealing with the gestures mentioned in the longest of the twenty chapters in this *Life,* the sixth one dedicated to Louis IX's "fervent devotion." It takes up twenty of the 143 pages of the Delaborde edition, not counting the thirteen-page introduction.

72. Guillaume de Saint-Pathus, *Vie de Saint Louis,* 32–52.

73. Ibid., 38–39.

74. Ibid., 39.

75. Ibid., 40.

76. Ibid., 42.

77. Ibid., 50.

78. Ibid., 51.

79. Ibid.

80. On the heretic's gestures, cf. Jean-Claude Schmitt, "*Gestus, gesticulatio.* Contribution à l'étude du vocabulaire latin médiéval des gestes," in *La Lexicographie du latin médiéval et ses rapports avec les recherches actuelles sur la civilisation du Moyen Âge* (Paris, 1981), 386 and n. 45; Emmanuel Le Roy Ladurie, *Montaillou, village Occitan de 1294 à 1324* (Paris, 1975), "Le geste et le sexe," 200–19.

81. "*Et sicut nos in parte vidimus et per probata audivimus et scimus, vita ejus non fuit solum vita hominis, sed super hominem*" (*Recueil des historiens des Gaules et de la France,* 23:149); "*Et hoc possumus secure asserere quod facies sua benigna et piena gratiarum docebat eum esse supra hominem*" (ibid., 153). Up until now, people had supposed that these expressions were unique in medieval literature. In fact, J.-C. Schmitt has brought it to my attention that in *La Légende dorée* (ed. Graesse, 449), Jacques de Voraigne uses the following phrase to describe Germain d'Auxerre: "*super hominem siquidem fuit omne, quod gessit.*"

This expression cannot be found in the original life of Guillaume d'Auxerre written by Constance de Lyon in the fifth century.

The expression *super hominem* then seems to belong to the vocabulary of the hagiography of the central Middle Ages, applied to saints who carried out certain kinds of miracles. However, Dante uses a similar expression to describe the twelfth-century mystic Richard de Saint-Victor, whom he said was, "more than a man [*più che viro*] when he entered a state of contemplation" (*Divine Comedy, Paradise,* X, v. 132). This encourages us to extend the idea beyond the realm of sainthood. Brother B. Beguin pointed out to me that the expression was used in the early Franciscan literature in regard to Saint Francis and the Friars Minor.

82. Guillaume de Saint-Pathus, *Vie de Saint Louis,* 133.

83. Ibid., 79–80.

84. Joinville, *Histoire de Saint Louis,* 172. I remind my readers of M. Zink's interpretation of this episode in his article, "Joinville ne pleure pas."

85. *"Sedebat enim quasi continue in terra super lectum"* (*Recueil des historiens des Gaules et de la France,* 23:149).

86. A fragment from this chronicle contained in French MS 4691 of the Bibliothèque nationale in Paris has been published in the *Recueil des historiens des Gaules et de la France,* 23:146.

87. Joinville, *Histoire de Saint Louis,* 115–16, 200. On the definition of the *prud'-homme* and the evolution of the notion that gradually supplants *sage* [wise] in the thirteenth century, cf. C. Brucker, *Sage et sagesse au Moyen Âge (XIIᵉ et XIIIᵉ siècles)* (Geneva, 1987).

88. Minstrel of Reims, 126.

89. Joinville, *Histoire de Saint Louis,* 16–19.

90. In his *credo,* Joinville describes the strands of honey that Samson tore from the lion's mouth: "the saints and the *prud'hommes* that God freed from Hell are signified by the strands that are sweet and profitable" (427).

91. Ibid., 217. I would like to thank Nicole Bériou for showing me the text of an unpublished sermon by Robert de Sorbon along with its very interesting commentary, "Robert de Sorbon, le prud'homme et le béguin."

92. Ibid., 20–23. This characteristic modesty in dress was also attributed to Philip Augustus and Louis VIII. It is still a commonplace idea about royalty. See Le Nain de Tillemont, *Vie de Saint Louis,* 3:178–79.

93. J. Le Goff, "Saint Louis à table: entre commensalité royale et humilité alimentaire," in *La Sociabilité à table. Commensalité et convivialité à travers les âges,* Actes du colloque de Rouen, 1990 (Rouen, 1992), 132–44.

94. Translated from Geoffroy de Beaulieu, *Vita,* 10–11. [This is my translation into English of Le Goff's translation into modern French.—Trans.]

95. See above, "Guillaume de Saint-Pathus," in Part III, ch. 2.

96. Guillaume de Saint-Pathus, 64. We can see Saint Louis' dietary concern for the health of the poor here, both in terms of bodily health and the health of the soul.

97. See the preceding section in this chapter, "Models and Personality."

98. Guillaume de Saint-Pathus, 79–80.

99. Ibid., 81. He observed the same charitable rite of feeding the poor overseas.

100. Ibid., 85–86. In the Dominican convent of Compiègne, he would also often go into the kitchen to order the food for the convent and would attend the meals that he brought from his own kitchen in the friars' refectory.

101. Ibid., 98–99.

102. Ibid., 105. The author highlights the fact that by doing this the king behaved as a "truly humble man," and saw "Our Lord Jesus Christ" himself in the poor man who ate his leftovers.

103. Ibid., 107.

104. Ibid., 109.

105. A certain dietary standard had been upheld during Saint Louis' month of captivity in the hands of the Muslims in Egypt. The only one of the king's servants to have avoided any disease was named Ysambart, and he cooked for the king when he was sick and prepared him bread made with meat and flour that he brought from the sultan's court.

106. Guillaume de Saint-Pathus, *Vie de Saint Louis,* 111. See also, Joinville, *Histoire de Saint Louis,* 367–69, and above, "The Return of a Grief-Stricken Crusader," in Part I, ch. 4.

107. This golden cup became a sort of relic within the royal family. In the inventory of the objects that belonged to Louis X taken after his death, we can read: "Item. The golden cup of Saint Louis that no one ever drinks from," in Delaborde, 120 n. 1.

108. Guillaume de Saint-Pathus, 119–22.

109. Joinville, *Vie de Saint Louis,* 13.

110. During the crusade, Joinville notes that in contrast to the king, "the barons who should have kept theirs [their wealth, their money] in order to make good use of it at the right time and in the right place, enjoyed giving great meals with an excess of meats" (95).

111. See above, "The 'Chivalry' of Brothers," in Part I, ch. 2.

112. Joinville, *Vie de Saint Louis,* 381.

113. Ibid., 367–69. See above, "The Return of a Grief-Stricken Crusader," in Part I, ch. 4.

114. Joinville, *Histoire de Saint Louis,* 369. See above, "Architecture: A Court Style?" in Part III, ch. 2.

115. Salimbene de Adam, *Cronica,* 1:318.

116. Ibid., 319.

117. Ibid., 321–22.

118. Ibid., 322. See above, "Salimbene of Parma," in Part II, ch. 7.

119. *Ad piscem*—a day without meat.

120. Matthew Paris, *Chronica majora,* 5:480–81.

121. "The 'Karolinus' of Egidius Parisiensis," ed. M. L. Colker, *Traditio* 29 (1973): 290, Book IV, v. 11–20++.

122. Éginhard, *Vita Caroli Imperatoris,* ed. Claudio Leonardi, 24:100.

PART III
Notes to Chapter 4

1. Georges Dumézil, *L'Idéologie tripartite des Indo-Européens* (Brussels, 1958). The final elaboration of the thesis appears in "À propos des trois orders," in *Apollon sonore et autres essais: vingt-cinq esquisses de mythologie* (Paris, 1982), 205–59; Jean Batany, "Des 'trois fonctions' aux 'trois états'," *Annales, E.S.C.* (1963): 933–38; J. Le Goff, *La Civilisation de l'Occident médiéval,* 290–95; idem, "Note sur société tripartite, idéologie monarchique et renouveau économique dans la Chrétienté du IXe au XIIe siècle" (1965), reprinted in *Pour un autre Moyen Âge,* 80–90. On the tri-functional ideology: Michel Rouche, "De l'Orient à l'Occident. Les origines de la tripartition fonctionnelle et les causes de son adoption par l'Europe chrétienne à la fin du Xe siècle," in *Occident et Orient au Xe siècle* (Paris, 1979), 321–55; Otto Gerhard Oexle, "Deutungsschemata der sozialen Wirklichkeit im frühen und hohen Mittelalter. Ein Beitrag zur Geschichte des Wissens," in *Mentalitäten im Mittelalter,* ed. Frantisek Graus (Sigmaringen, 1987), 65–117.

2. Adalbéron de Laon, *Poème au roi Robert,* trans. and ed. with introduction by Claude Carozzi (Paris, 1979).

3. Georges Duby, *Les Trois Ordres ou l'imaginaire du féodalisme* (Paris, 1974); J. Le Goff, "Les trois functions indo-européennes, l'historien et l'Europe féodale," *Annales, E.S.C.* (1979): 1184–1215.

4. See J. Le Goff, "Note sur société tripartite," 642; Daniel Dubuisson, "Le roi indo-européen et la synthèse des trois functions," *Annales, E.S.C.* (1978): 21–34.

5. Boniface VIII, 159.

6. On the coronation ceremony, see below, "The Royal Coronation," in Part III, ch. 9.

7. See the remarkable book by Ludwig Buisson, *Ludwig IX, der Heilige, und das Recht* (Freiburg, 1954), ch. 3, "Der König und die iustitia," 87–130.

8. Boniface VIII, 149.

9. Ibid., 154.

10. See above "The Meeting with Hugh of Digne," in Part I, ch. 4.

11. Joinville, *Histoire de Saint Louis,* 363.

12. Ibid., 277–83.

13. Guillaume de Saint-Pathus, *Vie de Saint Louis,* 118–19. See below, "'You Are Only the King of the Friars'," in Part III, ch. 8

14. Guillaume de Saint-Pathus, *Vie de Saint Louis,* 151–52.

15. For the context, see above, "The Uncompromising Dispenser of Justice," in Part I, ch. 4, and "Words of Faith," in Part III, ch. 3.

16. Guillaume de Saint-Pathus, *Vie de Saint Louis,* 135. See above "The Uncompromising Dispenser of Justice," for my detailed account of this sensational exemplary event that caused such a stir.

17. On the opposition between the hierarchical tendency and the egalitarian tendency in the thirteenth century, see P. Buc, *L'Ambiguïté du livre.*

18. J. Le Goff, "Millénarisme."

19. See L. Buisson, *Ludwig IX*, ch. 5, "Der König und der Fried," 183–248.

20. See below, "The Royal Coronation," in Part III, ch. 9, and L. Buisson, *Ludwig IX*, 131.

21. Boniface VIII, 149.

22. *Enseignements*, ed. D. O'Connell, 189.

23. Ibid., 189.

24. Guillaume de Saint-Pathus, *Vie de Saint Louis*, 73–74.

25. Joinville, *Histoire de Saint Louis*, 375–77.

26. Ibid., 377–79.

27. J. Le Goff, "Du ciel sur la terre: la mutation des valeurs." See my critique of what some have called "secularization" understood as a collaboration of the earth with heaven in the conduct of the world's affairs. This gives us hierarchy and partnership, and the central Middle Ages drew significant advantages from these egalitarian practices existing within a non-egalitarian structure. On the case of feudal relations of vassalage: J. Le Goff, "Le rituel symbolique de la vassalité."

28. See above, "The Peace with Aragon," in Part I, ch. 4.

29. Guillaume de Nangis, *Gesta Ludovici IX*, 400.

30. Boniface VIII, 152–53. In his *Louis VII* (347), Yves Sassier also applies the expression *rex pacificus* to Saint Louis' great-grandfather, although it was only with Saint Louis that this royal commonplace took on an explicitly eschatological meaning.

31. The Minstrel of Reims, 126.

32. C. T. Wood, "The Mise of Amiens and Saint Louis' Theory of Kingship."

33. See above, "The Conquering King," in Part I, ch. 2.

34. Joinville, *Histoire de Saint Louis*, 59.

35. See above, "The Voyage and the Campaign in Egypt," in Part I, ch. 3.

36. See P. Contamine, *La Guerre au Moyen Âge*.

37. See above, "The Voyage and the Campaign in Egypt," in Part I, ch. 3.

38. Matthew Paris, *Chronica majora*, 5:626, 636.

39. Joinville, *Histoire de Saint Louis*. See above, "The 'Chivalry' of Brothers," in Part I, ch. 2.

40. J. Le Goff, "Le dossier de sainteté de Philippe Auguste."

41. Saint Louis' beauty had been underscored so much by his biographers that it was made the topic for an entry in the index of volume 23 of the *Recueil des historiens des Gaules et de la France*—"*Qua forma fuerit Ludovicus IX*," 1025.

42. See above, "Salimbene of Parma," in Part II, ch. 7.

43. Boniface VIII, 149.

44. *Recueil des historiens des Gaules et de la France*, 23:173. Also, see above, "The Portrait of the King," in Part II, ch. 10

45. Cf. above, "Architecture: A Court Style?" in Part III, ch. 2.

46. Boniface VIII, 149. On the poor and poverty in the Middle Ages, see the fundamental works of M. Mollat, *Les Pauvres au Moyen Âge* (Paris, 1978) and *Études sur l'histoire de la pauvreté*, ed. Mollat, 2 vols. (Paris, 1974).

47. Boniface VIII, 150.

48. Guillaume de Saint-Pathus, *Vie de Saint Louis,* 79–90 and 89 in particular.

49. Joinville, *Histoire de Saint Louis,* 381.

50. Ibid., 391–95.

51. R.-H. Bautier, "Les aumônes du roi aux maladreries, maisons-Dieu et pauvres établissements du royaume," 44.

52. Xavier de la Selle, "L'aumônerie royale aux XIIIᵉ–XIVᵉ siècles," paper read at the colloquium on "Les Capétiens et Vincennes au Moyen Âge," acts forthcoming. On the royal hôtel, see below, "His Household and Entourage," Part III, ch. 6.

53. André Duchesne, *Historiae Francorum scriptores* (Paris, 1649), 5:438–40. This text has appeared more recently in the *Layettes du Trésor des chartes,* vol. 4, no. 5638 (1902). The executors of his will were the bishops of Paris and Évreux, the abbots of Saint-Denis and Royaumont, and two of his chaplains.

54. A. Murray, *Reason and Society in the Middle Ages.*

55. See below, "The Royal Coronation," in Part III, ch. 9.

56. See above, "Guillaume de Saint-Pathus's *Life* of Saint Louis," in Part II, ch. 3.

57. Lucette Valensi, "Anthropologie économique et histoire: l'oeuvre de Karl Polanyi," *Annales, E.S.C.* (1974): 1311–19; S. C. Humphrey, "History, Economics, and Anthropology: The Work of Karl Polanyi," *History and Theory* 8 (1969): 165–212.

58. Philippe Contamine et al., *L'Économie médiévale* (Paris, 1993), 222.

59. J. Baldwin, *Philippe Auguste*; Gérard Sivery, *L'Économie du royaume de France au siècle de Saint Louis* (Lille, 1984).

60. Guy Fourquin, *Les Campagnes de la région parisienne à la fin du Moyen Âge* (Paris, 1964).

61. Marc Bloch, *Rois et serfs. Un chapitre d'histore capétienne* (Paris, 1920).

62. G. Sivery, *L'Économie du royaume de France,* 33.

63. P. Buc, *L'Ambiguïté du livre,* 239.

64. T. Bisson, "The Problem of Feudal Monarchy: Aragon, Catalonia and France."

65. G. Sivery, *L'Économie du royaume de France,* 32.

66. See above, "Conflicts with the Bishops," in Part I, ch. 1

67. See below, "Saint Louis and the Church," in Part III, ch. 8.

68. Charles Petit-Dutaillis, *Les Communes françaises. Caractères et évolution des origines au XVIIIᵉ siècle* (Paris, 1947). J. Schneider, "Les villes du royaume de France au temps de Saint Louis."

69. A. Giry, ed., *Documents sur les relations de la royauté avec les villes en France,* 85–88.

70. W. C. Jordan, "Communal Administration in France 1257–1270," 309.

71. Philippe de Beaumanoir, *Coutumes de Beauvaisis,* ed. A. Salmon, 2nd ed. (1970), 2:266–70.

72. A. Serper, "L'administration royale de Paris au temps de Louis IX."

73. *Le Livre des métiers d'Étienne Boileau,* ed. R. de Lespinasse and F. Bonnardot (Paris, 1879).

74. N. de Wailly, ed., *Joinville et les Enseignements à son fils* (Paris, 1872), 26–28, 52.

75. Albert Rigaudière. *Gouverner la ville au Moyen Âge* (Paris, 1993), 7–8.

76. Ibid., 60. This appears in the outstanding clarification introduced in the chapter, "Qu'est-ce qu'une bonne ville dans la France du Moyen Âge?" 53–112.

77. A. Sayous, "Les mandats de Saint Louis sur son trésor pendant la septième croisade."

78. The bibliography on usury is extensive. Gabriel Le Bras' article on "Usure" in the *Dictionnaire de théologie catholique* (vol. 15 [1950], col. 2336–72) is essential. For the bibliography, I also refer readers to my essay, *La Bourse et la Vie. Économie et religion au Moyen Âge* (Paris, 1986).

79. See below, "Saint Louis and the Jews," in Part III, ch. 8.

80. Ibid. The two key texts are from Deuteronomy 23:19–20: "*Non foenerabis fratri tuo ad usuram pecuniam . . . sed alieno*" (You shall not lend money on interest to your brother in usury . . . but to the foreigner [you may]), and the Gospel of Luke 6:34–35: "*Mutuum date, nil inde sperantes*" (Lend without expecting anything in return). In his wonderful book, *The Idea of Usury. From Tribal Brotherhood to Universal Otherhood* (Princeton, 1949; repr. 1969), Benjamin N. Nelson situates the evolution of attitudes toward usury in a movement from "tribal fraternity" to a "universal altruism." In 1268, Saint Louis mentioned "foreign usurers" (*alienigene usurari*). These were the ones they repressed. The problem of usury was caught up in a general process of integration and exclusion within Christendom. See, R. I. Moore, *La Persécution*. On Saint Louis' monetary measures, see above, "The 'Good' Money," in Part I, ch. 4.

81. See above, "The 'Good' Money."

82. R. Folz, *Les Saints Rois du Moyen Âge en Occident*.

83. P. Michaud-Quantin, "La politique monétaire royale à la Faculté de théologie de Paris en 1265."

84. T. Bisson, *Conservation of Coinage*.

85. On *necessitas* as a political principle, see P. Buc, *L'Ambiguïté du livre*, 260–71.

86. A. Rigaudière, "Réglementation urbaine et législation d'État dans les villes du Midi français aux XIIIᵉ et XIVᵉ siècles," in *Gouverner la ville*, 113–59.

87. The earliest conflicts in the Parisian labor market arose in the 1250s. Bronislaw Geremek points to the conflict opposing the master and attendant fullers as the earliest known to have taken place: *Le Salariat dans l'artisanat parisien aux XIIIᵉ–XVᵉ siècles* (Paris and the Hague, 1968), 102.

88. John Baldwin has effectively shown that the "fair price" (*juste prix*) of the scholastics was nothing other than the market price. See John Baldwin, *The Mediaeval Theories of the Just Price. Romanists, Canonists, and Theologians in the XIIth and XIIIth Centuries* (Philadelphia, 1959).

89. In a work that I have already cited (*L'Économie du royaume de France au siècle de Saint Louis*), G. Sivery has formulated the hypothesis that Saint Louis' France was in possession of a two-tiered economy—a fragile traditional economy threatened with famine and another "new" economy that reacted in cycles to the development of large-scale trade and urban dynamism. According to the hypothesis, Saint Louis

"discovered" this new economy. Henri Dubois has judiciously critiqued this hypothesis in the *Revue historique* 109 (1985): 472–73.

90. It does however appear in a concealed form in the works of Gilbert de Tournai.

91. See J. Le Goff, *La Bourse et la Vie.*

PART III
Notes to Chapter 5

1. For example, T. Bisson, "The Problem of the Feudal Monarchy."

2. Jean-Philippe Genet, ed., *État moderne: genèse, bilan et perspective* (Paris, 1990). J. Krynen's excellent work (*L'Empire du roi*) somewhat rushes the march to royal absolutism in France and minimizes the relevance of the forces that tended to slow this development. See Albert Rigaudière's balanced and outstanding presentation of this issue, *Pouvoirs et institutions dans la France médiévale. Des temps féodaux aux temps de l'État,* vol. 2 (Paris, 1994).

3. This is G. Duby's position in his great survey, *Le Moyen Âge (987–1460),* in *Histoire de France,* vol. 1.

4. Some American medievalists have recently claimed that the Capetian king did not begin by relying on the feudal system in order to assure the triumph of the monarchical state system under him as a result, but that instead he began by establishing his royal power and only after that used it to take advantage of the feudal system and to use the feudal system to reinforce his own royal power. T. Bisson ("The Problem of the Feudal Monarchy") and J. Baldwin (*Philippe Auguste*) have situated the decisive moment in this development under the rule of Philip Augustus in whom Bisson sees "the first feudal king of France." In his *Monarchie féodale en France et en Angleterre,* without sufficiently proving this, C. Petit-Dutaillis had already claimed that Saint Louis' reign had been "the apogee of the feudal monarchy." Two German historians, H. Koller and B. Töpfer (*Frankreich, ein historischer Abriss* [Berlin, 1985]), have adopted this claim without providing any further proof: "Saint Louis made an essential contribution to the pursuit of reinforcing the monarchy." J. Richard entitled one of the chapters of his *Saint Louis,* "La Transformation des structures de la royauté féodale." On the subject of the "feudal politics" of the great Capetians, Roger Fédou writes: "One of the 'secrets' of their success consisted in making maximum use of the resources of feudal law in order to prepare or legitimate their conquests at the expense of the lesser feudal rulers," *L'État au Moyen Âge* (Paris, 1971), 64.

5. If I may, I refer my readers to J. Le Goff, "Le Moyen Âge," in *Histoire de la France,* ed. A. Burguière and J. Revel, vol. 2.

6. Jean-Marie Augustin, "L'aide féodale levée par Saint Louis et Philippe le Bel," *Mémoires de la Société pour l'histoire du droit* 37, no. 6 (1980): 59–81.

7. *Coutumes de Beauvaisis,* ed. A. Salmon, vol. 2, no. 1499 (1900).

8. C. T. Wood, "The Mise of Amiens and Saint Louis' Theory of Kingship."

9. Thomas N. Bisson, "Consultative Functions in the King's Parlements (1250–1314)," *Speculum* 44 (1969): 353–73.

10. Ibid., 361.

11. On the christological horizon of this expression, see below, "His Household and Entourage," in Part III, ch. 6, and above, "Familiar Speech," in Part III, ch. 3

12. Guillaume de Saint-Pathus, *Vie de Saint Louis,* 71: "And thus the saint king formed his household to do good." See below, "His Household and Entourage."

13. See above, "The Child Heir," in Part I, ch. 1, and below, "His Grandfather," in Part III, ch. 6.

14. See below, "The Royal Coronation," in Part III, ch. 9, and above, "The Coronation of the Child King," in Part I, ch. 1.

15. See above, "Conflicts with the Bishops," in Part I, ch. 1.

16. G. Campbell, "The Protest of St. Louis."

17. See his criticism of ill-considered and vain episcopal excommunications, below, "Saint Louis and the Church," in Part III, ch. 8.

18. *Enseignements,* ed. D. O'Connell, 189.

19. Geoffroy de Beaulieu, *Vita,* 12.

20. This is the original meaning of "augustus"—"he who augments."

21. Georges Duby, *La Société aux XIᵉ et XIIᵉ siècles dans la région mâconnaise* (Paris, 1953); *L'Économie rurale et la vie des campagnes dans l'Occident médiéval,* 2 vols. (Paris, 1962).

22. M. Bloch, *La Société féodale.*

23. J. Schneider, "Les villes du royaume de France."

24. See below, "Saint Louis and the Jews," in Part III, ch. 8.

25. On Saint Louis' monetary reforms, see above, "The 'Good' Money," in Part I, ch. 4, and "Currency," Part III, ch. 4.

26. "*Carissimae Dominae et matri reginae concessimus et voluimus quod ipsa in hac nostrae peregrinationis absentia plenariam habeat potestatem recipiendi et attrahendi ad regni nostri negoia,* quod sibi placuerit et visum fuerit *attrahere*" (F. Olivier-Martin, *Études sur les régences,* 1:87).

27. "*removendi etiam quos viderit removendos, secundum* quod ipsi videbitur bonum esse" (ibid.).

28. Albert Rigaudière, "'*Princeps legibus solutus est*' (*Dig.,* I, 3, 31) et '*Quod principi placuit legis habet vigorem*' (*Dig.,* I, 4, 1) à travers trois coutumiers du XIIIᵉ siècle," in *Hommages à Gérard Boulvert* (Nice, 1987), 438–39. From customary law, this text draws on the idea of the collective enjoyment of a good by a community in accordance with that community's customs, but the idea takes on a more general, abstract value at the level of the entire group of the kingdom's subjects. From Roman law, it upholds the idea of public utility but adapts this notion to the society of a Christian monarchy. Finally, it refers to the Aristotelean concept of the common good but in the form given by the scholastic theologians of the thirteenth century (notably, Thomas Aquinas after 1248) who reworked it within the framework of Saint Augustine's *City of God.*

29. *"Baillivos etiam instituere valeat, castellanos, forestarios et alios in servitium nostrum vel regni nostri ponere et amovere, prout viderit expedire,"* in F. Olivier-Martin, *Études sur les régences.*

30. *"Dignitates etiam et beneficia ecclesiastica vacantia conferre, fidelitates episcoparum et abbatum recipere et eis regalia restituere, et eligendi licentiam dare capitulis et conventibus vice nostra"* (ibid.).

31. This is Jacques Krynen's hypothesis. J. Verger does not believe that Philip Augustus intervened in this way either, see "Des écoles à l'université: la mutation institutionnelle," 844.

32. M. Boulet-Sautel, "Le concept de souveraineté chez Jacques de Révigny."

33. G. Fourquin, *Les Campagnes de la région parisienne à la fin du Moyen Âge,* 152.

34. José Luis Romero, *La Revolucion burguesa en el mondo feudal* (Buenos Aires, 1969).

35. See below, Part III, ch. 10.

36. Guillaume de Saint-Pathus, *Vie de Saint Louis,* 79.

37. See my essay, "Du ciel sur la terre."

38. Upon learning of the death of his father Charles VII, Louis XI left almost immediately after for a hunt.

39. I should add that although this remark very probably corresponds to the reality, it is still a hypothesis. I do not know of any document that shows or declares that Saint Louis never hunted. On the other hand, there are eyewitnesses who assert that no one had ever seen him play "games of chance of similar games" nor "any dishonest games" (Guillaume de Saint-Pathus, *Vie de Saint Louis,* 133).

40. See P. Buc, *L'Ambiguïté du livre,* 113. There is an incredible collection of sources on hunting and the related ideological stakes of power in this work. On hunting in the Middle Ages, see the article, "Chasse" by Alain Guerreau that is forthcoming in *Les Caractères originaux de la civilisation de l'Occident médiéval,* ed. J. Le Goff and J.-C. Schmitt, with a bibliography of primary sources. On Byzantium, see Évelyne Patlagean, "De la chasse et du souverain," in *Homo Byzantinus. Papers in Honor of Alexander Kazhdan,* Dumbarton Oaks Papers, no. 46 (1992): 257–63. The royal hunt was an act of prowess and a substitute for victory in war as it was in Antiquity.

41. Jonas d'Orléans' text can be found in Migne's *Patrologie latine,* vol. 106, col. 215–28.

42. Yves de Chartres, *Décret* in Migne, *Patrologie latine,* vol. 161, bk. 1, col. 808–10.

43. The text was published by Denifle and Chatelain in the *Chartularium Universitatis Parisiensis,* vol. 1, no. 71, 128–29. It is also quoted by H. Grundmann in his article, "*Sacerdotium-Regnum-Studium,*" and quoted and commented by P. Buc in *L'Ambiguïté du livre,* which I am following here. From the same author, see "Pouvoir royal et commentaires de la Bible (1150–1350)," *Annales, E.S.C.* (1989): 691–713.

44. The theme of *majestas* was also and perhaps mainly expressed in thirteenth-century art and literature, although according to the particular methods of these imaginary arts. See Alain Labbé, *L'Architecture des palais et jardins dans les chansons de geste. Essai sur le thème du roi en majesté* (Paris and Geneva, 1993). On the king in twelfth-

and thirteenth-century literature, see the wonderful book by Dominique Boutet, *Charlemagne et Arthur ou le roi imaginaire* (Paris, 1993). On *majestas* seen from a juridical-theological point of view, see the works in progress by Jacques Chiffoleau and Yann Thomas: J. Chiffoleau, "Sur le crime de majesté médiéval," in *Genèse de l'État moderne en Méditerranée* (Rome, 1993), 182–213.

45. See below, "Saint Louis' Sainthood," in Part III, ch. 9.

46. Robert J. Schneider has conducted a remarkable analysis of this text in a conference held at the University of Groningen in 1987. He has been nice enough to share its content with me, "*Rex imago trinitatis*: Power, Wisdom, and Goodness in the *De morali principis institutione* of Vincent Beauvais." I am following his argument here.

47. "*Magna regna, magna latrocinia.*"

48. This is the theme of the "return to the line of Charlemagne" (*reditus ad stirpem Karoli*), see above, "The Brief Reign of the Father," in Part I, ch. 1.

49. Ralph E. Gerry, *The Juristic Basis of Dynastic Right to the French Throne* (Baltimore, 1961), 7; E. H. Kantorowicz, *The King's Two Bodies.*

50. S. Mochy Onory, *Fonti canonistiche dell'idea moderna dello stato* (Milan, 1951).

51. A. Rigaudière, "'*Princeps legibus solutus est*'."

52. See above, Part II, ch. 1.

53. A. Rigaudière, "'*Princeps legibus solutus est*'," 441.

54. M. Boulet-Sautel, "Le concept de souveraineté chez Jacques de Révigny," 25. By the same author, see also, "Jean de Blanot et la conception du pouvoir royal au temps de Saint Louis," 57–68.

55. Ibid., 23. See above, "Saint Louis and the Law."

56. A. Rigaudière, "'*Princeps legibus solutus est*'," 444.

57. Philippe de Beaumanoir, *Coutumes de Beauvaisis,* ch. 49, § 1515. See also, A. Rigaudière, "'*Princeps legibus solutus est*'," 449 and n. 70.

58. Charles Petit-Dutaillis, "L'établissement pour le commun profit au temps de Saint Louis," *Annuario de Historia del Derecho español* (1933): 199–201.

59. Joseph R. Strayer, "The Laicization of French and English Society in the Thirteenth Century" (1940), reprinted in *Medieval Statecraft and the Perspectives of History* (Princeton, 1971), 251–65. Georges de Lagarde's impressive work supports views that seem equally debatable to me, *La Naissance de l'esprit laïque au déclin du Moyen Âge,* 3rd ed. (Louvain and Paris, 1956–1970).

60. Elizabeth A. R. Brown, "Taxation and Morality in the XIIIth and XIVth Centuries: Conscience and Political Power and the Kings of France," *French Historical Studies* 8 (1973): 1–28; reprinted in *Conscience and Casuistry in Early Medieval Europe,* ed. E. Lites (Cambridge and Paris, 1988).

61. See above, "The Stories of the Minstrel of Reims," in Part II, ch. 4; "Conscience," Part II, ch. 10; and below, "His Conscience," in Part III, ch. 7.

62. If the "absolutist" process studied remarkably by J. Krynen continued under Saint Louis, it sped up only after his rule.

63. See above, "Saint Louis and Space," in Part III, ch. 1.

64. See above, "Salimbene of Parma," in Part II, ch. 7.

65. Guillaume de Saint-Pathus, *Vie de Saint Louis,* 45–46.

66. Ibid., 89.

67. Ibid., 89–91.

68. Ibid., 117–18. See below for the conclusion to this passage that, for me, seems to provide the key for an in-depth understanding of Saint Louis' behavior.

69. See below, "His Household and Entourage," in Part III, ch. 6.

70. J. Krynen (*L'Empire du roi*) has presented the question of whether there was any potential Machiavellianism in medieval political practices.

71. See the epigraph to this book.

72. N. D. Fustel de Coulanges, "Saint Louis et le prestige de la royauté," in *Leçons à l'impératrice* (Colombes, 1970), 176

73. Matthew Paris, *Chronica majora,* 5:307.

74. Joinville, *Histoire de Saint Louis,* 35.

75. Ibid., 35.

76. I owe this pertinent remark to Bernard Guenée.

77. Montesquieu, *De l'esprit des loix,* bk. 28, ch. 29: "Fausser sans combattre" means that one appeals a seigniorial judgment to the king without having to request a judiciary combat, as used to be the case. The proper sense of *"fausser"* here is "to redress." We should remember here that Saint Louis suppressed the "battle wagers," the judiciary duel as a method of proof.

78. F. Lot and R. Fawtier, *Insitutions royales,* 332–33.

79. Ibid., 333.

Part III
Notes to Chapter 6

1. See the excellent work by A. W. Lewis, *Le Sang royal,* ch. 4, "Le développement du sentiment dynastique."

2. *Recueil des historiens des Gaules et de la France,* 23:168. On Louis VIII, see the favorable portrayal by G. Sivery, *Louis VIII le Lion* (Paris, 1995). This work includes an interesting chapter on Gilles de Rome's *Carolinus,* "Un programme politique offert au prince Louis," 29–52.

3. See above, "A Difficult Minority," in Part I, ch. 1.

4. J. Le Goff, "Philippe Auguste dans les exempla," in *La France de Philippe Auguste,* 145–46.

5. See above, "The Child Heir," in Part I, ch. 1

6. Guillaume de Saint-Pathus, *Vie de Saint Louis,* 137–38.

7. Ibid., 67–68. See above "The Child Heir," for Joinville's version of this anecdote. See also, above, "The Great Alliance of the Altar and the Throne," in Part III, ch. 5.

8. Philippe Mouskès, *Chronique rimée,* 2:431–32, v. 23861–84. Also quoted by A. Erlande-Brandenburg *Le Roi est mort,* 18.

9. See above, "David and Solomon," in Part II, ch. 5.

10. Élie Berger, *Histoire de Blanche de Castille* (Paris, 1895); Régine Pernoud, *La Reine Blanche*.

11. Geoffroy de Beaulieu, *Vita,* 4.

12. Georges Duby, *Mâle Moyen Âge* (Paris, 1968; repr. 1990).

13. Geoffroy de Beaulieu, *Vita,* 4.

14. *Tota virago,* in other words, a man-woman (*vir*), strong and combative.

15. *Masculinum animum.*

16. Geoffroy de Beaulieu, *Vita,* 4–5.

17. Boniface VIII, 155.

18. See above, "Was Saint Louis a Calculating King?" in Part III, ch. 5.

19. Guillaume de Saint-Pathus, *Vie de Saint Louis,* 13.

20. See above, Part I, ch. 1. I am presenting the previously reported events in chronological order here from the perspective of Blanche de Castile.

21. G. Sivery, *Marguerite de Provence,* 125.

22. On a mother's role in her son's religious formation, see Jean Delumeau, ed., *La Religion de ma mère. Le rôle des femmes dans la transmission de la foi* (Paris, 1992).

23. See above, "The Coronation of the Child King," in Part I, ch. 1.

24. Joinville, *Histoire de Saint Louis,* 43.

25. I have described this exceptional situation in its chronological place among the events in Part I, ch. 2. I have also commented on it through my discussion of a miniature in Part II, ch. 10, "The Portrait of the King."

26. See above, "The King's Illness and His Vow to Crusade," in Part I, ch. 2.

27. Joinville, *Histoire de Saint Louis,* 63.

28. See below, Part III, ch. 10.

29. In his study on *Le Langage et l'image au Moyen Âge. Signification et symbolique* (Paris, 1982), François Garnier notes that outstretched arms signify "an emotional attitude" (223).

30. Joinville, *Histoire de Saint Louis,* 331.

31. Ibid., 333.

32. Ibid.

33. On the apanages, see A. W. Lewis, *Le Sang royal.* I also take the liberty of referring to my article, "Apanage," in the *Encyclopaedia Universalis.*

34. A. Lewis, *Le Sang royal,* 213.

35. Jeanne the daughter of Saint Louis' uncle Philip Hurepel died without heir in 1252. Alphonse de Poitiers and Charles d'Anjou each claimed a third of her lands on the grounds that they were her nephews, but their fate was left in suspense until 1258 when a tribunal that consulted a group of *"prud'hommes"* gave them all to the king.

36. I am following A. W. Lewis's outstanding examination of these relations in *Le Sang royal,* 299.

37. I have tried to demonstrate this in examining the relations between lord and vassal in "Le rituel symbolique de la vassalité," in *Pour un autre Moyen Âge,* 349–420.

38. L. d'Achéry, *Spicilegium,* 2:4, *Miscellanea Epistularum,* no. 87, 549.

39. A. W. Lewis, *Le Sang royal,* 235–38.

40. See above, "The Conquering King," in Part I, ch. 2.

41. P. E. Riant, "1282: déposition de Charles d'Anjou pour la canonisation de Saint Louis," 175. Robert d'Artois was killed on the battlefield at Mansourah. The Church never recognized him as a martyr. Alphonse de Poitiers died of an illness in Italy on his return from the crusade of Tunis, and the Church had even less regard for his claim to martyrdom.

42. These references can be found in A. W. Lewis, *Le Sang royal,* 341 n. 98.

43. J. Richard, *Saint Louis,* 135.

44. Matthew Paris, *Chronica majora,* 5:280. In a page that engages a violent ideological confrontation between English and French interests, Matthew Paris opposes Robert with the example of a young knight *prud'homme* who belonged to the English royal family, Guillaume Longuépée, the count of Salisbury, who was a true hero who died fighting. According to him, it is Longuépée and not Robert d'Artois who should be considered a true martyr, especially with the help of the great English saint, Saint Edmond. Edmond Rich (Edmond of Abingdon) was archbishop of Canterbury in 1233. He came to France in 1240, perhaps on his way to Rome. He stayed in the Cistercian abbey of Pontigny where he died that same year. Considered a "martyr" who died in exile, he was canonized in 1246.

45. J. Richard, *Saint Louis,* 138.

46. E. Boutaric, *Saint Louis et Alphonse de Poitiers.*

47. Rutebeuf, *Oeuvres complètes* (Paris, 1990), 2:391–99.

48. Daniel Borzeix, René Pautel, Jacques Serbat, *Louis IX (alias Saint Louis) et l'Occitanie* (Pignan, 1976): this work is an example of the pro-Occitan delirium. Jacques Madaule, *Le Drame albigeois et l'unité française* (Paris, 1973) is sympathetic to the Occitans, but strives for objectivity.

49. The basic information on this can be found in J. Richard, *Saint Louis,* 455 ff.

50. See above, "Louis IX Crusading for the Second Time," in Part I, ch. 4.

51. Joinville, *Histoire de Saint Louis,* 221. See above, "The King's Flaws" in Part II, ch. 9.

52. See above, "The Flemish Inheritance," in Part I, ch. 4, and, for the details, J. Richard, *Saint Louis,* 329.

53. André Vauchez, *La Spiritualité au Moyen Âge occidental, VIIIᵉ–XIIᵉ siècle,* "Le Christianisme au féminin" (Paris, 1994), 158–68.

54. On the failed attempts to establish a royal religion centered around royal princesses in the West, see above, "His Sister and Brothers," in Part I, ch. 4. On the success of these attempts in Central Europe and particularly in Hungary, see Gabor Klaniczay, "La Sainteté des souverains. La sainteté dynastique hongroise et la typologie de la sainteté en Europe médiévale," a forthcoming thesis.

55. Joinville, *Histoire de Saint Louis,* 39.

56. On Queen Marguerite, see G. Sivery, *Marguerite de Provence.*

57. M. Zink, "Joinville ne pleure pas."

58. See above, "The King's Flaws," in Part II, ch. 9.

59. Joinville, *Histoire de Saint Louis,* 347.

60. Guillaume de Saint-Pathus, *Vie de Saint Louis,* 34.

61. *Enseignements,* ed. D. O'Connell, 188.

62. G. Sivery, *Marguerite de Provence,* 210.

63. Joinville, *Histoire de Saint Louis,* 333.

64. Jean-Louis Flandrin, *Un temps pour embrasser. Aux origines de la morale sexuelle occidentale (VIᵉ–XIᵉ siècles)* (Paris, 1983).

65. Guillaume de Nangis, *Gesta Ludovici IX,* 402.

66. "Saint" Thibaud died in 1247. Le Nain de Tillemont, *Vie de Saint Louis,* 2:393–94; A. Duchesne, *Historiae Francorum Scriptores* (Paris, 1636), 1:406.

67. See above, "The Limited Testimony of the *Exempla,*" in Part II, ch. 4.

68. See above, Part I.

69. Ibid.

70. I am following A. Lewis here, *Le Sang royal,* 222–24.

71. Rutebeuf, *Oeuvres complètes,* 2:381–90.

72. Geoffroy de Beaulieu, *Vita,* 23.

73. See above, "His Sister and Brothers," in Part I, ch. 4.

74. Again, we can see that he only became truly interested in them when they were grown.

75. Joinville, *Histoire de Saint Louis,* 381.

76. This is an allusion to the relic of the Crown of Thorns in the Sainte-Chapelle.

77. C. Bynum, *Jesus as Mother*; J. Le Goff, "Le vocabulaire des catégories sociales chez saint François d'Assise et ses biographes au XIIIᵉ siècle."

78. *Enseignements,* ed. D. O'Connell, 191.

79. Guillaume de Saint-Pathus, *Vie de Saint Louis,* 36.

80. Ibid., 37.

81. *Epistola publicata super obitum Ludovici noni regis,* in A. Duchesne, *Historia Francorum Scriptores* (1649), 5:440.

82. Matthew Paris, *Chronica majora,* 5:436.

83. The king's *hôtel* (manor) underwent a thorough reorganization under Saint Louis. See Élisabeth Lalou in the forthcoming *Actes du colloque de Vincennes sur les Capétiens.*

84. Guillaume de Saint-Pathus, *Vie de Saint Louis,* 124.

85. Ibid., 130.

86. Joinville, *Histoire de Saint Louis,* 33. See above, "Familiar Speech," in Part III, ch. 3.

87. Raoul Manselli, "*Nos qui cum eo fuimus,*" in *Contributo alla questione francescana* (Rome, 1980).

88. Ernst H. Kantorowicz, "Mysteries of State" (1955), French translation, "Mystères de l'État. Un concept absolutiste et ses origines médiévales," in *Mourir pour la patrie* (Paris, 1984).

PART III
Notes to Chapter 7

1. See *Histoire de la France religieuse,* ed. J. Le Goff and R. Rémond, vol. 1.

2. Cf. below, "Saint Louis' Sainthood" and "His Miracles and His Life," in Part III, ch. 9.

3. L. K. Little, "Saint Louis' Involvement with the Friars." I am following Little's argument here.

4. Matthew Paris, *Chronica majora,* 3:520.

5. *Le scuole degli ordini mendicanti (secoli XIII–XIV),* Convegno del Centro di studi sulla spiritualità medievale 17 (1975; repr. Academia Tudertina, Todi 1978).

6. Some venture that Robert de Sorbon was also one of his confessors. See above, "The King and his Intellectuals," in Part III, ch. 2.

7. Jacques-Guy Bougerol, "Saint Bonaventure et le roi Saint Louis," in *San Bonaventura, 1274–1974* (Grottaferratta, 1973); 2:469–93.

8. Eudes Rigaud, *Registrum visitationum archiepiscopi rothomagensis,* ed. Théodose Bonnin (Rouen, 1852); new edition *The Register of Eudes of Rouen,* ed. J. F. Sullivan (1964). Eudes Rigaud died when he was still archibishop of Rouen in 1274. Saint Louis had not been able to make him a cardinal.

9. See above, "The Mendicant Orders," in Part II, ch. 2.

10. See below, "'You are Only the King of the Friars'," in Part III, ch. 8.

11. This anecdote is reported without any given reference in G. G. Coulton, *From Saint Francis to Dante* (London, 1907), 405. It is also quoted by L. K. Little, "Saint Louis' Involvement with the Friars," 21.

12. *Enseignements,* ed. D. O'Connell, 185–86.

13. See, notably, Guillaume de Saint-Pathus, *Vie de Saint Louis,* 23–25.

14. Joinville, *Histoire de Saint Louis,* 23.

15. Ibid., 25.

16. Alberto Tenenti, *La Vie et la mort à travers l'art du XVe siècle* (Paris, 1953); J. Delumeau, *La Peur en Occident.*

17. Joinville, *Histoire de Saint Louis,* 23.

18. Ibid.

19. Ibid., 27.

20. Ibid., 25.

21. Guillaume de Saint-Pathus, *Vie de Saint Louis,* 23–24; Guillaume de Nangis, *Gesta Ludovici IX,* 381.

22. Joinville, *Histoire de Saint Louis,* 45.

23. P. M. Gy and J. Le Goff, "Saint Louis et la pratique sacramentelle," *La Maision-Dieu* 197 (1994): 118–20.

24. Guillaume de Saint-Pathus, *Vie de Saint Louis,* 52–53.

25. Ibid., 53.

26. Geoffroy de Beaulieu, *Vita,* 15.

27. Ibid.

28. See above, "Books of Images," in Part III, ch. 2.

29. Geoffroy de Beaulieu, *Vita,* 15.

30. See J.-G. Bougerol, "Saint Bonaventure et le roi Saint Louis."

31. Joinville, *Vie de Saint Louis,* 15. See above, "Familiar Speech," in Part III, ch. 3.

32. Ibid., 15–17.

33. On his table manners, see above, Part III, ch. 3.

34. Geoffroy de Beaulieu, *Vita,* 10.

35. Raoul Manselli, "L'anno 1260 fu anno gioachimitico?" in *Il movimento dei disciplinati nel settimo centenario del suo inizio.*

36. Geoffroy de Beaulieu, *Vita,* 10.

37. On Purgatory, see Jacques Chiffoleau, *La Comptabilité de l'au-delà. Les hommes, la mort et la religion dans la région d'Avignon à la fin du Moyen Âge* (Rome, 1980).

38. Guillaume de Saint-Pathus, *Vie de Saint Louis,* 123.

39. Even Matthew Paris recognized this in his discussion of a problem to which he was very sensitive himself—the question of the respective rights of the English and the French in Normandy: "But, as the purity of conscience of His Royal Highness the king of France was not satisfied by these arguments, this dubious question was put before the bishops of Normandy to decide" (*Chronica majora,* 4:646).

40. Guillaume de Saint-Pathus, *Vie de Saint Louis,* 123.

41. Geoffroy de Beaulieu, *Vita,* 14. For the entire passage and Michelet's commentary on it, see below, "The Suffering of Tears Denied," in Part III, ch. 10.

42. Matthew Paris, *Chronica majora,* 4:524.

43. See the last chapter of this book, "The Suffering King, The Christ King."

44. This is the topic of Guillaume de Pathus's thirteenth chapter: "On Vigor and Patience."

45. Matthew Paris, *Chronica majora,* 5:203.

46. Ibid., 5:482.

47. Joinville, in D. O'Connell, *Les Propos de Saint Louis,* 116–17.

48. Boniface VIII, 150.

49. Joinville, *Histoire de Saint Louis,* 211.

50. This is Joinville, who was quite familiar with the king and his fits of anger. He was thinking that he would be able to give Philippe de Nemours and the people who tricked the Saracens reason to regret it.

51. Guillaume de Saint-Pathus, *Vie de Saint Louis,* 127–28.

52. P. M. Gy and J. Le Goff, "Saint Louis et la pratique sacramentelle."

53. Ibid., 112.

54. Ibid., 112–13.

55. Guillaume de Saint-Pathus, *Vie de Saint Louis,* 39.

56. Ibid., 39.

57. See M. Ruben's beautiful book, *Corpus Christi.*

58. See above, "The Marriage of Louis IX (1234)," in Part I, ch. 2.

59. P. M. Gy and J. Le Goff, "Saint Louis et la pratique sacramentelle," 112.

60. The texts of the period almost never mention confirmation, and, of course, ordination is reserved for the priests.

61. Cf. *La Prière au Moyen Âge, Senefiance,* no. 10 (Aix-en-Provence, 1991). I am employing the content from my essay here, "Saint Louis et la prière," which was first presented at Father Pierre-Marie Gy's seminar at the École normale supérieure in the rue d'Ulm and then later published in the essays published for my mentor and friend Michel Mollat du Jourdain, *Horizons marins, itinéraires spirituels (V^e–XVIIIe siècles),* vol. 1, *Mentalités et sociétés,* ed. Henri Dubois, Jean-Claude Hocquet, and André Vauchez (Paris, 1987), 85–94.

62. Boniface VIII, 158.

63. Ibid., 159.

64. D. O'Connell, *Les Propos de Saint Louis,* 186.

65. Joinville, *Histoire de Saint Louis,* 331.

66. Ibid., 407.

67. Geoffroy de Beaulieu, *Vita,* 13–14. I am repeating many of the elements that I grouped around the theme of Saint Louis' use of time above (Part III, ch. 1, "Circular and Liturgical Time"), arranging them around the theme of prayer here. This section on prayer contains additional details that were not previously mentioned, and I treat the theme of his gestures in prayer here in greater depth than in "Gestures of Religious Devotion," in Part III, ch. 3.

68. We know that the edicts of 1254 and 1256 charged the royal functionaries with repressing gambling, among other things, not only in the royal domain but also throughout the entire kingdom. See above, "The Kingdom's Reformer," in Part I, ch. 4. On Saint Louis' possible aversion to hunting, see "Saint Louis Does Not Hunt," in Part III, ch. 5.

69. Cf. P. Saenger, "Silent Reading." See also, by the same author, *Manières de lire médiévales,* in *Histoire de l'édition française* (Paris, 1982), 1:130–41.

70. On the affirmation of the individual in the twelfth and thirteenth centuries, see above, "History and the Individual," in Part II, ch. 10.

71. J.-C. Schmitt, *La Raison des gestes.* In particular, see ch. 8 in Schmitt, "De la prière à l'extase."

72. *Enseignements,* ed. D. O'Connell, 190–91.

73. J. Le Goff, "Saint Louis et les corps royaux," in *Le Temps de la réflexion,* vol. 3 (1982). Saint Louis twice mentions the deliverance of the souls of his ancestors in his *Enseignements* for his son (ch. 18).

74. J. Le Goff, *La Naissance du Purgatoire.*

75. There is a rich bibliography on this. I will only mention those works that deal with its problematic aspects: Nicolas Huyghebaert, *Les Documents nécrologiques,* in *Typologie des sources du Moyen Âge occidental,* vol. 4 (Turnhout, 1972); Karl Schmidt and Joachim Wollasch, "Die Gemeinschaft der Lebenden und Verstorbenen in Zeugnissen des Mittelalters," *Frühmittelalterliche Studien* 1 (1967): 365–405; J.-L. Lemaître, "Les obituaires français. Perspectives nouvelles," *Revue d'histoire de l'Église de France* 64 (1978): 69–81; Karl Schmidt and Joachim Wollasch, eds., *Memoria. Das geistliche Zeugniswerk des liturgischen Gedenkens im Mittelalter* (Munich, 1984); Otto Gerhard Oexle, "Memoria und Memorialüberlieferung im früheren Mittelalter," *Frühmittelalterliche*

Studien 10 (1976): 70–95. Michel Lauwer's wonderful thesis has not yet been published, "La Mémoire des ancêtres, le souci des morts. Fonction et usage du culte des morts dans l'Occident médiéval (diocèse de Liège, XIe–XIIIe siècles)," Paris, 1992. On Saint Louis and the dead, see above, "Saint Louis and the Royal Bodies," in Part I, ch. 4, and "The Children," in Part III, ch. 4.

76. *Prier au Moyen Âge. Pratiques et expériences (V^e–XVe siècles)* (Brépols, 1991).

77. Father Gy has been kind enough to point out to me that Saint Louis' practice of prayer closely resembled the Dominican practice of prayer in the thirteenth century on all but two points: first, with regard to the incredible importance he granted to prayer for the dead; second, in his propensity for praying for a long time, an especially long time for individual prayer, whereas the Dominican constitutions recommend that prayers be said *breviter et succincte*—a phrase repeated twice at the beginning of the constitutions. Cf. Roger Creytens, "Les constitutions des frères Prêcheurs dans la rédaction de S. Raymond de Penafort," *Archivum Fratrum Praedicatorum* 189 (1948): 30. In order to more specifically describe Saint Louis' practice of prayer in this regard, we would have to consult the ordinary from the chapel of the king of France. We possess a manuscript of this text from the late fourteenth and early fifteenth centuries—MS Paris, B.N., cod. Lat. 1435. Cf. Jean Dufrasne, *Les Ordinaires manuscrits des églises séculaires conservés à la Bibliothèque nationale de Paris,* dactylograph (Institut catholique, Institut supérieur de liturgie, 1959), 125–34.

78. *Recueil des historiens des Gaules et de la France,* 20:29.

79. J. Le Goff, *La Bourse et la vie.*

80. Guillaume de Saint-Pathus, *Vie de Saint Louis,* 72–73.

81. Geoffroy de Beaulieu, *Vita,* 14.

82. Guillaume de Saint-Pathus, *Vie de Saint Louis,* 89.

83. Ibid., 54.

84. Joinville, *Histoire de Saint Louis,* 381.

85. See above, "Saint Louis and the Third Function," in Part III, ch. 4.

86. J. Le Goff, "Saint Louis, croisé idéal?"

87. W. C. Jordan has very well understood the importance of these gestures; see *Louis IX and the Challenge of the Crusade,* 105 ff.

88. See above, "The King of Relics," in Part I, ch. 2.

89. P. Alphandéry and A. Dupront, *La Chrétienté et l'idée de croisade,* 425. See also, *"Militia Christi" e Crociata nei secoli XI–XIII* (Mendola, 1989; repr. Milan, 1992).

Part III
Notes to Chapter 8

1. The relations between Saint Louis and the Church is the subject of an outstanding article by Father Y. Congar, "L'Église et l'État sous le règne de Saint Louis."

2. *Enseignements,* ed. D. O'Connell, 188.

3. Joinville, *Histoire de Saint Louis,* 395–97.

4. *Enseignements,* ed. D. O'Connell, 188. See above, "The Great Alliance of the Altar and the Throne," in Part III, ch. 5.

5. See above, "Conflicts with the Bishops," in Part I, ch. 1.

6. See above, "The King, the Pope, and the Emperor," in Part I, ch. 2, and "His Conscience," in Part III, ch. 7. The fundamental study on this is still Élie Berger's *Saint Louis et Innocent IV.*

7. This document has been preserved in a version given by Matthew Paris. Living in a country where hostility to the pontifical curia was even greater than it was in France, the Benedictine Englishman may have hardened this letter's tone. This is the topic of an excellent study by Father G. J. Campbell, "The Protest of Saint Louis." He describes this letter as a "wild document."

8. Y. Congar, "L'Église et l'État sous le règne de Saint Louis," 271. The major text that espouses this opinion is J. Strayer's "The Laicization of French and English Society in the XIIIth Century." This theory was generalized in the seductive pages of G. de Lagarde's *La Naissance de l'esprit laïque au Moyen Âge.* This text seems to engage the reflection on the political thought and structures of the late Middle Ages on erroneous grounds. In a somewhat strange article ("The Uses of Heterodoxy: the French Monarchy and Unbelief in the XIIIth Century") R. E. Lerner determines that the thirteenth-century Capetians had "a policy of tolerating anti-clerical or heretical movements" (202). He mainly bases this judgment on Philip Augustus's attitude toward the Jews and the heresy of the university scholar Amaury de Bène, and on Blanche of Castile's attitude in the affair of the shepherds in 1251 (see above, "The Affair of the Shepherds," in Part I, ch. 3). As for Saint Louis, he refers to his resistance to episcopal excommunications and his protest to the pope in 1247. Although Saint Louis' attitude did harbor a desire for "the development of a new order opposed to the universal pretensions of the Church and supporting the exercise of national authority" (202), I do not see any relation between this policy and the supposed tolerance toward "heterodoxy" or "unbelief." It is my impression that this article is largely based on concepts that did not exist in the thirteenth century.

9. Primat, in *Recueil des historiens des Gaules et de la France,* 23:68.

10. *Enseignements,* ed. D. O'Connell, 190.

11. Guillaume de Saint-Pathus, *Vie de Saint Louis,* 26.

12. R. I. Moore, *La Persécution.*

13. R. I. Moore, "Heresy as Disease," in *The Concept of Heresy in the Middle Ages (11th–13th Century),* ed. W. Lordeaux and D. Verhelst (Louvain and the Hague, 1976); Boniface VIII, 258.

14. See above, "The Cistercian Model and the Mendicant Model," in Part III, ch. 7.

15. Joinville, *Histoire de Saint Louis,* 29–31.

16. Ibid.

17. He also called them "sons of the shadows" in opposition to Christians who were "sons of the light." In any case, this was the expression used by Geoffroy de Beaulieu in an argument attributed to the king (*Vita,* 15).

18. Matthew Paris, *Chronica majora,* 5:310.

19. D. O'Connell, *Les Propos de Saint Louis,* 81–82.

20. B. Z. Kedar, *Crusade and Mission.*

21. A. Miquel, *Ousâma, un prince syrien face aux croisés.*

22. Guillaume de Saint-Pathus, *Vie de Saint Louis,* 151.

23. Geoffroy de Beaulieu, *Vita,* 16–17.

24. The major surveys are the article by Margaret Wade-Labarge, "Saint Louis et les juifs," in *Le Siècle de Saint Louis* (Paris, 1970), 267–75, and the very brief studies by Jacques Madaule, "Saint Louis et les juifs," *L'Arche,* no. 165 (November–December, 1970): 58–61, and Bernard Blumenkranz, "Louis IX ou Saint Louis et les juifs," *Archives juives* 10 (1973–1974): 18–21. See also, S. Menache, "The King, the Church and the Jews," *Journal of Medieval History* 13 (1987): 223–36.

25. Gérard Nahon, "Une géographie des Juifs dans la France de Louis IX (1226–1270)," in *The Fifth World Congress of Jewish Studies,* vol. 2 (Jerusalem, 1972), 127–32, with a map: "Among the entire group of locations, ninety-eight have some Jewish presence. Twenty-three are located in the bailiwick of Tours, thirteen in the seneschalcy of Beaucaire, eleven in the constabulary of Auvergne, ten in the seneschalcy of Poitou-Limousin, nine in the bailiwick of Vermandois, nine in the provostship of Paris, six in the seneschalcy of Carcassonne, five in the seneschalcy of Saintonge, three in the bailiwick of Caen, three in the bailiwick of Gisors, three in the seneschalcy of Tours and Albigeois, one in the bailiwick of Cotentin, one in the seneschalcy of Agenais and Quercy. Are these cities, towns, or villages? When we consider the actual numbers of their populations, we find that twenty-two locations have less than one thousand inhabitants, thirty-seven have fewer than five thousand, and forty have more than five thousand. Jews therefore lived in villages (twenty-two percent), towns (twenty-seven percent), and cities (forty percent). On the other hand, the locations where Jews have clients but no residences include fifty-one villages (for thirty-six of them), towns (for thirteen), and cities (only two). Practically seventy percent of the locales that have no Jews are villages, while seventy-seven percent of localities with a Jewish presence are towns or cities. Although a certain rural Jewish population is still present, a trend toward the urbanization of the population clearly appears. The presence of a Jewish populace frequently coincides with the presence of an administrative center."

26. Michel Roblin, *Les Juifs de Paris* (Paris, 1952); William C. Jordan, *The French Monarchy and the Jews. From Philip Augustus to the Last Capetians* (Philadelphia, 1989), 9.

27. G. Nahon, "Une géographie des Juifs dans la France," 132.

28. Guillaume de Chartres, *De Vita et Miraculis,* 34. Aryeh Grabois has brought this declaration to my attention. However, it seems to me that he interprets it in a way that is too favorable to Saint Louis. In fact, his protection was a right to exercise punishment, and we may apply the adage "spare the rod, and spoil the child" to him because Saint Louis did not like the Jews.

29. R. I. Moore, *La Persécution.*

30. Claudine Fabre-Vassas, *La Bête singulière. Les juifs, les chrétiens, le cochon* (Paris, 1994). See also, Noël Coulet, "Juif intouchable et interdits alimentaires," in *Exclus du*

système dans la littérature et la civilisation médiévales (Aix-en-Provence and Paris, 1978). This work deals mainly with the fifteenth and sixteenth centuries.

31. Paul Rousset, "La conception de l'histoire à l'époque féodale."

32. N. Cohn has quite accurately recalled that the Romans had made this accusation against the Christians.

33. G. Langmuir, "*Judei nostri* and the Beginning of Capetian Legislation," *Traditio* 14 (1960).

34. Here I am following the excellent study by Gérard Nahon, "Le crédit et les Juifs dans la France du XIIIᵉ siècle," *Annales, E.S.C.* 24 (1969): 1121–1449. See also, Aryeh Grabois, "Du crédit juif à Paris au temps de Saint Louis," *Revue des études juives* 129 (1970).

35. A. Grabois, "Le crédit juif à Paris," 7–8.

36. See W. C. Jordan, *The French Monarchy and the Jews.*

37. G. Nahon, "Le crédit et les Juifs," 142. In this article, Nahon also goes over the more general opinion expressed by Raymond de Roover according to which the Church doctrine on usury had more serious repercussions on the history of banking than previously believed, "New Interpretations of the History of Banking," *Cahiers d'histoire mondiale* (1954): 38–76.

38. Guillaume de Chartres, *De Vita et de miraculis,* 34; for Gérard de Nahon's translation, 30–31.

39. See above, in this section.

40. Luigi Aurigemma, *Le Signe zodiacal du scorpion dans les traditions occidentales de l'Antiquité gréco-latine à la Renaissance* (Paris, 1976).

41. S. Schwarzfuchs, "De la condition des Juifs en France aux XIIᵉ et XIIIᵉ siècles," *Revue des études juives,* Memorial Maurice Liber, 125 (1966): 223; G. Langmuir, "*Tanquam servi.* The Change in Jewish Status in French Law about 1200," in *Les Juifs dans l'histoire de France,* First International Colloquium of Haïfa (Leyden, 1980).

42. *Layettes du Trésor des chartes,* vol. 4, no. 922, 350.

43. *Ordonnances des rois de France,* 1:36.

44. Ibid., 1:197.

45. The translated texts have been published by Gérard Nahon in "Les ordonnances de Saint Louis sur les juifs," *Les Nouveaux Cahiers* 23 (1970): 26–29.

46. W. C. Jordan, *The French Monarchy and the Jews,* 133.

47. G. Nahon, "Les ordonnances de Saint Louis sur les Juifs," with original documents translated from Latin and Hebrew.

48. The "characters" here are the written signs of Hebrew, which were considered magical.

49. See the following pages here.

50. G. Nahon, "Le crédit et les Juifs."

51. William C. Jordan, "Jewish-Christian Relations in Mid-Thirteenth-Century France: An Unpublished *Enquête* from Picardy," *Revue des études juives* 138 (1979): 47–54.

52. W. C. Jordan, *The French Monarchy and the Jews,* 161–62.

53. P. Fournier and P. Guébin, *Enquêtes administratives d'Alphonse de Poitiers* (Paris, 1959); M. Jurselin, "Documents financiers concernant les mesures prises par Alphonse de Poitiers contre les Juifs (1268–1269)," *Bibliothèque de l'École des chartes* 68 (1907): 130–49.

54. W. C. Jordan, *The French Monarchy and the Jews,* 162–68.

55. See Adin Steinaltz, *Introduction au Talmud* (Paris, 1994).

56. Yvonne Friedman, "Les attaques contre le Talmud (1144–1244), de Pierre le Vénérable à Nicolas Donin," a paper presented at the international colloquium on *Le Brûlement du Talmud à Paris en 1244,* which was held in Paris on May 2–3, 1994. I participated in this colloquium and am using the proceedings here, which are forthcoming. The main works on the "judgment" of the Talmud in Paris in 1240 are: Gilbert Dahan, "Rashi sujet de la controverse de 1240," *Archives juives* 14 (1978): 43–54; I. Loeb, "La controverse de 1240 sur le Talmud," *Revue des études juives,* vols. 1, 2, and 3 (1880–1881); J. Rembaum, "The Talmud and the Popes: Reflection on the Talmud Trials of the 1240s," *Viator* (13): 203–21; J. Rosenthal, "The Talmud on Trial," *Jewish Quarterly Review,* n.s. 47 (1956–1957): 58–76 and 145–69; Alberto Temko, "The Burning of the Talmud in Paris. Date: 1242," *Commentary* 20 (1955): 228–39. A century earlier, the abbot of Cluny Pierre le Vénérable had harshly attacked the Talmud, although he was not familiar with the modern versions and can in no way "be held responsible for the burning of the Talmud."

57. Nicolas de Donin's history and motives are disputed and not very well known. For some, he was at least in the beginning a "heretical" Jew instead of a convert. He supposedly wanted to protest the Talmud's emergence at the expense of the Bible just as certain Christians like the great thirteenth-century Franciscan university scholar Roger Bacon contested the importance granted in the Christian universities to the twelfth-century Parisian bishop Pierre de Lombard's *Sentences* to the detriment of direct readings of Holy Scripture. Some have even ventured that Nicolas Donin must have been in contact with certain Parisian Franciscan milieus that favored a return to Holy Scripture shorn of its glosses and scholastic commentaries.

58. I am following Andre Tuilier's paper here, "La condemnation du Talmud par les maîtres universitaires parisiens au milieu du XIIIᵉ siècle, ses causes et ses conséquences politiques et idéologiques," presented at the colloquium of Paris in May, 1994 (proceedings forthcoming).

59. Aryeh Grabois, "Une conséquence du brûlement du Talmud: la fondation de l'école talmudique d'Acre," act of the colloquium of Paris, May 1994.

60. The count of Brittany had expelled all the Jews there in 1236.

61. From G. Nahon's translation in "Les ordonnances de Saint Louis."

62. Guillaume de Saint-Pathus, *Vie de Saint Louis,* 10.

63. G. Nahon, "Les ordonnances de Saint Louis," 28.

64. G. Nahon, "Une géographie des Juifs," 131.

65. G. Nahon, "Les ordonnances de Saint Louis," 32–33.

66. Ibid., 25.

67. To an abbot and a knight who were talking about discussions that they had with Jews, the king replied: "I can also tell you that no one should debate with them [the Jews] if he is a very good cleric. But, when any layman hears anyone maligning the Christian law, he should only defend it with his sword and he should thrust it into his enemy's stomach as far as it can go" (Joinville, *Histoire de Saint Louis,* 31); see above, "Saint Louis and the Heretics," in Part III, ch. 8.

68. From a discussion that I had with Aryeh Grabois.

69. G. Nahon, "Les ordonnances de Saint Louis," 25.

70. See J. Le Goff, *La Bourse et la Vie.*

71. For my interpretation of this entire group of measures, see above, "The Kingdom's Reformer," in Part I, ch. 4.

72. G. Nahon, "Les ordonnances de Saint Louis," 28.

73. Ibid., 23. In some cases, Jews organized, resisted, and escaped from the pogrom. This was the case of the Jews in Niort.

74. G. Langmuir, "Anti-Judaism as the Necessary Preparation for Anti-Semitism," *Viator* 2 (1971): 383–90.

75. See above, "The King's Flaws," in Part II, ch. 9, and "His Wife," in Part III, ch. 6.

76. Guillaume de Saint-Pathus, *Vie de Saint Louis,* 37–38.

77. Ibid., 71.

78. Ibid., 39.

79. See above, "The Good Use of Time," in Part III, ch. 1.

80. See above, "Saint Louis on Display for His Subjects," in Part III, ch. 5, and below, Part III, ch. 10.

81. Geoffroy de Beaulieu, *Vita,* 6.

82. Ibid., 6.

83. Guillaume de Saint-Pathus, *Vie de Saint Louis,* 109–10.

84. Guillaume de Nangis, *Gesta Ludovici IX,* 406.

85. See above, "The Uncompromising Dispenser of Justice," in Part I, ch. 4; "Words of Faith," in Part III, ch. 3, and "The First Function," in Part III, ch. 4.

86. Geoffroy de Beaulieu, *Vita,* 11.

87. Guillaume de Saint-Pathus, *Vie de Saint Louis,* 88–89.

88. Cf. above, "The English Benedictine, Matthew Paris," in Part II, ch. 7.

89. Matthew Paris, *Chronica majora,* 3:325.

90. Ibid., 336.

91. Ibid., 4:198 (*franc = libre* [free]).

92. See above, "The Franco-English Peace," in Part I, ch. 4.

93. See above, "The Uncompromising Dispenser of Justice," in Part I, ch. 4, and "The First Function" in Part III, ch. 4.

94. "Chanson sur les établissements du roi Saint Louis," *Bibliothèque de l'École des chartes* 1 (1840): 370–74.

95. Gérard Sivery, "Le mécontentement dans le royaume de France et les enquêtes de Saint Louis," *Revue historique* 545 (1983): 3–24.

96. On Saint Louis' relations with the Mendicant friars, see above, Part II, ch. 2, and L. K. Little, "Saint Louis' Involvement with the Friars." .

97. Rutebeuf was particularly violent. See the list of his grievances against Saint Louis in Jean Dufournet, "Rutebeuf et les moines mendiants," *Neuphilologische Mitteilungen* 85 (1984): 165–66. This article includes a bibliography on this subject.

98. I have already discussed it as an example illustrating the king's clemency, see above, "The First Function," in Part III, ch. 4.

99. Guillaume de Saint-Pathus, *Vie de Saint Louis,* 118–19.

100. L. Carolus-Barré, *Le Procès de canonisation,* 248. On Thomas de Cantimpré and Saint Louis, see above, "Guillaume de Saint-Pathus," in Part II, ch. 2.

PART III
Notes to Chapter 9

1. This charisma only partially corresponds to Weber's concept of charismatic domination because Saint Louis' charismatic prestige not only came from his own personality, it was based on the objective prestige of the royal function and on the Christian principles defined by the Mirrors of the Princes that imposed limits on the influence of personality. His charisma fed off the divine image and the religious model.

2. The great book that produced the modern treatment of the whole problematic of medieval royalty is M. Bloch's *Les Rois thaumaturges.*

3. This is the *ordo* contained in the Latin MS 1246 in the Bibliothèque nationale in Paris. I date it from around 1250, as does Jean-Claude Bonne, in agreement with Richard Jackson and François Avril. See above, "Books of Images," in Part III, ch. 2, and my article "A Coronation Program for the Age of Saint Louis: The Ordo of 1250," and the article by Jean-Claude Bonne, "The Manuscript of the Ordo of 1250 and Its Illuminations," in *Coronations,* ed. J. M. Bak, 46–57 and 58–71. J.-C. Bonne and I are preparing an edition of this *ordo* with commentary.

4. A. Dupront, *Du sacré.*

5. In the Middle Ages, the name *"écrouelles"* (scrofulous) or *"scrofules"* was given to various kinds of swelling of the glands and purulent skin conditions.

6. J. Le Goff, "Le miracle royal," see the next section of this chapter below.

7. The royal dubbing should be distinguished from chivalric dubbing. We may recall that Saint Louis had been dubbed as a child at Soissons just before the coronation at Reims. See J. Richard, "L'adoubement de Saint Louis."

8. See J. Le Goff, "Reims, ville du sacre," especially 118–22.

9. Hervé Pinoteau, "La tenue de sacre de Saint Louis IX, roi de France. Son arrière-plan sybolique et la *renovatio regni Iuda,*" *Itinéraires* 162:120–66, reprinted in *Vingt-cinq ans d'études dynastiques* (Paris, 1982), 447–504; idem, "Les insignes du pouvoir des Capétiens directs," *Itinéraires* 323 (May 1988): 40–53.

10. Anne Lombard-Jourdan, *Fleurs de lys et oriflamme. Signes célestes du royaume de France* (Paris, 1991).

11. In one text that I have examined above, Saint Louis presents himself as a kind of "external bishop" for the Jews, but the expression is not pronounced.

12. First practiced in the eighth century at Pepin's coronation, this rite was only introduced into episcopal ordination in the ninth century: the anointment of bishops therefore imitated the anointment of kings and not the other way around.

13. I have attempted to demonstrate this in a recent study "Le miracle royal"; idem, "Le mal royal au Moyen Âge: du roi malade au roi guérisseur," *Mediaevistik* 1 (1988): 101–9. Fred Barlow uses similar arguments to support the thesis that royal laying-on-hands in England only became institutionalized with Henry III, "The King's Evil," *English Historical Review* (1980): 3–27.

14. Louis' reputation as a healer spread throughout Christendom. A certain Lanfranchino living in Montassenti near Siena was suffering from scrofula and departed for France in 1258 in order to be "touched" by the king (Odile Redon, in *Archeologia medievale* 14 [1987]: 390–93).

15. A separate treatment still needs to be worked out for the throne.

16. Or, *sede vacante,* by its suffragant, usually the first one, the bishop of Soissons.

17. This is a milestone in the formation of what J. Krynen has called *L'Empire du roi.*

18. See above, "The First Function," in Part III, ch. 4.

19. A. Vauchez, *La Sainteté en Occident.*

20. R. Folz, "La sainteté de Louis IX d'après les textes liturgiques de sa fête."

21. A. Vauchez, *Les Laïcs au Moyen Âge.*

22. J.-L. Flandrin, *Un temps pour embrasser.*

23. R. Folz, *Les Saints Rois du Moyen Âge en Occident.*

24. J. Le Goff, "Saint Louis, croisé idéal?"

25. See above, "The *Eruditio Regum et Principum* by Gilbert de Tournai," in Part II, ch. 6. Although there is no doubt that they had no influence on the king and his reign, to these five Mirrors of the Princes we can add the *De eruditione principum* by the Dominican Guillaume Perraut (ca. 1265), and, with more of a stretch, the *De regimine principum* composed for the king of Cyprus by Thomas Aquinas who began it around 1265, whereas it was completed by Ptolemée de Lucques in 1304. I discuss the *De morali principis institutione* on the next page.

26. Sverre Bagge, *The Political Thought of the King's Mirror* (Odense University Press, 1987); Einar Mar Jonsson, "La situation du *Speculum regale* dans la littérature occidentale," *Études germaniques* (October-December 1987): 391–408.

27. I owe these specific observations to the text of R. J. Schneider's lecture, "*Rex imago Trinitatis*: Power, Wisdom and Goodness in the *De morali principis institutione* of Vincent de Beauvais," given at the University of Groningen on January 23, 1987. I extend my warm thanks to J. Schneider for his willingness to send me the unpublished text of this lecture as well as the one cited just below. See above, "Mirrors of the Thirteenth Century," in Part II, ch. 6, and "An Encyclopedist in the Service of the King: Vincent de Beauvais," in Part III, ch. 2. On Vincent de Beauvais' *opus politicum,* see Part III, ch. 2, same section.

28. This text would have been lost if Vincent de Beauvais had not reproduced it in bk. 29 of his *Speculum historiale.*

29. See above, Part II, ch. 6. Robert J. Schneider, "Vincent de Beauvais on Political Legitimacy and the Capetian Dynasty: The Argument of the *De morali principis institutione,*" lecture given at the 22nd International Congress of Medieval Studies, "The Capetian Millenium: 987–1987," Kalamazoo, May 8, 1987.

30. On the king as an "image of God," see above, Part II, ch. 6. On this trifunctionality, see above, Part III, ch. 4. Despite its relative success among authors of Mirrors of the Princes, the concept of the king as an "image of God" mainly circulated among theologians and probably also in the common mentality of the time.

31. See above, "Louis and Josiah," in Part II, ch. 5.

32. See above, Part II, ch. 8.

33. Cf. J. W. Baldwin, *Philippe Auguste et son gouvernement,* 491–95, and J. Le Goff, "Le dossier de sainteté de Philippe Auguste."

34. See the remarkable study by R. Floz, *Les Saints Rois du Moyen Âge en Occident.*

35. Alain Boureau, "Saint Louis," in *Histoire des saintes et de la sainteté chrétienne,* vol. 6, *Au temps du renouveau évangélique* (1054–1274), ed. André Vauchez (Paris, 1986), 196–205.

36. See above, "The *Prud'homme,*" in Part III, ch. 3.

37. In *La Sainteté,* A. Vauchez has shown that this conception of miracles was only slowly and rather imperfectly imposed over the course of the thirteenth century.

38. I am reproducing the essential information from my study on this topic, "Saint de l'Église et saint du people." See the excellent study carried out from a slightly different perspective, which parallels mine, a history of the body (which I also undertake in the following and final chapter of this book) by S. Chennaf and O. Redon, "Les miracles de Saint Louis."

39. "After the burial of the holy bones, there was no lack of divine miracles; God was swift in making his [new] saint the beneficiary of miracles" (*Recueil des historiens des Gaules et de la France,* 20:25).

40. *De Vita et de Miraculis,* 28.

41. Boniface VIII, 23:159.

42. Innocent III's position is articulated in the bull for the canonization of Saint Homebon (January 12, 1199), edited by O. Hageneder and A. Haidacher, *Das Register Innocenz III* (Graz and Cologne, 1964), 1:761–64. "According to the true evidence, although only final perseverance is required for a soul to reach sainthood in the triumphant Church, since 'the person who has persevered until the end will be saved,' two things are required in the militant Church in order for someone to pass as a saint: virtue in manners and truth in the signs of sainthood, in other words works of piety in life, and miracles accomplished after death" (A. Vauchez, *La Sainteté en Occident,* 42–43).

43. *Recueil des historiens des Gaules et de la France,* 23:150.

44. Guillaume de Saint-Pathus, *Les Miracles de Saint Louis,* 171–74.

45. For example, Guillaume de Chartres: "*ac de miraculis quae circa ejus sepulcrum et alias*" (*De Vita et de Miraculis,* in *Recueil des historiens des Gaules et de la France,* 20:28).

46. By delocalization, I mean the trend of situating miracles in places other than those marked by the presence of the saint or his relics in his own lifetime. Cf. A. Vauchez, *La Sainteté en Occident,* "Du tombeau à l'image: le lieu de l'invocation," 519–29.

47. The record shows that there were twelve inhabitants of Saint-Denis, twenty-five Parisians, twenty individuals residing in Île-de-France or the outlying areas, and two from regions that were a bit further away—a knight of Hainaut from the diocese of Arras and a swineherd valet from Ranton near Loudun in Vienne and the diocese of Poitiers.

48. For example, there is the miracle (42) for Jehanne de Sarris (near Crécy-en-Brie), the wife of Jehan le Charpentier, who one night in 1276 lost the use of her legs and feet. After a month, "as she was poor and had no one who would help her, not even her husband who did not want to give her what she needed," she was brought to the hospital in Paris. After spending a period of time there, she wanted to go home and went back on crutches with her husband's help, but he did not want to take care of her again, so she went "with great difficulty" (on crutches) to beg at the church of Saint-Merri in Paris. When she heard about the miracles that took place at Saint Louis' tomb, she decided to go to Saint-Denis and to survive there on what she could earn for herself. She "begged enough to make three *sous*," and with this money, she made the difficult journey to Saint-Denis (still on crutches) with the help of one of her daughters. She offered a "candle of her own height [*de sa longueur*]" at the king's tomb, and after four days she began to feel better. After nine days, she was able to return to Paris, "standing on her own two feet without the aid of any cane or crutches and without needing anyone to help her." She was in good health after that "and did her work like any other saintly woman" (Guillaume de Saint-Pathus, *Les Miracles de Saint Louis,* 131–34).

49. Geoffroy de Beaulieu, *Vita,* ch. 35, "*Quod in tangendo infirmos signum sanctae crucis super addidit,*" the allusion consists of eight lines in the *Recueil des historiens des Gaules et de la France,* 20:20. Guillaume de Saint-Pathus briefly alluded to it twice in his *Vie de Saint Louis* because these were examples of healing that the king accomplished during his life: "*Chascun jour, au matin, quand il avoit oy ses messes et il revenoit en sa chambre, il fesoit apeler ses malades des escroeles et les touchoit*" (Each day in the morning when he had heard his mass and came back to his room, he would summon the sick people who were suffering from scrofula and touch them), ed. Delaborde, 99. Again, we read, "*Et par bonc tens li benoiez rois et de coutousme que quant il avoit ses messes oyes et il a [voit] touchié ses malades du mal des escroeles*" (And sometimes when he had heard his masses, the blessed king had the custom of touching his people who were sick with the disease of the scrofulous), ibid., 142. I have kept the original Old French, which is not too difficult to understand here.

50. Guillaume de Saint-Pathus, *Les Miracles de Saint Louis,* 188.

51. Boniface VIII, in *Recueil des historiens des Gaules et de la France,* 23:159.

52. H.-F. Delaborde thought that this should perhaps be read as *fortissima* in reference to the expression "*goutte flestre*" (gouty fistula) from the French translation of the *Miracles,* but, as *flestre* signifies "fistula" and in the manuscript of the sermon (from Chartres) *a gutta forma* appears under *fistulati,* this hypothesis does not seem very convincing (H.-F. Delaborde, "Une oeuvre nouvelle de Guillaume de Saint-Pathus," 277).

53. I have kept the Roman numerals from the original manuscript. H.-F. Delaborde points out that the original text reads *timore* and not *tumore,* and does not decipher the abbreviation *sil,* which is still a mystery to me (ibid., 277).

54. The difficulty of determining the exact definition of the category of the miracles mentioned in a certain number of cases and the difficulty of defining the category of paralytics in particular have prevented me from identifying the five miracles that are not accounted for in the sermon.

55. Guillaume de Saint-Pathus, *Les Miracles de Saint Louis,* 1–2.

56. Pierre-André Sigal, "Maladie, pèlerinage et guérison au XIIᵉ siècle. Les miracles de Saint-Gibrien à Reims," *Annales, E.S.C.* 24 (1969): 1–27; A. Vauchez, *La Sainteté en Occident,* 549–52.

57. Piero Camporesi, *Il pane selvaggio* (1980); French translation, *Le Pain sauvage. L'imaginaire de la faim de la Renaissance au XVIIIᵉ siècle* (Paris, 1981).

58. Jacques Paul, "Miracles et mentalité religieuse populaire à Marseille au début du XIVᵉ siècle," *La Religion populaire en Languedoc du XIIIᵉ à la moitié du XIVᵉ siècle. Cahiers de Fanjeaux* 11 (Toulouse): 61–90.

59. Here, we might recall Joinville's famous dream in which Saint Louis appeared to him after his death and asked him to place a statue of him in the chapel in his castle. Cf. M. Zink, "Joinville ne pleure pas." We should note that Saint Louis' appearance in dreams to people who knew him seems to have been a *topos* in the years following the king's death.

60. One text that has recently been discovered confirms this. This is the archbishop of Toledo D. Gonzalo Pérez's response to a questionnaire on Saint Louis' miracles from Boniface VIII. (The miracles were the ones that had already been assembled in the course of the inquiry, notably in 1282; see above, "Toward Canonization," in Part I, ch. 5.) The questionnaire was drawn up in Rome in the first months of 1297. Gonzalo Pérez finds that Saint Louis had two of the virtues the Church had recognized in saints since Innocent III, the *virtuositas operationum* (virtuous actions) and the *continuatio vel continuitias actionum* (perseverance in goodness). A man of great culture, among other arguments the archbishop of Toledo also draws on Aristotle's *Nicomachean Ethics.* He possessed a manuscript of this text that was written at Viterbo in 1279 after Saint Louis' death. As for the third characteristic of sainthood, the *claritas se evidentia miraculorum* (the light or evidence of miracles), he is satisfied to state that it appeared clearly in Louis IX's case, although without adding anything else. He thus avoided taking any position on these miracles and did not grant them any real significance. I extend my thanks to P. Lineham and F. J. Hernandez for discovering and publishing this text with their excellent commentary, "*Animadverto*: A Recently Discovered *Consilium* Concerning the Sanctity of King Louis IX."

61. Boniface VIII, in *Recueil des historiens des Gaules et de la France,* 23:151.

62. A. Vauchez, *La Sainteté en Occident,* "Mentalité hagiographique et mentalité commune," 615–22.

63. See above, "The History of the Relics," in Part I, ch. 5. I recall the astonishing account that Matthew Paris gives of Saint Louis' anger upon being presented with the member of a saint's body at the abbey of Pontigny. Matthew Paris died in 1259.

PART III
Notes to Chapter 10

1. Robert Folz, "Trois saints rois 'souffre-passion' en Angleterre: Oswin de Deira, Ethelbert d'Est-Anglie, Edouard le Martyr," *Comptes rendus de l'Académie des inscriptions et belles-lettres* (1980): 36–49. R. Folz includes Saint Louis in his book, *Les Saints Rois du Moyen Âge en Occident.* I do not agree with this great scholar on several important points. It is true that "between the sixth and thirteenth centuries the type of the saint king evolved in the same measure that royalty itself was consolidated," although I do not think that there was such a close relation between these two phenomena. "The sanctified king gradually replaced the martyr who wore the royal crown because of the way he used his power" (21). However, in claiming that "it is striking to notice that the first kings to be considered saints had been completely lacking in that royal 'virtue' that created victory or success that was hypothetically recognized in some of their pagan forbearers," I do not think that he places this important remark in the best light. Victory was still an attribute of the royal image, but the content of this success changed within Christendom as it came to consider martyrdom as the most beautiful type of victory. This was still the predominant concept at the time of Saint Louis' canonization. Nevertheless, between the "passion-suffering" kings and Saint Louis there was a profound difference characteristic of the age that marked a break with tradition, whereas R. Folz insists instead on what he interprets as continuity between these two concepts of royal sainthood. Saint Louis' suffering was a daily suffering in his heart and body, accepted with patience or sought out with zeal, and not a dramatic event entirely imposed from the outside. His suffering became a value and only rejoined the Christ of the Passion in the end. His was the suffering of a man who accepted his human condition and made it into an element of his power instead of an assault on this power, an increase and not a decrease in prestige. It was not the concept of royalty that changed as much as the concept of suffering and attitudes toward the body.

2. Joinville, *Histoire de Saint Louis,* 40–41. This passage can be found in Part I, ch. 1 of Joinville's text. A very suggestive special issue of the review *Médiévales* has been devoted to the different forms of suffering in the Middle Ages: *Du bon usage de la souffrance,* no. 27 (Autumn 1994).

3. One of the royal investigators' main tasks was to gather complaints against unfair exactions, which was supposed to lead to restitutions made by the king. Along with repentance, the restitution of usuries by the usurer or his heirs was the essential

condition for his salvation. The many thirteenth-century treatises "on restitutions" (*De restitutionibus*) are among the most interesting on lending practices and church doctrine on this matter. Saint Louis insisted heavily on his duty to make restitution in his *Enseignements* for his son. See Joinville, *Histoire de Saint Louis,* 19.

4. Geoffroy de Beaulieu, *Vita,* 14.

5. See above, "The Children," in Part III, ch. 6.

6. Guillaume de Chartres, *De Vita et de Miraculis,* 33. "It happened once in a parlement that a woman who was extravagantly dressed [*non modicum curiose*], came into the king's chamber after the court's ruling on her affair and got herself noticed by the king. She was actually extremely beautiful and reputed for her beauty according to the deceitful age and the false judgment of the people of the age when it comes to the vain beauty of the body. Completely devoted in his heart to God, the king wanted to talk to her personally about her salvation. He called on Brother Geoffroy [de Beaulieu] who was there and said to him: 'I want you to be with me and for you to hear what I am going to say to this lady present here who has asked to speak with me personally.' When the other affairs had been dispatched, this lady was still there alone with the king and the friar, and the king told her: 'Madame, I only want to remind you about one thing for your salvation. People have said that you were once a beautiful lady, but, as you know, what you once were has already passed. So, reflect on the fact that this beauty was vain and useless and that it has faded fast like a flower that rapidly withers and does not last. And you cannot call it back, whatever care and diligence you put into it. Take care then to acquire another beauty, not the beauty of the body, but that of the soul. Thanks to this kind of beauty, you will please our Creator and redeem the wrongs you committed in the time of that past beauty.' The lady took in these words without any reaction. She then improved and conducted herself with more humility and honesty." On the relations that a saint who was very close to Saint Louis had with women, see the beautiful work by Jacques Dalarun, *Francesco: un passagio. Donna et donne negli scritti nelle leggende di Francesco d'Assisi* (Rome, 1994). The model of the female temptress that a man was supposed to turn away from belongs to the monastic tradition.

7. Guillaume de Saint–Pathus, *Vie de Saint Louis,* 142–43. "When a woman who belonged to the best society of Pontoise and the lineage of Pierrelaye had been arrested by the saint king's sergeants because, according to what people said, she had her husband killed by a man she loved with an evil love, according to what people say, and had him thrown into a latrine when he was dead, the lady recognized the fact during the trial, and the saint king wanted justice to be done for this action, although the queen of France and the countess of Poitiers [her sister-in-law, the wife of her brother Alphonse], and some of the other ladies of the Kingdom and some of the Minor and Preaching friars begged the king to spare the woman's life because she showed such great contrition and repentance. The friends and cousins of this lady, the queen, and the other people mentioned supplicated the king that, if she absolutely had to die, her execution not be held at Pontoise. The king asked His wise and noble Grace Simon de Nesle his opinion, and His Grace Simon de Nesle answered that the public execution of justice would be a good thing. So, the

saint king ordered the woman to be burned at the castle of Pontoise, and she was burned publicly."

8. Ibid., 144.

9. *Enseignements,* ed. D. O'Connell, 186.

10. Georges Daumet, "Une femme-médecin au XIIIᵉ siècle," *Revue des études historiques* (1918): 69–71.

11. Henri Stein, "Pierre Lombard médecin de Saint Louis," *Bibliothèque de l'École des chartes* 100 (1939): 63–71.

12. Guillaume de Saint-Pathus, *Vie de Saint Louis,* 132–33.

13. Here, I am going back over texts that I have already cited either in their chronological order or from some other perspective, but I am now examining them from the perspective of the body and Saint Louis' pain.

14. There is an excellent pathological and nosological record on Saint Louis in the now dated work of Dr. Auguste Brachet, *Pathologie des rois de France* (Paris, 1903), despite the unconvincing character of the author's argument, which attempts to prove the hereditary nature of epilepsy that it claims to have afflicted Louis XI and caused the madness of Charles VI, attempting to find the least sign of madness or physiological degeneration for all the Capetian kings since Hugh Capet. My readers can find a summary of this work in Appendix 1. On the relations between sainthood and disease, cf. C. L. B. Trub, *Heilig und Krankheit,* in *Bochumer historische Schriften,* vol. 19 (Stuttgart, 1978). See also, Claude Gauvart, "Les maladies des rois de France," *L'Histoire,* special issue: *Les maladies ont une histoire,* no. 74 (1984): 93–95. Of course, the chroniclers and biographers reported Louis VI's "stomach spasms" [*flux de ventre*], the obesity that reached pathological proportions at the end of the lives of Philip I (1060–1108) and Louis VI (1108–1137), the disease that was falsely identified as a sweating fever [*la suette*] that afflicted Philip Augustus and Richard the Lion-Hearted during the crusade of 1191, and the fragile health of Louis' father, Louis VIII (1223–1226). However, all these bodily ills are described as weaknesses and handicaps, whereas Saint Louis' illnesses were interpreted as merits worthy of the aura of sainthood.

15. Boniface VIII, 155.

16. Guillaume de Saint-Pathus, *Vie de Saint Louis,* 71.

17. Ibid., 21.

18. Joinville, *Histoire de Saint Louis,* 60.

19. Ibid., 6.

20. Guillaume de Saint-Pathus, *Vie de Saint Louis,* 116.

21. Joinville, *Histoire de Saint Louis,* 10.

22. Eudes Rigaud, in *Recueil des historiens des Gaules et de la France,* 21:581.

23. Joinville, *Histoire de Saint Louis,* 400.

24. Guillaume de Saint-Pathus, *Vie de Saint Louis,* 113.

25. Boniface VIII, 156.

26. *"Sic vir totus in fide fixus, et totus in spiritum absorptus, quando magis erat malleis adversitatis et infirmatis adtribus, eo plus fervorem emittens, in se perfectionem fidei declarabat"* (Guillaume de Chartres, *De Vita et de Miraculis,* 36).

27. For his son, he wrote: "If Our Lord sends you *persecution, disease,* or any other *suffering,* you must tolerate it in good nature, and you should thank him and acknowledge him, because you have to understand that he did this for your own good" (D. O'Connell, *Les Propos de Saint Louis,* 186). To his daughter, he wrote: "Dear daughter, if you are ever subjected to any *suffering* or *sickness* or anything else . . . suffer it in good nature, and thank Our Lord for it and acknowledge him for it, because you should believe that it is for your own good and that you have *merited* it" (ibid., 193).

28. To his son: "if you have *malaise de coeur,* tell it to your confessor" (ibid., 193).

29. "And with all this, the blessed king comforted the sick man and told him *that he had to suffer this disease in good patience, and that it was his purgatory in this world,* and that it was better to suffer from this disease in this world than to suffer something else in the age to come" (Guillaume de Saint-Pathus, *Vie de Saint Louis,* 95).

30. See J. Le Goff, *La Naissance du Purgatoire.*

31. Joinville, *Histoire de Saint Louis,* 16.

32. Cf. G. G. Meersseman, *Dossier de l'ordre de la pénitence au XIIIe siècle* (Freiburg, 1961); idem, "Disciplinati e penitenti nel Duecento," in *Il movimento dei Disciplinati nel settimo centenario del suo inizio,* 43–72; Ida Magli, *Gli uomini della penitenza* (Milan, 1977).

33. Saint Louis' hair shirts and disciplinary objects were kept in the abbey of Lys near Melun after his death.

34. Guillaume de Saint-Pathus, *Vie de Saint Louis,* 122–23.

35. "*Carnem ipsam quasi assidui asperitate cilicii . . . edomans . . . districtis etenim corpus atterebat jejuniis . . . post ejus reditum supradictum, non in pluma vel paleis jacuit sed super ligneum lectum portabilem, mataratio simpli superjecto, stramine nullo supposito decumbebat*" (Boniface VIII, 158).

36. Joinville, *Histoire de Saint Louis,* 134.

37. "There, we lost our brave and illustrious brother the count of Artois, worthy of eternal memory. It is with bitterness in our heart that we remember this painful loss, although we must rejoice in it instead, for we believe and hope that he has gone to the celestial country, having received the martyr's crown, and that he enjoys the rewards that are granted to the martyred saints there" (D. O'Connell, *Les Propos de Saint Louis,* 165).

38. Joinville, *Histoire de Saint Louis,* 330. See above, "His Mother," in Part III, ch. 6.

39. Geoffroy de Beaulieu, *Vita,* 17.

40. Joinville, *Histoire de Saint Louis,* 114.

41. Matthew Paris, *Chronica majora,* 8:89; D. O'Connell, *Les Propos de Saint Louis,* 139.

42. Matthew Paris, *Chronica majora,* 8:64–65; see D. O'Connell, *Les Propos de Saint Louis,* 102. I quoted this text in its entirety and in its chronological place in Part I.

43. Joinville, *Histoire de Saint Louis,* 216.

44. D. O'Connell, *Les Propos de Saint Louis,* 171.

45. Ibid., 169.

46. Guillaume de Saint-Pathus, *Vie de Saint Louis,* 23.

47. Guillaume de Chartres, *De Vita et de Miraculis,* 30.

48. Boniface VIII, 149–50, 156.

49. This very deep, very cruel trait of Saint Louis' has been perfectly understood by these two great historians and psychologists of the biological—Michelet and Roland Barthes. In the 1833 version of his *Histoire de France* (vol. 2, bk. 4, ch. 8, in *Oeuvres complètes,* vol. 4, ed. P. Viallaneix [1974], 586), Michelet quotes the confessor, actually the translation into Old French that Guillaume de Saint-Pathus had made of Geoffroy de Beaulieu's passage in Latin, and in his famous preface to the 1869 edition of the *Histoire de France* writes: "This gift that Saint Louis requested and failed to obtain, I had it: 'the gift of tears'." Roland Barthes comments on Michelet's interest in Saint Louis' inability to cry in the following way: "Another medium for incubation: tears. Tears are a gift; Saint Louis asked God to give them to him in vain. Michelet understood the fertile force of tears, not mental or metaphoric tears but tears of salt and water that swell up in one's eyes and run down one's face and into one's mouth, because tears are the liquid milieu of warm expansion, which people know is nothing other than the true genitive power" (*Michelet par lui-même* [Paris, 1965], 157). Michelet sees tears as characteristic of the Gothic Middle Ages: "A tear, a single one, cast down on the foundations of the Gothic church, suffices to evoke it" (Preface of 1869 in *Oeuvres complètes,* vol. 4, 167). This idea is developed in "La passion comme principe d'art au Moyen Âge": "Here is the whole mystery of the Middle Ages, the secret of its inexhaustible tears and its profound genius. Precious tears—they ran in limpid legends, in marvelous poems, and accumulating and rising toward the heavens they crystallized in the form of gigantic cathedrals that tried to rise up to the Lord!" (Michelet, *Histoire de France* in *Oeuvres complètes,* vol. 4 [Paris, 1974], 593).

50. See above, "Worship and Asceticism," in Part III, ch. 7. This passage can be found in Michelet's beautiful text quoted in the preceding footnote (4:586). Here is Geoffroy de Beaulieu's original Latin text (*Vita,* 14): "*Lacrymarum gratiam plurimum affectabat, et super hoc defectu confessori suo pie et humiliter conquerebatur, familiariter ei dicens, quod quando in letania dicebatur;* Ut fontem lacrymarum nobis dones, *devote dicebat: 'O Domine, fontem lacrymarum non audeo postulare, sed modicae lacrymarum stillae mihi sufficerent ad cordis mei ariditatem et duritiam irrigandam.' Aliquando etiam confessori suo familiariter recognovit,* quod quandoque Dominus in oratione aliquas lacrymas sibi dedit; *quas cum sentiret per genuas suaviter in os influere, non solum cordi, sed gustui suo dulcissime sapiebant.*"

51. P. Viallaneix edition, 590–93.

52. Guillaume de Saint-Pathus, *Vie de Saint Louis,* 104.

53. Ibid., 86.

54. Ibid., 99.

55. Ibid., 86.

56. Geoffroy de Beaulieu, *Vita,* 11.

57. Guillaume de Chartres, *De Vita et de Miraculis,* 52.

58. D. O'Connell, *Les Propos de Saint Louis,* 186–87.

59. Ibid., 193.

60. Guillaume de Saint-Pathus, *Vie de Saint Louis,* ch. 9 on "his love for his fellow man," ch. 10 on "his compassion for his fellow man," and ch. 11 on "his humility," 59–111.

61. Ibid., 74–75.

62. Ibid., 93–96.

63. Ibid., 107–8.

64. Boniface VIII, 150.

65. Ibid., 157.

66. Geoffroy de Beaulieu, *Vita,* 4–5.

67. Joinville, *Histoire de Saint Louis,* 42.

68. Ibid.

69. D. O'Connell, *Les Propos de Saint Louis,* 186.

70. On the origins of this image and the worship of the cross, see the outstanding study by M.-C. Sepière, *L'Image d'un Dieu souffrant. Aux origines du crucifix* (Paris, 1994). There are quite a few studies on the emergence of the worship of the Christ of the Passion and the crucified Christ from the eleventh to the thirteenth century. I refer my readers to Galienne Francastel, *Le Droit au trône. Un problème de prééminence dans l'art chrétien du IVe au XIIe siècle,* ch. 8, "Le Christ souffrant et la Vierge triomphante" (Paris, 1973). For Saint Louis himself, see the revealing words related by Guillaume de Saint-Pathus, above, "Criticisms and Resistance," in Part III, ch. 8.

71. Matthew Paris, *Chronica majora,* 6:202; D. O'Connell, *Les Propos de Saint Louis,* 91.

72. Ibid., 171.

73. Joinville, *Histoire de Saint Louis,* 430.

74. Matthew Paris, *Chronica majora,* 5:147; in D. O'Connell, *Les Propos de Saint Louis,* 147, the same chronicler gives a slightly different version of Louis' words here: "Either we will make these Tartars go back . . . to the Tartarean realms they came from . . . or they will be the ones who deliver us all to heaven."

75. Guillaume de Saint-Pathus, *Vie de Saint Louis,* 101.

76. Geoffroy de Beaulieu, *Vita,* 3–4.

77. Ibid., 23.

78. Boniface VIII, 159.

79. Joinville, *Histoire de Saint Louis,* 406.

80. Ibid., 4.

81. Luc de Heusch, "The Sacrificial Body of the King," in *Fragments for a History of the Human Body,* ed. M. Féher, vol. 3 (New York, 1989), 387–94.

Notes to the Conclusion

1. See A. Lewis, *Le Sang royal.*

2. One example of this anachronistic, un-nuanced type of condemnation of Louis IX's politics in the Occitan Midi can be found in the pamphlet by D. Borzeix, R. Pautal, and J. Serbat, *Louis IX (alias Saint Louis) et l'Occitanie.* J. Madaule identifies

the royal administration's excesses in the Midi and aligns the government of the entire kingdom on this model, but also determines that "despite this wrong, Louis IX's government was excellent overall: he made peace reign in a country that had hardly known it since the time of the Romans, and that would soon lose it again; he healed the wounds created by a religious and political war that had lasted nearly thirty years" (*Le Drame albigeois et l'unité française*).

3. M. Zink, *La Subjectivité littéraire*.

4. Jacques Chiffoleau, "Pour une histoire de la religion et des institutions médiévales," *Cahiers d'histoire* (1991): 3–21.

5. E. H. Kantorowicz, *L'Empereur Frédéric II*.

6. See above, "Salvation and Necessity," in Part III, ch. 4.

List of Abridged Titles

Boniface VIII   See Documents on the Canonization

Enseignements (ed. D. O'Connell)   See Saint Louis' Enseignements

Geoffroy de Beaulieu, *Vita*   See Biographies and Hagiographies

Guillaume de Chartres, *Vita et de Miraculis*   See Biographies and Hagiographies

Guillaume de Nangis, *Chronicon*   See Chronicles

Guillaume de Nangis, *Gesta Ludovici IX*   See Biographies and Hagiographies

Guillaume de Saint-Pathus,   See Biographies and Hagiographies
   Les Miracles de Saint Louis

Guillaume de Saint-Pathus,   See Biographies and Hagiographies
   Vie de Saint Louis

Joinville, *Histoire de Saint Louis*   See Biographies and Hagiographies

Layettes du Trésor des chartes   See Acts and Administrative and
                                                        Legislative Documents

Le Nain de Tillemont, *Vie de Saint Louis*   See Biographies and General Works

Matthew Paris, *Chronica majora*   See Chronicles

Ordonnances des rois de France   See Acts and Administrative and
                                                        Legislative Documents

Salimbene de Adam, *Cronica*   See Chronicles

N.B. All the translations of the biographies that I give in this book with the exception of Joinville's and any contrary notices are mine.

Bibliography

PRIMARY SOURCES

Acts and Administrative and Legislative Documents

As for Louis VIII and Philip III, there is no published edition of Saint Louis' Acts. This creates a large gap in the recorded acts of thirteenth-century French royalty that extends from 1223 to 1285.

The chancery register kept by Friar Guérin (d. 1227), Philip Augustus's main advisor, bishop of Senlis, Keeper of the Seals under Louis VIII and at the beginning of Saint Louis' minority, is kept in the Archives nationales (JJ26). It was used until 1276. Saint Louis brought a copy of it to Egypt, which is now kept in the Bibliothèque nationale (MS Latin 9778). He may have also brought the register to Tunis in 1270.

The charters and other acts have been published in the *Layettes du Trésor des chartes,* vol. 2, *1223–1246,* edited by A. Teulet (Paris, 1866); vol. 3, *1246–1262,* edited by J. De Laborde (Paris, 1875); vol. 4, *1262–1270,* edited by Élie Berger (Paris, 1902).

The acts of the Parlement beginning in 1254 have been published in the *Olim ou registres des arrêts rendus par la cour du roi sous les règnes de Saint Louis, Philippe le Hardi, etc.,* edited by Arthur Beugnot, vol. 1, *1254–1273* (Paris, 1839). Edgar Boutaric has presented an analysis of it in *Actes du Parlement de Paris,* vol. 1, *1254–1299* (Paris, 1863).

There are only a few remaining fragments from the royal accounting records that were destroyed in the fire at the Chambre des comptes in 1737. These fragments (the accounts of the royal Hôtel from 1231, 1234, 1238, 1248, and 1267; the records of the tithe levied from the clergy for the crusade; a recapitulation of the expenses for the crusade of 1248; expenses for the army; and lists of crusaders' names) were published by Natalis de Wailly in the *Recueil des historiens des Gaules et de la France,* vol. 21 (Paris, 1855), and vol. 22 (Paris, 1865). The records from the investigations decreed by Saint Louis were published by Léopold Delisle in the *Recueil,* vol. 24 (Paris, 1904).

The lists of Saint Louis' voyages and visits (*Itinera et Mansiones*) have also been published in the *Receuil,* vol. 22.

The edicts have been published in a rather unsatisfactory form by Eusèbe de Laurière in the *Ordonnances des rois de France de la troisième race,* vol. 1 (Paris, 1723). Study of this work should be complemented by Jourdan, Decrusy, and Isambert, *Recueil général des anciennes lois françaises . . .* (Paris, 1822–1833), which is equally subject to caution.

Biographies and Hagiographies

Geoffroy de Beaulieu. *Vita et sancta conversatio piae memoriae Ludovici quondam regis Francorum.* In *Recueil des historiens des Gaules et de la France,* vol. 20. 3–27.
Guillaume de Chartres. *De Vita et Actibus Inclytae Recordationis Regis Francorum Ludovici et de Miraculis quae ad ejus Sanctitatis Declarationem Contingerunt.* In *Recueil des historiens des Gaules et de la France,* vol. 20. 27–41.

Guillaume de Nangis. *Gesta Ludovici IX.* French and Latin versions in *Recueil des historiens des Gaules et de la France,* vol. 20. Edited by C. F. Daunou and J. Naudet. Paris, 1840. 312–465

Guillaume de Saint-Pathus. *Vie de Saint Louis* (preserved in its French version). Edited by Henri-François Delaborde. Paris, 1899.

——*La Vie et les Miracles de Monseigneur Saint Louis.* Edited by Percival B. Fay. Paris, 1931.

Delaborde, Henri-François. "Une oeuvre nouvelle de Guillaume de Saint-Pathus" (a sermon on Saint Louis). *Bibliothèque de l'École des chartes* 63 (1902): 263–88.

Jean de Joinville. *Histoire de Saint Louis.* Edited by Natalis de Wailly. (I quote the edition of 1874 with translation in modern French.) N. L. Corbett has published a reconstructed version of Joinville's text based on a single fourteenth-century manuscript in order to produce something closer to the original, *La Vie de Saint Louis. Le témoignage de Jehan, seigneur de Joinville,* edited by Naamon (Sherbrooke, Canada, 1977). Extracts from the work in modern French have been presented by A. Duby, *Saint Louis par Joinville* (Paris, 1963). A partial modern translation of Joinville has been published in *Historiens et Chroniqueurs du Moyen Âge* (Paris, 1963), 195–366. A new edition and translation by Jacques Monfrin, with introduction, has just been published—Joinville, *Vie de Saint Louis* (Paris, 1995). I was not able to consult this edition for this work.

Chronicles

Philippe Mouskès. *Chronique rimée de Philippe Mouskès.* Edited by F. de Reiffenberg. 2 vols. Brussels, 1836–1838.

Matthew Paris. *Chronica majora.* Edited by Henry R. Luard. 7 vols. London, 1972–1973.

Salimbene de Adam (de Parme). *Cronica.* Edited by G. Scalia. 2 vols. Bari, 1966.

Primat. In *Les Grandes Chroniques de France,* vol. 1. Edited by J. Viard. Paris, 1920. A French translation (from the first half of the fourteenth century) by Jean de Vignay of Primat's Latin Chronicle is in *Recueil des historiens des Gaules et de la France,* vol. 23, 1–106.

Guillaume de Nangis. *Chronicon.* Edited by H. Géraud. 2 vols. Paris, 1843–1844. Also in *Recueil des historiens des Gaules et de la France,* vol. 20, 544–586, and vol. 21, 103–123.

The Minstrel of Reims. *Récits d'un ménestrel de Reims au XIIIe siècle.* Edited by Natalis de Wailly, 1876.

Saint Louis' Enseignements

The primitive text of Saint Louis *Enseignements* for his son and daughter has been published by Henri-François Delaborde, "Le texte primitif des enseignements de Saint Louis à son fils," *Bibliothèque de l'École des chartes* 73 (1912).

An effort to reconstitute the original version is by David O'Connell, *The Teachings of Saint Louis. A Critical Text* (Chapel Hill, 1972). See the French translation in D. O'Connell, *Les Propos de Saint Louis,* preface by Jacques Le Goff (Paris, 1974).

Miscellaneous Documents

Their sources are indicated where they are cited in the text. They come from:

D'Achery, Luc. *Spicilegium sive collectio veterum aliquot scriptorum.* New edition in 3 vols. Paris, 1723.

Duchesne, André. *Historiae Francorum Scriptores,* vol. 5. Paris, 1649.

Durand, E., and U. Martène. *Thesaurus novus anecdotorum,* vol. 1. Paris, 1717.

Documents on the Canonization

Although its principle can be contested, a remarkable attempt to reconstitute the original document has been made by Louis Carolus-Barré, *Reconstitution du procès de canonisation de Saint Louis (1272–1297),* published posthumously. Edited by H. Platelle. Rome: École française de Rome, 1995. The texts utilized by Guillaume de Saint-Pathus are presented in French translation.

The two sermons and Boniface VIII's bull for the canonization (August, 1297) have been published in the *Recueil des historiens des Gaules et de la France,* vol. 23, 148–60.

Comte, P. E. Riant. "Déposition de Charles d'Anjou pour la canonisation de Saint Louis." In *Notices et documents publiés par la Société de l'histoire de France à l'occasion de son cinquantième anniversaire,* 155–176. Paris, 1884.

Delaborde, Henri-François. "Fragments de l'enquête faite à Saint-Denis en 1282 en vue de la canonisation de Saint Louis." In *Mémoires de la Société de l'Histoire de Paris et de l'Île-de-France,* vol. 23, 1–71. 1896.

A Mirror of the Princes offered to Saint Louis:

Gilbert de Tournai. *Eruditio regum et principum (1259).* Edited by A. de Poorter. In *Les Philosophes belges,* vol. 9. Louvain, 1914.

An Anthology of translated sources:

O'Connell, David. *Les Propos de Saint Louis.* With introduction by Jacques Le Goff. Paris, 1974.

Literature

Dufournet, Jean. *Rutebeuf. Poèmes de l'infortune et poèmes de la croisade.* Paris, 1979.

Moos, Peter von. "Die Trotschrift des Vincenz von Beauvais für Ludwig IX. Vorstudie zur Motiv und Gattungsgeschichte der consolatio." *Mittelateinisches Jahrbuch* 4 (1967): 173–219.

Rutebeuf. *Oeuvres complètes.* Edited by Michel Zink. 2 vols. Paris, 1990.

Art

Branner, Robert. *The Manuscript Painting in Paris during the Reign of Saint Louis. A Study of Styles.* Berkeley: University of California Press, 1977

———. "Saint Louis et l'enluminure parisienne au XVIIe siècle." In *Septième centenaire de la mort de Saint Louis,* Acts of the colloquia held at Royaumont and Paris, May 1970, 69–84. Paris, 1976.

Leniaud, Jean-Michel, and Françoise Perrot. *La Sainte-Chapelle.* Paris, 1991.

Le Psautier de Saint Louis. Graz: Akademische Druck-und-Verlagsanstalt, 1972. (Facsimile.)

Songs

Leroux de Lincy, Adrien, ed. "Gent de France, mult estes esbahie." *Bibliothèque de l'École des chartes* 1 (1840).

Meyer, W., ed. "Wie Ludwig IX der Helige das Kreuz nahm." In *Nachrichten der königlichen Gesselschaft der Wissenschaften zu Göttingen* (1907): 246–57.

Paris, Gaston. "La Chanson Composée à Acre." *Romania* 22 (1893).

Exhibitions (Catalogues)

Au temps de Saint Louis. Museum of Melun (dactylograph), 1970.

La France de Saint Louis. Salle des gens d'armes du palais, Paris, October 1970–January 1971.

Le Mariage de Saint Louis à Sens en 1234. Museum of Sens, 1984.

Saint Louis à la Sainte-Chapelle. Direction générale des Archives de France, Paris, May–August, 1960.

ON SAINT LOUIS' ENVIRONMENT

Alphandéry, Paul, and Alphonse Dupront. *La Chrétienté et l'idée de croisade.* 2 vols. Paris, 1954–1959. New edition with postscript by M. Balard, Paris, 1995.

Barbey, J. *tre roi. Le roi et son gouvernement en France de Clovis à Louis VI.* Paris, 1992.

Barlow, Fred. "The King's Evil." *English Historical Review* (1980): 3–27.

Beaune, Colette. *Naissance de la nation France.* Paris, 1985.

Berges, Wilhelm. *Die Fürstenspiegel des hohen und späten Mittelalters.* Leipzig, 1938.

Bloch, Marc. *Les Rois thaumaturges.* Preface by J. Le Goff. Third edition. Paris, 1985.

Bogyay, T. von, J. Bak, and G. Silagi. *Die heiligen Könige.* Graz, 1976.

Bourin-Derreau, M. *Temps d'équilibre, temps de rupture.* Paris, 1990.

Buc, Philippe. *L'Ambiguïté du Livre. Prince, pouvoir et peuple dans les commentaires de la Bible au Moyen Âge.* Paris, 1994.

Bulst, N., and J.-P. Genet, eds. *La Ville, la bourgeoisie et la genèse de l'État moderne (XIIe–XVIIe siècles).* Paris, 1988.

Burns, R. I. "Christian Islamic Confrontation in the West: The Thirteenth Century Dream of Conversion." *The American Historical Review* 76 (1971): 1386–1434.

Cazelles, Raymond. *Paris de la fin du règne de Philippe Auguste à la mort de Charles V (1223–1380).* In *Nouvelle histoire de Paris,* vol. 3. Paris, 1972.

Comprendre le XIIIe siècle. Edited by Danièle Alexandre-Bidon and Pierre Guichard. Lyon, 1995.

Contamine, Philippe, ed. *L'État et les aristocraties (France, Angleterre, Écosse, XIIe–XVIIe siècles).* Paris, 1989.

———. *La Guerre au Moyen Âge.* Third edition. Paris, 1992.

Contamine, Philippe, et alii. *L'Économie médiévale.* Paris, 1993.

Culture et idéologie dans la genèse de l'État moderne. Rome, 1985.

Droits savants et pratiques françaises du pouvoir (XIe–XVe siècles). Edited by Jacques Krynen and Albert Rigaudière. Bordeaux: Presses universitaires de Bordeaux, 1992.

Duby, Georges. *Le Temps des cathédrales. L'art et la société (980–1420).* Paris, 1976.

Duby, Georges, and Robert Mandrou. *Histoire de la civilisation française.* Vol. 1. Paris, 1967.

Duggan, A. J., ed. *Kings and Kingship in Medieval Europe.* London: King's College, 1993.

Durchhardt, H., R. A. Jackson, and D. Sturdy, eds. *European Monarchy.* Stuttgart, 1992.

Erlande-Brandenburg, Alain. *Le Roi est mort. Étude sur les funérailles, les sépultures et les tombeaux des rois de France jusqu'à la fin du XIIIe siècle.* Paris, 1975.

Faral, Edmond. *La Vie quotidienne au temps de Saint Louis.* Paris, 1942.

Folz, Robert. *Les Saints Rois du Moyen Âge en Occident (V^e–XIIIe siècles).* Brussels, 1984.

Fossier, R. *La Société médiévale.* Paris, 1991.

Fossier, R., et alii. *Le Moyen Âge.* Vol. 2, *L'Éveil de l'Europe (950–1250)*; vol. 3, *Le Temps des crises (1250–1520).* Paris, 1990.

Genet, Jean-Philippe. *État moderne. Genèse: bilan et perspectives.* Paris, 1990.

Genet, Jean-Philippe, with B. Vincent, eds. *État et Église dans la genèse de l'État moderne.* Madrid, 1986.

Génicot, Léopold. *Le XIIIe siècle européen.* Paris, 1988.

Gorski, K. "Le Roi-Saint, un problème d'idéologie féodale." *Annales, E.S.C.* (1969).

Guenée, Bernard. "État et nation au Moyen Âge." *Revue historique* 237 (1967): 17–30.

———. "La fierté d'être capétien en France, au Moyen Âge." *Annales, E.S.C.* (1978): 450–77. Reprinted in *Politique et histoire au Moyen Âge,* 341–368. Paris, 1981.

———. *Histoire et culture historique dans l'Occident médiéval.* Paris, 1991.

Guérout, Jean. "Le palais de la Cité à Paris des origines à 1417. Essai topographique et archéologique." In *Paris et Île-de-France. Mémoires de la Fédération des sociétés historiques et archéologiques de Paris et de l'Île-de-France* 1 (1949): 57–212; 2 (1950): 21–204; 3 (1951): 7–101.

Histoire de la France urbaine. Edited by Georges Duby. Vol. 2, *La Ville médiévale,* edited by J. Le Goff. Paris, 1980.

Histoire de la France rurale. Edited by Georges Duby. Vol. 1, *Des origines à 1340.* Paris, 1975.

Histoire de la France. Edited by André Burguière and Jacques Revel. Vol. 2, *L'État et les pouvoirs,* edited by Jacques Le Goff. Paris, 1989.

Histoire de la France religieuse. Edited by Jacques Le Goff and René Rémond. Vol. 1, *Des dieux de la Gaule à la papauté d'Avignon,* edited by Jacques Le Goff. Paris, 1988.

Jordan, William Chester. *The French Monarchy and the Jews from Philip Augustus to the Last Capetians.* Philadelphia: University of Pennsylvania Press, 1989.

Kantorowicz, Ernst H. *The King's Two Bodies. A Study in Medieval Theology.* Princeton, 1957. French translation: *Les Deux Corps du roi.* Paris, 1989.

Krynen, Jacques. *L'Empire du roi. Idées et croyances politiques en France, XIIIe–XVe siècles.* Paris, 1993.

Lafaurie, J. *Les Monnaies des rois de France. De Hugues Capet à Louis XII.* Paris and Bâle, 1951.

Lamarignier, Jean-François. *La France médiévale. Institutions et sociétés.* Paris, 1991.

Lecoy de la Marche, Albert. *La France sous Saint Louis et sous Philippe le Hardi.* Paris, 1893.

Le Goff, Jacques. "La genèse du miracle royal." In *Marc Bloch aujourd'hui. Histoire comparée et sciences sociales,* directed and edited by H. Atsma and A. Burguière, 147–58. Paris, 1990.

———. "Portrait du roi idéal." *L'Histoire* 81 (September 1985): 70–76.

———. "Reims, ville du sacre." In *Les Lieux de mémoire,* vol. 2, *La Nation,* edited by P. Nora, 1:89–184. Paris, 1986.

———. "Le roi enfant dans l'idéologie monarchique de l'Occident médiéval." In *Historicité de l'enfance et de la jeunesse,* 231–50. International Congress of Athens. Athens, 1986.

Le Siècle de Saint Louis. Paris, 1970.

Lewis, Andrew W. *Royal Succession in Capetian France: Studies on Familial Order and the State.* Cambridge, MA: 1981. French translation: *Le Sang royal. La famille capétienne et l'État. France, X^e–XIVe siècles.* Paris, 1986.

Lorcin, Marie-Thérèse. *La France au XIIIe siècle.* Paris, 1975.

Lot, Ferdinand, and Robert Fawtier, eds. *Histoire des institutions françaises au Moyen Âge.* Vol. 2, *Les Institutions royales.* Paris, 1958.

McGovern, J. F. "The Rise of the New Economic Attitudes. Economic Humanism, Economic Nationalism during the Later Middle Ages and the Renaissance, A.D. 1200–1550." *Traditio* 26 (1970): 217–53.

Mirot, L. *Manuel de géographie historique de la France.* 2 vols. Paris, 1948–1950.

Nora, Pierre, ed. *Les Lieux de mémoire.* Vol. 2, *La Nation.* Paris, 1986.

Pange, J. *Le Roi très chrétien.* Paris, 1949.

Paul, Jacques. *Histoire intellectuelle de l'Occident médiéval.* 2 vols. Paris, 1973.

Petit-Dutaillis, Charles. *La Monarchie féodale en France et en Angleterre, X^e–XIIIe siècles.* Paris, 1933. New edition, Paris, 1971.

Rigaudière, Albert. *Gouverner la ville au Moyen Âge.* Paris, 1993.

———. *Pouvoirs et institutions dans la France médiévale.* Vol. 2, *Des temps féodaux aux temps de l'État.* Paris, 1994.

Rigaudière, Albert, with André Gouron, eds. *Renaissance du pouvoir législatif et genèse de l'État.* Montpellier, 1987.

Saenger, P. "Prier de bouche et prier de coeur." In *Les Usages de l'imprimé,* edited by Roger Chartier, 191–227. Paris, 1987.

———. "Silent Reading: Its Impact on Late Medieval Script and Society." *Viator* 13 (1982): 367–414.

Schramm, Percy Ernst. *Der König von Frankreich. Das Wesen der Monarchie vom 9. bis zum 16. Jahrhundert.* 2 vols. Weimar, 1939. New edition, 1960.

Spiegel, Gabrielle M. *The Chronicle Tradition of Saint-Denis: A Survey.* Brookline, MA, and Leyden, 1978.

Strayer, Joseph R. "France: The Holy Land, the Chosen People and the Most Christian King." In *Action and Conviction in Early Modern Europe,* 3–16. Princeton, 1969.

———. *Medieval Statecraft and the Perspectives of History.* Princeton, 1971. French translation: *Les Origines médiévales de l'État moderne.* Paris, 1979.

Tessier, Gaston. *La Diplomatique royale française.* Paris, 1962.

Topfer, B. "Staatliche Zentralisation im regionalen und im national-staatlichen Rahmen in Frankreich vom 13 bis zum 15 Jahrhundert." *Jahrbuch für Geschichte des Feudalismus* 11 (1987): 159–73.

Vauchez, André. *La Sainteté en Occident aux derniers siècles du Moyen Âge.* Rome, 1981.

Zink, Michel. *La Subjectivité littéraire. Autour du siècle de Saint Louis.* Paris, 1985.

BIOGRAPHIES AND GENERAL WORKS ON SAINT LOUIS

The Most Important Works

La Vie de Saint Louis, roi de France, written by Louis Sébastien Le Nain de Tillemont (d. 1698), published by J. de Gaulle. 6 vols. Paris: Société de l'Histoire de France, 1847–1851. (This is still fundamental for its use of sources that no longer exist today and the grandeur of its conception.)

The important biographies of Saint Louis are:

Jordan, William C. *Louis IX and the Challenge of the Crusade: A Study in Rulership.* Princeton, 1979.

Langlois, Charles Victor. *Saint Louis, Philippe le Bel: les derniers Capétiens directs (1226–1328).* Book 3, volume 2 of *L'Histoire de France depuis les origines jusqu'à la Révolution,* edited by Ernest Lavisse. Paris, 1901; reprint, Paris, 1978.

Richard, Jean. *Saint Louis, roi d'une France féodale, soutien de la Terre sainte.* Paris, 1983, second edition, Paris, 1986.

Saint-Denis, Alain. *Le Siècle de Saint Louis.* Paris, 1984. (An outstanding recent comprehensive summary.)

Septième centenaire de la mort de Saint Louis. Actes des colloques de Royaumont et de Paris (21–27 mai 1970). Edited by Louis Carolus-Barré. Paris, 1976.

Le Siècle de Saint Louis. Edited by R. Pernoud. Paris, 1970.

Wallon, Henri-Alexandre. *Saint Louis et son temps.* 2 vols. Paris, 1875.

Valuable Works

Bailly, *Saint Louis.* Paris, 1949.

Beer, J. de. *Saint Louis.* Paris, 1984.

Benouville, G. de. *Saint Louis ou le printemps de la France.* Paris, 1970.

Bordeaux, H. *Un précurseur. Vie, mort et survie de Saint Louis, roi de France.* Paris, 1949.

Boulenger, Jacques Romain. *La Vie de Saint Louis.* Paris, 1929.

Cristiani, Mgr. *Saint Louis, roi de France.* Paris, 1959.

Evans, J. *The History of Saint Louis.* Oxford, 1938.

Eydoux, Henri-Paul. *Saint Louis et son temps.* Paris, 1971.

Faure, F. *Histoire de Saint Louis.* 2 vols. Paris, 1966.

Goyau, G. *Saint Louis.* Paris, 1928.

Guth, P. *Saint Louis.* Paris, 1960.

Klein, C. *Saint Louis, un roi au pied du pauvre.* Paris, 1970.

Labarge, M. W. *Saint Louis.* London, 1968.

Lecoy de la Marche, Albert. *Saint Louis, son gouvernement et sa politique.* Paris, 1889.

Levis-Mirepoix, duc de. *Saint Louis, roi de France.* With preface by G. Walter, "Saint Louis, fou du Christ." Paris, 1970.

Levron, J. P. *Saint Louis ou l'apogée du Moyen Âge.* Paris, 1969.

Madaule, Jacques. *Saint Louis de France.* Paris: 1943.

Mousset, J. *Saint Louis.* Paris, 1950.

Olivier-Martin, F. *Saint Louis.* In *Hommes d'État,* vol. 2, 131–212. Paris, 1937.

Pernoud, Régine. *Un chef d'État. Saint Louis, roi de France.* Paris, 1960.

Sertillanges, P. *Saint Louis.* Paris, 1918.

Sivery, Gérard. *Saint Louis et son siècle.* Paris, 1983.

Studies on Particular Topics

Augustin, Jean-Marie. "L'aide féodale levée par Saint Louis et Philippe le Bel." *Mémoires de la Société pour l'histoire du droit et des anciens pays bourguignons, comtois et romands* 38 (1981): 59–81.

Babelon, Jean-Pierre. "La monnaie de Saint Louis." In *Le Siècle de Saint Louis,* edited by R. Pernoud, 83–92. Paris, 1970.

———. "Saint Louis dans son palais de Paris." In *Le Siècle de Saint Louis,* edited by R. Pernoud, 45–56. Paris, 1970.

———. "Saint Louis et le traité de Paris." In *Le Siècle de Saint Louis,* edited by R. Pernoud, 227–29. Paris, 1970.

Bastin, Julia. "Quelques propos de Rutebeuf sur le roi Louis IX." *Bulletin de l'Académie royale de langue et littérature française* 38, no. 1 (1960): 5–14.

Bautier, Robert-Henri. "Les aumônes du roi aux maladreries, maisons-Dieu et pauvres établissements du royaume. Contribution à l'étude du réseau hospitalier et de la fossilisation de l'administration royale de Philippe Auguste à Charles VII." *Actes du 97ᵉ Congrès national des sociétés savantes* (Nantes, 1972) in *Bulletin philologique et historique* (1975): 37–105.

Beaune, Colette. "La légende de Jean Tristan, fils de Saint Louis." *Mélanges de l'École française de Rome. Moyen Âge, Temps modernes* 98, no. 1 (1986): 143–60.

Bemont, Charles. "La campagne de Poitou, 1242–1243. Taillebourg et Saintes." *Annales du Midi* 5 (1893): 289–314.

Berger, Élie. *Histoire de Blanche de Castile*. Paris, 1895.

———. *Saint Louis et Innocent IV. Étude sur les rapports de la France et du Saint Siège*. Paris, 1893.

Bisson, Thomas N. "Consultative Functions in the King's Parlements (1250–1314)." *Speculum* 44 (1969): 353–73.

Bougerol, Jacques-Guy. "Saint Bonaventure et le roi Saint Louis." In *San Bonaventura (1274–1974)*, vol. 2, 469–93. Grottaferrata, 1973.

Boulet-Sautel, Marguerite. "Le concept de souveraineté chez Jacques de Révigny." In *Actes du congrès sur l'ancienne université d'Orléans (XIIIᵉ–XVIIIᵉ siècles)*, 17–27. Orléans, 1982.

———. "Jean de Blanot et la conception du pouvoir royal au temps de Louis IX." In *Septième centenaire*, 57–68.

Boureau, Alain. "Saint Louis." In *Histoire des saints et de la sainteté*, edited by A. Vauchez, vol. 6, *Au temps du renouveau évangélique*, 196–205. Paris, 1986.

Boutaric, Edgar. *Saint Louis et Alphonse de Poitiers. Étude sur la réunion des provinces du Midi et de l'Ouest à la Couronne et sur les origines de la centralisation administrative*. Paris, 1870.

Brachet, Auguste. *Pathologie mentale des rois de France*. Edited by A. Brachet née Korff. Paris, 1903.

Branner, Robert. *The Manuscript Painting in Paris during the Reign of Saint Louis. A Study of Styles*. Berkeley: University of California Press, 1977.

Brown, Elizabeth A. R. "Burying and Unburying the Kings of France." In *Persons in Groups. Social Behaviour as Identity Formation in Medieval and Renaissance Europe*, edited by R. C. Trexler, 241–66. Binghamton, 1985.

———. "The Chapels and Cult of Saint Louis at Saint-Denis." *Mediaevalia* 10 (1984): 279–331.

———. "Philippe le Bel and the Remains of Saint Louis." *Gazette des Beaux Arts* (1980–1981): 175–82.

———. "Taxation and Morality in the XIIIth and XIVth Centuries: Conscience and Political Power and the Kings of France." *French Historical Studies* 8, no. 1 (Spring 1973): 1–28.

Buc, Philippe. "David's Adultery with Bathsheba and the Healing Powers of the Capetian Kings." *Viator* 23 (1993): 101–20.

Buisson, Ludwig. *König Ludwig IX der Helige und das Recht*. Freiburg, 1955.

———. "Saint Louis et l'Aquitaine (1259–1270)." In *Actes de l'Académie nationale des sciences, belles-lettres et arts de Bordeaux*. 4th series, vol. 26, 15–33. Bordeaux, 1972. Reprinted in *Lebendiges Mittelalter*, 251–69. Cologne and Böhlau, 1988.

———. "Saint Louis, Justice et Amour de Dieu." *Francia* 6 (1978): 127–49.

Cahen, Claude. "Saint Louis et l'Islam." *Journal asiatique* 258 (1970): 3–12.

Campbell, Gerard J. "The Attitude of the Monarchy towards the Use of Ecclesiastical Censures in the Reign of Saint Louis." *Speculum* 35 (1960): 535–55.

Carolus-Barré, Louis. "Les enquêtes pour la canonisation de Saint Louis, de Grégoire IX à Boniface VIII, et la bulle *Gloria, laus* du 12 août 1287." *Revue d'histoire de l'Église de France* 57 (1971).

———. "La Grande ordonnance de 1254 sur la réforme de l'administration et la police du royaume." In *Septième centenaire,* 85–96.

———. "Le prince héritier Louis et l'intérim du pouvoir royal de la mort de Blanche (novembre 1252) au retour du roi (juillet 1254)." *Comptes rendus de l'Académie des inscriptions et belles-lettres,* 1970.

———. "Saint Louis dans l'histoire et la légende." *Annuaire-bulletin de la Société de l'histoire de France,* 1970–1971.

———. "Saint Louis et la translation des corps saints." In *Études d'histoire du droit canonique dédiées à M.G. Le Bras,* vol. 2. Paris, 1965.

Cazelles, Raymond. "Une exigence de l'opinion depuis Saint Louis: la réformation du royaume." *Annuaire-bulletin de la Société de l'histoire de France* 469 (1963): 91–99.

———. "La réglementation royale de la guerre privée, de Saint Louis à Charles V." *Revue historique de droit français et étranger* (1960): 530–48.

Chaplais, Pierre. "Le traité de Paris de 1259 et l'inféodation de la Gascogne allodiale." *Le Moyen Âge* (1955): 121–37.

Chennaf, Sarah, and Odile Redon. "Les miracles de Saint Louis." In *Gelis,* edited by Jacques and Odile Redon, *Les Miracles, miroirs des corps,* 53–85. Paris, 1983.

Cole, P., D.L. D'Avray, and J. Riley-Smith. "Application of Theology to Current Affairs: Memorial Sermons on the Dead of Mansurah and on Innocent IV." *The Bulletin of Historical Research,* 63, no. 152 (1990): 227–47.

Congar, Yves. "L'Église et l'État sous le règne de Saint Louis." In *Septième centenaire,* 257–71.

Coornaert, E. "Les corporations au temps de Saint Louis." *Revue historique* (1936).

Delaborde, Henri-François. "Instructions d'un ambassadeur envoyé par Saint Louis à Alexandre IV à l'occasion du traité de Paris (1258)." *Bibliothèque de l'École des chartes* (1888): 530–34.

———. "Joinville au conseil tenu à Acre en 1250." *Romania* 23 (1894).

Delaruelle, Étienne. "L'idée de croisade chez Saint Louis." *Bulletin de littérature ecclésiastique* (1960). Reprinted in *L'Idée de croisade au Moyen Âge.* Turin, 1980.

———. "Saint Louis devant les Cathares." *Septième centenaire,* 273–80.

Dimier, Louis. *Saint Louis et Cîteaux.* Paris, 1954.

Dufeil, M.M. "Le roi Louis dans la Querelle des mendiants et des Séculiers (université de Paris, 1254–1270)." In *Septième centenaire,* 281–89.

Erlande-Brandenburg, Alain. "Le tombeau de Saint Louis." *Bulletin monumental* 126 (1968): 7–30.

Favier, Jean. "Les finances de Saint Louis." In *Septième centenaire,* 133–40.

Fawtier, Robert. "Saint Louis et Frédéric II." In *Convegno internazionale di Studi Federiciani.* Palermo, 1950.

Fietier, Roland. "Le choix des baillis et sénéchaux aux XIIIᵉ et XIVᵉ siècles (1250–1350)." *Mémoires de la Société pour l'histoire du droit et des institutions des anciens pays bourguignons, comtois, et romands,* 29 (1968–1969): 255–74.

Folz, Robert. "La sainteté de Louis IX d'après les textes liturgiques de sa fête." *Revue d'histoire de l'Église de France* 57 (1971): 30–45.

François, M. "Initiatives de Saint Louis en matière administrative: les enquêtes royales." In *Le Siècle de Saint Louis,* 210–14.

Gavrilovitch. *Étude sur le traité de Paris de 1259 entre Louis IX, roi de France, et Henri III, roi d'Angleterre.* Paris, 1899.

Giesey, Ralph E. "The Juristic Basis of Dynastic Right to the French Throne." *Transactions of the American Philosophical Society.* New series, vol. 51, part 5. Philadelphia, 1961.

Giordanengo, Gérard. "Le pouvoir législatif du roi de France (XIᵉ–XIIIᵉ siècles): travaux récents et hypothèses de recherche." *Bibliothèque de l'École des chartes* 147 (1989): 283–310.

Grabois, Aryeh. "Du crédit juif à Paris au temps de Saint Louis." *Revue des études juives* (1970): 5–22.

Griffiths, Q. "New Men among the Lay Counsellors of Saint Louis' Parlement." *Medieval Studies* 32–33 (1970–1971): 234–72.

Guilhiermoz, P. "Saint Louis, les gages de batailles et la procédure civile." *Bibliothèque de l'École des chartes* 48 (1887): 11–20.

———. "Les sources manuscrites de l'histoire monétaire de Saint Louis." *Le Moyen Âge,* 34 (1923).

Halliam, E. M. "Philip the Fair and the Cult of Saint Louis. Religion and National Identity." *Studies in Church History* 18 (1982): 201–14.

Haseloff, Arthur. "Les Psautiers de Saint Louis." *Mémoires de la Société des antiquaires de France* 59 (1898): 18–42.

Jordan, William Chester. "Communal Administration in France 1257–1270. Problems Discovered and Solutions Imposed." *Revue belge de philologie et d'histoire* 59 (1981): 292–313.

———. "*Persona* et *gesta:* The Image and Deeds of the Thirteenth Century Capetians. 2. The Case of Saint Louis." *Viator* 19 (1988): 209–18.

———. "The Psalter of Saint Louis. The Program of the Seventy-Eight Full Page Illustrations." *Acta: The High Middle Ages* 7 (1980): 65–91.

———. "Supplying Aigues-Mortes for the Crusade of 1248: The Problem of Restructuring Trade." In *Order and Innovation (Mélanges J. Strayer).* Princeton, 1976.

Labande, Edmond-René. "Quelques traits de caractère du roi Saint Louis." *Revue d'histoire de la spiritualité* 50, no. 2 (1974): 135–46.

———. "Saint Louis pèlerin." *Revue d'histoire de l'Église de France* 57 (1971).

Labarge, M. W. "Saint Louis et les juifs." In *Le Siècle de Saint Louis,* 267–74.

Langlois, C. V. "Doléances recueillies par les enquêteurs de Saint Louis." *Revue historique* 92 (1906).

Lecoy de la Marche, Albert. "Saint Louis, sa famille et sa cour d'après les anecdotes contemporaines." *Revue des questions historiques* 22 (1877): 465–84.

Le Goff, Jacques. "Les gestes de Saint Louis." In *Mélanges Jacques Stiennon,* 445–59. 1982.

———. "Ludwig IX der Heilige und der Ursprung der feudalen Monarchie in Frankreich." *Jahrbuch für Geschichte des Feudalismus* 14 (1990): 107–14.

———. "Un roi souffrant: Saint Louis." In *La Souffrance au Moyen Âge (France, XIIᵉ–XVᵉ siècles). Les Cahiers de Varsovie* (1988): 127–36.

———. "Royauté biblique et idéal monarchique médiéval. Saint Louis et Josias." In *Les Juifs au regard de l'histoire. Mélanges Bernhard Blumenkranz,* 157–68. 1985.

———. "La Sainteté de Saint Louis. Sa place dans la typologie et l'évolution chronologique des rois saints." In *Les Fonctions des saints dans le monde occidental (IIIᵉ–XIIIᵉ siècles),* colloquium of l'École française de Rome, 1988, 285–93. Rome, 1991.

———. "Saint de l'Église et saint du peuple. Les miracles officiels de Saint Louis entre sa mort et sa canonisation (1270–1297)." In *Histoire sociale, sensibilités collectives et mentalités. Mélanges Robert Mandrou,* 169–80. 1985.

———. "Saint Louis and the Mediterranean." *Mediterranean Historical Review* 5, no. 1 (1990): 21–43.

———. "Saint Louis à table: entre commensalité royale et humilité alimentaire." In *La Sociabilité à table. Commensalité et convivialité à travers les âges,* colloquium of Rouen, 1990, 132–44. Rouen, 1992.

———. "Saint Louis a-t-il existé?" *L'Histoire,* no. 40 (December 1981).

———. "Saint Louis, croisé idéal?" *Notre histoire,* no. 20 (February 1986): 42 ff.

———. "Saint Louis et les corps royaux." In *Le Temps de la réflexion,* 255–84. Paris, 1982.

———. "Saint Louis et la parole royale." In *Le Nombre du temps. En hommage à Paul Zumthor,* 127–36. Paris, 1988.

———. "Saint Louis et la pratique sacramentelle." Dialogue with Pierre Marie Gy. *La Maison-Dieu* 197, no. 1 (1994): 99–124.

———. "Saint Louis et la prière." *Horizons marins, itinéraires spirituels (Vᵉ–XVIIIᵉ siècles),* vol. 1 *Mentalités et sociétés.* Studies collected by Henri Dubois, Jean-Claude Hocquet, and André Vauchez. *Mélanges Michel Mollat,* 85–94. Paris, 1987.

———. "Saint Louis et la mer." In *L'uomo e il mare nella civiltà occidentale: da Ulisse a Cristoforo Colombo,* colloquium of Genoa, 11–24. Genoa, 1992.

Lerner, Robert E. "The Uses of Heterodoxy, the French Monarchy and Unbelief in the XIIIth Century." *French Historical Studies* 4 (1965): 189–202.

Lineham, Peter, and Francisco Hernandez. "*Animadverto*: A Recently Discovered *Consilium* Concerning the Sanctity of King Louis IX." *Revue Mabillon* 66, new series 5 (1994): 83–105.

Little, Lester K. "Saint Louis' Involvement with the Friars." *Church History* 33, no. 2 (June 1964): 125–48.

Longnon, Auguste N. *Documents parisiens sur l'iconographie de Saint Louis.* 1882.

Michaud-Quantin, Pierre. "La politique monétaire royale à la faculté de théologie de Paris en 1265." *Le Moyen Âge* 17 (1962): 137–51.

Michel, R. *L'Administration royale dans la sénéchaussée de Beaucaire au temps de Saint Louis.* Paris, 1910.

Mollaret, H. H., and J. Brossolet. "Sur la mort de Saint Louis." *La Presse médicale* 74, no. 55 (December 25, 1966): 2913–2916.

Mollat, Michel. "Le 'passage' de Saint Louis à Tunis. Sa place dans l'histoire des croisades." *Revue d'histoire économique et sociale* 50 (1972): 289–303.

Monfrin, Jacques. "Joinville et la mer." In *Études offertes à Félix Lecoy*, 445–68. Paris, 1973.

———. "Joinville et la prise de Damiette (1249)." *Comptes rendus de l'Académie des inscriptions et belles-lettres* (1976): 268–85.

Musset, Lucien. "Saint Louis et la Normandie." *Annales de Basse-Normandie* (1972): 8–18.

Nahon, Gérard. "Le crédit et les juifs dans la France du XIIIᵉ siècle." *Annales, E.S.C.* (1964): 1121–1148.

———. "Une géographie des Juifs dans la France de Louis IX (1226–1270)." In *The Fifth World Congress of Jewish Studies,* vol. 2, 127–32. Jerusalem, 1972.

———. "Les ordonnances de Saint Louis et les juifs." *Les Nouveaux cahiers* 23 (1970).

Parent, M. "Les Assemblées royales en France au temps de Saint Louis." In *Positions des thèses de l'École des chartes,* 155–61. Paris, 1939.

Pelicier, P. "Deux lettres relatives à Louis IX." *Bulletin du Comité des travaux historiques. Histoire et Philologie* (1892): 229–31. (On the conflicts between the bishop and the bourgeois of Châlons.)

Pernoud, Régine. *La Reine Blanche.* Paris, 1972.

Petit, E. "Saint Louis en Bourgogne et principalement dans les contrées de l'Yonne." *Bulletin de la Société des sciences historiques et naturelles de l'Yonne* (1893): 576–91.

Pinoteau, Hervé. "La tenue du sacre de saint Louis IX roi de France, son arrière-plan symbolique et la renovatio regni Juda." *Itinéraires,* no. 162 (1972): 120–66.

———, with C. Le Gallo. *Héraldique de Saint Louis et de ses compagnons.* Paris, 1966.

Pognon, E. "Les arbitrages de Saint Louis." In *Le Siècle de Saint Louis,* 221–26.

Pontal, Odette. "Le différend entre Louis IX et les évêques de Beauvais et ses incidences sur les conciles (1232–1248)." *Bibliothèque de l'École des chartes* 123 (1965).

Richard, Jean. "L'adoubement de Saint Louis." *Journal des savants* (1988): 207–17.

———. "Une ambassade mongole à Paris en 1262." *Journal des savants* (1979).

———. "La fondation d'une église latine en Orient par Saint Louis: Damiette." *Bibliothèque de l'École des chartes* 120 (1962). Reprinted in *Orient et Occident au Moyen Âge.* London, 1976.

———. "La politique orientale de Saint Louis. La croisade de 1248." In *Septième centenaire,* 197–208.

———. "Sur les pas de Plancarpin et de Rubrouck. La lettre de Saint Louis à Sartaq." *Journal des savants* (1977).

Sablou, J. "Saint Louis et le problème de la fondation d'Aigues-Mortes." In *Hommages à André Dupont,* 256–65. Montpellier, 1974.

Sadler, Donna L. "The King as Subject, the King as Author: Art and Politics of Louis IX." In *European Monarchy,* edited by H. Durchhardt, R. A. Jackson, and D. Sturdy, 53–68.

Sayous, André. "Les mandats de Saint Louis sur son trésor pendant la septième croisade." *Revue historique* 167 (1931).

Schneider, Jean. "Les villes du royaume de France au temps Saint Louis." *Comptes rendus de l'Académie des inscriptions et belles-lettres* (1971).

Serper, Arié. "L'administration royale de Paris au temps de Louis IX." *Francia* 7 (1979): 123–39.

Sivery, Gérard. *Les Capétiens et l'argent au siècle de Saint Louis.* Paris, 1995.

———. *L'Économie du royaume de France au siècle de Saint Louis.* Lille, 1984. (See the review by H. Dubois, *Revue historique* 109, no. 1 [1985]: 472–73.)

———. "L'équipe gouvernementale, Blanche de Castille et la succession de Louis VIII en 1226." *L'Information historique* (1979): 203–11.

———. *Marguerite de Provence. Une reine au temps des cathédrales.* Paris, 1987.

Slattery, M. *Myth, Man and Sovereign Saint. King Louis IX in Jean de Joinville's Sources.* New York, Bern, and Frankfurt, 1985.

Sommers Wright, Georgia. "The Tomb of Saint Louis." *Journal of the Warburg and Courtauld Institute* 34 (1971): 65–82.

Stahl, Harvey. "Old Testament Illustration during the Reign of St. Louis: The Morgan Picture Book and the New Biblical Cycles." In *Il Medio Oriente e l'Occidente nell'arte del XIIIe secolo. Atti del XXIV congresso internazionale di storia dell'arte,* edited by H. Belting, 79–93. Bologna, 1982.

Stein, Henry. "Pierre Lombard, médecin de Saint Louis." *Bibliothèque de l'École des chartes* (1939): 63–71.

Strayer, Joseph. *The Administration of Normandy under Saint Louis.* 1932.

———. "La conscience du roi. Les enquêtes de 1258–1262 dans la sénéchaussée de Carcassonne-Béziers." In *Mélanges Roger Aubenas.* Montpellier, 1974.

———. "The Crusades of Louis IX." In *History of the Crusades,* edited by K. M. Setton, vol. 2, 487–521. London, 1962.

Tardif, J. "Le procès d'Enguerran de Coucy." *Bibliothèque de l'École des chartes.* 1918.

Tuilier, André. "La fondation de la Sorbonne, les querelles universitaires et la politique du temps." *Mélanges de la Bibliothèque de la Sorbonne* 3 (1982): 7–43.

———. "La révolte des pastoureaux et la querelle entre l'université de Paris et les ordres Mendiants." In *Actes du 99ᵉ congrès national des sociétés savantes,* Besançon, 1974, Section of philology and history, vol. 1, 353–67. 1977.

Uitti, K. D. "Nouvelle et structure hagiographique: le récit histioriographique nouveau de Jean de Joinville." In *Mittelalterbilder aus neuer Perspektive,* edited by E. Ruhe and R. Rehrens, 380–91. Munich, 1985.

Wood, Charles T. *The French Apanages and the Capetian Monarchy, 1224–1328.* Cambridge, MA, 1966.

———. "The Mise of Amens and Saint Louis' Theory in Kingship." *French Historical Studies* 6 (1969–1970): 300–10.

———. "*Regnum Francie*: A Problem in Capetian Administrative Usage." *Traditio* 23 (1967): 117–47.

Zink, Michel. "Joinville ne pleure pas, mais il rêve." *Poétique* 33 (February 1978): 28–45.

Jerzy Prsiaka has written an interesting "Ludwik Swiety. Portret hagiograficzny idealnegi wladcy" (Saint Louis. A Hagiographical Portrait of the Ideal Ruler) in Polish. This is an unpublished doctoral thesis at the University of Warsaw, 1994, directed by H. Samsonowicz.

Index

A prolific medievalist of international renown, Jacques Le Goff (1924 –) is the former director of studies at the L'École des Hautes Études en Sciences Sociales, Paris. Among his honors is the Dr. A. H. Heineken Prize for History, bestowed in 2004 by the Royal Netherlands Academy of Arts and Sciences to Le Goff for "fundamentally changing our view of the Middle Ages." He was also among the recipients of the 2007 Dan David Prize in recognition of contributions to his discipline.